The SAGE Handbook of Leadership

Second Edition

The **Second Edition** of **The SAGE Handbook of Leadership** provides not only an in-depth overview the current field of leadership studies, but also a map into the future debates, innovations and priorities of where the field will move to. Featuring all new chapters from a global community of leading and emerging scholars, each chapter offers a comprehensive, critical overview of an aspect of leadership, a discussion of key debates and research, and a review of the emerging issues in its area.

Featuring an innovative structure divided by prepositions, this brand-new edition moves away from essentializing boundaries, and instead seeks to create synergies between different schools of leadership. A key feature of the second edition, is the attention to sensemaking (exploring the current themes, structures and ideas that comprise each topic) and sensebreaking (disrupting, critiquing and refreshing each topic). Suitable for students and researchers alike, this second edition is a critical site of reference for the study of leadership.

PART 1: Between: Leadership as a Social, Socio-cognitive and Practical Phenomenon

PART 2: About: Exploring the Individual and Interpersonal Facets of Leadership

PART 3: Through: Leadership Seen Through Contemporary Frames

PART 4: Within: Leadership as a Contextually Bound Phenomenon

PART 5: But: A Critical Examination of Leadership

The SAGE Handbook of Leadership

Second Edition

Edited by
Doris Schedlitzki, Magnus Larsson,
Brigid Carroll, Michelle C. Bligh
and Olga Epitropaki

SAGE

Los Angeles | London | New Delhi
Singapore | Washington DC | Melbourne

SAGE Publications Ltd
1 Oliver's Yard
55 City Road
London EC1Y 1SP

SAGE Publications Inc.
2455 Teller Road
Thousand Oaks, California 91320

SAGE Publications India Pvt Ltd
B 1/I 1 Mohan Cooperative Industrial Area
Mathura Road
New Delhi 110 044

SAGE Publications Asia-Pacific Pte Ltd
3 Church Street
#10-04 Samsung Hub
Singapore 049483

Editor: Ruth Stitt
Assistant Editor: Jessica Moran
Production Editor: Zoheb Khan
Copyeditor: Joy Tucker
Proofreader: Genevieve Friar
Indexer: KnowledgeWorks Global Ltd
Marketing Manager: Alison Borg
Cover Design: Ginkhan Siam
Typeset by KnowledgeWorks Global Ltd
Printed in the UK

At SAGE we take sustainability seriously. Most of our products are printed in the UK using responsibly sourced papers and boards. When we print overseas we ensure sustainable papers are used as measured by the PREPS grading system. We undertake an annual audit to monitor our sustainability.

Editorial Arrangement and Introduction © Michelle C. Bligh, Brigid Carroll, Olga Epitropaki, Magnus Larsson and Doris Schedlitzki, 2023

Chapter 1 © Jean-Louis Denis, Nancy Côté, Élizabeth Côté-Boileau, 2023
Chapter 2 © Lucia Crevani, Inti J. Lammi, 2023
Chapter 3 © Magnus Larsson, Frank Meier, 2023
Chapter 4 © Catherine R. Holt, Allan Lee, 2023
Chapter 5 © Daan van Knippenberg, 2023
Chapter 6 © Birgit Schyns, Gretchen Vogelgesang Lester, 2023
Chapter 7 © Joshua Pearman, Emily Gerkin, Dorothy R. Carter, 2023
Chapter 8 © Teresa Almeida, Nelson Campos Ramalho, Francisco Esteves, 2023
Chapter 9 © Reinout E. de Vries, Jan L. Pletzer, Amanda M. Julian, Kimberley Breevaart, 2023
Chapter 10 © Olga Epitropaki, Bryan P. Acton, Karolina W. Nieberle, 2023
Chapter 11 © Ashlea C. Troth, Peter J. Jordan, Neal M. Ashkanasy, 2023
Chapter 12 © Marian Iszatt-White, 2023
Chapter 13 © Jay A. Conger, 2023
Chapter 14 © David V. Day, Darja Kragt, 2023
Chapter 15 © Yiannis Gabriel, 2023
Chapter 16 © H. A. Martinez, Richard E. Boyatzis, 2023
Chapter 17 © Joanne B. Ciulla, 2023
Chapter 18 © Brad Jackson, Steve Kempster; Chaturi Liyanage, Sudong Shang, Peter Y. T. Sun, 2023
Chapter 19 © Marianna Delegach, Ronit Kark, Dina Van Dijk, 2023
Chapter 20 © Jackie Ford, Julia Morgan, 2023
Chapter 21 © Viviane Sergi, 2023
Chapter 22 © Donna Ladkin, 2023
Chapter 23 © Simon Kelly, 2023
Chapter 24 © Owain Smolović-Jones, David Hollis, 2023
Chapter 25 © Chellie Spiller, Amber Nicholson, 2023
Chapter 26 © Suze Wilson, 2023
Chapter 27 © Kent K. Alipour, Susan Mohammed, 2023
Chapter 28 © Martyna Śliwa, 2023
Chapter 29 © Burak Oc, Joseph A. Carpini, 2023
Chapter 30 © Stephen Allen, Dermot O'Reilly, 2023
Chapter 31 © Vanessa Iwowo, Peter Case, Samantha Iwowo, 2023
Chapter 32 © Stewart Clegg, Ace V. Simpson, Miguel Pina e Cunha, Arménio Rego, 2023
Chapter 33 © Ralph Bathurst, Michelle Sitong Chen, 2023
Chapter 34 © Brigitte Biehl, Suvi Satama, 2023
Chapter 35 © Lester Levy, Kevin B. Lowe, 2023
Chapter 36 © Laura G. Lunsford, Art Padilla, 2023
Chapter 37 © Mats Alvesson, Martin Blom, Thomas Fischer, 2023
Chapter 38 © Jennifer L. Sparr, David A. Waldman, Eric Kearney, 2023
Chapter 39 © Gail T. Fairhurst, David Collinson, 2023
Chapter 40 © Leah Tomkins, 2023
Chapter 41 © Celina McEwen, Alison Pullen, Carl Rhodes, 2023
Chapter 42 © Nancy Harding, 2023
Chapter 43 © Suzanne Gagnon, Wendy Cukier, Mohamed Elmi, 2023

Apart from any fair dealing for the purposes of research, private study, or criticism or review, as permitted under the Copyright, Designs and Patents Act, 1988, this publication may not be reproduced, stored or transmitted in any form, or by any means, without the prior permission in writing of the publisher, or in the case of reprographic reproduction, in accordance with the terms of licences issued by the Copyright Licensing Agency. Enquiries concerning reproduction outside those terms should be sent to the publisher.

Library of Congress Control Number: 2022951317

British Library Cataloguing in Publication data

A catalogue record for this book is available from the British Library

978-1-5297-6906-7

EDITORIAL ADVISORY BOARD

Stephen Kempster, Lancaster University, UK
Ronald Riggio, Clairemont McKenna College, USA
Leah Tomkins, The Open University, UK
Carole J. Elliott, Sheffield University, UK
Ralph Bathurst, Massey University, New Zealand
Gareth Edwards, University of the West of England, UK
Deanne den Hartog, University of Amsterdam, the Netherlands

Week 1 71-85   Oct 23-29
Week 2 203-214   Oct 30
Week 3 53-70   Nov 6
Week 5 136-150   Nov 20
Week 6 165-178   Nov 27

Contents

List of Figures and Tables xi
Notes on Editors and Contributors xiii
Introduction xxx

PART 1 BETWEEN: LEADERSHIP AS A SOCIAL, SOCIO-COGNITIVE AND PRACTICAL PHENOMENON

1 Pluralism in studies on plural leadership: Analysis and perspectives 3
   Jean-Louis Denis, Nancy Côté and Élizabeth Côté-Boileau

2 Leadership and practice theories: Reconstructing leadership as a phenomenon 16
   Lucia Crevani and Inti José Lammi

3 Leadership in interaction 28
   Magnus Larsson and Frank Meier

4 The quality of relationships: An exploration of current leader–member exchange (LMX) research and future possibilities 40
   Catherine R. Holt and Allan Lee

5 Embodying who we are: Social identity and leadership 52
   Daan van Knippenberg

6 Romance of leadership 63
   Birgit Schyns and Gretchen Vogelgesang Lester

7 What is 'functional' about distributed leadership in teams? 72
   Joshua Pearman, Emily Gerkin and Dorothy R. Carter

8 Followership 83
   Teresa Almeida, Nelson Campos Ramalho and Francisco Esteves

PART 2 ABOUT: EXPLORING THE INDIVIDUAL AND INTERPERSONAL FACETS OF LEADERSHIP

9 Leadership as contextualised personality traits 99
   Reinout E. de Vries, Jan L. Pletzer, Amanda M. Julian and Kimberley Breevaart

10 Implicit leadership and followership theories: From the leader/follower *within and between* to leaders/followers *in plural and in flux* 115
   Olga Epitropaki, Bryan P. Acton and Karolina W. Nieberle

11	Leadership, emotion regulation and sense-making *Ashlea C. Troth, Peter J. Jordan and Neal M. Ashkanasy*	129
12	Authentic leadership or authenticity in leadership? Finding a better home for our leadership aspirations *Marian Iszatt-White*	142
13	Redefining followership: Towards an expansive construct of the 'followers' of charismatic leaders in entrepreneurial organisations *Jay A. Conger*	154
14	Leadership development: Past, present and future *David V. Day and Darja Kragt*	164
15	Psychoanalytic approaches *Yiannis Gabriel*	178
16	Leadership beyond the leader to relationship quality *H. A. Martinez and Richard E. Boyatzis*	190
17	The myth of the passions: Reason, emotions and ethics in leadership *Joanne B. Ciulla*	202
18	Responsible leadership: From theory building to impact mobilisation *Brad Jackson, Steve Kempster, Chaturi Liyanage, Sudong Shang and Peter Y. T. Sun*	212
19	Self-regulatory focus and leadership: It's all about context *Marianna Delegach, Ronit Kark and Dina Van Dijk*	227

PART 3 THROUGH: LEADERSHIP SEEN THROUGH CONTEMPORARY FRAMES

20	Critiquing leadership and gender research through a feminist lens *Jackie Ford and Julia Morgan*	247
21	Problematising communication and providing inspiration: The potential of a CCO perspective for leadership studies *Viviane Sergi*	262
22	Leading as aesthetic and artful practice: It's not always pretty *Donna Ladkin*	274
23	Process theory approaches to leadership *Simon Kelly*	285
24	Technology and leadership *Owain Smolović Jones and David Hollis*	296
25	Indigenous leadership as a conscious adaptive system *Chellie Spiller and Amber Nicholson*	309

26	Leadership through history: Rethinking the present and future of leadership via a critical appreciation of its past *Suze Wilson*	322
27	Temporal considerations in leadership and followership *Kent K. Alipour and Susan Mohammed*	335
28	Rebuilding leadership theory through literature *Martyna Śliwa*	346

PART 4   WITHIN: LEADERSHIP AS A CONTEXTUALLY BOUND PHENOMENON

29	How and why is context important in leadership? *Burak Oc and Joseph A. Carpini*	359
30	Leadership within 'alternatives' *Stephen Allen and Dermot O'Reilly*	371
31	Leadership and culture *Vanessa Iwowo, Peter Case and Samantha Iwowo*	383
32	From 'leadership' to 'leading': Power relations, polyarchy and projects *Stewart Clegg, Ace V. Simpson, Miguel Pina e Cunha and Arménio Rego*	395
33	In defence of hesitant leadership: An ancient Chinese perspective *Ralph Bathurst and Michelle Sitong Chen*	406
34	Popular culture and leadership *Brigitte Biehl and Suvi Satama*	418
35	The impact of context on healthcare leadership *Lester Levy and Kevin B. Lowe*	432

PART 5   BUT: A CRITICAL EXAMINATION OF LEADERSHIP

36	On destructive leadership *Laura G. Lunsford and Art Padilla*	447
37	Leadership and its alternatives *Mats Alvesson, Martin Blom and Thomas Fischer*	459
38	Paradoxes in agentic and communal leadership *Jennifer L. Sparr, David A. Waldman and Eric Kearney*	471
39	Leadership dialectics *Gail T. Fairhurst and David L. Collinson*	484
40	Care and caring leadership: Positive attractions and critical asymmetries *Leah Tomkins*	498

| 41 | Politicising the leader's body: From oppressive realities to affective possibilities
Celina McEwen, Alison Pullen and Carl Rhodes | 509 |
| 42 | Leadership as (new) material(ities) practices: Intra-acting, diffracting and agential-cutting with Karen Barad
Nancy Harding | 521 |
| 43 | Leadership representation: A critical path to equity
Suzanne Gagnon, Wendy Cukier and Mohamed Elmi with acknowledgement to Tomke Augustin | 534 |

Index   548

List of Figures and Tables

FIGURES

Figure 1.1	Evolution of the number of scholarly publications on 'plural leadership' and related concepts, using Publish or Perish software and Google Scholar search (1969–2021).	4
Figure 8.1	Followership approached from a power-based perspective	84
Figure 8.2	Some followership assumptions and examples of topics to be addressed	84
Figure 8.3	Evolution of publications	85
Figure 10.1	*Web of Science* Core Collection search of the term 'implicit leadership theories' and 'implicit followership theories' in all fields (n = 479 and n = 79) records, respectively. 28 June 2021.	120
Figure 11.1	Publications listed in *Web of Science* that include 'Leader*' and 'Emotion*' in the title	130
Figure 11.2	Leaders' emotion regulation options and followers' interpretation of those options (adapted from Troth et al. 2018)	131
Figure 18.1	Theoretical Framework	216
Figure 18.2	Four-Level Model of Organisational Consciousness	221
Figure 19.1	Three organisational environmental contexts and leadership styles in the lens of regulatory focus theory	228
Figure 29.1	The effect of contextual factors on leadership and its four elements	361
Figure 34.1	Dance practice. Photographer: Sakari Viika	422
Figure 34.2	Charismatic leader (*Game of Thrones*, US, S08E08, 2019, HBO, YouTube)	423
Figure 34.3	Leadership and loneliness (*Game of Thrones*, US, S06E10, 2014, HBO, YouTube)	425
Figure 34.4	'Guilty of being a dwarf'. (GoT, USA, S04E06, 2014, HBO, YouTube)	425
Figure 34.5	A new role model @Lizzobeeating https://www.instagram.com/p/COGJr33MH7h/	428
Figure 37.1	The usefulness of leadership as a managerial response to subordinates' task related issues	467
Figure 38.1	The meta-paradox of agency and communion in leadership with examples of leader traits, orientations and behaviours	473
Figure 38.2	Model of 'both-and' leadership and followership	477
Figure 43.1	Overall representation on boards of directors across sectors	538

TABLES

Table 7.1	Exemplar findings from research on team leadership distribution across people, roles and time	74
Table 9.1	Descriptions and example items of the generic and contextualised HEXACO domains	104
Table 10.1	Guidelines for developing an agent-based model for studying the role of ILTs/IFTs	124

Table 12.1	Mapping of academic papers against evolutionary stages (2000–2021)	146
Table 12.2	Cultural orientations of lead authors for conceptual papers on AL (2000–2021)	147
Table 18.1	Studies addressing relationship between positive leadership styles and social outcomes	215
Table 27.1	Noteworthy temporal characteristics for leadership research (adapted from Alipour et al., 2017)	338
Table 29.1	Most commonly used study designs and measurement of contextual factors, along with presence of meta-analytic evidence	365
Table 30.1	Three lenses on types of organisations and social relations in contemporary society	373
Table 32.1	How power, leadership and designs co-evolve	396
Table 39.1	Dialectical leadership/followership empirical research	486
Table 43.1	Women on Boards and in CEO positions, 2020, world comparison	537

Notes on the Editors and Contributors

THE EDITORS

Doris Schedlitzki is Professor in Organisational Leadership at London Metropolitan University. Doris's main research focus is on leadership and explores the areas of cultural studies of leadership, discourse and leadership, leadership as identity, psychoanalytic approaches to leadership and the role of national language within cultural leadership studies. Recent publications include articles and special issues in *Leadership, Scandinavian Journal of Management, Management Learning, International Journal of Management Reviews, Human Relations, International Journal of Management Education*, as well as a textbook on leadership entitled *Studying Leadership: Traditional and Critical Approaches* (2013, currently in its third edition) and an edited book on *Worldly Leadership* (2012).

Magnus Larsson is Senior Lecturer at the Department of Business Administration, Lund University School of Economics and Management, Sweden. His main research focus is leadership and leadership development, particularly from organisational and interactional perspectives. Recent publications include articles and special issues in *Leadership, Human Relations, Management Learning, International Journal of Business Communication, Journal of Management Development*, as well as textbook chapters and a chapter on 'Leadership in interaction' in *The Routledge Companion to Leadership* (2016).

Brigid Carroll is a Professor in the Department of Management and International Business and holds the Fletcher Building Employee Educational Fund Chair in Leadership at the University of Auckland in New Zealand. She teaches broadly in the area of leadership, organisational theory and qualitative research methods at undergraduate, postgraduate and executive level and does extensive cross-sector leadership development work with corporate, community, professional and youth organisations. Ongoing research themes revolve around identity work, power, responsibility and resistance, leadership development, distributed and collective leadership, cross-system governance and discursive/narrative approaches. Ultimately Brigid is interested in leadership as a discourse, identity and practice and in exploring how it is constructed and shaped between people, spaces and artefacts in different organisational contexts. She has published in *Organization Studies, Human Relations, Academy of Management Learning and Education, Management Learning* and *Leadership* and has co-edited three books on leadership.

Michelle C. Bligh is Dean of the School of Social Science, Policy, and Evaluation and a Professor of Organizational Behavior at Claremont Graduate University in Claremont, California. Her research interests focus on charismatic leadership, gender, interpersonal influence and followership. She has been published in over two dozen academic journals, and she was recognised by *Leadership Quarterly* as one of the top-50 most cited authors of the last decade. She also serves on the editorial review boards of *Leadership Quarterly* and *Group and Organization Management* and as Associate Editor of Leadership. Dr Bligh has taught leadership and change management around the globe, including Europe, Asia, North

America and Latin America. She regularly consults with organisations in the areas of leadership development, followership, organisational culture and change management in a variety of industries, including law enforcement, finance, healthcare and real estate.

Olga Epitropaki is Professor of Management and Deputy Executive Dean (Research) at Durham University Business School. Her research interests include implicit leadership theories, leader–member exchanges, creative leadership and leader identity. Her research has been published in top refereed journals, such as the *Academy of Management Annals*, *Journal of Applied Psychology*, *Personnel Psychology*, *Journal of Management*, *Leadership Quarterly*, and *Journal of Organizational Behavior*, among others. She is Senior Associate Editor of *Leadership Quarterly* and a member of several editorial boards. She has an edited book *Creative Leadership: Prospects and Contexts* (2018) and is Series Editor of Contemporary Perspectives on Relationship-based Leadership (IAP). She is the founder and organiser of the annual Interdisciplinary Perspectives in Leadership symposium (www.leadership-symposium.com).

THE CONTRIBUTORS

Bryan Acton is an Assistant Professor of Leadership/Organizational Behavior at Binghamton University School of Management. His research has been published in top refereed journals, such as Leadership Quarterly and Journal of Business and Psychology. His research expertise relates to studying the process of how collective leadership emerges in groups, as well as improving the measurement of leadership. He also has expertise in advanced quantitative methodologies, including agent-based computational modelling, as well as advanced statistical modelling such as machine learning. In addition to research interests, Bryan has a passion for the R statistical programming language; he teaches workshops on how to build tools and applications for research using R.

Stephen Allen is Lecturer in Organisation Studies at the University of Sheffield. By working at the intersections of ideas about sustainability, reflexivity and leadership his interdisciplinary research explores how people make sense of and attempt to organise for socio-ecological sustainabilities. He has published articles in *British Journal of Management*, *Management Learning* and *Scandinavian Journal of Management*, among others. His recently published book *Being and Organizing in an Entangled World: Sociomateriality and Posthumanism* is available open access from MayFly Books.

Kent K. Alipour is an Assistant Professor of Management at East Carolina University. His research focuses on leadership and teams, adopting a multilevel lens. Dr Alipour is passionate about utilising research to solve organisations' real-world problems. He earnt his doctorate in industrial-organisational psychology from Pennsylvania State University.

Teresa Almeida is an Invited Assistant Professor at ISCTE Business School in Portugal, and Researcher at the Business Research Unit, IUL. Teresa has been developing research focused on organisational leaders and followers. She is particularly interested in studying followers' profiles and resistance mechanisms that may help organisations curb destructive leadership processes. Her research interests also include the study of human reactions to artificial intelligence decision-making systems.

Mats Alvesson works at Lund University and Stockholm School of Economics. He has done much research on identity, leadership, power, organisational culture, managerial work, functional stupidity, wilful ignorance, qualitative method etc. Recent books include *The Triumph of Emptiness* (2022), *Re-imagining the Research Process* (2021, with J. Sandberg), *Reflexive Leadership* (2016, with Martin Blom and Stefan Sveningsson), *The Stupidity Paradox* (2016, with André Spicer), *Managerial Lives* (2016, with Stefan Sveningsson).

NOTES ON THE EDITORS AND CONTRIBUTORS

Neal M. Ashkanasy OAM, PhD is Professor of Management in the UQ Business School at the University of Queensland, Australia, where he graduated with a PhD in 1989. He studies emotion in organisations, leadership, culture, ethical and sustainable behaviour, and the physical environment of work. He has published in journals such as the *Academy of Management Journal and Review*, *Journal of Management* and *Journal of Applied Psychology*. He served as Editor-in-Chief of the *Journal of Organizational Behavior*, Associate Editor for the *Academy of Management Review* and *Academy of Management Learning and Education*.

Tomke Jerena Augustin is a Postdoctoral Fellow at the Asper School of Business, University of Manitoba, Winnipeg, Canada. Dr Augustin earnt her PhD from the School of Business and Economics, University of Tübingen, Germany, in 2020 and was international graduate trainee at McGill University, Montreal, Canada. Her research considers multilingual and multicultural individuals, equity, diversity and inclusion in organisations, social innovation and entrepreneurship. She was a finalist for the Best Paper Award of the Academy of Management Annual Meeting 2020, and regularly presents her work at the Academy of International Business and the European Group for Organizational Studies.

Ralph J. Bathurst lectures in management and leadership at Massey University's Albany Campus, New Zealand. His research in the aesthetics of leadership focuses on music performance and composition. This and other arts inform his interests in sustainability and corporate social responsibility, as well as Chinese philosophy and what we can learn from ancient texts today.

Brigitte Biehl (Biehl-Missal) is Professor for Media and Communication Management in the School of Popular Arts, SRH Berlin University of Applied Sciences, Germany. She was Guest Professor for Gender and Queer Studies in Leadership at the Faculty of Business Administration and Economics, FernUniversität in Hagen, Germany, and continues working there as a researcher. She is the director of the SRH institute 'Institut für Weiterbildung in der Kreativwirtschaft IWK' which applies experiential learning methods for professional development. She is widely published on aesthetics, art and leadership. Her contributions appeared in *Gender, Work and Organization*, *Journal of Management Studies*, *Management Learning* and *Culture and Organization*. She has written five books, including *Dance and Organization* (2017) and, most recently, *Leadership in Game of Thrones* (2021).

Martin Blom is an Associate Professor in Strategic Management at Lund University School of Economics and Management, Sweden. His research is primarily centred around corporate governance, leadership/followership and strategy. Recent publications appear in journals such as *Human Relations*, *Corporate Governance: An International Review* and *Leadership*.

Richard E. Boyatzis is Distinguished University Professor of Case Western Reserve University in the departments of Organizational Behavior, Psychology and Cognitive Science, OH. He has a BS in Aeronautics and Astronautics from MIT and PhD in Social Psychology from Harvard. His more than 200 scholarly and 50 practitioner articles examine sustained, desired change on leadership, competencies, emotional intelligence, competency development, coaching, neuroscience and management education. His Coursera MOOCs have over 1.5 million visitors, enrolled from 215 countries. His nine books include: the international bestseller *Primal Leadership* (2001, with Daniel Goleman and Annie McKee) and *Helping People Change* (2019, with Melvin Smith and Ellen Van Oosten).

Kimberley Breevaart is an Associate Professor of Organisational Psychology at the Erasmus University Rotterdam in the Netherlands. Her main research topic is leadership: she studies destructive leadership, day-to-day leadership and the relations between personality, leadership, work engagement and burnout. She recently published *The Barriers Model of Abusive Supervision* (2021), in which she and her co-authors outline the most important barriers that prevents victims of abusive supervision from escaping. She is Section Editor at *Stress and Health*, and she is on the editorial board of *Organizational Psychology Review* and *European Journal of Work and Organizational Psychology*.

Joseph A. Carpini is a Lecturer of Organisational Behaviour and Human Resource Management at the University of Western Australia, Business School. His research interests rest at the intersection of individual work performance and mental health. Specifically, his research examines the antecedents and consequences of different forms of work performance and employee mental health. His work has been published in the *Academy of Management Annals*, as well as multidisciplinary outlets including *BMJ Open* and *Early Interventions in Psychiatry*. He is an award-winning researcher and educator, passionate about improving workplaces through evidence-based practice.

Dorothy R. Carter (PhD, Georgia Institute of Technology, 2016) is an Associate Professor of Organizational Psychology at Michigan State University. She directs the Leadership, Innovation, Networks, and Collaboration (LINC) Laboratory. The LINC Lab investigates the factors underpinning the effectiveness of teams and larger organisational systems working in contexts such as the military, medicine, scientific collaboration and space exploration. Dr Carter's research has appeared in a variety of top outlets including *Journal of Applied Psychology*, *Journal of Management*, *American Psychologist* and *Leadership Quarterly*. Her programme of research is funded by the National Science Foundation, the Army Research Institute, the National Institutes of Health and the National Aeronautics and Space Administration.

Peter Case is Professor of Organisation Studies, Bristol Business School, University of the West of England, and also holds a part-time chair at the College of Business, Law and Governance, James Cook University, Australia. His research encompasses leadership studies, organisation development, international development and global health. For the past nine years Peter has acted as a programme management consultant for the Bill and Melinda Gates Foundation-funded Malaria Elimination Initiative, advising on projects in sub-Saharan Africa and the Greater Mekong Sub-region. Peter has published widely in the fields of leadership studies, organisation studies, international development and global health.

Michelle Sitong Chen is a Lecturer in Sustainability at the University of Auckland Business School, New Zealand. She has worked as a lecturer and senior tutor over the past six years across New Zealand tertiary institutions such as Massey University, Unitec Institute of Technology and Whitireia and Wellington Institute of Technology. Her PhD research is about helping Chinese and New Zealand organisations in managing tensions arising from sustainability.

Joanne B. Ciulla is Professor of Leadership Ethics, Director of the Institute for Ethical Leadership at Rutgers Business School, NJ, and Professor Emerita of the Jepson School of Leadership Studies, University of Richmond. She has held the UNESCO Chair in Leadership Studies and been a visiting professor in the Netherlands, United Kingdom, South Africa and Australia. A philosopher by training, Ciulla has published extensively on ethics in leadership and business. She is the recipient of Lifetime Achievement Awards for her scholarship from the International Leadership Association and the Society for Business Ethics and received the Eminent Scholar Award from the Network of Leadership Scholars. She is a past president of the International Society of Business, Ethics and Economics and the Society for Business Ethics. Ciulla serves on the *Business Ethics Quarterly*, *Leadership Quarterly* and *Leadership* boards.

Stewart Clegg is a Professor at the University of Sydney School of Project Management and the John Grill Institute for Project Leadership as well as being an Emeritus Professor at the University of Technology Sydney. He currently holds visiting positions at the University of Stavanger Business School, Norway; Nova School of Business and Economics, Carcavelos, Portugal. He is a leading authority on power relations but has published widely on many topics, usually with an interest in power relations.

David L. Collinson is Distinguished Professor of Leadership and Organisation at Lancaster University Management School. Previously at the universities of Manchester, Warwick, St Andrews and South Florida, he is the Founding Co-Editor of the *Leadership* journal and Founding Co-Organiser of the International Studying Leadership Conference (both with K. Grint). David's publications focus on critical approaches to leadership, management and organisation. His primary research interests explore leadership and followership dialectics; power, identities and insecurities; gender, men and masculinities; conformity, dramaturgy and resistance; and humour, positivity and Prozac leadership. He has published 13 books and over 100 articles and chapters in journals and books, including *Organization Studies*, *Human Relations*, *Journal of Management Studies*, *Work, Employment and Society*, *Organization*, *Gender, Work and Organization*, *Leadership* and *Leadership Quarterly*.

Jay A. Conger is the Henry R. Kravis Chaired Professor of Leadership Studies at Claremont McKenna College, CA. Author of 15 books and over 100 articles and book chapters, he researches charismatic leadership, influence, executive leadership, boards of directors, organisational change, empowerment and the training and development of leaders. His most recent book *The High Potential's Advantage* (1998) describes the distinguishing characteristics of high-potential leadership talent. His most notable book on charismatic leadership is entitled *Charismatic Leadership in Organizations* (1998, co-authored with Rabindra Kanungo). He is the co-author of the Conger-Kanungo Scale of Charismatic Leadership, a widely used assessment for research on the topic.

Nancy Côté is Associate Professor in the Department of Sociology at Université Laval, Quebec, Canada, and FRQS Research Scholar and member of VITAM, a sustainable health research centre where she co-leads the research axis on environment and health. She holds a doctorate in Applied Human Sciences from the University of Montreal, Canada. Her work is at the crossroads of the sociology of work, professions and organisations. Her current research focuses on the transformations of healthcare organisations and their effects on the work experience of professionals and managers in this sector. She is particularly interested in governance and leadership, new modes of collaboration and redefinition of professional roles in health systems and organisations. She has developed an expertise in research conducted in partnership with healthcare organisations.

Élizabeth Côté-Boileau is Assistant Professor in Management and Strategy at the Department of Health Management, Evaluation and Policy, School of Public Health (ESPUM), University of Montreal, Quebec, Canada, and Researcher at the Research Center for Public Health (CReSP). Her research mainly focuses on health systems reforms, with a particular interest in changes in governance, leadership and accountability. She conducts interdisciplinary qualitative research that combines health sciences, social studies and organization theories. Her most recent publications have appeared in the Journal of Health Organization and Management, Health Policy, Health Economics, Policy and Law and the International Journal of Health Policy and Management.

Lucia Crevani is Professor in Business Administration with specialisation in Organization and Leadership, Editor (Leadership) of *Journal of Change Management: Reframing Leadership and Organizational Practice* and Director of Research for Industrial Economics and Organization at Mälardalen University, Sweden, where she is a member of the NOMP research group. What fascinates her is the everyday practices and interactions that make organisational processes develop in certain ways. She thus focuses on developing the leadership as practice stream of research and contributing to processual understandings of organising and place, as well as of organisational change and technology. Her ambition is also to contribute to increased inclusion and justice in organising practices.

Wendy Cukier is Founder of the Diversity Institute at Toronto Metropolitan University, Research Lead of the Future Skills Centre of Canada and Academic Director of the national Women Entrepreneurship Knowledge Hub. She is the co-author of the bestseller, *Innovation Nation: Canadian Leadership from Java to Jurassic Park* (2002) and former vice-president of Research and Innovation at Toronto Metropolitan University. Dr Cukier is one of Canada's leading experts in disruptive technologies, innovation processes, the skills gap, and future skills and their critical intersections with diversity and inclusion. She has more than 200 published papers. She is the principal investigator on many successful grants in support of research to advance theory as well as policy outcomes to drive equality in Canada. She serves on a host of boards in the private and non-profit sectors.

Miguel Pina e Cunha is the Fundação Amélia de Mello Professor at Nova School of Business and Economics. His research focuses mainly on organisation as positive and paradoxical. He recently co-authored *Positive Organizational Behavior* (2020) and *Paradoxes of Power and Leadership* (2021).

David V. Day holds appointments as Professor of Psychological Science, Steven L. Eggert '82 P'15 Professor of Leadership and Academic Director of the Kravis Leadership Institute at Claremont McKenna College, CA. Day is a Fellow of the American Psychological Association, Association for Psychological Science, International Association of Applied Psychology and the Society for Industrial and Organizational Psychology. He has published more than 100 peer-reviewed journal articles, books and book chapters, many pertaining to the core topics of leadership and leadership development. In 2010 he received the Walter F. Ulmer Research Award from the Center for Creative Leadership for outstanding, career-long contributions to applied leadership research.

Reinout E. de Vries is Full Professor in the department of Experimental and Applied Psychology at the Vrije Universiteit Amsterdam. His main research interests are in the areas of personality, communication styles and leadership at work. Recent work focuses on the Situation-Trait-Outcome Activation (STOA) model, Three Nightmare Traits (TNT) and the automatic assessment of personality. Instruments that he has constructed or co-developed, such as the Dutch translation of the HEXACO-PI-R, the six-dimensional Communication Styles Inventory (CSI), the Brief HEXACO personality Inventory (BHI) and the Circumplex Leadership Scan (CLS) are widely used in academia and practice. More information and publications of Reinout de Vries can be obtained through the Vrije Universiteit Amsterdam website, Google Scholar and/or ResearchGate.

Marianna Delegach is a Senior Lecturer of Organizational Psychology at Sapir Academic College, Israel. Marianna received her PhD in Organizational and Social Psychology from Bar-Ilan University and had experience as an organisational consultant with private and public organisations sectors. Marianna's research focuses on employees' motivation and organisational leadership. She has published her research in scholarly journals, including *Academy of Management Discoveries*, *Journal of Applied Psychology*, *European Journal of Work and Organizational Psychology*, *Human Resource Development Review* and *International Journal of Stress Management*.

Jean-Louis Denis is Full Professor in Health Policy and Management, School of Public Health (ESPUM), University of Montreal, Quebec, Canada, Researcher at the University of Montreal Hospital Research Centre (CRCHUM) and Research Fellow at the Centre de recherché en droit public (CRDP). He holds the Canada Research Chair (Tier 1) on design and adaptation of health systems. His research programme is located at the intersection of applied health services research, organisational studies and policy research. Dr Denis is a Member of the Academy of Social Sciences of the Royal Society of Canada (2002), Fellow of the Canadian Academy of Health Sciences (2009) and Fellow of the UK Academy of Social Sciences (2019). His work has been published in journals like *Milbank Quarterly*, *Implementation Science*, *Journal of Health Politics, Policy and Law*, *Human Relations*, *Organization Science*, *Public Administration*, *Journal of Public Administration Research and Theory* and *Academy of Management Annals*. He is co-editor of the Organizational Behaviour in Healthcare series at Palgrave.

Dina Van Dijk is an Associate Professor of Organizational Behavior (OB) at the Department of Health Systems Management, the Faculty of Health Sciences and the Guilford-Glaser Faculty of Business and Management at Ben-Gurion University of the Negev, Israel. She received her PhD from the School of Business Administration of the Hebrew University. Her main area of research is work motivation; she is interested specifically in the role that self-regulatory focus plays in various organisational phenomena, such as leadership, feedback interventions, health behaviours and employees' well-being. Dina's work has been published in top OB journals such as *Academy of Management Review*, *Academy of Management Annals* and *Journal of Organizational Behavior*.

Mohamed Elmi is the Acting Executive Director at the Diversity Institute, Toronto Metropolitan University, Canada. The Diversity Institute conducts and coordinates multidisciplinary, multi-stakeholder research to address the needs of diverse Canadians, the changing nature of skills and competencies, and the policies, processes and tools that advance economic inclusion and success. Dr Elmi has several journal articles and other publications in these and related areas. He holds a PhD in Information Systems from the University of Cape Town. Prior to this, Dr Elmi completed his MA thesis in International Development Studies at Saint Mary's University in Halifax, Nova Scotia, and a BA (Hons) in Political Science from the University of New Brunswick.

Olga Epitropaki is Professor of Management and Deputy Executive Dean (Research) at Durham University Business School. Her research interests include implicit leadership theories, leader–member exchanges, creative leadership and leader identity. Her research has been published in top refereed journals, such as *Academy of Management Annals*, *Journal of Applied Psychology*, *Personnel Psychology*, *Journal of Management*, *Leadership Quarterly* and *Journal of Organizational Behavior*, among others. She is Senior Associate Editor of *Leadership Quarterly* and a member of several editorial boards. She is the founder and organiser of the annual Interdisciplinary Perspectives in Leadership symposium (www.leadership-symposium.com).

Francisco Esteves is a Visiting Professor at the Faculty of Human Sciences, Catholic University of Portugal, in Lisbon, and Senior Professor at the Department of Psychology and Social Work, Mid Sweden University, Östersund, Sweden. He is the coordinator of the international PhD programme in Emotion Psychology at the Catholic University of Portugal. Francisco's main research interests have been the study of emotional processing and the relationship between cognitive and emotional components of human information processing – in particular, research in clinical psychology (mainly related to anxiety and eating disorders) and psychology in the workplace and economy (e.g., decision-making and leadership).

Gail T. Fairhurst is a Distinguished University Research Professor of Organizational Communication at the University of Cincinnati, USA. She specialises in organisational and leadership communication processes, including those involving paradox, dialectics, problem-centred leadership and framing. She is the author of three books, including *Discursive Leadership: In Conversation with Leadership Psychology* (2007) and the forthcoming, *Organizational Paradoxes: A Constitutive Approach* (with L. Putnam). She has also published over 90 articles and chapters in management and communication journals and books, including *Academy of Management Annals*, *Academy of Management Journal*, *Academy of Management Review*, *Organization Science*, *Organization Studies*, *Human Relations* and *Management Communication Quarterly*. She is a Fellow of the International Communication Association, Distinguished Scholar of the National Communication Association and Fulbright Scholar.

Thomas Fischer is Assistant Professor of Responsible Leadership at the University of Geneva. His research focuses mostly on the conceptualisation and measurement of leadership styles as well as on how managers talk about their leadership. His work has been published in the *Journal of Management* and *Leadership Quarterly*.

Jackie Ford is Professor of Leadership and Organisation Studies at Durham University Business School. Her research interests include critical feminist, psychosocial and interdisciplinary approaches that recognise specific gender, wider diversity and ethical dimensions, and ways in which leadership and management research and practice impact on working lives and identities. She has co-authored a monograph on leadership and co-edited a textbook on critical leadership studies and has published in a range of scholarly journals including *British Journal of Management*, *Human Relations*, *Journal of Management Studies*, *Leadership*, *Management Learning*, *Organization*, *Organization Studies*, *Sociology* and *Work Employment and Society*.

Yiannis Gabriel is Emeritus Professor at the University of Bath, where he held a Chair in Organisational Theory. Earlier, he held chairs at Imperial College and Royal Holloway, University of London. Yiannis is known for his work into leadership, management learning, organisational storytelling and narratives, psychoanalytic studies of work, and the culture and politics of contemporary consumption. He is the author of ten books, numerous articles and maintains an active blog in which he discusses music, storytelling, books, cooking, pedagogy and research outside the constraints of academic publishing (www.yiannisgabriel.com/). Recently, he has been developing the concept of narrative ecology and writing about conspiracy theories and nostalgia as elements of post-truth political cultures. His enduring fascination as a researcher and educator lies in what he describes as the unmanaged and unmanageable qualities of life in and out of organisations. His most recent book is *Music and Story: A Two-Part Invention* (2022).

Suzanne Gagnon is Associate Professor, Canada Life Chair, and Associate Dean, Professional Graduate Programs, at the Asper School of Business, University of Manitoba, Canada. Her research focuses on identity, inclusion, power and leadership in private and public sector organisations, gender and entrepreneurship, and strategic change. Her work is published in leading management and organisation journals. She sits on the editorial boards of *Organization Studies*, *Leadership* and *Management Learning*. Dr Gagnon holds several competitive grants for her work including from the Social Sciences and Humanities Research Council of Canada. She is a member of the National Advisory Board for the Women Entrepreneurship Knowledge Hub. She joined the Asper School from McGill University where she was a faculty member for 14 years. She holds a PhD from Lancaster University and an MSc from Oxford University.

Emily Gerkin is pursuing her PhD in the Organizational Psychology Program at Michigan State University. Her research focuses on leadership, team and multi-team system effectiveness. Her graduate education is supported by funding from the National Aeronautics and Space Administration and the Army Research Institute. Emily earnt her BA in Psychology at the University of St Thomas, MN, and her MS in Industrial-Organizational Psychology at the University of Georgia.

Nancy Harding is Professor of Human Resource Management at University of Bath's School of Management, an unfortunate job title for someone who is against management, loathes the idea that people are 'resources' but is interested in 'the human'. After working first as a typist and on factory production lines she became a mature student, got addicted to academia and is still there 40 years later. Her research and teaching focus on critical approaches to understanding organisations, with a particular interest is working lives. She has published papers in many of the expected academic journals, has written two sole-authored books, with a third planned but long delayed, and has co-authored three books. Her greatest accolade to date came from her grandsons, who used to think that she was 'amazing'. Now grown, they are far more discriminating and no longer think she walks on water.

David Hollis is a Lecturer in Organization Studies at Sheffield University Management School. His research is largely ethnographic and utilizes Communication as Constitutive of Organization (CCO) and other performativity perspectives to show how seemingly innocuous everyday practices and discourses become exploitative. David's research has been published in Organization Studies and De Gruyter Mouton's Handbook of Management Communication.

Catherine R. Holt is a PhD candidate and Research Assistant at the University of Exeter Business School. Her research focuses on leadership and specifically examines leader–follower relationships through mixed methodologies. Her background is in sociolinguistics, and she is particularly interested in introducing more discursive approaches to the study of management.

Marian Iszatt-White is a Senior Lecturer in Leadership at Lancaster University Management School. She received her PhD from Lancaster University in 2006, under the auspices of the Centre for Excellence in Leadership. Her research interests revolve around the practice turn in leadership and its implications for 'aspirational' forms of leadership (such as authentic leadership) and leadership development. Her recent research has utilised leadership as emotional labour as a lens for critiquing the authentic leadership (AL) construct and in 2020 she published a review of the AL literature in the *International Journal of Management Reviews*. Marian has published four books, including a postgraduate leadership textbook (now in its third edition) and an edited volume on leadership as emotional labour. She serves on the editorial boards of *Management Learning* and the *Journal of Management Studies*, is an Associate Editor for *Leadership* and is Co-Editor-in-Chief of the *International Journal of Management Reviews*.

Samantha Iwowo is Principal Academic in Film and Directing at Bournemouth University. Her research straddles the fields of film and postcolonial critique, with particular interests in film studies and practice, viewed through a postcolonial reader. Drawing on Bhabha's notions of 'mimicry', 'sly civility' and Saidian Orientalism, her doctoral thesis unearthed problematic vestiges of the Colonial Film Unit in neo-Nollywood and contributes to the development of conceptual knowledge frameworks for the advancement of African film and transnational cinema. She is also a director who commenced her career as a commissioned screenwriter with South Africa's largest cable network, M-Net; from 2013–14 she wrote several episodes of the daily drama series *Tinsel* (2008–present). She has published 50 screenplays, including the internationally celebrated feature *Oloibiri* (2016) which premiered at the Cannes Film Festival. Her most recent film, *The Tyrant* (forthcoming) takes a pertinent view on African leadership and is a biopic on Zimbabwean dictator Robert Mugabe. She has directed four films.

Vanessa Iwowo is Assistant Professor in Organisational Psychology at Birkbeck, University of London and Visiting Senior Fellow to the LSE Firoz Lalji Institute for Africa, where she leads on the Programme for African Leadership (PfAL). Her research focuses on ways of enhancing leadership development in cross-cultural contexts with a particular interest in Africa. Her interests lie in the critical study of processes, interactions and power relationships through which knowledge is generated and disseminated, particularly in the fields of leadership development and management education. Her work in critical leadership studies has received recognition in the form of several awards including Academy of Management (AoM) CMS Best Dissertation Prize, the Emerald Literati Award for Excellence *Highly Commended Paper* and the AoM Best Critical Paper. She is a recipient of the British Academy/Leverhulme Trust Fellowship awarded for her research on gender and leadership development in Africa.

Brad Jackson is Professor of Leadership and Governance at the University of Waikato Management School/Te Raupapa, New Zealand. He serves as the Programme Director for the Waikato-based Community and Enterprise Leadership Foundation (CELF) programme. Brad has co-authored seven leadership books, including *A Very Short, Fairly Interesting and Quite Cheap Book About Studying Leadership* (2007), and co-edited two others including the first edition of *The SAGE Handbook of Leadership* (2011). Brad's current research explores the inter-relationship between leadership and governance practices in promoting and sustaining social and economic innovation and the application of place-based approaches to foster cross-sectoral leadership development and education.

Peter J. Jordan is a Professor of Organizsational Behaviour at the Griffith Business School, Griffith University, Australia. Peter has published in leading international journals including the *Academy of Management Review*, *Journal of Organizational Behavior*, *Human Relations* and *Leadership Quarterly*. He has also been awarded grant funding for his research from the Australian Research Council. Peter is on the editorial board of a number of journals. His current research interests include emotional intelligence, discrete emotions in organisations, leadership and teams, and employee entitlement in organisations. Prior to working at Griffith University, he worked for the federal government in strategic and operational planning.

Amanda Julian is the Chief Research Officer at Monark, in Calgary, AB, Canada. She holds a PhD in Industrial-Organizational Psychology from the University of Calgary and has experience working with client organisations to deliver leadership assessment and development solutions, primarily at the executive level. In her current role at Monark, she is responsible for overseeing the development of a leadership training platform, leveraging technology to scale leadership development to all levels of an organisation. She has previously published research in the area of personality; including topics such as personality measurement, and relations among personality traits and work-related variables, such as employee compensation preferences.

Ronit Kark is a Full Professor of Leadership and Organizational Psychology in the Department of Psychology at Bar-Ilan University, Israel, and was the founder and former director of the Gender in the Field Graduate Program. She is also Faculty at the University of Exeter Business School and an affiliated scholar at the Center for Gender in Organizations at Simmons College, Boston. She received her PhD from the Hebrew University of Jerusalem and completed her postdoctoral studies at the University of Michigan. Her research interests include leadership and followership, positive relationships, identity and identification processes, gender and leadership, and leading for creativity. Her work has been published in leading journals including: *Academy of Management Review*, *Academy of Management Annals*, *Academy of Management Discoveries*, *Leadership Quarterly*, *Journal of Applied Psychology*, *Journal of Occupational and Organizational Psychology*, *Journal of Organizational Behavior*, *Organization* and *Academy of Management Learning and Eductaion*. Professor Kark is an Associate Editor at the *Leadership Quarterly* and also has served on the editorial boards of *Academy of Management Review*, *Academy of Management Journal*, *Academy of Management Discoveries*, *Frontiers in Psychology* and *International Journal of Management Reviews*. She has been awarded several prestigious prizes for her work.

Eric Kearney is a Professor of Organisational Behaviour at the University of Potsdam, Germany. He received his doctorate degree in Management from the TU Berlin and he has taught at universities and business schools in Europe, the US, South America and China. His main research interests are leadership and teamwork. His work has examined, for example, the effects of visionary and empowering leadership behaviours and of team diversity, respectively. His work has been published in leading outlets including the *Academy of Management Journal*, *Journal of Applied Psychology*, *Organization Science*, *Leadership Quarterly*, and *Organizational Behavior and Human Decision Processes*.

Simon Kelly is Senior Lecturer at University of Huddersfield, where he researches and teaches in the areas of leadership, ethics and organisation studies. His research explores the relationship between leadership and notions of the heroic to consider the intellectual, practical and ethical potential of rethinking leadership as shared collective action. Simon's research has been published in academic journals including *Human Relations*, *Organization*, *Journal of Business Ethics*, *Leadership* and *Gender, Work and Organization*.

Steve Kempster is Professor of Leadership Learning and Development at Lancaster University Management School and is an Associate Partner of the Regenerative Alliance. He has published broadly on leadership learning, leadership of purpose and responsible leadership, including five books and many articles and chapters. Steve leads the Good Dividends project (www.gooddividends.com) – formed from an interdisciplinary group of academics drawn from five universities in Europe and Australasia – with the objective of enabling business leaders to develop their business models towards realising 'good dividends' and becoming regenerative. His latest book is *Good Dividends: Responsible Leadership of Business Purpose* (2019, with Thomas Maak and Ken Parry).

Darja Kragt is a Lecturer in Work Psychology at the University of Western Australia School of Psychological Science. Her research is focused in investigating the role of identity in leadership and leadership development. Her research has been published in several high-quality, peer-reviewed journals. Darja is particularly interested in understating the effect of explicit and implicit identity on leadership attitudes, behaviours and effectiveness. Darja is passionate about teaching others how to become better leaders and has facilitated many leadership development workshops and programmes for professionals, MBAs and executives. Her other research interests include identity processes in retirement transition and volunteering with emergency services. Before coming to Australia, Darja worked and researched at Maastricht University in the Netherlands.

Donna Ladkin is Professor of Inclusive Leadership at Birmingham Business School, University of Birmingham, UK. A philosopher by background, Donna's work has explored how phenomenology and aesthetics can inform the practice of leadership in books such as *Rethinking Leadership: A New Approach to Old Leadership Questions* (2010). Her appreciation of organisational ethics as a practice, rather than a set of rules of conduct is offered in her recent text, *Mastering Ethics in Organizations* (2021). She is currently engaged in a critical appraisal of leadership theorising from a race perspective, and is working to include forgotten and overlooked voices in both her writings on leadership and organisational ethics.

Inti José Lammi is a Senior Lecturer in Organization and Management at Mälardalen University, Sweden, where he is a member of the NOMP research group. His research interests are social theory, digital transformation and organisational change processes. Additionally, Inti is interested in contemporary practice and process theories and the methodological implications of drawing on such theories when approaching organisational phenomena. He is currently studying the challenges of implementing inclusive leadership models in public sector organisations and virtual work arrangements in high-security organisations.

Magnus Larsson is Associate Professor at the Department of Organization at Copenhagen Business School (CBS), Denmark. He has a PhD in Psychology from Lund University, Sweden. His research primarily focuses leadership as an interactional phenomenon, and leadership development practices. Magnus teaches the Executive MBA and other master programmes at CBS. His publications appear in *Human Relations*, *Management Learning*, *Leadership*, *Journal of Change Management*, *Journal of Leadership* and *Organization Studies*, among others.

Allan Lee is a Senior Lecturer at the University of Exeter Business School. Before working at Exeter, he was at Alliance Manchester Business School. Allan's research focuses on leadership and particularly the relationship between leaders and their followers. His research has appeared in journals such as *Journal of Management*, *Leadership Quarterly*, *Journal of Organizational Behavior*, *Personnel Psychology* and *Journal of Occupational and Organizational Psychology*.

Lester Levy is Professor in Digital Health Leadership at the Auckland University of Technology (AUT) and is the Ministerial appointed Chair of the New Zealand Health Research Council. Lester's multi-decade career across medicine, academia, business and governance has seen him serve on 26 boards of directors across the public and private sectors. He has been Chair of 16 of these boards and deputy Chair of three. At various times he has been a chair, chief executive and entrepreneur in the healthcare sector. The focus of Lester's academic career has been leadership, change and disruption and he has taught and researched leadership for over two decades. Lester's current research interests focus on the contextual leadership challenges and opportunities presented by digital health adoption. In the 2013 Royal New Year's Honours Lester was appointed a Companion of the New Zealand Order of Merit for services to health and education.

Chaturi Liyanage is a doctoral researcher and a teaching assistant at the Lancaster University Management School (LUMS). Her research currently focuses on meaningful work, with a specific emphasis on unravelling the processual dynamics of meaningful work. Prior to joining LUMS she worked as a qualitative researcher and consultant in Sri Lanka. She received her MA in Social Research from the University of York, her MSc in Organisational Psychology from the University of Coventry and her BSc in Economics and Management from the University of London.

Kevin B. Lowe is Professor in Leadership at the University of Sydney Business School. He serves on several leading editorial boards including as Editor of the Annual Yearly Review at *Leadership Quarterly*, the leading journal in the field of leadership. Other professional roles include service on the Board of Directors of the International Leadership Association, the Board of Directors of the Australia and New Zealand Academy of Management, the Harvard Business Review Advisory Council and as an Executive Panellist for *McKinsey Quarterly*. Kevin's research has twice won the Best Paper of the Year Award from *Leadership Quarterly*, as well as winning the Article of the Decade Award from both *Leadership Quarterly* and *Journal of International Business Studies*. Prior to academia Kevin worked in financial forecasting and planning roles for Baxter (healthcare) and NextEra Energy (world's largest utility company).

Laura G. Lunsford is an expert in mentoring and leadership. A US Fulbright Scholar to Germany, she has authored over 50 peer-reviewed articles, chapters and books on these topics, including *The Mentor's Guide: Five Steps to Build a Successful Mentor Program (2nd Ed)* (2021). Lunsford's books include the textbook, *Leadership 2nd Edition*, *The SAGE Handbook of Mentoring* (2017) and *Mentoring Undergraduate Students* (2017). She co-authored one of the National Academy of Sciences most downloaded reports *The Science of Effective Mentorship in STEMM* (2019). She is a Professor of Psychology and an Assistant Dean at Campbell University. Her BA and PhD are from North Carolina State University and her MS is from University of North Carolina Greensboro. A board member of the International Mentoring Association, she is on the editorial board of the *International Journal of Mentoring and Coaching in Education*.

Hector Martinez is a Lecturer in the Management Department at the University of Kentucky Gatton College of Business and Economics. His research has focused on motivation, and in particular the impact of coaching on employee engagement, performance and meaningfulness of work. By applying Boyatzis's coaching model around sustainable change (intentional change theory), his approach to teaching is both positive and appreciative, looking to help students identify and realise their future ideal self. In the classroom, his courses are structured using the experiential learning theory (Kolb, 1984), with the intent of providing students with an engaging and transformative learning experience. Before Gatton he was an Assistant Professor at INCAE Business School in Costa Rica and taught courses at Case Western Reserve University in Cleveland, OH. In addition, he is a certified coach and facilitates executive education programmes. At Gatton he is teaching courses in Leadership, Negotiations, Small Business and HR Management. Hector has a PhD in Organizational Behavior from Case Western Reserve University, an MBA from INCAE Business School and a BA in Literature from New College of Florida.

Celina McEwen is a Research Fellow at UTS Business School, University of Technology Sydney. She is a researcher in the sociology and anthropology of professional practice and education. Her work has been conducted across several fields with a focus on leadership diversity practices, the aged care sector workforce, and workplace learning. Celina's books and edited books include *Educating Deliberate Professionals: Beyond Reflective and Deliberative Practitioners* (2016, edited with Franziska Trede) and *Education for Practice in a Hybrid Space: Enhancing Professional Learning with Mobile Technology* (2019, with Franziska Trede, Lina Markauskaite and Susie Macfarlane), published with Springer.

Frank Meier is currently Postdoctoral Researcher in the Department of Organization at Copenhagen Business School (CBS), Denmark. His academic interests include leadership, leadership development and the leadership of digital transformation, often observed from a communicative as constitutive, CCO perspective. Frank teaches primarily at executive masters at CBS and is doing various cross-sector leadership development work. His research has appeared in journals such as *Human Relations*, *Leadership* and *Scandinavian Journal of Management*.

Susan Mohammed is Professor of Industrial and Organizational (I-O) Psychology at the Pennsylvania State University. Her research focuses on teams, temporality and leadership, with special emphasis on team cognition, team composition and diversity, and the integration of time in team and leadership constructs. Dr Mohammed received her PhD in I-O Psychology from Ohio State University.

Julia Morgan has spent the last nine years working for Bradford University School of Management teaching across all areas of leadership, organisational behaviour, human resource management and business management. Her research interests are centred around gender and leadership, informed by critical leadership and management studies. Prior to moving into academia, she gained 20 years' experience working within the executive search industry, predominantly in a leadership capacity. Throughout her academic career Julia has continued to be passionate about and engage in practice, organisational development and impact through leadership research, engagement and consultancy where she still performs a range of consultancy projects and leadership development and coaching activities for a small number of client organisations.

Amber Nicholson is from the iwi of Ngāruahine of Taranaki, Aotearoa/New Zealand. She is a Lecturer at the Auckland University of Technology in the Management Department with research interests in Māori concepts of well-being, economies of mana, kaitiakitanga, sustainability and leadership. Amber's doctoral research explores ways to enhance well-being through recognising and honouring the ancestral landscapes in which business operates.

Karolina Nieberle is an Assistant Professor in Psychology and Behavioural Science at Durham University. Karolina is passionate about leadership and followership, and her research has implications for how to build, support and sustain successful leadership processes in teams and organisations. Her research particularly focused on questions such as how leader identities form and change, how followers affect leadership and how leadership is shared among multiple team members. In addition to her research interests, Karolina engages as a workshop trainer on topics related to leadership and well-being at work.

Burak Oc is an Associate Professor at the Melbourne Business School, Australia. In life, he is troubled by the way that powerful individuals in organisations exploit their power or status either for even more power or to pursue their own self-interest at the expense of others. In his research he explores the antecedents and consequences of this phenomenon. To this end, he conducts research in three streams: leadership, power, and organisational justice and behavioural ethics. His research has been published in *Journal of Applied Psychology*, *Organizational Behavior and Human Decision Processes*, *Journal of Management*, *Leadership Quarterly* and other outlets. He currently serves on the editorial boards at *Journal of Organizational Behavior* and *Organizational Behavior and Human Decision Processes*, and chairs one of the university-wide research ethics committees. His other service to the field includes serving as a member of best paper and best symposium committees, and as a symposium organiser and discussant.

Dermot O'Reilly is Senior Lecturer in the Department of Organisation, Work and Technology at Lancaster University. His research interests revolve around questions of power in life, culture, value, organising, learning and leading. He has published in the journals *Organisation Studies*, *Public Administration*, *Leadership*, *British Journal of Management* and *Management Learning*, among others.

Art Padilla earnt his bachelor's degree at N.C. State University and his PhD at University of North Carolina Chapel Hill. He served as Professor and Head of the Management department at North Carolina State University and taught at the Eller College of Management, University of Arizona and at the University of North Carolina Chapel Hill. He served as Academic Vice-President in the 17-campus University of North Carolina. He was awarded two Fulbright scholarships and was a Brookings Institution Fellow in Washington, DC. He writes about leadership and management, both in professional journals and in the *Washington Post*, *New York Times* and *Chronicle of Higher Education*. Presidential search committees at several universities have used his 2005 book, *Portraits in Leadership*. His manuscript on the Toxic Triangle is one of the most cited papers in *Leadership Quarterly* and he co-authored a textbook *Leadership*.

Joshua Pearman is a PhD student in the Organizational Psychology Program at Michigan State University. His research interests include personality, team dynamics, expertise and computational modelling. His graduate education is supported by funding from the National Aeronautics and Space Administration and Army Research Institute. Joshua completed his BS in Psychology at the University of Oregon, and his MS in Industrial-Organizational Psychology at the University of Georgia.

Jan Luca Pletzer is an Assistant Professor of Organisational Psychology at the Erasmus University Rotterdam in the Netherlands. His research focuses on the relations of broad and narrow personality traits with a wide variety of different outcomes in an organisational context, such as contextual performance, well-being, or leadership, often using meta-analytic methods. For example, he has published several meta-analyses that examine the extent to which personality traits predict outcomes such as workplace deviance or organisational citizenship behaviour. Jan is on the editorial boards of *Organizational Psychology Review*, *Stress and Health* and *International Journal of Selection and Assessment*.

Alison Pullen, is a Professor of Gender, Work and Organisation at Macquarie University, Sydney and Visiting Professor at Bath University and the Open University. Over the course of her career, Alison's research has been concerned with analysing and intervening in the politics of work as it concerns gender discrimination, identity politics and organisational injustice. While pursuing this agenda, Alison has become a prolific contributor to leading journals in the fields of organisation theory, gender studies and management studies, including leadership and diversity. Alison is joint Editor-in-Chief of *Gender, Work and Organization*, Associate Editor of *Organization* and sits on the editorial board of *Organization Studies*, among other journals. She is co-editor of the Routledge series Women Writers in Management and Organization Studies and on the International Editorial Board of the book series Feminist Perspectives on Work and Organisation, Bristol University Press.

Nelson Campos Ramalho is an Associate Professor at the department of Human Resources and Organisational Behaviour at ISCTE Business School in Portugal and is a researcher at the Business Research Unit – IUL. Nelson's research interests cover leadership as well as political behaviour in organisations. He has co-authored papers on these topics as well as book chapters on political psychology and organisational behaviour. He has experience in managing university knowledge transfer units since 2009 and has coordinated several projects and studies (both executive and scientific coordination) bridging community and business, both in national and international settings.

Arménio Rego is a Professor at the Católica Porto Business School, Portugal, and member of the Business Research Unit (ISCTE-IUL, Portugal). He has published in journals such as *Human Relations*, *Journal of Business Ethics*, *Journal of Occupational Health Psychology*, *Journal of Management*, *Organization Studies* and *Leadership Quarterly*.

Carl Rhodes is Professor of Organization Studies and Dean of UTS Business School, University of Technology Sydney. Carl researches the relationship between business and society in the nexus between liberal democracy and contemporary capitalism. His most recent books are *Woke Capitalism: How Corporate Morality is Sabotaging Democracy* (2022), *Organizing Corporeal Ethics* (2022, with Alison Pullen), *Disturbing Business Ethics* (2019) and *CEO Society: The Corporate Takeover of Everyday Life* (2018, with Peter Bloom).

Suvi Satama is a Postdoctoral Researcher in Management and Organisation at the Turku School of Economics, University of Turku, Finland. Currently, Suvi's curiosity leads her to study embodied experiences and vulnerabilities at work and her passion lies in exploring unconventional research topics. She is interested in applying creative research methods, such as visual methods, to the study of organisational phenomena. Her previous work has appeared, for example, in *Human Relations*, *Organization*, *Management Learning*, *Leadership*, *Gender, Work and Organization* and *Culture and Organization*.

Birgit Schyns is Professor of Organisational Behaviour at Neoma Business School and membre associé laboratoire C2S (Cognition, Santé, Société) Université de Reims Champagne Ardenne, France. She received her PhD in psychology from the University of Leipzig and subsequently worked in academic positions in the Netherlands and the UK. She has published widely on topics including antecedents and consequences of exchange relationships between leaders and their followers and factors influencing followers' perception of leadership (e.g., mood, personality, implicit leadership theories). She has been Associate Editor *of European Journal of Work and Organizational Psychology* (2007–12), *British Journal of Management* (2009–14) and *Applied Psychology: An International Review* (2017–20) and currently undertakes that role for *Zeitschrift für Psychology* [*Journal of Psychology*] as well as being a member of several editorial boards (including *Leadership Quarterly* and *Group and Organization Management*).

Viviane Sergi is Professor in Management in the Department of Management at ESG UQAM in Montreal, Canada. Her research interests include process thinking, performativity, project organising, the transformation of work and leadership. Her recent studies have explored how communication is, in various settings, constitutive of organisational phenomena, such as new work practices, strategy and leadership. She also has a keen interest for methodological issues related to qualitative research. Her work has been published in journals such as *Academy of Management Annals*, *Human Relations*, *Scandinavian Journal of Management*, *Strategic Organization*, *Long Range Planning*, *M@n@gement* and *Qualitative Research in Organizations and Management*.

Sudong Shang is a Lecturer at Griffith Business School, Griffith University, Australia. His expertise is in work–life balance, employees' well-being, leadership and immigrants' acculturation. Prior to joining Griffith Business School, he worked as a research fellow at Waikato Management School, New Zealand. He was involved in research projects on transforming leader's social capital, human capital and reputational capital into serving non-profit sector, and leader's morality. He actively engages in research and publication in these areas, and has publications in many international journals.

Ace V. Simpson is Reader in Human Resource Management and Organisational Behaviour at Brunel Business School, Brunel University London. His main research focus is on the cultivation of organisational compassion, which he studies through the lens of power. Ace's research has been published in journals such as the *Academy of Management Review*, *Journal of Management*, *Journal of Business Ethics* and *Management Learning*. Ace is also co-author of *Positive Organizational Behaviour* (2020) and the *Elgar Introduction to Organizational Paradox* (2021).

Martyna Śliwa is Professor of Business Ethics and Organisation Studies at Durham University Business School. She studies leadership and organisations drawing on insights from different disciplines and perspectives, including: ethics and aesthetics; equality, diversity, inclusion and respect; and language, linguistic diversity and translation. Martyna's research has been published in journals such as the *British Journal of Management*; *ephemera*; *Gender, Work and Organization*; *Human Relations*; *Journal of International Business Studies*; *Management Learning*; *Organization* and *Organization Studies*. She currently serves as Co-Editor-in-Chief of *Management Learning* and the Vice-Chair of the British Academy of Management for Equality, Diversity, Inclusivity and Respect.

Owain Smolović Jones is Director of the Research into Employment, Empowerment and Futures academic centre of excellence at the Open University, where he is also a Senior Lecturer. His research focuses on leadership from below, particularly from workers. He is particularly interested in how space and technology mediate and generate domination, leadership and resistance. Owain is the co-author of *Leadership: Limits and Possibilities*, second edition, with Keith Grint.

Jennifer L. Sparr is a senior researcher and lecturer at the Center for Leadership in the Future of Work at the University of Zurich, Switzerland. She received her doctorate degree from the University of

Konstanz. Her research focuses mainly on paradox, leadership, organisational change and innovation. Her research has been published in outlets such as *Academy of Management Perspectives*, *Academy of Management Collections*, *Journal of Applied Behavioral Science*, *Journal of Change Management*, *Journal of Business and Psychology*, *European Journal of Work and Organizational Psychology* and *Leadership and Organizational Development Journal*, as well as practitioner-oriented outlets.

Chellie Spiller, of Māori and European NZ lineage, is based at the University of Waikato Management School, Aotearoa/New Zealand. Her research explores wayfinding, authentic and collective leadership, diversity and inclusion, and how leaders, situated within economies of well-being, can be 'paradigm warriors' who are a force for deep systemic change. Chellie's books include *Wayfinding Leadership: Groundbreaking Wisdom for Developing Leaders* (2015); *Reflections on Authentic Leadership: Concepts, Coalescences and Clashes* (2013); and *Practical Wisdom, Leadership and Culture: Indigenous, Asian and Middle-Eastern Perspectives* (2020). Recent journal articles include 'Paradigm warriors: advancing a radical ecosystems view of collective leadership' in *Human Relations* (2020) and 'The field of race and leadership' in *Leadership* (2021). Chellie is currently 2022 Atlantic Institute Leader-in-Residence, Oxford University; 2022 Fellow International Leadership Association and lead researcher on a large-scale project investigating Māori economies of well-being. She was a Fulbright Senior Scholar at the Harvard Kennedy School and the University of Arizona.

Peter Y. T. Sun serves as an Associate Professor in the Waikato Management School, The University of Waikato, Hamilton, New Zealand. Peter is the Founding Trustee for the Community and Enterprise Leadership Foundation (CELF), an organisation that brings leaders from different sectors of the community together. Peter comes to academia after extensive experience in industry. His research interests are in the areas of leadership, knowledge management and organisational learning, and he has published in many international refereed journals such as the *Leadership Quarterly, Journal of Management Studies, Management Learning, and International Journal of Management Reviews.*

Leah Tomkins is an independent writer, researcher and consultant. Current academic affiliations include a Visiting Fellowship at the University of Oxford (The Bodleian) and Visiting Professor at the University of the West of England (UWE). A key focus of her work is bridging the gap between academia and practice, drawing on her in-depth experience of leadership – warts and all – including at Accenture, the UK Cabinet Office and London's Metropolitan Police Service. Leah has written extensively on the topic of caring leadership, and has edited a book on the subject, *Paradox and Power in Caring Leadership: Critical and Philosophical Reflections* (2020). She is currently Associate Editor and inaugural Social Media Editor for the journal *Leadership*.

Ashlea Troth is a Professor of Organizational Behavior and the Deputy Director of the Work Organization and Wellbeing Research Centre at the Griffith Business School, Griffith University, Australia. Her research interests include multilevel and multimethod approaches to examining emotional regulation and emotional intelligence in workplaces, and the impact of these phenomena on well-being and performance outcomes. She is also interested in the day-to-day work experiences of frontline managers and the role of their emotional regulation strategies on well-being when performing a range of tasks. She has published in leading journals such as the *Journal of Organizational Behavior, Leadership Quarterly* and *Human Resource Management Journal*.

Daan van Knippenberg is Houston Endowment Professor of Management at the Jones Graduate School of Business, Rice University. Daan's areas of expertise include leadership, diversity & inclusion, team performance, and creativity & innovation. He is a former Editor-in-Chief of *Academy of Management Annals* and *Organizational Psychology Review*, and a former Associate Editor of *Academy of Management Journal, Organizational Behavior and Human Decision Processes*, and *Journal of Organizational Behavior*. Currently, he is a Senior Editor for *Journal of Leadership & Organizational Studies*.

Gretchen Vogelgesang Lester is an Associate Professor at San Jose State University, CA. She has earnt a Lucas Graduate Fellowship for her work on multi-domain leadership and 360-degree coaching. She also serves on the leadership team for the Network of Leadership Scholars, a community of leadership researchers that fosters interconnectivity and linkages among leadership scholars from different fields. Dr Vogelgesang Lester's research interests include leader identity development, transparency in leader communication, leadership in multiple domains, trust and leadership development. She has published papers in *Academy of Management Learning and Education*, *Leadership Quarterly*, *Journal of Management Inquiry*, *Journal of Leadership and Organization Studies* and co-authored an award-winning article in *Journal of Management Education*.

David A. Waldman is a Professor of Management in the W. P. Carey School of Business and Co-Executive Director of the Global Center for Technology Transfer at Arizona State University. He is heralded as being one of the top-ten leadership researchers in the world, as demonstrated in his recently receiving the Network of Leadership Scholars' Eminent Leadership Scholar award in 2020. Many of his research efforts have been interdisciplinary in nature, including the neuroscience of leadership, responsible leadership and leadership that accompanies technology transfer and entrepreneurship. Professor Waldman's accomplishments include over 130 articles, five books, over 37,000 cites, and grants approximating $2 million. He is on the editorial review boards of the Academy of Management Journal, Academy of Management Review, Academy of Management Perspectives, Journal of Applied Psychology, Personnel Psychology and The Leadership Quarterly. He is a Fellow of the Academy of Management, American Psychological Association and the Society for Industrial and Organizational Psychology.

Suze Wilson is a Senior Lecturer in the School of Management at Massey University, Tamaki Makaurau/Auckland, Aotearoa/New Zealand. Her research into leadership explores issues of history, context, power, gender, identity, ethics, crisis and leadership development and has appeared in journals such as *Leadership*, *Journal of Business Ethics*, *Organizational Dynamics* and *Organization*. She has also authored or edited several books, including *Thinking Differently About Leadership* (2016), *Revitalizing Leadership* (2017) and *After Leadership* (2018).

We would like to thank **Amanda Sterling** for her outstanding support of the editorial team.

Introduction

Michelle C. Bligh, Brigid Carroll,
Olga Epitropaki, Magnus Larsson
and Doris Schedlitzki

AMBITION AND PURPOSE OF THE SECOND EDITION

We welcome you as collaborator and co-pilot on this journey exploring the variety and richness of leadership scholarship in its being and becoming in this 2nd edition of *The SAGE Handbook of Leadership*. We will canvas the familiar and known, enquiring into the enduring relevance of now settled traditions, and travel into unfamiliar territory towards new ways of understanding a field that is diverse and alive with possibility. Suitable for students and researchers alike, this *Handbook* provides a retrospective and prospective overview of the state of knowledge on leadership as a multidisciplinary field. Our commitment to providing an inclusive overview of the field is reflected in a set of original chapters by teams of leading and emerging scholars from around the world and across disciplines.

Building on the ideas explored in the first edition in 2011 this work takes an innovative turn. For, where handbooks tend to emphasise topical and disciplinary boundaries between different approaches and perspectives, here we have overcome the problem of essentialising boundaries, by focusing on ontologies, epistemologies, methodologies, subjectivities and theories that allow for sense-making and sense-breaking. Indeed, a special feature of this *Handbook* is the attempt to create synergies and dialogue across the different leadership camps, schools and approaches and to pay attention to the sites, nodes and streams where perspectives might diverge and cluster beyond entrenched differences. Authors have responded to the same invitation which we offer readers: to understand where we are today (*sense-making* of the field) and where we might go in the future (*sense-breaking* with tradition). Therefore, each chapter offers a comprehensive, critical overview of an aspect of leadership, a discussion of key debates and research, and a review of the emerging issues in its area.

Sense-making: Where are We Now?

Leadership studies as a field of research and practice has significantly developed over the last ten years in ontological, epistemological and methodological terms, taking place within and across many disciplines, languages and contexts. New insights have enabled a deeper understanding of important aspects of leadership, on the one hand, and sharper problematisation/identification of paradoxes (such as the continuing leader-centrism at the same time as increasing attention to followers, processes, practices, relationships, interactions), on the other. The sheer breadth and diversity of the field is reflected in the variety of different approaches that chapter authors have taken when conceptualising the very phenomenon of leader/ship. While some are underpinned by and rooted in different ontological and epistemological paradigms that lead them to focus on the leader, others are concerned with the activity of leading and/or the process of leadership. To enable the reader's sense-making of this diverse field, we have chosen to organise chapters into five sections through the use of prepositions: 'Between', 'About', 'Through', 'Within' and 'But'. When taken together – 'between', 'about', 'through', 'within' and 'but' – speak to the proliferation of leadership research into all aspects of contemporary life, and ask salient questions about the concept's utility, longevity and conceptual power.

The Between section focuses on leadership as something happening in relationships, interaction and practice, and mobilises a range of ways to conceptualise this between-ness. Leadership is here considered as including plural actors (Denis, Côté and Côté-Boileau) and as being a team function (Pearman, Gerkin and Carter). Our general tendency to romanticise leadership and leaders is critically discussed (Schyns and Vogelgesang Lester), and the constitutive role of followership is consequently explored (Almeida, Ramalho and Esteves). The phenomenon in between is explored through well-established traditions as a relationship (Holt and Lee) and as a matter of social identity (van Knippenberg), as well as through emerging approaches focusing on practice (Crevani and Lammi) and interactions (Larsson and Meier). Each chapter pursues a particular angle on the leadership relationship, offering sharpness and depth, and demonstrating impressive developments over the last decade. Together they constitute a breadth of approaches to conceptualise and explore leadership as in some sense happening in the social sphere in-between people, and encourage us to appreciate that this space is dependent on contributions from the individuals (be that in terms of social identities or in terms of romanticisation) and also constitutes an ontological arena in its own right.

The chapters in the About section share a focus on research that enquires into the question of what it is *about* the person or individual that can be associated with leadership. Authors draw from a wide range of disciplines and ontologies to explore different individual and interpersonal facets of the leader and follower involved in the process of leadership. This includes explorations of personality and contextualised personality traits (DeVries, Pletzer, Julian and Breevaart), implicit leadership and followership theories (Epitropaki, Acton and Nieberle), the role of context in self-regulation (Delegach, Kark and Van Dijk) and the importance of understanding emotions and emotion regulation within the leadership process (Troth, Jordan and Ashkanasy). Others raise questions of reason, empathy and ethics as they are linked to emotions and emotional intelligence in leadership (Ciulla), explore notions of authenticity (Iszatt-White), charisma (Conger), relationship quality (Martinez and Boyatzis) and responsible leadership (Jackson, Kempster, Liyanage, Shang and Sun). Finally, this section introduces how psychoanalysis may enable a deeper understanding of relations between leaders and followers, the romanticisation of leadership and dysfunctional forms of leadership (Gabriel) and explores current practices and future opportunities for leader development (Day and Kragt). The breadth and diversity of these chapters is testament to the movement and developments in this more traditional field of leadership studies. It shows increasingly critical conversations and avenues that call for careful considerations of context, practice and ethics when researching and conceptualising leadership from an individual or interpersonal perspective.

The Through section takes a predominantly processual approach to leadership and explores the tangible and intangible actors (both human and non-human) *through* which leadership is accomplished. This section therefore explores the significance of artefacts, spaces, texts and technologies alongside phenomena of gender, race, embodiment and aesthetics. It activates the metaphor of a lens or a frame and the process of looking or approaching leadership 'through' a particular and distinctive set of concepts or constructs. Those include feminism (Ford and Morgan), materiality (Sergi), aesthetics and artful practice (Ladkin), process theory (Kelly), technology (Smolović-Jones and Hollis), indigenous theories and practice (Spiller and Nicholson), history (Wilson), temporality (Alipour and Mohammed) and literary fiction (Śliwa). The power of these lenses/frames is in their sharpness, focus and depth. Each chapter provides a deep dive into one contemporary and central phenomenon. What results are fascinating excavations of the territories that leadership both shapes and is shaped by. The invitation to gaze through a particular lens or a frame is an invitation to pay attention to a dimension that traditionally has often been overlooked, overshadowed, or evaded in leadership studies. The opportunity to engage with multiple lenses and frames opens up a kaleidoscope of different forms, patterns and interactions which of course continue to locate leadership as such a potent, contested and expansive field of contemporary study.

The chapters in the Within section highlight the role of context and address how context enables and bounds leadership. They map how specific environmental (omnibus) and situational (discrete) contextual factors influence leadership enactment (Oc and Carpini), explore the meaning of leadership in alternative forms of organising such as cooperatives and social movements (Allen and O'Reilly) and delve into the practice and development of leadership in specific contexts such as healthcare (Levy and Lowe). They revisit existing discourses on leadership, national culture and symbolism (Iwowo, Case and Iwowo) and invite us to reflect on popular culture as a representation of leadership (Biehl and Satama). They further address power dynamics and relations in context (Clegg, Simpson, Pina e Cuhna and Rego) and distil modern wisdom about the leader's power and leadership practice from ancient texts (Bathurst and Chen). Each chapter offers a unique lens to examine leadership 'within' and the opportunity for a more systematic and holistic understanding of leadership intricacies. Taken together, they invite us to think beyond heroic representations of individual leaders and beyond common elements of leadership (leaders, followers, influence, effectiveness). Instead, they ask us to embrace context not as a mere canvas in front of which leadership takes place, but as a foundational property of leadership enactment.

Finally, the chapters in the But section take a predominantly processual approach to defining and studying leadership and stretch the reader's understanding of the complexity of leadership by considering dark sides (Lunsford and Padilla), issues of equality and diversity (Gagnon, Cukier and Elmi), paradoxes (Sparr, Waldman and Kearney), leadership dialectics (Fairhurst and Collinson) and alternatives to leadership (Alvesson, Blom and Fischer). They further encourage us to consider the ethics of care in leadership (Tomkins) and challenge us to look more critically upon notions of embodiment (McEwen, Pullen and Rhodes) and materiality (Harding) in leadership. While each chapter takes a different path and focuses on the complexities of leadership and the role of individuals and systems of thought, power and language, they share a common purpose: to unravel and contest overly simplified notions of the leader, to question the positivity and potential for unchecked power dynamics in and by the language of leadership.

Sense-breaking: Where Next?

To move the field of leadership studies forward, we have ensured that all chapters make space for reflections on how future research can constructively break sense with tradition in order to advance our understanding of leadership. For us as an editorial team and leadership researchers, this includes 1) 'busting' the still-persistent assumption of positivity and neutrality of leadership (moral, ethical, political, cultural), 2) stopping the call for 'more' leadership in favour of 'other' (than) leadership and 3) breaking the 'closed system' mentality that surrounds a lot of leadership research in favour of its entanglement in more 'open systems'.

With the aim to focus on leadership seen as something involving two or more people and as something of a social accomplishment, the Between section invites a range of sense-breaking themes to the field of leadership studies. The section demonstrates both that the space 'in between' is highly complex, and that there is a wide range of approaches available to conceptualise leadership in terms of such a space. While fragmentation of the field of leadership studies is an obvious risk, the section offers a strategy for bridging and integration. The chapters invite a range of questions about how various aspects of leaders, acts of leading and the broader context might play a role in this space in between and, turning the tables, how individual characteristics and contextual forces might be triggered or mobilised in and through social relationships. The section thus challenges us to critically examine both how we conceptualise leadership and how various elements might play together to produce the complex phenomenon of leadership. Moreover, the section urges us to embrace a range of different methodologies, while carefully specifying the phenomena to study.

Exploring a wide range of individual and interpersonal perspectives on leadership, the chapters in the About section offer numerous sense-breaking opportunities for leadership research. This includes a call for considerations of diversity, inclusion and shared/collective forms of leadership in more established areas of leadership studies such as implicit leader and follower theories. It also encourages researchers to continue to develop emerging areas, such as that of responsible leadership and emotion regulation as a part of the leadership process, as well as to reflect on implications for leader development. Authors highlight the need to continue to bridge the gap between research and practice, to consider the role of context, relationality and paradox in leadership, and to reflect carefully on questions of ethics. Chapters have also highlighted paucity in areas of research such as that of stability and lifespan in leadership personality research, which could bring further insight into the environmental impact on and age-related dynamics of particular leadership traits, behaviours and styles. Overall, these sense-breaking themes suggest that the future lies in the intersection of the individual and the social, and in processual explorations of leadership that consider both stability and paradox, regulation and irrationality.

There are a number of sense-breaking patterns evident in the Through section. First, a plea to research leadership as close to movement, accomplishment, action and undertaking as possible given all those happen 'through' a myriad of technological intermediaries, micro-interactions, engagement with artefacts and symbols and flows of human and non-human encounters. We still overlook too much that is intertwined through what can be framed as leadership. Second, we as researchers need to rethink our own categorisations, given that we lack the language for leadership processes which involve mutuality, reciprocity and fluidity, struggle with the interpolation of seemingly contradictory states such as compliance and resistance, and pull short in discovering emancipatory and generative alternatives 'through' resources such as art, literature and history. Finally, the chapters in this section aim to pull us 'through' our attachment to overly individualistic, masculine and rationalist crutches towards more exploration of the non-rational (desire, fantasy, craving), ecological (sustainability, relationality, connection) and revolutionary (social equality, justice, democracy).

The chapters in the Within section demonstrate the need for leadership studies to acknowledge that context changes the meaning of leadership. They invite us to explore and discover different and alternative spaces and contexts to uncover diversity in conceptualisations and manifestations of leadership and resistance to leadership. This includes embracing new methodologies that are enabling us to look for leadership in these spaces with care, an open mind and attention to social, cultural, historical and political roots and dynamics. For example, there is rich potential for new theoretical, methodological and empirical insights through a focus on popular culture, particularly into emotions, power and inter-corporeal dynamics in different work contexts. There is further the potential for a radical empowerment of alternative forms of leadership by challenging current leadership norms through adopting an ancient political, philosophical or spiritual lens. Focusing on power dynamics, we are encouraged to focus on social relations and explore how the dialectic between power structures and individual authority shapes leadership as a relational process.

In light of the aim of the But section to bring further complexity and criticality to our discussions of leadership, the chapters are naturally focused on sense-breaking with other traditions of leadership, at times even suggesting a search for alternatives to leadership. They raise important questions and concerns for the study of leadership that need to be taken further. These include a call for a rethinking of the way we conceptualise and study leadership to embrace dialectical thinking that enables a focus on paradoxes rather than seeking to compartmentalise and tame the issue of power dynamics in leadership relations. The avenues for research opened up in this section further include calls for studies into diversity and representation that consider dynamics of intersectionality and critically explore issues of embodiment. Finally, there is encouragement to explore and add to our understanding of, on the one hand, destructiveness in leadership and, on the other, potential for caring leadership.

In sum, leadership scholars have covered wide-ranging and diverse terrain over the last 12 years. We have attempted to provide an innovative and useful organisation of this landscape to encourage reflection and exploration. Through processes of sense-making and sense-breaking, each chapter provides a unique piece of the puzzle, helping to acknowledge where we have been and highlight new directions to discuss and debate. As you contemplate leadership Between, About, Through, Within and But, we welcome you as collaborator and co-pilot as we embark on more than a decade of exploration in leadership studies.

PART 1

Between: Leadership as a Social, Socio-cognitive and Practical Phenomenon

Pluralism in Studies on Plural Leadership: Analysis and Perspectives

Jean-Louis Denis, Nancy Côté and Élizabeth Côté-Boileau

INTRODUCTION

Conceptions of leadership that look beyond formally appointed *individual* leaders and leader–follower dyads date back to the mid-20th century (Benne & Sheats, 1948; Follett, 1924; Gibb et al., 1954). Pioneering work on 'political leadership in a plural society' appeared in political and sociological studies in the early 1970s, and was later pursued by scholars interested in empirical manifestations of leadership emanating from multiple individuals (Denis et al., 1996; Hambrick & Mason, 1984; Heenan et al., 1999; Leng, 1969). However, until the mid-1990s, leadership studies were still predominantly rooted in a culture that valued the role of individual leaders as shapers of organisations (Yammarino et al., 2012). It was not until the turn of the millennium that leadership in the plural became a main focus among organisational and management scholars, with a growing body of work appearing after 2010 (Denis et al., 2012; White et al., 2014). Plural leadership is a broad concept that incorporates studies on 'shared', 'distributed', 'collective', 'collaborative', 'integrative', 'relational' and 'post-heroic' leadership forms (Denis et al., 2012). Plural leadership is more a perspective than a precisely defined approach to the study of leadership.

In previous work (Denis et al., 2012; Lusiani et al., 2016), we distinguish forms of plural leadership according to variations around formality, hierarchy and power. A high degree of formality is seen when a group of individuals is assigned a formal position of leadership in an organisation and shares the leadership role. When informality predominates, plural leadership emerges almost at random from the day-to-day interactions of individuals. More collective forms of leadership can also manifest in situations where influence is concentrated among leaders who exert influence over others, or in situations where a plurality of leaders exert mutual influence on each other. It should also be noted that achieving more plural forms of leadership is not easy, as tensions can emerge within the constitution and activation of leadership roles in organisations (Denis et al., 2001).

Attention to plural forms of leadership is associated with increasing interest in new organisational forms, manifest in the expansion of professionalised and knowledge-based organisations at the end of the 20th century (Empson & Alvehus, 2020; Greenwood & Prakash, 2017; Uhl-Bien et al., 2007). In highly professionalised settings, power, authority and legitimacy are structurally diffuse and spread across groups that control critical expertise (Denis et al., 2007).

Representations of leadership phenomena have also evolved alongside broader theoretical developments in social science and organisation studies, such as the practice turn (Cetina et al., 2005), constructionist approaches (Barge, 2014; Fairhurst & Grant, 2010) and complexity theory (Uhl-Bien & Arena, 2018). Overall, research into plural forms of leadership responds to the call for a more realistic assessment of actors' agency in organisations, with attention to how the capacity for action of a wide set of individuals develops within and across organisations through day-to-day interactions (Lok & Willmott, 2019; Reed, 2003). In this chapter, we use Publish or Perish software and Google Scholar platforms to empirically trace the evolution of scholarly publications on the theme of plural leadership over the past 50 years (finding 40 articles explicitly on 'plural leadership' published between 1969 and 2021, with over 993 citations). We then look at related and precursor concepts such as 'shared leadership', 'collective leadership', 'distributed leadership' and/or 'conjoint agency' (finding 981 publications, with 147,946 citations). Figure 1.1 illustrates the evolution of scholarly publications in these areas (see Table 1.1 for metrics). We see two distinct productive streams of work that initially developed in parallel and represent the bedrock on which further conceptualisations of plural leadership develop.

Shared leadership is rooted in literature on team-based leadership by authors such as Manz and Sims (1993, 2001) and Pearce et al. (2000, 2002, 2008, 2009). Shared leadership emanates from a designated leader and other group members who share leadership roles. The leaders are involved in a process of reciprocal influence and share the knowledge necessary to achieve common goals. Studies on shared leadership regard organisational structure as the basis through which plurality in leadership is achieved (Gibeau et al., 2020).

In contrast, distributed leadership is fundamentally relational, and sees informal leadership roles develop in parallel with formal roles (Spillane, 2012). Distributed leadership differs from shared leadership in that leadership is held not only by designated leaders within the organisation, but also by many individuals who do not necessarily hold formal leadership roles. The practice of distributed leadership is constituted and shaped by continuous interactions between leaders and followers, and attention is paid to both the context in which leadership is enacted and the expression of joint agency (Gronn, 2002, 2003).

These two streams are precursors to work undertaken after 2010 that seeks to decode various representations of leadership in the field (Ospina et al., 2020) and provide a

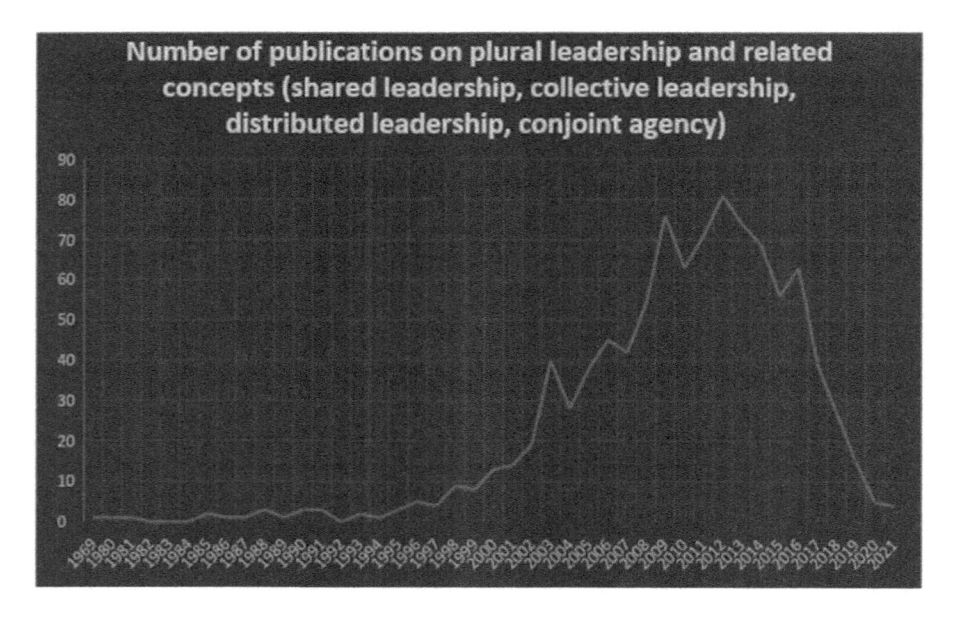

Figure 1.1 Evolution of the number of scholarly publications on 'plural leadership' and related concepts, using Publish or Perish software and Google Scholar search (1969–2021).

critical reading of discourse on plural leadership (Alvesson & Spicer, 2014; Collinson, 2017; Bromley & Meyer, 2021). The growing prominence of studies looking at leadership from a practice perspective (Alvesson & Sveningsson, 2003; Raelin, 2016, 2017) also stimulates interest in plurality based on distributed agency and on leadership as an emergent property of organisations or systems. The decline of publications on plural leadership observed after 2013, and more markedly after 2016, is puzzling. It may be a natural response to the rapid growth rate of publications in previous years, when post-heroic representations of leadership became fashionable and more widely accepted as a legitimate lens for leadership studies. Between 2010 and 2020, scholars in the field also appear to want to take stock of the proliferation of works and concepts around plural leadership, exemplified by four highly cited reviews on the topic (Crevani & Endrissat, 2016; Denis et al., 2012; Fitzsimons et al., 2011; Ospina et al., 2020).

In Part I of this chapter, we explore the scholarship on plural leadership. In Part II, we focus on three lines of enquiry to address some of the limitations in current approaches to plural leadership in organisations and propose possibilities for further theoretical and empirical developments.

PART I: VARIATIONS IN REPRESENTATIONS OF PLURAL LEADERSHIP

Studies of plural leadership can be classified according to various representations about where leadership lies, namely in individuals or in interactions, and according to their emphasis on theoretical or empirical developments. In this section, we first deal with the distinction between entitative and relational approaches to plural leadership. We then consider studies of plural leadership according to their predominant theoretical and empirical focus.

Plurality in two Modes: Entitative and Relational

There is a fundamental distinction in the literature between two (ontological) representations of leadership: entitative and relational (see Chapter 3, Leadership in interaction). The entitative approach focuses mostly on the embodiment of leadership in individuals where the characteristics and attributes of individual leaders are the focus of attention. The relational approach considers leadership in a more decentred way, where the interactions between individuals in organisations shape leadership in organisations (Denis et al., 2012).

Entitative perspective on plural leadership

The entitative form of leadership encompasses studies that situate leadership primarily in entities, meaning individual leaders and by extension their practices and the technologies used to influence others in organisations (Drath, 2001; Drath et al., 2008; Pye, 2005; Schedlitzki & Edwards, 2021). Plurality in leadership is based here on assembling skills, attributes and behaviours that are distributed among a diversity of individuals (Uhl-Bien, 2006). Individuals in leadership roles become part of a leadership constellation (Denis et al., 2001). From an entitative viewpoint, emphasis is placed on the role of social and cognitive processes within and between leaders that culminate (or not) in situations of plural leadership (Dachler & Hosking, 1995; Lichtenstein et al., 2006; see also Chapter 23).

By focusing on individual characteristics and behaviour, research adopting the entitative approach focuses mainly on *typical leadership behavior and the assessment about which leadership style is the most effective (in a particular situation, across cultures, etc.)* (Crevani & Endrissat, 2016, p. 25). A variance approach to the study of plural leadership is privileged where attention is focused on predictors of effective leadership behaviours in context.

Despite the predominance of the entitative approach in leadership studies, many scholars are critical regarding its limited capacity to take into account the volatility of individual leadership positions and roles in organisations and their dependence on context or situational factors (Hosking, 2011; Fitzsimons et al., 2011). These considerations emphasise the importance of relations between individuals in the development of organisational leadership.

Relational perspective on plural leadership

From a relational perspective, leadership is not primarily embedded in individuals, but emerges instead from the day-to-day interactions of individuals in organisations (Lichtenstein et al., 2006). Two main bodies of work exemplify the attention paid to relationality in leadership studies: the relational approach (Crevani & Endrissat, 2016;

Gronn, 2002; Spillane, 2012) and the leadership-as-practice approach (LAP) (Raelin, 2017). These works adopt a *strong process* perspective (Chia & Tsoukas, 2003) with *a view of leadership and organisation as human social constructions that emanate from the rich connections and interdependencies of organisations and their members* (Uhl-Bien et al., 2007, p. 655). Leadership is thus conceived as a kind of unplanned practice in organisations (Denis et al., 2012) shaped by cultural, historical and political contexts (Fitzsimons et al., 2011). Pushed to the extreme, the relational approach proposes a more tacit and amorphous (invisible) representation of plural leadership, which raises questions around the distinction between leadership and other forms of interaction in organisations.

Many authors conclude that researchers adhering to a relational perspective have not yet developed a methodological agenda to fully grasp the importance of process and interactions in the development of plural leadership (Fitzsimons et al., 2011; Denis et al., 2012; Ospina et al., 2020). They invite researchers to adopt more diverse methodologies than those used in studies based on an entitative perspective, such as case study research (Crevani et al., 2007; Vine et al., 2008). The study by Crevani (2011) on the development of leadership through conversations at work is an example of methodological creativity in this area.

Combining representations of leadership

Some researchers present a less dichotomous vision of leadership studies by insisting on the importance of both entitative and relational representations (Crevani and Endrissat, 2016; Pullen & Vachhani, 2013; Ropo & Salovaara, 2019; Sergi, 2016). For Crevani and Endrissat, the relational approach to leadership recognises the importance of *individuals and how they relate to each other, how they construct relationships with each other, how they (re)construct their identities in relationships* (Crevani & Endrissat, 2016, p. 37).

Another stream of work sees relationships between actors in an organisational structure as opportunities and constraints to enacting leadership (Fitzsimons et al., 2011). Leadership is thus presented as combining an actor's cognitive capacity and position within an organisational or network structure, and opportunities arising in a given context, which may or may not culminate in plural leadership. Fitzsimons and colleagues (2011) also refer to leadership as a response to the need to adapt to changing environments that builds on the psychosocial needs of individuals. Emotions in organisations are considered a force that propels connections among individuals and the development of more plural forms of leadership.

Approaches that combine entitative and relational representations of leadership expand our understanding of the roles of interactions and agency (individual, collective) in the emergence of plurality in leadership. Processual thinking and methodologies are mobilised to look at leaders and leadership in organisations as dynamic phenomena in leadership studies.

Two Entry Points for the Study of Plural Leadership: Theoretical and Empirical

Another duality that emerges from the analysis of scholarship on plural leadership concerns the different ways researchers study and construct the phenomenon. We observe two main streams in research on plural leadership: one is theoretically focused and conceptually driven, and another is more empirically focused and aims to support the practice of plural leadership in and across organisations. In the next sub-section, we examine how plural leadership studies have evolved alongside research on emerging theoretical frames and analysis of practices in and around organisations.

Theoretically driven studies on plural leadership

As organisational and management scholars looked for pluralism in theory by the late 1990s, the notion of plural leadership emerged to recognise the multiple ideas, actors, reflexive experiences and disciplines at play in shaping and solving complex organisational problems (Rouleau, 2011). Various theoretical perspectives have been used to operationalise plural leadership as a specific field of enquiry, such as 'symbolic interactionism', constructionist approaches (Barge, 2014; Fairhurst & Grant, 2010; Hosking, 2011), practice theory (Raelin, 2017), critical theory (Alvesson & Spicer, 2014; Collinson, 2017), complexity theory (Uhl-Bien & Arena, 2018) and post-structural and postmodern theory (Ford, 2010; Zoller & Fairhurst, 2007), among others. In general, these theoretical frames aim to problematise the manifestations of plural leadership in organisations and to avoid prescription.

We identify several examples of theoretically informed studies on plural leadership. First, Uhl-Bien and colleagues (2008) developed 'complexity leadership theory', where leadership is either adaptive, enabling or administrative within organisations. Leadership is conceived as a mix of formal and informal relations dedicated to strengthening cohesiveness, interdependency and coordination among organisational actors. Building on Uhl-Bien and colleagues (2008), Yammarino and colleagues (2012) later developed the concept of 'network leadership', highlighting the role of 'soft' (informal) relationships in spreading leadership capacities. More recently, Opsina and colleagues (2020) drew on this body of work to explore manifestations of plural leadership, at both group (in the tradition of shared leadership) and system level (in the tradition of distributed leadership). The authors argue that plural leadership can only be found in the multiple processes involved in leading an organisation, and not in individual attributes or entities.

Building on a range of pre-existing theories, theoretically driven studies of plural leadership expand and clarify the conceptual foundations of this domain of enquiry. However, theoretical refinements have been considered insufficient by some scholars, raising questions of how leadership in the plural is enacted in practice. This led to a revival of empirically driven research on plural forms of leadership.

Empirically driven studies on plural leadership

An important body of research uses empirical observations as an entry point for the study of plural leadership. The focus on empirical studies and their implications for understanding plurality in leadership are described in reviews by Denis and colleagues (2012) and Crevani and Endrissat (2016).

The review performed by Denis and colleagues (2012) identifies four distinct streams of work in plural leadership studies: sharing leadership for team effectiveness; pooling leadership capacities at the top to direct others; spreading leadership within and across levels over time; and producing leadership through interaction. The *sharing leadership* stream refers to mutual leadership in groups. Both vertical leadership and self-elected leaders contribute to shared leadership in teams. Contexts such as task interdependence and complexity induce the need for shared leadership (Uhl-Bien et al., 2007; Yammarino et al., 2012). Key contributors to this work are Huxham and Vangen (2000), Alvarez and Svejenova (2005), Spillane (2006), Denis et al. (1996), Denis et al. (2001) and Gronn (1999, 2002).

These researchers inform the work of Schuh et al. (2013), who look at ethical (moral) versus authoritarian leadership interactions and behaviours in the context of subordinate–supervisor dyads. The authors find that producing transformational leadership through interactions is a contextually driven phenomenon that is not determined by individual characteristics and actions, but rather by the way behaviours, morals and structures create spaces to lead change in organisations. In their study, White and colleagues (2014) explore how cross-boundary leadership interactions are triggered differently in 'routine' and 'non-routine' situations in health and social care organisations. In routine situations, plural leadership spreads more easily and widely through stabilised channels of interaction, while in non-routine (disruptive) situations, leadership in the plural is increasingly controlled and limited by hierarchical sources of power and accountability structures. Gibeau and colleagues (2020) look at how, in the context of co-management in healthcare, co-leadership dyads bridge expertise and provide legitimacy in professionalised settings.

Empirical studies based on a LAP perspective, while emphasising the importance of interactions among organisational members, tend to focus on individual leadership practices and behaviours. Individual leadership practices are conceived as generators of direction within organisational processes and dynamics (Crevani, 2011; Packendorff et al., 2014; Nicolini, 2012). For example, Jian (2022) studies the role of empathy as a leadership practice that contributes to the emergence of plural leadership in organisations.

Theoretical and empirical contributions

A wide range of theoretical and empirical studies enriches scholarship on plural leadership. Theory-driven research contributes to our understanding of plural leadership as a collectively and relationally bounded concept that can be found in leaders, attributes, groups and systems of relations. Empirical work on plural leadership helps us understand how 'leading in the plural' manifests in practice and comes to be through deliberate and purposeful efforts by organisational actors. Mixing empirical and theoretical insights deepens our understanding of plural leadership.

For instance, Sergi and colleagues' (2021) recent review of business and general press publications in the early months of the Covid-19 crisis reveals that 'romanticised' manifestations of leadership (e.g., 'heroic' leadership) are more explicitly brought forward and valued than more diffuse, plural and decentred forms of leadership (Sergi et al., 2021). The authors call for enhanced theoretical development around the distinction between 'leading' and 'leadership' in organisations and societies to help raise awareness of less traditional forms and experiences of leadership.

In addition, Fairhust and colleagues (2020, pp. 598–599) identify three main empirical gaps in the collective leadership literature: the need to *decipher collective leadership configurations and its power-based foundations; the need to establish how leadership is made relevant in a collective setting; and the need for collective leadership researchers to adopt strong process models*.

Denis and colleagues (2012) identify limitations in studies of plural forms of leadership, noting a relative neglect of conflictual situations or tensions and an overemphasis on shared goals and direction. They also note a lack of attention to the differential ability of organisational actors to participate in plural forms of leadership due to asymmetrical power relationships. The question of power appears insufficiently problematised. Finally, the authors see a constant demarcation between work that focuses on pluralising leadership and work on channelling pluralism in organisations. Pluralising leadership implies deliberate strategies by individual leaders to create more collective forms of leadership in organisations (co-management, for example) to respond to growing complexities. Channelling pluralism refers to social and somewhat more fluid processes of leading to reconcile competing values, interests and distributed agency with demands for leadership. Moreover, the authors mention that discourse promoting plural leadership may mask new forms of organisational control. The socio-political substrate and signification of plural forms of leadership need to be further investigated. In Part II, we propose to expand the content and boundaries of plural leadership studies around three lines of enquiry that may help transcend the limitations or shortcomings identified in the field of plural leadership studies.

PART II: NOVEL IDEAS AND PROMISING PERSPECTIVES

Two core tensions emerge from our analysis of prior work on plural leadership. A first relates to consensual versus conflicting goals in organisations and the prospects for joint and collaborative agency. Plurality of leadership often implies that preferences are transcended in leadership configurations, and that conflicting goals are dysfunctional (Bromley & Meyer, 2021; Chreim, 2015; Sergi et al., 2012; Youngs, 2017). A second set of tensions, between entitative and relational approaches, is emphasised in Part I. Recent enthusiasm for relational and processual views contributes to rehabilitating the role of actors and agency in plural leadership studies. In this section, we explore dimensions involved in the problematisation of plural leadership as conjoint or collaborative agency (Crevani, 2011), and as a phenomenon that is both entitative and relationally driven. We propose three lines of enquiry around plural forms of leadership: 1) plurality of the self and plural leadership, 2) plural leadership as a manifestation of power and control and 3) resistance and the construction of pluralism.

Line of Enquiry 1: Plurality of the Self and Plural Leadership

A first line of enquiry focuses on the identity of individuals or aspiring leaders and explores the notion of multiple identities and the plurality of the self as consequential for plural leadership. Works on identity construction in organisations emphasise how individuals act as a repository of multiple identities (Ramarajan, 2014). Identity is conceived here as an ongoing process of negotiation to accommodate perceived tensions and inconsistencies in organisations (Alvesson & Willmott, 2002; Brown, 2015; Gill & Caza, 2018). Competing identities can emerge from 'the work of others' (external to oneself) implying that identity is not only the property or the work of the individual, but also of power and control structures within organisations (DeRue & Ashford, 2010; Lawrence & Phillips, 2019, pp. 94–95). It is expected that changes in the environment and in the experience of work impact the way individuals enact their multiple identities and the reconciliation among them. Individuals engage in inter-identity work in reaction to environmental changes in order to restore a viable arrangement among potentially competing intrapersonal identities (Ramarajan, 2014). Unsuccessful self-identity work may lead to a sense of 'alienation' in the workplace (Rouleau, 2011). From an entitative standpoint, the assemblage of competing sources of identity may represent a challenge to the formation of functional or collaborative leadership. In a similar vein, Chreim and colleagues (2020) study counter-institutional identities and argue that, for some individuals and groups, marginal identities can help gain and affirm leadership in organisations. Individuals with opposing identities may or may not refrain from taking leadership roles, depending on organisational context and opportunities to manifest overt resistance (Courpasson et al., 2012).

Recognition of pluralism in individual identity, and by extension in groups, supports the value of diversity in leadership. Complex patterns of identity related to gender, culture, social status and position inevitably intersect with occupational identities and influence the development of leadership configurations. The network of intrapersonal identities brings richness to plural forms of leadership, but creates dilemmas for the articulation and orchestration of leadership configurations (Ford, 2020). Plurality in leadership seeks to deal with latent tensions and orchestrate potentially diverging views and perspectives in leadership configurations. Moreover, the dissolution of physical, geographic and material organisational boundaries and the concomitant development of new organisational forms (e.g., meta-organisations, digitalised organisations) increase the heterogeneity of individual identities (Coun et al., 2019; Pratt & Rafaeli, 2013). For instance, Waring and colleagues (2014) demonstrate that networked interactions in healthcare are influenced by local socio-cultural boundaries, and underline the importance of shared mental models rather than shared structural arrangements to achieve coordination and joint agency.

An identity perspective on plural leadership considers a broad range of work on diversity, inclusivity and equity in organisations. Superposition of complex identities may make agreement around shared orientations or initiatives challenging. Plural leadership can be an opportunity to promote diversity and inclusion in organisations, which are currently underdeveloped in plural leadership studies (see Chapter 25, Indigenous leadership as a conscious adaptive system).

Line 2 of Enquiry: Plural Leadership as a Manifestation of Power and Control

A second line of problematisation considers discourses and practices associated with plural forms of leadership as emerging manifestations of control or power in contemporary organisations. For Collinson (2020; see Chapter 41, Politicising the leader's body: from oppressive realities to affective possibilities), situations of leadership take root in situations of collective interdependency within and across organisations. Manifestations of leadership (individual or collective) are an expression of situated power where actors continuously negotiate their identities and relationships to access leadership status and recognition. These ongoing negotiations occur within a structural context that allocates authority and delineates agentic capacities. Organisations are a mediated space where local or situated activities and broader social determinants are reconciled at least superficially. From a critical perspective, attention must be paid to dysfunctional or damaging aspects of pluralising leadership in organisations.

Many authors call for critical studies on leadership (Alvesson & Spicer, 2014; O'Reilly & Reed, 2010, 2011). The notion of leaderism as an ideological matrix to transform organisations suggests that leadership is a notion in need of problematisation. In a study of university governance, Youngs (2017) sees the appeal for collective and distributed leadership as a means of glossing over conflictual organisational arrangements and inducing cooperation within a collective of interdependent actors in asymmetrical relationships (Collinson, 2020). Organisations are not conceived as arenas of consensus where efforts at communication and inclusiveness, through emerging leadership configurations, dissipate hierarchies and asymmetry in power relations (Bromley & Meyer, 2021; Tourish, 2018). For these authors, enrolling leaders in developing and organising plural leadership essentially aims to cloak fundamental incompatibilities of interests and values in a veil of consensual politics, allowing organisational elites to control organisations (Bromley & Meyer, 2021; Youngs, 2017).

Calls for more plural forms of leadership have expanded in a context of emerging complex organisational forms inhabited by professionals, experts or knowledge workers, where heroic forms of leadership are at once widespread and insufficient to reflect emerging norms of participation and inclusiveness (Collinson, 2017; Tourish, 2018). In collective leadership, sources of disruptive power in organisations are domesticated through more collective or collaborative work and build on assumptions derived from growing neoliberalism (Bromley & Meyer, 2021). Using the label of hyper-management, Bromley and Meyer (2020) see the collaborative spirit of contemporary management and leadership as an expression and institutionalisation of discourse about the salience of purposeful, self-determined and empowered individuals in organisations. Individual leaders, and by extension the collectivity of leaders, are instruments of unification beyond what is required in terms of skills and expertise to lead and achieve organisational goals. For instance, management tools and digital systems are increasingly considered allies to ('hyper') managerialist leadership approaches, exerting an endogenous form of control and surveillance in and around organisations (De Vaujany et al., 2021; see Chapter 24, Technology and leadership).

This perspective on plural forms of leadership may appear severe at first. However, it has the benefit of alerting academics and practitioners to the ideological underpinnings of calls to reconceive leadership from a pluralistic standpoint and see leadership as one modality of control in organisations. In addition, by paying attention to collective or distributed leadership, critical leadership studies create bridges with the neo-institutionalist approach to organisations (Greenwood et al., 2011). The harmonisation of competing institutional logics is considered essential in many sectors (health, higher education) and more plural and collaborative forms of leadership are conceived as a plausible, if challenging, response. Adjusting and harnessing the agency of a wide set of autonomous actors (Meyer, 2010) to secure cooperation and collaboration is seen as a fundamental problem in liberal democracies. Leadership discourse and practices associated with pluralism can thus be seen as one plausible response to this challenge and as a manifestation of soft power in contemporary organisations (Courpasson, 2000).

One of the insufficiently explored issues in scholarly work on plural leadership is how the search for new and more differentiated and legitimate forms of control within organisations impacts on the plausibility, functionality, viability and contributions of pluralism in leadership. Another is how the incorporation into leadership configurations of actors who are not identified as members of organisational elites impacts on the development of less invasive and more visible forms of control within organisations (Lockett et al., 2012). The next section will partly address this issue by looking at the interface between plural forms of leadership and organisational resistance.

Line 3 of Enquiry: Resistors as Actors in Plural Leadership

This third line of enquiry is a sub-text of the broader theme of plural leadership as power and control. Resistance in organisations is defined as situations of collective action where individuals or groups that do not have full access to institutionalised forms of influence develop oppositional strategies to voice their views and demands (Briscoe & Gupta, 2016). Resistors can contribute to expanding plural leadership, while at the same time inducing instability in leadership configurations. Here, individuals invite themselves, through acts of resistance, into the world of leadership and exert demands to create leadership arrangements that are more responsive to their claims (Ferlie et al., 2005). Through boundary work, they exert pressure to assure a more inclusive approach to leadership (Lawrence & Phillips, 2019). As an example, throughout the Covid-19 pandemic, citizens, public, private and state actors advocated for greater social justice, equity, political transparency and scientific independence in public policy in different parts of the world (Shafik, 2021). In situations where plural forms of leadership are conceived as control, it is the more powerful organisational actors who invite others to engage in joint leadership. When claims for pluralism in leadership come from organisational resistors, it is the less advantaged groups that insist on more plural and open forms of leadership (Theoharis, 2007; Theoharis, 2004). Power and resistance are considered mutually constitutive (Mumby et al., 2017) and resistors will impose inclusive principles on emerging forms of plural leadership in organisations (see Chapter 43, Leadership representation: A critical path to equity). Plural leadership inhabited by resistors is analogous to social movements in organisations (Wamsley & Zald, 1973; Wood & Zald, 1966), where individuals or groups work to create a space where oppositional forces can be more explicitly or safely expressed (Courpasson et al., 2012; Zietsma & Lawrence, 2010).

This line of enquiry sees in plural leadership an opportunity for organisational members to redress situations that are considered dysfunctional and disruptive of decency at work. Studies by Courpasson and colleagues (2012) look at how middle managers provisionally take control of the organisational agenda in situations where senior managers agree to temporarily suspend prevalent power relations in the organisation. In such situations, middle managers become de facto participants in plural forms of leadership. In other situations, resistors promote innovative practices through a set of demands and tactics, reminiscent of the practice turn in leadership studies, to create a safe space for alternate approaches (Zietsma & Lawrence, 2010). While resistors can invite themselves into emerging plurality in leadership, their participation in leadership constellations is still conditional on consent from organisational elites (Cartwright, 1965).

When studying plural forms of leadership, consideration for phenomena of resistance in organisations provides an opportunity to pay more attention to fluid configurations, where leaders are provisionally conferred a leadership role. Heterogeneity and instability appear as significant attributes of plural forms of leadership. Organisational elites cannot fully control the development and manifestations of plural leadership, which is a contested terrain featuring power asymmetries and claims to reorder predominant logics. Through resistors, plural forms of leadership become inhabited by a wider range of actors who challenge organisational elites and privileged sources of power.

CONCLUSION

In a recent paper, Cloutier and Langley (2020) look at strategies to develop process theories without empirical enquiry. They use as one starting point the distinction between weak and strong process approaches: *While the first may indeed incorporate the notion of change and evolution of time, it views processes as 'happening to things' that nevertheless retain their unique identity over time. In contrast, from a 'strong' process ontological perspective, process is viewed as all encompassing: things are seen as momentary instantiations of processes* (Cloutier & Langley, 2020, p. 1). They suggest that theorising from a process perspective can focus on practices, activities and entanglements that stabilise a conceptual entity – in our case plural leadership. While they are most interested in the pay-off of strong process theorisation, at the end of the paper they introduce the notion of disentanglement, where the framing of agents and objects plays a key role in process theorisation. Our assessment of scholarly work on plural leadership brings us to a similar place. Strong process and weak process combine in an unexpected way, which supports the importance of both entitative and relational approaches in leadership studies. Our assessment of the field suggests that entities have a role in the formation of plural leadership, and that it is important to understand how these entities participate in the unfolding of leadership and its relational dynamics. We suggest that the role of agents needs to be restored to reconcile immanence with the specificity and tractability of plurality in leadership. While entitative representations of leadership have often been associated with heroic leadership, our analysis builds on a more polysemic notion of the role of entity in shaping plural leadership. Agents are conceptualised in our review as complex social entities that bring pluralism to plurality of leadership, a view that calls for a more critical look at leadership studies. Immanent expressions of leadership are also the result of agentic capacities that influence the unfolding of processes and practices associated with the emergence of plural forms of leadership.

Based on our review of the field, we advocate anchoring studies on plural leadership strongly within the more critical stream of organisational scholarship. The predominance of consensual politics as an overarching matrix to approach plurality of leadership appears counter-productive. The veil of consensual politics makes it difficult to address the various potentialities of plural forms of leadership in organisations and society. Overall, we delineate two main representations of plural leadership: plural leadership as revelatory of a renewal of forms of control in organisations to align actors with hierarchy and structural determinism; and plural leadership as a contested terrain where resistors demand active participation in leadership. This second representation opens the possibility of multiple co-existing leadership configurations within and across organisations, where actors seek to maintain or transform manifestations of plural leadership.

In terms of *practical implications*, we emphasise that individuals who are mobilised within plural leadership forms are consequential. Depending on their relational abilities and reflexivity, they nurture, to a greater or lesser extent, the development and sustainability of more collective forms of leadership. In addition, as suggested in our treatment of the relation between plurality of the self and plural leadership, individuals are potential carriers of diversity and inclusivity in organisations and consequently of plurality in leadership.

We also suggest that plural forms of leadership can be analogous to leaderism and hyper-management in organisations. Individuals engaged in plural leadership forms need to adopt a reflexive posture and ask how effectively plurality enables new forms of collaboration within organisations and contributes to the expansion of their own agentic capacities. One may argue that a call for plural leadership is essentially a political statement in organisations that can be oppressive or emancipative depending on the malleability of prevalent structures and power relationships. These considerations bring us to the significant role of resistors or more marginal organisational actors in the development of plural leadership forms. Again, this is only plausible in situations where actors, through their reflexive stance, challenge the distribution of opportunities and power that shape the organisational context.

Another important insight from our analysis is that plural leadership is an achievement. It is effortful to develop and sustain because of the social substrate of the organisation. Aspiring leaders face conflicts and contradictions that emerge from attempts to achieve cooperation among individuals or groups that have very different experiences of organisational life. If the notion of plural forms of leadership implies greater heterogeneity among leadership roles and situations, it will necessarily raise tensions and contradictions among aspiring leaders.

FUNDING

Canada Research Chair on Health System Design and Adaptation (Jean-Louis Denis)
Research Scholar FRQS (Nancy Côté)

REFERENCES

Alvarez, J.L., & Svejenova, S. (2005). *Sharing executive power: Roles and relationships at the top*. Cambridge: Cambridge University Press.

Alvesson, M., & Spicer, A. (2014). Critical perspectives on leadership. *The Oxford Handbook of Leadership and Organizations* (pp. 40–56). Oxford University Press.

Alvesson, M., & Sveningsson, S. (2003). Managers doing leadership: The extra-ordinarization of the mundane. *Human Relations*, 56(12), 1435–1459.

Alvesson, M., & Willmott, H. (2002). Identity regulation as organizational control: Producing the appropriate individual. *Journal of Management Studies*, 39(5), 619–644.

Barge, J. K. (2014). Pivotal leadership and the art of conversation. *Leadership*, 10(1), 56–78.

Benne, K. D., & Sheats, P. (1948). Functional roles of group members. In S. Tubbs (Ed.), *Shared Experiences in Human Communication* (pp. 155–163). Routledge.

Briscoe, F., & Gupta, A. (2016). Social activism in and around organizations. *Academy of Management Annals*, 10(1), 671–727.

Brock, D. M. (2008). The reconstructed professional firm: A reappraisal of Ackroyd and Muzio (2007). *Organization Studies*, 29(1), 145–149.

Bromley, P., & Meyer, J. W. (2021). Hyper-management: Neoliberal expansions of purpose and leadership. *Organization Theory*, 2(3), 26317877211020330.

Brown, A. D. (2015). Identities and identity work in organizations. *International Journal of Management Reviews*, 17(1), 20–40.

Cartwright, D. (1965). Influence, leadership, control. *University of Illinois at Urbana-Champaign's Academy for Entrepreneurial Leadership Historical Research Reference in Entrepreneurship*. University of Illinois.

Cetina, K. K., Schatzki, T. R., & Von Savigny, E. (2005). *The Practice Turn in Contemporary Theory*. Routledge.

Chia, R., & Tsoukas, H. (2003). Everything flows and nothing abides: towards a 'rhizomic' model of organizational change, transformation and action. *Process Studies*, 32(2), 196–224.

Chreim, S. (2015). The (non) distribution of leadership roles: Considering leadership practices and configurations. *Human Relations*, 68(4), 517–543.

Chreim, S., Langley, A., Reay, T., Comeau-Vallée, M., & Huq, J. L. (2020). Constructing and sustaining counter-institutional identities. *Academy of Management Journal*, 63(3), 935–964.

Cloutier, C., & Langley, A. (2020). What makes a process theoretical contribution? *Organization Theory*, 1(1), 2631787720902473.

Collinson, D. (2017). Critical leadership studies: A response to Learmonth and Morrell. *Leadership*, 13(3), 272–284.

Collinson, D. L. (2020). 'Only connect!': Exploring the critical dialectical turn in leadership studies. *Organization Theory*, 1(2), 2631787720913878.

Coun, M., Peters, P., & Blomme, R. (2019). Taking the leadership role: Understanding leadership across team and organizational boundaries in view of the changing employment relationship. *Journal of Leadership Studies*, 12(4), 65–68.

Courpasson, D. (2000). Managerial strategies of domination: Power in soft bureaucracies. *Organization Studies*, 21(1), 141–161.

Courpasson, D., Dany, F., & Clegg, S. (2012). Resisters at work: Generating productive resistance in the workplace. *Organization Science*, 23(3), 801–819.

Crevani, L. (2011). *Clearing for action: Leadership as a relational phenomenon* (PhD Thesis). KTH Royal Institute of Technology.

Crevani, L., & Endrissat, N. (2016). Mapping the leadership-as-practice terrain: Comparative elements. In J. A. Raelin (Ed.), *Leadership-as-Practice* (pp. 21–49). Routledge.

Crevani, L., Lindgren, M., & Packendorff, J. (2007). Shared leadership: A post-heroic perspective on leadership as a collective construction. *International Journal of Leadership Studies*, 3(1), 40–67.

Dachler, H. P., & Hosking, D.-M. (1995). The primacy of relations in socially constructing organizational realities. In D.-M. Hosking, H. P. Dachler & K. J. Gergen (Eds.), *Management and Organization: Relational Alternatives to Individualism* (pp. 1–28). Avebury/Ashgate.

De Vaujany, F.-X., Leclercq-Vandelannoitte, A., Munro, I., Nama, Y., & Holt, R. (2021). Control and surveillance in work practice: cultivating paradox in 'new' modes of organizing. *Organization Studies*, 42(5), 675–695.

Denis, J.-L., Lamothe, L., & Langley, A. (2001). The dynamics of collective leadership and strategic change in pluralistic organizations. *Academy of Management Journal*, 44(4), 809–837.

Denis, J.-L., Langley, A., Cazale, L., Denis, J.-L., Cazale, L., & Langley, A. (1996). Leadership and strategic change under ambiguity. *Organization Studies*, 17(4), 673–699.

Denis, J.-L., Langley, A., & Rouleau, L. (2007). Strategizing in pluralistic contexts: Rethinking theoretical frames. *Human Relations*, 60(1), 179–215.

Denis, J.-L., Langley, A., & Sergi, V. (2012). Leadership in the plural. *Academy of Management Annals*, 6(1), 211–283.

DeRue, D. S., & Ashford, S. J. (2010). Who will lead and who will follow? A social process of leadership identity construction in organizations. *Academy of Management Review*, 35(4), 627–647.

Drath, W. H. (2001). *The Deep Blue Sea: Rethinking the Source of Leadership*. Jossey-Bass.

Drath, W. H., McCauley, C. D., Palus, C. J., Van Velsor, E., O'Connor, P. M., & McGuire, J. B. (2008). Direction, alignment, commitment: Toward a more integrative ontology of leadership. *Leadership Quarterly*, *19*(6), 635–653.

Empson, L., & Alvehus, J. (2020). Collective leadership dynamics among professional peers: Co-constructing an unstable equilibrium. *Organization Studies*, *41*(9), 1234–1256.

Fairhurst, G. T., & Grant, D. (2010). The social construction of leadership: A sailing guide. *Management Communication Quarterly*, *24*(2), 171–210.

Ferlie, E., Fitzgerald, L., Wood, M., & Hawkins, C. (2005). The nonspread of innovations: The mediating role of professionals. *Academy of Management Journal*, *48*(1), 117–134.

Fitzsimons, D., James, K. T., & Denyer, D. (2011). Alternative approaches for studying shared and distributed leadership. *International Journal of Management Reviews*, *13*(3), 313–328.

Follett, M. P. (1924). *Creative Experience*. Longmans, Green.

Ford, J. (2020). Leadership and identities: Towards more critical relational approaches. *The Oxford Handbook on Identities in Organizations* (pp. 750–765). Oxford University Press.

Gibb, C. A., Lindzey, G., & Aronson, E. (1954). *Handbook of Social Psychology*. Addison Wesley.

Gibeau, É., Langley, A., Denis, J.-L., & van Schendel, N. (2020). Bridging competing demands through co-leadership? Potential and limitations. *Human Relations*, *73*(4), 464–489.

Gill, C., & Caza, A. (2018). An investigation of authentic leadership's individual and group influences on follower responses. *Journal of Management*, *44*(2), 530–554.

Goldring, L.(2002). The power of school culture. *Leadership*, *32*(2), 32–35.

Greenwood, R., & Prakash, R. (2017). 25 years of the professional partnership (P2) form: Time to foreground its social purpose and herald the P3? *Journal of Professions and Organization*, *4*(2), 112–122.

Greenwood, R., Raynard, M., Kodeih, F., Micelotta, E. R., & Lounsbury, M. (2011). Institutional complexity and organizational responses. *Academy of Management Annals*, *5*(1), 317–371.

Gronn, P. (1999). Substituting for leadership: The neglected role of the leadership couple. *Leadership Quarterly*, *10*(1), 41–62.

Gronn, P. (2002). Distributed leadership as a unit of analysis. *Leadership Quarterly*, *13*(4), 423–451.

Gronn, P. (2003). *The New Work of Educational Leaders: Changing Leadership Practice in an Era of School Reform*. Sage.

Hambrick, D. C., & Mason, P. A. (1984). Upper echelons: The organization as a reflection of its top managers. *Academy of Management Review*, *9*(2), 193–206.

Heenan, D. A., Bennis, W. G., & Bennis, W. (1999). *Co-leaders: The Power of Great Partnerships*. University of Texas Press.

Hosking, D. M. (2011). Moving relationality: Meditations on a relational approach to leadership. *The SAGE Handbook of Leadership* (pp. 455–467). Sage.

Huxham, C., & Vangen, S. (2000). Leadership in the shaping and implementation agendas: How things happen in a collaboration (not quite) joined-up world. *Academy of anagement Journal*, *43*(6), 1159–1175.

Jian, G. (2022). From empathic leader to empathic leadership practice: An extension to relational leadership theory. *Human Relations*, *75*(5), 931–955.

Kort, E. D. (2008). What, after all, is leadership? 'Leadership'and plural action. *Leadership Quarterly*, *19*(4), 409–425.

Lawrence, T. B., & Phillips, N. (2019). *Constructing Organizational Life: How Social-Symbolic Work Shapes Selves, Organizations, and Institutions*. Oxford University Press.

Leng, H.-S. (1969). *Political Leadership in a Plural Society: Penang in the 1960's*. Australian National University.

Lichtenstein, B. B., Uhl-Bien, M., Marion, R., Seers, A., Orton, J. D., & Schreiber, C. (2006). Complexity leadership theory: an interactive perspective on leading in complex adaptive systems. *Emergence: Complexity and Organization*, *8*(4), 2–12.

Lockett, A., Currie, G., Waring, J., Finn, R., & Martin, G. (2012). The role of institutional entrepreneurs in reforming healthcare. *Social Science & Medicine*, *74*(3), 356–363.

Lok, J., & Willmott, H. (2019). Embedded agency in institutional theory: Problem or paradox? *Academy of Management Review*, *44*(2), 470–473.

Lusiani, M., Denis, J.-L., & Langley, A. (2016). Plural leadership in health care organizations. *The Oxford Handbook of Health Care Management* (pp. 210–230).

Manz, C.C. and Sims, H.P. Jr (1993). *Business without Bosses: How Self-Managing Teams Are Building High Performance Companies*. New York: Wiley.

Manz, C.C. and Sims, H.P. Jr (2001). *The New Superleadership: Leading Others to Lead Themselves*. San Francisco, CA: Berrett-Koehler.

Meyer, J. W. (2010). World society, institutional theories, and the actor. *Annual Review of Sociology*, *36*, 1–20.

Mumby, D. K., Thomas, R., Martí, I., & Seidl, D. (2017). Resistance redux. *Organization Studies*, *38*(9), 1157–1183.

Nicolini, D. (2012). *Practice theory, work, and organization: An introduction*. OUP Oxford.

O'Reilly, D., & Reed, M. (2010). 'Leaderism': An evolution of managerialism in UK public service reform. *Public Administration*, 88(4), 960–978.

O'Reilly, D., & Reed, M. (2011). The grit in the oyster: Professionalism, managerialism and leaderism as discourses of UK public services modernization. *Organization Studies*, 32(8), 1079–1101.

Ospina, S. M., Foldy, E. G., Fairhurst, G. T., & Jackson, B. (2020). Collective dimensions of leadership: Connecting theory and method. *Human Relations*, 73(4), 441–463.

Packendorff, J., Crevani, L., & Lindgren, M. (2014). Project leadership in becoming: A process study of an organizational change project. *Project Management Journal*, 45(3), 5–20.

Pearce, C.L. and Sims, H.P. (2000). Shared leadership: toward a multi-level theory of leadership. In Beyerlein, M.M., Johnson, D.A. and Beyerlein, S.T. (eds), *Advances in Interdisciplinary Studies of Work Teams: Team Development*, Vol. 7. Greenwich, CT: JAI Press, pp. 115–139.

Pearce, C.L. and Sims, H.P. (2002). The relative influence of vertical vs. shared leadership on the longitudinal effectiveness of change management teams. *Group Dynamics: Theory, Research and Practice*, 6, pp. 172–197.

Pearce, C.L., Conger, J.A. and Locke, E.A. (2008). Shared leadership theory. *Leadership Quarterly*, 19, pp. 622–628.

Pearce, C.L., Manz, C.C. and Sims, H.P. Jr (2009). Where do we go from here? Is shared leadership the key to team success? *Organizational Dynamics*, 38, pp. 234–238.

Pratt, M. G., & Rafaeli, A. (2013). Artifacts and organizations: Understanding our 'object-ive' reality. In M. G. Pratt & A. Rafaeli (Eds.), *Artifacts and Organizations* (pp. 295–304). Psychology Press.

Pullen, A., & Vachhani, S. (2013). *The Materiality of Leadership*. Sage.

Pye, A. (2005). Leadership and organizing: Sensemaking in action. *Leadership*, 1(1), 31–49.

Raelin, J. A. (2016). Introduction to leadership-as-practice: Theory and application. In J. A. Raelin (Ed.), *Leadership-as-Practice* (pp. 1–17). Routledge.

Raelin, J. A. (2017). Leadership-as-practice: Theory and application – An editor's reflection. *Leadership*, 13(2), 215–221.

Ramarajan, L. (2014). Past, present and future research on multiple identities: Toward an intrapersonal network approach. *Academy of Management Annals*, 8(1), 589–659.

Reed, M. (2003). The agency/structure dilemma in organization theory: Open doors and brick walls. *The Oxford Handbook of Organization Theory* (pp. 289–309). Oxford University Press.

Ropo, A., & Salovaara, P. (2019). Spacing leadership as an embodied and performative process. *Leadership*, 15(4), 461–479.

Rouleau, L. (2011). *Théories des organisations: Approches classiques, contemporaines et de l'avant-garde*. Puq.

Schedlitzki, D., & Edwards, G. (2021). *Studying Leadership: Traditional and Critical Approaches*. Sage.

Sergi, V. (2016). Who's leading the way?: Investigating the contributions of materiality to leadership-as-practice. In J. A. Raelin (Ed.), *Leadership-as-Practice* (pp. 110–131). Routledge.

Sergi, V., Denis, J.-L., & Langley, A. (2012). Opening up perspectives on plural leadership. *Industrial and Organizational Psychology*, 5(4), 403–407.

Sergi, V., Lusiani, M., & Langley, A. (2021). Highlighting the plural: Leading amidst romance (s). *Journal of Change Management*, 21(2), 163–179.

Shafik, M. (2021). *What We Owe Each Other*. Princeton University Press.

Spillane, J. P. (2006). Towards a theory of leadership practice: A distributed perspective. In *Rethinking schooling* (pp. 208–242). Routledge.

Spillane, J. P. (2012). *Distributed Leadership* (Vol. 4). John Wiley & Sons.

Theoharis, G. (2007). Social justice educational leaders and resistance: Toward a theory of social justice leadership. *Educational Administration Quarterly*, 43(2), 221–258.

Theoharis, G. T. (2004). *At No Small Cost: Social Justice Leaders and their Response to Resistance*. University of Wisconsin-Madison.

Tourish, D. (2018). Dysfunctional leadership in corporations. In P. Garrard (Ed.), *The Leadership Hubris Epidemic* (pp. 137–162). Springer.

Uhl-Bien, M. (2006). Relational leadership theory: Exploring the social processes of leadership and organizing. *Leadership Quarterly*, 17(6), 654–676.

Uhl-Bien, M., & Arena, M. (2018). Leadership for organizational adaptability: A theoretical synthesis and integrative framework. *Leadership Quarterly*, 29(1), 89–104.

Uhl-Bien, M., & Marion, R. (2009). Complexity leadership in bureaucratic forms of organizing: A meso model. *Leadership Quarterly*, 20(4), 631–650.

Uhl-Bien, M., Marion, R., & McKelvey, B. (2007). Complexity leadership theory: Shifting leadership from the industrial age to the knowledge era. *Leadership Quarterly*, 18(4), 298–318.

Vine, B., Holmes, J., Marra, M., Pfeifer, D., & Jackson, B. (2008). Exploring co-leadership talk through interactional sociolinguistics. *Leadership*, 4(3), 339–360.

Wamsley, G. L., & Zald, M. N. (1973). The political economy of public organizations. *Public Administration Review*, 62–73.

Waring, J., Marshall, F., Bishop, S., Sahota, O., Walker, M. F., Currie, G., ... & Avery, T. J. (2014). An ethnographic study of knowledge sharing across the boundaries between care processes, services and organisations: the contributions to 'safe' hospital discharge. *Health Services and Delivery Research*, 2(29).

White, L., Currie, G., & Lockett, A. (2014). The enactment of plural leadership in a health and social care network: The influence of institutional context. *Leadership Quarterly*, *25*(4), 730–745.

Wood, J. R., & Zald, M. N. (1966). Aspects of racial integration in the Methodist Church: Sources of resistance to organizational policy. *Social Forces*, *45*(2), 255–265.

Yammarino, F. J., Salas, E., Serban, A., Shirreffs, K., & Shuffler, M. L. (2012). Collectivistic leadership approaches: Putting the 'we' in leadership science and practice. *Industrial and Organizational Psychology*, *5*(4), 382–402.

Youngs, H. (2017). A critical exploration of collaborative and distributed leadership in higher education: Developing an alternative ontology through leadership-as-practice. *Journal of Higher Education Policy and Management*, *39*(2), 140–154.

Zietsma, C., & Lawrence, T. B. (2010). Institutional work in the transformation of an organizational field: The interplay of boundary work and practice work. *Administrative Science Quarterly*, *55*(2), 189–221.

ZOLLER, Heather M. et FAIRHURST, Gail T. Resistance leadership: The overlooked potential in critical organization and leadership studies. *Human Relations*, 2007, vol. 60, no 9, p. 1331–1360.

Leadership and Practice Theories: Reconstructing Leadership as a Phenomenon

Lucia Crevani and Inti José Lammi

INTRODUCTION

This chapter focuses on the study of leadership and practice with the aim to foreground how different strands of practice theory have contributed to an understanding of leadership as phenomenon by providing a specific orientation and sensibility. Practice theories have been one way of answering the need for accounting for the processual, relational and interactional character of leadership. In fact, practice theories not only offer the theoretical and methodological tools to understand leadership as a social accomplishment – but also, as we will argue, as a material accomplishment.

Conceptualising leadership in terms of practice is not new (Follett, 1919; Hosking, 1988). However, what is exactly implied in such conceptualisation can vary. In broad terms, practice can be understood to designate what people do together. Building on such a general idea, leadership scholars have increasingly focused on *how leadership is performed and enacted in a distributed way through situated everyday actions*. Leadership is thus not necessarily what leaders do. Rather, it is the practical collective accomplishment of direction in organising that is in focus. However, there is not one theory of practice but multiple, which implies that multiple lines of enquiry are imaginable for practice studies of leadership.

In this chapter, we describe how leadership studies have benefitted by (re)attending to practice theories. Practice theories are not presented as more valid theoretical alternatives than dominant leadership theories. Rather, we elaborate on how these theories have offered the possibility to develop new understandings of leadership by reimagining the study of this phenomenon.

The first section of the chapter presents an introduction to practice theories and their entrance in leadership studies. Then, in the second section, we illustrate what studies mobilising practice theories have contributed to. In the third section we dig into a discussion of the different positionings that researchers drawing on practice theories have taken, in order to provide the reader with the possibility to navigate the sensitising framework that these theories provide. The chapter ends with a discussion of criticalities and possibilities, including the possible need to advance our methodological tools.

PRACTICE THEORIES

A Brief Genealogy of Practice Theories

In this chapter we review the theoretical and analytical peculiarity of practice theories in relation to the study of leadership. The commonsensical interpretation of the notion of practice as that opposite to theory is not our point of departure. Practices are *meaning-making, order-producing and reality-shaping activities* (Nicolini & Monteiro, 2017, p. 114). These can, as Reckwitz (2002) proposes, be understood in two senses. On the one hand, the concept of practice is often evoked to designate activity in general – for example, as praxis. On the other hand, it is also common to speak of practice to designate specific sets of organised actions (Schatzki, 1996, 2002; Shove et al., 2012) – for example, practices. These two senses of discussing practices are not opposite notions. Practice scholars can refer to praxis and engage in analysing the process of bringing about social phenomena such as strategy or technology. At other times, scholars might analyse one particular set of organised actions – for example, certain work or meeting practices – and do so with granularity. For leadership, this means either discussing how leadership emerges in action widely speaking, for instance by following how a certain course for collective action emerges, or to alternatively focus on specific practices that play a role in the enactment of leadership, as for instance the preparation of a meeting room in which furniture and objects are arranged so that authority is produced in a specific way. We will clarify this further below.

It is difficult to account for practice theories without accounting for the theoretical discussion and disagreement between conceptual paradigms that preceded them. Reasons for being interested in practice, as either praxis or practices, stem from the two-decades old 'turn to practice' within the social sciences that reflected the rise of practice theorising as a separate line of thought (Schatzki et al., 2001). Arguably, this turn stretches further back (Miettinen et al., 2009). For our purposes we will briefly discuss what has been called 'classical' practice theory (Sandberg & Tsoukas, 2015), namely the work of Giddens (1979, 1984) and Bourdieu (1977, 1990). Both are commonly cited for having challenged two dominating ways of studying social phenomena at their time. On the one hand, the structuralist – and functionalist – approach that often entailed conceptually and analytically privileging large or 'deep structures' beyond human intention and control. On the other hand, the subjectivist, phenomenological stream of research that conceptually and analytically privileged individual intentions and experiences alone.

Both these approaches were problematised for creating the classical agency/structure-debate dividing scholars into two camps. On the one hand, those marshalling individualist voluntarism risked overlooking the contextual constraints of social action. On the other hand, static, deterministic, forms of analysis risked treating people as 'cultural dopes', only able to heed and reinforce structure unreflexively. In both Bourdieu's and Giddens' work, one finds appeals to consider the 'in-between', the space where agency and structure necessarily are interlinked: practice. It is in practice and across practices that structure comes to matter, when norms and resources that pre-date any instance of practising are mobilised in time/space by individuals and thus re-enacted. By arguing that actors were reflexive but that their action fundamentally presupposed some form of structure, both theorists argued that what mattered was not structure nor agency in abstract terms, but rather what could be pictured *in situ*, in practice. Realising this point, classical practice theorists also argued that it was possible to also account for how structures could change. Participation in practices presupposes structure but is not predetermined by extant norms and resources during actual practising. Giddens argued for the notion of a duality of structure to suggest that structure is both a means for actors to engage socially and an outcome of practical doing. This distinctive set of thinking is often tied to classical practice theorising but comes in different forms across the social sciences – for example, in ethnomethodology (Garfinkel, 1967; Suchman, 2007), feminist theorising of situated knowledge (Haraway, 1988) and posthumanist perspectives (Latour, 2005; Pickering, 1995).

Both leadership studies and the closely linked field of organisation and management studies (OMS) have been informed by practice theories through their conceptual affordances. Traces are in the efforts to go beyond agency/structure as a dichotomy, but also in efforts to conceptually attend to the challenges of organisational practice – and to come close to the actual practice rather than being limited to abstract notions that risk being devoid of practical relevance (Sandberg & Tsoukas, 2011). The work of Orlikowski (2000), Orr (1996), Feldman (2000), Barley (1996) and Gherardi (2001) offers important examples what new insight we have gained about phenomena such as work, routines, rules, knowledge and technology by exploring the 'in-between' – practice – within the realm of organisations. Since the turn two decades ago, the appeal of these theories has also fostered new research directions, many

Practice Theories in Leadership Studies

Shortly after the 'turn to practice', leadership studies followed with their own version of the 'turn' (examples are Carroll et al., 2008; Crevani et al., 2010; Raelin, 2007, 2011). Carroll et al. (2008), for instance, argued for translating the philosophical underpinnings of practice theories into leadership studies to critically reassess the meaning of leadership and leadership development. In relation to this, Crevani et al. (2010) articulated a set of basic assumptions on the nature of leadership, how to develop knowledge on it and how to deal with normative aspects to move researchers' attention from individuals to everyday social interactions and what these interactions achieve in practice. This 'turn' also included a shift in how leadership scholars approached the theory/practice divide, with calls to attend to practice-based learning in relation to leadership (Raelin, 2007). In these terms, doing leadership implied learning in the midst of action, learning where reflection and uncertainty could have a role to play for practitioners that would develop their own tools. In parallel, there also were attempts at articulating leadership in terms of desirable sets of inclusive leadership practices, as for instance with the normative notion of leaderful practice (Raelin, 2011). Hence, elements that were brought to the fore in this 'turn' included the importance of understanding non-heroic work and non-deliberate actions, as well as the need for developing knowledge of practical relevance and reframing how leadership development programmes were designed.

This 'turn' took place in the context of a broader set of developments motivated by dissatisfaction with the way leadership had been traditionally studied, practised and taught. Formally shared forms of leading were increasingly becoming legitimated among practitioners and their merits acknowledged by researchers (Pearce & Conger, 2002). Also, scholars, in particular those interested in professional and pluralistic organisations (such as hospitals or schools), increasingly started to characterise leadership as distributed, collective, postheroic, relational, plural, characterised by complexity (see Brown & Hosking, 1986; Fletcher, 2004; Cunliffe & Eriksen, 2011; Denis et al., 2001; Uhl-Bien et al., 2007). This also sparked an interest for interrogating the nature of the phenomenon of leadership by reflecting on its relational as well as its processual character (Barker, 1997; Drath et al., 2008; Wood, 2005) and its location in everyday interactions (Larsson & Lundholm, 2010).

All these developments led to a context ripe for pursuing new avenues of research. Practice theories proved capable of offering *a unique orientation* to the study of leadership: one way of answering the need to account for the processual, relational and interactional character of the phenomenon by providing the theoretical and methodological tools to understand it as a social accomplishment. This meant de-emphasising the focus on individual agency typical of leadership notions and contextualising individual actions in wider bundles or texture of practices (Simpson, 2016). Concretely, this implied the need to look for situations in which leadership may emerge, rather than studying individuals identified as leaders before they even act. Is a CEO giving a speech in a room filled with employees or is a manager having a delicate conversation with a subordinate doing leadership? We do not know before the situation has unfolded and we can say whether direction has emerged or not. In order to do that, we need to pay attention to not only what the CEO or manager is doing, but also what others, including objects and spaces, are doing and have been doing over time.

In sum, the translation of practice theories into leadership studies entailed primarily a way of going beyond individualist explanations. The appeal of practice theories was the possibility to approach the in-between of social life and individuals in action and to, in many cases, simultaneously charge the notion of practice with important normative and critical implications regarding the 'who' and 'how' of leadership. This has led to an understanding of what practice means for leadership studies focused on relationality, processuality, distributedness and situatedness. Studies exploring and making sense of these aspects of leadership need certain methodological orientations. As we will discuss below, researchers mobilise practice theories in different ways that, in turn, require different methods.

LEADERSHIP STUDIES BUILDING ON PRACTICE THEORIES: EMERGING INSIGHTS RECONSTRUCTING THE PHENOMENON

The mobilisation of practice theories in the study of leadership presented an opportunity to reconstruct the phenomenon of leadership. In this section, we emphasise interconnected reframings that brought the 'in-between' to the fore resulting in interesting avenues in leadership research.

Decentring Leadership

The first reframing we point to is the *decentring leadership from specific individuals*. The classical unit of analysis of leadership studies, the leader, is challenged when leadership is envisioned as accomplished in actions and interactions among several actors. There are two ways of interpreting this decentring. In its less challenging form, this means recognising that more people are involved in producing direction and that they can come from different hierarchical levels; in its more radical form, this means that objects, places, technologies are also seen as critical relata, even as actors, involved in the accomplishment of leadership. This means thinking of leadership beyond individual leaders (see also Chapter 1, Pluralism in studies on plural leadership), if thinking of leaders at all. It means focusing on accounting for the role played by different actors in producing direction. Decentring also implies giving relations conceptual and analytical priority. Reality – and leadership – can be seen as being produced and reproduced through relations (Ospina and Foldy, 2010). This means treating individuals as embedded in and transformed in fields of relations (foregrounding interdependence), rather than considering them as autonomous entities (foregrounding independence).

Focusing on practice thus has enabled us to, for example, explore the so-called leadership in the plural (see Chapter 1, Pluralism in studies on plural leadership, and Denis et al., 2012) by for instance analysing how different configurations of leadership roles may emerge and with which consequences. As an example, Chreim (2015) shows what happens when managers become part of an ambiguous leadership space, as in the case of a merger with units including managers from both merging companies. Authority and responsibilities are negotiated and distributed through practices of framing each other, shaping relations (for instance in terms of mutual accommodation) and configuring role definitions (for instance as complementary). This results in leadership spaces ranging from vacant spaces (no one takes initiatives to enact leadership) to overcrowded spaces (where work for configuring the roles of the people in the space is considered to take too much energy, at the expense of other work). Whereas researchers may still centre their studies on formal leaders, these actors are not understood as the ones in charge, but as part of an assemblage or configuration of actors accomplishing leadership (Vivier and Sanchez, 2020). This also implies opening up for the possibility to include nonhuman actors in such an assemblage (see also Chapter 21, Problematising communication and providing inspiration).

Expanding Leadership

The second reframing is *expanding leadership* to pay attention to more dimensions of practice than the discursive dimension that many studies of leadership have foregrounded. These dimensions include materiality and embodiment. Someone engaging in a practice necessarily engages with their body, – for example by manual labour, typing on a computer, or speaking with their voice in front of audience. This, in tandem, occurs with objects that practices critically depend on. Giving a PowerPoint presentation critically depends on a computer and certain software, after all. Not only objects but also affect, atmospheres and the space where interacting and relating happens matter for accomplishing of leadership.

Technologies, artefacts and workspaces are therefore considered as important elements in interactions producing leadership, which means that suited concepts and methods to capture and make sense of them are needed. Inspiration may come from various streams of research such as, among others, science and technology studies, affect theory, phenomenology, human geography. These methodologies can imply a foregrounding of the body and what the body experiences as central to how leadership unfolds (see also Chapter 22, Leadership as aesthetic and artful practice). For instance, *living bodies serve as tangible media through which various forms of leadership practices are negotiated, fractured, resisted or integrated* (Küpers, 2013, p. 336). In this view, responsiveness is embodied and relations cannot be instrumentally controlled (Küpers, 2013).

Not only the body, but also the situation is understood as co-constituting leadership. The context of leadership is not a static container, but integral part of the performance of leadership. Atmospheres are, for instance, clearly important when it comes to influencing, producing direction and engaging. We have all experienced, in one way or another, how a meeting atmosphere can be tense, energic, frightening. But as social scientists, we are mostly trained to reproduce what is done with words and we are not used to making full use of our body and what it senses while observing. Interestingly, expanding leadership enquiry means acknowledging the embodied nature of knowledge. An example is provided by Salovaara's work (2014) that in an affective way explores the role of space and place through a video that guides us through different environments, from an elevator to a chapel. The concept of 'spacing leadership' is then proposed to express how leadership is produced in an embodied process between people and space. Building on a relational and processual understanding of space, in which we shape space as much as space shapes us, Ropo and Salovaara (2019) bring to the fore the role played by the senses, feelings and memories in the production of leadership when performing space. In other words, space contributes to leading through human embodied experiences. See also Chapter 21, Problematising communication and providing inspiration for similar discussions.

The notion of sociomateriality – that is, understanding the social and the material as constitutively entangled (Orlikowski and Scott, 2008) – has inspired not only Ropo and Salovaara's work, but also an increasing number of scholars. By means of an autoethnography, Case and Śliwa (2020) follow, for instance, the process in which the first author learns how an assemblage of humans and non-humans (including furniture, paintings, flags) contributes to produce leadership in a context unfamiliar to him. This enables him to more actively participate in organising such an assemblage and constructing his own positioning in it in order to participate in leadership practice and to exercise power. This is an example of how attending to non-humans does not mean disregarding the role of humans and their capacity to learn. Moreover, it also brings to the fore how politics and power are articulated in the flow of practice, as assemblages are ordered and reordered. This may also mean that individuals should consider taking responsibility for the assemblages they become part of and act within (Andersson et al., forthcoming).

To be considered is also that, in Endrissat and von Arx's words, leadership practice is *context-shaped but also context-shaping* (2013, p. 300). They show how historically grown practices, such as consensus practices, both constitute the premises for practising leadership and are reproduced in such practising (Endrissat and von Arx, 2013). To some extent, thus, individual intentionality is 'preconfigured' by those practices that constitute the context, at the same time as such a context is ongoingly reconstructed.

Of course, practice is not the only way of approaching the materiality and sensuality of leadership. See Chapter 21, Problematising communication and providing inspiration, Chapter 22, Leadership as aesthetic and artful practice, and Chapter 24, Technology and leadership, as examples of other approaches to these matters.

Redefining Leadership

The third reframing is *redefining leadership* and its very meaning. This follows from developing a different understanding of where leadership happens and how it happens, as a consequence of both decentring and expanding leadership. In some research traditions as well as in organisational life there may be a tendency to reproduce leadership in terms of somewhat grandiose acts taking place at a specific time and place, and leading to affecting the way organisational members act in a certain direction. Leadership is thus traditionally understood as exercised by a leader on followers. Meindl and colleagues have, for instance, talked of the 'romance of leadership' as how people tend to create heroes when making sense of how things develop (1985). Sergi et al. (2021) have recently shown how, even when going from appreciating male heroes to praising the way in which female leaders handled a crisis, there still is a tendency to attribute achievements that have a collective character to single individuals and to put our hope in their hands. However, practice theories have enabled researchers to instead bring to the fore the mundane, decentred and expanded character of leadership.

Leadership is then conceptualised as the complex, unfolding outcome of interactions involving assemblages of human and non-human actors. It is in the emergence of interactions that direction may be produced and thus agency is to be found in the practising itself, implicating the need to unpack the 'consequentiality of everyday practices' (Feldman and Orlikowski, 2011). Emergence, given the processual character of leadership, is thus a key concept. Processes are often understood in terms of variance between two stable states, start and end. Practice theories focus instead on what happens in the emergent flow of action, positing that the world is in an ongoing state of becoming. This effort includes not only identifying different kinds of doings taking place in organisations, but also interpreting what such doings accomplish. A processual understanding is open to divergence, contradictions and tensions in the ongoing production of direction – that is, of leadership. Understanding process in this way also implies that agency emerges in the practising itself, depending on how it plays out, and it is not solely a matter of individual intentionality (Simpson, 2016; Crevani, 2018; see Chapter 23, Process theory approaches to leadership).

What follows is thus that a romantic and heroic view of leadership is challenged by a more mundane but also more inclusive view of leadership (see Chapter 3, Leadership in action). Studying practice enables, for instance, exploration of how community leadership, an informal kind of leadership, is sustained in everyday practices, such as those of service maintenance in an informal settlement in South Africa (Vivier and Sanchez, 2020). In this context of informality, and the related power-laden practices and inequalities, individuals gain and maintain legitimacy as community leaders due to their positioning as intermediaries between the city and the local community in the ongoing enactment of practices of service maintenance. Community leadership may thus be understood as a broad collective form of agency, enabled and constrained by informality, emerging in at times contradictory everyday practices that position community leaders as intermediaries.

Oborn et al. (2013) offer another example by exploring how leadership comes to be distributed *across sociomaterial practices which together (re) configure policy coalitions and context* in health policy development (p. 253) This is a complex context characterised by multiple stakeholders with divergent interests. As the authors describe, *leadership enactment entails engaging with materiality – for example, offices, meeting rooms, desks, computers, reports, email distribution lists. [...] multiple actors, data sheets, structures of accountability, specialized knowledge, technological resources, protocols and workshop rooms come together to enact leadership in formulating policy* (Oborn et al., 2013, p. 256). A process of transformation is therefore possible precisely because leadership is relationally distributed. Agency is produced in the contingent enactment of a distributed assemblage. Resolving conflict is thus achieved by manipulating the assemblage – for example, by incorporating a scientific paper that enables the legitimate reframing of an issue.

LEADERSHIP STUDIES BUILDING ON PRACTICE THEORIES: DIFFERENCES ACROSS SELECTED DIMENSIONS

Whereas the section above presented what kind of insight on the phenomenon of leadership has been developed through an orientation informed by practice theories, this section delves into the complexity of adopting such an orientation. Practice theories offer a rich sensitising and partly eclectic framework (Reckwitz, 2002; Gherardi, 2019a). Whereas this may be a strength, it is also demanding for the reader to navigate the diverse landscape of leadership studies that build on practice theories.

Below we suggest some ways of navigating this landscape. It is important to consider this multidimensional complexity to fully appreciate the range of studies that have been conducted, as well as which possibilities lie ahead. These dimensions are to be understood as ranges of positions, rather than linear distinctions, and are necessarily based on simplifications that do not do justice to the richness of details in the original works. Still, this may be a reasonable compromise in order to illustrate the main differences in leadership studies building on practice theories. We also want to point out that some dimensions are not to be treated as either/or. For instance, attention may be paid to the human-oriented 'social' and to the 'material' character of leadership to different degrees, but also be symmetrically balanced in socio-material theorising. Whereas these dimensions may be found in social sciences in general, we focus on these here as vividly actualised in leadership studies building on practice theories.

View: Entitative - Relational

The first dimension relates to how the researcher views reality. The entitative view posits that reality is composed of discrete and stable elements that interact with each other in performing leadership practices. As such, individuals have agency and can be studied in themselves. The relational view sees instead individuals as provisory stabilisations of ever-evolving relations. Individuals do not exist as separated entities but are rather produced and reproduced in relation; they co-evolve with other humans and non-humans (humans and non-humans co-constitute each other). The former position has dominated leadership studies in general and is found in many studies of leadership practices in which we follow individuals acting (for instance, Case and Śliwa, 2020). The latter position is sustained by the leadership approaches articulated in relational constructionism (Hosking, 1988), pragmatism and performativity (see Simpson, 2016, for a discussion), but was already anticipated by Mary Parker Follett's distinction between *power over* and *power with* (1924). Simpson (2016) calls such a view *leadership in the flow of practice* and provides a vivid narrative of the rugby team All Blacks' leadership paying attention to the *wholistic and continuous nature of the collective effort that transforms the meanings of situations* (Simpson, 2016, p. 172).

Worldview: Flat - Tall

Another dimension lies in a discussion not often explicit within studies of leadership building on practice theories. An interest in practices has often been accompanied by an interest in flat worldview (Latour, 2005) – that is, a worldview that conceives of the world as only composed of a plenum of interactions and/or practices (cf. Schatzki, 2016). This implies that 'large' social phenomena can be understood simply by tracing how practices interlink with one another. Only practices matter. This 'flat' understanding is common in studies focusing on the everyday practising, such as Ropo and Salovaara's work on leadership and spatial practices (2019), but also in studies conceptualising leadership as accomplished by heterogeneous assemblages (see, for instance, the case of leadership in policy formulation studied by Oborn et al., 2013).

In contrast, classical practice theorising often entailed an interest in larger social systems and structures, but approached these by attending to practices (e.g., Giddens, 1984). Such a worldview is 'tall'. In recent theorising, this has taken the shape of explaining the link between particular practices and wider institutional change (Smets et al., 2017). In leadership studies building on practice theories, a 'tall' worldview may thus mean sensitising scholars to investigate two particular concerns with leadership. First, it has helped, and can further help, to understand the relationship between particular instances of leadership and the wider discourses and taken-for-granted notions – the deeper, alternatively, the macro structures of leadership – that considerably define leadership. A second concern is that the bigger picture also can help to understand structural inequalities that define the asymmetric nature of 'classic' leadership. To solely focus on a situated occurrence of leadership may lead to losing track of these wider structures – for example, gender, class, ethnicity/race – that have prefigured the situation (see, for instance, the analysis done of learning leadership practices in a foreign country by Case and Śliwa, 2020). Consequently, critical studies of leadership may further build on the sensitising nature of a 'tall' worldview. See for instance, Chapter 41 Politicising the leader's body: From oppressive realities to affective possibilities and Chapter 43 Leadership representation: A critical path to equity.

Focus: Emergence - Patterns

The third dimension interrogates the meaning the researcher gives to practice and therefore what focus the enquiry has. As described at the beginning of the chapter, practice can be mobilised for focusing on praxis, on how leadership emerges in action in the continuous becoming of the world. Alternatively, it can be mobilised to focus on specific practices – that is, on specified recurrent patterns of actions that make up the structuring of organisational life. The former position sees leadership appearing in the changing direction of flow, in transforming a situation, and has, for instance been mobilised for identifying turning points in the flow of talk bringing together the past and the future with performative effects (Simpson et al., 2018). The latter position involves the identification of leadership practices and the analysis of what they do. For instance, Dovey et al. (2017) explore a number of practices in a television production setting creating *a form of 'interstitial glue' to bind [...] creative interests together without ever having to make the power of the broadcaster overt* (p. 33). These positions can be combined, of course, to suggest an interest in a number of practices and the emerging qualities of leadership.

Scope: Concentrated - Diluted

One central question when doing research on leadership and practice is if it is meaningful to talk of leadership without even mentioning leaders. Is it still leadership? How distributed can it become? And on the other hand, are there leaders without leadership being performed? Practice theories have been mobilised in order to contextualise how individuals enact leadership in relation to other individuals, in a specific place, together with certain objects, thus reconstructing and concentrating the locus of leadership to specific individuals and their doing (for instance, Case and Śliwa, 2020). But practice also enables a consideration of objects and places as actors participating in the producing of direction, thus diluting the locus of leadership to all those relations and actions that affect organising processes by directing them, meaning that assemblages are accomplishing leadership (for instance, Ropo and Salovaara, 2019, in relation to space or Oborn et al., 2013, in relation to a variety of objects and practices). This does not mean diminishing the importance of humans, their actions, their reflections and learning. It rather means that scholars can develop new knowledge on the unfolding of organising and how it is oriented by going beyond the focus on specific individuals and their doings.

Character: Material - Social

Leadership has predominantly been studied as a social phenomenon taking shape in relations and interactions, often focusing on meaning-making processes and communication in terms of discursive practices. The social character of leadership has been explored in a discursive way by interviewing and observing people, and accounting for what they say. The material character of the phenomenon has, however, increasingly gained researchers' interest. Materiality can take many forms, as above described, and includes attention to bodies, artefacts, spaces and places and technologies. When engaging with materiality, scholars often focus on one kind of materiality at a time. De Paoli et al. (2014) provide a rare case of attending to both the body and digital technologies. There are also different ways of conceiving of the relation between the social and the material and consequent avenues of research. How the social and the material influence each other is one possible avenue to pursue, whereas unpacking the effect of practices that are sociomaterial (that is both material and social at the same time) in character is another. If we take leadership enacted in a virtual meeting, in the first case we may look at how the technology affects the social interaction, whereas in the second case we may focus on the effects of doings that are sociomaterial in character, such as acknowledging each other's contributions (by, for instance, giving a yellow thumb up or nodding in a zoom meeting).

Term: Actor - Analyst

This dimension refers to a methodological question of how researchers know that what they are analysing is leadership. The matter is complicated in leadership studies by the earlier-mentioned issue with the romance of leadership (Meindl et al., 1985), leading to leadership ideals rarely corresponding to everyday practice. Doing leadership and talking about leadership can thus diverge. Consequently, there might be a concern in using emic concepts – that is, what people say they do – rather than to consider etic concepts – that is, the concepts used by the analyst to understand. Both positions are keen on understanding actor's meaning-making processes and experiences without aiming at any objective representation of reality due to the situated nature of research they enact. But research privileging the analyst's use of the term may focus on practices that the actors involved would have not called leadership. Positions that privilege the actor's use of the term are often grounded in a phenomenological sensitivity which means a commitment to accounting for the lived leadership experience of those studied (Raelin, 2021).

Ambition: Descriptive - Normative

Acknowledging the situated nature of knowledge development is integral to orientation and sensibility in doing research coming from practice theories. Although researchers do not position themselves outside the world they study, they may articulate different kinds of ambitions for their enquiries. On the one hand, there have been many contributions aimed at developing insight on leadership practice and its consequences without any explicit ideological positioning. On the other hand, we also have normative contributions clearly stating an aim for new conventions for practising leadership (for instance, Raelin, 2011; By, 2021). This is often done based on an ideological position privileging inclusion and democracy over individuals invested with power to command and control others. Somewhere in the middle we find studies of social change – they conceptualise leadership in collective terms given that social change is seen as achieved through bridging across different actors' trajectories (Ospina and Foldy, 2010). In all cases, issues of power, ideology and ethics intersect in complex ways, something that still needs to be further explored in order to detail more precisely what practice theories contribute in relation to criticism posed from a critical management studies point of view (Collinson, 2018; see Chapter 18, Responsible leadership).

Concluding, there is a multitude of ways in which practice theories have renewed and enriched the study of leadership. Some of the dimensions presented in this section touch on themes developed more at length in this book – for instance, the plurality of leadership in Chapter 1, leadership in interaction in Chapter 3, spaces/materiality in Chapter 21, process theories in Chapter 23, technology and media in Chapter 24, to mention a few. These dimensions also relate to the task of empirically exploring practices, which necessarily builds on the choices to be made. Largely, scholars of practice tend to draw on qualitative method in order to come close to the practising itself, whether zooming in on specific interactions or following organising processes over time. Observations and interviews are thus common, often building on an ethnographic sensibility. Recent developments in social sciences – for instance, affective ethnography or multimodal analyses – provide an increasingly rich, but also demanding, methodological 'toolbox' (Gherardi, 2019b). Finally, having produced empirical material, the particular analytical task of mobilising practice theories in writing presents further challenges. Efforts might mobilise multiple definitions of practice simultaneously in varying eclectic senses (Nicolini, 2012; Nicolini & Monteiro,

2017; Gherardi, 2019a) or, alternatively, they might emphasise a more delimited appreciation of the theoretical concept of practice (Lammi, 2018).

LEADERSHIP AND PRACTICE THEORIES: MOVING FORWARD

After having described ways in which practice theories have and may further contribute to leadership studies, we conclude this chapter by discussing how practice theories may be crucial in further developing knowledge on contemporary leadership at a time of profound changes in organisations and society. Flexibilisation, digitalisation, the use of alternative workplaces and increased focus on intra- and interorganisational collaboration are some of the developments reconfiguring the in-between where leadership takes shape. Developing knowledge in this changing context may benefit from engaging with contemporary practice research and reimagining method along the lines we have presented. Not least, we hope researchers will follow the phenomenon of leadership wherever it may take place during these contemporary changes.

There is an issue, however, that we have not touched upon. The scholar interested in decentering leadership from individuals will have to also consider how their research can do leadership justice. Practice theories suggest the importance of the vividity, intensity, fluidity of organisational life. How can we hope to accommodate such aspects in our accounts? Practice theories present the researcher with new challenges because of the very richness they provide. In a similar way, how can we decentre from individuals and expand and redefine leadership development efforts? This is also an important issue to further consider (Carroll and Smolović Jones, 2018). Moreover, reframing leadership also leads to a reconsideration of critical issues such as responsibility and ethics. These have yet to find the central place in leadership studies that they may deserve. Positing that leadership is distributed, as practice theories suggest, is not to be understood as no one needing to take responsibility or being responsible, for instance. Rather, *ethics is too important to discuss only a formal leader's role* (Andersson et al., forthcoming). Formal leaders may be positioned in a privileged way, but other people also contribute to producing direction. Practice theories enable focus on actions and relations, and which courses of action are made possible, as well as which are closed down (Andersson et al., forthcoming). Responsibility for which worlds are produced is therefore an obligation that we may argue all people share in organisations – it is not within a person, but rather in-between. To what extent, how and what to do about it are questions to be further explored. At a time in which digital technologies increasingly are entangled with humans in organisations, it may be even more urgent to unpack what these new assemblages accomplish and with what consequences.

Finally, as we initially discussed, practice theories have travelled and been translated across the social sciences, including organisation and management studies and studies of leadership. Leadership scholars are thus not only appropriating a toolbox, but also innovating it. As much as practice theories can help understand leadership, leadership might help us better understand organisational practices. Leadership, whether as specific practices or emergent production of direction, plays a role in configuring contemporary organisational practices such as remote work or the automation of white-collar work. More so, leadership scholars have mobilised a specific style in attending to practice that is distinct from studies of practice in organisation and management studies. Notably, an attention to practice has meant for some scholars the possibility to reframe leadership in a more democratic and inclusive fashion. This is a uniquely strong feature of practice studies of leadership that other practice scholars do not necessarily engage with to the same extent. As such, our final suggestion is that leadership scholars should not only consider how practice theories can help them better understand leadership, but also be open to consider how their particular approach to leadership might enrich practice studies widely speaking.

REFERENCES

Alvehus, J. (2019). Emergent, distributed, and orchestrated: Understanding leadership through frame analysis. *Leadership*, *15*(5), 535–554.

Andersson, C., Crevani, L., & Hallin, A. (forthcoming). Leadership as care-ful co-directing change: A processual approach to ethical leadership for organisational change. In R. T. By, B. Burnes & M. Hughes, *Organizational Change, Leadership and Ethics*. Routledge.

Barker, R. A. (1997). How can we train leaders if we do not know what leadership is?. *Human Relations*, *50*(4), 343–362.

Barley, S. R. (1996). Technicians in the workplace: Ethnographic evidence for bringing work into organizational studies, *Administrative Science Quarterly*, *41*(3), 404–441.

Barley, S. R., & Tolbert, P. S. (1997). Institutionalization and structuration: Studying the links between action and institution, *Organization Studies*, 18(1), 93–117.

Bourdieu, P. (1977) *Outline of a Theory of Practice*. Cambridge University Press.

Bourdieu, P. (1990) *The Logic of Practice*. Reprinted. Stanford University Press.

Brown, M. H., & Hosking, D. M. (1986). Distributed leadership and skilled performance as successful organization in social movements. *Human Relations*, 39(1), 65–79.

By, R. T. (2021). Leadership: In pursuit of purpose. *Journal of Change Management*, 21(1), 30–44.

Carroll, B., Levy, L., & Richmond, D. (2008). Leadership as practice: Challenging the competency paradigm. *Leadership*, 4(4), 363–379.

Carroll, B., & Smolović Jones, O. (2018). Mapping the aesthetics of leadership development through participant perspectives. *Management Learning*, 49(2), 187–203.

Case, P., & Śliwa, M. (2020). Leadership learning, power and practice in Laos: A leadership-as-practice perspective. *Management Learning*, 51(5), 537–558.

Chreim, S. (2015). The (non)distribut on of leadership roles: Considering leadership practices and configurations. *Human Relations*, 68(4), 517–543.

Collinson, M. (2018). So what is new about leadership-as-practice? *Leadership*, 14(3), 384–390.

Crevani, L. (2018). Is there leadership in a fluid world? Exploring the ongoing production of direction in organizing. *Leadership*, 14(1), 83–109.

Crevani, L., Lindgren, M., & Packendorff, J. (2010). Leadership, not leaders: On the study of leadership as practices and interactions. *Scandinavian Journal of Management*, 26(1), 77–86.

Cunliffe, A. L., & Eriksen, M. (2011). Relational leadership. *Human relations*, 64(11), 1425–1449.

Denis, J. L., Lamothe, L., & Langley, A. (2001). The dynamics of collective leadership and strategic change in pluralistic organizations. *Academy of Management Journal*, 44(4), 809–837.

Denis, J. L., Langley, A., & Sergi, V. (2012). Leadership in the plural. *Academy of Management Annals*, 6(1), 211–283.

De Paoli, D., Ropo, A., & Sauer, E. (2014). Disappearing bodies in virtual leadership? In D. Ladkin, S. Taylor and F. O. Walumbwa (Eds.), *The Physicality of Leadership: Gesture, Entanglement, Taboo, Possibilities* (Vol. 6, pp. 59–79). Emerald.

Dovey, K., Burdon, S., & Simpson, R. (2017). Creative leadership as a collective achievement: An Australian case. *Management Learning*, 48(1), 23–38.

Drath W. H., McCauley C. D., Palus C. J., Van Velsor E., O'Connor P. M. G., & McGuire J. B. (2008). Direction, alignment, commitment: Toward a more integrative ontology of leadership. *Leadership Quarterly*, 19(6), 635–653.

Endrissat, N., & von Arx, W. (2013). Leadership practices and context: Two sides of the same coin. *Leadership*, 9(2), 278–304.

Feldman, M. S. (2000). Organizational routines as a source of continuous change. *Organization Science*, 11(6), 611–629.

Feldman, M., & Orlikowski, W. (2011). Theorizing practice and practice theory. *Organization Science*, 22(5), 1240–1253.

Fletcher, J. K. (2004). The paradox of postheroic leadership: An essay on gender, power, and transformational change. *Leadership Quarterly*, 15(5), 647–661.

Follett, M. P. (1919). Community is a process. *Philosophical Review*, 28(6), 576–588.

Follett, M. P. (1924) *Creative Experience*. Longman, Green.

Garfinkel, H. (1967) *Studies in Ethnomethodology*. Polity Press.

Gherardi, S. (2001). From organizational learning to practice-based knowing. *Human Relations*, 54(1), 131–139.

Gherardi, S. (2017). One turn ... and now another one: Do the turn to practice and the turn to affect have something in common? *Management Learning*, 48(3), 345–358.

Gherardi, S. (2019a). *How to Conduct a Practice-Based Study: Problems and Methods*. Edward Elgar.

Gherardi, S. (2019b). Theorizing affective ethnography for organization studies. *Organization*, 26(6), 741–760.

Giddens, A. (1979) *Central Problems in Social Theory: Action, Structure and Contradiction in Social Analysis*. Macmillan (Contemporary social theory).

Giddens, A. (1984) *The Constitution of Society: Outline of the Theory of Structuration. 1*. Paperback edn. University of California Press.

Haraway, D. (1988) Situated knowledges: The science question in feminism and the privilege of partial perspective. *Feminist Studies*, 14(3), 575–599.

Hosking, D. M. (1988). Organizing, leadership and skilful process. *Journal of Management Studies*, 25(2), 147–166.

Kempster, S., & Jackson, B. (2021). Leadership for what, why, for whom and where? A responsibility perspective. *Journal of Change Management*, 21(1), 45–65.

Küpers, W. M. (2013). Embodied inter-practices of leadership: Phenomenological perspectives on relational and responsive leading and following. *Leadership*, 9(3), 335–357.

Lammi, I. J. (2018). *A practice theory in practice: Analytical consequences in the study of organization and socio-technical change* (Doctoral dissertation, Företagsekonomiska institutionen, Uppsala University).

Larsson, M., & Lundholm, S. E. (2010). Leadership as work-embedded influence: A micro-discursive analysis of an everyday interaction in a bank. *Leadership*, *6*(2), 159–184.

Latour, B. (2005) *Reassembling the Social: An Introduction to Actor-Network-Theory*. Oxford University Press (Clarendon lectures in management studies).

Meindl, J. R., Ehrlich, S. B., & Dukerich, J. M. (1985). The romance of leadership. *Administrative Science Quarterly*, *30*(1), 78–102.

Miettinen, R., Samra-Fredericks, D., & Yanow, D. (2009). Re-turn to Practice: An Introductory Essay. *Organization Studies*, 30(12), 1309–1327.

Nicolini, D. (2012) *Practice Theory, Work, and Organization: An Introduction*. Oxford: Oxford University Press.

Nicolini, D., & Monteiro, P. (2017). The practice approach: For a praxeology of organisational and management studies. In A. Langley & H. Tsoukas (Eds.), *The SAGE Handbook of Process Organization Studies* (pp. 110–126). Sage.

Oborn, E., Barrett, M., & Dawson, S. (2013). Distributed leadership in policy formulation: A sociomaterial perspective. *Organization Studies*, *34*(2), 253–276.

Orlikowski, W. J. (2000) Using technology and constituting structures: A practice lens for studying technology in organizations. *Organization Science*, *11*(4), 404–428.

Orlikowski, W. J. (2007). Sociomaterial practices: Exploring technology at work. *Organization Studies*, *28*(9), 1435–1448.

Orlikowski, W. J., & Scott, S. V. (2008). 10 Sociomateriality: Challenging the separation of technology, work and organization. *Academy of Management Annals*, *2*(1), 433–474.

Orr, J. E. (1996) *Talking About Machines: An Ethnography of a Modern Job*. ILR Press.

Ospina, S., & Foldy, E. (2010). Building bridges from the margins: The work of leadership in social change organizations. *Leadership Quarterly*, *21*(2), 292–307.

Pearce, C. L., & Conger, J. A. (2002). *Shared Leadership: Reframing the Hows and Whys of Leadership*. Sage.

Pickering, A. (1995) *The Mangle of Practice: Time, Agency, and Science*. University of Chicago Press.

Raelin, J. (2007). Toward an epistemology of practice. *Academy of Management Learning & Education*, *6*(4), 495–519.

Raelin, J. (2011). From leadership-as-practice to leaderful practice. *Leadership*, *7*(2), 195–211.

Raelin, J. (2021). Leadership-as-practice: antecedent to leaderful purpose. *Journal of Change Management*, *21*(4), 385–390.

Reckwitz, A. (2002). Toward a theory of social practices: A development in culturalist theorizing. *European Journal of Social Theory*, *5*(2), 243–263.

Ropo, A., & Salovaara, P. (2019). Spacing leadership as an embodied and performative process. *Leadership*, *15*(4), 461–479.

Salovaara, P. (2014). Video: Leadership in spaces and places. *Organizational Aesthetics*, *3*(1), 79–79 [sic].

Sandberg, J., & Tsoukas, H. (2011). Grasping the logic of practice: Theorizing through practical rationality. *Academy of Management Review*, *36*(2), 338–360.

Sandberg, J., & Tsoukas, H. (2015). Practice theory: What it is, its philosophical base, and what it offers organization studies. In R. Mir, H. Wilmott & M. Greenwood (Eds.), *The Routledge Companion to Philosophy in Organization Studies* (pp. 184–198). Routledge.

Schatzki, T. R. (1996). *Social Practices: A Wittgensteinian Approach to Human Activity and The Social*. Digitally printed version, paperback reissue. Cambridge University Press.

Schatzki, T. R. (2002). *The Site of The Social: A Philosophical Account of The Constitution of Social Life and Change*. Pennsylvania State University Press.

Schatzki, T.R. (2005) 'Peripheral vision: The sites of organizations', *Organization Studies*, 26(3), pp. 465–484.

Schatzki, T.R. (2006) 'On Organizations as they Happen', Organization Studies, 27(12), pp. 1863–1873.

Schatzki, T.R. (2016) 'Practice Theory as Flat Ontology', in G. Spaargaren, D. Weenink, and M. Lamers (eds) *Practice Theory and Research: Exploring the dynamics of social life*. 1st edn. Abingdon, Oxon: Routledge, pp. 28–42. Available at: https://doi.org/10.4324/978131565690.

Schatzki, T. R. (2019). *Social Change in a Material World: How Activity and Material Processes Dynamize Practices*. Routledge.

Schatzki, T. R., Knorr-Cetina, K., & Savigny, E. von (Eds.) (2001). *The Practice Turn in Contemporary Theory*. Routledge.

Sergi, V., Lusiani, M., & Langley, A. (2021). Highlighting the plural: Leading amidst romance(s). *Journal of Change Management*, *21*(2), 163–179.

Shove, E., Pantzar, M., & Watson, M. (2012). *The Dynamics of Social Practice: Everyday Life and How it Changes*. Sage.

Simpson, B. (2016). Where's the agency in leadership-as-practice? In J. Raelin (Ed.), *Leadership-as-practice: Theory and Application* (pp. 159–177). Routledge.

Simpson, B., Buchan, L., & Sillince, J. (2018). The performativity of leadership talk. *Leadership*, *14*(6), 644–661.

Smets, M., Aristidou, A., & Whittington, R. (2017). Towards a practice-driven institutionalism. In R. Greenwood, C. Oliver, T. B. Lawrence & R. E. Meyer (Eds.), *The SAGE Handbook of Organizational Institutionalism*. 2nd edition (pp. 365–391). Sage.

Smets, M., Morris, T. I. M., & Greenwood, R. (2012) From practice to field: A multilevel model of practice-driven institutional change. *Academy of Management Journal*, *55*(4), 877–904.

Suchman, L. A. (2007). *Human–Machine Reconfigurations: Plans and Situated Actions*. 2nd edition. Cambridge University Press.

Uhl-Bien, M., Marion, R., & McKelvey, B. (2007). Complexity leadership theory: Shifting leadership from the industrial age to the knowledge era. *Leadership Quarterly*, *18*(4), 298–318.

Vivier, E., & Sanchez-Betancourt, D. (2020). Community leaders as intermediaries: How everyday practices create and sustain leadership in five informal settlements in Cape Town. *Leadership*, *16*(6), 738–756.

Wood, M. (2005). The fallacy of misplaced leadership*. *Journal of Management Studies*, *42*(6), 1101–1121.

Zammuto, R. F., Griffith, T. L., Majchrzak, A., Dougherty, D. J., & Faraj, S. (2007). Information technology and the changing fabric of organization. *Organization Science*, *18*(5), 749–762.

Leadership in Interaction

Magnus Larsson and Frank Meier

Most readers would agree that interaction is integral to all conceptions of leadership. Nevertheless, the scholarly literature on leadership has included very few observational studies of what Goffman calls *strips of everyday, actual doings involving flesh-and-blood individuals in face-to-face dealings with one another* (cited in Gronn, 1983, p. 19). In the seminal work 'Talk as the work: The accomplishment of school administration', Gronn made an early and strong case for both observing and investigating workplace interactions because *the power to control must be worked at linguistically and worked at never-endingly as an ongoing everyday activity* (1983, p. 20). However, only at the turn of the millennium did a body of leadership in interaction literature truly begin to emerge. As much of this literature was published in linguistic and discourse-oriented journals such as *Journal of Pragmatics*, *Discourse and Communication* and *Text & Talk*, it had initially a limited impact on leadership studies. In 2007 Fairhurst's landmark publication *Discursive Leadership* (2007a) paved the way for more studies to appear in decidedly organisational and leadership-oriented journals. Ultimately, the publication of a special *Leadership* issue on leadership in interaction (Clifton et al., 2020) evidences the maturation of this field and the increasing cross-pollination between linguistics, discourse and communication studies, on the one hand, and leadership studies on the other.

In this chapter we present the characteristics defining the field of leadership in interaction studies and discuss the main methodological and theoretical approaches. We also explore four key empirical themes permeating the literature: roles and actions; the construction of leader and follower identities; the accomplishment of influence and the organising of action; and leadership and materiality. Next, we briefly discuss how studies of interaction highlight and problematise the concept of leadership. Finally, we outline and discuss significant contributions made in this line of research, as well as sketch out a horizon for future possibilities.

WHAT IS LEADERSHIP IN INTERACTION?

Leadership in interaction has a distinctive methodological orientation and perspective on the ontological location of leadership. Methodologically, studies in this field are based on observations and audio or video recordings of work interactions in a variety of organisations. Interaction in this context means any verbal or non-verbal interpersonal exchange, either face-to-face or technologically mediated. Such studies focus on so-called naturally occurring interactions, which is to say interactions neither orchestrated nor provoked by the researcher, as would be the case with research interviews or experiments (Atkinson & Silverman, 1997; Heritage & Clayman, 2010).

Ontologically, studies of interaction treat leadership as located in social interaction and in relationships. This means that they do not treat interactions as signs or evidence of phenomena in other loci, such as individual orientations, perceptions, motivations, or organisational structures. Instead, the phenomenon of interest is seen as ontologically located in the interaction itself. In this way, power or cognition, for instance, cannot operate behind the backs of those interacting – see Garfinkel's well-known rejection of the human as a 'cultural dope' (1967, p. 68) – but must be shown by the analyst to make a difference within the interaction. Such an imperative thereby directs the researcher's effort *to locate leadership in everyday organisational practice for research to credibly grant it any role in the shaping of organizational reality* (Larsson, 2017, p. 173).

Studies of interaction thus respond to the criticism levelled at social psychology, arguing that it no longer studies behaviours but only self-reports and reports of experiences of behaviours, acquired through interviews and surveys as opposed to observations (see Baumeister et al., 2007). In social psychology, however, the notion of behaviours typically refers to classes of actions categorised by a researcher and decontextualised from the specific situations, whereas studies of interaction tend to focus on the very situated nature of actions and on how *conduct is built out of the details of the particular social settings in which it is occasioned* (Sidnell, 2017, p. 321), with contributions being dependent on what the current, unfolding situation offers.

Beyond these shared characteristics, studies of leadership in interaction are informed by a variety of methodological and theoretical approaches. As such, these studies do not constitute a distinct **theoretical** tradition, instead being centrally characterised by their focus on the empirical exploration of social interactions through observations and recordings.

THEORETICAL AND METHODOLOGICAL APPROACHES

Beyond focusing on observed or recorded work interactions, this line of leadership studies draws on a number of theoretical and methodological approaches, the most common of which are described below.

Building on the sociological tradition of ethnomethodology (Garfinkel, 1967; Llewellyn & Hindmarsh, 2010; Rawls, 2008), **conversation analysis** (CA) (Heritage & Clayman, 2010; Sacks 1992) focuses on the methods and mechanisms interactants utilise to collaboratively produce a sequence of interaction. The approach operates on a principle of attentiveness to what is demonstrably relevant to the participants in an interaction (Schegloff, 1997) – that is, how they themselves make sense of and reflexively contribute to the evolving interaction. A rich technical vocabulary and body of research have developed from the approach since its first use in the early 1960s.

Developed in linguistics rather than sociology, **interactional sociolinguistics** (Gumpertz, 1982) shares the linguistic orientation to how interaction is reflexively produced in situ and a linguistic interest in how linguistic practices differ between various communities and groups.

More **interpretative approaches**, inspired by ethnography and Goffmanian sociology (Goffman, 1982; Hammersley & Atkinson, 1995), similarly focus on the observed interaction described above, but tend to give primacy to the analyst's (often theoretically founded) gaze and interpretation. Whereas studies oriented at CA and sociolinguistics examine the details of short stretches of interaction, interpretative studies often scrutinise developments and shifts over time (Meschitti, 2018; Sarangi & Roberts, 2008; Simpson et al., 2018).

Communication as constitutive of organisations (CCO) Cooren, 2010; Taylor & van Every, 2000) builds on CA and shares its and interactional sociolinguistics' commitment to closely observing conversations. Drawing on speech act theory (Austin, 1962) and actor-network theory (Latour, 2005), the approach also takes an interest in how texts and other artefacts partake in conversations (Taylor, 1999), thus seeking to uncover how leadership occurs within a network of human and other-than-human actants. Accordingly, anything other or absent can be made present in a conversation, thereby allowing action to *scale up from interaction to organization* (Cooren & Fairhurst, 2008, p. 117).

EMPIRICAL THEMES IN STUDYING LEADERSHIP IN INTERACTION

Studies of leadership in interaction have explored numerous empirical aspects of leadership. For the purpose of this overview, we have identified four themes in the empirical studies:

- roles and actions
- the construction of leader and follower identities

- the accomplishment of influence and organising of action
- an emerging theme on materiality and leadership.

They all share the use of recorded naturally occurring interactions – that is, work interactions not orchestrated by the researcher (such as a research interview). These recordings are subsequently analysed with a close attention to the interactional details.

The below example from Baxter (2014, pp. 33–34) illustrates the type of material typically used in this line of research. We will use this extract to show the analytical focus of the four empirical themes identified in the literature.

Extract 3.1 'That's the magic'

72	Lucy	I like where you're going with this but what I think you
73		should do (.) is have one standing up there (*points to*
74		*parts of tower*)
75	Julie	yep yep
76	Lucy	one standing up there
77	Julie	yep yep
78	Lucy	and do as I said that matchstick thing and do another one
79		standing up
80	Julie	do you want to come and build?
81	Lucy	yeah I guess I could do that (.) I'm pretty rubbish at
82		rolling
83	Julie	I'll roll and you can build (*gets up and moves away*)
84	Georgina	can you hold this here for a moment (*looking at Katarina*)
85		so I can
86	Katarina	so what is (.) so what is it now? (*looking at Lucy*)
87	Lucy	um it will be the green one otherwise it isn't going to
88		look um very (.) attractive (.) unless we have one there
89		and have two like a blue one either side and then we'll
90		go red on top of that
91	Georgina	it's so random
92	Lucy	it's all right↑(.) it's going to look good eventually (3)
93	Georgina	(*looking at Lucy*) wh-what's going to happen at the next
94		level? (.) how are you going to do the next level?
95	Lucy	that's the magic
96	Georgina	oh is that right? (*Ge and Lucy both laugh*)
97	Lucy	we'll find a way (.) okay (.) so (.) next maybe there's a
98		better idea if we stick them to this bit here?
99	Georgina	okay

This is a relatively detailed transcript of a short sequence of interaction. We should emphasise that, ideally, the recording, not the transcript, is the object of analysis. Although the transcript is an important analytical and presentational tool, the aim is to stay as close to the core phenomenon of interaction as possible. Because the analysis aims to be close to the (seemingly messy) original phenomenon, interactionally oriented researchers also generally avoid coding procedures, as coding serves to reduce the complexity of the data for the benefit of analysis (Heritage & Clayman, 2010; Llewellyn & Hindmarsh, 2018).

In this extract, we see how a group of MBA students collaborate on a group task to build a paper tower, in a pedagogical rather than regular work context. The research interest concerns the emergence of leadership – *what an emerging leader 'looks and sounds like' within a woman-only team* (Baxter, 2014, p. 28). After unpacking a wealth of interactional details, Baxter notes the subtle emergence of a leader in this extract: *In her extended response (lines 87–90), Lucy has effortlessly stepped into the leadership role: she supplies the answer, with reasons, and gives an indirect, collective command ('we'll go red on top of that')* (p. 34).

As the extract makes obvious, even an interactional sequence as short as this one contains abundant details and can be explored in a variety of ways. We will put this extract in the context of each of the respective empirical themes selected: roles and actions; the construction of leader and follower identities; the accomplishment of influence and organising of actions; and materiality and leadership.

EMPIRICAL THEMES

Roles and Actions

A range of studies either focus on what a person in a formal leader/manager role does or take leadership to be the performance of particular actions or activities. Studies focusing on individuals in particular roles have explored the detailed actions of formal managers, meeting chairs and such professionals as medical doctors, among others. Baxter (2017), for instance, investigated the communication problems experienced by a female manager; Ladegaard (2012) analysed rudeness as a discursive strategy employed by managers in Hong Kong; and Chalupnik and Atkins (2020) showed how medical doctors that made mitigated rather than direct requests when delegating tasks to an emergency team were evaluated more positively.

The role of chairing meetings in organisations, often but not always performed by a formal manager, has drawn particular attention. Contemporary organisations use a meeting format to handle a wide range of issues, and the conduct of the chair is often considered key to these meetings' productiveness (Angouri & Marra, 2010; Pomerantz & Denvir, 2007). The role of the chair is typically associated with particular rights and obligations, including not only managing the right to speak, but also summarising the discussion and moving the agenda forward. Studies demonstrate that such rights are always enacted with attention to contextual factors, such as the type of meeting and who is present (Pomerantz & Denvir, 2007; Holmes & Marra, 2004), and to the meeting participants' acceptance of actions. As such, the authority vested in the chair is always negotiated and at stake. Moreover, the chair has been shown to employ a wide range of tactics to manage conflicts (Holmes & Marra, 2004) and develop consensus (Wodak et al., 2011). For instance, in a study by Wodak et al. (2011) the use of more egalitarian leadership styles tended to be associated with more durable consensus.

Another approach has been to focus on types of actions instead of particular roles. Rather than assuming that actions are performed in particular roles or positions, these studies of interaction enables an exploration of who performs actions, as well as when and with what consequences. Many such studies draw on interactional sociolinguistics and build on Holmes and Marra (2004). In this paper, the authors view leadership as the discursive performance of task- and relationship-oriented actions. These dimensions were originally identified in the classic Ohio and Michigan studies (Fleishman, 1953; Likert, 1961; Yukl, 2012) as categories of behaviours performed by managers. Studies of interaction drawing on these categories are thus essentially grounded in a role perspective. The above extract from Baxter (2014) aptly illustrates this research orientation. Baxter identifies a specific participant as stepping into an emerging leadership role, signified by her issuing directives and requests (lines 78–79 and 89–90) and (politely) evaluating others' suggestions (lines 72–73).

A focus on types of actions rather than roles further opens the possibility of exploring the extent to which given actions are both distributed and collaboratively produced. For instance, Vine et al. (2008) looked into how pairs of individuals performed co-leadership by collaboratively performing task- and relationship-oriented actions, typically distributing them so that each individual concentrated on one type of behaviour.

Studying types of actions can challenge taken-for-granted assumptions about effective collaboration in specific situations. For instance, conventional wisdom suggests that in medical emergencies directness ('put a drain in') is more efficient than indirectness ('let's make sure we've got the chest drain trolley' (Chalupnik & Atkins, 2020, p. 86)). In a study of emergency team simulations, Mesinioti et al. (2020) also showed that directness and taking control over interaction worked to position senior medical doctors as leaders. However, in another study of such simulations, Chalupnik and Atkins (2020) showed the opposite to be true: doctors making indirect requests and considering interpersonal dynamics, for instance, by using politeness markers such as 'please', completed their tasks faster and were given higher marks for their leadership effectiveness. Chalupnik and Atkins argue that these results constitute *a significant counterargument for the claim that the employment of authoritative leadership necessarily facilitates more effective and efficient communication, particularly in urgent settings* (p. 88). Their results suggest that attention to relational aspects and team rapport does not necessarily conflict with the need for efficient communication.

These studies indicate that interaction and the accomplishment of leadership are also complex in situations seemingly easily characterised as urgent. While richly detailing how acts aimed to establish interactional dominance are actually produced, they also help to problematise a leadership approach focused only on the actions or behaviours of one party (typically the leader) and attempts to link these actions to various outcomes. In minutely probing both discursive and physical actions, the studies reveal considerable variability in the performance of even single type of action, a finding implying that far more than the single observed actions contribute to the observed outcomes, such as efficient communication or swift medical treatment.

The focus on types of actions rather than predetermined roles aligns well with the recent and growing interest in shared, distributed and collective leadership (Ospina et al., 2020). Examining how actions 'indexed for leadership' (Choi & Schnurr, 2014, p. 14) are performed, studies have shown the distribution of leader roles to be situated and at times rapidly shifting. Studying a team with no formal leader, Choi and Schnurr (2014) showed how a range of persons took turns performing leadership tasks, forming various constellations depending on the immediate context and the task at hand. Similarly, Van de Mieroop et al. (2020) showed how at meetings participants other than just the formal chair or leader could claim the right to decide the next steps in the meeting underway. Van de Mieroop et al. (2020) further showed how such rights were shifted collaboratively, with the formal chair occasionally endorsing and supporting an emerging informal leader. Studies like these substantiate and flesh out assumptions about shared and collective leadership as flexible and adaptive (see Chapter 1, Pluralism in studies on plural leadership). Moreover, as the notions of shared and collective leadership can suffer from a certain romanticism (see Chapter 1, Pluralism in Studies on Plural Leadership), studies of interaction also help to balance this. For instance, in a CCO-inspired study of a municipal team, Holm and Fairhurst (2018, p. 716) noted how sharing leadership involved a complex pattern of claims and grants of authority, and how vertical leadership actually helped *contain the excesses of shared leadership*, thus contributing to a constructive work process.

What is more, studies of types of actions in interaction both complement and partly challenge network-oriented studies of shared leadership (Carson et al., 2007; DeRue et al., 2015), which deploy questionnaires to explore how patterns of role distribution emerge over time. Such patterns might provide a framework for interaction, but the actual performance of shared leadership is clearly rapidly shifting and flexible. Emphasising the moment-by-moment evolving collaboration, studies of interaction elucidate the highly adaptive and flexible distribution of roles accomplished within short timeframes, whereas network-oriented studies tend to focus on somewhat longer timeframes.

The Construction of Leader and Follower Identities

In studies of interaction, identity is treated as located in the interaction, as being a negotiated understanding of who a person is, rather than a more individually held self-concept (Antaki & Widdicombe, 1998):

> *Orientation to who is who in relation to whom, and their relative rights and obligations, is thus visible in the structure of talk and so identities, and thus the organization, are said to be talked into being. The upshot of such an approach is that identity is considered to be something that people 'do', rather than something that they 'have'.*
> (Van de Mieroop et al., 2020, p. 496)

Instead of seeing inner notions of self as causing or motivating social action, such an interactional concept of identity paves the way for exploring how identities are claimed, accepted, resisted and generally negotiated in the midst of social activities. Returning to the extract from Baxter (2014), we observe that an identity focus would note how the evaluative comment in lines 72–73 serves as a claim on a leader identity in the sense of setting a direction for the work. Moreover, Julie's positive response in lines 75 and 77 as well as the invitation to actively participate in the building (line 80) serves as an acceptance and reinforcement of the leader identity, thus also demonstrating how it is collaboratively established and negotiated.

Being a generally well-known type of interaction research, studies of leadership identity also abound. This body of literature demonstrates that establishing an interactional identity as a leader – and at times a follower – can be accomplished through a vast range of resources and mechanisms, including control over the agenda (Svennevig, 2012; Van Praet, 2009), control over topic shifts (Walker & Artiz, 2014), and access to symbolic resources such as knowledge (Nielsen, 2009) or feedback (Svennevig, 2011). Some of the previously mentioned studies of actions and roles also discuss these aspects in terms of identities.

For instance, establishing dominance in a medical treatment team can be analysed as a means of claiming a leader identity (Mesinioti et al., 2020) or of accomplishing a leader and a co-leader identity via face-work in the case of disagreement (Schnurr & Chan, 2011).

A recent development emanating from the CA tradition involves using the rising interest in deontic and epistemic authority to discuss leader and follower identities. Deontic authority refers to the situated right to decide on the actions of others (Stevanovic et al., 2014). For instance, on the one hand, the chair of a meeting is conventionally entitled to decide on the next speaker (Angouri & Marra, 2010). Epistemic authority, on the other hand, concerns knowledge claims and access to knowledge domains (Heritage, 2012; Stivers et al., 2011). A high level of epistemic authority refers to a speaker's being seen as more knowledgeable, typically by having direct access to a knowledge domain, say, something he or she can see directly on a computer screen. Conversely, a lower epistemic authority is associated with not having direct access to a given domain, such as what another person did yesterday or saw on his or her computer screen. Drawing on the concept of deontic authority, Van de Mieerop (2019) showed how a complex interplay between a formal superior, the meeting chair and other participants served to establish leadership in corporate meetings. Participants were shown to *shift in and out of the construction* (p. 613), a finding emphasising how highly flexible and situated the interactional identity construction process is. Studies like this validate and accentuate DeRue and Ashford's (2010) earlier distinction between what they call relational recognition and individual internalisation – that is, between interactional identities and individual identities. However, whereas DeRue and Ashford are principally interested in how individual identities are developed through processes of relational recognition, interactional studies focus strictly on the interactional identities, exploring their complexities and dynamics. Importantly, to this end, studies of interaction can draw on a distinct methodology and analytical approach, without relying on the actors' self-reports – as social psychological identity studies tend to do.

Most studies of identity in interaction focus on leader identity while often acknowledging that follower identities are simultaneously constructed in the interaction. More directly focusing on followership, Larsson and Nielsen (2021) demonstrated some of the practical problems and risks surrounding claiming a followership identity. They showed how follower identities, like leader identities, need to be tied to the task at hand, and risk failure if that task is misinterpreted.

Identities need not be only individual. Taking interactional identities to be established by categorisation in interaction and drawing on notions like teaming (Djordjilovic, 2012), some studies focus on how collective identities play a role in leadership processes. In a study of interactions in a bank, Larsson and Lundholm (2013) showed how the leadership influence process depended on the construction of a small, situated collective comprised of not just an abstract *'we' but of 'we working on this task'* (p. 1123). Arvedsen and Hassert (2020) note how virtual collaboration affords different situated identities for individuals at different locations and, in a more ethnographic study of an R&D team, Smith et al. (2018) noted how shifting constructions of team identity helped different individuals emerge as leaders.

Influence and Organising of Action

Although the previously discussed studies shed light on a range of important topics, they only indirectly address the influence processes taken to be at the core of leadership. Positions, roles and identities all play a role in the accomplishment of influence and organising but cannot fully explain how leadership effects are produced. The study of influence and organising concerns scrutinising how the resources offered by positions, roles, identities and particular types of actions are actually employed and put to use in interaction. In other words, whereas questions regarding how positions and identities are established ask how a particular interactional field is structured and configured, questions regarding influence and organising are more clearly future-oriented, seeking answers about the outcome and how it is produced. Moreover, studying influence and organising is necessarily oriented towards the recipients of actions – for instance, those who might emerge as followers – rather than towards the originators of the actions and the resources available to them (communicative skills, access to information, etc.).

Returning to Extract 3.1, we see that orienting to influence could put the focus on the interactional mechanisms through which the suggestion made in lines 72–73 (*what I think you should do [...] is have one standing up there*) is accepted. The analysis could note the interweaving of acceptance tokens (in lines 75 and 77) with Lucy's further development of the suggestion (lines 76 and 78), followed by not just the acceptance but also the actual implementation of the suggestion in line 81.

As this analytical comment illustrates, a focus on demonstrated effects is characteristic of empirical studies of influence, as they endeavour to analytically show the accomplishment of influence rather than to assume influence is an inherent quality of certain types of behaviours. Analysing the interactions of a management team, Clifton (2009), for instance, shows how summaries can be a resource for influence, as a particular version of what has been said is offered and, when accepted, helps to move the conversation forward. Wåhlin-Jacobsen (2020) showed how managers substantially influenced employees' suggestions during formal voice activities by subtly reframing the issue discussed. Larsson and Lundholm (2013) further demonstrate the importance of sequence and timing in their analysis of the influence effects of resisting closure of an issue, as well as of how a stepwise elaboration of an issue was persuasive. The key characteristic of this elaboration is how the target of influence is invited to contribute and step by step co-construct the new position (in this case, a different perspective on an overdrawn bank account).

Studies of interaction also demonstrate how influence can be accomplished through mechanisms and practices beyond what is typically considered influence tactics. For example, in a study by Watson and Drew (2017) on humour and influence, laughter was produced at various points in a work group consisting of participants from different parts of the organisation. Producing laughter through humour obviously entails drawing on elements of the situation at hand and is thus highly temporal and situated. Laughter here was conducive to team work: *the principal function of humor [was] to draw forth shared laughter which then serve[d] to align the group* (p. 323). As such, group participants were able to position themselves as more or less influential, for instance, by pursuing a story throughout sequences of multi-person overlapping talk. Here, this made constructing an interactional identity as leader closely connected to influence: a leader identity was constructed through the use of humour to influence the group, and the established identity enabled subsequent influence on the group's work.

Watson and Drew's (2017) study demonstrates an often-implicit assumption in studies focusing on identity construction as leader and follower: that constructing such identities might have influence implications. Studying interaction, rather than simply perceptions and assessments (DeRue et al., 2015), allows the consequences of identity ascriptions to be explored in detail, thus showing how and when such identities provide the resources for accomplishing influence. Rather than assume that interactional identities have influence functions, one can instead empirically explore and analyse the relationship between such identities and interactional outcomes.

Closely connected to influence is the organising of action. Studies of leadership in interaction have been able to demonstrate some central mechanisms through which leadership results in actions being organised and committed to. Decision-making is one way commitment to actions is shaped and mobilised. In a classic study, Huisman (2001) showed decision-making to be a fluid and diverse process, and decisions to exist only as post-hoc sense-making. In other words, there is no generally identifiable feature of interaction, or observable action that constitutes a decision. Instead, what team members subsequently treat as a decision can vary from setting to setting. Similarly, in Clifton's studies (2006, 2009) summaries, particularly when made by the meeting chair, were practically treated as decisions (although without being explicitly labelled as such) and served to move the conversation on.

The fact that the decision-making process concerns how actions are shaped and commitments mustered in interaction make it varied and context-dependent. This is one area where the reflexive nature of interactional accomplishment is visible. By reflexive nature we mean not only how participants utilise the resources at hand, including roles and relationships, but also what the conversation has yielded thus far (Heritage & Clayman, 2010; Meschitti, 2018). For example, studying decision-making in simulated business meetings, both Halvorsen and Sarangi (2015) and Du-Babrock and Chan (2018) drew on a distinction between activity roles, referring to an actor's relation to the activity at hand (such as being a chair), on the one hand, and discourse roles, or the relationship *between the participant and the utterance in question* (Du-Babcock & Chan, 2018, p. 500), on the other. Du-Babcock and Chan noted that *[i]t is only when the participants start to enact other discourse roles (such as the meeting chair to review the progress of the discussion and an assessor to identify agreed and disagreed points and to modify the given options), the discussion moves toward a direction leading to consensus* (p. 512). In other words, flexibly building on what has so far emerged and being able to relate to this in varied ways seems to be an important aspect of mobilising commitment to a particular line of action.

Why, then, can people be expected to act in accordance with what has been said? Larsson and Lundholm (2013) highlight that identities constructed in interaction not only address the question of who one is in this context, but are also infused with rights and obligations. Such interactional identities go beyond generic categories – for example, leader, medical doctor, or in their study professional banker – to instead be situated identities connected to a particular task and the interpersonal obligations tied to that task. Interactionally constructed identities might tie individuals together in small, task-based 'operational unit[s]'

(Larsson & Lundholm, 2013, p. 1121) and organise future action through obligations beyond a person's own commitment and intention. Their study thus provides substance to the general claim that leadership is closely connected to organising (Drath et al., 2008; Hosking, 1988; Pye, 2005). Further, it demonstrates that constructing these organising obligations demands considerable interactional work that reflexively builds on what has so far emerged (Meschitti, 2018).

The Materiality of Leadership in Interaction

Any work interaction involves more than linguistic elements. Bodily movements, space and material artefacts (like texts and information technology) are typically instrumental in accomplishing work tasks. Using notions like sociomateriality (Hindmarsh & Llewellyn, 2018) and multimodal interaction analysis, scholars have recently turned their sights on such aspects as bodily movements and the use of physical objects (Mondada, 2011). This trend has also come to include the study of leadership in interaction.

For instance, in the extract from Baxter (2014), Lucy's suggestion in lines 72–74 is partly accomplished through the bodily act of pointing, and in line 83 Julie's getting up and moving away helps her to claim a follower role and grant a leader role to Lu as well as to engage in the suggested action. Physical movements clearly contribute both to the establishment of leader and follower relationships and to the process of accomplishing influence and organising actions.

Drawing on video recordings, Mesinioti et al. (2020) noted how the particular physical positions medical doctors occupied in the emergency room contributed to the establishment of a leader role in the given interaction. Positioning themselves by the side of the bed helped the senior doctors to establish their expertise and influence others' actions. Similarly, Van de Mieroop (2019) and Van de Mieroop et al. (2020) used multimodal interaction analysis to explore the distribution of leader identities and positions in various settings.

Not just bodies but also physical aspects of the environment can be important to the leadership process. In a study of virtual teams, Arvedsen and Hassert (2020) showed how the technological environment shaped the conditions for accomplishing leadership in online interactions. For instance, during a presentation at a video conference, control over the cursor was key to influencing others and establishing the direction of the discussion.

In leadership processes more broadly, artefacts might aid in establishing positions of domination (leadership roles and identities) and influence. Drawing on the theoretical tradition of CCO, Holm and Fairhurst (2018) explored how the use of various authorising resources such as texts established and balanced vertical and shared readership by bringing a range of authorisation artefacts into play. The resulting configuration of leadership figures thus became hybrid in the sense of being constituted by both humans and artefacts (Grint, 2005). Clearly, the attention to physical aspects of interaction and the role of artefacts and space brings a wealth of resources useful for unpacking the situated and hybrid nature of leadership in interaction.

The Concept of Leadership

These empirical themes generate a range of theoretical questions, most centrally the question of how the concept of leadership is understood (Clifton et al., 2020; Schnurr & Schroeder, 2019). In work interactions the primary challenge with the concept of leadership lies in the fact that people are preoccupied with the details and practicalities of their work tasks. Whatever we as analysts take to be leadership is rarely the focus of participants' attention. In the empirical material, leadership is simply less clearly present than the practical work task.

Some methodologies offer a way of avoiding this engagement with the practical task by shifting the focus to participants' perceptions, experiences, assessments and the like, or even by asking the respondents what they themselves consider leadership to be. At times, this approach can therefore make leadership seem to be *something that floats ethereally above task accomplishment as some metalevel commentary* (Fairhurst, 2007b, p. 59), or something that exists only in the minds of individuals.

In studies of interaction, however, the task at hand has a powerful presence, for which reason the analyst must identify what in all the messy engagement with and talk about the task at hand constitutes relevant leadership aspects.

We can identify at least three different ways that leadership is understood in studies of interaction. These loosely correspond to our first three empirical themes:

- leadership as a role or a type of action
- leadership as the establishment of leader and follower identities (and interactional dominance)
- leadership as the accomplishment of influence and organising of action (establishment of commitment and obligations).

Each of these conceptualisations offers possibilities for challenging and developing leadership theory. Taking a role or action perspective on leadership demonstrates, for instance, the dependence of any role or action on both the specific situation and the collaboration and acceptance of others. Studies on negotiating identities support DeRue and Ashford's (2010) suggestion that relational identities cannot be reduced to individual identities, as well as offer a wealth of material on how relational identity is negotiated. Influence-oriented studies similarly challenge a view of influence as an inherent property of classes of actions, again demonstrating a need to take the relationship into account. Moreover, studies on organising action are beginning to unravel a theoretical understanding of how leadership might contribute to changes in organisations' practices (as well as why they are difficult and take time).

Taken together, studies of interaction suggest that whatever one considers leadership to be, it is collaboratively negotiated and produced. Theoretically, leadership is thus reasonably located – at least partly – in interactions and relationships, rather than in individuals or social structures (Fairhurst, 2007b; Uhl-Bien, 2006). However, this is not intended as an argument for analytically relying on what participants understand the concept of leadership to mean. On the contrary, leadership as a concept is essentially an analyst's concern, something the participants in an interaction perform rather than articulate. The mechanisms and practices of leadership are *seen but unnoticed* (Garfinkel, 1967, p. 10) aspects of the interaction, handled but not focused on, and as such outside the actors' awareness.

These empirical studies offer ample material to challenge and develop the theoretical understanding of leadership as a concept. Most agree that interpersonal influence processes (Ashford & Sitkin, 2019; Rost, 1991; Yukl, 2012) and the establishment of leader and follower positions (Uhl-Bien & Carsten, 2018) lie at the heart of leadership. How these are accomplished, remains, however, less fully theorised than the factors influencing the process and the various resources at play (cognitions, knowledge, styles, prototypes, individual identities, etc.).

Ways Forward

In this section we envision some future lines of research where leadership in interaction might make some novel contributions to leadership studies, at times based on relevant theoretical questions from other subfields of leadership studies and aimed at identifying how detailed analyses of situated leadership practice might answer such questions.

LMX (Graen & Uhl-Bien, 1995) and studies of leadership as practice (Raelin, 2016), among others, share the relational aspect of leadership emphasised in studies of interaction. LMX has made significant progress bringing important qualities of leadership relationships to light, and studies of interaction might aid in developing a theoretical understanding of the mechanisms for realising such relationships. Similarly, although studies of leadership as practice forcefully promote a processual perspective on leadership, the actual production and accomplishment of these processes remain less theoretically developed. The preference for questionnaire-based studies in LMX and for interpretative observation in studies of leadership as practice might benefit from a supplement of more detailed analysis of interaction, which could advance theory development.

More individual-oriented traditions could also benefit from studies of interaction. In line with trait activation theory (Tett et al., 2021), personality traits have different effects depending on how they are activated in specific situations. Studies of interaction could help show how, when and in what sense personality traits are mobilised in leadership situations. Narcissism and the dark sides of leadership, for example, are a growing area of interest where a combination of destructive leaders, participating followers and conducive environments are argued to produce destructive outcomes (Padilla et al., 2007). Studies of interaction could help untangle the mechanisms at work in such adverse situations.

Finally, digitalisation can play an obvious role in the evolution of leadership – understood as influence processes – for example, through the introduction of virtual teams or artificial intelligence (AI). Although strong hyperbole undergirds the organisational benefits touted in the trend, situated interactional studies may provide some keys to understanding how these phenomena elicit or even format new leadership practices. For instance, Parry et al. (2016) theoretically discuss how an AI-based leadership decision system could impact human identity and organisational ethics, whereas interactional studies might explicate how organisational conversations appropriate and (de-)authorise AI-generated input, and thus how leadership and followship identities are bestowed on humans and, indeed, non-human agents. Finally, leadership in interaction could reveal which mechanisms and methods realise leadership and how they involve not only talk and the body, but also space, artefacts and the affordances of digital technology itself.

REFERENCES

Angouri, J., & Marra, M. (2010). Corporate meetings as genre: A study of the role of the chair in corporate meeting talk. *Text & Talk*, *30*(6), 615–636.

Antaki, C., & Widdicombe, S. (1998). *Identities in Talk*. Sage.

Arvedsen, L. D., & Hassert, L. O. (2020). Accomplishing leadership-in-interaction by mobilizing available information and communication technology objects in a virtual context. *Leadership*, *16*(5), 546–567.

Ashford, S. J., & Sitkin, S. B. (2019). From problems to progress: A dialogue on prevailing issues in leadership research. *Leadership Quarterly*, *30*(4), 454–460.

Atkinson, P., & Silverman, D. (1997). Kundera's *Immortality*: The interview society and the invention of the self. *Qualitative Inquiry*, *3*(3), 304–325.

Austin, J. L. (1962). *How to Do Things with Words*. Oxford University Press.

Baumeister, R. F., Vohs, K. D., & Funder, D. C. (2007). Psychology as the science of self-reports and finger movements: Whatever happened to actual behavior? *Perspectives on Psychological Science*, *2*(4), 396–403.

Baxter, J. (2014). 'If you had only listened carefully …': The discursive construction of emerging leadership in a UK all-women management team. *Discourse & Communication*, *8*(1), 23–39.

Baxter, J. (2017). Resolving a gender and language problem in women's leadership: Consultancy research in workplace discourse. *Discourse & Communication*, 11(2), 141–159.

Carson, J. B., Tesluk, P. E., & Marrone, J. A. (2007). Shared leadership in teams: An investigation of antecedent conditions and performance. *Academy of Management Journal*, *50*(5), 1217–1234.

Chalupnik, M., & Atkins, S. (2020). 'Everyone happy with what their role is?': A pragmalinguistic evaluation of leadership practices in emergency medicine training. *Journal of Pragmatics*, *160*, 80–96.

Choi, S., & Schnurr, S. (2014). Exploring distributed leadership: Solving disagreements and negotiating consensus in a 'leaderless' team. *Discourse Studies*, *16*(1), 3–24.

Clifton, J. (2006). A conversation analytical approach to business communication: The case of leadership. *Journal of Business Communication*, *43*(3), 202–219.

Clifton, J. (2009) Beyond taxonomies of influence: 'Doing' influence and making decisions in management team meetings. *Journal of Business Communication*, 46(1), 57–79.

Clifton, J., Larsson, M., & Schnurr, S. (2020). Leadership in interaction: An introduction to the special issue. *Leadership*, *16*(5), 511–521.

Cooren, F. (2010). *Action and Agency in Dialogue: Passion, Incarnation and Ventriloquism*. John Benjamins.

Cooren, F., & Fairhurst, G. T. (2008). Dislocation and stabilization: How to scale up from interactions to organization. In L. L. Putnam & A. M. Nicotera (Eds.), *Building Theories of Organization: The Constitutive Role of Communication* (pp. 117–152). Routledge.

DeRue, D. S., & Ashford S. J. (2010). Who will lead and who will follow? A social process of leadership identity construction in organizations. *Academy of Management Review*, *35*(4), 627–647.

DeRue, D. S., Nahrgang, J. D., & Ashford, S. J. (2015). Interpersonal perceptions and the emergence of leadership structures in groups: A network perspective. *Organization Science*, *26*(4), 1192–1209.

Djordjilovic, O. (2012). Displaying and developing team identity in workplace meetings: A multimodal perspective. *Discourse Studies*, *14*(1), 111–127.

Drath, W. H., McCauley, C. D., Palus, C. J., Van Velsor E., O'Connor P. M. G., & McGuire J. B. (2008) Direction, alignment, commitment: Toward a more integrative ontology of leadership. *Leadership Quarterly*, 19(6), 635–653.

Du-Babcock, B. & Chan, A. C. (2018). Negotiating consensus in simulated decision-making meetings without designated chairs: A study of participants' discourse roles. *Discourse & Communication*, *12*(5), 497–516.

Fairhurst, G. T. (2007a). *Discursive Leadership: In Conversaion with Leadership Psychology*. Sage.

Fairhurst, G. T. (2007). Liberating leadership in Corporation: After Mr. Sam: A response. In F. Cooren (Ed.), *Interacting and organizing: Analyses of a management meeting* (pp. 53–71). Lawrence Erbaum Associates.

Fleishman, E. A. (1953). The description of supervisory behavior. *Journal of Applied Psychology*, *37*(1), 1–6.

Garfinkel, H. (1967). *Studies in Ethnomethodology*. Prentice Hall.

Goffman, E. (1982), *Interaction Ritual: Essays on Face-to-Face Behavior*. Pantheon.

Graen, G. B., & Uhl-Bien, M. (1995). Relationship-based approach to leadership: Development of leader-member exchange (LMX) theory of leadership over 25 years: Applying a multi-level multi-domain perspective. *Leadership Quarterly*, *6*(2), 219–247.

Grint, K. (2005). *Leadership: Limits and Possibilities*. Palgrave Macmillan.

Gronn, P. C. (1983). Talk as the work: The accomplishment of school administration. *Administrative Science Quarterly*, *28*(1), 1–21.

Gumpertz, J. J. (1982). *Discourse Strategies*. Cambridge University Press.

Halvorsen, K., & Sarangi, S. (2015). Team decision-making in workplace meetings: The interplay of activity roles and discourse roles. *Journal of Pragmatics*, *76*, 1–14.

Hammersley, M., & Atkinson, P. (1995). *Ethnography. Principles in Practice* (2nd edn). Routledge.

Heritage, J. (2012). Epistemics in action: Action formation and territories of knowledge. *Research on Language and Social Interaction*, 45(1), 1–29.

Heritage, J., & Clayman, S. (2010). *Talk in Action: Interactions, Identities, and Institutions*. John Wiley & Sons.

Hindmarsh, J., & Llewellyn, N. (2018). Video in sociomaterial investigations: A solution to the problem of relevance for organizational research. *Organizational Research Methods*, 21(2), 412–437.

Holm, F., & Fairhurst, G. T. (2018). Configuring shared and hierarchical leadership through authoring. *Human Relations*, 71(5), 692–721.

Holmes, J., & Marra, M. (2004). Leadership and managing conflict in meetings. *Pragmatics*, 14(4), 439–462.

Hosking, D. M. (1988). Organizing, leadership and skilful processes. *Journal of Management Studies*, 25(2), 147–166.

Huisman, M. (2001). Decision-making in meetings as talk-in-interaction. *International Studies of Management & Organization*, 31(3), 69–90.

Ladegaard, H. J. (2012). Rudeness as a discursive strategy in leadership discourse: Culture, power and gender in a Hong Kong workplace. *Journal of Pragmatics*, 44(12), 1661–1679. https://doi.org/10.1016/j.pragma.2012.07.003.

Larsson, M. (2017). Leadership in interaction. In J. Storey, J. Hartley, J.- L. Denis, P. 't, Hart & D. Ulrich (Eds.), *The Routledge Companion to Leadership* (pp. 173–193). Routledge.

Larsson, M., & Lundholm, S. E. (2013). Talking work in a bank: A study of organizing properties of leadership in work interactions. *Human Relations*, 66(8), 1101–1129. 10.1177/0018726712465452.

Larsson, M., & Nielsen, M. F. (2021). The risky path to a followership identity: From abstract concept to situated reality. *International Journal of Business Communication*, 58(1), 3–30.

Latour, B. (2005). *Reassembling the Social: An Introduction to Actor-Network-Theory*. Oxford University Press.

Likert, R. (1961). *New Patterns of Management*. McGraw-Hill.

Llewellyn, N., & Hindmarsh, J. (2010). *Organisation, Interaction and Practice: Studies of Ethnomethodology and Conversation Analysis*. Cambridge University Press.

Meschitti, V. (2018). The power of positioning: How leadership work unfolds in team interactions. *Leadership*, 15(5), 621–643. 1742715018808905.

Mesinioti, P., Angouri, J., O'Brien, S., et al. (2020). 'Get me the airway there': Negotiating leadership in obstetric emergencies. *Discourse & Communication*, 14(2), 150–174.

Mondada, L. (2011). Understanding as an embodied, situated and sequential achievement in interaction. *Journal of Pragmatics*, 43(2), 542–552.

Nielsen, M. F. (2009). Interpretative management in business meetings: Understanding managers' interactional strategies through conversation analysis. *Journal of Business Communication*, 46(1), 23–56. 10.1177/0021943608325752.

Ospina, S. M., Foldy, E. G., Fairhurst, G. T., & Jackson, B. (2020) Collective dimensions of leadership: Connecting theory and method. *Human Relations*, 73(4), 441–463.

Padilla, A., Hogan, R., & Kaiser, R. B. (2007). The toxic triangle: Destructive leaders, susceptible followers, and conducive environments. *Leadership Quarterly*, 18(3), 176–194.

Parry, K., Cohen, M., & Bhattacharya, S. (2016). Rise of the machines: A critical consideration of automated leadership decision making in organizations. *Group & Organization Management*, 41(5), 571–594.

Pomerantz, A., & Denvir, P. (2007). Enacting the institutional role of chairperson in upper management meetings: The interactional realization of provisional authority. In F. Cooren (Ed.), *Interacting and Organizing* (pp. 31–52). Lawrence Erlbaum.

Pye, A. (2005). Leadership and organizing: Sensemaking in action. *Leadership*, 1(1), 31–50.

Raelin, J. A. (2016). *Leadership-as-Practice: Theory and Application*. Routledge.

Rawls, A. W. (2008). Harold Garfinkel, ethnomethodology and workplace studies. *Organization Studies*, 29(5), 701–732.

Rost, J. C. (1991). *Leadership for the Twenty-First Century*. Praeger.

Sacks, H. (1992) *Lectures on Conversation*. Blackwell.

Sarangi, S., & Roberts, C. (2008). The dynamics of interactional and institutional orders in work-related settings. In S. Sarangi & C. Roberts (Eds.), *Talk, Work and Institutional Order* (pp. 1–60). De Gruyter Mouton.

Schegloff, E. A. (1997). Whose Text? Whose Context? *Discourse & Society*, 8(2), 165–187.

Schnurr, S., & Chan, A. (2011). Exploring another side of co-leadership: Negotiating professional identities through face-work in disagreements. *Language in Society*, 40(02), 187–209. 10.1017/S0047404511000030.

Schnurr, S., & Schroeder, A. (2019). A critical reflection of current trends in discourse analytical research on leadership across disciplines: A call for a more engaging dialogue. *Leadership*, 15(4), 445–460.

Sidnell, J. (2017). Action in interaction is conduct under a description. *Language in Society*, 46(3), 313–337.

Simpson, B., Buchan, L., & Sillince, J. (2018). The performativity of leadership talk. *Leadership*, 14(6), 644–661.

Smith, P., Haslam, S. A., & Nielsen, J. F. (2018). In search of identity leadership: An ethnographic study of emergent influence in an interorganizational R&D team. *Organization Studies*, *39*(10), 1425–1447.

Stevanovic, M., & Peräkylä, A. (2014). Three orders in the organization of human action. *Language in Society*, *43*(2), 185–207.

Stivers, T., Mondada, L., & Steensig, J. (2011). *The Morality of Knowledge in Conversation*. Cambridge University Press.

Svennevig, J. (2011). Leadership style in managers' feedback in meetings. In J. Angouri & M. Marra (Eds.), *Constructing Identities at Work* (pp.17–39). Palgrave.

Svennevig, J. (2012). The agenda as resource for topic introduction in workplace meetings. *Discourse Studies*, *14*(1), 53–66.

Taylor, J. R. (1999). What is 'organizational communication'? Communication as a dialogic of text and conversation. *Communication Review*, *3*(1–2), 21–63.

Taylor, J. R., & van Every, E. J. (2000). *The Emergent Organization: Communication as Its Site and Surface*. Lawrence Erlbaum Associates.

Tett, R. P., Toich, M. J., & Ozkum, S. B. (2021). Trait activation theory: A review of the literature and applications to five lines of personality dynamics research. *Annual Review of Organizational Psychology and Organizational Behavior*, *8*, 199–233.

Uhl-Bien, M. (2006). Relational leadership theory: Exploring the social processes of leadership and organizing. *Leadership Quarterly*, *17*(6), 654–676.

Uhl-Bien, M., & Carsten, M. (2018). Reversing the lens in leadership: Positioning followership in the leadership construct. In I. Katz, G. Eilam-Shamir, R. Kark & Y. Berson (Eds.), *Leadership Now: Reflections on the Legacy of Boas Shamir* (pp. 195–222). Emerald.

Van de Mieroop, D. (2019). A deontic perspective on the collaborative, multimodal accomplishment of leadership. *Leadership*, *16*(5), 592–619. 10.1177/1742715019893824.

Van de Mieroop, D., Clifton, J., & Verhelst, A. (2020) Investigating the interplay between formal and informal leaders in a shared leadership configuration: A multimodal conversation analytical study. *Human Relations*, *73*(4), 490–515.

Van Praet, E. (2009). Staging a team performance: A linguistic ethnographic analysis of weekly meetings at a British embassy. *Journal of Business Communication*, *46*(1), 80–99. 10.1177/0021943608325754.

Vine, B., Holmes, J., Marra, M., Pfeifer, D., & Jackson, B. (2008) Exploring co-leadership talk through interactional sociolinguistics. *Leadership*, *4*(3), 339–360. 10.1177/1742715008092389.

Walker, R. C., & Artiz, J. (2014). *Leadership Talk: A Discourse Approach to Leader Emergence*. Business Expert Press.

Watson, C., & Drew, V. (2017) Humour and laughter in meetings: Influence, decision-making and the emergence of leadership. *Discourse & Communication*, *11*(3), 314–329.

Wodak, R., Kwon, W., & Clarke, I. (2011) 'Getting people on board': Discursive leadership for consensus building in team meetings. *Discourse & Society*, *22*(5), 592–644. 10.1177/0957926511405410.

Wåhlin-Jacobsen, C. D. (2020). Open or closed? A social interaction perspective on line managers' reactions to employee voice. *Management Communication Quarterly*, *34*(1), 32–57.

Yukl, G. (2012). Effective leadership behavior: What we know and what questions need more attention. *Academy of Management Perspectives*, *26*(4), 66–85.

The Quality of Relationships: An Exploration of Current Leader–Member Exchange (LMX) Research and Future Possibilities

Catherine R. Holt and Allan Lee

INTRODUCTION

Leader–member exchange (LMX) focuses on the quality of the dyadic relationship between a leader (i.e., manager, supervisor, etc.) and follower (i.e., member, subordinate, employee, etc.). A central premise of LMX is the recognition that a leader will have varying relationship qualities with each follower (Dansereau et al., 1975). Low-quality relationships are characterised by minimal levels of trust and respect, whereas high-quality relationships embody trust, commitment, shared respect and feelings of mutual obligation (Graen & Uhl-Bien, 1995; Uhl-Bien & Maslyn, 2003). Early longitudinal studies found evidence that there is a process of relationship development that occurs in the initial part of the leader–follower relationship (Graen et al., 1982; Scandura & Graen, 1984). It has been suggested that newly formed dyads progress through three stages in which their roles within the relationship become established: role-taking, role-making and role-routinisation (Graen & Scandura, 1987). Studies of the development process propose that perceptions of relationship quality form quickly within the initial stages, and then remain relatively stable throughout the course of the relationship (Liden et al., 1993; Nahrgang et al., 2009).

LMX is a prominent and significant approach to studying the dyadic leader–follower relationship. Empirical research continues to demonstrate that relationship quality is theoretically important because high-quality leader–follower relationships are associated with outcomes that are beneficial to employees and organisations. Studies have also examined the antecedents of LMX, demonstrating that there are a wide range of factors that influence LMX relationship quality – from contextual considerations such as team size (Schyns et al., 2005), to individual differences, such as relationship attachment styles developed during childhood (Richards & Hackett, 2012). After nearly half a century of scholarship, LMX still remains a dynamic and progressive method of exploring the dyadic relationship and leadership more generally.

In this chapter, we provide an overview of LMX research and a discussion of current developments and emerging research areas. First, we introduce a wealth of research that has explored the antecedents, mediators, moderators and outcomes associated with LMX quality. In the next section we demonstrate how the study of LMX has grown to consider other aspects of the relationship and introduce emerging concepts such as LMX ambivalence, which challenges the way we understand the LMX quality continuum and suggests that we can simultaneously have both positive and negative feelings towards our relationships (Lee et al., 2019b). In addition, we review team-level studies of LMX and the advances in LMX differentiation which explore social comparisons that followers make about other team members' leader–follower relationships (e.g., Vidyarthi et al., 2010). In the next section, we consider areas of LMX that have been repeatedly critiqued, such as the commonly used measurements and how the studies are designed. Finally, we review the attempts to resolve these issues and suggest areas for future study, such as utilising mixed method approaches to help us understand more about the micro-level dynamics of the LMX relationship.

LMX QUALITY

The vast majority of research examining LMX has focused on measuring the quality of the leader–follower relationship (i.e., LMX quality) by gathering followers' evaluations. This work typically utilises the seven-item measure developed by Graen and Uhl-Bien (1995), although other instruments have also been developed and used (see Liden et al., 2015). Using these measures scholars have examined antecedents and outcomes that are theoretically associated with LMX quality, often examining proposed mediators and moderators of these relationships. The sections below will briefly summarise this large body of work.

Consequences of LMX Quality

Much research effort has focused on examining the outcomes associated with LMX quality. Outcomes that are posited to result from LMX quality tend to fit into the following categories: follower job attitudes, behaviours, well-being and emotions. Hundreds of studies report a positive relationship between LMX quality and beneficial outcomes (see reviews by Dulebohn et al., 2012; Martin et al., 2016). For example, LMX quality, rated by followers or leaders is positively associated with follower's in-role and extra-role performance (see meta-analysis by Martin et al., 2016). Similarly, LMX quality is positively related to job attitudes such as job satisfaction and organisational commitment (see review by Epitropaki & Martin, 2016). A number of studies have highlighted the effects of LMX quality at the team level. Specifically, researchers have tended to explore either the effects of average LMX quality within a team on, for example, team performance (e.g., Boies, & Howell, 2006), or the effects of LMX variation within teams (e.g., Li & Liao, 2014). Further discussion of the latter is provided later in this chapter.

Mediators

To explain the association between LMX and outcomes such as job attitudes and behaviours, scholars have drawn on several theoretical frameworks, such as social exchange theory and self-determination theory (Martin et al., 2016). Each theoretical framework is associated with explanatory mechanisms that are operationalised in the form of mediating variables; thus, scholars examine the indirect effect between LMX and follower outcomes by measuring these mediating variables.

A framework that is often used to explain the effects of LMX is social exchange theory (e.g., Blau, 1964). Although different views of social exchange have developed, theorists agree that social exchange entails a series of interactions between parties (e.g., a leader and follower) that generate obligations (Emerson, 1976). Accordingly, it is argued that the better the quality of the LMX relationship, the more driven followers are to invest in the social exchange relationship with the leader (Erdogan & Enders, 2007). This process is posited to flow from a norm of reciprocity which decrees that resources received should be repaid (Gouldner, 1960). Scholars have contended that to reciprocate high-quality LMX relationships, it is likely that followers will go beyond required in-role behaviour (i.e., in-role job performance) and engage in extra-role behaviour, known as organisational citizenship behaviour (OCB), to retain a balanced social exchange (e.g., Ilies et al., 2007). In support of this idea, research demonstrates that felt obligation generated from high-quality LMX relationships mediates the relationship between LMX quality, OCB (Lee et al., 2019c; Lemmon & Wayne, 2015), pro-social behaviour (Kim & Qu, 2020) and creativity (Pan et al., 2012). Building on the reciprocity principles of social exchange, Liao and colleagues (2019) investigated episodic resource transactions that involve the giving and taking of resources from both leaders and followers. By studying resource exchanges over a period of two weeks, the authors examined micro-exchange dynamics in leader–member dyads. Their findings suggested followers repay leaders only when what they have received is more than what they have given in an episodic transaction.

Social exchange theory also leads to the expectation that trust in the leader is a key mediator between LMX and follower outcomes. Indeed,

LMX has been defined as a trust-building process (e.g., Bauer & Green, 1996). Specifically, as social exchanges proceed, the leader and follower develop trust with each other so that there is an expectation that the positive exchanges will continue (Sue-Chan et al., 2012). As such, trust in leader has been found to mediate the relationship between LMX quality and follower outcomes such as in-role and extra-role performance (Martin et al., 2016). However, LMX researchers view trust as a mediator with caution because the dominant LMX measures (LMX-7 and LMX-MDM) include items that are highly related to the concept of trust (Liden & Maslyn, 1998).

Self-determination theory (Deci & Ryan, 1985) is another relevant theoretical framework for understanding the effects of LMX. Self-determination theory helps us to understand human motivation, and states that people are motivated by both external rewards such as money and acclaim, and internal factors such as developing knowledge and mastering skills. In order to achieve and encourage these motivations a leader should support an individual's experience of autonomy, competence and relatedness. Research has demonstrated that these three components are closely associated with high LMX relationships and found that LMX was positively related to followers' motivation and sense of psychological empowerment (e.g., Aryee & Chen, 2006; Kim & George, 2005). Motivation and empowerment have been repeatedly found to mediate the relationship between LMX and employee outcomes, such as performance (Kim et al., 2015; Martin et al., 2016) and employee voice (Wang et al., 2016).

Moderators

Although studies have shown significant relationships between LMX and beneficial follower outcomes, the effect sizes of these associations have been heterogeneous (Martin et al., 2016). Thus, a key question is *when* does LMX quality have more or less of an impact. To answer this, researchers have found a wide range of moderating variables that exacerbate or attenuate the association between LMX quality and follower outcomes. The range of moderators studied makes a succinct summary difficult, but they can be broadly categorised as attributes of the follower (e.g., personality), the leader (e.g., whether they are seen as a representative of the wider organisation), or aspects of the team, organisational, or wider cultural context (e.g., job characteristics). To illustrate, one study found that LMX was only positively related to in-role performance when leaders perceived they had high levels of organisational support (Erdogan & Enders, 2007). Other studies suggest that followers react differently to their LMX relationship based on their characteristics. For instance, Ozer (2008) showed that the LMX–job performance relationship was stronger when followers' locus of control was internal as opposed to external. This growing area of research suggests that the effects of LMX quality are contingent on many factors.

Antecedents of LMX Quality

Given the apparent benefits of developing a high-quality LMX relationship, a substantial amount of research effort has been devoted to uncovering antecedents of LMX quality (see review by Nahrgang & Seo, 2015). These antecedents can largely be categorised as 1) leader and member attributes, 2) attributes of the relationship, 3) leader and member actions and behaviours, or 4) contextual characteristics (Nahrgang & Seo, 2015).

The first category 'leader and member attributes', often include personality characteristics such as extraversion, agreeableness and positive and negative affectivity (see Schyns, 2015). The second category 'attributes of the relationship', includes variables connected to the relationship between a leader and follower, such as perceived similarity, interaction frequency, affect or liking. Research has, for example, examined similarity in attributes between the leaders and followers and how such similarity influences the relationship that develops. Early work in this area suggested that the degree of compatibility between leader and member would contribute to the quality of LMX relationship that forms (Dienesch & Liden, 1986; Graen & Cashman, 1975). One category of similarity relates to the extent to which leaders and followers are similar with regards to personality. For instance, Zhang and colleagues (2012) explored the congruence between a leader and follower's proactive personality (i.e., the extent to which individuals take action to influence their environments). Results of their study found that followers reported lower-quality LMX and poorer work outcomes when their proactive personality was lower than their leaders. A further area of research that considers attributes of the leader–follower relationship is the analysis of relationship attachment styles. Attachment styles are believed to form in early childhood and are related to the parental support a child received (Bowlby, 1969); it is thought that these early messages from childhood shape the way individuals deal with all types of relationships during adulthood, including how they interact in a work environment. In a study of 150 leader–follower dyads, Richards and Hackett (2012) found that if a leader or follower reported themselves as having attachment insecurity (i.e., attachment anxiety and avoidance in relationships) this was a key predictor of lower evaluations of the LMX relationship.

The third category of antecedents refers to the actions or behaviours of leaders or followers. For instance, Sluss and Thompson (2012) studied newcomers to organisations and discovered that leaders who provided more guidance, advice and role-modelling developed more positive LMX relationships. Others have explored the transactional behaviours of leaders and their influence on LMX – reporting that contingent rewards were positively associated with LMX quality, whereas non-contingent punishment was negatively related to LMX (Wayne et al., 2002).

The fourth category of antecedents is related to contextual factors. In their discussion of LMX development, Dienesch and Liden (1986) highlighted that contextual factors such as work group composition, leader's power and organisational policies and culture also influence the LMX process. Supporting the importance of contextual factors, studies show that the number of employees reporting to a supervisor was negatively related to the quality of LMX (Green et al., 1996; Schyns et al., 2005). Studies of work climate have explored the extent to which the work unit emphasises human relations, teamwork and cohesion and have found that this type of climate helps to foster high-quality LMX relationships (Aryee & Chen, 2006; Cogliser & Schriesheim, 2000).

BEYOND LMX QUALITY: RECENT TRENDS IN THE CONCEPTUALISATION OF LMX

LMX scholars have underlined the need to go beyond focusing purely on LMX quality. At the individual level, the concepts of LMX ambivalence and LMX importance have emphasised the necessity to examine other properties of the leader–follower relationship. At the dyadic level, research examining LMX agreement has indicated that agreement between leaders and follower in terms of LMX quality is also important to consider. Finally, at the group level, LMX differentiation and related constructs recognise the prominence of the group context for understanding LMX relationships. These three areas will be discussed in turn below.

Individual Level

As highlighted above, LMX research typically measures the overall quality of the LMX relationship, assuming that followers (or leaders) evaluate their relationship on a continuum ranging from low to high quality. This approach simplifies the nature of interpersonal relationships. For instance, this reliance on a high–low quality dichotomy overlooks the fact that many leader–follower relationships are not evaluated as purely positive or negative. In fact, relationship scholars have long acknowledged that interpersonal relationships in any domain (e.g., friendships) are prone to eliciting ambivalence whereby simultaneously positive and negative thoughts and feelings co-exist (e.g., Fingerman et al., 2008; Uchino et al., 2004). One of the earliest accounts of relational ambivalence can be found in Freud's musings on the coexistence of seemingly contradictory intimate emotions, such as love and hate and affection and hostility (Freud, 1918). Such accounts are consistent with findings showing that individuals in abusive relationships may concurrently hold strong feelings of love and hate for each other (e.g., Patzel, 2006). Leadership scholars too have shown that abusive behaviour can occur within otherwise high-quality LMX relationships (Lian et al., 2012). More generally, studies have demonstrated that ambivalent perceptions can exist, for example, within romantic relationships (e.g., Uchino et al., 2014), friendships (e.g., Holt-Lunstad et al., 2007) and co-worker relationships (Pratt & Doucet, 2000). However, compared to the vast amount of research on positive or negative relationships, ambivalent relationships are noticeably understudied, especially in workplace settings (Methot et al., 2017). To address this issue, Lee and colleagues (2019b) introduced the construct of LMX ambivalence, defining it as *the subjective experience of coexisting positive and negative thoughts towards the leader–follower relationship* (p. 1928). Because ambivalence violates people's fundamental consistency motives (Festinger, 1957) it is often experienced as undesirable, unpleasant and physiologically arousing (e.g., Van Harreveld et al., 2009). Applying this reasoning to the leader–follower relationship, Lee et al. (2019b) found that LMX ambivalence was distinct from overall LMX quality and had a negative association with follower performance. This effect was mediated by negative emotions elicited by LMX ambivalence. Similarly, Dechawatanapaisal (2021) reported a negative relationship between LMX ambivalence and career commitment, while Herr and colleagues (2019) showed that followers who evaluated their supervisor in terms of both positive and negative behaviours (i.e., ambivalence) had higher levels of distress and stress-related endocrine dysregulation. This nascent research highlights the importance of considering ambivalence within LMX relationships and the need for further research to better understand the negative and potentially positive consequences (Rothman et al., 2017).

As well as assuming that LMX relationships fall on a continuum from high to low quality, researchers have also tended to presume that the LMX relationship is always important to followers. However, research conducted by Lee and colleagues (2019c) challenged this assumption by arguing that followers do not always perceive their LMX relationship as personally important or valuable. The authors measured LMX importance – a meta-perception indicating whether followers view their LMX relationship as personally important to them. They found that when a follower stated high levels of both LMX quality and LMX importance these concepts interacted to create a greater feeling of obligation to their leader, which in turn led to increased OCB. This novel finding may account for the unexplained variation in LMX quality and OCB found in previous meta-analyses (see Ilies et al., 2007; Martin et al., 2016), which showed that even though followers had high LMX they still displayed varying levels of OCB. Taken together, the findings related to LMX ambivalence and LMX importance highlight the need for more research, at the individual level, that goes beyond LMX quality and considers other aspects of the LMX relationship.

Dyadic Level

LMX research highlights that leaders and followers develop unique dyadic relationships, so there is a theoretical expectation that both members of the dyad would view the relationship in a similar manner (Graen & Uhl-Bien, 1995). However, despite LMX emphasising the reciprocity and the pattern of exchanges between leaders and followers, LMX has tended to be assessed from either the leader's or follower's perspective, which seems to mask a surprisingly high level of disagreement between leader and follower ratings (Gerstner & Day, 1997; Sin et al., 2009). Loignon et al., (2019) state that agreement between leader and follower reports of LMX share as little as 8–13 per cent of the variance in LMX perceptions.

Research suggests that follower outcomes are maximised when leaders and followers are in agreement regarding LMX quality, and outcomes suffer when assessments of relationship quality are not aligned (Cogliser et al., 2009; Markham et al., 2010; Matta et al., 2015; Sherman et al., 2012). Importantly, and somewhat counterintuitively, this includes agreement on both high-quality and low-quality ratings. In other words, it is more favourable for leaders and followers to agree that they have a low-quality relationship than for just one member of the dyad to evaluate the relationship as high quality.

Scholars have speculated about the reasons for LMX disagreement, from leader narcissism to leaders not meeting a follower's implicit expectations (van Gils et al., 2010) or because of the way LMX is typically measured (e.g., Epitropaki et al., 2020). An often-cited explanation for LMX disagreement is linked to leader overestimation; where leaders could be providing high ratings due to viewing the questionnaire as a reflection of their own competence as a manager (Sin et al., 2009). In their meta-analysis Sin et al. (2009) found only weak support that leaders inflated their ratings and concluded that this was not a leading cause of LMX disagreement. Some research has empirically examined antecedents of LMX agreement. Sin et al. (2009) found that agreement between leader- and follower-rated LMX increased with the length of tenure and dyadic intensity, and Jackson and Johnson (2012) reported that leaders with strong relational identities or dyads that had similar relational identities were more likely to have LMX agreement. They recommend that organisations seek to foster strong relational and collective identities between employees to enhance LMX agreement and benefit from its positive organisational outcomes.

Group Level

As highlighted previously, a central tenet of LMX research is that a leader will typically develop different-quality relationships with each of their various followers. Indeed, empirical research has demonstrated that most leaders have different-quality relationships with each member of their team (e.g., Liden & Graen, 1980) – a process known as LMX differentiation. A key tenet of LMX differentiation is that followers are conscious of the variation in the quality of exchanges within a workgroup and are aware of each other's LMX quality with the leader (Duchon et al., 1986). This awareness comes from regular interactions, observations, casual discussions and shared events, which create opportunities for both conscious and unconscious social comparisons (Vidyarthi et al., 2010). Thus, the quality of LMX is not shaped in isolation from surrounding contexts and an important theoretical question concerns how different LMX relationships within a team affect followers' and teams' outcomes. LMX differentiation has been studied in three distinct ways (Martin et al., 2018):

- as individual perceptions of within-group variation (e.g., Choi et al., 2020);
- as individuals' relative position within their own group (e.g., Hu & Liden, 2013; Vidyarthi, et al., 2010);
- as within-group variation in LMX quality (e.g., Auh et al., 2016).

At the group level, research often shows inconsistent findings that tend to be influenced by moderators (see review by Martin et al., 2018). However, meta-analytic investigation has reported that LMX differentiation has negative associations with collective harmony and solidarity of the team, as indicated by a consistent negative relationship with emergent states and group processes (Yu et al., 2018). For instance, studies have highlighted that LMX differentiation within a team is associated with relationship conflict (Auh et al., 2016; Choi et al., 2020; Zhou & Shi, 2014) and reduced team cohesion (Chiniara & Bentein, 2018). As such, LMX differentiation is often associated with poorer team performance (e.g., Choi et al., 2020; Li & Liao, 2014; Manata, 2020).

As well as exploring the group-level consequences of LMX differentiation, scholars have also focused on how individual followers react to perceiving a better or worse LMX relationship than their teammates with whom they share the same leader. Relative LMX (RLMX) refers to the actual level of one's own LMX quality as compared with the average LMX within the team. RLMX is calculated by subtracting the mean LMX of a group from each follower's LMX score. Higher RLMX scores suggest that a follower is better than average in terms of LMX quality. As such, followers with high RLMX relationships are argued to be more likely to make downward social comparisons whereby they compare themselves with those who are worse off (e.g., Hu & Liden, 2013), although this comparison is implied rather than directly tested. A more direct measure of LMX social comparison (LMXSC) was developed by Vidyarthi and colleagues (2010). The authors' LMXSC scale asks respondents to indicate how their manager treats them compared to other members of the work team with high scores indicating a downward comparison. Although complicated by contextual factors, downward comparisons are often associated with the experience of more positive emotions (Lyubomirsky & Ross, 1997) and greater self-confidence (Hakmiller, 1966). Thus, in accordance with social comparison theory, studies measuring RLMX and downward LMXSC typically report positive associations with follower outcomes. For instance, at the individual-level, RLMX and LMXSC has shown positive associations with job performance (e.g., Henderson et al., 2008; Hu & Liden, 2013; Lapointe et al., 2020; Lee et al., 2019a; Singh & Vidyarthi, 2018; Vidyarthi et al., 2010, 2016), organisational citizenship behaviour (e.g., Bakar & Connaughton, 2019; Henderson et al., 2008; Hu & Liden, 2013) and positive job attitudes (e.g., Choi et al., 2020; Singh & Vidyarthi, 2018; Hu & Liden, 2013). In contrast to downward LMXSC, only two studies have explored the effects of upward LMXSC. Tse and colleagues (2018) found that upward LMXSC elicited hostile emotions and provoked individuals to direct harmful behaviour towards their co-worker. Similarly, Latif et al. (2020) used social comparison theory to show that an individual's feelings of envy mediated the relationship between upward LMXSC and knowledge-hiding behaviour.

Criticisms of LMX and Future Research Directions

Despite its popularity there have been notable critiques of the LMX construct (Dienesch & Liden, 1986; Gerstner & Day, 1997; Schriesheim et al., 1999). Most recently Gottfredson et al. (2020) highlighted issues related to its conceptualisation and measurement as well as the design of studies used to test LMX. In this section we will briefly review some of the recurring complaints levelled at the construct and make some suggestions for ways forward.

Lack of Theoretical Clarity and Measurement Issues

LMX has been criticised for being conceptually unclear due to the theoretical associations that have emerged during its development (Gottfredson et al., 2020; Schriesheim et al., 1999). For example, LMX has been traditionally built on the foundations of social exchange theory, referring to the exchange and reciprocation of services between individuals. However, with reference to LMX, the theory is often used to explain not only the exchange of services but also the negotiation of exchanges within a role development process, which is wider than the original social exchange theory developed by Blau (1964). In addition, the measurement of LMX tends to focus more on the overall quality of the relationship and lacks overt statements about the underlying social exchange process. Therefore, scholars have questioned whether common scales such as LMX-7 are measuring what the underlying LMX concept describes (Colquitt et al., 2014; Gottfredson et al., 2020; Liden & Maslyn, 1998).

Graen and colleagues trialled many item scales in the late 1970s and 1980s (two-item to 16-item scales), before recommending LMX-7 as a universal scale (Graen & Uhl-Bien, 1995). LMX-7 focuses on questions that measure the quality and effectiveness of the relationship, such as *how well does your leader recognize your potential?* and *how well does your leader understand your job problems and needs?* (Graen & Uhl-Bien, 1995, p. 237). It could be argued that there are underlying aspects of the relationship exchange present in the LMX-7 measure; for example, it would have taken time, energy and attention for the leader to understand the follower's needs. However, the exchange process is mostly inferred and not directly measured (Gerstner & Day, 1997). Recognition of this limitation led Bernerth and colleagues (2007) to create and validate a leader–member social exchange (LMSX) measure, in the hope of developing a scale that more accurately establishes the social exchange element of LMX. Items such as *My manager and I have a two-way exchange relationship* and *I have a balance of inputs and outputs with my manager* (Bernerth et al., 2007, p. 1003) focus on the reciprocal nature of the exchange, whereas LMX-7 requires that the leader and follower independently rate aspects of their mutual relationship. Although Bernerth and colleagues' (2007) scale appears to be more aligned to the LMX construct, very few scholars have adopted this measure, with most favouring the well-established LMX-7 scale or Liden and Maslyn's (1998) multidimensional measure called LMX-MDM, which includes affect, loyalty, contribution and professional respect.

While the exchanges that occur between leaders and followers may not be well captured by the popular LMX scales, some research has sought to examine these exchanges as antecedents to LMX quality (e.g., Seers et al., 2006). For instance, in an aforementioned study, Liao and colleagues (2019) quantitatively analysed discrete exchanges between leaders and followers to calculate each resource transaction. Building on the social exchange principles of equity and reciprocity, they found that followers 'repay' leaders only when they have received more than they have contributed, known as resource contribution surplus. Future research on the exchange of contributions seems a logical place to build our understanding of LMX exchange dynamics and strengthen our theoretical understanding of LMX.

A topical new direction which would provide substantial value to our understanding of LMX theory is increased integration with other methodologies. This coincides with a recent critique of quantitative leadership research, which highlights that the field relies too heavily on questionnaires, and queries if this method suitably captures real-world dynamics (Fischer et al., 2020). LMX questionnaires only measure the leader or follower's perceptions of the quality of the relationship, so there are limitations to our interpretations and analyses. Fischer et al. (2020) suggest that new methodologies are needed within the leadership field to capture what leaders are actually doing at a micro-level. Focusing only on quantitative data will create limits to our understanding of LMX, whereas a mixed method approach can bring the data to life with real-world narratives about relationship quality and social exchanges.

A mixed methods approach to assessing the exchange process within LMX could help our understanding of both the measurement issues and the LMX concept. Omilion-Hodges and Baker (2017) undertook a study to understand relationship quality through leader communication exchange. An interesting quote from a participating manager illuminated the leader–member exchange within her team. She openly admits to viewing the exchange as a 'reward system' and withholding support from followers who were not communicating their progress.

> *If one of my employees doesn't make an effort to talk to me, to reach out or keep me in the loop, I'm too busy to track them down. I can tell you they're not the first one on my list to get a reward like my time or support.*
> (Omilion-Hodges & Baker, 2017, p. 126)

This study relied on focus groups but demonstrates that mixed method studies collecting LMX-7 data and leader–follower communication exchanges at a micro-level could really enhance our understanding of LMX quality and social exchanges within leader–follower relationships. Unlike the Liao et al. (2019) study which concluded that managers must first create a resource contribution surplus, the manager in this study seems to be suggesting she has a different strategy. Drawing on the work of the previous chapter (Chapter 3, Leadership in interaction), combining a quantitative LMX measure with the collection of leader–follower interactions could be very informative for the theoretical development of LMX. As Larsson (2017) recognises, more work needs to be done to connect studies which analyse micro-interactions, such as conversation analysis and critical discourse analysis, to ongoing theoretical problems in the leadership field. This is an exciting time for cross-discipline projects, and many opportunities exist for engagement with LMX and current theoretical challenges.

Poor Study Design

Another criticism of LMX research relates to study design, an issue that has been highlighted within the leadership literature more generally (e.g., Eden, 2021; Fischer et al., 2021; Hughes et al., 2018). Briefly, the concerns revolve around the extent to which researchers can establish a causal relation between LMX and the proposed antecedents, mediators and outcomes. To illustrate, researchers typically posit that higher-quality LMX causes better follower job performance. Conversely, one could argue that followers who are better performers will be treated better by their leaders. Equally, both explanations may be true, or some unmeasured variable could explain both LMX quality and follower performance. Establishing causality within survey research is problematic, if not impossible, because of endogeneity bias (see Antonakis et al., 2010; Hughes et al., 2018) – an issue that most field studies must confront. As we have already noted many of the criticisms of LMX can be addressed through drawing on alternative methodologies and study designs. The issue of endogeneity can be systematically addressed with the use of methodologies such as randomised controlled experiments (Antonakis et al., 2010; Hughes et al., 2018), which would answer Fisher et al.'s (2020) call for the 'rediscovery of experimentation' as a methodology to study leadership.

Lack of Longitudinal Data

A further area of criticism that LMX has faced is the lack of longitudinal studies and a paucity of data supporting relationship development and the exchange processes within that development (Dienesch & Liden, 1986; Graen & Uhl-Bien, 1995). Several early LMX studies suggest that the perceived effectiveness of the relationship tends to form very quickly over the first two weeks of the relationship, and then remains stable (Bauer & Green, 1996; Liden et al., 1993; Nahrgang et al., 2009). Yet there have been very few longitudinal studies that confirm these findings and track the progress of new dyads in organisations. There is still much that is unknown about relationship development and the stability of LMX over time.

Undertaking some longitudinal case studies involving LMX and a second methodology could help us understand how relationship quality is formed and how stable it remains. For instance, two theoretical models of LMX development (Dienesch & Liden, 1986; Graen & Scandura, 1987) and one empirical study (Bauer & Green, 1996) suggest that a pivotal variable that signifies the initial stability in relationship quality could be the delegation of tasks by the leader. Additional methodologies would be able to track task delegation in detail and confirm its significance or suggest alternative signals of relationship stability.

CONCLUSION

We hope that this chapter has demonstrated the continued and unrelenting progress of the LMX concept and stimulated fresh ideas for future advancements. It is apparent that despite nearly half a century of research on the leader–follower relationship, interest in the study of LMX has not diminished. From our perspective some of the most interesting emerging trends are the introduction of new study designs and cross-discipline potential. Specifically, new methodologies will bring advancements to our understanding of the dyadic and team relationships at a micro-level. We are excited for the next decade of LMX research and hope it will bring more clarity around conceptual speculations and a broader understanding of how high-quality LMX can be developed and fostered within organisational settings.

REFERENCES

Antonakis, J., Bendahan, S., Jacquart, P., & Lalive, R. (2010). On making causal claims: A review and recommendations. *Leadership Quarterly*, *21*(6), 1086–1120.

Aryee, S., & Chen, Z. X. (2006). Leader–member exchange in a Chinese context: Antecedents, the mediating role of psychological empowerment and outcomes. *Journal of Business Research*, *59*(7), 793–801.

Auh, S., Bowen, D. E., Aysuna, C., & Menguc, B. (2016). A search for missing links: Specifying the relationship between leader–member exchange differentiation and service climate. *Journal of Service Research*, *19*(3), 260–275.

Bakar, H. A., & Connaughton, S. L. (2019). Relative leader–member exchange within work groups: The mediating effect of leader–member conversation quality on group-focused citizenship behavior. *International Journal of Business Communication*, August, 1–23.

Bauer, T. N., & Green, S. G. (1996). Development of leader–member exchange: A longitudinal test. *Academy of Management Journal*, *39*(6), 1538–1567.

Bernerth, J. B., Armenakis, A. A., Feild, H. S., Giles, W. F., & Walker, H. J. (2007). Leader–member social exchange (LMSX): Development and validation of a scale. *Journal of Organizational Behavior*, *28*, 979–1003.

Blau, P. M. (1964). *Exchange and Power in Social Life*. Wiley.

Boies, K., & Howell, J. M. (2006). Leader–member exchange in teams: An examination of the interaction between relationship differentiation and mean LMX in explaining team-level outcomes. *Leadership Quarterly*, *17*, 246–257.

Bowlby, J. (1969). *Attachment and Loss: Vol. 1. Attachment*. Basic Books.

Chiniara, M., & Bentein, K. (2018). The servant leadership advantage: When perceiving low differentiation in leader–member relationship quality influences team cohesion, team task performance and service OCB. *Leadership Quarterly*, *29*(2), 333–345.

Choi, D., Kraimer, M. L., & Seibert, S. E. (2020). Conflict, justice, and inequality: Why perceptions of leader–member exchange differentiation hurt performance in teams. *Journal of Organizational Behavior*, *41*(6), 567–586.

Cogliser, C. C., & Schriesheim, C. A. (2000). Exploring work unit context and leader–member exchange: A multi-level perspective. *Journal of Organizational Behavior*, *21*(5), 487–511.

Cogliser, C. C., Schriesheim, C. A., Scandura, T. A., & Gardner, W. L. (2009). Balance in leader and follower perceptions of leader–member exchange: Relationships with performance and work attitudes. *Leadership Quarterly*, *20*(3), 452–465.

Colquitt, J. A., Baer, M. D., Long, D. M., & Halvorsen-Ganepola, M. D. K. (2014). Scale indicators of social exchange relationships: A comparison of relative content validity. *Journal of Applied Psychology*, *99*(4), 599–618.

Dansereau, F., Graen, G., & Haga, W. J. (1975). A vertical dyad linkage approach to leadership within formal organizations: A longitudinal investigation of the role making process. *Organizational Behavior & Human Performance*, *13*(1), 46–78.

Dechawatanapaisal, D. (2021), Effects of leader–member exchange ambivalence on work attitudes: a moderated mediation model. *Journal of Management Development*, 40, 35–51.

Deci, E. L., & Ryan, R. M. (1985). *Intrinsic Motivation and Self-determination in Human Behavior*. Plenum.

Dienesch, R. M., & Liden, R. C. (1986). Leader–member exchange model of leadership: A critique and further development. *Academy of Management Review*, *11*(3), 618–634.

Duchon, D., Green, S. G., & Taber, T. D. (1986). Vertical dyad linkage: A longitudinal assessment of antecedents, measures, and consequences. *Journal of Applied Psychology*, *71*(1), 56–60.

Dulebohn, J. H., Bommer, W. H., Liden, R. C., Brouer, R. L., & Ferris, G. R. (2012). A meta-analysis of antecedents and consequences of leader–member exchange: Integrating the past with an eye toward the future. *Journal of Management*, *38*(6), 1715–1759.

Eden, D. (2021). The science of leadership: A journey from survey research to field experimentation. *Leadership Quarterly*, *32*(3), 101472.

Emerson, R. M. (1976). Social exchange theory. *Annual Review of Sociology*, *2*, 335–362.

Epitropaki, O., & Martin, R. (2016). LMX and work attitudes: Is there anything left unsaid or unexamined? In T. N. Bauer & B. Erdogan (Eds.), *The Oxford Handbook of Leader–Member Exchange* (pp. 139–156). Oxford University Press.

Epitropaki, O., Marstand, A. F., van der Heijden, B., Bozionelos, N., Mylonopoulos, N., Van der Heijde, C., Scholarios, D., Mikkelsen, A., Marzec, I., & Jedrzejowicz, P. (2020). What are the career implications of 'seeing eye to eye'? Examining the role of leader–member exchange (LMX) agreement on employability and career outcomes. *Personnel Psychology*, 1–32.

Erdogan, B., & Enders, J. (2007). Support from the top: Supervisors' perceived organizational support as a moderator of leader–member exchange to satisfaction and performance relationships. *Journal of Applied Psychology*, *92*(2), 321–330.

Festinger, L. (1957). *A Theory of Cognitive Dissonance* (Vol. 2). Stanford University Press.

Fingerman, K. L., Pitzer, L., Lefkowitz, E. S., Birditt, K. S., & Mroczek, D. (2008). Ambivalent relationship qualities between adults and their parents: Implications for the well-being of both parties. *Journals of Gerontology Series B: Psychological Sciences and Social Sciences*, *63*(6), 362–371.

Fischer, T., Hambrick, D. C., Sajons, G. B. & Van Quaquebeke, N. (2020). Beyond the ritualized use of questionnaires: Toward a science of actual behaviors and psychological states. *Leadership Quarterly*, *31*(4), I–III.

Fischer, T., Tian, A., Lee, A., & Hughes D. (2021). Abusive supervision: A systematic review and fundamental rethink. *Leadership Quarterly*, 101540.

Freud, S. (1918 [1914]). From the history of an infantile neurosis. *Standard Edition 17* (pp. 3–122). Hogarth Press.

Gerstner, C. R., & Day, D. V. (1997). Meta-analytic review of leader–member exchange theory: Correlates and construct issues. *Journal of Applied Psychology*, *82*(6), 827–844.

Gottfredson, R. K., Wright, S. L., & Heaphy, E. D. (2020). A critique of the leader–member exchange construct: Back to square one. *Leadership Quarterly*, *31*(6), Article 101385.

Gouldner, A. W. (1960). The norm of reciprocity: A preliminary statement. *American Sociological Review*, *25*, 161–178.

Graen, G., & Cashman, J. F. (1975). A role-making model in formal organizations: A developmental approach. In J. G. Hunt & L. L. Larson (Eds.), *Leadership Frontiers* (pp. 143–165). Kent State University Press.

Graen, G. B., Liden, R. C., & Hoel, W. (1982). Role of leadership in the employee withdrawal process. *Journal of Applied Psychology*, *67*(6), 868–872.

Graen, G. B., & Scandura, T. A. (1987). Toward a psychology of dyadic organizing. *Research in Organizational Behavior*, *9*, 175–208.

Graen, G. B., & Uhl-Bien, M. (1995). Relationship-based approach to leadership: Development of leader–member exchange (LMX) theory of leadership over 25 years: Applying a multi-level multi-domain perspective. *Leadership Quarterly*, *6*(2), 219–247.

Green, S. G., Anderson, S. E., & Shivers, S. L. (1996). Demographic and organizational influences on leader–member exchange and related work attitudes. *Organizational Behavior and Human Decision Processes*, *66*(2), 203–214.

Hakmiller, K. L. (1966). Threat as a determinant of downward comparison. *Journal of Experimental Social Psychology*, *1*, 32–39.

Henderson, D. J., Wayne, S. J., Shore, L. M., Bommer, W. H., & Tetrick, L. E. (2008). Leader–member exchange, differentiation, and psychological contract fulfillment: A multilevel examination. *Journal of Applied Psychology*, *93*(6), 1208–1219.

Herr, R. M., Van Harreveld, F., Uchino, B. N., Birmingham, W. C., Loerbroks, A., Fischer, J. E., & Bosch, J. A. (2019). Associations of ambivalent leadership with distress and cortisol secretion. *Journal of Behavioral Medicine*, *42*(2), 265–275.

Holt-Lunstad, J., Uchino, B. N., Smith, T. W., & Hicks, A. (2007). On the importance of relationship quality: The impact of ambivalence in friendships on cardiovascular functioning. *Annals of Behavioral Medicine*, *33*(3), 278–290.

Hu, J. I. A., & Liden, R. C. (2013). Relative leader–member exchange within team contexts: How and when social comparison impacts individual effectiveness. *Personnel Psychology*, *66*(1), 127–172.

Hughes, D. J., Lee, A., Tian, A. W., Newman, A., & Legood, A. (2018). Leadership, creativity, and innovation: A critical review and practical recommendations. *Leadership Quarterly*, *29*(5), 549–569.

Ilies, R., Nahrgang, J. D., & Morgeson, F. P. (2007). Leader–member exchange and citizenship behaviors: A meta-analysis. *Journal of Applied Psychology*, *92*(1), 269.

Jackson, E. M., & Johnson, R. E. (2012). When opposites do (and do not) attract: Interplay of leader and follower self-identities and its consequences for leader–member exchange. *Leadership Quarterly*, *23*(3), 488–501.

Kim, B., & George, R. T. (2005). The relationship between leader–member exchange (LMX) and psychological empowerment: A quick casual restaurant employee correlation study. *Journal of Hospitality & Tourism Research*, *29*(4), 468–483.

Kim, T. Y., Liu, Z., & Diefendorff, J. M. (2015). Leader–member exchange and job performance: The effects of taking charge and organizational tenure. *Journal of Organizational Behavior*, *36*(2), 216–231.

Kim, H., & Qu, H. (2020). Effects of employees' social exchange and the mediating role of customer orientation in the restaurant industry. *International Journal of Hospitality Management*, *89*, Article 102577.

Lapointe, É., Vandenberghe, C., Ayed, A. K. B., Schwarz, G., Tremblay, M., & Chenevert, D. (2020). Social comparisons, self-conceptions, and attributions: Assessing the self-related contingencies in leader–member exchange relationships. *Journal of Business and Psychology*, *35*(3), 381–402.

Larsson, M. (2017). Leadership in interaction. In J. Storey, J. Hartley, J-L. Denis, P. Hart & D. Ulrich (Eds.), *The Routledge Companion to Leadership* (pp. 173–193). Routledge. Routledge Companions in Business, Management and Accounting.

Latif, K., Tariq, H., Khan, A. K., Weng, Q., Butt, H. P., Obaid, A., & Sarwar, N. (2020). Loaded with knowledge, yet green with envy: Leader–member exchange comparison and coworkers-directed knowledge hiding behavior. *Journal of Knowledge Management*, *24*(7), 1653–1680.

Lee, A., Gerbasi, A., Schwarz, G., & Newman, A. (2019a). Leader–member exchange social comparisons and follower outcomes: The roles of felt obligation and psychological entitlement. *Journal of Occupational and Organizational Psychology*, *92*(3), 593–617.

Lee, A., Thomas, G., Martin, R., & Guillaume, Y. (2019b). Leader–member exchange (LMX) ambivalence and task performance: The cross-domain buffering role of social support. *Journal of Management*, *45*(5), 1927–1957.

Lee, A., Thomas, G., Martin, R., Guillaume, Y., & Marstand, A. F. (2019c). Beyond relationship quality: The role of leader–member exchange importance in leader–follower dyads. *Journal of Occupational and Organizational Psychology*, *92*(4), 736–763.

Lemmon, G., & Wayne, S. J. (2015). Underlying motives of organizational citizenship behavior: Comparing egoistic and altruistic motivations. *Journal of Leadership & Organizational Studies*, *22*(2), 129–148.

Li, A. N., & Liao, H. (2014). How do leader–member exchange quality and differentiation affect performance in teams? An integrated multilevel dual process model. *Journal of Applied Psychology*, *99*(5), 847–866.

Lian, H., Ferris, D. L., & Brown, D. J. (2012). Does taking the good with the bad make things worse? How abusive supervision and leader–member exchange interact to impact need satisfaction and organizational deviance. *Organizational Behavior and Human Decision Processes*, *117*(1), 41–52.

Liao, Z., Liu, W., Li, X., & Song, Z. (2019). Give and take: An episodic perspective on leader–member exchange. *Journal of Applied Psychology, 104*(1), 34–51.

Liden, R. C., & Graen, G. (1980). Generalizability of the vertical dyad linkage model of leadership. *Academy of Management Journal, 23*(3), 451–465.

Liden, R. C., & Maslyn, J. M. (1998). Multidimensionality of leader–member exchange: An empirical assessment through scale development. *Journal of Management, 24*(1), 43–72.

Liden, R. C., Wayne, S. J., & Stilwell, D. (1993). A longitudinal study on the early development of leader–member exchanges. *Journal of Applied Psychology, 78*(4), 662–674.

Liden, R. C., Wu, J., Cao, A. X., & Wayne, S. J. (2015). Leader–member exchange measurement. In T. N. Bauer & B. Erdogan (Eds.), *The Oxford Handbook of Leader–Member Exchange* (pp. 29–54). Oxford University Press.

Loignon, A. C., Gooty, J., Rogelberg, S. G., & Lucianetti, L. (2019). Disagreement in leader–follower dyadic exchanges: Shared relationship satisfaction and investment as antecedents. *Journal of Occupational and Organizational Psychology, 92*(3), 618–644.

Lyubomirsky, S., & Ross, L. (1997). Hedonic consequences of social comparison: A contrast of happy and unhappy people. *Journal of Personality and Social Psychology, 73*(6), 1141–1157.

Manata, B. (2020). The effects of LMX differentiation on team performance: Investigating the mediating properties of cohesion. *Journal of Leadership & Organizational Studies, 27*(2), 180–188.

Markham, S. E., Yammarino, F. J., Murry, W. D., & Palanski, M. E. (2010). Leader–member exchange, shared values, and performance: Agreement and levels of analysis do matter. *Leadership Quarterly, 21*(3), 469–480.

Martin, R., Guillaume, Y., Thomas, G., Lee, A., & Epitropaki, O. (2016). Leader–member exchange (LMX) and performance: A meta-analytic review. *Personnel Psychology, 69*(1), 67–121.

Martin, R., Thomas, G., Legood, A., & Dello Russo, S. (2018). Leader–member exchange (LMX) differentiation and work outcomes: Conceptual clarification and critical review. *Journal of Organizational Behavior, 39*(2), 151–168.

Matta, F. K., Scott, B. A., Koopman, J., & Conlon, D. E. (2015). Does seeing 'eye to eye' affect work engagement and organizational citizenship behavior? A role theory perspective on LMX agreement. *Academy of Management Journal, 58*(6), 1686–1708.

Methot, J. R., Melwani, S., & Rothman, N. B. (2017). The space between us: A social-functional emotions view of ambivalent and indifferent workplace relationships. *Journal of Management, 43*(6), 1789–1819.

Nahrgang, J. D., & Seo, J. J. (2015). How and why high leader–member exchange (LMX) relationships develop: Examining the antecedents of LMX. In T. N. Bauer & B. Erdogan (Eds.), *The Oxford Handbook of Leader–Member Exchange* (pp. 87–118). Oxford University Press.

Nahrgang, J. D., Morgeson, F. P., & Ilies, R. (2009). The development of leader–member exchanges: Exploring how personality and performance influence leader and member relationships over time. *Organizational Behavior and Human Decision Processes, 108*(2), 256–266.

Omilion-Hodges, L., & Baker, C. (2017). Communicating leader–member relationship quality. *International Journal of Business Communication, 54*, 115–145.

Ozer, M. (2008). Personal and task-related moderators of leader–member exchange among software developers. *Journal of Applied Psychology, 93*(5), 1174–1182.

Pan, W., Sun, L. Y., & Chow, I. H. S. (2012). Leader–member exchange and employee creativity: Test of a multilevel moderated mediation model. *Human Performance, 25*(5), 432–451.

Patzel, B. (2006). What blocked heterosexual women and lesbians in leaving their abusive relationships. *Journal of the American Psychiatric Nurses Association, 12*(4), 208–215.

Pratt, M., & Doucet, L. (2000). Ambivalent feelings in organizational relationships. In S. Fineman (Ed.), *Emotion in Organizations* (pp. 204–226). Sage.

Richards, D. A., & Hackett, R. D. (2012). Attachment and emotion regulation: Compensatory interactions and leader–member exchange. *Leadership Quarterly, 23*(4), 686–701.

Rothman, N., Pratt, M., Rees, L., & Vogus, T. (2017). Understanding the dual nature of ambivalence: Why and when ambivalence leads to good and bad outcomes. *Academy of Management Annals, 11*, 33–72.

Scandura, T. A., & Graen, G. B. (1984). Moderating effects of initial leader–member exchange status on the effects of a leadership intervention. *Journal of Applied Psychology, 69*(3), 428–436.

Schriesheim, C. A., Castro, S. L., & Cogliser, C. C. (1999). Leader–member exchange (LMX) research: A comprehensive review of theory, measurement, and data-analytic practices. *Leadership Quarterly, 10*(1), 63–113.

Schyns, B. (2015). Leader and follower personality and LMX. In T. N. Bauer & B. Erdogan (Eds.), *The Oxford Handbook of Leader–Member Exchange* (pp. 119–135). Oxford University Press.

Schyns, B., Paul, T., Mohr, G., & Blank, H. (2005). Comparing antecedents and consequences of leader–member exchange in a German working context to findings in the US. *European Journal of Work and Organizational Psychology, 14*(1), 1–22.

Seers, A., Wilkerson, J. M., & Grubb III, W. L. (2006). Toward measurement of social exchange resources: Reciprocal contributions and receipts. *Psychological Reports*, *98*(2), 508–510.

Sherman, K. E., Kennedy, D. M., Woodard, M. S., & McComb, S. A. (2012). Examining the 'exchange' in leader–member exchange. *Journal of Leadership & Organizational Studies*, *19*(4), 407–423.

Sin, H. P., Nahrgang, J. D., & Morgeson, F. P. (2009). Understanding why they don't see eye to eye: An examination of leader–member exchange (LMX) agreement. *Journal of Applied Psychology*, *94*(4), 1048–1057.

Singh, S., & Vidyarthi, P. R. (2018). Idiosyncratic deals to employee outcomes: Mediating role of social exchange relationships. *Journal of Leadership & Organizational Studies*, *25*(4), 443–455.

Sluss, D. M., & Thompson, B. S. (2012). Socializing the newcomer: The mediating role of leader–member exchange. *Organizational Behavior and Human Decision Processes*, *119*(1), 114–125.

Sue-Chan, C., Au, A. K., & Hackett, R. D. (2012). Trust as a mediator of the relationship between leader/member behavior and leader–member-exchange quality. *Journal of World Business*, *47*(3), 459–468.

Tse, H. H., Lam, C. K., Gu, J., & Lin, X. S. (2018). Examining the interpersonal process and consequence of leader–member exchange comparison: The role of procedural justice climate. *Journal of Organizational Behavior*, *39*(8), 922–940.

Uchino, B. N., Holt-Lunstad, J., Smith, T. W., & Bloor, L. (2004). Heterogeneity in social networks: A comparison of different models linking relationships to psychological outcomes. *Journal of Social and Clinical Psychology*, *23*(2), 123–139.

Uchino, B. N., Smith, T. W., & Berg, C. A. (2014). Spousal relationship quality and cardiovascular risk: Dyadic perceptions of relationship ambivalence are associated with coronary-artery calcification. *Psychological Science*, *25*(4), 1037–1042.

Uhl-Bien, M., & Maslyn, J. M. (2003). Reciprocity in manager–subordinate relationships: Components, configurations, and outcomes. *Journal of Management*, *29*(4), 511–532.

Van Gils, S., Van Quaquebeke, N., & Van Knippenberg, D. (2010). The X-factor: On the relevance of implicit leadership and followership theories for leader–member exchange agreement. *European Journal of Work and Organizational Psychology*, *19*(3), 333–363.

Van Harreveld, F., Rutjens, B. T., Rotteveel, M., Nordgren, L. F., & Van Der Pligt, J. (2009). Ambivalence and decisional conflict as a cause of psychological discomfort: Feeling tense before jumping off the fence. *Journal of Experimental Social Psychology*, *45*(1), 167–173.

Vidyarthi, P. R., Liden, R. C., Anand, S., Erdogan, B., & Ghosh, S. (2010). Where do I stand? Examining the effects of leader–member exchange social comparison on employee work behaviors. *Journal of Applied Psychology*, *95*(5), 849–861.

Vidyarthi, P. R., Singh, S., Erdogan, B., Chaudhry, A., Posthuma, R., & Anand, S. (2016). Individual deals within teams: Investigating the role of relative i-deals for employee performance. *Journal of Applied Psychology*, *101*(11), 1536–1552.

Wang, D., Gan, C., & Wu, C. (2016). LMX and employee voice: A moderated mediation model of psychological empowerment and role clarity. *Personnel Review*, *45*(3), 605–615.

Wayne, S. J., Shore, L. M., Bommer, W. H., & Tetrick, L. E. (2002). The role of fair treatment and rewards in perceptions of organizational support and leader–member exchange. *Journal of applied psychology*, *87*(3), 590–598.

Yu, A., Matta, F. K., & Cornfield, B. (2018). Is leader–member exchange differentiation beneficial or detrimental for group effectiveness? A meta-analytic investigation and theoretical integration. *Academy of Management Journal*, *61*(3), 1158–1188.

Zhang, Z., Wang, M. O., & Shi, J. (2012). Leader-follower congruence in proactive personality and work outcomes: The mediating role of leader–member exchange. *Academy of Management Journal*, *55*(1), 111–130.

Zhou, M., & Shi, S. (2014). Blaming leaders for team relationship conflict? The roles of leader–member exchange differentiation and ethical leadership. *Nankai Business Review International*, *5*(2), 134–146.

Embodying Who we are: Social Identity and Leadership

Daan van Knippenberg

Leadership is an inextricably intertwined element of human groups. Whether the social group considered is as small as a three-person team or as large as a nation, a group with formal boundaries like an organisation or an informal group of friends, leadership structures are an integral part of group life. Especially in the context of organisations, which are formed to pursue a purpose, leadership is a salient factor expected to impact group (team, organisation) functioning (Selznick, 1957; van Knippenberg, 2020). Not surprisingly, leadership enjoys a long history in research in organisational behaviour (Judge et al., 2002). What is surprising is how little attention research has historically paid to the notion that an important influence on leadership effectiveness – leadership's success in mobilising and motivating group members to pursue group objectives (van Knippenberg, 2019) – is how the leader is perceived through the lens of the group membership shared by leader and members. If leadership fundamentally is a group process, how is the leader perceived as a group member and how does this impact leadership effectiveness?

The social identity theory of leadership was developed to address this issue (Hogg, 2001; van Knippenberg & Hogg, 2003). Building on social identity theory and its core notion that our group memberships influence our sense of identity (Tajfel & Turner, 1986), the core concept in the social identity theory of leadership is *leader group prototypicality* – the extent to which the leader is perceived to embody the group identity (Hogg, 2001). In this chapter, I take stock of this perspective in leadership research, reviewing research on leader group prototypicality. What this review shows is that the social identity theory of leadership received strong support in the roughly 25 years that it has been subject of empirical tests (Hogg et al., 2012; Steffens et al., 2021; van Knippenberg, 2011). It also captures how the social identity theory of leadership is well embedded in a broader 'follower-centric' perspective on leadership (Meindl, 1995; Shamir et al., 2007). I then review recent developments of the theory and close with two issues for which future research would be particularly valuable.

SOCIAL IDENTITY, ORGANISATIONAL BEHAVIOUR AND LEADERSHIP

Our group memberships are part of who we are – they are reflected in our mental representation of ourselves (our self-concept or identity). The extent to which a group membership is part of self-conception – the extent to which one *self-categorises* as a member of the group – is captured by the concept of social identification (Hogg, 2003; Tajfel & Turner, 1986; Turner et al., 1987). Social identifications (e.g., organisational identification, team identification) are a key element in understanding the psychology of group membership. Through social identification we judge the self in terms of what we understand to be group-defining attributes (Turner et al., 1987).

We have mental representations of the groups in which we are a member, capturing what we see as defining of the group in terms of what members have in common and what differentiates the group from other groups (part of what defines group identity is distinctiveness from 'outgroups'; Turner et al., 1987). These mental representations, or *group prototypes*, are not neutral but value-laden; they reflect the subjective perception of important group characteristics including group beliefs, norms, values, interests and aspirations (Turner et al., 1987). Social identification means that one views oneself in terms of one's mental representation of group identity and thus also in terms of such value-laden elements (Turner et al., 1987). This is why social identifications are so useful in understanding behaviour: they impact perceptions, attitudes and actions because they lead individuals to internalise the group's social reality and to be motivated to serve the group's best interest (Ashforth & Mael, 1989). Through social identification, group identity not only becomes self-describing, but also self-guiding.

Originally developed as a theory of intergroup relations (Tajfel & Turner, 1986), social identity theory has developed over the years into a broad-ranging theory of how social identifications influence a range of group membership-related phenomena, with increasing emphasis on group membership per se rather than the intergroup dimension. As part of this development, social identity theory built a distinct presence in organisational behaviour (Ashforth & Mael, 1989; Haslam, 2004; van Knippenberg & Hogg, 2018), where it is used to understand a range of issues including the employee–organisation relationship (Riketta, 2005; Tavares et al., 2016), work motivation and performance (Hekman et al., 2016; van Knippenberg, 2000) and responses to organisational change (Giessner et al., 2011; van Knippenberg, van Knippenberg, Monden, & De Lima, 2002), among others. Part of this development of the social identity perspective in organisational behaviour is the social identity theory of leadership (Hogg, 2001; van Knippenberg & Hogg, 2003).

Core to the social identity theory of leadership is the concept of leader group prototypicality. Leader group prototypicality captures the extent to which the leader is perceived to embody group identity – that is, to be similar to the group prototype (Hogg, 2001). Leader group prototypicality thus is a perception, not an objective attribute; it is in the eye of the beholder and determined in reference to individuals' subjective mental representation of the group (team, organisation, etc.). (Note that Eisenberger et al., 2010, reinvented the proverbial wheel in proposing the concept of supervisor organisational embodiment to refer to leader group prototypicality; following earlier reviews I do not treat this as a separate perspective; Steffens et al., 2021; van Knippenberg, 2011.)

Leader group prototypicality is important to group members' openness to leader influence. The more group prototypical the leader is, the more the leader is trusted to represent group norms, values and aspirations, and have the group's best interest at heart (van Knippenberg & Hogg, 2003) – trust in the leader's group-serving intentions is a key mediating mechanism (Giessner & van Knippenberg, 2008; van Knippenberg & van Knippenberg, 2005). As a result, more group prototypical leaders are better positioned to mobilise and motivate group members in the pursuit of group objectives and thus to be effective as a leader. These effects of leader group prototypicality obtain to the extent that members identify with the group. This is because group norms, values, interest and aspirations are more subjectively meaningful and important to members, the more they identify with the group and see these group attributes as integral to who they are. A core element in the social identity theory of leadership therefore is the proposition that the relationship of leader group prototypicality with indicators of leadership effectiveness is stronger the stronger members' group identification (Hogg, 2001).

The other core element in this analysis is that leader group prototypicality feeds into member trust in the leader's group-serving intentions; embodying the group identity, group prototypical leaders are trusted to act in the group's best interest. This is important because group members internalise group interests to the extent that they identify with the group (van Knippenberg, 2000). Accordingly, a key element in their responses to leadership is the extent to which the leader is perceived to act with the group's best interest at heart. Leader group prototypicality engenders such trust in the leader's group-serving motivation and thus renders members open to leader influence and more accepting of leader actions. Less group prototypical leaders, in contrast, rely more on the actual display of group-serving behaviour (actions that serve the group and show the leader's commitment to group interests) to gain such trust in their group-serving motivations. Thus, leader group prototypicality substitutes for such group-serving behaviour such that less group prototypical leaders' effectiveness is driven more by group-serving behaviour (van Knippenberg & Hogg, 2003).

LEADER GROUP PROTOTYPICALITY: EVIDENCE AND EXTENSIONS

Turning to a review of the evidence, I first consider evidence speaking to the core of the theory: the relationship of leader group prototypicality with indicators of leadership effectiveness and the moderating roles of member social identification and leader group-serving behaviour. I then consider how the social identity theory of leadership is positioned vis-à-vis other follower-centric leadership theories (Eagly & Karau, 2002; Eden & Leviatan, 1975; Lord & Maher, 1991; Meindl, 1995). Such theories in essence posit that responses to leadership are informed by leaders' perceived similarity to leadership prototypes (i.e., as opposed to group prototypes in the social identity theory of leadership) and therefore beg the question how the social identity theory of leadership should be seen relative to those perspectives. Next, I review two further developments of the theory that concern fundamental elements in the effects of leader group prototypicality: the uncertainty reduction function of social identity and the extent to which group prototypes should be understood to reflect an aspirational ideal-type of the group or a more descriptive reflection of the in-practice state of affairs. Finally, I outline two other developments that stand out more as 'unresolved issues' in need of theory development and research: the interactive effects of leader group prototypicality and leader fairness, and the role of leader agency in engendering perceptions of leader group prototypicality.

Leader Group Prototypicality: Core Evidence

Before reviewing the evidence, it is instructive to reflect on leadership effectiveness. From the idea that core to leadership is mobilising and motivating the pursuit of collective objectives, it stands to reason to understand leadership effectiveness first and foremost in terms of the collective's success in achieving these objectives, or at least in terms of leadership's success in motivating efforts in pursuit of these objectives (Stam et al., 2014; van Knippenberg, 2020). In the practice of leadership research, the dependent variables used to assess the effectiveness of leadership rarely concern such collective goal achievement, however. More typically, indications of leadership effectiveness are seen in group members' subjective evaluations of leadership, in job-related attitudes such as job satisfaction and organisational commitment and in performance-related behavioural outcomes such as in-role performance or creativity (van Knippenberg, 2019). There is a case that in work organisations, performance-related outcomes likely are instrumental in achieving collective objectives. There is also a case that, all other things being equal, group members more positively evaluating leadership and with more positive job attitudes are more likely to invest in the pursuit of collective objectives. It is important to realise, however, that these outcomes cannot be equated with the pursuit of collective objectives. In that sense, the leadership field does a poor job when it comes to assessing the outcomes it should be studying and instead has inadvertently created a research tradition of relying on proxy indicators. With these considerations as a backdrop, we turn to a review of the evidence.

There is a variety of studies yielding consistent evidence of positive relationships of leader group prototypicality and indicators of leadership effectiveness. Such evidence is found in laboratory experiments as well as in surveys in the field (e.g., Hains et al., 1997; Pierro et al., 2005). It is found in evidence concerning perceptual indicators of effectiveness such as leadership evaluations (as per the Barreto & Hogg, 2017, meta-analysis confirming such effects meta-analytically) or job attitudes such as job satisfaction and turnover intentions (e.g., Cicero et al., 2007), as well as in behavioural indicators of leadership effectiveness such as follower performance and creativity (Hirst et al., 2009; van Knippenberg & van Knippenberg, 2005). Consistent evidence in support of the theory is also found in studies from countries spread out over different continents (Australia, the Americas, Asia and Europe; van Knippenberg, 2011). While the vast majority of studies inspired by the social identity theory of leadership concern the effectiveness of people in formal leadership positions, there are also a few studies that established that the analysis applies to emergent leadership (more group prototypical members are more likely to emerge as leaders; Fielding & Hogg, 1997; van Knippenberg et al., 2000). Quantitatively capturing the consistency of evidence over studies, a meta-analysis of $k = 128$ effect sizes by Steffens et al. (2021) confirmed the positive relationship of leader group prototypicality and indicators of leadership effectiveness. Steffens et al. also observed that this effect size averaged over indicators of leadership effectiveness ($r = .38$) is larger than the average effect size in leadership research ($r = .29$) as established in a review of meta-analytic evidence by Paterson et al. (2016).

The earliest tests of the theory also established that leader group prototypicality is more strongly related to leadership effectiveness the higher member social identification (Hains et al., 1997; Hogg et al., 1998). Later studies too show evidence of this moderating role of identification either in straightforward replication (Cicero, Bonaiuto et al., 2008) or in three-way interactions with for instance leader behaviour (e.g., Platow & van Knippenberg, 2001) or follower traits (e.g., Pierro et al., 2005). The Steffens et al. (2021) study confirmed this moderation effect meta-analytically.

Platow and van Knippenberg (2001) were the first to test the proposition that leader group prototypicality substitutes for leader group-serving behaviour in a study focusing on the decisions leaders made in allocating resources between the own group and another group. Other studies showed that this finding was not limited to the experimental set-up used by Platow and van Knippenberg nor to the particular operationalisation of group-serving behaviour. It was for instance also shown to hold for leader self-sacrifice in pursuit of group goals (van Knippenberg & van Knippenberg, 2005), leader group-serving rhetoric (Platow et al., 2006), and leader success versus failure on behalf of the group (Giessner & van Knippenberg, 2008; Giessner et al., 2009). The moderating role of leader group-serving behaviour was also confirmed in the Steffens et al. (2021) meta-analysis.

In sum, the core of the social identity theory of leadership received considerable support. This support is not contingent on research method used but derives from the lab and the field, is not contingent on the indicator of leadership effectiveness but draws on a range of perceptual and behavioural indicators, and is not contingent on national setting but draws on evidence from across the world.

Social Identity Theory of Leadership and Other Follower-centric Theories

At its core, the social identity theory of leadership is a follower-centric theory – a theory that puts the subjective experience of followers centre-stage as opposed to leader-centric theories that have leader attributes and behaviour as the central focus (Shamir et al., 2007). The core concept in the social identity theory of leadership, leader group prototypicality, is well aligned with this follower-centric perspective in that leader group prototypicality is a subjective perception and not a leader attribute that exists separate from subjective mental representations (also leaders can have a sense of their group prototypicality, but that too is subjective; Giessner et al., 2013). In contrast to the social identity theory of leadership and its focus on mental representations of group identity, however, other follower-centric perspectives on leadership revolve around the notion of mental representations of leadership (Epitropaki et al., 2013). The notion of mental representations of leadership lies at the core of leadership categorisation theory (Lord & Maher, 1991), role congruity theory (Eagly & Karau, 2002), research on implicit leadership theories (Eden & Leviatan, 1975) and the romance of leadership (Meindl et al., 1985). Regardless of whether these mental representations are referred to as leadership prototypes (Lord & Maher, 1991), leadership stereotypes (Eagly & Karau, 2002), or implicit leadership theories (Eden & Leviatan, 1975), they are understood to reflect subjective beliefs about leadership that form a judgement standard against which (potential) leaders are assessed. The more (potential) leaders in their characteristics or actions match implicit beliefs about leadership, the more perceivers attribute leadership qualities to them. This for instance explains why certain traits are associated with leadership judgements (Eden & Leviatan, 1975; Epitropaki et al., 2013; Lord & Maher, 1991), why gender is associated with leadership judgements (Eagly & Karau, 2002) and why change (versus stability) is associated with leadership judgements (Meindl et al., 1985).

The social identity theory of leadership is similar to these perspectives in concerning the notion that responses to leadership are informed by subjective mental representations, but different in focusing on mental representations of the membership group rather than of leadership. These need not concern mutually excluding reference standards. Responses to leadership can be informed by both leader similarity to a group prototype and to a leadership prototype (leadership stereotype, implicit leadership theory). Even so, this begs the question how these two perspectives should be seen in relationship to each other. The first studies testing the social identity theory of leadership addressed this issue (Hains et al., 1997; Hogg et al., 1998). Hogg (2001) argued that people judge leaders against leadership stereotypes even when they do not feel personally involved with the leader, for instance because it concerns the leader of another group or because they identify with the group to only a small degree. The more they identify with the group, however, the more the group prototype gains in prominence relative to the leader stereotype as the standard against which the leader is judged. That is, with higher identification, the consideration of the extent to which the leader represents what the group stands for and has the group's best interest at heart gains in importance, but the more abstracted leadership prototype does not. This is what studies testing this proposition showed: with stronger identification, leader group prototypicality was a stronger predictor of leadership effectiveness, whereas the influence of leader stereotypicality was not moderated by identification (Hains et al., 1997 Hogg et al., 1998; Platow & van Knippenberg, 2001).

As noted in the introduction to this chapter, the social identity theory of leadership is positioned as a unique perspective in recognising that responses to leadership are informed by perceptions of the leader as a group member. This positioning comes into sharper focus when the social identity theory of leadership is positioned vis-à-vis other follower-centric perspectives on leadership that all put mental representations of leadership centre-stage. In that sense, tongue in cheek-ish, one might argue that the social identity theory of leadership is the most follower-centric of follower-centric perspectives in not even concerning mental representations of leadership.

Group Prototypicality and Uncertainty Reduction

Closely intertwined with the notion that group members anchor on the group prototype as reflecting shared social reality is the notion that group identification fulfils an uncertainty reduction function (Hogg, 2007). This notion recognises that categorisation is a process that helps us understand the world around us by being able to classify the objects, people, etc., we encounter in ways that inform how to respond to and interact with them (e.g., recognising a chair as a chair and knowing one can sit in it; recognising a train conductor as such and knowing one can ask her for information about the train's arrival time at the next station). Categorisations are also informative about ourselves because our group memberships are part of who we are – we also *self-categorise* (Turner et al., 1987). Anchoring on the shared identity and shared social reality (beliefs, norms, values, aspirations and interest) associated with those group memberships can reduce uncertainty because one can understand oneself, the situation one is in and how to respond to the situation from this shared reality. Accordingly, the more one is faced with an uncertain situation, or the more one desires to reduce uncertainty, the more one may anchor on one's group membership to inform one's responses (e.g., act in accordance to group norms; Hogg, 2007). A recent development in the social identity theory of leadership is to study the implications of this uncertainty reduction function for leader group prototypicality.

Pierro et al. (2005) argued that because a desire to reduce uncertainty motivates group members to anchor on group identity, member desire to reduce uncertainty increases the influence of leader group prototypicality (as reflecting the extent to which the leader is seen to embody group identity). To put this proposition to the test, they focused on trait differences in need for closure, the desire to reduce uncertainty by quickly reaching closure on judgements, decisions and actions (Kruglanski, 1989). They found that need for closure moderated the relationship of leader group prototypicality and a range of indicators of leadership effectiveness, such that leader group prototypicality was more strongly related to indicators of leadership effectiveness for followers with a higher need for closure (a stronger desire to reduce uncertainty). Further establishing that this is a social identity effect, Pierro et al. (2007) found that the interactive influence of leader group prototypicality and need for closure was stronger with stronger identification with the group.

Need for closure is not only a trait, but can also be situationally induced (Kruglanski, 1989). Focusing on such situational influences, Cicero et al. (2007) studied the moderating role of job stress and Cicero et al. (2010) the moderating role of role ambiguity. For both, the argument was essentially that they are associated with uncertainty. Because uncertainty is an averse psychological state, such uncertainty can be assumed to invite a desire to reduce uncertainty. Accordingly, both job stress and role ambiguity should be associated with stronger relationships of leader group prototypicality and indicators of leadership effectiveness. That was exactly what these studies found.

The uncertainty reduction function of leader group prototypicality should hold for issues to which group identity is relevant. It may be particularly salient in organisational change contexts because a key concern with organisational change often is that it threatens valued social identity – that it is perceived to change group identity in ways that are seen as undesirable (Rousseau, 1998; van Knippenberg et al., 2002). Therefore, effective leadership of change would speak to this issue to reduce concerns with such identity threats. Venus et al. (2019) showed for instance that leadership of change is more effective in overcoming resistance to change when leader change communication is not only change-oriented, but also focused on continuity of the valued identity, conveying that the change does not alter the essence of the valued identity. Van Knippenberg and Hogg (2003) argued that leader group prototypicality can fulfil a similar function in that embodying group identity and being trusted to have the group's best interest at heart, group prototypical leaders are perceived as guardians of group identity. That is, in a change context, leader group prototypicality may lead group members to perceive the leader not only as an agent of change, but also as an agent of continuity. This gives more group prototypical leaders an advantage in leading change in that their group prototypicality leads members to trust that the leader ensures continuity of the value identity. Studies assessing support for organisational change as an indicator of leadership effectiveness yielded support for this proposition in positive effects of leader group prototypicality that were moderated by leader self-serving behaviour (van Knippenberg & van Knippenberg, 2005), by follower need for closure and identification (Pierro et al., 2007) and by change magnitude (i.e., stronger effect for more disruptive change; van Knippenberg et al., 2008).

Clarifying the Nature of Group Prototypes: Ideal or Average?

In their meta-analysis, Steffens et al. (2021) raised the issue that studies of leader group prototypicality vary in the extent to which they operationalised leader group prototypicality more as a reflection of the ideal-type of the group or more as a reflection of the average group member. The issue here is that individuals and groups are in part defined by their aspirations – part of who we are is also who we want to be. Who we are includes what we aim to accomplish and believe is desirable; it is not limited to our current level of accomplishment and current actions (Stam et al., 2014). This notion is reflected in the distinction between descriptive and injunctive norms (Cialdini et al., 1991): group norms not only reflect 'what is', but also 'what should be'. Descriptive norms reflect what group members on average are and do; injunctive norms reflect what group members ideally would be and do. Descriptive and injunctive norms are not independent. What we typically do is guided by what we believe we should do, and what we believe we should do is informed by what most of us do (if group members typically behave in a certain way, this suggests that behaving in that way is appropriate). Descriptive norms and injunctive norms are not the same, however, in that what we believe and value is aspirational and need not be reflected in our current accomplishments and actions. The question Steffens et al. (2021) raised concerns how important this ideal, aspirational element of group identity is to the influence of group prototypes and leader group prototypicality.

This is an underdeveloped element in the social identity theory of leadership in that it is not fully articulated to what extent group prototypes, and thus leader group prototypicality, should be understood as descriptive or injunctive. Studies that are relatively articulate in this respect put the emphasis on the injunctive understanding of group prototypes (e.g., Steffens et al., 2013; van Knippenberg, 2011). Many studies of leader group prototypicality do not address the issue conceptually, however, and studies differ in the extent to which operationalisations of leader group prototypicality anchor on the notion of group prototypes as ideal-types or reflecting the 'average group member' (Steffens et al., 2021). Whether the effects of leader group prototypicality concern the extent to which leaders embody the group ideal or the average group member concerns the very nature of leader group prototypicality effects and thus is worth addressing.

Steffens et al. (2021) argued that an ideal-type conception of leader group prototypicality is the more conceptually accurate understanding in the context of the social identity theory of leadership and should be more strongly related to leadership effectiveness than an average group member understanding. The rationale for this proposition is that the influence of leader group prototypicality derives first and foremost from the most value-laden group attributes: what we see as desirable and aim to accomplish. By their very nature, such attributes are aspirational in being something we strive for and not something we necessarily have fully achieved. In support of this analysis, Steffens et al. (2021) established meta-analytically that the relationship of leader group prototypicality and indicators of leadership effectiveness is stronger for prototypicality operationalisations that put more emphasis on the ideal ($r = .56$) than for operationalisations that put more emphasis on the average ($r = .35$).

Leader Fairness: Enhancing or Substituting Effects?

There is a long tradition in studying organisational justice (Colquitt et al., 2001). This work has sparked a growing recognition that leaders are an important source of the experience of organisational justice. How fair leaders are in the way they treat followers is an important influence on leadership effectiveness (van Knippenberg et al., 2007a). As part of the broader stream of research on leader fairness, this inspired a series of studies of interactive effects of leader group prototypicality and leader procedural or interactional fairness.

In this line of research, there are two different arguments for such interactive effects. On the one hand, there is the argument that how fairly one is treated by the leader is an important influence on trust in the leader (Lind & Tyler, 1998). Accordingly, leader group prototypicality would substitute for leader fairness because it invites trust in the leader (and trust in the leader in turn feeds into leadership effectiveness). On the other hand, there is the argument that leader fairness conveys a social evaluation: how one is treated by an authority is informative of one's standing with the authority (Koper et al., 1993). From this perspective, leader group prototypicality would enhance the effect of leader fairness because the social evaluation conveyed by fairness of treatment carries more weight the more it is perceived to reflect one's standing with the group more broadly (and positive evaluations of one's standing feed into leadership effectiveness; van Knippenberg et al., 2004).

Both these perspectives on leader group prototypicality by leader fairness interactions received support. Studies by Janson et al. (2008) and Ullrich et al. (2009) found evidence for the substituting effect of leader group prototypicality in the interaction with leader fairness. Both these studies replicated the finding over samples and Ullrich et al. (2009) moreover across methods (an experiment and a survey). In contrast, other studies report evidence for the enhancing effect of leader group prototypicality in the interaction with leader fairness (De Cremer et al., 2010; Koivisto & Lipponen, 2015; Koivisto et al., 2013; Lipponen et al., 2005; Seppälä et al., 2012). These studies too include replications across samples and methods. So, the evidence for the substitution effect as well as the enhancing effect is reasonably robust. There is no clear pattern to these diverging findings; findings for both substituting and enhancing effects hold across cultures, methods and leader procedural and interactional fairness.

This thus is a challenge for future research to determine when leader group prototypicality substitutes for the effects of leader fairness and when it enhances these effects. This seems to be an issue of determining when a concern with leader trustworthiness is salient and when a concern with one's standing with the leader and the group the leader represents is salient. Such research is important not only because it would address an apparent inconsistency in the evidence base, but also because it can speak to multiple mechanisms involved in the effects of leader group prototypicality and the contingencies of these mechanisms (van Knippenberg & Dwertmann, 2022).

Underscoring the point that this concerns a broader issue, the evidence for substituting and enhancing interaction effects of leader group prototypicality and other elements of leadership is not limited to interactions with leader fairness. I already reviewed the evidence for substituting interaction effects of leader group prototypicality and different instantiations of leader group-serving behaviour and how these too are linked to trust in the leader. There is also evidence of enhancing interaction effects of leader group prototypicality and leader–member exchange (LMX, reflecting the quality of the leader–member relationship) on follower perceptions of their relationship with the organisation (Eisenberger et al., 2010; Eisenberger et al., 2014). Addressing the issue of enhancing versus substituting interactions for leader fairness thus likely lays the groundwork for broader-ranging conceptual development of the social identity theory of leadership.

Leader Agency and Leader Group Prototypicality

As outlined in the previous, the social identity theory of leadership is a follower-centric theory. At its core lie follower perceptions of leadership and leader group prototypicality is not seen as an attribute independent of subjective perceptions. It is a relevant question, however, what leader attributes may feed into leader group prototypicality perceptions. Arguably most pertinent to understanding leadership effectiveness from this perspective is the question whether leaders have agency in influencing such perceptions. Rather than having to make do with however followers perceive them, can leaders shape followers' perceptions of their group prototypicality and thus increase their effectiveness? Qualitative research by Reicher and Hopkins (2001, 2003) suggests they can and do – which also suggests that some leaders are at least implicitly aware of the advantage of being perceived as group prototypical.

Reicher and Hopkins analysed political leadership from several countries, studying such leaders as Thatcher, Sukharno and Ghandi. My core take-away from their analysis is that these leaders were able to be effective as political leaders in part by creating an image of themselves as group prototypical. They seemed to do so through one or both of two kinds of actions. The first type of action concerned how they presented themselves in reference to a presumably shared understanding of group identity. They took actions to suggest they were group prototypical by such behaviours as adopting symbols of group identity (e.g., items with a strong connection to national history or mythology) and referencing national identity and history in their public speaking in reference to themselves and the course of action they advocated. The second type of actions aimed to influence the perception of group identity such that their personal characteristics and advocated course of action would be perceived as prototypical of that identity. Recognising that group identity is not an objective given but a social construction, they would talk about national identity in ways that suggested an understanding of national identity that was well aligned with who they personally were and what they were advocating. Reicher and Hopkins for instance described how in the Scottish elections, both Labour Party and Conservative Party candidates referenced the harsh Scottish climate to suggest that historically Scots are a people with qualities that are well aligned with the policies their party was advocating. Simply put, the differences between the two kinds of actions is whether the attempt targets perceptions of leader group prototypicality taking an understanding of group identity as a given or targets perceptions of group identity taking characteristics of the leader as a given. Both tactics can be used in conjunction to align what can be claimed about oneself and about group identity.

One could argue that there are important differences between the political leadership context analysed by Reicher and Hopkins and the leadership in organisations that has been the focus here. However, their analysis is well aligned with insights from qualitative studies of how organisational leadership shapes the understanding of organisational change and organisational identity to mobilise support for change. In this literature too it is recognised that group (organisational) identity is a social construction that can be influenced by leadership (van Knippenberg, 2016). Here too, qualitative analyses point to the importance of leader rhetoric and the adoption of symbols representing the envisioned identity (Chreim, 2005; Corley & Gioia, 2004; Gioia & Chittipeddi, 1991). Such leadership is focused on shaping how followers make sense of the ambiguities of organisational identity (Ashforth et al., 2011; Ravasi & Schultz, 2006). While these analyses do not address the role of leader group prototypicality, it is easy to see that more group prototypical leaders can be more influential in shaping follower understanding of organisational identity; being seen to embody organisational identity gives credibility and legitimacy in staking claims about how to understand organisational identity (van Knippenberg, 2020). Conversely, leaders can gain support for their change leadership when they are able to convey a sense of organisational identity that makes the leader and the change efforts come across as well aligned with organisational identity.

Bridging the body of quantitative research speaking to the effects of leader group prototypicality and the much smaller body of qualitative research that speaks to leader agency in shaping follower perceptions of leader group prototypicality and group identity would be an important step towards a theory that captures social identity and leadership processes as a dynamic interplay between leaders and group members rather than prioritising a follower-centric or a leader-centric perspective.

CONCLUSION

The social identity theory of leadership represents a unique perspective in leadership research. A review of empirical work shows that the theory is well supported by a substantive and diverse body of evidence. What a review of the evidence also shows is that there are issues that are valuable to address to develop the theory further. Specifically, I identified two issues as particularly valuable to address in future research: developing theory to capture when leader group prototypicality enhances and when it substitutes for the effects of other elements of leadership, and bridging the main body of quantitative research on the effects of leader group prototypicality and the much more modest body of qualitative research on leader agency in influencing follower perceptions of leader group prototypicality and group prototypes. Future research to advance our understanding of these issues is both important in developing the social identity theory of leadership and in embedding the theory within the broader landscape of leadership theories.

REFERENCES

Ashforth, B. E., & Mael, F. (1989). Social identity theory and the organization. *Academy of Management Review*, *14*, 20–39.

Ashforth, B. E., Rogers, K. M., & Corley, K. G. (2011). Identity in organizations: Exploring cross-level dynamics. *Organization Science*, *22*, 1144–1156.

Barreto, N. B., & Hogg, M. A. (2017). Evaluation of and support for group prototypical leaders: A meta-analysis of twenty years of empirical research. *Social Influence*, *12*, 41–55.

Chreim, S. (2005). The continuity–change duality in narrative texts of organizational identity. *Journal of Management Studies*, *42*, 567–593.

Cialdini, R. B., Kallgren, C. A., & Reno, R. R. (1991). A focus theory of normative conduct: A theoretical refinement and re-evaluation of the role of norms in human behavior. In L. Berkowitz (Ed.), *Advances in Experimental Social Psychology* (Vol. 24, pp. 201–234). Academic Press.

Cicero, L., Bonaiuto, M., Pierro, A., & van Knippenberg, D. (2008). Employees work effort as a function of leader group prototypicality: The moderating role of team identification. *European Review of Applied Psychology, 58*, 117–124.

Cicero, L., Pierro, A., & van Knippenberg, D. (2007). Leader group prototypicality and job satisfaction: The moderating role of job stress and team identification. *Group Dynamics, 11*, 165–175.

Cicero, L., Pierro, A., & van Knippenberg, D. (2010). Leadership and uncertainty: How role ambiguity affects the relationship between leader group prototypicality and leadership effectiveness. *British Journal of Management, 21*, 411–421.

Colquitt, J. A., Conlon, D. E., Wesson, M. J., Porter, C. O. L. H., & Ng, K. Y. (2001). Justice at the millennium: A meta-analytic review of 25 years of organizational justice research. *Journal of Applied Psychology, 86*, 425–445.

Corley, K. G., & Gioia, D. A. (2004). Identity ambiguity and change in the wake of a corporate spin-off. *Administrative Science Quarterly, 49*, 173–208.

De Cremer, D., van Dijke, M., & Mayer, D. M. (2010). Cooperating when 'you' and 'I' are treated fairly: The moderating role of leader prototypicality. *Journal of Applied Psychology, 95*, 1121–1113.

Eagly, A. H., & Karau, S. J. (2002). Role congruity theory of prejudice toward female leaders. *Psychological Review, 109*, 573–598.

Eden, D., & Leviatan, V. (1975). Implicit leadership theory as a determinant of the factor structure underlying supervisory behavior. *Journal of Applied Psychology, 60*, 736–741.

Eisenberger, R., Karagonlar, G., Stinglhamber, F., Neves, P., Becker, T. E., Gonzales-Morales, M. G., & Steiger-Mueller, M. (2010). Leader–member exchange and affective organizational commitment: The contribution of supervisor's organizational embodiment. *Journal of Applied Psychology, 95*, 1085–1103.

Eisenberger, R., Shoss, M. K., Karagonlar, G., Gonzalez-Morales, M. G., Wickham, R. E., & Buffardi, L. C. (2014). The supervisor POS–LMX–subordinate POS chain: Moderation by reciprocation wariness and supervisor's organizational embodiment. *Journal of Organizational Behavior, 35*, 635–656.

Epitropaki, O., Sy, T., Martin, R., Tram-Quon, S., & Topakas, A. (2013). Implicit leadership and followership theories 'in the wild': Taking stock of information-processing approaches to leadership and followership in organizational settings. *Leadership Quarterly, 24*, 858–881.

Fielding, K. S., & Hogg, M. A. (1997). Social identity, self-categorization, and leadership: A field study of small interactive groups. *Group Dynamics, 1*, 39–51.

Giessner, S. R., Ullrich, J., & van Dick, R. (2011). Social identity and corporate mergers. *Social and Personality Psychology Compass, 5*, 333–345.

Giessner, S. R., & van Knippenberg, D. (2008). 'License to fail': Goal definition, leader group prototypicality, and perceptions of leadership effectiveness after leader failure. *Organizational Behavior and Human Decision Processes, 105*, 14–35.

Giessner, S. R., van Knippenberg, D., & Sleebos, E. (2009). License to fail? How leader group prototypicality moderates the effects of leader performance on perceptions of leadership effectiveness. *Leadership Quarterly, 20*, 434–451.

Giessner, S. R., van Knippenberg, D., Sleebos, E. P., & van Ginkel, W. P. (2013). Team-oriented leadership: The interactive effects of leader group prototypicality, accountability, and team identification. *Journal of Applied Psychology, 98*, 658–667.

Gioia, D. A., & Chittipeddi, K. (1991). Sensemaking and sensegiving in strategic change initiation. *Strategic Management Journal, 12*, 433–448.

Hains, S. C., Hogg, M. A., & Duck, J. M. (1997). Self-categorization and leadership: Effects of group prototypicality and leader stereotypicality. *Personality and Social Psychology Bulletin, 23*, 1087–1100.

Haslam, S. A. (2004). *Psychology in Organisations: The Social Identity Approach* (2nd edn). Sage.

Hekman, D. R., van Knippenberg, D., & Pratt, M. G. (2016). Channeling identification: How perceived regulatory focus moderates the influence of organizational and professional identification on professional employees' diagnosis and treatment behaviors. *Human Relations, 69*, 753–780.

Hirst, G., van Dick, R., & van Knippenberg, D. (2009). A social identity perspective on leadership and employee creativity. *Journal of Organizational Behavior, 30*, 963–982.

Hogg, M. A. (2001). A social identity theory of leadership. *Personality and Social Psychology Review, 5*, 184–200.

Hogg, M. A. (2003). Social identity. In M. R. Leary & J. P. Tangney (Eds.), *Handbook of Self and Identity* (pp. 462–479). Guilford.

Hogg, M. A. (2007). Uncertainty-identity theory. In M. P. Zanna (Ed.), *Advances In Experimental Social Psychology* (Vol. 39, pp. 69–126). Academic Press.

Hogg, M. A., Hains, S. C., & Mason, I. (1998). Identification and leadership in small groups: Salience, frame of reference, and leader stereotypicality effects on leader evaluations. *Journal of Personality and Social Psychology, 75*, 1248–1263.

Hogg, M. A., van Knippenberg, D., & Rast, D. E. III. (2012). The social identity theory of leadership: Theoretical origins, research findings, and conceptual developments. *European Review of Social Psychology, 23*, 258–304.

Janson, A., Levy, L., Sitkin, S., & Lind, A. E. (2008). Fairness and other leadership heuristics: A four-nation study. *European Journal of Work and Organizational Psychology, 17*, 251–272.

Judge, T. A., Bono, J. E., Ilies, R., & Gerhardt, M. (2002). Personality and leadership: A qualitative and quantitative review. *Journal of Applied Psychology, 87*, 765–780.

Koivisto, S. & Lipponen, J. (2015). A leader's procedural justice, respect and extra-role behaviour: The roles of leader in-group prototypicality and identification. *Social Justice Research, 28*, 187–206.

Koivisto, S., Lipponen, J., & Platow, M. J. 2013. Organizational and supervisory justice effects on experienced threat during change: The moderating role of leader in-group representativeness. *Leadership Quarterly, 24*, 595–607.

Koper, G., van Knippenberg, D., Bouhuijs, F., Vermunt, R., & Wilke, H. (1993). Procedural fairness and self-esteem. *European Journal of Social Psychology, 23*, 313–325.

Kruglanski, A. W. (1989). *Lay Epistemics and Human Knowledge*. Plenum.

Lind, E. A., & Tyler, T. R. (1988). *The social psychology of procedural justice*. New York: Plenum Press.

Lipponen, J., Koivisto, S., & Olkkonen, M. E. 2005. Procedural justice and status judgements: The moderating role of leader ingroup prototypicality. *Leadership Quarterly, 16*, 517–528.

Lord, R. G., & Maher, K. J. (1991). *Leadership and Information Processing: Linking Perceptions and Performance*. Unwin Hyman.

Mathieu, J. E., Hollenbeck, J. R., van Knippenberg, D., & Ilgen, D. R. (2017). A century of work groups in the Journal of Applied Psychology. *Journal of Applied Psychology, 102*, 452–467.

Meindl, J. R. (1995). The romance of leadership as a follower-centric theory: A social constructionist approach. *Leadership Quarterly, 6*, 329–341.

Meindl, J. R., Ehrlich, S. B., & Dukerich, J. M. (1985). The romance of leadership. *Administrative Science Quarterly, 30*, 78–102.

Paterson, T. A., Harms, P. D., Steel, P., & Credé, M. (2016). An assessment of the magnitude of effect sizes evidence from 30 years of meta-analysis in management. *Journal of Leadership and Organizational Studies, 23*, 66–81.

Pierro, A., Cicero, L., Bonaiuto, M., van Knippenberg, D., & Kruglanski, A. W. (2005). Leader group prototypicality and leadership effectiveness: The moderating role of need for cognitive closure. *Leadership Quarterly, 16*, 503–516.

Pierro, A., Cicero, L., Bonaiuto, M., van Knippenberg, D., & Kruglanski, A. W. (2007). Leader group prototypicality and resistance to organizational change: The moderating role of need for closure and team identification. *Testing, Psychometrics, Methodology in Applied Psychology, 14*, 27–40.

Platow, M. J., & van Knippenberg, D. (2001). A social identity analysis of leadership endorsement: The effects of leader ingroup prototypicality and distributive intergroup fairness. *Personality and Social Psychology Bulletin, 27*, 1508–1519.

Platow, M. J., van Knippenberg, D., Haslam, S. A., van Knippenberg, B., & Spears, R. (2006). A special gift we bestow on you for being representative of us: Considering leader charisma from a self-categorization perspective. *British Journal of Social Psychology, 45*, 303–320.

Ravasi, D., & Schultz, M. (2006). Responding to organizational identity threats: Exploring the role of organizational culture. *Academy of Management Journal, 49*, 433–458.

Reicher, S., & Hopkins, N. (2001). *Self and Nation*. Sage.

Reicher, S., & Hopkins, N. (2003). On the science and art of leadership. In D. van Knippenberg & M. A. Hogg (Eds.), *Leadership and Power: Identity Processes in Groups and Organizations* (pp. 197–209). Sage.

Riketta, M. (2005). Organizational identification: A meta-analysis. *Journal of Vocational Behavior, 66*, 358–384.

Rousseau, D. M. (1998). Why workers still identify with organizations. *Journal of Organizational Behavior, 19*, 217–233.

Seppälä, T., Lipponen, J., & Pirttilä-Backman, A. M. (2012). Leader fairness and employees' trust in coworkers: The moderating role of leader group prototypicality. *Group Dynamics, 16*, 35–49.

Selznick, P. (1957). *Leadership in Administration*. University of California Press.

Shamir, B., Pillai, R., Bligh, M. C., & Uhl-Bien M. (2007). *Follower-Centered Perspectives on Leadership: A Tribute to the Memory of James R. Meindl*. Information Age.

Stam, D., Lord, R. G., van Knippenberg, D., & Wisse, B. (2014). An image of who we might become: Vision communication, possible selves, and vision pursuit. *Organization Science, 25*, 1172–1194.

Steffens, N. K., Haslam, S. A., Ryan, M. K., & Kessler, T. (2013). Leader performance and prototypicality: Their inter-relationship and impact on leaders' identity entrepreneurship. *European Journal of Social Psychology, 43*, 606–613.

Steffens, N. K., Munt, K. A., van Knippenberg, D., Platow, M. J., & Haslam, S. A. (2021). Advancing the social identity theory of leadership: A meta-analytic review of leader group prototypicality. *Organizational Psychology Review, 11*, 35–72.

Tajfel, H., & Turner, J. C. (1986). The social identity theory of intergroup behavior. In S. Worchel & W. Austin (Eds.), *Psychology of Intergroup Relations* (pp. 7–24). Nelson-Hall.

Tavares, S., van Knippenberg, D., & van Dick, R. (2016). Organizational identification and 'currencies of exchange': Integrating social identity and social exchange perspectives. *Journal of Applied Social Psychology, 46*, 34–45.

Turner, J. C., Hogg, M. A., Oakes, P. J., Reicher, S. D., & Wetherell, M. S. (1987). *Rediscovering the Social Group: A Self-categorization Theory.* Blackwell.

Ullrich, J., Christ, O., & van Dick, R. (2009). Substitutes for procedural fairness: Prototypical leaders are endorsed whether they are fair or not. *Journal of Applied Psychology, 94*, 235–244.

van Knippenberg, B., & van Knippenberg, D. (2005). Leader self-sacrifice and leadership effectiveness: The moderating role of leader prototypicality. *Journal of Applied Psychology, 90*, 25–37.

van Knippenberg, D. (2000). Work motivation and performance: A social identity perspective. *Applied Psychology: An International Review, 49*, 357–371.

van Knippenberg, D. (2011). Embodying who we are: Leader group prototypicality and leadership effectiveness. *Leadership Quarterly, 22*, 1078–1091.

van Knippenberg, D. (2016). Making sense of who we are: Leadership and organizational identity. In M. G. Pratt, M. Schultz, B. E. Ashforth & D. Ravasi (Eds.), *The Oxford Handbook of Organizational Identity.* Oxford University Press.

van Knippenberg, D. (2019). The social psychology of personality and leadership: A person-in-situation perspective. In K. Deaux & M. Snyder (Eds.), *Oxford Handbook of Personality and Social Psychology* (2nd edn, pp. 777–802). Oxford University Press.

van Knippenberg, D. (2020). Meaning-based leadership. *Organizational Psychology Review, 10*, 6–28.

van Knippenberg, D., De Cremer, D., & van Knippenberg, B. (2007). Leadership and fairness: The state of the art. *European Journal of Work and Organizational Psychology, 16*, 113–140.

van Knippenberg, D., & Dwertmann, D. J. G. (2022). Interacting elements of leadership: Key to integration but looking for integrative theory. *Journal of Management, 48*(6), 1695–1723.

van Knippenberg, D., & Hogg, M. A. (2003). A social identity model of leadership effectiveness in organizations. *Research in Organizational Behavior, 25*, 243–295.

van Knippenberg, D., & Hogg, M. A. (2018). Social identifications in organizational behavior. In D. L. Ferris, R. E. Johnson & C. Sedikides (Eds.), *The Self at Work: Fundamental Theory and Research* (pp. 72–90). Routledge.

van Knippenberg, D., van Knippenberg, B., & Bobbio, A. (2008). Leaders as agents of continuity: Self continuity and resistance to collective change. In F. Sani (Ed.), *Self-continuity: Individual and Collective Perspectives* (pp. 175–186). Psychology Press.

van Knippenberg, D., van Knippenberg, B., De Cremer, D., & Hogg, M. A. (2004). Leadership, self, and identity: A review and research agenda. *Leadership Quarterly, 15*, 825–856.

van Knippenberg, D., van Knippenberg, B., & Giessner, S. R. (2007). Extending the follower-centered perspective: Leadership as an outcome of shared social identity. In B. Shamir, R. Pillai, M. C. Bligh & M. Uhl-Bien (Eds.), *Follower-centered Perspectives on Leadership: A Tribute to the Memory of James R. Meindl* (pp. 51–70). Information Age.

van Knippenberg, D., van Knippenberg, B., Monden, L., & de Lima, F. (2002). Organizational identification after a merger: A social identity perspective. *British Journal of Social Psychology, 41*, 233–252.

van Knippenberg, D., van Knippenberg, B., & van Dijk, E. (2000). Who takes the lead in risky decision making? Effects of group members' individual riskiness and prototypicality. *Organizational Behavior and Human Decision Processes, 83*, 213–234.

Venus, M., Stam, D., & van Knippenberg, D. (2019). Visions of change as visions of continuity. *Academy of Management Journal, 62*, 667–690.

Romance of Leadership

Birgit Schyns and Gretchen Vogelgesang Lester

The second most important job in the country.
Niall Edworthy, on the job of
England football manager

The world of sports gives us wonderfully illustrative examples of what *romance of leadership* is and what its consequences can be for the leaders in question. Here leaders are hailed as the one crucial reason for team performance while other factors are ignored (Schyns et al., 2016). The consequence of the intense pressure from fans and media is obvious: *There's only two types of manager. Those who've been sacked and those who will be sacked in the future.* (Howard Wilkinson). There are many cases across different sports, where success or failure is attributed to the coach (leader), regardless of the complexity of the situation, the health of the players, external competitive forces and the state of the fandom – a perfect metaphor for how romance of leadership explains such phenomena in other domains. We see the same pattern in business, where scandals often result in the public firing or forced retirements of CEOs such as Martin Winterkorn of VW (Glinton & Gotbaum, 2018) and Bill Stumpf of Wells Fargo (Crimmons & Freifield, 2017), while performance above expectations is also attributed to CEOs such as Elon Musk at Tesla and SpaceX and Jeff Bezos at Amazon and Blue Origin. Such attribution suggests we have a romantic image of leadership when we use leaders to explain the performance of organisations or teams over other factors – regardless of a leader's actual impact and ignoring other influence factors (Meindl et al., 1985). The leader thus reflects a larger-than-life image, a figurehead and often a scapegoat (Gamson & Scotch, 1964). Romance of leadership is at the same time an implicit *leadership* theory (see Chapter 8, Followership) as it makes assumptions about leaders' influence and also an implicit *organisational* theory as it makes assumptions about the functioning of an organisation (Schyns & Meindl, 2005).

In this chapter, we present romance of leadership as a process that people use to make sense of organisational performance. We also seek to differentiate the conditions under which romance of leadership thrives and thereby explore its boundary conditions. We highlight misunderstandings of the theory due to misalignment between the theory and methods of operationalisation. From its inception through today, romance of leadership examines how people retroactively make sense of organisational events, such as unexpected performance (Meindl, 1995). In this sense, romance of leadership is a cognitive short-cut that ignores the complexities behind organisational performance. The original research was conceived as a critique not only of the way we as a society romanticise leaders, but also on the leader focus of leadership research (Meindl, 1995), paving the way for more follower-centric approaches to leadership. However, along the way, romance of leadership has been over-interpreted, morphing from a retrospective analysis of responsibility to a prediction for how organisations and their members will operate.

In order to return to the tenets of the theory, we will first define romance of leadership, complete a brief historical review of the research to this point, and present a current understanding of the field. We will then present how more recent research challenges past evidence and can stimulate researchers to reconsider and understand the boundary conditions of romance of leadership. We conclude by recommending new directions for research into romance of leadership.

DEFINITION OF ROMANCE OF LEADERSHIP

Romance of leadership was originally conceptualised as an over-attribution to leaders for responsibility over organisational performance (Meindl, 1990); this implicit organisational theory, or lay-theory, about how organisations achieve performance is also an implicit leadership theory as it views the leader as the source of organisational performance (Meindl, 1990; Schyns & Meindl, 2005). The concept was introduced in the 1980s as a critique of the prevailing view of leaders as larger-than-life figures often regarded as the only explanation for company performance. Meindl (1990) called it *an alternative to conventional wisdom* (p. 159) and a fundamental attribution error.

Individuals get caught up in the excitement and mystery of leadership and may tend to set leaders upon pedestals leading to an outsized idea of the influence of leaders (Meindl et al., 1985). In that sense, romance of leadership is an implicit leadership theory (ILT). ILTs are defined as *assumptions, beliefs, and expectations regarding the causes, nature, and consequences of leadership* (Lord & Emrich, 2000) (covered in more detail in Chapter 8, Followership). Each individual carries their own unique implicit leadership theories – basically, their picture of what a typical leader is like (Schyns & Schilling, 2011). These ILTs are formed through experiences, behavioural models, cultural understandings, representations of leaders in the media, fiction and non-fiction content and role models, and might change through exposure to different managers and leaders. Romance of leadership is a specific ILT in that it idealises leaders and the influence they have. As such, romanticising leaders prevents us from taking into account other factors that influence performance.

Concurrently, implicit organisation theories (IOTs) are lay ideas about how organisations function. Humans often attribute more power to leaders as part of their IOTs – that is, the functioning of the organisation is largely assumed to rely on leaders. Early romance of leadership research findings support this notion. Here, participants rated organisations better when leaders were mentioned to be responsible for the success of a company than when other explanations such as the market, the government, or the human capital within the organisation were introduced (Meindl & Ehrlich, 1987).

As research into the construct continued, additional evidence provided support that romance of leadership can also be a social construction *within* an organisation. Thus, while the first studies focused on the attribution of responsibility to the leader from individuals outside the organisation (Meindl et al., 1985; Meindl & Ehrlich, 1987), follow-up studies (Meindl, 1995) explored followers' social construction processes with regards to romance of leadership. Thus, the research sought to understand how people make sense of the complex events occurring within organisations, particularly in regards to the overestimation of the impact of leaders. The research in this era coincided with the rise of the 'superstar' CEO, a leader with charisma drawing attention from institutional and ordinary investors alike due to personal charisma as much as business acumen (Khurana, 2002). This shift in attention to the CEO as a personality is troubling given the continued difficulty in tying such leadership to organisational performance (Khurana, 2002). The next section will detail the different empirical approaches to studying romance of leadership.

HISTORICAL REVIEW: EMPIRICAL EVIDENCE

The stream of research on romance of leadership has incorporated many different methodologies. Researchers have used archival data, experiments and field studies, while also using quantitative and qualitative approaches.

Archival Studies

The first series of studies relating to romance of leadership (Meindl et al., 1985) contained three archival studies. The assumption driving the archival studies was that interest in leadership varies with firm, industry and government performance. First, the authors explored the relationship that the popular press makes between performance and leadership. In the following two studies, they investigated if the interest in researching leadership is linked to variations in the national economy. They found that mention of leadership in the *Wall Street Journal* is related to overall economic and industry performance, so the leadership narrative is tied closely to very good or very bad performance. They confirmed the same tendency with regard to thesis topics in the *Business Periodical Index*. This evidence provides support that there is a tendency to romanticise leaders on a societal level; however, the findings cannot ultimately conclude whether press coverage drives the relationship, or if company performance drives up interest in leadership.

Using a similar methodology, Bligh and Meindl (2004) analysed 257 popular leadership books (based on their sales ranking). Their first observation is in line with the prevalence of a general romance of leadership tendency in society. That is, there are a large number of popular press books available on leadership, highlighting the popularity of the topic. The authors identified seven clusters of topics through their analysis, the largest of which coincides with the romance of leadership idea – namely leading change. The underlying assumption is that leaders have the power to change organisations. Another interesting finding relates to the great interest in biographical books about leaders, again highlighting the interests in (and likely over-attribution to) a single person in an organisation and their influence. To conclude, archival studies on romance of leadership present evidence that this phenomenon exists, notably when leaders are seen and evaluated by individuals outside the organisation.

Experimental Studies

In addition to the three archival studies, the first publication on romance of leadership (Meindl et al., 1985) also contained three experimental studies. In the 1985 study (as well as in most subsequent research), participants read organisational descriptions and financial indicators and subsequently indicated who or what was most responsible for the performance. Business students attributed a higher share of responsibility to leaders than other factors when the performance of an organisation was described as increasing or decreasing. A further series of studies used two scenarios to link the tendency to romanticise leadership (using the romance of leadership scale) to 1) the attribution of responsibility to leaders and 2) the probability of turnaround depending on a described leader's experience (Schyns & Hansbrough, 2012). The results indicated that individuals with a higher tendency to romanticise leaders are indeed more likely to attribute responsibility to leaders when the cause of organisational performance is ambiguous.

Following up on their original experimental studies, Meindl and Ehrlich (1987) presented participants with vignettes describing a successful company and varied the cause for the success, namely, participants either read a vignette presenting the leader, employees, the market, or government policies as a reason for the company success. Overall, they found that participants rated the company more positively when the leader was presented as the cause for the company's success. Recently, Hammond et al. (2021) used the same vignettes in an attempt to replicate the results. However, the predicted differences were not significant.

Clarifying which circumstances show a clear romance of leadership helps us to consider boundary conditions of the concept. Looking at the differences between the Meindl et al. (1985) studies, which were replicated (Schyns & Hansbrough, 2012), and the Meindl and Ehrlich (1987) experiments, which were not (Hammond et al., 2021), we detect critical design differences. When directly asked who is responsible for the company performance, the participants picked the leader; however, when asked to rate the company's performance, the cause for success presented was less relevant. That is, a successful company is a good company regardless of the reason but when asked for a reason, individuals often point to the leader. In a sense, the approach may demand a cognitive short-cut and, when it does, the short-cut is to choose the leader over the other options. Another important finding here is that to decrease the tendency for individuals to romanticise leadership, offering multiple explanations for performance could limit the attribution error.

Further, we can speculate that the individual difference of one's tendency to romanticise leadership is relevant when it comes to attributing responsibility to leaders for specific situations (Schyns & Hansbrough, 2012). Research presenting vignettes and asking participants to judge the likelihood of success supports this idea (Felfe & Petersen, 2007; Hermann & Felfe, 2009). In these studies, individual-level romance of leadership influenced how far leadership descriptions (as opposed to descriptions of other factors) influenced the probability of project success ratings. That is, while the tendency to attribute performance to leaders seems widespread, some individuals are more prone to this attribution error than others.

In most of the studies reported so far gender was not an experimental condition – that is, in most romance of leadership studies, a male leader was presented. In a quest to find out if romance of leadership also applies to female leaders, another experimental study (Kulich et al., 2007) varied the gender of the presented leader. They found that male and female leaders did not differ in terms of the attribution of charisma or leadership ability, but the amount of conferred bonus differed with a stronger romance of leadership effect for male (given a larger bonus) as opposed to the female leader (given a smaller bonus).

In summary, experimental studies on romance of leadership show that the effect is particularly prevalent when leaders are evaluated directly (rather than when company performance is evaluated), that the effect is stronger when participants are high in individual-level romance of leadership and that the results regarding gender difference depend on which outcome measure is used.

Field Studies

Meindl (1990) was particularly sceptical regarding charisma (see Chapter 13, Redefining followership) attributed to leaders. According to him, charisma embodies *hyper-romanticism* (p. 192) and is linked more to the observers than to the leaders. Several studies have been conducted to examine the link between individual-level romance of leadership and ratings of charisma (e.g., Awamleh & Gardner, 1999). A meta-analysis including an overall sample size of $N = 3,312$ participants shows a positive relationship between individual-level romance of leadership and ratings of charismatic/transformational leadership ($r = .25$; 95 per cent confidence interval .22 to .28), supporting Meindl's (1990) assumption (Schyns et al., 2007). In addition, research into crisis context provides evidence that charisma is vulnerable to romance of leadership effects; two studies found that crisis indeed influenced charisma ratings in the political context (Bligh et al., 2004a and b). Similar to the experimental research, where unexpected performance seems particularly prone to attribution attempts, these studies imply that crisis could serve as a boundary condition for romance of leadership.

LEADERS AS THE SOURCE OF ROMANCE OF LEADERSHIP

While most research into romance of leadership explores attributions of observers of leadership such as the general public or followers, considering how crisis is related to romance of leadership in a political context (Bligh et al., 2004a and b) evokes the question as to the extent to which leaders can influence romance of leadership. In the political context, for example, a rhetoric of crisis might contribute to attributions of charisma – potentially activating the tendency for observers to over-attribute responsibility to leaders. Testimony from the Chief Advisor to the Prime Minister of the United Kingdom recently highlighted this quote from then Prime Minister Boris Johnson regarding the Covid-19 pandemic: *Chaos isn't that bad. Chaos means everyone has to look to me to see who's in charge.* As far back as 1977, Pfeffer argued that effective leaders succeed by associating themselves with company success and distancing themselves from company failure. This hints at the notion that leaders themselves can play on romance of leadership – that is, influence the attribution of responsibility to themselves (see e.g., Gray & Densten, 2007). Investigating leaders' or leaders-to-be's romance of leadership, Felfe and Schyns (2014) found that romance of leadership is positively related to motivation to lead. This means that motivated individuals seeking leadership opportunities might use romance of leadership to their advantage to inflate their impact on outcomes, particularly in times of crisis. Related to this notion of leaders wielding romance of leadership, Steffens and Haslam (2020) suggest that narcissistic leaders might find romance of leadership an attractive idea as it creates a façade that leaders are individuals with extraordinary capabilities.

INFLUENCE ON LEADERSHIP RESEARCH

While even now, nearly 40 years of research into the phenomenon of romance of leadership, the empirical research on romance of leadership is mixed, the idea itself has had a huge influence on leadership research and practical approaches to leadership. Certainly, the body of research into romance of leadership has warned leadership researchers not to glorify leaders; this is arguably where romance of leadership has had its biggest influence. Hence, we start our overview of the influence of romance of leadership with the topic of succession – that is, where leaders are replaced based on the notion that they are responsible for bad performance and that a new leader can single-handedly turn an organisation around.

Succession

Research into leadership succession has invoked romance of leadership, particularly in the professional sports domain. Schyns and colleagues (2016), in analysing lessons learnt from football (soccer), outline that the revolving door of football managers in European leagues as a sign of scapegoating is very much in line with romance of leadership's notion of over-attribution of performance to leaders. This phenomenon also occurs when business organisations are caught acting in an unethical manner or receive bad press (see CEO terminations in firms investigated by *60 Minutes*; Cooper, 2015; Bar-On & Stahl, 2014). This is in line with Meindl's (1990) conceptualisation of romance of leadership as an implicit organisational theory (Schyns & Meindl, 2005), implying that one of the main issues in over-attributing performance to leaders is the failure to acknowledge the complexity that lies behind organisational performance. Romance of leadership is a short-cut that many use to quickly make sense of performance, and perhaps swiftly show decisive action to placate stakeholders in times of distress. This, in turn, can lead organisations to replace leaders without addressing their actual problems (as highlighted in the very beginning in European football).

Followership

Another area of research that has been influenced by romance of leadership is research into followership, that is, the influence of followers on the process of leadership. In a way, this can be seen as a natural consequence of romance of leadership. Most empirical studies focus on the general tendency of individuals and society to romanticise leaders and thus invite us to reconsider the emphasis we put on leaders. This, as a consequence, directs the focus to other factors relevant to organisational performance, such as followers. This is also reflected in current research on post-heroic leadership (e.g., Collinson et al., 2018). Romance of leadership might be one of the reasons behind the growing interest in researching leadership as a process that includes leaders and followers. Indeed, a book related to the legacy of James Meindl's research (Shamir et al., 2007) is called *Follower-Centered Perspectives on Leadership*. Topics covered include follower attribution, sense-making and perceptions of leadership. Arguably, focusing on followers shifts the attention, but is, at the same time, only a limited application of romance of leadership. Collinson et al. (2018) note that at least some research into followership falls into the trap of substituting romanticising leaders with romanticising followers, mainly by discounting the barriers that followers face to expressing their discontent (e.g., in the context of Chaleff's [1995] reference to the courageous follower).

Charisma

As noted above, romance of leadership has influenced the research approach to charisma. While Weber (1921) alluded to the relevance of follower perceptions to leaders' charisma, large swaths of research regard charisma or transformational leadership as situated in the leader rather than the follower. With the findings that charisma and romance of leadership are highly correlated (Schyns et al., 2007), romance of leadership theory has encouraged researchers to consider charisma more as an attribution by others than a characteristic of the leader, in line with Meindl's (1990) conceptualisations. A recent review of follower-centric perspectives on charismatic leadership (Ito et al., 2020) draws upon Meindl's legacy in terms of charisma research (Meindl, 1990).

Implicit Leadership Theories

Romance of leadership is both an implicit theory about organisations (in the sense of a cognitive short-cut that explains how organisations function) and an implicit theory about leaders (in a sense of the scope that leaders are given in influencing organisations). A recent study invoked the idea of romance of leadership when investigating two different types of implicit leadership theories – that is, implicit theories about leadership versus management (Kniffin et al., 2020). Here the authors argued and found that implicit theories about leadership and management differed in terms of the contents ascribed to them. While leaders inspire, motivate and guide, managers budget, hire and supervise. Given this, we conclude that leadership is more romanticised than management.

Post-heroic Leadership

As a response to the questioning of leaders as the origin of company performance, another stream of research building on romance of leadership calls for an end to the heroic notion of leaders and leadership (e.g., Collinson et al., 2018; Ladkin 2020). Drawing on criticism of charismatic leadership as an example of romance of leadership, Collinson and colleagues (2018) argue that the issue continues even in more recent theories of leadership, such as spiritual, authentic and servant leadership. In addition to achieving extraordinary performance (as claimed by charismatic leadership researchers), these theories highlight the normatively positive way in which followers are influenced, thus making leadership something even more romanticised. At the same time, using the example of Donald Trump, a former US president, Ladkin (2020) warns that the romance of leadership continues to be prevalent in the way today's leaders are regarded and that such leaders even play on this concept and encourage their followers to romanticise them. Thus, evidence from both theory and practice of leadership shows that the romance is not over yet.

Recently, Guthey et al. (2021) explain why this might be the case. They subsume romance of leadership under *affective rationality* which they define as *a discourse for validating social action based on the conviction that emotions make their own kind of sense and constitute their own form of legitimacy apart from any appeal to formally rational utility or to substantively rational beliefs and values* (p. 9). That is, emotions rather than rational analysis take precedence when interpreting leadership.

LEADERLESS MOVEMENTS

Some recent social movements seem to reject strong leadership or dominance as the base for political or environmental/social issues. Often joined by young protesters (e.g., Arab spring, Hong Kong protests and Fridays for Future), one might consider if the romance of leadership is over for younger generations who may be disenchanted with leaders. However, even these seemingly leaderless movements have emergent leaders such as Asmaa Mahfouz, Joshua Wong Chi-fung, or Greta Thunberg. While their leadership emerged due to passion about an issue, their followers might inadvertently romanticise them (rather than the issue they stand for) and thus place undue pressure on them to lead by example.

This reflects Collinson and colleagues' (2018) warning that we have to be careful not to romanticise only leaders' influence but also how they achieve this influence. There is a risk of romanticising even reluctant leaders due to the ethical nature of the change they want to achieve. It is, for example, hard to imagine that Greta Thunberg foresaw her lonely school strike turning her into the symbol for addressing climate change across the globe – with all the pressure and scrutiny for her every action that comes with it. Here, romance of leadership results from followers' buy-in to what the leader is trying to achieve.

At the same time, populist leaders continue to wield romance of leadership through their presentation of themselves as infallible. They encourage their followers to romanticise them by actively building an image of themselves. This even goes as far as denying past actions if it does not fit their current façade. In an era of 'post-truth' and social media, some leaders have curated an image of themselves as larger-than-life, clearly reflecting romance of leadership.

Overall, romance of leadership continues to influence research into leadership and followership. While, in some ways, leadership has been less romanticised, newer theories might re-romanticise leadership. In practice, it seems that our views of leaders have not changed and indeed a recent reoccurrence of populism might indicate that we are in an era where leadership is increasingly more rather than less romanticised. At the same time, we need to be careful not to replace romanticising leaders with romanticising followers and thereby underestimating the risks that 'heroic' followers face.

Boundary Conditions

Crisis

Even the first papers on romance of leadership acknowledged that the phenomenon is particularly strong when performance is very high or very low, implying that 'surprising' performance shifts require explanations – and leaders are used as a simple one. Several papers imply that crisis is an important factor in romance of leadership. In investigating the job selection context, Emrich (1999) found that more leadership was attributed to candidates from troubled rather than tranquil groups. In the context of a study linking social identity and romance of leadership, Haslam and colleagues (2001) found that crisis turnaround invoked more romance of leadership than crisis decline, hinting at moderating factors when examining romance of leadership in the context of crisis, namely time and the outcome. However, crisis is not always an objective state; it can also be influenced by the leaders themselves. It appears that, similar to external threats creating a stronger in-group identity, promoting oneself as the person able to deal with a threat can increase romance of leadership. As Bligh and colleagues (2004a and b) showed, crisis can increase charisma ratings. This also leaves open the question of the extent to which leaders may manufacture crises to enhance romance of leadership in the hope of creating stronger followership.

Gender

A final question asks how this mechanism works for male versus female leaders. As noted above, the research findings available regarding gender effects for romance of leadership are mixed (Kulich et al., 2007). Here, romance of leadership for female leaders seems to depend on the outcome investigated. An interesting exploration of female romance of leadership occurred at the outset of the Covid-19 crisis. Here, maybe unexpectedly so, female leaders were hailed to be better at navigating this health crisis (Henley, 2020; Sorkin, 2020). One question is whether or not this reflects better leadership or if there is an element of romance of leadership, as this positive press for women leaders does not take into account the complexity of leading in a crisis, nor does it acknowledge the context in which these leaders operate. For example, would taking into account the size and density of a population decrease the effect of gender – for example, the difference between leading a small, not very densely populated island (New Zealand, female leader) versus leading a nation with many bordering countries that is densely populated (France, male leader)? Or does taking into account the woman leader's education background and its fit to the crisis explain why female leaders were more successful during this health crisis – for example, the difference between being a leader with a science degree (Germany) versus a classics degree (the UK)? Certainly, further research is needed to examine if the Covid-19 crisis is a rare case of female romance of leadership (and, if so, why), or if women were more successful at guiding their countries through this crisis. Is it also possible that, for female leaders, different conditions exist under which they are attributed responsibility for outcomes? Maybe a health crisis is something that is considered to be a calling for female leadership more than, for example, a political conflict or an economic crisis. Possibly the type of crisis (health versus economic/conflict) requires a different response (e.g., solidarity versus hardness), which is more in line with the female leadership stereotype and thus romanticises female leaders. Future research should continue to explore the conditions under which romance of leadership is likely to emerge.

CONCLUSION AND OUTLOOK

In this chapter, we have employed romance of leadership as a sense-making approach that leadership observers use to explain performance and that leaders themselves can play on to achieve success. Decades of research provide evidence that this is a worthy pursuit, but we present aspects of the theory that require reconsideration to clarify the boundary conditions of the theory. The findings are mixed when looking at romance of leadership as an over-attribution versus a social construction, and also when exploring different contexts. We recommend that future research continues to use this delineation and consider the relevant context. If we can question underlying assumptions and ensure that as many perspectives as possible are considered (individual-differences in the tendency to romance leadership, organisation membership, followership, identity, charisma, status, gender, etc.), we can continue to study and predict the conditions under which romance of leadership will materialise to educate leaders and followers alike.

REFERENCES

Awamleh, R., & Gardner, W. L. (1999). Perceptions of leader charisma and effectiveness: The effects of vision content, delivery, and organizational performance. *Leadership Quarterly*, *10*(3), 345–373.

Bar-On, S., & Stahl, L. (2014). Sticker shock: Why are glasses so expensive? *60 Minutes*. Columbia Broadcasting System. Internet resource.

Bligh, M.C., & Meindl, J. R. (2004). The Cultural Ecology of Leadership: An Analysis of Popular Leadership Books. In D. M. Messick & R. M. Kramer, (Eds.) *The Psychology of Leadership: New Perspectives and Research*, pp. 11–52. LEA Press.

Bligh, M. C., Kohles, J. C., & Meindl, J. R. (2004a). Charting the language of leadership: A methodological investigation of President Bush and the crisis of 9/11. *Journal of Applied Psychology, 89*, 562–574. https://doi.org/10.1037/0021-9010.89.3.562

Bligh, M. C., Kohles, J. C., & Meindl, J. R. (2004b). Charisma under crisis: Presidential leadership, rhetoric, and media responses before and after the September 11th terrorist attacks. *Leadership Quarterly, 15*(2), 211–239.

Bligh, M. C., Kohles, J. C., & Pillai, R. (2011). Romancing leadership: Past, present, and future. *Leadership Quarterly, 22*, 1058–1077. http://dx.doi.org/10.1016/j.leaqua.2011.09.003

Bligh, M. C., & Schyns, B. (2007). Leading question: The romance lives on: Contemporary issues surrounding the romance of leadership. *Leadership, 3*, 343–360.

Chaleff, I. (1995). *The Courageous Follower: Standing Up to and for Our Leaders*. Barrett.

Collinson, D., Smolovic Jones, O., & Grint, K. (2018). 'No more heroes': Critical perspectives on leadership romanticism. *Organization Studies, 39*, 1625–1647. https://doi.org/10.1177/0170840617727784

Cooper, A. (2015). Lumber liquidators. *60 Minutes*. Columbia Broadcasting System. Internet resource.

Crimmons, C. & Freifeld, K. (2017). 'Best banker in America' blamed for Wells Fargo sales scandal. *Reuters*. https://www.reuters.com/article/us-wells-fargo-accounts/best-banker-in-america-blamed-for-wells-fargo-sales-scandal-idUSKBN17C18P

Emrich, C. G. (1999). Context effects in leadership perception. *Personality and Social Psychology Bulletin, 25*(8), 991–1006.

Felfe, J., & Petersen, L. E. (2007). Romance of leadership and management decision making. *European Journal of Work and Organizational Psychology, 16*, 1–24. https://doi.org/10.1080/13594320600873076

Felfe, J. & Schyns, B. (2014). Romance of leadership and motivation to lead. *Journal of Managerial Psychology, 29*, 850–865. https://doi.org/10.1108/JMP-03-2012-0076

Gamson, W. A., & Scotch, N. A. (1964). Scapegoating in baseball. *American Journal of Sociology, 70*(1), 69–72.

Glinton, S., & Gotbaum, R. (2018). Former Volkswagen CEO indicted over emissions testing scandal. *NPR*. https://www.npr.org/sections/thetwo-way/2018/05/04/608374639/former-volkswagen-ceo-indicted-over-emission-testing-scandal

Gray, J. H., & Densten, I. L. (2007). How leaders woo followers in the romance of leadership. *Applied Psychology, 56*, 558–581. http://dx.DOI.org/10.1111/j.1464-0597.2007.00304.x

Guthey, E., Ferry, N. C., & Remke, R. (2021). Taking leadership fashions seriously as a vehicle for leadership learning. *Management Learning*, 13505076211009674.

Hammond, M. M., Schyns, B., Lester, G. V., Clapp-Smith, R., & Thomas, J. S. (2021). The romance of leadership: Rekindling the fire through replication of Meindl and Ehrlich. *Leadership Quarterly*, 101538.

Haslam, S. A., Platow, M. J., Turner, J. C., Reynolds, K. J., McGarty, C., Oakes, P. J., Johnson, S., Ryan, M. K., & Veenstra, K. (2001). Social identity and the romance of leadership: The importance of being seen to be 'Doing it for us.' *Group Processes & Intergroup Relations, 4*, 191–205. https://doi.org/10.1177/1368430201004003002

Henley, J. (2020). Female-led countries handled coronavirus better, study suggests. *Guardian*. https://www.theguardian.com/world/2020/aug/18/female-led-countries-handled-coronavirus-better-study-jacinda-ardern-angela-merkel

Herrmann, D., & Felfe, J. (2009). Romance of Leadership und die Qualität von Managemententscheidungen (Romance of leadership and the quality of management decision-making). *Zeitschrift für Arbeits- und Organisationspsychologie A&O, 53*, 163–176. https://doi.org/10.1026/0932-4089.53.4.163

Ito, A., Harrison, J., Bligh, M., & Roland-Levy, C. (2020). A follower-centric perspective on charismatic leadership: An integrative review and agenda for future research. In J. P. Zúquete (Ed.), *Routledge International Handbook of Charisma* (pp. 324–336). Routledge.

Khurana, R. (2002). The curse of the superstar CEO. *Harvard Business Review, 80*(9), 60–66.

Kniffin, K. M., Detert, J. R., & Leroy, H. L. (2020). On leading and managing: Synonyms or separate (and unequal)? *Academy of Management Discoveries, 6*(4), 544–571.

Kulich, C., Ryan, M. K., & Haslam, S. A. (2007). Where is the romance for women leaders? The effects of gender on leadership attributions and performance-based pay. *Applied Psychology: An International Review, 56*, 582–601. https://doi.org/10.1111/j.1464-0597.2007.00305.x

Ladkin, D. (2020). What Donald Trump's response to COVID-19 teaches us: It's time for our romance with leaders to end. *Leadership, 16*(3), 273–278.

Lord, R. G., & Emrich, C. G. (2000). Thinking outside the box by looking inside the box: Extending the cognitive revolution in leadership research. *Leadership Quarterly, 11*(4), 551–579.

Meindl, J. R. (1990). On leadership: An alternative to the conventional wisdom. *Research in Organizational Behavior, 12*, 159–203.

Meindl, J. R. (1995). The romance of leadership as a follower-centric theory: A social constructionist approach. *Leadership Quarterly, 6*, 329–341. https://doi.org/10.1016/1048-9843(95)90012-8

Meindl, J. R., Ehrlich, S. B., & Dukerich, J. M. (1985). The romance of leadership. *Administrative Science Quarterly, 30*, 78–102. http://dx.DOI.org/10.2307/2392813

Meindl, J. R., & Ehrlich, S. B. (1987). The romance of leadership and the evaluation of organizational performance. *Academy of Management Journal, 30*, 91–109. http://dx.doi.org/10.2307/255897

Schyns, B., Felfe, J., & Blank, H. (2007). Is charisma hyper-romanticism? Empirical evidence from new data and a meta-analysis. *Applied Psychology, 56*, 505–527. https://doi.org/10.1111/j.1464-0597.2007.00302.x

Schyns, B., Gilmore, S., & Dietz, G. (2016). What lessons can we learn from football about leadership and management? In C. Peus, S. Braun, & B. Scyns (Eds.), *Leadership Lessons from Compelling Contexts* (pp. 95–128). Emerald.

Schyns, B., & Hansbrough, T. (2012). The romance of leadership scale and causal attributions. *Journal of Applied Social Psychology, 42*, 1870–1886. http://dx.doi.org/10.1111/j.1559-1816.2012.00922.x

Schyns, B., & Meindl, J. R. (Eds.) (2005). *Implicit Leadership Theories: Essays and Explorations*. IAP.

Schyns, B., & Schilling, J. (2011). Implicit leadership theories: Think leader, think effective? *Journal of Management Inquiry, 20*(2), 141–150.

Shamir, B., Pillai, R., Bligh, M. C., & Uhl-Bien, M. (2007). *Follower-centered Perspectives on Leadership: A Tribute to the Memory of James R. Meindl*. IAP.

Sorkin, A. (2020). The global struggle to control the coronavirus. *New Yorker.* https://www.newyorker.com/magazine/2020/04/27/the-global-struggle-to-control-the-coronavirus

Steffens, N. K., & Haslam, S. A. (2022). The narcissistic appeal of leadership theories. *American Psychologist, 77*(2), 234.

Weber, M. (1921). *Gesammelte politische schriften.* Drei Masken Verlag.

What is 'Functional' About Distributed Leadership in Teams?

Joshua Pearman, Emily Gerkin and Dorothy R. Carter

As organisations continue to rely on team-based work structures to accomplish key objectives, facilitating team effectiveness has become an essential aspect of organisational leadership (Morgeson et al., 2010; Zaccaro et al., 2001, 2008). Research on teams often relies on a *functional* view of leadership (McGrath, 1962) which positions 'effective' team leadership as *the process of team need satisfaction in the service of enhancing team effectiveness* (Morgeson et al., 2010, p. 4). Prior work from a functional perspective has significantly advanced understanding of the leader–team interface by identifying key leadership behaviours, such as information search and structuring, information use in problem-solving, or managing personnel and material resources, that support team functioning across phases of team performance (Zaccaro et al., 2001). Traditionally, studies of team leadership have assumed these functions will be fulfilled within teams by 'formal' leaders (e.g., a manager) who sit at the top of the team hierarchy and wield authority by assigning tasks and determining how the team should accomplish those tasks.

However, the leadership literature is increasingly recasting team leadership as a *collective* or *distributed* endeavour involving multiple team members who may or may not occupy formal positions of authority (Carson et al., 2007; D'Innocenzo et al., 2016; Klein et al., 2004; Mehra et al., 2006; Pearce & Conger, 2002). As Contractor and colleagues (2012) noted, different aspects of the team leadership *role* are often distributed among multiple *people*, simultaneously or across *time*. For example, a team's leadership structure might shift from a highly centralised form where one individual handles nearly all leadership responsibilities to a more decentralised structure where leadership responsibilities are accomplished by multiple people and/or multiple people are granted leadership authority.

This chapter synthesises the growing body of research exploring associations between leadership distribution structures – across people, roles and time – and team performance in order to better understand what is 'functional' about distributed leadership in teams. We characterise distributed leadership as a problem of organised complexity, such that elements contributing to leadership distribution are both independent and connected.

A FUNCTIONAL VIEW OF TEAM LEADERSHIP

Effective teamwork is essential to organisational success. Unfortunately, many teams fail to achieve outcomes that are 'greater' than their constituent parts (DeChurch & Mesmer-Magnus, 2010; Kozlowski, 2018; Kozlowski & Ilgen, 2006; LePine et al., 2008; Mathieu et al., 2008). Therefore, organisations need leaders to fulfill certain *functions* in order to ensure that teams perform synergistically (Burke et al., 2006; Carson et al., 2016; Fleishman et al., 1991; Morgeson et al., 2010; Zaccaro et al., 2001). Functional views of team leadership rely on the *input–process–output* model (IPO; Hackman, 1987; Ilgen et al., 2005; McGrath, 1962). The IPO model positions leaders and leadership behaviours as key inputs to team functioning that impact the *team behavioural processes* (e.g., communication, coordination, backup behaviour, conflict management) and *psychological states* (e.g., trust, cohesion, psychological safety) to shape team performance (Chiocchio & Essiembre, 2009; DeChurch & Mesmer-Magnus, 2010; Edmondson, 1999; Frazier et al., 2017; Grossman et al., 2021; LePine et al., 2008; Niler et al., 2021).

Research on team leadership as well as the broader leadership literature have identified a variety of leadership behaviours that are functional for teams and thus constitute key elements of the team leadership 'role'. For example, leadership scholars have long argued that the leadership role involves both task- and relational-oriented behaviours (e.g., Fleishman, 1953, Fleishman & Harris, 1962, Stogdill et al., 1963). Yukl (2012) organised leadership behaviours into four categories: task-, relations-, change- and externally-oriented leadership. *Task-oriented* leadership describes the management of resources to most efficiently achieve a group's mission, and therefore involves behaviours such as planning, clarifying, monitoring and problem-solving. *Relations-oriented* leadership involves the development of team members' skills and organisational commitment through interpersonal behaviours such as supporting, developing, recognising and empowering. *Change-oriented* leadership is necessary for teams and organisations to learn and adapt to external factors, involving advocating for change, envisioning change, encouraging innovation and facilitating collective learning. Finally, *Externally-oriented* leadership focuses on preparing team members for outside events, such as networking, monitoring external phenomena and representing the team when interacting with other entities.

Focusing more specifically on *team* leadership behaviours, Zaccaro and colleagues (2001) identified four overarching categories of leader behaviours that shape team performance through affective/motivational, behavioural and cognitive states (Fleishman et al., 1991): information search, information use, personnel management and material management. *Information search* refers to primarily externally oriented behaviours such as acquiring, organising and evaluating information, and task/relational-oriented behaviours such as providing feedback to team members. *Information use* refers to behaviours such as identifying team needs and requirements, planning, coordinating and communicating. Information use behaviours overlap primarily with task-based leadership behaviours and serve to enable goal attainment in teams. *Personnel management* includes behaviours such as obtaining, allocating, developing and motivating personnel. Personnel management behaviours can constitute task-, relational and change-oriented leadership behaviours and serve to motivate and coordinate teams. Lastly, *material management* involves obtaining, allocating, maintaining and monitoring material resources. Material management is critical for facilitating action in teams.

Building on these arguments, Contractor et al., (2012) identified four key objectives of team leadership: navigation, engineering, social integration and liaison with external entities. *Navigation* refers to the need for leadership to enable the collective to establish and maintain a clear purpose and direction. *Engineering* refers to the need for leadership to structure the collective and the task and coordinate the contributions of members. *Social integration* refers to the need to maintain a healthy and productive social environment in the team. The final objective, fulfilled when leaders play a *liaison* role, is to develop and maintain productive relationships with external stakeholders; fulfilling this role can involve leaders acting as advocates and/or ambassadors for the team.

LEADERSHIP AS A COLLECTIVELY ENACTED TEAM FUNCTION

Research on team leadership through a functional lens has often focused on the role that *formal* team leaders or managers play in supporting team effectiveness. However, such top-down views of team leadership approach the process of leading teams as a *problem of simplicity*. According to Sayama (2015), problems of simplicity narrow down a system so that it can be explained and restricted by the influence of only a few variables. On the opposite end of the spectrum, a problem of *disorganised complexity* is one where all variables being examined are considered independent of one another, resulting in completely random behaviour.

Between these two ends are problems of *organised complexity*, where a system is composed of both independent and connected components. Viewing team leadership as a problem of simplicity emphasises a formal leaders' ability to *control* the entire situation and/or the behaviours of all team members. Yet, leading teams – with their independent, yet connected, team members – is actually a problem of organised complexity where even formal leaders lack complete control over team functioning and performance (Hackman, 2012; McGrath et al., 2000).

To better reflect the complexity of leadership, researchers are increasingly depicting leadership as an emergent and relational process that may or may not involve formal authority (Carter et al., 2015; Contractor et al., 2012; DeRue & Ashford, 2010; Osborn et al., 2002; Pielstick, 2000; Wheelan & Johnston, 1996). Accompanying these shifts in conceptualisations of leadership is a growing body of research on *distributed* or *collective* leadership in teams which seeks to identify the patterns of leadership that can occur within teams as one or more *person* assumes responsibility for some or all aspects of the leadership *role* – simultaneously or over *time* (Contractor et al., 2012). Extending arguments from functional leadership theory, research on team leadership has begun to consider what is 'functional' about leadership distribution by linking patterns of collective leadership – across people, roles and time – to team performance and other outcomes. In the following sections, we briefly review prior research investigating these three elements of leadership distribution (i.e., people, roles and time; see Table 7.1).

People

The first element of leadership distribution, *people*, refers to the idea that the team leadership role might be accomplished by one or more team member. These 'leaders' may or may not occupy

Table 7.1 Exemplar findings from research on team leadership distribution across people, roles and time

Leadership distribution component	Key finding(s)	Exemplar citations
People	Distributed leadership patterns are often more effective than more centralised leadership patterns	(Carson et al., 2007; Ensley et al., 2006; Hoch et al., 2013; Mehra et al., 2006)
	The effectiveness of leadership distribution depends on the level of interdependence of the task, how performance is measured and task complexity	(Carnabuci et al., 2018; D'Innocenzo et al., 2016; Nicolaides et al., 2014)
	Antecedents of leadership distribution include individual characteristics and team-level factors (e.g., coaching, psychological states)	(Bell et al., 2018; Judge et al., 2002; Carson et al., 2007)
People x roles	Relational-oriented leadership is best shared, whereas task-oriented leadership is best centralised	(Wang et al. 2014)
	People have unique aptitudes towards different leadership functions	(Albrecht & Hall, 1991; Bales, 1950; Contractor et al., 2012; Seers et al., 2003)
	Another factor in distributing leadership is determining which member can best meet the demands of the team	(Carson et al., 2007; Marks et al., 2001; Marrone et al., 2010; Morgeson et al., 2010; Yukl, 2012)
People x time	Leadership might be like a baton that shifts over time, such that one person is in charge at any given moment but who that is can change	(Aime et al., 2014; Klein et al., 2004; Pearce & Conger, 2002)
	Matching leadership responsibility to changing task demands is beneficial	(Friedrich et al., 2009; Woolley et al., 2008)
	Factors including a lack of flexibility or a lack of willingness to relinquish or assume authority can prevent leadership rotation	(Hollenbeck et al., 2015; Park & DeShon, 2018)

formal positions of authority. A key assumption pervading research on team leadership distribution across people is that there are certain patterns of distribution that are more 'functional' than others.

Depicting leadership distribution among people. One way of describing how leadership is distributed among team members is by examining different distribution patterns across the spectrum of influence, varying from concentrated to decentralised. For example, Mehra et al. (2006) identified four patterns of leadership distribution in teams: *leader-centred, distributed, distributed–coordinated,* and *distributed–fragmented.* Leader-centred refers to the traditional vertical hierarchy, where a single leader influences the rest of the team. In a team with fully distributed leadership, each member could hypothetically lead every other member. Alternatively, in the distributed–coordinated structure two or more members of the team are viewed as leaders, with one member leading in a formally appointed role and the other member(s) contributing as informal leader(s). Finally, in the distributed–fragmented structure, the team splits into smaller subgroups to accomplish multiple tasks. In this structure, each subgroup has its own leader.

Others have suggested leveraging social network analytic approaches to operationalise and describe the pattern of leadership distribution in teams (Balkundi et al., 2009; Balkundi & Harrison, 2006; Balkundi & Kilduff, 2006; Carter et al., 2015; Denis et al., 2012; Katz et al., 2004; Sparrowe, 2014; Zhang & Peterson, 2011; Zohar & Tenne-Gazit, 2008). Mayo et al. (2003) proposed examining collective leadership by using decentralisation and density metrics. Carson et al. (2007) applied these density metrics to develop leadership sociograms of a team, capturing varying levels of shared leadership through network ratings. D'Innocenzo et al. (2016) performed a meta-analysis that showed studies which conceptualised shared leadership in terms of network metrics (e.g., density, decentralisation) instead of traditional aggregate leadership metrics amplified the shared leadership–team performance relationship and captured greater nuance. More recently, Carnabuci et al. (2018) provided an overview of network representations of leadership beyond density and decentralisation, such as symmetry, transitivity, cyclicity and popularity.

Often, social network studies investigating the distribution of leadership in teams will assess leadership using short (e.g., one-item) sociometric/round-robin items such as 'Who regards whom as his or her leader?' (Carnabuci et al., 2018) or 'To what degree does your team rely on this individual for leadership?' (Carson et al., 2007). These types of network items are grounded in assumptions that: 1) people are leaders when *others* grant them leadership authority and 2) a key aspect of the leadership 'role' is to gain the buy-in of potential followers. Indeed, these items assume that occupying a position of 'leadership' in teams is a co-constructed relational process whereby certain individuals become 'leaders' through claiming influence and others become 'followers' through granting influence (DeRue & Ashford, 2010). This exchange of influence is supplemented by research on followership, as Almeida et al. (Chapter 8, Followership) note that followers can affect their leader's behaviour through expressing their discontentment and revoking influence.

What patterns of leadership distribution are functional? Research on leadership distribution often implies that moving from a vertical hierarchy towards a more distributed leadership structure will support team performance. Ensley et al. (2006) compared shared and vertical leadership in venture teams, finding that shared leadership explained unique variance in the venture's performance above and beyond vertical leadership. This research is supplemented by findings regarding the effectiveness of shared leadership in teams from other industries (Carson et al., 2007; Hoch et al., 2013; Mehra et al., 2006), as well as findings from meta-analyses indicating shared leadership predicts team performance (D'Innocenzo et al., 2016; Nicolaides et al., 2014).

However, the literature also suggests there are a number of boundary conditions which limit or enhance the effectiveness of leadership distribution in teams. For example, Nicolaides et al. (2014) found that shared leadership was more strongly related to team performance for more interdependent tasks, whereas tasks that were less interdependent did not show as strong a benefit. Moreover, the shared leadership–performance relationship was stronger in subjective performance measures compared to objective performance measures. Another key quality is task complexity, as D'Innocenzo et al. (2016) observed that as tasks became more complex the relationship between shared leadership and performance decreased significantly.

People x Roles

The second element of leadership distribution, *roles*, reflects the notion that teams can distribute responsibility for different *aspects* of leadership behaviours or functions to some or all team members. Indeed, according to Seers et al. (2003), 'collective leadership' describes *the extent to which more than one individual can effectively operate in a distinctively influential role within the same interdependent role system* (p. 79). Moving beyond the mere pattern of leadership distribution in teams, research on functional team leadership has begun to explore associations between patterns of *who does what* (i.e., people x roles) and team performance.

What patterns of leadership role *distribution are functional?* Prior research suggests at least three key factors that determine what is 'functional' with regard to leadership distribution across people x roles: 1) the nature of the leadership role; 2) the people; and 3) the demands of the team.

The nature of the leadership role. For shared leadership to be effective, teams must consider how the nature of the leadership role matches to the task at hand. One effective paradigm for organising leadership roles is through a taxonomy containing two orientations: task-oriented and person-oriented (Fleishman et al., 1991). Task-oriented leaders emphasise the achievement of team goals by engaging in behaviours such as clarifying task requirements, initiating structure and allocating responsibilities to team members. In contrast, person-oriented leaders are concerned with resolving member conflict, developing trust within the team and motivating team members through interpersonal processes. Homan et al. (2020) proposed that effective leaders can adapt their orientation to complement the team's problems, whereas leaders only capable of one orientation had the potential to worsen problems due to the mismatch. These orientations also affect shared leadership processes. In a meta-analysis by Wang et al. (2014), the authors found that shared leadership was more strongly related to attitudinal and behavioural outcomes, which included the development of team satisfaction, commitment, cohesion and other motivational factors. However, shared leadership showed a weaker relationship with both subjective and objective performance outcomes. These findings indicate that in ceteris paribus task-oriented leadership behaviours may show greater benefits from more centralised leadership models, whereas person-oriented leadership behaviours may be more optimised in decentralised leadership models.

Capabilities of team members. When distributing leadership roles in a team, it may be important to consider the team member's aptitude towards the specific role. Many teams include individuals who possess unique competencies and skill sets, equipping them to lead different tasks. For example, one member may be highly task-oriented, excelling at coordinating the team's specific goals and increasing overall task competence. In comparison, another member could be more relationally oriented, focusing on building trust within the team and meeting socio-emotional needs (Albrecht & Hall, 1991; Bales, 1950; Carson et al., 2007). Teams also need leaders that are change-oriented (Carter et al., 2020; Yukl, 2012), as they emphasise the importance of innovation in an organisation.

Morgeson et al. (2010) suggested that certain roles are better suited to formal versus informal leaders, involving behaviours in transition and action phases. The transition phase involves preparing for the action phase, including defining the mission, setting expectations for the team, training, sense-making and providing feedback to members from a prior task. Afterwards, the team moves into an action phase, where the leader monitors the team's performance, provides resources, supports the team's social climate and challenges the team. Morgeson et al. (2010) proposed that formal leaders are positioned to engage in task-oriented behaviours, as they define the task's parameters and initiate structure. In contrast, informal leaders are positioned to engage in person-oriented behaviours, such as managing the team's social climate and providing crucial feedback to other team members. Team members might self-select themselves into different leadership roles depending on their individual differences and social functions within the group (Bales, 1950). For instance, a team may select the most competent expert on the subject matter as the 'task leader', and then delegate the 'social leader' role to the most liked team member (Contractor et al., 2012). Teams that have members who clearly excel in different leadership orientations from each other may show the greatest benefit to their overall performance (Seers et al., 2003).

Demands of the team. The distribution of leadership across roles can also be affected by the demands of the team. Leadership behaviours are designed to address these demands, often organised into action and transition phases or through person- and task-oriented goals (Fleishman et al., 1991; Morgeson et al., 2010). Morgeson et al. (2010) introduced a taxonomy for separating these behaviours based on whether a leader is internal/external to the team or formal/informal in their authority, but the taxonomy has yet to be empirically validated. Furthermore, this taxonomy suggests that leadership distribution across roles is made even more complex through moderators related to a team's demands, including external factors such as a task's requirements.

How leadership is distributed across these orientations can be further understood through their associated motivations and behaviours for influencing a team. The motivations and behaviours of these orientations are summarised in research on transition and action phases (Marks et al., 2001; Morgeson et al., 2010) and leadership taxonomies (Carson et al., 2007; Marrone, 2010; Yukl, 2012). Therefore, functional leadership can be understood through the distribution of leadership across roles.

People x Time

The final element of leadership distribution, *time*, reflects the notion that patterns of leadership distribution (across people and roles) may shift over time. For example, Pearce and Conger (2003) argue that multiple team members can *rise to the occasion to exhibit leadership and then step back at other times to allow others to lead* (p. 2). Similarly, Klein et al. (2004) argue that team leadership is like a 'baton' that can be passed from person to person over time.

What is functional about leadership distribution across time? For the most part, prior research investigating patterns of leadership distribution over time has tended to assume that at any given moment, the leadership structure is centralised around one or a few key individuals, yet who those individuals are will shift over time. For example, Erez et al. (2002) argued that when a team rotates the entire leadership role among its members on a routine basis there will be a greater investment in the team's success. During leader rotation, a team is still operating in a traditional, top-down hierarchical manner, but is also sharing leadership by alternating which member is the formal leader at different points in time. Cycling the leadership role in self-managed teams can amplify each member's voice and promote cooperation (Erez et al., 2002), thereby increasing overall performance. Likewise, Friedrich et al. (2009) proposed that in addition to cycling the leader role through a round-robin approach, teams can also change leaders depending on which member is most qualified to solve a given problem. Teams in more complex situations might benefit from distributing leadership based on which member has the relevant expertise to solve a given problem (Friedrich et al., 2009).

These arguments informed Aime et al.'s (2014) concept of power heterarchies in teams, defined as a *relational system in which the relative power among team members shifts over time as the resources of specific team members become more relevant (and the resources of other members become less relevant) because of changes in the situation or task* (p. 328). Power heterarchies draw on Emerson's (1962) theory of power-dependence, which posits that a group member will acquire power because of their access to resources or their competencies that reduce group vulnerability and uncertainty. The key implication of this line of research is that not only can multiple leaders emerge and share leadership in a team, but they may also take turns being the leader in order to ensure there is an optimal match between the leaders' skills and the problem at hand.

Situation-driven leadership authority is particularly relevant when a team is composed of multiple subject matter experts (Klein et al., 2004; Woolley et al., 2008), or is operating under extreme conditions (Driskell et al., 2018). These groups are sometimes referred to as 'extreme action teams', which Sundstrom et al. (1990) describe as *highly skilled, specialized teams cooperating in brief performance events that require improvisation in unpredictable circumstances* (p. 121). Although leadership is shared across members and deindividualised in such teams, their performance is still best when there is only one leader at any given moment. Klein et al. (2004) observe that surgery teams operate in a system of dynamic delegation, which involves the senior leader actively delegating and withdrawing the leadership role to other team members. By leveraging their flexible structure, teams can enhance their ability to adapt by being prepared to rotate leaders on a situational basis.

Flexibility to share leadership in a team. Another important factor that determines the functionality of leadership distribution over time is the level of *flexibility* in the team. Cycling the leadership role requires the team to be able to reorganise their behaviours; therefore, anything that inhibits flexibility will interfere with the benefits of rotating leaders. For example, a key condition is the timing of the group formation (Park & DeShon, 2018), such that newly formed teams may struggle more to distribute leadership compared to more experienced teams that have already developed one or more informal leaders. In newly formed teams, members may not be comfortable with suddenly assuming responsibility and guiding the team's actions. Therefore, teams may have to rely on a single member that can guide the team until they gain the experience necessary to transition from one leader to another in a seamless manner. Problems with flexibility in a team can also manifest when the current leader is asked to cede their authority to another team member. Hollenbeck et al. (2015) propose an opponent process theory of leadership, such that disagreement about leadership styles can lead to conflict affecting leadership succession in a team. However, a leader can be unwilling to yield their authority once they have attained it, and therefore wield their authority and access to upper level leaders to prevent leadership succession from occurring. This is complemented by Epitropaki et al. (Chapter 10, Implicit leadership and followership theories), who argue that a team member's self-schemas as both leader and follower affects their ability to switch roles and yield or assume authority. Examinations of how leadership is distributed across time should therefore include a discussion of members' unwillingness to assume or relinquish power.

ADVANCING FUTURE RESEARCH ON FUNCTIONALLY DISTRIBUTED LEADERSHIP IN TEAMS

Our review of the extant literature considered the question of 'what is functional?' with regard to how leadership is distributed across people, roles and time in teams. Prior research demonstrates that *some* level of sharing in responsibility for leadership – particularly across time and in accordance with task demands and members' capabilities – can improve team flexibility, learning, creativity, motivation and overall performance (Carson et al., 2007; Currie & Spyridonidis, 2019; D'Innocenzo et al., 2016; Erkutlu, 2012; Hoch, 2013; Liu et al., 2014; Mehra et al., 2006; Nicolaides et al., 2014; Pearce & Sims, 2002; Small & Rentsch, 2010; Wang et al., 2014). However, different forms of leadership distribution can also vary in effectiveness depending on the context of a team. Therefore, it is necessary to examine how the unique patterns of distributed leadership across people, roles and time impact team effectiveness in conjunction across these elements. Rather than focus on a single functional leader, future work could integrate complex systems science to examine 'functional teams' that vary in patterns of distributed leadership depending on contextual factors that include the individual team members, the task, the time and the environment of the team as a whole. Developing a model of distributed leadership will inform our understanding of functional teamwork.

How do the different elements of people, roles and time interact with each other to affect patterns of distributed leadership? Current research investigates how these elements independently affect distributed leadership (Aime et al., 2014; Carson et al., 2007; Contractor et al., 2012; Morgeson et al., 2010). The pattern of shared influence within each element is affected by various boundary conditions, such as the nature of the task or the demands of the team (D'Innocenzo et al., 2016; Morgeson et al., 2010; Nicolaides et al., 2014). Yet, distributed leadership is still not examined as a problem of organised complexity, as there is a dearth of work on how teams are affected when they distribute leadership based on two or more of these factors. Understanding the complexity of distributed leadership opens up new research questions. For emergence, why do certain patterns of distributed leadership emerge at certain points in a team's lifespan? For team effectiveness, what patterns of distribution across people, roles and time together embody functional leadership? Answering these questions will require a more holistic approach and new methods in studying distributed leadership. In empirical data collection efforts, researchers must employ study designs that include multiple time points for measurement, have multiple raters assessing the team and encode multiple behaviours at the level of the individual and the team. Capturing this data will reveal how teams make decisions to share influence across different people and according to specific roles. Furthermore, it will reveal how the pattern of leadership distribution is dynamic over time points. Alipour and Mohammed (Chapter 27, Temporal considerations in leadership and followership) describe how temporal characteristics can affect leadership in unique ways depending on how they are operationalised, thereby introducing further complexity to how time influences the distribution of leadership. Another approach is to apply agent-based models and other computationally intensive methods to model emergence. Through computational modelling, researchers can identify why specific patterns of distributed leadership emerge over time instead of alternative patterns.

Developing our understanding of distributed leadership may require that researchers revisit established theories in organisational psychology and teams literature. For example, research on transition and action stages in team leadership provides a foundation for key leadership behaviours (Fleishman et al., 1991). Morgeson et al. (2010) suggest that within these transition and action stages, a leader may be more optimised for specific behaviours depending on whether they are an informal or formal source of authority. Yet, how many informal leaders are good for a team? When should the leadership role move between the formal and informal leader? Alternatively, Hackman and Morris (1975) proposed that task strategy, member effort and member knowledge and skills interact and play a role in how group interaction processes influence group task performance. Building on this research, McGrath (1962) developed the Task Circumplex, which is composed of four key stages: generate plans and ideas; choose alternatives; resolve conflicts of viewpoints and interests; and perform action tasks. Each stage links with an interpersonal behaviour. The first stage, generate, includes coming up with shared values and goals in the team. The second stage, choose, involves agreeing on the generated values and goals and developing a consensus on policy. The third stage, negotiate (or resolve), requires members to develop norms that guide behaviour and assign roles in the team. In the fourth and final stage, execute, members establish and maintain their team cohesion. Depending on the stage, different team members' roles may show variety in their ability to be an effective leader. For example, a person-oriented leader can excel at stages that involve resolving interpersonal conflict or motivating the team, whereas a task-oriented leader would be suited to developing the goals of the team and helping everyone execute their tasks. Therefore, a key question remaining is how do leaders dynamically share influence depending on the needs of the team?

Finally, future research should also consider how the larger context of the team affects what patterns of leadership are functional at certain points in time. Oc and Carpini (Chapter 29, How and why is context important to leadership?) advance a taxonomy of macro-level omnibus and micro-level discrete contextual factors, providing an overview of the dimensions examined in both context types. The discrete factors can be viewed as a subset of the omnibus contextual factors, thereby raising the question of how these two factors interact to affect leadership processes. Beyond examining the effects of specific contextual factors, Morgeson et al.'s (2015) event system theory describes how certain situations will become salient to teams or organisations depending on the event's strength, which is determined by its novelty, disruptiveness and criticality. For example, a team will be severely affected by the unexpected turnover of a member. Alternatively, changes in the organisation's leadership can trigger downward effects that alter the functioning and culture of teams. Salient events produce impactful, exogenous shocks that significantly affect how teams operate. Leveraging an event-oriented perspective could help explain significant sources of variability that influence the distribution of leadership in teams.

CONCLUSION

A functional leaders' goal is to meet the needs of the team. As these needs increase in number and complexity, researchers have emphasised the importance of considering functional teams over functional leaders. Consequently, scholarly definitions of leadership have transitioned from emphasising an individual functional leader to viewing it as an evolving and distributed team process. People will influence those around them through both formal and informal mechanisms, and in turn be influenced by their peers. The same is true in teams – any member is capable of leading their fellow members. Over the past 30 years, research on collective team leadership has surged. Yet, much is still not known about the true complexity of distributed leadership. Therefore, we encourage future research to fully consider how leadership across people, roles and time intertwine to shape functioning and effectiveness.

REFERENCES

Aime, F., Humphrey, S., DeRue, D. S., & Paul, J. B. (2014). The riddle of heterarchy: Power transitions in cross-functional teams. *Academy of Management Journal*, 57(2), 327–352. https://doi.org/10.5465/amj.2011.0756

Albrecht, T. L., & Hall, B. 'J.' (1991). Facilitating talk about new ideas: The role of personal relationships in organizational innovation. *Communication Monographs*, 58(3), 273–288. https://doi.org/10.1080/03637759109376230

Bales, R. F. (1950). *Interaction Process Analysis: A Method for the Study of Small Groups* (pp. xi, 203). Addison-Wesley.

Balkundi, P., Barsness, Z., & Michael, J. H. (2009). Unlocking the influence of leadership network structures on team conflict and viability. *Small Group Research*, 40(3), 301–322. https://doi.org/10.1177/1046496409333404

Balkundi, P., & Harrison, D.A. (2006). Ties, leaders, and time in teams: Strong inference about network structure's effects on team viability and performance. *Academy of Management*, 49(1), 49–68. https://doi.org/10.5465/amj.2006.20785500

Balkundi, P., & Kilduff, M. (2006). The ties that lead: A social network approach to leadership. *Leadership Quarterly*, 17(4), 419–439. https://doi.org/10.1016/j.leaqua.2006.01.001

Bell, S. T., Brown, S. G., Colaneri, A., & Outland, N. (2018). Team composition and the ABCs of teamwork. *American Psychologist*, 73(4), 349–362. https://doi.org/10.1037/amp0000305

Burke, C. S., Stagl, K. C., Klein, C., Goodwin, G. F., Salas, E., & Halpin, S. M. (2006). What type of leadership behaviors are functional in teams? A meta-analysis. *Leadership Quarterly*, 17(3),

288–307. https://doi.org/10.1016/J.LEAQUA.2006.02.007

Carnabuci, G., Emery, C., & Brinberg, D. (2018). Emergent leadership structures in informal groups: A dynamic, cognitively informed network model. *Organization Science*, *29*(1), 118–133. https://doi.org/10.1287/orsc.2017.1171

Carson, J. B., Tesluk, P. E., & Marrone, J. A. (2007). Shared leadership in teams: An investigation of antecedent conditions and performance. *Academy of Management Journal*, *50*(5), 1217–1234. https://doi.org/10.5465/amj.2007.20159921

Carson, J., Tesluk, P. E., & Marrone, J. A. (2016). Shared leadership in teams: An investigation of antecedent conditions and performance. *IEEE Engineering Management Review*. https://doi.org/10.5465/AMJ.2007.20159921

Carter, D. R., DeChurch, L. A., Braun, M. T., & Contractor, N. S. (2015). Social network approaches to leadership: An integrative conceptual review. *Journal of Applied Psychology*, *100*(3), 597–622. https://doi.org/10.1037/a0038922

Carter, D. R., Cullen-Lester, K. L., Jones, J. M., Gerbasi, A., Chrobot-Mason, D., & Nae, E. Y. (2020). Functional leadership in interteam contexts: Understanding 'what' in the context of why? where? when? and who? *Leadership Quarterly*, *31*(1), 101378. https://doi.org/10.1016/j.leaqua.2019.101378

Chiocchio, F., & Essiembre, H. (2009). Cohesion and performance: A meta-analytic review of disparities between project teams, production teams, and service teams. *Small Group Research*, *40*(4), 382–420. https://doi.org/10.1177/1046496409335103

Contractor, N. S., DeChurch, L. A., Carson, J., Carter, D. R., & Keegan, B. (2012). The topology of collective leadership. *Leadership Quarterly*, *23*(6), 994–1011. https://doi.org/10.1016/j.leaqua.2012.10.010

Currie, G., & Spyridonidis, D. (2019). Sharing leadership for diffusion of innovation in professionalized settings. *Human Relations*, *72*(7), 1209–1233. https://doi.org/10.1177/0018726718796175

DeChurch, L. A., & Mesmer-Magnus, J. R. (2010). Measuring shared team mental models: A meta-analysis. *Group Dynamics: Theory, Research, and Practice*, *14*(1), 1–14. https://doi.org/10.1037/a0017455

Denis, J. L., Langley, A., & Sergi, V. (2012). Leadership in the plural. *Academy of Management Annals*, *6*(1), 211–283. https://doi.org/10.5465/19416520.2012.667612

DeRue, D. S., & Ashford, S. J. (2010). Who will lead and who will follow? A social process of leadership identity construction in organizations. *Academy of Management Review*, *35*(4), 627–647. https://doi.org/10.5465/amr.35.4.zok627

D'Innocenzo, L., Mathieu, J. E., & Kukenberger, M. R. (2016). A meta-analysis of different forms of shared leadership–team performance relations. *Journal of Management*, *42*(7), 1964–1991. https://doi.org/10.1177/0149206314525205

Driskell, T., Salas, E., & Driskell, J. E. (2018). Teams in extreme environments: Alterations in team development and teamwork. *Human Resource Management Review*, *28*(4), 434–449. https://doi.org/10.1016/j.hrmr.2017.01.002

Edmondson, A. (1999). Psychological safety and learning behavior in work teams. *Administrative Science Quarterly*, *44*(2), 350–383. https://doi.org/10.2307/2666999

Emerson, R.M. (1962). Power-dependence relations. *American Sociological Review*, *27*(1), 31–41. https://doi.org/10.2307/2089716

Ensley, M. D., Hmieleski, K. M., & Pearce, C. L. (2006). The importance of vertical and shared leadership within new venture top management teams: Implications for the performance of start-ups. *Leadership Quarterly*, *17*(3), 217–231. https://doi.org/10.1016/j.leaqua.2006.02.002

Erez, A., Lepine, J. A., & Elms, H. (2002). Effects of rotated leadership and peer evaluation on the functioning and effectiveness of self-managed teams: A quasi-experiment. *Personnel Psychology*, *55*(4), 929–948. https://doi.org/10.1111/j.1744-6570.2002.tb00135.x

Erkutlu, H. (2012). The impact of organizational culture on the relationship between shared leadership and team proactivity. *Team Performance Management: An International Journal*, *18*(1/2), 102–119. https://doi.org/10.1108/13527591211207734

Fleishman, E. A. (1953). Leadership climate, human relations training, and supervisory behavior. *Personnel Psychology*, *6*(2), 205–222. https://doi.org/10.1111/j.1744-6570.1953.tb01040.x

Fleishman, E. A., & Harris, E. F. (1962). Patterns of leadership behavior related to employee grievances and turnover. *Personnel Psychology*, *15*(2), 43–56. https://doi.org/10.1111/j.1744-6570.1962.tb01845.x

Fleishman, E. A., Mumford, M. D., Zaccaro, S. J., Levin, K. Y., Korotkin, A. L., & Hein, M. B. (1991). Taxonomic efforts in the description of leader behavior: A synthesis and functional interpretation. *Leadership Quarterly*, *2*(4), 245–287. https://doi.org/10.1016/1048-9843(91)90016-U

Frazier, M. L., Fainshmidt, S., Klinger, R. L., Pezeshkan, A., & Vracheva, V. (2017). Psychological safety: A meta-analytic review and extension. *Personnel Psychology*, *70*(1), 113–165. https://doi.org/10.1111/peps.12183

Friedrich, T. L., Vessey, W. B., Schuelke, M. J., Ruark, G. A., & Mumford, M. D. (2009). A framework for understanding collective leadership: The selective utilization of leader and team expertise within networks. *Leadership Quarterly*, *20*(6), 933–958. https://doi.org/10.1016/j.leaqua.2009.09.008

Grossman, R., Nolan, K., Rosch, Z., Mazer, D., & Salas, E. (2021). The team cohesion-performance relationship: A meta-analysis exploring measurement approaches and the changing team landscape. *Organizational Psychology Review*, 20413866211041156. https://doi.org/10.1177/20413866211041157

Hackman, J. R. (1987). The design of work teams. In J. W. Lorsch (Ed.), *Handbook of Organizational Behavior* (pp. 315–42). Prentice-Hall.

Hackman, J. R. (2012). From causes to conditions in group research. *Journal of Organizational Behavior*, 33(3), 428–444. https://doi.org/10.1002/job.1774

Hackman, J. R., & Morris, C. G. (1975). Group tasks, group interaction process, and group performance effectiveness: A review and proposed integration. In L. Berkowitz (Ed.), *Advances in Experimental Social Psychology* (Vol. 8, pp. 45–99). Academic Press. https://doi.org/10.1016/S0065-2601(08)60248-8

Hoch, J. E. (2013). Shared leadership and innovation: The role of vertical leadership and employee integrity. *Journal of Business and Psychology*, 28(2), 159–174. https://doi.org/10.1007/s10869-012-9273-6

Hollenbeck, J. R., DeRue, D. S., & Nahrgang, J. D. (2015). The opponent process theory of leadership succession. *Organizational Psychology Review*, 5(4), 333–363. https://doi.org/10.1177/2041386614530606

Homan, A. C., Gündemir, S., Buengeler, C., & van Kleef, G. A. (2020). Leading diversity: Towards a theory of functional leadership in diverse teams. *Journal of Applied Psychology*, 105(10), 1101. https://doi.org/10.1037/apl0000482

Ilgen, D. R., Hollenbeck, J. R., Johnson, M., & Jundt, D. (2005). Teams in organizations: From input-process-output models to IMOI models. *Annual Review of Psychology*, 56(1), 517–543. https://doi.org/10.1146/annurev.psych.56.091103.070250

Judge, T. A., Bono, J. E., Ilies, R., & Gerhardt, M. W. (2002). Personality and leadership: A qualitative and quantitative review. *Journal of Applied Psychology*, 87(4), 765–780. https://doi.org/10.1037/0021-9010.87.4.765

Katz, N., Lazer, D., Arrow, H., & Contractor, N. (2004). Network theory and small groups. *Small Group Research*, 35(3), 307–332. https://doi.org/10.1177/1046496404264941

Klein, K. J., Ziegert, J. C., Knight, A. P., & Xiao, Y. (2004). A leadership system for emergency action teams: Rigid hierarchy and dynamic flexibility. *Academy of Management Journal*, 47(6), 1–55.

Kozlowski, S. W. J. (2018). Enhancing the effectiveness of work groups and teams: A reflection. *Perspectives on Psychological Science*, 13(2), 205–212. https://doi.org/10.1177/1745691617697078

Kozlowski, S., & Ilgen, D. R. (2006). Enhancing the effectiveness of work groups and teams. *Psychological Science in the Public Interest: A Journal of the American Psychological Society*. https://doi.org/10.1111/j.1529-1006.2006.00030.x

LePine, J. A., Piccolo, R. F., Jackson, C. L., Mathieu, J. E., & Saul, J. R. (2008). A meta-analysis of teamwork processes: Tests of a multidimensional model and relationships with team effectiveness criteria. *Personnel Psychology*, 61(2), 273–307. https://doi.org/10.1111/j.1744-6570.2008.00114.x

Liu, S., Hu, J., Li, Y., Wang, Z., & Lin, X. (2014). Examining the cross-level relationship between shared leadership and learning in teams: Evidence from China. *Leadership Quarterly*, 25(2), 282–295.

Marks, M. A., Mathieu, J. E., & Zaccaro, S. J. (2001). A temporally based framework and taxonomy of team processes. *Academy of Management Review*, 26(3), 356–376. https://doi.org/10.5465/amr.2001.4845785

Marrone, J. A. (2010). Team boundary spanning: A multilevel review of past research and proposals for the future. *Journal of Management*, 36(4), 911–940. https://doi.org/10.1177/0149206309353945

Mathieu, J., Maynard, M. T., Rapp, T., & Gilson, L. (2008). Team effectiveness 1997–2007: A review of recent advancements and a glimpse into the future. *Journal of Management*, 34(3), 410–476. https://doi.org/10.1177/0149206308316061

Mayo, M., Meindl, J. R., & Pastor, J.-C. (2002). Shared leadership in work teams: A social network approach. In C. L. Perace & J. A. Conger (Eds.), *Shared Leadership: Reframing the Hows and Whys of Leadership* (pp. 193–214). Sage. https://doi.org/10.4135/9781452229539

McGrath, J. E. 1962. *Leadership Behavior: Some Requirements for Leadership Training*. US Civil Service Commission.

McGrath, J. E., Arrow, H., & Berdahl, J. L. (2000). The study of groups: Past, present, and future. *Personality and Social Psychology Review*, 4(1), 95–105. https://doi.org/10.1207/S15327957PSPR0401_8

Mehra, A., Smith, B. R., Dixon, A. L., & Robertson, B. (2006). Distributed leadership in teams: The network of leadership perceptions and team performance. *Leadership Quarterly*, 17(3), 232–245. https://doi.org/10.1016/j.leaqua.2006.02.003

Morgeson, F. P., DeRue, D. S., & Karam, E. P. (2010). Leadership in teams: A functional approach to understanding leadership structures and processes. *Journal of Management*, 36(1), 5–39. https://doi.org/10.1177/0149206309347376

Morgeson, F. P., Mitchell, T. R., & Liu, D. (2015). Event system theory: An event-oriented approach to the organizational sciences. *Academy of Management Review*, 40(4), 515–537. https://doi.org/10.5465/amr.2012.0099

Nicolaides, V. C., LaPort, K. A., Chen, T. R., Tomassetti, A. J., Weis, E. J., Zaccaro, S. J., & Cortina, J. M. (2014). The shared leadership of teams: A meta-analysis of proximal, distal, and moderating relationships. *Leadership Quarterly*, 25(5), 923–942. https://doi.org/10.1016/j.leaqua.2014.06.006

Niler, A. A., Mesmer-Magnus, J. R., Larson, L. E., Plummer, G., DeChurch, L. A., & Contractor, N. S. (2021). Conditioning team cognition: A meta-analysis. *Organizational Psychology Review*, 11(2), 144–174. https://doi.org/10.1177/2041386620972112

Osborn, R. N., Hunt, J. G., & Jauch, L. R. (2002). Toward a contextual theory of leadership. *Leadership Quarterly*, 13(6), 797–837. https://doi.org/10.1016/S1048-9843(02)00154-6

Park, G., & DeShon, R. P. (2018). Effects of group-discussion integrative complexity on intergroup relations in a social dilemma. *Organizational Behavior and Human Decision Processes*, 146, 62–75. https://doi.org/10.1016/j.obhdp.2018.04.001

Pearce, C. L., & Conger, J. A. (2002). *Shared Leadership: Reframing the Hows and Whys of Leadership*. Sage.

Pearce, C. L., & Sims Jr, H. P. (2002). Vertical versus shared leadership as predictors of the effectiveness of change management teams: An examination of aversive, directive, transactional, transformational, and empowering leader behaviors. *Group Dynamics: Theory, Research, and Practice*, 6(2), 172. https://doi.org/10.1037/1089-2699.6.2.172

Pielstick, C. D. (2000). Formal vs informal leading: A comparative analysis. *Journal of Leadership Studies*, 7(3), 99–114. https://doi.org/10.1177/107179190000700307

Sayama, H. (2015). *Introduction to the Modeling and Analysis of Complex Systems*. State University of New York. http://opensuny.org/

Seers, A., Keller, T., & Wilkerson, J. M. (2003). Can team members share leadership. In C. L. Pearce & J. A. Conger (Eds.), *Shared Leadership: Reframing the Hows and Whys of Leadership* (pp. 77–102). Sage. https://dx.doi.org/10.4135/9781452229539

Small, E. E., & Rentsch, J. R. (2011). Shared leadership in teams. *Journal of Personnel Psychology*, 9(4), 203–211. https://doi.org/10.1027/1866-5888/a000017

Sparrowe, R. T. (2014). Leadership and social networks: Initiating a different dialog. In D. V. Day (Ed.), *The Oxford Handbook of Leadership and Organizations* (pp. 434–454). Oxford University Press.

Stogdill, R. M., Goode, O. S., & Day, D. R. (1963). The leader behavior of corporation presidents. *Personnel Psychology*, 16(2), 127–132. https://doi.org/10.1111/j.1744-6570.1963.tb01261.x

Sundstrom, E., De Meuse, K. P., & Futrell, D. (1990). Work teams: Applications and effectiveness. *American Psychologist*, 45(2), 120–133. https://doi.org/10.1037/0003-066X.45.2.120

Wang, D., Waldman, D., & Zhang, Z. (2014). A meta-analysis of shared leadership and team effectiveness. *Journal of Applied Psychology*. https://doi.org/10.1037/a0034531

Wheelan, S. A., & Johnston, F. (1996). The role of informal member leaders in a system containing formal leaders. *Small Group Research*, 27(1), 33–55. https://doi.org/10.1177/1046496496271002

Woolley, A. W., Gerbasi, M. E., Chabris, C. F., Kosslyn, S. M., & Hackman, J. R. (2008). Bringing in the experts: How team composition and collaborative planning jointly shape analytic effectiveness. *Small Group Research*, 39(3), 352–371. https://doi.org/10.1177/1046496408317792

Yukl, G. (2012). Effective leadership behavior: What we know and what questions need more attention. *Academy of Management Perspectives*, 26(4), 66–85. https://doi.org/10.5465/amp.2012.0088

Zaccaro, S. J., Heinen, B., & Shuffler, M. (2008). Team leadership and team effectiveness. In E. Salas, G. F. Goodwin & C. S. Burke (Eds.), *Team Effectiveness in Complex Organizations* (pp. 117–146). Routledge.

Zaccaro, S. J., Rittman, A. L., & Marks, M. A. (2001). Team leadership. *Leadership Quarterly*, 12(4), 451–483. https://doi.org/10.1016/S1048-9843(01)00093-5

Zhang, Z., & Peterson, S. J. (2011). Advice networks in teams: The role of transformational leadership and members' core self-evaluations. *Journal of Applied Psychology*, 96(5), 1004–1017. https://doi.org/10.1037/a0023254

Zohar, D., & Tenne-Gazit, O. (2008). Transformational leadership and group interaction as climate antecedents: A social network analysis. *Journal of Applied Psychology*, 93(4), 744–757. https://doi.org/10.1037/0021-9010.93.4.744

8

Followership

Teresa Almeida, Nelson Campos Ramalho and Francisco Esteves

INTRODUCTION

The best way to introduce this topic is to recall Ronald Riggio's (2020) question, 'Why followership?'. An immediate answer is that there are no leaders without followers (Hollander, 1993). However, followership's relevance goes far beyond that. This chapter will start by highlighting followership as a natural social phenomenon that has always been there; its function in balancing the expression of leadership; and its essential role in leadership-as-a-process.

An important conceptual clarification must be made upfront as to the nature of leadership/followership since it changes according to the theoretical perspective, which makes it prone to confusion. Departing from Uhl-Bien et al.'s (2014) classification, we propose that an analysis to the power dynamics (primacy of agency, and direction of influence) clarifies how leader, follower, supervisor, subordinate, leadership and followership concepts relate. Across six theoretical perspectives (i.e., from evolutionary to constructionist, Uhl-Bien et al., 2014; Bastardoz & Van Vugt, 2019, see Figure 8.1) the primacy of agency ranges from being systemic, to becoming centred on both leader and follower, independently of the formal position. Concomitantly, the direction of influence also starts by being systemic deterministic, to become downwards, upwards and, finally, horizontal. Context is also explicitly acknowledged as an important dimension within the relational perspective (e.g., Padilla et al., 2007). In light of this power dynamics, leader equals supervisor (formal leader) and follower equals subordinate across all perspectives until the informal role is considered (Uhl-Bien & Carsten, 2018), and this overlap is fully rejected in the constructionist perspective.

After taking stock, the chapter challenges some theoretical/methodological assumptions. In Figure 8.2, we present the challenged assumption, their underlying idea and, within brackets, the specific examples that we bring to discussion. To close the chapter, we identify two important limitations within followership: the lack of measures and the lack of attention to followership development in business schools.

FOLLOWERSHIP: GOING BEYOND FOLLOWERS AND FOLLOWING

Broadly taken, followership refers to the impact of followers in the leadership process (Uhl-Bien

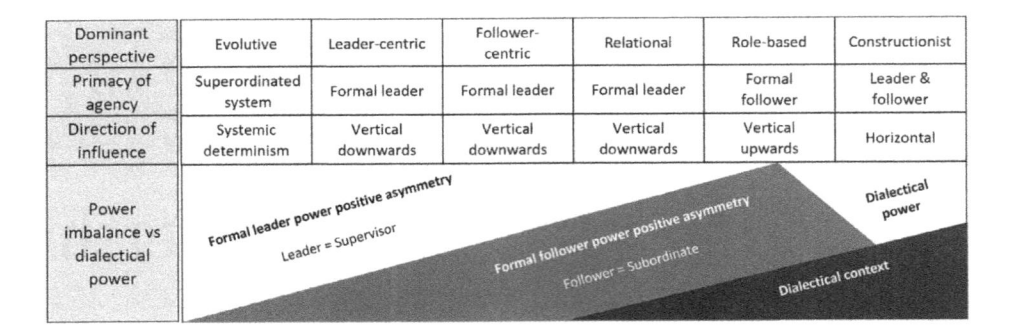

Dominant perspective	Evolutive	Leader-centric	Follower-centric	Relational	Role-based	Constructionist
Primacy of agency	Superordinated system	Formal leader	Formal leader	Formal leader	Formal follower	Leader & follower
Direction of influence	Systemic determinism	Vertical downwards	Vertical downwards	Vertical downwards	Vertical upwards	Horizontal
Power imbalance vs dialectical power	Formal leader power positive asymmetry; Leader = Supervisor		Formal follower power positive asymmetry; Follower = Subordinate			Dialectical power; Dialectical context

Figure 8.1 Followership approached from a power-based perspective

---

Theoretical/methodological assumptions

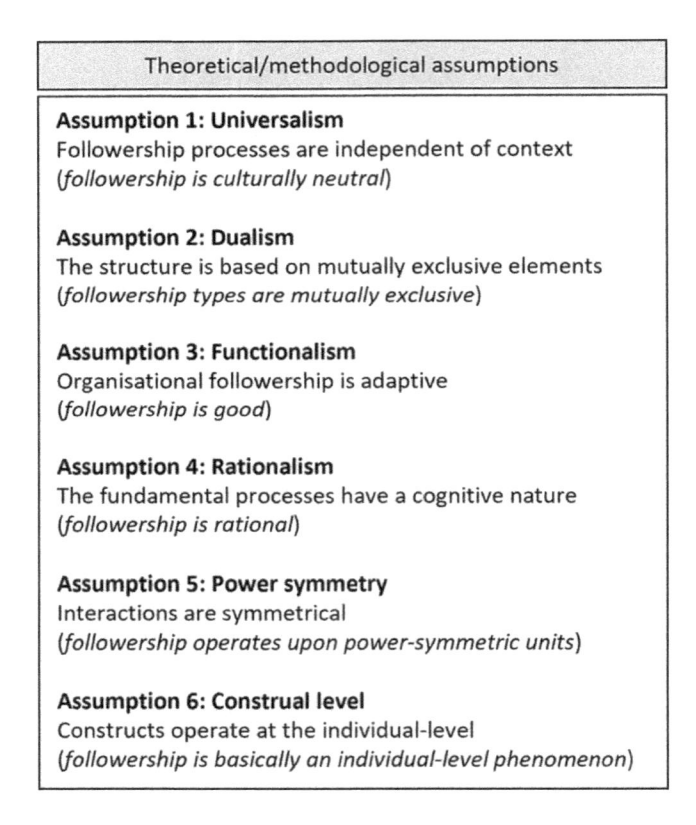

Assumption 1: Universalism
Followership processes are independent of context
(*followership is culturally neutral*)

Assumption 2: Dualism
The structure is based on mutually exclusive elements
(*followership types are mutually exclusive*)

Assumption 3: Functionalism
Organisational followership is adaptive
(*followership is good*)

Assumption 4: Rationalism
The fundamental processes have a cognitive nature
(*followership is rational*)

Assumption 5: Power symmetry
Interactions are symmetrical
(*followership operates upon power-symmetric units*)

Assumption 6: Construal level
Constructs operate at the individual-level
(*followership is basically an individual-level phenomenon*)

Figure 8.2 Some followership assumptions and examples of topics to be addressed

---

et al., 2014). This simple claim brings out two major ideas: a) leadership is not a person – it is a process; and b) followers (both actively and passively) take part in and co-shape that process (Kellerman, 2016). Although the conceptual debate on followership, its nature and impact has been gaining attention ever since Robert Kelley's seminal work in 1988, it can be considered a recent topic compared to the long history of leadership research (e.g., Baker, 2007). It is surprising, then, that something required for a process to occur has been overlooked for so long. In Uhl-Bien and Carsten's (2018, p. 211) words, *that does not mean followership is not there, or not foundational. It just means that we are not using a lens that sees it.*

Although the prevalence of followership and its importance are acknowledged, investment in followership research remains scarce compared to leadership studies. This becomes clear when searching the words *leader*, *leadership*, *follower* and *followership* as topic records in the Web of Science database.

As evidenced in Figure 8.3, the ratios found for follower:leader and followership:leadership are, respectively, 1:5 and 1:160, which reveals the gap between the two fields. Another noteworthy piece of evidence is that the ratio between leadership/leader is approximately 1, but followership/follower is well below 1. Contrasting the follower–followership and follower–leadership pairs suggests that followers have been overwhelmingly studied within the larger leadership framework. Furthermore, over 60 per cent of the studies on followership have been developed since 2017, indicating its relative recency. However, followership has always been around us. This is clearly supported if we look beyond any conceptual debate and see followership as a social phenomenon. According to this idea, under certain conditions, a group accepts the influence of another agent – that is, a leader (Bastardoz & Van Vugt, 2019) – which is considered the best strategy to pursue collective goals. So, accepting to follow a leader has emerged as an evolutionary adaptive strategy (Kellerman, 2012; Van Vugt, 2006) which is supported by studies showing these dynamics across species (Bastardoz & Van Vugt, 2019; Smith, 2017).

FOLLOWER(SHIP) BALANCES LEADER(SHIP)

As an adaptive process, followership carries a critical purpose: regulating the leader's behaviour to ensure that he or she works to accomplish the group's goals (Bastardoz & Van Vugt, 2019). An extreme example of the group working together to ensure they only keep the leader as long as it is the right agent occurs in a beehive. According to Vollet-Neto et al. (2017), when the queen bee no longer serves the beehive's interests because reproduction became defective, she is killed by the group and replaced by another queen.

We should then acknowledge that followers can develop tactics or strategies to influence those in formal power positions (Van Vugt & von Rueden, 2020). This means that the asymmetric power relation assumed in leadership (Collinson, 2005) can be rebalanced once followers engage in counter-power behaviours (Yukl & Gardner, 2020).

In contrast to other contexts, such as those with animals where natural leadership processes emerge, human leadership does not necessarily stem from natural group processes or sanctioning. In human leadership, even when the group indicates the leaders, it is possible that such leaders, at a given time, no longer act in line with the group's interests (Burke, 2006). Still, unlike bees, the group might not be able to dethrone such a leader.

So, it is essential to develop mechanisms that allow to control and express discontentment when the leader does not perform well. This idea is not new, and many examples of the importance of

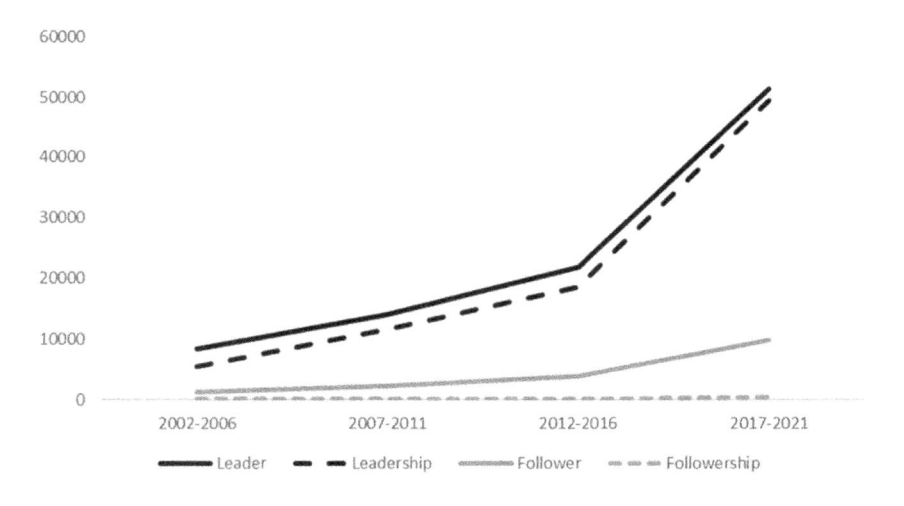

Figure 8.3 Evolution of publications

curbing the leaders' behaviours have been fully described, such as when Winston Churchill's wife rescued him when he started to derail by confronting him with truths that others would not dare (Hyde, 2018). This idea restores a very old, universal and institutional mechanism aimed to prevent destructive behaviours by those in power: the jester (Otto, 2007). Entertaining the court was but a means to fulfil a much more important purpose: to mirror the truth, in the form of satire, about the behaviour of those in power and their surroundings. These are but some examples that show the relevance of not leading alone. When we think about these dynamics at work, shouldn't followership be in charge of this?

Followership and/or Leadership?

Leadership is not leader position-exclusive, nor is followership follower position-limited. This is supported by a constructionist approach, and it can be observed when followers engage in leading behaviours (Riggio, 2014). It is due to the dynamic (and not static) imbalanced power relationship between those in leading and follower positions (Collinson, 2005) that, at some point, followers can influence leaders.

So, from a power-based process view, although there is an imbalanced relationship, the apparently powerless subordinate can always decide about his or her own behaviour, create counterpower and steer the system using uncertainty zones (Crozier & Friedberg, 1980), opening room for both downward and upward influence (Oc & Bashshur, 2013; Yukl & Tracey, 1992). Leadership is thus a play where both leaders and followers can act.

From what has been described, it is clear that we must acknowledge followers as agents in the process for both leadership and followership to occur. So, in line with the idea of the invisible leader proposed by Mary Parker Follet (1949), formal leaders and followers are expected to work together for the collective good (Riggio, 2014). As it will be described in this work, although not the pioneer (Baker, 2007), it was Kelley (1988) who gave the stage to followers as active agents. Since then, research on followership has established itself as a main perspective on its own. Two main and related reasons help explain the slow evolution of this field: 1) the word 'follower' holds a negative connotation (Kelley, 2008; Riggio, 2020); and 2) followership emerges from leadership studies, which have been traditionally leader-centric (Oc & Bashshur, 2013). This means that, for a long time, mainstream leadership studies treated followers as mere recipients (Shamir, 2007; Thoroughgood et al., 2018), which, in turn, helped to increase the negative connotation of the word follower. According to this idea, to follow is meaningless and powerless – and no one wishes to fulfil such a role (Hoption et al., 2012).

Within the evolution of perspectives, the leader-centric approaches overvalue the leader's characteristics and take them as the major influencers of the followers' attitudes, behaviours and performance (Shamir, 2007). This idea is well illustrated by trait-related approaches (Jago, 1982; Kirkpatick & Locke, 1991), and it is not difficult to understand its origin if we consider that for many years the survival of the species was associated with physical traits (Riggio & Riggio, 2010). As mentioned, followers were mere recipients, even when some approaches started to consider that the leader's behaviour should fit the type of follower (e.g., maturity level, Hersey, et al., 1979; traits, Matthews et al., 2021; Schmitt et al., 2021; or needs, De Vries et al., 2002).

Although leader-centric trait-based theories remain relevant (Zaccaro et al., 2018), a novel emphasis on followers' cognitions emerged stating followers' implicit theories on leadership should be considered (Chapter 10, Implicit leadership and followership theories). The most remarkable example of this approach is the *romance of leadership* (Meindl, et al., 1985; Meindl, 1995), which paved the way for the follower-centric perspectives. It helps explain, for example, the attribution of charisma (Bligh & Schyns, 2007) related to the mobilisation of masses (Grabo et al., 2017). Although considers the relevance of including followers in the process (Kohles et al., 2012), it does not really allow for analysis of their active role in the process as agents of influence. According to Uhl-Bien et al. (2014), we can then describe the relational view, according to which followers are part of the mutual-relational leadership process, but their role is not emphasised. For example, the dyadic perspective illustrated by the leader–member–exchange theory (LMX, Dansereau et al., 1975; Gerstner & Day, 1997) illustrates this approach. The definitive focus on followers comes with followership, which recognises (emphasises) the importance of these elements in the leadership process. It can be seen according to two lenses: the position one holds (role) or as a social process (Uhl-Bien et al., 2014).

So, followership emerged as research advanced, and academics started to see followers as a heterogeneous group where both active and passive followers can co-exist (e.g., Collinson, 2006; Kelley, 1988). Some of these classifications were developed under the role-based approach and started to 'reverse the lens' (Shamir, 2007) in leadership studies. For example, several followers' typologies, behaviours and cognitive role-orientations have been described (e.g., Carsten & Uhl-Bien, 2012; Kellerman, 2008; Sy, 2010; Tepper et al., 2001). Within this perspective, it is also possible to find an emphasis on an informal role-based approach (Uhl-Bien & Carsten, 2018) that opens the way to a promising view on leader and follower role-switching (Sy & McCoy, 2014). Moreover, a developmental perspective on followership is worth noting since people in organisations occupy formal roles that may change over time.

Overall, the role-based approach draws attention to the importance of followers as differentiated agents that can be moved by different purposes (e.g., their implicit theories, level of engagement with the leader). This idea of behavioural drivers in followership has been discussed by critical leadership studies (CLS) addressing the nature of followership (Blom & Lundgreen, 2020; Collinson, 2017; Learmonth & Morell, 2017) and is linked to another critical issue on the topic: follower's agency or volition. Once this volition is linked to the purpose of taking a leading behaviour (as an expression of the wish to follow the common good), a constructionist approach to leadership needs to be considered. In such an approach, leadership emerges from the interaction between the individuals (Uhl-Bien et al., 2014). Within this dynamic process, people grant and claim leader and follower roles in a dynamic process where roles can alternate, not being necessarily linked to formal positions (DeRue & Ashford, 2010). More recently Epitropaki et al. (2017) presented an extensive review on both leadership and followership identity processes, where they explain how the same person may create a follower or a leader identity. Another example – which comes from a different perspective, while still within a constructionist approach – focuses on how different followers' identities are developed and how they impact leadership (Collinson, 2006).

It is then possible to argue that followership theory is necessary to better understand leadership. More than that, these *are two sides of the same construct* (Uhl-Bien & Carsten, 2018, p. 197). In other words, we have moved from a leader-centric approach to a perspective where both leaders and followers are central players in the construction of the leadership process. So, leadership or followership? Isn't it just a matter of perspective?

Why (Do We Need) Followership?

As described, given its adaptive nature, followership (through followers' behaviours) should curb the leader's behaviours when they are not aligned with or when they threaten the collective good. Those behaviours can be described as destructive once the leader behaves unethically or ineffectively (Kellerman, 2012). There are many classifications of destructive behaviours, such as abusive supervision (Tepper, 2000), petty tyranny (Ashforth, 1997), toxic leadership (Lipman-Blumen, 2005), exploitative leadership (Schmid et al., 2019) and destructive leadership (Einarsen et al., 2007), among others.

Two main reasons make this phenomenon critical: its consequences and prevalence. First, destructive leaders have a great impact due to the negative consequences of their behaviours on followers, the organisation and themselves (Mackey et al., 2021; Schyns & Schilling, 2013; Tepper et al., 2006; Webster et al., 2016). Second, although studies based on the perception of abusive supervision tend to present low mean values (e.g., Ju et al., 2019; Schyns et al., 2018; Tepper, 2000), other studies show that there is an important prevalence of destructive behaviours (33.5–61 per cent) by leaders in organisations (Aasland et al., 2010). It is then reasonable to ask why followership is not acting according to its adaptive nature designed to curb destructiveness.

A possible answer is that leaders at organisations take a formal position whose continuance is not affected by followers (i.e., organisations create an artificial context where leaders do not emerge naturally), and there are no natural (and sometimes no formal) mechanisms to stop the leader's behaviours. Although adverse, this can be considered a critical context to examine followership. In such an adverse context, in which practices to balance leaders' behaviours are not easy to implement, those who resist can be seen as the ones who want to take part in a change process (Collinson, 2006). However, within this specific context, studies have been focusing on followers that enable the leader's behaviours (Lipman-Blumen, 2005; Schyns et al., 2018; Thoroughgood et al., 2012). This aligns with the toxic triangle model (Padilla et al., 2007), where destructive leadership is a process that depends on the leaders, followers and the context to occur. In line, Thoroughgood et al. (2018, p. 627) highlight the dialectical nature of destructive leadership, conceptualising it as a *dynamic, co-creational process between leaders, followers, and environments, the product of which contributes to group and organisational outcomes*. These models explain how destructive leadership is developed but do not foresee a way to stop the process. By extending followership research and considering that followers behave within a complex and complete behavioural spectrum, with different motivations, followership can be better understood and claim its importance as a powerful tool for organisations.

It is not meaningless to notice that 'why followership?' should now be taken as 'why do we need followership?'. Followership is not just relevant due to its inherent and inevitable existence; it can now be conceived as an organisational asset. And this becomes even more critical in contexts that represent a severe threat to leadership.

FOLLOWERSHIP: WHAT'S NEXT?

Assumptions pervade organisational research and, just as they lay the ground upon which theory develops and empirical research thrives, so too are these assumptions inherently limiting (Weick, 2014) since they tend to operate below the level of conscious scrutiny (Eacott, 2018). In this section, we highlight some assumptions that permeate followership research. Some echo those highlighted a decade ago by Collinson (2011) and are still waiting to be answered, while others are emerging.

These assumptions are not universally taken as there are publications that explicitly or tacitly go beyond them; however, they do tend to prevail in the field and, for such reason, it is timely to explicitly challenge them. These assumptions are: 1) followership is culturally neutral, 2) followership types are mutually exclusive, 3) followership is good, 4) followership is rational, 5) followership operates upon power-symmetric units and 6) followership is basically an individual level. There is then a call for more cross-cultural research, more complexity in profiling and conceiving followers' types and interaction, more scrutiny of perverse dynamics of followership, more focus on affective processes and more group-level design research.

Challenging Universalism: Followership Across Cultures

Because IFT are a product of cognitive schemata on the idealised behaviour of followers (Carsten et al., 2010) and these schemata must rely on the societal and normative beliefs (Ajzen & Fishbein, 2005), it is but evident that followership research benefits from taking into account the societal culture that sustains such norms. Surprisingly, this is yet under-researched in such areas as IFT (Lord et al., 2020). Novel conceptual proposals have been made – for example, the conceptual model designed by Urbach et al. (2021) that focuses on proactive work behaviour, one dimension of the followership prototype; also the exploration of epistemic dominance in followership research by Blair and Fox-Kirk (2021). There might be limits to the construct modulation as some conceptions advocate radically different followership prototypes. Zhou et al.'s (2015) scale on followership in the Chinese context may provide such an example. While items such as *I will not openly disagree with the leader* may be understood due to the *mianzi* cultural value, items such as *I will sacrifice my spare time and even my health to accomplish the tasks assigned by the leader* will raise doubts if one needs to target the construct of 'followership' or if 'obedience' can serve the purpose. This needs further clarification.

Challenging Dualism: A Dialectical View on Followership

People in general, are often assumed to behave consistently (for a critique of leadership-as-practice and interaction perspectives, see Chapter 2, Leadership and practice theories, and Chapter 3, Leadership in interaction). This assumption was fuelled by the idea that traits predict consistent behaviour across similar situations (Sherman et al., 2010). However, as Chaleff (2017) claims, evaluating a behavioural profile should not be tied to any deterministic idea. That is, the follower can choose, at each moment, which behaviour to have as human behaviour is neither deterministic nor stochastic. This goes in line with Collinson's (2006) proposal that followers, as chameleons, can develop *dramaturgical selves* (to adjust to contingencies), as well as empirical findings suggesting followers may display inconsistent behaviours (Almeida et al., 2021).

The expectation of consistency implies the notion of dichotomisation (e.g. follower/subordinate), which is one of the topics under scrutiny by the critical leadership studies. Overcoming the dichotomy and mutual exclusiveness implies a dialectical approach (Collinson, 2020) and data analysis techniques that discard this assumption, such as latent profile analysis (Coyle & Foti, 2021; Woo et al., 2018). This opens doors to mirroring ambidextrous leadership research within a followership approach, which is greatly under-explored with the exception of rare studies (e.g., Luu et al., 2018).

Challenging Functionalism: The Destructive Side of Followership

The co-production of leadership has been conceived as an adaptive mechanism because followers can add to leaders' capacity, can strengthen positive decisions and can also sanction or block the destructive ones (Carsten & Uhl-Bien, 2013; Carsten et al., 2018). Followers can be the balancing mechanism that compensates for the wrongdoing or insufficiencies of leaders (Bastardoz & Van Vugt, 2019; Chaleff, 2009) but they can also resist a good leader (if an instrumental self-interested intention takes over even at the expense of the collective good). Moreover, they can follow a destructive leader, thus enabling a destructive leadership process (Padilla et al., 2007; Thoroughgood et al., 2012).

Resisting a good leader might bring detrimental effects, such as delaying process implementation, as often reported in situations of resistance to change (Stouten et al., 2018). However, the effects of following a destructive leader are covert and undetectable until the magnitude of the destruction becomes undisguisable. Due to the lack of sanction, destructive leaders have an open way to exert their nefarious effect without intermediate red flags, such as those that would emerge from whistleblowing or contradictory voicing (Morrison, 2014), or gossiping (e.g., Dijkstra et al., 2014). Another intriguing possibility is that leaders become bad because of destructive followers' influence. This raises questions about the locus of control, accountability and countering strategies. The dark side of followership has gained ground on research (e.g., Offerman, 2004; Schyns et al., 2019; Solas, 2016; Thomas et al., 2016), but it definitely deserves greater attention.

Challenging Rationalism: Emotion-Based Followership

Emotions made a late entry in organisational research but have gained momentum since the 1990s. With a larger delay, emotions have been the least-researched mechanism underlying theorisation on leadership among the four (and has evolved from traits to include behaviour, cognition and affect) proposed by Hernandez et al. (2011).

Followership mimicked this evolution with extant research stressing followers' traits (e.g., Tepper et al., 2001), cognitions (e.g., Carsten et al., 2018) and behaviours (e.g., Ahmad et al., 2021). These are intertwined, as evidenced by Thomas Sy's (2010, p. 73) definition of IFT referring to *individuals' personal assumptions about the* **traits** *and* **behaviors** *that characterise followers* (our bold). Although much remains to be explored in these domains, the emotional dimension is clearly the most under-researched in followership. Emotional intelligence gained much attention (Martin, 2015), but this is only a facet of emotions' larger role in human behaviour. An early conceptual contribution in this line was given by Tee et al. (2013), which called attention to collective follower emotions, and also by the inspirational large scope review by Elfenbein (2016), who stressed socio-emotional followership. Although emotions have been increasingly acknowledged in organisations and leadership studies, they are mostly absent in followership studies (cf. Ashkanasy & Dorris, 2017) and their prevalence in human behaviour and collective processes calls for more research.

Challenging Power Symmetry: Differential Followership

Ever since the inception of dyadic perspectives on leadership (e.g., VDL, Liden & Graen, 1980), the focus on the relationship between leaders and followers has highlighted differential relationships (e.g. falling into an ingroup versus outgroup). Thus, being a follower does not mean the same for everyone as the consequences for falling into one or the other group are greatly dissimilar (Henderson et al., 2009). This LMX (Chapter 4, The quality of relationships) differentiation (Chen et al., 2015) has multiple and inconsistent outcomes (Buengeler et al., 2021), which have motivated much enquiry. This debate could also occur in followership studies if more attention is given to differential followership theory – that is, vertical upward influence (e.g., Xu et al., 2019) and horizontal peer-to-peer influence (e.g., Waller et al., 2016).

Challenging the Construal Level: Group-Level Followership

Followership from a role-based perspective, seen as hierarchically upwards influence (Carsten et al., 2010) or 'upwards leadership' (Crossman & Crossman, 2011), admits the possibility of a one-to-one influence process but does not preclude the collective nature of this influence. From a constructionist view, this collective nature of followership is inherent as it occurs from a mutual social influence process, characterised by granting and claiming leader and follower roles, in which collective endorsement plays a part (DeRue & Ashford, 2010). The collective nature of leadership/followership is also presented in DeRue's (2011) description of shared leadership/followership. For an extensive view on the perspective of leadership as a team function, see Chapter 7, What is 'functional' about distributed leadership in teams? Albeit this collective nature is almost a taken-for-granted in most – if not all – publications on followership, measures are not truly treated as a group-level construct.

Whenever a collective phenomenon occurs within a group (such as the emergent states resulting from a mutual influence process, as seen in followership), the group itself may become the unit of theory and analysis instead of each composing individual (Chan, 2019). An approach to this group-level measurement has been recently rehearsed by Wang (2021), who refers to team followership based on a scale of followership targeting the team (instead of 'my supervisor' has used 'my team members') but without explicit demonstration of its aggregability at the team level. A consensus approach can also be adopted by having teams discussing followership-related constructs and providing a single common answer (Quigley et al., 2007). Still, the conceptual, theoretical and methodological advances made in team-level research lay the ground for a promising future group-level followership research.

Within this discussion it is worth noting that, once we conceive subgroups inside teams, we must also consider these subgroups and their impact on leaders, the organisation and how the subgroups differentially interact to produce followership. Alongside LMX differentiation, member–member exchange (MMX) differentiation or team-member exchange (TMX, in line with Seers, 1989) may claim a more central place in followership research.

Adding to these assumptions, there are two visible limitations within the followership field of research and application: 1) the need for followership measures and 2) the lack of investment in followership development.

The Need for Measures

Despite the rich production of theoretical proposals in the followership field (e.g., Carsten et al., 2010; Chaleff, 2009; Collinson, 2006; Howell & Mendez, 2008; Kellerman, 2008; Kelley, 1988; Pigors, 1934; Potter & Rosenbach, 2006; Steger et al., 1982; Sy, 2010; Zaleznik, 1965) there is yet a modest number of instruments that can be used for hypothetico-deductive tests.

Most measures have been developed within the role-based approach. The most widely used scale is Kelley's (1992), which assesses the type of follower (sheep, yes-people, alienated, effective and survivors) from the product of two orthogonal axes: the level of critical/uncritical thinking crossed with activity/passivity. Later, Chaleff (2009) proposed a typology of the courageous follower that motivated a measure by Eugene Dixon, who developed a scale covering the five dimensions of courageous followers.

Within implicit followership theories (IFT), Sy (2010) developed an instrument to assess, primarily (but not exclusively), leaders' IFT comprising a followership prototype and a followership antiprototype. A novel approach to IFT was taken by Junker et al. (2016) that developed an implicit ideal follower theory scale reflecting ideal versus counter-ideal and task versus relationship axes. Another scale that developed a follower-based IFT was published by Yang et al. (2020) and it structures mirrors Sy's (2010) dimensions identifying positive and negative prototypes. Related to IFT, Carsten and Uhl-Bien (2012) presented a scale to assess the orientation for the co-production of leadership. These beliefs in leadership co-production were found to be associated with important behaviours in the followership context, such as constructive resistance, voice, obedience and upward delegation (Carsten et al., 2018).

Overall, the array of existing instruments, of which these are good examples, is already nurturing valuable hypothetic-deductive research. However, judging from the vast rich theoretical proposals, there is much room for development here.

Developing Followers in Business Schools

The ability to critically analyse every single 'truth' is the watermark of a scientific ethos. The recurrent production of self-critique scholarly publications targeting the schools themselves is but proof of this scientific ethos. However, in leadership studies, normative pressures go hand-in-hand with a functionalist view of management and, thus, leadership has claimed only a small share of critical analysis (Alvesson, 2019). So, this has been more the exception than the rule, and it is the driving force of CLS. In the recurrent ritual of criticising business schools (e.g., Bennis & O'Toole, 2005; Cheit, 1985; Collinson & Tourish, 2015; Mabey & Mayrhofer, 2015; Pfeffer & Fong, 2002), leadership training deserves a central role. For leadership development, see Chapter 14, Leadership development. The separation between leading and managing is long used to understate why being a leader outperforms being a manager, but this is a misconception (Kniffin et al., 2020). Likewise, the hidden power play that takes becoming-a-leader as evidence of a successful management student has the intrinsic cost of downgrading the status of those that became followers. As Riggio (2014, p. 16) highlighted, *in a culture where everyone wants to be a leader, and few are happy embracing the follower role, follower development is a tough sell.* Although scholars have highlighted the lack of followership training programmes (e.g., Kelley, 2008; Riggio, 2014), this situation lingers (Riggio, 2020) as the topic is seemingly not yet being taken seriously, especially because, for many, followership is common sense, and everyone allegedly knows how to follow (Agho, 2009). Followership theory is showing otherwise, and business schools gain from giving it due attention.

CONCLUSION

Summing up, followership is a promising field of research and application – not only because it is building momentum, but also because theory may benefit from challenging many assumptions or highlighting blind spots, often unnoticed in literature. Additionally, it opens the way to start crossing research fields. Just to name a few examples, defying the dualistic nature of followership invites an identity formation approach (e.g., Larsson & Nielsen, 2021). Questioning the universal nature of followership draws attention to the relevance of integrating cross-cultural studies in this field of research (Blair & Fox-Kirk, 2021). The study of diversity can be approached from a TMX approach. Power-focused research may also offer explanatory mechanisms for good and bad followership.

If the assumptions explored are proven to be faulty, and more attention is given to the identified limitations, then future research may conclude that: a cross-cultural view cast new light upon the variations and limits of followership as a construct; followership types already integrated complex behaviours; destructive followership was documented and strategies devising its prevention were successfully designed; emotional processes at group level played a critical role in explaining followership; followership theorising entailed complex power-asymmetric dynamics; followership was tackled from multilevel theorising and testing; hypothetic-deductive approaches and measuring made a difference; and business schools gained from giving followership its true status, both in their research and particularly in teaching. Business schools may notice that followership training is not the same as training to follow.

REFERENCES

Aasland, M., Skogstad, A., Notelaers, G., Nielsen, M., & Einarsen, S. (2010). The prevalence of destructive leadership behaviour. *British Journal of Management, 21*(2), 438–452.

Agho, A. (2009). Perspectives of senior-level executives on effective followership and leadership. *Journal of Leadership & Organizational Studies, 16*(2), 159–166.

Ahmad, M., Klotz, A., & Bolino, M. (2021). Can good followers create unethical leaders? How follower citizenship leads to leader moral licensing and unethical behavior. *Journal of Applied Psychology, 106*(9), 1374–1390.

Ajzen, I. & Fishbein, M. (2005). The influence of attitudes on behavior. In D. Albarracín, B. T. Johnson & M. P. Zanna (Eds.), *The Handbook of Attitudes* (pp. 173–221). Lawrence Erlbaum.

Almeida, T., Ramalho, N., & Esteves, F. (2021). Can you be a follower even when you do not follow the leader? Yes, you can. *Leadership, 17*(3), 336–364.

Alvesson, M. (2019). Waiting for Godot: Eight major problems in the odd field of leadership studies. *Leadership, 15*(1), 27–43.

Ashforth, B. (1997). Petty tyranny in organizations: A preliminary examination of antecedents and consequences. *Canadian Journal of Administrative Sciences/Revue Canadienne des Sciences de l'Administration, 14*(2), 126–140.

Ashkanasy, N., & Dorris, A. (2017). Emotions in the workplace. *Annual Review of Organizational Psychology and Organizational Behavior, 4*, 67–90.

Baker, S. (2007). Followership: The theoretical foundation of a contemporary construct. *Journal of Leadership & Organizational Studies, 14*(1), 50–60.

Bastardoz, N., & Van Vugt, M. (2019). The nature of followership: Evolutionary analysis and review. *Leadership Quarterly, 30*(1), 81–95.

Bennis, W., & O'Toole, J. (2005). How business schools have lost their way. *Harvard Business Review, 83*(5), 96–104.

Blair, A., & Fox-Kirk, W. (2021). The colonization of cross-cultural leadership and followership research. In Y. Tolstikov-Mast, F. Bieri & J. L. Walker (Eds.), *Handbook of International and Cross-Cultural Leadership Research Processes: Perspectives, Practice, Instruction.* Routledge. https://doi.org/10.4324/9781003003380-17

Bligh, M., & Schyns, B. (2007). Leading question: The romance lives on: Contemporary issues surrounding the romance of leadership. *Leadership, 3*(3), 343–360.

Blom, M., & Lundgren, M. (2020). The (in)voluntary follower. *Leadership, 16*(2), 163–179.

Buengeler, C., Piccolo, R., & Locklear, L. (2021). LMX differentiation and group outcomes: A framework and review drawing on group diversity insights. *Journal of Management*, *47*(1), 260–287.

Burke, R. (2006). Why leaders fail: Exploring the dark side. In R. Burke & C. Cooper (Eds.), *Inspiring Leaders* (pp. 239–248). London: Routledge.

Carsten, M., & Uhl-Bien, M. (2012). Follower beliefs in the co-production of leadership: Examining upward communication and the moderating role of context. *Zeitschrift Fur Psychologie/Journal of Psychology*, *220*(4), 210–220.

Carsten, M., & Uhl-Bien, M. (2013). Ethical followership: An examination of followership beliefs and crimes of obedience. *Journal of Leadership & Organizational Studies*, *20*(1), 49–61.

Carsten, M., Uhl-Bien, M., & Huang, L. (2018). Leader perceptions and motivation as outcomes of followership role orientation and behavior. *Leadership*, *14*(6), 731–756.

Carsten, M., Uhl-Bien, M., West, B., Patera, J. & McGregor, R. (2010). Exploring social constructions of followership: A qualitative study. *Leadership Quarterly*, *21*(3), 543–562.

Chaleff, I. (2009). *The Courageous Follower: Standing Up to and for Our Leaders* (3rd edn). Berrett-Koehler.

Chaleff, I. (2017). In praise of followership style assessments. *Journal of Leadership Studies*, *10*(3), 45–48.

Chan, D. (2019). Team-level constructs. *Annual Review of Organizational Psychology and Organizational Behavior*, *6*, 325–348. https://doi.org/10.1146/annurev-orgpsych-012218-015117

Cheit, E. (1985). Business schools and their critics. *California Management Review*, *27*(3), 43–62.

Chen, X., He, W., & Weng, L. (2015). What is wrong with treating followers differently? The basis of leader–member exchange differentiation matters. *Journal of Management*, *44*(3), 946–971.

Collinson, D. (2005). Dialectics of leadership. *Human Relations*, *58*(11), 1419–1442.

Collinson, D. (2006). Rethinking followership: A post-structuralist analysis of follower identities. *Leadership Quarterly*, *17*(2), 179–189.

Collinson, D. (2011). Critical leadership studies. In A. Bryman, D. Collinson, K. Grint, B. Jackson & M. Uhl Bien (Eds.), *Handbook of Leadership Studies* (pp. 181–194) Sage.

Collinson, D. (2017). Critical leadership studies: A response to Learmonth and Morrell. *Leadership*, *13*(3), 272–284.

Collinson, D. (2020). 'Only connect!': Exploring the critical dialectical turn in leadership studies. *Organization Theory*, *1*, 1–22. https://doi.org/10.1177/2631787720913878

Collinson, D., & Tourish, D. (2015). Teaching leadership critically: New directions for leadership pedagogy. *Academy of Management Learning & Education*, *14*(4), 576–594.

Coyle, P., & Foti, R. (2021). How do leaders vs followers construct followership? A field study of implicit followership theories and work-related affect using latent profile analysis. *Journal of Leadership & Organizational Studies*, 15480518211053529. https://doi.org/10.1177/15480518211053529

Crossman, B., & Crossman, J. (2011). Conceptualising followership: A review of the literature. *Leadership*, *7*(4), 481–497.

Crozier, M., & Friedberg, E. (1980). *Actors and Systems: The Politics of Collective Action*. University of Chicago Press.

Dansereau, F. Jr, Graen, G., & Haga, W. (1975). A vertical dyad linkage approach to leadership within formal organizations: A longitudinal investigation of the role making process. *Organizational Behavior and Human Performance*, *13*(1), 46–78.

De Vries, R. E., Roe, R. A., & Taillieu, T. C. (2002). Need for leadership as a moderator of the relationships between leadership and individual outcomes. *Leadership Quarterly*, *13*(2), 121–137.

DeRue, D. S. (2011). Adaptive leadership theory: Leading and following as a complex adaptive process. *Research in Organizational Behavior*, *31*, 125–150. https://doi.org/10.1016/j.riob.2011.09.007

DeRue, D., & Ashford, S. (2010). Who will lead and who will follow?: A social process of leadership identity construction in organizations. *Academy of Management Review*, *35*(4), 627–647.

Dijkstra, M., Beersma, B., & van Leeuwen, J. (2014). Gossiping as a response to conflict with the boss: Alternative conflict management behavior? *International Journal of Conflict Management*, *25*(4), 431–454.

Eacott, S. (2018). *Beyond Leadership: A Relational Approach to Organizational Theory in Education*. Springer.

Einarsen, S., Aasland, M., & Skogstad, A. (2007). Destructive leadership behaviour: A definition and conceptual model. *Leadership Quarterly*, *18*(3), 207–216.

Elfenbein, H. (2016). Emotional division-of-labor: A theoretical account. *Research in Organizational Behavior*, *36*, 1–26. https://doi.org/10.1016/j.riob.2016.11.001

Epitropaki, O., Kark, R., Mainemelis, C., & Lord, R. (2017). Leadership and followership identity processes: A multilevel review. *Leadership Quarterly*, *28*(1), 104–129.

Gerstner, C., & Day, D. (1997). Meta-Analytic review of leader–member exchange theory: Correlates and construct issues. *Journal of Applied Psychology*, *82*(6), 827–844.

Grabo, A., Spisak, B., & van Vugt, M. (2017). Charisma as signal: An evolutionary perspective on charismatic leadership. *Leadership Quarterly*, *28*(4), 473–485.

Henderson, D., Liden, R., Glibkowski, B., & Chaudhry, A. (2009). LMX differentiation: A multilevel review and examination of its antecedents and outcomes. *Leadership Quarterly, 20*(4), 517–534.

Hernandez, M., Eberly, M., Avolio, B., & Johnson, M. (2011). The loci and mechanisms of leadership: Exploring a more comprehensive view of leadership theory. *Leadership Quarterly, 22*(6), 1165–1185.

Hersey, P., Blanchard, K., & Natemeyer, W. (1979). Situational leadership, perception, and the impact of power. *Group & Organization Studies, 4*(4), 418–428.

Hollander, E. (1993). Legitimacy, power, and influence: A perspective on relational features of leadership. In M. Chemers & R. Ayman (Eds.), *Leadership Theory and Research: Perspectives and Directions* (pp. 29–47). Academic Press.

Hoption, C., Christie, A., & Barling, J. (2012). Submitting to the follower label. *Zeitschrift für Psychologie, 220*(4), 221–230.

Howell, J., & Mendez, M. (2008). Three perspectives on followership. In R. Riggio, I. Chaleff & J. Lipman-Blumen (Eds.), *The Art of Followership: How Great Followers Create Great Leaders and Organizations* (pp. 25–40). Jossey-Bass.

Hyde, G. (2018). Influential partnerships: A possible role for a modern-day court jester. In P. Garrard (Ed.), *The Leadership Hubris Epidemic* (pp. 179–192). Palgrave Macmillan.

Jago, A. (1982). Leadership: Perspectives in theory and research. *Management Science, 28*(3), 315–336.

Ju, D., Huang, M., Liu, D., Qin, X., Hu, Q., & Chen, C. (2019). Supervisory consequences of abusive supervision: An investigation of sense of power, managerial self-efficacy, and task-oriented leadership behavior. *Organizational Behavior and Human Decision Processes, 154*, 80–95. https://doi.org/10.1016/j.obhdp.2019.09.003

Junker, N., Stegmann, S., Braun, S., & Van Dick, R. (2016). The ideal and the counter-ideal follower: Advancing implicit followership theories. *Leadership & Organization Development Journal, 37*(8), 1205–1222.

Kellerman, B. (2008). *Followership: How Followers are Creating Change and Changing Leaders*. Harvard Business School Press.

Kellerman, B. (2012). *The End of Leadership*. Harper Business.

Kellerman, B. (2016). Leadership: It's a system, not a person! *Daedalus, 145*(3), 83–94.

Kelley, R. (1988). In praise of followers. *Harvard Business Review, 66*(6), 141–148.

Kelley, R. (1992). *The Power of Followership: How to Create Leaders People want to Follow and Followers who Lead Themselves*. Doubleday.

Kelley, R. (2008). Rethinking followership. In R. Riggio, I. Chaleff & J. Lipman-Blumen (Eds.), *The Art of Followership: How Great Followers Create Great Leaders and Organizations* (pp. 5–16). Jossey-Bass.

Kirkpatrick, S., & Locke, E. (1991). Leadership: Do traits matter? *Academy of Management Perspectives, 5*(2), 48–60.

Kniffin, K., Detert, J., & Leroy, H. (2020). On leading and managing: Synonyms or separate (and unequal)? *Academy of Management Discoveries, 6*(4), 544–571.

Kohles, J. C., Bligh, M. C., & Carsten, M. K. (2012). A follower-centric approach to the vision integration process. *Leadership Quarterly, 23*(3), 476–487.

Larsson, M., & Nielsen, M. F. (2021). The risky path to a followership identity: From abstract concept to situated reality. *International Journal of Business Communication, 58*(1), 3–30.

Learmonth, M., & Morrell, K. (2017). Is critical leadership studies 'critical'? *Leadership, 13*(3), 257–271.

Liden, R., & Graen, G. (1980). Generalizability of the vertical dyad linkage model of leadership. *Academy of Management Journal, 23*(3), 451–465.

Lipman-Blumen, J. (2005). *The Allure of Toxic Leaders: Why We Follow Destructive Bosses and Corrupt Politicians – And How We Can Survive Them*. Oxford University Press.

Lord, R., Epitropaki, O., Foti, R., & Hansbrough, T. (2020). Implicit leadership theories, implicit followership theories, and dynamic processing of leadership information. *Annual Review of Organizational Psychology and Organizational Behavior, 7*, 49–74.

Luu, T., Rowley, C., & Dinh, K. (2018). Enhancing the effect of frontline public employees' individual ambidexterity on customer value co-creation. *Journal of Business & Industrial Marketing, 33*(4), 506–522.

Mabey, C., & Mayrhofer, W. (Eds.) (2015). *Developing Leadership: Questions Business Schools Don't Ask*. Sage.

Mackey, J., Ellen III, B., McAllister, C., & Alexander, K. (2021). The dark side of leadership: A systematic literature review and meta-analysis of destructive leadership research. *Journal of Business Research, 132*, 705–718. https://doi.org/10.1016/j.jbusres.2020.10.037

Martin, R. (2015). A review of the literature of the followership since 2008: The importance of relationships and emotional intelligence. *Sage Open, 5*(4), 1–9.

Matthews, S. H., Kelemen, T. K., & Bolino, M. C. (2021). How follower traits and cultural values influence the effects of leadership. *Leadership Quarterly, 32*(1), 101497.

Meindl, J. (1995). The romance of leadership as a follower-centric theory: A social constructionist approach. *Leadership Quarterly, 6*(3), 329–341.

Meindl, J., Ehrlich, S., & Dukerich, J. (1985). The romance of leadership. *Administrative Science Quarterly*, *30*(1), 78–102.

Morrison, E. (2014). Employee voice and silence. *Annual Review of Organizational Psychology and Organizational Behavior*, *1*(1), 173–197.

Oc, B., & Bashshur, M. (2013). Followership, leadership and social influence. *Leadership Quarterly*, *24*(6), 919–934.

Offerman, L. (2004). When followers become toxic. *Harvard Business Review*, *82*(1), 54–60.

Otto, B. (2007). *Fools are Everywhere: The Court Jester Around the World*. University of Chicago Press.

Padilla, A., Hogan, R., & Kaiser, R. (2007). The toxic triangle: Destructive leaders, susceptible followers, and conducive environments. *Leadership Quarterly*, *18*(3), 176–194.

Parker Follett, M. (1949). *Freedom and Coordination: Lectures in Business Organization*. https://mpfollett.ning.com/mpf/follett-writings

Pfeffer, J., & Fong, C. (2002). The end of business schools? Less success than meets the eye. *Academy of Management Learning & Education*, *1*(1), 78–95.

Pigors, P. (1934). Types of followers. *Journal of Social Psychology*, *5*(3), 378–383.

Potter, E., & Rosenbach, W. (2006). Followers as partners: The spirit of leadership. In W. Rosenbach & R Taylor (Eds.), *Contemporary Issues in Leadership* (pp. 153–158). Westview Press.

Quigley, N., Tekleab, A., & Tesluk, P. (2007). Comparing consensus- and aggregation-based methods of measuring team-level variables: The role of relationship conflict and conflict management processes. *Organizational Research Methods*, *10*(4), 589–608.

Riggio, H., & Riggio, R. (2010). Appearance-based trait inferences and voting: Evolutionary roots and implications for leadership. *Journal of Nonverbal Behavior*, *34*(2), 119–125.

Riggio, R. (2014). Followership research: Looking back and looking forward. *Journal of Leadership Education*, *13*(4), 15–20.

Riggio, R. (2020). Why followership? *New Directions for Student Leadership*, *167*, 15–22. https://doi.org/10.1002/yd.20395

Schmid, E., Pircher Verdorfer, A., & Peus, C. (2019). Shedding light on leaders' self-interest: theory and measurement of exploitative leadership. *Journal of Management*, *45*(4), 1401–1433.

Schmitt, A., Den Hartog, D. N., & Belschak, F. D. (2021). Understanding the initiative paradox: The interplay of leader neuroticism and follower traits in evaluating the desirability of follower proactivity. *European Journal of Work and Organizational Psychology*. https://doi.org/10.1080/1359432X.2021.1950690

Schyns, B., & Schilling, J. (2013). How bad are the effects of bad leaders? A meta-analysis of destructive leadership and its outcomes. *Leadership Quarterly*, *24*(1), 138–158.

Schyns, B., Neves, P., Wisse, B., & Knoll, M. (2018). Turning a blind eye to destructive leadership: What's wrong with leadership? In. R. Riggio (Eds.), *What's Wrong with Leadership? Improving Leadership Research and Practice* (pp. 189–206). Routledge.

Schyns, B., Wisse, B., & Sanders, S. (2019). Shady strategic behavior: Recognizing strategic followership of Dark Triad followers. *Academy of Management Perspectives*, *33*(2), 234–249.

Seers, A. (1989). Team-member exchange quality: A new construct for role-making research. *Organizational Behavior and Human Decision Processes*, *43*(1), 118–135.

Shamir, B. (2007). From passive recipients to active co-producers: Followers' roles in the leadership process. In B. Shamir, R. Pillai, M. Bligh & M. Uhl-Bien (Eds.), *Follower-centered Perspectives on Leadership: A Tribute to the Memory of James R. Meindl* (pp. 9–39). Information Age.

Sherman, R., Nave, C., & Funder, D. (2010). Situational similarity and personality predict behavioral consistency. *Journal of Personality and Social Psychology*, *99*(2), 330–343.

Smith, J. (2017). Non-human leadership. In T. K. Shackelford & V. A. Weekes-Shackelford (Eds.), *Encyclopedia of Evolutionary Social Science*. Springer International. https://doi.org/10.1007/978-3-319-16999-6_2714-1

Solas, J. (2016). The banality of bad leadership and followership. *Society and Business Review*, *11*(1), 12–23.

Steger, J., Manners, G., & Zimmerer, T. (1982). Following the leader: How to link management style to subordinate personalities. *Management Review*, *71*(10), 22–28.

Stouten, J., Rousseau, D. & deCremer, D. (2018), Successful organizational change: Integrating the management practice and scholarly literatures. *Academy of Management Annals*, *12*(2), 752–788.

Sy, T. (2010). What do you think of followers? Examining the content, structure, and consequences of implicit followership theories. *Organizational Behavior and Human Decision Processes*, *113*(2), 73–84.

Sy, T., & McCoy, T. (2014). Being both leaders and followers. In L. M. Lapierre & M. K. Carsten (Eds.), *Followership: What is it and Why do People Follow?* (1st edn, pp. 121–140). Emerald.

Tee, E., Paulsen, N., & Ashkanasy, N. (2013). Revisiting followership through a social identity perspective: The role of collective follower emotion and action. *Leadership Quarterly*, *24*(6), 902–918.

Tepper, B. (2000). Consequences of abusive supervision. *Academy of Management Journal*, *43*(2), 178–190.

Tepper, B., Duffy, M., & Shaw, J. (2001). Personality moderators of the relationship between abusive supervision and subordinates' resistance. *Journal of Applied Psychology*, *86*(5), 974–893.

Tepper, B., Uhl-Bien, M., Kohut, G., Rogelberg, S., Lockhart, D., & Ensley, M. (2006). Subordinates' resistance and managers' evaluations of subordinates' performance. *Journal of Management*, *32*(2), 185–209.

Thomas, T., Gentzler, K., & Salvatorelli, R. (2016). What is toxic followership? *Journal of Leadership Studies*, *10*(3), 62–65.

Thoroughgood, C., Padilla, A., Hunter, S., & Tate, B. (2012). The susceptible circle: A taxonomy of followers associated with destructive leadership. *Leadership Quarterly*, *23*(5), 897–917.

Thoroughgood, C., Sawyer, K., Padilla, A., & Lunsford, L. (2018). Destructive leadership: A critique of leader-centric perspectives and toward a more holistic definition. *Journal of Business Ethics*, *151*(3), 627–649.

Uhl-Bien, M., & Carsten, M. (2018). Reversing the lens in leadership: Positioning followership in the leadership construct. In I. Katz, G. Eilam-Shamir, R. Kark & Y Berson (Eds.), *Leadership Now: Reflections on the Legacy of Boas Shamir* (Monographs in Leadership and Management, Vol. 9, pp. 195–222). Emerald.

Uhl-Bien, M., Riggio, R., Lowe, K., & Carsten, M. (2014). Followership theory: A review and research agenda. *Leadership Quarterly*, *25*(1), 83–104.

Urbach, T., Den Hartog, D., Fay, D., Parker, S., & Strauss, K. (2021). Cultural variations in whether, why, how, and at what cost people are proactive: A followership perspective. *Organizational Psychology Review*, *11*(1), 3–34.

Van Vugt, M. (2006). Evolutionary origins of leadership and followership. *Personality and Social Psychology Review*, *10*(4), 354–371.

Van Vugt, M., & von Rueden, C. R. (2020). From genes to minds to cultures: Evolutionary approaches to leadership. *Leadership Quarterly*, *31*(2), 101404. https://doi.org/10.1016/j.leaqua.2020.101404

Vollet-Neto, A., Oliveira, R. C., Schillewaert, S., Alves, D. A., Wenseleers, T., Nascimento, F. S., Imperatriz-Fonseca, V. L., & Ratnieks, F. L. W. (2017). Diploid male production results in queen death in the stingless bee Scaptotrigona depilis. *Journal of Chemical Ecology*, *43*(4), 403–410.

Waller, M., Okhuysen, G., & Saghafian, M. (2016). Conceptualizing emergent states: A strategy to advance the study of group dynamics. *Academy of Management Annals*, *10*(1), 561–598.

Wang, L. (2021). The impact of narcissistic leader on subordinates and team followership: Based on 'Guanxi' perspective. *Frontiers in Psychology*, *12*, 2580. https://doi.org/10.3389/fpsyg.2021.684380

Webster, V., Brough, P., & Daly, K. (2016). Fight, flight or freeze: Common responses for follower coping with toxic leadership. *Stress and Health*, *32*(4), 346–354.

Weick, K. (2014). The work of theorizing: The context of discovery. In R. Swedberg (Ed.). *Theorizing in Social Science* (pp. 177–194). Stanford University Press.

Woo, S., Jebb, A., Tay, L., & Parrigon, S. (2018). Putting the 'person' in the center: Review and synthesis of person-centered approaches and methods in organizational science. *Organizational Research Methods*, *21*(4), 814–845.

Xu, A., Loi, R., Cai, Z., & Liden, R. (2019). Reversing the lens: How followers influence leader–member exchange quality. *Journal of Occupational and Organizational Psychology*, *92*(3), 475–497.

Yang, Y., Shi, W., Zhang, B., Song, Y., & Xu, D. (2020). Implicit followership theories from the perspective of followers. *Leadership & Organization Development Journal*, *41*(4), 581–596.

Yukl, G., & Gardner, W. (2020). *Leadership in Organizations* (9th edn). Pearson Education

Yukl, G., & Tracey, J. (1992). Consequences of influence tactics used with subordinates, peers, and the boss. *Journal of Applied Psychology*, *77*(4), 525–535.

Zaccaro, S. J., Kemp, C., & Bader, P. (2018). Leader traits and attributes. In J. Antonakis, A. T. Cianciolo & R. J. Sternberg (Eds.), *The Nature of Leadership* (3rd edn, pp. 29–55). Sage.

Zaleznik, A. (1965). The dynamics of subordinacy. *Harvard Business Review*, *43*(3), 119–131.

Zhou, W., Song, J., & Li, H. (2015). The definition, structure and measurement of followership in Chinese context. *Chinese Journal of Management*, *12*(3), 355–363.

PART 2

About: Exploring the Individual and Interpersonal Facets of Leadership

Leadership as Contextualised Personality Traits

Reinout E. de Vries,[†] Jan L. Pletzer,
Amanda M. Julian and Kimberley Breevaart

INTRODUCTION

Scholars who are interested in leadership face a bewildering task when having to select one of the many leadership models and questionnaire operationalisations (Bass & Bass, 2009; Yukl, 2012). The many available leadership models vary in a number of ways, such as the leadership characteristic that is targeted (e.g., behaviours, styles, traits, values, tactics, strategies, competencies, skills, etc.), the breadth of the model (from focusing on a single construct to a 'full range' of leadership attributes) and the target that is being rated (e.g., self-ratings, [subordinate or supervisory] observer ratings, group ratings). The task of selecting a leadership instrument is further complicated by the widespread presence of the 'jingle-jangle fallacy' in leadership research, either having the same term used for a leadership attribute that is different (jingle fallacy) or having a different term used for a leadership attribute that is the same (jangle fallacy). As an example of the latter, Mackey et al. (2021; see also Schyns and Schilling, 2013) list no fewer than 21 different terms that have been used to operationalise virtually indistinguishable destructive leadership behaviours.

Clearly, an integration of leadership models and operationalisations is called for. In the current chapter, we offer such an integration by arguing that the most important leader characteristics proposed by scholars are instances of what we will call 'contextualised leadership traits'. We define contextualised leadership traits as *the relatively stable intrapersonal structure of individual differences that are manifested through a set of influencing acts of a person – who has gained position power through a process of legitimation – towards an individual or a group of individuals*. First, the definition stresses the usual three important elements in leadership – that is, that leadership is exhibited by (1) a person who is in a 'legitimate' (but not necessarily formal) position in which they (2) influence (3) an individual or a group of individuals. Second, and important for the remainder of this chapter, the definition posits that these influencing acts are based on (4) an underlying structure of individual differences and (5) that these acts are relatively stable, two assumptions that are shared with assumptions held in personality research. Consequently, by turning to personality models, on which there is a great deal of consensus, an integration of leadership models and operationalisations can be achieved. Such an integration offers clear advantages by allowing leadership scholars to use one unifying framework to integrate past and future research, similar to the integration in personality research which has been achieved by the introduction of the Big Five (Goldberg, 1990) and its successor, the HEXACO (Ashton et al., 2014) model of personality.

In the following – second – section ('Sense-making: The case for leadership traits'), we argue that the assumptions and empirical findings in leadership research support a contextualised leadership trait approach. In the third section ('The structure of leadership traits'), we explore the dimensional space of contextualised leadership traits, arguing that these fall within the space of the six-dimensional HEXACO model of personality (Ashton & Lee, 2020; Ashton et al., 2014), and we provide some preliminary results on the self–other agreement and convergent validity of a recently constructed contextualised HEXACO instrument that measures leadership, the HEXACO-Lead (Julian, 2021). In the fourth section ('The effects of leadership traits'), we provide an overview of the most important findings with respect to leadership styles – that can be regarded as contextualised leadership traits – and their relations to leadership emergence and attitudinal and performance outcomes. Last, in the final section ('Sense-breaking: Summary and future research'), we summarise the main findings and we propose potential fruitful avenues for future research that may further our knowledge about leadership. We conclude by stating that a contextualised leadership trait approach may offer a way out of the wilderness of leadership models and operationalisations by focusing on the most relevant traits that are brought to light by personality researchers.

SENSE-MAKING: THE CASE FOR LEADERSHIP TRAITS

In this section, we discuss our reasons for conceptualising leadership as contextualised (from personality to leadership) traits. We focus on personality traits and not on other individual differences, such as physical traits, or individual differences associated with knowledge, skills and abilities (KSAs; Hoffman et al., 2011). Although physical traits, such as physical formidability, height and attractiveness (Knapen et al., 2017; Little & Roberts, 2012), have been found to be important in leadership, studies of physical traits do not face the same kinds of conceptualisation and operationalisation problems that are present in studies on psychological traits. With respect to KSAs, operationalisations should be based on test performance (e.g., items with 'right' or 'wrong' answers) and such operationalisations are rare in the leadership literature (for exceptions, see Hoffman et al., 2011). That is, personality trait-like attributes – exemplified in questionnaires that measure styles, strategies, behaviours, acts, etc. – are most common in leadership research. We first define what personality is and we discuss – and provide empirical evidence for – four main arguments to call leadership trait-like: a) the amount of content overlap of leadership-style (and behaviour, strategy, act, etc.) items with personality trait items, b) the amount of trait variance in leadership, c) the temporal stability of leadership and d) its heritability and genetic overlap with personality.

Personality Defined

In line with other definitions (e.g., Larsen et al., 2021, p. 3), personality is defined here as *the relatively stable intrapersonal structure of traits and mental processes manifested by interpersonal variability and intrapersonal temporal and cross-situational consistency in a person's responses to the physical, mental, and social environment*. That is, personality is (1) structured (the architecture of 'traits' and 'mental processes'), (2) relatively stable across time and situations ('intrapersonal consistency') and (3) makes individuals different from each other ('interpersonal variability') in (4) their reactions ('responses') to (5) the internal and external (physical and social) world ('environment'). In other words, personality describes the set of stable characteristics that determine our thoughts, feelings and behaviours. This definition is more encompassing than the earlier-mentioned contextualised leadership trait definition, but the two definitions overlap substantially in the sense that both cover the structuredness and stability of a person's responses in their environment. Note that the 'structure' part of the personality definition includes 'mental processes' and not only outwardly manifested traits. Operationalisations of leadership most often do not contain references to mental processes because they are not observable for subordinates, who are most frequently used as raters of leadership. Furthermore, the personality definition refers to both the variability between persons and the consistency within persons in their responses to the environment, which make it possible to speak of a person's unique 'style' or 'behavioural pattern'. Without this part, it would be impossible to distinguish – across situations and time – the behaviour of one person from another. Last, the definition delineates the (physical, mental and social) environment in which personality is expressed. Note that the leadership environment is a subset of the personality environment because the leadership environment refers to much more confined social – and not physical and mental – situations in which a person has gained position power in a group of individuals.

Content Overlap Personality: Leadership

In the following, we focus on the similarities between personality trait and leadership-style conceptualisations and operationalisations. We use 'leadership style' as a shorthand for different leadership (style, behaviour, strategies, etc.) conceptualisations because these tend to share a similar way of operationalising constructs (e.g., through the rating of usual behaviours and/or enacted values/preferences in situations). Although there is no widely accepted definition of leadership style, trait definitions (such as the above contextualised leadership trait definition) are very similar to generic (and person-oriented) 'style' definitions that stress *a way of doing something, especially one that is typical of a person* (retrieved on 4 August 2021 from https://dictionary.cambridge.org/dictionary/english/style). The 'typical of a person' part is in line with the interpersonal variability and intrapersonal situational and temporal consistency part associated with traits that is incorporated in the personality definition, and thus the conceptualisations of (personality) traits and (leadership) styles strongly overlap.

Not only do the conceptualisations overlap, but, more importantly, leadership items are highly similar to personality items. The main difference between leadership items and personality items is that the former refer to much more narrow (most often: hierarchical social) situations. That is, leadership items are personality items designed for a particular context (i.e., they are *contextualised* items). For example, adjectives that are considered prototypical of leadership, such as dynamic, trustworthy and organised (Lord & Maher, 1993), are a subset of adjectives that define the personality space (Ashton et al., 2004; De Vries, 2008). Similarly, leadership scales, such as the Multifactor Leadership Questionnaire (MLQ; Bass & Avolio, 1999) and the Supervisory Behavior Description Questionnaire (SBDQ; Fleishman, 1953), contain items such as *Talks optimistically about the future* (MLQ) and *Criticizes poor work* (SBDQ), that can be considered contextualised behavioural expressions of personality operationalisations such as *On most days, s/he feels cheerful and optimistic* and *People sometimes say that s/he is too critical of others* (both from the HEXACO Personality Inventory; Lee & Ashton, 2006). That is, although leadership items are often more situationally specific than personality items, there is a large degree of content overlap between the two domains.

Trait Variance in Personality and Leadership

Another piece of evidence for the similarity of leadership styles and personality comes from research using the social relations model (SRM; Kenny, 1994). The SRM distinguishes between four sources of variance in round-robin ratings (where members of a group rate each other): target variance (associated with rater consensus on a person's trait), perceiver variance (associated with a rater's overall perceptual bias when rating all other group members), relationship variance (associated with each unique dyadic relationship) and error variance. That is, when people in a group rate each other on personality, apart from error variance, people agree on some part of the rating of a person (target variance), another part of that rating is determined by a rater's overall biases in rating others (perceiver variance, which is in the 'eye of the beholder') and yet another part of the rating is determined by the unique relationship that each person has with another person in the group (relationship variance).

Using the HEXACO Personality Inventory, and when correcting for the error variance component, De Vries (2010) found the following percentages for the three substantive variance components: 47 per cent (target), 18 per cent (perception) and 35 per cent (relationship). That is, most variance in the ratings of personality is target variance, associated with observable traits, but there is still a substantial amount of relationship variance. That is, people in a group tend to agree on somebody's personality for most part (target variance), but the ratings also depend to a considerable extent on the way people have a unique relationship with each other (relationship variance). If leadership was in the eye of the beholder or mostly driven by unique dyadic relationships, we would expect higher levels of perception and relationship variance, which is not the case. In fact, in a synthesis of leadership studies conducted using the SRM, Livi et al. (2008) actually found high levels of target variance in leadership (again, when correcting for error variance), that is: 57 per cent (target), 15 per cent (perception) and 28 per cent (relationship variance). Thus, if anything, there does not seem to be much evidence based on SRM research that leadership is any less trait-like than personality.

Temporal Stability of Personality and Leadership

Yet another piece of evidence comes from longitudinal research on the temporal stability of personality and leadership. Personality has been found to be highly stable across time. For instance, when correlating personality across two points in time, Costa and McCrae (1994) reported a stability correlation (r) of .64 across an average 17-year period of Big Five scales. Similarly, Thielmann and De Vries (2021) reported an average .77 ten-year stability correlation for middle-aged adults and an average of .73 3.5-year stability correlation among students for the six HEXACO personality domain scales.

In contrast to the many studies on personality, there are surprisingly few studies on the temporal stability of leadership, and the following three studies that are summarised suffer from notable methodological limitations. The first study, by Van Dierendonck et al. (2004), measured subordinate-rated leadership behaviours four times, each spaced five months apart. The average correlation across all possible six combinations of measurements was .68. In the second study, by Skogstad et al. (2014), four leadership styles were measured across two occasions in two studies, respectively six months and two years apart. The average temporal consistencies were respectively .57 and .45 (.66 and .55, when using latent variables). In the third study, by Nielsen et al. (2019), transformational and laissez-faire leadership were measured six months apart with temporal consistency correlations of .61 and .50, respectively. Although, on average, these figures are slightly lower than those found for personality, it should be noted that team membership was not consistent across time points (Van Dierendonck et al., 2004) or – in an unknown number of cases – an altogether other leader may have been rated by the subordinate (Nielsen et al., 2019; Skogstad et al., 2014), most likely attenuating the observed correlations. Because it is difficult to study the same subordinate–supervisor dyads across longer periods of time, the level of long-term temporal stability of leadership styles is unclear. However, given the robust, but conservative, estimate of temporal stability, the findings do make clear that – similar to personality – leadership styles are generally highly stable across time.

Heritability and Genetic Overlap of Personality and Leadership

A final – and important – piece of evidence comes from behavioural genetics studies on personality and leadership. Based on more than 50 years of twin studies on personality, the average influence of heritability, shared environment and non-shared environment (plus measurement errors) across the Big Five personality traits has been estimated to be 45 per cent, 5 per cent and 50 per cent, respectively (Johnson et al., 2008). A recent study using the HEXACO personality model shows an almost equal amount of heritability (specifically: additive genetic variance) – that is, an average of 43 per cent across different traits (De Vries et al., 2022).

Again, there have been only few behavioural genetic studies on leadership, but the available evidence shows that leadership has a similar, or even higher, level of heritability. That is, Li et al. (2012) showed that 48 per cent of the variance in transformational leadership was accounted for by additive genetic factors. In Johnson et al. (2004), 57 per cent of the variance in transformational leadership – and 47 per cent of the variance in transactional leadership – was accounted for by additive genetic factors (the remaining variance in both studies was explained by non-shared environmental factors). Most importantly, Johnson et al. (2004) also showed that personality and leadership styles share a large amount of genetic variance, with conscientiousness ($r = .58$), openness to experience ($r = .56$) and extraversion ($r = .23$) having significant positive genetic relations with transformational leadership, and conscientiousness ($r = -.49$), extraversion ($r = -.46$) and agreeableness ($r = -.23$) having significant negative genetic relations with transactional leadership. In contrast, there was almost no overlap in environmental variance between personality and leadership styles. Consequently, not only are leadership styles at least just as heritable as personality, personality and leadership also show strong genetic overlap, supporting the stance that leadership is trait-like and, thus, that leadership styles can be considered contextualised personality traits.

3. THE STRUCTURE OF LEADERSHIP TRAITS

The previous section ('Sense-making: The case for leadership traits') has shown that – definitionally – leadership styles can be equated to traits, that leadership items are a subset of personality items, that the trait variance of leadership and personality is highly similar, that leadership is just as stable and heritable as personality and, most importantly, that there are strong genetic relations between personality and leadership styles.

This latter finding flies in the face of meta-analyses on the relations between personality and leadership, which have been described as 'weak' (Bono & Judge, 2004, p. 906). Similar weak links (e.g., with r's in the .10–.20 range) have been reported in other studies relating personality to leadership styles (e.g., De Hoogh et al., 2005; Deinert et al., 2015; DeRue et al., 2011; Judge & Bono, 2000; Lim & Ployhart, 2004). In a recent meta-analysis, Do and Minbashian (2020) also reported weak correlations between the Big Five personality dimensions openness to experience ($r = .15$), conscientiousness ($r = .11$), extraversion ($r = .23$), agreeableness ($r = .15$) and emotional stability ($r = .19$) and transformational leadership. Although extraversion has repeatedly emerged as one of the strongest personality predictors of constructive leadership, meta-analytic evidence (Mackey et al., 2021) indicates that it does not significantly predict destructive leadership ($\rho = -.03$). Correlations of openness to experience ($\rho = -.08$), conscientiousness ($\rho = -.18$), agreeableness ($\rho = -.15$) and neuroticism ($\rho = .17$) with destructive leadership are, however, similar to those for constructive leadership. Taken together, these findings mimic what Bono and Judge (2004) already concluded based on their meta-analytic findings: Links between personality and leadership styles are weak. As a consequence of these findings, Bono and Judge (2004) have suggested that leadership styles may be less trait-like than expected or that other traits may explain leadership better than the Big Five personality traits used in their meta-analysis.

The Self–Other Agreement Problem

However, De Vries (2012) has argued – and shown – that there is a relatively straightforward reason for the weak personality–leadership relations. In all of the above studies, leadership styles have been measured using subordinate observer ratings, whereas personality has been measured using leader's self-ratings, introducing the so-called self–other agreement problem. That is, correlations between two different constructs measured using two different sources face a *ceiling effect* whereby such correlations cannot be higher than the correlation between the same construct rated by two different sources (e.g., heterotrait-heteromethod correlation ≤ monotrait-heteromethod correlation, in which *trait* is the construct being measured and *method* is the source providing the ratings). For example, the correlation between transformational leadership rated by subordinates and leader's extraversion, rated by the leaders themselves (a heterotrait-heteromethod correlation, in which there are two traits [transformational leadership and leader's extraversion] and two rating sources [subordinates and leaders]) cannot be higher than the correlation between the ratings of transformational leadership rated by subordinates and leaders (a monotrait-heteromethod correlation, in which there is one trait [transformational leadership] and two rating sources [subordinates and leaders]).

Although monotrait-heteromethod correlations (or: self–other agreement correlations) of a personality construct are notably high among people who are highly acquainted (e.g., averaging in the $r = .50$–70 range among family members, close friends, or partners; Connelly & Ones, 2010; De Vries et al., 2008), they are substantially lower in work settings (e.g., .25–.30; Connelly & Ones, 2010; De Vries et al., 2008). The level of self–other agreement on leadership constructs has been found to be even somewhat lower than that of personality – that is, an average of .24 in Warr and Bourne (1999) and .16 in Ostroff et al. (2004). These correlations using the same construct put an effective ceiling on the correlations between different constructs measured using different sources, whereby in a work setting correlations between different constructs measured using different sources (heterotrait-heteromethod correlations) cannot logically surpass the .20–.30 boundary imposed by these relatively weak self–other agreement (monotrait-heteromethod) correlations.

In an empirical study using self- and subordinate-rated leader personality and leadership styles, De Vries (2012) showed, using an instrumental variable approach, that the relations between personality and leadership styles are actually mostly strong to very strong, with HEXACO honesty–humility significantly related to ethical leadership ($\beta = .50$), extraversion significantly related to charismatic leadership ($\beta = .76$), agreeableness significantly related to supportive leadership ($\beta = .74$) and conscientiousness significantly related to task-oriented leadership ($\beta = .33$). That is, like in the above-mentioned genetic study (Johnson et al., 2004), there seems to be a strong link between personality and leadership styles. Given such strong links between personality and leadership, and given the empirical evidence that leadership styles are contextualised traits, the question remains which personality traits are most closely related to which leadership styles. For that question, we first have to turn to the dimensional space spanned by personality. That is, what are the most important personality dimensions?

The Structure of Personality

The question of the optimal dimensional structure of personality has vexed personality researchers for more than a century. Based on Galton's (1884) suggestion, personality scholars have turned to the lexicon to find the most important words (most often adjectives) that distinguish individuals from one another in their personality traits. By the 1990s, a near consensus was reached by the establishment of the Big Five model of personality (Goldberg, 1990). However, a reanalysis of the – at that time – available lexical studies has shown that the most encompassing cross-culturally replicable factor solution contains six instead of five personality dimensions (Ashton et al., 2004). These six dimensions are known by the HEXACO acronym for honesty–humility, emotionality, extraversion, agreeableness, conscientiousness, and openness to experience (Lee & Ashton, 2004; Ashton & Lee, 2020). The HEXACO model explains a full additional factor in comparison with the Big Five (Ashton & Lee, 2018) and captures variance associated with honesty–humility that is not well-captured by the Big Five. Additionally, two of the HEXACO dimensions, emotionality and agreeableness, are rotated variants of Big Five neuroticism and agreeableness, with HEXACO agreeableness containing variance associated with irritability that is more closely associated with Big Five neuroticism, and HEXACO emotionality containing variance associated with sentimentality that is more closely associated with Big Five agreeableness. Table 9.1 includes descriptions and example items for each of the six HEXACO domains.

The Structure of Leadership

Only few lexical studies have been conducted on leadership. Instead of departing from the lexicon, Offermann et al. (1994) had 115 students list up to 25 traits or characteristics of a leader (i.e., based on their implicit leadership theory [ILT]), resulting in a list of 160 terms. These 160 terms were further narrowed to 41 terms comprising eight factors: sensitivity, dedication, tyranny, charisma, attractiveness, masculinity, intelligence and strength. Using a similar design, Offermann and Coates (2018) complemented these eight factors with a

Table 9.1 Descriptions and example items of the generic and contextualised HEXACO domains

Domain	Description	Generic HEXACO-PI-R example item	Contextualized HEXACO-Lead example item
Honesty–humility	The tendency to be sincere, fair, modest and to avoid being greedy	If I knew that I could never get caught, I would be willing to steal a million dollars. (R; Fairness)	If I knew that I could never get caught, I would be willing to take credit for my subordinates' work or ideas. (R)
Emotionality	The tendency to be fearful, anxious, sentimental and dependent on others	I sometimes can't help worrying about little things (Anxiety)	My subordinates would say that I worry a lot at work.
eXtraversion	The tendency to be sociable, bold, lively and to have self-esteem in social interactions	On most days, I feel cheerful and optimistic. (Liveliness)	Compared to other leaders, I tend to be more optimistic.
Agreeableness	The tendency to be gentle, flexible, patient and to easily forgive others	People sometimes tell me that I am too critical of others (R; Gentleness)	I have been told I can be too critical of my team's performance. (R)
Conscientiousness	The tendency to be organised, diligent, perfectionistic and prudent	I often push myself very hard when trying to achieve a goal (Diligence)	I often push both myself and my team very hard when trying to achieve a goal.
Openness to experience	The tendency to be inquisitive, creative, unconventional and to appreciate aesthetics	I would enjoy creating a work of art, such as a novel, a song, or a painting. (Creativity)	I enjoy when my team takes on projects requiring creativity.

Note: Descriptions are based on the lower-order facets of the HEXACO domains; example items of the generic HEXACO-PI-R are reproduced from www.hexaco.org (R = Recoded; between brackets the specific facet is also noted); and example items of the HEXACO-Lead are from Julian (2021).

ninth factor, which they named creativity. In a follow-up study of the 1994 study by Epitropaki and Martin (2004), the earlier 41 items were best captured by six factors: sensitivity (cf. agreeableness), intelligence (cf. openness to experience), dedication (cf. conscientiousness), dynamism (cf. extraversion), tyranny (cf. low honesty–humility) and masculinity (cf. low emotionality). Even more recently, Keshet et al. (2020) used the lexicon and identified – after a number of pruning steps – 393 adjectives than can be used to identify effective and ineffective leaders. A factor analysis using 248 leader self-ratings and 307 subordinate observer ratings identified respectively five and four leadership factors, named corruption/tyranny (cf. low honesty–humility), calculated/competency (cf. conscientiousness), weakness (cf. emotionality), positive energy (cf. extraversion) and – in the leader self-ratings only – aggression (cf. low agreeableness). Thus, although there is yet no direct empirical evidence to establish to what extent the leadership lexical factors overlap with the personality factors, the content of the items in these factors suggest a strong overlap between the two (personality and leadership) domains.

The Construction of a Contextualised Leadership Questionnaire

Based on these findings, which demonstrate that leadership dimensions show a high level of semantic overlap with personality dimensions, and given the fact that leadership styles can be regarded as contextualised personality, a logical next step would be to construct a contextualised leadership questionnaire. Contextualisation of a personality measure can be accomplished by instructing respondents to think of a particular context when completing the assessment, by adding a 'tag' at the end of each scale item (e.g., for a workplace context, adding the tag 'at work' to the end of each item) or by completely rewriting each item to fit within a particular context (see Holtrop et al., 2014). Several HEXACO personality items contain contextual information, and therefore instructions or a tag would obscure the content of such items (Holtrop et al., 2014; Julian, 2021). Furthermore, the complete contextualisation ('rewriting') method leads to the highest level of criterion-related validity (Holtrop et al., 2014), and thus this method was employed in the creation of the HEXACO-Lead (Julian, 2021), a contextualised leadership inventory based on the HEXACO model. To construct the HEXACO-Lead, seven subject matter experts created contextual examples for items from the full HEXACO-PI-R (Lee & Ashton, 2004). The examples were used to generate an initial pool of contextualised items, which was subsequently refined using a working student sample (see Julian, 2021, for the full procedure and Table 9.1 for example items).

Self–Other Agreement of the HEXACO-Lead

In an initial study using the 92-item HEXACO-Lead (Julian, 2021), a sample of leaders ($N = 445$), as well as a subset of their subordinates ($N = 165$, nested within 79 leaders and aggregated to the leader level for analyses), completed self- and observer report versions (respectively) of the HEXACO-Lead, the HEXACO-60 (Ashton & Lee, 2009) and various leadership styles (i.e., transformational, contingent reward, ethical and supportive leadership styles). As mentioned earlier in this chapter, self–other agreement among leaders and subordinates tends to be lower for leadership styles relative to personality traits (De Vries, 2012). When compared with the generic HEXACO personality scales, results using a matched leader–subordinate sample ($n = 77$–78) showed that the HEXACO-Lead had similar – or even slightly higher – self–other agreement (i.e., mean self–other convergent correlation for HEXACO-Lead scales was .43, compared to .40 for the HEXACO-60 scales). Importantly, self–other agreement correlations were higher for the contextualised HEXACO-Lead and the generic HEXACO personality measure when compared to those for the leadership styles (i.e., mean correlation of .20 for leadership styles). That is, similar to findings in prior research using generic personality scales (De Vries, 2012), leadership-style measures seem to contain much less systematic variance than contextualised and generic personality measures, as evidenced by the lower level of self–other convergent correlations in leadership-style measures.

Validity of the HEXACO-Lead

Apart from self–other agreement, the ability of the HEXACO-Lead to predict several leadership styles, compared to the generic HEXACO-60, was also examined (Julian, 2021). For these analyses, the larger leader sample was used which contained self-report personality and leadership-style data ($n = 436$). Results showed that the HEXACO-Lead consistently produced a larger multiple correlation coefficient across all four self-rated leadership-style measures, relative to the HEXACO-60 (e.g., when calculating the difference in multiple R values between the two measures when leadership styles are regressed on them, i.e., $R_\text{diff} = R_\text{HEXACO-LEAD} - R_\text{HEXACO-60}$), though the differences among the two estimates varied greatly in size ($R_\text{diff} = .03$ to $R_\text{diff} = .12$). That is, the R_diff was significant for supportive leadership only, suggesting that the HEXACO-Lead outperformed the generic HEXACO-60 in the prediction of this leadership style, but it did not for the other three leadership styles. Importantly, the differences among the contextualised and generic measures in this study are in the range of what could be expected based on prior meta-analytic research comparing validities of contextualised versus non-contextualised personality measures (Shaffer & Postlethwaite, 2012). The pattern of consistently higher self–other agreement and stronger prediction (though not always statistically significant) of leadership styles offered by the HEXACO-Lead shows the potential benefit of a complete contextualisation of personality to leadership.

In summary, findings from the HEXACO-Lead research offer additional evidence that self–other agreement among leaders and subordinates is higher for both contextualised and generic personality relative to leadership-style measures (De Vries, 2012), and also slightly higher for contextualised leadership traits relative to generic personality traits. Moreover, this research supports a consistent pattern of higher validity in the relation with self-rated leadership styles for the contextualised HEXACO-Lead, relative to the generic HEXACO-60 measure. Although the findings using the HEXACO-Lead are encouraging, more research is needed to further examine the impact of contextualisation on self–other agreement and on personality–leadership-style relations, and to investigate the incremental validity of the HEXACO-Lead in the prediction of organisational criteria beyond generic personality and leadership styles.

4. THE EFFECTS OF LEADERSHIP TRAITS

In the previous section ('The structure of leadership traits'), we demonstrated that lexical studies on personality and leadership show high levels of content convergence, and subsequently argued and showed that leadership can best be assessed using a contextualised personality questionnaire. In addition, we reviewed evidence indicating that the generally weak personality–leadership correlations observed in meta-analyses are due to low self–other agreement in ratings of personality and leadership (outcomes). In the current section, we provide a more detailed overview of the relations of both leaders' personality traits and their leadership styles with leadership outcomes (i.e., leadership emergence, leadership effectiveness and various follower outcomes/perceptions), which are often attenuated as well because of the self–other agreement problem. We will argue that future research may benefit from focusing on contextualised leadership traits to increase the predictive validity in a number of important leadership outcomes.

Leadership Emergence and Effectiveness

The study of individual differences to explain and predict leadership emergence and effectiveness is the longest-standing research topic in the leadership field (Zaccaro et al., 2018). In their 2002 review, Judge et al. showed that all Big Five traits were related to leadership emergence and effectiveness (except that agreeableness did not predict leadership emergence), with a combined multiple correlation of .53 for leadership emergence and .39 for leadership effectiveness. Extraversion emerged as the most predictive trait, whereas agreeableness was the least predictive trait for both criteria. Similarly, Ensari et al. (2011) meta-analytically demonstrated that extraversion (Fisher's $z = .33$), conscientiousness (Fisher's $z = .19$), openness to experience (Fisher's $z = .17$) and emotional stability (e.g., reversed neuroticism; Fisher's $z = .12$) were significantly related to leadership emergence in initially leaderless groups. In another meta-analysis, Ilies et al. (2004) showed that intelligence in combination with the Big Five personality traits had a multiple correlation of $R = .57$ with leadership emergence. Although some of the correlations for personality traits with leadership emergence and effectiveness were relatively weak, the reviewed findings in combination with the attenuation due to the self–other agreement problem indicate that personality traits, and most notably extraversion, play a crucial role in predicting who emerges as a leader and how effective they are.

Research linking different leadership styles to leadership emergence is scarce, likely because leadership styles are usually only assessed once someone has already emerged as a leader, but correlations of the few available studies are generally of similar magnitude as those for the relations of personality traits with leadership emergence. For example, López-Zafra et al. (2008) found that participants who scored high, compared to low, on transformational leadership were more likely to emerge as leaders. Similarly, Mitchell et al. (2019)

found that both task-oriented (cf. conscientiousness, $r = .33$) and relationship-oriented leadership behaviours (cf. extraversion and agreeableness, $r = .35$) were positively related to leadership emergence (although the relation for the latter was curvilinear). Another key finding with regard to leadership emergence is that individuals who communicate more frequently and more forcefully (cf. extraversion) are more likely to emerge as leaders (Acton et al., 2019; Gerpott et al., 2019).

Relations of different leadership styles with perceived leadership effectiveness are generally stronger than those of personality traits. For example, Hoch et al. (2018) and Breevaart and Zacher (2019) found a relation between transformational leadership and leader effectiveness ($\rho = .79$ and $r = .92$ respectively) that even suggests that the two constructs are hard to separate empirically. Similar, albeit slightly weaker, correlations were found in other meta-analyses (Dumdum et al., 2013; Judge & Piccolo, 2004) and for other constructive leadership styles (e.g., Banks et al., 2016; Kim et al., 2018). With regards to negative leadership styles, Breevaart and Zacher (2019) found that laissez-faire leadership was negatively related to perceived leadership effectiveness ($r = -.41$). Next to the fact that these correlations are likely inflated because followers confound their leader's effectiveness with how much they like their leader, these strong correlations can also be explained by the fact that both are usually rated by the follower, dissolving the self–other agreement problem. Overall, leaders' personality and leadership styles seem to exhibit similar correlations with both leadership emergence and effectiveness.

Follower Outcomes/Perceptions

Follower outcomes are often regarded as the most crucial outcomes influenced by leaders because they ultimately determine organisational success. Although little research exists, some studies have examined how leaders' personality traits relate to different follower outcomes (keep in mind that some of the following correlations are based on personality traits rated by leaders and outcomes rated by followers, creating the self–other agreement problem which attenuates these correlations). For example, leaders' extraversion and agreeableness both correlated .18 with followers' perception of LMX (Dulebohn et al., 2012), and leaders' narcissism significantly predicted followers' counterproductive work behaviour directed at leaders ($r = .57$; Braun et al., 2018). DeRue et al. (2011) reported that leaders' agreeableness ($\rho = .22$) and emotional stability ($\rho = .08$) correlated significantly with followers' satisfaction with their leader, whereas correlations for leaders' openness to experience, conscientiousness and extraversion were non-significant. All of these outcomes can be regarded as leader-directed outcomes.

Very few studies have correlated leaders' personality traits with followers' general attitudes, but DeRue et al. (2011) report only non-significant meta-analytic correlations for leaders' Big Five traits with followers' job satisfaction. These meta-analytic correlations are, however, based on only two studies, highlighting the need for more research to examine how leaders' traits correlate with attitudes of followers, such as turnover intentions or organisational commitment. Similarly, very few studies examined relations between leaders' personality and followers' performance outcomes. DeRue et al. (2011), based on $k = 1-5$ studies, found that leaders' conscientiousness ($\rho = .31$) related positively to followers' group performance, whereas correlations for agreeableness ($\rho = .20$) and openness to experience ($\rho = .13$) were modestly sized but non-significant (which can likely be attributed to low statistical power). The current evidence therefore seems to indicate that leaders' personality traits do affect followers' attitudes and performance, but more research is clearly needed.

The relations of different leadership styles with various follower outcomes have been examined abundantly in past decades. Similar to the relations we reviewed above for leaders' personality with follower outcomes, findings for leadership styles generally indicate that relations are strongest for leader-directed outcomes (e.g., trust in leader, satisfaction with leader), followed by attitudinal outcomes (e.g., job satisfaction, organisational commitment) and ultimately by performance outcomes (e.g., job performance, organisational citizenship behaviour). For example, Hoch et al. (2018), who compared effect sizes for the most commonly studied constructive leadership styles (i.e., authentic, ethical, servant and transformational leadership), reported the strongest correlations for trust in the leader ($\rho = .65-.71$; i.e., across the four leadership styles), followed by different positive attitudinal outcomes ($\rho = .39-.66$) and ultimately by various behavioural and performance outcomes of followers ($\rho = .12-.45$).

Again: The Self–Other Agreement Problem

Taken together, these findings indicate that there is strong overlap in the relations of leader personality and of leadership styles with the different leadership outcomes we reviewed here. In other words, leader personality traits exhibit correlations with follower outcomes in a similar magnitude as leadership styles do. An important reason for these correlations that are often interpreted as being weak to medium-sized is the self–other agreement problem described in the previous section ('The structure of leadership traits'). That is, in most studies, leaders report on the predictor variable (i.e., personality), whereas subordinates rate the outcome variable (e.g., leadership effectiveness, attitudinal outcomes). As we noted above, research shows that in work settings, self–other agreement on leadership ($r = .24$; Warr & Bourne, 1999), leadership behaviour ($r = .16$; Ostroff et al., 2004) and personality ($r = .30$; De Vries et al., 2008) is quite low, which can explain the weak relations between leader-rated personality and subordinate-rated outcome variables. Supportive of this claim, correlations are much higher for subordinate-rated leadership-style and subordinate-rated (leader-directed, attitudinal and performance related) outcome variables.

Based on the evidence reviewed above, leaders' extraversion is a particularly important trait as it predicts both leadership emergence and effectiveness as well as various follower outcomes/perceptions (e.g., LMX). Conscientiousness also plays an important role in predicting both leadership emergence and effectiveness. Whereas agreeableness seems to be of little relevance in explaining leadership emergence, agreeable leadership does seem to be relevant for maintaining happy and healthy relationships with subordinates (i.e., high LMX and low abusive supervision). Although there is little research linking honesty–humility to organisational outcomes, given that honesty–humility has been positively linked to ethical leadership and negatively linked to abusive supervision (Breevaart & De Vries, 2017; De Vries, 2012), and given that dishonest leaders may provide counterproductive examples, thereby triggering low honesty–humility traits in their subordinates (De Vries, 2018), it seems likely that honesty–humility is an important leadership trait. Future research should therefore examine how leaders' honesty–humility relates to different follower outcomes.

SENSE-BREAKING: SUMMARY AND FUTURE RESEARCH

In the previous sections, we argued and showed that the most commonly used leadership constructs (i.e., those pertaining to behaviours or styles) can be regarded as contextualised (from personality to leadership) traits. First, we demonstrated that there is a strong overlap between leadership and personality definitions and items, and that personality and leadership constructs have similar levels of target variance, stability over time and heritability. Furthermore, behavioural genetics studies show strong genetic – and weak environmental – overlap between personality and leadership. Second, we argued that the relatively weak personality–leadership relations in past studies are due to the self–other agreement problem in work settings and that the leadership lexical space is – like the personality space – spanned by a maximum of six factors that align with the HEXACO personality factors. Using a contextualised leadership inventory, the HEXACO-Lead, it was shown that, when compared to leadership styles measures, complete contextualisation of a personality questionnaire results in substantially higher self–other (leader self-rating–subordinate observer rating) agreement. Additionally, the HEXACO-Lead showed slightly – but consistently – higher validity in the prediction of leader-rated leadership-style measures than generic HEXACO personality. Third, we delved into the literature on the relations between personality and leadership styles, on the one hand, with leadership emergence and attitudinal and effectiveness outcomes, on the other hand. This section showed that leaders' personality traits exhibit similar (albeit attenuated due to the self–other agreement problem) correlations with follower outcomes as various leadership styles, providing further evidence that leadership can best be conceptualised using contextualised personality traits. Based on the relations with various leader, subordinate and organisational outcomes, the most important contextualised leadership traits appear to be extraversion, conscientiousness, agreeableness and – although less research has been conducted on this trait – honesty–humility. In the remaining, we highlight a number of areas that have been underdeveloped in leadership research on which findings in personality psychology can shed light. That is, the contextualised leadership traits approach may open up a number of avenues for future research that may further our knowledge about leadership.

Lifespan Leadership Research

As the second section (Sense-making: The case for leadership traits) has shown, there is a paucity of research on leadership stability. We were able to locate three articles; in those, the maximum number of years that leaders were followed was only two years. No true lifespan research has yet been conducted on the stability and development of leadership styles, probably because it is almost impossible to obtain data from the same subordinates across such a vast space of time. When using different raters, scholars have to realise that the stability coefficients are likely to be much lower than what is usually found in personality research. A large cross-cohort study using HEXACO self-ratings shows that there are important age trends in traits that are associated with leadership styles (Ashton & Lee, 2016). That is, given the large changes in honesty–humility (e.g., close to 1 *SD* between 18 and 70 years), one might expect convergent changes in ethical leadership and (less) abusive supervision, with older leaders showing on average more ethical leadership and less abusive supervision than younger leaders. Extraversion, which we have shown is the strongest leadership predictor (e.g., Bono & Judge, 2004; De Vries, 2012; Do & Minbashian, 2020), also shows an upward trend, especially with respect to the facets social self-esteem and social boldness, two potentially important leadership traits. Agreeableness, which is positively related to supportive leadership and negatively to abusive supervision (Breevaart & De Vries, 2017; De Vries, 2012), shows a 'U-shaped' trend, with its lowest point around 40 (at the age that most people have young children). It would be interesting to see whether this trend is also present for supportive leadership. Finally, conscientiousness shows a gradual age-related increase, which may result in more consistent and complete leader planning behaviours. Although some leadership studies have investigated leader age and its relation with leadership styles (e.g., Oshagbemi, 2004, 2008), most leadership studies do not report correlations between leader age and leadership styles. That is, until a meta-analysis and/or large-scale age-related and preferably longitudinal leadership-style study is conducted, it is unclear what are the most important age-related leadership-style changes and whether these coincide with personality changes across the lifespan.

Age-related changes are important for another reason. Recent behavioural genetics research (Kandler et al., 2021) has shown a decline in additive genetic effects and an increase in environmental effects on personality across the lifespan. This is accompanied by an increase in stability of personality, which is most stable around the age of 50 (Specht et al. 2011). If these trends are true for leadership as well, it may mean that leadership styles are 'set in plaster' – that is, formed by environmental forces across time, but increasingly less malleable as time goes by. It may also mean that there is a critical period for leadership training before leadership styles are 'set in stone'. Future research might like to investigate whether there is such a critical period and at what age leadership-style changes are harder to realise.

Volitional Leadership Change

Another area of research that is important for leadership training is research that has focused on volitional change. Thielmann and De Vries (2021) have shown that personality feedback may increase volitional personality change, especially for those who are low on honesty–humility, conscientiousness and agreeableness (e.g., the three nightmare traits, De Vries, 2018). Studies on volitional change in personality have shown that programmes designed to elicit specific behavioural changes can be successful if people are motivated to change (Hudson & Fraley, 2015). As far as we know, there have been no studies looking at volitional leadership change, although in the aforementioned study especially increases in extraversion were found among those who desired to become more extraverted. A subsequent study (Hudson et al., 2019) found that desire to change was not a sufficient condition to evoke lasting personality change, but that it had to be complemented with successful behavioural change implementations. It is yet unknown to what extent feedback, volitional change motivations and/or successful behavioural change implementations have an impact on lasting leadership-style changes.

Person–Supervisor Fit

Using (contextualised) personality measures in leadership research may be also advantageous because it makes it easier to 'match' the questions posed to leaders and subordinates when investigating person–supervisor fit (P–S fit). P–S fit has been most closely related to satisfaction with the supervisor (Kristof-Brown et al., 2005), but further investigations are warranted into the nature of this relation. In terms of personality, the question is on which personality traits P–S fit is more likely to relate to supervisor satisfaction and, in turn, positive attitudes towards the job and the organisation. Some hints may be provided by research showing that, in general, people who are befriended tend to be similar – and assume similarity – on two of the six HEXACO traits: honesty–humility and openness to experience (Lee et al., 2009). Research on preferences for ethical leadership has shown that people high on honesty–humility are more likely to prefer to work for an ethical leader, whereas this was less true for those low on honesty–humility (Ogunfowora, 2014). Because honesty–humility and openness to experience are the dimensions of personality that are most closely related to values (Lee et al., 2009), it is not unlikely that these two play an important role in the attitudes that leaders and subordinates have towards each other.

The Role of Leader Liking

That brings us to another important area that is underrepresented in leadership research – that is, the role of liking and the personal relationships between leaders and subordinates. As we have highlighted in the second section (Sense-making: The case for leadership traits), apart from target variance, there is also a substantial amount of relationship variance in personality and leadership (e.g., 35 per cent in De Vries, 2010, and 28 per cent in Livi et al., 2008). It is highly likely that this variance is determined by the extent of liking between leaders and subordinates. Staggeringly high correlations (with $|r| \geq .80$) between leader affect questionnaires (measuring leader [dis-]liking) and leadership styles (e.g., abusive supervision, authentic leadership and leader–member exchange [LMX]) have been observed (Martinko et al., 2018), showing that at least some leadership-style questionnaires do not measure much else than leader (dis-)liking. Such findings may be another reason why researchers should turn to more evaluatively neutral contextualised trait questionnaires (Julian, 2021). Furthermore, social relations analyses (Kenny, 1994) should be used to clarify the nature of the relations between leadership styles or contextualised traits and liking – that is, whether this is mainly through the relationship variance or whether there is also target variance (e.g., a leader's extraversion) associated with leader liking.

Incremental Validity of Leadership

That brings us to a last important point. For leadership-style studies to show that they add value in the prediction of leadership outcomes (e.g., leader emergence, leader effectiveness and subordinate attitudes and performance), leadership scholars have to show that leadership-style measures add variance in the prediction of these outcomes beyond liking, generic personality traits and cognitive ability measures (e.g., objectively measured emotional intelligence, Mayer et al., 2003), while at the same time taking into account the self–other agreement problem noted in the third section (The structure of leadership traits). Only when researchers are able to show that leadership-style measures have incremental validity in the prediction of organisational and attitudinal outcomes when combined with leader liking, leader personality and leader ability measures, may we be able to conclude that such measures are a worthwhile addition at the disposal of scholars.

Conclusion

The leadership field has been plagued by a bewildering number of leadership conceptualisations. In this chapter, we have offered an integrative solution for the current state of affairs by conceptualising leadership styles as contextualised personality. In this chapter, we have outlined why such an integrative solution is warranted (i.e., because of the theoretical, conceptual, operational, and empirical overlap between personality and leadership) and what benefits it may provide. A preliminary study using a fully contextualised leadership measure, the HEXACO-Lead, shows the advantages of using a contextualised leadership measure by offering higher levels of self–other agreement than leadership-style measures. Integrating leadership-style measures with existing personality trait measures into an overarching contextualised leadership trait model, such as the HEXACO-Lead, may ultimately result in a more parsimonious and unified leadership field, something that all leadership scholars should strive for.

REFERENCES

Acton, B. P., Foti, R. J., Lord, R. G., & Gladfelter, J. A. (2019). Putting emergence back in leadership emergence: A dynamic, multilevel, process-oriented framework. *The Leadership Quarterly*, *30*(1), 145–164. https://doi.org/10.1016/j.leaqua.2018.07.002

Ashton, M. C., & Lee, K. (2009) The HEXACO-60: A short measure of the major dimensions of personality. *Journal of Personality Assessment*, *91*, 340–345. http://dx.doi.org/10.1080/00223890902935878

Ashton, M. C., & Lee, K. (2016). Age trends in HEXACO-PI-R self-reports. *Journal of Research in Personality*, *64*, 102–111. https://doi.org/10.1016/j.jrp.2016.08.008

Ashton, M. C., & Lee, K. (2018). How well do Big Five measures capture HEXACO scale variance? *Journal of Personality Assessment*, *101*(6), 567–573. https://doi.org/10.1080/00223891.2018.1448986

Ashton, M. C., & Lee, K. (2020). Objections to the HEXACO model of personality structure: And why those objections fail. *European Journal of Personality*, *34*(4), 492–510. https://doi.org/10.1002/per.2242

Ashton, M. C., Lee, K., & De Vries, R. E. (2014). The HEXACO honesty–humility, agreeableness, and emotionality factors: A review of research and theory. *Personality and Social Psychology Review*, *18*(2), 139–152. https://doi.org/10.1177/1088868314523838

Ashton, M. C., Lee, K., Perugini, M., Szarota, P., De Vries, R. E., Di Blas, L., Boies, K, & De Raad, B. (2004). A six-factor structure of personality-descriptive adjectives: Solutions from psycholexical studies in seven languages. *Journal of Personality and Social Psychology*, *86*(2), 356–366. https://doi.org/10.1037/0022-3514.86.2.356

Banks, G. C., McCauley, K. D., Gardner, W. L., & Guler, C. E. (2016). A meta-analytic review of authentic and transformational leadership: A test for redundancy. *The Leadership Quarterly*, *27*(4), 634–652. https://doi.org/10.1016/j.leaqua.2016.02.006

Bass, B. M. & Avolio, B. J. (1999). *Manual for the Multifactor Leadership Questionnaire D(Form 5X)*. Mind Garden.

Bass, B. M., & Bass, R. (2009). *The Bass Handbook of Leadership: Theory, Research, and Managerial Applications*. Simon & Schuster.

Bono, J. E., & Judge, T. A. (2004). Personality and transformational and transactional leadership: A meta-analysis. *Journal of Applied Psychology*, *89*, 901–910. https://doi.org/10.1037/0021-9010.89.5.901

Braun, S., Aydin, N., Frey, D., & Peus, C. (2018). Leader narcissism predicts malicious envy and supervisor-targeted counterproductive work behavior: Evidence from field and experimental research. *Journal of Business Ethics*, *151*(3), 725–741. https://doi.org/10.1007/s10551-016-3224-5

Breevaart, K. & De Vries, R. E. (2017). Supervisor's HEXACO personality traits and subordinate perceptions of abusive supervision. *The Leadership Quarterly*, *28*, 691–700. https://doi.org/10.1016/j.leaqua.2017.02.001

Breevaart, K., & Zacher, H. (2019). Main and interactive effects of weekly transformational and laissez-faire leadership on followers' trust in the leader and leader effectiveness. *Journal of Occupational and Organizational Psychology*, *92*(2), 384–409. https://doi.org/10.1111/joop.12253

Connelly, B. S. & Ones, D. S. (2010). An other perspective on personality: Meta-analytic integration of observers' accuracy and predictive validity. *Psychological Bulletin*, *136*, 1092–1122. https://doi.org/10.1037/a0021212

Costa, P. T. Jr, & McCrae, R. R. (1994). Set like plaster? Evidence for the stability of adult personality. In T. F. Heatherton and J. L. Weinberger (Eds.), *Can Personality Change?* American Psychological Association.

De Hoogh, A. H. B., Den Hartog, D. N., & Koopman, P. L. (2005). Linking the Big Five-factors of personality to charismatic and transactional leadership: Perceived dynamic work environment as a moderator. *Journal of Organizational Behavior*, *26*, 839–865. https://doi.org/10.1002/job.344

De Vries, R. E. (2008). What are we measuring? Convergence of leadership with interpersonal and non-interpersonal personality. *Leadership*, *4*, 403–417. https://doi.org/10.1177/1742715008095188

De Vries, R. E. (2010). Lots of target variance: An update of SRM using the HEXACO Personality Inventory. *European Journal of Personality*, *24*(3), 169–188. https://doi.org/10.1002/per.764

De Vries, R. E. (2012). Personality predictors of leadership styles and the self–other agreement problem. *The Leadership Quarterly*, *23*(5), 809–821. https://doi.org/10.1016/j.leaqua.2012.03.002

De Vries, R. E. (2018). Three nightmare traits in leaders. *Frontiers in Psychology*, *9*, 871. https://doi.org/10.3389/fpsyg.2018.00871

De Vries, R. E., Lee, K., & Ashton, M. C. (2008). The Dutch HEXACO Personality Inventory: Psychometric properties, self–other agreement, and relations with psychopathy among low and high acquaintanceship dyads. *Journal of Personality Assessment*, *90*(2), 142–151. https://doi.org/10.1080/00223890701845195

De Vries, R. E., Wesseldijk, L. W., Karinen, A. K., Jern, P., & Tybur, J. M. (2022). Relations between HEXACO personality and ideology variables are mostly genetic in nature. *European Journal of Personality*, *36*(2), 200–217. https://doi.org/10.1177/08902070211014035

Deinert, A., Homan, A. C., Boer, D., Voelpel, S. C., & Gutermann, D. (2015). Transformational leadership sub-dimensions and their link to leaders' personality and performance. *The Leadership Quarterly*, *26*(6), 1095–1120. https://doi.org/10.1016/j.leaqua.2015.08.001

DeRue, D. S., Nahrgang, J. D., Wellman, N., & Humphrey, S. E. (2011). Trait and behavioral theories of leadership: An integration and meta-analytic test of their relative validity. *Personnel Psychology*, *64*, 7–52. https://doi.org/10.1111/j.1744-6570.2010.01201.x

Do, M. H., & Minbashian, A. (2020). Higher-order personality factors and leadership outcomes: A meta-analysis. *Personality and Individual Differences*, *163*, 110058. https://doi.org/10.1016/j.paid.2020.110058

Dulebohn, J. H., Bommer, W. H., Liden, R. C., Brouer, R. L., & Ferris, G. R. (2012). A meta-analysis of antecedents and consequences of leader-member exchange: Integrating the past with an eye toward the future. *Journal of Management*, *38*(6), 1715–1759. https://doi.org/10.1177/0149206311415280

Dumdum, U. R., Lowe, K. B., & Avolio, B. J. (2013). A meta-analysis of transformational and transactional leadership correlates of effectiveness and satisfaction: An update and extension. In B. J. Avolio & F. J. Yammarino (Eds.), *Transformational and Charismatic Leadership: The Road Ahead 10th Anniversary Edition* (p. 39–70). Emerald.

Ensari, N., Riggio, R. E., Christian, J., & Carslaw, G. (2011). Who emerges as a leader? Meta-analyses of individual differences as predictors of leadership emergence. *Personality and Individual Differences*, *51*(4), 532–536. https://doi.org/10.1016/j.paid.2011.05.017

Epitropaki, O., & Martin, R. (2004). Implicit leadership theories in applied settings: Factor structure, generalizability, and stability over time. *Journal of Applied Psychology*, *89*(2), 293–310. https://doi.org/10.1037/0021-9010.89.2.293

Fleishman, E. A. (1953). The description of supervisory behavior. *Journal of Applied Psychology*, *37*(1), 1–6. https://doi.org/10.1037/h0056314

Galton, F. (1884). The measurement of character. *Fortnightly Review*, *42*, 179–185.

Gerpott, F. H., Lehmann-Willenbrock, N., Voelpel, S. C., & Van Vugt, M. (2019). It's not just what is said, but when it's said: A temporal account of verbal behaviors and emergent leadership in self-managed teams. *Academy of Management Journal*, *62*(3), 717–738. https://doi.org/10.5465/amj.2017.0149

Goldberg, L. R. (1990). An alternative 'description of personality': The Big-Five factor structure. *Journal of Personality and Social Psychology*, *59*(6), 1216–1229. https://doi.org/10.1037/0022-3514.59.6.1216

Hoch, J. E., Bommer, W. H., Dulebohn, J. H., & Wu, D. (2018). Do ethical, authentic, and servant leadership explain variance above and beyond transformational leadership? A meta-analysis. *Journal of Management*, *44*(2), 501–529. https://doi.org/10.1177/0149206316665461

Hoffman, B. J., Woehr, D. J., Maldagen-Youngjohn, R., & Lyons, B. D. (2011). Great man or great myth? A quantitative review of the relationship between individual differences and leader effectiveness. *Journal of Occupational and Organizational Psychology*, *84*(2), 347–381. https://doi.org/10.1348/096317909X485207

Holtrop, D., Born, M. P., De Vries, A., & De Vries, R. E. (2014). A matter of context: A comparison of two types of contextualized personality measures. *Personality and Individual Differences*, *68*, 234–240. https://doi.org/10.1016/j.paid.2014.04.029

Hudson, N. W., Briley, D. A., Chopik, W. J., & Derringer, J. (2019). You have to follow through: Attaining behavioral change goals predicts volitional personality change. *Journal of Personality and Social Psychology*, *117*(4), 839–857. https://doi.org/10.1037/pspp0000221

Hudson, N. W., & Fraley, R. C. (2015). Volitional personality trait change: Can people choose to change their personality traits? *Journal of Personality and Social Psychology*, *109*(3), 490–507. https://doi.org/10.1037/pspp0000021

Ilies, R., Gerhardt, M. W., & Le, H. (2004). Individual differences in leadership emergence: Integrating meta-analytic findings and behavioral genetics estimates. *International Journal of Selection and Assessment*, *12*(3), 207–219. https://doi.org/10.1111/j.0965-075X.2004.00275.x

Johnson, A. M., Vernon, P. A., & Feiler, A. R. (2008). Behavioral genetic studies of personality: An introduction and review of the results of 50+ years of research. In G. J. Boyle, G. Matthews & D. H. Saklofske (Eds.), *The SAGE Handbook of Personality Theory and Assessment*, *1* (pp. 145–173). Sage.

Johnson, A. M., Vernon, P. A., Harris, J. A., & Jang, K. L. (2004). A behavior genetic investigation of the relationship between leadership and personality. *Twin Research and Human Genetics*, *7*(1), 27–32. https://doi.org/10.1375/twin.7.1.27

Judge, T. A., & Bono, J. E. (2000). Five-factor model of personality and transformational leadership. *Journal of Applied Psychology*, *85*, 751–765. https://doi.org/10.1037/0021-9010.85.5.751

Judge, T. A., Bono, J. E., Ilies, R., & Gerhardt, M. W. (2002). Personality and leadership: A qualitative and quantitative review. *Journal of Applied Psychology*, *87*(4), 765. https://doi.org/10.1037/0021-9010.87.4.765

Judge, T. A., & Piccolo, R. F. (2004). Transformational and transactional leadership: A meta-analytic test of their relative validity. *Journal of Applied Psychology*, *89*(5), 755–768. https://doi.org/10.1037/0021-9010.89.5.755

Julian, A. (2021). *Not to be taken out of context: The development and validation of a contextualized measure of leader personality*. Unpublished doctoral dissertation. University of Calgary.

Kandler, C., Bratko, D., Butković, A., Vukasović Hlupić, T., Tybur, J. M., Wesseldijk, L., De Vries, R. E., Jern, P., & Lewis, G. J. (2021). How genetic and environmental variance in personality traits shift across the lifespan: Evidence from a cross-national twin study. *Journal of Personality and Social Psychology*, *121*(5), 1079–1094. https://doi.org/10.1037/pspp0000366

Kenny, D. A. (1994). *Interpersonal Perception: A Social Relations Analysis*. Guilford.

Keshet, N. S., Oreg, S., Berson, Y., De Vries, R. E., & Hoogeboom, M. (2020). *The structure of leaders' personality: A lexical study*. Presentation at the IOBC 2020 conference, Tel-Aviv.

Kim, M., Beehr, T. A., & Prewett, M. S. (2018). Employee responses to empowering leadership: A meta-analysis. *Journal of Leadership & Organizational Studies*, 25(3), 257–276. https://doi.org/10.1177/1548051817750538

Knapen, J. E. P., Blaker N. M., & Pollet T. V. (2017). Size, skills, and suffrage: Motivated distortions in perceived formidability of political leaders. *PLoS ONE*, 12(12): e0188485. https://doi.org/10.1371/journal.pone.0188485

Kristof-Brown, A. L., Zimmerman, R. D., & Johnson, E. C. (2005). Consequences of individuals' fit at work: A meta-analysis of person–job, person–organization, person–group, and person–supervisor fit. *Personnel Psychology*, 58(2), 281–342. https://doi.org/10.1111/j.1744-6570.2005.00672.

Larsen, R., Buss, D., Wismeijer, A., Song, J., & Van den Berg, S. M. (2021). *Personality Psychology: Domains of Knowledge about Human Nature (3d edn)*. McGraw-Hill.

Lee, K., & Ashton, M. C. (2004). Psychometric properties of the HEXACO personality inventory. *Multivariate Behavioral Research*, 39(2), 329–358. https://doi.org/10.1207/s15327906mbr3902_8

Lee, K., & Ashton, M. C. (2006). Further assessment of the HEXACO Personality Inventory: Two new facet scales and an observer report form. *Psychological Assessment*, 18(2), 182–191. https://doi.org/10.1037/1040-3590.18.2.182

Lee, K., Ashton, M. C., Pozzebon, J. A., Visser, B. A., Bourdage, J. S., & Ogunfowora, B. (2009). Similarity and assumed similarity in personality reports of well-acquainted persons. *Journal of Personality and Social Psychology*, 96(2), 460–472. https://doi.org/10.1037/a0014059

Li, W. D., Arvey, R. D., Zhang, Z., & Song, Z. (2012). Do leadership role occupancy and transformational leadership share the same genetic and environmental influences? *The Leadership Quarterly*, 23(2), 233–243. https://doi.org/10.1016/j.leaqua.2011.08.007

Lim, B. C., & Ployhart, R. E. (2004). Transformational leadership: Relations to the five-factor model and team performance in typical and maximum contexts. *Journal of Applied Psychology*, 89, 610–621. https://doi.org/10.1037/0021-9010.89.4.610

Little, A. C., & Roberts, S. C. (2012) Evolution, appearance, and occupational success. *Evolutionary Psychology*, 10(5). https://doi.org/10.1177/147470491201000503

Livi, S., Kenny, D. A., Albright, L., & Pierro, A. (2008). A social relations analysis of leadership. *The Leadership Quarterly*, 19(2), 235–248. https://doi.org/10.1016/j.leaqua.2008.01.003

López-Zafra, E., Garcia-Retamero, R., & Landa, J. M. A. (2008). The role of transformational leadership, emotional intelligence, and group cohesiveness on leadership emergence. *Journal of Leadership Studies*, 2(3), 37–49. https://doi.org/10.1002/jls.20074

Mackey, J. D., Ellen III, B. P., McAllister, C. P., & Alexander, K. C. (2021). The dark side of leadership: A systematic literature review and meta-analysis of destructive leadership research. *Journal of Business Research*, 132, 705–718. https://doi.org/10.1016/j.jbusres.2020.10.037

Martinko, M. J., Mackey, J. D., Moss, S. E., Harvey, P., McAllister, C. P., & Brees, J. R. (2018). An exploration of the role of subordinate affect in leader evaluations. *Journal of Applied Psychology*, 103(7), 738–752. https://doi.org/10.1037/apl0000302

Mayer, J. D., Salovey, P., Caruso, D. R., & Sitarenios, G. (2003). Measuring emotional intelligence with the MSCEIT V2.0. *Emotion*, 3(1), 97–105. https://doi.org/10.1037/1528-3542.3.1.97

Mitchell, T. D., Hu, J., & Johnson, L. (2019). Diminishing returns of leadership behaviors on leadership emergence. *Small Group Research*, 50(6), 759–773. https://doi.org/10.1177/1046496419870600

Nielsen, M. B., Skogstad, A., Gjerstad, J., & Einarsen, S. V. (2019). Are transformational and laissez-faire leadership related to state anxiety among subordinates? A two-wave prospective study of forward and reverse associations. *Work & Stress*, 33(2), 137–155. https://doi.org/10.1080/02678373.2018.1528307

Offermann, L. R., & Coats, M. R. (2018). Implicit theories of leadership: Stability and change over two decades. *The Leadership Quarterly*, 29(4), 513–522. https://doi.org/10.1016/j.leaqua.2017.12.003

Offermann, L. R., Kennedy, J. K. Jr, & Wirtz, P. W. (1994). Implicit leadership theories: Content, structure, and generalizability. *The Leadership Quarterly*, 5(1), 43–58. https://doi.org/10.1016/1048-9843(94)90005-1

Ogunfowora, B. (2014). The impact of ethical leadership within the recruitment context: The roles of organizational reputation, applicant personality, and value congruence. *Leadership Quarterly*, 25(3), 528–543. https://doi.org/10.1016/j.leaqua.2013.11.013

Oshagbemi, T. (2004). Age influences on the leadership styles and behaviour of managers. *Employee Relations*, 26(1), 14–29. https://doi.org/10.1108/01425450410506878

Oshagbemi, T. (2008). The impact of personal and organisational variables on the leadership styles of managers. *International Journal of Human Resource Management*, 19(10), 1896–1910. https://doi.org/10.1080/09585190802324130

Ostroff, C., Atwater, L. E., & Feinberg, B. J. (2004). Understanding self–other agreement: A look at rater and ratee characteristics, context, and outcomes. *Personnel Psychology*, *57*, 333–375. https://doi.org/10.1111/j.1744-6570.2004.tb02494.x

Schyns, B., & Schilling, J. (2013). How bad are the effects of bad leaders? A meta-analysis of destructive leadership and its outcomes. *The Leadership Quarterly*, *24*(1), 138–158. https://doi.org/10.1016/j.leaqua.2012.09.001

Shaffer, J. A., & Postlethwaite, B. E. (2012). A matter of context: A meta-analytic investigation of the relative validity of contextualized and noncontextualized personality measures. *Personnel Psychology*, *65*(3), 445–494. https://doi.org/10.1111/j.1744-6570.2012.01250.x

Skogstad, A., Aasland, M. S., Nielsen, M. B., Hetland, J., Matthiesen, S. B., & Einarsen, S. (2014). The relative effects of constructive, laissez-faire, and tyrannical leadership on subordinate job satisfaction. *Zeitschrift für Psychologie*, *222*(4), 221–232. https://doi.org/10.1027/2151-2604/a000189

Specht, J., Egloff, B., & Schmukle, S. C. (2011). Stability and change of personality across the life course: The impact of age and major life events on mean-level and rank-order stability of the Big Five. *Journal of Personality and Social Psychology*, *101*(4), 862–882. https://doi.org/10.1037/a0024950

Thielmann, I., & De Vries, R. E. (2021). Who wants to change and how? On the trait-specificity of personality change goals. *Journal of Personality and Social Psychology*, *121*(5), 1112–1139. https://doi.org/10.1037/pspp0000304

Van Dierendonck, D., Haynes, C., Borrill, C., & Stride, C. (2004). Leadership behavior and subordinate well-being. *Journal of Occupational Health Psychology*, *9*(2), 165–175. https://doi.org/10.1037/1076-8998.9.2.165

Wang, G., Oh, I. S., Courtright, S. H., & Colbert, A. E. (2011). Transformational leadership and performance across criteria and levels: A meta-analytic review of 25 years of research. *Group & Organization Management*, *36*(2), 223–270. https://doi.org/10.1177/1059601111401017

Warr, P., & Bourne, A. (1999). Factors influencing two types of congruence in multirater judgments. *Human Performance*, *12*, 183–210. https://doi.org/10.1080/08959289909539869

Yukl, G. (2012). Effective leadership behavior: What we know and what questions need more attention. *Academy of Management Perspectives*, *26*(4), 66–85. https://doi.org/10.5465/amp.2012.0088

Zaccaro, S. J., Green, J. P., Dubrow, S., & Kolze, M. (2018). Leader individual differences, situational parameters, and leadership outcomes: A comprehensive review and integration. *Leadership Quarterly*, *29*(1), 2–43. https://doi.org/10.1016/j.leaqua.2017.10.003

10

Implicit Leadership and Followership Theories: From the Leader/Follower *Within and Between* to Leaders/Followers *in Plural and in Flux*

Olga Epitropaki, Bryan P. Acton and Karolina W. Nieberle

Reality is created by the mind; we can change our reality by changing our mind.

Plato

INTRODUCTION

How do we evaluate leaders and followers? Are leadership and followership phenomena 'in the eye of the beholder'? Scholarly work on implicit leadership and followership theories (ILTs/IFTs) has tried to address these questions and specifically cast light on the perceptual processes underlying leadership and followership (Lord et al., 1984; Lord et al., 2020; Lord & Maher, 1991; Sy, 2010).

We know from social-cognitive research that human beings rely on cognitive simplification to cope with information complexity (e.g., Fiske & Taylor, 1984; Galambos et al., 1986). Individuals are naturally inclined to use a similar process to classify people as leaders and/or followers (Lord, 1985; Lord, et al., 1984; Sy, 2010). Perceptual targets are categorised as leaders (followers) based on their perceived match with the characteristics of the leader (follower) category or prototype – that is, the implicit leadership and followership theories the perceiver holds in memory. ILTs and IFTs are thus defined as cognitive structures or schemas specifying the traits that characterise leaders and followers, respectively (Lord et al., 1984; Sy, 2010). They are developed via socialisation and past experiences and facilitate sense-making during interactions with actual leaders or followers (e.g., Epitropaki et al., 2013; Lord et al., 2020).

Research on leadership schemas spans nearly a half-century (Eden & Leviatan, 1975; Lord, 1985; Lord et al., 1984; Rush et al., 1977). Early work was mainly 'follower-centric' as the emphasis was placed on followers' perceptions and mental representations of leaders (i.e., ILTs). The ILTs field developed in sync with other 'follower-centric' perspectives such as the romance of leadership (Meindl, 1995) and social identity (Tajfel & Turner, 2004) that are thoroughly discussed in other chapters of this volume (see, e.g., Chapter 6, Romance of leadership, and Chapter 5, Embodying who we are). The introduction of followership schemas ten years ago (Shondrick & Lord, 2010; Sy, 2010; Van Gils et al., 2010) has infused new energy in the field and has shifted the conversation towards the importance of *both* leadership and followership perceptions and the co-enactment of leader–follower roles (Uhl-Bien et al., 2014).

Our chapter is organised in the following manner. First, we offer an overview of the theoretical foundations and existing research on ILTs/IFTs and further highlight emerging areas of study. Then, we critically approach current ILTs/IFTs research, indicate possible limitations and further attempt to dispel common misconceptions such as the implicit–explicit dichotomy, schemas as a source of bias and prototype fit as a restrictive process, among others. Next, we focus on two exciting areas for future ILTs/IFTs research, specifically, diversity and inclusion and shared leadership. Finally, we highlight novel methodological approaches (i.e., agent-based computational modelling) that can significantly extend our understanding of leadership and followership schemas as dynamic phenomena.

THEORETICAL FOUNDATIONS OF ILTs/IFTs

It was originally Eden and Leviatan (1975) who introduced the term *implicit leadership theories* (ILTs) to describe the effects of raters' implicit knowledge structures on leadership behavioural ratings. The role of schemas on leadership ratings was further supported by Rush et al. (1977), who found a similar factor structure of leadership ratings between participants with no information about a leader and participants rating of actual leaders. But ILTs research took off as an independent field of study with the influential work of Robert Lord and colleagues (e.g., Lord, 1985; Lord et al., 1984; Lord & Maher, 1991). Leadership was viewed as a *within follower* phenomenon – that is, a perceptual construction based on schemas stored in memory (rather than a leader trait or behaviour). Thus, the role of followers as active co-creators of leadership processes was highlighted.

A key theory that has tried to explain this perceptual construction process was the *leader categorisation theory*, the most popular theory in the ILTs/IFTs field. According to Lord and colleagues (Lord et al., 1984; Lord & Maher, 1991), perceptual targets are categorised as leaders through a *recognition-based process* and a *perceived match* between observed characteristics and the traits of the cognitive category 'leader' that the follower holds in memory. This matching process is automatic and can involve processing an entire set of traits or a gestalt (Smith & Foti, 1998). People can use *prototypes* or *exemplars* in their matching process (Smith & Zárate, 1992). In the case of prototypes, followers compare the traits of the target individual to those of the leadership or followership category in memory, whereas, in the case of exemplars, they categorise the target individual based on their perceived similarity to a person most representative of the category. An equivalent *follower categorisation process* has also been proposed in the case of IFTs (Sy, 2010).

The leadership categorisation approach has been highly influential and underlies a significant body of empirical work on ILTs and IFTs (e.g., Epitropaki et al., 2013; Junker & van Dick, 2014; Lord et al., 2020). Later, Medvedeff and Lord (2007), as well as Shondrick and Lord (2010), applied the principles of *adaptive resonance theory* (ART; Grossberg, 2013) to emphasise the role of context in leadership perceptual processes. According to ART when external stimuli are perceived (e.g., the direct manager or a direct report), they are automatically compared to leadership/followership categories in memory. When a successful match with a category and resonance occurs, the target is classified as a leader (or follower). However, if there is a mismatch, the process will reset to search for another relevant category (e.g., non-leader) or a category that has nothing to do with leadership (e.g., gender) (Medvedeff & Lord, 2007). Furthermore, the process of matching perceptual targets to schemas will be monitored by the *vigilance parameter*, an individual difference that reflects tolerance (or strictness) in prototype matching. The use of ART in the ILTs/IFTs literature has pointed to the dynamic interaction among schemas, individual differences (reliance on schemas) and context.

The connectionist perspective (Brown & Lord, 2001; Hanges et al., 2000; Lord et al., 2001) has strongly emphasised the dynamic and complex nature of leadership and followership schemas.

Lord et al. (2001) argued that categories or schemas could be understood in terms of neural networks. A schema is a recurring network composed of many interconnected traits that receive information from person perceptions, behavioural input and contextual constraints. According to the connectionist model, schemas are sensitive to context, can vary within and between individuals and can be generated in real time as a response to contextual factors (e.g., culture). At the same time, connectionist models allow for ILTs/IFTs generalisability and stability over time. The broader set of traits that composes the schema network can be generalisable; however, different combinations of these traits may be activated in different contexts. Although there is still limited empirical research testing the theoretical propositions of the connectionist approach in applied settings (Braun et al., 2018; Foti et al., 2008; Sy et al., 2010), it is an important theory in the ILTs/IFTs domain. It highlights the dynamic nature of schemas and resolves some of the mixed findings of past research regarding schema generalisability, stability and change (e.g., Epitropaki & Martin, 2004). It also emphasises the role of context in the perceptual construction of leadership. Novel methodologies, such as agent-based computational modelling, which we will extensively present in a later section, can capture this dynamic nature of leadership and followership schemas and extend empirical research on connectionist models.

ILTs/IFTs RESEARCH

Early ILTs research had mainly focused on three key themes: a) the impact of leadership schemas on leader behaviour ratings (Eden & Leviatan, 1975; Rush et al., 1977); b) the content of ILTs – in terms of specific traits and factor structure (Lord et al., 1984; Offermann et al. 1994); and c) ILTs generalisability in different contexts (Bryman, 1987; Nye & Forsyth, 1991). A few studies further tried to cast light on the origins of leadership schemas by examining personality and parental traits as ILTs antecedents (e.g., Keller, 2003). Gradually ILTs research moved to applied settings and sought to understand the influence of leadership schemas on leader–follower relationships and transformational/charismatic leadership perceptions, as well as job attitudes and performance (Bass & Avolio, 1989; Engle & Lord, 1997; Epitropaki & Martin, 2005; Johnson et al., 2012). Several organisational studies have looked at congruence and the prototype matching proposed by leadership categorisation theory (Lord & Maher, 1991), either in the form of individual-level congruence (leader-to-prototype matching; Epitropaki & Martin, 2005) or dyadic-level congruence (leader–follower prototype matching; Engle & Lord, 1997; Riggs & Porter, 2017). Studies have generally shown that individual- and dyadic-level congruence on positive (or prototypical) ILTs matter for leader–member exchanges, attitudinal and performance outcomes. The more recently developed research on followership schemas tackled similar themes such as IFTs content and factor structure (Sy, 2010) and congruence and prototype fit (Wang & Peng, 2016). (The interested reader can find more detailed descriptions of early ILTs research and ILTs/IFTs studies in organisational settings in the reviews by Epitropaki et al., 2013 and Lord et al., 2020).

In addition to the topics presented above, there is an exciting new line of enquiry that has gained traction in more recent ILTs and IFTs research – that is, leadership and followership *self-schemas* and their importance for leader development (e.g., Bray et al., 2014; Van Quaquebeke et al., 2011). The critical role that schemas can play in leadership development has been consistently highlighted in several conceptual papers (Liu et al., 2020; Lord et al., 2020; Murphy & Johnson, 2011). Epitropaki et al. (2017) especially highlighted the role of ILTs/IFTs in leader/follower identity processes. They defined leader (follower) identity as *a sub-component of one's working self-concept that includes* leadership [followership] *schemas, leadership experiences and future representations of oneself as a leader* [follower] (p. 107, emphasis added). They, thus, pointed to the central role of schemas as core components of leader/follower identities. Lord et al. (2020) further indicated the role of self-categorisation processes ('self-to-prototype' and 'self-to exemplar' comparisons) for leader/follower identity salience. Individuals who perceive a match between their own ILTs and their enacted leadership will be more likely to view themselves as leaders. When a mismatch is perceived, leader identity salience will decrease. In general, examining ILTs/IFTs self-categorisation processes is a promising line of enquiry for future leadership development research to pursue.

In an experimental study, Guillén et al. (2015) showed that both self-to-exemplar comparisons (i.e., self-comparisons with influential leaders of the past or present) and self-to prototype comparisons (i.e., comparisons with more general representations of leadership) related positively to motivation to lead. Hoyland et al. (2021), using young adult samples from UK and Japan, found self ILTs to be related to leadership self-efficacy and motivation to lead and further found gender and socioeconomic status to be important moderators. Schyns et al. (2020) showed that congruence between ILTs and implicit self-schemas on different characteristics (such as dynamism, integrity and intelligence) was related to leadership self-efficacy and indirectly to motivation to lead. No prior studies have examined IFTs self-perceptions.

ADDRESSING COMMON MISCONCEPTIONS ABOUT ILTs/IFTs RESEARCH

ILTs research may have been around for almost 50 years but when compared with leadership theories of the same era, it does not appear to be the most popular leadership research strand. A keyword search in the *Web of Science* reveals 497 records for 'implicit leadership theories' and 79 records for 'implicit followership theories'. In contrast, keyword searches for theories that appeared in the literature at the same time as ILTs revealed 8,832 records for 'transformational leadership', 2,155 records for 'charismatic leadership' and 3,241 records for 'leader–member exchange'. There are a few misconceptions that we believe have stifled progress in the ILTs field (especially in the early years) and we address them below.

Can We Measure Implicit Constructs?

Psychological research on implicit phenomena had generally suffered a major setback in the 1960s after the publication of Arthur Koestler's (1967) *The Ghost in the Machine*, which heavily criticised measurement of implicit constructs via explicit methodologies (e.g., introspection and self-report measures) (Bargh & Chartrand, 2000). A strict dichotomy between implicit and explicit processes (either–or) was put in place (Johnson & Hasher, 1987) with negative implications for research on implicit constructs. Although this dichotomy was later refuted (Bargh, 1994), the use of explicit measures to assess ILTs and IFTs remains a common criticism that researchers face when studying prototypes in applied settings.

In the context of ILTs and IFTs 'implicit' reflects the fact that they operate in implicit (preconscious) fashion, but they may also be processed explicitly (consciously) (Lord & Maher, 1991). Whereas implicit processing is the default mode, explicit processing is possible in situations where there are opportunities for reflection and sufficient motivation (Bargh, 1994). Although individuals may be unaware that particular schemas have been activated in a specific moment and influence their behaviour and action tendencies, they can still have schema content awareness. In other words, individuals can lack impact awareness but still be able to access their leadership and followership schemas through conscious introspection (Gawronski et al., 2006). The use of both explicit and implicit methodologies (e.g., Uhlmann et al., 2012) when studying ILTs and IFTs has been previously recommended (Epitropaki et al., 2013).

Are ILTs/IFTs Just Sources of Bias and Measurement Error?

Early ILTs research had indeed focused on schemas as a source of bias and error in leadership behaviour measurement (Eden & Leviatan, 1975; Rush et al., 1977), leading to the impression that ILTs are just 'noise' in leadership measurement. However, later research showcased their practical importance for leader–follower relations and practices in organisational settings (Engle & Lord, 1997; Epitropaki & Martin, 2005). Lord et al. (2020) recently stressed that *prototypes are not just a source of rating error. They facilitate sensemaking by allowing raters to apply general knowledge learned through experience (e.g., semantic memory) to make sense of stimuli* (p. 52). Prototypes help us categorise leaders and followers and make sense of our organisational experiences and leader–follower interactions. However, we must note that despite their importance, prototypes cannot help us accurately evaluate observed leadership/followership behaviours. This is because accuracy in behavioural assessment depends on episodic memory (Hansbrough et al., 2015) whereas ILTs/IFTs are semantic memory structures that underlie leadership/followership perceptions and expectations (Lord et al., 2020). If there are limited opportunities for specific interactions with leaders/followers (i.e., creation of episodic memories), perceivers may inevitably overly rely on schemas and semantic memory to not only categorise others as leaders (followers) (which is the key role of ILTs/IFTs) but also to evaluate leader and follower behaviours (with error).

Does the Prototype Matching Process Resemble a 'Procrustean Bed' for Leaders and Followers?

The prototype–actual leader (follower) matching process proposed by leader (follower) categorisation theory has also been viewed as rigid and restrictive. Like Procrustes in the Greek myth who tied his victims to a bed and stretched or cut off their legs to make them fit it, schemas have been criticised for robbing people of their individuality by requiring them to match the abstract prototype. Social perceivers have been characterised as 'cognitive misers' (Fiske & Taylor, 1984), 'mental sluggards' (Gilbert & Hixon, 1991) and 'efficiency experts' (Macrae et al., 1994) who resort to categorical knowledge at the expense of individuating information. Rejecting these characterisations, Spears and Haslam (1997) offered a different (and more appropriate in our opinion) metaphor for the social perceiver, that of a 'meaning seeker'. Prototypes are important sense-making mechanisms that help perceivers make sense of leadership and followership experiences and information. ILTs/IFTs research has never proposed schemas as absolute benchmarks that someone must fit into if they wish to be successful leaders. Instead, it has highlighted the power of implicit categorisation processes and the significance of both leaders and followers being aware of the role of schemas in their evaluations and decisions (Epitropaki & Martin, 2005). Understanding how prototypes influence our and others' perceptions, and under which conditions, can have important implications for our developmental leadership journey and the way we lead and follow in organisational settings. Recent connectionist perspectives (Lord & Brown, 2001) have further challenged this 'Procrustean' misconception by highlighting the dynamic, context-sensitive, fluid nature of leadership and followership schemas that can be constructed 'on the fly' in different contexts.

Ideal, Typical, Effective or Simply Leader (Follower)?

Another point of debate has been the stimulus word (e.g., ideal, typical, effective) one should use when asking participants to reflect on their ILTs/IFTs. Some researchers have argued in favour of 'ideal' (e.g., Junker & van Dick, 2014) whereas others favoured 'effective' (e.g., GLOBE). However, none of the commonly used ILTs scales (except the GLOBE questionnaire measuring CILTs) has proposed using additional stimuli words to make participants think of ideal, typical or effective leaders. ILTs are cognitive categories with a similar hierarchical structure to other person- or object-categories (Rosch, 1978) and develop around an abstract set of attributes shared by different types of leaders. Lord et al. (1984) viewed ILTs as being organised hierarchically into three levels: *superordinate* (containing characteristics that distinguish leaders from non-leaders), *basic* (contextualised prototypes that describe different types of leaders, e.g., business, political, military) and *subordinate* (contextualised prototypes within each category, e.g., in the category 'business leader' one can distinguish among senior, middle-level and line managers). A similar hierarchical structure has been hypothesised in the case of IFTs (Epitropaki et al., 2013).

Existing trait scales have adhered to the Roschean conceptualisation of prototypes evoking mainly the superordinate category 'leader' or basic levels of that category (e.g., business leader). When generating the first list of 59 ILT traits, Lord et al. (1984) asked people to think of a 'leader' focusing on the superordinate level of the prototype hierarchy. Gerstner and Day (1994) used the same list of 59 attributes and asked participants to think of a 'business leader' focusing on the basic-level of the prototype hierarchy (i.e., a specific leadership context). Offermann et al. (1994), in the instructions of their 41-item scale, also asked participants to think of a 'business leader'. It is important to note that Offermann et al. (1994) did compare among three stimuli: 'business leader', 'effective leader' and 'supervisor', and found the same eight-factor structure across all three conditions. However, there were mean differences between the 'supervisor' stimulus condition and the other two. Generally, participants rated supervisors lower on positive traits (e.g., sensitivity, dedication, charisma). No mean differences were found between 'business leader' and 'effective leader' conditions in most dimensions (except for strength and tyranny). Later, Epitropaki and Martin (2004) also used 'business leader' in the instructions of their 21-item scale following Offermann et al. (1994). In the most recent 47-item ILTs scale, Offermann & Coats (2017) once again used 'business leader' in the participants' instructions. In the case of the IFTs scale (Sy, 2010), participants are asked to think how characteristic a list of 18 traits are of followers, thus focusing on the superordinate category 'follower'.

By adding extra stimuli (e.g., 'ideal', 'effective', 'business') one narrows down the 'leader' or 'follower' category to a basic or subordinate level of the hierarchy (or to a specific exemplar) by providing more contextual information. We would, thus, argue that using the word 'ideal' or 'effective' is not better (or worse) than using the general stimulus 'leader' – it just captures a different level of the schema hierarchy. Whereas superordinate (leader) or basic-level (e.g., business leader) stimuli would normally suffice when measuring leader/follower prototypes, there are cases when the researcher may decide to narrow down participants' recognition process to a lower category level or a specific exemplar (e.g., ideal or effective leader). In general, researchers need to choose the stimulus that best fits the purpose and scope of their study as different stimuli words activate different levels of the category hierarchy or exemplars and may thus capture different aspects of the leadership/followership schemas.

EXPANDING THE LENS

Although some of the above misconceptions have perhaps slowed down early ILTs research, we observe a significant growth in the field in the last ten years (see Figure 10.1).

One possible explanation for this growth is the introduction of IFTs (Sy, 2010) that reinvigorated the field. Furthermore, methodological advances have made easier the testing of the propositions of leader categorisation theory that relate to prototype matching and congruence, such as the wider application of polynomial regression analyses.

As the field moves forward, a substantial body of the conceptual and the theoretical propositions of the latest approaches (such as the connectionist models) remain untested. This is an important gap and opportunity for future research. Research in emerging areas (such as self-schemas and identity) needs to continue and new avenues can be explored. We specifically focus on two promising areas for future ILTs/IFTs research: a) diversity and inclusion and b) shared leadership.

ILTs/IFTs AND DIVERSITY AND INCLUSION

There is significant scope in examining ILTs/IFTs in the context of inclusive leadership and diversity research (Ferdman et al., 2021). Early ILTs research focused mainly on the cultural generalisability of leadership prototypes. For example, the GLOBE study examined *culturally endorsed* ILTs (CILTs) in 62 countries GLOBE and identified 29 universally positive and negative leader attributes (e.g., honest, intelligent, ruthless) and 35 culturally contingent leader characteristics (e.g., compassionate, domineering) (e.g., House et al., 2002). Sy et al. (2010) addressed the issue of *race* and found ILTs differences between Asian Americans and Caucasian Americans. Whereas the leadership perceptions of Asian Americans were based on a competent leader prototype (i.e., intelligence and dedication), Caucasian Americans' perceptions were based on an agentic leader prototype (i.e., dynamism, masculinity and tyranny). Race (black versus white) was also studied by Rosette et al. (2008); they found 'being white' to be part of a leadership prototype, and that fit with this prototype affected evaluations of leadership effectiveness. Rosette and Livingston (2012) examined gender in addition to race and found black women leaders to suffer double jeopardy and be evaluated more negatively than black men and white women, under conditions of organisational failure. Under conditions of organisational success, black women,

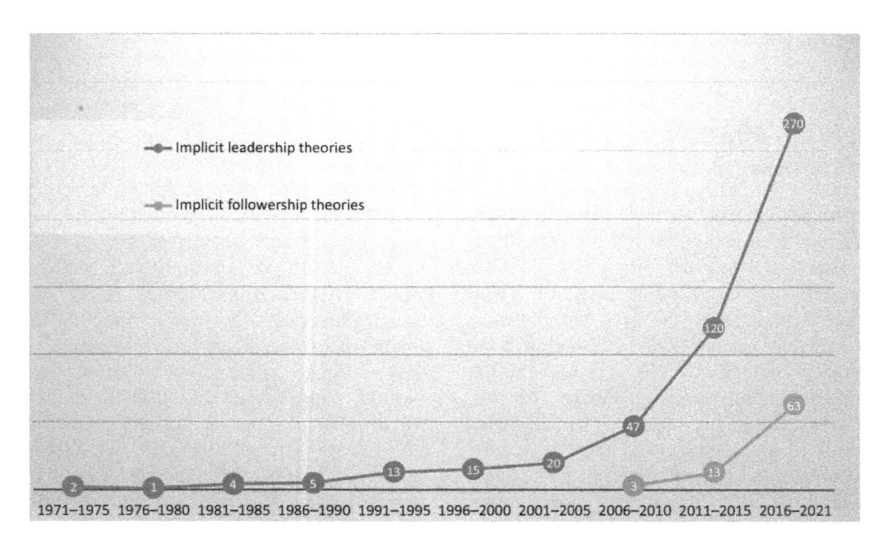

Figure 10.1 *Web of Science* Core Collection search of the term 'implicit leadership theories' and 'implicit followership theories' in all fields (n = 479 and n = 79) records, respectively. 28 June 2021.

black men and white women were evaluated comparably to each other, but always less favourably than white men.

Numerous past studies have examined gender and leadership perceptions (e.g., Ayman & Korabik, 2010; Duehr & Bono, 2006; Heilman et al., 1989; Schein, 1973; Schein & Mueller, 1992) and generally showed a backlash effect for women leaders due to an incongruity between gender and leader perceptions (Eagly & Karau, 2002; Heilman, 2001). Recently, Braun et al. (2018) challenged some of these assumptions in relation to authentic leadership and found women to be perceived as more authentic leaders.

In contrast, leadership perceptions related to LGBTQ leaders have not been examined by prior research (Fassinger et al., 2010). The double jeopardy (Beale, 1970) effect found in the case of black women leaders (Rosette & Livington, 2012) could potentially underlie perceptions of LGBTQ leaders, due to misalignment with typical leader characteristics, such as male, white, heterosexual and able-bodied (e.g., Cunningham & Macrae, 2011; Rosette & Livingston, 2012). Other scholars have argued for intersectional invisibility. Multiple minority identities may allow individuals to 'escape' the stereotype of each single minority identity (Livingston et al., 2012; Purdie-Vaughns & Eibach, 2008). Violating leader typicality on more than one dimension could possibly result in a positive effect. In an unpublished experimental study, Westcott (2017) found homosexual male leaders to be perceived as more transformational than heterosexual male leaders and further evaluated as more effective. No significant effects were found for homosexual women leaders.

Regarding disability, there is limited research examining perceptions of leaders with disabilities. In an unpublished doctoral thesis including two experiments, Marchioro (2000) examined disability and leadership perceptions. In the first experiment that only presented participants with background materials about the applicants, he found disabled applicants to receive lower leader ratings. However, in the second experiment that utilised a 2x2 design (disabled/non-disabled and prototypical/antiprototypical leadership behaviours) and the participants had the chance to view a video of the person, the results were very different. The disabled leader was rated higher on leadership and overall performance, was liked more and was perceived to be more charismatic when exhibiting prototypical leadership behaviours. In the antiprototypical leadership condition, the disabled leader was rated lower or similar to the non-disabled leader.

Diversity and the intersectionality of identities are important topics for future ILTs/IFTs research to address. How do individuals perceive leaders of different races, gender and disability? What leadership and followership schemas are more salient for perceivers belonging to these diverse groups? Following ART propositions, do perceivers classify leaders with high intersectionality of identities in different, not related to leadership, categories altogether that may have higher salience (Medvedeff & Lord, 2007)? Are gender, race and disability contextual constraints that influence the activation of specific trait nodes in the ILTs/IFTs neural network in accordance with the propositions of connectionist perspectives (Hanges et al., 2000)?

ILTs/IFTs in Plural: Shared Leadership Schemas

The strong emphasis of ILTs/IFTs on *individuals* limits the scientific understanding of the schemas that guide leadership perceptions and behaviours *in plural* (Lord et al. 2020, Shondrick et al. 2010). Leading collectively has become a strong endeavour in practice as evidenced by the *New Work* revolution (e.g., flattened collaborative structures, self-managed teams, agile teamwork) that breaks its way through entrepreneurial start-ups and established businesses alike. Similarly, scholars point to leadership as an adaptive process as leadership and followership roles dynamically switch (DeRue, 2011), with *multiple* individuals mutually leading one another to the achievement of shared goals (Denis et al., 2012; Pearce & Conger, 2003). This challenges the traditional distinction between those who lead and those who follow and, accordingly, the implicit theories that individuals hold about leaders(hip) and followers(hip). When sharing the lead, leadership and followership are inherently interdependent. Shared leadership requires considering ILTs and IFTs in concordance rather than in isolation. Simultaneously exploring ILTs and IFTs will help to understand how individuals recognise who leads and who follows when leadership is shared and how they manage the tension of being both a leader and a follower.

An individual's ability to manage the dual tension of being both a leader and a follower is crucial for shared leadership. That is, self-schemas as leaders and followers are vital for intrapersonal role switching to occur. Interpersonal differences in the capability to switch between leader and follower roles depend upon the centrality of leader and follower self-schemas relative to each other (Sy & McCoy, 2014). At the same time, the repeated experience of shared leadership may inform integrated leader and follower (self-)schemas (Adriasola &

Lord, 2020). Individuals may no longer distinguish between leaders and followers but hold implicit schemas that capture the co-existence, co-activation of leadership and followership prototypes in shared settings. The relevant schemas may capture existing schemas that are similar in both ILT and IFT (e.g., motivated) and further capture (new) overlapping aspects that apply to both leaders *and* followers (e.g., active engagement, reliability, transparency, tolerance, flexibility).

We see schemas that inform shared leadership as a promising extension for future research. When sharing the lead, are individuals who are seen as leaders also seen as followers? Are individuals who share the lead relying on the traditional differentiation between 'leaders' and 'followers' or do they hold an integrated superordinate schema level? Are individuals with a strong leader identity less likely to flexibly switch to followership roles as part of shared leadership? It is also important to examine how leader*ship* as a collective patterning of relational processes (Acton et al., 2019; Carter et al., 2015) is cognitively represented. Which implicit schemas guide the patterning of leader–follower interactions over time? And how do these schemas interplay to inform the sharing of leadership?

The implicit beliefs about how leadership should be arranged and to which extent leadership is a shared property (i.e., leadership structure schemas; DeRue and Ashford, 2010) may inform the extent to which individuals grant leadership to others as well as claim leadership for themselves when they hold no formal managerial responsibilities (DeRue & Ashford, 2010). Further theoretical work emphasised individuals' schemas of social network structures and interpersonal ties as relevant for leadership in plural. Balkundi and Kilduff (2006) proposed that the mental representations of social ties that individuals hold facilitate and constrain their actions within their social environment. Similarly, Scott et al. (2018) integrated social network perspectives of leadership into ILTs/IFTs to propose that individuals' implicit assumptions about the team network in general (e.g., hierarchical, distributed) and their own role in that network (e.g., the level of influence and activation) will shape the emergence and effectiveness of leadership at the collective level.

While much is known about when and why shared leadership is effective (e.g., D'Innocenzo et al., 2016; Nicolaides et al., 2014; Wang et al., 2014; Wu et al., 2020), little is known about the implicit theories that guide *the process of sharing leadership* in teams (Denis et al., 2012, Lord & Shondrick, 2011, Shondrick et al., 2010). Leadership scholars more generally have previously advocated turning the focus in leadership research more to relationships and relational interactions (Uhl-Bien, 2006). This view gains increasing relevance for shared leadership, a phenomenon that is grounded in multiple and distributed influence processes that happen – often simultaneously – between the members of a team (Acton et al., 2019; Carter et al., 2015). Individuals' implicit schemas are fundamental for understanding perception and behaviour in social interactions. Accordingly, individuals' assumptions about *how* the sharing of leadership takes place (i.e., schemas about the multiple relational processes that constitute shared leadership) are a key for leadership in plural. We thus see a need for future research to broaden the scope of ILTs/IFTs to include schemas that capture the relational processes that constitute shared leadership.

One promising extension to ILT and IFT research may be to incorporate relational schemas. Instead of focusing on person-based attributes such as schema content, relational schemas emphasise the relationship and the interactional processes that happen between actors (Baldwin, 1992). While the relevance of relational schemas has been acknowledged by ILT researchers (Epitropaki et al. 2013, Foti et al. 2017, Thomas et al. 2013), we see it as a particularly promising extension when it comes to leadership in plural. Carnabuci et al. (2018) relied on the notion of relational schemas and demonstrated that when there is no formal leader, a group's leadership network dynamically evolved based on individual team members behaving in accordance with their relational schemas. Relational schemas inform individuals' expectations about how the patterned leadership relationships around them should look. In groups, individuals will align their attributions and behaviours to these expectations in that they form (and dissolve) those leadership relations that were consistent (inconsistent) with their schematic expectations. At a collective level, these intra-individual cognitive meachnisms (i.e., individuals' schematic expectations that informed their relationship formation and dissolution) inform the evolution of informal leadership structures.

A recent work by Nieberle et al. (2021) uncovered how shared leadership is mentally represented by tapping into both the content and the structure of team members' social-cognitive schemas of shared leadership. Via inductive coding, the authors revealed schemas that describe the individual (e.g., claiming leadership), team-related (e.g., granting leadership) and managerial processes (e.g., stimulating and initiating) involved when team members share the lead. In a second step, via network analysis, the authors demonstrated how these schemas interplay with each other to inform a dense cognitive network of shared leadership schemas.

The findings suggest that how shared leadership happens to a great extent resides in team members' schemas of individual–team interaction as well as the motivating and enabling processes associated with managerial leadership.

STUDYING DYNAMIC ILTs/IFTs IN PLURAL

Prior ILT and IFT research has used experimental and congruence methodologies to capture leader and follower categorisation processes (Epitropaki et al., 2013). However, such methodologies cannot fully capture the dynamic nature of ILTs and IFTs proposed by connectionist models (Lord et al., 2001) or the shared leadership schemas dynamics discussed above. In this section, we focus on one new methodology – agent-based computational modelling – and outline its ability to address many of the challenges in current ILT/IFT research. We then present a brief walkthrough of how an agent-based model (ABM) might be created, using one specific concept discussed earlier: how ILTs/IFTs might influence the collective leadership process. A guide to the ideas discussed in this section is outlined in Table 10.1.

ABM represents a form of computational modelling that uses computer simulations to build and test mathematical models (Gilbert & Bankes, 2002). It provides a tool for researchers to test 'narrative theories' – which are dominant in the social sciences – by first formalising theoretical assumptions, followed by testing them via simulation. As such, computational models allow the researcher to test whether the core assumptions of a theory 'check out' (Vancouver & Colton, 2020). While multiple approaches to computational modelling exist, ABM is particularly strong for its ability to simulate dynamic multi-level phenomena (Conte & Paolucci, 2014). The basic idea of ABM is to 'grow' a system from the bottom-up by first selecting the lower-level elements (agents), then deciding how they interact with each other (interactional rules) and finally assessing what develops from this process (collective outcome). This represents the *three core components of any ABM*; we now briefly cover each, within the context of ILT/IFTs.

Agents

Agents represent the individual-level entities that make up the core of the collective system. Agents can be many things, including ants in an ant colony, cars in a traffic system, or cells in a body. In this chapter, we use agents to represent ILT/IFTs. As we focus on ILTs within collectives, agents are people within a collective. However, agents could also be individual dimensions within a single individual's ILT. In this case, it would be up to the modeller to assign specific agent characteristics to each team member. A central decision that the researcher should ask about agent characteristics is *how should the agent variable be represented in the model?* In the case of ILTs, the choice might be at what level should ILTs be represented. We list a further set of questions that the modeller might address at the agent level in Table 10.1.

Interactional Rules

Within ABMs, after defining the agents, the next step is to define what agents do and how do they do it? Interactional rules represent what complexity theorists might describe as the core process mechanisms. Studying ILTs in a team context likely concerns what the team members do over time. As an example of how one might do this, Grand and colleagues (2016) used ABM to model the emergence of team cognition. To do so, agents could 1) encode information about the environment, 2) share information with others, or 3) decode information shared with them. Ultimately, these rules led to knowledge integration and collective learning. To study ILTs within the collective, we recommend a similar approach as Grand and colleagues (2016) by purposely choosing the most simple and well-defined processes in the literature. We list a more expanded set of questions to help guide this model-building stage in Table 10.1.

Collective Context

The final core piece of any ABM is the role of context as an influence on agents' behaviour. While the interactional rules can be thought of as the bottom-up catalyst of emergence, the context represents the top-down influence in the system. In the case of ILT/IFT research, this would most closely align with a connectionist perspective, where the environment modulates ILTs that a person is interacting within. This type of model is commonly used in ABMs, where the modeller might compare a model with no contextual element compared to one where there is a top-down influence (Kozlowski et al., 2016). We list an expanded set of questions to help guide this model-building stage in Table 10.1.

Table 10.1 Guidelines for developing an agent-based model for studying the role of ILTs/IFTs

Questions to ask

Agents
1. Are there specific 'types' of agents, or only one 'type'?
2. What are the most essential properties of agents that should be included in the model?
3. Which properties of an agent are static and which are dynamic?
4. Do you have empirically collected data on the agent properties to use for assigning agent features?
5. What level of complexity should the agent properties be represented at?

Interactional rules
1. What are the most essential process mechanisms that drive the phenomena under study?
2. How much time does each iteration in the simulation represent?
3. Step-by-step, what happens at each time point in the simulation?
4. Which agents are allowed to perform actions at each step and what determines the order in which actions are performed?
5. What assumptions are you making about the topic in your model?

Contextual influence
1. Are there any environmental variables represented in the simulation?
2. Do agents 'learn' from the global environment by adapting to changes?
3. Are there 'network effects', in that the social structure influences the behaviour of individuals?
4. Are there goals or objectives associated with the collective environment that agents operate within?
5. Are there any 'shocks' or important environmental events that occur over time? When do they occur?

Despite the strengths of agent-based modelling and what we view as great opportunities for future research, it is important to acknowledge that this is only one methodological tool in a much larger toolbox that can be applied to ILT/IFT research. As many have noted in the past, the strength of models is largely dependent on the quality of theories that drive them (Vancouver & Weinhardt, 2012). One outcome of this review is that the role of ILTs/IFTs in leadership processes is both undertheorised and understudied. This statement coincides with core reflections in other chapters in this book that establishing leadership relationships generally neglects the importance of process mechanisms. With this in mind, one recommendation we have is that agent-based models be paired with the empirical study of collective leadership interactions (Chapter 3, Leadership in interaction). No simulation can replace the complete insights gained from observing real leaders and followers. As such, we recommend a similar approach to Grand and colleagues (2016), where they paired the results of an agent-based simulation with an experiment studying real teams over time.

CONCLUSION

Our chapter aimed to extend ILTs and IFTs beyond individual schemas and self/other perceptions. After offering a comprehensive summary of existing ILTs/IFTs theory and research, we emphasised emerging areas of interest for ILTs/IFTs research, such as diversity, inclusion and shared leadership. We broadened the ILTs/IFTs scope beyond the *within and between* level by highlighting more dynamic, *in plural* conceptualisations of schemas. We further presented a novel methodology (i.e., agent-based computational modelling) as a powerful tool for studying ILTs and IFTs as dynamic, shared phenomena.

REFERENCES

Acton, B. P., Foti, R. J., Lord, R. G., & Gladfelter, J. A. (2019). Putting emergence back in leadership emergence: A dynamic, multilevel, process-oriented framework. *Leadership Quarterly*, 30, 145–164.

Adriasola, E., & Lord, R. G. (2020). From a leader and a follower to shared leadership: An identity-based structural model for shared leadership emergence. In Z. Jaser (Ed.), *The Connecting Leader: Serving Concurrently as a Leader and a Follower* (pp. 31–66). Information Age.

Ayman, R. & Korabik, K. (2010). Leadership. Why gender and culture matter. *American Psychologist*, 65, 157–170.

Baldwin, M. W. (1992). Relational schemas and the processing of social information. *Psychological Bulletin*, *112*(3), 461–484.

Balkundi, P., & Kilduff, M. (2006). The ties that lead: A social network approach to leadership. *Leadership Quarterly*, *17*(4), 419–439.

Bargh, J. A. (1994). The four horsemen of automaticity: Awareness, intention, efficiency, and control in social cognition. In R. S. Wyer Jr & T. K. Srull (Eds.), *Handbook of Social Cognition: Basic Processes: Applications* (pp. 1–40). Lawrence Erlbaum.

Bargh, J. A., & Chartrand, T. L. (2000). The mind in the middle: A practical guide to priming and automaticity research. In H. T. Reis & C. M. Judd (Eds.), *Handbook of Research Methods in Social and Personality Psychology* (pp. 253–285). Cambridge University Press.

Bass, B. M., & Avolio, B. J. (1989). Potential biases in leadership measures: How prototypes, leniency, and general satisfaction relate to ratings and rankings of transformational and transactional leadership constructs. *Educational and Psychological Measurement*, *49*(3), 509–527.

Beale F. (1970). Double jeopardy: To be Black and female. In Bambara T. C. (Ed.), *The Black woman: An anthology* (pp. 90–100). New York, NY: Signet.e

Braun, S., Peus, C., & Frey, D. (2018). Connectionism in action: Exploring the links between leader prototypes, leader gender, and perceptions of authentic leadership. *Organizational Behavior and Human Decision Processes*, 149, 129–144.

Bray, B. C., Foti, R. J., Thompson, N. J., & Wills, S. F. (2014). Disentangling the Effects of Self Leader Perceptions and Ideal Leader Prototypes on Leader Judgments Using Loglinear Modeling With Latent Variables. *Human Performance*, *27*(5), 393–415.

Bryman, A. (1987). The generalizability of implicit leadership theory. *The Journal of Social Psychology*, 127(2), 129–141.

Carnabuci, G., Emery, C., & Brinberg, D. (2018). Emergent leadership structures in informal groups: A dynamic, cognitively informed network model. *Organization Science*, *29*(1), 118–133.

Carter, D. R., DeChurch, L. A., Braun, M. T., & Contractor, N. S. (2015). Social network approaches to leadership: An integrative conceptual review. *Journal of Applied Psychology*, *100*(3), 597–622.

Conte, R., & Paolucci, M. (2014). On agent-based modeling and computational social science. *Frontiers in Psychology*, *5*, 668. https://doi.org/10.3389/fpsyg.2014.00668

DeRue, D. S. (2011). Adaptive leadership theory: Leading and following as a complex adaptive process. *Research in Organizational Behavior*, *31*, 125–150.

DeRue, D. S., & Ashford, S. J. (2010). Who will lead and who will follow? A social process of leader identity construction in organizations. *Academy of Management Review*, *35*, 627–647.

Denis, J. L., Langley, A., & Sergi, V. (2012). Leadership in the plural. *Academy of Management Annals*, *6*(1), 211–283.

D'Innocenzo, L., Mathieu, J. E., & Kukenberger, M. R. (2016). A meta-analysis of different forms of shared leadership–team performance relations. *Journal of Management*, *42*(7), 1964–1991.

Duehr, E. E., & Bono, J. E. (2006). Men, women, and managers: are stereotypes finally changing?. *Personnel Psychology*, *59*(4), 815–846.

Eagly, A. H., & Karau, S. J. (2002). Role congruity theory of prejudice toward female leaders. *Psychological Review*, *109*(3), 573–598.

Eden, D., & Leviatan, U. (1975). Implicit leadership theory as determinant of the factor structure underlying supervisory behavior scales. *Journal of Applied Psychology*, *60*, 736–741.

Engle, E. M., & Lord, R. G. (1997). Implicit theories, self-schemas, and leader-member exchange. *Academy of Management Journal*, *40*, 988–1010.

Epitropaki, O., Kark, R., Mainemelis, C., & Lord, R.G. (2017). Leadership, followership and identity processes: A multilevel review. *Leadership Quarterly*, *28*, 104–129.

Epitropaki, O., & Martin, R. (2004). Implicit leadership theories in applied settings: Factor structure, generalizability and stability over time. *Journal of Applied Psychology*, *89*, 293–310.

Epitropaki, O., & Martin, R. (2005). From ideal to real: A longitudinal study of the role of implicit leadership theories on leader–member exchanges and employee outcomes. *Journal of Applied Psychology*, *90*(4), 659–676.

Epitropaki, O., Sy, T., Martin, R., Tram-Quon, S., & Topakas, A. (2013). Implicit leadership and followership theories 'in the wild': Taking stock of information-processing approaches to leadership and followership in organizational settings. *Leadership Quarterly*, *24*, 858–881.

Fassinger, R. E., Shullman, S. L., & Stevenson, M. R. (2010). Toward an affirmative lesbian, gay, bisexual, and transgender leadership paradigm. *American Psychologist*, *65*(3), 201–215.

Ferdman, B.M., Prime, J., & Riggio, R.E. (2021). *Inclusive Leadership: Transforming Diverse Lives, Workplaces, and Societies*. Routledge.

Fiske, S. T., & Taylor, S. E. (1984). *Social Cognition*. Addison-Wesley.

Foti, R. J., Hansbrough, T. K., Epitropaki, O., & Coyle, P. T. (2017). Dynamic viewpoints on implicit leadership and followership theories: Approaches, findings, and future directions. *Leadership Quarterly*, *28*, 261–266.

Foti, R. J., Knee Jr, R. E., & Backert, R. S. (2008). Multilevel implications of framing leadership

perceptions as a dynamic process. *Leadership Quarterly, 19*, 178–194.
Galambos, J. A., Abelson, R. P., & Black, J. B. (1986). *Knowledge Structures.* Lawrence Erlbaum.
Gawronski, B., Hofmann, W., & Wilbur, C. J. (2006). Are 'implicit' attitudes unconscious? *Consciousness and Cognition: An International Journal, 15*(3), 485–499.
Gerstner, C. R., & Day, D. V. (1994). Cross-cultural comparison of leadership prototypes. *Leadership Quarterly, 5*(2), 121–134.
Gilbert, D. T., & Hixon, J. G. (1991). The trouble of thinking: Activation and application of stereotypic beliefs. *Journal of Personality and Social Psychology, 60*(4), 509–517.
Gilbert, N., & Bankes, S. (2002). Platforms and methods for agent-based modeling. *Proceedings of the National Academy of Sciences, 99*(suppl 3), 7197–7198.
Grand, J. A., Braun, M. T., Kuljanin, G., Kozlowski, S. W. J., & Chao, G. T. (2016). The dynamics of team cognition: A process-oriented theory of knowledge emergence in teams. *Journal of Applied Psychology, 101*(10), 1353–1385.
Grand, J. A., Braun, M. T., Kuljanin, G., Kozlowski, S. W. J., & Chao, G. T. (2016). The dynamics of team cognition: A process-oriented theory of knowledge emergence in teams. *Journal of Applied Psychology, 101*(10), 1353–1385.
Grand, J. A., Braun, M. T., Kuljanin, G., Kozlowski, S. W. J., & Chao, G. T. (2016). The dynamics of team cognition: A process-oriented theory of knowledge emergence in teams. *Journal of Applied Psychology, 101*(10), 1353–1385.
Grossberg, S. (2013). Adaptive resonance theory: How a brain learns to consciously attend, learn and recognize a changing world. *Neural Networks, 37*, 1–47.
Guillén, L., Mayo, M., & Korotov, K. (2015). Is leadership a part of me? A leader identity approach to understanding the motivation to lead. *Leadership Quarterly, 26*(5), 802–820.
Hanges, P. J., Lord, R. G., & Dickson, M. W. (2000). An information-processing perspective on leadership and culture: A case for connectionist framework. *Applied Psychology: An International Review, 49*(1), 133–161.
Hansbrough, T. K., Lord, R. G., & Schyns, B. (2015). Reconsidering the accuracy of follower leadership ratings. *Leadership Quarterly, 26*, 220–237.
Heilman, M. E. (2001). Description and prescription: How gender stereotypes prevent women's ascent up the organizational ladder. *Journal of Social Issues, 57*(4), 657–674.
House, R., Javidan, M., Hanges, P., & Dorfman, P. (2002). Understanding cultures and implicit leadership theories across the globe: An introduction to project GLOBE. *Journal of World Business, 37*(1), 3–10.
Hoyland, T., Psychogios, A., Epitropaki, O., Damiani, J., Mukhuty, S., & Priestnall, C. (2021). A two-nation investigation of leadership self-perceptions and motivation to lead in early adulthood: The moderating role of gender and socio-economic status., *Leadership and organization development journal, 42* (2), 289–315.
Johnson, M. K., & Hasher, L. (1987). Human learning and memory. *Annual Review of Psychology, 38*, 631–668.
Johnson, S. K., Sy, T., & Kedharnath, U. (2012). *What lies beneath: The role of schema in charismatic leadership.* Unpublished manuscript.
Junker, N. M., & van Dick, R. (2014). Implicit theories in organizational settings: A systematic review and research agenda of implicit leadership and followership theories. *Leadership Quarterly, 25*, 1154–1173.
Keller, T. (2003). Parental images as a guide to leadership sensemaking: An attachment perspective on implicit leadership theories. *Leadership Quarterly, 14*, 141–160.
Koestler, A. (1967). *The Ghost in the Machine.* Hutchinson.
Kozlowski, S. W. J., Chao, G. T., Grand, J. A., Braun, M. T., & Kuljanin, G. (2016). Capturing the multi-level dynamics of emergence: Computational modeling, simulation, and virtual experimentation. *Organizational Psychology Review, 6*(1), 3–33.
Liu, Z., Venkatesh, S., Murphy, S. E., & Riggio, R. E. (2020). Leader development across the lifespan: A dynamic experiences-grounded approach. *Leadership quarterly,* N/A, [101382]. https://doi.org/10.1016/j.leaqua.2020.101382
Livingston, R. W., Rosette, A. S., & Washington, E. F. (2012). Can an Agentic Black Woman Get Ahead? The Impact of Race and Interpersonal Dominance on Perceptions of Female Leaders. *Psychological Science, 23*(4), 354–358.
Lord, R. G. (1985). An information processing approach to social perceptions, leadership perceptions and behavioral measurement on organizational settings. In B. M. Staw & L. Cummings (Eds.), *Research in Organizational Behavior,* (pp. 87–128). JAI Press.
Lord, R. G., & Brown, D. J. (2001). Leadership, values, and subordinate self-concepts. *The Leadership Quarterly, 12*(2), 133–152.
Lord, R. G., Brown, D. J., Harvey, J. L., & Hall, R. J. (2001). System constraints on leadership perceptions, behavior and influence: An example of connectionist level processes. In M. Hogg & R. Tinsdale (Eds.), *Blackwell Handbook of Social Psychology: Vol. 3. Group processes* (pp. 283–310). Blackwell.

Lord, R. G., Epitropaki, O., Foti, R., & Keller-Hansbrough, T. (2020). Implicit leadership and followership theories and dynamic processing of leadership information. *Annual Review of Organizational Psychology and Organizational Behavior, 7*, 49–74.

Lord, R. G., Foti, R. J., & De Vader, C. L. (1984). A test of leadership categorization theory: Internal structure, information processing, and leadership perceptions. *Organizational Behavior and Human Performance, 34*(3), 343–378.

Lord, R. G., & Maher, K. J. (1991). *Leadership and Information Processing: Linking Perceptions and Performance*. Unwin Hyman.

Lord, R. G., & Shondrick, S. J. (2011). Leadership and knowledge: Symbolic, connectionist, and embodied perspectives. *Leadership Quarterly, 22*(1), 207–222.

Macrae, C. N., Bodenhausen, G. V., Milne, A. B., & Jetten, J. (1994). Out of mind but back in sight: Stereotypes on the rebound. *Journal of Personality and Social Psychology, 67*(5), 808–817.

Marchioro, C. A. (2000). *The effect of leader disability on leadership perceptions* (Unpublished doctoral dissertation). University of Akron, Ohio.

Medvedeff, M. E., & Lord, R. G. (2007) Implicit leadership theories as dynamic processing structures. In B. Shamir, R. Pillai, M. C. Bligh & M. Uhl-Bien (Eds.), *Follower-centred Perspectives on Leadership* (pp. 19–50). Information Age.

Meindl, J. R. (1995). The romance of leadership as a follower-centric theory: A social constructionist approach. *Leadership Quarterly, 6*(3), 329–341.

Murphy, S. E., & Johnson, S. K. (2011). The benefits of a long-lens approach to leader development: Understanding the seeds of leadership. *The Leadership Quarterly, 22*(3), 459–470.

Nicolaides, V. C., LaPort, K. A., Chen, T. R., Tomassetti, A. J., Weis, E. J., Zaccaro, S. J., & Cortina, J. M. (2014). The shared leadership of teams: A meta-analysis of proximal, distal, and moderating relationships. *Leadership Quarterly, 25*(5), 923–942.

Nieberle, K. W., Braun, S., Epitropaki, O., Kark, R., & Frey, D. (2021). *Dare to share the lead: The social-cognitive building blocks of shared leadership*. Working manuscript.

Nye, J. L., & Forsyth, D. R. (1991). The effects of prototype-based biases on leadership appraisals: A test of leadership categorization theory. *Small Group Research, 22*, 360–379.

Offermann, L. R., & Coats, M. R. (2017). Implicit theories of leadership: Stability and change over two decades. *Leadership Quarterly, 29*, 513–522.

Offermann, L. R., Kennedy, J. K., & Wirtz, P. W. (1994). Implicit leadership theories: Content, structure, and generalizability. *Leadership Quarterly, 5*(1), 43–58.

Pearce, C. L., & Conger, J. A. (Eds.. (2003). *Shared Leadership: Reframing the Hows and Whys of Leadership*. Sage.

Purdie-Vaughns, V., & Eibach, R. P. (2008). Intersectional invisibility: The distinctive advantages and disadvantages of multiple subordinate-group identities. *Sex Roles: A Journal of Research, 59*(5-6), 377–391.

Riggs, B., & Porter, C. (2017). Are there advantages to seeing leadership the same? A test of the mediating effects of LMX on the relationship between ILT congruence and employees' development. *Leadership Quarterly, 28*, 285–299.

Rosch, E. (1978). Principles of categorization. In E. Rosch & B. B. Lloyd (Eds.), *Cognition and Categorization* (pp. 27–48). Lawrence Erlbaum.

Rosette, A. S., Leonardelli, G. J., & Phillips, K. W. (2008). The white standard: Racial bias in leader categorization. *Journal of Applied Psychology, 93*(4), 758–777.

Rosette, A. S., & Livingston, R. W. (2012). Failure is not an option for Black women: Effects of organizational performance on leaders with single versus dual-subordinate identities. *Journal of Experimental Social Psychology, 48*(5), 1162–1167.

Rush, M. C., Thomas, J. C., & Lord R. G. (1977). Implicit leadership theory: A potential threat to the internal validity of leader behavior questionnaires. *Organizational Behavior and Human Performance, 20*, 93–110.

Scott, C. P. R., Jiang, H., Wildman, J. L., & Griffith, R. (2018). The impact of implicit collective leadership theories on the emergence and effectiveness of leadership networks in teams. *Human Resource Management Review, 28*(4), 464–481.

Schein, V. E. (1973). The relationship between sex role stereotypes and requisite management characteristics. *Journal of Applied Psychology, 57*, 95–100.

Schein, V. E., & Mueller, R. (1992). Sex role stereotyping and requisite management characteristics: A cross cultural look. *Journal of Organizational Behavior, 13*(5), 439–447.

Schyns, B., Kiefer, T. & Foti, R. J. (2020). Does thinking of myself as leader make me want to lead? *The role of congruence in self-theories and implicit leadership theories in motivation to lead, Journal of vocational behavior, 122*, p. 103477.

Shondrick, S. J., Dinh, J. E., & Lord, R. G. (2010). Developments in implicit leadership theory and cognitive science: Applications to improving measurement and understanding alternatives to hierarchical leadership. *Leadership Quarterly, 21*, 959–978.

Shondrick, S. J., & Lord, R. G. (2010). Implicit leadership and followership theories: Dynamic structures for leadership perceptions, memory and leader-follower processes. In G. P. Hodgkinson & J. K.

Ford (Eds.), *International Review of Industrial and Organizational Psychology* (25, pp. 1–33). Wiley.

Smith, E. R., & Zárate, M. A. (1992). Exemplar-based model of social judgment. *Psychological Review*, 99(1), 3–21.

Smith, J. A., & Foti, R. J. (1998). A pattern approach to the study of leader emergence. *Leadership Quarterly*, 9, 147–160.

Spears, R., & Haslam, S. A. (1997). Stereotyping and the burden of cognitive load. In R. Spears, P. J. Oakes, N. Ellemers & S. A. Haslam (Eds.), *The Social Psychology of Stereotyping and Group Life* (pp. 171–207). Blackwell.

Sy, T. (2010). What do you think of followers? Examining the content, structure and consequences of implicit followership theories. *Organizational Behavior and Human Decision Processes*, 113, 73–84.

Sy, T., & McCoy, T. (2014). Being both leaders and followers: Advancing a model of leader follower role switching. In L. M. Lapierre & M. K. Carsten (Eds.), *Followership: What is it and Why do People Follow?* (1st edn, pp. 121–140). Emerald.

Sy, T., Shore, L. M., Strauss, J., Shore, T. H., Tram, S., Whiteley, P., & Ikeda-Muromachi, K. (2010). Leadership perceptions as a function of race-occupation fit: The case of Asian Americans. *Journal of Applied Psychology*, 95, 902–919.

Tajfel, H., & Turner, J. C. (2004). The social identity theory of intergroup behavior. In J. T. Jost & J. Sidanius (Eds.), *Political Psychology: Key Readings* (pp. 276–293). Psychology Press.

Thomas, G., Martin, R., Epitropaki, O., Guillaume, Y., & Lee, A. (2013). Social cognition in leader-follower relationships: Applying insights from relationship science to understanding relationship-based approaches to leadership. *Journal of Organizational Behavior*, 34(S1), S63–S81.

Uhl-Bien, M. (2006). Relational leadership theory. *Leadership Quarterly*, 17(6), 654–676. https://doi.org/10.1016/j.leaqua.2006.10.007

Uhl-Bien, M., Riggio, R. E., Lowe, K. B., & Carsten, M. K. (2014). Followership theory: A review and research agenda. *Leadership Quarterly*, 25, 83–104.

Uhlmann, E. L., Leavitt, K., Menges, J. L., Koopman, J., Howe, M., & Johnson, R. E. (2012). Getting explicit about the implicit: A taxonomy of implicit measures and guide for their use in organizational research. *Organizational Research Methods*, 15(4), 553–601.

Van Gils, S., Van Quaquebeke, N., & van Knippenberg, D. (2010). The X-factor: On the relevance of implicit leadership and followership theories for leader–member exchange agreement. *European Journal of Work and Organizational Psychology*, 19, 333–363.

Vancouver, J. B., & Colton, C. E. (2020). *Computational Modeling: Getting Dynamic Theory Correct*. Edward Elgar.

Vancouver, J. B., & Weinhardt, J. M. (2012). Modeling the mind and the milieu: Computational modeling for micro-level organizational researchers. *Organizational Research Methods*, 15, 602–623.

van Quaquebeke, N., van Knippenberg, D., & Eckloff, T. (2011). Individual differences in the leader categorization to openness to influence relationship: The role of followers' self-perception and social comparison orientation. *Group Processes & Intergroup Relations*, 14(5), 605–622.

Wang, D., Waldman, D. A., & Zhang, Z. (2014). A meta-analysis of shared leadership and team effectiveness. *Journal of Applied Psychology*, 99(2), 181–198.

Wang, X., & Peng, J. (2016). The effect of implicit–explicit followership congruence on benevolent leadership: Evidence from Chinese family firms. *Frontiers in Psychology*, 7, Article 812.

Westcott, D. (2017). *Coming Out of the Role Congruity Closet: The Effect of Leadership Style, Gender and Sexual Orientation on Leadership Perceptions*. Unpublished MSc dissertation, Durham University.

Wu, Q., Cormican, K., & Chen, G. (2020). A meta-analysis of shared leadership: antecedents, consequences, and moderators. *Journal of Leadership & Organizational Studies*, 27(1), 49–64.

Leadership, Emotion Regulation and Sense-making

Ashlea C. Troth, Peter J. Jordan and Neal M. Ashkanasy

Research on the role of emotion-related phenomena (e.g., emotional intelligence, emotional contagion, discrete emotions) in leadership processes has proliferated since the publication of key articles by Ashkanasy and Tse (2000) and George (2000). We conducted a search of the literature to understand how leadership and emotions research has grown, and found the field has expanded from just a handful of articles in 2000 to almost 80 in 2020 (Figure 11.1). Our search also revealed that an increasing number of leadership and emotions articles focus specifically on leadership and emotion regulation (ER). The major aim of this chapter is therefore to discuss the place of emotions, and more specifically ER, in leadership and to provide guidance for future practitioners and researchers.

Our specific research questions are: 1) How do leaders regulate their own emotions at the *individual level* (i.e., use strategies to modify or maintain their own emotional experiences and expressions)? 2) How do leaders regulate their own and others' emotions at the *interpersonal level* (e.g., use strategies to regulate the emotional experiences and expressions of followers)? 3) How can leaders encourage their followers to regulate their own emotions (cf. Troth et al., 2018)? To address these questions, we also examine how a leader's ER might support leader and subordinate sense-making (defined by Maitlis & Christianson, 2014, as an individual's need to understand their expectations in an organisational context). We conclude that, through the use of ER at the individual and interpersonal level, leaders should be able to interpret (or reinterpret) the meaning of their own emotional responses to organisational events, or at least enable their subordinates to do so.

Ashkanasy and Tse (2000) and George (2000) originally promoted the idea that leadership involves ER processes whereby leaders consciously or unconsciously use strategies to manage their own and their subordinates' experience and expression of emotion – with consequences for performance, attitudes and health. For instance, a leader might attempt to reframe subordinates' feelings of anxiety or anger in the face of organisational change as a means to engender enthusiasm and optimism. Alternatively, a leader might deliver negative performance feedback that initiates subordinate disappointment or embarrassment (precipitating either performance improvement or decline). Overall, the topic of leader ER is important to understand because such regulation is likely to have significant outcomes for the leaders themselves, their employees and the organisations in which they work (see Niven et al., 2019; Vasquez et al., 2020).

Leadership and Emotion Publications

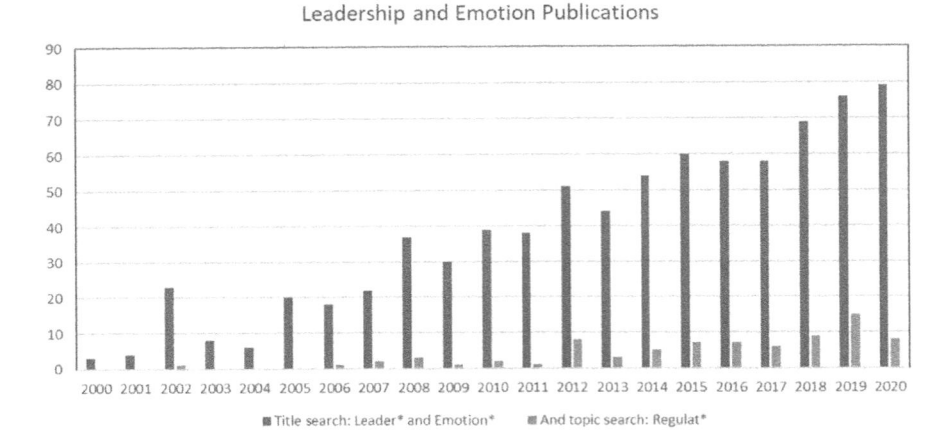

Figure 11.1 Publications listed in *Web of Science* that include 'Leader*' and 'Emotion*' in the title

A small but growing body of empirical work suggests further that leaders' use of interpersonal ER influences the quality of work relationships (Niven et al., 2012a; Niven et al., 2019) as well as employees' task performance (Vasquez et al., 2020) and discretional performance (such as their citizenship behaviour, see Little et al., 2012; Niven et al., 2019). In these instances, leader ER can also be conceived as supporting subordinate sensemaking (or attempts to make sense of increasing ambiguity or uncertainty) when events differ from expectations (Weick et al., 2005). These are all critical aspects of the roles of leaders in modern workplaces that we address in this chapter.

Before proceeding further, however, we need to acknowledge that the notion of leadership entailing regulation of emotion in both leaders and followers is not new (see Gates, 1995, for a historical review); and is in fact embedded in a range of different leadership styles. Shamir et al. (1993), for example, discuss ER as a central component of charismatic leadership. More recently, this idea has become more deeply embedded in the leadership literature in the form of, for example, emotional contagion (Sy et al., 2005), emotional labour (Humphrey et al., 2008) or as emotional intelligence (Antonakis et al., 2009; Dasborough et al., 2022). For instance, Arnold et al. (2015) linked emotion labour to transformational leadership. Nonetheless, while there appears a consideration of ER as a broad concept (i.e., akin to the leaders managing their own emotions), we argue that a more nuanced approach (e.g., interpersonal ER which may involve both leaders and followers) may have been overlooked.

In the following sections of this chapter, we begin by overviewing our conceptualisation of leadership and emotions. We then present Ashkanasy's (2003a) five-level model of emotion (FLME) in organisations (see also Ashkanasy & Dorris, 2017; Ashkanasy & Humphrey, 2011a, b) as a useful framework for researchers and practitioners to think about the myriad ways emotion and leadership are intertwined. Our focus is on individual (leader) and interpersonal (leader and follower) ER at the lower levels of the FLME – and what this means for leadership and sense-making. To round off, we highlight a relatively new framework: the Troth et al. (2018) 2x2 categorisation of interpersonal ER at work, which we adapt to the context of leadership (Figure 11.2). We conclude by considering future directions for researchers and implications for practitioners.

LEADERSHIP

For the purposes of this chapter, we adopt Yukl and Gardner's (2019) general definition of leadership as an influence process (which may include the salience of interpersonal ER), where the leader interprets group or organisational goals (which may include sense-making), motivates and coordinates followers to achieve those goals, and then marshals the necessary internal and external resources to maximise the chances that the goals will be met. In essence, this definition presents leadership as a form of human capital mobilisation, enacted within

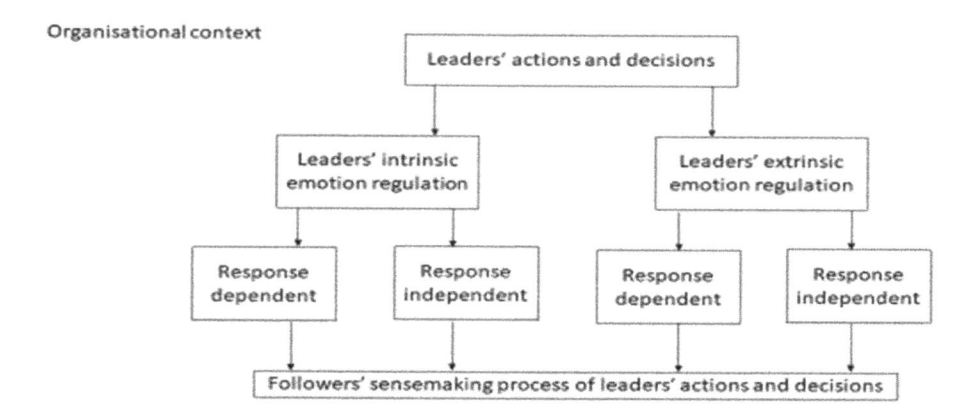

Figure 11.2 Leaders' emotion regulation options and followers' interpretation of those options (adapted from Troth et al. 2018)

the context of a particular societal and organisational context. Notably, a corollary of this definition is that such leadership must intrinsically adopt a follower-centric approach (Meindl, 1990).

In this regard, and as Ashkanasy and Tse (2000) point out, emotions play a critical role in leadership processes, especially in the context of transformational leadership (Bass & Riggio, 2006) and leader–member exchange (LMX: Graen & Uhl-Bien, 1995). Leaders both convey emotions to their followers (via contagion, see Sy et al., 2005) and receive emotions from their followers (Tee et al., 2013) via an interactive process (Dasborough et al., 2009). In this respect, Gooty et al. (2010) conclude that leadership is, at its core, an intrinsically emotional exchange process. We therefore view ER (both individual and interpersonal) strategies to be inexorably part of these processes, particularly when attempting to achieve some form of sense-making or sense-breaking (i.e., how individuals and organisations redirect existing cognitive associations to form new meanings for the self or others; cf. Giuliani, 2016).

in that organisation (Weiss & Cropanzano, 1996). Drawing on the ideas of Weick et al. (2005), Maitlis et al. (2013) argue that emotions are a sense-making tool to help individuals develop an explanation of situations and events. Indeed, effective interpersonal ER could form a conduit in some instances through which leaders guide their followers to make sense of the emotions they attach to various organisational events such as mergers or restructuring. A leader, for example, might seek to help temper subordinates' negative emotional reactions to new colleagues by helping subordinates to reframe using cognitive reappraisal (e.g., try to find out different information about the other person) or attentional deployment (e.g., try to reduce or neutralise their negative feelings by focusing concentration elsewhere). Such strategies can be conceived as a form of sense-making. We argue that greater understanding of the potential of ER in this regard can be achieved by examining this phenomenon through the lens of Ashkanasy's (2003a) FLME.

EMOTIONS

Emotion research has an extensive history across a range of different disciplines including psychology (Plamper, 2015), sociology (Stearns, 2008) and anthropology (Reddy, 1999). The main reason that emotions have emerged as a focus in business research is the premise that they provide signals to leaders about their organisations; and drive the attitudes and behaviour of the individuals working

EMOTIONS AND LEADERSHIP IN THE FLME

As we noted earlier, Ashkanasy and his colleagues (Ashkanasy & Jordan, 2008; Ashkanasy & Humphrey, 2011b) outline a framework for emotions and leadership that captures how emotions work at multiple levels in organisations, based on the FLME. This approach is based on the notion that emotions in general, and more especially in the context of leadership, need to be considered at five different levels of analysis: 1) at the within-person level, where positive and negative emotions can vary moment-by-moment and day-by-day for an individual; 2) at a between-persons level, where personal dispositions, abilities (e.g., emotional intelligence) and attitudes can play a pivotal role for that individual; 3) at the level of interpersonal relationships, where emotional displays, perceptions and exchanges (e.g., LMX) take place, which introduce the reactions of other people into this process; 4) at the level of teams and groups, where group affective tone (cf. Collins et al., 2013) and emotional contagion (Johnson, 2009) come into the equation; and 5) at the organisational level (Ashkanasy & Härtel, 2014) involving both deeply embedded and perennial affective culture as well as a more ephemeral climate that varies in line with organisational-level affective events (Ashton-James & Ashkanasy, 2008). At each of these five levels, the reactions of leaders can play a major role in determining outcomes at work.

In terms of ER, researchers who have looked at leadership at Level 1 of the FLME (within-person temporal variations) include Jordan and Lindebaum (2015), who proposed a theoretical model for understanding the use of scripts by leaders in relation to managing their own emotions across situations. Arnold et al. (2015) conducted empirical work at around the same time and found relationships between leadership styles and ER (in this case as emotion labour) in different situations. Also focusing on emotional labour, Edelman and van Knippenberg (2017) found that ER techniques (surface and deep acting) which are important processes for maintaining a professional demeanour could be improved by training for leaders. Clearly, based on this evidence, how leaders manage their own emotions across situations is important.

At Level 2 of the FLME (between-persons), Ashkanasy and Jordan (2008) identify two approaches: 1) trait and 2) behavioural. In terms of traits, despite the long-held view that leaders are *born rather than made* (see Stogdill, 1974), more recent twin research (Arvey et al., 2006) has established that the nature-nurture balance is roughly 50-50. Much of the recent behaviourally focused research on trait affective leadership have instead focused on emotional intelligence, where some scholars (e.g., Ashkanasy & Dasborough, in Antonakis et al., 2009) maintain that emotional intelligence is a critical skill for leadership effectiveness, while others (e.g., Antonakis, in the same article) maintain that emotional intelligence plays no role, and can even result in the *curse of emotions* (p. 250) effect, where over-emphasis on emotions is detrimental to good leadership (see Dasborough et al., 2022, for a more recent update on this debate). Nevertheless, the issue here is that central to understanding Level 3 is the idea that leaders differ in their ability to manage emotions at work.

At Level 3 of the FLME (interpersonal relationships) more research is evident. For instance, Chuang et al. (2012) found that transformational leaders can enable followers to amplify positive emotions to enhance customers' experiences. In another study, Fisk and Friesen (2012) found that the quality of leader–member exchanges (LMX) influences employee satisfaction through emotional labour. Specifically, deep acting (seeking actually to feel an expressed emotion) appears to be important to enable followers to function effectively in low-quality exchanges; while surface acting (pretending to feel an expressed emotion) is antithetical to prosocial behaviour in high-quality relationships (Fisk & Friesen, 2012). On this basis, how leaders are perceived and interact with individual followers (i.e., enact ER) is a critical component of effective leadership.

Research on leadership and emotions has also been conducted at Level 4 of the FLME (groups and teams), which deals with the manner in which leaders interact with members of their teams. Research conducted on this topic includes the effects of downward ER of the leader towards their team (Sy et al., 2005) and upward ER of the team influencing the leaders' emotions (Tee et al., 2013). In this regard, Sirén and her associates (2020) demonstrated the importance of ER as a key factor enabling leader emergence in nascent venture teams. Again, the evidence tells us that emotions become important for leaders when dealing with groups of people and teams at work.

At Level 5 of the FLME (the organisation as a whole), research has tended to focus on how leaders can shape the climate and culture of the organisation (Ashkanasy & Härtel, 2014), and especially how they can help determine what de Rivera (1992) refers to as *a palpable phenomenon* (p. 197) of emotion across the whole organisation. Ashkanasy and Härtel (2014) argue further that an organisation's positive and/or negative emotional climate can vary with time depending upon the organisation's leader's response to both internal and external affective events (see also Ashton-James & Ashkanasy, 2008). While an under-researched phenomenon, the emotional climate of an organisation can often be directly linked to the leadership of that organisation.

In this chapter, our focus regarding ER and leadership is primarily on Levels 2 and 3 of the FLME although, as Ashkanasy (2003b) emphasises, all five levels are closely interconnected (see also Ashkanasy & Dorris, 2017). This is especially true in the context of organisational sense-making, where employees seek to make sense of their world within a given group (i.e., Level 4) or organisational (i.e., Level 5) context.

Emotion Regulation and Leadership at the Individual Level of Analysis (Levels 1 and 2 in the FLME)

As we noted earlier, ER research has been primarily conducted at these levels. According to Lawrence et al. (2011), the main approach to workplace ER at the individual level has been to use one of three theoretical perspectives: 1) Gross's (1998) ER process model (Gross 2013), 2) emotional labour (Grandey et al., 2013; Humphrey et al., 2015), or 3) Mayer and Salovey's (1997) ability model of emotional intelligence (see Côté, 2014 for a review). We note, however, that the most frequently used ER model in the workplace literature is Gross's (1998) *process model* and this will be the focus of our chapter.

These strategies can be either antecedent-focused (prior to full development of an emotional experience) or response-focused (after a discrete emotion has been experienced). Gross (1998) identified four categories of antecedent ER strategies: 1) situation selection, 2) situation modification, 3) attentional deployment and 4) cognitive change (e.g., cognitive reappraisal), together with a fifth response-focused category of response modulation (e.g., expressive suppression). More recently, authentic expression of emotion without modification (see Lawrence et al., 2011) has come to be recognised as a valid ER response-focused strategy.

In terms of application to leadership, Williams (2007) offers examples of how managers or leaders might use the different Gross strategies in effective ways to reduce their feelings of threat, especially when they need to make sense of situations they experience on a daily basis (Maitlis & Christianson, 2014). For example, in terms of *situation selection* (reducing their own negative feelings of fear or trepidation), a leader might modify a threat-inducing situation by changing the environment, for example, by holding a meeting at a restaurant instead of a boardroom. In terms of *attentional deployment* (reducing their own feelings of an emotion, for instance boredom or apathy), a leader might redirect their attention to a part of a project that they enjoy as a means to reduce their negative affect and increase their enthusiasm. *Cognitive reappraisal* could be used effectively by a leader to reframe the way they think about chairing board meetings from one of defending their position to members and evoking their own feelings of threat, to seeing it as an opportunity for collaboration to increase their own positive affect during the meeting. Finally, an example of *expressive suppression* (or modulation of the leaders' emotional display despite fully feeling the emotion) might be a leader telling themselves to 'not show any emotion' when going into a high-stakes meeting. Together with the research showing these different types of ER strategies have different health and performance outcomes (see Gross & John, 2003; John & Gross, 2004) and are context-dependent (English et al., 2017), understanding ER suggests potential ways to educate and to train current and future leaders to make sense of and more intentionally choose ways to regulate their emotions.

Leadership and Interpersonal Emotion Regulation (Level 3 in the FLME)

While ER research has been primarily conducted at the individual level of analysis, researchers (e.g., see Côté et al., 2013; Kafetsios et al., 2014a, b; Little et al., 2012; Niven et al., 2012a; Zaki & Williams 2013) are beginning to recognise the critical importance of ER as an interpersonal phenomenon – especially in leadership contexts (which inherently concern relationships). Indeed, evidence continues to emerge that both leaders' and employees' perceptions of workplace events shape their emotional experiences and expressions as well as the emotional experiences and expressions of others (Lawrence et al., 2011; Vasquez et al., 2020).

In this chapter, we draw upon Troth and colleagues' (2018) framework, grounded in the work of Zaki & Williams (2013), to consider four types of interpersonal ER processes that can be used by leaders and consider how this applies to the leadership context and is a potential tool for sense-making (for the leader and their followers). We argue that the Troth et al. (2018) 2x2 categorisation scheme can be adapted to consider interpersonal ER distinctions in the leadership context (see Figure 11.2) according to one of four types: 1) ER seen as a purely extrinsic process; 2) differentiation of extrinsic interpersonal from intrinsic individual ER; 3) co-occurring intrinsic and extrinsic interpersonal ER; or 4) interpersonal co-regulation, where both interactants seek simultaneously to regulate their own and the other's emotions.

In the following sections, we outline the 2x2 taxonomy first proposed by Zaki and Williams (2013) and developed further by Troth and her colleagues (2018). We then discuss in more detail each of the four types of processes.

The first distinction in this view of ER is the extent to which the target of a regulation is *intrinsic* or *extrinsic* (Gross, 2013; Zaki & Williams, 2013). The second is the extent to which interpersonal regulation strategies are *response-dependent* or *response-independent* (Hofmann, 2014; Zaki & Williams 2013).

Distinction 1: Intrinsic Versus Extrinsic ER

Intrinsic strategies. These encompass *the process by which individuals influence which emotions they have, when they have them and how they experience and express these emotions* (Gross, 1998, p. 275). By intrinsic, consistent with Gross, we mean regulation in which individuals regulate their own emotions. For example, leader might reduce their own negative feelings (e.g., trepidation, anxiety) about giving negative performance feedback to subordinates by reframing the episode as an opportunity to develop and to mentor subordinates. This should then increase the leader's own positive feelings of enthusiasm and satisfaction. Intrinsic regulation can also refer to episodes where individuals utilise social interactions with others to regulate their own experiences (Hofmann, 2014; Zaki & Williams, 2013). For example, leaders might increase their feelings of enthusiasm about a new organisational initiative by associating themselves with peers or employees who tend to be more optimistic and positive about new ideas in general. In essence, intrinsic ER enables individuals (in this case leaders) to achieve the right emotional state to make sense of a situation. Indeed, Antonakis's observation (in Antonakis et al., 2009) about the potential *curse of emotions* for leaders could, we argue, be premised on the leader considering or experiencing emotions without intrinsic regulation.

Extrinsic strategies. These come into play when a person attempts to regulate another person's emotion (Gross, 2013; Hofmann, 2014; Zaki & Williams, 2013). This might also include repeated episodes in which a person attempts to regulate another person's emotions and requires feedback from the target to know that this regulatory goal has been attained (e.g., Ashkanasy & Humphrey, 2011b; Gracia & Ashkanasy, 2014; Zaki & Williams, 2013). For example, a leader might attempt to reduce subordinates' negative affect by cheering them up with praise or humour (Niven et al., 2009). Again, in terms of sense-making, a leader being able to help individuals to regulate their emotions is an important part of the leader's role to maintain workplace emotional stability (i.e., to deal with situations that may arise at work). Extrinsic ER by leaders enables followers to create space for a sense-making process to be completed.

Distinction 2: Response Dependence versus Independence

Response-dependent ER. This refers to a dynamic regulation process between the leader and follower in the sense that verbal and/or non-verbal feedback loop(s) from followers (receivers) act as a signal back to the leaders (senders) to either maintain or to modify their ER strategy, and vice versa from leader to follower (e.g., Ashkanasy & Humphrey, 2011a; Zaki & Williams, 2013). As such, this is a regulation process in which no feedback loop is overtly considered (e.g., Little et al., 2012; Zaki & Williams 2013). Each may be of use for both leaders and followers in the sense-making process. For example, in engaging in response-dependent ER, the leader might receive signals back for followers that his or her attempts at promoting a specific emotional state are not working (e.g., telling followers to move on after receiving bad news without giving them space to make sense of the situation).

Response-independent ER. This form of ER is often used by leaders in crisis situations to control situations (e.g., calls for calm to resolve a crisis). It is independent because leaders do not depend on the response of another (e.g., followers) to fulfil the regulatory goal (see Troth et al., 2018). For example, a leader might use other-focused actions or conversation content (e.g. verbally reframing an email about a reduction in work hours to emphasise the minimisation of job losses) to regulate follower emotions (e.g., to reduce anger or fear) while engaging in the sense-making process.

Having discussed the two key distinctions in ER theory we now outline the four ER processes defined by the two distinctions.

Extrinsic Interpersonal Emotion Regulation

The most dominant approach to conceptualising and examining interpersonal ER phenomena in the workplace is to view it as a wholly extrinsic process, where only another's emotion is regulated (Gross, 2013; Little et al., 2012; Williams 2007). While extrinsic regulation processes can occur both consciously and unconsciously (Gross, 2013), the focus of extrinsic interpersonal ER model is on how an individual (e.g., a leader) intentionally regulates (or, more darkly, 'manipulates') the emotions of others using different regulation strategies. Auvinen and colleagues (2013) argue that what distinguishes intentional regulation or influence from manipulation is really the motivation and method of influence (e.g., calming others down in a volatile situation may require influence, whereas getting them enthusiastic for a project and hiding the benefits for the leader may be manipulation). For example, in terms of helping followers to make sense of changes in the workplace, leaders may focus on positive messaging and reasons behind by the initiative to reduce resistance to change. In terms of sense-making, this would enable followers to conceptualise the change as low impact or as an opportunity.

Researchers taking an extrinsic approach have variously employed Gross's (1998) ER process, emotional labour, or emotional intelligence to guide the development of their models. Scholars utilising this framework to conceptualise interpersonal strategies to achieve extrinsic ER goals specifically in a leadership context frequently reference work by Little and her colleagues (e.g., Little et al., 2012; Little et al., 2016) who all build on the work of Williams (2007). These researchers developed an interpersonal emotional management measure (Little et al., 2012) to assess how leaders' use of different ER strategies (as perceived by their followers) influences perceptions of leader–follower relationship quality and follower citizenship behaviours and job satisfaction. These interpersonal ER strategies map directly from four of Gross's individual strategy categories that we described earlier: 1) situation modification, 2) attention deployment, 3) cognitive reappraisal and 4) response modulation.

In terms of a leader using *situation modification*, Little et al. (2012) give the example of a vice-president who, to deal with the anger and frustration felt by clerical employees, worked behind the scenes to ensure the transfer of their difficult boss. In terms of *attentional deployment*, a manager might divert the topic of conversation from threats to opportunities or use appropriate humour in a meeting to improve followers' emotions. In terms of *cognitive change/reappraisal* – perhaps most closely aligned with sense-making (in terms of perspective-making) – a leader faced with disgruntled staff during organisational disruption could reappraise/reframe the situation by highlighting the greater business sustainability and job security for staff in order to provide a sense-making rationale for the change but also to influence the emotions of the employees about the change. Finally, a leader, when confronted with a situation involving violations of expectations, might attempt to *suppress* follower reactions by telling them to 'relax' or to 'calm down' as a means to enable followers to make sense of the situation and subsequently to resolve that situation.

In sum, researchers taking the extrinsic ER approach have tended to conceptualise interpersonal ER as extrinsic and response-independent (i.e., not contingent upon the response of the target to fulfil the regulatory goal). This approach focuses on the leader (sender) using other-focused actions or conversation content to regulate the subordinate's emotions.

Differentiating Extrinsic Interpersonal from Intrinsic Individual ER

In the next approach, researchers differentiate between ER at the individual versus interpersonal level in terms of intrinsic (own-individual) versus extrinsic (other-interpersonal) processes respectively. These scholars (e.g., Hallam et al., 2014; Niven et al., 2009; Niven et al., 2011; Niven et al., 2012a; Niven et al., 2012b) reason that intrinsic ER strategies are inherently individual in nature (see also Gross, 2013). Niven and her colleagues are the main proponents of this approach (Niven et al., 2009; Niven et al., 2011; Niven et al., 2012a; Niven et al., 2012b). Their focus is on controlled (conscious) interpersonal regulation, where individuals seek actively to manipulate the emotional experiences of self and others via four main types of interpersonal ER strategies: 1) intrinsic affect-improving; 2) intrinsic affect-worsening; 3) extrinsic affect-improving, or 4) extrinsic affect-worsening.

Niven and her associates provide many examples of negative feedback, criticism and bullying as examples of affect-worsening extrinsic regulation strategies. They suggest social support provision (e.g., emotional, positive reappraisal) and the use of humour can be considered as examples of affect-improving extrinsic strategies. More recently, Niven et al. (2019) tested elements of these types of strategies in the context of leadership – in conjunction with how followers' perceive the underlying motives (e.g., prosocial or egoistical) of their leader for engaging in the ER of their follower. They found complex and unexpected effects; for example, improving employees' affect does not necessarily lead to favourable employee outcomes if the employee attributes their leaders IER strategies towards them as self-serving. This demonstrates the importance of perceived motives or intentions behind a leader's ER efforts towards their followers. For followers assessing these, motivations is a key part of the sense-making process, especially when events at work initiated by a leader necessitate the followers needing to make sense of the situation.

Co-occurring Extrinsic and Intrinsic Interpersonal Emotion Regulation

While the co-creation of leadership has been a topic for many scholars (Lord et al., 1999), as Troth et al. (2018) note, a less common approach to interpersonal ER is to consider how intrinsic and extrinsic ER processes might co-occur within a relationship context (e.g., Rimé, 2007, 2009; Zaki & Williams 2013), a truly interpersonal-level approach. Scholars addressing this approach argue that it is important to distinguish between two types of interpersonal ER processes: intrinsic interpersonal regulation, in which an individual tries to initiate social contact with another to regulate her or his own emotional experiences, and extrinsic interpersonal regulation, where an individual attempts to regulate another's emotional experiences and expressions. This contrasts strikingly with the differentiated approach insofar as, in this case, interpersonal ER processes are seen simultaneously to involve both the regulation of the actor's own emotional experiences (intrinsic) *and* the regulation of the target's emotional experiences (extrinsic) – that can be either feedback-dependent or response-independent. Thus, in essence, ER strategies enacted during intrinsic regulation while focused on the actor's own emotions come to be viewed as interpersonal in nature. For example, in the leadership context, where both parties need to deal with organisational change, the leader might endeavour to regulate their own and their employee's emotions *within* the interaction simultaneously in response to the emotion-eliciting change. Depending on the strategies chosen, this could impact interpretation of the situation and possibly result in a mutually acceptable response to the situation.

This combined intrinsic and extrinsic approach encapsulates a social sharing of emotions and is a much more comprehensive and broad view of interpersonal ER. To understand this view further, it is useful to refer again to Zaki and Williams's (2013) framework (that builds on Rimé's, 2009, conceptualisation of interpersonal ER). Zaki and Williams distinguish between intrinsic and extrinsic ER strategies by focusing on those responses that are overtly interpersonal in nature (e.g., empathy, social support, emotion expression, prosocial behaviour), and whether or not these strategies form part of either response-dependent (i.e., rely on the particular qualities of another person's feedback) or response-independent processes (i.e., occur in the context of social interactions, but do not require that another person respond in any particular way).

An example of this type of co-occurring ER may be seen when charismatic leaders address their followers. Such leaders are likely to amplify their own positive emotions about a course of action or a vision while at the same time using emotive language (for instance, invoking passion) to regulate their followers' experience of that announcement. The employee's potential change in emotional expression (as a reaction to the sense-making they engage in based on the leader's actions) in turn might then partially shape the leader's subsequent emotional expressions to further regulate the employee's emotions. Equally, when delivering bad news, especially regarding violated expectations, leaders may suppress their negative emotions and communicate the news to followers in a way designed to impart a slow consideration (a form of sense-making) of the impact of the bad news to assist the followers in suppressing panic or sadness and make sense of the situation.

Interpersonal Co-Regulation of Emotion

Troth et al. (2018) note that the ways in which interpersonal ER has been conceptualised in research to date still falls short of encapsulating the dynamic processes involved in many interpersonal ER encounters. This final approach to interpersonal ER focuses specifically on a two-way flow of emotion between two individuals, where the partners seek to help each other actively and dynamically to manage their emotional expressions and states (e.g., see Butler & Randall, 2013; Saxbe & Repetti, 2010; Troxel, 2013). Also known as *affective attunement* or *emotional synchrony*, these authors refer to this reciprocal process as *co-regulation of emotion* in line with Butler and Randall's (2013) terminology. This label captures the reciprocal nature of the process. Thus, during co-regulation, one person attempts to enhance or suppress their personal emotion based on the reactions of another person who, in turn, seeks to enhance or suppress his or her own personal emotion. Thus, co-regulation is an interactive and dynamic process of mutual ER. Indeed, this is akin to the dynamic process that is often involved in sense-making. Of the three broad approaches we have addressed so far in this chapter, Zaki and Williams's (2013) response-dependent (intrinsic and extrinsic) processes seem most closely to align to this concept of co-regulation.

This notion of interpersonal ER has clear applicability (and implications) for workplace affective relationships such as leader–follower relations.

There is plenty of evidence, for example, to show close affective workplace relationships often emerge in the context of mentoring or when teams are working under pressure to meet deadlines or when colleagues work together for significant periods of time (e.g., see McAllister, 1995). Butler and Randall (2013) discuss how the co-regulation construct encapsulates the constant interchange of emotions between individuals that provides a degree of emotional stability for those involved. An important feature of co-regulation is that it is a unique dyadic-level phenomenon that cannot be reduced to the behaviours or experiences of the individuals involved (Butler & Randall, 2013). In this regard, the emphasis is not on the actor's or the target's ER, but rather on the ways in which both partners attempt to influence each other in a recursive pattern of mutual regulation.

Importantly, Troth and her colleagues (2018) identify co-regulation as a distinct form of interpersonal ER. They draw on Butler and Randall's (2013) argument that many regulatory efforts are targeted at changing either a social partner's emotions or the emotional tone of the relationship, and that these efforts constitute specific examples of interpersonal ER (i.e., extrinsic approach; individual intrinsic/extrinsic interpersonal approach), rather than co-regulation *per se* (see also Niven et al., 2009). To illustrate, a team leader making a team member feel guilty so they will comply with demand is a form of extrinsic interpersonal regulation, not co-regulation. That is, extrinsic interpersonal regulation does not require a bi-directional process (unlike co-regulation). However, an interactive process that results in emotional progression and growth of understanding between individuals (e.g., supporting an employee emotionally through a difficult change process via listening, conveying empathy, providing distractions) is seen as leading to co-regulation because, in this instance, emotions change over time between the leader and follower.

In summary, interpersonal co-regulation describes the leader and followers working together to help each other to regulate their respective emotional states and displays. This process can be described as a *spiral* of emotionality (Fredrickson & Joiner, 2002, p. 172; see also Dasborough et al., 2009). These may involve escalation or de-escalation of emotions where each party relies on the other's reactions to decide the next step in ER. For leaders this may involve information-sharing during change designed to moderate the emotions followers experience during the change process. The follower's reactions then assist the leader to decide on the next step in the change process and the level of emotionality involved in that process.

FUTURE DIRECTIONS FOR EMOTION REGULATION AND LEADERSHIP RESEARCH

As can be seen in our review, there has been significant research examining ER and leadership. In the following, we identify some potential lines of research that may serve to continue this emerging interest in the role of ER in leadership research, with a focus on the heretofore little explored aspect of how ER affects follower's sense-making.

Our first suggestion is that future researchers need to develop further the idea of ER at both the individual and at the interpersonal level. Such development should have the potential to support leaders in the sense-making process, especially in the context of emotion-producing events (e.g., change, conflict, etc.). This applies especially in the context of understanding leaders' use of ER (for self and followers) and how this can affect changing employee perspectives or impacts of expectations not met. For example, are different ER strategies more effective than others when leaders attempt to support followers in sense-making processes that are underpinned by affect? From a practical perspective, this means leaders need increased awareness and knowledge about how ER and interpersonal ER are forms of conscious (or unconscious) sense-making that are available for them to utilise.

Our second suggestion for future research is to seek to understand how leaders should be trained not only about how to ER others, but also how their ER of their own emotions (intrinsic ER) affects their own sense-making of situations. Possibly, this might link to the idea of *emotions as social information* (the EASI model, see Van Kleef, 2009). Associated with this idea, researchers in the future might consider how different ER strategies such as cognitive reappraisal or situation selection can produce different sense-making outcomes.

A third potential area for future research concerns the notion that a leader's use of interpersonal ER might backfire if the leader's motives are seen by followers to be self-motivated (as opposed to prosocial, cf. Niven et al., 2019). In this case, attempts to assist employees to engage in sense-making via ER might be seen as disingenuous. Thus, from a practical perspective, it is important that leaders understand the importance of authentic ER.

Our fourth suggestion for future research is that we still need to improve our conceptualisation and measurement of ER and interpersonal ER and, at the interpersonal level, the idea that

ER can be bi-directional. For example, Tee and his colleagues (2013) found, leaders' emotional experience (regulation), and thus sense-making, is also influenced by their own followers. While this research represents a start, the reciprocal model of ER (first mooted by Dasborough et al., 2009) remains for the most part unexplored.

Our fifth and final suggestion for future research concerns the two uppermost levels in the FLME: ER at the group and organisational level. While Ashkanasy and his colleagues (Ashkanasy & Jordan, 2008; Ashkanasy & Humphrey, 2011b) suggest that ER at these levels can play an important role, empirical research at these levels remains scant. This is especially true at the organisational level, where sense-making can be seen to play a central role (cf. Maitlis & Christianson, 2014).

REFERENCES

Antonakis, J., Ashkanasy, N. M., & Dasborough, M. T. (2009). Does leadership need emotional intelligence? *Leadership Quarterly*, 20, 247–261. https://doi.org/10.1016/j.leaqua.2009.01.006.

Arnold, K. A., Connelly, C. E., Walsh, M. M., & Martin Ginis, K. A. (2015). Leadership styles, emotion regulation, and burnout. *Journal of Occupational Health Psychology*, 20, 481–490. https://doi.org/10.1037/a0039045

Arvey, R. D., Rotundo, M., Johnson, W., Zhang, Z., & McGue, M. (2006). The determinants of leadership role occupancy: Genetic and personality factors. *Leadership Quarterly*, 17, 1–20. https://doi.org/10.1016/j.leaqua.2005.10.009

Ashforth, B. E., & Humphrey, R. H. (1995). Emotion in the workplace: A reappraisal. *Human Relations*, 48, 97–125. doi: 10.1177/001872679504800201

Ashkanasy, N. M. (2003a). Emotions in organizations: A multilevel perspective. In F. Dansereau and F. J. Yammarino (Eds.), *Research In Multi-Level Issues, Volume 2: Multilevel Issues in Organizational Behavior and Strategy* (pp. 9–54). Elsevier Science. https://doi.org/10.1016/s1475-9144(03)02002-2

Ashkanasy, N. M. (2003b). Emotions at multiple levels: An integration. In F. Dansereau and F. J. Yammarino (Eds.), *Research In Multi-Level Issues, Volume 2: Multilevel Issues in Organizational Behavior and Strategy* (pp. 71–81). Elsevier/JAI Press. https://doi.org/10.1016/s1475-9144(03)02005-8

Ashkanasy, N. M., & Dorris, A. D. (2017). Organizational behavior. In O. Braddick (Ed.), *The Oxford Research Encyclopedia of Psychology*. Oxford University Press. https://doi.org/10.1093/acrefore/9780190236557.013.23

Ashkanasy, N. M., & Härtel, C. E. J. (2014). Positive and negative affective climate and culture: The good, the bad, and the ugly. In B. Schneider & K. Barbera (Eds.), *The Oxford Handbook of Organizational Culture and Climate* (pp. 136–152). Oxford University Press. https://doi.org/10.1093/oxfordhb/9780199860715.013.0008

Ashkanasy, N. M., & Humphrey, R. H. (2011a). A multi-level view of leadership and emotions: Leading with emotional labour. In A. Bryman, D. Collinson, K. Grint, B. Jackson, & M. Uhl-Bien, M. (Eds.), *The SAGE Handbook of Leadership* (pp. 363–377). Sage.

Ashkanasy, N. M., & Humphrey, R. H. (2011b). Current emotion research in organizational behavior. *Emotion Review*, 3, 214–224. https://doi.org/10.1177/1754073910391684

Ashkanasy, N. M., & Jordan, P. J. (2008). A multi-level view of leadership and emotion. In R. H. Humphrey. (Ed.), *Affect and Emotion: New Directions in Management Theory and Research* (pp. 17–39). Information Age.

Ashkanasy, N. M., & Tse, B. (2000). Transformational leadership as management of emotion: A conceptual review. In N. M. Ashkanasy, C. E. J. Härtel, & W. J. Zerbe (Eds.), *Emotions in the Workplace: Research, Theory, and Practice* (pp. 221–235). Quorum.

Ashton-James, C. E., & Ashkanasy, N. M. (2008). Affective events theory: A strategic perspective. In W. J. Zerbe, C. E. J. Härtel, & N. M. Ashkanasy (Eds.), *Research on Emotion in Organizations* (vol. 4, pp. 1–34). Emerald/JAI Press. https://doi.org/10.1016/s1746-9791(08)04001-7

Auvinen, T. P., Lämsä, A. M., Sintonen, T., & Takala, T. (2013). Leadership manipulation and ethics in storytelling. *Journal of Business Ethics*, 116(2), 415–431.

Bass, B. M., & Riggio, R. E. (2006). *Transformational Leadership*, 2nd edn. Erlbaum.

Becker, W. J., & Cropanzano, R. (2014). Good acting requires a good cast: A meso-level model of deep acting in work teams. *Journal of Organizational Behavior*, 36, 232–249.

Butler, E. A., & Randall, A. K. (2013). Emotional coregulation in close relationships. *Emotion Review*, 5, 202–210.

Chuang, A., Judge, T. A., & Liaw, Y. J. (2012). Transformational leadership and customer service: A moderated mediation model of negative affectivity and emotion regulation. *European Journal of Work and Organizational Psychology*, 21, 28–56. https://doi.org/10.1080/1359432X.2010.532911

Collins, A. L., Lawrence, S. A., Troth, A. C., & Jordan, P. J. (2013). Group affective tone: A review and future research directions. *Journal of Organizational Behavior*, 34, S43–S62. https://doi.org/10.1002/job.1887

Côté, S. (2014). Emotional intelligence in organizations. *Annual Review of Organizational Psychology and Organizational. Behavior*, 1, 459–488. https://doi.org/10.1146/annurev-orgpsych-031413-091233

Côté, S., Van Kleef, G. A., & Sy, T. (2013). The social effects of emotion regulation in organizations. In A. A. Grandey, J. M. Diefendorff & D. E. Rupp (Eds.), *Emotional Labour in the 21st Century: Diverse Perspectives on the Psychology* (pp. 288–294). Routledge.

Dasborough, M. T., Ashkanasy, N. M., Humphrey, H. H., Harms, P. D., Credé, M., & Wood, D. (2022). Does leadership still not need emotional intelligence? Continuing 'the great EI debate'. *Leadership Quarterly* This is now published as vol. 33, article no. 101539. https://doi.org/10.1016/j.leaqua.2021.101539

Dasborough, M. T., Ashkanasy, N. M., Tee, E. E. J., & Tse, H. H. M. (2009). What goes around comes around: How meso-level negative emotional contagion can ultimately determine organizational attitudes toward leaders. *Leadership Quarterly*, 20, 571–585. https://doi.org/10.1016/j.leaqua.2009.04.009

de Rivera, J. (1992). Emotional climate: Social structure and emotional dynamics. In K. T. Strongman (Ed.), *International Review of Studies on Emotion* (vol. 2, pp. 197–218). Wiley.

Edelman, P. J., & van Knippenberg, D. (2017). Training leader emotion regulation and leadership effectiveness. *Journal of Business and Psychology*, 32, 747–757. https://doi.org/10.1007/s10869-016-9471-8

English, T., Lee, I. A., John, O. P., & Gross, J. J. (2017). Emotion regulation strategy selection in daily life: The role of social context and goals. *Motivation and Emotion*, 41, 230–242. https://doi.org/10.1007/s11031-016-9597-z

Fisk, G. M., & Friesen, J. P. (2012). Perceptions of leader emotion regulation and LMX as predictors of followers' job satisfaction and organizational citizenship behaviors. *Leadership Quarterly*, 23, 1–12. https://doi.org/10.1016/j.leaqua.2011.11.001

Fredrickson, B. L., & Joiner, T. (2002). Positive emotions trigger upward spirals toward emotional well-being. *Psychological Science*, 13, 172–175. https://doi.org/10.1111/1467-9280.00431

Gates, G. (1995). A review of literature on leadership and emotion: Exposing theory, posing questions, and forwarding an agenda. *Journal of Leadership Studies*, 2, 98–110. https://doi.org/10.1177/107179199500200408

George, J. M. (2000). Emotions and leadership: The role of emotional intelligence. *Human Relations*, 53(8), 1027–1055.

Gooty, J., Connelly, S., Griffith, J., & Gupta, A. (2010). Leadership, affect and emotions: A state of the science review. *Leadership Quarterly*, 21, 979–1004. https://doi.org/10.1016/j.leaqua.2010.10.005

Gracia, E., & Ashkanasy, N. M. (2014). Emotional labour as a dynamic process in service organizations: Development of a multi-perspective, multilevel model. In W. J. Zerbe, N. M. Ashkanasy & C. E. J. Härtel (Eds.), *Research on Emotion in Organizations* (vol. 10, pp. 331–365. Emerald/JAI Press. https://doi.org/10.1108/S1746-979120140000010021

Graen, G. B., & Uhl-Bien, M. (1995). Relationship-based approach to leadership: Development of leader–member exchange (LMX) theory of leadership over 25 years: Applying a multi-level multi-domain perspective. *Leadership Quarterly*, 6, 219–247. https://doi.org/10.1016/1048-9843(95)90036-5

Grandey, A. A., Diefendorff, J. M., & Rupp, D. E. (2013). Bringing emotional labour into focus: A review and integration of three research lenses. In A. Grandey, J. Diefendorff & D. Rupp (Eds.), *Emotional Labour in the 21st Century: Diverse Perspectives on Emotion Regulation at Work* (pp. 3–27). Routledge.

Gross, J. J. (1998). The emerging field of emotion regulation: An integrative review. *Review of General Psychology*, 2, 271–299. https://doi.org/10.1037/1089-2680.2.3.271

Gross, J. J. (2010). The future's so bright, I gotta wear shades. *Emotion Review*, 2, 212–216. https://doi.org/10.1177/1754073910361982

Gross, J. J. (2013). Emotion regulation: Taking stock and moving forward. *Emotion*, 13, 359–365. https://doi.apa.org/doi/10.1037/a0032135

Gross, J. J., & John, O. P. (2003). Individual differences in two emotion regulation processes: Implications for affect, relationships, and well-being. *Journal of Personality and Social Psychology*, 85, 348–362. https://doi.org/10.1037/0022-3514.85.2.348

Giuliani, M. (2016). Sensemaking, sensegiving and sensebreaking: The case of intellectual capital measurements. *Journal of Intellectual Capital*, 17, 218–237. https://doi.org/10.1108/JIC-04-2015-0039

Hallam, G.P., Webb, T.L., Sheeran, P., Miles, E., Niven, K., Wilkinson, I.D., Hunter, M.D., Woodruff, P.W., Totterdell, P. and Farrow, T.F. (2014). The neural correlates of regulating another person's emotions: An exploratory fMRI study. *Frontiers in Human Neuroscience*, 8, 376–388.

Hofmann, S. G. (2014). Interpersonal emotion regulation model of mood and anxiety disorders. *Cognitive Therapy and Research*, 38, 483–492.

Humphrey, R. H., Pollack, J. M., & Hawver, T. (2008). Leading with emotional labour. *Journal of Managerial Psychology*, 23, 151. https://doi.org/10.1108/02683940810850790

Humphrey, R. H., Ashforth, B. E., & Diefendorff, J. (2015). The bright side of emotional labour. *Journal of Organizational Behavior*, *36*(6), 749–769.

John, O. P., & Gross, J. J. (2004). Healthy and unhealthy emotion regulation: Personality processes, individual differences, and life span development. *Journal of Personality*, *72*, 1301–1334. https://doi.org/10.1111/j.1467-6494.2004.00298.x

Johnson, S. K. (2009). Do you feel what I feel? Mood contagion and leadership outcomes. *Leadership Quarterly*, *20*, 814–827. https://doi.org/10.1016/j.leaqua.2009.06.012

Jordan, P. J., & Lindebaum, D. (2015). A model of within person variation in leadership: Emotion regulation and scripts as predictors of situationally appropriate leadership. *Leadership Quarterly*, *26*(4), 594–605.

Kafetsios, K., Athanasiadou, M., & Dimou, N. (2014a). Leaders' and subordinates' attachment orientation, emotion regulation and affect at work: A multilevel analysis. *Leadership Quarterly*, *25*, 512–527.

Kafetsios, K., Hantzara, K., Anagnostopoulos, F., & Niakas, D. (2014b). Doctors' attachment orientations, emotion regulation strategies, and patient satisfaction: A multilevel analysis. *Health Communication*, *29*, 205–214.

Lawrence, S. A., Troth, A. C., Jordan, P. J., & Collins, A. L. (2011). A review of emotion regulation and development of a framework for emotion regulation in the workplace. In P. L. Perrewé & D. C. Ganster (Eds.), *Research in Occupational Stress and Well-being* (vol. 9, pp. 197–263. Emerald. https://doi.org/10.1108/s1479-3555(2011)0000009010

Little, L. M., Gooty, J., & Williams, M. (2016). The role of leader emotion management in leader–member exchange and follower outcomes. *Leadership Quarterly*, *27* 85–97. https://doi.org/10.1016/j.leaqua.2015.08.007

Little, L. M., Kluemper, D., Nelson, D. L., & Gooty, J. (2012). Development and validation of the interpersonal emotion management scale. *Journal of Occupational and Organizational Psychology*, *85*, 407–420. https://doi.org/10.1111/j.2044-8325.2011.02042.x

Lord, R. G., Brown, D. J., & Freiberg, S. J. (1999). Understanding the dynamics of leadership: The role of follower self-concepts in the leader/follower relationship. *Organizational Behavior and Human Decision Processes*, *78*(3), 167–203.

McAllister, D. J. (1995). Affect- and cognition-based trust as foundations for interpersonal cooperation in organizations. *Academy of Management Journal*, *38*, 24–59.

Maitlis, S., & Christianson, M. (2014). Sensemaking in organizations: Taking stock and moving forward. *Academy of Management Annals*, *8*, 57–125. https://doi.org/10.5465/19416520.2014.873177

Maitlis, S., Vogus, T. J., & Lawrence, T. B. (2013). Sensemaking and emotion in organizations. *Organizational Psychology Review*, *3*, 222–247. https://doi.org/10.1177/2041386613489062

Mayer, J. D., & Salovey, P. (1997). What is emotional intelligence? In P. Salovey & D. J. Sluyter (Eds.), *Emotional Development and Emotional Intelligence* (pp. 3–31). Basic Books.

Meindl, J. R. (1990). On leadership: An alternative to the conventional wisdom. In B. Staw & L. L. Cummings (Eds.), *Research in Organizational Behavior* (vol. 12, pp. 159–203). JAI Press. https://doi.org/10.2307/2393214

Niven, K., Totterdell, P., & Holman, D. (2009). A classification of controlled interpersonal affect regulation strategies. *Emotion*, *9*, 498–509. https://doi.org/10.1037/a0015962

Niven, K., Holman, D. & Totterdell, P. (2012a). How to win friendship and trust by influencing people's feelings: An investigation of interpersonal affect regulation and the quality of relationships. *Human Relations*, *65*, 777–805.

Niven, K., Totterdell, P., Holman, D., & Headley, T. (2012b). Does regulating others' feelings influence people's own affective well-being? *Journal of Social Psychology*, *152*, 246–260.

Niven, K., Totterdell, P., Stride, C. B., & Holman, D. (2011). Emotion regulation of others and self (EROS): The development and validation of a new individual difference measure. *Current Psychology*, *30*, 53–73.

Niven, K., Troth, A. C., & Holman, D. (2019). Do the effects of interpersonal emotion regulation depend on people's underlying motives?. *Journal of Occupational and Organizational Psychology*, *92*, 1020–1026. https://doi.org/10.1111/joop.12257

Plamper, J. (2015). *The History of Emotions: An Introduction*. Oxford University Press.

Reddy, W. M. (1999). Emotional liberty: Politics and history in the anthropology of emotions. *Cultural Anthropology*, *14*, 256–288. https://www.jstor.org/stable/656565

Rimé, B. (2007). Interpersonal emotion regulation. In J. J. Gross (Ed.), *The Handbook of Emotion Regulation* (pp. 466–485). Guilford.

Rimé, B. (2009). Emotion elicits the social sharing of emotion: Theory and empirical review. *Emotion Review*, *1*(1), 60–85.

Saxbe, D., & Repetti, R. L. (2010). For better or worse? Coregulation of couples' cortisol levels and mood states. *Journal of Personality and Social Psychology*, *98*, 92–103.

Shamir, B., House, R. J., & Arthur, M. B. (1993). The motivational effects of charismatic leadership:

A self-concept based theory. *Organization Science*, *4*, 577–594. https://doi.org/10.1287/orsc.4.4.577

Sirén, C., He, V. F., Wesemann, H., Jonassen, Z., Grichnik, D., & von Krogh, G. (2020). Leader emergence in nascent venture teams: The critical roles of individual emotion regulation and team emotions. *Journal of Management Studies*, *57*, 931–961. https://doi.org/10.1111/joms.12563

Stearns, P. N. (2008). History of emotions: Issues of change and impact. In M. Lewis, J. M. Haviland-Jones & L. F. Barrett (Eds.), *Handbook of Emotions* (3rd edn, pp. 17–31). Guilford.

Stogdill, R. M. (1974). *Handbook of Leadership: A Survey of Theory and Research*. Free Press.

Sy, T., Côté, S., & Saavedra, R. (2005). The contagious leader: Impact of the leader's mood on the mood of group members, group affective tone, and group processes. *Journal of Applied Psychology*, *90*, 295–305. https://doi.org/10.1037/0021-9010.90.2.295

Tee, E. Y. J., Ashkanasy, N. M., & Paulsen, N. (2013). The influence of follower mood on leader mood and task performance: Evidence for an affective, follower-centric perspective of leadership. *Leadership Quarterly*, *24*, 496–515. https://doi.org/10.1016/j.leaqua.2013.03.005

Troth, A. C., Lawrence, S. A., Jordan, P. J., & Ashkanasy, N. M. (2018). Interpersonal emotion regulation in the workplace: A conceptual and operational review and future research agenda. *International Journal of Management Reviews*, *20*, 523–543. https://doi.org/10.1111/ijmr.12144

Troxel, W. M. (2013). Comment: Butler and Randall's 'emotion coregulation in close relationships'. *Emotion Review*, *5*, 211–212.

Van Kleef, G. A. (2009). How emotions regulate social life: The emotions as social information (EASI) model. *Current Directions in Psychological Science*, *18*, 184–188. https://doi.org/10.1111/j.1467-8721.2009.01633.x

Vasquez, C. A., Niven, K., & Madrid, H. P. (2020). Leader interpersonal emotion regulation and follower performance. *Journal of Personnel Psychology*, *19*, 97–101. https://doi.org/10.1027/1866-5888/a000249

Weick, K. E, Sutcliffe, K. M, & Obstfeld, D. (2005). Organizing and the process of sensemaking *Organization Science*, *16*, 409–421. https://doi.org/10.1287/orsc.1050.0133

Weiss, H. M., & Cropanzano, R. (1996). Affective events theory: A theoretical discussion of the structure, causes, and consequences of affective experiences at work. In B. M. Staw & L. L. Cummings (Eds.), *Research in Organizational Behavior* (vol. 18, pp. 1–74). JAI Press.

Williams, M. (2007). Building genuine trust through interpersonal emotion management: A threat regulation model of trust and collabouration across boundaries. *Academy of Management Review*, *32*, 595–621. https://doi.org/10.2307/20159317

Yukl, G., & Gardner, W. L. III. (2019) *Leadership in Organizations*, 9th edn. Pearson.

Zaki, J., & Williams, W. C. (2013). Interpersonal emotion regulation. *Emotion*, *13*, 803–810. https://doi.org/10.1037/a0033839

Authentic Leadership or Authenticity in Leadership? Finding a Better Home for Our Leadership Aspirations

Marian Iszatt-White

INTRODUCTION: HISTORICAL BACKGROUND AND THE EMERGENCE OF THE AL CONSTRUCT

The clamour for leaders to be authentic in enacting their roles is now widely heard in both the academic literature and popular media. Yet the authentic leadership (AL) construct remains deeply problematic and arguably impossible to enact. This introduction traces the historical background to the development of the AL construct and its theoretical forebears in leadership research, as a precursor to evaluating its current status.

As discussed in more detail below, the notion of authenticity has a long history in the fields of product origination and tourist attractions (see Gardner et al., 2011, for a historical overview), but it first entered the leadership lexicon in the late 1990s as a response to the apparent failure of transformational and charismatic leadership to deliver the promised counterweight to brewing ethical crises in business and more broadly. A number of high-profile corporate scandals that spanned the globe – accounting fraud at Enron Corporation in America, obtaining contracts by bribery at BAE Systems in Saudi Arabia and large-scale financial fraud at Satyam Systems in India – have all come to light since the turn of the century but there were much earlier scandals too. The flight of CEO Asil Nadir after the collapse of Polly Peck in 1991, money laundering and regulatory fraud by BCCI spanning the 1980s and accounting fraud at Barlow Clowes in 1988 started to raise concerns much earlier that powerful leaders were not always a force for good. One response to these concerns was a tighter formulation of what it meant to be transformational. Based on a distinction between 'personalised' and 'socialised' forms of leadership, Bass (1998) coined the term pseudo-transformational leadership to refer to those leaders who transform others in pursuit of their own goals, versus authentic transformational leadership, which was said to transcend individual interests in favour of the interests of others (Howell and Avolio, 1993). This distinction was further developed by Bass and Steidlmeier (1999), who delineated four components said to constitute authentic transformational leadership and grounded authenticity in moral foundations (May et al., 2003).

The 1980s had also seen the decline of manufacturing and the rise of service industries around the globe, privatisation of key industries such as rail and power in the UK and a radical change of personal horizons and perceptions following the invention of the internet. By the 1990s the prospects presented by the aspirational 1980s had been dashed and most of the major world economies had seen a dramatic economic downturn, with clamorous calls for a new kind of leadership to solve the world's problems, both economic and environmental. Against this backdrop, AL emerged as an antidote to the resultant delayering, restructuring and redundancies which demotivated employees as well as an aspirational focus for hard-pressed managers. The honours for initiating the construct are shared between three key sources. Luthans and Avolio's (2003) chapter on authentic leadership development brought together their respective interests in transformational leadership (e.g. Avolio, 1999) and positive organisational behaviour (Luthans, 2002) while George (2003; George & Sims, 2007) focused on how leaders could discover their 'True North'. Price (2003), building on Bass and Steidlmeier (1999) to make an overt connection between ethical behaviour and authenticity, was potentially the first to suggest 'authentic leadership' as an idea in its own right. These early sources were extended by May et al. (2003), to offer AL as a positive construct, and by Gardner and Schermerhorn (2004), who drew together the preceding ideas through case studies of prominent leaders to offer the connectivity of AL with organisational performativity. Avolio et al. (2004) synthesised the various strands, suggested how AL connects with follower attitudes, behaviours and performance, and were instructive and foundational to the trajectory of AL research.

As already noted, the development of AL was explicitly positioned as a response to the troubled world and loss of faith in previous forms of leadership, said to have resulted in an *ethical corporate meltdown* (May et al., 2003, p. 247). The construct grew out of attempts to answer the question *what are the factors that influence ethical decision-making processes and behaviours of leaders [...] and why* [do] *they choose to deceive their followers, shareholders and the general public?* (May et al., 2003, p. 247). Northouse (2010, p. 205) supported the appeal of AL as a response to disillusionment with past leadership scandals when he suggested that:

> *Upheavals in society have energised a tremendous demand for authentic leadership. The destruction on 9/11, corporate scandals at companies like WorldCom and Enron and massive failures in the banking industry have all created fear and uncertainty. People feel apprehensive and insecure [...] they long for bona fide leadership they can trust and for leaders who are honest and good. People's demand for leadership makes the study of authentic leadership timely and worthwhile.*

Building on this demand, the close-knit coterie of early AL writers was quickly able to gather a following for the notion of authenticity as a valuable underpinning of modern leadership. Their avowedly instrumentalist and functionalist orientation sought to meet the desired outcomes of AL for followers, alongside an alignment with enhanced organisational performance. It drew heavily on the humanistic tradition in psychology, and particularly the work of Carl Rogers' (1959) person-centred counselling approach aimed at helping people to develop into 'fully functioning' individuals – that is, able to encounter the reality of their world and deal with it honestly and without fear or delusion – and Maslow's (1968) idea of self-actualisation. Hence authentic leaders were framed as *being anchored by their own deep sense of self* (Avolio and Gardner, 2005, p. 329) and capable of owning their own personal experiences (Harter, 2002).

The launch of AL as a recognisable entity came in June 2004 with the inaugural Authentic Leadership Development Summit, entitled 'Stretching Across the Academic-Practice Divide: Crossing Borders on Authentic Leadership Perspectives' and hosted by the University of Nebraska-Lincoln's Gallup Leadership Institute and the Gallup Organisation. Despite its newness, the press release for the event heralded the 'renewal' of AL as an area of business study and its 'resurgence' as a field of scholarship. It also offered a surprisingly concrete set of criteria for so nascent a construct. These criteria found resonance in the desires of the time: as Guthey has noted (2013) leadership research has a significant role to play in the production and reproduction of popular leadership ideas and the rise of 'fashionable' approaches as cultural products. Such fashions rarely require an in-depth understanding of the underpinning research or a critical consideration of their tenets to drive their popularity.

A special issue (SI) in *The Leadership Quarterly* followed the next year. The SI provided a range of outlines of the emerging AL theory, not yet a fully fledged construct but certainly a series of aligned definitions and perspectives. Key elements developed in the SI were informed by the tenets of positive psychology. Various constructs were offered and suggestions made with regard to discriminant validity with respect to transformational leadership, ethical leadership, servant leadership and spiritual leadership, for many of which authentic leadership claimed to be the 'root construct' (Avolio and Gardner, 2005). Within the

SI, Cooper et al. (2005) were a lone voice arguing for the development of AL to proceed carefully: they cautioned against a rush towards *designing strategies for authentic leadership development* and suggested that *careful consideration needs to be given to (1) defining and measuring the construct, (2) determining the discriminant validity of the construct,* [and] *(3) identifying relevant construct outcomes (i.e. testing the nomological network)* (2005, p. 477). The SI acted as a vehicle for legitimising the concept and elaborating on earlier definitions and arguments (see for example Harter, 2002; May et al., 2003; Avolio et al., 2004), at the same time as encouraging further research into its dimensions. In particular, Cooper et al. (2005) encouraged the need for qualitative research in the early stages of theory development *as a useful way of identifying specific dimensions […] when there is little extant research on which to base hypothesis* [and to] *relate authentic leadership to its key antecedent, moderating, mediating and dependent variables* (2005, p. 479). Gardner et al. (2005) highlighted the paucity of empirical papers examining discriminant validity with regard to transformational leadership and ethical leadership.

While the SI (alongside an edited collection of chapters that were not accepted for the SI itself) demonstrated considerable alignment between definitions of AL, Gardner et al. (2011) described the period which followed (between 2005 and 2008) as problematic for researchers seeking to operationalise AL due to the lack of an accepted instrument for measurement. In this context the appearance of the Authentic Leadership Questionnaire (ALQ) (Walumbwa et al., 2008) was of much significance for the construct's subsequent development and popularity. The ALQ was and remains centred on four dimensions: self-awareness – four questions; transparency – five questions; internal moral compass – four questions; and balanced processing – three questions. It was grounded in Avolio, Gardner, Luthans, May, Walumbwa and colleagues' (Avolio and Gardner, 2005; Gardner et al., 2005; Walumbwa et al., 2008) perspective of AL, which in turn derived from Kernis and Goldman's (2006) *multiple components of authenticity* (Gardner et al., 2011, p. 1134). Since its appearance in 2008, the ALQ has remained largely untested and unchallenged in the literature (see Avolio et al., 2018, Neider and Schriesheim, 2011, and Randolph-Seng and Gardner, 2012, for the only exceptions). Despite Gardner et al.'s (2005) observation that *further assessment of the ALQ's construct validity is needed, as well as alternative […] approaches to operationalizing the construct* (2011, p. 1133), it is telling that these alternatives are yet to materialise.

THE CURRENT STATE OF EVOLUTION OF THE AL CONSTRUCT

What, then is the current standing of authentic leadership as a construct and what claims have been made for its impact on organisational outcomes? These questions are considered using Reichers and Schneider's (1990) three-stage model of construct evolution. This framework was first utilised by Gardner et al. (2011) in their review of the field, and still stands as useful 'scaffolding' for exploring the development and current state of our understanding of authentic leadership. Reichers and Schneider's (1990, pp. 6–8) delineation of the three stages of construct evolution can be summarised as follows:

1. Concept introduction and elaboration – during which concepts are borrowed or 'displaced' (Morey and Luthans, 1985) in order to invent new ones, which are then interpreted and modified to suit their new context (Schön, 1963). Attempts are made to legitimise the concept and offer preliminary data to 'prove' it describes a real phenomenon.
2. Concept evaluation and augmentation – during which critical reviews of the concept appear, attempting to address faulty conceptualisation, inadequate operationalisation and equivocal empirical results. 'Improved' reconceptualisations of the construct also appear.
3. Concept consolidation and accommodation – when one or two definitions and operationalisations become generally accepted and research interest declines. Acceptance of the construct is signalled by its inclusion in more general models, where it appears as a mediator/moderator or contextual variable.

Reichers and Schneider's (1990) acknowledgement that the evolutionary stages are not strictly chronological and that boundaries can be fuzzy is strongly reflected in the history of AL. Papers relating to all three stages of 'evolution' began appearing almost immediately after its inception, and multiple aspects of construct development occurred within a relatively compressed period of time. The clear positivist/quantitative bias in Reichers and Schneider's worldview is also reflected in the extant AL literature, with the absence of grounded, qualitative research and the consequent disconnect from practice being notable in both. So, what, then, can we say about the current state – and status – of authentic leadership?

In the broadest possible context, 'authenticity' has been subject to two very different symbolic interpretations (Carroll and Wheaton, 2009): 'type authenticity', which refers to whether an entity is true to its associated type, category or genre, and 'moral authenticity' where *the issue concerns whether the decisions behind the enactment and operation of an entity reflect sincere choices (i.e. choices true to one's self) rather than socially scripted responses* (Carroll and Wheaton, 2009, p. 255). Type authenticity – associated most commonly with product origination and tourist attractions – is relatively easy to assess and establish via a number of recognised authentication processes that confirm the innate qualities of the 'product' and its right to be described as belonging to a particular type. Moral authenticity, with its inherent relationship to people and roles, has proved somewhat more complex to pin down. For example, Harter (2002, p. 382) tells us that authenticity occurs when *one acts in accord with the true self, expressing oneself in ways that are consistent with inner thoughts and feelings*. On this view, authenticity is clearly a property of that which is claiming to be authentic, and arises as a natural or spontaneous occurrence. Yet, as most leaders will know to their cost, it is possible to have authentic intentions and yet appear inauthentic, or to effectively 'fake' authenticity for others and yet not feel it (this disconnect is explored in more detail later in the chapter). In relation to leadership authenticity, such issues of intention versus attribution (Martinko et al., 2007) are particularly salient, but were largely absent from the 'introduction and elaboration' stage of AL construct evolution and have not featured prominently in AL research since.

Notwithstanding these complexities, the notion of authenticity – borrowed or displaced from positive psychology – was accepted as largely unproblematic by scholars seeking to launch a new form of 'positive' leadership, and a generally accepted definition of AL, complete with imported ethical overtones, was arrived at within five years of its emergence in 2003. Aligned with its generally accepted operationalisation and measure – both arising from Walumbwa et al.'s (2008) construction, 'validation' and subsequent mass propagation of the ALQ – authentic leadership is thus said to be:

a pattern of leader behaviour that draws upon and promotes both positive psychological capacities and a positive ethical climate, to foster greater self-awareness, an internalised moral perspective, balanced processing of information, and relational transparency on the part of leaders working with followers, fostering positive self-development.

(Walumbwa et al., 2008, p. 94)

Reflective of its idealised normative and functionalist aims of delineating a style of leadership capable of producing measurable organisational outcomes (Avolio et al., 2004; Gardner and Schermerhorn, 2004), authentic leaders are said to be *transparent about their intentions and* [to] *strive to maintain a seamless link between espoused values, behaviours and actions* (Luthans and Avolio, 2003, p. 242). Based on this definition/operationalisation Antonakis (2017) drew attention to the 'loaded' nature of authenticity within AL (i.e., its definition includes the outcomes it is seeking to deliver in a way that is positively and morally valenced), its origin in the ideological agenda surrounding the construct and the tautologies and circular theorising that resulted.

This conceptual infrastructure became embedded in the literature relatively quickly, while failing to grapple with more substantive issues of its theoretical underpinnings and philosophical antecedents. As such, the 'evaluation and augmentation' stage of evolution, when it would be expected that critical reviews of the emerging construct would lead to improved conceptualisations and operationalisations, was relatively light. Even now, the AL construct is yet to be thoroughly grounded in empirical research from a qualitative, practice perspective: a 'bottom-up' approach that would add significant value to the more reductionist, quantitative research that has dominated the field. Its key proponents appear to have ducked the challenge, among others, as to whether a psychometric with only four key components (Walumbwa et al., 2008) can comprehensively capture the complexities of what it means to be an authentic leader in the messy world of practice. The rush to perceived maturity is illustrated in Table 12.1, which maps the 171 academic papers published between January 2000 and March 2021 (based on a search using the *Web of Science* social sciences citation index and utilising the words 'authentic' and 'leadership' as search terms in the field of 'topic') against the key stages of Reichers and Schneider's (1990) construct evolution model.

Within the development period of the AL construct, it has been common for papers to combine antecedents and consequences (stage 1) with mediators and moderators (stage 2) of AL (Hsieh and Wang, 2015; Ling et al., 2017; Malik and Dhar, 2017; Valsania et al., 2016) or characteristics and components (stage 2) (Gatling et al., 2016). Similarly, AL antecedents and consequences have often been considered at the same time as treating AL as a mediator or moderator for other variables (stage 3) (Agote et al., 2016; Liang, 2017; Monzani et al., 2016) or when comparing AL with other leadership theories as part of a meta-analytic

Table 12.1 Mapping of academic papers against evolutionary stages (2000–2021)

	Stage 1: introduction and elaboration	Stage 2: evaluation and augmentation	Stage 3: consolidation and accommodation
Conceptual/theoretical	38		
Antecedents/consequences	89		
Comparing with other theories	14		
Critical of definition or operationalisation		27	
Validity of empirical findings		2	
Characteristics/components		35	
Mediators/moderators		63	
Accepted definitions/measures			129
Meta-analytic studies			8
AL as mediator/moderator in other theories			23

review (Banks et al., 2016 – comparison with transformational leadership) (stage 3). A relatively small proportion of the papers exploring stage 2 themes were actually critical of the existing definition/operationalisation (27/171) or components/characteristics (35/171), with much of the research contributing to this stage being of a more 'technical' nature – that is, exploring the mediators and moderators of the accepted construct. The inclusion of AL and its components as contextual variables in wider research (stage 3) is clear evidence of the assumed consolidation of the construct and its accommodation into wider theorising, as is the appearance of meta-analytic reviews of previous work (stage 3), while the empirical warranting of where AL sits within the leadership lexicon and the implications of its philosophical grounding remain relatively light. Significantly, calls for further warranting and philosophical exploration by Cooper et al. (2005) failed to gain traction, despite having been made nearly 20 years ago. No empirical work has been based on any of the critical papers relating to AL.

It is telling to note that there were only two papers during this period seeking to validate earlier empirical findings, both of which have appeared as recent additions to the extant literature. Indeed, all the empirical papers adopt definitions/operationalisations of AL either directly derived from the ALQ (Walumbwa et al., 2008) or more broadly from the positive psychology related writing by the same team of authors, both of which have passed into the popular narrative of what it means to be an authentic leader. Overall, what emerges from Table 12.1 is a broad overlapping of the three 'stages', with multiple aspects of construct development occurring within a relatively compressed period of time. While Reichers and Schneider (1990) did acknowledge the existence of fuzzy boundaries between the stages, this suggests an overly rapid progression (in evolutionary rather than chronological terms) of the construct's development, with the consequent potential for a lack of sufficient interrogation and robustness. This can be seen as akin to putting the roof on a house before the foundations have firmly set and can be expected to result in similar instability in the resultant edifice. The retraction of three quantitative papers, all published in US journals and arising from methodological concerns which the authors were unable to satisfy, has further damaged academic perceptions of the AL construct, although its popular status has been largely unaffected.

EXISTENTIALIST AND PSYCHODYNAMIC CRITIQUES OF AL

Building on the conclusions of the previous section – centred around the notion that the AL construct has short-circuited the need for a thorough and robust process of construct evolution – this section explores the key critiques of AL and the perceived consequences of the failure to address them. As noted above, there is a positivist/quantitative skew in the distribution of empirical studies in the AL field. This, in itself, is not problematic and represents a reasonable pattern of work aimed at sketching out the nomological network of the construct. What is more significant, perhaps, is the cultural distribution of conceptual authors within the field, and the parallel distribution of conceptual underpinnings. Table 12.2 sets out the distribution of the 38 conceptual papers published between January 2000 and March 2021 according to the nationality of the lead author and the theoretical underpinnings utilised to ground the AL construct.

Table 12.2 shows that the US writers on AL are deeply imbedded in the somewhat superficial and potentially one-sided views of authenticity deriving from positive psychology (Avolio and Gardner, 2005; Gardner et al., 2005; May et al., 2003; Price, 2003), while the more critical conceptualisations mostly originated in Europe and Australia. These critiques sought to expound a more complex, political and contested understanding of authenticity, based on existentialist and psychoanalytic perspectives, and to problematise the notion of a 'self' to which an authentic leader can be 'true' (Ladkin and Taylor, 2010). As discussed below, these critiques of the dominant AL discourse failed to gain traction against – or at least be properly addressed by – the construct's positivist, American founding fathers. This perhaps owes something to the 'politics of publishing' (Li and Parker, 2012) and the consequent potential for perspectives critical of an influential 'centre' ground within the literature – in this case, a positive psychological stance developed within a positivist framework – to find themselves marginalised in terms of citation patterns and influence. Critiques from Asia and the rest of the world focused largely on the suitability of a Western theoretical framework for application in Eastern contexts, thus introducing a more situated and cultural element to the understanding of authenticity.

The critiques of AL came from a variety of perspectives, but all sought to problematise the normative, positive psychological roots of the construct. For example, Ford and Harding (2011) drew on object relations theory to argue that authentic leadership as a reflection of the 'true self' is impossible and that the AL construct *contains the seeds of its own destruction* (2011, p. 464). In being predicated on leaders sacrificing their subjectivity to that of the organisational collective, AL by definition requires them to be *in*authentic – to privilege their collective or organisational self over their individual self. From a psychoanalytic perspective, this suggests the potential for destructive dynamics within the organisation generally and deleterious impacts on those leaders subjected to its expectations and whose imperfections as individuals are not acknowledged. Also from a psychoanalytic perspective, Costas and Taheri (2012) problematised the possible implications of AL as a model of post-heroic, non-authoritarian leadership seeking to displace traditional hierarchical, authoritarian leadership theories. Drawing on insights from the work of Lacan, they critically discussed the potential of AL to foster more emancipatory subject-authority relations in organisations and concluded by highlighting the dangers they perceived as arising from the enactment of AL's operating principles. Its categorical emphasis on love, harmony and completeness as a substitute for symbolic authority had, they contended, the potential to generate paranoid dependency in followers and reinstate leaders to the position of a *fantasy figure akin to the Freudian primal father* (Costas and Taheri, 2012, p. 1211).

Algera and Lips-Wiersma (2012) offered an existentialist perspective on authenticity, suggesting that insufficient focus had been accorded to the ontological question of what it means to be authentically human as a necessary precursor to what it means to be an authentic leader. Their concern was that by dismissing the complexities raised by existential authenticity – relating to inevitability, personal meaning, goal/value congruence and intrinsic ethicality – as awkward but essentially minor obstacles to implementation, the resultant theorising had been limited and inconsistent. In addition, they suggested that the importance of being true to *self-in-relationship* (Erickson, 1995, p. 139) rather than merely true to self as an aspect of authenticity means that more attention needs to be paid to the relational and structural aspects of AL rather than the individual and psychological ones. Also, from an existentialist perspective, Lawler and Ashman (2012) echoed this latter point by drawing on Sartre to reject the current AL focus on an 'inner' or 'true' self in favour of the need to consider context and both subjective and intersubjective experience in the practice of authentic leadership. Both these critiques were concerned with the failure of AL to appreciate tensions and complexities inherent in its practical enactment by fallible humans.

Another critique concerns the lack of contextualised empirical research, which has already been noted above. Of the few qualitative papers that explore the construct directly, most tend to focus on specific elaborations – for example, developing the Western AL construct for application to a Chinese context (Zhang et al., 2012) or

Table 12.2 Cultural orientations of lead authors for conceptual papers on AL (2000–2021)

	USA/CAN	EUR/AUS	Asia/RoW
Positive psychology	7		
Existentialist	0	2	
Psychoanalytic		2	
Other critical	4	9	4
Other	3		1
Peripheral	3	3	

considering gender issues in relation to AL (Liu et al., 2015) – rather than testing its validity. It is striking that there has been no contextual examination of the suggested dimensions that shape the AL construct despite repeated encouragement (Cooper et al., 2005; Gardner et al., 2011). The underlying concern here is that normative and idealised core assumptions underpinning the AL construct have not been developed through grounded, empirical research, but rather posited on the basis of ideas borrowed from elsewhere and shoehorned into a reductionist psychometric.

PROBLEMATISING THE AL CONSTRUCT THROUGH AN EL LENS

Notwithstanding this concern, the emergence of more qualitative empirical papers in recent years is at last shedding light on the complexity of authentic leadership in practice, and the challenges to the AL construct (as operationalised by the ALQ) that this represents. Of the four components, it is the notion of an internal moral compass and the requirement for relational transparency that are receiving the most attention. This section illustrates this new strand of theorising through a review of how the performance of emotional labour (EL) in leadership has been utilised as a lens through which to view these components, to surface the paradoxes inherent in the construct and to consider their implications for practising leaders.

The requirement for leaders to perform emotional labour (Hochschild, 1983) as a routine part of enacting their role is widely accepted in the leadership literature (Connelly and Gooty, 2015; Humphrey et al., 2008), as is the distinction between general social/professional emotion management and the intentional employment of emotions as a tool of enacting a leadership role which constitutes emotional labour. This acknowledgement of EL within the practice of leadership (Iszatt-White, 2009, 2012) is not surprising, given our understanding of leadership as a social influence process (Yukl, 2002) and the requirement to use affective as well as rational skills to achieve organisational goals. Yet the challenges this represents to the AL construct were for a long time neglected within the literature. An example of work seeking to rectify this omission is Iszatt-White et al.'s (2021) interrogation of emotional labour as a fundamental aspect of leadership practice as a means of holding the concept of authentic leadership up to scrutiny. In addition to the explication of a series of rationales through which leaders were able to 'square the circle' between the requirement to perform emotional labour as a routine tool of enacting their leadership role and the desire to appear (and feel) authentic, these authors also surface what they describe as a fundamental paradox in the construction of AL.

The rationales used to justify performing EL without feeling inauthentic related to its being part of how they appeared professional and consistent as a leader; an accepted tool for achieving valued organisational goals; and beneficial to both themselves and others, particularly in a hostile environment. Collectively, these rationales are said to demonstrate that participants saw emotional labour as integral to their sense of themselves as authentic leaders. This resonates with ideas of a *deeper level of authenticity – where identity resides* (Humphrey et al., 2015, p. 754) and with deep acting's effort to *conjure up a sincere performance* (Bolton and Boyd, 2003, p. 290). The rationales thus implicitly construct authenticity as a situated and subjective phenomenon: true to the self, yes, but a more fluid and contingent self (Tomkins and Nicholds, 2017) than this phrase implies. Significantly, the ability to hold competing ethical systems in play simultaneously, rather than choosing between them, suggests a more complex understanding of the ethical component of what it means to be authentic than the possession of an 'internal moral compass' (Walumbwa et al., 2008). Specifically, managers appeared to shift seamlessly from the deontological elements of 'being true' – grounded in notions of standards of professionalism that they are obliged to portray – and more teleological elements – where the achievement of valued goals as ends justifies the in-the-moment presentation of an inauthentic self through the performance of emotional labour as legitimate means. This ability to shift ethical ground in the practice of leadership places a question mark over the efficacy of including an 'internal moral compass' (Walumbwa et al., 2008) as a component of what it means to be authentic as a leader.

The inclusion of 'relational transparency' (Walumbwa et al., 2008) as the *most fundamental element of authentic leadership* (Ciulla, 2013, p. 156) was also scrutinised through the lens of EL. Specifically, it was argued that if authenticity is concerned with the 'true self' and relational transparency requires the showing of that true self, then the routine performance of emotional labour must perforce require leaders to be inauthentic. The utilisation of emotional labour as an accepted 'means' for accomplishing values-driven 'ends', with little or no apparent tension or dissonance for the leaders in this study, was suggested as demonstrating that relational transparency was largely irrelevant for these leaders. And if leaders could feel authentic while intentionally being less than transparent in their relationships with others, then this also undermines the relevance of authenticity more widely for them. The acceptance of emotional labour as a routine tool of the leadership role was likewise seen as suggesting the impossibility of enacting authenticity as specified by the AL construct.

In a final coup de grâce to the AL construct, Iszatt-White et al. (2021) went on to propose a fundamental paradox of 'authentic inauthenticity' as enacted by practising leaders. Their argument here was that in accepting emotional labour as a routine part of their leadership practice, and an essential tool for the accomplishment of valued goals, practising leaders constructed authentic leadership as *requiring* them to be *inauthentic* in order to lead effectively. They saw an 'inextricable symbiosis' between authenticity and inauthenticity, and a need to recognise that not all inauthenticity should be viewed as bad. That leaders' implicit inauthenticity did not appear to produce *feelings* of inauthenticity – rather, that it was interwoven with their experience of being authentic as a leader – was at the heart of their call for a more complex social construction of authenticity in leadership than that currently underpinning the AL construct. Any such definition or construction would, they claimed, need to address the centrality of inauthenticity to authentic leadership at the same time as combating perceptions of irrelevance and/or impossibility.

AUTHENTICITY IN LEADERSHIP RATHER THAN AUTHENTIC LEADERSHIP

The apparent disconnect between the experiencing of authenticity and the actions/interactions in which this experience is embedded has serious implications for the future of the AL construct. Together with the serious epistemological and existential questions already raised by earlier scholars, these concerns cast doubt on the usefulness and appropriateness of AL as a home for our leadership aspirations. As suggested by Algera and Lips-Wiersma (2012), the unquestioning adoption of the ALQ as a measure of authentic leadership by the leadership development industry has effectively reduced it to a mere 'technique' which has abandoned its ontological roots in favour of ease of implementation. As such, it is failing to meet its normative goals and has lost its place as a 'central organising principle' (Driscoll and Wiebe, 2007) for leadership research. Drawing on the work of Jacques Ellul, Driscoll and Wiebe (2007) draw attention to the manner in which AL is treated as a *totality of methods rationally arrived at and having absolute efficiency* (2007, p. 333) supported by a *closed fraternity of its practitioners* who *have their own discourse and are obsessed with facts and results* (2007, p. 334).

There have, of course, been attempts to reclaim a more robust theoretical grounding for AL. For example, the call for papers for a 2021 Special Issue on authentic leadership in the *Leadership* journal sought to provoke the development of a more nuanced understanding of what it means to be authentic as a leader, grounded in rich, qualitative data, at the same time as calling for more critical attention to be paid to the notion of authenticity in leadership rather than authentic leadership per se. In making this call, the editors highlighted attempts that had already been made to reground AL more solidly or to problematise its historical roots in positive psychology. Nyberg and Sveningsson (2014) questioned the assumption that an authentic leader's 'true self' is morally good as well as the notion that leader authenticity necessarily leads to good outcomes for either the leader or the organisation. Relatedly, Nicholson and Carroll (2013) sought to reconceive authenticity as a social virtue in order to reframe what is meant by the authentic self and the relationship of this self to others. They went on to ask what this means for the purpose of authenticity and for its role in leadership and leadership development. Work by Shaw (2010), critiquing past attempts to delineate authenticity and the authentic self, using narrative theory, drew attention to the tendency of such approaches to replicate existing paradigms rather than open up new possibilities. And Kempster et al. (2019), drawing on emotional labour as a lens to unpack the components of the AL construct from a practice perspective, proposed the repositioning of authenticity as 'fidelity to purpose'. Also noted in this SI was Gardiner's (2015) Arendtian analysis of the ways in which authenticity unfolds within specific relational contexts, and the implicit problematisation of the previous 'one size fits all' approach to delimiting authentic leadership. All of these approaches have value in retaining a focus on the importance of authenticity in the practice of leadership, while seeking to weaken our reliance on the AL construct as the appropriate way of capturing this phenomenon.

CONCLUSION: ADVOCACY VERSUS ENQUIRY IN THE SEARCH FOR ASPIRATIONAL LEADERSHIP

In concluding, it is perhaps worth commenting on how we arrived at where we are with regard to AL, and reflecting on some of the pitfalls of developing (and promulgating) new aspirations for leadership. As noted previously, there is a case for arguing that the theory of AL has declined into a management or leadership development 'fashion' (Jackson and Guthey, 2007), with a significant commercial element (Guthey, 2017), very much to its detriment and to the detriment of practising leaders. As Abrahamson (1996, p. 263) observes, *management fashions [...] are cultural commodities deliberately produced by fashion setters in order to be marketed to fashion followers*: the drawbacks of popular appeal were always inherent in the normative and instrumentalist aims of the original founders of AL's decision to develop the construct in the format that they did. In their bid to produce an antidote to what had gone before it can be argued that attempts at robust construct development – for example, through responding to and addressing critiques from existentialist and other perspectives – become distracted or diluted to the detriment of AL's status and usefulness. The tensions between advocacy (the normative and functionalist promulgation of a not-necessarily epistemologically robust construct) versus enquiry (the bottom-up, practice-based understanding of what it means to be authentic as a leader in practice) is proposed as an important consideration in any critical retrospective on the development and 'success' of AL. The apparent rush to achieve construct maturity (Reichers and Schneider, 1990) and the promotion of a reductionist psychometric instrument in the face of a clearly messy and 'non-reductionist' field of practice are perhaps now taking their toll. And as noted by Fineman (2006, p. 281), the *positive scholars' quest for positive change and learning is likely to be a truncated, single-loop mission if the stress, anxiety, anger, pessimism and unhappiness of life and work are silenced or marginalized.*

The previous *SAGE Handbook of Leadership*, published in 2011, suggested that authentic leadership was an idea whose *time ha*[d] *come* as a *powerful response to the entrenched scepticism and suspicion towards established leaders and* [as something which] *accords with a general desire for selfless, enlightened leadership* (2011, p. 361). The still unaddressed challenges to AL – and other 'positive' forms of leadership for which it was claimed as the root construct (Avolio and Gardner, 2005) – highlighted in this chapter, which call into question both its epistemological underpinnings and its feasibility/desirability in practice, might lead us to conclude that it is now an idea whose time has gone by. As a final note, it is worth considering whether the emergence of new candidates for our leadership aspirations – sustainable (Hargreaves and Fink, 2006), responsible (Pless and Maak, 2011), as purpose (Kempster et al., 2011), etc. – may be suffering from another tension currently prevalent in leadership scholarship, that of confusing leadership research (empirically grounded theorisation of how to do leadership better) with leadership philosophising (more speculative conceptualising of what leadership is for).

REFERENCES

Abrahamson, E. (1996). Management fashion. *Academy of Management Review*, *21*(1) 254–285.

Agote, L., Aramburu, N., & Lines, R. (2016) Authentic leadership perception, trust in the leader, and followers' emotions in organizational change processes. *Journal of Applied Behavioural Science*, *52*(1), 35–63.

Algera, P. M., & Lips-Wiesma, M. (2012). Radical authentic leadership: Co-creating the conditions under which all members of the organization can be authentic. *Leadership Quarterly*, *23*(1) 118–131.

Antonakis, J. (2017). Charisma and the 'new leadership'. In J. Antonakis & D. V. Day (Eds.), *The Nature of Leadership (3rd edn)* (pp. 56–81). Sage.

Avolio, B. J. (1999). *Full Leadership Development: Building Vital Forces in Organizations*. Sage.

Avolio, B. J., & Gardner, W. L. (2005). Authentic leadership development: Getting to the root of positive forms of leadership. *Leadership Quarterly*, *16*(3), 315–338.

Avolio, B. J., Gardner, W. L., Walumbwa, F. O., Luthans, F., & May, D. R. (2004). Unlocking the mask: A look at the process by which authentic leaders impact follower attitudes and behaviours. *The Leadership Quarterly*, *15*(6), 801–823.

Avolio, B. J., Wernsing, T., & Gardner, W. L. (2018). Revisiting the development and validation of the authentic leadership questionnaire: Analytical Clarcifications. *Journal of Management*, *44*(2) 399–411.

Banks, G. C., McCauley, K. D., Gardner, W. L., & Guler, C. E. (2016). A meta-analytic review of authentic and transformational leadership: A test for redundancy. *Leadership Quarterly*, *27*(4), 634–652.

Bass, B. M. (1998). The ethics of transformational leadership. In J. Ciulla (Ed.), *Ethics: The Heart of Leadership* (pp. 169–92). Preager.

Bass, B. M., & Steidlmeier, P. (1999). Ethics, character, and authentic transformational leadership behaviour. *Leadership Quarterly*, *10*(2), 181–217.

Bolton, S. C., & Boyd, C. (2003). Trolley dolly or skilled emotion manager? Moving on from

Hochschild's Managed Heart. *Work, Employment and Society, 17*(2), 289–308.

Bryman, A., Collinson, D., Grint, K., Jackson, B., & Uhl-Bien, M. (Eds.) (2011). *The SAGE Handbook of Leadership.* Sage.

Carroll, G. R., & Wheaton, D. R. (2009). The organisational construction of authenticity: An examination of contemporary food and dining in the US. *Research in Organisational Behaviour, 29*, 255–282.

Ciulla, J. B. (2013). Essay: Searching for Mandela: The saint as a sinner who keeps on trying. In D. Ladkin & C. Spiller (Eds.), *Authentic Leadership: Clashes, Convergences and Coalescences* (pp. 169–92). Edward Elgar. (pp. 152–175).

Connelly, S., & Gooty, J. (2015). Leading with emotion: An overview of the special issue on leadership and emotions. *Leadership Quarterly, 26*, 485–488.

Cooper, C. D., Scandura, T. A., & Schriesheim, C. A. (2005). Looking forward but learning from our past: Potential challenges to developing authentic leadership theory and authentic leaders. *Leadership Quarterly, 16*(3), 475–493.

Costas, J., & Taheri, A. (2012). 'The return of the primal father' in Postmodernity? A Lacanian analysis of authentic leadership. *Organization Studies, 33*(9), 1195–1216.

Driscoll, C., & Wiebe, E. (2007). Technical spirituality at work: Jacque Ellul on workplace spirituality. *Journal of Management Inquiry, 16*(3), 334–348.

Erickson, R. J. (1995). The importance of authenticity for self and society. *Symbolic Interaction, 18*(2), 121–144.

Fineman, S. (2006). On being positive: Concerns and counterpoints. *Academy of Management Review, 31*, 270–291.

Ford, J., & Harding, N. (2011). The impossibility of the 'true self' of authentic leadership. *Leadership, 7*(4), 463–479.

Gardiner, R. (2015). *Gender, Authenticity and Leadership: Thinking with Arendt.* Palgrave Macmillan.

Gardner, W. L., Avolio, B. J., Luthans, F., May, D. R., & Walumbwa, F. (2005). 'Can you see the real me?' A self-based model of authentic leader and follower development. *Leadership Quarterly, 16*(3), 343–372.

Gardner, W. L., Cogliser, C. C., Davis, K. M., & Dickens, M. P. (2011). Authentic Leadership: A review of the literature and research agenda. *Leadership Quarterly, 22*(6), 1120–1145.

Gardner, W. L., & Schermerhorn Jr, J. R. (2004). Performance gains through positive organizational behaviour and authentic leadership. *Organizational Dynamics, 33*(3), 270–281.

Gatling, A, Kang, H. J. A., & Kim, J. S. (2016). The effects of authentic leadership and organizational commitment on turnover intention. *Leadership and Organization Development Journal, 37*(2), 181–199.

George, W. (2003). *Authentic Leadership: Rediscovering the Secrets to Creating Lasting Value.* Jossey-Bass.

George, W., & Sims, P. (2007). *True North: Discover Your Authentic Leadership.* Jossey-Bass.

Guthey, E. (2013). The production of leadership fashions. *Academy of Management Proceedings, 2013*(1) 12214.

Guthey, E. (2017). *What makes for a 'good' leadership development provider?* Paper presented at the 33rd European Group for Organizational Studies Colloquium, Copenhagen Business School, 6–8 July.

Harter, S. (2002). Authenticity. In C. R. Snyder, & S. J. Lopez (Eds.), *Handbook of Positive Psychology* (pp. 382–394). Oxford University Press.

Hargreaves, A., & Fink, D. (2006). *Sustainable Leadership for Sustainable Change.* Jossey-Bass.

Hochschild, A. (1983). *The Managed Heart: Commercialization of Human Feeling.* University of California Press.

Howell, J. M., & Avolio, B. J. (1993). The ethics of charismatic leadership: Submission or liberation? *Academy of Management Executive, 6*(2), 43–54.

Hsieh, C.-C., & Wang, D.-S. (2015). Does supervisor-perceived authentic leadership influence employee work engagement through employee-perceived authentic leadership and employee trust? *International Journal of Human Resource Management, 26*(18), 2329–2348.

Humphrey, R. H., Ashforth, B. E., & Diefendorff, J. M. (2015). The bright side of emotional labour. *Journal of Organizational Behaviour, 36*(6), 749–769.

Humphrey, R. H., Pollack, J. M., & Hawyer, T. (2008). Leading with emotional labour. *Journal of Managerial Psychology, 23*(2), 151–168.

Iszatt-White, M. (2009). Leadership as emotional labour: the effortful accomplishment of valuing practices. *Leadership, 5*(4), 447–467.

Iszatt-White, M. (2012). Leadership as emotional labour: So what's new? In M. Iszatt-White (Ed.), *Leadership as Emotional Labour: Management and the 'Managed Heart'* (pp. 14–36). Routledge.

Iszatt-White, M., Stead, V., & Elliott, C. (2021). Impossible or just irrelevant? Unravelling the 'authentic leadership' paradox through the lens of emotional labour. *Leadership, 17*(4), 464–482. doi: 10.1177/1742715021996928

Jackson, B., & Guthey, E. (2007). Putting the visual into the social construction of leadership. In B. Shamir, R. Pillai, M. C. Bligh & M. Uhl-Bien (Eds.), *Follower-centered Perspectives on Leadership: A Tribute to the Memory of James R. Meindl* (pp. 167–186). Information Age.

Kempster, S., Iszatt-White, M., & Brown, M. (2019). Authenticity in leadership: Reframing relational transparency through the lens of emotional labour. *Leadership*, *1,5*(3) 319–338.

Kempster, S., Jackson, B., & Conroy, M. (2011). Leadership as purpose: Exploring the role of purpose in leadership practice. *Leadership*, *7*(3), 317–334.

Kernis, M. H., & Goldman, B. M. (2006). A multicomponent conceptualization of authenticity: Theory and research. *Advances in Experimental Social Psychology*, *38*, 283–357.

Ladkin, D., & Taylor, S. S. (2010). Enacting the 'true self': Towards a theory of embodied authentic leadership. *The Leadership Quarterly*, *21*(1) 64–74.

Lawler, J., & Ashman, I. (2012). Theorizing leadership authenticity: A Sartrean perspective. *Leadership*, *8*(4), 327–344.

Li, E. Y., & Parker, M. (2012). Citation patterns in organization and management journals: Margins and centres. *Organization*, *20*(2), 299–322.

Liang, S.-G. (2017). Linking leader authentic personality to employee voice behaviour: A multi-level mediation model of authentic leadership development. *European Journal of Work and Organizational Psychology*, *26*(3) 434–443.

Ling, Q., Liu, F., & Wu, X. (2017). Servant versus authentic leadership: Assessing effectiveness in China's hospitality industry. *Cornell Hospitality Quarterly*, *58*(1), 53–68.

Liu, H., Cutcher, L., & Grant, D. (2015). Doing authenticity: The gendered construction of authentic leadership. *Gender, Work and Organization*, *22*(3), 237–255.

Luthans, F. (2002). The need for and meaning of positive organizational behaviour. *Journal of Organizational Behaviour*, *23*(6), 695–706.

Luthans, F., & Avolio, B. (2003). Authentic leadership: A positive development approach. In K. S. Cameron, J. E. Dutton & R. E. Quinn (Eds.), *Positive Organizational Scholarship* (pp. 241–258). Berrett-Koehler.

Malik, N., & Dhar, R. L. (2017). Authentic leadership and its impact on extra role behaviour of nurses. *Personnel Review*, *46*(2) 277–296.

Martinko, M. J., Harvey, P., & Douglas, S. C. (2007). The role, function, and contribution of attribution theory to leadership: A review. *The Leadership Quarterly*, *18*, 561–585.

Maslow, A. (1968). *Towards a Psychology of Being*. Van Nostrand.

May, D. R., Chan, A. Y. L., Hodges, T. D., & Avolio, B. J. (2003). Developing the moral component of authentic leadership. *Organizational Dynamics*, *32*(3), 247–260.

Monzani, L., Braun, S., & van Dick, R. (2016). It takes two to tango: The interactive effect of authentic leadership and organizational identification on employee silence intentions. *German Journal of Human Resource Management*, *30*(3–4), 246–266.

Morey, N. C., & Luthans, F. (1985). Refining the displacement of culture and the use of scenes and themes in organizational studies. *Academy of Management Review*, *10*, 219–229.

Neider, L. L., & Schriesheim, C. A. (2011). The Authentic Leadership Inventory (ALI): Development and empirical tests. *The Leadership Quarterly*, *22*(6) 1146–1164.

Nicholson, H., & Carroll, B. (2013). Essay: So you want to be authentic in your leadership: To whom and for what end? In D. Ladkin & C. Spiller (Eds.), *Authentic Leadership: Clashes, Convergences and Coalescences* (pp. 286–302). Edward Elgar.

Northouse, P. G. (2010). *Leadership: Theory and Practice (5th edn)*. Sage.

Nyberg, D., & Sveningsson, S. (2014). Paradoxes of authentic leadership: Leader identity struggles. *Leadership*, *10*(4) 437–455.

Pless, N. M., & Maak, T. (2011). Responsible leadership: Pathways to the future. *Journal of Business Ethics*, *98*, 3–13.

Price, T. L. (2003). The ethics of authentic transformational leadership. *Leadership Quarterly*, *14*(1), 67–81.

Randolph-Seng, B., & Gardner, W. L. (2012). Validating measures of leader authenticity: Relationships between implicit/explicit self-esteem, situational cues, and leader authenticity. *Journal of Leadership and Organizational Studies*, *20*(2), 214–231.

Reichers, A. E., & Schneider, B. (1990). Climate and culture: An evolution of constructs. In B. Schneider (Ed.), *Organizational Climate and Culture* (pp. 5–39). Jossey-Bass.

Rogers, C. R. (1959). A theory of therapy, personality, and interpersonal relationships, as developed in the client-centered framework. In S. Koch (Ed.), *Psychology: A Study of a Science (Vol. 3)* (pp. 184–256). McGraw-Hill.

Schön, D. A. (1963). *Invention and the Evolution of Ideas*. Social Science Paperbacks.

Shaw, J. (2010). Papering the cracks with discourse: The narrative identity of the authentic leader. *Leadership*, *6*(1), 89–108.

Tomkins, L., & Nicholds, A. (2017). Make me authentic, but not here: Reflexive struggles with academic identity and authentic leadership. *Management Learning*, *48*(3), 253–270.

Valsania, S. E., Moriano, J. A., & Molero, F. (2016). Authentic leadership and intrapreneurial behaviour: Cross-level analysis of the mediator effect of organizational identification and empowerment. *International Entrepreneurship and Management*, *12*, 131–152.

Walumbwa, F. O., Avolio, B. J., Gardner, W. L., Wernsing, T. S., & Peterson, S. J. (2008). Authentic leadership: Development and validation of a theory-based measure. *Journal of Management*, *34*(1), 89–126.

Yukl, G. (2002). *Leadership in Organizations (5th Edn)*. Prentice-Hall.

Zhang, H., Everett, A. M., Elkin, G., & Cone, M. H. (2012). Authentic leadership theory development: theorizing on Chinese philosophy. *Asia Pacific Business Review*, *18*(4), 587–605.

Redefining Followership: Towards an Expansive Construct of the 'Followers' of Charismatic Leaders in Entrepreneurial Organisations

Jay A. Conger

While aspects of followership have been explored in the literature on charismatic leadership in organisations (e.g., Conger & Kanungo, 1998; Howell & Shamir, 2005; Ito et al., 2020; Shamir et al., 1993), it remains a poorly understood subject (Bligh 2011; Uhl-Bien et al., 2014). Moreover, the research perspective to date is primarily leader-centric. For example, the extant literature examines *how leaders impact their followers rather than how followers influence their leaders* (Ito et al., 2020). The aim of this chapter is to critique, refresh and expand our current notions of the construct of 'followership' and to reinforce the need for more follower-centric perspectives. I will do so by examining three classes of stakeholders who can be considered as 'followers', but whom researchers have overlooked. My goal is to challenge the field's framing of 'followers' as the *organisational members* of a charismatic leader. As defined by the *Oxford English Dictionary*, the term *follower* describes *a person who supports or admires a particular individual*. Our three classes of *external followers* meet and exceed this criteria. Similar to organisational members, these stakeholders not only support and admire the leader, but they also make significant resource and career commitments. With this examination, I hope to address Meindl's (1993) concern that in 'romancing the leader' we have overlooked the broader contextual and relational dynamics beyond the individual leader.

Specifically, I will examine the roles of three groups of *external* stakeholders: investors, the media and business partners. Similar to organisational members, these stakeholders are influenced by the referent power of the charismatic leader. Their commitments validate the leader, their charisma and their organisational vision. As importantly, these stakeholders' actions facilitate a virtuous cycle of positive influence which reinforces the organisational or internal followers' perceptions of their leader's charisma. They in essence play a 'contagion' role as proposed by Mayo and Pastor (2007). For example, a journalist from a widely recognised publication who writes an effusive media story affirms the beliefs of organisational members that their leader is a visionary individual worthy of being followed. Their publication may also favourably influence investors who in turn commit funds to the charismatic leader's venture.

To explore this expansive construct of followership, the chapter draws upon the recent and rich documentation of two charismatic entrepreneurs – Elizabeth Holmes of Theranos and Adam Neumann of WeWork (Carreyrou, 2018; Wiedeman, 2020).

Both of these leaders have been the recipients of extensive investigations due to the scale of their ventures, their claims for revolutionising their industries and ultimately scandals associated with their tenure as CEOs. A brief description of each leader and their venture follows. As such, this chapter's conclusions may prove to be primarily relevant to charismatic entrepreneurs rather than the charismatic leaders of mature complex organisations or of social and political movements.

ELIZABETH HOLMES: FOUNDER OF THERANOS

Elizabeth Holmes was the founder and chief executive of Theranos, a now-defunct health technology company (Carreyrou, 2018). The company claimed to have revolutionised blood testing. Their method required only tiny volumes of blood from essentially a finger prick. This was in sharp contrast to current approaches requiring multiple tubes of blood to be drawn from patients. Blood samples, in turn, had to be divided up across specialised machines in a variety of off-site laboratories resulting in greater costs and time delays. Theranos's approach differentiated itself from the status quo along three lines: 1) minimum invasiveness, 2) speed of assessment and 3) far lower costs.

On the basis of its revolutionary claims, Theranos would raise upwards of $945 million from an impressive list of investors, including media mogul Rupert Murdoch, Oracle founder Larry Ellison, Walmart's Walton family and the billionaire family of former US Secretary of Education Betsy DeVos. At its peak, the company was described as such a disruptive force within healthcare that it reached an internal valuation of $9 billion. *Forbes* would name Holmes the youngest and wealthiest self-made female billionaire in America on the basis of the valuation of her company in 2015 (Sorvino, 2015). Later in that same year, a series of journalism and regulatory investigations, however, revealed doubts about the company's technology claims and whether Holmes had misled investors and regulators. Through a series of damning exposes, the *Wall Street Journal* documented that Theranos's flagship testing device, the Edison, was completely unreliable (Carreyrou, 2015). While claiming to be using Edison to conduct its blood tests, the firm in secret had been using commercially available machines made by other manufacturers along with outside laboratories. In a number of cases, the test results were forged. Following these revelations of potential fraud, *Forbes* revised its published estimate of Holmes's net worth down to zero in 2016 (Herper, 2016) and *Fortune* named her as one of the *world's most disappointing leaders* (Fortune Editors, 2016). Two years later, the US Securities and Exchange Commission charged Holmes and her company of 'massive fraud' through false or exaggerated claims about the accuracy of the company's blood-testing technology. Theranos ceased its operations by September of 2018.

Holmes would settle the charges by paying a $500,000 fine, returning 18.9 million shares to the company, and relinquishing her voting control of Theranos. A federal grand jury indicted Holmes and the company's chief operating officer Ramesh Balwani on nine counts of wire fraud and two counts of conspiracy to commit wire fraud for distributing blood tests with falsified results to consumers. In January of 2022, she was found guilty of four of the 11 federal charges.

In examining the media's coverage of Holmes, the term 'charismatic' was consistently used to describe her leadership. She embodied the baseline attributes of charismatic leaders (Conger & Kanungo, 1998): 1) a revolutionary vision, 2) compelling confidence in her product and vision, 3) inspirational rhetoric, 4) a strong appeal to values and 5) unconventional behaviour. She also leveraged the narrative of the successful Silicon Valley entrepreneur – dropping out from Stanford University to start a technology company at age 19. The only missing element was that she did not start her venture in a garage. Playing off of predetermined images of leaders' traits (Eden & Leviatan, 1975), she intentionally 'channelled' Steve Jobs – wearing a black turtleneck sweater just as Jobs did and taking lessons to deepen her voice pitch. *Inc.* magazine exclaimed: *You'd have to look awfully hard not to see Steve Jobs in Elizabeth Holmes*. Theranos advisor Channing Robertson, a Stanford chemical engineering professor, told *Fortune* in 2014: *When I finally connected with what Elizabeth fundamentally is, I realized that I could have just as well been looking into the eyes of a Steve Jobs or a Bill Gates.* (Parloff, 2014).

ADAM NEUMANN: CEO AND CO-FOUNDER OF WEWORK

The second case study (Wiedeman, 2020) is Adam Neumann, an Israeli-American businessman, best known as the co-founder of WeWork – a real-estate company offering flexible, shared work spaces. At the age of 29, Adam opened his first shared-workspace business called Green Desk with a friend Miguel McKelvey. Two years later, he co-founded WeWork with Miguel, serving as its CEO from 2010 to 2019, and his wife Rebekah. Prone to hyperbole, Neumann described WeWork as the *largest physical social network in the world*. He even claimed that the company would one day solve the problems associated with public education and orphaned children. The company's SEC (Securities and Exchange Commission) Form S-1 paperwork (required in order to go public) boldly stated: *We dedicate this* [WeWork] *to the energy of we – greater than any one of us, but inside all of us.*

In 2014, WeWork was described by *Forbes* as *the fastest-growing lessee of office space in New York* and *the fastest-growing lessee of new space in America* (Konrad, 2014). A year later, WeWork doubled its number of working spaces – with 51 locations across the US, Europe and Israel. By January of 2016, WeWork was selected as one of *Fortune*'s three 'unicorn' companies (venture capitalists use the term 'unicorn' to describe a privately held company with a valuation over $1 billion), boasting an internal valuation of $10 billion (Nusca, 2016). That year, the company raised $1.7 billion in private capital. Around 2017, WeWork started to attract the attention of the SoftBank Group Corp., which initially invested over $1 billion into the company. The same year, WeWork expanded into India, China and Southeast Asia, reaching a valuation of $20 billion. By 2018, WeWork moved onto college campuses, raised an additional $900 million in funding and secured a further $3 billion from SoftBank … achieving an internal valuation of $47 billion.

Hoping to capitalise on its rapid growth and favourable press, WeWork filed for an initial public offering (IPO) in 2019. The release of the actual IPO prospectus paradoxically would end Adam Neumann's tenure as CEO. The document revealed a bleak picture of the company's financial state: $900 million in losses in the first half of 2019 and $47 billion in lease obligations. While its revenue was doubling annually, the company was losing $1 for every dollar it made in revenue. In addition, aspects of its corporate governance violated standard good practices. As a result, WeWork lowered its asking price from an initial valuation of $65 billion down to $10 billion before deciding on 16 September to postpone its stock offering. Two days later, a *Wall Street Journal* article chronicled a number of incidents of questionable judgements by Neumann (Brown, 2019). Six days following that article, he was ousted from his job as CEO. With the arrival of the Covid pandemic, WeWork would post a $2.1 billion loss.

While Neumann never faced criminal charges, he engaged in highly questionable business practices. The most serious was the overselling of the company's business model. Other examples include the fact that he sold the 'We' trademark to his own private business for $5.9 million, involved unqualified family members in the operations and purchased a $60 million private jet often used for his family's vacations.

In media reports, Neumann was consistently described as a charismatic leader. Describing his removal from the CEO office, the headline of a 25 September 2019 *Fortune* article stated: 'The remarkable rise – and epic fall – of WeWork's charismatic, controversial founder Adam Neumann' (Mashayekhi, 2019). He embodied the baseline attributes of charismatic leaders (Conger & Kanungo, 1998): 1) a revolutionary vision, 2) compelling confidence in his vision, 3) inspirational rhetoric, 4) a strong appeal to values and 5) unconventional behaviour.

THE MOTIVES OF EXTERNAL STAKEHOLDERS TO 'FOLLOW' CHARISMATIC ENTREPRENEURS

Throughout the literature, one of the most foundational dimensions of charismatic leadership is an inspiring strategic vision and its compelling articulation (Conger & Kanungo, 1998). Exploring the motives of followers who are *external* to the leader's organisation, the appeal of the vision appears to take precedence in influence and attribution processes. For investors, the media and business partners, the promises of the leader's vision are the sources of attraction to 'following' the charismatic leader – though each class of stakeholders does so for different reasons. The leaders' behaviours act to enhance their credibility as visionaries but may not be the dominant motive for external stakeholders to 'follow'. It appears to be the appealing vision, its compelling articulation and the unique rewards of wealth creation, new business opportunities and public recognition that promote followership.

In contrast, organisational members may find the role modelling, unconventionality, high affect intensity and empowerment practices of their charismatic leader as appealing as their leaders' visions (Conger & Kanungo, 1998). As such, future research may discover that certain theories positing why organisational followers are susceptible to charismatic leadership (Ito et al., 2020) may have limited or no applicability to external followers of charismatic entrepreneurs. For example, one theory hypothesises that organisational crises engender followers' attributions of charisma (Pillai & Meindl, 1998). Another theory hypothesises that low self-esteem and low self-concept clarity favour the engagement of some followers in charismatic relationships (Howell & Shamir, 2005). In the cases of Theranos and WeWork, it was the perceptions of opportunity not crisis that promoted follower attributions of charisma. As the two organisations slipped into crisis, their leaders lost their charismatic appeal. In contrast to the low self-esteem theory, the external followers of Holmes and Neumann were highly successful investors or company executives or journalists who most likely had high self-esteem and self-concept clarity. Where the overlap between internal and external followers may exist is in the areas of social contagion (Mayo and Pastor, 2007) and implicit leadership theories (Eden & Leviatan, 1975; Shamir, 1995).

Given the vision's predominance in the influence process, we will briefly summarise the organisational visions of our two case study leaders. WeWork's vision can be traced back to the 'co-working' movement started in 2005 by Brad Neuberg, a software engineer in San Francisco (https://www.coworkingresources.org/blog/history-of-coworking). As a freelancer, he wanted to find a happy medium between the solitude of freelancing and the cubicles of modern workplaces. He invited other freelance engineers to join him in a community-oriented workspace called San Francisco Coworking Space. His model built upon an earlier concept called the business incubator. Started in the 1970s, 'incubators' were shared work offices where entrepreneurs gathered in a low-cost space and were provided with a set of shared services such as secretarial assistance, copy equipment, meeting rooms and kitchen facilities. By the time Adam Neumann and his business partner started Green Desk, the amenities of co-working spaces had already been established: conference rooms, happy hours, good coffee. During 2012, Adam Neumann repositioned what had been a boutique office space company to the co-working model but with a marketing twist (Wiedeman, 2020). At a company event that year, he announced *Starting tomorrow, we're going to be the world's first physical social network*. Drawing upon popular associations with 'social media', Adam's spin was that WeWork was a technology company similar to Facebook with the promise of exponential growth from network effects. This would set the stage for a much larger potential base of investors who would normally not have an interest in real-estate investments. Technology companies attracted large investments ten to 20 times their income towards the end of the 2009 financial crisis. In contrast, real-estate companies would typically bring in investments at the most five times their income. While the high technology company valuations were not always justified, investors believed that technology companies could grow rapidly by leveraging network effects – a benefit that could not be harnessed by real-estate companies because of their high overhead costs.

Elizabeth Holmes's vision of Theranos offered a similar promise – the opportunity to scale a business dramatically. Her pitch (Carreyrou, 2018) was more visceral. In interviews, Holmes likened the traditional blood drawing methods to vampirism and torture experiments that aliens might devise. The biggest problem plaguing traditional blood testing was the need for an unpleasant syringe and multiple vials of blood to be drawn. She implied that a widespread aversion to needles was preventing people from getting blood tests and learning about their health. Added to this was the difficulty of scheduling, since blood testing requires the approval of a physician. Finally, traditional blood tests are expensive. Holmes often cited that a typical cholesterol blood test alone could cost over $50. She claimed that Theranos would perform that same test for $3. Combined – the use of a syringe, the inconvenience and the cost – these factors resulted in fewer people getting their blood tested using traditional methods. In aggregate, Holmes argued that many conditions often went undiagnosed because between 40 and 60 per cent of people who are directed to get their blood tested did not. As a result, diabetes, sexually transmitted diseases and other conditions remained undiagnosed until it was too late. Theranos's methodology promised to completely alter this landscape of blood testing and would ultimately result in saving more lives.

INVESTORS AS FOLLOWERS: THE CHARISMATIC LEADER AS A WEALTH ENHANCER

For entrepreneurial charismatic leaders, investors provide the lifeblood of their nascent ventures. Without their financial backing, the leader's revolutionary vision is unlikely to become a reality. For this reason, we begin our analysis with this essential class of external followers.

Theranos and WeWork were perceived as 'unicorns' by their investor followers. The term 'unicorn' describes a privately owned start-up with a valuation of over $1 billion. From the standpoint of venture capitalists, this valuation indicates that the start-up is already a revolutionary force within its marketplace. It also ensures rich financial returns, especially if the venture goes on to become a publicly traded company. For example, Facebook had a 'conservative' $10 billion valuation in 2009, and it soared to a publicly traded market capitalisation of $321 billion within a few short years. For investors, the driving motive to follow a charismatic entrepreneurial leader is wealth accumulation.

Theranos and WeWork were fortunate to have been launched during the second decade of the 21st century – an era favourable to speculative investments in start-ups. Thanks to historically low interest rates and the growth of non-traditional fundraising sources, it was an easy time to raise money privately. For example, venture capital funds grew dramatically in the US during this time – from $17.5 billion in 2004 to $74.5 billion in 2020 (statista.com). Private equity, banks and mutual fund companies joined the rush to invest in potential unicorns, further pushing up valuations. In this low-interest-rate and slow-growth environment, even established companies like Apple, Facebook and Google found it easier to grow through acquisitions instead of investing internally – buying unicorns themselves. National legislation in the form of the Jobs Act of 2012 was a further facilitator. Before the Jobs Act, a private firm with 500 investors was required to list publicly on a stock exchange. The Act changed the threshold to 2,000 investors. Regulatory shifts like the Jobs Act made it easier for small companies to grow privately and to reach high internal valuations given a much larger pool of internal investors.

A powerful driver behind the dramatic increase in start-up funding was investors' fears of 'missing out' on the next Amazon or Apple. This fear led investors to overlook critical risk factors and fund promising unicorn candidates without proper due diligence. Further fuelling the dramatic growth of 'unicorns', investors and venture capital firms had adopted an investment strategy known as 'blitzscaling', starting in the early 2000s (Yeh and Hoffman, 2018). Under this approach, a new venture expands at a high rate to rapidly grow market share and push away competitors as fast as possible – the expansion is driven by large funding rounds from investors. Both Elizabeth Holmes and Adam Neumann leveraged this tactic of blitz-scaling to build their visions of the future. For example, it is estimated that Theranos raised somewhere between $900 million and $1.3 billion in funding. WeWork would raise billions of dollars … $4.4 billion alone from the Japanese investment firm SoftBank.

To get a sense of the potential investment returns, one can look at the internal valuations of the two ventures. While there are varied approaches to valuing an entrepreneurial venture, investor funding and valuations often move in parallel. For example, one year after its funding, Theranos raised $6.9 million and gained a $30 million valuation. By 2007, the company raised another $43.2 million resulting in a $197 million valuation. By 2014, Theranos received over $400 million in funding and was valued at $1 billion. Similarly, WeWork received $6.3 million from investors in its early days and was reported to have a $15 million valuation. By 2012, some $32 million in funding was received from seven investors which resulted in a valuation of $215 million. In 2017, 12 investors provided an additional $582 million in funding. After this round, WeWork's valuation was estimated at $20 billion. As mentioned earlier, its valuation would reach $47 billion at its zenith.

In both cases, Holmes and Neumann fostered investor momentum through the reputations of their early investors – leveraging a 'contagion' effect (Meindl, 1993). These individuals served to reassure the next round of investors – in essence creating a virtuous cycle of investment. For example, Elizabeth Holmes convinced Tim Drapper, the father of a childhood friend, to invest $1 million in her start-up (Carreyrou, 2018). Tim's venture firm, known as DFJ, had a reputation for lucrative earlystage investments such as the web-based email service Hotmail. Another family connection – a long-time friend of her father's – was a retired corporate turnaround specialist Victor Palmieri. Interviews with both individuals describe how impressed they were by her vision of applying the principles of nano- and microtechnology to the field of health diagnostics and her personal vision. More prestigious investors would follow: media mogul Rupert Murdoch, Oracle Chairman and founder Larry Ellison, famous venture capitalists including Donald Lucas and Dixon Doll and the wealthy heirs of the Amway, Walmart and Cox Communications. As these more prestigious investors stepped in, it created greater credibility for Holmes, her vision and the potential returns on the investment. For example, following Rupert Murdoch's investment, Theranos raised a $9.1 million Series B funding round led by ATA Ventures and a $28.5 million Series C, both in 2006.

Erin Griffith noted in a *New York Times* article how these investors were so swept up in Holmes's compelling vision and enthusiasm that they ignored red flags that in hindsight were obvious (Griffith, 2021):

In 2014, Dan Mosley, a lawyer and power broker among wealthy families, asked the entrepreneur Elizabeth Holmes for audited financial statements of Theranos, her blood testing start-up. Theranos never produced any, but Mr Mosley invested $6 million in the company anyway – and wrote Ms Holmes a gushing thank-you email for the opportunity. Bryan Tolbert, an investor at Hall Group, said his firm invested $5 million in Theranos in 2013, even though it did not have a detailed grasp of the start-up's technologies or its work with pharmaceutical companies and the military. And Lisa Peterson, who handles investments for Michigan's wealthy DeVos family, said she did not visit any of Theranos's testing centers in Walgreens stores, call any Walgreens executives or hire any outside experts in science, regulations or legal matters to verify the start-up's claims. In 2014, the DeVos family invested $100 million into the company.

Similarly, Adam Neumann's vision of WeWork attracted well-known property investor Mortimer Zuckerman of Boston Properties as well as a venture capital firm called Benchmark Partners (Wiedeman, 2020). Benchmark was known for its selectivity and for investing only in ventures that could scale significantly. They had turned a $6.7 million investment in eBay into a $5 billion stake. In what could be described as a 'contagion', these investors were followed by highly visible investment firms such as J. P. Morgan Chase & Co., T. Rowe Price Associates, Wellington Management, Goldman Sachs Group and the Harvard Corporation. On 9 March 2016, the company raised $430 million in new rounds of financing from Legend Holdings and Hony Capital, valuing the company at $16 billion. By the autumn of that year, WeWork had raised $1.7 billion in private capital. In 2017, Japanese investment fund SoftBank invested $4.4 billion in the firm. In 2018 and 2019, they invested another $6 billion. By the end of 2019, SoftBank's investments in WeWork totalled $18.5 billion.

When interviewed and asked why he invested, Masayoshi Son, the founder of SoftBank, explained that he was drawn to Neumann's drive and WeWork's expanding growth prospects, believing the company would be a good fit as for his Vision Fund. For example, while most US technology companies had failed to make meaningful inroads in China, WeWork already had 115 buildings across 12 cities in Greater China, about 15 per cent of the company's total office space locations. In addition, WeWork's revenue had more than quadrupled to $1.82 billion from 2016 to 2018, according to its S-1 filing. In just the first half of 2019, sales had reached $1.53 billion (Alex Shreman, CNBC, 25 September 2019). These dramatic growth rates became the proof points of Adam's vision – that a real-estate company could replicate the growth rates of a technology firm.

JOURNALISTS AS 'FOLLOWERS': THE CHARISMATIC LEADER AS A 'SCOOP'

The media plays a significant role in ensuring visibility and in turn credibility for charismatic leaders and their visions. They play a vital role in 'contagion effects' (Meindl, 1993). Journalists are always on the lookout for a compelling news story. Charismatic leaders and their bold visions are reliable sources. The journalists' motive to 'follow' is the personal recognition for their journalistic talents. In rarer cases, it is the opportunity to write a bestselling book and reap its financial awards. Journalists stake an element of their career success on their ability to get a 'scoop'. A scoop is an exclusive news story. Good scoops attract a great deal of attention for the journalists and their news outlets. For example, most major newspapers and media outlets strive to get as many scoops as possible to add to their prestige and visibility. When a journalist releases a major story ahead of other journalists, he or she is said to have 'scooped' the competition. These stories can range from celebrity scandals to outbreaks of war and pandemics. If a journalist develops a reputation for their high-quality scoops, he or she will typically be in great demand from the major media outlets. This stature allows the journalist greater leeway to pursue projects and stories of personal interest (McMahon, 2022). In the case of both Theranos and WeWork, journalists were able to leverage their stories on these leaders into scoops as well as bestselling books, bringing further personal recognition as well as financial rewards.

For example, the first major scoop regarding Elizabeth Holmes occurred on 12 June 2014. On that date, *Fortune* magazine published an article by Roger Parloff discussing the growth of Theranos and the company's mission. In it, Holmes boasted the company employed 700 employees and was aggressively moving towards its mission of making lab testing more accessible. Holmes discussed the lower cost of Theranos's lab tests and discussed its partnership with Walgreens. She told the interviewer that Theranos planned to roll out testing in all of the Walgreen locations. The interview praised the firm, celebrating many of Theranos's achievements, without a real discussion of the downsides. Writing for the *Washington Post*, Paul

Farhi later summarised the impact of this one article (Farhi, 2021):

> The story was 5,500 words of pure rapture about a Silicon Valley company few had ever heard of and its intriguing chief executive. Theranos, declared Fortune magazine in 2014, appeared to be on the verge of revolutionizing the health care industry with a wondrous new technology for diagnosing diseases with just a few drops of blood. The magazine's cover put a human face on the company's alleged breakthroughs. Theranos's founder, a young woman named Elizabeth Holmes, stared at readers with serene blue eyes and a Mona Lisa smile. 'This CEO Is Out for Blood,' the headline read. Emblematic of the gushy, overly credulous business and tech journalism ascendant at the time, Fortune's story touched off a media stampede that transformed Holmes, then 30, into a business superstar.

Similarly, a 5 November 2014 article by Alex Konrad in *Forbes* was one of the first to describe WeWork. The article opened with a story about Mort Zuckerman, the 77-year-old billionaire chairman of Boston Properties (a real-estate development firm with $19.6 billion-worth of prime office buildings in major metropolitan areas). He shared his reflections on meeting Adam Neumann: *Adam understood in a very serious way that we are in a new culture […] I found it extraordinarily creative and original after being in this business for God knows how many years* (Konrad, 2014). By 2015, WeWork had become the anchor tenant for a $300 million redevelopment co-owned by Boston Properties in the Brooklyn Navy Yard. The article's scoop included this description:

> WeWork's founders have been content to stay quiet about their story until now, swearing investors to secrecy. No longer. Over the next 12 months the company expects to triple its membership from 14,000 to 46,000 and expand to 60 locations from 21 today and 9 just a year ago. WeWork's first location four years ago was just 3,000 square feet in SoHo with creaky floorboards and walls powerwashed by its founders. Now WeWork is the fastest-growing lessee of new office space in New York and next year will become the fastest-growing lessee of new space in America as it spreads to cities such as Austin and Chicago, not to mention London, Amsterdam and Tel Aviv.
>
> (Konrad, 2014)

The secret was out. *Forbes* readers were the first to learn about the industry disrupter called WeWork.

On 2 October 2017, another *Forbes* article touted 'WeWork's $20 billion office party: The crazy bet that could change how the world does business' (Bertoni, 2017). It described SoftBank's decision to invest $3 billion in WeWork which produced a $20 billion valuation for the firm. A separate $1.4 billion was to be spread across three new entities expanding WeWork across Asia: WeWork Japan, WeWork Pacific, WeWork China. WeWork would now be worth more than its early partner commercial real-estate giant Boston Properties.

What makes these media or journalist followers unique is that they can benefit when the charismatic leader fails as well as succeeds. Chronicling the fall of Theranos and Holmes, journalist John Carreyrou's bestselling book *Bad Blood: Secrets and Lies in a Silicon Valley Startup* (2018) sold over a million copies. The book received critical acclaim, winning the 2018 Financial Times and McKinsey Business Book of the Year Award. Published in the autumn of 2020, Reeves Wiedeman's *Billion Dollar Loser: The Epic Rise and Spectacular Fall of Adam Neumann and WeWork* similarly became a bestseller and was chosen as a *New York Times Editors'* Choice, *Newsweek's* Must Read Nonfiction and *Publishers Weekly* Top Ten for Business.

BUSINESS PARTNERS AS FOLLOWERS: THE CHARISMATIC LEADER AS THE PURVEYOR OF GROWTH OPPORTUNITIES

Similar to investors, business partners can become 'followers' of charismatic entrepreneurs in the belief that they offer a unique business opportunity or compelling solution to an ongoing challenge that a firm faces. For example, Elizabeth Holmes impressed two early clients – Safeway grocery stores and Walgreens pharmacies – with the potential of in-store blood-testing centres that could deliver test results in 30 minutes. Both companies were searching for growth opportunities. The idea was simple. Shoppers could do a quick finger-prick blood test. While the results were being processed, they could do their shopping and then receive their tests results at the end of their visit. Depending on the test results, they might end up purchasing prescription drugs or other medications on their way out. While Walgreens had a significant pharmacy business, grocery stores like Safeway had been moving aggressively into prescription drugs and vaccine provisions. Theranos's in-store labs offered more means to capture sales for both firms.

Walgreens' executives were so impressed with Holmes's vision that the company poured $140 million into a joint venture. Safeway spent close to $400 million into remodelling 969 stores to build Theranos patient service centres. The partnership with Walgreens involved in-store testing centres at 40 locations with an eventual national roll-out. Internal presentations by Theranos to Walgreens reflected the promise of the *Lowest cost, highest quality testing from a finger-stick* with a *State of the art result turnaround* of four to 24 hours. Not surprisingly, these partnerships proved fraught with delays and fraud. After John Carreyrou's expose in 2015 and the start of government investigations, the two retailers withdrew their deals, abruptly ending Theranos's first public experiments.

During the courtroom trial of Elizabeth Holmes, Safeway chief executive Steven Burd testified that he saw the partnership as a business opportunity to expand the company's health offerings. He described how impressed he had been with Holmes, whom he felt was charismatic, decisive and smart. Similarly, the chief financial officer of Walgreens, Wade Miquelon, testified that Theranos was one of the *most exciting companies that we have seen* (Somerville, 2021). In an email to his CEO from March 2010, Miquelon said that Theranos *may have found the lead pony* among firms that offered rapid diagnostic tests.

As mentioned earlier, Boston Properties was a business partner with WeWork in the Brooklyn Naval Yard project. A 675,000-square-foot building was designed to cater to the technology and creative industries in Brooklyn. The $380 million building, named Dock 72, aimed to increase Brooklyn's competitiveness and spur thousands of new jobs. At the time, a press release from the Brooklyn Navy Yard Development Corporation exclaimed that this project would play a critical role in urban redevelopment and job creation (Boston Properties, 2016):

'From start-ups to expanding firms, this new workspace is going to put thousands of New Yorkers to work and help launch the next great wave of home-grown innovation. We are growing the Navy Yard's capacity for manufacturing, tech and the maker economy faster than any time in its modern history. We are thrilled to work with Boston Properties, Rudin Development and WeWork to bring this new space online and keep building on the Navy Yard's incredible success story,' said NYC Deputy Mayor for Housing and Economic Development Alicia Glen.

'The tenants that occupy this new building will contribute to the modern industrial ecosystem of the Yard – where technology, design and manufacturing converge. The shared work space will nurture hundreds of small businesses and spark the next generation of large-scale employers in the Yard,' said BNYDC President and CEO David Ehrenberg. *'Furthermore, this type of large, private-sector investment signals a watershed moment in the growth of the Brooklyn Navy Yard. Thanks to this vote of confidence from respected investors and developers and this partnership with WeWork, BNYDC will be able to attract additional top creative and industrial firms that will create thousands of jobs for local residents.'*

In summary, the visions of the charismatic leaders of Theranos and WeWork held out the promise of compelling growth opportunities that would differentiate their venture partners from the competition.

CONCLUSION

The aim of this chapter has been to illustrate that our construct of what constitutes the 'followers' of charismatic leaders is too narrow. While organisational members play a pivotal role in attributing charisma to a leader, they are but one of several classes of 'followers'. There are at least three overlooked categories with pivotal if not essential roles to play with charismatic entrepreneurs – investors, the media and business partners. These followers' contributions vary, and yet all are foundational to the rise and success of charismatic leaders of new ventures. As suggested in this chapter, contagion effects appear particularly pronounced. Research is needed to examine the motives and self-concepts that encourage each category to attribute charisma to a leader and to commit investments in the leader and their vision.

Future research should explore how external followers who occupy central positions within their stakeholder networks influence others' perceptions of charisma and in turn foster a contagion. In both the cases of Theranos and WeWork, influential investors appear to have heightened the credibility of the leader and their vision. One prominent investor's decision to invest in the venture of a charismatic leader led peers to make similar investments. What makes these cases more compelling is that the contagion effects were so strong that future investors often failed to do their own due diligence. Contagion effects also appear to occur across the three distinct follower networks. For example, the attribution of charisma to a leader by a journalist may spread the content of the leader's vision to potential business partners and investors. These contagion dimensions are ripe areas for research investigations.

Another potential research topic is related to the articulation of the leader's vision. Given that the vision plays a more central role in influencing the commitments of external stakeholders, research needs to examine the attributes of highly resonant visionary communications. Are there distinct frames of perspective that make the leader's vision particularly compelling to external followers? From the WeWork case study, it was clear that Neumann's linking his vision to the concept of social networks made it far more attractive to investors. It also allowed him to raise significantly greater amounts of investment capital. In addition, are there certain appeals to values that make the leader's vision more attractive? For example, Holmes described her product as a humane way to get blood tests. It would result in far more individuals proactively learning about their health and addressing underlying health conditions – essentially, saving lives. She often spoke about her quest to live a purposeful life and do something for the greater good of society.

Another research question is whether concrete proofs of the vision are needed to reassure external stakeholders that the vision is not an imaginary ideal conjured up by the charismatic leader. For example, the rapid expansion and popularity of WeWork facilities served as 'proof of concept' for investors. Theranos forged test results to create the illusion that their testing machine Edison was a viable product. I suspect that charismatic entrepreneurial leaders may require initial successes and tangible 'proofs of concept' to attract external followers, especially investors and business partners.

Given that the external stakeholders are more often 'distant' from the leader, what dynamics foster the attributions of charisma at a distance versus close up? Shamir (1995) posited that there were fundamental differences in distant versus close charismatic leadership. Since the external followers are primarily in a position of distance from the leader, this area of study – while largely overlooked in the literature to date – becomes more salient as we expand our notions of followers.

In summary, we are only scratching the surface of followership and charismatic leadership. From the standpoint of future research, the aim of this chapter is fourfold: 1) to broaden our perspective on what constitutes a 'follower' of a charismatic leader, 2) to identify the varying roles that external followers play, 3) to hypothesise the motives that encourage the three classes of external followers to not only attribute charisma but to make significant investments of various forms and 4) to speculate on the role of contagion effects across the networks of the distinct classes of external followers.

REFERENCES

Akhtar, A. (2019). Adam Neumann built a global coworking empire. These are the cities with the most WeWork offices, and how much they cost. *Business Insider*, 22 October. https://www.businessinsider.com/global-cities-with-the-most-wework-offices

Auletta, K., & Denby, D. (2014). Blood, simpler. *New Yorker*, 15 December. https://www.newyorker.com/magazine/2014/12/15/blood-simpler

Bertoni, S. (2017). WeWork's $20 billion office party: The crazy bet that could change how the world does business. *Forbes*, 2 October. https://www.forbes.com/sites/stevenbertoni/2017/10/02/the-way-we-work/

Boston Properties (2016). Boston Properties, Rudin Development and WeWork to develop new high performance workspace at Brooklyn Navy Yard. *Inc.* 6 July. http://ir.bostonproperties.com/news-releases/news-release-details/boston-properties-rudin-development-and-wework-develop-new-high/

Bligh, M. C. (2011). Followership and follower-centred approaches. In A. Bryman, K. Grint, B. Jackson, B. Uhl-Bien & D. Collinson (Eds.), *The SAGE Handbook of Leadership*. Sage.

Brown, E. (2019). How Adam Neumann's over-the-top style built WeWork. 'This is not the way everybody behaves'. *Wall Street Journal*, 18 September. https://www.wsj.com/articles/this-is-not-the-way-everybody-behaves-how-adam-neumanns-over-the-top-style-built-wework-11568823827

Carreyrou, J. (2015). Hot Startup Theranos has struggled with its blood-test technology *Wall Street Journal*, 16 October. https://www.wsj.com/articles/theranos-has-struggled-with-blood-tests-1444881901

Carreyrou, J. (2018). *Bad Blood, Secrets and Lies in a Silicon Valley Startup*. Penguin Random House.

Conger, J. A., & Kanungo, R. N. (1998). *Charismatic Leadership in Organizations*. Sage.

Eden, D. & Leviatan, U. (1975). Implicit leadership theory as a determinant of the factor structure underlying supervisory behavior scales. *Journal of Applied Psychology*, 60, 736–741.

Farhi, P. (2021). The magazine story that made Elizabeth Holmes famous could now help send her to prison. *Washington Post*, 16 December.

https://www.washingtonpost.com/lifestyle/media/elizabeth-holmes-fortune-cover-theranos/2021/12/15/f2332ed8-5841-11ec-a808-3197a22b19fa_story.html

Fortune Editors (2016). The world's 19 most disappointing leaders. *Fortune*, 31 March. https://fortune.com/2016/03/30/most-disappointing-leaders/

Fortune (2014). Elizabeth Holmes mission: full interview *Fortune MPW*, 8 October. YouTube. https://www.youtube.com/watch?v=YecjzEScXqU

Fortune (2015). Elizabeth Holmes defends Theranos amid media scrutiny at Fortune's Global Forum. *Fortune*, 2 November. YouTube. https://www.youtube.com/watch?v=A8qgmGtRMsY

Griffith, E. (2021). What red flags? Elizabeth Holmes trial exposes investors' carelessness. *New York Times*, 4 November. https://www.nytimes.com/2021/11/04/technology/theranos-elizabeth-holmes-investors-diligence.html

Herper, M. (2016). From $4.5 billion to nothing: Forbes revises estimated net worth of Theranos founder Elizabeth Holmes. *Forbes*, 1 June. https://www.forbes.com/sites/matthewherper/2016/06/01/from-4-5-billion-to-nothing-forbes-revises-estimated-net-worth-of-theranos-founder-elizabeth-holmes/

Howell, J. M., & Shamir, B. (2005). The role of followers in the charismatic leadership process: Relationships and their consequence. *Academy of Management Review*, 30, 96–112.

Ito, A., Harrison, J., Bligh, M., & Roland-Levy, C. (2020). An integrative review and agenda for future research. In J. P. Zuquete (Ed.), *Routledge International Handbook of Charisma*. Routledge.

Konrad, A. (2014). Inside the phenomenal rise of WeWork. *Forbes*, 5 November. https://www.forbes.com/sites/alexkonrad/2014/11/05/the-rise-of-wework/

Mashayekhi, R. (2019). The remarkable rise – and epic fall – of WeWork's charismatic, controversial founder Adam Neumann. *Fortune*, 25 September. https://fortune.com/2019/09/25/the-remarkable-rise-and-epic-fall-of-weworks-charismatic-controversial-founder-adam-neumann/

Mayo, M., & Pastor, I. (2007). Leadership embedded in social networks: Looking at inter-follower processes. In B. Shamir, N. Rajagopalan, M. C. Bligh, & M. Uhl-Bien (Eds.), *Follower-centered Perspectives on Leadership: A Tribute to the Memory of James R. Meindl*, Information Age.

McMahon, M. (2022). In journalism, what is a scoop? (with pictures). *Language Humanities*, 19 March. https://www.languagehumanities.org/in-journalism-what-is-a-scoop.htm

Meindl, J. R. (1993). Reinventing leadership: A radical, social psychological approach. In J. K. Murnighan (Ed.), *Social Psychology in Organizations: Advances in Theory and Research*. Prentice Hall.

Nusca, A. (2016). Three unicorns to bet on. *Fortune*, 22 January. https://fortune.com/2016/01/21/unicorns-hype-valuations/

Parloff, R. (2014). This CEO is out for blood. *Fortune*, 12 June. https://fortune.com/2014/06/12/theranos-blood-holmes/

Pillai, R., & Meindl, J. R. (1998). Context and charisma: A 'meso' level examination of the relationship of organic structure, collectivism, and crisis to charismatic leadership. *Journal of Management*, 24, 643–671

Shamir, B. (1995). Social distance and charisma: Theoretical notes and an exploratory study. *Leadership Quarterly*, 6(1), 19–47.

Shamir, B., House, R. J., & Arthur, M. B. (1993). The motivational effects of charismatic leadership: A self-concept based theory. *Organization Science*, 4, 577–594.

Somerville, H. (2021). Former Walgreens CFO describes how Theranos wooed him. *Wall Street Journal*, 13 October.

Sorvino, C. (2015). America's richest women 2015. *Forbes*, 29 September. https://www.forbes.com/sites/chloesorvino/2015/09/29/americas-richest-women-2015/

Uhl-Bien, M., Riggio, R. E., Lowe, K. B., & Carsten, M. K. (2014). Followership theory: A review and research agenda. *Leadership Quarterly*, 25, 83–104.

Wiedeman, R. (2019). How did WeWork's Adam Neumann build a $47 billion company? *Intelligencer*, 10 June. https://nymag.com/intelligencer/2019/06/wework-adam-neumann.html

Yeh, C., & Hoffman R. (2018). *Blitzscaling: The Lightening-Fast Path to Building Massively Valuable Companies*. Currency.

Wiedeman, R. (2020). *Billion Dollar Loser: The Epic Rise and Spectacular Fall of Adam Neumann and WeWork*. Back Bay Books.

Leadership Development: Past, Present and Future

David V. Day and Darja Kragt

INTRODUCTION

In the first edition of this *Handbook*, Day (2011) concluded that leadership development was losing its perceived quality and added value in organisations. To overcome this negative trend, researchers and practitioners were urged to support more evidence-based approaches to leadership development. As a field of research distinct from the voluminous leadership literature, leadership development has advanced significantly over the past decade, but comparatively little seems to have changed in practice. Despite a wealth of programmes, new interventions and purportedly innovative approaches – as well as billions of dollars spent on leader development annually – we have little evidence that these programmes are achieving the intended results. Simply put, the considerable investments made in developing organisational leaders and leadership do not seem to have improved things. The quality of workplace leadership remains relatively poor, with 60 per cent of employees reporting that their superiors frequently and consistently display destructive leadership behaviours in the preceding six months (Aasland et al., 2010).

Leadership development remains a significant concern for organisations. As of this past year, 55 per cent of CEOs report that developing future generation of leaders is their primary critical concern, while a staggering 85 per cent of senior executives lack confidence in their own leadership team's ability to successfully navigate through disruptive times (Odgers Berndtson, 2020). According to another survey, only 48 per cent of leaders and 28 per cent of HR professionals believe that their organisations have high-quality leaders (DDI, 2021). In this chapter, we again urge academics and practitioners to close the gap between research and practice. We do so by reviewing significant advances in leadership development theories and empirical research over the last decade (or so) with an overarching goal of translating these scholarly advancements into sound, actionable advice for practitioners. In addition, we address questions related to what the added value is of adopting sense-making and sense-breaking in this mix and what do these processes look like in the context of leadership development?

Day (2011) identified leader and leadership development as demonstrably different concerns (also see Day, 2000). Leader development refers to the development of individual's knowledge, skills and abilities (KSAs), whereas leadership development focuses on building social structures and processes that enable more collective forms of leadership. This distinction continues to inform the literature by sharpening the focus of research, theory and practice on the appropriate level of analysis. Most of what will be discussed here is related to leader development, except for those sections in which shared, team, or collective leadership development are discussed mainly as nascent areas of research. We use the term 'leader development' to refer to the development initiatives targeted at individual leaders and the term 'leadership development' to refer to initiatives targeted at groups, teams, or other collectives.

In terms of understanding the history and evolution of the field, Vogel and colleagues (2021) conducted a bibliometric review of the leadership development literature. Bibliometric methods use available data in the form of documents on a given topic to discern how a particular field of study has evolved. Specific methods include publication counts and trend analysis, co-citation analysis, co-authorship analysis and keywords co-occurrence analysis (Zhang et al., 2021). The results of the Vogel et al. review identified leadership styles, leader identity, authentic leadership and learning/goal-setting theories as dominant domains related to leadership development.

Overall, the Vogel et al. (2021) review concluded that leadership development knowledge has evolved around one main storyline, focusing on practice and influential leadership theory. Note that there is no bibliometric data suggesting any strong influence of leadership *development* theory. Most theoretical influences are traceable to mainstream leadership theories, with an apparent assumption that development would be merely the application of whatever was the most compelling leadership theory. This implicit assumption has been a major restrainer to moving forward both the science and practice of leadership development.

THEORETICAL PERSPECTIVES ON LEADER AND LEADERSHIP DEVELOPMENT

Day (2011) identified three major theoretical perspectives that underpinned the leader development literature, namely, leader skills, leader identity and authentic leadership. A decade later these three perspectives remain relatively influential but to different degrees. Leader skills remains the dominant focus and approach in leader development. On the one hand, whereas identity-based perspectives have seen increased theoretical and empirical interest, the literature on authentic leadership is relatively stagnant in terms of new empirical insights. On the other hand, new foci have emerged on shared and collective forms of leadership, with additional theoretical perspectives being offered. In this section, we review the most prominent advancements in theorising about leader and leadership development around two main themes: leader identity and team (collective) leadership development.

Leader Identity

The idea that leader identity (or self-perception as a leader) underpins the development of KSAs regarding leadership has been informing the leader development literature over the last decade. Another way of thinking about leader identity is as a sense-making mechanism. If someone thinks of the self as at least partly grounded in a leader identity, it frames how that person makes sense of experiences that might be leveraged as developmental opportunities. In terms of how it has been discussed traditionally, one stream of literature has focused on identifying how leader identity is developed at the individual level, but within broader social interactions. For example, DeRue and Ashford (2010) proposed that identity is co-constructed in organisations when individuals claim and grant leader and follower identities through their social interactions. Claiming refers to the actions people take to assert their identity, whereas granting refers to the actions that a person takes to bestow an identity to someone else. The construction of identity occurs when claiming–granting is reciprocated with granting–claiming by other organisational members. Over time, the adopted identities become internalised, but also relationally and collectively endorsed within an organisational context.

Focusing on first-time leaders, Maurer and London (2018) identified a shift from individual contributor to an organisational leader as a major identity challenge. Building on a grounded theory approach to developing a leader identity by Komives and colleagues (2005), Maurer and London described different degrees of identity shift – from incremental to substantial to radical – that depend on and are influenced by organisational policies and resources. Organisations should focus on providing resources and rewards to new leaders who are successfully shifting their role identity to that of an innovative leader for a given collective. Maurer and London (2018) identify identity destruction (a form of sense-breaking) as a legitimate part of role shifting, whereby an identity as an individual contributor is replaced by identity as a leader.

Based on these core ideas regarding the development of an individual's leader identity, a significant body of work has focused on understanding how leader identity develops and the ways in which it supports development at different levels and across different domains. Extending an integrative framework of leader development offered by Day et al. (2009), Day and Dragoni (2015) proposed a multilevel summary framework of leadership development processes and outcomes at both individual leader and team (i.e., collective) leadership levels.

At the individual level, proximal outcomes of development were proposed in the form of self-views such as leadership self-efficacy, self-awareness and leader identity, in addition to leadership KSAs. A novel contribution offered by this framework was the incorporation of the distal outcomes of development informed by human development theories of dynamic skills theory (Fischer, 1980) and constructive-developmental theories (McCauley et al., 2006). At the individual level, distal outcomes of development include dynamic skills and abstractions, and meaning-making structures and processes. Given that leader development is thought to transpire over lengthy time scales – months and even years rather than days or weeks – thinking about the developmental outcomes in relatively short (i.e., proximal) and long (i.e., distal) terms helps to develop a richer criterion space for leader development research.

Hammond and colleagues (2017) proposed an interesting extension to the idea of leader identity development by advocating for a holistic or 'whole person' approach to leader development. The essence of their thinking is that leaders develop in different domains outside the immediate work environment. Their cross-domain leader development model posits that leaders develop through a combination of the characteristics of an experience and understanding connections and disconnections of that experience. Leader identity aids in integrating these connections and disconnections from multiple domains into a coherent sense of self-as-a-leader, which enhances sense-making ability.

Recognising the multilevel nature of leader emergence, Acton and colleagues (2019) introduced a process-oriented framework incorporating leader identity. Two categories of leadership emergence mechanisms are proposed: self-structures and enacted structures. Self-structures refer to cognitions related to how individuals produce, process and make sense of information about the self (i.e., leader identity). Enacted structures refer to the behaviours, expressions and communications that are performed to support an ongoing social construction process between leaders and followers. This distinction further refines the leader emergence construct in potentially important ways for future researchers to use.

Central to leader emergence are processes of sense-making and sense-giving, which facilitate the development of a shared reality of leadership (we return to this point in the section on collective leadership). Leader emergence starts at the individual level, whereby leadership self-structures are activated if the social context is favourable, an individual is motivated and they have prior experience in a similar context. At the relational level, leadership perceptions of a specific individual are driven by implicit leadership theories – that is, specific self-structures that refer to followers' prototypes or expectations of leaders. Enacted structures at the relational level describe a pattern of interactions in the leader–follower dyad, which determine whether leadership identity is activated. Acton et al. (2019) suggest that both an activation of individual self-structure *and* leadership perception (i.e., attribution) by the follower must occur in order for leader identity to be activated. Interestingly, the authors suggest that these processes occur simultaneously across all dyads. Hence, at the collective level, an activation of leader identity is possible when the individual's self-structures are activated and they are perceived as a leader by other group/team members.

Focusing on leader development across multiple domains and over the lifespan, Liu and colleagues (2021) introduced an interdisciplinary framework of the critical developmental experiences at each stage in the lifespan. The framework involves multiple experiential windows or stages in the lifespan that present unique opportunities for leader development. For example, adulthood (30–60 years of age) is described as a purpose-driven stage, in which individuals are concerned with discovering a sense of meaning and purpose in their life. Critical developmental experiences at this stage include formal development programmes, developmental challenges at work, marriage and parenthood, as well as other purpose-seeking activities, such as meditation. Similar insights are offered across the lifespan. The framework further specifies the mediating role of an experience processing system and leader self-view system that support leader development. An experience processing system consists of experiential learning through deliberate practice and contextualised application. A leader self-view system involves leader identity, self-awareness and self-efficacy. Liu et al. (2021) also consider individual differences as a foundation for leader development, thus pointing to the necessity of considering how genetic and other influences impact an individual's development. This enhances an individualised perspective on leader development.

Team and Collective Leadership Development

In the last decade, there has been an increased attention on the development of shared, team-based and collective approaches to developing leadership capacity (i.e., leadership development; Day, 2000). As noted in the previous sections, many integrative frameworks of leadership development discuss the interplay between an individual and collective. For example, Acton et al. (2019) described a number of processes that occur at the collective level that support individual leader emergence. Furthermore, Day and Dragoni (2015) discuss proximal outcomes of leadership development at the team level, including psychological safety, knowledge of team members' expertise, shared mindsets and team learning, which are thought to indicate the potential for long-term development at a distal level in terms of enhancing the outcome of collective leadership capacity. These authors also acknowledge how individual-level leader development can serve as inputs into more collective or team-based development of leadership capacity at a different level of analysis.

Recognising that leadership development traditionally adopts an individualistic focus, Clarke (2013) drew on complexity science to present a relational model of leadership development that goes beyond the individual. Complexity science frames leadership as a property of a social system, more specifically, defined as a system capacity for adapting to change, dealing with ambiguities and responding more effectively to complex problems. Complexity leadership development compromises four key dimensions: network conditions, shared leadership, organisational learning and leader behaviours. The network conditions dimension implies that organisational members must communicate and knowledge-share effectively to achieve synergies from interactions between information and expertise. Shared leadership is important in complexity leadership development as it ensures contribution from members at all levels, resulting in better ideas and superior problem-solving. Organisational learning emphasises the importance of co-creation, which can facilitate adaptation and innovation.

These system-level dimensions are supported by an individual leader's knowledge and skills in seven major areas (e.g., supporting shared leadership, developing the system's network, building social capital). Interestingly, both formal and informal leaders are seen as critical to harness the effects of distributive intelligence. This is because the complexity perspective posits that the more often differing patterns and sources of leadership are planned and aligned, the greater the likelihood of positive leadership outcomes. A question that this approach raises is whether developing more effective individual leaders will result in enhanced shared and collective capacity for leadership. This highlights a need for more research on collective leadership development to best determine how the aggregation processes work across levels of analysis (Kozlowski & Klein, 2000).

Despite early recognition of the importance of collective leadership (Day et al., 2004), there is a lack of research progress on the *how* of collective leadership development. One noteworthy contribution discussed different perspectives and approaches that can help both researchers and practitioners to understand how to implement collective leadership development. Eva and colleagues (2021) developed a multi-perspective framework by integrating five dominant perspectives on collective leadership development – person-centred, social networks, social-relational, socio-material and institutional. These perspectives are arranged on a 2x2 visual framework with two key dimensions of ideology (normative versus critical) and centricity (context-centric versus consultant-centric). On the one hand, for example, social-relational perceptive is normative because it is focused on improving the level of communication and relationships among leaders, rather than redefining those relationships. An example of this is appreciative enquiry, which is an organisation development intervention that relies on a number of pre-defined tools to facilitate a conversation with organisational members about collective leadership. On the other hand, a socio-material perspective is more critical as it seeks to examine and disrupt current organisational practices. For example, *action learning sets* can be used to map and refine the routines of collective leadership work, and because this process is unique to an organisation, it is also mostly context-specific. Recognising that each perceptive has its own weaknesses, Eva et al. (2021) advocate for a multi-perspective approach to collective leadership development that is neither static nor linear. They present two case studies in which collective leadership development was facilitated through multiple perspectives in the framework.

Finally, Raelin (2018) argued that whereas collective leadership is increasingly noted, individual leadership perspectives still seem to prevail in popular culture, particularly in Western societies. This may be because collective leadership contradicts the leader-centric perspective that so-called great leaders have inherently great leadership traits (e.g., charismatic, intelligent, visionary). Raelin sees collective leadership as highly beneficial as the world becomes more unpredictable, complex and interdependent. Collaboration is essential to make optimal decisions in organisations as globalisation increases and technology advances rapidly. Collective leadership can be developed by targeting individual-, interpersonal- and system-level factors. At the individual level, people must offer contributions but also be open to challenge from others. Interpersonally, employees must interact to learn different perspectives and encourage innovation. Teams and organisations can encourage members to form and agree to rules for knowledge-sharing and group work. Top-level leaders should encourage organisations and individuals across levels to develop this collective leadership perspective through regular practice rather than direction.

Overall, despite growing interest in the practice of collective leadership development, there is a need for informative theoretical contributions elaborating on the process behind the emergence and sustenance of such leadership forms. Central to all discussions of collective leadership is the individual leader as the enabler and cornerstone of collective leadership. Ironically, this perspective focusing on the leader might continue to reinforce leader-centric approaches to leadership and its development that this stream of literature seems to be actively pushing against.

RESEARCH ON LEADER AND LEADERSHIP DEVELOPMENT

Significant advances have been made in the empirical science of leader and leadership development in the last decade. The majority of this research remains focused on individual development, as opposed to team and collective development. The next section reviews what are considered to be contributions to the literature that are especially helpful in understanding the processes underpinning leader and leadership development.

Longitudinal Studies and Trajectories of Leader Development

A strong empirical focus has been on examining development over time, particularly using a personal trajectory approach adopted by Day and Sin (2011). What is of interest in this research contribution is charting and understanding the personal trajectories of individuals engaged with leader development initiatives. This research uncovered a curvilinear overall trajectory of development in leadership effectiveness that first declined before becoming positive and linear. In addition, Day and Sin found that leader identity served as a time-varying covariate of leader development, thus providing some empirical support for the importance of identity development in understanding leader development processes. Studying development from the perspective of personal trajectories has uncovered some interesting and unpredicted forms of development, specifically that developmental outcomes might first decline before showing positive growth.

Miscenko and colleagues (2017) mapped the trajectories of leader identity development and, similar to the findings of Day and Sin (2011), noted that leader identity developed in a curvilinear (J-shaped) pattern. That is, initial losses were followed by gains over time. They also examined the complex and intertwined relationship between the development of leader identity and leadership behaviours. On one side, leader identity is said to direct an individual's behaviour and interactions when engaged in leadership roles and processes (Day et al., 2009), meaning that forming a stronger leader identity should support gains in leadership behaviours. But based on self-perception theory (Bem, 1972), which suggests that individuals derive information about their attributes and beliefs from observing their own behaviour, engaging in leadership behaviour should lead to strengthening of identity.

To test these competing explanations, Miscenko et al. (2017) collected weekly data on 98 postgraduate students engaged in a seven-week leadership course at a Dutch business school. Using a sophisticated and innovative longitudinal modelling framework (Latent Change Score analysis; McArdle, 2009), they tested a series of possible lead–lag relationships between leadership behaviour and identity. Their results showed that, consistent with self-perception theory, previous changes in leaders' consideration behaviour were significantly and negatively related to subsequent changes in leader identity. Furthermore, previous level, but not changes in leader's initiating structure behaviour, were significantly related to the changes in leader identity.

An extension of this trajectory-oriented research on leader development was conducted with a sample of high-potential senior executives across five different programme cohorts (Kragt & Day, 2020). Participants were engaged in a five-month leadership development programme designed around the core principles of action learning in which an emphasis was placed on developing while working in project teams to deliver against a strategic imperative of the organisation. Relevant findings from the research include evidence that leadership competencies (as rated independently by programme coaches) did not all change in the same way or follow identical trajectories. Leader identity was again modelled as a time-varying covariate and, despite evidence of a ceiling effect in participant ratings of leader identity, it was a positive covariate for approximately half of the rated competencies. The results of the study support the assertion that personal trajectories of development are relevant for participants in leader development initiatives across populations including college students (i.e., emerging leaders), graduate students and experienced senior executives, and that leader identity is an important consideration in the developmental trajectories of these different groups.

Focusing on a different component of leader's cognition, Quigley (2013) investigated the development of leadership self-efficacy (i.e., self-confidence in engaging in leadership activities) over a four-day immersive business simulation involving MBA work teams. Individual differences in cognitive ability and personality characteristics were examined in terms of their relationships with development. The focus of the paper was on antecedents of the underlying change trajectory, rather than the trajectory itself. The trajectory in leadership efficacy was estimated using growth curve modelling. Cognitive ability (operationalised as GMAT score) and extraversion were found to be significantly and positively related to the intercept values (i.e., starting level) of leadership efficacy. Agreeableness, emotional stability and openness to experience were found to predict the cubic slope (i.e., change) of leadership efficacy. The results are counterintuitive because emotional stability and openness to experience were found to negatively relate to change in efficacy. Unfortunately, no guidance is provided as to how to interpret these unexpected findings.

Another study on leader development adopting a personal trajectory methodology examined how military cadets develop when participating in a formal leadership training programme (Kwok et al., 2021). A novel feature of this study is that it considered both leader identity and leadership self-efficacy as important parts of an individual's self-concept. Whereas identity describes the content and frame of one's self-image, self-efficacy involves the more evaluative aspect of the self (Schaubroeck et al., 2012). Kwok et al. (2021) followed 240 cadets in the Royal Canadian Air Cadet Program enrolled in a six-week leadership development training course. They surveyed participants on leader efficacy, leader identity, learning goal orientation (LGO) and motivation to lead (MTL). Results suggested that leadership efficacy developed linearly over the course of the programme, whereas leader identity developed quadratically, suggesting leader identity grows at first before plateauing over time. Also, participants lower on MTL had greater changes in leadership self-efficacy over time, which was also moderated by LGO. Alternatively, cadets high and low on LGO seemed to develop their leader identity equally via different trajectories over time. This research suggests that developmental trajectories for leadership efficacy and leader identity development are different in their impact on leader development. A meaningful contribution of the Kwok et al. (2021) findings is in recognising the self is a multi-dimensional structure and charting a way for future investigations into how different parts of self-systems develop and operate interdependently (Hannah et al., 2008).

Finally, whereas previous research has predominantly focused on leader's current self-perception as a leader, Jennings and colleagues (2022) considered how a future or possible leader self (Markus & Wurf, 1987) may alter present work behaviour. They surveyed students in a professional MBA course three times per day for ten days. They found that participants who reported reflecting more on their best possible leader self subsequently enacted more leader-congruent behaviours, and perceived themselves to be more leader-like compared with those who reflected less on their best possible leader self. Furthermore, on days when participants reflected on their best possible leader self they became more helpful to colleagues, possibly because of the positive affect that was generated through reflecting on one's best self. Being more helpful towards colleagues in turn helped participants perceive themselves as more leader-like.

Overall, a strong focus on identity and related cognitions has helped the field of leader development shift from completely behavioural approaches to including more cognitive approaches. This corresponds with greater attention on sense-making as crucial part of development and indeed helped researchers to make more sense about what processes underlie and support ongoing leader development. We now have good evidence that supports the importance of considering leader identity and other self-views (Day & Dragoni, 2015) in leader development processes. Yet a current limitation of this research is a gap in how identity is conceptualised and measured. Indeed, leader identity is an implicit cognition and as such involves spontaneous information processing, especially under high cognitive load conditions (e.g., the workplace; Epitropaki et al., 2017). Thus, solely relying on explicit (e.g., self-rated) measures to assess leader identity contributes to only a partial understanding of its role in guiding leader behaviours.

Additional Recent Research on Leader Development

An interesting empirical study investigated the relationship between over-parenting (i.e., parents engaged in excessive control over the lives of their child) on adolescent leader emergence using a multi-source rating approach (Liu et al., 2019). Leader emergence was examined via peer, teacher and parent ratings, and actual emergence as measured through leadership roles of participants. Junior high school students ($N = 1255$) and their parents, peers and teachers completed a survey indicating their perception of leader emergence of a focal student. Results demonstrated that over-parenting was negatively correlated with perceived and actual adolescent leader emergence. The mechanism for this relationship was hypothesised to be self-esteem. Over-parenting reduced adolescent self-esteem, resulting in reduced leadership self-efficacy and a subsequent reduction in leader emergence. The self-esteem of female participants was more strongly affected by over-parenting and leader emergence was more strongly related to leader self-efficacy than for males. Ultimately, over-parenting may inhibit adolescent leadership emergence by protecting a child from what are perceived to be overly demanding experiences. Nonetheless, it is challenging experiences that best forge development as a leader (McCall, 2010). In an ironical twist of faith, overly protective parents may be inadvertently reducing the leadership potential of their offspring by depriving them of the chance to learn the valuable lessons of experience at an early age.

Research on Team and Collective Leadership Development

The leadership space is (slowly) moving away from viewing leadership through an individual lens and towards views of processual leadership, defined in terms of ongoing social interaction among all members of a given collective. Another way of conceptualising this phenomenon is as collective leadership development (Day & Dragoni, 2015). Despite increasing interest in the topic, processual or collective leadership can be difficult to achieve in practice.

Schweiger et al. (2020) examined potential barriers to processual leadership development by analysing leadership development of a cohort of EMBA students over two years. Although the study had a small sample size (with 33 trainees recruited initially and only 14 trainees who completed all study surveys, all of whom were male), the data collection involved many additional data sources, including written and verbal reflections, group observation notes and related qualitative measures. The findings are of particular interest here because the trainees' sense of self-as-a-leader and the associated process of sense-making were found at the core of two hindering patterns that continue to uphold a leader-centric meaning of leadership, thus effectively inhibiting the development of a more collective approach to leadership. The first pattern sees trainees striving for control and power to avoid ambiguity and insecurity. These trainees make sense of self-as-leader dependent on being superior in terms of being more prepared, more knowledgeable, more attentive, more observing, faster and more flexible than others. The second pattern sees trainees struggling with their self-expectations (and self-doubt) of living up to the daunting requirements of being a heroic leader. The sense-making involves acceptance of the ambiguity and complexity, but also inability to let go of the heroic expectations that represent the sense of self-as-leader. Both of these patterns inhibit application of collective leadership approaches in real-life workplace situations. Hence, the authors suggest modelling collective leadership within the context of a diverse range of situations, along with opportunities for practice.

Cullen-Lester and colleagues (2017) investigated how leadership is related to social networks in organisations and how networks might be leveraged to develop more collective forms of leadership. The authors presented a model explaining three networking-enhancing leadership development strategies and how these can improve the leadership capacity of leaders and collectives. The first approach is for individuals to develop social competence, which aligns with the traditional leader development focus. The focus on social competence requires development to target individuals to improve their KSAs and social skills. The second approach is for individuals to shape networks, which focuses on developing abilities to understand, leverage and modify social networks. The final approach is for collectives to co-create networks, which aligns with leadership being a result of interaction patterns. Leadership development interventions should help collectives modify their own social networks in ways that enable collective leadership emergence. Most study participants agreed that developing individual knowledge, skills and abilities (KSAs), social skills and interpersonal relationships are important components of more collective leadership development.

Several additional studies have focused on team leadership development. A case study by the Center for Creative Leadership (CCL) investigating the use of the Direction–Alignment–Commitment (DAC) framework (McCauley & Palus, 2021). Developed by CCL researchers, the DAC framework holds a relational view of leadership moving from leadership as leader actions to leadership as interactions between people that create purpose for those with shared work. The authors of this study found the framework was used most in training programmes and client interactions. It is also used for group or organisational development and views leadership as a collective position. CCL staff members indicated that the DAC framework has encouraged them to view leadership as a collective role of shared beliefs and practices. The framework is used by directing a group to focus on where they need to go (direction), what results they need to achieve (alignment) and overcoming what is standing in the way (commitment). Limitations of the DAC framework also exist and include the lack of deep understanding in how the framework operates, lack of guidance on how to best enact the framework, not targeting concepts specifically related to leadership and a lack of empirical support.

Relatedly, Lorinkova and Bartol (2021) examined how shared leadership changes over time within a team, and how this change was related to a team's performance. Study 1 consisted of observing 31 teams in a Master's level HR management course. Study 2 surveyed project teams in a mid-sized telecommunications and IT networking company in Eastern Europe. Study 3 observed 272 undergraduate students separated into 65 teams. The teams were observed during a ten-week project, with course instructors unaware of the study hypotheses. Taken together, results across the three studies suggested that shared leadership changes over time approximating an inverted U-shape, with shared leadership peaking around mid-way through the team's lifecycle. Shared leadership then gradually decreases towards the end of the performance cycle. Interestingly, this change in shared leadership was positively related to team performance. That is, the changes that occur in shared leadership tendencies through a team's lifecycle appear to improve performance, or at least covary with performance gains. Also, smaller teams, those with good social support, and those with high familiarity had more shared leadership throughout the entire lifecycle. Developmental efforts could target supporting teams in developing familiarity and a strong support climate that would enable more shared leadership emergence.

PRACTICE CONCERNS IN LEADER AND LEADERSHIP DEVELOPMENT

A primary remaining concern is the lack of integration of evidence-based research insights into leader and leadership development practice and the near absence of rigorous evaluation of practitioner-led programmes. A brief review of the available literature is presented below in the hope of providing guidance and motivation to enhance evidence-based practices in leader and leadership development.

Evaluation

Rigorous evaluation of leader and leadership development initiatives remains a rare undertaking among practitioners, although it may well be the case that evaluation efforts are not published as they are considered proprietary. But from what is available in the literature, the methods of evaluation used by academics and practitioners seem to differ substantially. Most of the evaluation studies among practitioners are focused on trainee reactions (i.e., so-called smile sheets). Yet, as observed by Lacerenza et al. (2017), academics rarely include reactions data in their experimental studies about the effectiveness of leadership development. Furthermore, studies reporting reactions tend to use a post-only study design, which is generally uninterpretable in identifying meaningful change. A suggestion for improving evaluation efforts in practice is to include other training outcomes (e.g., individual learning, behavioural transfer and organisational results). In this section, we provide a brief overview of several scholarly approaches to programme evaluation that should also appeal to practitioners.

Velasco and colleagues (2019) proposed that goal attainment should be adopted as a measure of leader development programme impact on individual change. Nonetheless, a difficulty in measuring goal attainment is that goals vary greatly in terms of nature, timeframe and domain. Hence, the authors propose a general scale of goal-directed behaviour (GDB) to measure goal progress, which leads to goal attainment. The GDB scale includes four dimensions: sharing information (i.e., making goals public), seeking information (i.e., accessing information to evaluate own goal progress), enacting the plan (i.e., moving from goal intention to action) and revising the plan (i.e., changing this plan where needed). The new scale allows researchers to evaluate programme effects as early as few months after setting the goals, thus offering an early indication of programme effectiveness.

As previously noted, researchers suggest that leadership training can result in positive work outcomes (Lacerenza et al., 2017), which is a strong causal claim. Martin et al. (2021) evaluated the extent to which this literature legitimately demonstrates causality. To do this, they examined studies based on a number of often ignored factors important in determining causality, including control variables, sample representation, condition randomisation, condition dependence, temporal design and author involvement. Their analysis found that the majority of studies included a control condition; however, sample representation was difficult to determine in most studies, and condition randomisation and independence were rarely achieved. Furthermore, temporal design was not often clearly justified, and lack of author involvement in the training was only clear in around a quarter of studies. Therefore, most leadership training research does not seem robust for making causal claims. Suggestions are offered in terms of how to better demonstrate causal relationships in research involving leadership training and development. An essential requirement is the use of control or comparison conditions and, whenever possible, active control conditions such as alternative leadership content, non-leadership content, or a waiting list (and not just a no-treatment control group). Researchers and practitioners should endeavour to recruit a representative sample of participants and, whenever possible, randomly assign them to different (independent) conditions. Evaluations should feature longitudinal design features in which outcomes are assessed at several points after training. Finally, evaluations should be conducted by an independent party and not the training providers themselves.

Temporal issues in evaluation efforts have received little attention (Joseph-Richard et al., 2021), creating significant knowledge gaps in understanding the effectiveness of interventions devoted to developing leaders and leadership. Although the consideration of time and the timing of when things occur is an important part of research focused on charting and understanding personal trajectories of development, there is relatively little or no attention given to this issue in practice when it comes to evaluation. The authors conducted a literature review combined with a case study evaluating a leader development programme offered to middle managers of a UK healthcare organisation. Their analysis suggested that using a temporal orientation in evaluating a leader development programme showed that outcomes emerge at different points in time, and that time did not affect participants' experience of the programme in the same way. It is recommended that programme evaluation include a temporal dimension to recognise when exactly certain outcomes emerge and whether this outcome changes throughout the programme.

More broadly, Wallace and colleagues (2021) extended the idea of multilevel development occurring over time to propose a novel model of evaluation for leadership development programmes. Similar to others, they argued that past evaluations have largely focused on individual leader outcomes (i.e., leader development), rather than collective results (i.e., leadership development). The framework includes three outcomes of development: performance, first-order learning and second-order learning outcomes. Performance outcomes capture changes in a leader's behaviour and subsequent changes in followers' performance. Therefore, performance of the group can indicate effectiveness of leader actions. First-order learning involves acquisition of different leadership competencies, such as intrapersonal, management, technical and collective competencies. Second-order outcomes include leadership maturation factors such as identity development, epistemic cognition of leadership and creating social network connections. This framework suggests that leadership development can impact the collective in a number of ways, thus including collective-level outcomes may help evaluate leader development interventions more comprehensively. Adopting this framework could be especially useful in guiding practitioners and scholars in designing programme evaluation and thinking about outcomes that are important to capture at different points in time.

Sustainability of Effects

In the absence of rigorous evaluation, a related concern is whether leadership development outcomes are sustained over time. For example, Joseph-Richard and colleagues (2021) observed an outcome decay in the healthcare organisation they studied, whereby initial leader engagement weakened over time and started to affect not only their own ward, but also other wards and departments whose workflow is interdependent. Similarly, Larsson and colleagues (2020) conducted repeated interviews with managers who were participating in a leadership development programme. They found that about a half of participating managers became disengaged with their organisation after the programme. Disengagement occurred because the programme allowed the participants to recognise problems in their organisation and become emotionally charged to blame the organisation for these problems. Further, a third of disengaged managers were seeking to leave their organisations altogether. This study illuminates an important area of leadership research which is currently under-investigated: unintended consequences of leadership development programmes (Vogel et al., 2021).

Effect of Trainers/Developers

Design and evaluation of leadership development programmes is often focused on participants and their anticipated outcomes. However, recent research highlighted that trainers have a pivotal role in training effectiveness and outcomes. A study of trainee reactions from more than 10,000 employees enrolled in professional development courses found that trainers matter more than previously thought and recommended that training theory should incorporate the role of the trainer in training effectiveness (Glerum et al., 2021).

More specifically, Luria and colleagues (2019) investigated the impact of trainers in a leader development programme. They followed 854 military cadets completing an officer training course and their 72 trainers for two years, which included a number of leadership exercises emulating real-world experiences. They found that with a highly effective trainer cadets who had high leadership potential before the programme showed greater effectiveness as leaders during the training. With an ineffective trainer, cadets had low levels of leadership effectiveness during training, regardless of leadership potential/emergence. Therefore, during leader development programmes trainers should model effective leadership effectively and consistently to help produce effective leaders.

There have been renewed calls for better understanding the beliefs that practitioners have about leadership development (and, indeed, the definition of leadership, as such) and how such beliefs impact the effectiveness of programmes and interventions (Vogel et al., 2021). For example, Kjellström and colleagues (2020) identified and categorised the different ways of understanding leadership development among leadership practitioners. They found six categories of understanding leader and leadership development increasing in complexity. Leadership development can be understood as one's own development, with feedback being an important resource. Another way of understanding one's development is by fulfilling a formal leadership role. Personal development views a leader holistically, with leadership consisting of a number of instrumental and soft skills. Integrating leader and organisational development is a view that emphasises alignment between leader development, the individual and the organisation as a whole. Collective leadership development distinguishes between leader and leadership development and views leadership as shared or collective in nature. Finally, human development – probably more accurately referred to as humankind development – is the most complex view in which someone understands leadership development to reflect wider perspectives broader than a single organisation. The specific perspective that a practitioner holds (often implicitly) will impact how they approach leadership development work and the outcomes of such work.

FUTURE DIRECTIONS IN THE SCIENCE AND PRACTICE OF LEADERSHIP DEVELOPMENT

In this contribution, we have provided an updated review of the available recent research and theory on leader and leadership development. The good news is that the fields of leader and leadership development have established their own unique contributions independent from the much larger leadership literature. There is active theorising about leader and leadership development. There are interesting and rigorous empirical studies associated with understanding the processes associated with developing leaders and leadership.

Despite substantial and significant advances on the scientific front, there is much less known about how evidence-based understandings are being adopted in the practice of leadership development (broadly construed to include leader development). One recent, noteworthy exception can be found in the evaluation work at PepsiCo (Church et al., 2021). The focus of the PepsiCo research team was on testing the general question as to whether the assessment of leadership potential adds value or otherwise enhances the talent review and classification process. A comprehensive assessment and development process based on multitrait-multimethod analysis was used to examine relationships between individual performance, assessed potential, designated potential and post-assessment promotion rates. Results suggested that assessed potential added unique incremental variance beyond performance in determining process outcomes in the form of designated potential and promotions. The authors conclude that a systematic assessment of leadership potential in organisations can be useful in making more informed talent management decisions. We encourage both scientists and practitioners to have a close read as to what careful, systematic evaluation in a multinational corporate setting contributes.

Kragt and Day (2020) also researched leader development as part of a corporate high-potential programme. Their results suggested that leader identity was shown to be a time-varying covariate supporting the development of a subset of leadership competencies among high-potential senior executives. These results were generally consistent with other research findings adopting similar longitundal personal trajectory analyses with undergraduate (Day & Sin, 2011) and graduate students (Miscenko et al., 2017). The findings also support the assertions that self-views are relevant proximal indicators of leader development along with leadership skills and competencies, even among experienced senior leaders.

Leadership Development Inclusiveness

An implicit tension emerging in the field is situated between developmental practices designed for high-potential senior leaders and what is emerging in the scholarly literature. Most corporate practices are centred around high-potential leaders – identifying, developing and selecting among designated employees for so-called corporate-critical roles (see Church et al., 2021, for example). Organisations tend to justify high-potential practices based on the need to best deploy relatively limited resources associated with succession management and leadership development. In other words, 'bets' are placed on who will rise to become strategic apex leaders in a highly competitive, and usually corporate, environment. Of course, the lucky 5–10 per cent of employees receiving the blessing (or bets) from current members of senior management get the benefit of more developmental attention that contributes to a form of self-fulfilling prophecy: Those designated as high-potential leaders get more opportunities to develop into high-potential leaders. But the larger issue that creates this purported tension involves how widely distributed leadership potential really is in organisations.

A much more limited practice involves making leadership development more inclusive through cultural changes targeted at becoming a deliberately developmental organisation (DDO; Kegan & Lahey, 2016). In this approach, development is considered everyone's job in supporting each other's development as well as their own. Although it may sound harsh, the high-potential culture is exclusive and elitist, whereas the DDO culture is inclusive and more egalitarian in terms of targeting the development of everyone in the organisation. That does not mean that a DDO organisation is run on democratic, one-person one-vote principles. Rather, it means that every employee's potential is considered worthy of resource investment in the organisation. It also does not mean that everyone in a DDO goes off to leader or leadership development programmes. What it does mean is that ongoing experience is highly leveraged and that developmental tools such as feedback and structured reflection are used liberally across organisational functions and levels. But this requires a different mindset as well as different shared values – the bedrock of organisational culture. This is where self-views come into play (especially the self-view of leader identity) and where we can potentially help translate scholarly advancements into evidence-based, actionable advice for practitioners.

Scholars in the field of leadership development have urged those in practice to recast their thinking to more fully leverage ongoing experiences (McCall, 2010). Internalising a leader identity and making it chronically salient, at least in the context of work, supports processes associated with experience-driven development. Identity represents key aspects of one's self-concept that are highly valued by an individual. Furthermore, what is highly valued is accorded resources, especially our most valuable resource of time. It is essentially a resource allocation process in which those aspects of the self that we identify with are given more attention and more time. Identity-based resource allocation works this way if someone identifies as a parent as well as if someone identifies as a leader. Sometimes identities conflict, which characterises the kinds of ethical dilemmas that are difficult to resolve cleanly (think work–family balance issues). It is also the case that identity is multifaceted for most people such that identifying as a parent does not mean that one cannot also identify as a leader. Identity salience is situational, but one thing is assured – that if someone does not think they are (or aspire to be) a leader then they will allocate little or no time to developing as a leader.

Identity-based leader development represents a subtle but significant shift in ownership of one's development. That shift is away from ownership by HR or other organisational functions to the self. Owning one's development means that someone takes primary responsibility for leveraging ongoing work experiences to practice and develop their leadership. It does not mean that development is a completely solitary endeavour; it is critical to include forms of social support as reinforcers of developmental change. It is also the case that those individuals with strong social identities – for example, a woman or person of colour – may find integrating a leader identity more difficult as it raises issues around intersectionality or the combination of various identities in defining the self (Crenshaw, 1989). As noted by others, leadership development is inherently identity work (Ely et al., 2011) and additional research is needed to examine intersectionality issues in leadership development processes (also see Day et al., 2021).

Sense-making and Sense-breaking

Intertwined with both high-potential and the more egalitarian developmental practices are issues associated with sense-making and sense-breaking. Essentially, the nature of the practices shapes how one views the self and the organisation. Although no research has been conducted that we could locate on sense-making/sense-breaking explicitly in leadership development, being designated as a high-potential leader (and most employees know if they have been selected for the designation) must shape their self-views in significant ways. Although someone might be more likely to fall prey to hubris or a sense of entitlement as a high-potential leader (or HiPo) it could also result in a heightened sense of organisational responsibility (or both). But how do these HiPos make sense of others who they work with that have not been designated or anointed in the same way? How possible is it to stay humble as a HiPo leader? These are just some of the many possible questions raised with regard to the interface between sense-making and leader development in high-potential systems. Regardless, of being a HiPo or a member of a DDO, one's identity as a leader is based partly on what that means to be a leader (Hammond et al., 2017). It seems likely – but awaiting empirical confirmation – that what it means to be a leader is a function of the organisational context (HiPo programme or not) and this shapes leadership behaviours.

Sense-breaking comes into play with identity change. It is often the case that as professionals progress in their respective careers, they are charged with more leadership responsibilities, yet being a leader is something that many had not anticipated or aspired to. Something that is needed in all cases of advancement to leadership roles is to 'let go to develop'. Specifically, individuals need to let go of an entrenched identity associated with a profession (e.g., accountant, engineer) and take on more of a leader identity. The identity change process sounds relatively straightforward but has proven to be difficult for those who have spent most of their adult lives honing their specific technical skills. In addition, research suggests that there is a substantial difficulty associated with subtractive changes (Adams et al., 2021) that might be associated with letting go to develop. Taking on a leader identity tends to correspond with the need to let go of other identity pieces that will be less helpful in a new role, which is increasingly difficult depending on how deeply entrenched one is in the existing professional identity.

Sense-making and sense-breaking are not explicit themes currently in the leadership development literature, but more implicitly underpin important processes in developmental change. Nonetheless, these are potentially very helpful concepts for those engaged in the practice of designing, implementing and evaluating leadership development initiatives.

CONCLUSIONS

In conclusion, the leadership development field is at a crossroads of sorts. The road of most practice-based approaches is firmly grounded in the belief of the existence of high-potential leadership talent that needs to be identified, nurtured, then deployed effectively in order to help organisations achieve their strategic objectives. These types of HiPo programmes are highly selective and focused on typically less than 10 per cent of the employee base, implicitly assuming that leadership potential is not widely distributed in the population.

The other road being forged by those working mainly in the trenches of science and evidence-based research offers a different perspective. In particular, identity-based approaches to development are based on the assumption that anyone can become a better leader the more that they engage in ongoing, dedicated leadership practice. It is also assumed that leadership can emerge from a collective as well as from an individual. The kind of practice taking place over an extended period of time is motivated in large part by leader identity. As noted previously in this section, people devote their time and other resources to things that they value most and these are things that are central to who they are – their identity. In this way, leadership development is more inclusive in that anyone can be *a* leader even if they cannot be *the* leader by virtue of title or formal role (Komives et al., 2006). Will science and practice continue down their separate and distinct roads, or can we find a common way forward? We sincerely hope the way forward is along a shared path of greater inclusivity, but we fear further separation of science and practice for the future of leadership development.

REFERENCES

Aasland, M. S., Skogstad, A., Notelaers, G., Nielsen, M. B., & Einarsen, S. (2010). The prevalence of destructive leadership behaviour. *British Journal of Management*, 21(2), 438–452.

Acton, B. P., Foti, R. J., Lord, R. G., & Gladfelter, J. A. (2019). Putting emergence back in leadership emergence: A dynamic, multilevel, process-oriented framework. *Leadership Quarterly*, 30(1), 145–164.

Adams, G. S., Converse, B. A., Hales, A. H., & Klotz, L. E. (2021). People systematically overlook subtractive changes. *Nature*, 592(7853), 258–+.

Bem, D. J. (1972). Self-perception theory. *Advances in Experimental Social Psychology*, 6, 1–62.

Church, A. H., Guidry, B. W., Dickey, J. A., & Scrivani, J. A. (2021). Is there potential in assessing for high potential? Evaluating the relationship between performance ratings, leadership assessment data, designated high-potential status and promotion outcomes in a global organization. *Leadership Quarterly*, 32(5), 101312.

Clarke, N. (2013). Model of complexity leadership development. *Human Resource Development International*, 16(2), 135–150.

Crenshaw, K. (1989). Demarginalizing the intersection of race and sex: A black feminist critique of antidiscrimination doctrine, feminist theory, and antiracist politics. *University of Chicago Legal Forum*, 1, 139–167.

Cullen-Lester, K. L., Maupin, C. K., & Carter, D. R. (2017). Incorporating social networks into leadership development: A conceptual model and evaluation of research and practice. *Leadership Quarterly*, 28(1), 130–152.

Day, D. V. (2000). Leadership development: A review in context. *Leadership Quarterly*, 11(4), 581–613.

Day, D. V. (2011). Leadership development. In A. Bryman, D. Collinson, K. Grint, B. Jackson & M. Uhl-Bien (Eds.), *The SAGE Handbook of Leadership* (pp. 37–50). Sage.

Day, D. V., & Dragoni, L. (2015). Leadership development: An outcome-oriented review based on time and levels of analyses. *Annual Review of Organizational Psychology and Organizational Behavior*, 2(1), 133–156.

Day, D. V., Gronn, P., & Salas, E. (2004). Leadership capacity in teams. *Leadership Quarterly*, 15(6), 857–880.

Day, D. V., Harrison, M. M., & Halpin, S. M. (2009). *An integrative approach to leader development: Connecting adult development, identity, and expertise*. New York: Psychology Press.

Day, D. V., Riggio, R. E., Tan, S. J., & Conger, J. A. (2021). Advancing the science of 21st-century leadership development: Theory, research, and practice. *Leadership Quarterly*, 32(5), 101557.

Day, D. V., & Sin, H. P. (2011). Longitudinal tests of an integrative model of leader development: Charting and understanding developmental trajectories. *Leadership Quarterly*, 22(3), 545–560. doi:10.1016/j.leaqua.2011.04.011

DDI (2021). *Development Dimensions International Global Leadership Forecast 2021*. https://www.ddiworld.com/glfsurvey

DeRue, D. S., & Ashford, S. J. (2010). Who will lead and who will follow? A social process of leadership identity construction in organizations. *Academy of Management Review*, 35(4), 627–647.

Ely, R. J., Ibarra, H., & Kolb, D. M. (2011). Taking gender into account: Theory and design for women's leadership development programs. *Academy of Management Learning & Education*, 10(3), 474–493.

Epitropaki, O., Kark, R., Mainemelis, C., & Lord, R. G. (2017). Leadership and followership identity processes: A multilevel review. *Leadership Quarterly*, 28(1), 104–129.

Eva, N., Cox, J. W., Herman, H. M., & Lowe, K. B. (2021). From competency to conversation: A multi-perspective approach to collective leadership development. *Leadership Quarterly*, 32(5), 101346.

Fischer, K. W. (1980). A theory of cognitive development: The control and construction of hierarchies of skills. *Psychological Review*, 87(6), 477.

Glerum, D. R., Joseph, D. L., McKenny, A. F., & Fritzsche, B. A. (2021). The trainer matters: Cross-classified models of trainee reactions. *Journal of Applied Psychology*, 106(2), 281.

Hammond, M. M., Clapp-Smith, R., & Palanski, M. (2017). Beyond (just) the workplace: A theory of leader development across multiple domains. *Acadmy of Management Review*, 42(3), 481–498.

Hannah, S. T., Avolio, B. J., Luthans, F., & Harms, P. D. (2008). Leadership efficacy: Review and future directions. *Leadership Quarterly*, 19(6), 669–692.

Jennings, R. E., Lanaj, K., Koopman, J., & McNamara, G. (2022). Reflecting on one's best possible self as a leader: Implications for professional employees at work. *Personnel Psychology*, 75(1), 69–90.

Joseph-Richard, P., Edwards, G., & Hazlett, S. (2021). Leadership development outcomes research and the need for a time-sensitive approach. *Human Resource Development International*, 24(2), 173–199.

Kegan, R., & Lahey, L. L. (2016). *An Everyone Culture: Becoming a Deliberatively Developmental Organization*. Harvard Business School Press.

Kjellström, S., Stålne, K., & Törnblom, O. (2020). Six ways of understanding leadership development: An exploration of increasing complexity. *Leadership*, 16(4), 434–460.

Komives, S. R., Longerbeam, S. D., Owen, J. E., Mainella, F. C., & Osteen, L. (2006). A leadership identity development model: Applications from a grounded theory. *Journal of College Student Development, 47*(4), 401–418.

Komives, S. R., Owen, J. E., Longerbeam, S. D., Mainella, F. C., & Osteen, L. (2005). Developing a leadership identity: A grounded theory. *Journal of College Student Development, 46*, 593–611.

Kozlowski, S. W. J., & Klein, K. J. (2000). A multilevel approach to theory and research in organizations: Contextual, temporal, and emerging processes. In K. J. Klein & S. W. J. Kozlowski (Eds.), *Multilevel Theory, Research and Methods in Organizations: Foundations, Extensions, and New Directions* (pp. 3–90). Jossey-Bass.

Kragt, D., & Day, D. V. (2020). Predicting leadership competency development and promotion among high-potential executives: The role of leader identity *Frontiers in Psychology, 11*, 1816.

Kwok, N., Shen, W., & Brown, D. J. (2021). I can, I am: Differential predictors of leader efficacy and identity trajectories in leader development. *Leadership Quarterly, 32*(5), 101422.

Lacerenza, C. N., Reyes, D. L., Marlow, S. L., Joseph, D. L., & Salas, E. (2017). Leadership training design, delivery, and implementation: A meta-analysis. *Journal of Applied Psychology, 102*(12), 1686–1718.

Larsson, M., Holmberg, R., & Kempster, S. (2020). 'It's the organization that is wrong': Exploring disengagement from organizations through leadership development. *Leadership, 16*(2), 141–162.

Liu, Z., Riggio, R. E., Day, D. V., Zhen, C., Dai, S., & Bian, Y. (2019). Leader development begins at home: Over-parenting harms adolescent leader emergence. *Journal of Applied Psychology, 104*(10), 1226–1242.

Liu, Z., Venkatesh, S., Murphy, S. E., & Riggio, R. E. (2021). Leader development across the lifespan: A dynamic experiences-grounded approach. *Leadership Quarterly, 32*(5), 101382.

Lorinkova, N. M., & Bartol, K. M. (2021). Shared leadership development and team performance: A new look at the dynamics of shared leadership. *Personnel Psychology, 74*(1), 77–107.

Luria, G., Kahana, A., Goldenberg, J., & Noam, Y. (2019). Leadership development: Leadership emergence to leadership effectiveness. *Small Group Research, 50*(5), 571–592.

Markus, H., & Wurf, E. (1987). The dynamic self-concept: A social psychological perspective. *Annual Review of Psychology, 38*(1), 299–337.

Martin, R., Hughes, D. J., Epitropaki, O., & Thomas, G. (2021). In pursuit of causality in leadership training research: A review and pragmatic recommendations. *Leadership Quarterly, 32*(5), 101375.

Maurer, T. J., & London, M. (2018). From individual contributor to leader: A role identity shift framework for leader development within innovative organizations. *Journal of Management, 44*(4), 1426–1452.

McArdle, J. J. (2009). Latent variable modeling of differences and changes with longitudinal data. *Annual Review of Psychology, 60*, 577–605.

McCall, M. W. (2010). Recasting leadership development. *Industrial and Organizational Psychology-Perspectives on Science and Practice, 3*, 3–19.

McCauley, C. D., Drath, W. H., Palus, C. J., O'Connor, P. M. G., & Baker, B. A. (2006). The use of constructive-developmental theory to advance the understanding of leadership. *Leadership Quarterly, 17*(6), 634–653.

McCauley, C. D., & Palus, C. J. (2021). Developing the theory and practice of leadership development: A relational view. *Leadership Quarterly, 32*(5), 101456.

Miscenko, D., Guenter, H., & Day, D. V. (2017). Am I a leader? Examining leader identity development over time. *Leadership Quarterly, 28*, 605–620.

Odgers Berndtson (2020). *Odgers Berndtson Leadership Confidence Index 2020*. https://www.odgersberndtson.com/media/9251/ob_index_report_eng_digital.pdf

Quigley, N. R. (2013). A longitudinal, multilevel study of leadership efficacy development in MBA teams. *Academy of Management Learning & Education, 12*(4), 579–602.

Raelin, J. A. (2018). What are you afraid of: Collective leadership and its learning implications. *Management Learning, 49*(1), 59–66.

Schaubroeck, J., Kim, Y. J., & Peng, A. C. (2012). The self-concept in organizational psychology: Clarifying and differentiating the constructs. In G. P. Hodgkinson & J. K. Ford (Eds.), *International Review of Industrial and Organizational Psychology 2012* (pp. 1–38). Wiley Blackwell.

Schweiger, S., Müller, B., & Güttel, W. H. (2020). Barriers to leadership development: Why is it so difficult to abandon the hero? *Leadership, 16*(4), 411–433.

Velasco, F., Batista-Foguet, J. M., & Emmerling, R. J. (2019). Are we making progress? Assessing goal-directed behaviors in leadership development programs. *Frontiers in Psychology, 10*, 1345.

Vogel, B., Reichard, R. J., Batistic, S., & Cerne, M. (2021). A bibliometric review of the leadership development field: How we got there, where we are, and where we are headed. *Leadership Quarterly, 32*(5), 101381.

Wallace, D. M., Torres, E. M., & Zaccaro, S. J. (2021). Just what do we think we're doing? The learning outcomes of leader and leadership development. *Leadership Quarterly, 32*(5), 101494.

Zhang, Y., Zhang, M., Li, J. T., Liu, G., Ynag, M. M., & Liu, S. (2021). A bibliometric review of a decade of research: Big data in business research – Setting a research agenda. *Journal of Business Research, 131*, 374–390.

15

Psychoanalytic Approaches

Yiannis Gabriel

The recent rise of populism and populist leaders across many countries has highlighted the power of emotional forces let loose by certain kinds of leadership. Individuals of questionable moral integrity and mental health have risen to positions of power on the back of questionable promises and downright lies, attracting mass following and precipitating extreme political processes, like the storming of the US Capitol in January 2021 (Eatwell & Goodwin, 2018; Foroughi et al., 2019; Muis & Immerzeel, 2017). Additionally, the Covid-19 pandemic unleashed extreme forms of anxiety and malaise that leaders have been called to address (Grint, 2020; Prasad, 2020; Wilson, 2020). As a result of these developments, there is a renewed interest in psychoanalysis as a discipline that addresses head on the unconscious and irrational dimensions of leadership, the relations that bind leaders and their followers together and, more generally, the psychological underpinnings of political phenomena.

In making sense of leadership, psychoanalysis intersects with numerous other traditions, including those stemming from political philosophy, ethics, critical theory and discursive approaches. Some core concepts in leadership theory, including charisma, narcissism, authoritarianism and transformational leadership, can be traced to psychoanalysis or have been incorporated in subsequent psychoanalytic discussions of leadership. In particular, psychoanalysis offers ways of developing or extending leadership insights deriving from social constructionist and relational approaches (e.g., Antonacopoulou & Gabriel, 2001; Smelser, 1998b; Ulus & Gabriel, 2018). At the same time, psychoanalysis and, more generally, psychodynamic approaches to leadership make a unique contribution of their own. Psychoanalysis urges us to look beyond the social construction of leadership and consider the possibility that leadership is constructed through fantasy, dream and myth; that it is a deeply emotional construct forged from insecurity, anxiety, fear, hope, love and other powerful emotions. In this regard, psychoanalytic approaches to leadership are *sense-breaking*, defying an accommodation within either social constructionist or objectivist frameworks. Psychoanalysis approaches leadership as a human construct without denying the objective reality of the bonds that tie leaders and followers together, the objective reality of leadership accomplishments and failures, the objective reality of claims and falsehoods propounded by leaders. It accepts contending accounts of reality and conflicting evaluations of it without reducing all facts to narratives and all accounts to stories.

The distinguishing feature of psychoanalytic approaches is the assumption of an unconscious dimension to social and individual life

(Chancer, 2013; De Board, 1977; Diamond, 1993; Gabriel, 1999; Obholzer, 1999). It is the assumption of the unconscious, as a large part of mental functioning at both individual and collective levels that provides psychoanalytic approaches with a cohesive and distinct physiognomy, whether studying leadership or other collective phenomena. The unconscious is the mental territory where dangerous and painful ideas and desires are consigned through different mechanisms of psychological defence. These mechanisms seek to protect people from anxiety-provoking thoughts and emotions. Thus, the psychoanalytic conceptualisation of the unconscious is irrevocably linked with the idea of psychological defence which can assume many forms. These include repression, the total screening of a dangerous or upsetting idea, emotion or desire from the conscious mind; regression, the assumption of an earlier form of mental functioning which denies or downplays the severity of current dangers; denial, the refusal to admit into consciousness an aspect of reality that is apparent to everyone else; rationalisation, the invention of plausible reasons or motives for deeply unsettling and irrational actions; projection, the expulsion of unwanted ideas, qualities and desires from the self and their attachment to another person, object or group; splitting, whereby an entity or an object can be split into two, one which is idealised and the other which is vilified. Defences operate in different ways – they can contain psychic conflict for a certain period holding back anxiety or other threatening emotions; they may trigger symptoms that are socially unacceptable, thus prompting further defences; or they may backfire altogether.

The activation of defence mechanisms makes the unconscious a source of resistance to specific ideas and emotions which present threats to our selfhood and our identity, individual and collective. Fantasies and delusions with little connection to reality become embedded in unconscious mental structures, individual and collective, resisting all attempts to correct them through logic, rationality or material evidence, if they fulfil deep unconscious desires or if they protect an individual or a group from deeply threatening anxieties. Yet, psychoanalysis also recognises the unconscious as a territory from which creative fantasies spring, as a source of imagination and creativity in scientific, artistic, economic and political spheres. In a well-known metaphor, Freud (1923) likened the unconscious to a horse whose energy and drive the ego seeks to control and redirect to social, economic, artistic, scientific and other creative ends.

Unconscious ideas, desires and emotions may be of a sexual nature but may also be related to ambition, envy, fear (of death, of failure, of rejection etc.), nostalgia, regret and so forth. These often reach consciousness in highly distorted or abstruse ways. Anger can be displaced from one target to another, fear can masquerade as defiance, anxiety can turn into aggression or, conversely, into passivity, disillusionment can fuel nostalgia. Fantasies are a vital element of the unconscious – they are mental representations which express unconscious wishes and desires as if they were already realised, yet often in a disguised and indirect manner (Levine, 2001; Moxnes, 1998; Smelser, 1998a). Fantasies are equally important in understanding the actions of people in and out of organisations: day-dreaming consumers, ambitious leaders, bullied employees, budding entrepreneurs, disaffected voters and so forth, are as liable to be guided and driven by their fantasies as by rational considerations of ends and means. Relations between leaders and their followers frequently stimulate powerful emotional experiences and are liable to unleash formidable fantasies. It is through its emphasis on emotions and fantasies that psychoanalysis has made its mark in the study of leadership (Cluley, 2008; Gabriel, 1997; Maccoby & Fuchsman, 2020; Stein, 2005).

The concept of the unconscious binds psychoanalytic approaches and gives them a distinct character. It also, however, presents an obstacle to the cross-fertilisation of these approaches with other approaches. The unconscious is not directly accessible through either observation or introspection and can sometimes be thought of as a mystical or obscure concept which resists any empirical study or validation. While unconscious phenomena are not directly observable, as will be seen in this chapter, their consequences whether in thoughts, emotions, or behaviours, individual and collective, are observable and can be studied. A fundamental part of this kind of study lies in *interpretation*, in other words in discovering deeper and significant meanings behind apparently irrational or random occurrences (Gabriel, 2018). Such interpretations can only be provisional and qualified, but they are not mere speculations. There are better and less good interpretations. There are plausible but spurious interpretations. There are wild and cautious interpretations. There are improbable but sound interpretations (Svensson, 2014) (Gabriel, 2018; Taylor, 1971). The art of interpretation is difficult and one that cannot be reduced to the simple application of a formula or a routine.

The success of an interpretation can be gauged using different criteria. Does a particular interpretation cast light on what was previously obscure? Does it account for an overall phenomenon as well as different aspects of it? Does it leave some loose ends that defy the interpretation? Does it fit with other interpretations of similar phenomena? Can it be subsumed or replaced by another simpler or more elegant interpretation? Psychoanalysis is not the only discipline relying on interpretations and one of the promising areas of cross-fertilisation between psychoanalytic and other leadership approaches lies in discovering interpretive lines from different disciplines that overlap, reinforce or qualify each other. In such instances, sense-breaking can give way to sense-co-creation, an effort that has often yielded fruitful insights (e.g., Devereux, 1955; Lindholm, 1988; Maccoby, 1976; Stein, 2007).

This chapter presents the core psychoanalytic insights into leadership. Following some early formulations by Freud, we explore the differences between leadership and management and examine leadership as the management of meaning and the management of emotions. We look closely at the relations between leaders and their followers, especially the tendency of the latter to idealise and identify with the former. We then examine why the leadership romance, the powerful bond that links leaders and their followers which in so many ways is akin to being in love, goes awry and fades for the followers; and, why leaders lapse into dysfunctional modes such as narcissism and authoritarianism. We conclude by addressing the different ways in which psychoanalysis enhances our understanding of leadership and deepens some of the insights generated by other approaches.

FREUD AND BION

Freud took leadership very seriously, both in his theoretical work and in his attempts to steer the movement that he founded away from schism, mysticism, quackery and dilettantism. Freud's leadership 'style' inspired great devotion among his followers, at times approaching deification; it also demanded unquestioned obedience, something that led to the alienation and subsequent departure from the fold of psychoanalysis of some of Freud's most creative disciples, including C. G. Jung, Alfred Adler and Otto Rank. Behind these painful separations lay a questioning of Freud's authority that inevitably led to bitter disputes between supporters and apostates. Instead of being viewed as scientific differences to be resolved through rational discourse, disagreements in psychoanalysis easily came to be viewed as rebellions against the authority of the father figure of psychoanalysis by his supporters and as questioning of his infallibility by his critics. This is not merely of historical interest. It helps explain the emphasis laid by psychoanalytic approaches to leadership on early life experiences as providing a template on which subsequent relations between leaders and followers unfold. Leaders can easily generate feelings of loyalty and devotion by assuming a parental position in the unconscious life of their followers (Oglensky, 1995). Such feelings can easily turn to resentment and disappointment when leaders fail to live up to the lofty expectations of their followers or are experienced as oppressive and tyrannical.

The theme of filial rebellion against an autocratic father is scattered throughout Freud's writings and is explored directly in *Totem and Taboo* (Freud, 1913). Using a hypothesis proposed by Darwin, Freud speculated that early human groups or primal hordes, like those of other primates, may have been dominated by a single powerful male, the primal father, who kept all females to himself and generated much fear, hostility and envy among other males, including his sons. At some point, this prehistoric band of brothers turned against the father and murdered him. Overwhelmed by guilt and fearful that the death of the father will lead to endless killings, they raised a totem animal, symbolic of the father, and agreed on two prohibitions or taboos – not to kill the totem animal outside ceremonial occasions and not to have sexual relations with members of the same totem clan. This murder of the primal father was not offered as a historical account of actual events, but rather as a hypothesis, accounting for the universal prohibition of incest and for what Freud viewed as the centrality of guilt in many religious beliefs and practices. The primal myth also provided a kind of phylogenetic equivalent of the Oedipus complex, mirroring its two core elements – killing the father and taking the mother for wife. As for leadership, it suggested that feelings of followers for their leader are invariably ambivalent – followers may love the leader, craving protection and support, but they also resent and envy the leader.

Freud's theory of group functioning highlights the importance of leaders. For Freud, leaderless groups are either ephemeral arrangements or, alternatively, they are led by an invisible symbolic leader. It is leadership that holds groups together, through the position that leaders occupy in the unconscious life of the followers. Using the Church and the army as examples, Freud argued that members of each group experience *an intense emotional tie* (Freud, 1921/1985, p. 123) to their leader and also to each other. The power of unconscious dynamics in groups is illustrated with the example of panic on the battlefield: when the leader falls, group members forsake the very relatedness that brought them together, as well as the task of battle, lose their minds and flee in fear.

Freud also proposes that the shared emotional experience of group members comes from a shared identification with and idealisation of the leader.

Each group member identifies with the leader; in so doing, each individual identifies with all other group members, who share the same relationship to the leader as themselves. This leads to a definition of a 'primary group' which has at its core the shared unconscious experience of group members:

> *A primary group [...] is a number of individuals who have put one and the same object in the place of their ego ideal and have consequently identified themselves with one another in their ego.*
> (Freud, 1921/1985, p. 147)

Groups represent a special type of love bond, one in which the sexual element has been replaced by an emotional attachment, in short one in which sexual energy (libido) becomes sublimated into social ties. Individuals in a group sacrifice the prospect of direct sexual gratification, but also their uniqueness and individuality, in return for the stability and protection of the group and its leader. The Freudian group is thus dominated by his conception of a powerful leader who embodies the qualities of the feared father of the archaic primal horde.

Groups, built on intense emotional ties, can lapse to psychological regression of childlike dependence on the leader. This may be tempered in the view of Wilfred Bion (1961), a British psychoanalyst, who dedicated much effort to understanding group dynamics, if groups can focus on a shared task. Bion's key contribution was to argue that regressive tendencies of groups are the result of excessive anxieties, which cause members to lose sight of the tasks they seek to accomplish and tips them into quasi-psychotic functioning dominated by destructive fantasies, collective delusions that severely distort their sense of proportion and reality. Bion identified three types of dysfunctional group modes that he termed 'basic assumptions', each associated with a type of leadership – dependency, fight–flight and pairing.

The importance of Bion's contribution lay in his view that group regression and dysfunction are consequences of leadership failures, and in particular the failure of leadership to contain anxiety and other potentially toxic emotions. In Bion's work we find a conception of the leader whose maternal qualities of caring and emotional sensitivity stand in juxtaposition to the Freudian conception of the leader as a stern father figure. We also have the first clear presentation of the argument that leading involves the management of emotion. Failure to manage anxiety effectively can lead to serious failures. Excessive anxiety leads to panic or fatalism while excessively low anxiety leads to complacency and decay. The containment of anxiety is then seen as an important leadership function by many authors (Fotaki, 2010; Hirschhorn, 1988; Menzies Lyth, 1988; Obholzer, 1999).

LEADERS AS MANAGERS OF EMOTION

Since its inception, psychoanalysis has emphasised the emotional qualities or personal, social and political life. Psychoanalysis approaches people, individually and in social groups primarily as feeling, dreaming and passionate beings, who only intermittently succumb to forces of reason, morality or expedience (Gabriel, 1999). Emotional labour for psychoanalysis is not only external, a form of deep or surface acting, as is currently conceptualised by social constructionist scholars following Hochschild (1983) and others (e.g., Bolton, 2005; Fineman, 1993); instead it is an ongoing inner and outer struggle to cope with, understand, tame and manage feelings, those of oneself and others. Arguing for such a psychoanalytic approach, Craib stresses that:

> *Individuals, people – men and women – are by definition engaged in at least two interlocking forms of emotional work: the 'internal' work of coping with contradiction, conflict and ambivalence and the 'external' work of reconciling what goes on inside with what one is 'supposed' or 'allowed' to feel.*
> (Craib, 1998, p. 113)

This is another point of a psychoanalytic argument acting as a sense-breaking device, disrupting the mainstream concept of emotional labour without dismissing it, but adding the important 'internal' dimension, one that was generally ignored or incorporated in generic terms like 'stress' or 'burnout'. In this way psychoanalytic approaches expand and reinforce other approaches that emphasise the management of emotion as a core feature of all powerful human relations, including those between parents and children, teachers and students, living partners and, of course, leaders and followers. Far from implying dissimulation and manipulation, management of emotion highlights the interactive nature of the leader–follower relation. In relating to their followers, leaders are liable to form deep emotional bonds. They may evoke powerful emotions, but also work with emotions, their own and those of their followers. This involves different aspects of emotional work, including the reading and decoding of emotions, their intensification and attenuation, channelling and containment.

The means by which leaders manage emotions revolve around the use of words and visible actions.

Leaders may influence emotions by using symbolic language, including stories and metaphors. Christ's use of the parables is an example of stories having powerful emotional effects. Churchill's use of metaphors, such as 'iron curtain' and 'cold war' set the emotional tone of post-World War II politics. The use of emotional language with powerful words, such as 'betrayal', 'war', 'victory', 'rebirth', 'downsizing', 'challenge' and so forth, is capable of stimulating strong emotions, as are less emotive words like 'change', 'modernisation' and 'merger' when used in particular contexts. In general, leaders manage emotions by offering explanations and interpretations that resonate with the experiences of their followers. The psychoanalytic contribution here lies in acknowledging that this 'resonance' is linked to unconscious wishes, desires and fantasies. Thus, a word that at a conscious level may seem innocent or commonplace, when uttered in the right context and at the right time, may unleash great emotional energy.

The management of emotions is a dangerous part of the leader's work. It can easily backfire. Words and actions regularly come back to haunt leaders. Once a genie is out of the bottle, it becomes impossible to put it back in. A word or an action that undermines the followers' trust in the leader will be difficult to reverse. What is especially damaging in this context is a visible discrepancy between what leaders say and what they do. This can easily give rise to cynicism and unleash strong negative emotions towards the leader or the organisation as a whole.

FOLLOWERSHIP

Considering the huge amount of scholarship dedicated to leaders, followers seem to be neglected by scholars and most other commentators (Collinson, 2006). In one way, this is to be expected. Understanding leadership has long been seen as a worthwhile quest. It promises to deliver the key for identifying leaders and leadership qualities and the basis of effective leadership training and development programmes. What use is understanding followership? Who would wish to train people to be good followers? This is the rub. Who could hope to be a good leader without understanding his/her followers?

As we have noted already, psychoanalytic approaches emphasise the relation between leaders and followers, a relation described by Burns as entailing *mutual stimulation and elevation* (1978, p. 4). Psychoanalytic approaches, however, argue that this relation is also liable to trigger powerful and at times unrealistic fantasies among followers. Where do followers' fantasies about their leaders originate? Some of them are rooted in their experiences, good and bad, of previous leaders, most especially the two important figures of authority that dominate most people's early lives, their mother and their father. To the eyes of the helpless and immature child, these figures appear immense and god-like, a 'primal mother' and a 'primal father' of myth and dream.

The qualities and characteristics attributed to these archetypal figures form the basis of some subsequent fantasies about leaders, through the process of transference, whereby feelings and relational patterns that individuals develop towards their parents at an early stage of dependency are later redirected or transferred to different figures of authority, such as teachers, analysts and leaders. Psychoanalyst Heinz Kohut (1971, 1976) has argued that some leaders are experienced by their followers as reincarnations of the primal mother, caring, giving and loving. Others are experienced as embodiments of the primal father, omnipotent, omniscient but also strict and terrifying. Kohut referred to the former as charismatic and to the latter as messianic. In the presence of charismatic leaders, followers are liable to feel inspired and elated, whereas in the presence of messianic leaders, they are liable to feel submissive and overawed.

The two types of leaders form very different types of relations with their followers. Charismatic are perceived as uniquely kind, smart and talented. Everything that they do or say appears to be fascinating, inspired and magnificent. They seem to have an aura around them, a field of energy that all those who enter experience as hugely invigorating. In their presence, their followers feel smarter and more talented, inspired and appreciated. Caring is an especially important quality of these leaders, since they are seen as setting great store by each and every one of their followers. Christ, in his capacity as good shepherd, is the archetype of such an all-caring, all-loving leader.

Messianic leaders are demanding, critical and confrontational. They place little store in maintaining a happy atmosphere and are blind to the sensitivities of their followers. And yet, precisely because they can make each person forget their narrow self-interests, they are capable of stirring them into great achievements. Followers of messianic leaders feel meek and sometimes even paralysed in the presence of their leaders. Such leaders inspire fear and awe, making their followers feel worthless and insignificant. Even so, such leaders can generate tremendous commitment, unleashing qualities of dedication, sacrifice and heroism in their followers. Their grip on their followers rests on an unshakeable conviction that, in spite of sacrifices and hardships, they can get them to the promised land and deliver them from their troubles. Leaders may discover that their own actions have limited ability to modify the way their followers imagine them to be by projecting such powerful fantasies onto them.

Kohut's account has received some support from my own study of follower fantasies through the medium of stories that followers tell about their leaders (Gabriel, 1997). A detailed analysis and interpretation of such stories revealed four recurring themes, each casting the leader in a particular role or its opposite.

1. First, the leader as someone who cares for his/her subordinates, either offering recognition and support or protection. The reverse of this fantasy is the leader who is indifferent to the plight of his/her subordinates and may even be an axeman, willing to sacrifice them in order to achieve his/her ambition.
2. Second, the leader as someone who is accessible, who can be seen and heard, even if his/her appearances constitute special occasions. Conversely, the leader as someone who is mysterious and aloof, distant and inscrutable.
3. Third, the leader as someone who is omnipotent, unafraid and capable of anything. Omnipotence sometimes extends to omniscience, especially an ability to read the minds of his/her subordinates and recognise true loyalty from flattery and sycophancy. Conversely, the leader as someone externally driven, afraid and fallible.
4. Fourth, the leader as someone who has a legitimate claim to power; conversely, the leader as an impostor, someone who usurped power and whose claims are fraudulent.

These themes are also encountered in numerous religious, mythological and other narratives, most especially when a follower has a chance to meet the leader face-to-face – when, in the Christian tradition, he/she comes face-to-face with God. They reflect fundamental fantasies which sometimes co-exist in the same story or the same experience of a leader.

Consistently with Kohut's distinction between charismatic and messianic leadership, the former two themes, highlighting caring and accessibility are qualities that once, in early infancy are associated with the mother figure. She was someone who cared for us and was available when we wanted her. She loved us fully and with no conditions, since after all we came out of her own body. In our eyes, she was prepared to do anything for us and, above all, she was prepared to love us, no matter what we did. The second two themes are linked with the other important figure of our early childhood, the father figure. To our childlike-like eyes, he seemed so big and powerful, so knowledgeable and strong. We depended on him for protection, but we were also more than a little afraid of him, since we were aware of his ability to punish. His love for us, unlike that of our mother, was much more conditional than our mother's, he was judgemental and perfectly able to make his dissatisfaction with our behaviour known to us. He was always ready to criticise and discipline. Yet, we accepted his criticism, punishment and discipline, because, after all, he was our rightful father. How much harder would similar treatment be in the hands of an uncle or a stepfather. In our father, we recognised rights that we would not find it easy to accord to others.

Subsequent relations with leaders frequently build on early experiences with people of our narrow family circle. A person who was maltreated by an authoritarian father figure, may later in life seek the protection of such a figure. Conversely, they may envisage a leader to be a punitive and harsh person, even if in reality the leader is not. While not everyone's parents act in the same manner, and not everyone grows up in a conventional family with a father and a mother, most people have powerful experiences with figures of authority in early life which they later revive in their contacts with leaders.

Instead of looking at the distinction between charismatic and messianic leaders as determined by the attributes of the leaders themselves, we would therefore be inclined to see it as the product of follower fantasies. A leader may be perceived as messianic by some followers, charismatic by others and as a mixture by yet others. He or she may be seen as an impostor, as caring or as aloof by different followers. In the course of rehearsing fantasies through jokes, stories and myths a few principal leadership fantasies may emerge, expressed in a shared folklore.

DYSFUNCTIONAL LEADERS

If the followers' relations with their leaders are shaped by past experiences, leaders themselves cannot escape from their own past – this sometimes prompts dysfunctional or toxic types of leadership that bring misfortune on leaders and followers alike. Leadership dysfunctions have been extensively discussed by both psychoanalytic (e.g., Hirschhorn, 1997; Kets de Vries & Miller, 1984; Sievers, 1994; Stein, 2005) and non-psychoanalytic writers (e.g., Alvesson & Sveningsson, 2003; Goldman, 2009; Grint, 2005; Lipman-Blumen, 2005; Tourish, 2013). What is unique about psychoanalytic contributions is that beyond the usual factors that may lead to dysfunctional leadership, like political corruption, failing institutions and so forth, they link such dysfunctions to the psychopathology of leaders and, in particular, unconscious forces that may suddenly find disruptive and irrational expressions. In this way, psychoanalytic approaches can cross-fertilise with mainstream approaches that highlight the devastating effects that dysfunctional leaders can have for their organisations but also for entire nations and societies, by asking questions like *What unconscious factors may account for the attraction of tyrannical leaders on their followers? What qualities in toxic leadership may be traced back to a leader's childhood or adolescence or to the followers' irrational fantasies and cravings? How do despotic leaders mobilise irrational fears and anxieties but also other emotions, such as nostalgia, envy, resentment, hate and even self-hate, to social ends? In what circumstances does charisma conceal a variety of psychological disorders, including sexual ones?*

There are various psychoanalytic studies and case studies of individual leaders that demonstrate the importance of examining unconscious factors in shaping up leader–follower relations and in promoting or checking abusive types of leadership. Some psychoanalytic studies of leadership focus on world historical figures from Moses (Freud, 1939) and Martin Luther (Erikson, 1958/1962) to Hitler (see several studies listed in Rosenbaum, 1999) and Donald Trump (Maccoby & Fuchsman, 2020). Dysfunctional leaders of organisations have attracted extensive attention by authors including Stein (2013), Goldman (2009), Hirschhorn (1997), Kets de Vries (1988) and others. In an influential book, Manfred Kets de Vries and Danny Miller (1984) argued that many organisational failures are the result of the leaders' own psychopathologies, many of them traceable to their childhoods. Indeed, they suggest organisational cultures can end up reflecting the individual pathologies of their leaders. For example, highly suspicious leaders, like Harold Geneen, the former CEO of ITT, may influence the ethos of their entire organisation, making it reactive, defensive and secretive. On the basis of their consultancy work with troubled organisations, Kets de Vries and Miller (1984) develop a typology of leadership dysfunctions and their counterparts in organisational culture, identifying five distinct types: paranoid; depressive; grandiose; compulsive; detached. Each type is associated with different fantasies that stand in the way of rational organisational functioning and a realistic assessment of opportunities and threats.

Along with other psychoanalytic authors, Kets de Vries and Miller (1984) offer a compelling explanation why the same qualities that bring success to a leader and an organisation can end up becoming counter-productive. Normality then crosses into neurosis, optimism becomes recklessness, resolve becomes pig-headedness, courage becomes bravado, caution becomes paralysis, firmness becomes cruelty. As long as leaders can keep a check on their neurotic tendencies, they may mobilise them in pursuit of organisational visions and goals. But once they lapse into neurotic behaviour, their effect on their organisation is negative and dramatically so. Many earlier victories and accomplishments are thus compromised and ruined.

Authoritarianism

Two of the most widely discussed types of leader pathologies are authoritarianism and narcissism. In a curious way, these two pathologies are almost the mirror image of each other. Authoritarianism, on the one hand, involves excessive emphasis on brute force and adherence to orders and regulations; it celebrates firmness and steadfastness and abhors fanciful ideas and initiatives. It usually leads to inflexible, fear-ridden organisations that are unable to compete in markets or environments where creativity, flexibility, imagination and flair are called for. Narcissism, on the other hand, involves excessive preoccupation with glamour, image and display. It celebrates creativity, beauty, freedom and spontaneity. It easily loses track of the difference between fantasy and reality and is liable to lead to dramatic and sudden failures, when the organisation discovers to its cost that there was a gulf between its grandiose aspirations and what it actually was able to deliver.

Authoritarianism is a well-established set of personality characteristics and the cause of numerous personality disorders. It is a type of leadership much in evidence in military dictatorships, military and police academies, prisons, boarding schools and other institutions that traditionally have been founded on the basis of a cast iron obedience to authority and a suppression of individual characteristics and needs. The study of authoritarianism originates in Freud's discussion of the anal obsessive character (Freud, 1905/1977), whose main features are stubbornness, orderliness, parsimony and control. Authoritarianism was the subject of the famous Berkeley study (Adorno et al., 1950), following World War II, when the question was asked how 'ordinary' people could have participated willingly in the Nazi atrocities. Adorno and his colleagues came up with a profile of an authoritarian character, a personality type, that formed the backbone of the Nazi regime, but is much in evidence in most countries and cultures. The key quality of this character is that as a follower they are obedient and quiescent, as a leader they demand unquestioned loyalty and obedience.

Authoritarian people are generally people who have not enjoyed much parental love in their childhood. Many had to fend for themselves and identified with images of powerful individuals, able to command, punish and humiliate others. As a result, they are people who in their adult lives tend to revere power and denigrate love; love is seen as a sign of weakness, a vulnerability. Authoritarian personalities reject and hate what they regard as effeminate, soft, unsuccessful and weak. They identify with what is strong and masculine. This is what draws them to institutions like the military, where these values have for a long time been held in high regard. Unfortunately, however, authoritarians do not generally make very good military leaders. According to a fascinating study by Dixon (1976), authoritarian leaders are responsible for some of the biggest military disasters. It is relatively easy to see why. They do not want to show any sign of weakness. They therefore are unwilling to change their mind (make a 'u-turn'), even when it is very clear that the chosen course of action is disastrous.

Authoritarians compound their self-destructive stubbornness with various other mistakes – they underestimate, stereotype and dismiss their enemies; they feel no compassion about the sufferings of their subordinates; they denounce and punish anyone who dares propose an alternative course of action ('defeatists and naysayers'); they dismiss cunning, technique and smartness in favour of courage ('sheer guts') to see them through to success. In business, authoritarian personalities can be as disastrous as in politics and the military – for nearly the same reasons. This is especially so when flair, flexibility, communication, empathy and imagination are vital for success.

Of course, there are some authoritarian leaders who have been successful, at least for a certain period of time. Few will question Hitler's successes in regenerating German industry (especially armaments), in restoring morale or, indeed, in conquering France. In particular, authoritarian leaders seem to rise and come into their own in moments of crisis, when there is a call for a 'strong man', when individuals appear willing to subordinate their individual interests to the general one.

In business too, authoritarian leaders can be successful – for a time. Henry Ford and Henry Ford II are good cases in point. Both enjoyed tremendous business success, until they met their nemesis in opponents whom they underestimated and dismissed. They both fell in love with a single winning idea and were unwilling to change their approach when times changed (Grint, 2000).

Narcissistic Leaders

Authoritarian leaders are less likely to be found leading cutting-edge businesses in entertainment, media, telecommunications, information, leisure, fashion, design and the arts sectors. They lack the imagination, flair and emotional sensitivity necessary for success in these sectors. They are too earth-bound and too rule-bound. They cannot make others feel good; they cannot communicate a dream. This is an environment in which narcissistic individuals can prosper.

Narcissism is a term coined by Freud (1914) to describe a person's self-love; narcissism can be a healthy and normal psychological phenomenon that enables us to feel worthy as human beings, able to attract the respect of others and of ourselves. Narcissism is the love we feel towards ourselves, or, more accurately, towards an image of ourselves we seek to attain. This is why narcissism can drive us towards achievement and success. A champion athlete, an artist, an entrepreneur, a creative writer can be driven by their narcissism to great accomplishments. Few things are as good for our narcissism as the acclaim of an enthusiastic audience.

But excessive narcissism can also cause our downfall. This is the narcissism which focuses not on achievement but on celebrity and image for their own sake. It is the narcissism that says *Admire me for who I am* rather than *Admire me for my achievements*. Achievement narcissism can easily degenerate into image narcissism when an individual, a leader or an organisation decide to rest on their laurels, seeking acclaim for their past achievements and disregarding their present failings (Gabriel, 1999).

If authoritarian personalities usually grow up in families with strict discipline and limited love, excessively narcissistic people grow up in families with a lot of love and admiration and limited discipline. They are likely to be only children or particularly pampered children. In their childhood they enjoy the unqualified worship of the only audience that counted, their parents. They grow up believing that they are special, unique and the centre of an adoring universe. They preserve many childlike qualities later in life – spontaneity, imagination, playfulness, moodiness and love of freedom. They continue to love performing in front of adoring audiences. Acclaim is their opiate, criticism throws them into tantrums, self-questioning and despair.

If narcissistic leaders are so uniquely attuned to the needs of today's organisations, why is narcissism seen as a potential organisational pathology? What are the risks of narcissistic leaders and organisations steeped in narcissism? The short answer is very simple. Narcissism of achievement easily degenerates into narcissism of pure image. Leaders become ever more concerned with public relations, celebrations and ceremonies, opulent buildings and grandiose undertakings, losing track of the organisational 'nuts and bolts', the machinery necessary to ensure the smooth running of an organisation. They become more and more preoccupied with preserving the image at all costs, cutting corners where not seen to maintain the organisation's profile. Gradually, they lose touch with reality altogether – their vision becomes a reality, whether it has been realised or not (Maccoby, 2000; Schwartz, 1990). This is the point where an organisation can suddenly collapse, leaving stakeholders wondering how they had suspected nothing about its rotting state. Organisations can recover from narcissistic leaders, but the cost of recovery is usually substantial, in broken lives and broken dreams, recrimination, scapegoating and subsequent need for discipline and rigour. Such organisations are often rife for a take-over by an authoritarian leader, who promises to restore order, proper procedures, accountability and discipline to the organisation. Thus the leader's narcissism can function effectively as a force inspiring and uniting the followers but equally may bring about an organisation's disintegration (Cluley, 2008).

Leadership dysfunctions often command attention following great disasters, military, political and economic. It is then tempting to interpret such failures as being the outcome of the leader's Achilles' heel – the soft spot in their personality (including authoritarianism and narcissism), disregarding social and political factors that may have been instrumental in bringing about such an outcome. Psychoanalysis is sometimes accused of reducing complex socio-political phenomena into emotional family dramas, dominated by the flawed personalities of their protagonists. There is some truth in this charge which, of course, applies not to psychoanalysis alone. It is always tempting to attribute success and failure to the outstanding personalities of leaders, something that Meindl and colleagues (1985) describe as the *leadership romance*. Psychoanalysis suggests that the personalities of leaders, including the dormant unconscious heritage from their past, can be significant factors accounting for successes and failures. As we noted earlier, it is important to recognise that the qualities accounting for success in one set of circumstances may become counter-productive when times change. Thus, some of the most skilful psychoanalytic accounts of organisational failure manage to transcend the social-psychological, the micro and the macro levels (e.g., Cluley, 2008; Fotaki, 2006; Hirschhorn, 1988; Sievers, 1999; Stein, 2007).

CONCLUSIONS

In this chapter we have examined some of the psychoanalytic themes in the study of leaders and leadership relations. The unifying feature of these themes is an emphasis on the unconscious dynamics underpinning leadership processes and relations even when these appear to unfold under the auspices of rationality and collective goal furtherance. We have noted, in line with Freud, that leadership involves a powerful relation between leaders and followers, one based on identification of followers with the leader and his/her idealisation. Following Bion's analysis of group dynamics, we emphasised that leaders fulfil vital emotional functions for their followers, paramount among which is the containment of anxiety and other toxic emotions. Both Freud and Bion emphasise the tendency of leaders to awaken in their followers unconscious fantasies and desires first experienced in childhood, mirroring early relations with parents, which act as templates for our subsequent encounters with authority and power. This view was elaborated by Kohut's theory of messianic and charismatic leaders, based on the primal father and primal mother respectively.

Leaders themselves are moved by fantasies of changing the world, having to tame their own delusions of grandeur, omnipotence and infallibility and stopping themselves from lapsing into dysfunctional modes, like narcissism and authoritarianism. Leaders must have a healthy narcissism, relishing the fame and glory which comes with success. This, however, makes them vulnerable to narcissistic disorders, where approval and admiration is all they crave for – in the interest of which, they can distort reality, disregarding obstacles and indulging in wishful thinking. Likewise, leaders must be able to maintain discipline and focus without crushing the creativity and drive of their followers, themselves lapsing into authoritarianism.

In this chapter, we noted several instances where psychoanalytic approaches cross-fertilise with other traditions of studying leadership. Overall, however, such instances are few and there is much greater scope for cross-fertilisation, in particular in studies of leadership dysfunctions and the dark aspects of leadership, of the role of positive and negative fantasies in leader–follower relations, and defensive processes such as idealisation, scapegoating and splitting that can often characterise these relations.

At the same time, it must be recognised that psychoanalytic approaches to leadership run counter to certain current trends and therefore act as sense-breakers; in particular, psychoanalytic approaches to leadership run counter to those emphasising dispersed, diffused leadership. Psychoanalytic approaches acknowledge the relational aspect of leadership, but in the last resort insist on the asymmetrical relation between followers and leaders, a relation that can never escape from the template of someone being set apart from the others, someone taking charge and responsibility for others, and someone who, ultimately, through words and actions, is capable of providing the basis on which the others identify with each other as followers. It will also be noted that psychoanalytic approaches resist the view that leadership is nothing but a social construct, a discursive construction or a word in the English language that many other languages fail to emulate. Psychoanalysis acknowledges that a person who is a leader to some, may be a tyrant to others, a joker to others and a non-entity to others. All the same, psychoanalysis would ultimately view such constructions as the products of very real and objective emotional and political dynamics that are part and parcel of social and organisational life.

We may now offer a tentative definition of leading as constructed from a psychoanalytic perspective. *Leading is imagining, willing, inspiring and driving*. This definition emphasises leaders as agents for change, engaged in relations with others. In the first instance, leading is imagining. Without imagination, no leadership. And imagination means being able to envisage new possibilities, new ideas, new methods, new alliances, new ways of using words and language and even new needs and desires. Leaders then are dreamers, drawing on their unconscious wishes to conjure up what to others may seem unrealistic, impossible or absurd possibilities. But leaders are not just dreamers. Many people have powers of imagination – creative artists and scientists, for example. While dreaming is an essential part of leading, it is not enough. In order to lead, a man or a woman must also have a strong will, a burning desire to see the dream become reality, the vision become fact. Willing means that the dream is not an 'idle' fantasy but becomes a strong motivator towards action. Imagining and willing together are essential for leadership. But again, they are not enough. An aspiring athlete may have the vision of himself climbing the podium of the Olympic Games to receive a golden medal; she may have the drive to train and practice with dedication to get there. But she is not a leader if she does not engage with others, if his vision does not become a shared vision, if it does not inspire and drive others. A leader will drive others by emotionally engaging with them, being able to communicate, elaborate and share a vision, inspiring them and winning them over, but also occasionally by cajoling and exhorting them. Engaging with others is a feature of all aspects of leading, including imagining. Leaders do not just sit and dream waiting for a vision to arrive. Still less do visions arise from vision statements carefully prepared by hired consultants. Instead, visions emerge from active engagement with others, understanding of collective aspirations and wishes and flights of imagination that push the bounds of possibility.

REFERENCES

Adorno, T. W., Frenkel-Brunswik, E., Levinson, D. J., & Sanford, R. N. (1950). *The Authoritarian Personality*. Harpers.

Alvesson, M., & Sveningsson, S. (2003). The great disappearing act: Difficulties in doing 'leadership'. *Leadership Quarterly*, 14, 359–381.

Antonacopoulou, E. P., & Gabriel, Y. (2001). Emotion, learning and organizational change: Towards an integration of psychoanalytic and other perspectives. *Journal of Organizational Change Management*, 14(5), 435–451.

Bion, W. R. (1961). *Experiences in Groups*. Tavistock.

Bolton, S. (2005). *Emotion Management in the Workplace*. Palgrave.

Chancer, L. S. (2013). Sociology, psychoanalysis, and marginalization: Unconscious defenses and disciplinary interests. *Sociological Forum*, 28(3), 452–468. doi:10.1111/socf.12033

Cluley, R. (2008). The psychoanalytic relationship between leaders and followers. *Leadership*, 4(2), 201–212.

Collinson, D. (2006). Rethinking followership: A post-structuralist analysis of follower identities. *Leadership Quarterly*, 17(2), 179–189.

Craib, I. (1998). *Experiencing Identity*. Sage.

De Board, R. (1977). *The Psychoanalysis of Organizations*. Tavistock.

Devereux, G. (1955). Charismatic leadership and crisis. In G. Roheim (Ed.), *Psychoanalysis and the Social Sciences* (pp. 145–157). International Universities Press.

Diamond, M. A. (1993). *The Unconscious Life of Organizations: Interpreting Organizational Identity*. Quorum Books.
Dixon, N. (1976). *On the Psychology of Military Incompetence*. Penguin.
Eatwell, R., & Goodwin, M. (2018). *National Populism: The Revolt Against Liberal Democracy*. Pelican.
Erikson, E. H. (1958/1962). *Young Man Luther: A Study in Psychoanalysis and History*. Norton.
Fineman, S. (1993). *Emotion in Organizations*. Sage.
Foroughi, H., Gabriel, Y., & Fotaki, M. (2019). Leadership in a post-truth era: A new narrative disorder? *Leadership*, 15(2), 135–151. doi:10.1177/1742715019835369
Fotaki, M. (2006). Choice is yours: A psychodynamic exploration of health policyrnaking and its consequences for the English National Health Service. *Human Relations*, 59(12), 1711–1744.
Fotaki, M. (2010). Why do public policies fail so often? Exploring health policy-making as an imaginary and symbolic construction. *Organization*, 17(6), 703–720. doi:10.1177/1350508410366321
Freud, S. (1913). *Totem and Taboo* (Standard edn. Vol. 13). Hogarth Press.
Freud, S. (1914). *On Narcissism* (Standard edn. Vol. 14). Hogarth Press.
Freud, S. (1921/1985). Group psychology and the analysis of the ego. In *Civilization, Society and Religion* (Vol. 12, pp. 91–178). Pelican Freud Library.
Freud, S. (1923). *The Ego and the Id* (Standard edn. Vol. 18). Hogarth Press.
Freud, S. (1939). *Moses and Monotheism*. Hogarth Press.
Gabriel, Y. (1997). Meeting God: When organizational members come face to face with the supreme leader. *Human Relations*, 50(4), 315–342.
Gabriel, Y. (1999). *Organizations in Depth: The Psychoanalysis of Organizations*. Sage.
Gabriel, Y. (2018). Interpretation, reflexivity and imagination in qualitative research. In M. Ciesielska & D. Jemielniak (Eds.), *Qualitative Methodologies in Organization Studies: Volume I: Theories and New Approaches* (pp. 137–157). Palgrave.
Goldman, A. (2009). *Destructive Leaders and Dysfunctional Organizations: A Therapeutic Approach*. Cambridge University Press.
Grint, K. (2000). *The Arts of Leadership*. Oxford University Press.
Grint, K. (2005). *Leadership: Limits and Possibilities*. Palgrave Macmillan.
Grint, K. (2020). Leadership, management and command in the time of the coronavirus. *Leadership*, 16(3), 314–319. doi:10.1177/1742715020922445
Hirschhorn, L. (1988). *The Workplace Within*. MIT Press.
Hirschhorn, L. (1997). *Reworking Authority: Leading and Following in the Post-Modern Organization*. MIT Press.
Hochschild, A. R. (1983). *The Managed Heart: Commercialization of Human Feeling*. University of California Press.
Kets de Vries, M. F. R. (1988). Prisoners of leadership. *Human Relations*, 41, 261–280.
Kets de Vries, M. F. R., & Miller, D. (1984). *The Neurotic Organization*. Jossey-Bass.
Kohut, H. (1971). *The Analysis of the Self*. International Universities Press.
Kohut, H. (1976). Creativity, charisma and group psychology. In J. E. Gedo & G. H. Pollock (Eds.), *Freud: The Fusion of Science and Humanism*. International Universities Press.
Levine, D. P. (2001). The fantasy of inevitability in organizations. *Human Relations*, 54(10), 1251–1265.
Lindholm, C. (1988). Lovers and leaders: A comparison of social and psychological models of romance and charisma. *Social Science Information*, 27(1), 3–45.
Lipman-Blumen, J. (2005). *The Allure of Toxic Leaders: Why We Follow Destructive Bosses and Corrupt Politicians – and How We Can Survive Them*. Oxford University Press.
Maccoby, M. (1976). *The Gamesman: New Corporate Leaders*. Simon & Shuster.
Maccoby, M. (2000). Narcissistic leaders: The incredible pros, the inevitable cons. *Harvard Business Review*, 78(1), 69–77.
Maccoby, M., & Fuchsman, K. (2020). *Psychoanalytic and Historical Perspectives on the Leadership of Donald Trump: Narcissism and Marketing in an Age of Anxiety and Distrust*. Routledge.
Meindl, J. R., Ehrlich, S. B., & Dukerich, J., M. (1985). The romance of leadership. *Administrative Science Quarterly*, 30(1), 78–108.
Menzies Lyth, I. (1988). *Containing Anxiety in Institutions: Selected Essays*. Free Association.
Moxnes, P. (1998). Fantasies and fairy tales in groups and organizations: Bion's basic assumptions and the deep roles. *European Journal of Work and Organizational Psychology*, 7(3), 283–298.
Muis, J., & Immerzeel, T. (2017). Causes and consequences of the rise of populist radical right parties and movements in Europe. *Current Sociology*, 65(6), 909–930. doi:10.1177/0011392117717294
Obholzer, A. (1999). Managing the unconscious at work. In R. French & R. Vince (Eds.), *Group Relations, Management, and Organization* (pp. 87–97). Oxford University Press.
Oglensky, B. D. (1995). Socio-psychoanalytic perspectives on the subordinate. *Human Relations*, 48(9), 1029–1054.
Prasad, A. (2020). The organization of ideological discourse in times of unexpected crisis: Explaining how Covid-19 is exploited by populist leaders. *Leadership*, 16(3), 294–302. doi:10.1177/1742715020926783

Rosenbaum, R. (1999). *Explaining Hitler: The Search for the Origins of his Evil*. Macmillan.

Schwartz, H. S. (1990). *Narcissistic Process and Corporate Decay*. New York University Press.

Sievers, B. (1994). *Work, Death and Life Itself*. Walter de Gruyter.

Sievers, B. (1999). Psychotic organization as a metaphoric frame for the socioanalysis of organizational and interorganizational dynamics. *Administration and Society*, *31*(5), 588–615.

Smelser, N. J. (1998a). Collective myths and fantasies: The myth of the good life in California. In N. J. Smelser (Ed.), *The Social Edges of Psychoanalysis* (pp. 111–124). University of California Press.

Smelser, N. J. (1998b). Depth psychology and the social order. In N. J. Smelser (Ed.), *The Social Edges of Psychoanalysis* (pp. 197–217). University of California Press.

Stein, M. (2005). The Othello conundrum: The inner contagion of leadership. *Organization Studies*, *26*(9), 1405–1419. doi:10.1177/0170840605055339

Stein, M. (2007). Oedipus rex at Enron: Leadership, Oedipal struggles, and organizational collapse. *Human Relations*, *60*(9), 1387–1410. doi:10.1177/0018726707082852

Stein, M. (2013). When does narcissistic leadership become problematic? Dick Fuld at Lehman Brothers. *Journal of Management Inquiry*, *22*(3), 282–293. doi:10.1177/1056492613478664

Svensson, P. (2014). Thickening thick descriptions: Overinterpretations in critical organizational ethnography. In E. Jeanes & T. Huzzard (Eds.), *Critical Management Research: Reflections from the Field* (pp. 173–188). Sage.

Taylor, C. (1971). Interpretation and the sciences of man. *Review of Metaphysics*, *25*(1), 3–51.

Tourish, D. (2013). *The Dark Side of Transformational Leadership: A Critical Perspective*. Routledge.

Ulus, E., & Gabriel, Y. (2018). Bridging the contradictions of social constructionism and psychoanalysis in a study of workplace emotions in India. *Culture and Organization*, *24*(3), 221–243.

Wilson, S. (2020). Pandemic leadership: Lessons from New Zealand's approach to Covid-19. *Leadership*, *16*(3), 279–293. doi:10.1177/1742715020929151

16

Leadership Beyond the Leader to Relationship Quality

H. A. Martinez and Richard. E. Boyatzis

INTRODUCTION

Leaders and organisational members feel and behave differently towards each other based on the quality of their relationships (Dansereau et al., 1975; Graen & Uhl-Bien, 1995). The relationship between emotional states and comportment – stemming from the leader–follower dyad – is well-noted in the OB literature, and led to the development of the leader–member exchange (LMX) construct (Dienesch & Liden, 1986). Over the last two decades, the LMX construct has prevailed as the most used measure in the leadership relationship literature (Anand et al., 2011), giving rise to a robust and influential line of research about leadership and relationship quality. However, while considerable research has found support for the role of the LMX in organisations, it has been widely recognised that the construct itself has numerous inaccuracies and inconsistencies in both its theory and its measurement scales (for a concise critique, see Gottfredson et al., 2020).

One of the key complications of the LMX – and quite possibly one of its great utilities for research – is its definition of the leader–follower relationship. The LMX defines the leader–member relationship as a dyad conduit for exchanges (Graen & Uhl-Bien, 1995). As such, the quality of the leader–follower relationship is assessed through satisfaction in reciprocity and the perceived benefit or cost of the exchanges. The trajectory of these exchanges provides information for both the leader and follower to interpret, helping to explain how and why two strangers at work can develop a working relationship of trust, influence, respect, liking and shared fate (Graen & Uhl-Bien, 1991, 1995; Graen & Schiemann, 1978; Schriesheim et al., 1999) (see Chapter 4, The quality of relationships, for an exploration of the current research and future possibilities of the LMX).

The problematic issue with this definition is that as it simplifies the leadership relationship, it excludes other contextual factors (e.g. social networks and organisational culture) that go beyond the dyad, yet also clearly encapsulate it and influence it (Anand et al., 2011). Indeed some researchers have noted that a social exchange framing misses the mark of the leadership relationship. They propose that the impact of the leadership relationship on followers is based on states of emotionality, inspiration, motivation and long-term sustainable change in followers (Boyatzis, & McKee, 2005). To better gauge the leadership relationship – this line of research posits – researchers need to assess and incorporate the relational and organisational context that lies beyond the individual actors (i.e., the dyad between leader and follower) in the relationship (Boyatzis & Rochford, 2020).

A possible way of approaching the context beyond the leadership dyad – and help to conceptualise and integrate the organisational factors that influence it – is the consensual validation lens (Weick, 1979; Munroe, 1955). This framing proposes that as the leader and the follower live through shared experiences, they develop a *common grammar* (Weick, 1979) that is elevated to a type of understanding about each other, reducing equivocation and uncertainty in the relationship. With reduced uncertainty, a shared vision can be established, grounded on a shared *common sense* (Weick, 1979). This common sense can be applied to future experiences, reducing the emotional stress, noise and anxiety generated by the uncertainty of being and performing in an organisational context (Carleton, 2016). This mutual understanding and shared common sense work as a type of lens that filters and influences the emotional experience of each person in the relationship. So, while the LMX captures key aspects of the transactional aspects of the leader–member relationship, it does not contemplate the emotional experience of the leader and follower and, perhaps more importantly, how the emotional competencies of both actors impact each other's perceptions, as well as the development of the leadership relationship within the organisational context (see Chapter 29, How and why is context important in leadership?, which provides a more extensive model of the factors that are important).

Developed in parallel to the LMX – yet conceptually distinct – the emotional competency research has focused considerable attention – more recently incorporating the use of neuroscience – on understanding how behaviours and emotions help performance at work, as well as impact the development and quality of the leader–follower relationship (Boyatzis, 2018). This research has conceptualised leadership as a relationship in which leaders and followers interact with each other, gaining a deeper understanding and awareness about each other's emotional states (both internally and through feedback), as well as learning about their values and the intentions behind the behaviours that each display within the organisational and relational context.

This framing relies on an understanding that behaviours represent and signify more than the function of the behaviour itself, but that those behaviours are explained by – and carry information about – the emotions, intentions and interactions among individuals in an organisational context (Boyatzis, 2018; Kolb, 1984; Lewin, 1936). In an organisational context, the relational environment within which employees most immediately engage is made up of their closest and most important relationships at work (Boyatzis, 2018). As such, the quality of these relationships has the most impact on how employees feel and behave at work. Within this relational context, emotions and emotional competencies are the main currency and filter for personal intent, providing information about each other, as individuals interact, perform and develop relationships within organisations. It is both through the interactions and the perceived intent behind those interactions that relationships are established and maintained, and thus their quality can be assessed. We propose that high-quality leader–follower relationships are constructed and developed by the trust that is established 1) through a developed shared vision, 2) compassion that provides understanding, support and caring and 3) relational energy that can be invested towards the realisation of the shared vision.

In this chapter, we will review research that attributes relational quality to the felt and interpreted quality of the repeated interactions between individuals (both leader and members) – guided by, and in response to, internal and external factors – leading to a relatively stable relational context that can be assessed and generates a substantial impact on organisational performance (Boyatzis & Rochford, 2020). We will first explain how the emotional and social intelligence of the leader and follower enables better leadership relationships. We will then review the notion of resonant relationships, which is grounded on positive emotional experiences and is characterised by renewal (i.e., parasympathetic nervous systems (PNS) arousal) and more effective and adaptive functioning at work. Then we will define the felt work-relational quality (i.e., relational climate) as a higher-order construct that is composed of: 1) the extent to which the organisational members share an explicit common mental image of the desired future, which provides a direction and objective(s) for aligned, coordinated and collaborative action (i.e., shared vision); 2) the interpersonal process of identifying the needs of other organisational members, empathising with them and acting to help them respond to those needs (i.e., compassion); and 3) the felt energy generated from relationships at work (i.e., energy). We will then address some of the factors that impact the leadership relationship and, finally, we propose coaching with compassion as a coaching approach that allows for all the components of relational climate to converge and establish an organisational culture of high-quality leadership relationships.

Through this chapter, we wish to break traditional assumptions about the leadership relationship in the field of organisational behaviour and complicate it by incorporating findings from new research that relies on neuroscience, providing new and different ways of assessing the mechanisms and impact of the leadership relationships at work. Through this sense-breaking, we propose a new sense-making, one that focuses on what really matters in the leader–follower dyad: a relationship quality that is assessed through a shared vision, a sense of compassion and a sense of energy to work towards the shared vision. We feel that the inclusion of these concepts in how the field understands leadership relationships is more representative of the dynamics of the leader–follower relationship in organisations, and can help in the development towards the future of this research stream.

ESI Competencies: The Foundations of Relationship Quality

Relationship quality from an LMX framing is based on the assessed quality of repeated exchanges, establishing a more commensurable – as opposed to an emotional – interpretation of a relationship. However, within the context of human relations, a person's emotional states hold a considerable impact on how experiences are understood and longer-term impressions are generated (Stanley & Burrows, 2001). Emotions direct attention to occurrences, thoughts and activities, which work to organise the processes related to perception and thinking (Stanley & Burrows, 2001). Within an organisational context, the emotional process, as well as the behaviours stemming from those emotions, cannot easily be attributed solely to the individual. Instead, the emotional state and comportment of an individual at work are informed by – and respond to – the organisational objectives, structures and incentives in the context (Boyatzis, 2018; Lewin, 1936).

However, the organisational context is filtered and understood through relationships at work (Boyatzis, 2018). Social network research has consistently established this link (Borgatti et al., 2009; Ibarra et al., 2005). As such, it is because of the role that relationships at work play in performance that researchers have included emotional intelligence – identified through emotional and social competencies (ESI) – as a key factor that explains a substantial and important variance in performance quality within organisations (Boyatzis, 2008).

ESI competencies (Boyatzis, 2018; McClelland & Boyatzis, 1982) are defined as the abilities that enable an individual to manage their emotional responses to perceptions – both internal (e.g., thoughts and emotions) and external (e.g., actions of others) – in the execution of work. These include competencies such as self-awareness, self-control and adaptability (Boyatzis, 2018; McClelland & Boyatzis, 1982). Beyond their role in self-management, ESI competencies can also be used to impact the emotional state and behaviour of others (Boyatzis, 2018; McClelland & Boyatzis, 1982). These include competencies such as empathy, influence and organisational awareness. People operationalise these competencies into action to perform with others in organisations, generating, developing and maintaining high-quality relationships – and high-performance levels (Boyatzis, 2018) – within the organisational context.

From this perspective, leaders who have worked to develop their ESI competencies are more likely able to: 1) be aware of and manage their emotional states; 2) recognise and understand the emotional states of others; 3) influence the negative and positive emotional states of followers; and 4) manage the relationship towards the establishment of high-quality positive relationships that help both leader and follower to perform successfully in organisations (McKee et al., 2008). Research on the role of emotional intelligence on leader effectiveness and follower performance is substantial (Chapter 11, Leadership, emotion regulation and sense-making, provides insight into how leaders regulate their emotions). Below we will review the role of positive emotions in developing high-quality relationships, which we call *resonant relationships*.

Resonant Relationships: Applied Relationship Quality

Several types of leadership relationships have been linked to the development and mastery of ESI competencies in people. These include mentoring, coaching and other helping relationships. These types of relationships are applied in leadership because they can be instrumental in coordinating collaboration (i.e., teamwork), negotiating and resolving disagreements (i.e., influence and conflict management), and can be a conduit in long-term sustainable change that facilitates performance (Boyatzis & McKee, 2005).

A type of overarching concept that has been proposed to link all of these leadership relationships is resonance (McKee et al., 2008). Resonance in a relationship has been characterised as the emergence of three factors: synchrony towards a shared vision (i.e., being in sync with another's emotional state and understanding of a purpose); compassion for each other (i.e., caring for each other's well-being); and playfulness (i.e., stimulate the PNS). When a resonant relationship emerges within an organisational context, individuals are more able to notice new possibilities in an environment, be more open to connecting with new people and be more open to face difficult issues (Boyatzis & Jack, 2018).

To assess the impact and scope of high-quality resonant leadership relationships and their role on performance, Boyatzis developed a measure of the positive and negative emotional attractors (PNEA) felt in a relationship (Boyatzis & Rochford, 2020). This measure focused on assessing the activation of the PNS, and the ability to sustain positive relationships (Boyatzis, 2018) through shared vision, shared compassion and shared positive mood, which activates the PNS and generates renewal from a physiological and psychological sense (Boyatzis & McKee, 2005; Boyatzis et al., 2006; Boyatzis, 2018). At this point, 39 longitudinal behaviour studies, two functional magnetic resonance imaging (fMRI) studies and two hormonal studies (see Boyatzis & Rochford, 2020, for details) have found that a positive coaching relationship leads to reports of higher relationship quality.

Relational Climate: Impact of Relationship Quality on Performance Constructs

More recently, Boyatzis and Rochford (Boyatzis et al., 2015; 2020) validated a comprehensive measure of relational climate to capture the quality of resonant leadership relationships in a given work context. Relational climate as a concept and measure assesses the *shared employee perceptions and appraisals of policies, practices, and behaviors affecting interpersonal relationships in a given context* (Mossholder et al., 2011, p. 36). While the concept of relational climate is relatively familiar in organisations, the field of research lacked a validated measure (Boyatzis & Rochford, 2020). In particular, the model Boyatzis and Rochford tested was grounded on communal sharing (Fiske, 1992; Mossholder et al., 2011). It was operationalised *as a second-order latent construct reflected by three first-order constructs: shared vision, compassion, and relational energy* (Boyatzis & Rochford, 2020, p. 1). Through these three factors, the leadership relationship reduces uncertainty and anxiety, provides mutual caring and cooperation and leverages enthusiasm for coordination and collaboration. The relational climate survey has been used in 36 studies and has been found to have an impact on employee effectiveness and innovation, citizenship behaviour (helping and voice) and engagement (Boyatzis & Rochford, 2020).

Shared Vision

Shared vision has been defined as *the extent to which members of an organization (or team or dyad) share a common mental image of a desirable future that provides a basis for action* (Boyatzis & Rochford, 2020, p. 2; Pearce & Ensley, 2004). The development of a shared vision is grounded on high-quality relationships (Boyatzis et al., 2015), that allow for an openness to share personal desires and motivations – by both the leader and follower – and reach levels of mutual acceptance and understanding that move the relationship beyond task motivation, or personal success (Berg, 2015). Instead, as a shared vision is collaboratively crafted and expressed, it plays a higher-level role in the relation climate, providing two avenues for impact in the workplace: the first impact is related to the emotional dimension of belonging, social identity and organisational culture (Boyatzis & Rochford, 2020; Pearce & Ensley, 2004; Fiske, 1992; Mossholder et al., 2011); while the second is related to the performance quality that is allowable through a mutually understood significance and meaning of the relational bonds (Allport, 1962; Boyatzis & Rochford, 2020; Leary et al., 1995; Weick, 1979). From this perspective, a shared vision in a relationship provides emotional and directional clarity for the contribution of both the leader and follower's effort, ability and hope. As such, a shared vision is quite different from an assigned task, or a vision provided by a supervisor.

To identify the impact of the development of a shared vision in organisations, some researchers have looked at family businesses, in particular how a shared vision can lead to organisational continuity and success across generations. Boyatzis et al. (2012) used a case study to see how two members of a family business developed high-quality relationships – using the intentional change theory – to develop a shared vision among its stakeholders, leading to greater involvement and organisational success. Related, Overbeke et al. (2015) found that a shared vision developed by fathers and daughters led to a greater probability that daughters would become the successors of their father's family business.

Compassion

Compassion is *an interpersonal process that involves noticing another person as being in need, empathizing with him or her, and acting to enhance his or her well-being in response to that need* (Boyatzis & Rochford, 2020, p. 2; Boyatzis et al., 2012). While the notion of compassion from a traditionally Western perspective implies a state of suffering or need that is alleviated through the charity of others, in an organisational setting, compassion holds a broader definition. Researchers have pointed out that the application of compassion in an organisational setting – beyond alleviating the suffering of others – can start from identifying a need or desire in someone through empathy and, through action, can lead to employee well-being (Dutton et al., 2006; Dutton et al., 2014; Boyatzis et al., 2012). In other words, the process of compassion can be attuned towards the development and potential of others, as opposed to the pain and hardship of another. In an organisational context, compassion is a process that incorporates ESI competencies, relationship quality and organisational resources, which links its application to high-quality leadership relationships. Through compassion, a leader can help followers identify a personal hoped-for future and link it to their current and future jobs roles, sparking hope, energy and excitement for their work (i.e., coaching with compassion; Boyatzis et al., 2006). Furthermore, because a leader holds greater resource authority within an organisation, the coach leader can then invest some of those resources in directions, tasks and roles that are more meaningful to the follower (e.g., job crafting).

Compassion at work has received considerable research (Dutton et al., 2014). Of particular note to the leadership relationship, coaching with compassion has been shown to be integral in how managers in an MBA programme develop their emotional and social intelligence (Boyatzis & Cavanagh, 2018). Coaching with compassion has also been found to be integral in follower openness to new ideas, positive affect and the default mode network (Boyatzis et al., 2012).

Relational Energy

Relational energy is *the extent to which relationships in an organization are a source of energy [...] that [...] result[s] in feelings of positive arousal, aliveness, and eagerness to act* (Boyatzis & Rochford, 2020, p. 3; Quinn & Dutton, 2005; Ryan & Frederick, 1997). While the idea of relational energy is a relatively new concept in organisational behaviour research, it is linked to emotional energy at the individual level, as well as arousal, positive affect, zest, vitality and a host of other terms that seem to capture the notion that an energetic force is created within an individual, which can be transformed into action or effort (Baker, 2019). However, relational energy has been identified as a particular type of energy force that is generated or depleted from social interactions (Quinn & Dutton, 2005; Baker, 2019). Some of the research on relational energy has used the LMX as its antecedent (Dutton 2003; Baker & Dutton, 2007). More current research has also linked this energy to perceived social support (Owens & Hekman, 2016).

Relational Climate as a Higher-Order Construct

Using the higher-order relational climate construct (including shared vision, compassion and relational energy), Kendall (2016) found that relational climate predicted product innovation and organisational citizenship behaviour (OCB) voice in technology-based firms. Berg (2015) found that relational climate predicted job engagement and OCB in non-profit organisations. Leah (2017) found that relational climate predicts economic performance in organisations across industries. Alharbi (2019) found that relational climate predicts work engagement in nursing students in Saudi Arabia. Barco (2019) found that relational climate predicts student engagement.

NEUROSCIENCE IN THE LEADERSHIP RELATIONSHIP

Emotional Contagion in the Leadership Relationship

Where the social exchange foundation of the LMX has led to assessing the transactional nature of the leadership relationship, the biological component of the emotional and social competencies research has led to the inclusion of neuroscience tools to assess the emotional impact of the leadership relationship. One of the paths towards this inclusion is emotional contagion. Beyond the conscious recognition by the follower of a leader's emotional cues, the leader can influence the follower's emotional state through emotional contagion (Hatfield et al., 1993; LeDoux, 2009). As a leader inspires and captures the hearts and minds of followers, emotional contagion can be seen as the process or mechanism through which some of the leader's emotional influence can reach a follower. Emotional contagion has been defined as the tendency towards an automatic synchronisation of one's emotional 'package' (i.e., conscious awareness; facial, postural and vocal expression; neurophysiological and autonomic nervous system [ANS] activity; and instrumental behaviours) with another person, leading to an emotional convergence between the two (Hatfield et al., 1993; Elfenbein, 2014).

This emotional convergence can emerge as an emotional response from both a conscious and unconscious process (LeDoux, 2009). LeDoux (2009) and other researchers have proposed that the brain is in a constant process of evaluating or appraising the emotional stimuli around it. This appraisal mechanism operates both consciously and unconsciously (LeDoux, 2009) and seems to underlie all the emotional responses and conscious feelings that emerge from emotional stimuli around the individual. LeDoux (2009) has proposed that there are two ways that an emotional response can be elicited from an emotional stimulus: some are hardwired by evolution, while others are learnt from personal experiences. As such, within the leader relationship, the leader's emotional influence on a follower can be understood as a type of learnt conditioning, through repeated interactions that are appraised both consciously and unconsciously. Furthermore, as emotional convergence (i.e., emotional contagion) is experienced repeatedly – possibly even intensified through positive organisational results – the potential for an almost conditioned activation of the empathic network (default mode network) can further impact and enhance the relationship quality between a leader and follower.

Further generating a positive leadership relationship quality is the activation of the PNS on both the leader and follower and its impact on stress and renewal. Stress is related to the activation of the sympathetic nervous system (SNS) (Boyatzis et al., 2021). The activation of the SNS is related to the earlier activation of the amygdala (from fear or defensiveness), as well as the secretion of hormones, which can – with repeated arousal – impair a person's cognitive, emotional and perceptual process (Boyatzis et al., 2021). The only antidote for the damage resulting from the secretion of the endocrines related to the activation of the SNS is an arousal of the PNS and its release of oxytocin and vasopressin (Boyatzis et al., 2021). Boyatzis et al. (2021) have proposed that an effective leader's functioning is directly related to the daily engagement of the PNS. This link has resulted in the development of the personal sustainability index (PSI) (Boyatzis et al., 2021).

The PSI looks to assess the balance between daily activities and the variety of those activities that activate the SNS (stress), and the activities and the variety of activities that activate the PNS (renewal). Related to the activation of the PNS through the leadership relationship are activities such as coaching, helping, talking about a shared vision or purpose and laughing with others (Boyatzis et al., 2021).

Strategy, Budgets, Learning and People: The Impact of the Organisational Context in the Leadership Relationship

As the integration of neuroscience provides theory and evidence to support the benefits of having high-quality leadership relationships, it has also provided some evidence as to the difficulty and complexity of developing a high-quality leadership relationship within an organisational context. Organisational neuroscience has identified that a brain responds to external stimulation by activating the appropriate task-positive network (i.e., a network of neural areas that work in coordinated or coherent activity) (Waldman et al., 2017). Before activation of a task-positive network, the brain is in a resting mode, which some have called the intrinsic brain (Waldman et al., 2017), or in contrast to the task-positive network, the default mode network (Buckner & Carroll, 2007). While the resting brain might imply an unactivated brain, actually the brain in the default mode network registers higher electrical energy than when in the task-positive network (Waldman et al., 2017). These two networks have been found to be anti-correlated, which has led to the coupling being called opposing domains.

The evidence for the antagonistic or opposing domains hypothesis for the brain is substantial (Buckner et al., 2008; Fox et al., 2005; Fransson, 2005; Golland et al., 2007; Greicius et al., 2003; Jack et al., 2013; Tian et al., 2007) and it has been linked to leadership and the types of tasks related to managing an organisation. Jack et al. (2013) found evidence that the two cognitive models (i.e., the task-positive and the default mode) are not only separate modes but also that they suppress each other. As one mode is activated, the other is shut down. In the same study, Jack et al. (2013) stated that these modes were activated by different task stimuli: solving a task related to causal/mechanical properties of inanimate objects activated the task-positive network, while reasoning about the mental states of other people led to the activation of the default mode. These findings have led Jack and others to also identify the default mode network as the empathic network (Friedman et al., 2015).

From a leadership perspective, these two networks seem to point to the traditional framing of the two roles of the leader: task leader and socio-emotional leader (Bales, 1958; Boyatzis et al., 2014). The link of the task-positive network to a task leader is intuitive, yet has substantial implications for the relationship between the leader and follower. The task-positive network is not only activated when working on inanimate objects (Jack et al., 2013), but also when the individual dehumanises others – or sees others in an objectifying way (Boyatzis et al., 2014). In other words, if a leader sees a follower as a resource for a task, then it is more likely that the leader is in a task-positive mode, even if people are involved. This has implications for the leadership relationship, as a leader's decisions – and their intentions – may be felt and understood by the follower, leading to the transactional perspective, much like the social exchange framing of the LMX. As such, a social exchange filter on the leadership relationship might in fact lead to the activation of the task-positive mode and allow leaders in organisations to treat other organisational members as dehumanised resources. Other organisational tasks that have been found to activate the task-positive mode – and benefit from it – include analytical, financial and budgetary tasks (Friedman et al., 2015).

Developing Resonant leaders: The Role of Coaching in the Leadership Relationship

A type of relationship that has received substantial research attention in the leadership literature is the coaching relationship (Ely et al., 2010, for a review). In the context of this chapter, coaching is a type of helping approach that can be incorporated into the leadership relationship. The relationship of a coach leader with a follower has been proposed by researchers as a type of influential, helping relationship that leverages relationship quality for performance and role development (Boyatzis et al., 2006; Goleman, 2006). Boyatzis (2015; Boyatzis et al., 2015; Boyatzis et al., 2018) proposed that the coaching relationship impacts followers through the emotional state of the relationship. In particular, a coaching approach that focuses on activating the follower towards their positive emotional attractors (PEA) activates neural systems that allow a coached follower to be open to change (Boyatzis et al., 2006). This is in contrast to a more task-focused, performance-centred coaching process.

One of the key aspects of the coaching relationship is its impact on change and development, which in the brain is realised through the creation of new neural pathways (Boyatzis and Jack, 2018). The primary process that leads to the development of new neural pathways in coached followers is through the emergence of a shared vision (Boyatzis, 2018). A shared vision between a coach leader and a follower implies a shared sense of purpose, which indicates a relationship quality that has allowed for an open and honest sharing of independent ideas that eventually led to an alignment of the components of the shared vision. This particular level of alignment eliminates the potential for the trivialisation of the visioned goal or task (Boyatzis, 2018). From a relational framing – and directly opposed to social exchange – a shared vision is not an exchange between two individuals where reciprocity and value are calculated from two sides, but instead a collaboration, mutually constructed and mutually significant. As mentioned earlier, the ESI competencies of both the leader and the follower impact how the emotionality and intentions of the shared vision development are established.

Research on shared vision has identified its impact on change and development. The degree of shared vision has been found to impact leadership effectiveness for next-generation leaders in family businesses (Miller, 2014), impact the creation of an effective family business culture (Neff, 2015), to predict championing behaviours in professional financial services (Clayton, 2015), to moderate the relationship between open-mindedness and learning capacity in university endowment officers (Lord, 2015) and employee engagement in work teams in consulting and manufacturing research and development (Mahon et at., 2014), as well as mediating the relationship between emotional and social intelligence on engagement (Pittenger, 2015). Quinn (2015) found that shared vision also mediated the effect of emotional and social intelligence and organisational citizenship behaviour in physician leaders. Of particular note, Khawaja (2011) studied the doctor–patient relationship and found that if doctors created a shared vision with their diabetic patients, this shared vision predicted treatment adherence as reported by the patient's caregivers.

Measuring Relationship Quality on Followers: fMRI Studies

Advances in neuroimaging have allowed neuroscience the possibility to describe and explain the neurological processes of thoughts, feelings and behaviour in the leadership relationship, allowing for a better understanding as to why some leaders are more effective than others (Boyatzis et al., 2021). From a relationship framing, studies incorporating neuroscience have begun to provide some evidence for the proposition that inspiring and supportive relationships activate an individual's openness to new ideas, as well as help to generate a more social orientation towards others (Boyatzis et al., 2012).

Boyatzis et al. (2012) used fMRI imaging scans to assess the neural mechanisms of how repeated interactions with leaders impacted the memories of followers. When followers recalled interactions with leaders with whom they had a resonant relationship – relationships *characterized by mutual positive emotions, a subjective sense of being in synchrony with one another, and physiological effects of PNS activation (e.g., rest and digest response)* (Boyatzis, et al., 2012, p. 261) – fMRI scans identified the activation of the *bilateral insula, right inferior parietal lobe, and left superior temporal gyrus, as well as regions associated with the mirror neuron system, default mode (i.e. social network), and positive affect* (2012, p. 259). In contrast, when followers were prompted to recall interactions with leaders whom they considered generated a dissonant relationship – relationships characterised by *negative emotions, interpersonal discord, and SNS activation (e.g., fight or flight response)* (Boyatzis et al., 2012, p. 261) – fMRI scans identified the *activation of the right anterior cingulate cortex and activated the right inferior frontal gyrus, bilateral posterior region of the inferior frontal gyrus, and bilateral inferior frontal gyrus/insula; regions associated with mirror neuron system and related to avoidance, narrowed attention, decreased compassion, and negative emotions* (2012, p. 259). While this was an exploratory study, the results displayed the significant activation or negative activation of 31 different brain regions for all subjects. Of particular note for the leadership relationship, this study found that recalling interactions with leaders in resonant relationships activated the 'default mode', which has been found to be the opposite of neural activation in goal-directed behaviour (Raichle & Snyder, 2007) and is involved combining emotional and cognitive processes (Raichle et al., 2001), as well as emotional activations that are cognitively demanding.

Coaching with Compassion: Impact on Followers

Recent studies on a particular type of coaching – coaching with compassion – have incorporated neuroscience to better understand its impact on emotions, behaviour and the brain. These studies have identified that coaching with compassion provides considerable benefits from performance-centred coaching (Boyatzis et al., 2013). The focus of this coaching approach is on the development of the person being coached, as opposed to coaching an employee for the benefit of the organisation in which they work (Boyatzis et al., 2013). Because of this focus, coaching with compassion is structured around the intentional change theory (Boyatzis, 2006), which places a priority on an expression of the person's ideal self – the most desired, exciting and motivating version of the possible selves (Boyatzis & Akrivou, 2006; Martinez et al., 2021).

The motivation and effort for sustainable change are linked to the image of the ideal self, allowing the person who is being coached to then identify their path towards operationalising the ideal self through the development of their identified strengths and opportunities (Boyatzis, 2006). At the centre of the process is the relationship between the coach and coachee. This relationship is not easily placed under the traditional leader–follower model, as the coach sometimes follows the coachee, responding and aligning to their emotional and cognitive states with the intent of providing help in their development; and other times provides greater guidance and direction through questions and feedback. Fundamental to the approach is the relationship quality between the two individuals, which is fostered by shared vision, compassion, relational energy and the activation of the PNS.

This coaching relationship integrates the application of emotional intelligence, resonance, shared vision, compassion and relational energy for the benefit of another. Furthermore, because the priority for the coach is the well-being of the other, there is a decreased sense of self-preoccupation, which in the context of the leadership relationship can help to reduce self-aggrandisement that can come from the traditional leadership role (Boyatzis et al., 2013). It has been proposed that the application of this type of coaching in organisations can lead to developing norms and relationships of caring and development across all levels of the organisation, helping establish in the organisation a culture of positive, developmental coaching that leads to better outcomes than deficit-based coaching, or coaching for compliance (Boyatzis et al., 2013).

IMPLICATIONS AND FUTURE DIRECTIONS

In this chapter, we have proposed that leadership is a relationship. The implications of the ideas that support our proposition are substantial. From a research perspective, relationships are the context for an employee's experience in an organisation; as such relationship quality is a moderator – or mediator – for an individual's behaviour. Researchers should move beyond transactional assessments and include relationship quality in models that explain behaviour and outcome dependent variables. Furthermore, as noted above, the transactional framing of the LMX that is traditionally used to measure the leadership relationship can actually lead leaders to objectify and dehumanise the follower, eroding the quality and impact of the leadership relationship. As the field of study progresses, further integration of neuroscience will provide a greater understanding of the mechanisms of how the leader and follower connect, leading to more precise interventions that will allow leaders to be more efficient in their relationship development with followers.

CONCLUSION

Social exchange theory and LMX have helped researchers to better understand relationships from a rational perspective, but not from an emotional framing. The leadership relationship is the basis for how employees understand the organisation and their role in that organisation. It has a substantial impact on how they feel and behave in the organisation and, of course, how they perform and complete their tasks. The co-construction of the relational context is necessary for the relationship quality, and the relationship quality impacts the co-construction of that context. How leaders engage with followers in their intent, their emotions and their actions matters, but less from a rational transaction analysis and more from a humanist perspective. Even in an organisational context, we respond to our common sense, to someone's compassion and their sense of fun because we can forgive – or even forget – what someone owes us from our last transactional exchange.

REFERENCES

Alharbi, M. (2019). *The role of emotional and social competencies: Assessment of work engagement and clinical performance in the clinical learning environment*. 28186580. Doctoral dissertation, Case Western Reserve University. ProQuest Dissertations.

Allport, G. W. (1962). The general and the unique in psychological science1. *Journal of Personality*, 30(3), 405–422.

Anand, S., Hu, J., Liden, R. C., & Vidyarthi, P. R. (2011). Leader–member exchange: Recent research findings and prospects for the future (pp. 311–325). *The SAGE Handbook of Leadership*. Sage.

Baker, W. E. (2019). Emotional energy, relational energy, and organizational energy: Toward a multilevel model. *Annual Review of Organizational Psychology and Organizational Behavior*, 6, 373–395.

Baker, W., & Dutton, J. E. (2007). Enabling positive social capital in organizations. In J. E. Dutton & B. R. Ragins (Eds.), *Exploring Positive Relationships at Work: Building a Theoretical and Research Foundation* (325345). Lawrence Erlbaum.

Bales, R. F. (1958). Task roles and social roles in problem-solving groups. In E. E. Maccoby, T. M. Newcomb & T. M. Hartley (Eds.), *Readings in Social Psychology* (pp. 437–447). Holt, Rinehart & Winston.

Barco, I. J. (2019). *Being an inspiring professor*. Unpublished doctoral dissertation, Case Western Reserve University.

Berg, J. L. (2015). The role of personal purpose and personal goals in symbiotic visions. *Frontiers in Psychology*, 6, 443.

Borgatti, S. P., Mehra, A., Brass, D. J., & Labianca, G. (2009). Network analysis in the social sciences. *Science*, 323(5916), 892–895.

Boyatzis, R. E. (2006). An overview of intentional change from a complexity perspective. *Journal of Management Development*, 25(7), 607–623.

Boyatzis, R. E. (2018). Measuring the impact of quality of relationships through the positive emotional attractor. In M. A. Warren & S. I. Donaldson (Eds.), *Toward a Positive Psychology of Relationships: New Directions in Theory and Research* (pp. 193–209). Praeger/ABC-CLIO.

Boyatzis, R. E., & Akrivou, K. (2006). The ideal self as the driver of intentional change. *Journal of Management Development*, 25(7), 24–642.

Boyatzis, R. E., & Cavanagh, K. V. (2018). Leading change: Developing emotional, social, and cognitive competencies in managers during an MBA program. In K. V. Keefer, J. D. A. Parker & D. H. Saklofske (Eds.), *Emotional Intelligence in Education* (pp. 403–426). Springer.

Boyatzis, R. E., Goleman, D., Dhar, U., & Osiri, J. K. (2021). Thrive and survive: Assessing personal sustainability. *Consulting Psychology Journal: Practice and Research*, 73(1), 27.

Boyatzis, R. E. & Jack, A. I. (2018). The neuroscience of coaching. *Consulting Psychology Journal: Practice and Research*, 70(1) 11–27.

Boyatzis, R. E. & McKee, A. (2005). *Resonant Leadership: Renewing Yourself and Connecting with Others Through Mindfulness, Hope, and Compassion*. Harvard Business Press.

Boyatzis, R. E., Passarelli, A. M., Koenig, K., Lowe, M., Mathew, B., Stoller, J. K., & Phillips, M. (2012). Examination of the neural substrates activated in memories of experiences with resonant and dissonant leaders. *Leadership Quarterly, 23*(2), 259–272.

Boyatzis, R. E., & Rochford, K. (2020). Relational climate in the workplace: Dimensions, measurement, and validation. *Frontiers in Psychology, 11*(85).

Boyatzis, R. E., Rochford, K., & Jack, A. I. (2014). Antagonistic neural networks underlying differentiated leadership roles. *Frontiers in Human Neuroscience, 8*, 114.

Boyatzis, R. E., Rochford, K., & Taylor, S. N. (2015). The role of the positive emotional attractor in vision and shared vision: Toward effective leadership, relationships, and engagement. *Frontiers in Psychology*, 670.

Boyatzis, R. E., Smith, M. L., & Blaize, N. (2006). Developing sustainable leaders through coaching and compassion. *Academy of Management Learning & Education, 5*(1), 8–24.

Boyatzis, R. E., Smith, M. L., & Beveridge, A. J. (2013). Coaching with compassion: Inspiring health, well-being, and development in organizations. *Journal of Applied Behavioral Science, 49*(2), 153–178.

Buckner, R. L., Andrews-Hanna, J. R., & Schacter, D. L. (2008). The brain's default network: Anatomy, function, and relevance to disease. *Annals of the New York Academy of Sciences, 1124*(1), 1–38.

Buckner, R. L., & Carroll, D. C. (2007). Self-projection and the brain. *Trends in Cognitive Sciences, 11*(2), 49–57.

Carleton, R. N. (2016). Fear of the unknown: One fear to rule them all? *Journal of Anxiety Disorders, 41*, 5–21.

Clayton, B. C. (2015). Shared vision and autonomous motivation vs financial incentives driving success in corporate acquisitions. *Frontiers in Psychology, 5*, 1466.

Dansereau F. Jr, Graen, G., & Haga, W. J. (1975). A vertical dyad linkage approach to leadership within formal organizations: A longitudinal investigation of the role making process. *Organizational Behavior and Human Performance, 13*(1), 46–78.

Dienesch, R. M., & Liden, R. C. (1986). Leader–member exchange model of leadership: A critique and further development. *Academy of Management Review, 11*(3), 618–634.

Dutton, J. E. (2003). *Energize your Workplace: How to Create and Sustain High-Quality Connections at Work*. John Wiley & Sons.

Dutton, J. E., Workman, K. M., & Hardin, A. E. (2014). Compassion at work. *Annual Review of Organizational Psychology and Organizational Behavior, 1*(1), 277–304.

Dutton, J. E., Worline, M. C., Frost, P. J., & Lilius, J. (2006). Explaining compassion organizing. *Administrative Science Quarterly, 51*(1), 59–96.

Elfenbein, H. A. (2014). The many faces of emotional contagion: An affective process theory of affective linkage. *Organizational Psychology Review, 4*(4), 326–362.

Ely, K., Boyce, L. A., Nelson, J. K., Zaccaro, S. J., Hernez-Broome, G., & Whyman, W. (2010). Evaluating leadership coaching: A review and integrated framework. *Leadership Quarterly, 21*(4), 585–599.

Fiske, A. P. (1992). The four elementary forms of sociality: Framework for a unified theory of social relations. *Psychological Review, 99*(4), 689.

Fox, M. D., Snyder, A. Z., Vincent, J. L., Corbetta, M., Van Essen, D. C., & Raichle, M. E. (2005). The human brain is intrinsically organized into dynamic, anticorrelated functional networks. *Proceedings of the National Academy of Sciences, 102*(27), 9673–9678.

Fransson, P. (2005). Spontaneous low-frequency BOLD signal fluctuations: An fMRI investigation of the resting-state default mode of brain function hypothesis. *Human Brain Mapping, 26*(1), 15–29.

Friedman, J., Jack, A. I., Rochford, K., & Boyatzis, R. (2015). Antagonistic neural networks underlying organizational behavior. In D. A. Waldman & P. A. Balthazard (Eds.), *Organizational Neuroscience* (Vol. 7, pp. 115–141). Emerald.

Goleman, D. (2006). The socially intelligent. *Educational Leadership, 64*(1), 76–81.

Golland, Y., Bentin, S., Gelbard, H., Benjamini, Y., Heller, R., Nir, Y., Hasson, U. & Malach, R. (2007). Extrinsic and intrinsic systems in the posterior cortex of the human brain revealed during natural sensory stimulation. *Cerebral Cortex, 17*(4), 766–777.

Gottfredson, R. K., Wright, S. L., & Heaphy, E. D. (2020). A critique of the leader–member exchange construct: Back to square one. *Leadership Quarterly, 31*(6), 101385.

Graen, G., & Schiemann, W. (1978). Leader–member agreement: A vertical dyad linkage approach. *Journal of Applied Psychology, 63*(2), 206.

Graen, G. B., & Uhl-Bien, M. (1991). The transformation of professionals into self-managing and partially self-designing contributors: Toward a theory of leadership-making. *Journal of Management Systems, 3*, 25–39.

Graen, G. B., & Uhl-Bien, M. (1995). Relationship-based approach to leadership: Development of leader–member exchange (LMX) theory of leadership over 25 years: Applying a multi-level multi-domain perspective. *Leadership Quarterly*, 6(2), 219–247.

Greicius, M. D., Krasnow, B., Reiss, A. L., & Menon, V. (2003). Functional connectivity in the resting brain: A network analysis of the default mode hypothesis. *Proceedings of the National Academy of Sciences*, 100(1), 253–258.

Hatfield, E., Cacioppo, J. T., & Rapson, R. L. (1993). Emotional contagion. *Current Directions in Psychological Science*, 2(3), 96–100.

Ibarra, H., Kilduff, M., & Tsai, W. (2005). Zooming in and out: Connecting individuals and collectivities at the frontiers of organizational network research. *Organization Science*, 16(4), 359–371.

Jack, A. I., Dawson, A. J., Begany, K. L., Leckie, R. L., Barry, K. P., Ciccia, A. H., & Snyder, A. Z. (2013). fMRI reveals reciprocal inhibition between social and physical cognitive domains. *NeuroImage*, 66, 385–401.

Kendall, L. D. (2016). *A theory of micro-level dynamic capabilities: How technology leaders innovate with human connection*. Doctoral dissertation, Case Western Reserve University. ProQuest Dissertations, 28078332.

Khawaja, M. S. (2011). *The mediating role of positive and negative emotional attractors between psychosocial correlates of doctor–patient relationship and treatment adherence in type 2 diabetes*. Doctoral dissertation, Case Western Reserve University. ProQuest Dissertations, 3497554.

Leah, J. (2017). *Positive impact: Factors driving business leaders toward shared prosperity, greater purpose and human wellbeing*. Doctoral dissertation, Case Western Reserve University. ProQuest Dissertations, 28099776.

Leary, M. R., Tambor, E. S., Terdal, S. K., & Downs, D. L. (1995). Self-esteem as an interpersonal monitor: The sociometer hypothesis. *Journal of Personality and Social Psychology*, 68, 518–530.

LeDoux, J. E. (2009). Emotion circuits in the brain. *Focus*, 7(2), 274–274.

Lewin, K. (1936). *Principles of Topological Psychology*. McGraw-Hill.

Lord, M. (2015). Group learning capacity: The roles of open-mindeness and shared vision. *Frontiers in Psychology*, 6, 150.

Mahon, E. G., Taylor, S. N., & Boyatzis, R. E. (2014). Antecedents of organizational engagement: Exploring vision, mood and perceived organizational support with emotional intelligence as a moderator. *Frontiers in Psychology*, 5, 1322.

Martinez, H. A., Rochford, K., Boyatzis, R. E., & Rodriguez-Chaves, S. (2021). Inspired and effective: The role of the ideal self in employee engagement, well-being, and positive organizational behaviors. *Frontiers in Psychology*, 12, 1641.

McClelland, D. C., & Boyatzis, R. E. (1982). Leadership motive pattern and long-term success in management. *Journal of Applied Psychology*, 67(6), 737.

McKee, A., Boyatzis, R. E., Johnston, F., & Johnston, F. (2008). *Becoming a Resonant Leader: Develop your Emotional Intelligence, Renew your Relationships, Sustain your Effectiveness*. Harvard Business Press.

Miller, S. P. (2014). Next-generation leadership development in family businesses: The critical roles of shared vision and family climate. *Frontiers in Psychology*, 5, 1335.

Mossholder, K. W., Richardson, H. A., & Settoon, R. P. (2011). Human resource systems and helping in organizations: A relational perspective. *Academy of Management Review*, 36(1), 33–52.

Munroe, R. L. (1955). *Schools of Psychoanalytic Thought: An Exposition, Critique, and Attempt at Integration*. Holt.

Neff, J. E. (2015). Shared vision promotes family firm performance. *Frontiers in Psychology*, 6, 646.

Overbeke, K. K., Bilimoria, D., & Somers, T. (2015). Shared vision between fathers and daughters in family businesses: The determining factor that transforms daughters into successors. *Frontiers in Psychology*, 6, 625.

Owens, B. P., & Hekman, D. R. (2016). How does leader humility influence team performance? Exploring the mechanisms of contagion and collective promotion focus. *Academy of Management Journal*, 59(3), 1088–1111.

Pearce, C. L., & Ensley, M. D. (2004). A reciprocal and longitudinal investigation of the innovation process: The central role of shared vision in product and process innovation teams (PPITs). *Journal of Organizational Behavior*, 25(2), 259–278.

Pittenger, L. M. (2015). Emotional and social competencies and perceptions of the interpersonal environment of an organization as related to the engagement of IT professionals. *Frontiers in Psychology*, 6, 623.

Quinn, J. F. (2015). The affect of vision and compassion upon role factors in physician leadership. *Frontiers in Psychology*, 6, 442.

Quinn, R. W., & Dutton, J. E. (2005). Coordination as energy-in-conversation. *Academy of Management Review*, 30(1), 36–57.

Raichle, M. E., MacLeod, A. M., Snyder, A. Z., Powers, W. J., Gusnard, D. A., & Shulman, G. L. (2001). A default mode of brain function. *Proceedings of the National Academy of Sciences*, 98(2), 676–682.

Raichle, M. E., & Snyder, A. Z. (2007). A default mode of brain function: A brief history of an evolving idea. *Neuroimage*, 37(4), 1083–1090.

Ryan, R. M., & Frederick, C. (1997). On energy, personality, and health: Subjective vitality as a dynamic reflection of well-being. *Journal of Personality*, 65(3), 529–565.

Schriesheim, C. A., Castro, S. L., & Cogliser, C. C. (1999). Leader–member exchange (LMX) research: A comprehensive review of theory, measurement, and data-analytic practices. *Leadership Quarterly, 10*(1), 63–113.

Stanley, R. O., & Burrows, G. D. (2001). Varieties and functions of human emotion. In R. L. Payne & C. Cooper (Eds.), *Emotions at Work: Theory, Research and Applications for Management* (pp. 3–19). Wiley.

Tian, L., Jiang, T., Liu, Y., Yu, C., Wang, K., Zhou, Y., Song, M., & Li, K. (2007). The relationship within and between the extrinsic and intrinsic systems indicated by resting state correlational patterns of sensory cortices. *Neuroimage, 36*(3), 684–690.

Waldman, D. A., Ward, M. K., & Becker, W. J. (2017). Neuroscience in organizational behavior. *Annual Review of Organizational Psychology and Organizational Behavior, 4*, 425–444.

Weick, K. E. (1979). *The Social Psychology of Organizing*. Addison-Wesley.

The Myth of the Passions: Reason, Emotions and Ethics in Leadership*

Joanne B. Ciulla

The misinterpretation of passion and reason, as if the latter were an independent entity, and not a state of the relationship between all of the various passions and desires; and as though every passion did not possess its quantum of reason.
(Nietzsche, *The Will to Power*, section 387)

INTRODUCTION

Philosophers, artists, psychologists and ordinary people have long regarded emotions or what some philosophers call 'the passions' as a part of human nature that needs to be controlled by reason. In ethics, emotions are usually considered an enemy within. Our feelings engage in a Manichean struggle with reason, which is why we enlist ethical principles, virtues, society, law and religion to beat them into submission. Philosopher R. C. Solomon (1993) calls this struggle between reason and emotion the *myth of the passions*, which designates *objective reality* and the cool hand of rationality as the masters and emotions as second-class citizens. The myth is embedded in our everyday conceptions of ourselves. We talk about feelings as if we are passive, helpless martyrs to them. Emotions happen. They carry us away and violate our free will. We fall in love, get paralysed by fear, plagued with remorse, haunted by guilt, felled by shame, seized by anger and struck by jealousy. Nevertheless, like Solomon, some believe emotions have a rich cognitive content that dispels the perception that they are *blind forces that have no selectivity or intelligence about them* (Nussbaum, 2003, p. 11).

Leadership is as much about emotion as it is about reason. Separating where feelings begin and reason ends is not easy and, I will argue, not wise. Those who assume the myth of emotions may be perplexed or disappointed when the relationship between leaders and followers defies logic, as is the case in polarised societies where truth is in the eye of the beholder. We fear emotions because they threaten us with 'irrational' harmful behaviour. Yet, are our emotions misguided more often than our thoughts? Are they any more dangerous than the detrimental products of rational minds? Consider the many rationally calculated acts of foolishness and cruelty that leaders and others have perpetrated in history and daily life.

In leadership studies, most research on emotion and leadership focuses on emotional intelligence (EI). Emotional intelligence is the ability to *identify, assess and control one's own emotions, the emotions of others and that of groups* (Goleman

1996, p. 4). Researchers use self-awareness, self-regulation, motivation, empathy and social skills to measure EI in leaders and others. If you put 'emotional intelligence and leadership' into Google Scholar, you find 1,500,000 articles. The idea of EI is also popular among practitioners and in public discourse because it offers a way to make sense of people. Nonetheless, EI also places boundaries on how we understand and research emotions in leadership.

This chapter offers an examination of three problems with EI that constrain our understanding of emotions in leadership by focusing on the individual, when emotions are also social constructions. The chapter will first challenge the notion that EI is a different form of intelligence from general intelligence. (For this chapter, I will refer to general intelligence as intelligence or general intelligence.) The American Psychological Association (APA) defines intelligence as *the ability to derive information, learn from experience, adapt to the environment, understand, and correctly utilise thought and reason* (APA, 2020). I argue that the line between EI and general intelligence is so fuzzy that it is a distinction without a difference. Separating EI from general intelligence conflates intelligence as an ability to know with knowledge about emotions. The second problem is that EI falls prey to the myth of the passions by separating emotions and reason. In doing so, EI fails to consider the intelligence of emotions or how emotions work in concert with reason. The third and most important problem with EI is that it can confuse or obscure the difference between leaders who lack EI with leaders who are unethical. Leaders who appear to not possess EI may simply not care about the well-being of their followers. As we will see, emotions influence ethical behaviour but are not independent determinants of it. After exploring these three problems, we look at why they matter for researchers, practitioners and those who want to make sense of leaders and followers in today's politically polarised world.

IS EMOTIONAL INTELLIGENCE DIFFERENT FROM INTELLIGENCE?

Background: The Passion for Emotional Intelligence

Leadership research examines a wide range of questions about emotions. The literature encompasses charismatic leadership, emotional labour, emotional contagion and dyadic leadership (Connelly & Gooty, 2015). The concept of emotional intelligence is not new (Riggio et al., 2002). It originated from a comment that Thorndike made in a 1920 *Harper's Magazine* article. Thorndike, a distinguished pioneer in research on general intelligence or IQ, expressed concern about the narrowness of instruments used to measure intelligence (Landy, 2005). He mused, *man has not some one amount of one kind of intelligence, but varying amounts of different intelligences* (Thorndike, 1920, p. 228). He concluded measuring people for their mechanical, social and abstract intelligence would be more practical. When Thorndike realised that the initial IQ test questions were too narrow and needed to measure other aspects of intelligence, he might have added them to the IQ test. Instead, he decided to call them different intelligences requiring different tests.

In 1937, Thorndike and Stein differentiated social intelligence from general intelligence. They note that one aspect of social intelligence is *the ability to understand and manage people* (Thorndike & Stein, 1937, p. 275), and Salovey and Mayer's (1990) seminal work on EI focused on this element of social intelligence. Like Thorndike and Stein's characterisation of social intelligence, they divide EI into knowledge about emotions in the self (intrapersonal) and others (interpersonal). Salovey and Mayer acknowledge the conflicting perspectives of researchers on emotion and reason. Noting, in one tradition, emotions are considered at war with reason and affect a *complete loss of cerebral control* and contain *no trace of conscious purpose* (p. 185). At the same time, another tradition sees *emotion as an organizing response because it adaptively focuses cognitive activities and subsequent action* (p. 186). In the first tradition, the idea of emotional intelligence is an oxymoron, which is why Salovey and Mayer embrace the second. *We view emotions as organized responses, crossing the boundaries of many psychological subsystems, including the physiological, cognitive, motivational, and experiential systems* (1990, p. 186). Nevertheless, Salovey and Mayer still embrace the myth of the passions. They write, *People who don't learn to regulate their emotions may become slaves to them* (1990, p. 201).

Goleman's book, *Emotional Intelligence: Why it Can Matter More Than IQ* (1996), popularised Salovey and Mayer's ideas. Goleman attempts to connect emotions with reason but instead separates reasoning about emotions from reasoning about other things. He too talks about *when passions overwhelm reason* (Goleman 1996, p. 4). Goleman (2001) says EI consists of self-awareness, self-regulation, motivation, empathy and social skill. The widespread use of 'emotional intelligence' appeals to common sense. We all know and experience people who do not care about the feelings of others or are boorish. In the popular use of the term, EI refers to people who are sensitive to others. Human resource professionals have embraced the idea of EI, partly because insensitive employees can poison the workplace.

Furnham (2006) compares the popularity of EI to Dale Carnegie's 1936 bestseller *How to Win Friends and Influence People* (1963). Carnegie's book offers readers advice on developing the people skills needed to get ahead in work and life. Given the book's enduring popularity, Carnegie's lessons resonate. Furnham notes the upbeat 'anyone can do it' motivational tone of EI. Although some researchers believe Goldman's work discredited serious EI research (Jordan & Troth, 2004), the fact that EI is popular is not grounds for condemning it. After all, saying certain employees lack EI sounds much better than calling them 'jerks' or worse.

The Emotional EI Debate in Leadership Studies

In leadership studies, the primary interest in EI concerns how it contributes to leader effectiveness. Usually, the working hypothesis is if leaders have EI, they will be effective leaders (Ashkanasy et al., 2005; George, 2000; Jin et al., 2017; Kanwal et al., 2017; Kerr et al., 2006; Prati, et al., 2003). EI is considered both a trait and an ability. The trait construct of EI measures self-reported perceptions of emotions, whereas ability EI measures emotion-related cognitive abilities (Petrides, 2011). This conceptual split between *descriptions* of what leaders *are* like and *prescriptions* of what they *should be* like frequently pop up in leadership research. Perhaps this is because leadership scholars are unconscious prisoners of the *Are leaders born or made?* question. Also, some cannot resist the lure of discovering the ideal traits of leaders.

Leadership scholars can be surprisingly emotional in their criticism and defence of EI. For example, Antonakis (2004) argues that EI is not more helpful in predicting leader effectiveness than the Big Five personality traits. He says researchers and practitioners have been *captivated* and *hoodwinked* by the *apparent magic* of EI and its ability to affect organisational performance by claims that are *unsubstantiated, exaggerated, misrepresented, or simply false* (2004, p. 171). I will not delve into the criticisms of the methodology and validity of EI research (see Conte, 2005). At this point, my concern is whether EI and general intelligence are different and, later in the chapter, the implications for understanding ethics in leadership.

In a lively exchange about EI with Ashkanasy and Dasborough, Antonakis maintains that you do not need EI to understand and manage other people's emotions. Instead, he says, *what makes leaders good depends on how intelligent they are* (Antonakis et al., 2009, p. 250). Assuming Solomon's 'myth of emotions', Antonakis sees emotions as a 'curse' because they can bog down leaders and get in the way of exercising intelligence. Ashkanasy and Dasborough rebut Antonakis's claim with neuroscience research on the relationship between emotion and reason. For example, Damasio (2005) describes cases where people have neurological conditions that destroy their ability to feel but not their IQ. When emotion is not part of the reasoning process, *reason turns out to be more flawed than when emotion plays bad tricks on our decisions* (Damasio, 2005, p. xii). Damasio concludes that emotions play diverse roles in reasoning and deliver crucial cognitive information. Hence, Damasio's work offers an empirical counterpoint to Antonakis's claim that emotions get in the way by showing that we cannot reason well without them. Yet, the debate does not end there.

Ashkanasy and Dasborough also submit that whether EI matters in leadership depends on your definition of effective leadership. General intelligence is more relevant if being effective is about achieving task goals. If we define leader effectiveness in relationships between leaders and followers, understanding emotions matter more. Nonetheless, this is not an either-or question. The general question about EI is whether it is separate from general intelligence and the knowledge we have about people and the world. Leadership researchers mostly want to know if EI is an antecedent of effective leadership. Antonakis says no, you only need IQ – people without emotional intelligence are just not intelligent. Ashkanasy and Dasborough say yes, you need both, which still begs the question of whether they are separate intelligences or if EI is an area of knowledge that we gain through our general intelligence.

Is EI an Intelligence or Knowledge?

The discussion about EI in leadership studies reflects the struggle between reason and emotion mentioned at the beginning of the chapter. Perhaps the only problem with EI is calling it an intelligence. If everything we know about and know how to do were an intelligence, we would talk, as

Gardner (2011) does, about multiple intelligences such as naturalist intelligence, linguistic intelligence, mathematical, musical intelligence, etc. He defines intelligence in three ways, all compatible with what philosophers mean by reason. First, intelligence is a property of humans; second, it is variable among people; and, third, it is how people carry out their goals and solve problems. Gardner says there *can never be a single irrefutable and universally accepted list of intelligence.* (Gardner, 2011, p. 64). Gardner is correct because his *intelligences* refer to areas of knowledge. Do we need musical intelligence to learn how to play the piano, or can any intelligent person learn? A person may have to practice, be talented, or both to play the piano. Yet, most people can use their general intelligence to learn how to play the piano.

Emotional intelligence and Gardner's multiple intelligences refer to knowledge about various things. Does general intelligence give us the potential to know anything, or is it limited to knowing only certain things? Philosophers call knowledge about the world propositional knowledge or knowledge that can be put into a true or false statement – for example, 'Tilly knows that Tom is sad.' This statement is only true if Tom is indeed sad. Some philosophers divide knowledge into *knowing how* and *knowing that* (Ryle & Dennett, 2000), but both can be forms of propositional knowledge (Stanley, 2010). For example, 'Tilly knows how to play the piano' is empirically verifiable. All we need do is listen to her play to see if it is true.

If EI is knowledge of emotions in the self and others, it is verifiable. If I know how to control my feelings and do not control them, then the statement 'I know how to control my emotions' is false. If I say, 'Tom is sad,' and Tom is actually happy, then it is false that I know how Tom feels. Some people may know more, have more experience and pay more attention to emotions than others, but they still employ the same tools of reasoning that constitute general intelligence. Just because some people are better at playing the piano and others are better at understanding emotions does not mean they possess a separate faculty of intelligence for each.

What some call 'intelligences' may be talents, proclivities, or, as Antonakis suggests, something about a leader's Big Five personality traits. If general intelligence is something all humans possess, then it is the machinery for obtaining knowledge about emotions, not the knowledge about emotions. Intelligence is not propositional in that it is not expressible in true or false statements. Only the information we use intelligence to get is propositional. We learn about how others feel through experience and other means. Granted, some people pay more attention to what others feel or to music, but this has more to do with their preferences, personalities, context and experience, and how they use their minds to know the world. Knowing different things does not mean people have other intelligences. We do not teach courses on intelligence. However, consultants and HR professionals sell programmes to teach EI, so it must be a kind of knowledge. Getting rid of the idea of EI as a separate intelligence clears the way for examining the role of emotions in general intelligence.

REASON AND INTELLIGENT EMOTIONS

Aristotle on Practising Emotions

For centuries, philosophers have examined the interplay between ethics, reason and emotions. When philosophers talk about reason, they refer to most aspects of the APA's definition of intelligence mentioned earlier (although rationalists and empiricists have different views on reason and knowledge). Philosophers have referred to emotions as feelings, passions, affections and sentiments. However, the origins of the word emotion show why it is relevant to leadership and ethics. Emotion comes from the Latin *movere*, or move, and the French word *émouvoir*, which means to agitate or excite (Oxford Languages). In psychiatry, there is no ambiguity about what emotion means. It is motivation (Gabriel, 1998). When we consider the big picture of our lives, the passions, which consist of emotions, moods and desires, move us to act and bestow meaning on our experiences (Solomon, 1993).

In contrast to Solomon, who says emotions give meaning to our lives, Aristotle believes life gives meaning to our feelings. Unconstrained by the Cartesian mind–body or the modern mind–brain dichotomy, Aristotle regards reason and emotion as one with ethical judgement and personal and social behaviour. As an empiricist, he says we learn how to have emotions from experience. Like virtues, there are right and wrong ways to have emotions. Aristotle writes:

> it is possible, for instance, to feel the emotions of fear, confidence, lust, anger, compassion, and pleasure and pain generally, too much or too little, and in either case wrongly; but to feel them when we ought, on what occasions, towards whom, why, and as, we should do, is the mean, or in other words the best state, and this is the property of virtue.
>
> (2003, *Book II*, Chapter 5)

Goleman (1996) cites this same passage and calls it *Aristotle's challenge*. However, instead of understanding Aristotle's statement as an experiential learning process, Goleman casts it as the *rare skill* of emotional intelligence (1996, p. xix). Yet, for Aristotle, knowing how to feel is not a skill; it is part of practical knowledge (*phronesis*). We learn how, what and why we feel over time, situation and experience. For example, extreme emotions like rage are appropriate and useful in the face of severe social injustice (Cherry, 2021) but less appropriate when you spill your coffee.

Aristotle believed our thoughts, decisions, actions and virtues must be accompanied by the right feelings that are appropriately felt. Because of this, we are responsible for how and what we feel regardless of the context. So, for Aristotle, emotions do not happen to us. We learn how to have them from society and the people around us. Hence, emotions are both personal and social constructions.

Emotions and Power

Aristotle's most extensive and provocative discussion of emotion in leadership and as a personal and social construction is in the *Rhetoric* ([4th c. BCE], 1984a). He sees emotions as part of persuasion and essential to forming social bonds, making ethical decisions, determining justice and getting and holding power. *The emotions are all those feelings that so change men as to affect their judgments, and that are also attended by pain or pleasure* (Aristotle, 1984a, p. 2194, 1378a 21). Contrary to the myth of emotions, Aristotle does not believe emotions occur against the backdrop of objective reality. Elements of what he calls *character type* also condition how and what we feel. For Aristotle, character types include a person's virtues and vices, personal choices, age and fortune (meaning birth, wealth and power) (1984a, p. 2213, 1388b 35-1389a 2). So, personality, talent and other things determine people's emotions and how they are socially constructed. (In modern terms, these would include the Big Five personality traits.)

Emotions occur in the context of the meanings we discover around us and depend on our identity, history and social context. Aristotle argues that power also affects the type and extent of emotions people experience. For example, he says a king has privileged access to feelings of magnanimity in a way that the pauper does not. Contemporary scholars such as Hirschman make a similar point. Hirschman says the most powerful people are *particularly well endowed with passions in comparison to lower orders and could therefore do harm on a huge scale* (1997, pp. 69–70). One example of this is lust for glory. Indeed, poor, powerless people may also lust for glory, but Hirschman's point is that their emotions would not be the same as a king's because their character type and context are different. In other words, because an angry king can do more damage than an angry commoner his anger has a larger dimension. So, even when a king has the same emotions as a commoner, he may feel them differently because their meaning and potential impact differ due to his power and context.

The king's emotions are distinctive and, according to Aristotle, they matter more. In the *Poetics* (1984b), Aristotle says the best tragedies are about people in powerful places because their misfortune is more significant than that of a commoner and does a better job of eliciting pity and fear from the audience. We see this today in how we regard leaders and celebrities. As Gross (2007) observes, *Princess Diana's death could provoke mourning across the world while the death of an indigent provokes apathy or, more accurately, nothing at all* (p. 4). He argues that institutions like poverty and slavery give the rich and powerful a broader emotional range that has nothing to do with their worth and everything to do with what he calls *the technologies of social emotion*. According to Gross, we have not democratised emotions. By this he means, for example, that subordinates cannot express the same range of emotions as those in power at work. Like Aristotle and Hirschman, Gross thinks our place in the social world shapes how we experience and express feelings.

Both Gross and Aristotle challenge the idea that emotional and, for that matter, social intelligence are distinct from general intelligence. Both talk about how we learn emotions and virtues and how they are rational and socially constructed. While we all feel love, anger and other emotions, we can experience them in different ways, depending on our personalities and social context. Hence, understanding the feelings of ourselves and others requires so much of our general intelligence to obtain and process the relevant empirical knowledge that it is challenging to discern what another intelligence would do. Furthermore, as Aristotle notes, through experience, we learn how to make our emotions intelligent, meaning we have them at the right time, the right way and towards the right people. It might well be that leaders who lack EI are, as Antonakis says, simply not intelligent, or as Aristotle argues, ignorant about the practice of emotions. It is also possible that leaders who seem deficient in EI are not deficient in empathy or other qualities of it but, as I will discuss later, simply unethical.

EMPATHY, EI AND ETHICS

Empathy

We usually think of empathy as knowing or understanding how someone feels. Sometimes people confuse empathy with moral concepts such as care, kindness, compassion, concern and sympathy. While empathy may result in ethical or at least admirable behaviour, you do not have to be empathetic to be kind or have compassion for others. When we empathise, we draw an analogy between what someone feels and our feelings in a similar situation. We imagine how they must feel, based on knowledge, observation and experience.

It is possible to understand how others feel even if someone is incapable of having feelings. For example, people with alexithymia cannot feel, describe, or identify emotions (Taylor and Bagby, 2000). In one case, a woman afflicted with alexithymia was unable to feel sad. Yet, she learnt about what made others sad and how to express sympathy in situations like the death of a spouse (Linder, 2021). Alexithymia raises epistemological questions about empathy: do you have to experience an emotion to understand it in others? And, to what extent can we know if the word someone uses for a feeling refers to the same feeling that we have when we use that word? For example, as Wittgenstein et al. (1991) famously asked, can we ever really know what someone means when using a word like 'pain' for a feeling?

The Downsides to Empathy

In his book *Against Empathy* (2016), Bloom challenges the idea that empathy results in good behaviour. What appears to be an empathetic response to someone is often a response to their emotional display, such as laughter or tears. He argues that empathy does not always motivate ethical behaviour. Sometimes our response to empathising with someone who suffers is to relieve the pain we share with them. So, if it pains you to see a homeless person out in the cold every day, rather than helping him, you avoid him by taking a different route to work. Empathy sometimes reinforces prejudices. Bloom says white people may believe that Black lives matter, but most of them find it easier to empathise with the plight of people like themselves than Black people. So, for Bloom, empathy does not always inspire intelligent decisions about our ethical obligations to other people. It can make us overrate the present because of how we feel and underrate the future, impacting a leader's ability to make ethical and strategic decisions. Bloom's argument that empathy can turn out badly takes us full circle to the tension between EI and general intelligence. He shows that empathy does not always motivate us to fill our obligations to others.

Passions and Intelligent Emotions

Hume has a different perspective on emotions. For him, emotions help determine what is ethical and unethical. Hume also acknowledges the tension between emotions and reason: *Nothing is more usual in philosophy, and even in common life, than to talk of the combat of passion and reason, to give the preference to reason, and assert that men are only so far virtuous as they conform themselves to its dictates* ([1739] Hume et al., 2000, Part III, section III). In contrast to Kant ([1985] Kant & Beck, 1989), who says ethics is about reason, Hume believes ethics is about emotions. He says emotions create our will (motivation) to act, and reason plays a supporting role by supplying the necessary information. Some psychologists agree. For example, Zajonc (1980) found that while emotions always come before cognition, they do not always follow it. Emotions sometimes tell us things before we know about them – for example, we say, 'I had a feeling that was true' before we find out if it is. Hume views the passions as intelligent emotions that tell us what is right and wrong. There are times when doing something does not feel right before knowledge and reason tell you why. Emotions constitute moral sentiments that facilitate moral judgements based on feelings of pleasure and pain, approval or disapproval, agreeable or disagreeable and love or hate. We discover what is good and evil by our emotional response to experience. Hence, for Hume, emotions respond to the social world and formulate knowledge of what is ethical and unethical.

A brain scan experiment illustrates what Hume means by intelligent emotions (Helmuth, 2001). Researchers took images of subjects' brains as they tried to solve the Trolley Problem. The Trolley Problem is an ethical dilemma where you must decide whether to switch the tracks of a runaway trolley. One direction kills one person or the other kills five. A third option is to stop the trolley by pushing a large man off a bridge, saving six people but killing the large man. When researchers presented the problem to subjects in magnetic resonance imaging machines, the areas of their brains associated with emotions lit up when offered the option of pushing the man off the bridge but not when considering the other options. The subjects, like my students, strongly felt it was wrong to push the man off the bridge, even though killing one person to save five or killing one person to save six encompass the same utilitarian logic. The experiment illustrates how emotions motivate moral action and are intelligent (or unintelligent) about right and wrong. Intelligent emotions are the 'gut feelings' we have about what is right or wrong that we cannot always put into words.

EI and Ethics

Defenders of EI would argue that those gut feelings we get about ethics are precisely what EI describes because they demonstrate self-knowledge about our feelings and those of others. I agree that EI describes a type of knowledge but have argued it is not an intelligence. The gut feeling is an intelligent emotion. It is intelligent because our general intelligence processes personal experience, social context and other information. It is not a different intelligence. Gut feelings lead to good or bad moral judgements and behaviour based on personality, knowledge and social context. As Aristotle and Hirschman note, the feelings of powerful people differ from powerless people because of their respective places in the world. While Hume's passions motivate ethical behaviour, the fundamental part of moral judgement and behaviour still rests on values, social norms and moral principles, which is why having the qualities articulated in EI does not mean leaders will behave ethically. If anything, regarding EI as a separate intelligence may potentially mask unethical behaviour in leaders.

It is sometimes tough to tell if leaders misbehave because they are unethical, lack relevant information, or are not intelligent (Ciulla, 2011). EI tells us that leaders who do not have EI are not in touch with their feelings and the feelings of others, do not have empathy, social skills and the ability to use emotions to motivate people. What is not clear is whether this is a failure of EI, fixable by education and training about emotions, or a paucity of virtues and commitment to moral principles. Using EI to assess leaders' behaviour can obscure unethical behaviour. Some leaders do not know or consider what they and other people feel because they do not care. Such leaders have an ethical deficiency that EI will not cure. Perhaps some leaders seem to lack empathy, but in Kantian terms they might fail to respect the dignity of human beings or not think they have a duty to treat others as rational agents who are ends-in-themselves. Such leaders would be morally deficient rather than lacking intelligence about emotions. They do not possess what Kant ([1785] Hume et al., 1989) calls *a good will*, meaning the rational desire to fill their duties to others and be fair, honest, just, etc.

Leaders may not know about people's feelings either because of narcissism or power difference. Moreover, leaders who fail to embrace their responsibilities to the people in their organisations may do so not because they are insensitive but because they either do not understand the moral obligations of leadership or want to fulfil those obligations. Leaders are responsible for looking after followers even if they do not empathise or understand their followers' feelings. They do not have to feel care *about* their followers if they know it is their duty to care *for* them and act on it (Ciulla, 2020). Feeling care for followers is an emotional response to them; however, leaders can also have strong feelings about their duty to care or do what feels right regardless of how they feel about others. As noted earlier, emotions are also social constructions. Leaders learn about their role, and this knowledge informs their theory and practice of how to fill it. Our knowledge about the world informs how we feel about what we do in it. Leaders may not have strong emotions about or empathy for their followers, but they may have strong emotions about their responsibilities to followers.

Without the appropriate virtues or habits of moral behaviour and commitment to promoting the organisation's well-being, EI may not lead to ethical leadership. There is nothing to keep leaders from using their EI to manipulate followers. Empathy is neither a necessary nor sufficient condition for ethical behaviour. And last, but not least, attributing the insensitive behaviour of leaders to a scarcity of EI, a deficiency they can fix, may obfuscate what is really a lack of moral virtues, values and commitments. A low IQ or EI is not a moral failing. People do not have to be intelligent or sensitive to be ethical. Still, since emotions are inseparable from intelligence and moral behaviour, we need to differentiate socially awkward or emotionally distant leaders from those who fail to respect people regardless of their lot in life. Hence, having EI does not necessarily mean that leaders or their leadership will be ethical. It might be more important to see if a leader has the intelligent emotions described by Aristotle than intelligence about emotions.

WHAT DOES THIS CRITIQUE OF EI MEAN FOR LEADERSHIP RESEARCH?

This chapter has critically examined three problems with EI as a means of understanding how it constrains our understanding of emotions in leadership. I first argued that EI is knowledge about emotions and not a separate intelligence. If we go back to the essential characteristics of EI – self-awareness, self-regulation, motivation, empathy and social skill (Goleman, 2001), – they all fall under the category of things that we know about or how to do. The second was that EI embraces the myth of the passions that puts emotions and reason in separate intelligences. Aristotle and Hume show how emotions can be intelligent and integrated parts of reason. Both see emotions as social constructions that we use our intelligence to derive from empirical knowledge about the world, whereas EI refers to emotions as personal abilities or traits. Lastly, focusing on EI can mask or deflect unethical behaviour in leaders.

At this point, a passionate defender of EI might argue, 'there's nothing new here, EI encompasses everything you have talked about'. To them, I would reply, no, EI is a descriptive and epistemological construct that seeks to describe something about a leader's traits, knowledge and ability. I have argued that EI is not a separate intelligence but merely part of regular intelligence. The EI literature also carries normative undertones yet having EI does not necessarily mean that a leader is ethical. These criticisms add up to my main point. First, dividing intelligences and embracing the myth of the passions inhibits understanding what is most significant about emotions, their part in reason and ethics. And, second, there is a danger in assessing leaders' good or bad behaviour based on EI, when it may be their possession or lack of ethical commitment. Lastly, regarding leadership studies, do we need 1.5 million articles on something that may be common sense? I agree with Humphrey et al. (2016) that leadership studies would benefit from the rich and varied research on emotions that would take us beyond the constraints of EI. Future research should explore the logic of emotions and attempt to understand the social life of emotions. To do so requires more empirical studies of their rationale and social dynamics.

The practitioner reading this chapter may wonder, what's in it for me? The issues I have discussed concerning ethics and EI have implications for leader development. As mentioned, EI, in a more generic sense, is useful for HR professionals. While weeding out or reforming insensitive people is valuable and desirable in organisations, having employees with diverse personalities and dispositions can also be beneficial. What is essential to know is whether the insensitive 'jerks' are unethical ones. Current and future leaders may not need to understand how they or others feel if they are ethical and polite. Teaching ethics and etiquette may be more practical than giving employee seminars on EI. After all, etiquette is about more than what fork to use. It concerns smoothing social interactions and making people feel comfortable (Ciulla, 1986). While good etiquette may not motivate people like emotions do, it can dampen down the noise so that diverse types of people can work together in organisations.

And, finally, a bored reader yawns and asks, 'In the larger scheme of things, so what? Doesn't this boil down to a quibble about calling EI an intelligence?' Separating EI from general intelligence may not be helpful when the relationship between emotions, reason and ethics matters more when trying to understand leadership in today's world. We have moved from the age of reason to the age of emotion. In this post-Enlightenment, post-modern, post-truth era, feelings, not facts, often determine who leads, what leaders do, how they lead and their relationships with followers. Where society is polarised, it is all too easy to say the choices of leaders and followers on the other side defy reason. They do not when you eschew the myth of emotions and the idea that EI is separate from general intelligence. Beneath their surface, emotions have intelligence. They inform ethical judgements and light up the meanings of our world's social and historical conditions. We cannot dismiss or ignore emotions in leadership studies. They explain what human behaviour means, and there is no meaning without them.

REFERENCES

Antonakis, J. (2004). On why 'emotional intelligence' will not predict leadership effectiveness beyond IQ or the 'Big Five': An extension and rejoinder. *Organizational Analysis*, *12*(2), 171–182. https://doi.org/10.1108/eb028991

Antonakis, J., Ashkanasy, N. M., & Dasborough, M. T. (2009). Does leadership need emotional intelligence? *Leadership Quarterly*, *20*(2), 247–261. https://doi.org/10.1016/j.leaqua.2009.01.006

American Psychological Association (APA) (2020). *APA Dictionary of Psychology*. APA. https://dictionary.apa.org/intelligence

Aristotle (1984a). *Rhetoric*. Trans. W. R. Roberts. Ed. Barnes, A. J. *The Complete Works of Aristotle: The Revised Oxford Translation. Volume II. Edited by Jonathan Barnes.* Princeton University Press, 2152–2269.

Aristotle (1984b). *Poetics*. Trans. R. Kassel. Ed. A. J. Barnes. *The Complete Works of Aristotle: The Revised Oxford Translation. Volume II. Edited by Jonathan Barnes.* Princeton University Press, 2316–2340.

Aristotle (2003). *Nichomachean Ethics*. Trans. D.P. Chase. Project Gutenberg eBook #8438. https://www.gutenberg.org/files/8438/8438-h/8438-h.htm#chap02

Ashkanasy, N. M., & Daus, C. S. (2005). Rumors of the death of emotional intelligence in organizational behavior are vastly exaggerated. *Journal of Organizational Behaviour*, 26(4), 441–452. https://doi.org/10.1002/job.320

Bloom, P. (2016). *Against Empathy: The Case for Rational Compassion*. Harper Collins.

Carnegie, D. (1963). *How to Win Friends and Influence People* (Revised edn). Pocket Books.

Cherry, M. (2021). *The Case for Rage: Why Anger is Essential to Anti-Racist Struggle*. Oxford University Press.

Ciulla, J. B. (1986). Elbows off the boardroom table. *Harvard Business Review*, 64(5), 46–50.

Ciulla, J. B. (1995). Leadership ethics: Mapping the territory. *Business Ethics Quarterly*, 5(1), 5–28. https://doi.org/10.2307/3857269

Ciulla, J. B. (2011). Ethics and effectiveness: The nature of good leadership. D. V. Day & J. Antonakis (Eds.), *The Nature of Leadership* (2nd edn, pp. 438–468). Sage.

Ciulla, J. B. (2020). Do leaders need to have tender hearts? Emotion and the duty to care. In L. Tomkins (Ed.), *Paradoxes of Leadership and Care: Critical and Philosophical Reflections*. Edward Elgar.

Connelly, S., & Gooty, J. (2015). Leading with emotion: An overview of the special issue on leadership and emotions. *Leadership Quarterly*, 26(4), 485–488. https://doi.org/10.1016/j.leaqua.2015.07.002

Conte, J. M. (2005). A review and critique of emotional intelligence measures. *Journal of Organizational Behavior*, 26(4), 433–440. https://doi.org/10.1002/job.319

Damasio, A. (2005). *Descartes' Error (text only) by A. Damasio*. Penguin (Non-Classics).

Furnham, A. (2006). Explaining the popularity of emotional intelligence. In K. R. Murphy (Ed.), *A Critique of Emotional Intelligence: What Are the Problems and How Can They Be Fixed?* Routledge.

Gabriel, Y. (1998). Psychoanalytic contributions to the study of the emotional life of organizations. *Administration and Society*, 30(3), 291–314.

Gardner, H. E. (2011). *Frames of Mind: The Theory of Multiple Intelligences* (3rd edn). Basic Books.

George, J. M. (2000). Emotions and leadership: The role of emotional intelligence. *Human Relations*, 53(8), 1027–1055. https://doi.org/10.1177/0018726700538001

Goleman, D. (1996). *Emotional Intelligence: Why It Can Matter More Than IQ*. Bloomsbury.

Goleman, D. (2001). What makes a leader? *Harvard Business Review on What Makes a Leader?* Harvard Business School Press. https://search-ebscohost-com.newman.richmond.edu/login.aspx?direct=true&db=nlebk&AN=79106&site=ehost-live

Gross, D. M. (2007). *The Secret History of Emotion: From Aristotle's Rhetoric to Modern Brain Science* (1st edn). University of Chicago Press.

Helmuth, L. (2001). Cognitive neuroscience: Moral reasoning relies on emotion. *Science*, 293(5537), 1971a–11972. https://doi.org/10.1126/science.293.5537.1971a

Hirschman, A. O., Adelman, J., & Sen, A. (2013). *The Passions and the Interests: Political Arguments for Capitalism before its Triumph (Princeton Classics, 2)* (Revised edn). Princeton University Press.

Hume, D., Norton, D. F., & Norton, M. J. (2000). *A Treatise of Human Nature (Oxford Philosophical Texts)* (New edn). Oxford University Press.

Humphrey, R. H., Burch, G. F., & Adams, L. L. (2016). The benefits of merging leadership research and emotions research. *Frontiers in Psychology*, 7. https://doi.org/10.3389/fpsyg.2016.01022

Jin, S., Seo, M. G., & Shapiro, D. L. (2017). How and when emotional intelligence aids leaders' effectiveness: An empirical test. *Academy of Management Proceedings*, 2017(1), 15882. https://doi.org/10.5465/ambpp.2017.15882abstract

Jordan, P. J. & Troth, A. C. (2004). Managing emotions during team problem solving: emotional intelligence and conflict resolution. *Human Performance*, 17(2), 195–218. https://doi.org/10.1207/s15327043hup1702_4

Kant, I., & Beck, L. W. (1989). *Foundations of the Metaphysics of Morals* (2nd edn). Pearson.

Kanwal, A. A., Yasmin, R., & Bhatti, O. K. (2017). Impact of leaders' emotional and cultural intelligence on leadership effectiveness: Mediating role of transformational leadership. *Journal of Management and Research*, 4(2), 1–38. https://doi.org/10.29145/jmr/42/040201

Kerr, R., Garvin, J., Heaton, N., & Boyle, E. (2006). Emotional intelligence and leadership effectiveness. *Leadership & Organization Development Journal*, 27(4), 265–279. https://doi.org/10.1108/01437730610666028

Landy, F. J. (2005). Some historical and scientific issues related to research on emotional intelligence. *Journal of Organizational Behavior*, 26(4), 411–424. https://doi.org/10.1002/job.317

Linder, J. (2021). My quest for sadness. *New York Times*, 28 June. https://www.nytimes.com/2020/10/13/well/mind/sadness-alexithymia-emotions.html?referringSource=articleShare

Nietzsche, F. Trans. Kaufmann, W., & Hollingdale, R. J. (1968). *The Will to Power*. Vintage.

Nussbaum, M. C. (2003). *Upheavals of Thought: The Intelligence of Emotions* (1st edn). Cambridge University Press.

Oxford Languages. https://languages.oup.com/google-dictionary-en/

Petrides, K. V. (2011). Ability and trait emotional intelligence. In T. Chamorro-Premuzic, S. von Stumm & A. Furnham (Eds.), *The Wiley-Blackwell Handbook of Individual Differences* (pp. 656–678). Wiley Blackwell.

Prati, L. M., Douglas, C., Ferris, G. R., Ammeter, A. P., & Buckley, M. R. (2003). Emotional intelligence, leadership effectiveness, and team outcomes. *International Journal of Organizational Analysis*, *11*(1), 21–40. https://doi.org/10.1108/eb028961

Riggio, R. E., Murphy, S. E., & Pirozzclo, F. J. (Eds.) (2002). *Multiple Intelligences and Leadership*. Lawrence Erlbaum.

Ryle, G., & Dennett, D. C. (2000). *The Concept of Mind* (1st edn). University of Chicago Press.

Salovey, P., & Mayer, J. D. (1990). Emotional intelligence. *Imagination, Cognition and Personality*, *9*(3), 185–211. https://doi.org/10.2190/dugg-p24e-52wk-6cdg

Solomon, R. C. (1993). *The Passions: Emotions and the Meaning of Life* (2nd edn). Hackett.

Stanley, J. (2010). Knowing (how). *Noûs*, *45*(2), 207–238. https://doi.org/10.1111/j.1468-0068.2010.00758.x

Taylor, G. J., & Bagby, R. M. (2000). An overview of the alexithymia construct. In R. Bar-On & J. D. A. Parker (Eds.), *The Handbook of Emotional Intelligence: Theory, Development, Assessment, and Application at Home, School, and in the Workplace* (pp. 40–67). Jossey-Bass.

Thorndike, R. L. (1920). Intelligence and its uses. *Harper's Magazine*, *140*, 227–235.

Thorndike, R. L., & Stein, S. (1937). An evaluation of the attempts to measure social intelligence. *Psychological Bulletin*, *34*(5), 275–285. https://doi.org/10.1037/h0053850

Wittgenstein, L., Anscombe, G. E. M., & Anscombe, E. (1991). *Philosophical Investigations: The German Text, with a Revised English Translation 50th Anniversary Commemorative Edition* (3rd edn). Wiley Blackwell.

Zajonc, Robert.B. (1980). Feelings and thinking, preferences need no inferences. *American Psychologist*, *35*(2), 15–175.

Responsible Leadership: From Theory Building to Impact Mobilisation

Brad Jackson, Steve Kempster, Chaturi Liyanage, Sudong Shang and Peter Y. T. Sun

INTRODUCTION

Although the literature has not generated a widely accepted definition of *responsible leadership* (RL), we argue that responsible leaders engage with multiple stakeholders (both internal and external to the organisation) in order to foster responsible change and development. The purpose of this chapter is to galvanise broader scholarly interest in understanding and critiquing the nascent research on RL. We are doing this in order to encourage the development of responsible leadership practices that can genuinely address the full gamut of social, economic, environmental and cultural challenges we all share in common. In making the case that RL is best not seen as a distinctive theory of leadership but rather as a particular orientation of leadership, we outline a series of five reorientations along the following dimensions that we believe are critical for both leadership scholars and leadership practitioners to consider and embrace:

- away from studying leadership behaviour, towards studying decisions, actions and outcomes;
- away from a preoccupation with leader(s) and followers, towards leader(s) and stakeholders (those internal and external to the organisation);
- away from a short-term focus towards a long-term focus;
- away from place-agnostic approach towards a place-centric approach;
- away from individualistic (and heroic) approaches to leading towards collaborative approaches with a strong emphasis placed upon stewardship.

In assimilating these dimensions, we note that RL should have a strong normative base with an underlying premise that those in leadership positions – that is, those with a disproportionate influence on sense-making, decisions and actions – need to be fully considerate of the leadership implications for the stakeholders with which they and their organisation engage. Kempster and Jackson (2021) recently gave prominence to the leader–stakeholder relationship in RL within the corporate context. They highlighted the importance for those in leadership positions to be clear about what they *seek to achieve, why, for whom, and where* in their leadership (2021, p. 46).

In essence, we argue that the fundamental objective of RL is to enhance the interest of others both within the organisation and those connected with and affected by the organisation. We highlight the salience of a wide range of stakeholders that have an interest in an organisation and can affect or be affected by the organisation. Without their support the organisation might cease to exist (Freeman & Reed, 1983). Traditionally, primary stakeholders in a typical corporation were recognised as being its investors, employees, customers and suppliers but more recently our recognition of stakeholder salience has been widened to include regulators, unions, professional associations, community and interest groups as well as the broader citizenry under a broader shift away from *shareholder capitalism* to *stakeholder capitalism* (Schwab, 2021).

The normative orientation that we shall develop in this chapter draws upon a utilitarian ethic – in which the greatest benefit is generated for the greatest number (Greene, 2015). We recognise that the criticism that is often levelled at this normative orientation is also shared with advocates of perhaps more mainstream leadership orthodoxy with which we critically take issue in this chapter (for example, transformational or authentic leadership, LMX, servant leadership, charismatic or trait-based leadership). These theories have also developed from a normative ideal in order to generate desired leader behaviours. In common with these theories, we seek not only to ground this utilitarian orientation within the realities of everyday routines and pressures within individual organisations, but we also strive to extend the sphere of concern to encompass the wider and more complex context of the grand challenges facing humanity which we argue are even more significant to leadership responsibilities.

Leadership studies have an essential need to connect its scholarship with helping to address the enormous challenges that face society, the environment and indeed humanity. Although there has been growing attention paid to the grand challenges in leadership studies, we sadly agree with Tourish's observation that *mainstream leadership theories are of little help, since an environment of radical uncertainty means that leaders have less information, expertise and resources to guide them than is often assumed* (2020, p. 262). Abundant data are available that point to the extraordinary crisis we face throughout this century and into the next. For example, there is as much carbon-dioxide in the atmosphere now as when the dinosaurs were wiped from the planet by a meteorite; the consequence then was a sea-level rise in excess of 10 metres! The major cities and countries will be severely impacted unless such carbon-dioxide can be extracted from the atmosphere, but carbon-dioxide levels continue to rise. The planetary boundary conditions for supporting life have been breached (Steffen et al., 2015). *The clock is ticking. We are not on life support yet; but in another 50 years, the world will need some extraordinary ventilators to keep our grandchildren alive* (Kempster & Jackson, 2021, p. 47).

We structure the chapter to first take an overview of the research and commentary on RL – highlighting where RL has convergence and divergence with prominent leadership theories such as authentic, ethical and transformational leadership. The overriding conclusion from our review is to assert that RL should be less focused on providing a distinctive (and competing) theory of leadership that is fixated on explicating the leader–follower axis and more focused on creating a compelling orientation for leading thought, influence and action towards enhancing stakeholder interests. RL can, therefore, be responsible for replacing the predominant leader–follower axis with an alternative considerably more generative and impactful leader–stakeholder axis.

The second part of the chapter explores the shift from the leader–follower focus to the leader–stakeholder focus by drawing on the conceptual lens which we describe as 'Us and Them'. An argument for a pragmatic utilitarian ethic is developed for the advancement of RL that offers place-based regenerative thinking for the advancement of stakeholders' value – that is, 'Us *with* Us'. We conclude the chapter by taking a systems view of the key challenges that RL faces. This offers a framework through which to integrate micro-, meso- and macro-perspectives on RL that will enable us to strengthen the position of RL within leadership studies.

MAKING SENSE OF THE RESPONSIBLE LEADERSHIP AND RELATED LITERATURES

Responsibility within leadership has been the subject of considerable research (e.g., Berns et al., 2009; Stahl & de Luque, 2014; Tsui, 2021; Waldman & Siegel, 2008). Despite its importance, scholars have bemoaned the lack of a comprehensive understanding of responsibility within leadership, which has impacted the progress of this important area of research (Tsui, 2021). We want to address two fundamental issues within the RL literature.

First, while the existing literature addresses responsibility within leadership using the term 'responsible leadership' (RL), there is no unifying understanding of what RL means and encompasses (Maak et al., 2016; Miska & Mendhall, 2018). Various scholars have provided differing definitions, as well as explanations, for RL. We can contrast the earliest definition provided by Maak and Pless (2006) who define RL as *a relational and ethical phenomenon, which occurs in social processes of interaction with those who affect or are affected by leadership and have a stake in the purpose and vision of the leadership relationship* (2006, p. 99) with one of the most recent definitions provided by Lin et al. (2020) who define RL as *a leader's ethical act of inspiring others through his/her motivating, communicating with, empowering and convincing employees to engage with responsible development and positive changes* (2020, p. 1). Our review of these different approaches to RL has led us to identify four broad orientations that are common to the way in which RL is conceptualised. Responsible leaders tend to: 1) adopt a multi-stakeholder orientation; 2) are moral and ethical and have altruistic motives; 3) seek to balance profit and societal outcomes; and 4) are able to influence and motivate subordinates to be involved in achieving common good for the organisation's wider stakeholders.

Guided by stakeholder theory, several leadership scholars have advocated for RL to be considered as a separate theoretical construct which is substantially different from and superior to other leadership styles (e.g., Maak & Pless, 2006; Pless & Maak, 2011). They differentiate RL from other styles of leadership based on the fact that: current leadership theories tend to focus on specific personality characteristics (e.g., charisma and authenticity – see Chapter 9, Leadership as contextualised personality traits, Chapter 12, Authentic leadership or authenticity in leadership? and Chapter 13, Redefining followership) through which leaders exercise power over their followers; current leadership theories are also value-free where morality is absent; current leadership theories are solely internally focused; and current leadership theories are void of purpose (Maak & Pless, 2006; Pless & Maak, 2011).

This brings us to the second issue we have identified with respect to RL. That is, responsibility is already implicitly subsumed within other positive leadership styles such as transformational, transactional, ethical, servant and shared leadership. Such leadership approaches have been empirically shown to result in socially responsible outcomes (see Table 18.1). They are also inherently moral and ethical in nature (Hoch et al., 2018). A growing body of existing work has discussed the relationships between these styles of leadership and corporate social responsibility (CSR). Further, we shall show that positive forms of leadership styles are related to the four orientations of RL that we have synthesised from the RL literature.

Drawing on the findings from the various empirical studies that are summarised in Table 18.1, we provide the following critique of the four orientations that have been offered as the primary basis for conceptualising RL as a distinct leadership theory.

Orientation 1: Adopting a multi-stakeholder approach. Our review reveals that other positive leadership styles also involve exercising a multi-stakeholder orientation in promoting CSR, which is the dominant orientation and outcome of RL. For example, transformational leaders have been observed to value building relationships with all stakeholders, and thus adopt a stakeholder perspective (Groves & LaRocca, 2011). Pless et al. (2012) argue that the transformational leadership style is well suited to leaders who have high accountability towards a broader group of stakeholders. Servant leaders are also theorised to go beyond employees to embrace stakeholders within the community and society (Liden et al., 2008).

Orientation 2: Moral and ethical with altruistic motives. Studies have shown that the moral values of ethical leaders are congruent with social responsibilities (based on universal values). Such values trickle down to the work units and to individual employees, resulting in a stronger ethical climate and greater trust in the organisation (Tourigny et al., 2019). Servant leaders are altruistically driven to consider the good of others, extending beyond the organisations to the community (Liden et al., 2008). For this reason, Christensen et al. (2014, p. 174) claim that servant leadership *is the only leadership style in which CSR is both foundational to the conceptual model and specified as an expected outcome of the model.* The moral and ethical qualities of leaders that are foundational to CSR are arguably more explicitly articulated in the positive forms of leadership styles than they are in the RL literature. This assertion is underlined in a recent empirical study by Lips-Wiersma et al. (2020), which measured RL by combining scores on transformational, ethical and shared leadership and argued that the combination best represents leaders' ethics and morality, especially in matters to do with social responsibility. This critical intersection between ethics, reason, and the passions of leaders is explored in considerable detail in Chapter 17, The myth of the passions.

Orientation 3: Balancing social and profit outcomes. Balancing social and profit orientations is an important behaviour of responsible leaders. A number of researchers have identified associations between positive leadership styles and enhanced economic performance of organisations (e.g., Liden et al., 2014; Wang et al., 2011) and the propensity for firms to purposefully engage in socially responsible behaviours (Groves &

Table 18.1 Studies addressing relationship between positive leadership styles and social outcomes

Type of leadership	Key points and references
Transformational leadership	• Dual leadership styles, involving transformational and transactional leadership styles, are needed to manage CSR complexities (Egri & Herman, 2000) • Transformational leadership relates to CSR (Du et al., 2013; Groves & LaRocca, 2011; Pless et al., 2012; Verissimo & Lacerda, 2015) • The intellectual stimulation component of transformational leadership relates to CSR (Waldman et al., 2006b)
Transactional leadership	• Transactional leadership is important to ensure CSR outcomes for the organisation (Benn et al., 2010; Pless et al., 2012; Stahl & de Luque, 2014; Strand, 2014)
Charismatic leadership	• Charismatic leadership relates to CSR (Vlachos et al., 2013) • CEOs with strong stakeholder values tended to be viewed by followers as highly visionary (Waldman et al., 2006a; de Luque et al., 2008)
Ethical leadership	• Employees' external CSR perception (looking outwards) is positively related to the ethical climate of the organisation but is fully mediated by their perception of top management's ethical leadership (looking upwards) (Hansen et al., 2016) • Ethical leadership relates to CSR (Pasricha et al., 2018; Stahl & de Luque, 2014; Tourigny et al., 2019; Zhu et al., 2014) • Ethical leadership is used as a moderator (De Roeck & Farooq, 2018)
Servant leadership	• Servant leadership strengthens socially responsible behaviours (Afsar et al., 2018; Luu, 2019) • Servant leadership is related to CSR (Pless et al., 2012)
Shared leadership	• Participative leadership results in positive CSR perceptions (Lythreatis et al., 2019) • Self- and shared leadership will diminish CSIR behaviour (Pearce & Manz, 2011; Pearce et al., 2014)

Note: CSR = corporate social responsibility; CSIR = corporate social irresponsibility.

LaRocca, 2011). In this way, it has been suggested that positive leadership behaviours achieve a balance between profit and social outcomes.

Orientation 4: Influencing and motivating subordinates to be involved. The ability of positive forms of leadership styles to motivate and influence subordinates to be involved is well established in the literature. Leaders do this by structuring the organisation to support CSR (Strand, 2014), and by influencing others through role modelling (Tourigny et al., 2019).

Given these relationships between existing positive leadership styles (i.e., transformational, transactional, ethical, servant and shared leadership) and the four responsibility orientations, we challenge the view that RL should be considered a unique and distinctive leadership approach. The RL literature has noted the need for responsible leaders to display a wide and complex range of behaviours (e.g., Egri & Herman, 2000; Pless, 2007). Our review shows that responsibility can be enacted through most positive forms of leadership styles. This suggests that a broad repertoire of behaviours that leaders can engage in to influence individuals within the organisation to become more responsible. They do not necessarily need to engage in a separate group of behaviours that are circumscribed by RL.

This leads us to question whether or not RL, as conceptualised in the extant literature, should be viewed as a distinct leadership theory (Miska & Mendenhall, 2018; Waldman & Balven, 2014). We recommend instead that future work should be geared to better understanding how leadership promotes responsibility within and beyond the organisation. To that end, we argue that RL is better viewed as a process, with antecedents, moderators and outcomes, operating at three levels, which is outlined in Figure 18.1.

Given that the current relevant research is somewhat incomplete, a more systematic examination of the antecedents, outcomes and boundary conditions (moderators) of responsibility in leadership is needed (Miska & Mendenhall, 2018). We argue that responsible outcomes are enabled through the effective combination of antecedents and moderators and the engagement with various forms of leadership (including the suggested positive approaches to leadership). There has been some limited work on understanding responsibility within leadership as a process, but more work is needed to build on previous

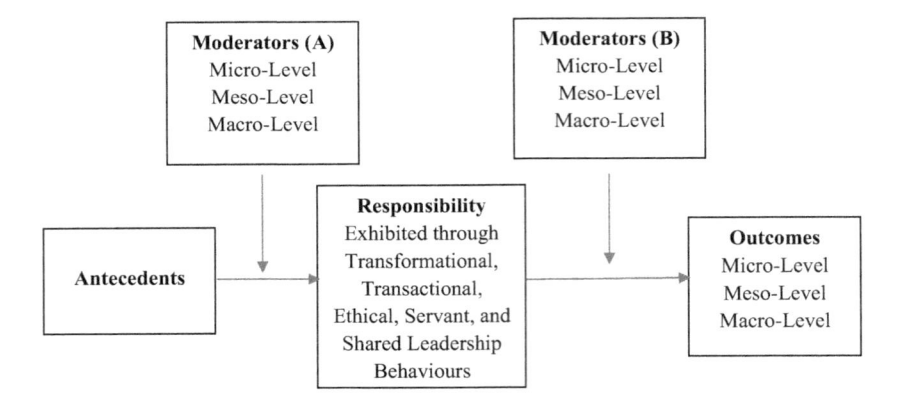

Figure 18.1 Theoretical Framework

attempts. For example, Stahl and deLuque (2014) discussed leaders' characteristics (antecedents) (e.g., leaders' personality traits and moral philosophies) and how they are moderated by proximal and distal contexts (e.g., national culture as a distal context and organisational code of conduct as a proximal context). Maak et al. (2016) theorised how leader value orientations (antecedents) lead to RL behaviours, which in turn lead to organisational engagement with CSR. These theoretical works have contributed to our understanding of the process of RL, but have limitations. Stahl and deLuque (2014) describe leaders' responsible behaviours as *doing good* and *avoiding harm*, but do not address how responsibility plays out in the organisational role behaviours of leaders. The theoretical work of Maak et al. (2016) is limited to considering a narrow set of leader's values (i.e., fiduciary duties and social welfare orientation). They also focus on leadership that drives organisational engagement only with political CSR. That is, *activities that are traditionally understood as governmental responsibilities (e.g., enforcing human rights, and providing public goods and services, such as education and infrastructure)* (2016, p. 464).

The moderators and outcomes are addressed at three levels: the micro (i.e., individual), meso (i.e., organisational) and macro (i.e., societal) levels (see Figure 18.1). There has been empirical work done to better understand how some of the components of the framework, shown in Figure 18.1, for responsibility in leadership works. For example, responsibility requires leaders to have a moral base (Groves & LaRocca, 2011) and a responsible orientation (Witt & Stahl, 2016) (i.e., antecedents). When responsibility is enacted, there appears to be a close association between it and the manifestation of meaningful work (Lips-Wiersma et al., 2020), as well as greater work engagement (Lin et al., 2020) (i.e., outcomes at the micro-level). In consequence, the organisation becomes an attractive place to work in and for (Voegtlin & Scherer, 2019). However, the leader's motivation to act responsibly is strengthened in a national culture with lower power distance and higher humane orientation (i.e., macro-level Moderator A) (Witt & Stahl, 2016). Further, it is noted that the outcome for the organisation is strengthened when there is a deliberate strategic choice made for social responsibility (i.e., meso-level Moderator B) (Maritz et al., 2011). Due to space constraints, we are unable to discuss all of the empirical work that has been conducted on explicating antecedents, moderators and outcomes. However, Figure 18.1 provides a framework to synthesise the existing empirical work on antecedents, moderators and outcomes.

Importantly, we argue that responsible outcomes are enabled through the effective combination of antecedents and moderators and the engagement with positive forms of leadership styles. Because responsibility can be enacted through various positive forms of leadership behaviours, these behaviours lead to outcomes at the micro, meso and macro levels, something insufficiently addressed in extant literature (Miska & Mendenhall, 2018). For example, transformational leadership behaviours are more effective at the meso level than other positive forms of leadership behaviours such as servant leadership (Van Dierendonck et al., 2014). Through visioning and the ability to motivate followers to embrace a common purpose, transformational behaviours are able to create a valued socially responsible identity for their organisation. Since leaders exercising transformational behaviours tend to occupy central positions in social networks (Bono & Anderson, 2005), as well as integrate the interests of various external stakeholders for the public good (Sun & Anderson, 2012), their behaviours are better able to create macro-level outcomes such as influencing political agendas and global governance mechanisms. Servant leadership behaviours, in contrast, are better at realising outcomes at the micro level because they are highly relational (Van Direndonck et al., 2014). By engaging with subordinates, leaders exercising servant leadership behaviours are better able to inculcate a community orientation in them (Liden et al., 2008). Shared leadership is also able to realise outcomes at the micro level by enabling employees to employ different CSR perspectives to manage CSR complexities (Benn et al., 2010), leading to positive internal CSR perceptions (Lythreatis et al., 2019). Therefore, these broad sets of positive leadership behaviours are able to realise responsible outcomes at different levels.

In summary, while some initial light has been cast on some of the antecedents for RL, an important need remains for a comprehensive understanding of the process and the nature of RL. Through our review of the RL literature, as well as the companion set of positive leadership theories, we have concluded that we are better to shift the focus of our work from advancing RL as a distinct theory of leadership which advocates for a distinctly different type of leadership behaviours within and between organisations. Rather we believe it is better to focus our attention on articulating RL as the responsibilities of leading, emphasising the understanding of the processes by which responsibility is enacted and pursued. This leads us to a guiding research question that we believe needs to shape the nomological network associated with the responsibility in leadership: how is responsibility enacted through leadership? An important set of ancillary questions related to this question are: what are leaders seeking to achieve, for whom, why and where? Addressing these questions, linked with an understanding of how responsibility is enacted, would substantially reorient leadership studies. Researchers would be seeking to understand how leaders embrace and address the great challenges of leadership. Such an orientation moves leadership studies away from an entrenched preoccupation with the leader–follower axis towards the potentially more enlightening leader–stakeholder axis (Kempster et al., 2019; Maak & Pless, 2006). Next, we examine the (re)orientation through the lens of 'Us and Them'.

RESPONSIBLE LEADERSHIP: SHIFTING FROM 'US *AND* THEM' TOWARDS 'US *WITH* THEM'

Out of the way it's a busy day I've got things on my mind;

For want of the price of tea and a slice the old man died.

These lyrics are from the 'Us and Them' song that anchored the emblematic *Dark Side of the Moon* album (Waters & Wright, 1973). They capture the essence of tribes competing, protecting and promoting themselves and those they affiliate with. Our metaphoric interpretation of a 'tribe' within the leadership lexicon are the leader–follower tribes: a sense of close relationships with a discrete set of people that leads to valuing Us as distinct from Them. For example, the theory of leader–member exchange (LMX) offers the notion of 'in' and 'out' groups and the respective positive or negative attributions associated with Us (the in-group members) and Them (the out-group others) (Graen & Uhl-Bien, 1995).

Leadership studies have historically been transfixed with the notion of leader–follower – indeed it is often incommensurate in many scholars' minds to consider leadership without followers (Kempster et al., 2020). The leader–follower relationship is explored in detail in Chapter 10, Implicit leadership and followership theories. Our RL orientation foregrounds the relationship between leaders and stakeholders: an emphasis to consider the questions outlined in the previous section – leadership for what, why and for whom? (Kempster & Jackson, 2021). An RL orientation seeks to encourage those leading to dissolve away the binary divide of Us and Them in a conscious effort to understand and relate to others and to work across tribal boundaries (Greene, 2015). A leader–stakeholder orientation seeks to understand what constitutes value for each of the stakeholders and to pursue action to realise such value. We shall now develop an argument for framing RL as Us *with* Them through the ethics of utilitarianism.

Ethics has been highlighted earlier as a prominent dimension of RL. Although we shall give prominence here to utilitarian ethics, this is but one of a number of ethical lenses through which to view leadership decisions and actions (see, for example, Chapter 17, The myth of the passions). Utilitarianism is associated with realising the 'greatest happiness' or the 'greatest good' – an outcomes orientation, often conflated (unfairly) with the phrase 'the end justifies the means'. The concerns with utilitarianism are important and we wish to address these upfront. Political history can highlight the abuses of leadership in the pursuit of the 'greatest good' (Sanders & Grint, 2019). In fact, certain scholars argue that embracing a utilitarian mindset may fuel 'tyrannical majoritarianism', where the majority's interests and wants are considered to be more important than that of the minorities (Udofia, 2017). Such abuses are also relevant in the business context where the rationalisation for unethical acts is justified in the pursuit of 'higher loyalties' – to advance the organisation (Anand et al., 2004). Utilitarianism leans towards an assessment of the greatest good – often linked with cost–benefit analysis in search of balancing the utility of an act in terms of calculating the value of the good against the harm across a range of stakeholders. Given the notion that leaders must grapple with 'bounded ethicality', such a calculation is typically fraught with difficulties and is highly subjective. Further, in such a calculation individual interests can be overlooked as their interests are no more than equal weight to everyone else – sacrificing one person to give benefit to many more. In this way, utilitarianism needs to be balanced against notions of justice and rights – most fundamentally, human rights. These concerns do require attention and need to be properly weighed. Yet they do not throw out the significant complementary value a utilitarian orientation can bring to the development of RL – particularly with addressing the Us and Them issue.

The ethical position of being in pursuance of the 'greatest good' was first articulated by the social commentator and philosopher Jeremy Bentham (1748–1832) and was associated with the hedonistic maximisation of pleasure and the minimisation of pain. In the 21st-century neoliberal consumption society, we may associate such hedonism with extrinsic goods. However, Bentham and, subsequently, John Stuart Mill (1806–73) were seeking to extend greatest happiness beyond extrinsic goods to embrace intrinsic valuable human needs such as friendship, trust and love (Crane et al., 2019) – similar to MacIntyre's (1985) thesis of external and internal goods. Mill's development of utilitarianism offers the idea of acts and rules: acts are associated with situations while rules look at underlying principles of an action that generate greater good for society over the long term. The long-term perspective provides a pragmatic embrace of Kantian deontological or categorical ethics – where someone acts according to rules or principles. It is to the long-term rule orientation of the greatest good that we shall develop here in understanding the application of utilitarianism to RL.

We have argued in this chapter that RL should be reoriented to the leader–stakeholder axis. A utilitarianist articulation would suggest that stakeholder interests (such as employees, suppliers, customers, community and the environment) would be viewed as valued independent constituents rather than as means of production or sources of revenue (Crane et al., 2019). Traditional framing of stakeholder management has been oriented to minimising the impact on business value – Us against Them. In contrast, RL would seek to understand and realise stakeholders' value as a core leadership responsibility (Kempster et al., 2019) – that is, Us *with* Them.

That being said, we need to emphasise balance and pragmatism as part of such a utilitarian responsibility. Where, for example, should the boundary be placed for utilitarian judgement? Should Steve (co-author) give up his subscription for Sky Sports (the benefit of which is for him and his family) and give that money to support a charity (the benefit would be to many more people)? And how does Steve assess the maximum benefit realised from particular charities? And which charities should he select? From the perspective of those in organisational leadership positions, what is the greatest good and for whom? As such, defining 'Us' is mired in complexity, and one may argue is partly dependent on the moral dilemma at play in a given scenario.

Greene (2015) advocates for a pragmatic utilitarian position that seeks to explore the greatest good through exploration of evidence. Rather than the absolute assertion of rights as the moral justification of action, utilitarianism demands that the evidence be tabled and considered. Some rights are supported by overwhelming evidence; other rights can be interpreted differently in particular contexts. Where rights are beyond debate (such as the right to life, or anti-slavery) there is a sense *that these matters have been settled* (Greene, 2015, p. 308). Where there is a dispute, we tend to move towards tribes and the assertion of belief. The pragmatic utilitarianist then seeks evidence for the argument for where the greatest benefit lies. In this way, the benefit the tribe seeks to derive, and for whom, becomes transparent. Translated to the context of an organisational leader, the approach would reflect seeking to understand how decisions and actions may generate benefits (i.e., value) for others (i.e., organisational stakeholders). We orient the pragmatist approach to frame the greatest benefit to the stakeholders within an organisation's ecosystem, as will be discussed subsequently. Echoing such views, Bazerman (2020) suggests that a pragmatic utilitarian mindset will help leaders to navigate the myriad of contradictions and tensions faced in organisations.

Given the premise of utilitarianism discussed thus far, one might well question how organisations can inculcate an 'Us with Them' utilitarian mindset among their stakeholders, particularly considering that we are biologically predisposed to take care of ourselves and our close circles (Greene, 2015). In this chapter, we propose two interrelated mechanisms that responsible leaders can tap into when developing an 'Us *with* Them' orientation: a) by drawing on Kempster et al.'s (2019) model of 'good dividends' we explore how a utilitarian notion in organisations can become manifest; and b), in line with this, we argue that fostering a sense of meaningfulness within and across these 'dividends' provide a useful mechanism for bridging the divide between 'Us and Them'.

The argument of orienting the utilitarianist principle towards a related ecosystem has been outlined in Kempster et al.'s book, *Good Dividends: Responsible Leadership of Business Purpose* (2019). The primary argument of this book is centred on the realisation that responsible business leadership is both normative and pragmatic. We should use capitalism to change capitalism through RL in pursuit of the good dividends. The notion of good dividends reflects the returns that are yielded from investing in six capitals – financial, human, social, reputational, operational and planet-community. The pursuit of utilitarianism is reflected in the association of stakeholders with the dividends (benefits) from the capitals. For example, employees with human capital, shareholders with financial capital, communities and the environment with planet-community capital, customers with reputational capital. Among these stakeholders, the responsible leader embraces a more centralised position (compared to the traditional hierarchical top-down position), which not only provides the leader with more access to resources but facilitates greater stakeholder engagement (Maak & Pless, 2006; Pless, 2007; Voegtlin et al., 2012, as cited in Frangieh and Yaacoub, 2017). Drawing on systems thinking, Kempster et al. (2019) suggest the interconnectivity of these dividends – including planet-community, which offers a reframing of the notion of business towards pragmatic utilitarianism – a business in pursuit of the greatest good to its stakeholders, hence the term 'good dividends'.

Building on this framework, we argue that fostering a sense of meaningfulness within the people dividend (i.e., employees), in particular, will help to galvanise energy towards inculcating an 'Us *with* Them' utilitarian mindset. While meaningful work has been defined in different ways, the definition provided by Bailey et al. (2017) is particularly relevant in developing our thesis: the authors define meaningful work as *work that is personally enriching and that makes a positive contribution* (2017, p. 1). This echoes Martela and Pessi's (2018) twofold conceptualisation of meaningful work: a) work having a broader sense of purpose (i.e., contributing towards a greater good) *and* b) self-realisation (i.e., the intrinsic value of work – authenticity, autonomy, self-expression etc.). Drawing from these definitions of meaningful work we argue that a utilitarian 'Us *with* Them' mindset can be fostered through an integration of authenticity *and* purpose-related meaningful work mechanisms. However, it is important to emphasise that such a conceptualisation of meaningfulness does not suggest that we eschew other sources of meaning like belongingness, autonomy or self-efficacy, for instance. Rather we make the argument that in transcending to the realm of 'Us *with* Them', work should be both purposeful (i.e., working towards a pro-social good), and rooted in one's beliefs, values and aspirations (i.e., authentic self). In other words, in this context, working towards a pro-social good is intrinsically driven. Activating such a dual state of meaningfulness could be particularly useful in transcending the boundary to the realm of 'Us *with* Them', as one is tapping into the inherent, biological drive to focus on the self (Greene, 2015), while working towards a pro-social cause. In fact, drawing parallels between meaning and morality, Wolf (2010) argues that individuals will not only strive to attain moral objectives but in fact it will be more rewarding, *for* they *will be doing so not out of obedience to duty but out of love* (2010, p. 62). In this way, meaningful work becomes a useful resource to bridge the divide between 'Us and Them' and 'Us with Them'. While the notion of meaningfulness discussed thus far revolved around employees' work, it could help to create a wave of meaningfulness across other stakeholders as well. When employees have a sense of meaning in their work, not only will employee well-being, satisfaction and engagement increase but employee commitment will also rise, as employees are now emotionally intertwined with their work (Steger et al., 2012). As such, it is likely that employees will act as purveyors of meaning, inspiring other stakeholders both within and outside their organisation. In this way, more and more stakeholders will embrace the utilitarian or regenerative mindset of 'Us with Them'.

In recent work, Kempster and Jackson (2021) have elaborated the good dividends argument to explicitly connect with the notion of ecosystems through the related concepts of regenerative organisations and regenerative capitalism:

A healthy plant, animal, or human must grow to full stature. One can even say something similar of a community [or business], *which, unless it reaches a certain threshold of size and productive capacity, cannot expect to provide the range of services required in order to offer a satisfying life to each of its* [stakeholders].

(Wallis, 2010, p. 39)

We have highlighted the end of the sentence where resonance with utilitarianism becomes readily manifest. Every organisation is rooted in its particular ecosystem. Many organisations may be degenerative – extractive from their ecosystem through exploiting others (and the planet) in the pursuit of maximising financial dividends (Fullerton, 2015) – in a sense responsible only to shareholders, a short-term orientation that utilises employees, suppliers, communities and the environment as a means of production and customers as consumption. By contrast, a regenerative organisation seeks to enhance others and the planet through being central to its related ecosystem. Kempster and Jackson argue that as a consequence of the Covid-19 pandemic *corporate leaders have become powerfully reminded that they, like their corporations, are an integral part of a very delicate global ecosystem that needs to be nurtured in a considerably more responsible manner* (2021, p. 62).

Maak and Pless (2019) advocate that RL should be considered from a steward orientation. They suggest that we are at a point where we need to decide whether to continue feeding the machine or *put aside our differences and act in the interest of humanity* (2019, p. 139). They are appealing to those in leadership positions to let go of the straitjacket tailored by the dominant 'Us and Them' relationship. Reinterpreting Hans Jonas, we need to *consider the global conditions of human life, the distant future, as an unprecedented moral concern* (2019, p. 141). RL is fundamentally concerned with the human condition. Drawing on utilitarianism's guiding principles to understand and realise the greatest happiness provides vital moral scaffolding: scaffolding from which those in powerful leadership positions can seek to enhance the happiness of others – the respective stakeholders – within their related ecosystem.

We thus arrive at 'Us with Them' as a foundational utilitarian principle to drive an alternative orientation to leadership: a responsible orientation operating within a particular ecosystem that can generate 'good dividends' for all related stakeholders – including communities and the planet. By emphasising dividends to the planet, we bring to the fore the need to consider not only 'Us' but 'Us in the future'. As Anand and Sen resolutely conclude:

> We cannot abuse and plunder our common stock of natural assets and resources leaving future generations unable to enjoy the opportunities we take for granted. We cannot use up, or contaminate, our environment as [those controlling resources] wish, violating the [utilitarian] *rights and the interests of future generations.*
> (Anand & Sen, 2000, p. 2020)

TOWARDS A PROGRESSION OF RESPONSIBLE CONSCIOUSNESS

The progress from 'Us *and* Them' to 'Us *with* Them' reflects a process of increasing consciousness beyond the organisation towards a responsible partner that seeks to develop a regenerative ecosystem. Building on the discussion developed thus far, we seek to capture this movement through a four-tier model of organisational consciousness, through which we argue that the responsible leader orientation of leader–stakeholder relationship falls within the outer circles of 'Us *with* Them' and 'Us *with* Future Us'.

As illustrated in Figure 18.2, the model is displayed in terms of concentric circles, indicating increasing levels of consciousness and transcendence as an organisation moves from the inner circle (Me *and* You) to the outer circles (Us *with* Them, and Us *with* Future Us). In other words, each level represents a degree of consciousness and transcendence from the organisation's perspective. In the centre circle (i.e., Me *and* You), each individual is concerned with his or her own position in the company and is wired to think of themselves first, possibly fuelled by a 'perform or perish' (or 'survival of the fittest') culture. Within this sphere, the emphasis is on the individual's needs and personal goals over the interests and needs of the group. As such, it is likely for employees to think of work as a mere transaction, as a means of furthering the self; hence employees and other stakeholders may be driven by materialistic, extrinsic rewards. Moreover, within such an orientation, leaders may distance themselves from the employees, perceiving them as mere pawns in the game called business, therein reflecting a leader–follower orientation as illustrated in the model. Thus, egotistic values are likely to become the foundation of a 'Me *and* You' organisational orientation, where the language used may revolve around 'I', 'me' and 'my'.

In the second circle (Us *and* Them), organisations adopt a more tribalistic mindset through which employees and leaders feel a sense of belonging by being part of a valued in-group, and hence are likely to be driven by organisational norms and values. In comparison with the previous sphere, organisations that resemble an 'Us *and* Them' orientation tend to be less independent and more interdependent, emphasising and embodying the values, beliefs and goals of the group. At this level, the leader–follower relationship is united by a shared organisational purpose that commonly views the out-group as an external entity. Thus, relationships within such an orientation are family-like, where it is not uncommon to hear phrases

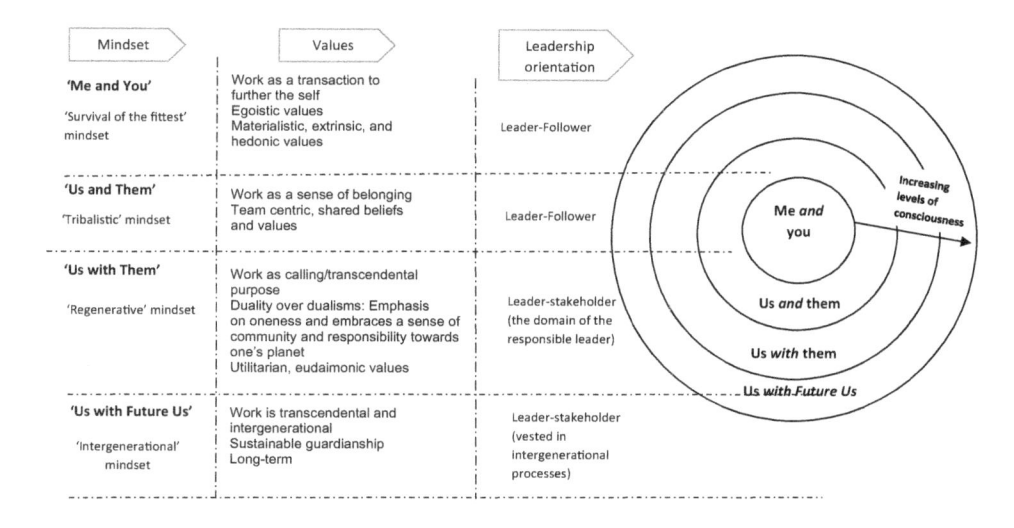

Mindset	Values	Leadership orientation
'Me and You' 'Survival of the fittest' mindset	Work as a transaction to further the self Egoistic values Materialistic, extrinsic, and hedonic values	Leader-Follower
'Us and Them' 'Tribalistic' mindset	Work as a sense of belonging Team centric, shared beliefs and values	Leader-Follower
'Us with Them' 'Regenerative' mindset	Work as calling/transcendental purpose Duality over dualisms: Emphasis on oneness and embraces a sense of community and responsibility towards one's planet Utilitarian, eudaimonic values	Leader-stakeholder (the domain of the responsible leader)
'Us with Future Us' 'Intergenerational' mindset	Work is transcendental and intergenerational Sustainable guardianship Long-term	Leader-stakeholder (vested in intergenerational processes)

Figure 18.2 Four-Level Model of Organisational Consciousness

like 'we are the best', therein fuelling a notion of 'our team' versus the rest. Such faux competition, coupled with unregulated capitalism, has created a breeding ground for corporations to increase profit – often ignoring the negative externalities created (Blakeley, 2016). For instance, the scandals witnessed at Enron, Siemens, Uber and Volkswagen are examples of the adverse repercussions of an 'Us *and* Them' and/or 'Me *and* You' competitive orientation that is often symptomatic of a tribalistic and/or individualist mindset.

At the outer circle (Us *with* Them), organisations are at a higher level of consciousness, where the focus is on realising the greater good for the greatest number of stakeholders. This changes the leadership orientation fundamentally, from that of the leader–follower to the leader–stakeholder relationship. Unlike the two other previous orientations the focus shifts towards the 'other', where the out-group which was previously perceived to be made of different types of individuals and entities is now conceptualised as similar, therein embracing a sense of oneness and coherence with one's community. Thus, in this realm, a sense of belonging is not to one's team/group but rather it is to one's community. In fact, at this level (and the next concentric circle – 'Us *with* Future Us'), responsible behaviours are perceived to be integral, non-negotiable aspects of an organisation's identity (Lehmann et al., 2010). For instance, Lehmann and colleague's case study of the Danfoss Group portrays an organisation *at an advanced stage of CSR development focusing on products and processes and employee relations* (2010, p. 153) even during times of financial crisis – therein alluding to a stakeholder orientation. Moreover, the authors found that the organisation's commitment and CSR capacity to learn were key catalysts that shaped their CSR practices (Lehmann et al., 2010). As such, we argue that it is this 'Us *with* Them' orientation that provides the fertile ground for a regenerative, purpose-led business model and is, thus, the domain of the responsible leader.

We can extend beyond the third level of consciousness to a fourth level. As an extension to 'Us *with* Them', when the good dividend focuses on the planet-community, the dividend spills over to future generations embracing the 'Them' as the 'Future Us'. This leads us to conceive a fourth 'Us *with* Future Us' concentric circle, where the mindset is intergenerational, purpose is transcendental and where long-term orientation and sustainable guardianship are key organisational values. While leadership orientation is still towards multi-stakeholders, the values that drive such engagement are intergenerational, leading to leadership that is collective and vested in intergenerational processes and purposes. For a greater elaboration of this level of consciousness, refer to Chapter 25, Indigenous leadership as a conscious adaptive system.

Research by Kempster and Halme (2019) illustrates three case studies of company-wide RL. The cases illustrate a progression from 'Us *with* Them' to 'Us *with* Future Us'. The third case is of St1; the owner, Mika Anttonen, comments on a carbon sink project underway in Morocco: *Biomass production would become established, local economies transformed. Communities enriched. Ecology transformed from desert to forest. This is about demonstrating the potential of what might be. We shall make the knowledge freely available* (2019, p. 104). A more prominent leader is former CEO of Unilever, Paul Poleman, who was named 'Captain Planet' by *Harvard Business Review* (Ignatius, 2012) – a title he earnt for his *audacious objectives* that abolished short-term reporting for long-term sustainable objectives. In his recent book, *Net Positive: How Courageous Companies Thrive by Giving More than they Take*, Poleman emphasises the need to go beyond sustainability initiatives by embracing *restorative, reparative and regenerative* values (Ignatius, 2021). In fact, in a recent interview with Poleman and HBR chief editor, Adi Ignatius, it was opined that net positive leaders should *take responsibility for their total impact on the world, lead with transparency, and focus on the long term. They aim for cooperative leadership, not just competitive leadership, because the world's problems are so immense that it is beyond the scope and ability of a single company to fix them* (Ignatius, 2021).

While we have enthusiastically advocated the merits of the fundamental shift in RL orientation to an 'Us *with* Them' and an even more ambitious 'Us *with* Future Us' perspective, we are mindful that this is not devoid of significant and serious challenges and risks. For it is inevitable that leaders will have to navigate a myriad of contradictions and tensions when operating in an 'Us *with* Future Us' (or 'Us *with* Them') orientation. In fact, it is likely that tensions may be interrelated (e.g., resolving one tension might strengthen, entangle or create other tensions), resulting in what Sheep et al. (2017) describe as *tensional knots*. This then raises the question as to how leaders should navigate and respond to such tensional knots. Exploring how RL navigates such tensions in practice is beyond the scope of this chapter and, in fact, there is a lacuna in the existing literature on how RL should navigate these myriad and often contradictory tensions in practice (Frangieh & Yaacoub, 2017). Nevertheless, we have outlined in this chapter two possible mechanisms through which responsible leaders can fuel an 'Us *with* Them'/'Us *with* Future Us' orientation – that is, through the pursuit of good dividends and meaningfulness. Future research should explore the role of the RL in fuelling this four-tier model of transcendence in practice, while exploring the boundary conditions through which this transition takes place.

CONCLUSION

We have outlined in this chapter how responsibility is present and addressed to varying extents in many prominent leadership theories, either explicitly or implicitly, and is not the preserve of RL theory. As a consequence, we have suggested that RL should not be viewed as a stand-alone theory but rather more specifically as a process, and more broadly as an orientation. This shift of perspective and focus we argue will have a far greater effect on the reach and impact of the leadership studies field. As a process, leadership researchers are encouraged to explore the antecedents, relationships, actions, contexts and outcomes associated with growing responsibility. As an orientation, we have suggested the necessity to build an ethical foundation for the leadership of responsibility that is associated with pragmatic utilitarianism; this emphasises the need to generate the 'greatest good' associated with pursuing a regenerative stakeholder ecosystem.

We made the assertion at the outset of this chapter that leadership is the most influential and, therefore, most important social process among humankind. Perhaps an enthusiastic and idealistic overstatement … but maybe not. What other form of agency imbued with institutional structural power has such scope for good or for bad in terms of the enhancement it can make to humanity? So, when we speak of leadership it is very difficult and indeed ultimately undesirable to separate out responsibility into a discrete theory of leadership. It is indeed a quintessential and timeless aspect of leadership – with power and influence inevitably comes responsibility.

When we consider power and responsibility, we should draw our chapter to a close with a special consideration of those who wield political influence. It has not been our intention to offer a unitarist apologia for contemporary capitalism and be naive and ignorant to the overarching influence of political economy in our exposition of RL and ideas of 'Us *with* Them'. We recognise that this is critical in the next phase of the elucidation of our RL framework and the development of RL practice. We would make the observation though that perhaps we are not so far off from a moment when developed and developing societies may not permit business leaders to have a licence to operate if it cannot be shown that society is better off because of the acts and deeds of the business. The global drive to promote ESG governance and integrated reporting by shareholder activists, institutional investors, professional and institutional bodies and government regulators provides grounds for some cautious encouragement. Related to this, the well-being economy is being pursued with some vigour in Scotland, Canada, Finland, Iceland, New Zealand and other nations. Research has not yet shown what forms of business and interrelated leadership will flourish in such an economy. We do humbly submit that the notion of RL that we have developed in this chapter in an effort to mobilise a reorientation within leadership studies will resonate strongly with all stakeholders in this brave new world.

REFERENCES

Afsar, B., Cheema, S., & Javed, F. (2018). Activating employee's pro-environmental behaviors: The role of CSR, organizational identification, and environmentally specific servant leadership. *Corporate Social Responsibility and Environmental Management*, 25, 904–911.

Anand, S., Ashforth, B. & Joshi, M. (2004). Business as usual: The acceptance and perpetuation of corruption in organisations, *Academy of Management Executive*, 19(4), 9–23.

Anand, S., & Sen, A. (2000). Human development and economic sustainability. *World Development*, 28(12), 2029–2049.

Angus-Leppan, T., Metcalf, L., & Benn, S. (2010). Leadership styles and CSR practice: An examination of sensemaking, institutional drivers and CSR leadership. *Journal of Business Ethics*, 93, 189–213.

Bailey, C., Madden, A., Alfes, K., Shantz, A., & Soane, E. (2017). The mismanaged soul: Existential labor and the erosion of meaningful work. *Human Resource Management Review*, 27(3), 416–430. 10.1016/j.hrmr.2016.11.001

Bazerman, M. H. (2020). A new model for ethical leadership. *Harvard Business Review*, September–October. https://hbr.org/2020/09/a-new-model-for-ethical-leadership

Benn, S., Todd, L. R., & Pendleton, J. (2010). Public relations leadership in corporate social responsibility. *Journal of Business Ethics*, 96, 403–423.

Berns, M., Townend, A., Khayat, Z., Balagopal, B., Reeves, M., Hopkins, M. S., & Kruschwitz, N. (2009). Sustainability and competitive advantage. *MIT Sloan Management Review*, 51, 19–26.

Blakeley, K. (2016). Responsible leadership: A radical view. In S. Kempster & B. Carroll (Eds.), *Responsible Leadership: Realism and Romanticism* (pp. 108–130). Routledge.

Bono, J. E., & Anderson, M. H. (2005). The advice and influence networks of transformational leaders. *Journal of Applied Psychology*, 90, 1306–1314.

Cheng, K., Wei, F., & Lin, Y. (2019). The trickle-down effect of responsible leadership on unethical pro-organizational behavior: The moderating role of leader–follower value congruence. *Journal of Business Research*, 102, 34–43.

Christensen, L. J., Mackey, A., & Whetten, D. (2014). Taking responsibility for corporate social responsibility: The role of leaders in creating, implementing, sustaining, or avoiding socially responsible firm behaviors. *Academy of Management Perspectives*, 28(2), 164–178.

Crane, A., Matten, D., Glozer, S., & Spence, L. (2019). *Business Ethic* (5th edn). Oxford University Press.

De Luque, M. S., Washburn, N. T., Waldman, D. A., & House, R. J. (2008). Unrequited profit: How stakeholder and economic values relate to subordinates' perceptions of leadership and firm performance. *Administrative Science Quarterly*, 53, 626–654.

De Roeck, K., & Farooq, O. (2018). Corporate social responsibility and ethical leadership: Investigating their interactive effect on employees' socially responsible behaviors. *Journal of Business Ethics*, 151, 923–939.

Du, S., Swaen, V., Lindgreen, A., & Sen, S. (2013). The roles of leadership styles in corporate social responsibility. *Journal of Business Ethics*, 114, 155–169.

Egri, C. P., & Herman, S. (2000). Leadership in the North American environmental sector: Values, leadership, styles, and contexts of environmental leaders and their organizations *Academy of Management Journal*, 43, 571–604.

Frangieh, C. G., & Yaacoub, K. H. (2017). A systematic literature review of responsible leadership. *Journal of Global Responsibility*, 8(2), 281–299. 10.1108/jgr-01-2017-0004.

Freeman, R. E., & Reed, D. I. (1983). Stockholders and stakeholders: A new perspective on corporate governance. *California Management Review*, 25(3), 88–106.

Fullerton, J. (2015). *Regenerative Capitalism: How Universal Principles and Patterns Will Shape Our New Economy*. Capital Institute.

Gond, J. P., Igalens, J., Swaen, V., & Akremi, A. E. (2011). The human resources contribution to responsible leadership: An exploration of the CSR–HR interface. *Journal of Business Ethics*, 98, 115–132.

Graen, G. B., & Uhl-Bien, M. (1995). Relationship-based approach to leadership: Development of leader–member exchange (LMX) theory over 25 years: Applying a multi-level, multi-domain perspective. *Leadership Quarterly*, 6, 219–247.

Greene, J. (2015). *Moral Tribes*. Atlantic.

Groves, K. S., & LaRocca, M. A. (2011). Responsible leadership outcomes via stakeholder CSR values: Testing a values-centered model of transformational leadership. *Journal of Business Ethics*, 98, 37–55.

Hansen, S. D., Dunford, B. B., Bradley, J. A., & Jackson, C. L. (2016). Corporate social responsibility, ethical leadership, and trust propensity: A multi-experience model of perceived ethical climate. *Journal of Business Ethics*, 137, 649–662.

Hoch, J. E., Bommer, W. H., Dulebohn, J. H., & Wu, D. (2018). Do ethical, authentic, and servant leadership explain variance above and beyond transformational leadership? A meta-analysis. *Journal of Management*, 44, 501–529.

Ignatius, A. (2012). Captain Planet. *Harvard Business Review*, June. https://hbr.org/2012/06/captain-planet

Ignatius, A. (2021). Former Unilever CEO Paul Polman says aiming for sustainability isn't good enough: The goal is much higher. *Harvard Business Review*, November. https://hbr.org/2021/11/former-unilever-ceo-paul-polman-says-aiming-for-sustainability-isnt-good-enough-the-goal-is-much-higher

Kempster, S. & Halme, M. (2019). Social innovation dividend: Leading stakeholders in value creation for all our futures. In S. Kempster, T. Maak & K. Parry (Eds.), *Good Dividends: Responsible Leadership of Business Purpose* (pp. 89–107). Routledge.

Kempster, S., & Jackson, B. (2021). Leadership for what, why, for whom and where? A responsibility perspective. *Journal of Change Management*, 21(1), 45–65.

Kempster, S., Maak, T., & Parry, K. (2019). *Good Dividends: Responsible Leadership of Business Purpose*. Routledge.

Kempster, S., Scheditzki, D. & Edwards, G. (2020). Where have all the followers gone? *Leadership*, 17(1), 118–128.

Lehmann, M., Toh, I., Christensen, P., & Ma, R. (2010). Responsible leadership? Development of CSR at danfoss, Denmark. *Corporate Social Responsibility and Environmental Management*, 17(3), 153–168.

Liden, R. C., Liao, C., & Meuser, J. D. (2014). Servant leadership and serving culture: Influence on individual and unit performance. *Academy of Management Journal*, 57, 1434–1452.

Liden, R. C., Wayne, S. J., Zhao, H., & Henderson, D. (2008). Servant leadership: Development of a multidimensional measure and multi-level assessment. *Leadership Quarterly*, 19, 161–177.

Lin, C. P., Huang, H. T., & Huang, T. Y. (2020). The effects of responsible leadership and knowledge sharing on job performance among knowledge workers. *Personnel Review*, 49(9), 1879–1896. https://doi.org/10.1108/PR-12-2018-0527

Lips-Wiersma, M., Haar, J., & Wright, S. (2020). The effect of fairness, responsible leadership and worthy work on multiple dimensions of meaningful work. *Journal of Business Ethics*, 161, 35–52.

Lythreatis, S., Mohammed, A., Mostafa, S., & Wang, X. (2019). Participative leadership and organizational identification in SMEs in the MENA region: Testing the roles of CSR perceptions and pride in membership. *Journal of Business Ethics*, 156, 635–650.

Luu, T. T. (2019). CSR and customer value co-creation behavior: The moderation mechanisms of servant leadership and relationship marketing orientation. *Journal of Business Ethics*, 155, 379–398.

Maak, T., & Pless, N. M. (2006). Responsible leadership in a stakeholder society: A relational perspective. *Journal of Business Ethics*, 66, 99–115.

Maak, T., & Pless, N. (2019). Responsible leadership: Reconciling people purpose and planet. In S. Kempster, T. Maak & K. Parry (Eds.), *Good Dividends: Responsible Leadership of Business Purpose* (pp. 30–36). Routledge.

Maak, T., Pless, N. M., & Voegtlin, C. (2016). Business statesman or shareholder advocate? CEO responsible leadership styles and the micro-foundations of political CSR. *Journal of Management Studies*, 53, 463–493.

MacIntyre, A. (1985). *After Virtue: A Study in Moral Theory*. Duckworth.

Maritz, R., Pretorius, M., & Plant, K. (2011). Exploring the interface between strategy-making and responsible leadership. *Journal of Business Ethics*, 98, 101–113.

Martela, F., & Pessi, A. B. (2018). Significant work is about self-realization and broader purpose: defining the key dimensions of meaningful work. *Frontiers in Psychology*, 9, 363.

Miska, C., & Mendenhall, M. E. (2018). Responsible leadership: A mapping of extant research and future directions. *Journal of Business Ethics*, 148, 117–134.

Pasricha, P., Singh, B., & Verma, P. (2018). Ethical leadership, organic organizational cultures and corporate social responsibility: An empirical study in social enterprises. *Journal of Business Ethics*, 151, 941–958.

Pearce, C. L., & Manz, C. C. (2011). Leadership centrality and corporate social ir-responsibility CSIR: The potential ameliorating effects of self and shared leadership on CSIR. *Journal of Business Ethics*, 102, 563–579.

Pearce, C. L., Wassenaar, C. L., & Manz, C. C. (2014). Is shared leadership the key to responsible leadership? *Academy of Management Perspectives*, 28, 275–288.

Pless, N. M. (2007). Understanding responsible leadership: Role identity and motivational drivers. *Journal of Business Ethics*, 74, 37–456.

Pless, N. M., & Maak, T. (2011). Responsible leadership: Pathways to the future. *Journal of Business Ethics*, 98, 3–13.

Pless, N. M., Maak, T., & Waldman, D. A. (2012). Different approaches toward doing the right thing: Mapping the responsibility orientations of leaders. *Academy of Management Perspectives*, 26(4), 51–65.

Sanders, P., & Grint, K.(2019). The interplay of the dirty hands of British area bombing and the wicked problem of defeating Nazi Germany in the Second World War: A lesson in leadership ethics. *Leadership*, 15(3), 271–295.

Schwab, K. (2021). *Stakeholder Capitalism*. Wiley.

Sheep, M. L., Fairhurst, G. T. & Khazanchi, S. (2017). Knots in the discourse of innovation: Investigating multiple tensions in a reacquired spin-off. *Organization Studies*, 38(3–4), 463–488. 10.1177/0170840616640845

Stahl, G. K., & de Luque, M.S. (2014). Antecedents of responsible leader behavior: A research synthesis, conceptual framework, and agenda for future research. *Academy of Management Perspectives*, 28, 235–254.

Steffen, W., Richardson, K., Rockström, J., Cornell, S. E., Fetzer, I., Bennett, E. M., Biggs, R., Carpenter, S. R., de Vries, W., de Wit, C. A., Folke, C., Gerten, D., Heinke, J., Mace, G. M., Persson, L. M., Ramanathan, V., Reyers, B., & Sörlin, S. (2015) Planetary boundaries: Guiding human development on a changing planet. *Science*, 347(6223). 10.1126/science.1259855

Steger, M. F., Dik, B. J., & Duffy, R. D. (2012). Measuring meaningful work. *Journal of Career Assessment*, 20(3), 322–337. 10.1177/1069072711436160

Strand, R. (2014). Strategic leadership of corporate sustainability. *Journal of Business Ethics*, 123, 687–706.

Sun, P. Y. T., & Anderson, M. H. (2012). Civic capacity: Building on transformational leadership to explain successful integrative public leadership. *Leadership Quarterly*, 23(3), 309–323.

Tourigny, L., Han, J., Baba, V. V., & Pan, P. (2019). Ethical leadership and corporate social responsibility in China: A multilevel study of their effects on trust and organizational citizenship behavior. *Journal of Business Ethics*, 158, 427–440.

Tourish, D. (2020) Introduction to the special issue: Why the coronavirus crisis is also a crisis of leadership. *Leadership*, 16(3), 261–272.

Tsui, A. S. (2021). Research responsible leadership. *Academy of Management Discoveries*, 7(2), 166–170. https://doi.org/10.5465/amd.2019.0244

Udofia, D. A. (2017). Leadership in the health sector: A discourse of the leadership model of utilitarianism. *Journal of Health Ethics*,13(1). http://dx.doi.org/10.18785/ojhe.1301.06

Van Dierendonck, D., Stam, D., Boersma, P., deWindt, N., & Alkema, J. (2014). Same difference? Exploring the differential mechanisms linking servant leadership and transformational leadership to follower outcomes. *Leadership Quarterly*, 25, 544–562.

Veríssimo, J. M. C., & Lacerda, T. M. C. (2015). Does integrity matter for CSR practice in organizations? The mediating role of transformational leadership. *Business Ethics: A European Review*, 24, 34–51.

Vlachos, P. A., Panagopoulos, N. G., & Rapp, A. A. (2013). Feeling good by doing good: Employee CSR-induced attributions, job satisfaction, and the role of charismatic leadership. *Journal of Business Ethics*, 118, 577–588.

Voegtlin, C. (2011). Development of a scale measuring discursive responsible leadership. *Journal of Business Ethics*, 98, 57–73.

Voegtlin, C. (2016). What does it mean to be responsible? Addressing the missing responsibility dimension in ethical leadership research. *Leadership*, 12, 581–608.

Voegtlin, C. & Scherer, G. (2019). New roles for business: Responsible innovators for a sustainable future. In A. McWilliams, D. E. Rupp, D. S. Siegel, G. K. Stahl & D. A. Waldman (Eds.), *The Oxford Handbook of Corporate Social Responsibility: Psychological and Organizational Perspectives*. Oxford University Press.

Waldman, D. A. (2011). Moving forward with the concept of responsible leadership: Three caveats to guide theory and research. *Journal of Business Ethics*, 98, 75–83.

Waldman, D. A., & Balven, R. (2014). Responsible leadership: Theoretical issues and research directions. *Academy of Management Perspectives*, 28, 224–234.

Waldman, D. A., & Siegel, D. (2008). Defining the socially responsible leader. *Leadership Quarterly*, 19, 117–131.

Waldman, D. A., de Luque, M. S., Washburn, N., & House, R. J. (2006a). Cultural and leadership predictors of corporate social responsibility values of top management: A GLOBE study of 15 countries. *Journal of International Business Studies*, 37, 823–837.

Waldman, D. A., Siegel, D. S., & Javidan, M. (2006b). Components of CEO transformational leadership and corporate social responsibility. *Journal of Management Studies*, *43*, 1703–1725.

Wang, G., Oh, I. S., Courtright, S. H., & Colbert, A. E. (2011). Transformational leadership and performance across criteria and levels: A meta-analytic review of 25 years of research. *Group and Organization Management*, *36*, 223–270.

Waters, R., & Wright, R. (1973). *Us and them (lyrics from Dark Side of the Moon)*. pink-floyd-lyrics.com

Witt, M. A., & Stahl, G. K. (2016). Foundations of responsible leadership: Asian versus Western executive responsibility orientations toward key stakeholders. *Journal of Business Ethics*, *136*, 623–638.

Wolf, S. (2010). *Meaning in Life and Why it Matters*. Princeton University Press.

Zhu, Y., Sun, L. Y., & Leung, A. S. M. (2014). Corporate social responsibility, firm reputation, and firm performance: the role of ethical leadership. *Asia Pacific Journal of Management*, *31*, 925–947.

19
Self-regulatory Focus and Leadership: It's All about Context

Marianna Delegach, Ronit Kark and Dina Van Dijk

INTRODUCTION

Over the last few decades, researchers have made many attempts to elucidate leadership using motivational theories in order to understand leader–follower dynamics (Gonzalez-Cruz et al., 2019). Regulatory focus theory offers one of the most overarching motivational frameworks, as it comprises inner-self constructs and operates on three distinct levels – the system, the strategic and the tactical. As such, it explains individuals' differences in end-state preferences and goal-striving strategies, as well as cognitions, moods and behaviours (e.g., Higgins, 1997; Wallace et al., 2016). In recent years, a growing body of research has highlighted the essential role of regulatory focus in appreciating leadership influence on followers. However, this accumulative body of research has largely overlooked contextual factors that can play a pivotal role in these relationships. Leadership influence on followers does not occur in a vacuum. Indeed, leaders are *tenants of time and context* (Bryman et al., 1996, p. 355); therefore, we cannot analyse leadership constructs in isolation from followers' characteristics, organisational features and global environment attributes. To narrow this gap, Kark and Van Dijk (2019) suggested a multilevel theoretical framework that offers leadership regulatory focus research a meta-theoretical foundation for gaining better insight into underlying patterns of context and time variability in manifestations of the leader–follower dynamic. In line with their framework, this chapter incorporates recent research on leadership–followership and regulatory foci and further develops the framework by emphasising the role of context. Accordingly, in the current chapter, we aim to make a better sense of regulatory focus and leadership/followership by suggesting that exploring a variety of contexts can have a sense-breaking effect on our understanding of the different ways in which the former is experienced and enacted by leaders, followers and in the interaction between them.

To set the scene for our proposed exploration, we begin the chapter with a brief discussion of regulatory focus and regulatory fit theories and their role in understanding leader–follower dynamics. Next, we present three broader aspects of context: the internal organisational context, focusing on task types, occupational types and organisational culture; the industry organisational environment, with an emphasis on environmental dynamism; and the general organisational environment, concentrating on global cultural contexts. In these sections, based on the literature review, we explain how these contexts can affect or elicit different regulatory foci and influence the leadership process as a whole. Moreover, at the end of each section, we provide practical suggestions and future research directions. Finally, we summarise the ideas raised in the chapter and provide a forward-looking agenda for advancing the understanding of the role of regulatory foci in leader–follower relationships in different contexts. A summary of the context-sensitive model, including its impact on employee regulatory foci and leadership styles, is presented in Figure 19.1.

REGULATORY FOCUS THEORY

Regulatory focus theory distinguishes between two independent self-regulations: promotion and prevention (Higgins, 1997). Promotion-focused individuals have a strong 'ideals' guide and strive to meet their ideals and hopes through an eager approach strategy that emphasises growth, advancement and accomplishment. This model of 'keeping your head in the clouds' (Kark & Van Dijk, 2019) manifests, on the tactical level, in choosing approach-related tactics: seeking self-enhancing experiences (Lanaj et al., 2012), searching for opportunities to increase the probability of positive rewards, making risky decisions (Crowe & Higgins, 1997), perceiving a demanding situation as a challenge (Delegach & Katz-Navon, 2021) and scanning the environment for success-related information (Lockwood et al., 2002). Because the promotion focus is sensitive to gains and non-gains, goal achievement activates strong positive emotions, such as cheerfulness and happiness, while the discrepancy between the current state and the goal activates low-engagement negative emotions such as dejection and sadness (Higgins, 1997).

In contrast, prevention-focused individuals have a strong 'ought' guide and strive to meet their security needs through a vigilant avoidance strategy that emphasises duties, obligations and responsibilities. This model of 'keeping one's feet on the ground' (Kark & Van Dijk, 2019) corresponds with approach-related tactics: risk aversion (Crowe & Higgins, 1997), avoidance of errors and negative consequences (Higgins, 1997), perceiving a demanding situation as a threat (Delegach & Katz-Navon, 2021), implementing limited in scope and responsible behaviours in task accomplishment (Meyer et al., 2004) and scanning the environment for failure-related information (Lockwood et al., 2002). Because the prevention focus is sensitive to losses and non-losses, failure to achieve 'ought' goals activates strong negative emotions, such as anxiety and agitation, while success activates low-engagement positive emotions, such as relaxation and calmness (Higgins, 1997).

Regulatory foci can be dispositional (i.e., chronic regulatory foci) and context-induced (i.e., situational regulatory foci; Brockner & Higgins, 2001). While one's chronic regulatory foci develop in early childhood in relation to early life

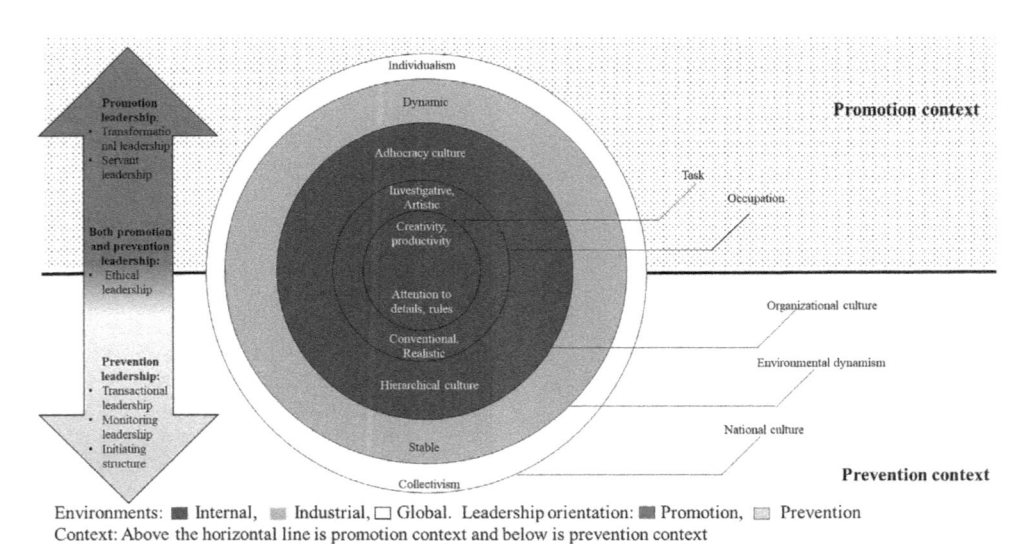

Environments: ■ Internal, ▨ Industrial, □ Global. Leadership orientation: ■ Promotion, ▨ Prevention
Context: Above the horizontal line is promotion context and below is prevention context

Figure 19.1 Three organisational environmental contexts and leadership styles in the lens of regulatory focus theory

experiences (Higgins, 1997), situational regulatory foci can be triggered by situational characteristics (Friedman & Förster, 2001). Different environment framing may cultivate different aspects of the self and, as a result, evoke situational promotion or prevention focus (Kark & Van Dijk, 2007).

Based on regulatory focus definitions, Kark and Van Dijk (2007) developed a conceptual framework that integrates regulatory focus theory into the leadership literature and suggests that a leader's dispositional regulatory focus is a major antecedent of leadership behaviours. In addition, their framework proposes that manager leadership style shapes followers' regulatory foci and, through that, contributes to a variety of organisational outcomes. This framework gained extensive research interest and support. First, the volume of research focused on leaders' dispositional regulatory focus and leadership behaviours has demonstrated that a leader's dispositional promotion focus contributes to transformational (Johnson et al., 2017) and authentic (Fladerer & Braun, 2020) leadership styles, while leaders' dispositional prevention focus contributes to a transactional leadership style (Johnson et al., 2017). Second, leaders as 'makers of meaning' and 'significant other' through symbols, rhetoric and role modelling may shape followers' regulatory foci (Brockner & Higgins, 2001). Leaders' behaviours represent salient interpersonal cues that shape followers' adaptive cognitive processes and influence their self-concept (Kark & Van Dijk, 2007). A vast body of recent literature supports this interpretation. For example, several field and experimental studies have demonstrated that transformational (Delegach et al., 2017; Kark et al., 2015; Kark et al., 2018; Van Dijk et al., 2020), servant (Neubert et al., 2008) and ethical (Neubert et al., 2013) leadership styles elicit followers' promotion focus and, as such, contribute to multiple positive organisational outcomes (e.g., extra-role voice behaviours, affective commitment, individual and team creativity). By contrast, transactional (Delegach et al., 2017; Kark et al., 2015; Kark et al., 2018), initiating structure (Neubert et al., 2008) and ethical (Neubert et al., 2013) leadership behaviours instil followers' prevention focus and, through that, contribute to organisational outcomes that differ in nature from the outcomes of promotion focus (e.g., compliance and conformal behaviours, continuance and normative commitments, in-role performance).

REGULATORY FIT THEORY

Extending regulatory focus theory, Higgins (2005) emphasised the importance of compatibility between individual characteristics and environmental attributes, thereby developing regulatory fit theory. Regulatory fit refers to the degree of congruence between individuals' regulatory orientation and the manner of their engagement in an activity. When environmental attributes match an individual's regulatory focus, they feel 'right' about their actions (Avnet et al., 2013); in turn, this experience leads to greater engagement in activities (Higgins, 2005). For example, an individual with a dominant promotion focus will feel more fit and, accordingly, more motivational strength and activity importance when a situation forces them to pursue promotion-framed (e.g., creativity tasks) versus prevention-framed goals (e.g., proof-reading). Field and experimental studies have provided evidence for regulatory fit theory and demonstrated that it contributes to job satisfaction (e.g., Kruglanski et al., 2007) and performance (e.g., Bianco et al., 2003), as well as lowering turnover intention (Hamstra et al., 2011).

In summary, the regulatory foci of leaders and followers affect the way the individuals choose to perceive, feel about and react in different situations; hence, a growing body of leadership literature encompasses the regulatory focus of leaders and followers to examine leadership effectiveness and leader ability to motivate followers. Most of these studies have explored the interplay between leadership and regulatory foci based on the followers' regulatory focus viewed either as being shaped by the leader's leadership style (e.g., Delegach et al., 2017; Johnson et al., 2017; Kark et al., 2015; Kark et al., 2018; Neubert et al., 2008; Neubert et al., 2013) or as a boundary condition of leadership effectiveness (e.g., DeCarlo et al., 2021; De Cremer et al., 2009; Graham et al., 2015; Hamstra et al., 2011; Hamstra et al., 2014b; Han & Hwang, 2019; Yadav & Dhar, 2021). Only a few studies have explored the regulatory focus of the leader as a chronic dispositional characteristic (e.g., Bush et al., 2021; Gamache et al., 2020; Hamstra et al., 2014a; Jiang et al., 2020; Wu et al., 2008) and to date, to the best of our knowledge, no studies have focused on the leaders' situational regulatory focus. This gap may suggest that scholars have tended to label leaders as having stable regulatory focus, which affects their leadership style and organisational outcomes (Kark & Van Dijk, 2019).

The contextual factors can weaken the explanatory power of dispositional antecedents of leadership styles regarding the emergence of leadership (Sternberg & Vroom, 2002). Moreover, the dynamic leader–follower regulatory focus interplay occurs in different organisational stages and contexts (Kark & Van Dijk, 2019); thus, it is essential to highlight the context's role in understanding leadership effectiveness. As Osborn et al. (2002) wrote, *Leadership and its effectiveness, in large part, are dependent upon the context. Change the context and leadership changes* (p. 797). Nevertheless, many leadership theories neglect this understanding and do not consider the influence of context on the leadership process (Boal & Hooijberg, 2000). In line with this perspective, most theoretical papers and review articles on leadership and context (Antonakis & Atwater, 2002; Osborn et al., 2002; Porter & McLaughlin, 2006; Shamir & Howell, 1999) have concluded that the effect of context on leadership is an under-researched area. Thus, understanding the role of context as a boundary condition of leader–follower influence makes it possible to draw a more comprehensive and accurate picture of leadership and its outcomes.

Thus, the goal of this chapter is to map and arrange an accumulative body of theories and studies into a context-sensitive framework for a better understanding of the leadership process. Specifically, we arrange our chapter using Hatch's (1997) organisational environment framework, which divides the organisational environment into three broader levels: an internal organisational environment that refers to inner organisational characteristics; an industry organisational environment that refers to industry-related factors, such as regulatory agencies, power of competitors and power of customers; and a general organisational environment that represents the external forces that can influence the attainment of organisational goals, such as national culture. On all three levels, we discuss the relevant organisational and environmental characteristics that can form a more nuanced perspective of leader–follower regulatory foci dynamics and their influence on organisational outcomes.

INTERNAL ORGANISATIONAL ENVIRONMENT LEVEL

Internal organisational environment refers to the set of conditions within organisational boundaries in which organisational members have to function to accomplish the organisational tasks and achieve their personal goals (Morris et al., 2008). Design components of the internal organisational environment, among others, include organisational structure, systems, processes and culture. On this level, we will discuss task types, occupational types and organisational culture as inner characteristics of the organisational environment that contribute to understanding employees' organisational life.

Task Type

Person–environment fit theories suggest that individuals who work in an environment congruent with their personality characteristics demonstrate better job performance and job attitudes than those who experience a misfit (Kristof-Brown et al., 2005). A person–task fit is a specific form of person–environment fit and refers to the match between an individual's characteristics and the task's features and demands (Finucane et al., 2005). A major personal characteristic that explains a person's needs, drivers and strategies for goal achievement is the regulatory focus. Higgins (2005) claimed that individuals strive for a match between their regulatory inclination and job-related activities. Consider, for instance, two employees, Emma, who has a high predominant promotion focus, and Mia, who has a high predominant prevention focus. Emma is mainly concerned with her aspirations and hopes, looking for developmental and growth opportunities as well as maximisation of positive outcomes, and uses the approach strategy to goal attainment. Thus, workplace activities that require growth behaviours and offer the possibilities to reach aspirations (e.g., product development, assimilation of new technology; Kluger & Van Dijk, 2010) would provide the regulatory fit for Emma's regulatory inclination. Mia strives to fulfil her duty and obligations. She concentrates on security needs and tries to minimise adverse outcomes while mainly using the avoidance strategy for goal attainment. Thus, workplace activities that demand accuracy, alertness and emphasise security (e.g., detecting errors, quality control; Kluger & Van Dijk, 2010) would provide a better fit for Mia's regulatory inclination.

A regulatory fit strengthens the individual's engagement in activities, makes them 'feel right' about what they are doing and intensifies their evaluative reaction to their experience (either positive or negative; Higgins, 2005). These responses, in turn, affect the individual's commitment, motivation and attitudes. For example, Park et al. (2015) surveyed 260 employees at a poultry processing plant whose primary duty was to carefully treat the plant products to prevent contamination (i.e., prevention-focused tasks). The research findings revealed that participants' prevention focus was positively associated with job satisfaction, task efficacy, task enjoyment, job effectiveness and job involvement.

Another noteworthy study focused on workplace stress to demonstrate the contribution of regulatory fit to workplace outcomes. The researchers (Parker et al., 2014) assumed that for promotion-focused individuals workplace autonomy could attenuate the relationship between the performance of high-demand tasks and stress reaction, as the autonomy provides them with a sense of progression. In contrast, autonomy can increase stress for prevention-focused individuals, whereas strict instructions and rules that provide structure and clear guidelines for task accomplishment could relieve stress. An experimental design study that combined psychological (i.e., anxiety, task dissatisfaction and task performance) with physiological (i.e., heart rate variability) measures confirmed the research hypotheses. Further support came from Freitas et al.'s (2002) research. Here, the authors assumed that a task with attractive distractions (e.g., a video clip) is congruent with prevention focus, as it requires temptation resisting, which is an avoidance strategy, whereas a task without distractions is more congruent with promotion focus, as it requires eagerness and approach strategy. Based on this assumption, Freital et al. (2002) demonstrated that promotion-focused individuals found tasks with no distractions to be more enjoyable, whereas prevention-focused individuals evaluated tasks with distractions as more enjoyable. Moreover, prevention-focused participants outperformed promotion-focused participants in the condition of task disruption; this association between participants' regulatory focus and task performance was mediated by task enjoyment.

Together, these research findings demonstrate that task characteristics play a central role as a contextual factor that binds the association between employee regulatory foci and workplace outcomes. This understanding might guide leaders on how to appropriately assign and construct activities for employees with different regulatory foci orientations and how to effectively use the regulatory dissimilarities between employees to achieve organisational goals. Moreover, the contingency and situational theories of leadership (Fiedler, 1964; House & Mitchell, 1974) recognise that leadership effectiveness depends on task characteristics and is a function of the fit between leadership style and task context. Accordingly, Mumford et al. (2002) suggest that ambiguous and complex tasks require leader creativity, while Pawar and Eastman (1997) propose that the boundary-spanning units which deal with tasks that cannot be standardised or routinised and have a high level of discretion in decision-making are more receptive to a transformational style of leadership.

Another possible direction in this stream of thinking is a perspective that views the task features as a contextual factor that primes different aspects of the self-regulatory foci; for example, a task that requires creativity and productivity can prime promotion focus. In contrast, a task that requires attention to detail and following rules can prime prevention focus. Following this consideration, Van Dijk and Kluger (2011), in a set of experimental studies, demonstrated that task type (error detection versus creativity) elicited participants' regulatory inclination, and that induced regulatory focus affected participants' response to type of performance feedback (negative versus positive).

In summary, managers in organisations can either frame the task to fit the employee's regulatory focus or change the employee's state regulatory focus to fit the task at hand. More specifically, managers can reframe tasks to offer more opportunities for achievement and personal growth and thus tailor the work environment for promotion-oriented employees. Similarly, they can redesign tasks to be more defined and structured, allowing a more secure and steady environment suited for prevention-oriented employees. Another way managers can shape tasks for employees in order to increase their motivation is by reframing employees' situational focus to fit the organisation's tasks. For example, if organisational tasks require caution, safety and precision, managers can frame their messages in a more prevention-oriented way by striving for safety, maintaining procedures and following instructions. In the same way, when tasks require creativity, imagination and enterprise, it is possible to frame promotional messages.

Additionally, recognising the role of task context on leader effectiveness and followers' outcomes revealed several important gaps that need to be addressed in future research. First, the tasks' attributes may prime either prevention or promotion foci; thus, examining which tasks are associated with each regulatory focus is essential. Second, studies should not treat employee tasks as 'regulatory-focus neutral' when researching leader–follower influence. Moreover, as the tasks' characteristics may shape the followers' different regulatory foci, they may also affect the leaders' and followers' situational regulatory focus, interplaying with the leader dominant leadership style or impacting it, as well as influence the followers' recipiency to the leader and the resulting outcomes.

Occupation Type

Another important extension of person–environment fit is a person–occupational fit, which refers to the correspondence between one's needs, skills, preferences and the usual demands of the individual's profession (Kristof-Brown et al., 2005). Individuals perceive environments as satisfying when environmental features resemble their personality. The greater the incongruence between an individual's personality characteristics and the environmental features, the more the individual experiences the environment as uncomfortable and destructive (Holland, 1997). Accordingly, the research demonstrated a positive contribution of person–occupation congruency to employees' well-being (Strauser et al., 2008) and professional success (Lee et al., 2015).

In general, vocational choices are not random but represent a self-concept extension (Westerman et al., 2002). Thus, based on regulatory focus theory, it is plausible that a dominant regulatory orientation may guide people's vocational choices and career preferences. The promotion and prevention focus distinction represents different underlying motives that drive individuals, and the different nature of goals and standards that individuals seek to achieve (Brockner et al., 2004). As such, regulatory focus theory can be highly relevant for determining an individual's vocational choices and the variability in how one's regulatory focus profile is associated with satisfaction and organisational outcomes in different occupations. Surprisingly, with the exception of Van Dijk and Kluger (2004), who assumed that artistic and investigative work environments are more likely to characterise promotion focus – while conventional and realistic work environments are more likely to characterise prevention focus – no systematic research has tried to draw theoretical and empirical connections between Holland's work on environment typology (1997), which defines six types of occupational work environments (realistic, investigative, artistic, social, enterprising and conventional [RIASEC]) and Higgins's (1997) regulatory focus theory.

Investigative and artistic environments are associated with openness to experience (Barrick et al., 2003) and encourage openness to change values while they correlate negatively with harm avoidance. Moreover, the artistic environment contradicts the value of traditionalism (Ackerman & Heggestad, 1997). Hence, it is possible to make relatively straightforward predictions that investigative and artistic environments fit promotion-focused individuals, who are characterised by positive affectivity, extraversion, openness to experience, optimism, agreeableness and self-efficacy (Gorman et al., 2012; Lanaj et al., 2012). Moreover, promotion focus is associated with openness to change (Kark & Van Dijk, 2007) and self-enhancement values and negatively related to conservation values (Leikas et al., 2009). Aligned with this prediction, in a cross-sectional study, Oren (2004) found that promotion-focused individuals tended to choose occupations characterised by a sense of self-fulfilment, challenge and autonomy.

A conventional environment encourages people to obey and maintain order as they reinforce efficiency, persistence, self-control and compliance (Holland, 1973). Such environments inspire control, traditionalism (Ackerman & Heggestad, 1997) and appreciate conscientiousness (Barrick et al., 2003). A realistic environment reinforces conforming, stability, thriftiness and practicality (Holland, 1973). Smith and Campbell (2009) found that conventional and realistic environments hold some common characteristics, such as straight company policies and rules. Thus, it is possible to assume that prevention-focused individuals will feel more comfortable (fit) in conventional and realistic environments as they are characterised by conscientiousness, negative affectivity (Gorman et al., 2012; Lanaj et al., 2012), conforming behaviours (Kark et al., 2015) and conservation values, and negatively associated with openness to change values (Leikas et al., 2009). In line with this finding, research revealed that prevention-focused individuals tended to choose occupations that provide security and stability (Oren, 2004).

In summary, understanding how regulatory foci predict occupational attraction has practical implications not only for recruitment and career counselling but also for leader–follower relationships and for the effect of leadership style on follower motivation. For example, in a cross-sectional study, Gilbert et al. (2015) found that a relational leadership style more strongly predicts a leader's perceived effectiveness for social service than for manufacturing samples. Thus, managers who lead functional departments should identify the predominant regulatory focus of their employees' occupational group and apply a corresponding leadership style. Further, the integration of leadership regulatory focus theory in vocational environment typology may provide several potential research directions. First, as we mentioned above, there is a lack of systematic research on the relationships between regulatory foci and the six interest types in the RIASEC hexagon. This integration would allow exploring leadership styles' effectiveness as a function of employees' dominant regulatory foci, viewing the latter either as a self-selection process based on occupational attraction or as shaped by the occupational environment.

In addition, the meta-analytical study conducted by Litano et al. (2016) demonstrated that in highly structured occupations, which offer little autonomy, the LMX relationships between leader and follower amplify the negative relationships between LMX and work interference with family, suggesting that in these occupations employees rely more heavily on their leaders to offer job autonomy as a work–family resource that buffers negative work–family experiences. Jepson (2009) conducted 105 interviews in chemical companies to gather the employees' perceptions of leadership and context. The results revealed that employees in the production plants (i.e., a task context characterised by strong structure and frequency of direct reports) preferred a supportive leadership style. Thus, it may be assumed that prevention-focused followers, who choose a more conventional environment characterised by a higher level of structure, are more likely to rely on LMX with the leader to function effectively. Future studies should investigate this direction.

Organisational Culture

Organisational culture represents the guideline of organisational life (Schneider et al., 2013) and reflects its underlying assumptions, expectations, taken-for-granted values, beliefs and behavioural norms (Cameron & Quinn, 2006; Schein, 2010). Hence, organisational culture is an essential social characteristic that affects organisational members' behaviours and performance outcomes (Hartnell et al., 2011). Although regulatory focus literature emphasises organisational culture as a main factor that shapes organisational members' regulatory focus (Brockner & Higgins, 2001), there is a paucity of empirical research that examines this proposition.

One of the more famous and widely used taxonomies of organisational culture is the competing values framework (Quinn & Rohrbaugh, 1983). This taxonomy conceptualises two dimensions of contradictory values that map distinct organisational culture clusters. The first dimension refers to a structure and differentiates flexibility and discretion versus stability and control. The second dimension refers to the organisation's focus and differentiates internal orientation and integration versus external orientation and rivalry (Cameron & Quinn, 2006). The overlay of these two dimensions creates four types of organisational culture: clan, adhocracy, hierarchy and market cultures. The clan culture (internal focus-flexible structure) emphasises shared values such as cohesion, collaboration, harmony and human resource development. The adhocracy culture (external focus-flexible structure) emphasises long-term goals, agility, risk-taking, autonomy, innovation and creativity. The hierarchy culture (internal focus-stability structure) is based on core values such as control, predictability, formalisation, consistency and order. Finally, the marker culture (external focus-stability structure) is based on competitiveness, achievement and productivity values.

Based on these definitions of cultural clusters, we can assume that the adhocracy culture can prime promotion focus. Driven by growth, variety and stimulation values, this culture has a strong focus on developing new and unique services, products and processes. Flexible organisational structure, long-term orientation and organisational focus on development and new resource acquisitions (Cameron & Quinn, 2006) facilitate proactivity and creativity in organisational members (Hartnell et al., 2011), encouraging them to deviate from the status quo and to take risks to fulfil customer needs (Büschgens et al., 2013). In contrast, organisations with a strong hierarchical culture cluster can shape employees' prevention focus. Driven by stability, rationality, efficiency and error omission, this culture focuses on maintaining smooth organisational functioning, process standardisation, rules, policies that structure organisational processes (Cameron & Quinn, 2006) and encourages caution, conformity and mistake avoidance. In line with this reasoning, Shin et al. (2016) explored team culture in 104 teams from 14 firms. Their research findings revealed that hierarchical and clan team cultures were associated with the team's prevention focus, and through that enhanced team performance, while adhocracy team culture was associated with the team's promotion focus, and via this quality enhanced creative performance.

These proposed relationships between organisational culture clusters and employees' regulatory foci are crucial to understanding leadership dynamics and leaders' influence on organisational members. First, organisational culture influences human resource composition: not only do organisational clusters have varying attractiveness to different individuals as a consequence of their personality characteristics (e.g., O'Reilly et al., 1991), but also organisational culture *as a sense-making* process (Weick, 1979) may shape organisational members' regulatory focus. Second, leaders have a critical role in organisational culture creation, reinforcement and maintenance (e.g., Schein, 2010). Although organisational founders establish organisational culture, subsequent top executives modify and change it (e.g., Kerr & Slocum, 2005) according to their beliefs, values and assumptions. Hence, Berson et al. (2008) found that the values of the firm's CEO contributed to organisational culture clusters and, by extension, to different organisational outcomes. For example, the authors found that the CEO characterised by security values (i.e., order, rules, predictability) contributed to bureaucratic culture and, as such, increased organisational efficiency and diminished employee satisfaction. In contrast, the CEO characterised by self-direction values (i.e., free thought, learning, exploring) contributed to innovation culture and, as such, to employee satisfaction and sales growth.

In conclusion, organisational leaders, especially top executives, must consider the organisational workforce's priorities and behaviours that are essential to organisational success and organisational strategy implementation and the underlying values that correspond to them. These values can be transmitted to employees through what Schein (2010) defined primarily as embedding mechanisms (e.g., resource allocation, role modelling, selecting and promoting processes) and secondarily as articulation and reinforcement mechanisms (e.g., organisational structure, organisational rituals, design of organisational space). In this respect, future research should examine whether and how organisational culture primes the employees' regulatory focus and, in this way, also affects their attitudes and behaviours. Furthermore, it should study the role of manager leadership styles as boundary conditions regarding these relationships.

Moreover, since leader-focused studies treat the leader's regulatory focus solely as a predisposition characteristic, the research on the potential of organisational culture to shape the leaders' regulatory focus and, through that, their leadership style is lacking. For example, Shamir & Howell (1999) suggested that a clan culture can lead to the emergence of charismatic leadership, while Waldman (1993) proposed that an organisational learning culture would be more responsive to transformational leadership. Bowers et al. (2017) provided a perceptive guide for effective organisational crisis response based on leadership style and organisational culture. They suggested that when an internal crisis occurs, the organisational culture predicts the effectiveness of leadership style. In the clan and adhocracy cultures, a transformational leadership style is needed, while in a hierarchy culture, a directive leadership style is also suggested as effective. In sum, as Porter and Mclaughlin (2006) pointed out, the emphasis on the interplay between culture and leadership exists more in the conceptual than in the empirical literature. Thus, future studies may provide a better understanding of how organisational culture shapes the leader's regulatory focus and how the interplay between organisational culture and leadership style contributes to different organisational outcomes.

INDUSTRY ORGANISATIONAL ENVIRONMENT LEVEL: ENVIRONMENTAL DYNAMISM

Different environment conditions require different leadership styles (e.g., Fiedler, 1964; Hersey & Blanchard, 1977), as leaders widely differ in their ability to match their talents to changing work conditions (Hambrick et al., 2005). Therefore, the interplay between the environment's characteristics and a leader's disposition shapes a leader's behaviours, decisions and priorities and, by extension, organisational strategy (Nadkarni & Chen, 2014). In this chapter, we highlight the role of environmental dynamism as a critical factor in an organisation's industrial environment, as it can create opportunities in the organisation's given market (Hakala, 2011); nowadays, an organisation's ability to respond correctly to these opportunities affects not only its success but also its survival.

Environmental dynamism refers to the extent to which an external organisational environment is unpredictable, unstable and subject to rapid change (Cooper et al., 2014). A dynamic environment is characterised by frequent shifts in customer preference, fluctuations in demand for services or products and continuous and fast technology changes (Jansen et al., 2009). In such an environment, the 'shelf life' of services or products is relatively short; thus, an organisation must continuously improve and update its products, services and markets, and develop new ones to remain relevant and competitive (Hou et al., 2019). A dynamic environment a priori includes high levels of uncertainty that contribute to stress, feeling of urgency and anxiety in the organisation (Waldman et al., 2001). Moreover, the rapid changes that characterise a dynamic environment bind the information flow and therefore limit an organisation's ability to make stable predictions of the future and of strategies that lead to organisational success (Hou et al., 2019). Hence, organisational dynamism compels organisations to be proactive, take more complex and risky strategic actions and make bolder decisions with a limited ability to determine their potential outcomes (Ruiz-Ortega et al., 2013). In such environments, top leaders with a promotion focus experience a regulatory fit, exhibiting creativity, flexibility and innovation in identifying new ways to facilitate effective organisational strategy (Wallace et al., 2010). Contrarily, a stable environment is characterised by low levels of change and uncertainty, and includes established routines and situations (Vera & Crossan, 2004). Its outcomes are predictable as the relevant information for estimating the probability of desired outcomes is available (Hmieleski & Baron, 2008). This environment demands different leadership emphases and styles (Jansen et al., 2009). Top leaders with a prevention focus may experience a better regulatory fit, demonstrating persistence and a slower, more cautious approach to decision-making (Wallace et al., 2010).

Following this notion, Waldman et al. (2001) demonstrated that charismatic leadership's positive contribution to organisational performance is limited to uncertain environments, while the association between charismatic leadership and organisational performance is negative when the environment is more stable. In the context of leader regulatory focus, several studies have demonstrated that environmental dynamism binds the relationship between leader regulatory focus and organisational outcomes. For example, Wallace et al. (2010), based on a sample of 70 CEOs, found that environmental dynamism strengthened the relationship between CEO promotion focus and firm performance and attenuated the relationship between CEO prevention focus and firm performance. Another study of 99 entrepreneurs in China revealed that environmental turbulence moderated the negative association between entrepreneurs' prevention focus and improvisational behaviours, such that, in a relatively stable environment, the entrepreneurs' prevention focus increased the occurrence of their spontaneous and creative behaviours (Hu et al., 2018). Additional research using a sample of 201 venture founders that also operated as top management team leaders demonstrated that, in a dynamic environment, entrepreneurs' chronic prevention (promotion) focus was negatively (positively) associated with the performance of the new ventures. These associations were mediated by the degree to which their new ventures deviated from the original business opportunity (Hmieleski & Baron, 2008). From these findings, we may conclude that for an organisation that operates in a dynamic environment a strategic leader with a promotion orientation is more beneficial and leads to better organisational outcomes.

However, dynamic environments require from a leader not only creativity, flexibility and agility in decision-making but also extensive monitoring of external and internal environments (Girod & Whittington, 2017). Moreover, during times of change, stability is essential and the two co-exist and are complementary in organisational life (Taylor-Bianco & Schermerhorn, 2006). Thus, leaders today must simultaneously manage change and continuity. Accordingly, several studies emphasised the diversity within the top management team as an essential characteristic that helps the organisation stay competitive in a dynamic environment (Richard et al., 2019). Interesting indirect support for this assumption comes from research on team innovation. Focusing on team composition, the authors demonstrated that the most innovative teams consisted not only of creative members but also of conformists, who contributed to team radical innovation by enhancing adherence to standards, reducing team conflicts and strengthening team potency (Miron-Spektor et al., 2011). Moreover, when the organisation faced environmental dynamism, it had to mobilise organisational members' motivation and efforts to implement changes and overcome their resistance to change. Taylor-Bianco and Schermerhorn (2006), based on paradox theory, suggested that in dynamic environments the diverse regulatory orientations of the TMT would lead to higher motivation by organisational members to implement changes as all employees would continually experience regulatory fit.

Complementing the above, the theoretical work of McMullen et al. (2009) suggests that the middle manager can affect the top managers' regulatory focus. As the organisation grows, top executives have to rely on the information that middle managers collect from different organisational functioning units to form an understanding of the inner organisational functioning and decide how to navigate the organisation through the environment. Some of these middle managers may be more prevention-focused (for example, managers in charge of competitive intelligence and external threats), while others may be more promotion-focused (for example, research and development managers) as a function of their main organisational tasks. The interactions between top and middle managers, and the information that the latter choose to provide to the former and its framing, may elicit different regulatory foci in top executives (Idson et al., 2000) and thus different responses to environmental opportunities.

In addition, top managers must consider contradictory organisational demands to decide how to allocate limited organisational resources. Some of these demands relate to the organisation's security needs (i.e., safety and protection), while others relate to nurturance organisational needs (i.e., development and growth). Hence, the top managers' predominant regulatory focus may explain the difference in their sensitivity to demands. For example, McMullen et al. (2009) suggested that the top managers' regulatory foci could be seen as a context condition that binds the use of the middle-level managers' surveillance information and top managers' attention to the threat. Thus, future research may explore these propositions. First, up until now the vast majority of research has studied CEO regulatory focus as a predictor of organisational effectiveness in different environmental conditions (e.g., Gamache et al., 2015; Gamache et al., 2020; Jiang et al., 2020; Kashmiri et al., 2019); future studies may examine the CEO team's regulatory composition as a more nuanced antecedent of organisational functioning. Second, since followers serve as a key source of validation for the leaders' behaviours (Howell & Shamir, 2005), future research may explore the middle managers' regulatory focus as a bottom-up 'cascade' that constrains their leaders' regulatory foci or buffers the influence and effectiveness of the latter's leadership style in the different industrial environments.

GENERAL ORGANISATIONAL ENVIRONMENT LEVEL: GLOBAL CULTURAL CONTEXT

The general organisational environment refers to all external forces that can influence the organisation's performance and operations and that lay beyond its influence (Cummings & Worley, 2014). Key factors that describe the general organisational environment are political, economic, legal, ecological, technological and sociocultural contexts (Bourgeois, 1980). In comparison to an industrial environment, a general environment is less direct and does not always have a short-term impact on the organisation. Indeed, a general organisational environment can affect the organisation by shaping the industrial environment, and its analysis can provide a guideline for building effective corporate strategy (Bourgeois, 1980).

This chapter focused on the social-cultural context as an essential general organisational environment characteristic. If we understand leadership as *the process of being perceived by others as a leader* (Lord & Maher, 1991, p. 11), leadership can be seen as a result of a social cognitive process that forms the perception of other social players (i.e., employees, co-workers) that she or he is a leader (House & Aditya, 1997). One of the main factors that shapes an individual's value system (Schwartz & Bardi, 2001) and cognitions and provides meaning to everyday experiences (Oyserman, 2016) is national culture. Accordingly, a growing body of cross-cultural leadership literature has emphasised the role of social culture in leadership attributes and the effectiveness of leadership styles (e.g., Dorfman et al., 2012). For example, one study found that idealised leadership styles varied across different cultural clusters and that leadership effectiveness was a function of congruence between a leaders' style and the culture-endorsed prototype of the leader (Dorfman et al., 2012). As Hofstede (2011) postulated, *ideas about leadership reflect the dominant culture of a country. Asking people to describe the qualities of a good leader is, in fact, another way of asking them to describe their culture* (p. 388).

According to House et al. (1997), culture *is distinctive normative systems consisting of modal patterns of shared psychological properties among members of collectives that result in compelling common affective, attitudinal, and behavioral orientations that are transmitted across generations and that differentiate collectives from each other* (pp. 539–540). Likewise, the cultural context in which individuals are socialised and form their self-view is an essential factor that fosters distinct self-regulatory orientations (Lee et al., 2000).

Most of the research tying regulatory focus to cultural context has focused on the individualism–collectivism dimension (e.g., Kark & Van Dijk, 2019). Individualism and collectivism are the 'deep structure' (Greenfield, 2000) that summarises fundamental dissimilarities in the strength of ties between an individual and their social group (Hofstede, 2011) and has been characterised as the most important cross-cultural difference (Triandis, 2001). In individualistic cultures, the ties between individuals are very loose, and the core unit is the individual as a distinct entity. Individuals strive to distinguish themselves from others through self-sufficiency and personal accomplishment (Heine & Lehman, 1999) and prioritise their personal goals over their inner group's goals (Triandis, 2001). They focus on their interests, achievements and preferences, and tend to define themselves through internal attributes such as traits, inspirations, experiences and attitudes that make them unique (Heine & Lehman, 1999). Thus, an individualistic culture cultivates in its members an independent self-view – a view of oneself defined by unique qualities and characteristics that distinguish them from others (Aaker & Lee, 2001).

Accordingly, individualistic culture appears to foster chronic promotion focus, emphasising the development of qualities and strengths that prove one's distinctiveness (Mesquita & Walker, 2003) and an approach towards positive outcomes (Elliot et al., 2001; Lockwood et al., 2005). Moreover, individuals from individualistic cultures are motivated mainly through positive models (Lockwood et al., 2005), are biased towards positive information (Elliot et al., 2001), have an approach strategy towards goal attainment (Elliot et al., 2001; Lockwood et al., 2005) and are more creative and innovative (Niu & Sternberg, 2003; Saeki et al., 2001) – all characteristics strongly associated with promotion motivation (e.g., Gorman et al., 2012; Lanaj et al., 2012).

In a collectivistic culture, ties between individuals are strong, and a core unit is a group as a relational entity. Individuals are supposed to look after the interest of their in-group, to 'fit' into it by maintaining their relationships with others (Heine & Lehman, 1999), and give priority to the goals of their in-groups over their self-goals (Triandis, 2001). Thus, the collectivistic culture appears to foster a chronic prevention focus. It emphasises eliminating negative or in-group characteristics, qualities and behaviours that might endanger intergroup relations or disappoint significant others (Mesquita & Walker, 2003), while violating social norms leads the individual to experience feelings of shame (Hofstede, 2011). Members of collectivistic cultures tend to focus on their responsibilities and obligations to others (Heine & Lehman, 1999) and prevent undesired outcomes (Elliot et al., 2001; Lockwood et al., 2005). Moreover, these individuals are motivated mainly through negative models (Lockwood et al., 2005), are biased towards information that is framed in avoidance terms (Elliot et al., 2001; Heine et al., 2000) and have an avoidant strategy towards goal attainment (Elliot et al., 2001; Lockwood et al., 2005). These characteristics are strongly associated with prevention motivation (e.g., Gorman et al., 2012; Lanaj et al., 2012).

In line with this reasoning, Lee et al. (2000), in an experimental design study, established the causal relationship between a collectivistic mindset and prevention orientation and an individualistic mindset and promotion orientation. Further, Aaker and Lee (2001) conducted four experiments demonstrating that priming an independent self-view encourages a promotion orientation and that priming an interdependent self-view enhances a prevention orientation. Another study conducted a meta-analytical procedure on four different samples (Lalwani et al., 2009), demonstrating that individualism positively contributed to promotion focus and, through that, to self-descriptive enhancement (i.e., a tendency to characterise oneself in an inflated manner and an unwillingness to admit one's own limitations with the aim to protect positive self-esteem; Paulhus, 1998). In contrast, collectivism positively contributed to prevention focus and, through that, to impression management (i.e., the desire to convey a positive self-image to others; Paulhus, 1998).

As we can see from the literature review presented above, culture has a vital role in shaping the idealised leadership style, leadership's perceived effectiveness and the regulatory inclination of societal members. Hence, understanding the conjunction effect of the national culture on leadership and regulatory foci is crucial and has significant implications for leadership research and for gaining a better understanding of leader–follower relationships and outcomes. Nevertheless, to date, the theoretical model and empirical studies on leadership regulatory focus relationships have mostly neglected the cultural dimensions.

Globalisation and liberalisation of business alter the organisational workforce's composition and increase the number of multinational corporations (Udin et al., 2017). Thus, globalisation of business creates more complex external and internal organisational contexts – an increase in the number of cultures, norms, assumptions and backgrounds of organisational members (Mazur, 2010) – and thus requires more globally 'prepared' leaders (Harvey et al., 2010). Leaders today must align their leadership style with the subsidiary's host culture and the followers' idealised leadership prototype (Dorfman et al., 2012) to motivate their employees and mobilise their efforts to meet organisational goals. Thus, understanding the inner motivation inclinations of followers and a leader's ability to provide the leadership behaviours that fit these motivations is essential to leadership effectiveness in the volatility, uncertainty, complexity and ambiguity (VUCA) environment.

Moreover, the complex cultural context suggests that the organisation's members may form plural cultural identities (Chen et al., 2016; Guan et al., 2020) when the context's different aspects are activated by situational cues, which leads to the salience of diverse cultural values and disparate emphases in working self-concept, relationality and cognitions (Oyserman & Lee, 2008). Thus, the integration of intrapersonal level leader–followers' regulatory focus literature and cultural priming literature can provide new venues for cross-national organisational research and potentially generate tools for managers of multinational corporations.

SUMMARY AND CONCLUSION

In the current chapter, we reviewed and made sense of the wide existing literature on leadership/followership and regulatory focus with regards to context. By adding the contextual perspective, we enabled a new sense-breaking aspect of this phenomenon that can change how we understand, theorise and empirically study the construct of regulatory focus within the arena of leadership and followership in organisations. The magnitude of this effort stems from two opposite but co-existing views on organisational functioning: contingency (i.e., Lawrence & Lorsch, 1967; Woodward, 1965) and paradox (Smith & Lewis, 2011) perspectives. On the one hand, numerous organisational diagnostic models (e.g., Galbraith, 2008; Waterman et al., 1980) build on the assumption that effective organisational functioning requires alignment of organisational subsystems and of the organisation and its external environments (Cummings & Worley, 2014). Congruence between organisational components partly determines organisational effectiveness and enables an organisation to respond effectively to environmental challenges (Middleton & Harper, 2004). We want to expand this notion and suggest that this alignment assumption may be elucidated by integrating regulatory fit theory into organisational development theory and practices. Different internal and external environment features may reframe employee reality in promotion or prevention terms. Situational characteristics that are incongruent with individuals' regulatory orientation or incongruence between regulatory contexts framed by different organisational features can impair an employee's ability to interpret a situation and understand what it requires of them, thus attenuating their motivation and productivity.

On the other hand, as the external organisational environment becomes more global and competitive, organisations must make continuous and concerted efforts to adhere to multiple demands and tensions, such as flexibility–efficiency (Adler et al., 1999), collaboration–control (Sundaramurthy & Lewis, 2003) and exploration–exploitation (Smith & Tushman, 2005). According to the paradox perspective, these tensions are a regular part of organisational life and can offer the organisation developmental opportunities and be harnessed as an energy source (Smith & Lewis, 2011). Managers must apprehend this paradox and not try to suppress it, as this paradox can be a powerful driver of organisational change and help design new organisational practices (Lewis, 2000). From this perspective, regulatory focus theory may also provide valuable insights. The regulatory focus is not only a stable individual disposition, but also can be induced by situational framing, while different regulatory foci are useful in different organisational contexts. Leaders who convey a message that activates followers' regulatory focus in line with contextual demands and recognise how to equalise these regulatory systems will be in a better position to manage organisational paradoxes and lead their followers through them.

In sum, the VUCA environment requires agile organisations and, as a consequence, agile leaders. Following Kotter (2012), two parallel organisational systems enable agility. The first is an organisational operating system that involves traditional hierarchy and processes. This system is characterised by stability, alignment and efficiency. The second is a more fluid, network-like model that allows the organisation to recognise opportunities and implement strategic changes. Thus, today's leaders must be armed with both regulatory focus orientations so they understand the requirements and complexities of their co-existence, or at least be aware of their dispositional regulatory orientation and the advantages of their less developed one.

In the empirical research area, future studies need to move away from the perspective of leader regulatory focus as a 'personal marker' that shapes the followers' regulatory foci, and adopt a more flexible view of this phenomenon as being itself moulded by contextual characteristics. Additionally, future research may address the dynamic perspective of context–leadership–regulatory focus relationships. The elements of context are not static but flux. Thus, a change in the context may lead to change in the followers' regulatory focus, which may change the followers' receptiveness to different leadership styles. Moreover, a change in followers' situational regulatory focus may shape the leaders' regulatory focus and, accordingly, their leadership style. This combination of top-down and bottom-up 'cascades' of regulatory foci, in which the predominant regulatory focus of the followers constrains their managers'/subordinates' influence in the given context, enables an understanding of the complexity of organisational dynamics. Moreover, the multiple contexts affect the leader–follower dynamic; thus, encompassing more than one context variable is needed to draw a better understanding of the role of different contextual elements on shaping the leaders'/followers' regulatory focus or its impact on organisational outcomes.

To conclude, context matters! Thus, it should be taken into account when studying leadership, followership, motivations in the form of self-regulatory focus and the interactions and dynamics among these components. Charting a wider and more nuanced framework of varied contexts at different levels is vital to move the study of leadership/followership and self-regulatory focus forward.

REFERENCES

Aaker, J. L., & Lee, A. Y. (2001). 'I' seek pleasures and 'we' avoid pains: The role of self-regulatory goals in information processing and persuasion. *Journal of Consumer Research*, *28*(1), 33–49.

Ackerman, P. L., & Heggestad, E. D. (1997). Intelligence, personality, and interests: Evidence for overlapping traits. *Psychological Bulletin*, *121*(2), 219–245.

Adler, P. S., Goldoftas, B., & Levine, D. I. (1999). Flexibility versus efficiency? A case study of model changeovers in the Toyota production system. *Organization Science*, *10*(1), 43–68.

Alderfer, C. P. (1969). An empirical test of a new theory of human needs. *Organizational Behavior and Human Performance*, 4(2), 142–175.

Agnihotri, A., & Bhattacharya, S. (2020). Chief executive officer regulatory focus and competitive action frequency. *Group & Organization Management*, 1059601120981411.

Antonakis, J., & Atwater, L. (2002). Leader distance: A review and a proposed theory. *Leadership Quarterly*, 13(6), 673–704.

Avnet, T., Laufer, D., & Higgins, E. T. (2013). Are all experiences of fit created equal? Two paths to persuasion. *Journal of Consumer Psychology*, 23(3), 301–316.

Barrick, M. R., Mount, M. K., & Gupta, R. (2003). Meta-analysis of the relationship between the five-factor model of personality and Holland's occupational types. *Personnel Psychology*, 56(1), 45–74.

Berson, Y., Oreg, S., & Dvir, T. (2008). CEO values, organizational culture and firm outcomes. *Journal of Organizational Behavior: The International Journal of Industrial, Occupational and Organizational Psychology and Behavior*, 29(5), 615–633.

Bianco, A. T., Higgins, E. T., & Klem, A. (2003). How 'fun/importance' fit affects performance: Relating implicit theories to instructions. *Personality and Social Psychology Bulletin*, 29(9), 1091–1103.

Boal, K. B., & Hooijberg, R. (2000). Strategic leadership research: Moving on. *Leadership Quarterly*, 11(4), 515–549.

Bourgeois III, L. J. (1980). Strategy and environment: A conceptual integration. *Academy of Management Review*, 5(1), 25–39.

Bowers, M. R., Hall, J. R., & Srinivasan, M. M. (2017). Organizational culture and leadership style: The missing combination for selecting the right leader for effective crisis management. *Business Horizons*, 60(4), 551–563.

Brockner, J., & Higgins, E. T. (2001). Regulatory focus theory: Implications for the study of emotions at work. *Organizational Behavior and Human Decision Processes*, 86, 35–66.

Brockner, J., Higgins, E. T., & Low, M. B. (2004). Regulatory focus theory and the entrepreneurial process. *Journal of Business Venturing*, 19(2), 203–220.

Bryman, A., Stephens, M., & a Campo, C. (1996). The importance of context: Qualitative research and the study of leadership. *Leadership Quarterly*, 7(3), 353–370.

Büschgens, T., Bausch, A., & Balkin, D. B. (2013). Organizational culture and innovation: A meta-analytic review. *Journal of Product Innovation Management*, 30(4), 763–781.

Bush, J. T., Welsh, D. T., Baer, M. D., & Waldman, D. (2021). Discouraging unethicality versus encouraging ethicality: Unraveling the differential effects of prevention-and promotion-focused ethical leadership. *Personnel Psychology*, 74(1), 29–54.

Cameron, K. S. & Quinn, R. E. (2006). *Diagnosing and Changing Organisational Culture Based on Competing Values Framework*. Jossey-Bass.

Chen, S. X., Lam, B. C., Wu, W. C., Ng, J. C., Buchtel, E. E., Guan, Y., & Deng, H. (2016). Do people's world views matter? The why and how. *Journal of Personality and Social Psychology*, 110(5), 743–765.

Cooper, D., Patel, P. C., & Thatcher, S. M. (2014). It depends: Environmental context and the effects of faultlines on top management team performance. *Organization Science*, 25(2), 633–652.

Crowe, E., & Higgins, E. T. (1997). Regulatory focus and strategic inclinations: Promotion and prevention in decision-making. *Organizational Behavior and Human Decision Processes*, 69(2), 117–132.

Cummings, T. G., & Worley, C. G. (2014). *Organization Development and Change*. Cengage Learning.

DeCarlo, T. E., Powers, T., & Sharma, A. (2021). Manager directives for salesperson ambidextrous selling and resulting job satisfaction: A regulatory focus perspective. *European Journal of Marketing*, 55(11), 3010–3032.

De Cremer, D., Mayer, D. M., Van Dijke, M., Schouten, B. C., & Bardes, M. (2009). When does self-sacrificial leadership motivate prosocial behavior? It depends on followers' prevention focus. *Journal of Applied Psychology*, 94(4), 887–899.

Delegach, M., Kark, R., Katz-Navon, T., & Van Dijk, D. (2017). A focus on commitment: The roles of transformational and transactional leadership and self-regulatory focus in fostering organizational and safety commitment. *European Journal of Work and Organizational Psychology*, 26(5), 724–740

Delegach, M., & Katz-Navon, T. (2021). Regulatory foci and well-being: Coping flexibility and stressor appraisal as explanatory mechanisms. *International Journal of Stress Management*, 28(2), 117–129.

Dorfman, P., Javidan, M., Hanges, P., Dastmalchian, A., & House, R. (2012). GLOBE: A twenty year journey into the intriguing world of culture and leadership. *Journal of World Business*, 47(4), 504–518.

Elliot, A. J., Chirkov, V. I., Kim, Y., & Sheldon, K. M. (2001). A cross-cultural analysis of avoidance (relative to approach) personal goals. *Psychological Science*, 12(6), 505–510.

Fiedler, F. E. (1964). A contingency model of leadership effectiveness. In L. Berkowitz, (Ed.), *Advances in Experimental Social Psychology*. Academic Press.

Finucane, M. L., Mertz, C. K., Slovic, P., & Schmidt, E. S. (2005). Task complexity and older adults' decision-making competence. *Psychology and Aging*, 20(1), 71–84.

Fladerer, M. P., & Braun, S. (2020). Managers' resources for authentic leadership – a Multi-study:

Exploration of positive psychological capacities and ethical organizational climates. *British Journal of Management*, *31*(2), 325–343.

Freitas, A. L., Liberman, N., & Higgins, E. T. (2002). Regulatory fit and resisting temptation during goal pursuit. *Journal of Experimental Social Psychology*, *38*(3), 291–298.

Friedman, R. S., & Förster, J. (2001). The effects of promotion and prevention cues on creativity. *Journal of Personality and Social Psychology*, *81*(6), 1001–1013.

Galbraith, J. R. (2008). Organization design. In J. W. Lorsch (Ed.), *Handbook of Organization Development*. JAI Press.

Gamache, D. L., McNamara, G., Mannor, M. J., & Johnson, R. E. (2015). Motivated to acquire? The impact of CEO regulatory focus on firm acquisitions. *Academy of Management Journal*, *58*(4), 1261–1282.

Gamache, D. L., Neville, F., Bundy, J., & Short, C. E. (2020). Serving differently: CEO regulatory focus and firm stakeholder strategy. *Strategic Management Journal*, *41*(7), 1305–1335.

Gilbert, G. R., Myrtle, R. C., & Sohi, R. S. (2015). Relational behavior of leaders: A comparison by vocational context. *Journal of Leadership & Organizational Studies*, *22*(2), 149–160.

Girod, S. J., & Whittington, R. (2017). Reconfiguration, restructuring and firm performance: Dynamic capabilities and environmental dynamism. *Strategic Management Journal*, *38*(5), 1121–1133.

González-Cruz, T. F., Botella-Carrubi, D., & Martínez-Fuentes, C. M. (2019). Supervisor leadership style, employee regulatory focus, and leadership performance: A perspectivism approach. *Journal of Business Research*, *101*, 660–667.

Gorman, C. A., Meriac, J. P., Overstreet, B. L., Apodaca, S., McIntyre, A. L., Park, P., & Godby, J. N. (2012). A meta-analysis of the regulatory focus nomological network: Work-related antecedents and consequences. *Journal of Vocational Behavior*, *80*, 160–172.

Graham, K. A., Ziegert, J. C., & Capitano, J. (2015). The effect of leadership style, framing, and promotion regulatory focus on unethical pro-organizational behavior. *Journal of Business Ethics*, *126*(3), 423–436.

Greenfield, P. M. (2000). Three approaches to the psychology of culture: Where do they come from? Where can they go? *Asian Journal of Social Psychology*, *3*(3), 223–240.

Guan, Y., Deng, H., & Zhou, X. (2020). Understanding the impact of the Covid-19 pandemic on career development: Insights from cultural psychology. *Journal of Vocational Behavior*, *119*, 103438.

Hakala, H. (2011). Strategic orientations in management literature: Three approaches to understanding the interaction between market, technology, entrepreneurial and learning orientations. *International Journal of Management Reviews*, *13*(2), 199–217.

Hambrick, D. C., Finkelstein, S., & Mooney, A. C. (2005). Executive job demands: New insights for explaining strategic decisions and leader behaviors. *Academy of Management Review*, *30*(3), 472–491.

Hamstra, M. R., Sassenberg, K., Van Yperen, N. W., & Wisse, B. (2014a). Followers feel valued: When leaders' regulatory focus makes leaders exhibit behavior that fits followers' regulatory focus. *Journal of Experimental Social Psychology*, *51*, 34–40.

Hamstra, M. R., Van Yperen, N. W., Wisse, B., & Sassenberg, K. (2011). Transformational–transactional leadership styles and followers' regulatory focus. *Journal of Personnel Psychology*, *10*, 182–186.

Hamstra, M. R., Van Yperen, N. W., Wisse, B., & Sassenberg, K. (2014b). On the perceived effectiveness of transformational–transactional leadership: The role of encouraged strategies and followers' regulatory focus. *European Journal of Social Psychology*, *44*(6), 643–656.

Han, M. C., & Hwang, P. C. (2019). How leader secure-base support facilitates hotel employees' promotive and prohibitive voices: Moderating role of regulatory foci. *International Journal of Contemporary Hospitality Management*, *31*(4), 1666–1683.

Hartnell, C. A., Ou, A. Y., & Kinicki, A. (2011). Organizational culture and organizational effectiveness: A meta-analytic investigation of the competing values framework's theoretical suppositions. *Journal of Applied Psychology*, *96*(4), 677–694.

Hartung, A. (2015). How bad leadership doomed Yahoo: CEO mistakes are costly. *Forbes*. https://www.forbes.com/sites/adamhartung/2015/12/06/how-bad-leadership-doomed-yahoo-ceo-mistakes-are-costly/?sh=ba654296dca9

Harvey, M., Mayerhofer, H., & Hartmann, L. (2010). Corralling the 'horses' to staff the global organization of 21st century. *Organizational Dynamics*, *39*(3), 258–268.

Hatch, M. J. (1997). *Organization Theory: Modern, Symbolic and Postmodern Perspectives*. Oxford University Press.

Heine, S. J., & Lehman, D. R. (1999). Culture, self-discrepancies, and self-satisfaction. *Personality and Social Psychology Bulletin*, *25*(8), 915–925.

Heine, S. J., Takata, T., & Lehman, D. R. (2000). Beyond self-presentation: Evidence for self-criticism among Japanese. *Personality and Social Psychology Bulletin*, *26*(1), 71–78.

Hersey, P., & Blanchard, K. H. (1977). *The Management of Organizational Behavior*. Englewood Cliffs.

Higgins, E. T. (1997). Beyond pleasure and pain. *American Psychologist, 52*, 1280–1300.

Higgins, E. T. (2005). Value from regulatory fit. *Current Directions in Psychological Science, 14*(4), 209–213.

Hmieleski, K. M., & Baron, R. A. (2008). Regulatory focus and new venture performance: A study of entrepreneurial opportunity exploitation under conditions of risk versus uncertainty. *Strategic Entrepreneurship Journal, 2*(4), 285–299.

Hofstede G. (2011). *Culture's Consequences: Comparing Values, Behaviors, Institutions, and Organizations Across Nations*. Sage.

Holland, J. L. (1973). *Making Career Choices: A Theory of Careers*. Englewood Cliffs.

Holland, J. L. (1997). *Making Vocational Choices: A Theory of Vocational Personalities and Work Environments*. Psychological Assessment Resources.

Hou, B., Hong, J., Zhu, K., & Zhou, Y. (2019). Paternalistic leadership and innovation: The moderating effect of environmental dynamism. *European Journal of Innovation Management, 22*, 562–582.

House, R. J., & Aditya, R. N. (1997). The social scientific study of leadership: Quo vadis? *Journal of Management, 23*(3), 409–473.

House, R. J., & Mitchell, T.R. (1974). Path–goal theory of leadership. *Journal of Contemporary Business, 3*, 81–97.

House, R. J., Wright, N. S., & Aditya, R. N. (1997). Cross-cultural research on organizational leadership: A critical analysis and a proposed theory. In P. C. Earley, & M. Erez (Eds.), *New Perspectives in International Industrial-Organizational Psychology* (pp. 535–625). New Lexington.

Howell, J. M., & Shamir, B. (2005). The role of followers in the charismatic leadership process: Relationships and their consequences. *Academy of Management Review, 30*(1), 96–112.

Hu, L., Gu, J., Wu, J., & Lado, A. A. (2018). Regulatory focus, environmental turbulence, and entrepreneur improvisation. *International Entrepreneurship and Management Journal, 14*(1), 129–148.

Idson, L. C., Liberman, N., & Higgins, E. T. (2000). Distinguishing gains from nonlosses and losses from nongains: A regulatory focus perspective on hedonic intensity. *Journal of Experimental Social Psychology, 36*(3), 252–274.

Jansen, J. J., Vera, D., & Crossan, M. (2009). Strategic leadership for exploration and exploitation: The moderating role of environmental dynamism. *Leadership Quarterly, 20*(1), 5–18.

Jaskiewicz, P., Luchak, A. A., Oh, I. S., & Chlosta, S. (2016). Paid employee or entrepreneur? How approach and avoidance career goal orientations motivate individual career choice decisions. *Journal of Career Development, 43*(4), 349–367.

Jepson, D. (2009). Leadership context: The importance of departments. *Leadership & Organization Development Journal, 30*(1), 36–52.

Jiang, W., Wang, L., Chu, Z., & Zheng, C. (2020). How does CEO regulatory focus matter? The impacts of CEO promotion and prevention focus on firm strategic change. *Group & Organization Management, 45*(3), 386–416.

Johnson, R. E., King, D. D., Lin, S. H. J., Scott, B. A., Walker, E. M. J., & Wang, M. (2017). Regulatory focus trickle-down: How leader regulatory focus and behavior shape follower regulatory focus. *Organizational Behavior and Human Decision Processes, 140*, 29–45.

Kark, R., Katz-Navon, T., & Delegach, M. (2015). The dual effects of leading for safety: The mediating role of employee regulatory focus. *Journal of Applied Psychology, 100*(5), 1332–1348.

Kark, R., & Van Dijk, D. (2007). Motivation to lead, motivation to follow: The role of the self-regulatory focus in leadership processes. *Academy of Management Review, 32*(2), 500–528.

Kark, R., & Van Dijk, D. (2019). Keep your head in the clouds and your feet on the ground: A multifocal review of leadership–followership self-regulatory focus. *Academy of Management Annals, 13*(2), 509–546.

Kark, R., Van Dijk, D., & Vashdi, D. (2018). Motivated or de-motivated to be creative? The role of self-regulatory focus in transformational and transactional leadership processes. *Applied Psychology: An International Review, 67*(1), 186–224.

Kashmiri, S., Gala, P., & Nicol, C. D. (2019). Seeking pleasure or avoiding pain: Influence of CEO regulatory focus on firms' advertising, R&D, and marketing controversies. *Journal of Business Research, 105*, 227–242.

Kerr, J., & Slocum, J. W. Jr (2005). Managing corporate culture through reward systems. *Academy of Management Perspectives, 19*(4), 130–138.

Kluger, A. N., & Van Dijk, D. (2010). Feedback, the various tasks of the doctor, and the feedforward alternative. *Medical Education, 44*(12), 1166–1174.

Kotter, J. (2012). Accelerate! *Harvard Business Review, 90*, 43–58.

Kristof-Brown, A. L., Zimmerman, R. D., & Johnson, E. C. (2005). Consequences of individuals' fit at work: A meta-analysis OF person–job, person–organization, person–group, and person–supervisor fit. *Personnel Psychology, 58*(2), 281–342.

Kruglanski, A. W., Pierro, A., & Higgins, E. T. (2007). Regulatory mode and preferred leadership styles: How fit increases job satisfaction. *Basic and Applied Social Psychology, 29*(2), 137–149.

Lalwani, A. K., Shrum, L. J., & Chiu, C. Y. (2009). Motivated response styles: The role of cultural values, regulatory focus, and self-consciousness in socially desirable responding. *Journal of Personality and Social Psychology, 96*(4), 870–882.

Lanaj, K., Chang, C.-H., & Johnson, R. E. (2012). Regulatory focus and work-related outcomes:

A review and meta-analysis. *Psychological Bulletin, 138*(5), 998–1034.

Lawrence, P. R., & Lorsch, J. W. (1967). Differentiation and integration in complex organizations. *Administrative Science Quarterly*, 1–47.

Lee, A. Y., Aaker, J. L., & Gardner, W. L. (2000). The pleasures and pains of distinct selfconstruals: The role of interdependence in regulatory focus. *Journal of Personality and Social Psychology, 78*, 1122–1134.

Lee, B., Lawson, K. M., & McHale, S. M. (2015). Longitudinal associations between gender-typed skills and interests and their links to occupational outcomes. *Journal of Vocational Behavior, 88*, 121–130.

Leikas, S., Lönnqvist, J. E., Verkasalo, M., & Lindeman, M. (2009). Regulatory focus systems and personal values. *European Journal of Social Psychology, 39*(3), 415–429.

Lewis, M. (2000). Exploring paradox: Toward a more comprehensive guide. *Academy of Management Review, 25*(4), 760–776.

Litano, M. L., Major, D. A., Landers, R. N., Streets, V. N., & Bass, B. I. (2016). A meta-analytic investigation of the relationship between leader–member exchange and work–family experiences. *Leadership Quarterly, 27*(5), 802–817.

Lockwood, P., Jordan, C. H., & Kunda, Z. (2002). Motivation by positive or negative role models: Regulatory focus determines who will best inspire us. *Journal of Personality and Social Psychology, 83*, 854–864.

Lockwood, P., Marshall, T. C., & Sadler, P. (2005). Promoting success or preventing failure: Cultural differences in motivation by positive and negative role models. *Personality and Social Psychology Bulletin, 31*(3), 379–392.

Lord, R. G., & Maher, K. J. (1991). Cognitive theory in industrial and organizational psychology. *Handbook of Industrial and Organizational Psychology, 2*, 1–62.

Marquis, C., & Battilana, J. (2009). Acting globally but thinking locally? The enduring influence of local communities on organizations. *Research in Organizational Behavior, 29*, 283–302.

Mazur, B. (2010). Cultural diversity in organisational theory and practice. *Journal of Intercultural Management, 2*(2), 5–15.

McMullen, J. S., Shepherd, D. A., & Patzelt, H. (2009). Managerial (in) attention to competitive threats. *Journal of Management Studies, 46*(2), 157–181.

Mesquita, B., & Walker, R. (2003). Cultural differences in emotions: A context for interpreting emotional experiences. *Behaviour Research and Therapy, 41*(7), 777–793.

Meyer, J. P., Becker, T. E., & Vandenberghe, C. (2004). Employee commitment and motivation: A conceptual analysis and integrative model. *Journal of Applied Psychology, 89*(6), 991–1007.

Middleton, P., & Harper, K. (2004). Organizational alignment: A precondition for information systems success? *Journal of Change Management, 4*(4), 327–338.

Miron-Spector, E., Erez, M., & Naveh, E. (2011). Team composition and innovation: The importance of conformists and attentive-to-detail members. *Academy of Management Journal, 54*(4), 740–760.

Morris, M. H., Kuratko, D. F., & Covin, J. G. (2008). *Corporate Entrepreneurship & Innovation*. Thomson South Western.

Mumford, M. D., Scott, G. M., Gaddis, B., & Strange, J. M. (2002). Leading creative people: Orchestrating expertise and relationships. *Leadership Quarterly, 13*(6), 705–750.

Nadkarni, S., & Chen, J. (2014). Bridging yesterday, today, and tomorrow: CEO temporal focus, environmental dynamism, and rate of new product introduction. *Academy of Management Journal, 57*(6), 1810–1833.

Neubert, M. J., Kacmar, K. M., Carlson, D. S., Chonko, L. B., & Roberts, J. A. (2008). Regulatory focus as a mediator of the influence of initiating structure and servant leadership on employee behavior. *Journal of Applied Psychology, 93*, 1220–1233.

Neubert, M. J., Wu, C., & Roberts, J. A. (2013). The influence of ethical leadership and regulatory focus on employee outcomes. *Business Ethics Quarterly, 23*(2), 269–296.

Niu, W., & Sternberg, R. J. (2003). Societal and school influences on student creativity: The case of China. *Psychology in the Schools, 40*(1), 103–114.

O'Reilly III, C. A., Chatman, J., & Caldwell, D. F. (1991). People and organizational culture: A profile comparison approach to assessing person–organization fit. *Academy of Management Journal, 34*(3), 487–516.

Oren, L. (2004). Regulatory focus as determinant of occupational status. In R. M. Afzalur & R. T. Golembiewski (Eds.), *Current Topics in Management* (pp. 117–132). JAI Press.

Osborn, R. N., Hunt, J. G., & Jauch, L. R. (2002). Toward a contextual theory of leadership. *Leadership Quarterly, 13*(6), 797–837.

Oyserman, D. (2016). What does a priming perspective reveal about culture: Culture-as-situated cognition. *Current Opinion in Psychology, 12*, 94–99.

Oyserman, D., & Lee, S. W. (2008). Does culture influence what and how we think? Effects of priming individualism and collectivism. *Psychological Bulletin, 134*(2), 311–342.

Park, E. S., Hinsz, V. B., & Nickell, G. S. (2015). Regulatory fit theory at work: Prevention focus' primacy in safe food production. *Journal of Applied Social Psychology, 45*(7), 363–373.

Parker, S. L., Laurie, K. R., Newton, C. J., & Jimmieson, N. L. (2014). Regulatory focus moderates the relationship between task control and physiological and psychological markers of stress: A work simulation study. *International Journal of Psychophysiology, 94*(3), 390–398.

Paulhus, D. L. (1998). Interpersonal and intrapsychic adaptiveness of trait self-enhancement: A mixed blessing? *Journal of Personality and Social Psychology, 74*(5), 1197–1208.

Pawar, B. S., & Eastman, K. K. (1997). The nature and implications of contextual influences on transformational leadership: A conceptual examination. *Academy of Management Review, 22*(1), 80–109.

Porter, L. W., & McLaughlin, G. B. (2006). Leadership and the organizational context: Like the weather? *Leadership Quarterly, 17*(6), 559–576.

Quinn, R. E., & Rohrbaugh, J. (1983). A spatial model of effectiveness criteria: Towards a competing values approach to organizational analysis. *Management Science, 29*(3), 363–377.

Richard, O. C., Wu, J., Markoczy, L. A., & Chung, Y. (2019). Top management team demographic-faultline strength and strategic change: What role does environmental dynamism play? *Strategic Management Journal, 40*(6), 987–1009.

Ruiz-Ortega, M. J., Parra-Requena, G., Rodrigo-Alarcón, J., & García-Villaverde, P. M. (2013). Environmental dynamism and entrepreneurial orientation. *Journal of Organizational Change Management, 26*, 475–493.

Saeki, N., Fan, X., & Van Dusen, L. (2001). A comparative study of creative thinking of American and Japanese college students. *Journal of Creative Behavior, 35*(1), 24–36.

Schein, E. H. (2010). *Organizational Culture and Leadership*. John Wiley & Sons.

Schneider, B., Ehrhart, M. G., & Macey, W. H. (2013). Organizational climate and culture. *Annual Review of Psychology, 64*, 361–388.

Schwartz, S. H., & Bardi, A. (2001). Value hierarchies across cultures: Taking a similarities perspective. *Journal of Cross-Cultural Psychology, 32*(3), 268–290.

Shamir, B., & Howell, J. M. (1999). Organizational and contextual influences on the emergence and effectiveness of charismatic leadership. *Leadership Quarterly, 10*(2), 257–283.

Shin, Y., Kim, M., Choi, J. N., & Lee, S. H. (2016). Does team culture matter? Roles of team culture and collective regulatory focus in team task and creative performance. *Group & Organization Management, 41*(2), 232–265.

Smith, T. J., & Campbell, C. (2009). The relationship between occupational interests and values. *Journal of Career Assessment, 17*(1), 39–55.

Smith, W. K., & Lewis, M. W. (2011). Toward a theory of paradox: A dynamic equilibrium model of organizing. *Academy of Management Review, 36*, 381–403.

Smith, W. K., & Tushman, M. L. (2005). Managing strategic contradictions: A top management model for managing innovation streams. *Organization Science, 16*(5), 522–536.

Sternberg, R. J., & Vroom, V. (2002). The person versus the situation in leadership. *Leadership Quarterly, 13*(3), 301–323.

Strauser, D. R., Lustig, D. C., & Çiftçi, A. (2008). Psychological well-being: Its relation to work personality, vocational identity, and career thoughts. *Journal of Psychology, 142*(1), 21–35.

Sundaramurthy, C., & Lewis, M. (2003). Control and collaboration: Paradoxes of governance. *Academy of Management Review, 28*(3), 397–415.

Taylor-Bianco, A., & Schermerhorn, J. (2006). Self-regulation, strategic leadership and paradox in organizational change. *Journal of Organizational Change Management, 19*, 457–470.

Triandis, H. C. (2001). Individualism–collectivism and personality. *Journal of Personality, 69*(6), 907–924.

Udin, S. H., Wahyudi, S. A. Y. S., & Wikaningrum, T. (2017). A systematic literature review of managing workplace diversity for sustaining organizational competitive advantage. *International Journal of Mechanical Engineering and Technology, 8*(12), 398–403

Van Dijk, D., Kark, R., Matta, F., & Johnson, R. E. (2020). Collective aspirations: Collective regulatory focus as a mediator between transformational and transactional leadership and team creativity. *Journal of Business and Psychology*, 1–26.

Van-Dijk, D., & Kluger, A. N. (2004). Feedback sign effect on motivation: Is it moderated by regulatory focus?. *Applied Psychology, 53*(1), 113–135.

Van Dijk, D., & Kluger, A. N. (2011). Task type as a moderator of positive/negative feedback effects on motivation and performance: A regulatory focus perspective. *Journal of Organizational Behavior, 32*(8), 1084–1105.

Vera, D., & Crossan, M. (2004). Strategic leadership and organizational learning. *Academy of Management Review, 29*(2), 222–240.

Waldman, D. A. (1993). A theoretical consideration of leadership and total quality management. *Leadership Quarterly, 4*(1), 65–79.

Waldman, D. A., Ramirez, G. G., House, R. J., & Puranam, P. (2001). Does leadership matter? CEO leadership attributes and profitability under conditions of perceived environmental uncertainty. *Academy of Management Journal, 44*(1), 134–143.

Wallace, J. C., Butts, M. M., Johnson, P. D., Stevens, F. G., & Smith, M. B. (2016). A multilevel model of employee innovation: Understanding the effects of regulatory focus, thriving, and employee involvement climate. *Journal of Management*, *42*(4), 982–1004.

Wallace, J. C., Little, L. M., Hill, A. D., & Ridge, J. W. (2010). CEO regulatory foci, environmental dynamism, and small firm performance. *Journal of Small Business Management*, *48*(4), 580–604.

Waterman, R. H., Peters, T. J., & Phillips, J. R. (1980). Structure is not organization. *Business Horizons*, *23*(3), 14–26.

Weick, K. E. (1979). *The Social Psychology of Organizing*. Random House.

Westerman, J. W., Nowicki, M. D., & Plante, D. (2002). Fit in the classroom: Predictors of student performance and satisfaction in management education. *Journal of Management Education*, *26*(1), 5–18.

Woodward, J. (1965). *Industrial Organization: Theory and Practice*. Oxford University Press.

Wu, C., McMullen, J. S., Neubert, M. J., & Yi, X. (2008). The influence of leader regulatory focus on employee creativity. *Journal of Business Venturing*, *23*(5), 587–602.

Yadav, A., & Dhar, R. L. (2021). Linking frontline hotel employees' job crafting to service recovery performance: The roles of harmonious passion, promotion focus, hotel work experience, and gender. *Journal of Hospitality and Tourism Management*, *47*, 485–495.

PART 3

Through: Leadership Seen through Contemporary Frames

20
Critiquing Leadership and Gender Research through a Feminist Lens

Jackie Ford and Julia Morgan

INTRODUCTION

There remains an enigma at the heart of studies of leadership. Hierarchical and traditional forms of leadership continue to attract considerable research focus, with undue attention being paid to the senior leader as organisational hero, romanticising their influence and neglecting other parties and contexts crucial to leadership. Such interest reinforces the model of leaders as power elites who manipulate organisational discourses through structural and cultural norms that are embedded in historical and (stereo)typically androcentric practices. The emergence of alternative leadership practices and behaviours that work more effectively in times of crises (such as during numerous economic and financial challenges in recent decades including 9/11, the banking crisis, major cyberattacks, Brexit and the Covid-19 pandemic) are posing a challenge to such tradition and lead to the quest for more inclusive, gendered, ethical, eclectic, reciprocal and contextually meaningful understandings of leadership. Looking at leadership through a gendered lens exposes assumptions relating to gender neutrality and makes possible an exploration of why people at work operate in the ways that they do, and why organisations are shaped and policies enacted in the ways that they are (Ely et al., 2003; Sinclair, 2019). Critical, feminist and psychoanalytic theorising on gender, work and organisation provide a challenge to contemporary writings, with recognition of the complex, more contested and less certain ways in which gender is studied, constructed, deconstructed and debated (Ford et al., 2008; Fotaki & Harding, 2018; see also Hearn, 2019).

This chapter presents an overview of key research and debates on gender and leadership. The first part examines traditional and influential approaches that present a broad outline. We highlight the ongoing under-representation of women that was originally documented in the first edition of this handbook (Carli & Eagly, 2011) and trace transitions in thinking on gender and leadership. The second part draws on critical, feminist and psychoanalytical theories to explore emerging issues and new possibilities for gender and leadership research that seek to disrupt, critique and refresh the subject. In exposing assumptions relating to gender neutrality, we consider why people at work operate in the ways that they do and why organisations are organised in gendered ways that perpetuate inequality and injustice – and reinforce masculine behavioural norms. Concluding sections dig deeper to look at micro-revolutionary change at local levels that challenge taken-for-granted assumptions and provide opportunities for analysis that gets to the heart of power, control, subjectivities and explorations of inequalities.

AN OVERVIEW OF APPROACHES

This provides the context to studies of gender within leadership and organisation theory, concluding with key transitions in thinking.

GENDER AND ORGANISATION THEORY

Despite extensive scholarship on gender and organisations, many accounts continue to ignore the relationship between organisational arrangements and gender, which leads some writers to suggest that the resounding silence on gender implicitly conveys that gender considerations are just not an issue (Jeanes et al., 2011; Fotaki & Harding, 2018). Feminist organisational analyses and the study of men and masculinities, however, have problematised the depiction of gender in organisations, and a range of theoretical perspectives have been adopted to expose such neglect. Such writings include explorations of essentialist and constructed accounts of gender; boundaries between families and work organisations; between processes of production and reproduction; the domination of gender power; and gender, class and race and the powers and paradox of sexuality. It is not only gendered considerations that are largely absent from study, but also other multiple-layered social identities such as race, ethnicity, age, social class, disability and sexuality.

Recent decades have witnessed progress in studies of gender and organisations, calling into question the assumed gender-neutral and gender-absent nature of organisational theory (Acker, 1998; Fotaki & Harding, 2018). In many ways, mainstream organisational theory continues to be constructed as non-gendered, although there remains ample evidence that it is written from the perspective, culture and discourse of a man with its *espoused theories of empiricism, rationality, hierarchy, leadership, management, and other masculinised concepts* (Hearn & Parkin 1993, p. 149; see also Hearn 2019; Knights, 2021). While men are portrayed as fitting organisational behaviour, women are associated with the 'feminine' characteristics of caring, nurturing and sharing that are deemed to be more appropriate for the domestic sphere and the reproduction of the home and the family. So, the cultural construction of femininity around body and emotions, and of masculinity around disembodiment and rationality, has made men the 'natural' inhabitants of organisational life, while positioning women as out of place in organisations (Gherardi, 1995; see also Ford, 2010; Ford et al., 2008; Ford et al., 2020). Furthermore, the presence of women in organisations calls for 'remedial' work that seeks to address the ambiguity that their position as *female occupants in a male world* creates (Gherardi, 1995). Such remedial work includes women making themselves acceptable in employment by being discrete and invisible; by requesting permission to speak in meetings; or other behaviours demonstrating a lack of assertiveness to repair the damage done by *infringement of the symbolic order of gender* (Gherardi, 1995, p. 141). These and other restrictive practices are still prevalent in organisational life (Beard, 2018; Fotaki & Harding, 2018) and are especially apparent in gendered accounts of leadership (Harding et al., 2011).

THE UNDER-REPRESENTATION OF WOMEN IN LEADERSHIP ROLES

Viewing organisations as gendered institutions allows us to explore the ways in which gender roles are ascribed to bodies and jobs in restrictive ways, which has led to women being segregated and marginalised from leadership positions of power and authority. While research has revealed that across the globe more women are ascending the hierarchical ladder (McKinsey Global Institute, 2015), the reality remains that the number of women in leadership positions of power and prestige is still significantly low. Indeed, proportions of women in senior management internationally declined in 2018 (Grant Thornton, 2018) and women remain a minority presence at board level (Vinnicombe et al., 2018), patterns mirrored across the professions. Women are under-represented at senior levels in engineering (Khilji & Pumroy, 2019), accounting (Castro & Holvino, 2016), medicine (Miller & Clark, 2008), law (Pringle et al., 2017), human resources (Webber, 2019a) and professorial academics (Catalyst, 2020).

These figures suggest that although the gender landscape of career progression has changed markedly since the 1970s women continue to experience considerable disadvantage (Bolton and Muzio, 2008; Durbin & Tomlinson, 2014). They earn less than their male counterparts (Webber, 2019b), face structural, cultural and informal barriers to career progress (Pringle et al., 2017) and suffer from attempting to conform with inflexible career structures (Miller & Clark, 2008). The Everyday Sexism Project, #MeToo movement and numerous studies reveal the persistence of sexual harassment and gendered inequalities (Vachhani & Pullen, 2019). Eradication of seemingly outdated prejudices, norms and antiquated modes of thinking is painfully slow. The coronavirus pandemic has illuminated questions of both leadership and the gender landscape – whether at global, national or local levels and across the political, economic and social contexts (Pullen & Vacchani, 2021; Wilson, 2020). But the seeds of what has been going on were sown long before the recent spotlight placed by the pandemic and this chapter seeks to explore some of these further.

GENDER AND LEADERSHIP: TRADITIONAL PERSPECTIVES

Traditional approaches to the study of gender and leadership tend to adopt a largely psychological perspective, grounded in research that explores the relationship between gender and leadership, with a particular essentialist focus on the question as to whether men and women lead differently (Eagly & Carli, 2003; Carli & Eagly, 2011). There appears a considerable bifurcation in the literature, with one strand finding no evidence of gender difference in leadership behaviours (Andersen & Hansson, 2011) and the other suggestive of significant difference, arguing that 'feminine' leadership behaviours present a female leadership advantage (Helgesen, 1990; Rosener, 1990). Such findings are further reinforced through research on transformational leadership (Bass, 1998), perceived as inspiring and nurturing subordinates' abilities through its reliance on trust and communication. Rosener (1990) argues that because men and women are socialised differently, they also lead differently. She suggests that women's style of leadership differs from that of men; and women are more likely to adopt transformational approaches which are perceived as being of greater significance in present-day organisations. Arguably much of this research is informed by stereotypical assumptions and judgements in relation to gender, frequently linked to gender role identity.

One of the enduring themes within the literature relates to such gender stereotypes and the ways in which these are played out in leadership practices. Gender role identity ascribes certain stereotypical traits to individuals; for men these tend to reflect agentic characteristics (such as competitive, dominant, assertive and ambitious) whereas women are perceived as displaying communal behaviours (such as compassion, kindness and nurturing). Much of this can be explained by drawing upon the influential and pervasive concept of role congruity theory (Eagly & Karau, 2002; Eagly & Carli, 2007). Grounded in social role theory, role denotes behavioural norms that are appropriate and consistent with gender stereotypes, and which are both prescriptive and descriptive in nature. A meta-analysis conducted by Koenig et al., (2011) of 69 previous studies demonstrates that stereotypes of successful leaders are still defined in masculine terms and remain in line with the mental model of 'think manager think male' (Schein, 1973). Such perceptions feed into and influence people's ideas of what a leader should be; where there is greater mismatch of role congruity, the more negative the attitudes will be towards women performing such roles.

Women leaders are therefore the target of two forms of bias, namely descriptive beliefs, which are expectations of what women do, and prescriptive beliefs, which are expectations of what women ideally do (Cialdini & Trost, 1998). Descriptive bias can be explained by Heilman's (2001) lack of fit model suggesting that the leadership role is inconsistent with attributes ascribed to women, leading to women experiencing greater likelihood of failure. Prescriptive bias occurs when a woman displays agentic leadership behaviours that accord with behaviours required to match the stereotypical leader, which are seen as violating gender role expectations and often lead to backlash effects (Heilman, 2012).

These assumptions feed into and influence the construction of gender binaries *that permeate organisations and shape our understandings of who can and should be leaders* (Elliott & Stead, 2018, p. 2). Research further suggests that women experience the 'double bind', where if women are perceived as being too communal they are criticised for not being agentic and when too agentic they are criticised for lacking communion (Eagly & Carli, 2007). When women progress to senior leadership roles the gaze upon them is both intense and highly disparaging. Such criticism has led to women leaders being labelled 'barracudas', 'battle-axes' (Still, 1994) and 'ice queen' (Heilman, 2001) and often having to endure pejorative characterisations such as *abrasive, arrogant, or self-promoting* (Ely et al., 2011, p. 482).

Empirical research has consistently supported the validity of backlash theory (cf. Williams and Tiedens, 2016), confirming how men as leaders can express dominance without incurring 'likeability' penalties whereas women cannot. The effect of the double bind can also be observed in the way women are criticised for power-seeking (Okimoto & Brescoll, 2010), self-promotion (Rivers & Barnett, 2013) or negotiating favourable employment treatment such as salary increases (Amanatullah & Tinsley, 2013). Women therefore tend to avoid these enacting behaviours for fear of social penalty and thereby deny themselves roles in senior leadership positions (Hoyt, 2010).

Barriers to Women's Progression

Early studies on women's absence from leadership roles have indicated multiple causes, some of which focused on the notion that a lack of qualified women creates a *pipeline problem* (Eagly and Karau, 2002) while other research explores the effects of the 'glass ceiling' or the 'labyrinths' that women face in their attempts to progress into leadership positions (Eagly & Carli, 2007). What is widely acknowledged is that a small rise in women's presence in leadership roles has done little to counteract the persistence of gender inequalities within organisations (Boni-Le Goff & Le-Feurve, 2017).

More recently, research has focused on gender-based organisation analysis as a means of identifying the major causes of inequality (Kumra, 2014). Such studies illuminate how implicitly gendered organisational and contextual structures, practices and behaviours can have differential outcomes for men's and women's careers. These are conceptualised as *demand-side* factors that relate to employer's actions and *supply-side* factors that refer to individual's choices and behaviour (Fernandez-Mateo & Kaplan, 2018). Empirical studies have considered the implications of demand- and supply-side perspectives, including gender pay gaps (Pucheta-Martinez & Bel-Oms, 2015); impacts on firms' performance (Martin-Ugedo & Minguez-Vera, 2017); and the under-representation of women in leadership (Gupta & Raman, 2014).

Demand-side factors tend to be operationalised within the organisational context and centre around issues such as gender discrimination (Mateos de Cabo et al., 2011; Hoobler et al., 2016), biased human capital perceptions (Ely et al., 2011) and lack of social and cultural capital (Seierstad, 2015; Terjesen et al., 2015). Many of these have been linked to earlier notions of the metaphorical labyrinth (Eagly & Carli, 2007) depicting the plethora of obstacles women face in navigating their way to more senior leadership roles.

Supply-side factors tend to relate to gender role theory, gender self-schema and work-family conflict (Gabaldon et al., 2016), and are influenced by a range of societal and labour-market influences. Supply-side factors are mobilised through presumed gender differences relating to values, motivations and aspirations, and in the absence of these being made explicit by women themselves they may be arbitrarily ascribed to their gendered identity.

Structural Barriers

Research interest has also turned to the structural framing of the gendered nature of organisations (Boni-Le Goff & Le-Feurve, 2017; Reskin & Roos, 1990). Reskin and Roos (1990) argue that because of patriarchal influences and homosocial preferences, women are placed behind men in employers' performance evaluations and consequently subordinated to men within labour markets. This notion of gender queues remains as pervasive as ever, seemingly institutionalised by organisations and submerged within exclusionary occupational strategies (Muzio et al., 2011). Such strategies are deployed specifically to protect the male prerogative of access to legitimate knowledge, and to maintain their authority and control (Witz, 1990).

There is much empirical evidence supporting the notion of institutionalised gender queues and occupational closure strategies that reinforce earlier patterns of gendered career disadvantage for women. Ford et al. (2020) explore the experiences of professional women working in the legal and human resource management sectors. Their findings reveal how women pioneers were often silenced by requirements to conform to male-dominated norms, values and practices governing masculine career pathways. Consequently, women adopt a predominately masculine language and set of practices that in turn constitute a significant barrier to effective resistance and preclude new ways of speaking about careers.

Other studies report that despite the professions' universal rhetoric of being committed to diversity and inclusion, law firms remain segmented by gender, in which the *most powerful and well remunerated positions remain overwhelmingly occupied by white men* (Sommerlad, 2016, p. 61). Such research identifies several recurring themes that contribute to women's lower status and marginalisation. These include the prevalence of hyper-masculine work cultures; deepening trends of work intensification; the heightened significance of client care and greater demands being placed on their time such that a harmonious work-life balance is impossible to achieve. Research findings have resulted in what is depicted as *boundary spanning roles* that adversely impact women's working conditions (Haynes, 2008; Sommerlad, 2016, p. 61; Tomlinson et al., 2013).

Homosocial Barriers

Homosociality is a concept that has been used to describe a preference for relations with the same gender (Gruenfield & Tiedens, 2005) and has informed organisational and gender scholarship as a way of explaining how men reproduce masculine hegemony (Gregory, 2009). Among the first authors to acknowledge the impact of homosocial behaviour and reproduction were Kanter (1977) and Lipman-Blumen (1976). Other studies have explored homosocial interaction in all male groups and how, through homosocial storytelling and humour, men are able to collectively define what makes a 'man' (Gregory, 2009). Homosociality as an unreflexive practice may explain why gender equality initiatives have had little success as they rarely focus on making men more aware of their own homosocial practice (Holgersson, 2013). When embedded in organisational structures and cultures, homosociality tends to lead to a homogenised and masculine work culture that simultaneously acts to reproduce men's dominance and generate barriers to women's progression.

These and other study findings raise several challenges for women, not least within recruitment, performance management and promotional evaluations where an observable social distinction such as gender becomes a status characteristic, where individuals (men) with the higher status characteristic, benefit from social advantages relative to other individuals (women).

TOWARDS NEW POSSIBILITIES FOR GENDER AND LEADERSHIP

We turn to more recent critical writings on leadership in our endeavour to disrupt, critique and seek new possibilities for research through gender to leadership. The emergent field of critical leadership studies (CLS) sets the context and, thereafter, we engage with critical feminist psychoanalytic theories to explore the emancipatory potential for new ways in which to research, conceptualise and practice leadership.

CRITICAL LEADERSHIP AND GENDER STUDIES

Critical studies of leadership create opportunities to generate research and theorising that draw from wider disciplinary perspectives. Such studies enable us to explore the subjective, the personal and the interpersonal, and about how people think, talk and dream about leadership (Collinson, 2011; Ford et al., 2008; Zoller & Fairhurst, 2007). CLS as a field of study is underpinned largely by critical theory, feminist, poststructuralist, psychoanalytic and social constructionist traditions and highlights the need to question leadership as a *normalizing template* (Alvesson & Spicer, 2012, p. 369), with a particular focus on exploring *what is neglected, absent or deficient in mainstream leadership research* (Collinson, 2011, p. 181). CLS not only provides a challenge to the assumed importance of leadership and the neglect of power asymmetries and gendered considerations (Ford, 2019), but also advances understandings of leadership that recognise it as a co-produced, indeterminate and discursive process that is embedded in context and culture (Ford, 2010; Learmonth & Morrell, 2017, 2019; Sutherland, 2019). Despite this emerging body of more critical study, the mainstream of leadership scholarship remains largely untouched, most especially in the US (Tourish, 2015; Wilson, 2020).

In addition to discursive CLS scholarship, a small but developing body of critical feminist literature focuses on leadership as an embodied, and thus material, practice (Ford et al., 2011; Ford et al., 2017). It explores such issues as bodily presence, body language, body work and embodied knowledge (Biehl, 2019; Fisher & Reiser Robbins, 2014; Ropo & Parviainen, 2001; Ropo & Sauer, 2008; Sinclair, 2011). Guthey & Jackson (2005) explore how photographs of leaders provide iconic representations of (otherwise immaterial) organisations, while Melina et al. (2013) seek both to conceptualise the relationship between the body and leadership and to explore ways in which to articulate and translate leaders' embodied knowledge. A special issue of *Leadership* (2013) focuses on embodiment, aesthetics and affect (Pullen & Vacchani, 2013). Its editors critique the dominance of *disembodied, over-cognitivised and pseudo-rational approaches* (p. 318) to understanding leadership and advocate research that embraces materiality, embodiment and corporeality. Ladkin's (2013) phenomenological account of felt and bodily based experiences emphasises the invisible intersubjective relations at the heart of leadership, interactions in which bodies, presumed gender and gender appearances are 'markers' used by employees to make sense of leaders and leadership (Muhr & Sullivan, 2013). Leadership can thus be interpreted as an emergent and creative process of inter-practices of leading and following (Kupers, 2013) that are embodied within space (Ropo et al. (2013), in ways akin to a musical performance where leader and follower bodies move and gesture to one another (Bathurst & Cain, 2013; see also Biehl, 2019).

These studies argue the merits of understanding leadership as corporeal practice. However, there is a need for recognition of not only bodies, but also other materialities such as technologies and places, as well as discourses, language, power and resistance, in the emergence of leadership (Ford et al., 2017; Pullen & Vacchani, 2013). More recently, scholars highlight further ways in which critical studies of gender are becoming more nuanced and diverse, with greater focus beyond the gender binary. This enables us to rethink the implications of gender, embodiment and fluidity in organising and managing. It disrupts our understanding of dualisms between sex (men and women), gender (masculinity and femininity) and mind/body and, in so doing, to analyse ways in which dominant power relations constitute heteronormativity throughout organisation history (McMurray and Pullen, 2020). A more recent body of scholarship that aims to disrupt persistent and harmful binaries that are discursively (re)produced within and through organisations can be found with queer theory (Rumens et al., 2018). Foundational to queer theory is the work of Foucault (1979, 1986, 1992). Most notably, Sedgwick (1991) and Butler (1990, 2004) interweave Foucault's ideas with those of other major theorists to challenge the ontologies of gender and to question the essentialist, given nature of grounding categorisations such as straight/gay, heterosexual/homosexual and, indeed, male/female.

Butler's challenge to social constructionist theories of gender shows that what is constructed is not so much identities but *regulatory fictions* which govern identities, and which order and organise the 'taken-for-granted' through which identities emerge. Thus, there is no core or essential centre that produces an authentic identity; rather it is the very performance of identity which produces that identity itself. In Butler's words, *there is no gender behind the expressions of gender* (1990, p. 25), for gender is constructed through the very *doing* of gender according to the norms of how a person with the relevant genitalia should behave. In other words, we dress up as male or female, move our bodies in a masculine or feminine way, conform to expectations (norms) of what it is to be male or female, never question this doing and this achieving of masculinity and femininity, and thereby *perform ourselves* as men or women (Harding et al., 2011).

Drawing on queer theory for the study of leadership enables us not only to question conventional leadership theory, but also to identify and illuminate forms of injustice. Queering leadership exposes ways in which the words 'leader' and 'leadership' confer powerful identities on the dominant leader and disempower the subordinate follower, but it also provides a language in which to challenge forms of oppression in organisations.

An early, critical contribution to leadership study is worthy of specific reference, as it suggests tangible ways, through feminist scholarship, to explore new formations of collective social action to replace the pervading leadership myth. Gemmill and Oakley (1992, p. 114) argue that while mainstream writers proclaim a positive subtext for leadership, they suggest it is *a serious sign of social pathology [...] a special case of an iatrogenic social myth that induces massive, learned helplessness among members of a social system.* This learnt helplessness can be seen through non-leaders being unable to imagine alternative viable options, along with accompanying feelings of despair and a reluctance to initiate any form of action. This leads to a deeper sense of social hopelessness and helplessness and the pursuit of a saviour (leader) or miraculous rescue (leadership) accelerates. In arguing that we should have less blind faith in the curative powers of leadership, Gemmill and Oakley propose a feminist conception of leadership that seeks to reconceptualise leadership and power relationships based on supportive and collaborative behaviours that encourage new ways of relating and working together. While research within leadership and organisation studies has been slow to respond to their call, more recent feminist scholarship advocates radical forms of ethical, relational leadership (Ford, 2019; Pullen & Vacchani, 2021; Sinclair, 2014) in which mutual empathy, reciprocal care, shared purpose and compassion are allowed to surface.

THE VALUE OF FEMINIST, CRITICAL THEORY IN STUDIES OF LEADERSHIP

Feminist theory affords several intellectual and practical values. First, it sustains social criticism by revealing subordination and the moral and political implications of that subordination. Making intellectual sense of the subordination of women has turned out to be a more encompassing project than political analyses of it may suggest, as it has exposed much of the male bias of the history of ideas and of society. It has enabled feminist scholars to reveal several distinct errors, notably sexism (taking men to be of greater value than women) and androcentrism (taking maleness or masculinity to be the norm for human-ness or humanity). Furthermore, feminist theories provide lenses through which ideas and social practices can be analysed and gender relations problematised (Flax, 1993). These theories have shown that much of what we do, and how we conceptualise what we do, is affected by gender. Finally, feminist theories offer emancipatory potential of what life, people and society would be like without the subordination of women. Feminist thinking opens possibilities to reconstruct ways of theorising leadership in organisations (Callas, 1991; Ford et al., 2008; Fotaki & Harding, 2018).

Casting a critical, feminist and psychoanalytic lens on gender and leadership enables us to expose the mythical character of self-determining, individualistic and autonomous ideas of subjectivity. Gender is one of the conditions of possibility of modern subjectivity: an *integral part of the process of becoming and being an individual subject* (Flax, 1993, p. 97). Our language and sets of social practices exist through which (gendered) subjectivity is constituted and by which individuals make sense of it to themselves and others. Since gendering is such a complex and over-determined process, it is not possible to be conscious of all its determinants, effects and consequences. In the very nature of going about our daily lives, of working and having relationships, our gendered selves are made to fit with and be intelligible to others. In this way, we are *inserted into pre-existing, gendered social locations and practices* (Flax, 1993, p. 97). So, questions of gender and other multiple-layered social identities are too important to ignore in writings on leadership.

Through exploring gender and leadership through a power lens we can better acknowledge the significance of social inequalities and potential injustices in the workplace. The role of agency is clearly central to such issues and a focus on social identities (including race, gender, class, age, sexuality, etc.) more readily accentuates structural, cultural and material issues in the workplace which in turn reinforce the significance of considering both micro- and macro-dynamics of power that inevitably influence the experiences of leadership in the workplace (Ospina & Foldy, 2009) and political contexts too (Pullen & Vacchani, 2021). Structural concerns include recognising that *social relations* at work are part of a deep-seated, broader system of relations between unequal social groups based on gender and/or class and/or race. Of central concern here is the creation by dominant groups of structures that serve the interests of these groups and seek to maintain this group's dominance. In relation to gender, for instance, differences are identified as an underlying social division in which women are systematically oppressed in order to service the interests of other more powerful social groups, particularly men but also whites and ruling classes (Halford & Leonard, 2001).

Unless we see gender as a *social relation*, rather than as an opposition of inherently different beings, we will not be able to identify the varieties and limitations of different women's (or men's) powers and oppressions within societies. Gender relations have tended to be ones of domination and, as a result, feminist theories should have a compensatory as well as a critical aspect (Flax, 1993). We need to recover and explore the aspects of social relations that have been suppressed, unarticulated, or denied within dominant (masculine) viewpoints. We need to regain and write the histories of women and others who identify as non-binary into the accounts and stories that cultures tell about themselves. Yet, we also need to think about how so-called women's activities are partially constituted by and through their location within the web of social relations that make up any society. That is, we need to know how these activities are affected but also how they effect, or enable, or compensate for the consequences of men's activities, as well as their implication in class, sex or race relations.

Critical, feminist, psychoanalytic informed theorising show how depictions of leadership are thoroughly embedded in relationships and experiences, in local context – and thus in social practices. Such writings offer much potential for developing sophisticated, innovative, highly informed analyses of organisations and working lives. To introduce some of these treasures to leadership thinking, we draw on Flax's and Benjamin's writings that offer new directions and possibilities for taking forward critical analyses of leadership studies. We suggest that they offer potential for new theoretical perspectives, a new politics and a new ethics of organisations that can stimulate different ways of thinking.

NEW DIRECTIONS AND POSSIBILITIES FOR RETHINKING GENDER THROUGH LEADERSHIP

We explore relational leadership through feminist, critical theorist and psychoanalysts Jessica Benjamin and Jane Flax, to offer a reimagining of the relational and ethical dynamic through gender to leadership.

Gender status is deeply personal and yet we continue to grapple with it as a social fact (Flax, 2004). In workplaces, we struggle with gender's normative and regulatory demands in the face of certain leadership privileges and power differentials, which are further compounded when illuminated through an intersectional lens. Exploring gender as a transitional space enables us to hold in mind the complexity of gender. As Flax (2004, p. 908) reminds us, gender *is a social fact; a socially constructed category; a possible site of intensely subjective fantasy, emotion, and meaning construction; and an effect of power with differential and asymmetric consequences inherent in varying positions within its grid.*

Similarly, Benjamin (1998) argues that gender is a complex achievement whose maintenance requires psychic energy. Drawing on psychoanalytic thought makes possible an exploration of how men and women internalise their gendered identities, it enables exploration of the ways in which the unconscious operates in the formation of the gendered psyche and provides a means of understanding the emotional investment that men and women may have in their identities, which may include anxiety and conflict that arises from them. Psychoanalysis offers additional resources with which to understand masculine and feminine identities that are not available through discourse theory. Lupton and Barclay (cited in Alsop et al., 2002, p. 156) propose that *one area which discourse theory has tended to overlook is an understanding of the inner world of the subject and the importance of emotional states, mutuality and intimate relations between people.* It is this *inner* world that is worthy of further exploration.

As Flax (1993, p. 123) has argued:

A social self would come to be partially in and through powerful, affective relationships with other persons. These relations with others and our feelings and fantasies about them, along with experiences of embodiedness also mediated by such relations can come to constitute an 'inner' self that is neither fictive or 'natural'. Such a self is simultaneously embodied, gendered, social and unique. It is capable of telling stories and of conceiving and experiencing itself in all these ways.

Flax (1981) suggests that gender is the first form of social differentiation. We learn from an early age that we are not persons, with a variety of characteristics that include gender, but male and female persons. Gender becomes part of who we are as individuals on the most deep, unconscious level. This would not necessarily be problematic except that gender carries with it such strong associations of superiority and inferiority. Expanding upon her earlier writings, Benjamin (1995) shows that the interactions between culture and psyche in the West contain a refusal to allow subjectivity to the woman. Such refusal results in the interplay of domination and submissions between man and woman or the masculine and feminine, or between the dominant (who stake a claim to rationality and are the seducers) and the submissive (who are cast as non-rational, emotional, nurturing and seduced).

Gender and Domination: Psychoanalytic Theories

Flax and Benjamin's writings have considerable explanatory potential in gendered explorations of leadership. Many theories of subjectivity and identity in management and organisation studies are influenced directly or indirectly by Hegel's thesis on the emergence of the modern Western subject. Benjamin's psychoanalytic writings build on Hegel's thesis and this is particularly pertinent to leadership studies because she argues that all encounters with others bring with them the potential for relationships of domination and subordination, and such relationships are fundamental to workplace encounters for, being hierarchical structures, they are inescapably places in which relationships of domination and submission – or powerful and powerlessness – are played out. Indeed, the very terms 'leaders' and 'followers' bespeak of a chain of command in which one is dominant and the other, the subordinate, must bend their will to that of the superior in the hierarchy. It is therefore particularly apposite for exploring the relational leadership dynamic as an encounter in which the leader becomes a leader only through their followers recognising them in that way.

It may be a rather obvious exploration of the association between gender and domination. As Benjamin (1988, p. 74) attests: *Men, after all, have everywhere dominated women […] yet even if we accept this logic, we would still want to understand how the subjugation of women takes hold in the psyche and shapes the pattern of domination.* The deep structure of gender complementarity has continued notwithstanding the increased flexibility of contemporary roles undertaken by men and women (Benjamin, 1995; Flax, 1981). The view of the mother as object and the man as adopting a defensive masculine stance resounds in our culture. In psychoanalytic discourse, the child relates to the mother as an object of his drives, and correspondingly devalues her independent subjectivity to an extent that recognition of woman as the other is seen as an exceptionally scarce event, a *moment of rare innocence, the recovery of lost paradise* (Benjamin, 1988, p. 75). The refusal of the man to recognise the other is further exacerbated by a woman's own acceptance of her lack of subjectivity and her continuing willingness to offer recognition without expecting it in turn as a complete self-denial.

Applying this to organisational and leadership roles, women participate in their own subjugation; they repress their sociability and their social agency and remain as slaves to the organisational master. Leadership scholars need to recognise this gendered nature of organisational life. The defensive masculine stance serves to promote a dualism of man as subject and woman as object, as part of what Benjamin depicts as the seemingly unavoidable situation in which the boy liberates himself in a situation of almost second birth from the woman who bore him. In this second birth, the fantasy of omnipotence and erotic domination begins.

As the absence of mutuality of recognition continues, the unequal complementarity is perpetuated in which the man plays the master and the woman plays the slave. Benjamin (1988, p. 81) contends that even when the roles are reversed and the woman plays the master to the man's slave, the sense of each *playing the other* is never lost. She argues that *gender continues, consciously and unconsciously to represent only one part of the polarised whole, one aspect of the self–other relationship*. This sustained lack of maternal subjectivity prevents women from experiencing the sense of successful destruction and survival that is needed in the interaction of individuals as social beings.

It is only when the woman (the mother in Benjamin's writing) feels entitled to be a person in her own right that she can ever be seen as such by others. This is important in relation to a feminist critique of organisations. As Benjamin (1998) notes the stereotype of the female as a career woman is that, for her to succeed, the career woman must clone herself on the man and thereby demonstrate that she is as disconnected and remote as a man (see also Flax, 1981). However, this yearning for individuation that is based on a denial of the need for others is not liberation for women, but rather a perpetuation of domination. The message for the future in leadership and organisation studies is a need to confront this continuing denial of recognition of the other and to experience again the lost tension between one individual and another. This requires rediscovering a tension that can only be sustained through the lived experience of mutuality of recognition of both leader and follower and the meeting together of separate minds. *What Jessica Benjamin refers to as a communion rather than a conquest of others. The mutuality of recognition requires not only a sense of confidence in one's own identity but also an understanding of the dependence of self on the other for one's own sense of self.*

Feminist psychoanalytic theorising provides a means through which to explore questions of subordination and domination that continue to be so important in studies of leadership. It provides a vocabulary of recognition and interaction and enables further exploration of subjectivity and intersubjectivity and a means through which to consider the relational, emotional, irrational, discursive and symbolic dimensions of people's working lives.

Relational encounters are thus crucial to explorations through gender to leadership. Daily experiences and interactions with colleagues in the workplace attest to the unique and multiple ways in which individuals bring a sense of their own subjective identity to the workplace – in all its myriad forms – as parents, siblings, friends, enemies and work colleagues, as well as through our social identities including gender, age, ethnicity, class, etc. All these factors can influence the relations with those around them. Thus, rather than focusing on styles of leadership and the heroic qualities of leaders, leadership is the collective and relational work of many people in an organisation. The focus thus shifts away from the omnipotent leader and towards followers *with* leaders in an interactive and relational dynamic, providing voice to all people in an organisation and harnessing the combined intelligence of the workforce as part of a process of building new relationships within, across and indeed outside the organisation. Such a refocus requires a radical reimagining of leadership theorising.

FEMINIST PSYCHOANALYSIS AND GENDERED THINKING IN LEADERSHIP STUDIES

Benjamin (1998, p. 22) argues that as *fundamentally social beings*, humans crave social stimulation, warmth and emotional interchanges from the beginning of life. This can be translated through to organisational life. In workplaces, there is ongoing need for emotional exchange, mutual acknowledgement, recognition and social contact. As active, social beings we need the interaction and recognition from others in order to make sense of who we are as well as how we relate to others. Her exploration of the centrality of the concepts of *recognition* and *intersubjectivity* has what can be perceived as a major contribution to making sense of and providing interpretive potential to studies of gendered leadership relationships.

Intersubjectivity

The notion of intersubjectivity in psychoanalysis is articulated in deliberate contrast to the logic of subject and object which predominates in Western philosophy and science. In Benjamin's (2004, p. 5) terms, intersubjectivity is *a relationship in which each person experiences the other as a 'like subject,' another mind who can be 'felt with,' yet has a distinct, separate center of feeling and perception*. Such intersubjectivity is explicitly political and ethical, in which the individual grows in and through the relationship to others. It offers a rich set of provocations about what we mean by freedom of individuals, describing the existence of a relationship between self and other in which the other subject is present as a subject in their own right and not merely as part of the subject's environment. It is through *reflexive recognition* by the other that we know ourselves. It is both through the confirming response of others and how we find ourselves that is important – and this is why psychoanalytic theory can speak for interpretations of organisational life and gendered leadership relations. It enables the *mutual recognition* of an inter-relationship and reciprocity between those in powerful and less powerful positions in the workplace.

Recognition

This mutuality of recognition is important as it contains the need to recognise as well as be recognised by the other. This inter-relationship is central – to see others as both like us and yet different from us, and to see the interaction and impact of the recognition on our sense of self. In an organisational setting, individuals at work require the existence of another, so that there is someone who recognises them. Benjamin refers to the dialectic of control in which if I completely control the other, then the other ceases to exist, and if the other completely controls me, then I cease to exist. Our own independent existence requires the recognition of the other, in the construction and maintenance of a tension between what Benjamin (1988, p. 53) refers to as *the contradictory impulses of both asserting the self and recognising the other*. This is important in relation to organisation studies generally, and to explorations of concepts of gendered leadership relations in workplaces. A lack of recognition of the self as a subject denies the contradictory desires for freedom and interdependence, for wanting to be both subordinated and free to leave at the same time.

For the leader to understand their leadership role, they need to both assert themself and recognise the other. If they fail to do this, then the outcome (according to Benjamin) is domination. The mutuality of recognition is central – wherein the subject accepts the premise that others are separate but nonetheless share like feelings and intentions. The subject is compensated for his loss of sovereignty by the pleasure of sharing and of the communication with another subject.

This emancipatory potential of Benjamin's idea of intersubjectivity and recognition thus offers *a rich set of provocations to re-think what we mean by freedom and equality* (Yeatman, 2015, p. 20). Benjamin's work enables us to shed light on workplace experiences of power asymmetries, domination and subordination, and of voicelessness and inferiority in the face of leadership encounters.

TOWARDS AN ETHICS OF RECIPROCAL CARE IN LEADERSHIP

Flax and Benjamin's theorising provides an opportunity to explore ways in which leadership thinking could be realigned to take account of the significance of the mutuality of recognition and to develop a gendered ethics of reciprocal care in leadership. Flax (2004) proposes the value of locating gender (and indeed race and other social identities) within and as a *transitional space*. This is a concept originally attributed to Winnicott (1971) in which questions such as *is this real or not*[?] are suspended and irrelevant (Flax, 2004, p. 908). Suspending the reality question or rejecting the construal of objective/subjective as a binary enables us to hold in mind the complexity of gender.

Winnicott (1971) describes the transitional space as a *third world*, an intermediate area that is neither subjective nor objective, neither purely inner nor outer. It bridges the gaps between self and other and inner and outer reality. This notion is closely related to Benjamin's (2004, p. 7) concept of *thirdness*, as *a quality or experience of intersubjective relatedness that has as its correlate a certain kind of internal mental space*. Benjamin's thirdness is built on intersubjectivity and mutual recognition; on attending to dominance and submission; and creating relational systems between supervisors and subordinates, executive managers and workers (Diamond, 2007; Ford, 2019). Through the concept of the third, Benjamin's feminist critique of patriarchal freedom creates both a challenge and an opportunity for a two-person, subject-to-subject approach to freedom. As Yeatman (2015, p. 5) attests, Benjamin's writings allow *the patriarchal subject to change his idea of what it means to be both a centre of subjective experience and free only if he recognizes the opportunity for him that is created by the refusal of women to continue to serve his narcissism*. So, the two-person concept of freedom comes about through challenging the notion of patriarchal individuality, such that women are no longer perceived as extensions or instruments of patriarchal self-assertion but rather as subjects in their own right, entitled to live (organisational) life as a self. These features of a transitional space provide opportunities to consider contextually specific, local and micro-levels of change for gendered leadership relations.

Building on Winnicott's transitional space, Benjamin's concept of *the third* enables mutual recognition between subjects in which each party acknowledges they are flawed human beings who each has a duty of care for the other. It is this transitional space that provides opportunity to refresh thinking on gender and leadership.

The Relational and Transitional Third

The concept of *the third* is a relational, transitional space between one subject and an *other* such that one is not completely determined by the other. This is an open space in which there are many different positions to move. Benjamin describes ways in which we move from a position of *one-ness* (the great individualist that has been nurtured by Western neoliberal cultures in recent decades) through to the position of *two-ness*. *Two-ness* is about doing to others what we would not want them to do to us. It is a position in which the other subject is not recognised as fully and fundamentally equivalent in the ethical sense. So we carry on misjudging, manipulating, neglecting and excluding. Benjamin describes this two-ness as being stuck in the extreme and partial, imaginary dualistic and populist identities of *us against them*; *us above them*; *doer and done to*; *perpetrator and victim*; *violator and violated*; *master and slave*; and in the case of leadership, *powerful leader and helpless follower*. Domination and submission is a breakdown in equal and mutual human relationships and it is through the notion of *the third* that we are able to move beyond this destructive dyad. Such authorship and agency of both parties is a relationship with some presence of *the third* in which each subject can express themself with a kind of freedom because there is a space between them and the other person in which they do not feel completely determined by the other.

To halt the cycle of domination and ongoing subordination, the relational space of *the third* enables a movement from the locked-in space of two-ness (and destruction) into the position of *the third* in which subjects can free up their minds and emotions. This position gives rise to the logic of paradox that requires our simultaneous need for recognition, acknowledgement and independence: that the other subject is outside of our control and yet we need them. But it goes further than that in allowing an open space that moves away from one living at the expense of the other and into a position of shared, responsible living together – through acknowledgement and mutual recognition. This is the opening-up of a co-created space in a shared relationship that recognises conflict and dissent and seeks to generate reciprocal contribution, understanding and generativity. In this way, it also demands acknowledging wrongdoing and opening up space for reparations. So, if each subject can be more courageous and consider how their actions make the other part react, then they can re-engage empathy for one another.

This is the direction in which ethically responsible and caring approaches to gendered accounts of leadership need to turn through reimagining the potential subject positions of powerful and powerless subjectivities in organisations. In a new era of leadership through gender theorising, there is a need for ethical and radically different relational forms – following the relational, transitional space of *the third* – that recognise the inherent dangers of the powerful effects of domination and submission in leader–follower and masculine/feminine thinking. Furthermore, it is also clearly beholden on those in the subordinate position in the dyad to ensure that if they suffocate their personal longings for recognition, they will extinguish all hopes for social and moral transformation within the workplace as well. Renouncing the victim position is a necessary step in the process of recognition and acknowledgement by another in relational encounters.

CONCLUDING THOUGHTS

Leadership is best viewed as collective, collaborative and relational work of many people in organisations. So, we also need to steer a course away from the dominance of the heroic, masculine leader figure that still haunts so many studies of leadership. We need to shift the association of power with the elite. Rethinking power decouples it from prestige and status and leadership. Rethinking leadership in this way creates more collaborative, relational forms and frees up space in which to reflect on gendered relationships. There is a need to escape from leadership approaches that continue the focus on the powerful and androcentric elite to the detriment of encouraging dissensus and co-created relations in the workplace. In addition, the subordinated other has a responsibility to claim their voice and value the contribution they make to the relationship. Too often, we hear of individuals feeling unable to speak or be recognised, thereby denying their sense of selfhood and what they can contribute. When working in a subordinate role, actively speaking up and speaking out is also crucial. So, we really do need understandings of gender and leadership that are more inclusive, ethical, eclectic and contextually meaningful. We need to develop a language that can challenge prevailing assumptions and structures of privilege.

Critical, feminist and psychoanalytical theorising enables us to articulate such a language and to think differently about gender and leadership. Benjamin's theories of intersubjectivity and recognition make visible the interdependencies between dominant and subordinate individuals; the power and powerlessness within such relations; and the damage that happens when leading and following are practised in a real dichotomy – in both positive and negative encounters. It exposes the damage that happens when leadership is practised in either enigmatic or noxious ways, calling for reimagining leadership such that gendered power asymmetries and interdependencies are recognised and acknowledged. Individuals, whether in dominant leader or subordinate follower roles, will experience leadership differently and this relationship will not always be one of equal partnership and communion. It is through the relational and transitional space of *the third* that we can move beyond the leader/follower dyad that has been so infused with masculine norms. Such authorship and agency of both parties is a relationship in which each subject can express themself with a kind of freedom because there is a space between each other in which they do not feel they are being determined by the other.

REFERENCES

Acker, Joan (1998). The future of gender and organizations: Connections and boundaries. *Gender, Work and Organization*, 5(4), 195–206.

Alsop, R, Fitzsimons, A. & Lennon, K. (2002) *Theorizing Gender*, Cambridge: Polity Press.

Alvesson M and Spicer A (2012) Critical leadership studies: the case for critical performativity. *Human Relations*, 65(3): 367–390.

Amanatullah, E. T., & Tinsley, C. H. (2013). Punishing female negotiators for asserting too much … or not enough: Exploring why advocacy moderates backlash against assertive female negotiators. *Organizational Behavior and Human Decision Processes*, 120(1), 110–122.

Andersen, J. A., & Hansson, H. (2011). At the end of the road? On differences between women and men in leadership behaviour. *Leadership & Organization Development Journal*, 32(5), 428–441.

Bass, B. (1998). *Transformational Leadership: Industrial, Military and Educational Impact*. Lawrence Erlbaum.

Bathurst, R & Cain, T (2013) Embodied leadership: The aesthetics of gesture, *Leadership* 9(3): 358–377.

Beard, M. (2018). *Women and Power: A Manifesto*. Profile.

Benjamin, J. (1988). *The Bonds of Love: Psychoanalysis, Feminism and the Problem of Domination*. Pantheon.

Benjamin, J. (1995). *Like Subjects, Love Objects: Essays on Recognition and Sexual Difference*. Yale University Press.

Benjamin, J. (1998). *Shadow of the Other: Intersubjectivity and Gender in Psychoanalysis*. Routledge.of thirdness. *Psychoanalytical Quarterly*, 73, 5–46.

Benjamin, J. (2004). *Beyond doer and done to: An intersubjective view*

Benjamin, J. (2018). *Beyond Doer and Done: Recognition Theory, Intersubjectivity and the Third*. Routledge.

Biehl, B. (2019). 'In the mix': Relational leadership explored through an analysis of techno DJs and dancers. Leadership 15(3): 339–359.

Boni-Le Goff, I. & Le Feuvre, N. (2017). *Professions from a Gendered Perspective*. Oxford Research Encyclopedia of Business and Management, Oxford: Oxford University Press doi:10.1093/acrefore/9780190224851.013.8

Bolton, S. and Muzio, D. (2008). The paradoxical processes of feminization in the professions. *Work, Employment and Society* 22(2): 281–299.

Brewis, J. (1999). How does it feel? Women managers, embodiment and changing public sector cultures. In S. Whitehead & R. Moodley (Eds.), *Transforming Managers: Gendering Change in the Public Sector*. UCL Press.

Butler, J. (1990). *Gender Trouble: Feminism and the Subversion of Identity*. Routledge, Chapman & Hall.

Butler, J. (2004). *Undoing Gender*. Routledge.

Calas, M. and Smircich, L. (1991) 'Voicing Seduction to Silence Leadership', *Organization Studies*, 12:4, 567–602.

Carli, L. & Eagly, A. (2011). Gender and leadership. In A. Bryman, D. L. Collinson, K. Grint, B. Jackson & M. Uhl-Bien (Eds.), *The SAGE Handbook of Leadership* (pp. 103–117). Sage.

Castro, M. and Holvino, E. (2016). Applying intersectionality in organizations: Inequality markers, cultural scripts and advancement practices in a professional service firm. *Gender, Work & Organization*, 23, 328–347.

Catalyst (2020), *Women in Academia*: https://www.catalyst.org/research/women-in-academia/

Cialdini, R., & Trost, M. (1998). Social influence: Social norms, conformity and compliance. In D. T. Gilbert, S. T. Fiske & G. Lindzey (Eds.), *The Handbook of Social Psychology* (pp. 151–192). McGraw-Hill.

Collinson, D. (2011). Critical leadership studies. In A. Bryman, D. L. Collinson, K. Grint, B. Jackson & M. Uhl-Bien (Eds.), *The SAGE Handbook of Leadership* (pp. 179–192). Sage.

Diamond, M. (2007). Organizational change and the analytic third: Locating and attending to unconscious organizational dynamics. *Psychoanalysis, Culture and Society, 12*, 142–164.

Durbin, S., & Tomlinson, J. (2014). Female part-time managers: Careers, mentors and role models. *Gender, Work & Organization, 21*(1), 308–320.

Eagly, A., & Carli, L. (2003). The female leadership advantage: An evaluation of the evidence. *Leadership Quarterly, 14*(6), 807–834.

Eagly, A., & Carli, L. (2007). Women and the labyrinth of leadership. *Harvard Business Review, 85*(62–71), 146.

Eagly, A., & Karau, S. (2002). Role congruity theory of prejudice toward female leaders. *Psychological Review, 109*(3), 573–598.

Elliott, C., & Stead, V. (2018). Constructing women's leadership representation in the UK press during a time of financial crisis: Gender capitals and dialectical tensions. *Organization Studies, 39*, 19–45.

Ely, R., Foldy, E., & Scully, M. (Eds.) (2003). *Reader in Gender, Work and Organization*. Blackwell.

Ely, R., Ibarra, H., & Kolb, D. (2011). Taking gender into account: Theory and design for women's leadership development programs. *Academy of Management Learning & Education, 10*(3), 474–493.

Fernandez-Mateo, I., & Kaplan, S. (2018). Gender and organization science: Introduction to a virtual special issue, *Organization Science*, INFORMS, *29*(6), 1229–1236.

Fisher, K., & Reiser Robbins, C. (2014). Embodied leadership: Moving from leader competencies to leaderful practice. *Leadership, 11*, 281–299.

Flax, J. (1981). A materialist theory of women's status. *Psychology of Women Quarterly, 6*(1), 123–136.

Flax, J. (1993). *Disputed Subjects: Essays on Psychoanalysis, Politics and Philosophy*. Routledge

Flax, J. (2004). What is the subject? Review essay on psychoanalysis and feminism in postcolonial time. *Signs, 29*(3), 905–923.

Ford, J. (2010). Studying leadership critically: A psychosocial lens on leadership identities. *Leadership, 6*, 1–19.

Ford, J. (2019). Rethinking relational leadership: Recognising the mutual dynamic between leaders and led. In B. Carroll, S. Wilson & J. Firth (Eds.), *After Leadership* (pp. 157–174). Routledge.

Ford, J., Atkinson, C., Harding, N., & Collinson, D. (2020). 'You just had to get on with it': Exploring the persistence of gender inequality through women's career histories. *Work, Employment and Society, 35*(1), 78–96.

Ford, J., Harding, N., Gilmore, S., & Richardson, S. (2017). Becoming the leader: Leadership as material presence. *Organization Studies, 38*(11), 1553–1571.

Ford, J., Harding, N., & Learmonth, M. (2008). *Leadership as Identity: Constructions and Deconstructions*. Palgrave Macmillan.

Fotaki, M., & Harding, N. (2018). *Gender and the Organization: Women at Work in the 21st Century*. Routledge.

Foucault, M. (1979). *The History of Sexuality*, Vol. 1. Allen Lane.

Foucault, M. (1986). *The History of Sexuality*, Vol. 2. Viking.

Foucault, M. (1992). *The History of Sexuality*, Vol. 3. Penguin.

Fournier, V., & Keleman, M. (2001). The crafting of community: Recoupling discourses of management and womanhood. *Gender, Work and Organization, 8*(3), 267–290.

Gabaldon, P., de Anca, C., Mateos de Cabo, R., & Gimeno, R. (2016). Searching for women on boards: An analysis from the supply and demand perspective. *Corporate Governance: An International Review, 24*, 371–385.

Gemmill, G., & Oakley, J. (1992). Leadership: An alienating social myth? *Human Relations, 45*(2), 113–129.

Gherardi, S. (1995). *Gender, Symbolism and Organizational Cultures*. Sage.

Grant Thornton (2018). *Women in Business: Beyond Policy to Progress*. Grant Thornton.

Gregory, M. (2009). Inside the locker room: Male homosociability in the advertising industry. *Gender, Work & Organization, 16*, 323–347.

Gruenfeld, D. and Tiedens, L. Z. (2005). "Organizational preferences and their consequences", in Fiske, S. T., Gilbert, D. T. and Lindzey, G. (eds.) *Handbook of Social Psychology*. New Jersey: John Wiley and Sons, 1252–1287.

Gupta, A., & Raman, K. (2014). Board diversity and CEO selection, *Journal of Financial Research, 37*: 495–517.

Guthey, E & Jackson, B (2005) CEO portraits and the authenticity paradox, *Journal of Management Studies, 42*(5): 1057–1082.

Halford, S. and Leonard, P. (2001) *Gender, Power and Organisations*, Basingstoke: Palgrave.

Harding, N., Lee, H., Ford, J and Learmonth, M. (2011) 'Leadership and charisma: A desire that cannot speak its name?' *Human Relations, 64* (7): 927–950.

Haynes, K. (2008). (Re)figuring accounting and maternal bodies: The gendered embodiment of accounting professionals. *Accounting, Organizations and Society*, 33(4–5), 328–348.

Hearn, J. (2019). So what has been, is, and might be going on in studying men and masculinities: Some continuities and discontinuities. *Men and Masculinities*, 22(1), 53–63.

Hearn, J., & Parkin, W. (1993). Organizations, multiple oppressions and postmodernism. In J. Hassard and M. Parker (Eds.), *Postmodernism and Organizations* (pp. 148–162). Sage.

Heilman, M. (2001). Description and prescription: How gender stereotypes prevent women's ascent up the organizational ladder. *Journal of Social Issues*, 57, 657–674.

Heilman, M. (2012). Gender stereotypes and workplace bias. *Research in Organizational Behavior*, 32, 113–135.

Helgesen, S. (1990). *The Female Advantage*. Doubleday.

Holgersson, C. (2013). Recruiting managing directors: Doing homosociality. *Gender, Work & Organization*, 20, 454–466.

Hoobler, J., Masterson, C., Nkomo, S., & Michel, E. (2016). The business case for women leaders: Meta-analysis, research critique, and path forward. *Journal of Management*, 44(6), 2473–2499.

Hoyt, C. (2010). Women, men, and leadership: Exploring the gender gap at the top. *Social and Personality Psychology Compass*, 4, 484–498.

Jeanes, E., Knights, D., & Yancey Martin, P. (Eds.) (2011). *Handbook of Gender, Work and Organization*. Wiley.

Kanter, R. (1977). *Men and Women of the Corporation*. Basic Books.

Khilji, S., & Pumroy, K. (2019). We are strong and we are resilient: Career experiences of women engineers. *Gender, Work & Organization*, 26, 1032–1052.

Knights, D. (2021). *Leadership, Gender and Ethics: Embodied Reasoning in Challenging Masculinities*. Sage.

Koenig, A., Eagly, A., Mitchell, A., & Ristikari, T. (2011). Are leader stereotypes masculine? A meta-analysis of three research paradigms. *Psychological Bulletin*, 37, 616–642.

Kumra, S. (2014). Gendered constructions of merit and impression management within professional service firms. In S. Kumra, R. Simpson & R. Burke (Eds.), *The Oxford Handbook of Gender and Organizations* (pp. 267–290). Oxford University Press.

Kupers, W. (2013). Embodied inter-practices of leadership. *Leadership*, 9, 335–357.

Ladkin, D (2013) "From Perception to flesh: A Phenomenological Account of the Felt Experience of Leadership", *Leadership*, Special Issue: The Materiality of Leadership, 2013 9(3), pp. 320–334.

Learmonth, M and Morrell, K (2017) Is critical leadership studies critical? *Leadership*, 13(3): 257–271.

Lipman-Blumen, J. (1976). Toward a homosocial theory of sex roles: An exploration of the sex segregation of social institutions. *Signs*, 1(3), part 2, 15–31.

McKinsey Global Institute (2015). *The Power of Parity: How Advancing Women's Equality can Add $12 Trillion to Global Growth*. September. https://kipdf.com/the-power-of-parity-how-advancing-women-s-equality-can-add-12-trillion-to-global_5b010f538ead0ebc0a8b463e.html

McMurray, R., & Pullen, A. (Eds.) (2020). *Gender, Embodiment and Fluidity in Organization and Management*. Routledge, Taylor and Francis Group (Routledge Focus on Women Writers in Organization Studies).

Martin-Ugedo, J., & Minguez-Vera, A. (2017). Female CEOs, returns and risk in Spanish publishing firms. *European Management Reveiew*, 15(1), 111–120.

Mateos de Cabo, R., Gimeno, R., & Escot, L. (2011). Disentangling discrimination on Spanish boards of directors. *Corporate Governance: An International Review*, 19, 77–95.

Melina, L., Burgess, G., Falkman, L., & Marturano, A. (Eds.) (2013). *The Embodiment of Leadership: A Volume in the International Leadership Association Series, Building Leadership Bridges*. Jossey-Bass

Miller, K., & Clark, D. (2008) 'Knife before wife': An exploratory study of gender and the UK medical profession. *Journal of Health Organization and Management Accounting Research*, 22, 238–253.

Muhr, S & Sullivan, K (2013) "None so queer as folk": Gendered expectations and transgressive bodies in leadership. *Leadership* 9(3): 416-435

Muzio, D., Kirkpatrick, I., & Kipping, M. (2011). Professions, organizations and the state: Applying the sociology of the professions to the case of management consultancy. *Current Sociology* 59. 805–824.

Okimoto, T., & Brescoll, V. (2010). The price of power: Power seeking and backlash against female politicians. *Personality and Social Psychology Bulletin*, 36(7), 923–936.

Ospina, S., & Foldy, E. (2009). A critical review of race and ethnicity in the leadership literature: Surfacing context, power and the collective dimensions of leadership. *Leadership Quarterly*, 20(6), 876–896.

Pringle, J., Harris, C., Ravenswood, K., Giddings, L., Ryan, I., & Jaeger, S. (2017). Women's career progression in law firms: Views from the top, views from below. *Gender, Work & Organization*, 24, 435–449.

Pucheta-Martinez, M., & Bel-Oms, I. (2015). The gender pay gap in company boards. *Industrial and Corporate Change*, 24(2), 467–510.

Pullen, A., & Vacchani, S. (2021). Feminist ethics and women leaders: From difference to intercorporeality. *Journal of Business Ethics*, 173(2), 233–243.

Pullen, A., & Vachhani, S., Aug 2013, The materiality of leadership, *Leadership*. 9, 3, p. 315-319

Reskin, B., & Roos, P. (1990). *Job Queues, Gender Queues: Explaining Women's Inroads into Male Occupations*. Temple University Press.

Rivers, C., & Barnett, R. (2013). *The New Soft War on Women: How the Myth of Female Ascendance Is Hurting Women, Men – and Our Economy*. Penguin.

Ropo, Arja & Parviainen, Jaana, 2001. "Leadership and bodily knowledge in expert organizations:: epistemological rethinking," *Scandinavian Journal of Management*, Elsevier, vol. 17(1), pages 1-18

Ropo, A., & Sauer, E. (2008). Corporeal leaders. In D. Barry & H. Hansen (Eds.), *The SAGE Handbook of New Approaches in Management and Organization* (pp. 469–478). Sage.

Ropo, A., Sauer, E., & Salovaara, P. (2013). Embodiment of leadership through material place. *Leadership*, 9, 378–395.

Rosener, J. (1990). Ways women lead. *Harvard Business Review*, 68(6), 119–125.

Rumens N, Moulin de Souza E, Brewis J, (2018) 'Queering Queer Theory in Management and Organization Studies: Notes toward queering heterosexuality' *Organization Studies* 40 (4) pp.593-612

Schein, V. E. (1973). The relationship between sex role stereotypes and requisite management characteristics. *Journal of Applied Psychology*, 57(2), 95–100.

Sedgwick, E. (1991) *Epistemology of the Closet*. Berkeley, CA: University of California Press.

Seierstad, C. (2015). Beyond the business case: The need for both utility and justice rationales for increasing the share of women on boards. *Corporate Governance: An International Review*, 24(4), 390–405.

Sommerlad, H. (2016). 'A pit to put women in': Professionalism, work intensification, sexualisation and work–life balance in the legal profession in England and Wales. *International Journal of the Legal Profession*, 23(1), 61–82.

Sinclair, A. (2011). Leading with body. In E. Jeanes, D. Knights and P. Yancey-Martin (Eds.), *Handbook of Gender, Work and Organization* (pp. 117–30). Wiley.

Sinclair, A. (2014). A feminist case for leadership. In J. Damousi, K. Rubenstein & M. Tomsic (Eds.), *Diversity in Leadership: Australian Women, Past and Present* (pp. 17–36). ANU Press.

Sinclair, A. (2019). Five movements in an embodied feminism: A memoir. *Human Relations*, 72(1), 144–158.

Still, L. (1994). Where to from here? Women in management: The cultural dilemma. *Women in Management Review*, 9(4), 3–10.

Sutherland, N (2019) Leadership without leaders: Understanding anarchist organising through the lens of Critical Leadership Studies, in Carroll, B. Ford, J. and Taylor, S. (eds) (2019) 2nd edn. *Leadership: Contemporary Critical Perspectives*. London: Sage. Pp 248-269

Terjesen, S., Aguilera, R. V. & Lorenz, R. (2015). Legislating a woman's seat on the board: Institutional factors driving gender quotas for boards of directors. *Journal of Business Ethics*, 128, 233–251.

Tomlinson, J., Muzio, D., Sommerlad, H., Webley, L., & Duff, L. (2013). Structure, agency and career strategies of white women and black and minority ethnic individuals in the legal profession *Human Relations*, 66, 245–269.

Tourish, D (2015) [Editorial] *Some announcements, reaffirming the critical ethos of Leadership, and what we look for in submissions*. Leadership, 11(2), pp. 135–141. ISSN 1742-7150

Vachhani, S., & Pullen, A. (2019). Ethics, politics and feminist organizing: Writing feminist infrapolitics and affective solidarity into everyday sexism. *Human Relations*, 72, 23–47.

Vinnicombe, S., Doldor, E., & Sealey, R. (2018). *The Female FTSE Board Report 2018*. Cranfield University.

Webber, A. (2019a). Diversity in HR: Is it really a 'white female' profession? *Personnel Today*. https://www.junglehr.com/2019/05/personnel-today-diversity-in-hr-is-it-really-a-white-female-profession/#:~:text=Unsurprisingly%2C%20the%20survey%20also%20found,female%20across%20the%20working%20population

Webber, A. (2019b). HR's gender pay gap: Female salaries grow, but still lag behind. *Personnel Today*. Available at: https://www.personneltoday.com/hr/gender-pay-gap-2019-widens/ (accessed 24 May 2019).

Williams, M., & Tiedens, L. (2016). The subtle suspension of backlash: A meta-analysis of penalties for women's implicit and explicit dominance behavior. *Psychological Bulletin*, 142(2), 165–197.

Wilson, S. (2020). Pandemic leadership: Lessons from New Zealand's approach to Covid-19. *Leadership*, 16(3), 279–293

Winnicott, D. W. (1971). *Playing and Reality*. Tavistock.

Witz, A. (1990). Patriarchy and professions: The gendered politics of occupational closure. *Sociology*, 24(4), 675–690.

Yeatman, A. (2015). A two-person conception of freedom: The significance of Jessica Benjamin's idea of intersubjectivity. *Journal of Classical Sociology*, 15(1), 3–23.

Zoller HM and Fairhurst GT (2007) Resistance leadership: the overlooked potential in critical organization and leadership studies. *Human Relations*, 6(9): 1331–1360.

21

Problematising Communication and Providing Inspiration: The Potential of a CCO Perspective for Leadership Studies

Viviane Sergi

INTRODUCTION

The case for the importance of communication in leadership is an obvious one. Think of a leader – not who that person is, but what they are doing; what comes up is either an exemplary case, or organisational situations when a leader is doing something for their organisation or people. Dig deeper into this image: what, specifically, is this person doing? Leading a virtual meeting, motivating a team, giving indications about what should be done next, making decisions, drafting an email that will be sent to the whole organisation? While these are only a few of the possible answers to this question, one can suggest with a fair degree of confidence that most, if not all, of the images that come to mind in relation to what a leader does imply a form of communication, understood in its common sense, either face-to-face or virtually, verbal and/or non-verbal, oral or written. The case for the intimate link between leadership and communication does not need to be made: it is so self-explanatory that it might no longer even need to be postulated. Communication is integral to practising leadership, to what leadership entails.

From this framing, issues become that of performance and improvement of skills. Indeed, the number of books written about 'how to communicate as a leader' is astounding, highlighting how one can work on one's speeches, delivery, tone, posture, rhetoric, aspirational qualities, empathy and the like – all with the assumption that in becoming a better orator, a better communicator, anyone in a leadership position might elevate themselves to become (and be perceived by others as) a 'good' leader. Furthermore, influencing – which can be considered as one of the key building blocks of what leadership is all about, and has been highlighted as the common denominator in the multitude of leadership definitions (Yulk, 1989, in Alvesson and Sveningsson, 2003) – is communicational in nature, just as are sharing a vision, uniting the troops and motivating teams, creating a sense of direction and setting organisational change in movement, among others.

There is nothing to debate about the place of communication in leadership, one could say. I would, however, object to such an observation. I would contest it not on its surface – communicating cannot be separated from leadership – but on what it overlooks. If communication is so central to leadership, shouldn't it be interrogated instead of simply being taken for granted? In other words, we might be jumping too quickly over a key question when we assume that we *already* know what communication is all about: the definition of communication itself. Not asking this question implies that we accept this commonly held answer: communication is about transmission of information and interpersonal communication. This answer can be understood as blackboxing communication and as such, it could prove fruitful to open it up, with the aim of reflecting on this intimate connection between communication and leadership.

This is of course not a new suggestion in the field of leadership. Indeed, associated with the rise of socio-constructionist research in leadership, a variety of studies have contributed to diversify how communication is treated in relation to leadership (Fairhurst and Connaughton, 2014). If the dominant view of communication in post-positivist research has been that of transmission, with a focus on effectiveness, socio-constructionist and critical leadership studies have diversified this view by conceptualising communication as the medium of negotiated meaning, relationality, power and dialogue, among others (Fairhurst and Connaughton, 2014). These different streams of research on leadership and communication have, each in their manner, challenged the idea that communication is essentially about transmission and interpersonal relationships. Yet, I suggest that it is still possible to extend enquiries at the intersection of leadership and communication by exploring the potential of the communication-centred perspective to study leadership.

Also named the communicative constitution of organisation (hereafter CCO), this perspective posits that there is much more about communication than what is usually postulated. Indeed, the core tenet of CCO is that communication is the medium through which organisations are brought to life, maintained and/or transformed. CCO does not deny that transmission is part of communication (Cooren, 2020b), but it proposes to go beyond this dimension. This perspective asks the fundamental, and ontological, question of what an organisation is, suggesting that communication is at least part of the answer. This moves communication from something that happens inside organisations to something that plays a role in creating and reproducing organisations. If the words 'communication' and 'organisation' are central to this perspective, the verb 'constitute' contains within itself the foundational proposition of the perspective: that communication is organising (Putnam and Nicotera, 2009).

In connection with this idea, CCO suggests moving the conception of communication from *explanandum* to *explanans* (Cooren, 2012) – in other words, making communication not a phenomenon to be explained but the explanation of what is observed and studied. This perspective views organisational phenomena – and, in fact, reality (see Cooren 2015 and 2018 for this enlarged view of communication) – as produced in communication, emerging from communicative acts and happening in communicative events. This perspective has strong and clear ontological implications for organisations, but also for a myriad of phenomena, including leadership. As I will discuss in these pages, CCO reconfigures how leadership is defined. At the same time, because of its premises, adopting this perspective also has clear implications for the concrete studies of leadership. Since this chapter is devoted to presenting the potential of CCO for the understanding and study of leadership, I will successively address the bases of CCO, how this perspective sheds light on and thus redefines leadership as a phenomenon and what such a renewed definition of leadership implies in terms of the methods used to study it.

It should be noted right from the start that I am not the first one to suggest taking inspiration from and building on CCO for extending our enquiry into this broad phenomenon that we label 'leadership'. Already in 2013, Tourish argued that a communication-centred perspective presented significant potential for understanding leadership in a finer way, and Fairhurst and Connaughton (2014) recognise its contribution to address materiality and non-human agency in leadership. A number of previous studies, although not necessarily explicitly CCO, can also be seen as resonating with the central ideas of CCO. I, among a few other researchers, have also proposed that CCO might represent a relevant theoretical basis from which to enquire into the materiality of leadership (Sergi, 2016). In recent years, a few CCO-inspired studies of leadership have been published, confirming the potential of its theoretical propositions, including a general overview of the different streams of CCO scholarship and their implications for the study of leadership (Bisel et al., 2022). This chapter will consider some of these studies in order to identify their main contributions and also to discuss what else could be, or remains to be, explored with this perspective. This will allow me to address the potential of CCO to be a stimulating theoretical framework for extending our understanding of leadership and for developing novel enquiries into this phenomenon that still, to this day, generates substantial discussion and debate, in research and in society alike.

THE COMMUNICATIVE CONSTITUTION OF ORGANISATION (CCO): MAIN IDEAS

Presenting a detailed overview of CCO is beyond the scope of this chapter, as its origin story points to a wide variety of conceptual and intellectual influences that cannot be reviewed in full here. Nonetheless, a few bases are needed to understand what it proposes, especially for readers who may not be familiar with this perspective (I suggest considering Cooren and Martine, 2016, and Schoeneborn and Vásquez, 2017, for more detailed accounts of this perspective's development). First, in terms of historical emergence, CCO originated from the field of organisational communication in the 1990s and gained its name around that time. While McPhee and Zaug's article (2000) may have been the first using the label *communication as constituting organisations*, other thinkers were also working on a similar root idea at the time. Notably, James Taylor and Elizabeth Van Every published at the same time as McPhee and Zaug their influential book *The Emergent Organization* (2000), which explored the nature of organisation, especially influenced by Giddens' structuration theory and Weick's sense-making. Their pioneering work would, with time, become identified as the starting point of the Montreal school of organisational communication. In parallel, a related line of enquiry around the organising properties of communication took inspiration from Niklas Luhmann's system thinking. In the years that followed, research around the central premise of CCO – that organisations are constituted in communication – diversified, which led to the consolidation of three main schools in CCO: one centred around McPhee's four flows model, a second one influenced by Luhmann's system thinking and the Montreal school, led by Taylor and Van Every, and then by Cooren and colleagues (Schoeneborn et al., 2014). Among these three perspectives, the Montreal school and the Luhmannian approach can be viewed as the two that have developed and blossomed the most since the mid-2000s. While Luhmann's approach is based, as its name implies, on Luhmann's thinking, the Montreal school is anchored in a combination of theoretical and philosophical influences, including American pragmatist philosophy, ethnomethodology, speech-act theory and Latour's actor-network theory. These schools should not be understood as separated or closed-off branches of enquiry, but rather as being in conversation with each other and open to cross-influence.

Today, CCO is a diversified stream of research, firmly located at the intersection of organisational communication and organisation studies, and one that has made numerous and important contributions to our understanding of organisations. These contributions derive from the manner by which CCO conceptualises organisations and organising, and also from the specific concepts that this perspective has developed, like those of ventriloquism (Cooren, 2010, 2012), presentification (Benoit-Barné and Cooren, 2009), materiality as mattering (Cooren et al., 2012) and, more recently, materialisation (Cooren, 2020b), organisationality (Dobusch and Schoeneborn, 2015) and its take on authority/authoring (Taylor and Van Every, 2014; Bourgoin et al., 2020). While all three schools of CCO have generated relevant insights that could be inspiring for enquiries into leadership, in this chapter I focus on and build more specifically on the Montreal school – most particularly on some of its original concepts. The (incomplete) list of influences of the Montreal school point to three of its core commitments: process ontology, performativity and relational agency. As I argue, these three commitments are worth adopting in the study of leadership – an argument that is not new and that has been made by a number of researchers over the last two decades. However, what I see as quite promising in this line of thinking is the specific potential of CCO, notably the Montreal school, emanating from its original concepts – a potential that could push our conceptualisation and understanding of leadership further. This will be the object of the next section of this chapter. But exploring this potential requires an understanding of the basic ideas of this communication-centred perspective.

As a theoretical perspective, CCO starts with the project of problematising communication, to attend to what communication is, in relation to organisation. It thus begins by moving the relationship between terms: questioning the generally accepted idea that communication happens 'inside' an organisation that would exist outside of it, it reverses the terms and proposes that the organisation is made in and through communication. Raising the seemingly simple question of the nature of organisation, CCO may be understood above all as an ontological project. Such a view of communication expands its role in organisations beyond the typical perspective in management and organisation studies, where it tends to be seen as an issue of transmission or limited to interpersonal communication. In this sense, the choice of verb in the perspective's name is not trivial: it highlights all the work that is needed to produce, sustain, or transform an organisation, while contending that this work is accomplished through communication (Putnam & Nicotera, 2009). Cooren et al. (2011; also summarised in Schoeneborn and Vásquez, 2017) present six premises of CCO, which taken together set the tone for what this perspective proposes.

- First, CCO enquiry focuses on communicative events; this premise directs researchers towards what happens in moments that may be deemed

local, while keeping visible the temporality and spatiality that are associated with what an event is.
- Second, CCO does not restrict communication to exchanges between human beings; rather, it asks the larger question of *what* is communicating, in any given event – which extends communication to material elements, ideas, bodies, etc.
- Third, CCO posits that communication is co-constructed, highlighting its relational and performative nature.
- Fourth, CCO attributes agency to anyone or anything acting in a situation – thus accepting a hybrid conception of agency, furthermore, making the decision of who or what is acting rests firmly on the analysis of specific communicative events.
- Fifth, CCO is resolutely empirically anchored – an approach that Cooren has defined as *never leaving the* terra firma *of interactions* (2006), p. 82, hence giving priority to actual action as it unfolds, as it is there that the constitutive and organising effects of communication are visible and can be observed and analysed.
- Sixth, CCO considers both organisation (noun/entitative view) and organising (verb/processual view), with the specificity of not submitting one term to the other. Indeed, CCO holds that both are always 'present at the scene' in communicative events. Recent works have even extended this duality to include another facet, that of organisationality – where organisation is considered in a third fashion, that of an adverb (Dobusch and Schoeneborn, 2015; Schoeneborn et al., 2019). This stimulating addition to the noun and verb views raises the question of degrees in relation to what an organisation is: in other words, this adverbial view allows us to consider to which degree an organisation is organisational. This points to the recognition that while organisations may present distinguishing features from other forms of social collectives, they are not all organisational to the same degree. Some organisations (e.g., a large bureaucracy) are more organisational than others (e.g., a temporary inter-organisational project) – but, in accordance with the previous premise, this should be submitted to empirical enquiry.

These six previously summarised premises speak clearly to the theoretical bases of what a communication-centred perspective proposes but should also be viewed as giving indications on methodological choices for conducting enquiries into the communicative constitution of organisations. In this sense, CCO can be regarded as a theory-method bundle, a set of ideas on phenomena that give a strong indication of how such phenomena need to be studied empirically, to attend to, and extend, its ideas (actor-network theory can also be viewed in a similar light). If recent publications in CCO have started to address methodological issues (see, for example, Nathues et al., 2021, for a presentation of a framework for guiding ventriloquial analysis), contributions on this topic remain limited (Boivin et al., 2017). Nonetheless, and as it is made visible in the above premises, communication-centred enquiries call for, at least at first glance, qualitative and up-close studies of situations. It is thus not surprising to note that several, if not most, CCO studies, especially those rooted in the Montreal school, opt for such detailed enquiries, often by building on ethnomethodology and conversation analysis. In these studies, extracts from actual communicative events (e.g., those taking place in meetings) are decorticated with the aims of exposing who and what is speaking, who and what is making a difference (Latour, 2005), how action unfolds and how organising (and/or disorganising; see Vásquez et al., 2016; Vásquez and Kuhn, 2019) is communicatively produced. It is thus not surprising to see that published CCO studies tend to focus on a limited number of vignettes that either reproduce the exact conversation that was captured, or a short moment of interaction with all its details.

This also goes for the limited CCO studies of leadership, as it can be seen in Clifton (2017), Clifton et al. (2021), and Meier and Carroll (2020), for example. More specifically, a key concept of the Montreal school, like that of ventriloquism (e.g., Cooren, 2010, 2012, 2020a; this concept is presented in the next section), cannot be easily separated from methodological choices; because ventriloquism asks, among other things, the question of who and what is speaking (not only who is speaking, but what animates speakers and what concerns are voiced through people, texts, etc.; what is invoked, evoked and convoked in situations), it demands a detailed attention to specific moments of interaction or to specific sites in order to answer the empirical questions raised by the concept. This analytical attention to situations is often located in ethnographic studies of organisational phenomena, which, given their immersive approach and long-lasting presence, allow for the generation of empirical material that lends itself to such detailed analysis. This is further facilitated with the popularisation of data-recording techniques in data collection and fieldwork.

However, while ethnographic methods and conversation analysis may appear to be the 'golden road' to collecting data and analysing communicative events from a CCO perspective, it should, however, be noted that they are not the sole methodological and analytical approach fitting with this perspective. Other approaches, such as photo and video methods (i.e., Wilhoit, 2018), among others, have been used and adapted in CCO enquiries and while they differ from conversation analysis, they remain committed to attending to the minutiae of how organisational phenomena are assembled and constituted in communication. This close connection should not, however, be seen as limiting or even excluding methodological possibilities. For example, if a vast majority of CCO enquiries are qualitative in nature, a few quantitative-inclined studies have been conducted, notably in relation to the Luhmannian approach (see, for example, the network analysis proposed by Blaschke et al., 2012). Nonetheless, with its keen interest (theoretically and empirically) in communicative events, talk and conversation, how action is unfolding in situations and what contributes to this action, and the assemblages of humans and other-than-humans[1], with the objective of attending to 'what' is produced and how it is achieved in communication, CCO strongly favours detailed, in situ and longitudinal approaches.

This explains why we can note the tendency in CCO scholarship to build its enquiries on the ethnographic tradition and/or with conversation analysis. Through a prolonged presence in a context, CCO researchers can gain a deeper understanding of the setting in which they are immersed, which helps them select key communicative events on which they will focus their analysis. Such a selection is fundamental in developing the analysis, deriving contributions and presenting empirical material especially in journal articles. While several CCO studies conducted in this fashion may appear, once published, as 'only' building on a handful of communicative events rendered as vignettes, which in turn are subjected to detailed analysis, these studies tend to rest on longer involvement in the field and on much richer empirical material than what is presented in the article, which informs in a notable way the researcher's selection of empirical material, its analysis and its interpretation.

These methodological choices were important to present before delving further in CCO and its potential for leadership studies, as they significantly colour the kind of data collection and analysis that is performed in current studies and will influence future studies taking inspiration from this perspective. I now turn to some of the specific concepts proposed by CCO to explore what we can learn about leadership from such a perspective, weaving in leadership studies that have adopted these concepts. I then discuss these theoretical implications and consider studies in leadership that build explicitly on CCO.

KEY CCO CONCEPTS AND STUDIES OF LEADERSHIP

It should first be noted that studies of leadership that explore this phenomenon with a clear and dominant anchoring in CCO are currently still limited. However, with their focus on communicative activities, practices and events, these leadership studies can be located somewhat proximally to a number of discursive studies of leadership. As Fairhurst and Uhl-Bien (2012) summarised in their overview of the types of organisational discourse analysis that can be conducted, discursive approaches to leadership cover a wide variety of studies, rooted in different theoretical perspectives. They identify four main types of organisational discourse analysis: interaction analysis, critical discourse analysis, conversation analysis and narrative analyses. While inspirations from critical discourse analysis and narrative analysis may be more distant (but not unconnected) from CCO, theoretical framing and analyses influenced by interaction analysis and conversation analysis are resolutely closer. In particular, conversation analysis has started to feature more prominently in leadership studies since the turn of the 2000s. Notable examples of this approach include studies from Fairhurst (2008), Larsson and Lundholm (2010, 2013), Meschitti (2019) and Vine et al. (2008). These studies approach leadership from the point of its enactment in situations, paying close attention to what is said by whom or to positioning and how the turns of conversation contribute to creating leadership. In this line, Schnurr and Schroeder (2019) have explicitly advocated for applied linguistics and pragmatics to advance discursive studies of leadership and Simpson et al. (2018) have proposed a performative conception of leadership talk. These studies may not theorise or analyse leadership from an explicitly CCO perspective, but with their close attention to leadership interactions, talk in situation and actual conversations they all share a sensitivity to communicative activities akin to that of CCO.

A similar observation could be made for studies that pay close attention to the materiality of leadership. Indeed, considering the active role that objects (understood in a very broad sense) play in how action unfolds and in the constitution of organisational phenomena in situ is one of the hallmarks of CCO. Some studies that explore the materiality of leadership (e.g., Mulcahy and Perillo, 2011) could thus be seen as located in close proximity to CCO. For example, with her exploration of how material actants co-produce leadership effects, Hawkins' (2015) work is very much aligned with CCO enquiry. What places it beside and not inside this perspective is that communication is not problematised (which is normal as this was not part of the focal points of her study). It is even possible to note proximities with a number of studies looking at leadership-as-practice (e.g., Crevani and Endrissat, 2016), and also with studies that define leadership processually (e.g., but differently, Crevani, 2018; Crevani et al., 2010; Cunliffe and Eriksen, 2011[2]; Hosking, 1988; Tourish, 2014).

Given that CCO is a perspective influenced by several streams of scholarship, it is not surprising to find connections with studies that may build on similar streams or that may enquire into the production of leadership from related assumptions (process ontology, relational agency and/or performativity). It should, however, be noted that all of the above-mentioned lines of enquiry into leadership are rather distinct from each other and, while they could be combined, they may or may not acknowledge each other. For example, not all studies that analyse leadership interaction through conversation analysis take non-human actors into consideration, and not all studies on leadership-as-practice focus on the discursive activities that surround and produce leadership. Furthermore, these studies do not problematise communication. These proximities illustrate that CCO-influenced leadership studies, present and future, do not stand as neatly separated from other enquiries currently pursued in the vast field of leadership, but belong to a constellation of studies that are loosely connected.

While tracing all the connections between CCO and the various streams of studies that are inspired by either similar ontological and epistemological anchoring or theories would be a stimulating project, I instead suggest considering two concepts originally developed by CCO scholars working in the Montreal school – that of ventriloquism and of materialisation – and exploring what a strong anchoring in this perspective could bring to leadership studies. As shown in the previous pages, I propose to proceed from CCO towards leadership, instead of working from the mass of leadership studies that could be, more or less, connected to CCO scholarship. Doing so will allow me to illustrate the conceptual potential of CCO, and also to discuss possible ways forward with this perspective. As evidenced by the subtitles of the two following sections, CCO proposes a different understanding of two elements that tend to be present in studies – including those on leadership – and that pay meticulous attention to unfolding actions and interaction in organised settings: talk and materiality. These concepts hold promise for advancing enquiries into leadership.

From 'Who is talking?' to ventriloquism. A novel idea first developed by Cooren (2010, 2015b) but that has since blossomed is that of ventriloquism, which he defines as *actions through which someone or something makes someone or something else say or do things* (2015b, p. 476). Ventriloquism has been developed to study agency and [t]*he advantage of adopting a ventriloqual vantage point is that we can observe how people implicitly or explicitly keep invoking, evoking, and convoking various forms of agency in their conversations* (Cooren, 2015b, p. 477). The elements that the ventriloquist invokes can be seen as enhancing their position and possibly their authority (e.g., someone invoking rules to justify a decision may be granted more authority in an organisational situation). It is in this sense that other-than-human elements are understood as making a difference. But the relationship is bidirectional:

> It is also possible to regard the ventriloquist as the one who is being ventriloquized for the very practice of ventriloquism creates a dynamic that transcends both the ventriloquist and the dummy. Hence, ventriloquism provides a useful metaphor for reconceptualizing communication, as human interactants do not only ventriloquize specific figures but are also ventriloquized (animated) by them (see Cooren, 2010). For example, when people are positioned (or position themselves) as speaking in the name of justice, commonsense, or freedom, it is as if justice, commonsense, or freedom were expressing itself in the interaction.
> (Cooren et al., 2013, p. 263)

Also, it should be noted that invoking, evoking, or convoking is not simply understood here as rational or intentional choices made by the people who are speaking: ventriloquism takes into consideration anything that animates ventriloquists, including emotions, motivations, attachments to ideas, or principles that appear in communicative events.

Ventriloquism is probably the CCO notion that has attracted the most interest in leadership studies up to now. It was featured in studies by Clifton (2017), Clifton et al. (2021) and Meier and Carroll (2020), revealing how different facets of leadership, such as leader identity, emerge through talk in situation and via the convocation of different other-than-human actants. Ventriloquial analyses of phenomena linked to leadership render visible empirically how these phenomena are accomplished in interaction and what plays a role in these processes, including artefacts but also other elements that may appear less tangible (ideas, concepts, emotions), showing and following how influence, authority, direction (among others) are assembled, rise, accumulate and orient what happens next – or not. Because space is limited here, I recommend that intrigued researchers turn to the above-mentioned studies, or other studies that build on ventriloquism, to see for themselves such empirical displays of the production of leadership.

From materiality to materialisation. A notable characteristic of the Montreal school is the importance given to materiality, which adds a significant layer to its attention to communicative events. This sensitivity to materiality can be understood as initially deriving from the theories that influenced the emergence of the Montreal school. This has led earlier contributions to address and develop the notion of hybrid agency, as listed in the premises of CCO. CCO locates agency in the assemblage of elements (human and anything else) that takes part in action. Such a hybrid conception leads to paying attention to everything that may be communicating, in an actual situation, as visible in the notion of ventriloquism. Furthermore, François Cooren has devoted part of his recent scholarship to reflecting on materiality and proposing a novel understanding of its place and role, first in the communicative constitution of organisation and, in later works, on reality (see 2012, 2015a, 2016, 2018, and 2020b, among others).

Starting with the recognition that, etymologically, the noun 'materiality' and the verb 'to matter' have the same etymological root of *materia*, Cooren et al. (2012) suggested how this play on materiality and mattering was inscribed in communication. Addressing materiality as mattering (and vice versa) can be understood as an entry point to reconfiguring how materiality and sociality are considered. Cooren has criticised how materiality has tended to be conceived in organisation studies, even by the researchers building on the notion of socio-materiality, arguing that the idea that 'the social' and 'the material' are intertwined rests on the implication that these dimensions still refer to distinct facets of reality (Cooren, 2016, 2018, 2020b). In an attempt to avoid this bifurcation (echoing Whitehead, 1920, as explained in Cooren, 2015a) between the social and the material, and rooting his proposal fully in a relational ontology, Cooren has been suggesting considering that materiality and sociality are features of any phenomenon:

> I argue that we should speak about materiality and sociality as essential features of everything that exists: emotions, ideas, words, but also rocks, technologies and architectures. [...] insisting on the sociality of anything amounts to focusing on the relations that sustain its existence and identity, while insisting on its materiality consists of highlighting what this thing is made of, which also leads us to acknowledge its relationality.
> (2018, p. 279)

In viewing materiality and sociality in this relational fashion, Cooren has posited communication as the fundamental process that links and establishes this constant relationship between materiality and sociality as translating into each other. Such a wide definition of communication locates it very closely to that of relation. Indeed, Cooren has suggested (2020b) that 'communication' and 'relation' can be understood in an almost synonymous manner. This extension of the concept of communication may not be shared by all researchers working in CCO, as some may consider that it widens the terms to a point where it becomes all-encompassing, hence losing its specificity. However, this relational conception transforms materiality from a noun into a verb, into a process. Indeed, Cooren invites researchers to address *materialisation*, rather than materiality. This shift is deeply consequential, as it opens up to the idea that everything has a material feature, *but to various degrees*. Moreover, making materiality into a process of materialisation implies that we can study how anything gradually materialises (or not) in situations, how anything becomes present (or recedes away) as action and interactions are unfolding. Combined with the concept of ventriloquism, materialisation thus offers conceptual tools to expose vividly how phenomena linked to leadership (e.g., the actual process of leading or leader identities) are assembled, uttered, stabilised or transformed over time, become influential, or retreat from the scene by attending not only to what is said by whom, but also in considering everything that communicates.

TAKING INSPIRATION FROM CCO: A FEW POSSIBILITIES

Taking inspiration from CCO has many possible implications for leadership studies. As I suggest, these extensions can take two forms: broadening a number of current theorisations on leadership through a reformulation of their ideas into CCO's terms and developing new perspectives on leadership by raising different questions through CCO's ideas.

Fundamentally, CCO built its premises on three important ontological bases: a processual, relational and performative view of reality, giving a key role to communication in the constitution of organisational phenomena on these bases. Whatever the direction taken, exploring leadership with a CCO perspective thus implies adhering to these ontological bases, and conferring communication with a significant role in how leadership is defined theoretically and accomplished empirically. Also, another obvious implication of CCO for leadership studies is in terms of methods. This may be the less-novel implication, as a number of studies are already making methodological choices akin to those that CCO studies make: considering what happens in situations and in interactions, focusing especially on talk and conversation and with the objective of attending to questions of 'what' and 'how' – namely, what is produced and how it is achieved through communication. What a CCO influence would add to these methodological choices would be, first, an impetus to question communication (take it seriously, as Cooren et al., 2013, have underlined) rather than taking it for granted; and, second, attention not only to who is speaking, but also to what is speaking through people, a consideration of whatever, human or not, takes part in what is unfolding.

More generally, what should be at the heart of a CCO enquiry of leadership is the assemblages of humans and other-than-humans emerging and engaged in the active production of leadership. This is where a distinction can be noted with studies that have opted for conversation analysis of leadership: most of these studies do not conceptualise leadership in this manner. Moreover, while these studies definitively attend to the minutiae of leadership production, either as emerging from the interaction between identified leaders and followers, or as being conceived in a decentred fashion, they mostly remain silent on their definition of communication. This is not an issue limited to leadership studies: in organisation studies in general, what communication *is* is rarely questioned. Communication is defined, explicitly or most often implicitly, as interpersonal communication. Problematising this common definition of communication by highlighting its organising properties may not radically alter methodological choices that have already been made by some researchers, but it certainly changes the questions asked and the analysis performed. If communication is no longer restricted to what is exchanged, verbally or textually, between two people, but rather as what constitutes the phenomenon we label 'leadership', it allows researchers to decentre it from human actors and to dig deeper into what generates, locally, this phenomenon. In this sense,

CCO provides theoretical tools to proceed to this decentring of leadership that has become an interest for some in the leadership community. It not only posits it in terms of definition (stating that leadership is a collective product), it also theorises that this decentring is communicationally produced. In other words, it locates a relational conception of leadership in communication. Doing so may broaden and invigorate current streams of studies, and it may also foster different questions motivating studies of leadership. Here are a few of these possibilities, going beyond what has already started to be explored from a CCO perspective.

A first possible inspiration that leadership studies could take from CCO would be to reformulate current focal points into CCO terms. Such reformulations could extend studies that conceptualise leadership as leadership *work* (e.g., Crevani, 2018; Meschitti, 2019). Furthermore, while studies in plural forms of leadership have grown over the last decades (see Denis et al., 2012, and Ospina et al., 2020, for overviews of this branch of leadership studies), how leading is actually collectively performed still requires more study. As already touched upon, studies of plural leadership could aspire to demonstrate how this pluralising happens and is assembled in actual situations (e.g., during meetings). This would not modify the premise of some of these studies – namely, that leadership is a collective phenomenon decentred for individuals – but it could document what this pluralising is made of, in various contexts and the variety of forms it can take, which could extend the work of Fairhurst and Cooren (2009).

Another stream of leadership studies that may benefit from taking inspiration from CCO is narrative enquiries of leadership. Conceptually speaking, narratives already share a proximity with CCO through their linguistic nature. However, narrative studies of leadership have not, for the most part, looked into the organising effects of narratives. In an organisation, what do narratives held about leadership and who 'the leaders' are achieve for this organisation? In other words, what do these narratives constitute, organisationally speaking? A CCO inspiration could add to current questions addressed through a narrative perspective. Moreover, leadership and who leaders ought to be and what they ought to do to be perceived as leaders are important topics, from a societal standpoint. Leadership can also then be conceived as materialised by a significant discourse in society. Again, based on some of their proximities, discourse analysis of leadership could find inspiration in CCO to expand on the performativity of such grand discourses on leadership. This project could be pursued through an attention to how elements of such discourses on leadership (e.g., commonly held ideas about what leadership is) intervene (e.g., are invoked and used) in organisations, play a role in communicative events and contribute (or not) to performing leadership locally. These studies could thus help in bridging more macro ('big D') and more micro ('small d'; Alvesson and Kärreman, 2000) discourse studies (as suggested by Cooren et al., 2013) and in showing the influence in organisation of social discourses on leadership, not only on how people conceive leadership and may define themselves as 'leaders', but also on how this is achieved.

Another example of studies that could be extended with a CCO perspective is that of leadership identity construction. Developed by DeRue and Ashforth (2010), this model of leadership proposes that leader and follower identities are socially constructed through a process of claiming and granting. These processes of claiming and granting lend themselves easily to a communication-centred redefinition: indeed, one could suggest looking at how, in situ, such claiming and granting is performed and what it generates, in terms of leadership effects. This could extend enquiries on identity issues in leadership, but could also allow us to explore other facets of leadership. Holm and Fairhurst (2018) provide a first illustration of this potential through their communication-centred study of the connections between hierarchical and shared leadership, in which claiming and granting processes play a key role.

Finally, I can also mention that studies that enquire into leaderless, non-hierarchical, or more horizontal organisation might find that CCO allows them to document and theorise leadership in a manner that goes beyond current dominant assumptions about leadership. As Sutherland et al. (2014) remind us, leaderless organisations are not leadership-less; but attending to leadership in such settings may require capturing its relational and processual emergence and production beyond a focus on the individual identification of 'leaders'. I hope to have demonstrated in these pages that it is exactly what CCO can allow us to do.

Beyond such extensions, CCO could also inspire researchers with different considerations. One key concern with leadership, especially when it is explored from the perspective of its enactment, as leading, is that of distinction with other processes. When looking at what people are doing in various situations, how can we establish what belongs to 'leadership' and what is rather connected to, for example, 'coordinating' or 'orienting'? This perennial question seems to haunt researchers adopting processual and practice perspectives on leadership. At the same time, the issue of what leadership is tends to be eschewed, at least partially, in many studies of leadership.

While I do not suggest that CCO studies could solve all the thorny issues pertaining to the definition of leadership, I consider that a constitutive perspective on leadership could develop relevant analyses because of its resolutely empirical grounding. Working from this bottom-up fashion, and clearly in line with ethnomethodology, a CCO enquiry into leadership would thus expose how 'leadership' is understood and produced in an organisational context. More importantly, by fully taking into consideration the organising properties of communications and presenting leadership as a category of organising (as argued, among others, by Hosking, 1988, and Crevani, 2018), a CCO conceptualisation of leadership might facilitate the distinction between what makes up leadership, understood processually, from other categories of organising effects. Working in the characteristically empirical fashion CCO strongly suggests, it may then be useful to prioritise what is made visible in communicative events and from local actors, and to conceptualise leadership, leading and leaders as local assemblages that do something related to direction in given situations.

Another implication of a CCO perspective on leadership, building particularly on its strong process ontology, is how it makes possible an enquiry into the *persistence* of leadership – in other words, its relative durability (or fragility). Such an enquiry would adopt a more longitudinal approach, considering how, from key moment to key moment, leadership materialises, and if it is sustained (or fades) over time. Such a more longitudinal approach could complement current studies that focus on specific situations or that opt for conversation analysis, by attending to how what is produced locally and situationally at a specific moment persists, or not, over time. This interest for the persistence of leadership could also take into consideration the issues of the effects attributed to leadership. CCO studies have traditionally attended to stability issues, especially those of organisations, but recent studies in CCO have started to address issues linked to disorganisation (see the edited collection on this topic by Vásquez and Kuhn, 2019). In parallel, leadership has not solely been studied as a 'positive' or beneficial phenomenon. Either through studies of narcissism and hubris (e.g., Sadler-Smith et al., 2017) or questionable, problematic and even plain negative effects for people and organisations, the dark side of leadership has been recognised and studied in an ample way[3]. I suggest that a CCO perspective could provide detailed accounts of the detrimental effects of leadership, by exposing the intricate mechanisms and assemblages through which these effects are produced.

A third – but not last! – extension that CCO could prompt in leadership studies concerns its evaluation. A CCO enquiry into the evaluation of leadership would move it from normative accounts of 'good' or 'bad' leadership and would instead question how such evaluations and attributions are made in organisational contexts. Combined with the specific sensitivity of valuation studies (which share a few roots with CCO through American pragmatism and actor-network theory), it would thus attend to what is assembled in such evaluation, locally and in relation to specific situations. This project could allow us to better trace the influence of leadership.

CONCLUDING REMARKS

As I have argued in these pages, CCO offers several sources of inspiration for leadership studies. First, by problematising communication and not taking it for granted and, second, either through its premises, its methodological commitments and/or through the novel concepts it has developed over the years, such a communication-centred perspective has the potential to refine and extend current enquiries into leadership. In concluding this chapter, I would like to acknowledge a criticism that has been directed at CCO scholarship: its relative lack of critical enquiries into organising processes and what they help maintain (Kuhn, 2021). However, as Kuhn demonstrates, this lack of attention does not derive from CCO's premises or positioning. Indeed, I argue that as a perspective it comes with all the conceptual tools necessary to address issues related to power and the effects of power in a detailed way.

The chosen verb present in its name, 'constituting', is not benign and alludes to the performative properties of communication. Beyond the already-mentioned studies on the organising effects of leadership discourses, a communicative and constitutive approach to leadership could appeal particularly to critical enquiries into leadership, by allowing the description of how leadership discourses naturalise hierarchies and asymmetries, or how consent (or dissent) is produced in actual conversations. As a stream of scholarship, CCO has developed a number of concepts over the years, and these concepts have now made their way into organisation studies. That most of the studies anchored in CCO have not questioned how dominant discourses and positions maintain their hold in organisations does not reveal a limit built into CCO theorising itself, but an unactualised potential. Hence, researchers enquiring critically into leadership may want to consider CCO and add it to their theoretical and methodological toolkits. In doing so (and possibly unintentionally), they may end up contributing both to leadership studies and to CCO scholarship, revealing that influences and inspirations always flow in multiple directions.

Notes

1 As argued in his 2020 article, Cooren now prefers this term to 'nonhuman,' as it enlarges our analytical view of what could be included under this label.
2 Interestingly, Cunliffe and Eriksen acknowledge the centrality of communication in a relational conception of leadership, but their approach is rooted in Bakhtin's dialogism, which leads them to explore the intersubjective production of living conversations and the ethical implications of such a relational conception.
3 When this chapter was written, a search with the expression 'dark side of leadership' on Google Scholar generated about 4,250 results. This of course does not include all the studies that document the excesses and damages of leaders of all kinds.

REFERENCES

Alvesson, M., & Kärreman, D. (2000). Varieties of discourse: On the study of organizations through discourse analysis. *Human Relations*, *53*(9), 1125–1149.

Alvesson, M., & Sveningsson, S. (2003). The great disappearing act: Difficulties in doing 'leadership'. *Leadership Quarterly*, *14*(3), 359–381.

Benoit-Barné, C., & Cooren, F. (2009). The accomplishment of authority through presentification. *Management Communication Quarterly*, *23*(1), 5–31.

Bisel, R. S., Fairhurst, G. T., & Sheep, M. L. (2022). CCO theory and leadership. In J. Basque, N. Bencherki & T. Kuhn (Eds.), *The Routledge Handbook of the Communicative Constitution of Organization* (pp. 297-309). Routledge.

Blaschke, S., Schoeneborn, D., & Seidl, D. (2012). Organizations as networks of communication episodes: Turning the network perspective inside out. *Organization Studies*, *33*(7), 879–906.

Boivin, G., Brummans, B., & Barker, J. R. (2017). The institutionalization of CCO scholarship: Trends from 2000 to 2015. *Management Communication Quarterly*, 31(3), 331–355.

Bourgoin, A., Bencherki, N., & Faraj, S. (2020). And who are you?: A performative perspective on authority in organizations. *Academy of Management Journal*, *63*(4), 1134–1165.

Clifton, J. (2017). Leaders as ventriloquists: Leader identity and influencing the communicative construction of the organisation. *Leadership*, *13*(3), 301–319.

Clifton, J., Fachin, F., & Cooren, F. (2021). How artefacts do leadership: A ventriloquial analysis. *Management Communication Quarterly*, *35*(2), 256–280.

Cooren, F. (2006). The organizational world as a plenum of agencies. In F. Cooren (Ed.), *Communication as Organizing: Empirical and Theoretical Explorations in the Dynamic of Text and Conversation* (pp. 81–100). Routledge.

Cooren, F. (2010). *Action and Agency in Dialogue. Passion, Incarnation and Ventriloquism*. J. Benjamins.

Cooren, F. (2012). Communication theory at the center: Ventriloquism and the communicative constitution of reality. *Journal of Communication*, *62*, 1–20.

Cooren, F. (2015a). In medias res: Communication, existence, and materiality. *Communication Research and Practice*, *1*(4), 307–321.

Cooren, F. (2015b). Studying agency from a ventriloqual perspective. *Management Communication Quarterly*, *29*(3), 475–480.

Cooren, F. (2016). Organizational communication: A wish list for the next fifteen years. In B. Czarniawska (Ed.) *A Research Agenda for Management and Organization Studies* (pp. 79-87). Edward Elgar Publishing

Cooren, F. (2018). Materializing communication: Making the case for a relational ontology. *Journal of Communication*, *68*(2), 278–288.

Cooren, F. (2020a). A communicative constitutive perspective on corporate social responsibility: Ventriloquism, undecidability, and surprisability. *Business and Society*, *59*(1), 175–197.

Cooren, F. (2020b). Beyond entanglement: (Socio-)materiality and organization studies. *Organization Theory*, OnlineFirst. https://doi.org/10.1177/2631787720954444

Cooren, F., Fairhurst, G., & Huët, R. (2012). Why matter always matters in (organizational) communication. In P. M. Leonardi, B. A. Nardi & J. Kallinikos (Eds.), *Materiality and Organizing: Social Interaction in a Technological World* (pp. 296–314). Oxford University Press.

Cooren, F., Kuhn, T., Cornelissen, J. P., & Clark, T. (2011). Communication, organizing and organization: An overview and introduction to the special issue. *Organization Studies*, *32*(9), 1149–1170.

Cooren, F., & Martine, T. (2016). Communicative constitution of organizations. In K. B. Jensen, R. T. Craig, J. D. Pooley & E. W. Rothenbuhler (Eds.), *The International Encyclopedia of Communication Theory and Philosophy* (pp. 1–9). Wiley-Blackwell.

Cooren, F., Matte, F., Benoit-Barné, C., & Brummans, B. H. J. M. (2013). Communication as ventriloquism: A grounded-in-action approach to the study of organizational tensions. *Communication Monographs*, *80*(3), 255–277.

Crevani, L. (2018). Is there leadership in a fluid world? Exploring the ongoing production of direction in organizing. *Leadership*, *14*(1), 83–109.

Crevani, L., & Endrissat, N. (2016). Mapping the leadership-as-practice terrain. In J. A. Raelin (Ed.), *Leadership-as-practice: Theory and Application* (pp. 21–49). Routledge.

Crevani, L., Lindgren, M., & Packendorff, J. (2010). Leadership, not leaders: On the study of leadership as practices and interactions. *Scandinavian Journal of Management*, *26*(1), 77–86.

Cunliffe, A. L., & Eriksen, M. (2011). Relational leadership. *Human Relations*, *64*(11), 1425-1449.

Denis, J. L., Langley, A., & Sergi, V. (2012). Leadership in the plural. *Academy of Management Annals*, *6*(1), 211–283.

DeRue, D. S., & Ashford, S. J. (2010). Who will lead and who will follow? A social process of leadership identity construction in organizations. *Academy of Management Review*, *35*(4), 627–647.

Dobusch, L., & Schoeneborn, D. (2015). Fluidity, identity, and organizationality: The communicative constitution of anonymous. *Journal of Management Studies*, *52*(8), 1005–1035.

Fairhurst, G. T. (2008). Discursive leadership: A communication alternative to leadership psychology. *Management Communication Quarterly*, *21*(4), 510–521.

Fairhurst, G. T., & Connaughton, S. L. (2014). Leadership: A communicative perspective. *Leadership*, *10*(1), 7–35. https://doi.org/10.1177/1742715013509396

Fairhurst, G. T., & Cooren, F. (2009). Leadership as the hybrid production of presence(s). *Leadership*, *5*(4), 469–490.

Fairhurst, G. T., & Uhl-Bien, M. (2012). Organizational discourse analysis (ODA): Examining leadership as a relational process. *Leadership Quarterly*, *23*(6), 1043–1062.

Hawkins, B. (2015). Ship-shape: Materializing leadership in the British Royal Navy. *Human Relations*, *68*(6), 951–971.

Holm, F., & Fairhurst, G. T. (2018). Configuring shared and hierarchical leadership through authoring. *Human Relations*, *71*(5), 692–721.

Hosking, D. M. (1988). Organizing, leadership and skilful process. *Journal of Management Studies*, *25*(2), 148–166.

Kuhn, T. (2021). (Re)moving blinders: Communication-as-constitutive theorizing as provocation to practice-based organization scholarship. *Management Learning*, *52*(1), 109–121.

Larsson, M., & Lundholm, S. E. (2010). Leadership as work-embedded influence: A micro-discursive analysis of an everyday interaction in a bank. *Leadership*, *6*(2), 159–184.

Larsson, M., & Lundholm, S. E. (2013). Talking work in a bank: A study of organizing properties of leadership in work interactions. *Human Relations*, *66*(8), 1101–1129.

Latour, B. (2005). *Reassembling the Social: An Introduction to Actor-Network Theory*. Oxford University Press.

McPhee, R. D., & Zaug, P. (2000). The communicative constitution of organizations: A framework for explanation. *Electronic Journal of Communication*, *10*(1/2), 1–16.

Meier, F., & Carroll, B. (2020). Making up leaders: Reconfiguring the executive student through profiling, texts and conversations in a leadership development programme. *Human Relations*, *73*(9), 1226–1248.

Meschitti, V. (2019). The power of positioning: How leadership work unfolds in team interactions. *Leadership*, *15*(5), 621–643.

Mulcahy, D., & Perillo, S. (2011). Thinking management and leadership within colleges and schools somewhat differently: A practice-based, actor-network theory perspective. *Educational Management Administration and Leadership*, *39*(1), 122–145.

Nathues, E., van Vuuren, M., & Cooren, F. (2021). Speaking about vision, talking in the name of so much more: A methodological framework for ventriloquial analyses in organization studies. *Organization Studies*, *42*(9), 1457–1476.

Ospina, S. M., Foldy, E. G., Fairhurst, G. T., & Jackson, B. (2020). Collective dimensions of leadership: Connecting theory and method. *Human Relations*, *73*(4), 441–463.

Putnam, L. L., & Nicotera, A. M. (2009). *Building Theories of Organization: The Constitutive Role of Communication*. Routledge.

Sadler-Smith, E., Akstinaite, V., Robinson, G., & Wray, T. (2017). Hubristic leadership: A review. *Leadership*, *13*(5), 525–548.

Schoeneborn, D., Blaschke, S., Cooren, F., McPhee, R. D., Seidl, D., & Taylor, J. R. (2014). The three schools of CCO thinking. *Management Communication Quarterly*, *28*(2), 285–316.

Schoeneborn, D., Kuhn, T. R., & Kärreman, D. (2019). The communicative constitution of organization, organizing, and organizationality. *Organization Studies*, *410*(4), 475–496.

Schoeneborn, D., & Vásquez, C. (2017). Communicative constitution of organizations. In C. R. Scott & L. Lewis (General Eds.); J. Barker, J. Keyton, T. Kuhn & P. Turner (Associate Eds.), *The International Encyclopedia of Organizational Communication*. Wiley-Blackwell.

Schnurr, S., & Schroeder, A. (2019). A critical reflection of current trends in discourse analytical research on leadership across disciplines: A call for a more engaging dialogue. *Leadership*, *15*(4), 445–460.

Sergi, V. (2016). Who's leading the way? Investigating the contributions of materiality to the study of leadership-as-practice. In J. A. Raelin (Ed.), *Leadership-as-practice: Theory and Applications* (pp. 110–131). Routledge.

Simpson, B., Buchan, L., & Sillince, J. (2018). The performativity of leadership talk. *Leadership*, *14*(6), 644–661.

Sutherland, N., Land, C., & Böhm, S. (2014). Anti-leaders(hip) in social movement organizations: The case of autonomous grassroots groups. *Organization*, *21*(6), 759–781.

Taylor, J. R. (1999). What is 'organizational communication'? Communication as a dialogic of text and conversation. *Communication Review*, *3*(1–2), 21–63.

Taylor, J. R., & Van Every, E. J. (2000). *The Emergent Organization: Communication as its Site and Surface*. Lawrence Erlbaum.

Taylor, J. R., & Van Every, E. J. (2014). *When Organization Fails: Why Authority Matters*. Routledge.

Tourish, D. (2013). *The Dark Side of Transformational Leadership: A Critical Perspective*. Routledge.

Tourish, D. (2014). Leadership, more or less? A processual, communication perspective on the role of agency in leadership theory. *Leadership*, *10*(1), 79–98.

Vásquez, C., & Kuhn, T. (2019). *Dis/organization as Communication: Exploring the Disordering, Disruptive and Chaotic Properties of Communication*. Routledge.

Vásquez, C., Schoeneborn, D., & Sergi, V. (2016). Summoning the spirits: Organizational texts and the (dis) ordering properties of communication. *Human Relations*, *69*(3), 629–659.

Vine, B., Holmes, J., Marra, M., Pfeifer, D., & Jackson, B. (2008). Exploring co-leadership talk through interactional sociolinguistics. *Leadership*, *4*(3), 339–360.

Whitehead, A. N. (1920). *The Concept of Nature*. Cambridge University Press.

Wilhoit, E. D. (2018). Affordances as material communication: How the spatial environment communicates to organize cyclists in Copenhagen, Denmark. *Western Journal of Communication*, *82*(2), 217–237.

Yukl, G. (1989). Managerial leadership: a review of theory and research. *Journal of Management*, *15*(2), 215–289.

Leading as Aesthetic and Artful Practice: It's not Always Pretty

Donna Ladkin

At its heart, leadership is an irrationally based, relational phenomenon. Young men and women do not willingly follow military leaders to their deaths in times of war because of logical enticements to do so, no matter how strongly they believe in a given ideology. Employees do not freely spend long, unpaid hours of discretionary time hunched over computer screens unless they have been hooked by something more than the belief that it 'makes sense' to do so. The magical ingredient, 'influence', which makes an individual a leader by virtue of being able to exercise it, is a many-faceted phenomenon. Although we might like to think of influence as something that can be easily explained, measured or distributed in a controlled fashion, its workings can be nefarious and shadowy. People are persuaded by fear and desire as often as they might be enticed by nobler drives. This chapter focuses on a particular fuel which drives influence in ways that might not always be apparent: aesthetic perception, and its role in leader–follower relations.

The chapter argues that prior to emotional engagement or reasoned argument, aesthetic perception is the spark that hooks potential followers' attention both to the possibility that an individual might best suit the situation in relation to their ability 'to lead' and to where that individual thinks it is important to go. Our sensory apparatus – eyes, ears, skin and intuition – are constantly scanning the environment, alerting us to changes in it. Operating below our habitual level of consciousness, our senses are attuned to potential dangers or delights which warrant a more conscious level of awareness. In this way, Baumgarten (1750), who is recognised for establishing aesthetics as a branch of philosophy, suggests that aesthetic perception – that is, perceiving through the senses – serves an important biological function, enabling us to stay safe in a world liable to change. The fact that it works at a pre-articulated, subliminal level (Postrel, 2003) is critical – its invisibility makes it powerful in ways that more rationally based types of influence can't approach. Leaders who are able to harness the power of aesthetic magnetism wield a mighty force.

Such a powerful capacity should be used with discretion. Most of the literature concerning the aesthetics or art of leadership (Hansen et al., 2007; Ladkin, 2008; Taylor, 2011) treats the aesthetic or the artful as a morally neutral dynamic. Artistry in one's practice of leading is seen as a capacity to be crafted and developed. This chapter offers a more cautionary account. If the aesthetic operates at a subliminal, often un-reflected-upon level of consciousness, and is at the core of influential power, then certainly the ends towards which that influence is being exercised need to be examined in order to remain within the realm of ethical relations. This point is worthy of emphasis: it is precisely because the aesthetic operates at a pre-rational level of consciousness that it is so powerful. Because of that power, rather than being encouraged without restriction, it should be subject to interrogation. The case study offered to illustrate the aesthetics of leadership in action – that of the insurrection which took place at the US Capitol on 6 January 2021 – serves as a cautionary tale of both the power of the aesthetic when it is used in leader relations and why that power needs to be used wisely.

As well as encouraging more careful consideration of leadership as an aesthetically based phenomenon, the chapter exercises sense-breaking by challenging the unquestioned reliance on leadership within our current context. 'More leadership' seems to be the answer to almost every societal difficulty we currently face. But if leadership is conceptualised fundamentally as an act of influence, the question arises as to why so many people either strive to influence others or hunger to be influenced by someone else. Does our current societal hunger for 'leadership' speak to a deeper gap in individual consciousness, an 'aesthetic craving' seeking to be filled? By considering what is fuelling our collective yearning for leadership, perhaps this phenomenon might take its rightful place as one of a number of answers to society's ills, rather than our collective go-to response.

The chapter begins with a description of events at the US Capitol on 6 January 2021. As an aside, it is interesting to note that when I agreed to write this chapter in mid- 2020, like the rest of us living in the US at the time, I had no idea what the presidential election of 2020 would bring. Given the former President's style of operating, I wondered what would occur should Biden prevail. As it became clear that the previous incumbent would not concede the election, and further that he was denying that he had lost (a move which subsequently earnt the moniker of 'The Big Lie'), like many Americans I worried what might happen as the inauguration approached. And like many Americans I watched events of 6 January unfurl with distress and horror. Once the riot at the Capitol had been dispelled, I had little appetite for ruminating over it, and what it meant about the state of leadership in the US.

However, as I began preparing to write this chapter I reread one of the first articles written about the aesthetics of leadership by the educationalist Daniel Duke. As I re-engaged with that article, published in 1986, the events of 6 January replayed themselves in my mind's eye. Almost everything that Duke had written could be seen to be in operation during that event. Bringing Duke's theoretically based article together with the experience of 6 January insurrection made me probe my assumptions about the aesthetic and how it relates to leadership more deeply. Whereas up until then I had held a rather benign and positive view about aesthetic leadership, I began to feel disquiet and unease. This chapter takes as its starting point that personal disquiet, in order to explore the extent to which it might expand the current conversation about aesthetics in leadership.

After setting the scene with a description of the events of 6 January, the chapter takes a step back to ask: what is meant by the term 'aesthetic', and how has it been associated with leadership? How does it relate to other ideas which have currency in the leadership studies canon, such as embodiment and meaning-making? The chapter then revisits the 6 January insurrection in order to consider how that elaborated understanding sheds further light both on that event and on how aesthetics within leadership work. The chapter ends by articulating the kinds of questions resulting from this exploration as well as suggesting how future research might elaborate on the ideas offered here. First, let us turn to events of 6 January 2021.

THE 6 JANUARY 2021 INSURRECTION IN THE US

Although Joe Biden won the US Presidential Election in November 2020 by more than 7 million popular votes and by an electoral college tally of 306 over Donald Trump's 232, Donald Trump refused to concede Biden's victory. As November wore on and ballot recounts were held in key battleground states of Arizona, Georgia and Michigan it became increasingly clear that Trump would not accept that Biden had fairly won. Instead, he insisted, mostly via the social media platform Twitter, on his version of events. He maintained that he had won in a 'landslide' and that the election had been stolen from him. Further stoking the agitation of his followers towards action, in a Tweet posted on 18 December Trump suggested that people should meet in Washington on 6 January, writing, *Big protest in DC on January 6th. Be there, will be wild.*

The 6th of January was when a Joint Session of the US Congress would convene to ratify the vote and announce Joe Biden as the 46th President of the United States, due to be inaugurated on 20 January, 2021. On that morning, thousands of people gathered in front of the White House for an event which Trump had dubbed the 'Save America' rally. Beginning at 12 noon Donald Trump addressed the crowds from behind a bullet-proof glass barrier. A YouTube clip of the event (see https://www.youtube.com/watch?v=JTjGuavtsVU&t=312s) shows Trump flanked by a phalanx of American flags with the White House centred behind him. His tone is measured, the rise and fall of his words resembling the cadence of a watered down version of a Southern preacher. He is oddly defiant yet fragile at the same time. As I watch him, the image that arises for me is that of the misunderstood bully. How many times have we, when seven years old, intoned the phrase 'it's not fair', when circumstances out of our control do something we feel is wrong? I know that feeling – it's hot and agitated and heavy at the same time. It sits in the middle of my chest and causes my throat to constrict. I read that same feeling of indignation and being wronged in Trump's stance, the way he seemed to fight to contain himself. I imagine that feeling was easily transmitted to those gathered before him, who themselves might have felt wronged, misconstrued and subject to events which were somehow not fair.

During Trump's speech, which lasted over an hour, he proclaimed, *We will never give up. We will never concede. It doesn't happen. You don't concede when there is a theft involved. We won this election and we won it by a landslide. This was not a close election.* Trump supporters' cheers are heard in the background. At 1.10, Trump ended his speech, saying, *We are going to the Capitol. We're going to try and give them* [the Republicans] *the kind of pride and boldness that they need to take back the country.* The crowd did indeed make its way to the Capitol building. President Trump did not join them, spending the following six hours in the White House instead.

According to reports in the *Washington Post* and the *New York Times,* protesters overwhelmed Capitol Police (who are more accustomed to directing tourists than holding back flak-suited mobsters intent on breaking into the building) shortly after 2pm. (For a detailed timeline of the day's events according to the *Washington Post*, see Tan et al., 2021.) Many of those who broke into the Capitol building were dressed in combat gear, and a number of them brandished high-quality military equipment for scaling walls. Make America Great Again signs, American flags, flags of Trump dressed as Rambo, men wearing Viking horns and animal skins were all in evidence.

A noose was erected outside the Capitol and chants of 'Hang Mike Pence', the Vice-President, began after Trump tweeted that Pence had been too cowardly to uphold the truth that day. Pence had indeed upheld his Constitutional duty to ratify the election results. The ongoing work of the joint houses stopped as senators, representatives and Vice-President Pence were bundled into safe places. The violence and breaking into officials' offices continued for four hours until police reinforcements from surrounding States and the National Guard arrived. In total, five people lost their lives as a result of the violence of the day, including Capitol Police Officer Brian Sicknick. Trump's response as the insurrection occurred was to Tweet, *These are the things and events that happen when a sacred landslide election victory is so unceremoniously and viciously stripped away from great patriots who have been badly and unfairly treated for so long. Go home with love and in peace. Remember this day forever.*

An Initial Analysis

In her book *Strangers in their Own Land* (Russell Hochschild, 2016) the sociologist Arlie Russell Hochschild provides an account of her five-year immersion in Louisiana where she sought to understand Tea Party enthusiasts. A liberal university professor from Berkeley, she attempts to cross over the 'empathy wall' to truly get to know Tea Party members' deep story – the underlying rationale for why they support far right policies. The book was published in 2016, before Trump was elected but while excitement for his candidacy was growing. She attended a number of rallies for the then candidate and tried to make sense of what his supporters were drawn to in their excitement over him.

In a passage which alludes to the aesthetic of Trump's campaign, she draws on the sociologist Emil Durkheim's ([1915] 1965) study of cults. She writes,

> People gather around what Durkheim calls a 'totem', a symbol such as a cross or a flag. Leaders associate themselves with the totem and charismatic leaders can become totems themselves. The function of the totem is to unify worshippers. Seen through Durkheim's eyes, the real function of the excited gathering around Donald Trump is to unify all the white, evangelical enthusiasts who fear that those cutting ahead in line are about to become a terrible, strange, new America. The source of the awe and excitement isn't simply Trump himself: it is the unity of the great crowd of strangers gathered around him […] what he gives participants is an **ecstatic high**.
>
> (Russell Hochschild, 2016, p. 226, emphasis is my own)

There are two points from this passage which I would like to elaborate on for what they say about the aesthetics of Trump's leadership. First, is the importance of the 'totem'. The totem is an artefact, something that can be seen, which is taken to symbolise a deeply held identity for those who connect with it. It is the aesthetic force of the totem to unify the sense of identification which holds its power. In this case the American flag is the totem, one which was accentuated by the sheer number of them flanking Donald Trump as he spoke to his followers at the start of the day. It is also important to note that Durkheim suggests the leader himself can become a totem, an idea which seems relevant in the case of Donald Trump. The second aspect of this quote which is telling from an aesthetic point of view is Durkheim's claim that it is the unity of the crowd, their *felt sense* of being part of something greater than their own individual experience, which gives participants an *ecstatic high*. An ecstatic high is first and foremost an aesthetic experience. It is pre-rational – it is not thought through. It is *felt*. Its power lies in its visceral immediacy. There is a truthfulness of experience about it which cannot be denied.

The attachment between Trump and his followers may be seen as extreme. However, I would argue that this kind of pull is on show at any successful political rally. Remember the thrill on the faces of Obama's supporters when he gave his acceptance speech after winning the presidential election in 2008. Any leader aspiring to influence others needs to be able to conjure up some degree of the kind of relational glue on show during Trump's rallies. A key element of that relational glue, I further suggest, is aesthetic. Let's turn now to examine how the term 'aesthetic' has been theorised in relation to leadership in more detail.

The Aesthetic in Relation to Leadership

For many people, the term 'aesthetic' refers to 'art' or the experience one has when engaging with art. We go to an art gallery or a concert if we want to have an 'aesthetic' experience. The term is also often associated with the aesthetic category of 'the beautiful', omitting the idea that aesthetic categories also encompass the ugly, the agitated and the dour as well as the harmonious or balanced (Strati, 1999). The way the term is being used here however, refers to its original meaning, rather than that of our contemporary times. The literary theorist Susan Buck-Morss reminds us that originally the term aesthetic had very little to do with art. Instead, the term originated from the Greek 'aisthitikos' which can be roughly translated as *that which is perceptive by feeling* (Buck-Morss, 2008, p. 6). Buck-Morss goes on to suggest that aesthetic perception serves the biological function of keeping us safe, and is closer to animal instinct than its subsequent association with questions of taste. Following from this, aesthetic perception is the kind of knowing which arises from our senses. Through our sight, hearing, taste, smell and touch we know the world directly. Visceral, aesthetic perception speaks the truth of our immediate experience. Furthermore, we are always having aesthetic experiences. At this very moment, should you choose to attend to the information your body is giving you, you can tell whether you are hot or cold, whether you are hungry, whether or not coffee is brewing nearby. Much of the time we filter out that sensory information, but it is always there should we choose to attend to it. It is that immediate, unjudged way of being in and knowing the world.

In relation to leadership, the term 'aesthetic' has been used to capture the pre-verbal apprehension that is in play between leaders and their followers (Ladkin & Taylor, 2010a). It is the 'feel' we have for another human being, the sense we are using to judge a new boss or colleague the first time we meet them. Are they open and friendly, or power-hungry and narcissistic? What does their posture say about the way they handle themselves? What is the 'vibe' they give off? This is the kind of aesthetic data we are honed into collecting.

Looking back in the organisational studies literature, references to aesthetic notions of balance and harmony within organisational workings are evident in Chester Barnard's writings as early as 1938. However, the idea of aesthetic leadership was not elaborated in a systematic way until the educationalist Daniel Duke published his article 'The aesthetics of leadership' (Duke, 1986). Writing in the mid-1980s, Duke's article was published at the brink of the rise of leadership studies as a discipline of its own. James MacGregor Burns's *Leadership* had been published in 1976, and Bernard Bass's notion of transformational leadership, which attempted to scientise leadership, had only just been published in 1985.

One can imagine that Duke was writing in response to attempts to nail leading down as a series of behaviours when he asserted, *The world of the leader often is portrayed as a rational one in which goals are set, resources are mobilized, plans are implemented, and problems are solved* (Duke, 1986, pp. 8–9). He goes on to declare that this is wrong, and to assert that leadership is a much less rational process than others have conjectured it to be. He argues that it is an irrational process with perception at its core, writing, *Leadership is, first and foremost, a perception invested with social meaning and value* (p. 10). Key within this claim is Duke's use of the word, 'perception'. Perception is sensory: we do it through our eyes, ears and bodies. By equating leading with perception Duke is claiming the aesthetic heart of leadership relations. Duke doesn't talk about the quality of that perception, or how it occurs. Importantly, however, and in contrast to theorists around him such as Bass or Gardner, he holds perception – and particularly followers' perceptions – at the core of his understanding of how leadership operates.

Duke goes on to focus on the meaning-making aspect of leading. Drawing from Eoyang's (1983) work on symbols, he stresses that symbolic meaning is characterised not as an independently attribute of the symbol but as an *attribute of the interaction of the symbol and the perceivers' previous experience and knowledge* (Duke, 1986, p. 12). This again places followers' perceptions front and centre to how leadership operates. Additionally, this view highlights the meaning-making dynamic at the heart of symbolic relations. For instance, on its own the American flag is merely a piece of cloth arranged in a certain pattern of red, white and blue. It is the meaning given that item within a particular culture, at a particular time in which the perceiver exists, that imbues this particular collection of cloth and colour with meaning.

Duke develops his argument by suggesting that leading incorporates four aspects, each imbued with its own aesthetic dimension. First he suggests that leaders need to provide followers with a sense of direction. What is different about Duke's rendering of this commonly heard aspect of leading is his insistence that the direction must be one that is meaningful to followers. The aesthetic job of the leader is to provide direction with meaning. In the case of the Capitol insurrection, Trump was very clear about the direction he wanted his followers to take and why marching on the Capitol was important. It was to 'right a wrong'; to win back a stolen election. From an even more compelling perspective, Trump framed what he was encouraging his followers to do as 'saving America' itself.

Second, Duke stresses the importance of engagement – that is, the sense followers have that they are involved, and that their involvement in something larger than their individual selves has meaning. Despite being a billionaire who is rumoured to have a gold-plated toilet, Trump is able to connect with those who have not done well through the system. Trump makes them feel like he 'gets' them in a way that few others have, particularly untrustworthy politicians who don't have their interests at heart. He is arch at playing the 'poor me', embattled little boy card which resonates with those in his base whose experience, despite working hard, is not being able to achieve the American dream.

Duke's third aspect – the importance of 'fit' between a leader and their context – is also evident in the relationship between Trump and his followers. Fit refers to the way in which an individual and the way they are perceived resonates with what followers perceive to be the needs of a particular moment. In relation to this aesthetic dimension, it is interesting to note that when Trump ran for President in 2000, his bid was spectacularly unsuccessful. (Similarly, Boris Johnson failed in his first bid to be Prime Minister of the UK in 2016.) Followers did not perceive that Trump was what the US needed in terms of a leader in 2000 and, similarly, in the immediate aftermath of the Brexit result in the UK, Johnson was not seen as a trustworthy candidate. Move forward 16 years in the US, after an African American had held the highest Office in the land and demographic shifts were beginning to be felt and Trump was seen as the answer to subterranean disquiet. It is interesting to note the way in which Trump's 'birthers' campaign against Obama's legitimacy to be President (which ran throughout Obama's eight years in office) spoke to a simmering unease among parts of the US population. The lies which were rehearsed about Obama's legitimacy somehow spoke to a powerful, *felt* reality experienced by a growing number of Americans, that it was somehow wrong that Obama should be President.

Duke's fourth dimension of aesthetic leadership is 'originality'. The leader has to be perceived as offering something new in some way, in order to capture followers' imaginations in a compelling way. Again, from an aesthetic perspective, Trump was like no politician ever encountered previously. Indeed, every show of politically incorrect behaviour, every dismissal of common courtesy or denial of tradition endeared Trump to his supporters even more. Each time Trump made ugly remarks about women, or mimicked the disabled, or called white supremacists 'very fine people' he re-enforced his uniqueness, the ways in which he was truly different from the political elite his base hate. His originality was further fortified by the aesthetic choices he often made at political rallies, in which he wore his Make America Great Again (MAGA) baseball cap, was known for punctuating speeches with fist-shaking and name-calling, and often arrived in his Trump aeroplane moments before he was due to speak.

These four aesthetic dimensions – direction, engagement, fit and originality – provide the basis for much subsequent work undertaken about the relationship between the aesthetic and leadership. The following section reviews the way this connection has been elaborated by other scholars.

How the Field Developed after Duke

A number of educationalists drew from Duke's work and developed it further by examining how the aesthetic played out within leading in school settings. However, it wasn't until late 2007, with the publication of Hansen et al.'s article 'Aesthetic leadership' in *Leadership Quarterly* (Hansen et al., 2007) that the idea was more broadly introduced to mainstream leadership thinking. In framing their interest in the arena, Hansen et al. identify two trends in leadership studies which presage attention to the aesthetic dimension of leading: the understanding of leadership as the 'management of meaning'; and through the burgeoning of relationally based approaches which focus on followers and their subjective experiences of leadership. By identifying these trends Hansen et al. echo Duke's work, particularly with its attention to the meaning-making aspect of aesthetic perception. In claiming the importance of the aesthetic within leadership theorising they argue that, *While previous leadership studies have largely taken an instrumental approach to what works, aesthetics also sheds light not only on what works, but what works aesthetically, what seems to agree with our tacit knowledge or implicit feelings and emotions regarding a particular context* (2007, p. 549). Their reference to tacit knowledge, feelings and emotions acknowledges the pre-rational ways in which leadership as an aesthetically based phenomenon occurs.

Theoretical development of the notion of aesthetic leadership has taken several distinct routes. For instance, Ladkin has identified how different types of leader enactments portray specific aesthetic qualities. In an early work she considers the ways in which charismatic leadership aligns itself with notions of the sublime (Ladkin, 2006), arguing that like the sublime, charisma often evokes a feeling of excitement coupled with fear in those who encounter it. Unlike beauty, which is experienced as wholly delightful, when encountering the sublime in forms such as a towering mountain, a wild storm, or a raging sea, the perceiver often experiences ambivalence and the fear of losing a sense of themselves. She argues that charismatic leaders can conjure up similar tensions in their followers. Later, she considers what might constitute 'beautiful leadership' by studying how the musician Bobby McFerrin engages a concert hall full of people without saying a word (Ladkin, 2008). Given that he never speaks during the concert, McFerrin's performance explicitly works at a pre-verbal level. Instead, his use of gestures and his overall demeanour provoke audience participation. Drawing from Plotinus's notions of the beautiful, she suggests that the mastery, coherence and aim towards a worthy purpose evident in McFerrin's leadership is indicative of beautiful leadership.

These forays into the beautiful and sublime categories of aesthetic leadership point to its generative capacity, its ability to entice followers towards worthy purposes. Such use of the aesthetic 'for good' is also apparent in the Prime Minister of New Zealand, Jacinda Ardern's taking part in an *ifoga* as an act of reparation for the Dawn Raids visited upon Pacific Islanders in New Zealand during the 1970s. During this ceremony, Ardern was covered by a large white mat, as a way of *seeking forgiveness by exposing herself to a kind of public humiliation* (Perry, 2021). Being willing to place herself, literally, into such a place of humiliation is an aesthetic act which carries power in a way that spoken apologies cannot. Such an act demonstrates how the aesthetic is intertwined with how leaders embody their roles.

Expanding on this notion further, Ladkin and Taylor have considered the role embodiment plays in creating a leader performance which is described as aesthetically *authentic* (Ladkin & Taylor, 2010a). Rather than being a question of the extent to which being authentic involves a leader acting in accordance with their *true self*, Ladkin and Taylor argue that authenticity is first and foremost an attribute given by followers to leaders who they feel are in some way *real*. They note humans' capacity to distinguish between smiles which are genuine (due to the involvement of involuntary muscles) and those that are forced (created through conscious voluntary muscular responses) as indicative of the tacit dynamic in play when both trying to create an authentic leadership performance and being read by others as doing so. Similarly scholars such as Sinclair (2014), Stephens (2014) and Bathurst and Williams (2014) elaborate on the overlaps between the way in which leaders embody their roles and the aesthetic they are perceived to exude.

A more systems-based understanding of aesthetic leadership is offered by Guillet de Monthuox et al. (2007). Drawing from Csikszentmihaly's (2003) work on *flow*, they suggest that flow is an aesthetic phenomenon in which individuals are absorbed holistically in a given activity and lose all awareness of time. In order to get the best from their followers, leaders are encouraged to intentionally create systems-based aesthetic experiences which can foster higher levels of productivity and well-being in those followers. Like the authors before them Guillet de Monthuox et al. do not discuss the possibility that flow experiences could be used for degenerative or unethical purposes.

Another body of work relating to aesthetic leadership has been developed by scholars looking at leadership as an art or craft which can be developed in similar ways to any embodied performance (Halpern Lubar, 2004; Ladkin & Taylor, 2010b; Taylor, 2011; Taylor & Ladkin, 2014). These writers assume that it is possible for individuals to present themselves in certain ways which will increase their chances of being identified as leaders and effectively influencing others. Whereas the argument being made here is that aesthetic judgement ultimately rests with those who are observing a leader or potential leader, these authors do highlight ways in which leaders can become more intentional about how they enact the leader role.

In ending this review of different approaches which have been taken in relation to leadership and aesthetics, it is important to cite two texts which summarise the field up until 2011. The first is Katz-Buonincontro's (2011) review of the literature concerning aesthetic leadership. Like Duke before her, Katz-Buonincontro is positioned within the context of educational leadership, and her concern is to understand the aesthetic qualities which have been most associated with leading. She identifies four such qualities prevalent within her review of 23 sources: emotional awareness and empathy, sensing and somatic attentiveness, interest in organisational beauty and the promotion of moral purpose. It is the relationship between aesthetic leading and promotion of moral purpose which I want to call into question.

Finally, Hansen and Bathurst's (2011) chapter 'Aesthetics and leadership' in the previous edition of this *Handbook* takes a slightly different approach from others mentioned so far by making the case for the importance of the aesthetic in generating transformational change. They argue that *large scale transformation involves inspiring followers to move toward a future state without knowing the precise shape of that future* (p. 255). For them, focus on the aesthetic as an important driver in achieving such change, is important because of its ability to work *beyond an instrumental* form of exchange. Claiming the power of the aesthetic to awaken a more critical form of consciousness, Hansen and Bathurst suggest that the holistic apprehension which aesthetic perception fosters can encourage followers to notice the structures and rituals that hold them in place. Highlighting the power of art such as Picasso's painting *Guernica* or the capacity of Greek tragedy to *help people see the light*, they write: *emancipation occurs as people within organizations feel, see, and discern the dominating structures within the enterprise* [which has the potential to] *liberate people from the damaging effects of organizational life* (p. 261).

Hansen and Bathurst's assertion is indicative of the way in which aesthetic leadership is held as a lofty ideal. Unerringly the aesthetic in relation to leadership is seen as a force for good, a creator of 'flow'. Hansen and Bathurst go as far as to suggest that aesthetic leadership can be the progenitor of critical, emancipatory consciousness. As noted by Edwards et al. (2019), there is a tendency in leadership theorising to focus on the 'beauty' of the phenomenon and ignore its ugly aspects, a trend which is particularly evident in aesthetic leadership scholarship. Although aesthetic engagement on the part of leaders can be used towards worthy ends, the events of 6 January, and indeed the ways in which the aesthetic was harnessed within regimes such as Nazi Germany or Stalin's Russia, extend our appreciation of its shadow side. The next section engages in sense-breaking by questioning the unchallenged assumption that the aesthetic within leadership is morally admirable, or at least morally neutral.

The Moral Dimension of Aesthetic Leadership

Let me begin this section by summarising the key points of the argument which have been made so far. The aesthetic is theorised here to be the kind of knowing arising from sensory perception which is occurring all the time. Distinct from authors such as Katz-Buonincontro or Hansen and Bathurst, I am suggesting that using an 'aesthetic orientation' in how one leads is not something that can be turned off and on like a switch. Followers are continuously accumulating sensory data – and making aesthetically based, pre-cognitive judgements whether the leader is intentionally trying to engage their followers aesthetically or not. This is such an important point, and differs so radically from much that is written about 'aesthetic leadership', that it is worth reiterating. We are all (whether we are acting as leaders or not) always giving off information which is perceived by others through their sensory apparatus. This information is judged by others in ways that we cannot control but which affects their willingness to assign us the label of 'leader' or to be influenced by us. Arising from our pre-cognitive, sensory experience, these perceptions are powerful because of the truth they hold (the sensory experiences we have do not lie). To date, the possibility of leaders honing the type of artistry used to intentionally engage followers from an aesthetic perspective has been encouraged. This is where my argument about aesthetic leadership takes a sharp turn.

Here, I align myself with a small group of theorists who address the moral issues associated with the aesthetic. For instance, Storsletten and Jakobsen (2014) draw from Kierkegaard's understanding of aesthetics to suggest that rather than being an ideal, because the aesthetic is based in human senses, it can too easily lead to uncontrollable desires and thus unethical actions. Kierkegaard believed that the realm of human behaviour associated with the aesthetic attracted us to that which we perceive to be *entertaining, exciting, or of interest* (quoted in Gardiner, 2002, p. 48). Things that are *entertaining, exciting or of interest* are not always morally sound.

Following from this problematisation, Kersten (2008) considers the way in which the aesthetic can result in morally questionable or wrong behaviours within organisations. Key to her argument is the understanding that the assignment of aesthetic categories is always born from the context in which we are situated, and is *often ideological* (p. 191). These words have particular resonance in relation to the 6 January 2021 insurrection. It is evident that the thousands of people who gathered in Washington D.C. that day and stormed the Capitol believed in the 'beauty' of their actions in relation to saving America.

Kersten (2008) draws from the work of the political theorist Kateb (2000) to elaborate the critical view she brings to understanding organisational aesthetics. Central to Kateb's thinking is the notion of *aesthetic craving*. Aesthetic craving is our desire for something more than the pleasure we enjoy from the artwork, the fashionable article of clothing, or the beautiful music. It involves making the absent (that which we would desire but which is not proximate) present. It is a psychological craving which bolsters our very experience of existing. It is the search for the rightness of a story we tell ourselves about ourselves, the world and our place in it. Importantly, aesthetic craving works on an unconscious level of awareness. Paraphrasing Kateb's work, Kersten argues that *the human desire for satisfying our aesthetic craving explains much of human behavior, both good and bad* (2008, p. 191). Of particular relevance to the argument being formed here are two key ways in which Kateb sees aesthetic craving expressing itself:

- Through the tendency of people to raise one culture above another, to impose one's own culture on others, and to readily destroy the culture of others;
- Through the tendency to preserve and advance a distinct group's identity, whether that is the identity of a tribe, nation or race.

(Kersten, 2008, p. 191)

There are two passages from Kersten and Kateb which seem to be particularly relevant to the notion of aesthetic leadership and how it can result in morally questionable outcomes. The first is as follows:

If the world does not conform to our specifications, we insist that it must be changed to fit our ideal of beauty, even at a cost. This then creates a politics in which aesthetic ideals become disconnected from morality and the ends justify the means.

(Kersten, 2008, p. 192)

The price of aesthetic craving – for a so-called 'perfect Aryan race', for 'ethnic cleansing' in China or Eastern Europe, for 'making America Great again' – has been untold human suffering and death, all in the name of an idealised notion of 'beauty'. Similarly, in the 'beautiful' reality which Trump wants to bring about (and it is startling how many times he actually uses the word 'beautiful' in his rhetoric) he won the 2020 election by a landslide. His intention, through his Save America rally and the subsequent storming of the Capitol, was to bring about that reality, regardless of the lie at its heart: that he lost the 2020 election. Moreover, his followers share the aesthetic craving for the reality he is painting.

Kateb offers another piece of the puzzle in terms of what goes on between Trump and his followers, in relation to his ability to perpetuate lies:

Strong leaders often exhibit hyperactive imaginations, making the absent present through a passion to alter reality based on a new description for it [...] They can persist despite the unprecedented scale of awful effects – only through the unconscious and uncontrolled aesthetic cravings which is what give shape to the imagination for the story about the world they wish to create.

(2000, p. 193)

A shiver ran up my spine as I read that passage. It was written in 2000, 20 years prior to events of 6 January 2021. Yet it describes Trump's proclivity to lie – but, more importantly, for his followers to accept his lies – in a way that I had found impossible to understand prior to reading Kateb's thoughts. There is an aesthetic craving for the visceral experience of belonging, for being understood, for not being left behind. There is a truth to that longing, it is viscerally felt. A leader who can detect that aesthetic craving and soothe it through a story which speaks directly to it exerts enormous influence. Interpreted through this lens, Trump is a master of working with the aesthetic dimension of leading. His very way of being – as an outsider battling against Washington's political 'elite', a hard-done-by business man who is only fighting for what is fair, a misunderstood boy who only says it like he sees it – reverberates with sufficient others' viscerally felt experiences to result in his having a formidable following. Furthermore, the intensity of the connection is such that his followers were willing to act on that connection, to storm the Capitol in order to achieve his vision for saving the country.

This analysis reveals the ways in which the connection between Donald Trump and his followers can be understood as primarily an aesthetically driven one. The connection is even more powerful for its pre-rational, unconscious rootedness in the truth of his followers' immediate, visceral, felt sense. This sensed reality overrides any rationally based information about votes cast or validated recounts. Trump's conviction that he has been wronged resonates with the many ways in which those who follow him have been wronged at the incontrovertible level of aesthetic sensibility.

The insurrection of 6 January demonstrates why aesthetically driven leadership should not be nurtured from within a vacuum. Rather, the purposes towards which such artistry will be used need to be questioned. What will such a powerful force be used in service of?

What Does this Analysis Say about Leadership Itself?

This chapter began with the assertion that leadership is an irrationally based relational phenomenon. What has been alluded to throughout the text is the suggestion that the dynamic at leadership's heart is essentially aesthetic. It is the felt sense flowing between individuals which results in some individuals being perceived to have the qualities required by a given situation 'to lead'. Kateb's notion of aesthetic craving provides new language to understand more about that attributional process. Driving it are perceptions about the extent to which a particular individual can satisfy others' unconscious craving for meaning, a story, a way of re-establishing a sense of belonging within the vicissitudes of a changing and uncertain world. Daniel Duke and others at the vanguard of writing about aesthetic leadership noted the importance of meaning-making within leadership. Kateb accentuates that importance by pointing to the visceral desire for such meaning-making, especially in relation to solidifying followers' identities.

Perhaps the analysis presented here provides a response to the question of why leadership seems to be the 'go to' answer for so many of our current crises. Leadership is the answer to our aesthetic craving for certainty, meaning and an ordered universe. To stretch this argument perhaps to its limit, it could be suggested that leadership itself has become a 'totem', a signifier imbued with irrational meaning and desire. We want the beauty and harmony provided by the overactive imagination of leaders such as Donald Trump who famously declared the Covid-19 virus would *miraculously disappear* in time for Easter 2020. We want to believe US President Joe Biden's version of a kinder America can be a reality, despite the intransigence of polarised ideologies which pervade the current political climate. We want to believe in the 'absent present' which leaders' visions of the future promise. And we want these things at the visceral, pre-rational level of felt sense, where our desires have the force of truth experienced in our gut. Understanding leadership in this way has implications for how we study, engage with and seek to develop this phenomenon, as described in the final section below.

Implications

As it has been conventionally theorised, leadership is offered as the magic bullet to cure each societal ill we face. Transformational leadership has the power to 'move followers beyond their moderate expectations', 'servant leadership' puts followers' needs first, authentic leaders are 'optimistic', morally upright and act in alignment with their (perfect) true selves.

Rather than trying to achieve these god-like feats, perhaps asking why we collectively crave such fantasies is a helpful developmental step. The dark side of aesthetic leadership shows us how leaders who can tap into followers' aesthetic cravings (especially for belonging and meaning) can result in ethically terrible outcomes: the wearing away of democratic processes, the demonisation of other human beings and genocide itself.

For those of us who study the phenomenon, this analysis suggests we pay greater attention to why leadership is needed in particular situations, as well as the ends to which it is directed. Often in conventional leadership scholarship, leadership in its many forms is theorised as if it happens in a vacuum. However, this aesthetically based analysis indicates the importance of context in determining the kind of leader followers yearn for and the purposes they are ready to support. As an essentially aesthetic phenomenon, more attention needs to be paid to what followers are, literally, sensing in the system and the ways in which those aesthetic perceptions are influencing their cravings.

Rather than encouraging potential leaders to develop their artistry and assuming that capacity will be used for beneficial ends, leadership developers might place ethics and responsibility principal to their developmental efforts. Lingering with questions of purpose and the ethics of holding influential power would be seen as central, rather than optional areas of concern. Additionally, leadership developers might incorporate more cautionary tales in their illustrations of how leadership happens rather than depending overwhelmingly on victory narratives.

Finally, for all of us who look to leaders when faced with the unknown, understanding that yearning is an instance of aesthetic craving might prompt us to reconsider what is truly needed in difficult circumstances. Rather than looking outward for our sense of certainty or identity, staying with our felt reality of where we actually experience our ground and how we maintain our own balance might be useful starting points. When we do turn our gaze outward, we might be more cautious and questioning about those whose visions offer easy answers or the comforts of nostalgia. Leadership as an aesthetically based phenomenon may indeed ease our cravings, but the question which this chapter aspires to prompt is: 'at what cost?'

REFERENCES

Bathurst, R, & Williams, L. (2014). Music beyond the chamber: NZTrio and embodied communities. In S. Ladkin, D. & Taylor (Eds.), *The Physicality of Leadership: Gesture, Entanglement, Taboo, Possibilities* (pp. 135–153). Emerald.

Baumgarten, A. G. (1750). *Aesthetica*. Laterza.

Buck-Morss, S. (2008). Aesthetics and anaesthetics: Walter Benjamin's artwork essay reconsidered. *October*, *62*, 3–41.

Csikszentmihaly, M. (2003). *Good Business, Leadership, Flow and the Making of Meaning*. Viking.

Duke, D. L. (1986). The aesthetics of leadership. *Educational Administration Quarterly*, *22*(1), 7–27.

Durkheim, E. ([1915]1965). *The Elementary Forms of Religious Life*. Free Press.

Edwards, G., Hawkins, B., & Schedlitzki, D. (2019). Bringing the ugly back: A dialogic exploration of ethics in leadership through an ethno-narrative re-reading of the Enron case. *Human Relations*, *72*(4), 733–754. https://doi.org/10.1177/0018726718773859

Eoyang, C. (1983). Symbolic transformation in belief systems. In D. Pondy, L. Frot, J. Morgan & G. Dandridge (Eds.), *Organizational Symbolism* (p. 115). JAI Press.

Gardiner, P. (2002). *A Very Short Introduction to Kierkegaard*. Oxford University Press.

Guillet de Monthoux, P., Gustafsson, C., & Sjostrand, S. E. (2007). *Aesthetic Leadership: Managing Fields of Flow in Art and Business*. Palgrave MacMillan.

Halpern, B.L., & Lubar, K. (2004). *Leadership Presence*. Penguin.

Hansen, H., & Bathurst, R. (2011). Aesthetics and leadership. In M. Bryman, A. Collinson, D. Grint, K. Jackson & B. Uhl-Bien (Eds.), *The SAGE Handbook of Leadership* (1st edn, pp. 255–264). Sage.

Hansen, H., Ropo, A., & Sauer, E. (2007). Aesthetic leadership. *Leadership Quarterly*, *18*, 544–560. https://doi.org/10.1016/j.leaqua.2007.09.003

Kateb, G. (2000). Aestheticism and morality: Their cooperaton and hostility. *Political Theory*, *28*(1), 5–38.

Katz-Buonincontro, J. (2011). How might aesthetic knowing relate to leadership? A review of literature. *International Journal of Education and the Arts*, *12*(SI 1.3), 2–18.

Kersten, A. (2008) When craving goodness becomes bad: A critical conception of ethics and aesthetics in organization. *Culture and Organization*, *14*(2), 182–202.

Ladkin, D. (2006). The enchantment of the charismatic leader: Charisma reconsidered as aesthetic encounter. *Leadership*, *2*(2), 165-179. https://doi.org/10.1177/1742715006062933

Ladkin, D. (2008). Leading beautifully: How mastery, congruence and purpose create the aesthetic of embodied leadership practice. *Leadership Quarterly*, *19*(1), 31–41. https://doi.org/10.1016/j.leaqua.2007.12.003

Ladkin, D., & Taylor, S. S. (2010a). Enacting the 'true self': Towards a theory of embodied authentic leadership. *Leadership Quarterly*, *21*(1), 64–74. https://doi.org/10.1016/j.leaqua.2009.10.005

Ladkin, D., & Taylor, S. S. (2010b). Leadership as art: Variations on a theme. *Leadership*, *6*(3) 235–241. https://doi.org/10.1177/1742715010368765

Perry, N. (2021). *New Zealand Apologizes for Historic Raids on Pacific People*. https://apnews.com/article/new-zealand-da13cc184aced872d1f36277a8293b7a

Postrel, V. (2003). *The Substance of Style: How the Rise of Aesthetic Value is Remaking Commerce, Culture and Consciousness*. HarperCollins.

Ropo, E., & Sauer, E. (2008). Corporeal leaders. In D. Barry & H. Hansen (Eds.), *New Approaches in Management and Organization* (pp. 469–478). Sage.

Russell Hochschild, A. (2016). *Strangers in their Own Land*. New Press.

Sinclair, A. (2014). On knees, breasts and being fully human in leadership. In D. Ladkin & S. Taylor (Eds.),

The Physicality of Leadership: Gesture, Entanglement, Taboo, Possibilities (pp. 177–197). Emerald.

Stephens, J. P. (2014). Leading a group by feeling: Teaching by the movement of learning. In D. Ladkin & S. Taylor (Eds.), *The Physicality of Leadership: Gesture, Entanglement, Taboo, Possibilities* (pp. 17–36). Emerald.

Storsletten, V. M. L., & Jakobsen, O. D. (2014). Development of leadership theory in the perspective of Kierkegaard's philosophy. *Journal of Business Ethics*, *128*(2): 337–349. https://doi.org/10.1007/s10551-014-2106-y

Strati, A. (1999). *Organization and Aesthetics*. Sage.

Tan, S., Shin, Y., & Rindler, D. (2021). *How one of America's ugliest days unraveled inside and outside the Capitol*. https://www.washingtonpost.com/nation/interactive/2021/capitol-insurrection-visual-timeline/

Taylor, S. S. (2011). *Leadership Craft, Leadership Art*. Palgrave MacMillan.

Taylor, S. S., & Ladkin, D. (2014). Leading as craftwork: The role of studio practices in developing artful leaders. *Scandinavian Journal of Management*, *30*(1): 95–103. https://doi.org/10.1016/j.scaman.2013.11.002

23

Process Theory Approaches to Leadership

Simon Kelly

INTRODUCTION

Open a leadership textbook or click on any online introductory resource and you will come across a description or definition of leadership that will look something like the following: *Leadership is the process of a leader influencing followers towards the achievement of a common goal*. There are many different variations on this theme, but some essential ingredients persist. Chief among these ingredients is some causal relationship between 'leaders', 'followers' and 'goals'. Whether the focus of a study is on the traits and character of a leader figure (Kirkpatrick & Locke, 1991; Zaccaro, 2007), the styles, behaviours or skills of that leader figure (Northouse, 2015), a leader's charisma (Avolio & Bass, 1994), their authenticity (Goffee & Jones, 2005), or the quality of the causal connection that binds leaders to followers (Graen & Uhl-Bien, 1995) there is a recognisable and seemingly inexhaustible playing out of the same tripodic refrain (Bennis, 2007; Wood & Case, 2006). This inexhaustibility of formulations and definitions means that leadership remains a source of fascination that refuses any final resolution in terms of what it is and how we might study and practise it. Any attempt to fix or finalise the nature of leadership, to place a limit on its possibilities, or in any way pin the concept down results in yet more interpretations and manifestations to suit each new context or requirements of the times. This ubiquitous quality is succinctly captured by James MacGregor Burns who, in the introduction to his 1978 book *Leadership*, stated that: *Leadership is one of the most observed and least understood phenomena on earth* (Burns, 1978, p. 2). Anything that is most observed – and therefore everywhere – but not understood, arguably requires our attention so that we might better appreciate the forces that shape and constrain our everyday lives. If leadership represents such a force then we need to understand it in any way that we can. In this chapter we take this statement by Burns as an invitation to examine the nature of leadership not just as personal quality or fixed state, but as part of this ongoing and ubiquitous flow of events – that is, leadership as process.

As we will see in the pages that follow, one of the challenges of turning our attention to something that is most observed and yet least understood is that such a phenomenon has a habit of exceeding and subverting our attempts at definition and categorisation. This is what makes something like leadership so enthralling as we all think that we will know it when we will see it, but upon closer inspection its nature and character slips out of sight. In my own research I suggest that this might be because we are asking the wrong questions about what leadership 'is' and that perhaps 'it' does not have any tangible coherence or cognitive, social, or material substance at all. Instead, leadership might not be an 'it' at all and exist in a kind of negative space which serves as a container or floating signifier for seeking to describe other things (see Kelly, 2014). In this chapter a similar perspective is adopted by looking at how notions of 'process' and 'process thinking' might offer productive ways of working at this problematic intersection of 'most observed'/'least understood'. In this chapter we look at process in three different but related ways: 1) the *epistemological* – process as theoretical lens for understanding and explaining leadership; 2) the *ontological* – process as the very nature of reality and our lived experience; and 3) the *axiological* – process as an invitation to engage differently with the ethical values we associate with leadership as a form of authority and influence. Overall, the aim of this chapter is to demonstrate how process thinking and thinking about process is not simply a new way to be a better leader or to motivate and manage people more effectively towards the accomplishment of a goal. Rather process thinking can provide some unique points of departure to revisit and revaluate the very foundations of leadership studies to then question why leadership matters, if it matters and how we might reorganise these foundations differently to provide new ways of conceiving what leadership in the 21st century might need to *be* right now and what it might need to *become* in the future.

UNDERSTANDING LEADERSHIP: PROPERTY OR PROCESS?

At first glance leadership and process might appear to be compatible and unproblematic concepts. After all, to lead and influence others towards a shared goal *is* a kind of process. Leading anyone requires plans, steps, stages, milestones to mark off accomplishments and so forth. However, one of the paradoxes of thinking about process this way is that our first attempt to conceive of process turns process (as in the continuous flow of events) into fixed stable entities that can be quantified and measured – that is, lists of typologies, categories, or segments. As Warren Bennis observed in 2007, the very formulation of what he called *the leadership tripod* comprising of *leaders*, *followers* and *shared goals* underpins and so limits much of what we presume leadership to be as it turns the dynamic process of leading and following into discrete bounded entities and causal relations. A good example of this tension between properties and processes of leadership is captured in an early paper by leadership psychologist Ralph Stogdill in 1950. Following his now famous review of trait research spanning the first decades of the 20th century (Stogdill, 1948), Stogdill suggested that a turn away from traits and leader-character was necessary. By 1950 Stogdill and his colleagues at Ohio State University were working towards an alternative way of researching leadership – one not based on measuring the traits of leaders, but on measuring the perceptions of followers about their leader's behaviour. In short, it was not who you *are* that mattered, but what you *do*; the new Leadership, Behavior Description Questionnaire (LBDQ) devised by Stogdill and his team would provide a new way of capturing a more holistic range of dynamic leadership qualities (Stogdill & Coons, 1957). As Stogdill argued, what really mattered was *influence upon the activities of the organization, rather than in terms of influence upon persons* (Stogdill, 1950, pp. 12–13). However, what could have been a radical paradigmatic shift in leadership research was quickly reabsorbed into the tripod metaphor when later in the same article Stogdill also provided his now famous definitional statement that: *Leadership may be considered as the process (act) of influencing the activities of an organized group in its efforts toward goal setting and goal achievement* (Stogdill, 1950, p. 4). What Stogdill, like so many leadership researchers overlooked, is the taken-for-granted use of the phrasing *the organisation* in his formulation of leadership as a process of influencing. Yet this definition, like Burns's assertion about most observed/least understood, provides those interested in process thinking with some valuable points of intervention.

What is important in Stogdill's 1950 definition is the progressive idea that leadership is a process of influence which arises through organisational activity *not* through influencing persons. Note also that there is nothing in Stogdill's formulation about distinct categories of 'leaders' or 'followers'. Instead, as Stogdill goes on to explain, leadership is what emerges at the intersection between organisation and influence. Rather than looking to heroic leaders as the source of influence, we should look instead to the organisation of activity as the source of influence, responsibility, and direction. As Stogdill's team at Ohio State proposed, effective leadership emerges in the space *between* leaders and followers through a combination of practices that produce observable effects like 'consideration' and 'initiating structure' (terms that would become more commonly known as 'people and task'). Later studies expanded on this theme such as Blake and Mouton's (1985) managerial grid in which notions of 'concern for people' versus 'concern for results' could be mapped out as potentialities through which leaders can better position themselves in relation to their followers' needs. Similarly, the contingency model of Fiedler (1967) developed this people versus task dynamic in a different direction by creating even more environmental factors that shape and constrain leader–follower relations around high and low *least preferred co-worker* (LPC) leader preferences matched against elements of situational favourableness. Later situational models such as that of Hersey and Blanchard (1988) pushed this fluidity even further by arguing that good leadership is the ability to blend a range of dynamic leader styles that seamlessly fit with the changing needs of the group.

However, while such studies and models contained the potential for a more expansive and process-oriented view of leadership, this was accompanied by an equal and opposite pull from another polarity that placed its focus on a return to the personal qualities of the leader figure. This is captured in calls in the late 1970s and throughout the 1980s and 1990s for more attention on leaders over managers, or the economic need to resolve a perceived crisis of transactional management by training up a new generation of transforming and charismatic leaders (Avolio & Bass, 1994; Burns, 1978; Kirkpatrick & Locke, 1991; Zalneznik, 1977). In many ways, the history of leadership studies can be characterised as an ongoing tug of war between two ideologies: leadership as a nonlinear shared processual activity versus leadership as a top-down causal tripod structure in which leadership results from the character or actions of the leader figure. Indeed, one of the valuable contributions of process thinking is that we can reflect on this ideological history of leadership studies as a productive ebbing and flowing of ideas (or what we might term 'epistemological' positions) organised around two irresolvable and mutually constitutive poles: collective versus individual; shared versus owned; top-down versus bottom-up; agency versus structure; unitarist versus pluralist; and so on.

As Jago (1982) noted, this ebbing and flowing of leadership epistemologies (knowledge building) and paradigms (worldviews) might be best approached not by seeking to resolve this tension or find a winning side, but by replacing an *either–or* mentality with *both–and*. In other words, leadership might be most usefully theorised processually as *both* shared *and* owned, *both* collective *and* individual, top-down *and* bottom-up, agency *and* structure, unitarist *and* pluralist and so on. For Jago this tension is best captured through the opposingly productive terms *property* versus *process*. Indeed, we could argue that the entire field of leadership studies and its expression in practice might be captured by this epistemological tension between property and process. However, one problem with this formulation is that – if taken too literally – it may suggest that property and process are two equal and opposite terms. As we will explore in the following sections, the world of 'process' that we must live with and within is not simply the other side of 'property' and it is not some other world we have a choice about engaging with or not. Instead, we are always living in process and the properties or categories we have constructed like 'leaders' and 'followers' and 'goals' may be nothing more than useful (and temporary) fictions for trying to map out and control an uncontrollable processual terrain.

EXPERIENCING PROCESS: IDEALLY ISOLATED SYSTEMS AND FALLACIES OF MISPLACED LEADERSHIP

Where process might be viewed as a useful theoretical or epistemological lens, some contemporary leadership researchers have sought to engage with process at what we might call the 'ontological' level as an objective reality that might be harnessed and exploited for the benefit of organisations and their leaders. A good example of this current trend for applied process thinking is captured in a recent review of the leadership and process literature by Fischer et al. (2017, p. 1727) in which the authors state: *We use the term process to refer to the mechanism that explains the causal relationship between inputs (e.g., leader behaviors) and outputs (e.g., performance), following an input–process–output logic.* In seeking to evaluate the instrumental value of process, the authors review 350 academic articles spanning 50 journals to develop a model of spatial and temporary components of leadership as process through which to leverage four interrelated organisational levels of individual, team, organisation and external environment.

Approaches such as those taken by Fischer et al. in which process is treated as a resource to exploit are instructive as they provide contemporary illustrations of what process philosopher Alfred North Whitehead once referred to as 'ideally isolated systems' (Whitehead, [1925] 1967, p. 58).

That is, a system of thought through which the complexity of the world (its very nature or ontological status) can be abstracted, reduced and reorganised as a model that comes to represent the world from which it was taken. For Whitehead this act of abstraction paved the way for modern science in that the world now becomes manageable and predictable as we mistake our models, categories, measures and maps for the world itself. Whitehead's work expands far beyond the confines of this chapter, but the lessons for understanding the relationship between leadership and process are succinctly captured in the parallel academic fields of postmodern organisational analysis by Robert Chia (1995, 1996) and later in the emerging field of critical leadership studies by Martin Wood (2005) – each of which provide a useful counterpoint to the idea that process is simply another form of managerial or leadership resource to be extracted and repurposed.

In transposing Whitehead's challenging philosophy onto discussions of organisation, Chia observes that we tend to think about and write about 'organisation' as if it is a discrete bounded entity with a fixed state. We even use phrasing like 'the' organisation or 'the' process to mark the boundaries of idealised isolated systems – something evident in Stogdill's earlier definitions in 1950 and also in Fischer et al.'s updated 21st-century take on discrete processes of leadership. Within this idealised system *the* organisation or *the* process can be made sense of as it is now bounded and potentially controllable. Here a machine metaphor is often invoked to further populate this organisation or fixed process with components and moving parts which produce predictable and measurable outcomes. As Chia states this is a very *modernist* conception of process:

> When modernists talk about 'process', they usually mean the various states of isolatable 'events/conditions' which lead towards an achievement or outcome. 'Process' in this modernist sense implies 'entities in process' or process in entities (e.g. strategic processes in organizations) not process in the constitution of entities. It does not refer to the precarious and tentative 'assemblages' of patternings or local orchestration of relationships which generate consequent effects that appear to be observable as discrete and isolatable stages/states. **In other words, modernists talk about process in static terms**.
>
> (Chia, 1995, p. 587 – my emphasis)

As we have seen, this modernist sensibility persists in contemporary attempts to transform process into 'a process' or 'sets' of processes that give a reassuring appearance of scientism, rationality and control. However, a belief in machine metaphors such as this can and do have their problems when it comes to understanding how leadership manifests in practice. In particular, the use of this kind of modernist storytelling can result in what process philosopher Alfred North Whitehead once termed the *fallacy of misplaced concreteness*.

According to Whitehead our knowledge of the world is always incomplete and always constructed through our need to find meaning. This need for meaning is so strong that we will even mistake our own human-made schemas and maps of the world for the world itself as this provides some temporary relief from life's inherent unpredictability. A contemporary example of this would be depending so much on a car satellite navigation system that you forget to look at the road! In other words, Whitehead is warning us that a blind dependence on a machine metaphor of inputs and outputs to represent a world of process may result in our manufacturing a simulated experience to match our expectations – think of the old proverb that *for the person with a hammer, every problem looks like a nail* and you might start to appreciate Whitehead's concern. Instead, for Whitehead the world of process is much more complex and fascinating:

> The occurrences of nature are in some way apprehended by minds […] But the mind in apprehending also experiences sensations which, properly speaking, are qualities of the mind alone [in contrast] Nature is a dull affair, soundless, scentless, colourless; merely the hurrying of material, endlessly, meaninglessly.
>
> ([1925] 1967, p. 54)

To be human for Whitehead is to exist in a world of process that we can only glimpse through our limited mental representations and schemas. Whitehead's famous *fallacy of misplaced concreteness* is the assumption that our vivid and imaginative representations of this world are all that the world is and can be.

Robert Chia (1995, pp. 590–591) builds on this notion of the fallacy of misplaced concreteness to demonstrate how it also shapes and limits our understanding of what constitutes phenomena like 'organisation' and that this fallacy develops through three distinct phases:

1 *reification* – we separate out a phenomenon by turning it from a verb/activity into a noun/entity and give it a life of its own.
2 *inversion* – we turn this act of reification back on itself to convince ourselves that our interest

in this abstraction was due to the independent existence of an entity itself rather than as a result of our reification.
3 *forgetting* – we solidify this process by forgetting that we ever engaged in reification and inversion in the first place. The entity now has independent being and its status as a separate thing is confirmed as having existed all along. Now all we need to concentrate on is how to study this novel and mysterious thing, and to decide on which elaborate research methods are best suited to discovering its inner workings.

To further illustrate our dislocated relationship with process, Chia (1995) draws on an example by David Bohm (1980, p. 29, in Chia, 1995) in which this fallacy of misplaced concreteness can even be observed in the ordinary language we use. Bohm suggests we look at the English language phrase 'It is raining' – an unremarkable phrase that is used to draw attention to the changing weather. However, when we work this through Whitehead's fallacy we can start to recognise the challenges of engaging with process by attending to the 'it' in this English language phrasing: *It is raining*. Think about this for a moment: who or what is the 'it' in this short sentence? What are we ascribing agency to by referring to a mysterious 'it' that has an ability to rain? Do we mean the clouds, the sky, a divine figure? This is unclear, but this is just one of many ways Bohm argues that we ascribe agency to something that empirically does not exist and through this kind of fallacy we develop further spurious causal relationships that produces an imagined outcome. Bohm then asks us to compare this to non-English languages like Mandarin Chinese where the more common phrasing might be something akin to *falling rain*. The first formulation requires the creation of a reified entity (a noun) that has an ability to create rain. In the second we have no requirement for reification and causality by using a verb and process language of *failing rain*.

If through language we commit the fallacy of misplaced concreteness just by remarking on the weather then consider the many other complex ways we turn process into entity, noun into verb, as we create a host of agentic forces that appear to have the power to do things or cause things to happen. As leadership scholar Martin Wood (2005) argues, the field of leadership studies is in many ways founded upon such fallacies as agency and causality is ascribed to special individuals who are thought to be the source of leading. However, committing the fallacy of misplaced concreteness – or as Wood reframes it: *the fallacy of misplaced leadership* – is not the problem. What really matters is that we do it without even realising it. Through habitual acts of *inversion* and *forgetting* we routinely act on our reifications as if they exist independently of our constructing them. We treat organisations as discrete bounded machines and humans as unproblematic resources to be exploited for their value. We treat as unproblematic our sorting of people into fixed categories of 'leader' and 'follower' with one having the higher status and higher value than the other. We then construct stories in which organisational success can be attributed to the inherent qualities of one category of person over another.

The lesson from Whitehead and others, however, is not to try to avoid committing this fallacy (as this might be impossible), but instead to remain cautious and vigilant in our uses of this fallacy and to always be critical and reflexive (playful even) in our production and mobilisation of our reifications. This sense of learning to live with our fallacies is nicely captured in the work of Hosking (1988) in which the author's approach to leadership returns to many of the interactional principles captured in that early Stogdill paper in 1950. Here Hosking calls for a radical change of strategy in which leaders as 'persons' is replaced with leadership-as-process (1988, p. 2) and in which the practice of leadership is captured not by quantifying the character of the leader or in the leveraging of processes, but in terms of encouraging collaboration, networking and skilful organising. As Hosking argued – borrowing the process language of Whitehead and others – the emphasis here should be on organising (as a verb) rather than the organisation (as a noun). While traditional top-down approaches to leadership may have their place, for Hosking skilful organising starts from a position that any recognisable leader figure should be properly understood as a temporary 'effect' (not a lasting cause) emerging out of an ongoing process of *organisational becoming* rather than as a distinct and special *being* who wields unique executive power over the world through force of personality or individual will.

NEW ONTOLOGIES OF LEADERSHIP

Two decades after Hosking's assertions about the need to take process seriously Drath et al. (2008) draw on a similar process approach to question the very status of leadership at the level of its essential nature or *ontology*. Starting with Bennis's (2007) critique of the leadership tripod as a product of our collective and problematic reification of leadership, Darth et al. develop an alternative ontological starting point which starts from a remarkably similar point to Stogdill (1950) in which they argue that leadership cannot and should not be uncritically attributed to the leader figure at the top of a reified tripod. Instead, they suggest that we focus on the combination of three phenomena that together intersect as a manifestation of leadership: *direction*; *alignment*; and *commitment* (DAC).

As Drath et al. argue, this is a radically different trinity of leadership qualities that do not work as a fixed tripod as there is nothing at the 'top' of an imaginary pyramidal structure holding these parts together. Instead, any organising activity which is directed in some way through an alignment of interests or perceived goals and underwritten by a commitment to this direction of travel and destination is a form of leadership. It might seem subtle, but just as Hosking's call for a focus on 'verbs' not 'nouns' and organising as a shared skilful process, a DAC ontology offers a similar creative space through which to consider the lived realities of leadership as an unfolding process or flow of events. However, as Crevani et al. (2010) caution, applying ideas like DAC are not sufficient unless we also stay alert to our committing of fallacies of misplaced leadership. Drawing on Wood's reformulation, Crevani et al. suggest that while we may have little choice but to experience the world through our constructed abstractions and reifications, this does not mean that we have to willingly engage with and practice *inversion* and *forgetting*. Instead, the very construction and mobilisation of reifications of leadership can become a topic of practical enquiry in itself.

A powerful example of this way of thinking comes from the work of Amy Fraher (2011) who – without discussing leadership at all – offers an innovative analysis of an event that took place in January 2009 when a passenger aircraft in New York city had to engage in an emergency landing in the Hudson River due to engine failure following a collision with a flock of geese. Fraher's interest in this story is not leadership-focused, so her approach to this case is not prefigured with reifications of what leadership is or should be. Instead, Fraher looks at two very different ways in which this event was experienced and narrated. One more visible version of this event is traced through the media coverage of the emergency water landing in which news media outlets across the US and the globe covered the heroic achievements and moral character of the aircraft's Captain – former military Airforce pilot Chesley Sullenberger. The story here centres on Sullenberger himself, how he managed to stay calm under pressure, his heroic actions that saved the passengers and crew, and the incredible skills that it personally took for him to successfully land a damaged passenger aircraft on water in one of the busiest cities in the world. Here Fraher actively works with the acts of reification in her analysis by investigating how the figure of Sullenberger becomes abstracted from the flow of events to become the causal factor and why so many other people, resources, materials and systems were subsequently excluded from this narrative. Fraher's conclusion is that this was never a story about what happened in terms of a sequence of events, it was a story about *hero-making* and the investment in a masculine hero archetype that America needed at the time – one which the aesthetic of Chesley Sullenberger fitted perfectly.

However, Sullenberger himself didn't want to be associated with this archetype and instead wanted to use his new-found media fame to draw attention to the role of teamwork and collaboration that took place between air traffic control, his co-pilot and crew, local ferry and emergency services and especially the success of training packages that were currently underfunded and facing further budget cuts. As Fraher observes, Sullenberger's desire to tell the untold story of teamwork that for him was responsible for this spectacular success was not welcome in the media and political landscape that preferred reified stories of old-fashioned heroes, daring deeds and happy endings. It is the tension between these two stories – *what we might recognise here as version of property versus process* – that is interesting for Fraher as it tells us something important about our relationship to the world and that sometimes our passionate attachment to our reifications is more highly valued than our ability to think critically. Hero stories are often one such reification that we cannot do without as they simplify the world, make it predicable and familiar. As Gemmill and Oakley (1992) argue, this all risks turning the study of leadership into a kind of *ghost dance* in which we engage in alienating practices of learned helplessness and divested responsibility by believing that there are such people as 'leaders' and that if we can only discern the 'right' way to identify and develop them then we can put our trust in their power to solve our problems for us. In contrast, concepts from process thinking like 'ideally isolated systems', 'fallacies of misplaced concreteness/leadership' and archetypal practices of hero-making allow us to recognise and potentially move beyond unhelpful reifications and towards more productive, inclusive and ethical understandings, decisions and forms of practical action based not on any fixed or final status of *being*, but on an endless unfolding process of *becoming*.

In the final section of this chapter, we move from themes of framing process thinking (*epistemology*) and the lived realities of process (*ontology*) to examine some of the ethical or *axiological* implications of our complex relationship with process. Here we deliberately step outside the formal academic field of leadership studies – with its historical canon and its pre-crafted reifications – to include some alternative and instructive examples of organisation, influence and responsibility that we can and arguably should incorporate into our understandings of leadership. We start by looking at the practice of movie-making and video production and then consider the shadow side of process thinking.

RETHINKING PROPERTY *AS* PROCESS

In 1964 American broadcaster CBC interviewed acclaimed film director Alfred Hitchcock for its television show *Telescope* (Media Film Professor, 2011). Hitchcock discusses what he calls *pure cinematics* and the power of editing in the movie-making process. To illustrate, Hitchcock describes a recorded scene (starring Hitchcock himself) which looks something like this:

> On the screen we see the face of an older man, his head and shoulders fill the frame. The man is gazing off to his right at something in the distance. There is an edit in the footage and the viewer now sees a woman sitting on some grass playing with a baby. Another edit, and we return to the gazing face of the man who is now slowly smiling.

As Hitchcock explains, the viewer might be expected to form an impression from this footage of this older man, perhaps says Hitchcock he is a *kindly man, he is sympathetic*. Hitchcock then changes the assembly of the edit and the footage plays again:

> On the screen we see the face of an older man, his head and shoulders fill the frame. The man is gazing off to his right at something in the distance. There is an edit in the footage and the viewer now sees a woman lying back on some grass wearing a bikini and staring up at the sun. Another edit, and we return to the gazing face of the man who is now slowly smiling.

Hitchcock then asks his interviewer and the audience to consider their impression of this man for a second time: *What is he now?* Hitchcock asks his interviewer. *He is a dirty old man. He is no longer a benign gentleman who loves babies [...] that's what film can do for you.*

The technique described by Hitchcock above is more commonly known in movie-making as the *Kuleshov Effect* named after Russian filmmaker Lev Kuleshov whose experimental films in the early 20th century demonstrated how meaning can be derived by fragmenting, reordering and disrupting the flow of a single piece of filmed footage. Contemporary movies and television shows do this regularly using 'the montage' to tell a complex story or show the passage of time in a short collection of carefully organised edits. However, this effect and Hitchcock's illustration of it during this interview also tell us something important about process, perception and judgement.

As Leo Tolstoy remarked in the opening of 'Book eleven' of his novel *War and Peace*: *absolute continuity of motion is incomprehensible to the human mind*. As we have seen in the previous sections, in order to make process comprehensible we (often unknowingly) engage in Whitehead's fallacy of *reification–inversion–forgetting*. Here Hitchcock similarly plays on our need to reify and construct meaning by using the Kuleshov Effect to create two very different impressions of the same person. Remember, the footage of the man gazing is unchanged. What has changed is *our impression* of him following the edited middle section of the short movie. Why is this important for students of leadership? Let's take the visual technique of the Kuleshov Effect and travel back a couple of decades to 1946, just two years before Ralph Stogdill published his famous review of leader trait studies in Ohio State, to the work of another US social psychologist called Solomon Asch based at that time in Brooklyn, New York. Unlike Stogdill, Asch was not interested in leadership. Instead, his concern was in impression formation, conformity and power.

In one famous experiment published in 1946, Asch carried out a study involving two groups of his psychology students. Each group was presented with an identical description of a person. This description listed this person's personal qualities, but with one important difference. As with Hitchcock's edit, a change had been made in that although each group had the same list of personal qualities, one group's list included the word *cold* whereas the other group's list included the word *warm*. For example:

energetic —assured — talkative — **cold** —ironical —inquisitive —persuasive

energetic —assured — talkative — **warm** —ironical —inquisitive —persuasive

(Adapted from Asch, 1946, p. 260)

What Asch found was that in forming an impression of this person the two student groups organised their impressions based around what appeared to be a 'central trait' – in this case *warm/cold*. In other words, if the person was thought to be cold then all of their other qualities would serve to support the students' judgement of the person as cold, calculating, ambitious and unsympathetic – and vice versa if *cold* was replaced with *warm*. In many variations of this experiment Asch found that not all descriptions of a person served this function as only some terms operated as central traits. These central traits would then interact with the other peripheral traits to form the overall impression of the person. Asch concluded that:

forming an impression is an organized process; that characteristics are perceived in their dynamic relations; that central qualities are discovered, leading to the distinction between them and peripheral qualities; that relations of harmony and contradiction are observed. **To know a person is to have a grasp of a particular structure**.
(Asch, 1946, p. 283 – my emphasis)

What Alfred Hitchcock and Solomon Asch are both describing here (albeit in very different contexts) is strikingly similar to Whitehead's process of reification as participants abstract or *reify* central traits from peripheral ones and give these central traits greater explanatory power. The central trait is then inverted so that it now explains the overall characteristics of the person. We do all of this so quickly that we are unaware that this calculation has even taken place. Instead, we believe that our reified judgement of a person is an accurate reflection of their inner character and true self rather than a product of a particular social structure or carefully crafted edit.

Such examples allow us to move beyond fixed 'property versus process' debates by rethinking some of the taken-for-granted assumptions we make about personality and character that have formed the very foundations of leadership research from early trait studies to contemporary schemas such as the Big Five personality traits. Instead, by remaining sensitive to the act of reification, we can draw on the likes of Solomon Asch's work to ask whether traits are a reliable indicator of the quality of person's character and their leadership potential or whether they are the product of an ongoing process of impression construction that is perceived by others and projected outwards. Similarly, we might question if the many biographies and autobiographies written about and by great leaders and businesspeople are reliable insights into their inherent moral character and their transformational leadership qualities, or whether they are the product of a collective desire for heroic archetypes, a susceptibility to the organising function of central traits, or a careful crafting of leadership accounts that rely on structural techniques of influence like the Kuleshov Effect.

LEADERSHIP AND THE SHADOW SIDE OF PROCESS

So far in this chapter we have focused on process thinking in broadly positive terms as a productive way of improving our understanding of leadership and complexity. However, there is also value in considering the other side of this by looking to the potentially harmful and destructive consequences of process. This is a theme tackled by Padilla et al. (2007) who suggest that to understand challenging topics like toxic and destructive leadership we must move beyond a strictly leader-centric focus. Instead, they argue that the presence of a toxic or destructive leader figure in an organisational setting is not enough on its own to cause systemic breakdown. Using a combination of historical examples and process-mapping similar to that of Fraher, the authors show how a leader figure always exists in a complex and dynamic relationship with *environmental factors* and the actions of what Padilla et al. term *susceptible followers*. As the authors assert, the decisions, actions, or agendas of a toxic leader (whether intentionally or unintentionally) have limited destructive potential on their own. It is only when the decisions and actions of the leader figure intersect with a wider organisational environment that is unstable, where there are perceived threats from 'outside', where there is a strong set of values that hold a group together and where usual checks, balances and regulations are suspended, that destruction and toxicity can spread. Yet even this is not enough for toxic leadership to take hold as all of these overlapping processes also require the presence and participation of followers who are either willing to *collude* with the toxic agenda of the leader, or who are forced to *conform* to this agenda due to a lack of ability to resist.

Without explicitly discussing the kind of process theory we have explored in this chapter, Padilla et al. offer important insights into what we could term the *shadow side of process* as they demonstrate how toxic leadership suffers from the same 'property versus process' divide that we discussed earlier. Just as reifying heroes may provide us with simplicity and reassurance, reifying individual villainous leaders similarly risks overlooking the untold stories of how toxicity spreads and is maintained through a neglect of complex and overlapping destructive elements and events. However, one aspect of Padilla et al.'s model does deserve closer scrutiny. This is the status the authors give to the *conformer* type of susceptible follower. Rather than taking Padilla et al.'s view that conformity arises through low self-esteem or a lack of power among followers, we might instead draw from outside the leadership canon to demonstrate how – when viewed through a process lens – every person has the potential to become a conformer. Moreover, this may have little to do with our moral character and everything to do with the flow of events that we might find ourselves enmeshed within.

Here we can turn to the work of the late sociologist Zygmunt Bauman and his book *Modernity and the Holocaust* (Bauman, 1989). As with earlier examples, this is not a leadership text and it makes for uncomfortable reading as Bauman asserts that what gave rise to atrocities like the Nazi Holocaust in Germany during the 1930s and 1940s was not the result of an evil elite or a single toxic leader, but the slow and subtle workings of something much more mundane – modern bureaucracy. To demonstrate this, Bauman analyses the experiments by social psychologist Stanley Milgram (1965; 1974) in which participants were recruited for what they thought was an experiment to test the effects of punishment on learning. What Milgram had actually devised was an experiment to test a person's ability to resist authority by asking participants to use an electric generator to administer shocks to another participant each time the question they asked was incorrectly answered. The experiment was overseen by the project experimenter (wearing a suitably authoritative white coat) and the participant was secretly observed by Milgram to see under what conditions they could be made to deliver harmful and even deadly electrical shocks to their fellow participant just because they were instructed to do so by the experimenter. As everyone who is familiar with these experiments will know, the whole experiment setting was fake. The experimenter and co-participant receiving the shocks were actors. The generator was not plugged into an electrical power source, and even the cries of pain from behind a screen when shocks were administered were audio recordings. However, what Milgram showed across the many variations of his experiment was that given the right circumstances over 60 per cent of his participants would severely harm or even think they had killed the other participant just because they could not refuse the authority of the experimenter. Curiously, resistance to authority did increase as the conditions of the experiment were altered. For example, increasing the visibility of and proximity between the participant and the person being shocked would increase resistance to authority – with the highest resistance to authority measured during a version of the experiment in which the participant had to place their hand in a protective glove and personally administer the shock by forcing the hand of the other participant on to an electrified metal plate (see Milgram, 1974).

For Bauman this controversial experiment offers important insights into the rise of fascism and authoritarianism in that conformity is not something that can be equated to a lack of moral character, but to the mobilisation of three intersecting processual factors:

1 *Authorisation* – responsibility is taken away from the individual and placed with those in power. You will therefore not be held responsible for your actions as you are just doing your job by following somebody else's orders. In this case Milgram's participants reported giving over their autonomy to the experimenter.
2 *Dehumanisation* – the person subjected to harm is made distant and their humanity removed. This Bauman argued, is easily achieved by separating somebody from the consequence of their actions and by turning people into data. In the case of the Milgram experiments the person being shocked was reduced to responses shared via a lightbulb and their distant cries of pain were heard from another room.
3 *Routinisation* – this part is key. Get the person to do parts 1) and 2) over and over again until they relinquish their own ability to think and commit to the multiple cycles of the task as simply a job to be completed. Milgram achieved this effect using a line of switches on his generator which increased the voltage incrementally as participants continued with the task.

Bauman's formulation for authoritarian control via his analysis of the Milgram experiments provides a powerful means of refining Padilla et al.'s concept of the susceptible follower as conformer. Conformity may not be a result of moral deficiency among a particular group, but instead represents an ever-present potential in all of us. What is required to produce conformity is frighteningly simple and only requires the right processual factors to click into place. We might also use this final example to reflect on our other process perspectives discussed in this chapter. For example, we might consider the risks of overlooking or undervaluing teamwork and followership in our theories and models of leadership. We might reflect on the processual factors that shape the impressions we form of other people, and we might also think carefully about the role of the material and non-human world in the processual production of influence. Indeed, as Milgram himself found, it was the careful design of the electrical generator with its series of switches that nudged participants further and further along a process of compliance until resistance to authority seemed impossible. After all, if you can clearly see the number of occasions that you have already shocked and harmed (perhaps even killed) another person then what moral ground is left for refusing the experimenter's orders?

CONCLUDING THOUGHTS

Process theory approaches to leadership allow us to step back from instrumental or outcome-based approaches for how to lead effectively and to reconsider some of the fundamental assumptions we make about the nature of leadership and why it matters. As this chapter has demonstrated, a turn to process allows for the inclusion of some unusual and unorthodox studies and examples that we might not typically encounter such as Whitehead's process philosophy, Fraher's analysis of hero-making and teamwork, Asch's configural model of traits and Milgram's experiments to test obedience to authority. Each of these examples offers a unique challenge to the traditional leadership tripod of *leaders–followers–goals* by allowing us to consider alternatives for how we might understand, practice and evaluate leadership. Underpinning each of these examples and studies is a commitment to understanding and appreciating process while recognising the dangers of seeking to control process, neglect process, or mistake our representations of process for the actual ebb and flow of events that shape and constrain our lives.

While the ideas in this chapter may be complex and challenging, they are also a starting point to learn more about how you might use process thinking yourself in your own explorations of leadership in order to:

1 Develop your own *epistemological* lens through which to become a critical and analytical reader of leadership texts, theories and models, and to become mindful of the risks and unintended consequences of committing fallacies of misplaced concreteness and misplaced leadership.
2 Embrace the *ontological* complexities of organisational process – beyond a need for leadership reifications – to look instead for the untold stories of human teamwork and collaboration, and the subtle non-human relationships that enable and constrain decisions, actions and outcomes.
3 Engage *axiologically* with the ethical dimensions of process by reflecting on its potential for enabling forms of toxic and destructive leadership, while also creating opportunities for opposing illegitimate authority, fostering responsible and critical followership, and building new strategies for constructive collective action.

REFERENCES

Asch, S. E. (1946). Forming impressions of personality. *Journal of Abnormal and Social Psychology*, *41*, 258–290.

Avolio, B. J., & Bass, B. M. (1994). *Improving Organizational Effectiveness Through Transformational Leadership*. Sage.

Bauman, Z. (1989). *Modernity and the Holocaust*. Cornell University Press

Bennis, W. (2007). The challenges of leadership in the modern world: Introduction to the special issue. *American Psychologist*, *62*(1), 2–5.

Blake, R. R., & Mouton, J. S. (1985). *The Managerial Grid III*. Gulf.

Bohm, D. (1980). *Wholeness and the Implicate Order*. Routledge.

Bryman, A. (1992). *Charisma and Leadership in Organizations*. Sage

Burns, J. M. (1978). *Leadership*. Harper and Row.

Chia, R. (1995) From modern to postmodern organizational analysis. *Organization Studies*, *16*(4), 579–604.

Chia R. (1996). The problem of reflexivity in organizational research: Towards a postmodern science of organization. *Organization*, *3*(1), 31–59.

Crevani, L., Lindgren, M., & Packendorff, J. (2010). Leadership, not leaders: On the study of leadership as practices and interactions. *Scandinavian Journal of Management*, *26*(1), 77–86.

Drath, W. H., McCauley, C. D., Palus, C. J., Van Velsor, E., O'Connor, P. M. G., & McGuire, J. B. (2008). Direction, alignment, commitment: Toward a more integrative ontology of leadership. *Leadership Quarterly*, *19*, 635–653.

Fiedler, F. E. (1967). *A Theory of Leadership Effectiveness*. McGraw-Hill.

Fischer, T., Dietz, J., & Antonakis, J. (2017). Leadership process models: A review and synthesis. *Journal of Management*, *43*(6), 1726–1753.

Fraher, A. (2011). Hero-making as a defence against the anxiety of responsibility and risk: A case study of US airways flight 1549. *Organisational and Social Dynamics*, *11*(1), 59–78.

Gemmill, G., & Oakley, J. (1992). Leadership: An alienating social myth. *Human Relations*, *45*(2), 113–29.

Goffee, R., & Jones, G. (2005). Managing authenticity. *Harvard Business Review*, *83*(12), 85–94.

Graen, G., & Uhl-Bien, M. (1995). Relationship-based approach to leadership: Development of leader–member exchange (LMX) theory of leadership over 25 years: Applying a multi-level multi-domain perspective. *Leadership Quarterly*, *6*(2), 219–247.

Hersey, P., & Blanchard, K. (1988). *Management of Organizational Behavior: Utilizing human Resources*, 5th edn. Prentice-Hall.

Hosking, D. M. (1988). Organizing, leadership and skilful process. *Journal of Management Studies*, *25*(2), 147–66.

Jago, A. (1982). Leadership: Perspectives in theory and research. *Management Science*, *28*(3), 315–336.

Kelly, S. (2014). Towards a negative ontology of leadership. *Human Relations*, *67*(8), 905–922.

Kirkpatrick, S., & Locke, E. (1991). Leadership: Do traits matter? *Academy of Management Executive*, *5*(2), 48–60.

Media Film Professor (2011). *Hitchcock Explains the Kuleshov Effect to Fletcher Markle on CBS Telescope, 1964* [video]. https://www.youtube.com/watch?v=96xx383lpiI

Milgram, S. (1965). Some conditions of obedience and disobedience to authority. *Human Relations*, *18*(1), 57–76.

Milgram, S. (1974). *Obedience to Authority: An Experimental View*. Harper & Row.

Northouse, P. (2015). *Leadership: Theory and Practice*. Sage.

Padilla, A., Hogan, R., & Kaiser, R. B. (2007). The toxic triangle: Destructive leaders, susceptible followers, and conducive environments. *Leadership Quarterly*, *18*(3), 176–194.

Spoelstra, S., & ten Bos, R. (2011). Leadership. In M. Painter-Morland and R. ten Bos (Eds.), *Business Ethics and Continental Philosophy*. Cambridge University Press.

Stogdill, R. M. (1948). Personal factors associated with leadership: A survey of the literature. *Journal of Psychology*, *25*, 35–71.

Stogdill, R. M. (1950). Leadership, membership and organization. *Psychological Bulletin*, *47*(1), 1–14.

Stogdill, R. M., & Coons, A. E. (1957). *Leader Behavior: Its Description and Measurement*. Ohio State University.

Tolstoy, L. ([1869] 1952). Book eleven: 1812, Chapter I & II. *War and Peace* (pp. 469–472). William Benton,.

Whitehead, A. N. ([1925] 1967). *Science and Modern World*. Cambridge University Press.

Whitehead, A. N. ([1929] 1985). *Process and Reality*. Ed. by D. R. Griffin & D. W. Sherburne. Free Press.

Wood, M. (2005). The fallacy of misplaced leadership. *Journal of Management Studies*, *42*(6), 1101–1121.

Wood, M., & Case, P. (2006). Editorial: Leadership refrains: Again, again and again. *Leadership*, *2*(2), 139–145.

Zaccaro, S. J. (2007). Trait-based perspectives of leadership. *American Psychologist*, *62*(1), 6–16.

Zaleznik, A. (1977). Managers and leaders: Are they different? *Harvard Business Review*, May–June, 67–78.

Technology and Leadership

Owain Smolović Jones and David Hollis

INTRODUCTION

In this chapter we try to accomplish four objectives. First, we aim to offer conceptual shape to what is a nascent and developing area of study. We do this by establishing definitional parameters around both technology and leadership that we hope will assist future scholars in more tightly shaping the kinds of practices that should be included under the heading of 'leadership and technology' studies – and, of course, which should be removed from consideration or critiqued as enacting something else under the guise of 'leadership'. These definitional parameters, we stress, are only valid for research that assumes a view of technology and leadership as constituted through socio-economic relations and practice. However, being clear on definitions is vital as it can help us to make more sense of the specific leadership dimensions of technology. It can also help us to reflect on any slippage in terminology between leadership and other types of practice (e.g., management), asking what interests such slippages serve.

Second, throughout the chapter we aim to embed consideration of technology and leadership within a context of social–political–economic relations and their manifestations in contemporary work and society. Under this objective we try to understand how technology can be deployed to manipulate, control and extract – sometimes under the guise of 'leadership'. We refer to the intensification of technology in the workplace to control and deskill as 'total management', an increasingly dominant organising logic that leadership must work through and against if it is to offer alternative futures for work and society. We also explore technology's promise to enhance participation, diversity and empowerment in leadership practices. Technologically mediated practice can defy conventional boundaries (geographical and organisational) to resist and provide democratic alternatives to the economic and political status quo (Bloom et al., 2021; Smolović Jones et al., 2021).

Third, we attempt to survey the landscape of studies of technology and leadership, applying a broad organising framework of 'leaders and technology' and 'leadership and technology' to assist further study in this area. However, we need to acknowledge that the vast majority of leadership studies tend to ignore technology at work and new forms of technologically mediated work (e.g., the gig economy and platform economy) as factors in the practice of leadership. This presents us with a mystery. Our case is that leadership studies, despite its fondness for 'post-industrial' rhetoric, remains stuck in assumptions of a working life that has largely ceased to exist – where technology is largely viewed as another passive tool in the hands of leaders, rather than as something that shapes practice and relations at work more profoundly.

Our fourth and final objective is to provide some initial thinking on how the terrain of studying technology and leadership could develop into the future. Future studies, we posit, should incorporate the diverse focus of leadership studies, embracing work, the social and the political. In the chapter overall we therefore try to maintain this diversity, bringing to view the practices of political leaders, employing organisations and social movements.

MAKING SENSE OF TECHNOLOGY AND LEADERSHIP

Technology

Both 'technology' and 'leadership' are slippery terms. Technologies can stand for any material configuration or object used for work purposes, no matter how seemingly basic – a hammer, a pen – or how sophisticated – innovative software, automated production machines. The social sciences have grappled with how to understand the influence and incorporation of technology in a variety of ways. Influential were early attempts by science and technology studies (STS) to problematise the nature of technology at work – technologies were not neutral tools but were socialised in particular ways within organisations, both shaping what kind of work could be done and being used to further the interests of certain social groups (Grint & Woolgar, 1997; Woolgar, 1992). Actor-network theory (ANT) and related post-humanist approaches are a continuation of the STS tradition. ANT examines the assemblages that form between humans and non-humans, and the affordances these make possible, in shaping social and work life (Latour, 2007). Relatedly, Marxism has always grappled with the role of technology in the workplace. Marx envisaged machines in production as shaped to suit the interests of capitalists, acting as technologies through which business owners could reduce their reliance on workers (Marx, 2004). Machines don't demand pay rises, better benefits or threaten strike action, after all. This basic proposition has been developed by Marxist political economists and sociologists since, with Braverman (1974), for example, making the case that production technologies tend to deskill workers and allow for a downward pressure on wages and terms of employment. More recently, workerist scholars in a Marxist tradition have explored how automated and platform forms of work can combine with a larger political–economic project to normalise the creation, diffusion and maintenance of precarious work (Woodcock, 2021).

This chapter is shaped by the influence of both post-humanism and Marxism insofar as we are interested in the influence of technology in its interaction with social processes to shape people's lives. We focus largely on digital technologies (including the production and reproduction of media), as these unquestionably bear a great influence on the lives of most people and will only become more important for work and society as automation technologies are further developed.

Leadership

We do not assume leadership to be synonymous with the acts or personalities of senior people within organisations. This also means that we refuse to equate technological leadership with the human resource, forecasting and decision-making technologies adopted by senior managers and executives. Rather, guiding us in the task of defining leadership in a tech-ubiquitous era is the seminal work of Grint (2005). For Grint, management may be complicated and sophisticated but is always concerned with systematising problems, making dealing with them routine – most obviously through the adoption of technology. Leadership, in Grint's terms, is concerned with collaborative forms of coordination and communication that seek to draw on a diverse range of inputs from across disciplines, hierarchies and work units to disrupt, pose difficult questions and ultimately break paradigms of settled practice and thought. However, we also need to understand a second side of leadership – that it can stand for practice that shapes meaning, operating at an aesthetic and discursive level to influence and exert control over people's imaginations. Hence, political leaders can be understood as doing leadership work when they shape people's perceptions through their rhetoric, or political parties through their use of imagery on social media (Smolović Jones et al., 2020).

This dual definition of leadership bears commonalities with theories of 'immaterial labour' (Hardt & Negri, 2001; Lazzarato, 2006). From this perspective the surplus value produced by workers is increasingly immaterial – meaning that it lies less in the physical product produced and more in the relations, collaboration and communication of the production process (Mumby, 2020). In Virno's (2004) terms, this means that work is more 'political', in the sense that we increasingly find that important aspects of our jobs involve talking to and convincing others. Such labour is fuelled by exponential leaps forward in digital technology, meaning that resources and input can be generated on a global scale and the circuits of creation amplified and accelerated. Similarly, leadership is increasingly presented in studies as something that happens in communication, practice or behaviours less concerned with material transaction and more connected to inspiring and influencing.

Before moving to the leadership and technology literature, however, we need to deal with what this chapter is not about – intensive technologically mediated management – as doing so will help us see with more clarity the spaces available for leadership and technology.

TECH-DRIVEN (DISRUPTIVE) LEADERSHIP OR TOTAL MANAGEMENT?

Casting an eye over where global wealth is accumulated, undoubtedly the past decades have witnessed the rise of tech giants. It would be easy, and misplaced, to simply account for the activity of such corporations as leadership, equating leadership to the success of individual people formally occupying executive positions. In meta-economic terms, there is an argument for stating that disruptive leadership processes are at work. Uber, Airbnb, Amazon and so on pride themselves as disruptors, drawing on a diverse range of talents and inputs of expertise to undermine and rewrite markets and consumer habits, with innovative tech the ostensive gateway to dominance. Digging deeper within these corporations, however, reveals a series of daily practices far more akin to management, or indeed management of the most totalising kind. In terms of the daily interactions of the majority of people with tech giants, it is such forms of management that matter more than the initial acts of disruptive leadership.

Total management can be defined as the use of technology to exert ever greater control over the movements, material conditions and thought processes of workers. It acts as a lever to diminish labour power and the costs and uncertainties associated with employing humans, maximising the accumulation of capital and power in the hands of a few. Amazon is the case study of distinction in relation to total management. The *Amazonification* of workplaces and economies (Alimahomed-Wilson, 2020, p. 69) is shorthand for describing the intensification of automation in the workplace in tandem with the generation of precarious employment. Within Amazon 'fulfilment centres' (warehouses), for example, movements are controlled through handheld devices that direct workers to and from shelving. In turn, goods are stored not through the logic of humans but through that of algorithms – grouped together according to purchasing habits rather than by category of use (Bridle, 2019). Workers are set tight targets and break times that are often insufficient to allow for walking to allocated rest and toilet facilities and back again (Bridle, 2019). Total management is increasingly a hallmark of employment relations. The surveillance of remote working is now commonplace – with keystrokes, time spent in front of computers and even the presence of phones or food on people's home desks monitored by algorithms and web cams (Walker, 2021). Such technology removes the discretion of managers through sending and logging evidence of infringements, and managers themselves, often not much better paid than the workers, subjected to potential disciplinary consequences if they do not act on the automatically generated evidence of worker infringements. Thus, we see technology enabling automation on a micro level of the processes of work but also at a more meta level, where norms of control and subservience to low wages and precarious conditions are normalised over time.

We therefore need to be careful not to be dazzled by the rhetoric of the tech industry and with technological developments in relation to work. Attributing leadership to senior tech figures but also directly to algorithms and robots is fraught with problems. Doing so without proper consideration of the practices enacted in reality risks romanticising leadership (Collinson et al., 2018), equating it with the positive attributes of socially desirable individuals and closing off potential for critique (Collinson, 2012). We need to consider what the place is for leadership and leadership research within the landscape of an ever totalising spread of technology and management. Do they: re-enforce these totalising trends? Exist outside them? Co-exist in, between and against them? Or act like they don't exist? Our answer in what follows concludes largely the latter but with glimpses of the other options occasionally visible.

Broadly speaking, we are left with two ways of interpreting the operation of leadership through technology: first, how technology is used to normalise, mystify and demystify dominant and opaque relations of power between leaders and the led; second, how technology can illuminate potentially creative modes of collective and/

or resistance leadership that can presage a more empowering future (Bloom et al., 2021). In the sections to come we view leaders and leadership as constituted through technology and socio-economic processes. We discard (but occasionally critique) studies that equate leadership to the personhood of senior executives and the technologies they deploy, but include studies that take seriously how technologies mediate how such leaders influence meaning. In the case of collective leadership practice, we adhere to Grint's (2005) definition, focusing on how technology mediates practice that challenges and disrupts status quo assumptions and the framing of meaning.

LEADERS AND TECHNOLOGY

In this section we are interested in exploring studies that seek to understand how leaders are portrayed, conveyed and indeed constituted through technology. Shaping our review is an interpretation of leaders socialised with technology in practice. Of significance is the semiotics of leaders, of interpreting leaders through technology as signs: images and texts that are produced and challenged in ways that shape our perceptions of certain leaders. The way leaders are viewed, related to and consumed has always been filtered through technology and media. Old tech such as the leader biography and portraiture usually set out to promote, but also to critically engage with or dismantle the mystique and reputation of leaders (Griffey & Jackson, 2010). Nevertheless, in an age of digital mediation and social media exposure, we can say that technology has never been more important in shaping who is regarded as a leader and what the rules of the game seem to be for earning and maintaining that status.

Leader Semiotics and Value Production

In an age of immaterial labour, the conversion of leaders into media signs is positioned, or assumed to be, a terrain of value production for corporations. Such semiotics are filtered through the more everyday and transient technologies of social media. Leaders and their corporations' cravings for eyeballs and *clicks* through *celebritisation* and *evangelisation* (Heavey et al., 2020, p. 1492) inform social media strategies that often trump whether messages hold any substantive value for recipients. Celebrity leaders such as Elon Musk and Jeff Bezos cultivate a certain image as entrepreneurial disruptors and adventurers, which customers are invited to admire. Mainstream and social media attributions perpetuate perceptions of CEOs as celebrities, which trigger a social contagion effect whereby a CEO's perceived leadership qualities and performance become largely locked into a circle of valorisation (cf., Bligh et al., 2011; Treadway et al., 2009).

Studies of leader semiotics can help us understand how such valorisation cycles are achieved – and challenged – in practice. Leaders and their teams expend great focus and energy on portraying their protagonists as authentic – recognising perhaps the contemporary moment where social media has, in theory, intensified the demand for leaders to reflect and share the experiences and everyday lives of followers. In such an attention economy (Marwick, 2015; Mumby, 2020), competitive advantage may be secured through appearing more relatable and in tune with the pressures and aspirations of everyday life. Hence, even bankers in the wake of the global financial crisis of 2007–2008 went to great lengths to portray themselves through media as authentic people, empathetic and suffering like everyone else (Liu, 2015; Liu et al., 2017). This drive for authentic positioning reflects the rise of what Rhodes (2021, p.1) terms *woke capitalism*, noting how corporations have co-opted and mutated the term 'woke' from black American culture. Billionaires, who have amassed fortunes squeezing labour costs and polluting the planet go to great lengths via social media to convey identities as philanthropic saviours. A cursory look at Jeff Bezos's Twitter feed, for example, communicates an image of a leader deeply concerned with poverty and climate change, eliding, of course, Amazon's status as a heavy polluter (Reynolds, 2020) and union-buster (Streitfeld, 2021). 'Woke' displays on social media, in Rhodes's terms, disguise a more sinister and dominant exercise of power over global economies and resources by a small elite (see also Heizmann & Liu, 2018). Such semiological archetypes, in the view of Bloom and Rhodes (2018) can establish aspirational identity norms that are dispersed, consumed and further spread through mainstream media, specialist business press and business schools. That such dispersion of leader-signs can be distinctly male – and how such views of being a leader can be challenged through technology is our next topic.

Leaders, Technology and Gender

That leadership tends to be associated with masculine norms of 'strength', 'decisiveness' and 'heroics' is by now well known (e.g., Ford et al., 2008). Such norms are communicated through mainstream culture but also bestselling leadership books, which tend to promote *heteronormative* views of leadership (Ferry, 2018, p. 603). Technology, particularly media and social media, has proliferated such norms. However, technology can also be leveraged to disrupt gendered norms, although research in this area remains nascent. Kelan (2013) presents an intervention with MBA students where images of prominent women business leaders were used as a means of facilitating discussion around the way in which industries sexualise and stereotype women leaders, drawing out possibilities for *displac*[ing] *some of the norms that exist around gender in the workplace* (p. 58). Similarly, Stead and Elliott (2019, p. 171) reflect on how media *power lists* of women leaders can provide important public pedagogical resources for deconstructing gendered norms of leadership. Specifically, they show that feminist ideals as portrayed by the media often proceed through narrow paths of individualist neoliberal norms of commanding resources, being a successful competitor and wielding power.

Leaders and Technology: Future directions, concluding remarks

In a field rich with possibility but light on studies, particularly missing at present are enquiries that go deeper into the economic relations generated through the semiotic representation of leaders through technology. Boje and Rhodes (2005) posit the emerging significance of the virtual leader construct, which is either the imitation or re-representation of a real leader virtually, or through the creation of a purely virtual leader (e.g., Ronald McDonald). They state that such figures serve an *economic function* (p. 409) in that they become omnipresent representations of corporations in times, spaces and areas of life where the flesh-and-blood leader cannot be so present or adaptable. Yet we need to understand more about how leaders in general are becoming more virtual and the implications this has on the economic relations that govern our lives. Such practices of enacting the identity of a leader are undoubtedly 'political', communicative and immaterial (Virno, 2004) but have serious material consequences in terms of how wealth is distributed and opportunities are unevenly offered within economies and societies. Such an emphasis suggests that the field is ripe for Marxist-inspired study that takes seriously the political economy of leader semiotics. We could obviously benefit from more in-depth analyses of the social media tactics of the wealthiest executives and how these interrelate with their corporate practices of wealth accumulation. Such studies can illuminate how a foregrounding of 'woke' celebrity CEOs (Rhodes, 2021) drives capital accumulation and glosses over the hidden dynamics of capital, which rely on extracting ever more surplus from workers so that 'leaders' may enjoy lives enriched by great wealth.

More prosaically, we could learn much from the forms of leadership enacted by social media influencers – the consuming habits and values they normalise and how these reflect back on the kind of leaders that societies increasingly seem to demand. Post-human analysis here seems particularly salient, exploring how influencers are constituted through technologically mediated processes that combine corporate, fashion and social justice discourses. Metrics such as views, reTweets and followers are regarded as influence proxies that enhance the status of social media influencers and tech-savvy corporations (Tur et al., 2021). The term 'follower' in relation to social media should particularly interest leadership scholars (Kempster et al., 2021) – the status such followers bestow in comparison to more traditional organisational followers; how social media leaders constitute themselves and their power in relation to 'followers'; the interdependency of global corporations and their economic influence with the 'authentic' presence of social media influencers; and, most importantly, the commercial power and wealth enabled by the accumulation of followers.

In methodological terms, the field could be enriched by more studies that take on in-depth analyses of social media activity of corporate 'leaders', virtual or otherwise. Too often perhaps researchers do not regard such work as 'real', lending more weight to the value of in-person research strategies. Yet as everyday life becomes increasingly shaped by online and digital experience, such assumptions appear ever less secure. Immersion in a scene of study is perfectly possible within online environments. One might track certain business leaders through their social media accounts and use such an anchor to branch out into related accounts and online communities – the interleaving of influencer eco-systems, customer and worker communities – to develop a rich picture of the reach and limitations of leaders in the digital realm. Analytically we are spoilt for choice, with the field of visual methods abounding in creative and incisive insight, connecting imagery to political, social and economic power (Bell et al., 2014). In particular, we urge more multimodal studies that seek to explore the power of visual grammar and how it is put to work in constituting a person's leadership (Liu et al., 2017). Finally, we should also bear in mind possibilities for research that seeks to glimpse behind the curtain of social media production. Much scope remains for interview-based or deeper ethnographic studies of the practices of the tech workers who assemble and distribute the semiotics of leaders – the dynamics of these industries and how the labour of such workers themselves is expropriated to serve the ends of capital accumulation.

LEADERSHIP AND TECHNOLOGY

We now explore how leadership as a practice – distinct from the formal status of individual leaders – is generated through, enhanced and undermined by, technology. Primarily, leadership studies tends to treat leadership practice as if it occurs in bounded and physically co-present groups that are tech-free. Yet we know from experience that this is now a limited perspective, perhaps heavily shaped by what people feel is possible and desirable to research, rather than how leadership is practised in reality. In this section we therefore discuss studies that seek to better understand how technology is adopted to practise leadership and how practices of leadership are shaped by technology. The relationship of mutual influence between leadership and technology was recognised as early as a review by Avolio and colleagues in 2001, in which they stated that *the repeated appropriation of information technology generates or transforms social structures, which over time become institutionalized* (p. 621). In this section we start our review in the workplace, zooming out into the political as we proceed. As a starting point, however, we first examine how studies have grappled with the effect technology has had on the operation of leadership within work teams.

Leadership, Technology and Teams

Digital technology has certainly affected how teams work together – challenging existing limitations by expanding the geography and diversity of input to team processes (Al-Ani et al., 2011). However, the extent to which technology is viewed in studies and practice as shaping leadership, and the degree to which the technology itself is seen as exercising agency over a leadership process, varies. Larson and DeChurch's (2020) review of the field highlights a continuum of approaches, from viewing technology as something distinct from social processes, which can be drawn upon and used to enhance pre-existing practice preferences, through to perspectives that offer more agency to technology. From this latter perspective the technology reshapes how leadership is practised, with technology ultimately capable of assuming the status of team-mate, and we eagerly await the first study of the leadership practice of artificial intelligence within teams.

Some studies have explored the effects technological innovations have had on team leadership. Arvedsen and Hassert's (2020) study of online meetings in commercial settings shows how participants in a leadership process draw on and balance a range of communicative resources – data, visuals, written and verbal talk – in sophisticated configurations that enable the generation of alignment, commitment and direction. Further, leadership enacted digitally can enhance its shared co-production, as digital spaces seem to hold more capacity for the smoothing out of hierarchical difference – wider access to digital resources can mean the significance of formal leaders receding. However, some digital technologies seem to enhance collaboration more than others – the more interactive they are, the more capacity for decentred leadership, achieved through greater access to resources and more transparency (Rhue & Sundararajan, 2014). This points to the fact that intensive use of technology and the knowledge-based nature of organisations does not necessarily equate to participative and collaborative forms of leadership. Indeed, Salovaara and Bathurst (2018) highlight how even in tech-heavy organisations with an ostensive commitment to cooperation and participation, the tendency to defer to hierarchical forms of power can persist.

From a post-human perspective, there remains room for further studies of how leadership practices and technology relationally emerge. Promising signs exist in the literature, with works shedding tired assumptions of leaders and technology as neatly separable phenomena and questioning the roles that human and technological affordances and assemblages play within leadership-in-interaction. The concept of affordances (*bundles of characteristics associated with material things, which emerge from the relationship of an object with other actants in a network*; Hawkins, 2015, p. 956) stands out as a germane path for leadership studies to furrow and to expand on. Arvedsen and Hassert's (2020) analysis of ICT objects' affordances (e.g., cursors and screensharing software), for example, reveals how technology can facilitate the collaborative accomplishment of leadership in team meetings. Other post-human studies show how within and through diverse assemblages, human and technological agency can activate distributed leadership, drawing on tech such as radiographic equipment, PowerPoint slides (Oborn et al., 2013) and videoconferencing tools (Mailhot et al., 2016).

A further fruitful line of enquiry in the loose post-human space may involve framing the relations between technology and leadership in more emergent, conjoint and communicatively constitutive terms (cf., Ashcraft et al., 2009; Cooren et al., 2011). Emerging at the *transdisciplinary intersection of organization studies and communication studies* (Blaschke et al., 2012, p. 882), communication as constitutive of organisation's (CCO) notion of materialisation (Cooren, 2020; Kuhn et al., 2017) holds the potential to develop post-human leadership thinking which, broadly speaking, conceives either of people drawing down technological affordances to accomplish leadership, or of human and technological agency as pregivens that 'awaken' within and through assemblages. Materialisation thinking, instead, conceptualises things – whatever (e.g., technology) or whoever they may be (like leadership or leaders) – as forever and always materialising within conjoint and constantly (re)enacted relations. While materialisation has recently borne novel insights into how bedfellows of leadership, such as power (Hollis et al., 2021) and authority (Bourgoin et al., 2020), conjointly materialise with technology, the notion may also evolve processual and relationally led understandings of leadership. Meier and Carroll's (2020) work marks a promising frontier in this area. Aided by CCO studies' development of the metaphor of ventriloquism, their analysis reveals how oscillating human and technological agency *make up* (2020, p. 1228) leaders and leadership within a leadership development programme. Who (people) or what (technology) exercises agency is a redundant question within such CCO analysis, with concepts such as materialisation and ventriloquism helping to collapse long-held dualisms of how leaders use or are serviced by technology. Technology and human leadership practice become inseparable.

Developing Leadership through Digital Technology

Some evidence exists suggesting that digital forms of leadership development may be effective at generating insight relevant to practice. This is a point elucidated by Carroll and Simpson (2012) and by Nicholson and Carroll (2013), who highlight the role of online discussion in leadership development programmes. Pacing contributions through digital discussion, where participants write amid daily experiences of work, can allow for play and provocation. Hence Carroll and Simpson (2012) point to practices of leadership generated online that increase the social capabilities of groups by kindling new modes of practice and thought, stretching preconceived notions and extending the span of insight across experiential engagements. Digital forms of development may also offer interesting ways of challenging power dynamics and exploring creative identity play in leadership (Nicholson & Carroll, 2013), in many ways mimicking the manner in which online life can invite identity experimentation. Such insights flag the fact that, paradoxically, although digital forms of developing leadership at first glance seem more removed from everyday organisational experience due to the mediating effects of technology, in practice they probably hold greater potential for meshing development with the experiences of work (Ladkin et al., 2009). This is because digital technology can offer more flexible and piecemeal engagement, allowing for organic insight in the midst of real organisational leadership experiences. Yet there is a darker side to the practice of leadership through technology, which we will now discuss.

Leadership, Power and Control

Power in leadership practice will continue to adapt as technology develops, enabling new forms of control but also of resistance. For example, the practice and development of leadership can be both enhanced, and undermined, by the use of tracking devices. Tracking devices can generate a plethora of data about the feelings, movements and productivity of workers. Avolio et al. (2014, p. 120) state that *leaders can use tracking technologies to learn more about the behaviours of followers or peers in the workplace and therefore react to those behaviours in more of a timely manner, providing guidance, recognition, manipulation or even criticism [...] When one's followers are rewarded on the basis of certain behaviours, tracking technology may make the monitoring and tracking of those behaviours easier to reinforce for good and bad purposes.* This is obviously a controversial area of practice and study, replete with ethical concerns that require fuller attention.

We can see how the consensual use of wearables to provide anonymised feedback could in theory enhance performance and responsiveness. Yet within the employment contract it is hard to foresee any situation where their use would not further entrench control, exploitation and alienation. In a global economy of chronic under-employment, a growing reserve army of labour, increasing wealth inequality and intensified casualisation, it is difficult to envisage how such technologies could do anything other than further disempower workers. We should add that such tracking technologies are already ubiquitous in the gig economy and service sector – for supermarket, call centre, delivery and warehouse workers, for example. Their use has nothing to do with leadership but everything to do with heavy managerial control. Whether the use of wearables is the future for the remainder of the labour market will be a matter of ongoing and pitched struggle. Avolio et al. (2014), however, despite some acknowledgement of 'privacy' concerns, prefer to focus on the productivity drawbacks of such technologies and their capacity for generating new forms of *loafing* and resistance (p. 120). Loafing was, of course, a term of pre-eminent importance to the founder of scientific management, F. W. Taylor ([1911] 1967), who wielded it and other synonyms like a weapon to engender widespread acceptance of the assumption that workers were inclined to exploit the bosses and shirk work. The answer to this tendency to loafing was the pooling of knowledge in the hands of management, the removal of judgement and discretion from workers, whose micro-movements would be measured and controlled from on high.

Aside from political and ethical concerns, which we will return to, what we note here is an all-too-easy slippage between leadership and management – where even the most controlling and disempowering forms of micro-management can be discussed in leadership terms. Who and what are being served by blurring distinctions between controlling forms of management and leadership rhetoric? The answer, we suspect, is corporate power, where the novelty and newness of technology is presented in liberating terms but implemented in ways that further entrench alienation and disempowerment. The slippage between management and leadership is all too common and needs a more careful and disciplined approach.

Few studies of technologically mediated resistance leadership in the workplace exist. An exception to the rule is the study by Smolović Jones et al. (2021) exploring workers' use of space in generating leadership. They draw attention to how technology and social media have been used to undermine and reconfigure the spaces of work and capital. Yet gig economy workers, lacking official employment status and dictated to by algorithms, are also able to exercise more flexibility in their resistance leadership, catching executives off guard. For example, Deliveroo food delivery drivers in Brighton did not need to follow the legally mandated bureaucracy for enacting strike action, as they were not classed as employees. Instead, they could simply collectively agree on a certain day not to log into their apps, bringing the company's operations to a standstill (Cant, 2019). Moreover, as the delivery app tended to push riders to routine and predictable parts of the city to await orders, workers were able to intercept and talk to colleagues who were either unaware of the strike action or who had not heard the arguments in its favour. This is an excellent example of leadership within our definition, as the workers collectively forced a reversal of their identities – from passive recipients of orders to agential subjects – through subversive use of officially mandated technologies. Undoubtedly were such actions to become commonplace, corporate interests would find a way of making them harder to achieve – through legislation and contractual obligations. Yet evident is an emerging terrain of technologically mediated resistance leadership and struggle, which is at present in a nascent stage and pregnant with possibilities for further research.

Political Leadership and Technology

Outside the direct employment relation, in many ways the leadership dynamics of technology are easier to identify. Digital technology has reshaped the nature of contemporary political leadership, particularly leadership from below (Gilani et al., 2020). Here we can turn to the struggles of resistance groups in the Gezi Park protests in Turkey (Eslen-Zia & Erhart, 2015), where digital activity and social media created a contagion effect of resistance leadership, with meaningful challenges to oppressive power spreading across and subverting identity boundaries. We can also note insurgent movements in and against mainstream political parties, which grew in and through digital media. For example, the campaigns of the socialist Jeremy Corbyn, which led to the capturing of the leadership of the mainstream UK Labour Party in 2015 and very nearly government power in 2017. As noted by Sinha et al. (2021), these campaigns were inspired by political values but their messages and control dispersed through digital networks of supporters. Evident here – as well as in Turkey, and before that the Arab Spring – was a hybrid form of political leadership, where reach was secured digitally and energy and commitment generated through collective moments of joy, as crowds and groups gathered in person to share hopes, debate and see for themselves the diverse people committed to radical social and economic change.

Black Lives Matter (BLM) is likewise an important example of dispersed digital leadership with hybrid features (Ruffin, 2020). The movement exploded through the digital sharing of the footage of the racist murder of George Floyd in 2020, which we, along with millions of others, watched on our devices, tearful and furious. Drawing on this potent affect, organisers emerged, many of whom had already gained experience through earlier BLM mobilisations (successful ones with wide support in the US, it should be noted), labour and other civil rights struggles. They were able to use social media and messaging services to draw people onto the streets, assemblies demanding change. In theory, digital technology holds the potential to enhance participation and inclusion. It can enable more flexibility, meaning that people can participate in movements and resistance leadership remotely, from their homes. In eliminating many of the physical boundaries to participation – inaccessible buildings, long formal meetings held at times that largely suit men with fewer home commitments and limited public transport options that hamper geographically remote and poorer urban people – digital technology can offer one powerful way of enhancing diversity in leadership practice. Yet the eruptions of activity and revolutionary energy witnessed around such political movements has thus far produced uneven and patchy results, some notable victories for the Left in Latin America the most obviously successful.

We should note the counter-movements of regressive politics that have emerged in parallel. The fascist alt-right, movements of patriarchal domination in Hungary and the reactionary nationalism of Donald Trump have all adopted digital technology as a means of disseminating propaganda and feeding powerful fantasies of domination and retribution (Goethals, 2021; Stead et al., 2021). Mingling here are forms of careful information management – the creation of media bubbles and sometimes more overt censorship of mass media – combined with a leadership of generating affective and manipulative rhetoric and imagery that can be widely shared. These well-funded networks rely on misinformation and manipulation, as well as upon the generation of envy and hostility towards anyone seeking racial, social or economic justice. They tend to receive stronger – if sometimes tacit – support from governmental, media and corporate actors.

For any meaningful challenge to the political and economic status quo to succeed, therefore, digital technology needs to enable sustained contagion, which Bloom et al. (2021) posit as organic leadership. By this they mean that any meaningful struggle will be rooted in particular and shared experiences – of oppression, trauma, joy, dispossession, empowerment. These are usually localised in particular communities, be these geographically situated or shared across specific experiences of workplace, racial or gendered oppression. These localised movements grow organically and generate their own leaders but for such leadership to scale up and make a broader social and economic impact they need to find commonalities with other movements and causes. Digital technology can facilitate connection, spread and learning, which over time may develop into movements more capable of enacting meaningful and sustained change.

Leadership and Technology: Future Directions, Concluding Remarks

As ripe as the field appears to be for studies that grapple with the intricacies of technology and leadership practice, we continue to have *relatively little understanding of the potential effects of these technologies on the leadership dynamic* (Avolio et al., 2014, p. 126). We therefore end this section by reflecting on some ways in which research on leadership and technology could proceed.

Turning to emergent and less established tech such as digital automation, robotics and artificial intelligence, we wonder whether leadership scholars, tacitly or otherwise, assume that this is not a valid terrain for them. As we indicated in our discussion of total management, we would hold some sympathy with such a position: the dominant thrust of these technologies is routinisation and the removal of discretion. Yet this does not mean that we cannot explore the leadership of workers in, around and against automating technology (Smolović Jones et al., 2021). Countless labour disputes are emerging globally where workers are resisting the alienating effects and downward pressure on wages and conditions brought about by automation and the capitalists who wield these technologies – tech, gig economy and precarious workers globally provide a plethora of rich possibilities for enquiry and understanding. Such campaigns themselves are often tech-savvy, using communication and organising platforms to influence consciousness and develop the agency of workers to step into leadership. Better understanding the campaigns of these workers may help to clarify the future of leadership practice for the majority of us, if workplaces and work become increasingly casualised, automated and precarious. We need more studies that tell us about the everyday practice of leadership in, through and against these technologies. Most obviously such research calls for rich Marxist theory that does not flinch from situating leadership in the structural position of workers in the process of capital accumulation. However, such struggles may also be illuminated through recourse to conceptual resources more rooted in post-structuralist analysis and dialectics that foreground the tensions and possibilities of resistance to offer alternative forms of power through the reimagining and redeployment of technology (Collinson, 2005; Sinha et al., 2021).

Bearing in mind the definitional care that needs to be applied towards leadership in relation to technology, we need to know more about the extent to which technology can enhance leadership practices more generally, beyond but including the experiences of work. Utopian discourse surrounding automation often promises liberating people from drudgery and dirty work, and enabling non-alienated forms of work, which engage people's intellectual and affective capacities. Yet in reality, evidence for this currently seems thin on the ground, with the tendency much more towards automation intensifying casualisation and underemployment (Benanav, 2020).

Therefore, where examples of technology being used to free people for more 'leaderful' practice (Raelin, 2011) exist, we need more empirical studies to spread learning about the practical use of digital technology. In particular, we need to understand how digital technology shapes, helps or hinders democratic forms of leadership, at work or elsewhere (Smolović Jones et al., 2016). However, in such studies we also need to be mindful of the dangers of assuming that democracy is a universally positive category, just as with leadership more generally (Collinson, 2012). As immaterial labour becomes more dominant at work, we need to consider both the positives and negatives of cooperation and participation through digital technology. As overt forms of digital surveillance can enclose spaces for workers, so we also ponder the extent to which digital technology might intensify a tyranny of participation for workers – forced to be always on call and always responsive to communication. We also need to recognise that most workplaces will not become hives of rich democratic practice, at least in the short-term, and are more likely to be directed by more instrumental logics. We therefore need to better understand how technology can help nurture novel forms of leadership in the interstices of totalising management – and again, thinking in terms of resistance and how it is practised in a multiplicity of ways, often ad-hoc and opportunistically.

Methodologically, as the nature of work and societies evolve, we are particularly interested in how digital technology may entail distinctive forms, structures and practices of collective leadership that escape the attention of currently dominant research strategies. Pre-eminent here are surely methodologies from post-humanism or Marxism that offer primacy to the role of materiality in everyday practice (Hawkins, 2015; Smolović Jones et al., 2021). We know from practice that collective leadership practised through digital or hybrid means performs spatial relations in ways that disrupt and connect in novel ways, potentially bringing leadership practice into people's homes and previously marginalised and overlooked communities. We also know that communication through digital technology is distinctive and models developed in studies of face-to-face interactions are unlikely to be easily transposable. Snatched dialogue between shifts or meetings, accelerated or stretched-out leadership talk over time, visuals, smileys, informal networks and so on, may all be hallmarks of a digital form of leadership that deserve more attention. Such demands seem to call forth the need for hybrid forms of ethnography, with researchers embedded in the face-to-face and online worlds of groups (Sutherland, 2018). Such studies need to focus on how the digital constitutes leadership longitudinally and (re)constitutes experience in the physical world.

Future research could fruitfully adopt more of an action orientation, seeking to implement and learn from technological interventions that offer the promise of more emancipated and inclusive leadership, necessitating close interdisciplinary collaboration between the worlds of leadership, engineering and computer science. Such research could be focused on capacity building to strengthen organisations – be they employers or trade unions – or to help enhance resistance in and to organisations. Action-oriented research into leadership and technology can also be more or less radically inclined: at the less radical end aimed at making practical interventions to enhance inclusion and agency; at the more radical end, engaging in struggle with workers and activists in enquiry against and with technology to inform larger struggles (Smolović Jones et al., 2021). All such research would make a valuable contribution to shaping this field of leadership and technology – our hardware is in need of multiple updates.

CONCLUDING REFLECTIONS

We conclude the chapter by summarising our thoughts and offering a provocation to consider the position of the academic researcher in the study of technology and leadership. Although we have offered a survey of some interesting studies of leadership and technology, the bigger picture is that leadership studies trails behind practice with regards technology. It largely maintains a preference for leadership that occurs in smaller co-present groups practised by humans with other humans. This tech-washing is concerning because the field seems in danger of becoming too detached from people's everyday experiences of work and life, which are both heavily and routinely technologically mediated. Can we really say that we are studying leadership practice if we do not offer more prominence to the use of technology, which fills the majority of people's working days, and only focus on face-to-face meetings and interactions? Or if we interview 'leaders' and do not delve deeper into how and through which mediums they communicate? Furthermore, studies of leadership outside office and corporate spaces are few and far between and we are left wondering whether the meta-conclusion that leadership studies has drawn is that blue collar and casualised workers do not practice leadership and/or are merely passive recipients of leadership who can therefore be safely ignored.

What do these conclusions say about the role of leadership scholars to date and the kind of stance we could adopt moving forwards? In a nutshell, we urge leadership researchers and educators to position themselves in more critical relation to the realities of technology in work and society. As Braverman (1974) and Marx (2004) noted, technological developments tend to intensify the downward pressure on wages and worker agency. This is achieved by technology making corporations less reliant on human beings, people who can resist the upward redistribution of wealth by demanding better pay and conditions. Thus a reserve pool of labour is created in society, people who are unemployed or under-employed (Benanav, 2020) – that is, overworked through trying to balance multiple precarious jobs while also expending emotional labour and health through self-marketing and networking. In parallel, the experience of being a worker is adapting, and experiences of being a precarious worker will be uneven – in some parts of the world, more akin to the industrial dynamics described vividly by Marx (back-breaking toil over long hours, child labour and so on); elsewhere more immaterial but nevertheless both precarious and demanding – hospitality and care work being exemplar cases.

Yet as capital accumulation intensifies and increasing portions of life become dominated by market logics, the pressure on university researchers to reproduce romanticised discourses of freedom and liberation in corporate life through digital technology will surely be intense. In times such as these, it is worth pausing and reflecting on who we are writing for. Workers are not abstract figures but our students and the people subjected to the leadership and management models we write about. Most of our students and wider reading audience, if we are ever lucky enough to reach one, will experience economic relations defined by insecure employment, an ever greater proletarianisation of previously professional and privileged jobs, expensive housing, stagnant wages and proliferating debt. At work, technology is leveraged to intensify inequality and the upward distribution of wealth, while removing the discretionary activity of ever greater portions of the labour force. Uncritically reproducing discourses of Silicon Valley liberation and disruption would be a dereliction of duty far removed from the work most people will be undertaking in practice. Yet our role as educators should likewise not be defined by pessimism and fatalism. In theory, digital technology can help usher in more autonomy and create work that is rewarding and flexible to human needs, rather than the abstract needs of the marketplace and employability logics. Leadership studies is perhaps uniquely positioned to offer a framework through which to move beyond totalising management and to rethink the possibilities for dignity, freedom and care offered by human beings working alongside and with technology. As leadership scholars we are in a powerful position to ensure this happens, just as the world grapples with how to leverage technology for emancipatory ends. So let's get to work.

REFERENCES

Al-Ani, B., Horspool, A., & Bligh, M. C. (2011). Collaborating with 'virtual strangers': Towards developing a framework for leadership in distributed teams. *Leadership*, 7(3), 219–249.

Alimahomed-Wilson, J. (2020). The Amazonification of logistics: E-commerce, labor, and exploitation in the last mile. In Alimahomed-Wilson, J. and Reese, E. (eds) *The cost of free shipping: Amazon in the global economy*. London: Pluto Press: 69–84.

Arvedsen, L. D., & Hassert, L. O. (2020). Accomplishing leadership-in-interaction by mobilizing available information and communication technology objects in a virtual context. *Leadership*, 16(5), 546–567.

Ashcraft, K. L., Kuhn, T. R., & Cooren, F. (2009). Constitutional amendments: 'Materializing' organizational communication. *Academy of Management Annals*, 3(1), 1–64.

Avolio, B. J., Kahai, S. S., & Dodge, G. E. (2001). E-leadership: Implications for theory, research, and practice. *Leadership Quarterly*, 11(4), 615–668.

Avolio, B. J., Sosik, J. J., Kahai, S. S., & Baker, B. (2014). E-leadership: Re-examining transformations in leadership source and transmission. *Leadership Quarterly*, *25*(1), 105–131.

Bell, E., Warren, S., & Schroeder, J. E. (2014). *The Routledge Companion to Visual Organization*. Routledge.

Benanav, A. (2020). *Automation and the future of work*. London: Verso.

Blaschke, S., Schoeneborn, D., & Seidl, D. (2012). Organizations as networks of communication episodes: Turning the network perspective inside out. *Organization Studies*, *33*(7), 879–906.

Bligh, M. C., Kohles, J. C., & Pillai, R. (2011). Romancing leadership: Past, present, and future. *Leadership Quarterly*, *22*(6), 1058–1077.

Bloom, P., & Rhodes, C. (2018). *CEO Society: The Corporate Takeover of Everyday Life*. Zed.

Bloom, P., Smolović Jones, O., & Woodcock, J. (2021). *Guerrilla Democracy: Mobile Power and Revolution in the 21st Century*. Bristol University Press.

Boje, D. M., & Rhodes, C. (2005). The virtual leader construct: The mass mediatization and simulation of transformational leadership. *Leadership*, *1*(4), 407–428.

Bourgoin, A., Bencherki, N., & Faraj, S. (2020). 'And who are you?': A performative perspective on authority in organizations. *Academy of Management Journal*, *63*(4), 1134–1165.

Braverman, H. (1974). *Labor and Monopoly Capital*. Monthly Review Press.

Bridle, J. (2019). *New Dark Age: Technology and the End of the Future*. Verso.

Cant, C. (2019). *Riding for Deliveroo: Resistance in the New Economy*. Polity.

Carroll, B., & Simpson, B. (2012). Capturing sociality in the movement between frames: An illustration from leadership development. *Human Relations*, *65*(10), 1283–1309.

Collinson, D. (2005). Dialectics of leadership. *Human Relations*, *58*(11), 1419–1442.

Collinson, D. (2012). Prozac leadership and the limits of positive thinking. *Leadership*, *8*(2), 87–107.

Collinson, D., Smolović Jones, O., & Grint, K. (2018). 'No more heroes': Critical perspectives on leadership romanticism. *Organization Studies*, *39*(11), 1625–1647.

Cooren, F. (2020). Beyond entanglement: (Socio-)materiality and organization studies. *Organization Theory*, *1*(3), 1–24.

Cooren, F., Kuhn, T., Cornelissen, J. P., & Clark, T. (2011). Communication, organizing and organization: An overview and introduction to the special issue. *Organization Studies*, *32*(9), 1149–1170.

Eslen-Ziya, H., & Erhart, I. (2015). Toward postheroic leadership: A case study of Gezi's collaborating multiple leaders. *Leadership*, *11*(4), 471–488.

Ferry, N. C. (2018). It's a family business!: Leadership texts as technologies of heteronormativity. *Leadership*, *14*(6), 603–621.

Ford, J., Harding, N., & Learmonth, M. (2008). *Leadership as Identity: Constructions and Deconstructions*. Palgrave Macmillan.

Gilani, P., Bolat, E., Nordberg, D., & Wilkin, C. (2020). Mirror, mirror on the wall: Shifting leader–follower power dynamics in a social media context. *Leadership*, *16*(3), 343–363.

Goethals, G. (2021). The 2020 election and its aftermath: Love, lies, and ensorceling leadership. *Leadership*, *17*(2), 240–250.

Griffey, E., & Jackson, B. (2010). The portrait as leader: Commissioned portraits and the power of tradition. *Leadership*, *6*(2), 133–157.

Grint, K. (2005). Problems, problems, problems: The social construction of 'leadership'. *Human Relations*, *58*(11), 1467–1494.

Grint, K., & Woolgar, S. (1997). *The Machine at Work: Technology, Work and Organization*. Polity.

Hardt, M., & Negri, A. (2001). *Empire*. Harvard University Press.

Hawkins, B. (2015). Ship-shape: Materializing leadership in the British Royal Navy. *Human Relations*, *68*(6), 951–971.

Heavey, C., Simsek, Z., Kyprianou, C., & Risius, M. (2020). How do strategic leaders engage with social media? A theoretical framework for research and practice. *Strategic Management Journal*, *41*(8), 1490–1527.

Heizmann, H., & Liu, H. (2018). Becoming green, becoming leaders: Identity narratives in sustainability leadership development. *Management Learning*, *49*(1), 40–58.

Hollis, D., Wright, A., Smolović Jones, O., & Smolović Jones, N. (2021). From 'pretty' to 'pretty powerful': The communicatively constituted power of facial beauty's performativity. *Organization Studies*, *42*(12), 1885–1907.

Kelan, E. K. (2013). The becoming of business bodies: Gender, appearance, and leadership development. *Management Learning*, *44*(1), 45–61.

Kempster, S., Schedlitzki, D., & Edwards, G. (2021). Where have all the followers gone? *Leadership*, *17*(1), 118–128.

Kuhn, T. R., Ashcraft, K. L., & Cooren, F. (2017). *The Work of Communication: Relational Perspectives on Working and Organizing in Contemporary Capitalism*. Routledge.

Ladkin, D., Case, P., Gaya Wicks, P., & Kinsella, K. (2009). Developing leaders in cyber-space: The paradoxical possibilities of on-line learning. *Leadership*, *5*(2), 193–212.

Larson, L., & DeChurch, L. A. (2020). Leading teams in the digital age: Four perspectives on technology and what they mean for leading teams. *Leadership Quarterly*, *31*(1), 1–18.

Latour, B. (2007). *Reassembling the Social: An Introduction to Actor-Network-Theory*. Oxford University Press.

Lazzarato, M. (2006). Immaterial labour. In P. Virno & M. Hardt (Eds.), *Radical Thought in Italy: A Potential Politics*. University of Minnesota Press.

Liu, H. (2015). Constructing the GFC: Australian banking leaders during the financial 'crisis'. *Leadership*, 11(4), 424–450.

Liu, H., Cutcher, L., & Grant, D. (2017). Authentic leadership in context: An analysis of banking CEO narratives during the global financial crisis. *Human Relations*, 70(6), 694–724.

Mailhot, C., Gagnon, S., Langley, A., & Binette, L. (2016). Distributing leadership across people and objects in a collaborative research project. *Leadership*, 12(1), 53–85.

Marwick, A. E. (2015). Instafame: Luxury selfies in the attention economy. *Public Culture*, 27, 137–160.

Marx, K. (2004). *Capital Volume 1*. Penguin.

Meier, F., & Carroll, B. (2020). Making up leaders: Reconfiguring the executive student through profiling, texts and conversations in a leadership development programme. *Human Relations*, 73(9), 1226–1248.

Mumby, D. K. (2020). Theorizing struggle in the social factory. *Organization Theory*, 1(2), 2631787720919440.

Nicholson, H., & Carroll, B. (2013). Identity undoing and power relations in leadership development. *Human Relations*, 66(9), 1225–1248.

Oborn, E., Barrett, M., & Dawson, S. (2013). Distributed leadership in policy formulation: A sociomaterial perspective. *Organization Studies*, 34(2), 253–276.

Raelin, J. (2011). From leadership-as-practice to leaderful practice. *Leadership*, 7(2), 195–211.

Reynolds, M. (2020). Jeff Bezos wants to fix climate change: He can start with Amazon. *Wired*, 18 February. https://www.wired.co.uk/article/jeff-bezos-climate-change-amazon

Rhodes, C. (2021). *Woke Capitalism: How Corporate Morality is Sabotaging Democracy*. Bristol University Press.

Rhue, L., & Sundararajan, A. (2014). Digital access, political networks and the diffusion of democracy. *Social Networks*, 36, 40–53.

Ruffin, H. G. (2020). Working together to survive and thrive: The struggle for black lives past and present. *Leadership*, 17(1), 32–46.

Salovaara, P., & Bathurst, R. (2018). Power-with leadership practices: An unfinished business. *Leadership*, 14(2), 179–202.

Sinha, P., Smolović Jones, O., & Carroll, B. (2021). Theorizing dramaturgical resistance leadership from the leadership campaigns of Jeremy Corbyn. *Human Relations*, 74(3), 354–382.

Smolović Jones, O., Briley, G., & Woodcock, J. (2021). Exposing and re-placing leadership through workers inquiry. *Leadership*, 18(1), 61–80. https://doi.org/10.1177/17427150211026431

Smolović Jones, O., Smolović Jones, S., & Grint, K. (2020). Understanding sovereign leadership as a response to terrorism: A post-foundational analysis. *Organization*, 27(4), 537–556.

Smolović Jones, S., Smolović Jones, O., Winchester, N., & Grint, K. (2016). Putting the discourse to work: On outlining a praxis of democratic leadership development. *Management Learning*, 47(4), 424–442.

Smolović Jones, S., Winchester, N., & Clarke, C. (2021). Feminist solidarity building as embodied agonism: An ethnographic account of a protest movement. *Gender, Work & Organization*, 28(3), 917–934.

Stead, V., & Elliott, C. (2019). Pedagogies of power: Media artefacts as public pedagogy for women's leadership development. *Management Learning*, 50(2), 171–188.

Stead, V., Elliott, C., & Gardiner, R. (2021). Leadership legitimacy and mobilization of capital(s): Disrupting politics and reproducing heteronormativity. *Leadership*, 17(6), 693–714.

Streitfeld, D. (2021). How Amazon crushes unions. *New York Times*, 16 March. https://www.nytimes.com/2021/03/16/technology/amazon-unions-virginia.html

Sutherland, N. (2018). Investigating leadership ethnographically: Opportunities and potentialities. *Leadership*, 14(3), 263–290.

Taylor, F. W. ([1911] 1967). *The Principles of Scientific Management*. Norton & Co.

Treadway, D. C., Adams, G. L., Ranft, A. L., & Ferris, G. F. (2009). A meso-level conceptualization of CEO celebrity effectiveness. *Leadership Quarterly*, 20(4), 554–570.

Tur, B., Harstad, J., & Antonakis, J. (2021). Effect of charismatic signaling in social media settings: Evidence from TED and Twitter. *Leadership Quarterly*, 1, 101476. https://doi.org/10.1016/j.leaqua.2020.101476

Virno, P. (2004). *A Grammar of the Multitude: For an Analysis of Contemporary Forms of Life*. Semiotext[e].

Walker, P. (2021). Call centre staff to be monitored via webcam for home working 'infractions'. *Guardian*, 26 March. https://www.theguardian.com/business/2021/mar/26/teleperformance-call-centre-staff-monitored-via-webcam-home-working-infractions

Woodcock, J. (2021). *The Fight Against Platform Capitalism: An Inquiry into the Global Struggles of the Gig Economy*. University of Westminster Press.

Woolgar, S. (1992). *Science: The Very Idea*. Routledge.

25

Indigenous Leadership as a Conscious Adaptive System

Chellie Spiller and Amber Nicholson

INTRODUCTION

Indigenous peoples make up 5 per cent of the global population, 15 per cent of the world's extreme poor and protect 80 per cent of the world's biodiversity (Raygorodetsky, 2018; World Bank, 2021). The UN Permanent Forum on Indigenous Issues (n.d.) explains thus: 'Indigenous' describes people who have a history of continuity with pre-invasion and pre-colonial societies that developed on their territories; they are the *inheritors and practitioners of unique cultures and ways of relating to other people and to the environment*. In many cases, colonisation rapidly oppressed Indigenous philosophies, values, ways of being and knowing, and superimposed other ideologies and practices. Despite the significant upheavals and subjugations imposed on Indigenous peoples, this has not succeeded in overwriting their ontologies and epistemologies (Hausdoerffer et al., 2021; Nicholson et al., 2015; Spiller et al., 2020; Verbos & Humphries, 2014).

Indigenous leadership reflects ancient, dynamic living systems of knowledge and experience. Founded on principles of kinship and affection between human and cosmological realms, Indigenous leaders, whether in community, political or corporate settings see themselves as stewards, tasked with caring for the well-being of social and ecological communities. Even though much of the world has *lost its way in caring for the planet*, says Waterhouse (in Raygorodetsky, 2018) *to find it again, we have great guides*:

> Indigenous peoples have mastered the art of living on the Earth without destroying it. They continue to teach and lead by example, from the restoration of eel grass and salmon by the Samish Nation, to the bison reintroduction by the Kainai Nation of the Blackfoot Confederacy, to the restoration of traditional 800-year old Hawaiian fish ponds. We must heed these lessons and take on this challenging task, if we want our grandchildren to have a future.

Indigenous leadership literature covers a wide gamut of discourse such as collective, relational, servant, gender, transformative, authentic, wayfinding, place-based and wisdom to name just a few of the theoretical frameworks within which Indigenous authors have situated their discussions. The intention of this chapter is not to deliver a comprehensive review – rather it is to introduce readers to some of the main seams. We do caveat our discussion by recognising the vast array of Indigenous societies with different creation stories, philosophies, ontologies, epistemologies and ways of being and acting in the world. Readers are encouraged to refer to the extensive reference list which has been purposefully gathered to provide pathways beyond this chapter. We hope there are many hours of pleasure tracing this illuminating far-reaching body of work. The places and cultures represented in this body of work is breathtaking (but obviously not exhaustive) and includes: Australian Aboriginal; Canadian Stó:lō; Hawaiian; Inuit; Māori of Aotearoa New Zealand; Native American tribes such as Blackfeet, Lakota, Sioux, Pueblo; and Peruvian Ayni to name but a few. As Kenny and Fraser (2012, p. 2) note *theorizing in this context is tough* due to the dazzling variety of Indigenous Peoples. Following Kenny and Fraser, our intention is not to *offer a general Indigenous theory of leadership* but rather, in this present work, it is to inspire leadership as a conscious adaptive system.

Apropos the invitation by the editors of this *Handbook of Leadership* to pay attention to *sense-making* (exploring the current structures, themes, meanings, epistemological and methodological positions, constituting each topic) and *sense-breaking* (disrupting, critiquing and refreshing each topic) we explore the idea of Indigenous leadership as a *conscious adaptive system*. A conscious adaptive system, we posit from an Indigenous standpoint, emerges from a steadfast awareness of systemic interconnectedness and interdependency. Respective Indigenous wisdom traditions appreciate that *the commons of human consciousness* (Loeffler, 2021, p. 130) is mutually constituted in relationship with all creation. Spiller (2021) describes this as I AM consciousness and draws links between Māori, ancient Celtic and African traditions. Our ontological, cosmogenealogical positioning of Indigenous leadership as a conscious adaptive system offers a powerful touchpoint for leadership studies and practice. We tap into complex adaptive systems theory and relational quantum physics to build the notion of a root ontology of belonging to the cosmos, in sacred kinship with all creation.

Such *sense-making* by Indigenous communities is guided by enduring *knowledge codes* (Spiller et al., 2020) that have been passed down through generations and manifested in features such as ceremony, ritual, arts, value systems and protocols. These adaptive knowledge codes are informed, refreshed and mastered through empirical observation by reading the signs in the environment and making sense of the relationship between things.

Sense-breaking is to reject the totalising rationalistic, individualistic stranglehold that engulfs, disconnects, alienates and is dispassionately indifferent to the energies that ply human experience and ecological lifeways on Earth. While this can be disconcerting for some, Indigenous ontologies embrace ambiguity, multiple truths and mystery (Nicholson, 2020), which allows a convergence of nature and science, of spiritual and cognitive, and of metaphoric and rational.

Indigenous peoples did not suffer the *epochal rupture*, as Josephson-Storm (2017) has argued in *The Myth of Disenchantment*, whereby Europeans constructed post-hoc typologies such as Renaissance, Modernity and bronze, golden ages – producing epistemic over-confidence and mass confirmation bias through Eurocentric reflexivity. The subsequent racialisation of science, including so-called organisation 'science', has resulted in an illusion of disciplinary norms, including in organisation and leadership studies, that bleed the world of meaning and create profound alienation, atomisation and conflict. In such a world the Indigenous 'other' has been marginalised, relicised and magicialised.

Many Indigenous cultures have survived in spite of the upheavals that engulfed them, railing against a totalising instrumental rationalism. Through it all these societies have retained their deep appreciation of interconnectedness, a sense of sacred ecology and a living cosmos, sustaining worldviews and practices that are integrative of mystery and meaning. Indigenous wisdom looks beyond the present use of resources and includes the relevance of ancestral associations and responsibilities, managing the relationship not only between humans and their ecological landscapes, but also relationships that transcend time and space.

Indigenous leadership scholars are driving change and transformation despite being systematically overlooked by the academy and silenced in much of the leadership canon (Gram-Hanssen, 2021; Spiller et al., 2020; Todd, 2016). This valuable repository of knowledge is sporadically clipped into discourse on topics such as sustainability or environmental concerns or enclaved as the comparative other for Western discourse, asked to explain how Indigenous leadership is relevant to the West, or how Western leaders can learn from Indigenous peoples, or indeed how Western leadership can be rehabilitated or revivified. Evans and Sinclair (2016) contest the assumption that all forms of leadership must be compared with the dominant Western leadership paradigm. Indigenous leadership cannot be shoehorned into extant Western literature even those that are beguilingly concordant such as collective, relational, servant and other communally oriented forms. The most Western theories can do is illuminate aspects of what is already there in Indigenous approaches.

The Western palate has its own taste for life, and supplying prescriptive answers is not our mission in this chapter. We provide stories, principles, practices, insights and encouragement to go back to the ontological beginning, a bedrock of belonging to the cosmos. This requires commitment to becoming a conscious adaptive system and be open to the world and a coachable spirit: each person aware of their influence on the whole.

As Josephson-Storm (2017) has argued, Europe and America are not as bereft of mystery, magic, miracles and meaning as believed – even though these ideas may be (explicitly) expelled from organisation 'science'. A key point he makes is that European *disenchantment* is an illusion because a significant proportion of the population across political, education and societal spectrums do search for an ensouled world through connection to nature, poetry, miracles and the mystical. Numerous leadership books and articles speak to these dimensions of the leader experience.

We can only hope that people from all walks of leadership life, scholars, students, practitioners alike, take up the challenge and join the vanguard of change. We believe turning to root ontologies is one way forward and can help support all life on Earth. In this great 'returning' (but not a romantic spiral) leaders are a movement through time, in service of a bigger purpose, and part of a collective human odyssey.

Moving forward in this chapter, we first set out the key tenets of Indigenous leadership which are organised across four dimensions. The first explores co-evolution, symbiotic exchange and stewardship. The second enquires into leadership in the context of place and community. The third dimension presents ancestral and cultural wisdom and the fourth dives into activism, resistance and resilience. While each of these dimensions will be of no major surprise to Indigenous scholars and practitioners, they are a necessary introduction to readers of this volume encountering Indigenous leadership for the first time.

The next section explores Indigenous ontology and epistemology, which acknowledges the sacred kinship between all things. This reverence of shared cosmogenealogies underpins the positioning of Indigenous leadership as a conscious adaptive system, which we believe offers a powerful turning point for leadership studies and practice. This section largely centres on Māori as this is the whakapapa (genealogy) of the two authors of this chapter and we acknowledge our cultural standpoint.

Three short cases furnish this work. We cameo the granting of legal personhood to the Whanganui River in Aotearoa NZ, an international precedent that enshrined stewardship from a Māori perspective. The story of Kurtal, a sacred waterhole and dwelling place of snake spirit, in the Kimberley region of Australia, depicts the devastating impact of environmental degradation on an Aboriginal community. We go behind the scenes of the Standing Rock Sioux protest against a pipeline and the way the leadership sought to galvanise and uplift people through ceremony and prayer. This triptych of cases is centred around water to draw attention to the plight of the world's waterways. As well as these cases we reference many other examples in our tapestry of Indigenous leadership.

There is much to be learnt from Indigenous leadership and we identify two coalescences in the discussion section which are drawn from complex adaptive systems theory and relational quantum physics. We conclude this chapter by encouraging scholars, students and practitioners to advance leadership as a conscious adaptive system.

KEY TENETS OF INDIGENOUS LEADERSHIP

Indigenous peoples are geographically diverse and culturally heterogeneous, however there are some key tenets we identified across a wide body of Indigenous leadership literature that provide touchstones of connection. Indigenous leadership ontologies have both evolved from and are embedded in extensive living histories. Indigenous leaders are often moving between worlds, attempting to reconcile the divergent leadership paradigms that often pit normative cultural ideals against intrusive agendas, albeit to varying degrees. The Harvard Project on Native American Indian Economic Development (n.d.) says *a particularly strong premium exists for indigenous leaders who can envision a new set of possibilities for the nation and build community capacities to reach them. Such leaders overcome the forces of inertia and decay if they can engage community support for change and development* (p. 6). What is important, the Harvard Project (n.d.) argue, is that cultural systems must be of practical use in the modern world, not enshrined in romantic ideals. Indigenous peoples must necessarily negotiate tensions amid various forces such as social, economic and technological.

Leadership, like any aspect of being human is fraught, messy, marred by disillusionment and the heartbreaking gap between reality and vision, a wrestle with despair and a clasp on hope. Indigenous leadership, as in any other society, is rife with tensions, conflicts, poor judgement, ill-chosen battles, sub-optimal outcomes, irreverent actions and self-aggrandising behaviour. It is often quotidian and sometimes extraordinary. Aforementioned caveats in place, we illuminate the remarkable resilience, courage and humility in the work of Indigenous leadership and present four dimensions: 1) co-evolution, symbiotic exchange and stewardship; 2) place and community; 3) ancestral and cultural wisdom; and 4) activism, resistance and resilience.

Co-Evolution, Symbiotic Exchange and Stewardship

Underpinning Indigenous worldviews is a deep sense of belongingness that flows from a belief in a sacred kinship with creation. Many cosmogenealogies tell of the ancestral descent of humans from the spiritual and natural landscapes, thus intimately intertwining human evolution with all that surrounds us (Cajete, 2000; Marsden, 2003; Spiller, 2021). Loeffler (2021, p. 130) explains *we humans are biologically kindred to all of the species that have ever lived on our planetary commons that we call Earth*:

> Each ecosystem is a self-regenerating system that includes all species cooperating within a geophysical habitat. The human species is but one of millions of species that might inhabit any ecosystem. Native peoples who still adhere to their respective traditional values intuitively recognize this systemic interconnectedness and thus honor their fellow species – plant, animal and otherwise – the true source of their ancestral wisdom, the commons of human consciousness.
>
> (p. 133)

The notion of *co-evolution* whereby human development occurs in symbiotic spiritual exchange with the world's life systems, engenders guiding ethics such as respect, reciprocity and interdependence (Intezari et al., 2020). Humans are not seen to own the land, but to belong to the earth. This responsibility shapes a profound commitment to Mother Earth justice; Indigenous peoples around the world *struggle without end* (Walker, [1990] 2004) to fight for the well-being of lands and waterways. As Kimmerer (2013, p. 209) notes *to be indigenous is to protect life on earth*. This can be seen in many Indigenous worldviews. For example, an Ayni Indigenous Peruvian outlook, Huambachano (2015), describes the *good living* principles that value equilibrium and harmony with cosmos, Pachamama Earth Mother and the human community. A Tewa Pueblo viewpoint talks to the dynamic relational balance between humans and the natural and spiritual communities (Cajete, 2016). Cajete (2000, p. 24) asserts, *to know yourself you must first know the earth*. For Māori, *to 'know' one's self is to know one's genealogy* (Murton, 2012, p. 94) and the connection of people and place underpins the obligation to protect, maintain and enhance the well-being and vitality of life systems that are both ancestors and kin, inherent with their own life energies (Nicholson et al., 2017).

Case Cameo: The Whanganui River, Aotearoa NZ

The proverb, *Ko te awa ko au, ko au te awa* (*The river is me; I am the river*) reflects the indivisible, symbiotic relationship between the river and local Māori. In 2017 the Whanganui River in Aotearoa NZ became the first river in the world to be conferred legal personhood with equal rights akin a person; two guardians were appointed by local Māori to speak on the river's behalf (New Zealand Parliament, 2017). The 290km long entity is recognised as an *indivisible and living whole, comprising the Whanganui River from the mountains to the sea, incorporating all its physical and metaphysical elements* (Hollingsworth, 2020). The river is an ancestor, spiritual mentor and healer, as well as a source of food and conveyance. Two Indian rivers have now been proclaimed legal entities, and Bangladesh has endowed all its rivers with legal rights.

The Whanganui River legislation is no recent modern day courtroom battle. Ever since the 1800s, when settlers arrived, one generation of Māori leaders after the next took up the fight and petitioned government to save their river kin. Decade after decade Indigenous leadership persevered throughout the upheavals of colonisation, settler land grabs, violent confiscations and bloody wars. The intergenerational leadership railed against the pollution from unfettered, unregulated industrialisation that muddied it from gravel extraction, and polluted it with toxic waste (Hollingsworth, 2020) thus, degrading the mauri, life force of the river.

Leaders continue to advocate for Earth Justice. One such leader, Jacinta Ruru, an expert in environmental and Māori law at Otago University, says:

> legal personhood represents a fundamental move from a Western to a Māori perspective – although new laws aren't always needed to change attitudes. The last hundreds of years has [sic] been all through this colonization process of dismantling Indigenous cultures and certainly not thinking of

them as having anything to add to us in the world order. That's really got to change. As we're starting to face really huge critical issues – climate change, adaptation, sea level rise, the ramifications of the collapse of the economy after Covid, we've got to look to all of the knowledges, we've got to be more embracing of as many knowledges and cultures as we can.

(Cited in Hollingsworth, 2020)

This longstanding fight for this river ancestor to be officially recognised for its inherent life force and life-giving capabilities highlights the wide-reaching scope of Indigenous leadership. More than protecting the river for the sake of the community, this law protects the river as a natural right. Intergenerational leadership ensured these river kin and their own spiritual life forces are protected and cherished.

Place and Community Leadership

The influential body of work by LaDuke (1999) on Indigenous ecological knowledge (IEK) reinforces and elevates the cultural and spiritual relationship between Indigenous peoples and their places and ecologies. Communities are both extensions and reflections of place. Cultural identities, core values and traditions are tied to particular landscapes, all of which carry ancestral legacies. Cajete (2000) explains that realisation of leadership stems from being of service to one's community and place.

Leadership is driven by the community, which also provides the purpose for its existence (Henry & Wolfgramm, 2018; Ruwhiu & Elkin, 2016). Belonging to a community requires active participation in the fullness of life. Even Indigenous leaders of organisations styled as corporations in the competitive capitalistic marketplace seek to make judicious decisions from an Indigenous sense-making standpoint, albeit these decisions often involve conscious compromises. Those leaders who subscribe to Indigenous traditions are aware that economic relationships are not separate to ecological, social, cultural and spiritual spheres (Dell et al., 2018). Many tribes and organisations have vast intergenerational plans that span many hundreds of years to ensure they are considering future generations in today's decision-making. Similarly, Indigenous leaders in urban contexts (Maracle et al., 2020) seek to transmit leadership ideals that have been established in ancestral times and are seen to still be very relevant today. Gambrell (2016) emphasises the *quiet leadership* of Lakota women leaders who shore up community resilience in the wake and face of hegemonic leadership tools of colonisation and assimilation. All these authors emphasise the shared, collectivist, consensus orientation of Indigenous leadership.

Kelly and Nicholson (2021, p. 2) tell us *our deepest human sense of belonging is rooted in our connection to place*. Often understated in the wider leadership literature, they emphasise that place is a fundamental tenet of Indigenous leadership. More than a physical geographical location, place is a cycle of spiritual, cultural and social processes that intertwine communities and their landscapes. They, Kelly and Nicholson, introduce the notion of ancestral leadership enshrined in mythology and cosmology, which is inherently tied to place. This profound sense of place sees humanity as both physically and spiritually belonging to the earth. Hawaiian academic Manulani Aluli Meyer (2008) explains that referring to land as Mother Earth is not a mere metaphor, it is an epistemological idea – the landscape shapes our very being and our consciousness. This outlook explicates why Indigenous peoples can be deeply affected by land loss and degradation, as it is experienced as a loss of soul, or a denigration of our relations (Cajete, 2000). Hēnare (2015, p. 205) explains the continuation of intergenerational trauma:

*the **tangi**, the weeping, is a declaration about and a reference to the tragedy of land loss and cultural identity. **Tangi** flows from the remnants of land in which resides the wounded soul handed down by ancestors. Such weeping is not just for the immediate material loss, but also for lost potential and the diminution of spiritual and cultural identity.*

Case Cameo: Kurtal, Australia

The story of Kurtal reveals a world of mysterious forces, power and immense intimacy, respect and communion between the Aboriginal community and sacred *jila* (living water). The documentary film *Putuparri and the Rainmakers* (Ma, 2015) tells the story of Aboriginal elders Nyilpirr Ngalyaku 'Spider' Snell and Dolly Juguja Snell who, with their grandson Putuparri Tom Lawford, journey from Fitzroy Crossing into the Great Sandy Desert of Western Australia to Spider's birthplace and site of the sacred jila water hole of Kurtal, some 80km east of Kulyayi (Well 42) on the Canning Stock Route in Western Australia. In Kurtal there dwells a kalpurtu, a powerful ancestral being regarded as a snake spirit:

Before they became snakes, however, these ancestral beings were men who made rain, shaped the features of the land and introduced practices of law into the jila Country. Many of the jila men were also companions who travelled the desert visiting one another, and creating the ceremonies and singing the songs still performed here today. One by one, the jila men ended their journeys at the springs that bear their names; as they entered them, they transformed into kalpurtu.

(National Museum Australia, n.d.)

Of the 200 permanent springs in jila country, 30 are believed to be dwelling places of kalpurtu. Over time the Kurtal jila is desecrated by others and becomes dirty, unhealthy, undrinkable. The elders are forsaken and Dolly says that with the death of Kurtal they are sick people, a people with no place for their spirits to go to when they pass: *when people who were born at Kurtal die, their spirit returns to the waterhole. Spider is one of the remaining elders born at Kurtal and a key custodian responsible for the practices that take place there* (Documentary Educational Resources, n.d.).

We bear privileged witness to the powerful, determined transmission of ritual, ceremony, dance and sacred knowledge from one generation to the next. We are reminded of the strength and resilience of 40,000 years of Indigenous leadership. Yunkaporta (2019, p. 254) explains the underlying meaning of a phrase *Aak ngamparam yimanang wunan* in the language of his Australian Aboriginal community which approximates in English *as being like our place*.

Ancestral, Cultural Wisdom

Knowledge is passed down through generations, validated and remembered by the community, maintaining a living connection to ancestors. This is an ongoing cyclical movement of time, where we – those in the present – are at the same time regarded as ancestors of the future; ancestors of the past are seen as stakeholders of the present. This keeps ancestral knowledge and traditions relevant and eternally new. Kenny and Fraser (2012, p. 3) note *we look to our ancestors as leaders* and they *guide us with deep respect for what they themselves have left behind. They communicate with us through dreams, through the teachings that have come down through the generations, through spirit.*

The rich, vast and varied *knowledge codes* (Spiller et al., 2020) transmitted in Indigenous communities around the world have been tested through the millennia in intimate relationship with direct experience of place. Knowledge codes are encapsulated through a plethora of mediums such as stories, parables, metaphor, symbol, the performing arts, ceremony and ritual (Intezari et al., 2020). Ceremony is a treasured, defining aspect of Indigenous life. Vision quests, sweat lodges, medicine wheel, dance, invocations and drumming are among the ways to cleanse, heal, celebrate, purify, honour and focus collective intention (Cajete, 2016). These codes orient leadership in communities, Kelly et al. (2014) explain how ancestral leadership is the translation and praxis of ancestral knowledge. Interlocking values systems, developed in intimate relationship with people and place, are endemic across Indigenous societies. For example, a study by Haar et al. (2019) surfaced five key values guiding Māori leaders: Whakaiti (humility); ko tau rourou and manaakitanga (altruism); tāria te wā and kaitiakitanga (time orientation and stewardship); whanaungatanga (collectivistic/relational orientation); and tikanga Māori (cultural authenticity).

Indigenous communities are the preserve of wayfinding traditions where for centuries cultures have read the signs in the world around them including the stars, sun and moon, the patterns formed by the winds on the oceans and sands, along with footprints and flight paths. Spiller et al. (2015) refer to Pacific leaders who read the stars, Australian Aboriginals who navigate the desert, Inuit who interpret the snow, Bedouin nomads who negotiate the sand dunes. Cajete (2000) and Kimmerer (2013) are among many Indigenous writers who highlight the impressively empirical, experiential and observation-based nature of Indigenous knowledge systems that accrues from one generation to the next.

In view of the dazzling heterogeneity of Indigenous societies, how leadership is formed and enacted is diverse and there is no 'one size fits all' approach. The Harvard Project on Native American Indian Economic Development (n.d.) studied Indigenous leadership and governance of American Indian tribes for 35 years, and its work points to the notion of 'cultural match'. It points out that one-size-fits-all policies are detrimental to native nations. Each society has developed its own ways of organising and governing itself including the pathways to leadership and exercise of power and authority, how wealth well-being outcomes are reached and distributed, what measures of success look like, how conflict is dealt with and so forth. For example, the Navajo Supreme Court is guided by traditional Navajo common-law and a traditional *peacemaker court* is available for conflict resolution. In Alaska, the village of Kake operates a peacemaking circle when sentencing minors. Black and Birmingham (2017, p. 126) note that the Cherokee have a women's council to make important decisions about *whether men were worthy of performing sacred duties, going to war, or holding public office*. Traditionally, while men are the Hodiyahnehsonh ('chiefly' leaders) in Iroquois or Haudenosaunee society, they are elected by women.

It ought to be noted that leaders within Indigenous communities are often referred to as 'chiefs'; however, some Indigenous scholars note that the term 'chief' is a European construct, devised so colonists could have a single point of negotiation (Black & Birmingham, 2017; Chamberlain et al., 2016). Black and Birmingham (2017) assert that while 'chief' persists today it is not a term traditionally used by clans – noting, in the Native American context, there are over 500 federally recognised tribes who are incredibly diverse, including geographically, linguistically, politically and culturally, that influence how leadership is enacted across a complex plethora of roles and responsibilities. Gladstone and Pepion (2016, p. 5) explain that in Blackfoot traditions, *a tribal chief was more a facilitator than a manager*, leading only with the mandate of the people. In Māori society the word *rangatira* captures the complexity of leadership as a collective endeavour – referring to weaving a group together where everyone is a thread in the textural whole and lends their own expertise and effort as situations and circumstances require (Spiller et al., 2020).

Activism, Resistance and Resilience

Indigenous leaders are forged in the fires of resistance, insistence and assertive action as they work at the frontline, interface, spaces in between and behind the scenes. In enterprises of all manner, they are navigating the forces of lore, commerce and culture. In community they are taking up warriorship against challenges such as addictions, despair, trauma, poor housing and economic hardship. Many are concerned about the loss of transmission between older and younger generations, urbanisation and drift, loss of language and culture. In the halls of power, they are battling hegemonic ideals of dominant societies that devastate ways of being, which impacts identity, purpose and meaning. Academics fight for voice and to dismantle structures that curtail freedom. Environmental degradation worries these societies. Chamberlain et al. (2016) chronicle the survival of Indigenous midwifery traditions amid various patriarchal regimes, including medicalisation and colonisation. The NDN collective is an Indigenous organisation committed to asserting Indigenous self-determination and power across Turtle Island. Pieratos et al. (2021, p. 53) note:

> Resistance and movement building are within our ancestral memory as Indigenous people, and our very survival is because of that historic resistance.

> Our survival today as culturally distinct Indigenous nations is still incumbent upon our commitment to ongoing resistance as colonized people fighting for justice and equity in our own lands.

As *paradigm warriors* Spiller et al. (2020, p. 522) capture the Indigenous ethos of leadership as those who see past the present-day reality to pursue the well-being of people and planet, even when faced with great resistance.

Case cameo: Standing Rock, USA

In cultural pockets all over the world Indigenous people are taking action – amassed, this is a formidable story of courage. A well-known case is the Dakota Access Pipeline, which carries a flow of oil across the Missouri River, a river entity that is of spiritual, cultural, environmental and economic significance to a number of Native American tribes, including Standing Rock Sioux whose reservation is less than a mile from the pipeline. The protest attracted peoples from all over the world, particularly from Indigenous nations who came to express solidarity and the stand against the pipeline. Standing Rock member Dave Archambault (2016) believes there was some 4,000 people on the camp, almost entirely Indigenous peoples from many different tribes.

Archambault, who was tribal chairman at the height of the protest, explains how he drew upon ceremony to galvanise people, create unity and replace despair with euphoria. He speaks to the ancestral wisdom that guided his leadership (Archambault, 2016):

> Sitting Bull is known for his famous quotes and his foresight, of being able to look out to the future [...] And if you look at the simple statements you can read into them. So, his spirit is still around and has always been around. If he says let's put our minds together and see what we can build for our children. That's the spirit that carries us forward.

The events and approach of Standing Rock Sioux inspired other Indigenous leaders, such as McLeod (as cited in Hect & McLeod, 2021, p. 77) who said that:

> When we went to Standing Rock, people seemed tuned into the idea that water is life, and water is sacred. That was coming from an Indigenous point of view, and I think that shift from protesting against something to praying for the protection of something was a real cultural moment. This happened because of Indigenous leadership.

LaDuke (2021, pp. 143–144) reminds people that advocating for Earth Justice is a leadership moment for everyone, not just a few who are willing to step into the fray:

> Standing Rock is not only a place, it is a state of mind, it is a thought, and it is an action […] For civil society is made, as democracy is made, by the hands of the people, and is not a spectator sport. While at one time slavery was legal, it is no longer, and soon we must free our Mother Earth from her slavery to an exploitative economy and ensure her rights […] As we saw at Standing Rock, unity, hope, a worldwide outpouring of love and support emboldens water protectors worldwide and that is something we will all need, along with our Mother. How that power is actualized is up to each of us, but acknowledging our responsibility for power is how we are accountable intergenerationally.

Sadly, the case cameos featured in this chapter only touch the surface of Indigenous leadership battles for spiritual and cultural recognition of natural ancestors. As well as Standing Rock, the Whanganui River and Kurtal, the Sápara of Ecuador are battling oil development in sacred territories. The Maasai in Tanzania, the Sengwer and Ogiek peoples in Kenya, the Biloxi-Chitimacha-Choctaw in Louisiana or the Inupiaq whaling community of Kivalina (Raygorodetsky, 2018), and many more, are seen and unseen protests. As the body of work in this chapter and far beyond it shows, Indigenous leadership is a phenomenal ongoing collective effort to improve the well-being of communities and ecologies.

INDIGENOUS ONTOLOGY AND EPISTEMOLOGY

Indigenous leadership rests on an ontological premise of relational cosmogenealogies. These genealogies tell the story of *woven universe* (Marsden, 2003) where nothing exists on its own: *we are all related, to the trees, soils, stars, seeds, and sacred sources of water and fire* (Hausdoerffer et al., 2021, p. 4). Yunkaporta (2019) emphasises that ours is not world comprised of *dead matter* as was *the ancient Greek mistake* and space as *lifeless and empty* but rather we inhabit a living, animated world that recognises, values and respects the sentiency in all things, including rocks.

Huambachano (2019) suggests that what connects Indigenous societies are shared practices of reciprocity between human and non-human entities, and the acknowledgement of the dynamic cyclical movement of life and energies. Cyclical thinking has no beginning and no end, with all cycles influencing each other. Yunkaporta (2019, p. 44) offers an exquisite explanation: *Creation time isn't a 'long, long ago' event, because creation is still unfolding now, and will continue to if we know how to know it.* Cyclical thinking recognises holism, multiple ways of knowing, appreciation of a process of unfolding, capacity to be with uncertainty, mystery and the unknown, and understanding the complex relationships between all things.

Another common thread across Indigenous worldviews is the paramountcy of energy, also thought of as spirit, emanating from a common centre, an originating coalescence of connectedness. It is in this central source that the potentiality of all things is held (Cajete, 2000; Peat, 1994; Spiller & Wolfgramm, 2015). In a Māori cosmogenealogy, it is Te Korekore where creation begins, and to which all eventually return.

i te kore, ki te pō, ki te ao mārama

out of nothingness, into the darkness, into the world of light

This maxim describes the perpetual journey of potential through and between Te Korekore – the void that is full of emptiness and possibilities – through Te Pō darkness – and into Te Ao Mārama – the world of life, light and enlightenment, the physical world in which we live. The life energies that are stirred within Te Korekore give life to landscapes and humans. These energies feed back into Te Korekore, binding all creative energy to this centre. Matua Pereme Porter (personal communication, September 2009) tells us that the task of the living is to reach into Te Korekore and release the potential within ourselves and interactions with others and circumstance to create more light in our world. It is the constant engagement with this realm beyond our senses that produces knowledge and wisdom (Nicholson, 2020). Te Ao Mārama is the world of making sense of what we know, the cyclical process of realising potential, in reflexivity with Te Korekore.

In this view, knowledge is a living energy, belonging to and derived from the cosmos and the landscape; and an Indigenous process of knowing draws on mind, body and spirit (Cajete, 2000; Meyer, 2008; Nicholson et al., 2015; Ruwhiu & Cone, 2010). In exploring Indigenous knowledges in the academy, Indigenous methodologies and philosophies illuminate the complexity and mystery of human leadership. For example, Dell (2021) talks about rongomātau, *feeling the knowing*, which acknowledges the emotionally absorbent being of the researcher – that is, that the researcher is not separate from the study. Spiller et al. discuss the concept of wānanga (Spiller et al., 2020). Wilson (2009) tells us that research is ceremony, a culmination of active participation and relationship-building that leads to an experience between people and their environment. Nicholson (2020) explicates Te Hihiri process, in which knowing is seen as a journey of experience and relationships. These methodologies highlight that when working within an Indigenous research paradigm, ontology, epistemology, methodology and axiology are interlocking components – that is, knowing is about being in relationships with place, centre and spirit.

DISCUSSION

A fundamental shift is required for many leaders to rehabilitate themselves and dwell within the world in sacred kinship. We can tackle our problems with the latest green technology, Western scientific approaches and treat problems as a vast experimentation project; however, we pour so much energy into focusing on fixing nature that we forget it is us who needs fixing. It is more making nature the problem not ourselves and acting upon the world, exerting our ideas of intervention. Nature knows how to heal; Māori have a word for this called rāhui – non-interference and giving time for ecosystems to heal themselves. Matua Rereata Makiha (personal communication, August 2017) explains that those who talk of restoring the mauri (life force) of things are not correct in their thinking, *Ehara koe i te atua* (*they do not have the spiritual power to do so*). What people are capable of doing is restoring the indicators of the life force, allowing the life force to flourish itself.

The case studies presented in this chapter highlight community, intergenerational leadership, a living cosmos of animated forces, a world where rivers, oceans and ecosystems are treated with respect as living entities, and the importance of taking responsibility for actions and impacts. The case studies also illuminate an ensouled, animated world filled with mystery, magic, miracles and meaning which, as Josephson-Storm (2017) has argued, curls its way in social and cultural circles even as it is swept under the carpet of 'organisation science'.

Indigenous worldviews make sense of human leadership through discussions of dynamic connections with the place and communities, sharing cosmogeneologies. These relationships are more than external factors of person; rather, the self emerges from a spiritual, ecological and socio-cultural interactions. As Spiller et al. (2011, p. 155) recite *I belong therefore I am, and so we become*. It is this interaction, the coming to being in relationship, the self-actualisation in relationship that is an ontological coalescence point which we believe begins with how we see ourselves in relationship with the world. To rehabilitate from the Cartesian split and waves of industrialisation, neo-liberal capitalism and globalisation, we encourage scholars, students and practitioners to do what Indigenous peoples have always done in the face of massive upheavals – be resilient and stay true to one another, move with wisdom, be protectors of Earth's life systems. Uphold reciprocity, stewardship, community and kinship values. The four dimensions presented above provide some insight; however, of course, there is nothing like learning, experiencing and partnering in actual relationship.

The Indigenous worldview is often at odds to Western standards that dominate scientific, educational and business discourse. Yet this dichotomy is also disputed by Indigenous and Western scholars alike (Bohm & Peat, 1987; Cajete, 2000; Hikuroa 2017; Marsden, 2003; Swimme & Berry, 1992). What Cajete (2000) calls *native science*, Royal (2009) terms *indigeneity* and Peat (1994) sees as *Indigenous science* are all references to Indigenous ancestral wisdom, and the experiential process of knowledge creation. As stated earlier, Indigenous ontologies are neither static nor fixated on finding the 'one' truth; therefore new knowledge that complements ancestral wisdom can be embraced. However, it has also been noted that it is not the role of those espousing Indigenous knowledges to validate these against Western concepts. Yet, mindful of warnings about using the tools of Western science to analyse and understand the foundations of Indigenous knowledge, or vice versa (e.g., Hikuroa, 2017), we detect some interesting connections at the interface of knowledge systems. In particular we turn to complex adaptive systems theory and relational quantum physics to develop our concept of leadership as a conscious adaptive system.

One approach to forge such connections may be in the literature that links leadership to complex adaptive systems (CAS). CAS are *aggregates of interacting subunits, or agents, which together produce complex and adaptive behavior patterns* (Boal & Schultz, 2007, p. 413). Lichtenstein et al. (2006, p. 2) link leadership to CAS, seeing leadership *an emergent event, an outcome of relational interactions among agents*. They explain that the complex dynamic process of leadership is a culmination of relational sense-making, that evolves from the *spaces between* people. Similarly, Boal and Schultz (2007, p. 411) talk of the emergence of self-organising systems and innovative behaviours from the interaction between agents at the *edge of chaos* who operate in the space between equilibrium and randomness, solidarity and chaos.

Indigenous knowledges often refer to these *spaces between*, the liminal threshold between light and dark, Earth and Sky, spiritual and cognitive, potential and being. In Māori thought, this space is referred to as wheiao (Barlow, 1991; Hēnare, 2015) or the pae (Salmond, 2017), the horizon or transitional state that connects all things and provides a way of linking past to present, ancestors gone and children to come. *The pae is a volatile, emergent space, now and then flashing out insights that create new kinds of order* (Salmond, 2017, p. 3). Ancient cosmogenealogies talk of chaos and creativity as generative forces that bring forth the universe (Cajete, 2000), as can be seen in the Māori creation story that begins and ends in Te Korekore.

However, while theoretical kinship can be found with complex adaptive systems, along with social-ecological systems theory (Berkes et al., 2008) and chaos theory (Boal & Schultz, 2007), in our view they lack explicit attention to consciousness, and spiritual and sacred kinships. These theories tend to treat people and energies as 'agents', 'variables' and 'aggregations', thus creating an indelible scientific, dispassionate, objectivising and disconnecting narrative. Indigenous wisdom, however, promotes creative participation and reciprocal experience with the surrounding environments.

We see glimmers of a partial root ontology that moves away from the mechanistic, atomised and disconnected through Rovelli's (2021) relational quantum theory. Rovelli makes the point that we need to stop talking about observation and observables, and begin to talk about interaction and relations. Relational quantum theory requires a relational way of viewing whereby properties are interpreted as things that come into interaction with something else. Economy, psychology, biology, he says, are all about relations. Agents are defined by the way they interact. This is in terms of not only physics, but also how societies work. This accords with the Indigenous *woven universe* wherein nothing exists on its own. Even though, as Rovelli (2021) laments, from his scientific perspective, that *this interconnection between all the components of the universe is disconcerting* (p. 93) wherein *even time exists only as a set of relations* (p. 147).

The convergence of ideas between the paradigms of relational quantum theory and Indigenous wisdom holds promise. The Indigenous wisdom traditions that embrace time as a perpetual present, interconnectedness and sacred kinship between all things seem entirely obvious (and comforting). In an Indigenous way of thinking, day and night, past and future, thought and feeling, mind and heart are not seen as binary pairs, but understood as a web of relationships. As Meyer (2008, p. 229) explains *The world is more than dual. It is whole.* Yunkaporta (2019, p. 91) puts this well when he says *people today will mostly focus on the points of connection, the nodes of interest like stars in the sky. But the real understanding comes in the spaces in between, the relational forces that connect and move the points.*

It is this liminal space of endless potential that we can imagine how Indigenous ontology can advance leadership conceptually and in practice. The strength of Indigenous leadership as we present it in this chapter is to recognise the spiritual dimension as fundamental to human experience. The knowledge codes passed down through cosmogenealogies, ceremonies and stories as outlined in this chapter present a leadership paradigm that is rooted in intimate relationships and experiential processes. It is the intangible spaces in between, emanating from the central void, that hold a plenitude of possibility that can be consciously and intentionally used to drive change and transformation. Energy is seen as creative, and a fundamental substance of the universe. Occurring in the higher realm of the *metaphoric mind* (Cajete, 2000), Indigenous thought accesses a spiritual dimension of time and potent space in which creative energies are available for humans to harness, consciously bringing potential into being. Through collaborative dialogues with the spiritual, natural and social communities, leaders can become 'in-sync' with a wider purpose and collective will. Thus, notions of emergence, adaptation and relational interactions resonate with Indigenous outlooks. More than a step-by-step guide on how to 'do' leadership, Indigenous knowledge codes urge us to 'sense' leadership: to see, to listen and to feel.

Leadership, as a conscious adaptive system, is thus part of this holistic, spiritually aware flow of creative energies in which human sense-breaking and sense-making takes place and wherein important actions are taken and decisions are made.

Acknowledgements: We thank the reviewers for their comments in strengthening this manuscript. We are especially grateful to Michelle Evans and Joseph Scott Gladstone for reviewing this work from their respective Indigenous perspectives.

REFERENCES

Archambault, D. (2016). *Interview Dave Archambault, APTN NationtoNation.* 25 November. https://www.youtube.com/watch?v=1rZoiwE5rqQ

Barlow, C. (1991). *Tikanga whakaaro: Key Concepts in Maori Culture*. Oxford University Press.

Berkes, F., Colding, J., & Folke, C. (2008). *Navigating Social-Ecological Systems: Building Resilience for Complexity and Change*. Cambridge University Press.

Black, S. L., & Birmingham, C. (2017). American Indian leadership practices. In D. M. Kennedy, C. F. Harrington, A. K. Verbos, D. Stewart, J. S. Gladstone & G. Clarkson (Eds.), *American Indian Business: Principles and Practices* (pp. 123–139). University of Washington Press.

Boal, K. B., & Schultz, P. L. (2007). Storytelling, Time, and Evolution: The Role of Strategic Leadership in Complex Adaptive Systems. *The Leadership Quarterly*, 18(4), 411–428.

Bohm, D., & Peat, D. (1987). *Science, Order, and Creativity*. Bantam Books.

Cajete, G. (2000). *Native Science: Natural Laws of Interdependence*.: Clear Light.

Cajete, G. (2016). Indigenous education and the development of indigenous community leaders. *Leadership*, 12, 364–376. doi: 10.1177/1742715015610412

Chamberlain, C., Fergie, D., Sinclair, A., & Asmar, C. (2016). Traditional midwifery or 'wise women' models of leadership: Learning from Indigenous cultures. *Leadership*, 12(3), 346–363.

Dell, K. (2021). Rongomātau–'sensing the knowing': An Indigenous Methodology Utilising Sensed Knowledge From the Researcher. *International Journal of Qualitative Methods*, 20, 16094069211062411

Dell, K., Staniland, N., & Nicholson, A. (2018). Economy of Mana: Where to next? *MAI Journal: A New Zealand Journal of Indigenous Scholarship*, 7(1), 1–15. doi:10.20507/MAIJournal.2018.7.1.5

Documentary Educational Resources (n.d.). *Kurtal: Snake Spirit*. https://store.der.org/kurtal-p721.aspx

Evans, M., & Sinclair, A. (2016). Containing, contesting, creating spaces: Leadership and cultural identity work among Australian Indigenous arts leaders. *Leadership*, 12(3), 270–292.

Folke, C. (2006). Resilience: The emergence of a perspective for social-ecological systems analyses. *Global Environmental Change*, 16(3), 253–267.

Gambrell, K. M. (2016). Lakota women leaders: Getting things done quietly. *Leadership*, 12(3), 293–307.

Gladstone, J. S., & Pepion, D. D. (2016). Exploring traditional indigenous leadership concepts: – spiritual foundation for Blackfeet leadership. *Leadership*, 13, 571–589. doi: 10.1177/1742715016638913

Gram-Hanssen, I. (2021). Individual and collective leadership for deliberate transformations: Insights from Indigenous leadership. *Leadership*, 1742715021996486.

Haar, J., Roche, M., & Brougham, D. (2019). Indigenous insights into ethical leadership: A study of Māori leaders. *Journal of Business Ethics*, 160(3), 621–640. doi: 10.1007/s10551-018-3869-3

Harvard Project on American Indian Economic Development (n.d.). Determinants of Development Success in the Native Nations of the United States*: An Introduction to the Research Findings of the Harvard Project on American Indian Economic Development*. http://nni.arizona.edu/application/files/9614/7940/9640/FINAL_2008_Five-Pager_English.pdf

Hausdoerffer, J., Hecht, B. P., Nelson, M. K., & Cummings, K. K. (Eds.) (2021). *What Kind of Ancestor Do You Want to Be?* University of Chicago Press.

Hecht, B. P., & McLeod, C. (2021). Interview: Caleen Sisk. In J. Hausdoerffer, B. P. Hecht, M. K. Nelson & K. K. Cummings (Eds.), *What Kind of Ancestor Do You Want to Be?* (pp. 73–83). University of Chicago Press.

Hēnare, M. (2015). Tapu, mana, mauri, hau, wairua. In C. Spiller & R. Wolfgramm (Eds.), *Indigenous Spiritualities at Work: Transforming the Spirit of Enterprise*. Information Age.

Henry, E., & Wolfgramm, R. (2018). Relational leadership: An indigenous Māori perspective. *Leadership*, 14, 203–219. doi: 10.1177/1742715015616282

Hikuroa, D. (2017). Mātauranga Māori: The ūkaipō of knowledge in New Zealand. *Journal of the Royal Society of New Zealand*, 47(1), 5–10.

Hollingsworth, J. (2020). *This River in New Zealand is Legally a Person. Here's How it Happened*. https://edition.cnn.com/2020/12/11/asia/whanganui-river-new-zealand-intl-hnk-dst/index.html

Huambachano, M. (2015). The Ayni principle. In C. Spiller & R. Wolfgramm (Eds.), *Indigenous Spiritualities at Work: Transforming the Spirit of Enterprise*. Information Age.

Huambachano, M. (2019). Traditional ecological knowledge and Indigenous foodways in the Andes of Peru. *Review of International American Studies*, 12(1), 87–110. doi: 10.31261/rias.6866

Intezari, A., Spiller, C. & Yang, S. (2020). *Practical Wisdom, Leadership and Culture: Indigenous, Asian and Middle-Eastern Perspectives*. Routledge.

Josephson-Storm, J. A. (2017). *The Myth of Disenchantment: Magic, Modernity, and the Birth of the Human Sciences*. University of Chicago Press.

Kelly, D., Jackson, B., & Hēnare, M. (2014). 'He āpiti hono, he tātai hono': Ancestral leadership, cyclical learning and the eternal continuity of leadership. In F. Khan, R. Westwood & G. Jack (Eds.), *Core-Periphery Relations and Organisation Studies*. Palgrave Macmillan.

Kelly, D., & Nicholson, A. (2021). Ancestral leadership: Place-based intergenerational leadership. *Leadership*, 18(1), 140–161. doi: 10.1177/17427150211024038

Kenny, C., & Fraser, T. N. (Eds.) (2012). *Living Indigenous Leadership: Native Narratives on Building Strong Communities*. UBC Press.

Kimmerer, R. (2013). *Braiding Sweetgrass: Indigenous Wisdom, Scientific Knowledge and the Teachings of Plants*. Milkweed Editions.

LaDuke, W. (1999). *All Our Relations: Native Struggles for Land and Life*. South End Press.

LaDuke, W. (2021). Essays: How to be better ancestors. In J. Hausdoerffer, B. P. Hecht, M. K. Nelson & K. K. Cummings (Eds.), *In What Kind of Ancestor Do You Want to Be?* (pp. 142–144). University of Chicago Press.

Lichtenstein, B. B., Uhl-Bien, M., Marion, R., Seers, A., Orton, J. D., & Schreiber, C. (2006). Complexity leadership theory: An interactive perspective on leading in complex adaptive systems. *Management Department Faculty Publications*. 8. https://digitalcommons.unl.edu/managementfacpub/8

Loeffler, J. (2021). Essays: Restoring Indigenous mindfulness within the commons of human consciousness. In J. Hausdoerffer, B. P. Hecht, M. K. Nelson & K. K. Cummings (Eds.), *In What Kind of Ancestor Do You Want to Be?* (pp. 130–137). University of Chicago Press.

Ma, N. (2015). *Putuparri and the Rainmakers*. Documentary film produced by Nicole Ma, John Moore, Australia.

Maracle, S., Bergier, A., Anderson, K., & Neepin, R. (2020). 'The work of a leader is to carry the bones of the people': Exploring female-led articulation of Indigenous knowledge in an urban setting. *AlterNative: An International Journal of Indigenous Peoples*, 16(4), 281–289.

Marsden, M. (2003). *The Woven Universe: Selected Writings of Rev. Māori Marsden*. Otaki, New Zealand: Estate of Rev. Māori Marsden.

Meyer, M. A. (2008). Indigenous and authentic: Hawaiian epistemology and the triangulation of meaning. In N. Denzin, Y. Lincoln & L. Smith (Eds.), *Handbook of Critical and Indigenous Methodologies*. Sage. doi: 10.4135/9781483385686

Murton, B. (2012). Being in the place world: Toward a Māori 'geographical self'. *Journal of Cultural Geography*, 29(1), 87–104. doi: 10.1080/08873631.2012.655032

National Museum Australia (n.d.). *The Jila Men*. https://www.nma.gov.au/exhibitions/yiwarra-kuju-canning-stock-route/artworks/the-jila-man

New Zealand Parliament (2017). *Innovative bill protects Whanganui River with legal personhood*. 28 March. https://www.parliament.nz/en/get-involved/features/innovative-bill-protects-whanganui-river-with-legal-personhood/

Nicholson, A. (2020). Te Hihiri: A process of coming to know. *Mai Journal*, 9(2), 133–142.

Nicholson, A., Spiller, C., & Hēnare, M. A. (2015). Arohia te rangi o te hihiri: Heeding the melody of pure and potent energy. In C. Spiller & R. Wolfgramm (Eds.), *Indigenous Spiritualities at Work: Transforming the Spirit of Enterprise* (pp. 273–298). Information Age.

Nicholson, A., Spiller, C., & Pio, E. (2017). Ambicultural governance: Harmonizing Indigenous and Western approaches. *Journal of Management Inquiry*, 1–17. doi:10.1177/1056492617707052

Panelli, R., & Tipa, G. (2007). Placing well-being: A Māori case study of cultural and environmental specificity. *EcoHealth*, 4(4), 445–460.

Peat, F. D. (1994). *Blackfoot Physics: A Journey into the Native American Universe*. Fourth Estate.

Pieratos, N. A., Manning, S. S., & Tilsen, N. (2021). Land back: A meta narrative to help indigenous people show up as movement leaders. *Leadership*, 17(1), 47–61.

Raygorodetsky, G. (2018). Indigenous peoples defend Earth's biodiversity: But they're in danger. *National Geographic*, 16 November. https://www.nationalgeographic.com/environment/article/can-indigenous-land-stewardship-protect-biodiversity-

Rovelli, C. (2021). *Helgoland: Making Sense of the Quantum Revolution*. Trans. Erica Segre and Simon Carnell. Riverhead.

Royal, C. (2009). *Mātauranga Māori: An introduction* [Lecture 1]. Macmillan Brown Lecture Series, 16 September. Macmillan Brown Centre for Pacific Studies, University of Canterbury.

Ruwhiu, D., & Cone, M. (2010). Advancing a pragmatist epistemology in organisational research. *Qualitative Research in Organizations and Management: An International Journal*, 5(2), 108–126. doi: 10.1108/17465641011068884

Ruwhiu, D., & Elkin, G. (2016). Converging pathways of contemporary leadership: In the footsteps of Māori and servant leadership. *Leadership*, 12, 308–323. doi: 10.1177/1742715015626326

Salmond, A. (2017). *Tears of Rangi: Experiments Across Worlds*. Auckland University Press.

Spiller, C. (2021). 'I AM': Indigenous consciousness for authenticity and leadership. *Leadership*, 17(4). doi: 10.1177/1742715021999590

Spiller, C., Barclay-Kerr, H., & Panoho, J. (2015). *Wayfinding Leadership: Ground-Breaking Wisdom for Developing Leaders*. Huia.

Spiller, C., Erakovic, L., Henare, M., & Pio, E. (2011). Relational well-being and wealth: Māori businesses and an ethic of care. *Journal of Business Ethics*, 98(1), 153–169.

Spiller, C., Maunganui Wolfgramm, R., Henry, E., & Pouwhare, R. (2020). Paradigm warriors: Advancing a radical ecosystems view of collective leadership from an Indigenous Māori perspective. *Human Relations*, 73(4), 516–543.

Spiller, C., & Wolfgramm, R. (Eds.) (2015). *Indigenous Spiritualities at Work: Transforming the Spirit of Business Enterprise*. Information Age.

Swimme, B., & Berry, T. (1992). *The Universe Story: From the Primordial Flaring Forth to the Ecozoic Era: A Celebration of the Unfolding of the Cosmos*. Harper Collins.

Todd, Z. (2016). An indigenous feminist's take on the ontological turn: 'Ontology' is just another word for colonialism. *Journal of Historical Sociology*, 29, 4–22. doi: 10.1111/johs.12124

UN Permanent Forum on Indigenous Issues (n.d.). Who are indigenous peoples? Factsheet. https://www.un.org/esa/socdev/unpfii/documents/5session_factsheet1.pdf

Verbos, A. K., & Humphries, M. (2014). A Native American relational ethic: An indigenous perspective on teaching human responsibility. *Journal of Business Ethics*, *123*(1), 1–9.

Walker, R. (1990/2004). *Ka whawhai tonu mātou: Struggle Without End* (Rev. edn). Penguin.

Wilson, S. (2009). *Research is Ceremony: Indigenous Research Methods*. Fernwood.

World Bank (2021). *Indigenous Peoples*. https://www.worldbank.org/en/topic/indigenouspeoples

Yunkaporta, T. (2019). *Sand Talk: How Indigenous Thinking Can Save the World*. Text.

26

Leadership through History: Rethinking the Present and Future of Leadership via a Critical Appreciation of its Past

Suze Wilson

INTRODUCTION

This chapter explores what the discipline of history and an historical sensibility can contribute to efforts to understand leadership. The concept of an historical sensibility is explained and key issues of historiography guiding how historians engage with the past and motivating their attention to matters that otherwise may be overlooked in efforts to study leadership are examined. Key features of Foucault's 'critical historical' approach are explained and then deployed, illustrating that the search for the 'essence' of leadership has a long and troubling history suggesting present-day efforts in this same vein thus warrant greater scrutiny. Barriers to, and opportunities for, deploying an historical lens are discussed. Overall, the chapter aims to explain and illustrate how history, and an historical sensibility, offers fertile opportunities through which we can think differently about the past, present and future of leadership.

Although this chapter's main title is 'leadership *through* history', this is not a history *of* leadership from times past. Rather, the aim here is to examine how both knowledge of the past and engagement with the kinds of questions and issues that historians address gives rise to insights *through* which we can better understand leadership. The chapter therefore explores how history and an historical sensibility can assist in developing a rich and broad perspective on the emergence, character, significance and effects of both past and present-day leadership theory and practice.

That history has relevance to building knowledge about leadership is not a novel idea. There are, after all, thousands of history books which focus heavily on the actions and character of leaders and their followers. As Gutmann puts it, history has value to leadership scholars and practitioners alike because *when looking for leadership insights, a real case is a good place to start* (2020a, p. 3). Harter goes further, arguing that *nowhere else do we encounter such an array of empirical examples* (2015, p. 39) as can be found in history. However, as an approach to carrying out research historical analysis stands in stark contrast to the hypothetical-deductive empirical studies focused on tightly defined constructs which these days tend to dominate leadership studies (Alvesson, 1996, 2017, 2019). Their strength lies in generating knowledge characterised by precision abstracted from context. But history's strength lies in helping us to develop a contextually rich breadth of perspective from which broad patterns shaping events and new or recurring trends can be more readily grasped, insights which may be especially useful in times when wicked

(Grint, 2010), adaptive (Heifetz, 1994; Heifetz & Linsky, 2017) problems have come to play such a central role in our existence.

As well as exploring core elements of how history is conventionally undertaken, through an illustrative *critical* historical analysis of efforts to determine the essence of leadership the chapter aims to demonstrate the value of such analyses in rethinking the past, present and future focus, shape, nature or direction of leadership theory and practice. This alternative way of engaging in analysis of the past and, simultaneously, the present, is informed by the work of philosopher Michel Foucault, who said of his scholarly endeavours: *The object was to learn to what extent the effort to think one's own history can free thought from what it silently thinks, and so enable it to think differently* (Foucault, 1985, p. 9). As a consequence, a Foucauldian lens treats as problematic commonplace assumptions that developments in our understanding of leadership via the use of scientific methods somehow inexorably bring us closer to 'the truth', or that newer leadership knowledge is somehow inevitably 'superior' to that of the past, be that in terms of accuracy, depth, breadth, sophistication or its moral standpoint. Through critically examining the history of efforts to locate the essence of leadership in some attribute of leaders, whether that be conceived as a divine gift, a trait or, more recently, a genetic marker or neurological characteristic, the chapter seeks to illustrate how doing so can enhance our capacity to *think differently* about the present state of play and prompt reflection about how we each might choose to contribute to leadership's future.

The chapter proceeds as follows. First, I introduce the concept of an historical sensibility and then discuss some selected key issues of historiography that inform how historians typically go about their work. I next turn to explain some key ideas in Michel Foucault's *critical history* approach, which is rooted in different concepts and questions from those used in more conventional historiography. One of its key aims is to help us *grasp the history of the present* (Foucault, 1977, p. 31), meaning the typically unacknowledged and unappreciated influence of times past on present-day understandings and practices. Using this approach, I then examine some critical junctures in the history of the search for the essence of leadership, illustrating how Foucauldian-inspired analyses can prompt opportunities to *think differently* about the past, present and future of leadership. The final section explores both barriers to and opportunities for the greater use of history as a means through which we can build our understanding of leadership.

INTRODUCING AN HISTORICAL SENSIBILITY AND SOME BASIC HISTORIOGRAPHIC CONSIDERATIONS

A foundational concept for what this chapter argues is that of an historical sensibility. By way of introductory comments, by this I mean the effort to grasp and place all manner of human thought and activity within its wider context, both chronologically and in relation to the social, political, cultural, economic, technological, organisational and intellectual milieu in which it takes place. Clearly a knowledge of history informs this sensibility; however, it is also not reducible to the mere possession of facts about the past. We need not become professionally trained historians to foster this sensibility within us: even a rudimentary grasp of how historians 'do history' helps focus our minds on different questions than might otherwise arise. More fundamentally, this sensibility is akin to an attitude, habit of mind or orientation motivating us to seek to understand 'why this particular idea, event, behaviour or practice, in this particular place, at this particular time'.

This effort to place matters in context helps foster a heightened appreciation and wide-angled grasp of their significance, enabling a richer set of insights as to their meaning, character, value and impact to be developed. It involves being attentive to a wide set of connections and influencing factors that shape the phenomena of focal interest, or which it shapes. It also enables us to de-essentialise ideas about leadership or leadership practices, meaning such matters are no longer presumed fixed or predetermined due to being rooted in 'nature', and to instead seek to locate them in their specific, bounded, historical setting. This anti-essentialist stance constitutes a counterpoint to those (many) leadership studies rooted in the ontological assumption that there exists some 'natural' and enduring truth about leadership, just waiting to be discovered (Alvesson, 1996; Collinson, 2011; Wilson, 2016).

This sensibility also comprises an anti-reductionist standpoint, a refusal to consider things in isolation of wider influences (Wren, 2011). Consequently, another part of its significance and value for leadership scholars is that an historical sensibility acts as a counterweight to the narrow focusing in on a few tightly specified variables, aiming for generalisable, context-free knowledge, typically underpinned by essentialist assumptions, which shape and govern many leadership studies today (Alvesson, 1996, 2019; Collinson, 2011; Wilson, 2016). This is not to say such work has no place or value. Rather my contention is that such efforts need to be both complemented and challenged by work that situates leadership in context – or, in other words, that we would be well served if an historical sensibility (and the grasp of history which that implies) was, as a matter of routine, paid greater heed when we attempt to understand leadership. As the chapter progresses, it continuously elaborates with greater specificity the kinds of considerations informing an historical sensibility and the kinds of questions it demands that we ask.

Having introduced this foundational concept, I now turn to explore *how* historical analysis is undertaken, informed by some basic historiographic considerations. 'Historiography' is the term used to refer to matters concerning how historical research ought to be undertaken and accounts of the past formulated.

Ongoing debate exists among historians about the purpose, role and function of historical research and how it should be undertaken and presented (Gaddis, 2002; Iggers, 2005). Accordingly, there are historians wedded to conventional scientific ambitions of creating 'objective' accounts of the past, some use social science theories to frame their analysis, while others adopt postmodern perspectives, disavowing grand narratives and demanding a reflexive sensitivity to the unavoidable interpretive choices made in formulating an historical account (Iggers, 2005). The same kinds of paradigmatic differences and debates, then, about how to understand social reality and generate credible knowledge about it which have shaped many other disciplines are also to be found among historians. Given these varying perspectives, what constitutes an historical lens (i.e., historical analysis and an historical sensibility) and what one might focus on when conducting historical analysis comprises a broad and diverse church.

While a diversity of perspectives exist about the 'how to' of historical analysis, there are also some concerns that historians of various stripes generally accept are important to bear in mind when it comes to interrogating the past. Assessing the credibility of archival source material and weighing up how that is to be interpreted are fundamental empirical concerns (Gaddis, 2002). Another basic concern is to limit the influence of 'presentism', wherein the past is interpreted by reference to present-day knowledge or perspectives unavailable to those whose time and place is being analysed (Spoerhase, 2008). To counter this, the aim is instead to understand events and individuals according to their historical context – to engage with the past on its own terms as much as is possible, in other words, rather than adjudging it through a contemporary lens.

According to Wren (2011) there are five key elements typically involved in historical analysis: change, causation, context, characters and connections. These *five Cs* inform the focus of historical analysis and attention to them is also pertinent to developing an historical sensibility (Wren, 2011, p. 68). Linked to this, he advocates that an historical lens itself brings a sixth *C* – that of an appreciation for complexity (p. 80) – which he contends is especially useful when it comes to understanding leadership, a point which complexity leadership scholars (e.g., Uhl-Bien & Arena, 2017) would likely endorse.

Working through each of these *five Cs*, analysis of *change* involves identifying trends, key events and developments over time. This in turn, aids in clarifying what has remained stable, which is also important to be mindful of. The focus on *causation* helps identify why changes have arisen and will typically consider multiple contributing factors, thus eschewing a reductionist stance. Analysis of matters of *context* – influences such as economic and political systems and conditions, demographic factors, cultural norms and the intellectual milieu – situates the issues of change and causation within their wider setting, helping to build a broad perspective of how and why things occurred as they did. The element of *characters* pertains to individuals or groups present in the time and place being examined, generating insights into matters such as their actions, intentions, life history, values or personality. The analysis of *connections* involves drawing together the four other elements and seeking to identify an overall pattern or patterns to the situation under consideration. The resultant effort to characterise the significance or meaning of events in an insightful way that acknowledges this diverse range of factors brings the final *C* of *complexity* into play.

All this involves collating, sifting, weighing up and interpreting empirical source material and the formation of a narrative that seeks to make sense of what happened in the past. Combined, these *six Cs* help reveal multiple influences leading to and arising from what did happen, as well as how other possible courses of action could have arisen: indeterminacy, complexity, interdependency and the long-run consequences of the choices made are therefore matters which an historical lens can help us to appreciate. These kinds of insights help to overcome tendencies to essentialise or naturalise leadership's form, function and effects or to generate bite-sized chunks of knowledge removed from their wider context. Instead, historical variability and the influence of contextual factors in what has been constituted as leadership in different times and places becomes evident, giving us a broader appreciation of its character, significance, causes and effects.

In sum, an historical sensibility motivates us to place leadership theory or practice in context, seeking to understand why it arises in particular ways at particular times and places. The discipline of history, meanwhile, is a broad church, paradigmatically speaking, affording researchers options that accommodate a variety of underpinning ontological, epistemological and axiological positions. Careful attention to the credibility and interpretation of source material, along with the effort to engage with the past on its own terms, are foundational considerations in generating credible analyses. Questions about the *six Cs* of change – causation, context, characters, connections and complexity – constitute the focal elements of much historical analysis, and aid in forming an historical sensibility. These historiographic considerations thus help to explain *how* to go about enhancing our understanding of leadership through history.

INTRODUCING FOUCAULT'S CRITICAL HISTORY PERSPECTIVE

The *critical historical* approach developed by Michel Foucault both extends and in some ways challenges the above understandings of how to undertake historical analysis by recourse to different concepts and through asking different questions. Here I will briefly highlight a few of his key ideas which guide the upcoming Foucauldian-inspired analysis of some aspects of the history of leadership thought.

As I noted earlier, Foucault turned to the past with the aim of uncovering what it is we *silently think*, in order that we might *think differently* (1985, p. 9). Accordingly, while he was deeply concerned to understand the past on its own terms, thereby avoiding the problem of presentism, his underlying purpose in so doing was to generate insights that would help call into question present-day understandings, most especially matters which are taken for granted as being normal, desirable, truthful or natural. Foucault considered common but problematic vanities of *we moderns* to be presumptions that today's world is more morally advanced than that of the past, that knowledge inexorably advances towards 'the truth' and that who we are today is therefore more enlightened and free than were our forebears (1978). All these beliefs Foucault seeks to challenge through looking to the past to reveal what he called *the history of the present* (1977, p. 31), meaning the often unacknowledged or hidden influences of the past on present-day understandings and practices.

A *strong* social constructionist orientation (Hacking, 1999) underpins Foucault's work, comprising efforts to reveal the historical and social situatedness and contingent character of what is claimed to be true, real and good, including about our very selves. This involves exploring what Foucault called *conditions of possibility*, contemporaneous factors rendering particular ideas credible or appealing at the time they emerged (1977, 1978). Conventional narratives where 'truth' is rooted in such matters in biology, fate, god, 'objective knowledge', 'progress', or some other essentialist or deterministic source are thus challenged by these considerations.

Foucault saw power, which he conceived of as a dynamic force with both repressive and enabling potentialities, as a motivating factor in all human endeavours and, hence, interwoven with all claims to knowledge (1980). Power is thus not limited to just formal authority, laws, rules or coercive force but, rather, is implicated in all relationships and all efforts to persuade others (or ourselves) as to what constitutes the truth, including practices derived from such truth claims. This means that in Foucauldian terms the analysis of knowledge is of necessity the analysis of power and vice versa, an understanding captured by his concept of *power/ knowledge* (1980).

Foucault's proposition is that social reality is brought into being by way of the discourses that shape our understanding of what is right, true and proper (1977, 1978). This ongoing construction of social reality includes the experience of what it is to be human, to have a sense of oneself and live one's life according to certain beliefs and adopt certain ways of living, and comes to take a particular form in a given time and place. Foucauldian analyses therefore trace the emergence and development of discourses over time, examining the nature and effects of their claims, all with a close eye as to matters of power implicated in those issues (1977, 1978). Of particular interest are expert discourses articulating prescribed and recommended ways of being human and through which processes of subjectivation – the ongoing effort of becoming and being a self – are mediated. A key element of Foucault's analysis of power, then, is that it is not simply an external, repressive force; as a consequence of whatever knowledge (and hence power) we come to accept as being truthful, we simultaneously discipline and empower ourselves according to its prescriptions, so as to be and become a certain kind of subject.

A FOUCAULDIAN-INSPIRED CRITICAL HISTORY: THE SEARCH FOR THE ESSENCE OF LEADERSHIP

Drawing on Foucault's insights, next I consider aspects of one influential strand of debate that can be found in the past and present of expert discourse about leadership, namely efforts to ground its existence in some kind of 'natural' capacity possessed by only a select few. This tradition of *essentialism* – meaning the attempt to locate leadership's essence in some attribute of leaders – has been identified as a common feature of many contemporary theories and is critiqued by those advocating a social constructionist foundation to leadership (Alvesson, 1996; Collinson, 2011; Grint, 1997). Here I consider some historical and contemporary claims of this nature so as to highlight more of the *history of the present* than is generally acknowledged or understood in such debates. The analysis considers the conditions of possibility for such claims, as well as their power/knowledge and subjectivating dynamics. While informed by Foucauldian concerns, the analysis also canvasses conventional historiographic considerations of change, causation, context, characters, connections and complexity (Wren, 2011). Its overall purpose is to illustrate how *through* an historical lens we can form a broader perspective on the past and present of leadership, using such insights to guide efforts to shape its future trajectories. The matters it examines are addressed in more detail in Wilson (2016).

The idea that some individuals are destined for leadership has a long but troubling history, in which such claims have repeatedly served elite, anti-democratic, authoritarian and/or patriarchal interests. In Classical-era Greece, Plato argued that God *added gold in the composition of those of you who are qualified to be Rulers* (Plato, 2007, 415a). Aristotle was just as direct, proposing that *from the hour of their birth, some are marked out for subjection, others for rule* (Aristotle, 2009, 1254a, 20). They were not alone, as a number of texts from this time and place combine to form this particular discourse (Wilson, 2016). According to its account of the truth leaders are exceptional, gifted individuals in innate possession of special characteristics and knowledge. They are expected to possess knowledge of, and make decisions about, a vast range of issues relating to the physical, economic, spiritual, moral, intellectual and cultural well-being of followers, whose own judgement was presumed fundamentally lacking. This knowledge base was to encompass such diverse issues as statecraft, warfare, crop management, seafaring, child-rearing technique and exercise regimes for pregnant women, among other matters. Overall, leaders were positioned in this discourse as a key force standing between order and chaos, morality and immorality, wisdom and foolishness, and without whose close supervision and direction followers would languish. In a society wracked by constant wars and where the state of science and technology offered little protection from natural forces, leadership was thus constituted as a foil against life's many difficulties.

Classical Greek scholarship relied on a combination of logical, metaphorical and analogous reasoning along with appeals to established mythological and religious beliefs, rather than empirical evidence, for its epistemological and methodological underpinnings. These factors provided the intellectual conditions of possibility for its account of leadership. This was brought into being by means of argumentation claiming to be concerned only with advancing the truth and goodness and eliminating falsehood and immorality. However, it was also an argument advanced by elites and which functioned to undermine the Athenian democracy: by asserting that most people innately lack the capacity for wise, ethical action and require a leader to make such decisions for them, the case for authoritarian rule was built (Wilson, 2016).

The subject of the leader constructed in this discourse was the most perfect of men, capable of overcoming all manner of challenges, driven only by a concern for the well-being of others and the pursuit of truth and morality. While the leader's powers were largely without limit, so too were the demands placed upon him: there was no scope for weakness, error or time off. To be such a leader was to know of oneself as a superior being, while others are weak, flawed and inadequate to contend with life's challenges. As a result, they need the leader to guide and direct them to follow the path he sets for them. Leaders here are constituted by an unshakeable self-confidence combined with the simultaneous suppression of personal desires, in order to fulfil their duty to others. As the leader comprises a role model for followers they are expected to conform themselves to his example as best as they can. The leader is tasked with making people better, to be as much like the leader as possible, hence leadership is constructed as an exercise in transformation akin to cloning. Many centuries later, proponents of transformational leadership would similarly claim that leadership success lies in transforming followers into leaders (Burns, 1978; Bass, 1985), replicating this cloning dynamic as the core impact of leadership (Wilson, 2016).

The notion that a chosen few are destined for leadership also found expression in medieval thought. A book genre known as 'mirrors for princes' – essentially the medieval equivalent of today's self-help guides and targeted directly at kings, princes and their key advisors – offers useful insights into the discourse on leadership at this time and place (see, for examples, Bodin, 2009; Calvin, 2010; Erasmus, 2010; James VI, 1950; Lipsius, 2004; Luther, 2010; Machiavelli, 2005). These texts upheld the so-called 'divine right of kings' to rule over others, reinforcing the institutionalised position that royalty were God's agents on earth, expressing his will through their actions.

In the 16th century, a range of factors combined to render princely leadership both more challenging and less certain than in prior centuries. The Reformation had the Christian church in turmoil, intensifying and complicating pre-existing dynastic tensions, territorial disputes and conflicts between church and state. The Renaissance saw long-established ideas and practices being questioned. Literacy rates and scientific knowledge grew rapidly, albeit the vast majority of the population remained highly vulnerable to crop failures, disease or warfare (Cameron, 2001). These developments all posed challenges for monarchical rule, hence scholars sought to articulate the virtues leaders needed to navigate such circumstances successfully.

A particular tension they grappled with was the realpolitik understanding that *those in the palace do not attain to the very first degree of mental and intellectual capacities* (Lipsius, 2004, p. 351) and that *a prudent prince has been a rare bird in the world since the beginning of time, and a just prince an even rarer bird* (Luther, 2010, p. 30). Yet at the same time, perhaps because it could be life-threatening to suggest otherwise, they also sought to portray princely leaders as *a sort of celestial creature, more like a divinity than a mortal, complete with every single virtue; born for the common good, sent indeed by the powers to alleviate the human condition by looking out and caring for everyone* (Erasmus, 2010, pp. 26–27). It appears the hope was that through setting out such ideals leaders might be motivated to live up to them.

As in the Classical Greece discourse, in 16th-century texts leaders were once again constituted as the most perfect of men, whom followers ought to obey due to their intrinsic and irremediable flaws. Virtues such as *integrity, prudence, clemency, moderation and innocence* (Calvin, 2010, p. 53), or *wisdom, a sense of justice, personal restraint, foresight, and concern for the public well being* (Erasmus, 2010, p. 5) were emphasised. A clear theme urging restraint by leaders when exercising their extensive powers is evident, meaning the discourse simultaneously functions both to legitimate and reinforce princely rule as natural, desirable and inevitable and, at the same time, to seek to tame its excesses. The explicit threat is that should a leader fail in their duties God's punishment will be more severe than for those less favoured by him, a claim clearly intended to motivate adherence to the prescribed virtues (Wilson, 2016).

A notable feature of this discourse, as with the Classical Greeks, is the wide range of knowledge and decision-making requirements it places on leaders, spanning practical, ethical/moral, secular and spiritual matters. They were expected to deal with strategic and tactical military issues, debates over Christian doctrine and all matters related to affairs of state. They required skills to detect flattery, solicit wise counsel and invoke both love and fear (Wilson, 2016). The subject of the leader constructed in this discourse is one who knows themselves to be an instrument of God's will, imbued with his divine grace and majesty, compelled to serve the greater good – and thus constantly needing to address all manner of secular and spiritual issues associated with the flourishing of the people and the State. For all that this is power without limitation, so too is it duty without end.

Moving forward in time again, modern efforts to create a scientific account of leadership really begin with Thomas Carlyle's 1840s lectures (1993), in which he analysed selected leaders through considering their biography and physiognomy (facial characteristics), style of speaking and sincerity of faith in God in order to determine their character. The empiricism in Carlyle's efforts mark him out as having a scientific rather than philosophical orientation, albeit that today the significance of his work is underestimated, largely because his 'science' is seen to be so profoundly flawed. As with earlier versions of the discourse on leadership, he too was an avowed advocate of the *naturalness* of inequality, the *morality* of obedience to those in authority and saw democratic forms of governance as dangerous. Decades later Hitler admired Carlyle's work and since the 1920s Carlyle has been understood as a proponent of *proto-fascist* thought (Goldberg, 1993). He is also the first leadership scholar of the modern age. This is our heritage, whether we like it or not.

In 1869 Francis Galton, influenced by the work of his more famous cousin Charles Darwin, sought to identify the inherited traits of those he saw as being men of *genius*. He examined factors such as race, place of birth, parental occupation, temperament, appearance, head size, perseverance, memory, impulsiveness and religious sensibilities (1892; 1970). Galton's influence on leadership studies is both substantive, inspiring a raft of subsequent trait studies (e.g. Cattell, 1906; Clarke, 1916; Ellis, 1904; Sorokin, 1925; Taussig & Joslyn, 1932; Thorndike, 1936; Visher, 1925) and methodological, being the first to use statistical modelling. Galton's core concern was to generate knowledge such that *it would be quite practicable to produce a highly-gifted race of men by judicious marriage during several consecutive generations* (1892, p. 45). Eugenic ambitions, including the racism that routinely implies (Gillham, 2001; Godin, 2007), are thus another disturbing feature of the history of modern efforts to ground the source of leadership in biological factors. Galton was an influential advocate within the eugenic movements, as were other leadership scholars at that time (Gillham, 2001; Godin, 2007). His influence was also long lasting: as late as 1932, for example, Taussig and Joslyn concluded that *natural inferiority* explained why labourer's sons were underrepresented among the ranks of America's business leaders, specifically citing Galton's work.

While Carlyle was, by Galton's time, discredited as lacking in scientific rigour, my own analysis nonetheless found considerable commonality between the characteristics he highlighted and those which trait scholars examined in the first half of the 20th century (Wilson, 2016). This lies not merely in the shared notion that leadership is the domain of the exceptional, gifted man: both also focused on matters that, at these times, were seen as desirable, gentlemanly, character attributes, thus infusing class- and gender-based social mores into their account of leadership. However, now absent from the discourse is the earlier concern to address the vast array of substantive issues that leaders needed to know so as to perform their duties. Now, rather than leadership scholars specifying the kinds of issues leaders needed to know about, as we saw when looking at ancient Greek and medieval era discourses, in modernity that substantive aspect of leadership practice disappears from focus. Instead, there is a distinctive narrowing of focus onto matters pertaining to who leaders are, rather than what issues leaders need to know about and make decisions on. Even through to the present day this psychologised orientation, this absence of attention to the substantive issues that leaders are expected to contend with, has become a marked feature of modern leadership studies. Where previously leadership scholars provided advice on how best to lead in respect of all manner of substantive issues, nowadays that role is largely limited to generic issues of leadership processes and behaviours.

In the post-World War II era Galton's influence, along with the connection between leadership studies and the eugenics movement, has been effaced from leadership textbooks, while Carlyle only occasionally attracts brief mention, usually absent any discussion of the political aspects of his thought. Northouse's influential *Leadership: Theory and Practice*, now in its ninth edition, for example, makes no mention of Galton in its discussion of trait studies. While Smith and Krueger's review of the field (1933) cited eugenicists Galton, Cattell and Ellis, Stogdill's influential review in 1948 did not. Indeed, convention now has it that inconsistent findings led to the turn away from the study of leader traits in the postwar era, something often credited to Stogdill's review (see, for example, Bass, 2008, Huczynski & Buchanan, 2006; Northouse, 2022). However, while Stogdill did argue both leader-related and situational factors deserved attention, he also reported a number of traits as having shown strong associations with leadership across multiple studies (1948). It is by no means clear, in other words, that the findings of Stogdill's famous review justify the turn away from traits and towards leader behaviours that occurred.

In fact, records show the Ohio State leadership studies where Stogdill worked had constructed a survey instrument comprising *nine dimensions or categories of leadership behaviour* as early as 1945 (Bowers & Seashore, 1966, p. 240). Stogdill's boss and project director, Carol Shartle, later acknowledged his prime interest was leader behaviour *from the outset* (1979). Given these moves precede Stogdill's review of the evidence – and that his review is far from being the definitive rebuttal of trait studies which it has since often been taken to be – what motivated this sudden turn away from traits and towards leader behaviour? My contention is that political considerations at the end of World War II rendered it untenable to sustain a focus on leader traits at that time. In the aftermath of the holocaust, the idea that leadership constituted a natural gift possessed only by a select few was just far too close in its underlying logic to that of the Nazi ideology of 'Aryan' supremacy. The turn to the leader behaviour, something presumed teachable and learnable rather than innate, provided a pragmatic way forward. And so it was that for some decades thereafter scholarly interest in locating the source of leadership in some natural capacity fell into almost complete abeyance (Wilson, 2016).

Recent years, however, have seen a resurgence in interest in the biological, neurological or evolutionary psychological foundations of leadership (see, for examples, Balthazard et al., 2012; Chaturvedi et al., 2012; King et al., 2009; Lee et al., 2012; Van Vugt & von Rueden, 2020). Among such efforts, in 2013 De Neve et al. reported their discovery of a particular *genetic marker*, named rs4950, which they found to have a *significant relationship* to *leadership role occupancy* (p. 46). In the centuries-long search for the essence of leadership, perhaps modern science had finally found the answer.

De Neve et al.'s study is, of course, but one example of a larger suite of mutually reinforcing efforts in recent years through which at least some elements of the field have circled back to its much earlier predilections of seeking to locate the essence of leadership in some particular attribute of leaders. This contemporary endeavour is rendered technically, politically and ethically possible via the wider normalisation in recent decades of deploying scientific knowledge to optimise the performative potential of our species and overcome adversities, such as diseases, which nature throws our way (Dean, 2010; Rose, 1990, 1996). Notably, many within the contemporary leadership studies community have strong commitments to the norms and methods of knowledge generation deployed in the natural sciences, seeing these as the template and gold standard for use when seeking the truth about leadership (Alvesson, 1996; Alvesson & Sveningsson, 2012; Antonakis et al., 2004). Where once leadership scholars turned to philosophy, history or literature, to an increasing extent the laboratory, along with its sophisticated mechanisms for detecting what the naked eye cannot see, now provides inspiration.

This scientific 'objectivism' now informs many within the field (Alvesson & Sveningsson, 2012). Meanwhile, the pervasive interest in optimising leaders' effectiveness also seen in leadership studies reflects and reinforces the core logic of what Foucault called *governmentality*, meaning efforts to *govern the conduct of conduct* by recourse to rationality and evidence (1991). This, he argued, enables the workings of power in ways that render its influence invisible yet pervasive, such that we come freely to subjectivate ourselves according to discourses of scientific truth. Accordingly, if through claims of engaging in science we come to declare with confidence to have discovered the biological foundations of leadership then, logically, this creates the potential – although this is by no means inevitable – to exclude from leadership roles on the grounds of 'scientific fact' those who lack the 'natural attributes' deemed necessary.

For a subject who comes to know themselves according to such claims, their right and duty to claim a leader identity and role would appear assured – much as it was in the medieval era when the 'divine right of kings' was accepted as the truth, or in Classical Greek times, when Aristotle and Plato argued some possessed a divine birthright to lead. These days, psychometric tests are already widely used in selection processes, so screening for genetic or neurological markers of leadership capacity could be argued as merely an extension of such methods. Perhaps as a consequence of such developments those lacking the desired attributes would also more readily accept their place in the scheme of things: a 'natural order' in which some are destined to lead and others to follow could yet emerge.

Our scholarly forebears – Plato, Aristotle, the medieval writers of 'mirrors for princes', and the likes of Carlyle and Galton – would likely be happy should this eventuate. Yet this recent resurgence of an interest in the biological foundations of leadership is rendered possible at least in part because too few understand the troubling history of such notions. These are propositions which have repeatedly in the past taken on raced, gendered, classed, anti-democratic and authoritarian characteristics. History's lesson is therefore that they require enormous caution as to their potential consequences. If that *history of the present* were better known perhaps these developments would be more thoroughly scrutinised.

BARRIERS TO AND OPPORTUNITIES FOR USING AN HISTORICAL LENS TO EXAMINE LEADERSHIP

Having illustrated what a critical historical lens can offer in terms of our understanding of the past, present and future of leadership, I now turn to explore some barriers that might deter leadership scholars from engaging with historical analysis, followed by consideration of the opportunities that such a lens offers.

There are a number of underlying beliefs or assumptions – matters that are often *silently thought* (Foucault, 1985, p. 9) – that I suggest may presently limit the use of an historical lens in the leadership studies field. Concerns about underlying assumptions and beliefs have often been the target of critically oriented leadership scholars, leading to the identification of leader-centrism, romanticism, entitism, essentialism, reductionism, white supremacism, elitism and sexism as commonplace features of leadership studies (see, for example, Alvesson, 1996, 2019, 2020; Alvesson & Sveningsson, 2012; Collinson, 2011; Gemmill & Oakley, 1992; Grint, 1999; Liu, 2020; Meindl et al., 1985; Sinclair, 2005, 2007; Tourish, 2013; Wilson, 2016). The scrutiny of often unstated assumptions offered here follows in this tradition, aiming in so doing to build the case for why greater engagement with historical analysis can enrich leadership studies. I examine three possible *silent* reservations that may impede the greater use of an historical lens in leadership research, theorising and practice.

The first is a belief that, empirically speaking, we live in a time of rapid, unprecedented change and, as a consequence, the past is simply of limited relevance to today's needs. It would, of course, be contrarian to dispute that change is not a significant feature of contemporary life. However, accepting this in no way diminishes the value an historical lens can offer – because other periods in the past have also encountered what was, at that time, 'unprecedented change'. In the 16th century, for example, major, disruptive change arose as a consequence of the Renaissance and the Reformation, unleashing fundamental shifts in how people understood reality, knowledge, God and the role of the Church and the State, with many consequences for the form, function and processes of leadership arising from this (Wilson, 2016). Accordingly, lessons exist in those experiences, such as how change arises and what consequences may flow out of different approaches to dealing with it that we would be foolish to ignore. If leadership scholars want to build their grasp of how change arises, especially given that leading to advance change is a central feature of transformational (Bass & Riggio, 2005), adaptive (Heifetz, 1994; Heifetz &Linksy, 2017) and complexity (Uhl-Bien & Arena, 2017) theories of leadership, just to name a few, then an historical lens offers many potential avenues for investigation.

Further, while accepting that change is a powerful feature of contemporary reality an historical lens helps in grasping that *many things* have nonetheless remained *relatively* stable, thereby affording us a more comprehensive grasp of reality which accounts for the co-existence of both change and relative stability. Important examples of relative stability that are of significance to leadership include that capitalism has been a key form of economic activity in many countries for several centuries and that most work organisations continue to use hierarchical distributions of power and authority: both these factors play an important role in shaping the nature and dynamics of leader–follower relationships in workplaces. Understanding of this matters for leadership research, theory and practice. Overall, only through adopting an historical lens can we grasp the long-run (Gaddis, 2002; Wren, 2011) nature of how changes arise, the effects of different ways of dealing with change and gain insight into what really is and is not changing.

A second belief that may influence what leadership researchers *silently think* is the idea that present-day concerns should take priority, because that is where we can make an impact. Yet here too, understanding the forces and events leading to our current situation, knowing the direction of influential trends, or learning how others in the past grappled with challenges bearing more than a passing similarity to our own can all enhance how we view current realities and offer ideas for how we might deal with them. The analysis offered earlier in this chapter, looking at past and present-day efforts to locate the essence of leadership in some attribute of leaders, illustrates how knowledge of the past can prompt us to rethink the present. As with the first concern, then, an historical lens can actually help in making sense of and dealing with current concerns, while the failure to consider such matters easily results in a distorted or limited grasp of current realities.

The third potential objection I suggest pertains to epistemological and/or methodological concerns for researchers: that one cannot study the dead with much accuracy, or, at least, with arguably less accuracy than one can study the living, hence we ought to focus our efforts on the living. It is of course true the dead cannot be interviewed, observed in action or fill in a questionnaire. However, while some degree of precision could be lost without the use of such methods, the dead allow us to more clearly grasp the longer-term consequences of their actions.

An example of this can be found in Amy Fraher's study of the fall of British rule in Singapore in December 1941. Despite an order from Churchill that the British Army facing the Japanese invading forces should fight *to the bitter end at all costs* (Fraher, 2020, p. 2) his generals in Singapore surrendered just five days later. Fraher's analysis of this historically significant incident affords us with multiple short- and longer-run implications and lessons including, for example, insights of relevance to multinational corporations today striving to contend with divisions between head office and regional operations.

Understanding the longitudinal effects of various ways of engaging in leadership is, frankly, a large gap in the field of leadership studies which history and an historical sensibility can help to address. Even for those that bring a temporal element to their analysis of leadership (e.g., Chreim, 2015), only rarely does that timeframe extend beyond a few months or years, likely due to the challenges involved in having extended periods of data gathering. The much greater time horizons that can be considered by recourse to an historical analysis thus offer an important and practicable means of generating insights into the longitudinal effects of leadership. Notably, these insights do not exclusively pertain to knowing what happened in the past but, rather, can be helpful for how we understand and approach contemporary challenges.

By surfacing here the assumptions and beliefs that may impede the use of an historical lens and subjecting them to critical review, hopefully the case for engagement with the past is made clearer and stronger. I now turn to offer some further ideas for how those interested to deploy an historical lens might proceed.

It is the case, of course, that there is a long history of using historiographic methods to examine leadership. Plutarch (AD 46–199) for example, wrote histories of 48 famous men, many of whom held leadership roles. Carlyle's 1840 *On Heroes, Hero Worship, and the Heroic in History*, the first modern-era leadership study, likewise deployed an historical lens as part of its analytic repertoire. Biographies of individual leaders are also a popular approach to doing history, albeit with generally little focus on theorising what such accounts can teach us about leadership. Still others, such as the Fraher study discussed above, deploy an historical lens in conjunction with other analytic methods or tools, aiming to draw out lessons of wider significance for leadership theory, research and practice. Other examples will be considered shortly.

As noted earlier, history as a discipline constitutes a broad church in which varying paradigmatic positions can be deployed. Overall, the potential range of issues to be explored and how one might go about doing this when undertaking historical research is therefore enormous. To give just a brief indication, researchers wanting to use an historical lens could examine matters such as are listed below, noting how these enable exploration of issues relating to one or more of the *six Cs* of change, causation, context, characters, connections and complexity (Wren, 2011):

- the different forms or styles of leadership that have arisen in various times and places in the past and the impacts of these;
- specific leaders or followers from the past, the nature of their roles, relationships and key behaviours, and the impacts of these matters;
- the different kinds of challenges leaders have faced in various times and places in the past, the strategies they used to address those challenges and the impacts of those;
- what was seen, and by whom, as constituting effective or ethical leadership in different times and places;
- how social, political, economic, legal, cultural, intellectual, technological or other systemic factors act to shape the kind of leadership that is possible and desirable in different times and places;
- developments in ways of conceptualising/theorising leadership over time and their connection with wider contextual influences;
- changes and continuities in ways of conceptualising/theorising leadership over time, in different places;
- similarities and differences in leadership across different times and places;
- what ideas about leadership have been 'lost' to history that were once influential (and which may yet have salience to present-day concerns).

Notably, this is far from being an exhaustive list of possibilities. Yet for all of the above topics there is enormous potential to research a particular time, place or people which has not yet been examined by leadership scholars. This scope for generating novel insights in a field where much recent work has been criticised for being trivial and dull (Tourish, 2015) means the time for an 'historical turn' in leadership studies is surely ripe.

Finally, I want to just briefly mention a few examples of work that illustrates the kinds of ideas explored in this chapter. An excellent place to look for inspiration would be work by Keith Grint. Deploying an historical lens to conduct case studies of leaders such as Henry Ford, Florence Nightingale, Richard Branson and Martin Luther King, Grint (1999) identifies how leadership involves the artful mastery of practices related to issues of identity, vision, tactics and persuasive communication. His examination of the D-Day landings analyses how this historically significant event illustrates the character of and differences and interdependencies between leadership, management and command as three modes of influencing collective effort (Grint, 2007). Other examples of work informed by an historical lens include Bert Spector's *Discourse on Leadership* (2016b) and my own *Thinking Differently about Leadership* (Wilson, 2016), both of which examine aspects of the history of leadership thought, guided also by varying approaches to discourse analysis. Gutmann (2020b) offers an edited collection of case studies of leadership in different times and places where a strategic challenge needed to be addressed which, being written by professional historians, exemplifies the kind of context-rich insights that historical analysis can offer. All these examples, in fact, illustrate different ways of 'doing history' depending on the nature of the research objective at hand and the specific paradigmatic and methodological choices a given researcher deploys. Overall, and to adapt a well known phrase, the whole of human history is your oyster when it comes to researching leadership. All you really need to get going is the curiosity to learn from the experiences of our forebears.

CONCLUSION

Developing an historical sensibility and building an understanding of our past offers multiple opportunities to enrich how we go about researching, theorising and practising leadership. This is the case despite the common belief we live in unprecedented times. At the very least, from learning what has come before we are better placed to avoid repeating past errors. Historiography offers a multiplicity of paradigms and approaches for researchers to deploy and invites us to consider issues of change, causation, context, characters, connection and complexity. Arising from this we have the potential to see the long-run effects of leadership that would otherwise be beyond our grasp.

The vast scope of human history affords expansive opportunities for generating novel findings in a field which, as demonstrated here, has vastly narrowed its scope of interests in recent centuries while also more recently circling back towards well-worn ideas rooting the essence of leadership in some special quality of leaders, seemingly unaware that historically such efforts have generated troubling effects. Informed by a Foucauldian critical history approach, the chapter has thus sought to illustrate the fascinating but also vexing history of how leadership has been discursively constituted, and the kinds of implications that can flow from such efforts. Overall, the proposition here is that the various ways of exploring leadership *through* history that exist can help us to gain a far deeper appreciation of the *history of the present* such that we are better placed to *think differently* about the past, present and future of leadership.

REFERENCES

Alvesson, M. (1996). Leadership studies: From procedure and abstraction to reflexivity and situation. *The Leadership Quarterly*, 7(4), 455–485.

Alvesson, M. (2017). Studying leadership: Taking meaning, relationality and ideology seriously. In J. Storey, J. Hartley, J.-L. Denis, P. t'Hart, & D. Ulrich (Eds.), *The Routledge Companion to Leadership* (pp. 67–88). Routledge.

Alvesson, M. (2019). Waiting for Godot: Eight major problems in the odd field of leadership studies. *Leadership*, 15(1), 27–43. 10.1177/1742715017736707

Alvesson, M. (2020). Upbeat leadership: A recipe for – or against – 'successful' leadership studies. *Leadership Quarterly*, 31(6), 101439. 10.1016/j.leaqua.2020.101439

Alvesson, M., & Sveningsson, S. (2012). Un- and repacking leadership: Context, relations, constructions, and politics. In M. Uhl-Bien & S. M. Ospina (Eds.), *Advancing Relational Leadership Research: A Dialogue Among Perspectives* (pp. 203–225). Information Age.

Antonakis, J., Cianciolo, A. T., & Sternberg, R. J. (Eds.). (2004). *The Nature of Leadership*. Sage.

Aristotle. (2009). *The Politics and the Constitution of Athens*. Ed. S. Everson. Cambridge University Press.

Balthazard, P. A., Waldman, D. A., Thatcher, R. W., & Hannah, S. T. (2012). Differentiating transformational and non-transformational leaders on the basis of neurological imaging. *Leadership Quarterly*, 23(2), 244–258. https://doi.org/10.1016/j.leaqua.2011.08.002

Bass, B. M. (1985). *Leadership and Performance Beyond Expectations*. Free Press.

Bass, B. M. (2008). *The Bass Handbook of Leadership: Theory, Research and Managerial Applications* (4th edn). Free Press.

Bass, B. M., & Riggio, R. E. (2005). *Transformational Leadership* (2nd edn). Lawrence Erlbaum.

Bodin, J. (2009). *On Sovereignty: Six Books of the Commonwealth*. Seven Treasures.

Bowers, D. G., & Seashore, S. E. (1966). Predicting organizational effectiveness with a four-factor theory of leadership. *Administrative Science Quarterly*, 11(2), 238–263.

Burns, J. M. (1978). *Leadership*. Harper & Row.

Calvin, J. (2010). *On Civil Government*. Ed. H. Hopfl. Cambridge University Press.

Cameron, E. (2001). The power of the word: Renaissance and Reformation. In E. Cameron (Ed.), *Early Modern Europe: An Oxford History* (pp. 63–101). Oxford University Press.

Carlyle, T. (1993). *On Heroes, Hero-Worship, and the Heroic in History*. Ed. M. Goldberg. Chapman & Hall.

Cattell, J. M. (1906). *American Men of Science*. Science Press.

Chaturvedi, S., Zyphur, M. J., Arvey, R. D., Avolio, B. J., & Larsson, G. (2012). The heritability of emergent leadership: Age and gender as moderating factors. *Leadership Quarterly*, 23(2), 219–232. https://doi.org/10.1016/j.leaqua.2011.08.004

Chreim, S. (2015). The (non)distribution of leadership roles: Considering leadership practices and configurations. *Human Relations*, 68(4), 517–543. 10.1177/0018726714532148

Clarke, E. L. (1916). *American Men of Letters: Their Nature and Nurture*. Columbia University.

Collinson, D. L. (2011). Critical leadership studies. In A. Bryman, D. L. Collinson, B. Jackson & M. Uhl-Bien (Eds.), *The SAGE Handbook of Leadership* (pp. 181–193). Sage

Dean, M. (1994). *Critical and Effective Histories: Foucault's Methods and Historical Sociology*. Routledge.

Dean, M. (2010). *Governmentality: Power and Rule in Modern Society* (2nd edn). Sage.

Decker, S., Hassard, J., & Rowlinson, M. (2021). Rethinking history and memory in organization studies: The case for historiographical reflexivity. *Human Relations*, 74(8), 1123–1155. 10.1177/0018726720927443

De Neve, J.-E., Mikhaylov, S., Dawes, C. T., Christakis, N. A., & Fowler, J. H. (2013). Born to lead? A twin design and genetic association study of leadership role occupancy. *Leadership Quarterly*, 24(1), 45–60.

Dixon, A., J., Webb, J., M., & Chang, C.-H. (2017). Biosensor approaches to studying leadership. In B. Schyns, R. J. Hall & P. Neves (Eds.), *Handbook of Methods in Leadership Research* (pp. 146–170). Edward Elgar. https://doi.org/10.4337/9781785367281.00014

Ellis, H. (1904). *A Study of British Genius*. Hurst and Blackett.

Erasmus (2010). *The Education of a Christian Prince*. Ed. L. Jardine. Cambridge University Press.

Foucault, M. (1977). *Discipline and Punish: The Birth of the Prison*. Trans. A. Sheridan. Penguin.

Foucault, M. (1978). *The History of Sexuality: Volume One: The Will to Knowledge*. Trans. R. Hurley. Random House.

Foucault, M. (1980). *Power/Knowledge: Selected Interviews and Other Writings by Michel Foucault 1972–1977*. Ed. C. Gordon. Pantheon.

Foucault, M. (1985). *The History of Sexuality: Volume Two: The Use of Pleasure*. Trans. R. Hurley. Vintage.

Foucault, M. (1991). Governmentality. In G. Burchell, C. Gordon & P. Miller (Eds.), *The Foucault Effect: Studies in Governmentality* (pp. 208–226). Harvester Press.

Fraher, A. L. (2020). Disobeying orders' as responsible leadership: Revisiting Churchill, Percival and the fall of Singapore. *Journal of Business Ethics*, 175, 247–263. 10.1007/s10551-020-04630-1

Gaddis, J. L. (2002). *The Landscape of History: How Historians Map the Past*. Cambridge University Press

Galton, F. (1892). *Hereditary Genius: An Inquiry into its Law and Consequences* (2nd edn). Macmillan.

Galton, F. (1970 (1875)). *English men of science: Their nature and nurture*. London: Frank Cass & Co.

Gemmill, G., & Oakley, J. (1992). Leadership: An alienating social myth? *Human Relations*, 45(2), 113–129.

Gillham, N. W. (2001). *A Life of Sir Francis Galton: From African Exploration to the Birth of Eugenics*. Oxford University Press.

Godin, B. (2007). From eugenics to scientometrics: Galton, Cattell, and Men of Science. *Social Studies of Science*, 37(5), 691–728.

Goldberg, M. (1993). Introduction. In Carlyle, T. (1993). *On Heroes, Hero Worship and the Heroic in History* (pp. xxi–lxxx). Chapman and Hall.

Grint, K. (Ed.) (1997). *Leadership: Classical, Contemporary and Critical Approaches*. Oxford University Press.

Grint, K. (1999). *The arts of leadership*. Oxford, UK: Oxford University Press.

Grint, K. (2007). *Leadership, Management and Command: Rethinking D-Day*. Palgave Macmillan.

Grint, K. (2010). The cuckoo clock syndrome: Addicted to command, allergic to leadership. *European Management Journal*, 28(4), 306–313. https://doi.org/10.1016/j.emj.2010.05.002

Gutmann, M. (2020a). Introduction: The value of the historical perspective for leadership studies. In M. Gutmann (Ed.), *Historians of Leadership and Strategy: Case Studies from Antiquity to Modernity* (pp. 1–14). Springer.

Gutmann, M. (2020b). *Historians on Leadership and Strategy: Case Studies from Antiquity to Modernity*. Springer.

Hacking, I. (1999). *The Social Construction of What?* Harvard University Press.

Harter, N. (2015). Introduction: History in the study of leadership. *Journal of Leadership Studies*, 9(2), 39–41. 10.1002/jls.21362

Heifetz, R. A. (1994). *Leadership without Easy Answers*. Harvard University Press.

Heifetz, R., & Linsky, M. (2017). *Leadership on the Line: Staying Alive Through the Dangers of Change*. Harvard Business Press.

Huczynski, A., & Buchanan, D. (2006). *Organizational Behaviour*. Prentice-Hall.

Iggers, G. G. (2005) *Historiography in the Twentieth Century: From Scientific Objectivity to the Postmodern Challenge*. Wesleyan University Press.

James VI (1950 [1599]). *Basilicon Doron*. William Blackwell & Sons.

King, A. J., Johnson, D. D. P., & Van Vugt, M. (2009). The origins and evolution of leadership. *Current Biology*, 19(19), R911–R916. https://doi.org/10.1016/j.cub.2009.07.027

Lee, N., Senior, C., & Butler, M. (2012). Leadership research and cognitive neuroscience: The state of this union. *Leadership Quarterly*, 23(2), 213–218. https://doi.org/10.1016/j.leaqua.2011.08.001

Li, W.-D., Ilies, R., & Wang, W. (2017). Behavioral genetics and leadership research. In B. Schyns, R. J. Hall, & P. Neves (Eds.), *Handbook of Methods in Leadership Research* (pp. 127–145). Edward Elgar. https://doi.org/10.4337/9781785367281.00013

Lipsius, J. (2004). *Politica: Six Books of Politics or Political Instruction*. Ed. J. Waszink. Royal Van Gorcum.

Liu, H. (2020). *Redeeming Leadership: An Anti-Racist Feminist Intervention*. Bristol University Press.

Luther, M. (2010). *On Secular Authority*. Ed. H. Hopfl. Cambridge University Press.

Machiavelli, N. (2005). *The Prince*. Ed. W. J. Connell. Bedford/St Martins.

Meindl, J. R., Ehrlich, S. B., & Dukerich, J. M. (1985). The romance of leadership. *Administrative Science Quarterly*, 30(1), 78–102.

Northouse, P. G. (2022). *Leadership: Theory and Practice* (9th edn). Sage.
Pietraszewski, D. (2020). The evolution of leadership: Leadership and followership as a solution to the problem of creating and executing successful coordination and cooperation enterprises. *Leadership Quarterly*, 31(2). 10.1016/j.leaqua.2019.05.006
Plato (2007). *The Republic*. Ed. M. Lane (2nd edn). Penguin.
Raffnsøe, S., Mennicken, A., & Miller, P. (2019). The Foucault effect in organization studies. *Organization Studies*, 40(2), 155–182. 10.1177/0170840617745110
Rose, N. S. (1990). *Governing the Soul: The Shaping of the Private Self*. Routledge.
Rose, N. S. (1996). *Inventing Our Selves: Psychology, Power, and Personhood*. Cambridge University Press
Shartle, C. L. (1979). Early years of the Ohio State University leadership studies. *Journal of Management*, 5(2), 127–134.
Sinclair, A. (2005). *Doing Leadership Differently: Gender, Power and Sexuality in a Changing Business Culture*. Melbourne University Press.
Sinclair, A. (2007). *Leadership for the Disillusioned: Moving Beyond Myths and Heroes to Leading that Liberates*. Allen & Unwin.
Smith, H. L., & Krueger, L. M. (1933). A brief summary of the literature on leadership. *Bulletin of the School of Education, Indiana University*, 9(4), 3–80.
Sorokin, P. (1925). American millionaires and multimillionaires: A comparative statistical study. *Journal of Social Forces*, 3(4), 627–640.
Spector, B. (2014). Flawed from the 'get-go': Lee Iacocca and the origins of transformational leadership. *Leadership*, 10(3), 361–379.
Spector, B. (2016a). Carlyle, Freud, and the great man theory more fully considered. *Leadership*, 12(2), 250–260.
Spector, B. (2016b). *Discourse on Leadership: A Critical Appraisal*. Cambridge University Press.
Spoerhase, C. (2008). Presentism and precursorship in intellectual history. *Culture, Theory and Critique*, 49(1), 49–72. 10.1080/14735780802024257
Stogdill, R. (1948). Personal factors associated with leadership: A survey of the literature. *Journal of Psychology*, 25, 35–71.
Taussig, F. W., & Joslyn, C. S. (1932). *American Business Leaders: A Study in Social Origins and Social Stratification*. Macmillan.
Thorndike, E. L. (1936). The relation between intellect and morality in rulers. *American Journal of Sociology*, 42(3), 321–334.
Tourish, D. (2013). *The Dark Side of Transformational Leadership: A Critical Perspective*. Routledge.
Tourish, D. (2015). Some announcements, reaffirming the critical ethos of leadership, and what we look for in submissions. *Leadership*, 11(2), 135–141. 10.1177/1742715015577889
Uhl-Bien, M., & Arena, M. (2017). Complexity leadership: Enabling people and organizations for adaptability. *Organizational Dynamics*, 46(1), 9–20. https://doi.org/10.1016/j.orgdyn.2016.12.001
Van Vugt, M., & von Rueden, C. R. (2020). From genes to minds to cultures: Evolutionary approaches to leadership. *Leadership Quarterly*, 31(2), 101404. https://doi.org/10.1016/j.leaqua.2020.101404
Visher, S. S. (1925). A study of the type of the place of birth and of the occupation of fathers of subjects of sketches in 'Who's Who in America'. *American Journal of Sociology*, 30(5), 551–557.
Wilson, S. (2016). *Thinking Differently about Leadership: A Critical History of Leadership Studies*. Edward Elgar.
Wren, J. T. (2011). Of history and leadership: The discipline of history and the understanding of leadership. In M. Harvey & R. E. Riggio (Eds.), *Leadership Studies: The Dialogue of Disciplines* (pp. 66–81). Edward Elgar.

27

Temporal Considerations in Leadership and Followership

Kent K. Alipour and Susan Mohammed

INTRODUCTION

Time matters, and it especially matters when the focus of the study is leadership.

(Day, 2014, p. 31)

Although time is omnipresent and impacts us all, its focus has been largely neglected within leadership research (Castillo & Trinh, 2018). This is unfortunate, as leadership does not occur in an a-temporal context, and leaders within organisations often navigate varying degrees of time pressure and deadlines (e.g., Mohammed & Nadkarni, 2011). Moreover, leaders and the leadership process are constantly evolving (e.g., McClean et al., 2019). Although it should be *difficult, if not impossible, to consider leadership without time playing a role*, a review of the leadership literature concluded that *the formal use of temporal variables in leadership research has been scarce and scattered* (Bluedorn & Jaussi, 2008, p. 657). In fact, four reviews on leadership and time within the past 15 years have criticised the failure of the literature to explicitly examine leadership in conjunction with temporality (Bluedorn & Jaussi, 2008; Castillo & Trinh, 2018; McClean et al., 2019; Shamir, 2011).

Temporality is a complex and multifaceted topic, as several dimensions of time exist (e.g., McClean et al., 2019). For instance, scholars have emphasised the need to examine leadership as a dynamic process (Castillo & Trinh, 2018). McClean and colleagues (2019, p. 479) bemoaned that *throughout its storied history, the leadership literature has predominantly treated leader behaviors as static.* Indeed, the need for longitudinal research is one of the most common refrains in future research sections of leadership articles. Although we strongly concur that leadership should be studied over time and measure lags, shifts, growth, decay, and ebbs and flows (McClean et al., 2019), reviews echoing this critical need are already numerous and vociferous (e.g., Castillo & Trinh, 2018; McClean et al., 2019; Shamir, 2011). Instead, we argue for considering other aspects of time in the leadership literature. Specifically, leaders and followers exhibit temporal characteristics that shape their perceptions and behaviours (Bluedorn & Jaussi, 2008). In addition, implicit theories regarding leaders' and followers' time-based traits can affect temporal expectations and behavioural patterns (Alipour et al., 2017). Moreover, leaders' actions are also inherently temporal and play a key role in managing the time-related resources of followers

(Mohammed & Alipour, 2014). Taken together, we illustrate the value of better understanding these three noted aspects of time (i.e., temporal individual differences, time-based expectations of leaders and followers, temporal leadership) by presenting the hypothetical scenario of Manager Max and Subordinate Sheila.

Manager Max and Subordinate Sheila

When Sheila's new boss, Max, made a habit of asking her to complete several time-consuming tasks right before the deadline, it was certainly not what Shiela expected of a business leader. As a monotasker who constantly worked ahead to avoid time pressure, Sheila assumed that Max would be better at planning, so she would not be saddled with so many last-minute tasks. Unfortunately, Max's urgent multitasking demands continued, and Sheila began to resent that she was not given enough time to showcase her best work. She brooded over Max's inconsiderate and unprofessional behaviour. Max, a multitasker who felt energised by time pressure, assumed that Sheila should be able to pick up the temporal slack and engage in whatever last-minute heroics were needed to complete tasks. Consequently, Max was confused by Sheila's negative reaction to his delegated tasks, and begrudged having to confront Sheila about her recent sub-par performance. As both their interpersonal and working relationship soured, Max wondered how he might effectively address his issues with Sheila.

Our Purpose

To further existing knowledge about temporal issues such as those highlighted above, we review extant literature and provide suggestions for future research. Notably, we examine temporal characteristics of leaders and followers, leaders' and followers' time-based inconsistencies, and temporal leader behaviours. By doing so, we draw attention to how leaders' temporal interactions with followers influence work- and time-related outcomes. Ultimately, we encourage future leadership work that incorporates a more thorough consideration of temporality, and we highlight fruitful temporal concepts for subsequent study.

For the sake of transparency, our approach for choosing the topics covered in this chapter was as follows. First, we engaged in an iterative process of searching management- and psychology-related academic databases that identified both leadership and temporal variables in the abstract. Second, we looked for articles with either time or temporality, in addition to leader(s) or leadership, as keywords. Third, we searched publications that had cited the above papers, as determined by Google Scholar. Finally, we performed a qualitative content analysis, in which we categorised leadership studies into three broad subgroups: temporal individual differences; time-based expectations of leaders and followers; and temporal leadership. Notably, the amalgamation of this research represents multiple leadership sub-literatures, each focusing on a different aspect of the leadership process, which we present below.

TEMPORAL INDIVIDUAL DIFFERENCES

Temporal individual differences refer to dispositional characteristics that explain how individuals think about, use, and prefer to use time (Mohammed & Harrison, 2013). Notably, leaders and followers may diverge with respect to their perceptions and utilisation of time, and these time-based differences can influence their interactions with each other, in addition to performance-related outcomes (Mohammed & Nadkarni, 2011). Below, we review four of the most commonly studied temporal individual differences (Mohammed & Harrison, 2013): time urgency (chronic hurriedness and preoccupation with deadlines), time perspective (temporal bias towards being past-, present-, or future-oriented), polychronicity (preference for multitasking) and pacing style (pattern of effort distribution towards meeting deadlines).

Time Urgency

Individuals high on time urgency strictly adhere to deadlines and exhibit other behaviours that pervade daily activities, such as eating fast, talking quickly, finishing others' sentences, and demonstrating impatience when forced to wait (Conte et al., 1998; Menon et al., 1996). Time-urgent individuals tend to believe that temporal resources are limited, and thus engage in behaviours to conserve these essential temporal resources (Conte et al., 1995). In turn, these individuals are often preoccupied with deadlines, the passage of time, and feel chronically rushed (e.g., Landy et al., 1991). Perceived time pressure and external deadlines typically impose restrictions on time urgent individuals' available time. Thus, time-urgent individuals may allocate a set amount of time to a new task, and then regularly track the time remaining while working toward completion (Rastegary & Landy, 1993; Waller et al., 2001). Time urgency has had high test-retest reliabilities and is regarded as a relatively stable personality trait influencing an individual's lifestyle and time-related decisions (Conte et al., 1995; Landy et al., 1991).

Time urgency has been included as one of the fundamental subdimensions characterising the Type A behaviour pattern (Koslowsky, 2012; Price, 1982). Individuals with a chronic feeling of being hurried and pressed for time (Landy et al., 1991) are often highly engaged workers, and have been found to have increased levels of job involvement, work speed, and job performance (e.g., Conte et al., 2001; Lee et al., 1990). Further, highly time-urgent individuals are frequently selected for formal leadership positions (Leroy et al., 2015), and may be successful in those positions by energetically, proactively, and efficiently synchronising their subordinates' efforts (Mohammed & Alipour, 2014).

Relatedly, in a sample of 129 small and medium-sized Chinese firms, more time-urgent CEOs were found to engage in more time-focused structuring, coordinating, and pace-managing behaviours (Chen & Nadkarni, 2017). However, when higher time-urgent leaders perceived themselves as having relatively high status, they were found to engage in more autocratic behaviours, which in turn increased subordinates' work stress and time pressure (Briker et al., 2021).

With respect to leaders' perceptions of followers, time patience may be considered particularly undesirable. That is, leaders may delegate important tasks to followers, and timely execution is often expected. Notably, highly time-patient individuals may be greatly concerned with the quality of their work, and prefer to take their time on tasks, as opposed to strictly adhering to deadlines. Thus, when time-urgent leaders must work interdependently with time-patient followers, workflow may be impeded due to slower than expected task pacing (Alipour et al., 2017).

Time Perspective

Time perspective, also called temporal focus (Bluedorn, 2002), refers to the relative importance of past, present, and future events in ongoing thought processes and decision-making (Shipp et al., 2009; Zimbardo & Boyd, 1999). Individuals with a present-time perspective are more carefree and focus on the 'here and now'. They tend to display interest in immediate gratification, engage in more risky endeavours, and make more short-term plans, whereas individuals with a future-time perspective are focused on making longer-term plans, setting goals that work towards a prospective vision, and contemplating future consequences of current actions or decisions (Ashkanasy et al., 2004). Future-oriented individuals are particularly aware of the idea that their actions today may influence distal outcomes. Finally, a past orientation refers to either a pessimistic and aversive or a nostalgic and sentimental view of the past (Thoms, 2004). Time perspective has been found to have high test-retest reliabilities in that individuals consistently exhibit the bias of focusing on one time frame over others (Keough et al., 1999). Because individuals demonstrate this cognitive bias in a stable manner, time perspective may be influential in the perception of task goals and how work is completed. For example, time perspective has been found to predict how individuals make task-related decisions with implications for information processing, planning, and task outcomes (e.g., Simons et al., 2004).

Polychronicity

Polychronicity is the proclivity towards working on multiple tasks simultaneously versus one task at a time (Konig & Waller, 2010). Therefore, it is conceptualised as the preference for engaging in monotasking or multitasking behaviour patterns to accomplish work. Individuals higher on polychronicity are characterised as working on multiple tasks at a time, effectively interspersing or merging tasks within a timeframe, and perceiving unscheduled events as routine to completing a task. On the opposite end of the continuum are monochromic individuals, who focus on one task at a time until completion. These individuals do not perform well when taking on more than one task simultaneously, and perceive unscheduled events as undesirable interruptions that impede the completion of their work (Bluedorn, 2002). Polychronicity is considered a stable individual trait with high test–retest reliability (e.g., Conte & Jacobs, 2003).

Further, polychronicity has been suggested to be a desirable trait in leaders, who often engage in multiple activities within a single minute (Mintzberg, 1990). For example, managers may juggle several responsibilities simultaneously such as phone calls, emails, meetings, and other interruptions, as is characteristic of many leadership positions (Tengblad, 2006). Moreover, highly polychronic managers may be more likely to welcome unscheduled visits from their subordinates, as they are more comfortable switching attention between tasks. Perhaps not surprisingly, polychronicity may be a characteristic that followers desire in their leader (Alipour et al., 2017).

Pacing style

Pacing style can be defined as the manner in which individuals distribute their effort over time in working towards deadlines (Gevers et al., 2015). It refers to a person's ideal allocation of time when working towards a time-based goal. Three pacing styles have predominantly received attention in extant literature (Gevers et al., 2006). First, the deadline-action style refers to a pacing style characterised by individuals performing most of the work near the deadline or before the time allotted for the task expires. Second, the early-action style refers to a pacing style characterised by individuals starting a task right away, or doing the bulk of the work upfront, allowing them to complete the task well in advance of the set deadline (Gevers et al., 2009). Notably, the early-action style is often referred to as the antithesis of the deadline-action style. Third, the steady-action style refers to a pacing style characterised by consistently working on a task at a constant pace, by spreading task activities out evenly over time. Unlike other temporal individual differences, pacing style has been found to have a moderate test-retest reliability. Regardless, it is still considered more stable than transitory states such as affect (Gevers et al., 2006). For a descriptive list of the temporal individual differences highlighted in this chapter, please see Table 27.1.

TIME-BASED INCONSISTENCIES BETWEEN LEADERS AND FOLLOWERS

Next, we highlight research on time-based inconsistencies between leaders and followers, which we divide into two subcategories: temporal implicit theories and temporal fit.

Table 27.1 Noteworthy temporal characteristics for leadership research (adapted from Alipour et al., 2017)

Construct	Description	Literature example
Time urgency	The extent to which individuals feel chronically hurried and are preoccupied with deadlines.	Mohammed & Harrison (2013)
Polychronicity	The degree to which individuals like to perform tasks simultaneously instead of sequentially (i.e., preference for multitasking).	Bluedorn et al. (1999)
Early pacing	Pacing styles (early, steady, deadline) refer to the manner in which individuals distribute their effort over time in working towards deadlines. Early-action pacers are characterised by starting a task immediately and doing the bulk of the work upfront, allowing them to complete the task well before the set deadline.	Gevers et al. (2006)
Steady pacing	Steady-action pacers are characterised by consistently working on a task at a constant pace, by spreading activity out evenly over time.	Gevers et al. (2006)
Deadline pacing	Deadline pacers are characterised by performing most of the work near the deadline or directly before the time allotted for the task expires.	Gevers et al. (2009)
Past perspective	Time perspective (past, present, future) refers to the relative importance of past, present, and future events in ongoing thought processes and decision-making. Individuals characterised by a past time perspective tend to focus on prior experiences and can have either pessimistic and aversive or nostalgic and sentimental views regarding past events.	Zimbardo and Boyd (1999)
Present perspective	Individuals characterised by a present time perspective tend to focus on the "here and now," and prefer to engage in short-term rather than long-term plans.	Thoms (2004)
Future perspective	Individuals characterised by a future time perspective tend to focus on making longer-term plans, setting goals that work towards a prospective vision, and contemplating future consequences of current actions and decisions.	Ashkanasy et al. (2004)
Synchrony preference	The degree to which individuals are willing to be temporally flexible in how they pace their activities in social contexts to synchronise with the pace of others.	Leroy et al. (2015)

Temporal Implicit Theories

Followers hold personal theories about the traits and behaviours that characterise leaders (Epitropaki et al., 2013). Similarly, leaders hold assumptions about the traits and behaviours characterising followers (Sy, 2010). Alipour and colleagues (2017) drew attention to the role of temporality in implicit theories, referring to them as temporal implicit leadership theories (TILTs) and temporal implicit followership theories (TIFTs). Importantly, these temporal implicit theories allow leaders and followers to form time-based expectations of one another, which encourage specific behaviours tied to the speed, pacing, and synchronisation of work efforts.

Leaders and followers may have differing TILTs and TIFTs, which generate conflicting expectations with respect to how each party should temporally manage a task. Further, although leaders and followers may begin to observe each other once an interdependent task has begun, any unexpected temporal behaviours demonstrated may be harmful to coordination and timely task completion. That is, the violation of time-based expectations may create misunderstandings between leaders and followers, resulting in temporal miscalculations and coordination breakdowns. Further exacerbating these issues is the fact that individuals are often unaware of their implicit theories (e.g., Epitropaki et al., 2013), which may obscure the cause of these problems and make them difficult for both leaders and followers to immediately identify, discuss, and solve (Alipour et al., 2017). Taken together, this research suggests that leaders' and followers' temporal characteristics (e.g., time patience, polychronicity) may shape their perceptions and expectations of one another, as well as their subsequent interactions and work-related behaviours (Alipour et al., 2017).

Temporal Fit

Research on leaders' and followers' temporal fit is, in part, derived from the leader–team fit literature (e.g., Carter & Mossholder, 2015; Cole et al., 2013). The notion of this research is that a leader's temporal characteristics can be viewed as aligned or misaligned with the respective characteristics of his/her followers. In other words, this work examines congruence (i.e., fit) or incongruence (i.e., misfit) between leaders' and followers' temporal characteristics, notes the degree of (in)congruence, and uses that information to predict work-related outcomes. Researchers have suggested that individuals prefer similarity (i.e., fit) between their own and others' temporal characteristics (Briker et al., 2020; Waller et al., 2001), which facilitates predictability. That is, temporal congruence may suggest, to the leader, that the team is functioning in an expected manner (Briker et al., 2020).

In contrast, greater dissimilarity (i.e., misfit) in temporal characteristics between leaders and followers may be associated with unexpected events and deleteriously impact perceptions (Alipour et al., 2017). Additionally, supervisors may perceive incongruence between their own and their team's temporal traits as a signal of potential time-related problems (e.g., coordination breakdowns, missed deadlines). This may be particularly likely in interdependent work contexts, as the way individuals utilise time and complete tasks can be readily observable (Alipour et al., 2017).

Relatedly, scholars have demonstrated that greater alignment between an individual and their team's temporal characteristics is associated with more favourable work experiences (Jansen & Kristof-Brown, 2005; Slocombe & Bluedorn, 1999). Additionally, researchers have examined time-based fit between formal leaders and their work teams, showing that (in)congruence between the leader's and their team's past temporal focus (i.e., the attention devoted to thinking about the past; Shipp et al., 2009) can influence the specific leadership styles utilised by the supervisor (Briker et al., 2020).

TEMPORAL LEADERSHIP

Temporal leadership refers to a pattern of *leader behaviours that aid in structuring, coordinating, and managing the pacing of task accomplishment* (Mohammed & Nadkarni, 2011, p. 492). These behaviours focus on task-oriented actions specific to managing followers' work, including building in time for contingencies, prioritising tasks, setting milestones, reminding followers of deadlines, scheduling followers' tasks, and pacing followers, so that work is completed on time (Mohammed & Nadkarni, 2011).

The most consistent finding and major conclusion across a growing number of studies is that temporal leadership positively predicts performance in team contexts (Maruping et al., 2015; Mohammed & Nadkarni, 2011; Santos et al., 2016; Yuan & Lo, 2018). Recent work has demonstrated temporal leadership's utility in predicting additional outcomes, including increasing corporate entrepreneurship (Chen & Nadkarni, 2017) and innovation (Zhang et al., 2021), while decreasing workplace deviance (Wan et al., 2021). In short, findings demonstrate the utility of temporal leadership for promoting desirable workplace outcomes.

Regarding mediating influences, temporal conflict (Santos et al., 2016), competency, and followership (Yuan & Lo, 2018) mediated the relationship between temporal leadership and performance. In addition, temporal leadership has been a moderating influence in multiple studies. For example, Mohammed & Nadkarni (2011) demonstrated that temporal leadership moderates the relationship between team temporal diversity and team performance, such that the impact of time urgency and pacing style diversity on team performance was more favourable when higher levels of temporal leadership were present. In another study, temporal leadership determined how time pressure affected team processes and performance by moderating the inverted U-shaped relationship between time pressure and team process, and by moderating the indirect effect of time pressure on team performance through team process (Maruping et al., 2015).

Rooted in time, interaction, and performance theory (McGrath, 1991; McGrath & Kelly, 1986; McGrath & Rotchford, 1983), research on temporal leadership has been primarily conducted in team contexts and has emphasised task behaviours. However, Alipour (2018) broadened beyond a team-based context to define temporal leadership as a behavioural style focused on influencing followers to efficiently utilise time. Building on functional leadership theory, he comprehensively conceptualised temporal leadership as having five dimensions: temporal tracking/monitoring, temporal intervention, temporal direction, temporal modeling and temporal encouragement. In addition to broadening the definition and conceptualisation, he expanded the operationalisation and nomological network of temporal leadership by developing and validating a multidimensional measure. The new, more holistic temporal leadership measure predicted incremental variance in leadership outcomes beyond several leadership styles, including consideration and initiating structure (Alipour, 2018).

FUTURE DIRECTIONS

Leaders' and Followers' Temporal Individual Differences

As a more recently proposed temporal individual difference relative to those highlighted earlier, synchrony preference captures the degree to which individuals are *willing to be temporally flexible in how they pace their activities in social contexts, to synchronize with the pace of others* (Leroy et al., 2015, p. 8). Specifically, individuals high on synchrony preference report flexibility in how they pace themselves to adjust to others, a willingness to 'go with the flow', proficiency in adapting to others' pace, and patience with others. Not only do they prefer to adapt their temporal behaviours to reach synchrony with others, but they also enjoy engaging in these behaviours to enhance social interactions (Leroy et al., 2015). As a stable individual difference, synchrony preference has been shown to predict behavioural flexibility in pacing behaviours and contribute to team synchrony (Leroy et al., 2015).

Given the synchronisation required for interdependent work activities, the synchrony preference of both the leader and follower are relevant to consider for dyadic outcomes. Because of the inherent power differential and greater dependency of followers (Snodgrass et al., 1998), subordinates would likely be expected to adapt more to managers than vice versa in the timing of work. However, temporal flexibility on the part of the leader in coordinating with followers' pacing is also an important consideration. Indeed, Leroy and colleagues (2015) found that individuals with the greatest likelihood of emerging as a team leader were high on both synchrony preference and time urgency. Given the paucity of work on synchrony preference, future research should examine its interaction with other temporal individual differences (e.g., time urgency, time perspective, polychronicity, pacing style).

Time-Based Inconsistencies between Leaders and Followers

Although empirical work on both implicit leadership (e.g., Epitropaki & Martin, 2005) and implicit followership (Sy, 2010) theories has been established, the same cannot be said of temporal implicit theories, which have been primarily highlighted via conceptual work (Alipour et al., 2017). Notably, TILTs and TIFTs may serve as antecedents of actual (or perceived) time-based inconsistency (e.g., misfit) between leaders and followers, which has been found to predict leaders' behaviours (Briker et al., 2020). More specifically, when a *leader's* time-related behaviours are inconsistent with a *follower's* time-related expectations, or vice versa, their interdependent and proximal outcomes may suffer (e.g., coordination quality, progress towards shared goals, task performance; Alipour et al., 2017). Unfortunately, empirical research focusing on the predictors, outcomes, and boundary conditions of TILTs and TIFTs is currently lacking.

Notably, synchrony preference may play a central role in allaying the difficulties caused by TILT/TIFT inconsistency. If a manager is expected to have an early-action style, but instead does most of his/her work right before deadlines (i.e., deadline-action pacing), high synchrony preference subordinates would be amenable to working at a quicker pace and longer hours prior to due dates to adapt to the manager. Consistent with the conceptualization of synchrony preference, the willingness to be temporally flexible would derive from a genuine desire to cooperate with others in the timing of work activities (Leroy et al., 2015).

Feeling in sync with others has been shown to increase the perception of liking and rapport, as well as the smoothness of interactions (Blount & Janicik, 2001; Lakin & Chartrand, 2003; Leroy et al., 2015), all of which can facilitate positive exchanges between leaders and followers (e.g., Dulebohn et al., 2012). Therefore, when there is a temporal mismatch between followers' behaviours and leaders' expectations, decrements in LMX quality are not expected to be as severe when followers' synchrony preference is higher. Consistent with this reasoning, synchrony preference was found to positively predict interpersonal facilitation, a dimension of contextual performance which improves morale and helps others improve performance (Leroy et al., 2015).

In contrast, individuals characterized by low synchrony preference inflexibly follow their own rhythm, and are unwilling to relinquish temporal control by adjusting to the pace of others (Leroy et al., 2015). This rigidity in maintaining one's work pace would likely exacerbate potentially low-quality exchanges from TILT/TIFT inconsistency. Consequently, TILT/TIFT inconsistency may be less negatively related to LMX quality when both leaders and followers are high on synchrony preference, and more negatively associated with LMX quality when both leaders and followers are low on synchrony preference.

Synchrony preference may similarly moderate the relationship between TILT/TIFT inconsistency and task performance. For instance, leaders' and followers' inaccurate temporal perceptions of one another may be associated with coordination failures and workflow gaps, resulting in unnecessarily rushed, unfinished, or poor-quality work. These undesirable problems would be *exacerbated/ameliorated* by *low/high* synchrony preference, respectively. Notably, the willingness to be temporally adaptable has been found to positively predict job dedication (Leroy et al., 2015), which includes devoting extra hours to complete tasks and taking the initiative to solve problems (Leroy et al., 2015). Therefore, high synchrony preference leaders/followers would eagerly and enthusiastically do what is necessary to pick up the temporal slack, resulting from TILT/TIFT inconsistency, to ensure effective performance. Supportive of this rationale, Leroy and colleagues (2015) reported that synchrony preference was positively related to one's contributions to interdependent tasks.

With respect to temporal fit, several additional temporal variables have yet to be studied. For example, although recent work has focused on leaders' and followers' temporal focus (e.g., Briker et al., 2020; Zhang et al., 2014), future work should expand our knowledge of (mis)fit on other temporal characteristics (e.g., time urgency, polychronicity). Moreover, rather than solely examining a single level of analysis, researchers might benefit from investigating multiple levels such as leader-team (i.e., team-level), leader-follower (i.e., dyadic-level), and leader or follower perceived (i.e., individual-level) temporal fit. Additionally, the assumption that all group members can be considered similar on a particular temporal characteristic, and can then be compared to their leader, on the same characteristic, may not be realistic. Such aggregate models can, at times, obscure differences between individual group members, as opposed to methodologically accounting for the fact that each of a leader's subordinates is unique.

Temporal Leadership

Because extant research has primarily focused on demonstrating relationships between temporal leadership and key outcomes to establish the predictive utility of the construct, more work needs to identify the antecedents of time-based leader behaviours. Additionally, further clarifying the specific contextual conditions under which temporal leadership is likely to successfully impact followers, and explaining why these effects exist, will help researchers and managers better grasp the utility of temporal leadership.

Given the demonstrated importance of temporal leadership in facilitating key outcomes such as performance and innovation (Maruping et al., 2015; Mohammed & Nadkarni, 2011; Santos et al., 2016; Yuan & Lo, 2018; Zhang et al., 2021), it may be worthwhile to train leaders to improve their temporal leadership behaviours. However, temporal leadership interventions should be conducted with an awareness that time-based differences between followers and leaders should be actively managed to minimise conflict (Mohammed & Schillinger, 2021). By understanding followers' temporal orientations, leaders can better match followers' time-based characteristics to tasks where possible. For example, assigning early pacers to start tasks, steady pacers to maintain project momentum over time, and deadline pacers to conclude tasks would represent thoughtful delegation from a leader. Relying on time-urgent individuals to monitor speed and time-patient members to monitor quality may also be helpful (Mohammed & Harrison, 2013). Moreover, leaders can foster an understanding of temporal dependencies among teammates, so that they recognise when others are waiting on others to complete work. Leaders can also be trained to recognise dysfunctional uses of time, assess whether the team is on track to meet deadlines, and adjust plans when necessary.

Joint Consideration of Temporal Themes

Rather than exploring temporal individual differences, time-based inconsistencies between leaders and followers, and temporal leadership in isolation, future leadership research may benefit from simultaneously considering how these themes impact work-related outcomes. More specifically, scholars may benefit from not only seeking to establish relationships between temporal constructs (e.g., temporal leadership) and outcomes (e.g., performance), but also better elucidating how (i.e., mediators) in addition to the conditions under which these relationships exist (i.e., moderators). In other words, by simultaneously accounting for different temporal variables (e.g., temporal individual differences, temporal leadership, leaders' and followers' temporal perceptions and expectations of one another) within a single model, we may gain a more holistic picture regarding the role of temporality for subsequent leadership theory and practical application.

Additional Temporal Themes

Although extant work has focused chiefly on the micro-orientation of temporal individual differences, the cultural temporal context reflects a macro-orientation. That is, time is regarded as culturally bound (Saunders et al., 2004), with countries differing on short- versus long-term orientation (Hofstede, 2001), clock (planned schedules and tight time allocation) versus event (scheduling is fluid) time (Saunders et al., 2004), slower versus faster pace (e.g., Levine & Norenzayan, 1999), and how much margin surrounds deadlines (e.g., White et al., 2011). Therefore, the intersection between national culture and leaders' and followers' experiences should also be considered. Further, cross-cultural research may provide more information about the effectiveness of temporal leadership across different regions.

Additionally, more insight into the development and evolution of temporal phenomenon is needed, in general. For example, how is temporal conflict communicated between leaders and followers with contrasting temporal individual differences? How are undesirable temporal outcomes triggered, exacerbated, ameliorated, and resolved? Similarly, do leaders enact different temporal behaviours across followers, depending on followers' unique temporal orientations (e.g., engage in more temporal leadership for time-patient than time-urgent followers)? Under what conditions is temporal leadership superior to other leadership styles?

Given the nascency of the research reviewed in this chapter, methodologies such as case studies, ethnographies, and interviews are especially appropriate (Edmondson & McManus, 2007) and may play a key role in answering these types of questions. Longitudinal case studies could help researchers understand how temporal differences emerge and change over time. Although extant work has been primarily survey-based, mixed-method studies combining quantitative and qualitative data may prove valuable in extracting real-world narratives about how temporal issues manifest in the leadership process.

Lastly, if we were to adopt a process view of leadership (i.e., leadership as a process involving influence toward a shared goal), we might propose that three broad groups of temporal variables are likely to be the general drivers of a leader's effectiveness:

1) Variables applicable to the leader involved (e.g., the leader's temporal leadership behaviours, temporal individual differences)
2) Variables applicable to the follower/followers involved (e.g., followers' temporal perceptions, temporal individual differences)
3) Variables applicable to the situational context/environment in which the leader in question is operating (e.g., the temporal characteristics of the task, temporal climate, temporal characteristics of the leader's supervisor)

Taken together, we might propose that the interaction of these three broad temporal variables, over time, is likely to determine the extent to which a leader is effective in the short and long term. Thus, future research on the temporal aspects of leadership should consider models that holistically sample from these three temporal groups. For instance, in contrast to leader-centric models, which would predominantly examine the characteristics (e.g., time urgency), perceptions, or behaviours (e.g., temporal leadership) of leaders, more process-focused models would also consider the temporal characteristics, perceptions, and behaviours of followers, in addition to key aspects of the temporal environment in which leadership is taking place (e.g., organizational temporal norms, temporal aspects of the national culture).

Practical Implications

Given that leaders and followers may be unaware of the impact of their preferences, perceptions, and behaviours, it is important to raise their awareness of each other's expectations and ideals. In other words, if leaders and followers explicitly communicate how they perceive, value, and utilise time, they may be more likely to behave in a manner consistent with each other's expectations (Alipour et al., 2017). Further, training interventions designed to teach leaders how to actively synchronise with followers and attend to followers' temporal characteristics may help both leaders and followers more quickly establish realistic temporal expectations regarding how tasks will be accomplished. Along this line of thinking, Schyns et al. (2011) developed a specific drawing exercise to help leaders and followers become more aware of each other's perceptions and desires. Moreover, organisations may benefit from temporal leadership by having managers remind subordinates of deadlines, coordinate task pacing, and form contingency plans (Mohammed & Nadkarni, 2011). Relatedly, managers can choose to reward efficient use of time, and teach subordinates how to prioritise work responsibilities, in addition to quickly intervening when obstacles threaten subordinates' timely task completion (Alipour, 2018).

CONCLUSION

In summary, although there have been several calls for examining how the leadership process unfolds over time (i.e., longitudinal methods), we seek to draw attention to 'other' conceptual aspects of time in the leadership literature. More specifically, we review three temporal sub-literatures of leadership (i.e., temporal individual differences, time-based expectations of leaders and followers, temporal leadership) and, in doing so, provide avenues for future research. Ultimately, we contend that a more holistic consideration of these sub-literatures, in addition to the situational context/environment in which the leadership process is occurring, may help to advance knowledge about leader–follower dynamics and the encompassing role that temporality plays in the process.

ACKNOWLEDGEMENTS

The contributions of the second author were supported by the National Center for Advancing Translational Sciences, National Institutes of Health, through Grant UL1 TR002014. The content is solely the responsibility of the authors and does not necessarily represent the official views of the NIH.

REFERENCES

Alipour, K. K. (2018). *Temporal leadership: A theoretically derived multidimensional measure and nomological network*. Unpublished dissertation, Pennsylvania State University.

Alipour, K. K., Mohammed, S., & Martinez, P. N. (2017). Incorporating temporality into implicit leadership and followership theories: Exploring inconsistencies between time-based expectations and actual behaviors. *Leadership Quarterly*, 28(2), 300–316.

Ashkanasy, Neal M., Vipin Gupta, Melinda S. Mayfield, and Edwin Trevor-Roberts. "Future orientation." (2004): 282–342.

Blount, S., & Janicik, G. A. (2001). When plans change: Examining how people evaluate timing changes in work organizations. *Academy of management Review*, 26(4), 566–585.

Bluedorn, A. C. (2002). *The Human Organization of Time: Temporal Realities and Experience*. Stanford University Press.

Bluedorn, A. C., & Jaussi, K. S. (2008). Leaders, followers, and time. *Leadership Quarterly*, 19(6), 654–668.

Briker, R., Walter, F., & Cole, M. S. (2020). The consequences of (not) seeing eye-to-eye about the past: The role of supervisor–team fit in past temporal focus for supervisors' leadership behavior. *Journal of Organizational Behavior*, 41(3), 244–262.

Briker, R., Walter, F., & Cole, M. S. (2021). Hurry up! The role of supervisors' time urgency and self-perceived status for autocratic leadership and subordinates' well-being. *Personnel Psychology*, 74(1), 55–76.

Carter, M. Z., & Mossholder, K. W. (2015). Are we on the same page? The performance effects of congruence between supervisor and group trust. *Journal of Applied Psychology*, 100(5), 1349.

Castillo, E. A., & Trinh, M. P. (2018). In search of missing time: A review of the study of time in leadership research. *Leadership Quarterly, 29*(1), 165–178.

Chen, J., & Nadkarni, S. (2017). It's about time! CEOs' temporal dispositions, temporal leadership, and corporate entrepreneurship. *Administrative Science Quarterly, 62*(1), 31–66.

Cole, M. S., Carter, M. Z., & Zhang, Z. (2013). Leader–team congruence in power distance values and team effectiveness: The mediating role of procedural justice climate. *Journal of Applied Psychology, 98*(6), 962.

Conte, J. M., & Jacobs, R. R. (2003). Validity evidence linking polychronicity and big five personality dimensions to absence, lateness, and supervisory performance ratings. *Human Performance, 16*(2), 107–129.

Conte, J. M., Landy, F. J., & Mathieu, J. E. (1995). Time urgency: Conceptual and construct development. *Journal of Applied Psychology, 80*(1), 178.

Conte, J. M., Mathieu, J. E., & Landy, F. J. (1998). The nomological and predictive validity of time urgency. *Journal of Organizational Behavior: The International Journal of Industrial, Occupational and Organizational Psychology and Behavior, 19*(1), 1–13.

Conte, J. M., Schwenneker, H. H., Dew, A. F., & Romano, D. M. (2001). Incremental validity of time urgency and other type A subcomponents in predicting behavioral and health criteria. *Journal of Applied Social Psychology, 31*(8), 1727–1748.

Day, D. R. 2014. Time and leadership. In A. J. ShippY. Fried (Eds.), *Time and work: How time impacts groups, organizations, and methodological choices*, vol. 2: 30–52. New York: Psychology Press.

Dulebohn, J. H., Bommer, W. H., Liden, R. C., Brouer, R. L., & Ferris, G. R. (2012). A meta-analysis of antecedents and consequences of leader-member exchange: Integrating the past with an eye toward the future. *Journal of management, 38*(6), 1715–1759.

Epitropaki, O., & Martin, R. (2005). From ideal to real: A longitudinal study of the role of implicit leadership theories on leader-member exchanges and employee outcomes. *Journal of Applied Psychology, 90*(4), 659.

Epitropaki, O., Sy, T., Martin, R., Tram-Quon, S., & Topakas, A. (2013). Implicit leadership and followership theories 'in the wild': Taking stock of information-processing approaches to leadership and followership in organizational settings. *Leadership Quarterly, 24*(6), 858–881.

Gevers, J. M., Rutte, C. G., & Van Eerde, W. (2006). Meeting deadlines in work groups: Implicit and explicit mechanisms. *Applied psychology, 55*(1), 52–72.

Gevers, J. M., Rutte, C. G., & Van Eerde, W. (2006). Meeting deadlines in work groups: Implicit and explicit mechanisms. *Applied psychology, 55*(1), 52–72.

Gevers, J., Mohammed, S., & Baytalskaya, N. (2015). The conceptualisation and measurement of pacing styles. *Applied Psychology, 64*(3), 499–540.

Gevers, J. M. P., Claessens, B. J. C., Van Eerde, W. & Rutte, C. G. (2009). Pacing styles, personality, and performance. In R. A. Roe, M. J. Waller & S. R. Clegg (Eds.), *Time in organizational research* (pp. 80–102). New York: Routledge

Jansen, K. J., & Kristof-Brown, A. L. (2005). Marching to the beat of a different drummer: Examining the impact of pacing congruence. *Organizational Behavior and Human Decision Processes, 97*(2), 93–105.

Keough, K. A., Zimbardo, P. G., & Boyd, J. N. (1999). Who's smoking, drinking, and using drugs? Time perspective as a predictor of substance use. *Basic and applied social psychology, 21*(2), 149–164.

König, C. J., & Waller, M. J. (2010). Time for reflection: A critical examination of polychronicity. *Human Performance, 23*(2), 173–190.

Koslowsky, M. (2012). Some new organizational perspectives on moderators and mediators in the stress–strain process: Time urgency, management, and worker control. In M. Erez, U. Kleinbeck & H. Thierry (Eds.), *Work Motivation in the Context of a Globalizing Economy* (pp. 314–324). Psychology Press.

Lakin, J. L., & Chartrand, T. L. (2003). Using nonconscious behavioral mimicry to create affiliation and rapport. *Psychological science, 14*(4), 334–339.

Landy, F. J., Rastegary, H., Thayer, J., & Colvin, C. (1991). Time urgency: The construct and its measurement. *Journal of Applied Psychology, 76*(5), 644.

Lee, C., Ashford, S. J., & Bobko, P. (1990). Interactive effects of 'Type A' behavior and perceived control on worker performance, job satisfaction, and somatic complaints. *Academy of Management Journal, 33*(4), 870–881.

Leroy, S., Shipp, A. J., Blount, S., & Licht, J. G. (2015). Synchrony preference: Why some people go with the flow and some don't. *Personnel Psychology, 68*(4), 759–809.

Levine, R. V., & Norenzayan, A. (1999). The pace of life in 31 countries. *Journal of Cross-Cultural Psychology, 30*(2), 178–205.

Maruping, L. M., Venkatesh, V., Thatcher, S. M., & Patel, P. C. (2015). Folding under pressure or rising to the occasion? Perceived time pressure and the moderating role of team temporal leadership. *Academy of management journal, 58*(5), 1313–1333.

Maruping, L. M., Venkatesh, V., Thatcher, S. M., & Patel, P. C. (2015). Folding under pressure or rising to the occasion? Perceived time pressure and the moderating role of team temporal leadership. *Academy of management journal, 58*(5), 1313–1333.

McClean, S. T., Barnes, C. M., Courtright, S. H., & Johnson, R. E. (2019). Resetting the clock on dynamic leader behaviors: A conceptual integration and agenda for future research. *Academy of Management Annals*, *13*(2), 479–508.

McGrath, J. E. (1991). Time, interaction, and performance (TIP): A theory of groups. *Small Group Research*, *22*(2), 147–174.

McGrath, J. E., & Kelly, J. R. (1986). *Time and Human Interaction: Toward a Social Psychology of Time*. Guilford Press.

McGrath, J. E., & Rotchford, N. L. (1983). Time and behavior in organizations. *Research in Organizational Behavior*, *5*, 57–101.

Menon, S., Narayanan, L., & Spector, P. E. (1996). The relation of time urgency to occupational stress and health outcomes for health care professionals. In C. D. Spielberger, I. G. Sarason, J. M. T. Brebner, E. Greenglass, P. Laungani & A. M. O'Roark (Eds.), *Stress and Emotion: Anxiety, Anger, and Curiosity*, Volume 16 (pp. 127–142). Taylor & Francis.

Mintzberg, H. (1990). Manager's job: Folklore and fact. *Harvard Business Review*, *68*(2), 163–176.

Mohammed, S., & Alipour, K. K. (2014). It's time for temporal leadership: Individual, dyadic, team, and organizational effects. *Industrial and Organizational Psychology*, *7*(2), 178–182.

Mohammed, S., & Harrison, D. A. (2013). The clocks that time us are not the same: A theory of temporal diversity, task characteristics, and performance in teams. *Organizational Behavior and Human Decision Processes*, *122*(2), 244–256.

Mohammed, S., & Nadkarni, S. (2011). Temporal diversity and team performance: The moderating role of team temporal leadership. *Academy of Management Journal*, *54*(3), 489–508.

Price, V. A. (1982). What is Type A? A cognitive social learning model. *Journal of Organizational Behavior*, *3*(1), 109–129.

Rastegary, H., & Landy, F. J. (1993). The interactions among time urgency, uncertainty, and time pressure. In A. J. Maule & O. Svenson (Eds.), *Time Pressure and Stress in Human Judgment and Decision Making* (pp. 217–239). Springer.

Santos, C. M., Passos, A. M., Uitdewilligen, S., & Nübold, A. (2016). Shared temporal cognitions as substitute for temporal leadership: An analysis of their effects on temporal conflict and team performance. *Leadership Quarterly*, *27*(4), 574–587.

Saunders, C., Van Slyke, C., & Vogel, D. R. (2004). My time or yours? Managing time visions in global virtual teams. *Academy of Management Executive*, *18*(1), 19–37.

Shamir, B. (2011). Leadership takes time: Some implications of (not) taking time seriously in leadership research. *Leadership Quarterly*, *22*(2), 307–315.

Shipp, A. J., Edwards, J. R., & Lambert, L. S. (2009). Conceptualization and measurement of temporal focus: The subjective experience of the past, present, and future. *Organizational Behavior and Human Decision Processes*, *110*(1), 1–22.

Simons, J., Vansteenkiste, M., Lens, W., & Lacante, M. (2004). Placing motivation and future time perspective theory in a temporal perspective. *Educational psychology review*, *16*(2), 121–139.

Slocombe, T. E., & Bluedorn, A. C. (1999). Organizational behavior implications of the congruence between preferred polychronicity and experienced work-unit polychronicity. *Journal of Organizational Behavior: The International Journal of Industrial, Occupational and Organizational Psychology and Behavior*, *20*(1), 75–99.

Snodgrass, S. E., Hecht, M. A., & Ploutz-Snyder, R. (1998). Interpersonal sensitivity: Expressivity or perceptivity?. *Journal of personality and social psychology*, *74*(1), 238.

Sy, T. (2010). What do you think of followers? Examining the content, structure, and consequences of implicit followership theories. *Organizational Behavior and Human Decision Processes*, *113*(2), 73–84.

Tengblad, S. (2006). Is there a 'new managerial work'? A comparison with Henry Mintzberg's classic study 30 years later. *Journal of Management Studies*, *43*(7), 1437–1461.

Thoms, P. (2004). *Driven by time: Time orientation and leadership*. Greenwood Publishing Group.

Waller, M. J., Conte, J. M., Gibson, C. B., & Carpenter, M. A. (2001). The effect of individual perceptions of deadlines on team performance. *Academy of Management Review*, *26*(4), 586–600.

Wan, W., Wang, A., & Li, L. (2021). Temporal leadership and employee workplace deviance: The role of perceived illegitimate tasks. *Social Behavior and Personality: An International Journal*, *49*(7).

Yuan, C. C., & Lo, S. H. (2018). Relationship among team temporal leadership, competency, followership, and performance in Taiwanese pharmaceutical industry leaders and employees. *Journal of Career Development*, *45*(3), 227–238.

Yuan, C. C., & Lo, S. H. (2018). Relationship among team temporal leadership, competency, followership, and performance in Taiwanese pharmaceutical industry leaders and employees. *Journal of Career Development*, *45*(3), 227–238.

Zhang, J., van Eerde, W., Gevers, J. M., & Zhu, W. (2021). How temporal leadership boosts employee innovative job performance. *European Journal of Innovation Management*, *24*(1), 23–42.

Zhang, W., Wang, H., & Pearce, C. L. (2014). Consideration for future consequences as an antecedent of transformational leadership behavior: The moderating effects of perceived dynamic work environment. *Leadership Quarterly*, *25*(2), 329–343.

Zimbardo, P. G., & Boyd, J. N. (1999). Putting time in perspective: A valid, reliable individual-differences metric. *Journal of Personality and Social Psychology*, *77*(6), 1271–1288. https://doi.org/10.1037/0022-3514.77.6.1271

28

Rebuilding Leadership Theory Through Literature

Martyna Śliwa

INTRODUCTION

In parallel to philosophers of science who have considered literary narrative as a sociological resource (Longo, 2015; Polkinghorne, 1988), for several decades now management and organisation studies (MOS) scholarship has drawn on literary fiction, and especially novels (e.g., Czarniawska-Joerges & Guillet de Monthoux, 1994; Griffin et al., 2018; Martin et al., 2018; Śliwa et al., 2015; Waldo, 1968) for the purposes of management education and research. Within this body of work, literary fiction has been proposed as an excellent vehicle especially for the study and pedagogy of leadership, with examples of application addressing topics such as the figure of the leader (Gosling & Villers, 2012), the power dynamics in leadership contexts (e.g., Knights & Wilmott, 1999), leadership ethics (e.g., Sucher, 2007) and explanation of post-heroic leadership theories (e.g., McManus & Perruci, 2015). Notwithstanding the many virtues that characterise extant writings that bring together literary fiction and leadership, these efforts have not yet succeeded in helping leadership scholars address the, arguably, most pressing challenges in leadership studies, and – in Carrol et al.'s (2019, n.p.) words – *construct the foundations of a more inclusive, participatory, bold, relational and social platform for leadership in the future*. This chapter offers reflections on why this might be the case and points to the need for leadership scholars to engage with more recent literary fiction that explores in complex and nuanced ways the relations between people and the phenomena contemporary society faces – from issues associated with gender, race, class and sexuality, to populism and threats to democracy, postcolonialism and migration, environmental degradation, and warfare.

In the chapter, I discuss the importance of literary fiction, and especially the novel, for management and organisation studies and, more specifically, for leadership education and research. I argue that scholars continue to be inspired by the novel, and see it as a vehicle for generating insights into managing, organising and leading. What I note though is that the novels selected by organisation studies and leadership scholars tend to reflect their own aesthetic preferences and the content of the literary canon into which they have been socialised; as a result, leadership scholars often tend to draw on classical literature. The chosen novels are, for good reason, applied in a way that serves the arguments that the researchers want to make. This approach to selecting and using novels also means that, in drawing on novels, MOS and leadership researchers and educators are not preoccupied with the current 'state of the art' in the broader world of novel-writing and publishing. They do not necessarily follow how the field has been evolving, which topics are seen at present as worthy of literary attention, which authors are considered to be the most interesting and promising – and, by implication, what new insights can be gained into how we understand and go about organising and leading. I argue that as scholars usually focus on the lessons that can be learnt about organisations and leadership from one literary novel at a time, we might be missing the chance to understand whether and what challenges to our thinking on leadership are posed by contemporary developments in the universe of literary fiction. Similarly, we might also be missing the opportunity to come up with creative solutions to what Alvesson (2019) refers to as the *Eight major problems in the odd field of leadership studies*. In proposing a shift towards greater engagement of leadership scholars with more recent literary fiction, I use the Booker Prize as an illustration of the evolution of literary novel-writing and reading over the past few decades, and argue that contemporary novels have a lot to offer in prompting us to reconsider how we understand leadership and come up with constructive alternatives following the process of *discarding, deconstructing,* [and] *starting again* (Carroll et al., 2019, n.p.) with leadership knowledge.

ORGANISATION STUDIES AND LITERARY FICTION

Turning to fiction in order to learn and theorise about organisations and organising remains a marginal approach (Holt & Zundel, 2014) within broader management and organisation studies research. Nevertheless, it has a long history and constitutes an established, even if still niche, endeavour. Already towards the end of the 1960s, Waldo (1968, 5), writing with a focus on public administration contexts, argued that fictional *literature helps to restore what the professional-scientific literature necessarily omits or slights: the concrete, the sensual, the emotional, the subjective, the valuational*. Similarly, a quarter of a century ago, Phillips (1995, 635) contended that *narrative fiction provides organizational analysis with an additional point of contact in the everyday world of real 'life'*. More recently, Longo (2015, 140) stated that a *fictional document is an instrument with which to probe into reality, testing certain features of the world as described in the text*, whereas Savage et al. (2018) have argued for the need to see fiction as a central concern in organisation studies.

In a Themed Section of the journal *Organization Studies* dedicated to the multiple connections between MOS research and literary fiction, Beyes et al. (2019, 1788) reflect on the interdependence of literature and organisation studies as forms of discourse as follows:

> the study of organization is contaminated by novels […] literary works influence the imagination of organizational scholars […] Novels can make us not only see new and different things but also see things differently. They have the power to affect the way we sense and, in this way, alter the very ways we perceive, study and write organization.

Novels, as Beyes et al. (2019) point out, are not simply an object of organisational analysis but can also fulfil the role of a medium of organisational thought. Beyes et al. (2019) elaborate on this point through reference to De Cock and Land's (2006) typology of three *modes of engagement* that can be discerned when analysing the relationship between literature and organisation. Mode One involves the application of literary theory to organisational literature in a way that aims to *problematise organization theory, thus enabling it to reinvigorate itself* (Czarniawska, 1999, 12). In Mode Two, literary genres are being deployed in the process of *production and presentation of organizational knowledge* (De Cock & Land, 2006, 520). Within Mode Three, literary fiction is used as an educational resource, with the view to helping students of management and organisation develop their knowledge and practice. Expanding De Cock and Land's (2006) distinction between the three modes of engagement, Śliwa and Cairns (2007) develop a discussion of the work that can be classified under Mode Three. They explain that it involves a consideration of novels from a realist perspective, and identify three levels at which management and organisation studies scholars apply the Mode Three-type of engagement with the 'novel as resource'. At the first level, novels serve as 'surrogate cases' of organisations; at second, as 'stories of organising', whereby an analogy is drawn between what is described in the novel and lived experience; and at third, as vehicles for organisational analysis, enabling *complex engagement with phenomena at a higher level of abstraction* (Śliwa & Carins, 2007, 312).

Śliwa and Cairns (2007) encourage the use of novels by management and organisation studies researchers and educators, highlighting that to mobilise literary fiction in their work, MOS scholars need not have the kind of competence in analysing literary texts that literary critics do. Drawing on DeVault (1990, 1999), Śliwa and Cairns (2007, 309) argue for the value of *lay reading* of novels *in order to facilitate the readers' processes of meso-theorising and critical reflection*. To DeVault (1990, 106), lay reading enables *experiment in the use of personal response as part of an archive for analysis*. While the *lay reading* differs from the *expert reading* of the literary critic, it does not mean that it is naive or lacking in critical analysis. Rather, lay reading acknowledges *the situated character of reading* (DeVault, 1999, 105) and considers the readers – including their demographic characteristics, circumstances and purposes of reading – as inseparable from interpretation. The lay reading approach, therefore, is particularly useful to organisation theory in that it offers:

> *the possibility of an inclusive, pluralist approach to learning that allows reading communities of students to reflect upon a range of theoretical perspectives from a starting point grounded in their own a priori knowledge and understanding of the world, as developed through reading literary fiction.*
>
> (Śliwa & Cairns, 2007, 321)

Such lay readings of literary fiction can offer ample opportunities for knowledge-building not only within the broadly understood field of management and organisation, but also in relation to a range of sub-disciplines, such as entrepreneurship (Loacker, 2021), project management (Bröchner, 2021), or, indeed, leadership (e.g., Martin et al., 2018; Śliwa et al., 2013). This broad applicability of literary fiction to research and education across different management-related disciplines gives rise to questions about which novels are chosen by MOS researchers and on what basis these choices are made. Loacker's (2021) recent discussion of entrepreneurship through the lens of Robert Musil's novel *The Man Without Qualities* is an example of an in-depth reflection on the selection of a specific oeuvre, whereby a lot of consideration was given to both the novel's content and to its author's knowledge and outlook on the world. Reading *The Man Without Qualities* has provided Loacker (2021, 2) with the opportunity *to develop a subtler understanding of the multi-faceted ambiguities accompanying 'total' orders such as entrepreneurship*. On the basis of her analysis, Loacker (2021) argues that *The Man Without Qualities* provides the first critique of entrepreneurship, as conceived by its early proponents from the Austrian School, such as von Mises and Schumpeter, whose ideas Musil would have been familiar with. Crucially, in addition to analysing the themes present in the novel, Loacker (2021) also draws attention to the importance of understanding how novels written by specific authors can be particularly valuable for our theorising. In analysing Musil's work, she reminds us that he was a polymath whose writings brought together literary, social and economic theory as well as philosophy. Following Harrington (2002, 59), she considers Musil,

> *as an exemplary kind of social theorist, a philosopher and critic of European civilization who exploits the literary devices of irony, ambivalence and aesthetics in order to communicate a particular style of thinking about the social conditions, ideologies and contradictory identities of modernity that could not otherwise be expressed in the abstract discursive language of social science.*

The issue of which authors' novels, and which novels, are chosen for the purpose of studying and educating students about management-related phenomena and concepts, as well as what insights into these phenomena are being generated on the basis of literary fiction is important for our ability to exploit more fully and more creatively the potential of novels to challenge our thinking about management and leadership, and to propose alternatives to the still dominant *masculine, linear rational and individualistic character of leadership as both a practice and a topic of research* (Knights, 2019, 7) in leadership studies. I elaborate on this in more detail in the sub-section below which discusses more specifically the uses of literary fiction in leadership education and research.

THE USE OF NOVELS IN LEADERSHIP STUDIES

Novels are used in leadership education because they are considered to have the capacity to invoke in students what leadership 'feels' like, and thus to vicariously experience it (Badaracco, 2006; Kajtár, 2015). Czarniawska-Joerges and Guillet de Monthoux (1994) argue for the use of fictional literature with students of leadership because of its complexity and concreteness, and its ability to portray 'ideal' types of leadership and to convey tacit knowledge about it. Currie (2016) contends that in learning about leadership from novels, students can develop their imagination as well as cognitive and emotional skills. It has also been suggested that when drawing on novels, leadership education can prompt students to ask critical and important questions (Hermida-Ruiz, 2008;

Warner, 2008) which otherwise they would have found difficult to generate and articulate.

In addition to offering a fruitful approach to leadership education, fictional narratives can also provide a basis of valid insights into leadership phenomena (Colton, 2020; Gosling & Villiers, 2012). Since leadership itself can be understood as *rooted in storytelling* (Nehls, 2012), narrative analysis should offer a promising approach to understanding leadership. In Colton's (2020) view, literary narratives provide particularly apt 'models' of leadership, in an analogous way to how equations, diagrams or physical representations provide fictional models that are widely used in the natural sciences. This is because, according to Colton (2020, 404), leadership concepts, both traditional and more recent ones, *present leadership as an irreducibly triadic relation that cannot be reduced to any series of dyadic relations, such as causal interactions*. In turn, the triadic relations that form leadership call for investigations *by means of other triadic relations* (Ketner et al., 1995, 275), and models of such triadic relations are plentiful in novels.

In a similar vein to Colton's (2020) argument, in Warner's (2011) view, literary fiction – even if it is yet to receive the attention it deserves from leadership scholars – has special relevance to leadership studies through its emphasis on emotions and ethical issues, its clear descriptions of events and settings, and the overall nuanced and insightful characterisation of humanity it offers. While both Colton's (2020) and Warner's (2011) observations are undoubtedly valuable, it is helpful to look more closely at the applications of literary fiction in leadership education and research, in order to build a picture of the kinds of insights into leadership and the novels on the basis of which these have been generated that have been gained to date.

Colton (2020) himself turns to *high fantasy* literary work for a portrayal of leadership. Following the contention that a *fruitful model of leadership can be found in J. R. R. Tolkien's stories and novels*, (Colton, 2020, 401), he draws attention to *The Silmarillon* and *The Lord of the Rings* as examples of narratives that present leadership as *practical wisdom* rather than craft. To Colton (2020), insights drawn from Tolkien's works can provide a response to the *Hitler problem* (Burns, 1978; Ciulla, 1995; Ciulla et al., 2018) in leadership studies which refers to the issue of whether bad leaders can be classified as leaders: based on Colton's reading of Tolkien, individuals who do bad things are still considered to be leaders, except that they are corrupt leaders. What is worth pointing out here is that the novels to which Colton (2020) refers were written throughout the 1930s and 1940s, and – notwithstanding Tolkien's excellent literary imagination and craft, and the popularity of his books – the myths which the books conjure up have been described as *profoundly conservative*, with a storyline which romanticises the idea of *return of the king to his rightful throne* which, in practice, means *the reassertion of a feudal social structure which had been disrupted by the 'evil'* (Walter, 2014, n.p.). Tolkien's books are marked by a nostalgia for *a more conservative society, one where people knew their place*, and, at the same time, they ignore *the brutality and oppression that were part and parcel of a world ruled by men with swords* (Walter, 2014, n.p.).

Another example of the use of fiction, albeit more contemporary, is provided by Vizmuller-Zocco (2016) who draws on examples of Italian literary fiction in order to move beyond anthropocentric views of leadership. Following her summary of existing ontologies and their concomitant definitions of leadership – which she categorises as belonging to one of two types: 1) a tripod consisting of leaders, followers and common goals; and 2) a focus on leadership outcomes, with an emphasis on direction, alignment and commitment – Vizmuller-Zocco (2016, 356) contends that *so far, no definition puts forth new types of technology as indispensable elements without which leadership could not function*. She proposes drawing on science fiction works as a *way to approach leadership of a more complex type, that is, the one that takes into account both human and possible future technological contributions to leadership* (Vizmuller-Zocco, 2016, 355; see also Parker et al., 1999).

Vizmuller-Zocco's (2016) analysis focuses on four novels, published in Italy and written by Italian authors, and which belong to the sub-genre of 'transhumanist fiction'. The author argues that 'transhumanist fiction' affords us a glimpse into a world where human leadership is replaced with technology as the latter both creates goals for individuals and fulfils them. In a transhuman future, in Vizmuller-Zocco's (2016, 357) words, *no one seems to be in charge. This type of society relies on the self-made man and woman who grope to find their own goals and look for ways to fulfil them on their own, or with minimal help from friends*. As Vizmuller-Zocco (2016) suggests based on the analysis of the selected novels, leadership in a transhuman society is difficult to discern and is associated with whoever controls technology, which, in turn, manages people – for example, by manufacturing consensus through deleting people's memories, or by gifting them *unspecified liquid born out of* [their] *DNA* Vizmuller-Zocco's (2016, 359) that enables the re-growth of previously lost limbs. Nevertheless, a technologically driven, transhuman society, as depicted in the four novels discussed by Vizmuller-Zocco (2016, 360) retains a number of characteristics associated with 'traditional' notions of leadership, including *charisma, authority, successful delegation of duties to skilled and skillful followers,* [and] *power,* as well as male dominance and a paternalistic style of leadership that selfishly demands unquestioning obedience from the followers. Altogether, the picture that emerges from the dystopian science-fiction novels analysed by Vizmuller-Zocco (2016) is one of undemocratic, coercive and sometimes violent ways of leading, devoid of ethically informed aspirations that would seek to accomplish broader humanitarian goals.

Both Colton (2020) and Vizmuller-Zocco (2016) discuss novels in which leadership is portrayed as individual-centric and hierarchical, as the domain of men and as an endeavour which justifies the use of violence. Arguably, to arrive at different conclusions about and visions of leadership, it would have been necessary to draw on other novels. However, Colton's (2020) and Vizmuller-Zocco's (2016) analyses are not unique within leadership writings that use literary fiction. For one, they can be seen as an illustration of a more general tendency observed by Martin et al. (2018): those leadership scholars who have drawn on literary fiction have primarily used texts written by men, and the texts used lack examples of women leaders and their experiences. Martin et al. (2018) also highlight that among the frequently cited examples of leadership in literature are Shakespeare's plays, whereas within the publicly available lists of literary fiction pieces composed by different leadership scholars and recommended for use in leadership education (e.g., Badaracco, 2006; McManus & Perrucci, 2015; Peters & Nesteruk, 2014; Sucher, 2007), women authors or protagonists constitute only a very small minority. As a consequence of such choices, the use of literary fiction in leadership research and education has contributed to the perpetuation of the framing and understanding of leadership in masculine terms (Sinclair & Evans, 2015). This, in Martin et al.'s (2018) view, is a key shortcoming because by excluding fiction that addresses women leaders' experiences, the research on leadership and literary fiction has not engaged with those aspects of the experience of leadership that have been documented as unique to women leaders, such as gender inequality and both conscious and unconscious biases against women (Eagly & Carli, 2007; Hoyt & Simon, 2016; Rhee & Sigler, 2015). What we can add to this is that neither has research that brings together leadership and literary fiction done much to engage with the experience of leadership of non-white people and members of other minority groups, or with more participatory, perhaps even 'leaderless' (Kempster & Parry, 2019) leadership contexts.

In summary, although a number of leadership scholars and educators have proposed using literary fiction both for leadership research and education purposes, these applications have primarily resulted in 'traditional' depictions of leadership, reflecting those typically found in leadership studies: what Carroll et al. (2019, n.p.) call *a field bounded by old or well-established ways of thinking and doing, engaging in limited critical assessment of its assumptions and making few excursions into new or exciting terrains,* and one in which *leadership has been portrayed as associated with the traits and actions of a specific individual, typically a white man, and with a model of a paternalistically governed, hierarchical and undemocratic society and organisation.* Moreover, the great majority of the literary texts drawn on by leadership scholars have been written by white men, and have been part of the canon of classical literature. This gives rise to some interesting questions: if leadership researchers and educators were to look for images of leadership in other examples of literary fiction, would it be possible to arrive at a different portrayal of leadership? Have the profiles of the authors of literary fiction changed over the past few decades and what are the concerns and worlds depicted by contemporary novelists? Below, I attempt to address these questions through a series of reflections on the evolution of the Booker Prize for International Fiction.

THE BOOKER PRIZE: THE EVOLVING WORLD OF FICTION

The Booker Prize holds a special place within the global *book prize culture* (Squires, 2004). It launched in 1969 as the Booker-McConnell Prize, with the aim to *promote the finest in fiction by rewarding the best novel of the year written by a citizen of the United Kingdom, the Commonwealth or the Republic of Ireland* (quoted in Morris, 2020, 262), with novels published in the UK eligible for the prize. Between 2002 and 2018, throughout the period of sponsorship by the Man Group, it was known as the Man Booker Prize. Since 2014, novels written by US citizens and published in the UK can be submitted to the Booker Prize competition. On a global level, the Booker is a highly prestigious award; in the UK, it tends to be the only literary prize that members of the general public are aware of. Being 'longlisted' or 'shortlisted' for the Booker guarantees an increase in the book sales and promises an additional income for the author from possible sales of film, TV and translation rights. As has been pointed out by its critics, the significance of the Booker also *reinforces London as the centre of cultural judgement about art production in the colonies* (Morris, 2020, 263; for further insights into the link between leadership and (post)coloniality, see e.g., Chapter 25, Indigenous leadership as a conscious adaptive system and Chapter 31, Leadership and culture).

Importantly in the context of this chapter, ever since its establishment in 1969, *the Booker has displayed an uncanny ability to reflect the broader social, political and economic changes that have taken place in Britain* (Norris, 2006, 140). For example, in the beginning, the panel of shortlisted authors comprised a group of renowned authors with impressive cultural, educational and social credentials. The winner was P. H. Newby who was Head of the BBC's Third Programme as well as an established novelist and literary critic. The other names on the shortlist included Iris Murdoch, who was an Oxford graduate, novelist and academic; Muriel Spark, another established novelist; Nicholas Mosley who was both an aristocrat and an Oxford graduate; and Barry England and Gordon Williams (Norris, 2006). Although, as noted by Todd (1996, 8), *the catchment area* [of authors eligible to enter] *comprises one quarter of the world's population*, all of the authors shortlisted in the first year of the Booker Prize were white and British (although Iris Murdoch had been born in Dublin to Irish parents, the family moved to London when she was a few weeks old). In other words, despite the competition's global aspirations, the authors on the 'leader board' of the Booker Prize were initially drawn from a narrow demographic group, traditionally associated with leadership in the British context – that is, white British elites.

Two years later, in 1971, the prize was awarded for the first time to a non-white author – V. S. Naipaul and ten years later to another non-white novelist, Salman Rushdie – for *Midnight's Children*. The 1981 award is considered especially historically significant in that, contrary to previous Booker winners that have dealt with the topic of India, it presented a perspective on India that was *not British but Indian, not that of the colonizer but of the colonized* (Todd, 1996, p. 82). Nevertheless, the evaluation of Rushdie's novel – as well as of other postcolonial fiction that has gained appreciation by Booker's judges – was carried out, in the process of selecting the Booker's winner, by members of a white British culture elite (Huggan, 2001). In Huggan's (2001) view, there was a link between the model of literary evaluation whereby the British elites judge the value of novels written by authors from the former colonies and the colonial history of the literary prize's sponsor, the company Booker McConnell, in the Caribbean, where for many years it exploited sugar workers in the British Guiana. To this, Frenkel (2008, 87) adds that – at least until the mid-2000s – the Booker propagated texts that *communicate a particular idea of history and culture* which he terms *postcolonial pathos*, and that *are intimately caught up in the mechanics of the empire*, whereby especially India and South Africa *are represented as being overwhelmed by their histories and marked by the triumph of loss or instability over love or redemption*. All this suggests that for many years, the leadership of the Booker Prize as an organisational phenomenon was performed in accordance with a 'traditional' Western approach to leadership, in the sense that it was not inclusive of non-dominant groups' perspectives and voices, and was characterised by sense- and decision-making kept in the hands of members of the ethnically and societally privileged group in the British context.

The evolution of the Booker Prize awards reflects the changing attitudes to age and sexuality within the British society, and a slow shift to a more inclusive approach to leadership. For many years, up until 2002 when the prize was given to the Canadian novelist Yann Martel (born in 1963), the Booker was typically awarded to older authors. For the first time, in 2004, the prize was given to a gay novel, *The Line of Beauty*, written by an openly gay author, Alan Hollinghurst. That year, the panel of judges was also chaired by an openly gay man, Chris Smith, who was the former UK Culture Secretary. Nevertheless, as Norris (2006) points out, the opening up of the Booker Prize to homosexual male authors did not mean that a similar extent of opening up was happening in relation to some of the other categories of social difference, especially class, which in the British context is inextricably connected to education within specific institutions (for further insights into related issues in the context of leadership, see Chapter 20, Critiquing leadership and gender research through a feminist lens, Chapter 41, Politicising the leader's body, and Chapter 43, Leadership representation). For example, all members of the judging panel that awarded the Booker to Hollinghurst, as well as the winning author himself, were Oxford-educated.

Both the prestige of the Booker and the controversies surrounding it have persisted over the years. In 2019, the prize was split between two novels: *The Testaments* by Margaret Atwood and *Girl, Woman, Other* by Bernardine Evaristo. Evaristo was the first black woman to ever have won the Booker – though in practice, she won half of the monetary prize and overall, possibly less than half of the in-store display space in bookshops, often dominated by or even exclusively given to Atwood's novel (Flood, 2019). Another controversy associated with the Booker has been the limited international diversity of the winners. Although the prize has been open to writers from all 53 Commonwealth countries (and since 2014 also to authors from the US), the circle of winners has only been represented by writers from eight Commonwealth countries outside the UK. The winners' list has been dominated by English writers, even though the English population comprises only 2.5 per cent of the Commonwealth population. Likewise, the narratives present in the shortlisted and winning novels have predominantly been those based on white experience. The history of the Booker is also marked by the lack of shortlisted novels written by Indigenous Australian writers and black South African writers, and by a very small number of black or Māori novelists, even if over the past few years, the number of black writers on the shortlist has increased, as exemplified by the inclusion of names such as Evaristo, Obioma, James or Edugyan among those recognised by the Booker judges. All this points to the persistence but also a slow thawing of the 'white elite' leadership model in the case of the Booker Prize.

In recent years, the Booker has come to be viewed as cultivating *a young, international, and racially-diverse cast of writers* (Eatough, 2021, p. 41). Over time, *the prize had morphed into something more like the Nobel Prize for Literature, the standard-bearer for international letters* (Holmes, 2021, 9), and in terms of the subject matter explored in the winning novels, the Booker has been described as favouring *intellectual engagement with the world* (Holmes, 2021, 11). In 2004, the Man Booker International Prize was created, to allow authors from outside the Commonwealth countries and literary works which were not originally published in English, as long as they have been translated into English. The International Booker showcases literary works written by authors from across the world, with awards between 2016 and 2020 given to writers from South Korea, Israel, Poland, Oman and the Netherlands.

The diversity of authors and topics that currently characterise the Booker Prize 'brand' is exemplified by the selection of shortlisted authors and novels. In 2020, the Booker shortlist – which could offer valuable inspiration to leadership scholars interested in advancing the field in a more inclusive, progressive and contemporarily relevant direction – included: 1) Douglas Stuart (the winner) – a debut novelist from a working-class Glaswegian background and an openly gay man, the author of *Shuggie Bain* – a novel about a young Scottish boy, inspired by the author's own upbringing and his mother's struggle with alcohol; 2) Avni Doshi – an American woman writer of ethnic Indian origin and the author of *Burnt Sugar* – an India-set story about a complex relationship between a daughter and her mother who has been diagnosed with Alzheimer's disease; 3) Brandon Taylor – an Alabama-born Black American gay man and the author of *Real Life* – a partly autobiographical campus novel about the experiences of a gay, black student studying towards a PhD in a predominantly white Midwestern university; 4) Diane Cook – a white American woman and the author of *The New Wilderness*, a dystopian story set in a world ravaged by climate change, about a mother's fight to save her daughter from perishing in that world; 5) Tsitsi Dangarembga – a Zimbabwean woman novelist and the author of *This Mournable Body* – a novel set in post-independence Zimbabwe, dealing with the condition of the Zimbabwean nation and the place of personal agency and responsibility for individuals' choices; and 6) Maaza Mengiste – an Ethiopia-born woman novelist currently living in New York and the author of *The Shadow King*, a novel about the African women soldiers in 1935 Ethiopia threatened by Mussolini's invasion.

As the Booker Prize 2020 shortlist suggests, regardless of the problematic nature of the 'institution' of book awards and especially the Booker (e.g., Holmes, 2021; Norris, 2006; O'Key, 2021) and its leadership, the recent developments in the world of literary fiction display a shift towards a greater diversity of the authors whose voices have been included as worth attending to as well as the subject matter of the books considered as deserving of recognition. In other words, the literary field has been redefining itself and undergoing a slow but sure decolonisation process, along with a serious and creative engagement with topics of import to 21st-century society. In the next section, I elaborate on the opportunities this self-redefinition of the literary field presents for the field of leadership studies which, as previously argued, continues to look for inspiration in the classical literary canon or in more contemporary novels which offer a vision of person-centric, hierarchical, undemocratic, white male-dominated leadership that does not provide an alternative to portrayals of leadership found in mainstream leadership studies.

THE LITERARY NOVEL AS A VEHICLE FOR ADDRESSING PROBLEMS WITH LEADERSHIP STUDIES

The first two sub-sections of this chapter have argued that management and organisation studies, and specifically leadership scholarship, has been drawing on literary fiction to advance both leadership research and education. Building on this, the third sub-section has suggested that the way in which leadership scholars have used literary fiction has been largely separated from – and not reflective of – the changes which the literary field has been undergoing over the past few decades. Then again, why would we worry about this? At the end of the day, is it fair and appropriate to expect leadership researchers and educators to be *au courant* with the developments in the world of fiction and, even if they were, then in what ways, if any, could this knowledge be expected to help with addressing the challenges that the field of leadership studies faces? I would like to propose affirmative answers to these questions, for two reasons. First, the discipline of leadership studies suffers from serious shortcomings and turning to contemporary fiction, in its diversity of the subject matter and authorship, might contribute to overcoming these. Second, critical leadership scholars have been grappling with the question of *whether and how leadership theory ought to be rebuilt* (Carroll et al., 2019, n.p.); here, again, drawing on some of the recent novels could certainly be of help.

Alvesson (2019, 27) offers a diagnosis of the key problematic aspects of leadership studies, which he systematises under eight labels: *Hollywood, Disneyland, closed system, two kinds of people, bees and the honeypot, reification, tautology and hyperreality problems*. In referring to *Hollywood*, Alvesson (2019, 29) points to the predilection of leadership theories to conform to a *hero mythology*, whereby *great leaders have a strong impact on mouldable followers*. In the depictions of leadership that are consistent with the hero mythology, organisational leaders are assumed to have the ability to *instill [sic] their values, beliefs, and assumptions within an organization* (Hartnell & Wallumbwa, 2011, 232). Drawing on examples of literary fiction which depict strong, male leaders as influencing, through their individual agency, the followers and the entire environment reinforces heroic views of leadership. However, turning to novels which present the embeddedness of all human action and reflection, and the ways in which what individuals do is inextricably linked to the actions of others and the broader historical, socioeconomic and cultural circumstances would help debunk the hero myth in leadership studies. In this regard, Douglas Stuart's *Shuggie Bain* offers an excellent analysis of such embeddedness through his depiction of how the lives of the novel's characters unfold against the backdrop of socioeconomic and cultural change in post-industrial Glasgow in the 1980s.

The *Disneyland ideology* is the label Alvesson (2019, 30) uses to describe leadership studies' *celebration of moral virtue as a key quality in effective leadership*. Authenticity and integrity are part of the moral virtue expected of and assumed about leaders, contributing to another myth about leadership which equips leaders with *messianic* qualities (Alvesson, 2011; Spoelstra & ten Bos, 2011; Tourish & Pinnington, 2002; also, Chapter 12, Authentic leadership or authenticity in leadership?, and Chapter 17, The myth of the passions). Again, there is a lot of scope for contributing to a more relational and multifaceted view of leadership drawing on novels that, unlike the classical Disney-style tales, dissect the moral complexity and ambiguity of human character, and show the capacity of people to act differently depending on circumstances. Among the 2020 Booker Prize shortlisted novels, Avni Doshi's *Burnt Sugar* could be drawn on by leadership scholars because, in its critical portrayal of life in an ashram, including the conduct of the guru and his followers, it questions the morality and ethics underlying leadership practice.

The *closed system* problem diagnosed by Alvesson (2019, 31) refers to how leadership studies scholars often treat leadership *as a closed system, made up* [of] *a limited, self-contained unit of a leader and a (or several) followers*. Again, to counter this problem, using novels that present the richness of context and address the multiple, historico-geographical, nonlinear interconnections between people, places, events and outcomes might help leadership scholars in moving away from the *closed system* view of leadership. An example of a novel that could be used by leadership scholars wishing to overcome the 'closed system' problem is Tsitsi Dangarembga's *This Mournable Body*. With its episodic structure and composition that experiments with a move away from the realist novel genre, the novel portrays the protagonist Tambu's life in contemporary Harare – and the different social worlds co-existing in the city – in a complex, contextualised and nonlinear way.

The fourth issue identified by Alvesson (2019, 32), *two kinds of people*, is described as the tendency of leadership studies to only present *two types of people: leaders and followers*. Such dichotomy, however, misrepresents the nature of human relations and identities. Obviously, literary fiction offers invaluable insights into the multiple ways people relate to one another, and contemporary fiction, with its diversity of characters – for example, in terms of ethnicity, race, gender, sexuality and age – deserves attention as a possible solution to the *two kinds of people* problem. Any of the six novels shortlisted for the 2020 Booker Prize could be drawn on by leadership scholars wishing to highlight the multiplicity and diversity of human relations and identities.

Further, Alvesson (2019) coins the term *bees and the honey pot* to describe another reason for his unease with leadership studies, namely, that due to the perceived high returns in career and financial terms for both academics and students, a lot of people are attracted to research, teaching and being trained in leadership, and a lot of very varied content becomes subsumed under the mega-discourse of leadership. As a result, the leadership discourse crowds out other possible discursive framings, such as *management, peer relations, professionalism, autonomy, co-workership, organizing processes or mutual adjustment* (Alvesson, 2019, 34). As a space within which complex and diverse types of relationships are described, and their difference examined, contemporary literary fiction provides multiple opportunities for exploring and pushing the boundaries of what we understand as leadership versus non-leadership. Again, any of the 2020 Booker Prize shortlisted novels could serve as a source of interrogation and insights into the nuanced phenomena that often get subsumed under the mega-discourse of leadership.

The fifth predicament that, according to Alvesson (2019, 34), the field of leadership studies suffers from is *reification – turning leadership into an 'it'*, or the fact that *all the popular leadership theories assemble a more or less complex, vague and varied qualities into a seemingly coherent, integrated and solid phenomenon becoming a suitable object for measurement*. The reification of leadership, in Alvesson's (2019) view, also makes it impossible to consider within leadership theories the *leadership according to whom?* question, and taking into account that different parties within the leadership relation will often have a different perspective and view on the aspects of leadership. Yet again, literary novels – and especially pieces of contemporary fiction that focus on matters of great importance to present-day society, and describe them as seen from the viewpoint of diverse characters, with different values and agendas – can help leadership scholars unsettle such reified, one perspective-based notions and elements of leadership. Diane Cook's book *The New Wilderness* which addresses the timely subjects of the climate crisis and human individualism and destructiveness, while half-way switching the narrative from one protagonist's (Bea, the mother) to another one's (Agnes, the daughter), is an inspirational example of such a novel.

Alvesson (2019, 35) also takes an issue with what he calls a *tautology* of *the good leads to the good* within leadership studies. He points out that very often, knowledge claims about leadership are made on the basis of conceptually and empirically weak research. This, for example, tends to be the case with questionnaire-based studies which, in Alvesson's (2019, 35) opinion, typically claim a connection between individuals' influence and positive outcomes on the basis of *highly subjective ratings of people evaluating leadership*. Of course, compared to questionnaire inventories, literary fiction provides a much more sophisticated way of capturing the ambiguities of influence, and the multiple and often indirect ways in which things, people and places are interconnected. They also have a unique ability to show how particular outcomes result from complex entanglements of external, structural conditions, existing relations of power, and individuals' agency. All of the 2020 Booker Prize shortlisted novels offer a complex account of such interconnections and entanglements.

Finally, Alvesson (2019, 36) identifies the eighth problem with leadership studies, which he labels *hyperreality – or who cares about reality?*. He challenges leadership studies scholars by expressing doubt about whether, when conducting empirical research, they are actually interested in organisational reality. Alvesson (2019, 36) argues that data derived from questionnaires or one-off interviews with individuals disconnected from one another *are usually distanced from actions, events, feelings, relations, articulations of opinions, etc. emerging in everyday life situations*. Valuable insights into such 'everyday life' phenomena, be it those occurring within organisational or other contexts, are offered by literary fiction. In particular, they can be found in contemporary novels as these have been written by authors who might have themselves experienced or at least observed them, as is the case, for example, with Brandon Taylor's novel *Real Life*, based on the author's own experience as a young black gay man on a PhD programme in a predominantly white university in the US, and Douglas Stuart's *Shuggie Bain*, drawing on the author's experience of growing up in Thatcher-era Scotland.

CONCLUSION

This chapter has argued for a more discerning engagement of leadership scholars with literary fiction. I have recommended, in particular, a turn towards more recent literary fiction, and especially towards fiction that would offer a different view of society – and leadership – to that found in 'traditional' leadership studies. Of course, this does not mean that there are no novels in the 'classical' canon that might help us reimagine leadership or that all contemporary fiction has this potential. Nevertheless, it is the contemporary novel that offers us a uniquely insightful glimpse into present-day world, together with its challenges which Carroll et al. (2019, n.p.) poignantly describe as:

> a number of catastrophes that can clearly be laid at leadership's door – global warming, polarisation of wealth and poverty, unresolved and often generational conflicts and wars, racism, sexism and fear of mistrust of 'the other' – to name but a few.

Contemporary literary fiction, written by diverse authors and exploring a broad range of societally relevant topics from a variety of perspectives can help us understand better these catastrophes and can inspire us to find new ways of addressing them through opening up new avenues for thinking about leadership.

REFERENCES

Alvesson, M. (2011). The leader as saint. In M. Alvesson & A. Spicer (Eds.), *Metaphors We Lead By: Understanding Leadership in the Real World* (pp. 51–75). Routledge.

Alvesson, M. (2019). Waiting for Godot: Eight major problems in the odd field of leadership studies. *Leadership*, 15(1), 27–43.

Badaracco, J. L. (2006). *Questions of Character: Illuminating the Heart of Leadership through Literature*. Harvard Business Review Press.

Beyes, T., Costas, J., & Ortmann, G. (2019). Novel thought: Towards a literary study of organization. *Organization Studies*, 40(12), 1787–1803.

Bröchner, J. (2021). Construction project management fiction: Individual values. *International Journal of Project Management*, 39(6), 594–604. doi: 10.1016/j.ijproman.2021.04.005.

Burns, J. M. (1978). *Leadership*. Harper Perennial Political Classics. HarperCollins.

Carroll, B., Firth, J., & Wilson, S. (2019). *After Leadership*. Routledge.

Ciulla, J. B. (1995). Leadership ethics: Mapping the territory. *Business Ethics Quarterly*, 5(1), 5–28.

Ciulla, J. B., Knights, D., Mabey, C., & Tomkins, L. (2018). Philosophical contributions to leadership ethics. *Business Ethics Quarterly*, 28(1), 1–14.

Colton, R. G. (2020). Modelling leadership in Tolkien's fiction: Craft and wisdom, gift and task. *Journal of Business Ethics*, 163, 401–415.

Currie, G. (2016). Models as fictions, fictions as models. *The Monist*, 99, 296–310.

Czarniawska, B. (1999). *Writing Management: Organization Theory as a Literary Genre*. Oxford University Press.

Czarniawska-Joerges, B., & Guillet de Monthoux, P. (Eds.) (1994). *Good Novels, Better Management: Reading Organizational Realities*. Routledge.

De Cock, C., & Land, C. (2006). Organization/literature: Exploring the seam. *Organization Studies*, 27, 517–535.

DeVault, M. L. (1990). Novel readings: The social organization of interpretation. *American Journal of Sociology*, 95(4), 887–921.

DeVault, M. L. (1999). *Liberating Method: Feminism and Social Research*. Temple University Press.

Eagly, A. H., & Carli L. L. (2007). *Through the Labyrinth: The Truth About Women Leaders*. Harvard Business School Press.

Eatough, M. (2021). 'Are they going to say this is fantasy?': Kazuo Ishiguro, untimely genres, and the making of literary prestige. *MFS: Modern Fiction Studies*, 67(1), 40–66.

Flood, A. (2019). Bernadine Evaristo doubles lifetime sales in five days after joint Booker win. *Guardian*, 22 October. https://www.theguardian.com/books/2019/oct/22/bernardine-evaristo-doubles-lifetime-sales-in-five-days-after-joint-booker-win

Frenkel, R. (2008). The politics of loss: Post-colonial pathos and current Booker Prize-nominated texts from India and South Africa. *Scrutiny2: Issues in English Studies in Southern Africa*, 13(2), 77–88.

Gosling, J., & Villiers, P. (Eds.) (2012). *Leadership in Literature*. Palgrave Macmillan.

Griffin, M., Learmonth, M., & Piper, N. (2018). Organizational readiness: Culturally mediated learning through Disney animation. *Academy of Management Learning & Education*, 17(1), 4–23.

Harrington, A. (2002). Robert Musil and classical sociology. *Journal of Classical Sociology*, 2(1), 59–75.

Hartnell, C., & Walumbwa, F. (2011). Transformational leadership and organizational culture: Toward integrating a multilevel framework. In N. Ashkanasy, C. Wilderom & M. Peterson (Eds.), *Handbook of Organizational Culture and Climate* (2nd edn) (pp. 131–144). Sage.

Hermida-Ruiz, A. (2008). The relevance of Don Quixote to leadership studies: Nostalgia, cynicism, and ambivalence. In J. B. Ciulla (Ed.), *Leadership at the Crossroads* (pp. 20–50). Praeger.

Holmes, C. (2021). The Booker Prize and the post-imperial British literature. *Oxford Research Encyclopaedia of Literature*. 26 May. doi: 10.1093/crefore/9780190201098.013.417

Holt, R., & Zundel, M. (2014). Understanding management, trade, and society through fiction: Lessons from *The Wire*. *Academy of Management Review* 39: 576–585.

Hoyt, C. L., & Simon, S. (2016). Gender and leadership. In P. G. Northouse (Ed.), *Leadership: Theory and Practice* (7th edn) (pp. 397–426). Sage.

Huggan, G. (2001). *The Postcolonial Exotic: Marketing the Margins*. Routledge.

Kajtár, L. (2015). What Mary didn't read: On literary narratives and knowledge. *Ratio, 39*(3), 327–343.

Kempster, S., & Parry, K. (2019). After leaders: A world of leading and leadership ... with no leaders. In B. Carroll, J. Firth & S. Wilson (Eds.), *After Leadership* (pp. 64–80). Routledge.

Ketner, K. L., Samway, P. H., & Percy, W. (1995). *A Thief of Peirce: The Letters of Kenneth Laine Ketner and Walker Percy*. University of Mississipi Press.

Knights, D., & Willmott, H. (1999). *Management Lives: Power and Identity in Work Organizations*. Sage.

Loacker, B. (2021). Entrepreneurship and the struggle over order and coherence: A thematic reading of Robert Musil's 'The Man Without Qualities'. *Culture and Organization, 27*(5), 403–422. doi: 10.1080/14759551.2020.1861451

Longo M. (2015). *Fiction and Social Reality: Literature and Narrative as Sociological Resources*. Ashgate.

McManus, R. M., & Perruci, G. (2015). *Understanding Leadership: An Arts and Humanities Perspective*. Routledge.

Martin, L., Edwards, M., & Sayers, J. (2018). A 'novel' discovery: Exploring women's literary fiction for use in management and leadership education. *Academy of Management Learning and Education, 17*(1), 24–40.

Morris P. (2020). The 'leftovers of empire': Commonwealth writers and the Booker Prize *Journal of Postcolonial Writing, 56*(2), 261–270.

Nehls, K. (2012). Leadership education: The power of storytelling. In J. D. Barbour, G. J. Burgess, L. Lid Falkman & R. M. McManus (Eds.), *Leading in Complex Worlds* (pp. 63–77). Jossey-Bass.

Norris, S. (2006). The Booker Prize: A Bourdieusian perspective. *Journal for Cultural Research, 10*(2), 139–158.

O'Key, D. (2021). Han Kang's *The Vegetarian* and the International Booker Prize: Reading with and against world literary prestige. *Textual Practice*. doi: 10.1080/0950236X.2021.1900376

Parker, M., Higgins, M., Lighfoot, G., & Smith, W. (1999). Amazing tales: Organization studies as science fiction. *Organization, 6*(4), 579–590.

Peters, T. D., & Nesteruk, J. (2014). Management as a liberal art: The legacy of the Hartwick Humanities in Management Institute. *Organizational Management Journal, 11*(3), 159–170.

Phillips, N. (1995). Telling organizational tales: On the role of narrative fiction in the study of organizations. *Organization Studies, 16*, 625–649.

Polkinghorne, D. E. (1988). *SUNY Series in Philosophy of the Social Sciences: Narrative Knowing and the Human Sciences*. State University of New York Press.

Rhee, K. S., & Sigler, T. H. (2015). Untangling the relationship between gender and leadership. *Gender in Management, 30*(2), 109–134.

Savage, P., Cornelissen, J., & Franck, H. (2018). Fiction and organization studies. *Organization Studies, 39*(7), 875–994.

Sinclair, A., & Evans, M. (2015). Difference and leadership. In B. Carroll, J. Ford & S. Taylor (Eds.), *Leadership: Contemporary Critical Perspectives* (pp. 130–149). Sage.

Śliwa, M., & Cairns, G. (2007). The novel as a vehicle for organizational inquiry: Engaging with the complexity of social and organizational commitment. *ephemera. theory & politics in organization, 7*(2), 309–325.

Śliwa, M., Sørensen, B. M., & Cairns, G. (2015). 'You have to choose a novel': The biopolitics of critical management education. *Management Learning, 46*(3), 243–259.

Śliwa, M., Spoelstra, S., Sørensen, B. M., & Land, C. (2013). Profaning the sacred in leadership studies: A reading of Murakami's *A Wild Sheep Chase*. *Organization, 20*(6), 860–880.

Spoelstra, S., & ten Bos, R. (2011). Leadership. In M. Painter-Morland & R. ten Bos (Eds.), *Business Ethics and Contemporary Philosophy* (pp. 181–198). Cambridge University Press.

Squires, C. (2004). A common ground? Book prize culture in Europe. *Javnost: The Public, 11*(4), 37–47.

Sucher, S. J. (2007). *Teaching the Moral Leader: A Literature-Based Leadership Course. A Guide for Instructors*. Routledge.

Todd, R. (1996). *Consuming Fictions: The Booker Prize and Fiction in Britain Today*. Bloomsbury.

Tourish, D., & Pinnington, A. (2002). Transformational leadership, corporate cultism and the spirituality paradigm: An unholy trinity in the workplace? *Human Relations, 55*(2), 147–152.

Vizmuller-Zocco, I. (2016). Science fiction and ontologies of leadership. *Rivista Internazionale Di Filosofia E Psicologia, 5*(3), 354–363.

Waldo, D. (1968). *The Novelist on Organization and Administration*. Institute of Government Studies.

Walter, D. (2014). Tolkien's myths are a political fantasy. *Guardian*. https://www.theguardian.com/books/booksblog/2014/dec/12/tolkiens-myths-are-a-political-fantasy

Warner, N. O. (2008). Of 'gods and commodores': Leadership in Melville's Moby-Dick. In J. B. Ciulla (Ed.), *Leadership at the Crossroads* (pp. 3–19). Praeger.

Warner, N. O. (2011). Leadership in literary perspective. In M. Harvey & R. E. Riggio (Eds.), *Leadership Studies: The Dialogue of Disciplines* (pp. 171–183). Edward Elgar.

PART 4

Within: Leadership as a Contextually Bound Phenomenon

29

How and Why is Context Important in Leadership?

Burak Oc and Joseph A. Carpini

Leadership can be defined as *a goal-influence process that occurs between a leader and a follower, groups of followers, or institutions* that directs effort towards the achievement of a shared objective (Antonakis & Day, 2018, p. 5). From this definition, we can distil four key elements of leadership: a) leaders, b) followers, c) influence and d) goals, motivation and performance. While leaders and followers are the main actors of leadership processes, how they influence each other has implications for group goals. However, most leadership research focuses on leaders, largely treating them as the sole driver of organisation success or failure (Kelley, 1988; Oc & Bashshur, 2013; Uhl-Bien et al., 2014). One upside of this overemphasis on leaders is a rich body of work on how dispositional characteristics and behaviours of leaders influence followers, the process between leaders and followers, and goals, motivations and performance of the group. The downside, of course, is the short shrift given to followers and other elements of leadership.

Where does this leave us with context of leadership? Although not part of the definition, context (along with followers) has become a prominent theme in leadership scholarship. This is because research has highlighted inconsistencies in the relationships between certain leader traits (e.g., extraversion) or behaviours (e.g., transformational leadership) and important leadership outcomes (e.g., individual and group performance). Such inconsistencies point to important contextual elements that shape the outcomes of leadership. Building on a rich tradition of contingency models recognising the interaction between individuals and their context, Fiedler (1978) pioneered the contingency theories of leadership. He claimed that a leader's leadership style by itself is not enough to understand why some groups of followers perform better than others, but rather that the suitability of the leadership style depends on leader, followers and situational factors. Other contingency theories followed in Fiedler's footsteps (e.g., Boyatzis, 1982; House & Mitchell, 1974; Vroom & Yetton, 1973) whereby followers were considered to be part of the leadership context. Even though this line of work generated a significant amount of research interest for almost a decade, context has, once again, fallen out of sight, largely overshadowed by new-age leadership theories (Day & Antonakis, 2012).

The good news is, though, increased desire to understand the impact of contextual factors in leadership in the past two decades (e.g., Johns, 2006; Rousseau & Fried, 2001) led researchers to reconsider the potential role that context might play in shaping leadership and its resultant outcomes (Hannah et al., 2009; Oc, 2018; Osborn et al., 2002; Porter & McLaughlin, 2006). In its entirety, contextual leadership explores the extent to which situational or contextual factors moderate the nature of the relationships among the main four elements of the leadership definition (Day & Antonakis, 2012; Liden & Antonakis, 2009; Oc, 2018).

Although interest in contextual leadership has been increasing, theoretical and empirical progress has been stifled somewhat due to a lack of agreement on which factors should be considered for the context of leadership. While some considered characteristics of market conditions or stages of an organisation's life cycle (e.g., Shamir & Howell, 1999; Osborn et al., 2002), others were interested to understand how leadership occurs in rather extreme contexts *where one or more extreme events are occurring or are likely to occur that may exceed the organization's capacity to prevent and result in an extensive and intolerable magnitude of physical, psychological, or material consequences to – or in close physical or psycho-social proximity to – organization members* (Hannah et al., 2009, p. 898).

To introduce some structure to this diverse body of research, Oc (2018) most recently used Johns's (2006) categorical framework to conceptualise the leadership context at two different levels, namely the omnibus context and the discrete context. Within this framework, he systematically reviewed the existing empirical research on the impact of contextual factors on leadership and its outcomes. In addition, he focused on how contextual factors represent their effects on leadership and its outcomes (e.g., affecting base rates, studied range of variables, and the nature of relationships as well as threatening the generalisability of findings). While the work by Oc (2018) pays significant attention to investigating the current structures, themes and meanings representing the context of leadership, his review offers less room for unsettling, critiquing and revitalising how contextual factors can be studied in leadership research. Thus, our main goal in this chapter is to focus on the latter and point to important theoretical gaps in the literature, methodological concerns and implications for contextualising leadership. Before we do so, this chapter will begin with a brief overview of the omnibus and discrete context of leadership.

THE OMNIBUS AND DISCRETE CONTEXT OF LEADERSHIP

Leadership occurs within a multilayered, multidimensional context, which Johns (2006) conceptualises at two different levels: a) the *omnibus context* and b) the *discrete context*. On one hand, the omnibus context includes contextual or environmental factors. These factors can be aptly summarised in the questions: *who* is being led, as well as *where* and *when* is leadership occurring? As Johns (2006) describes it, the omnibus context represents *an entity that comprises many features or particulars* [and] *refers to context broadly considered* (p. 391). On the other hand, Johns (2006) considers the discrete context as specific situational variables including the *task*, *social* and *physical* aspects of context, which either directly affect elements of leadership or moderate relationships between them. Although not included in Johns's conceptualisation of the discrete context, but in accordance with previous research on contextual leadership (Hannah et al., 2009; Porter & McLaughlin, 2006) and other areas of organisational research (e.g., teams: Marks et al., 2001), the *temporal* context should also be incorporated.

Next, using the same taxonomy, we turn our attention to *sense-breaking* which draws out what we consider to be the most pressing theoretical and methodological opportunities in the study of contextual leadership. In doing so, where relevant, we briefly discuss common empirical findings with respect to how omnibus and discrete contextual factors influence different elements of leadership (i.e., leaders, followers, influence, goals/performance) and the theoretical arguments and methodologies used to explain and test these findings. We begin by considering four important theoretical gaps, then turn our attention to three methodological concerns.

Important Theoretical Gaps in the Literature

Does research focus on the four elements of leadership equally? The simple answer is 'no'. As summarised in Figure 29.1, research examining the effect of omnibus and discrete contextual factors developed differently, resulting in four distinct trends. First, leader-related criterion variables are the most studied outcomes of omnibus contextual factors. Specifically, this research examines how the congruence between leaders and the omnibus, macro context of leadership predicts leader's leadership behaviours, leader emergence and so on. Concerning is the fact that these efforts fail to include theoretically relevant mediators in theorised models. This begs the question whether omnibus contextual factors act as distal predictors in these theoretical models with more proximal meso, micro and individual underlying mechanisms

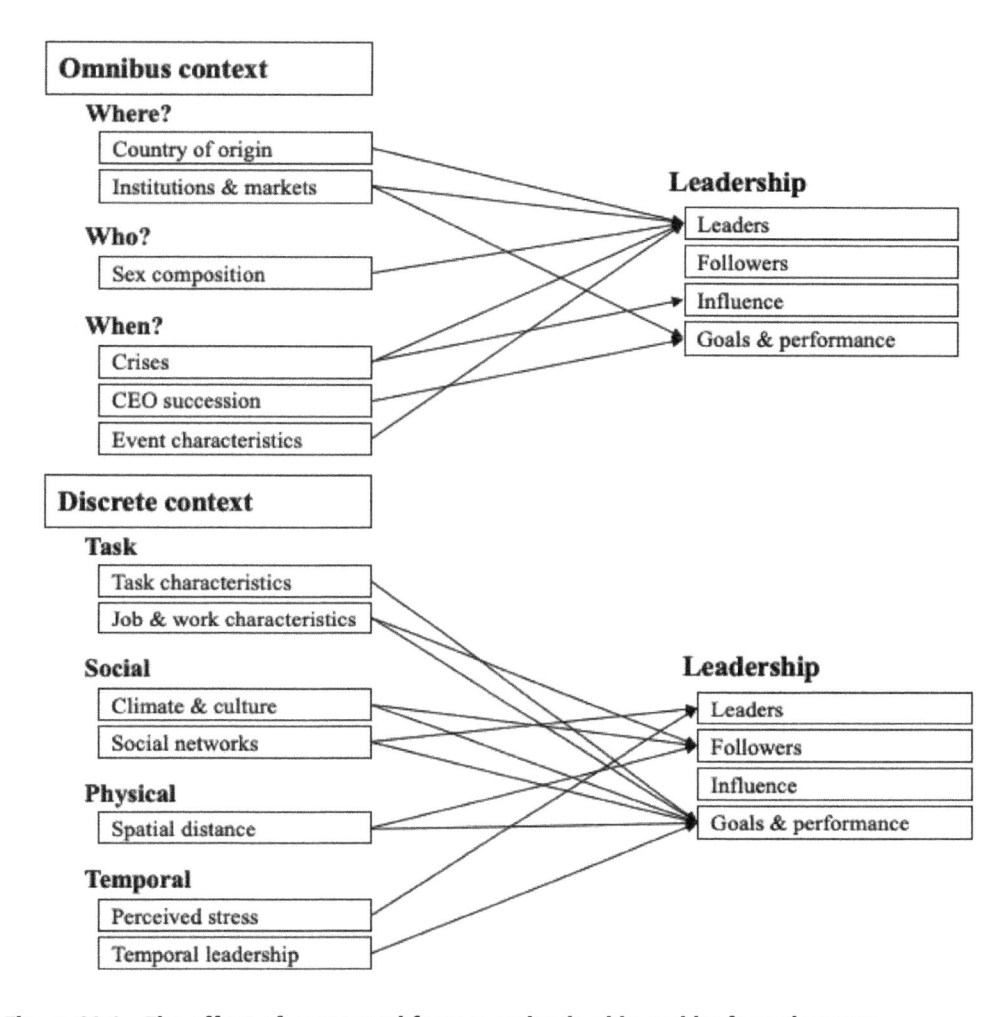

Figure 29.1 The effect of contextual factors on leadership and its four elements

Note: The arrows represent frequent cases (greater than 75 per cent of the studies).

explaining the hypothesised relationships. Elaborating the mediating mechanisms across different levels will provide a rich framework for future research and will help enhance the predictive ability of theories. Indeed, there is often a fine line in theorising unmeasured mediators versus not providing enough conceptual justification. In the absence of empirical data, we wonder whether bolstering theorising is enough.

Second, follower-related criterion variables are the least studied outcomes of omnibus contextual factors. We fear that the reason why there is a lack of emphasis on the potential effects of omnibus context on followers can be explained by the fact that research dedicated to followership – that is *the nature and impact of followers and following in the leadership process* (Uhl-Bien et al., 2014, p. 89) – is a relatively new area and measurement instruments to identify various followership typologies and styles have been scarce. On the other hand, implicit followership theories (IFTs), which focus on how leaders and followers classify followers based on their traits and behaviours and how well they match prototypes of followers (Sy, 2010), can help generate further research. An interesting finding in this research is that a leader's IFT can lead to a Pygmalion effect. Using leader–follower dyads, Whiteley et al. (2012) showed that leaders' positive IFTs strongly related to leaders having higher performance expectations than their followers, liking their followers more and building higher-quality exchange relationships with them, all of which related to better follower performance. If so, we wonder whether omnibus contextual factors such as cultural differences can feed into leader's own expectations leading to confirmation of those expectations.

Third, it is follower performance that is the most studied outcome of discrete contextual factors. In other words, researchers theorised and tested how the omnibus context affects leaders themselves, and how discrete context shapes the performance of followers. Major theoretical frameworks such as social identity theory (Tajfel, 1974) and social learning theory (Bandura, 1977) as well as contingency leadership theories (e.g., Fiedler's contingency model: Fiedler, 1978; path–goal theory: House, 1971) are the usual suspects for such focus. These theories help researchers easily theorise the impact of discrete contexts on follower performance. Yet, there may be missed opportunities, in particular around the effect of physical characteristics such as 'the sick building syndrome' (poor indoor air quality and lack of personal control; Crawford & Bolas, 1996), to improve our understanding of how the more understudied aspects of discrete context can shape follower performance.

Fourth, it is influence that is the least studied outcome of the discrete contextual factors. It is however difficult to explain why researchers chose not to pay greater attention to how discrete contextual factors shape the influence process between leaders and followers. There is in fact theoretical work that can inform empirical research. For instance, Oc and Bashshur (2013) argue that the extent to which followers, through social influence, can shape how leaders act depends on several follower-related factors including physical distance between the leader and followers (i.e., the physical context), the number of followers in a group and the unity among followers (i.e., the social context), as well as the frequency of leader–follower interactions (i.e., the temporal context). This work can also be extended to the potential effect followers might have on leader's self-concepts (Lord & Brown, 2001) and contribute to a better understanding of the role that discrete contextual factors play as leaders and followers co-produce leadership (DeRue & Ashford, 2012).

Do the omnibus and discrete contexts speak to each other? Another question that needs to be explored is how the omnibus context and the discrete context relate to each other. According to both Johns (2006) and Oc (2018), discrete contextual factors can be described as a subset of omnibus contextual factors such that they can help explain different features of the omnibus context. Thus, discrete contextual factors can be theorised as the underlying mechanisms driving the effects of omnibus contextual factors on leadership and its outcomes. For instance, if we want to understand whether leaders engage in different leadership behaviours in different types of organisations (i.e., the *where* dimension of the omnibus context), we may want to explore whether those differences are driven because of differences in social and physical characteristics of the discrete context as a function of the type of organisation, the omnibus context. In bringing the omnibus and discrete contexts together, we address theoretical gaps related to the potential mediators between the omnibus context and various criteria.

The potential impact of the *when* dimension of the omnibus context of the temporal dimension of the discrete context can serve as another good example of the benefits of such an approach. While existing research explores how charisma and charismatic rhetoric affects leader outcomes in times of crises (e.g., Davis & Gardner, 2012; Williams et al., 2012; Williams et al., 2009), research does not explore how crises might affect leader's perceived stress or interact with leader's temporal dispositions (Chen & Nadkarni, 2017; Mohammed & Nadkarni, 2011) to predict leadership effectiveness. Examining temporal leadership as the underlying mechanism and the temporal dispositions of leaders and followers as the moderators that explain how crises affect leaders and followers is another 'low-hanging fruit'. Similarly, considering leadership from an event-driven concept and time as the limited resource leaders have, we know that leaders do not necessarily devote enough time to activities directly related to leadership (e.g., Alvesson & Sveningsson, 2003; Holmberg & Tyrstrup, 2010). It will be theoretically interesting to see how omnibus and discrete contextual factors along with leader's temporal dispositions may shape how much time leaders save for leadership activities which in turn shape leadership outcomes. The following questions are other examples of thought experiments helping us learn more about the impact and interaction of the *when* dimension of the omnibus context with the discrete context factors on leadership. For instance, can CEO succession or characteristics of events at the omnibus level shape the social networks at the discrete level? How will institutional or market changes affect the task context of leadership? Will leaders and followers differ in terms of temporal dispositions depending on their country of origin and whether temporal leadership is conceptualised differently in an Asian context as opposed to a Western context?

In addition to the main effects, we can also explore the interaction of omnibus and discrete contextual factors. For instance, one can examine whether the relationship between social and physical characteristics of the discrete context and the type of behaviours leaders engage in can change depending on the type of organisation. Thus, considering the omnibus context and the discrete context in a nested manner, with the omnibus context being the higher-level variable, will help better pinpoint top-down effects. Such an approach represents leadership as a complex multilevel system (Oc, 2018) and mimics more contemporary areas of leadership research that assert that *leadership is multi-level, processual, contextual and interactive* (Uhl-Bien & Marion, 2009, p. 631). Therefore, several key theoretical questions in the contextual leadership may be better answered by a multilevel approach, that can also help us test boundary conditions of some of the relationships researchers heavily explored in the past. For example, will the effects of sex composition on leader emergence and leader effectiveness weaken or strengthen as the spatial distance increases? How would temporal leadership change the relationship between institutional/market forces and organisational performance? Should we theoretically expect organisational or national culture to moderate the relationship between CEO succession and organisational performance (you can find some hints in Chapter 19, Self-regulatory focus and leadership)?

Can one create profiles of context? To date, the primary approach to exploring the effect of contextual factors on leadership is to examine the consequences of each contextual factor in conjunction with leader and follower characteristics (Oc, 2018). This analytic method describes a *variable-centred* approach in which the impact of context on leadership via unique and different relations is demonstrated (as we discuss in the section above). For example, variable-centred approaches (i.e., correlation, regression) frequently test linear relationships among theorised variables, overlooking the possibility for these variables to associate in new and different ways to affect leadership outcomes. Even though interaction terms can be used to describe how two or three different constructs coalesce in variable-centred approaches, such analytic approaches fail to discover the presence of unique and distinct subgroups of context that show different patterns of the studied variables, especially when a relatively small number of contexts characterise a subgroup.

Variable-centred approaches fail to explain whether certain situations or contexts with unique combinations of characteristics exist and affect how leadership unfolds. For instance, the theoretical works by Osborn et al. (2002) and Hannah et al. (2009) took a stab at defining dimensions of different types of contexts. Such theoretical efforts suggest that different types of leadership contexts likely exist, and a *context-centred* approach needs to be employed to investigate whether there are distinct subpopulations of contextual factors that conjointly within context affect leadership. Similarly, doing so can help us better understand whether leaders might engage in initiating structure and consideration behaviours at different intensities across contexts. To do so, research can adopt inductive approaches to form context profiles using latent profile analysis (LPA, e.g., Gabriel et al., 2015). Instead of using interaction terms of multiple contextual factors or analyses and potentially creating artificial categories of context, approaches like LPA can form categories based on heterogeneity observed in the data (Morin et al., 2011). Indeed, whereas traditional variable-centred analyses report averaged estimates of the observed relationships in the data, person-centred analyses consider subpopulation effects based on quantitative and qualitative differences (Morin et al., 2011). Research seeking to identify such typologies may provide the impetus for theoretical development surrounding the dimensionality of the omnibus and discrete contexts.

What happened to the contextualisation? One of the critical steps of understanding how context can shape leadership is contextualising where the leadership unfolds. Rousseau and Fried (2001) described contextualisation as the *linking of observations to a set of relevant facts, events or point of view that make possible research and theory that form part of a larger whole* (p. 1) and identified six issues related to selecting the right research setting and assessment tools: 1) construct comparability, 2) points of view, 3) representativeness, 4) range restriction, 5) time and 6) levels. While we believe contextualisation of leadership research can be the focus of another review or meta-analysis, readers can find an excellent example in Chapter 35, The impact of context on healthcare leadership. Inspired by the recent novel coronavirus pandemic and its implications on health systems across and within countries, the authors provide an intellectually engaging and demanding conversation (rich with metaphors) around the context in healthcare. In doing so, they similarly touch on the distinction between external (i.e., omnibus) and internal (i.e., discrete) factors of the healthcare context and identify the importance of leading change in rapidly changing, complex healthcare settings.

Can leadership shape its own context? Existing research in organisational theory can shed light on this question. On one hand, consistent with environmental determinism, organisational theories attempt to describe the organisations' strategic choices, behaviour and outcomes by almost exclusively studying characteristics of the organisation's external environment (e.g., Betton & Dess, 1985;

Hannan & Freeman, 1977). These theories suggest that scarce environmental resources force organisations to continuously adapt to benefit from external environmental changes (also known as institutional logics, that inform how organisations make sense of and respond to situations; Hatch & Cunliffe, 2013). For instance, using the arguments rooted in environmental determinism, Delegach et al. (Chapter 19, Self-regulatory focus and leadership) make a compelling case for how environmental determinism can shape an important boundary condition for leader regulatory focus and organisational outcomes. On one hand, leaders with a promotion focus on advancement, accomplishments and aspirations (Higgins, 1997) can help their organisations perform better in dynamic market conditions, which forces organisations and those leading them to be more proactive, follow more complex strategic goals and end up making risky decisions (Ruiz-Ortega et al., 2013). On the other hand, leaders with a prevention focus on safety, responsibilities and obligations (Higgins, 1997) likely shine in more stable environments but may be ill-suited to more dynamic and uncertain business contexts. In contrast, several others expanded the view to also consider how organisations actively attempt to navigate and change their environments either by establishing inter-organisational alliances or by altering their institutional context (e.g., Thornton & Ocasio, 1999).

Although in this chapter we focus on the effect of contextual factors on leadership and its four elements, it becomes clear that the interesting question is whether or how leadership will change its own context (in particular the omnibus context) in a way similar to how organisations do. To help develop new theory in this area, we will need to reverse the lenses and have both leadership and followership research assign leaders and followers to a more active role (where possible). For instance, rather than studying the effects of crises or event characteristics, can research think of ways leaders and followers themselves a priori affect the base rates of organisational crises or CEO succession or restrict the range of event characteristics. What are the traits and/or behavioural qualities that help leaders prevent being exposed to certain types of crises or avoid forced succession? Similarly, what is the role that followers could play in diminishing the duration, urgency, magnitude, or even nature of disruptive events in organisations before they occur? For instance, in one of the few attempts Chizema et al. (2015) explore the impact of institutional forces (i.e., women's representation in politics, economic environment and religiosity) on the occurrence of female directors on corporate boards. Can we reverse the lenses here and ask ourselves what may be the characteristics of these female directors that in turn affect the institutional forces? Work on the context of leadership would be made richer if researchers reverse and broaden their lenses to consider these issues.

Methodological concerns

What can be said about the commonly employed study design and measurement of key constructs? Before we reflect on the robustness and the rigour with which the research on contextual leadership has progressed so far, we first want to spotlight two relatively important limitations that challenge the validity of findings in the field: a) study design and b) measurement. In particular, our aim is to consider whether the literature on contextual leadership suffers from potential problems of endogeneity so that future research takes the necessary steps to improve scientific and practical merit of research concerning the impact of context on leadership while considering these issues.

As it is evident from Table 29.1, cross-sectional, survey-based field studies are the most frequently used study designs. This should come as no surprise given that it is relatively hard to mimic leadership contexts, especially the omnibus contextual factors, in experimental laboratory studies. One possible avenue forward is the use of high-quality vignette studies for unravelling the unique effects of various contextual factors at both the omnibus and discrete levels. Experimental vignette studies *consist of presenting participants with carefully constructed and realistic scenarios to assess dependent variables including intentions, attitudes, and behaviors, thereby enhancing experimental realism and also allowing researchers to manipulate and control independent variables* (Aguinis & Bradley, 2014, p. 351). However, scholars should carefully consider the realism and representativeness of their manipulations (Highhouse, 2009) because using non-consequential tasks in low-stakes scenarios can produce offbeat effect sizes (e.g., Ma et al., 2017) and threatens the external validity of such studies (e.g., Hertwig & Ortmann, 2001). Thus, coupling vignette studies with other methodologies may help triangulate findings, bolster theoretical development and contribute to research that generalises.

An additional under-utilised methodology is the use of archival datasets. Archival data *entails capitalizing on research data that are already in existence* and includes such data as company records, government research archives, sports data, media-communications, historiometry, stock exchange information and O*NET (Barnes et al.,

Table 29.1 Most commonly used study designs and measurement of contextual factors, along with presence of meta-analytic evidence

Omnibus context	Dimensions	Study design	Measurement	Meta-analysis
Where?	Country of origin	Survey	Categorical variables	
	Institutional forces	Survey	Proxies	
	Market forces	Archival	Leader-rated psychometric scales	
Who?	Sex composition	Experimental Survey	Categorical variables	☑
When?	Crises	Survey Archival	Follower-rated psychometric scales Categorical variables	
	CEO succession	Survey	Categorical variables	☑
	Event characteristics	Survey	Leader- and follower-rated psychometric scales	

Discrete context	Dimensions	Study design	Measurement	Meta-analysis
Task	Task characteristics	Experimental Survey	Categorical variables Follower-rated psychometric scales	☑
	Job/Work characteristics	Experimental Survey	Categorical variables Follower-rated psychometric scales	☑
Social	Climate/Culture	Survey	Follower-rated psychometric scales	
	Social networks	Survey	Network measures	☑
Physical	Spatial distance	Survey	Follower-rated psychometric scales Categorical variables	☑
Temporal	Stress	Experimental Survey	Categorical variables Leader-rated psychometric scales	☑
	Temporal leadership	Survey	Follower-rated psychometric scales	

2018, p. 1454). An analysis of leadership-related scholarship by Antonakis et al. (2014) found only 10 per cent of articles published in top-tier social science included archival data. Archival datasets can allow researchers to identify the temporal order between study variables and eliminates the problem of reverse causality. For example, archival datasets can be used to understand the effect of the *when* dimension of the omnibus context and, in particular, the crises and institutional forces (e.g., Bligh & Hess, 2007; Scully et al., 1994). Datasets such as Archigos (originated from the Greek term for rule; Goemans et al., 2009), CHISOLS (i.e., change in source of leader support; Mattes et al., 2016), LEAD (i.e., the leader experience and attribute descriptions; Ellis et al., 2015) or DPI (i.e., database of political institutions; Beck et al., 2001) contain valuable information such as modes of leader transition and political institutions, and allow researchers to explore the effect of leaders in tandem with institutions on policy change across different time points in the history. Additionally, highly relevant, quantified and downloadable information about the discrete context is available through O*NET including physical proximity, level of competition and the level of work structure (see 'Work context'), all of which can be considered as discrete context, that offers an untapped opportunity for innovative research in this area.

Research concerning the effect of contextual factors on leadership has used a wide range of leader- and follower-rated psychometric scales as well as categorical variables (e.g., dummy coding for country of origin, coding events in archival datasets, dummy variables for the experimental conditions). While we will consider the psychometric measures in detail later, the categorical variables merit some attention.

Categorical variables are employed for at least three different purposes. First, they are used as objective measures representing the context. For instance, studies used nominal categorical variables to represent country of origin as an objective description of the omnibus context. They either compare Eastern countries to Western countries (e.g., Dorfman et al., 1997; Fu & Yukl, 2000) or use the same categories as proxies for cultural differences while showing separately how those cultural factors differ across countries (e.g., Ensari & Murphy, 2003). A similar creation of nominal categories also exists for sex composition – that is, groups of male majority, female majority groups, or equal sex composition (Eagly & Karau, 1991; Eagly et al., 1992) – as well as type of crises, incidents, or periods of time (e.g., Bligh & Hess, 2007; Davis & Gardner, 2012). Second, nominal categorical variables are frequently used to operationalise experimental conditions designed to test the effects of discrete contextual factors. In these studies, categories created represent treatment and control conditions. Third, and finally, ordinal categories are created to convert actual continuous measures of contextual factors. For instance, Howell and colleagues in two different studies converted physical distance between followers and leaders into a five-point scale ranging from 1 (*very close*) to 5 (*very distant*) and then further to a dichotomous variable (close versus distant) to ensure that their categorisation of physical distance included the majority of study participants (Howell et al., 2005). Although a pragmatic solution to a measurement issue, one should reflect as to the cost and benefits of such decisions given that the categorisation of otherwise continuous variables can increase measurement error (Liu et al., 2010).

When more objective operationalisations of contextual variables are not feasible, use of psychometric scales becomes a suitable method. Task- and job-related characteristics from Hackman and Oldham's (1976) Job Diagnostic Survey, the physical distance dimension of Kerr and Jermier's (1978) substitutes for leadership scale and Mohammed and Nadkarni's (2011) temporal leadership measure are some of the most used scales to measure discrete contextual factors. Researchers also frequently change or adapt some of the items, use a subset of items of scales or combine them with items from one or multiple scales. This frequently happens when there is no validated or widely used scale, the items provide poor contextual fit, or researchers want to reduce participant fatigue. While these strategies can be methodologically meaningful and reasonable, the fact that researchers rarely compare the psychometric properties of the new and original scale is somewhat problematic. As such, we recommend future research include an empirical consideration of how the new or revised measures relate to the established measures so the knowledge generated from the research can be integrated within the nomological network. Additionally, scholars should be encouraged to report all the revised items to ensure transparency and replicability either in-text or using online supplementary offerings (Carpini et al., 2017).

We next return to whether we believe that the findings in this field are prone to endogeneity concerns and how research can improve its practices in its pursuit of reporting unbiased, robust estimates of contextual factor effects.

Should we be concerned about endogeneity? From a methodological perspective, we consider the issue of endogeneity to be the most pressing as it poses a serious threat to the internal validity of research. While by no means a unique issue to contextual leadership research, we contend future scholars may want to pay special attention to certain threats more than others because of the nature of contextual factors. With this said, there is some good news that merits consideration. That is, we consider the issue of endogeneity in the study of contextual leadership an opportunity for future research. We now turn our attention to two primary issues before considering the 'good news'.

The first issue is that research has frequently studied either the main effect of contextual factors or their interaction effects with other factors on leadership, yet fails to include mediating variables in their theoretical models and analyses. Although absence of any underlying mechanisms may be a limitation, establishing causal relationships among study variables in mediation models is more difficult than it is presently represented in the current leadership literature. In fact, study designs that involve survey or even experimental studies that test mediational models without manipulating mediating variable(s) raise concerns about making causal inferences among study variables in the theorised model. In fact, analyses can be compromised if the mediating variable is endogenous (Antonakis et al., 2010). For instance, omitted variables, along with other potential threats, can create endogeneity and bias the estimation of causal effects of mediating variable(s) on the dependent variable. There are at least two potential solutions. On one hand, researchers can carry out endogeneity tests to see whether there is any empirical evidence to suggest that mediating variables are endogenous (i.e., they are systematically related to unobserved antecedents of dependent variables). This again may happen because of omitted variable bias as well as measurement errors in the dependent variables or reverse causality (Antonakis et al., 2010). Results of both the Hausman test and Durbin–Wu–Hausman endogeneity tests can help researchers reveal whether there is an endogeneity problem in their studies. If there is a problem, an instrumental variable approach may prove useful (Gennetian et al., 2008). On the other hand, researchers can employ a *experimental-causal-chain* design (Spencer et al., 2005, p. 846). When there is the chance to manipulate and measure a suggested psychological process (which involves at least two causal relationships), an examination of this process using a series of experiments is superior to relying on mediational analyses (Antonakis et al., 2010; Spencer et al., 2005). We strongly suggest leadership researchers consider the methodological solutions proposed by Spencer and colleagues (2005).

The second issue is that researchers have generally employed experimental studies to examine the effects of contextual factors, in particular discrete contextual factors, and have not considered issues of endogeneity. Even though randomised experiments can be considered the highest standard of causal evidence (Rubin, 2008), they are not immune to issues of endogeneity (Sajons, 2020). There are several reasons scholars should take note of this issue. For instance, assume that a researcher aims to understand the effect of temporal leadership on leadership effectiveness and manipulates temporal leadership. However, because perceptions of expressed leadership behaviours are manipulated, it is likely that such perceptions will be affected by a diverse range of omitted variables (e.g., personality traits, demographics). If known to researchers, they can control for the effects of these omitted variables; however, they may be sometimes unknown to researchers, or it may be simply unfeasible to include them all. There is then the so-called *post hoc ergo propter hoc* fallacy (Sajons, 2020, p. 1). We, researchers, like to think that when the explanatory variable happens before the outcome variable, the outcome variable must be caused by the explanatory variable. In fact, *omitted variables tend to correlate with themselves over time, and also with the outcome variable* (Sajons, 2020, p. 1). The use of experimentally randomised instrumental variables is an important solution to endogeneity problems (Sajons, 2020).

Where to from here? While issues related to endogeneity, study design and measurement are all pressing (see Antonakis et al., 2010; Sajons, 2020), we outline several avenues for overcoming these challenges and point to the possibility of theoretically rich and empirically sound research in the future. First and foremost, we believe that scholars must begin by asking themselves: *To what extent might omitted selection play a role in studying the effects of contextual factors?* Although one might consider context as a relatively exogenous factor (e.g., crises can be considered as exogenous shocks, opening doors to the use of regression discontinuities; Antonakis et al., 2010), the fact a) that the selection process into a group can be endogenous and b) that the samples recruited may not be representative (because leaders or followers might self-select themselves into specific context) potentially creates endogeneity bias in estimating the effect of contextual factors on leadership. For instance, sex composition of groups and CEO succession can be subject to such biases. Questioning the extent to which such unobserved factors may be influencing results is an important first step in designing better research and developing deeper theory.

In addition, most of the empirical research fails to include theoretically important control variables while simultaneously using cross-sectional study designs that are prone to common-method variance problems (e.g., Bernerth & Aguinis, 2016). We also fail to explore heteroscedasticity and assume that standard errors are normally distributed. Bligh and Hess (2007) as well as Chung and Luo (2008) are some of the few, noteworthy exceptions. Finally, using rather imperfect scales as explanatory variables and not including measurement error terms in our models biases the estimates of models exploring the effect of contextual factors on leadership.

The answers to some of these problems are quite simple and straightforward. The study design that we employ becomes critical. We will need to be aware of the advantages and disadvantages of using field and experimental studies. While field studies help us with external validity or generalisability of our findings, they are prone to threats to internal validity or threats to consistent estimates. In contrast, experimental studies are protected from threats to internal validity to a greater extent but can generate external validity concerns. In contrast, Highhouse (2009, p. 555) tempers the polarisation of research design concerns between field and laboratory studies because, when researchers are *caught up in the distinctiveness of the research setting,* [it] *implies that we are testing effects in settings rather than testing theories that should apply to multiple (especially organizational) settings.* As such, researchers should attend to ensuring issues of endogeneity are adequately addressed in both research settings as a primary concern. Moreover, a combination of field and laboratory studies may be, unsurprisingly, a compelling approach for future research.

Taken together, the next important question is the number and type of studies needed if we want to rigorously test our theorised model. If we aim to explain the underlying mechanisms of the theorised relationships, we will need to either use instrumental variable approaches, if the mediator(s) is (are), endogenous, or employ an experimental-causal-chain design (Spencer et al., 2005). Depending on the theorised model, we may need multiple studies to test our model in a progressive fashion. We may also need to perform experimental studies while incorporating Sajons's (2020) suggestions to address the issues around endogeneity. However, if an experimental manipulation of a contextual variable is not feasible, we then need to ascertain whether our model suffers from endogeneity, and if so, find and use instruments. If we cannot find instruments (which is not an easy task on its own), we need to highlight this as a limitation of the field study and consider performing quasi-experiments (which is also not an easy task). While we may sound like economists or econometricians, we echo Antonakis and colleagues' (2010) observation that economics underwent a similar period of research adjustment where scholars had to advance their methodological practices, particularly when trying to establish causal inferences. We are aware that these approaches will certainly result in us devoting more time and effort to generating our research but, at the expense of quantity, we will be able to offer higher-quality research. While leadership research has taken the lead in this quest, we hope that other fields of organisational behaviour will join the cause.

REFERENCES

Aguinis, H., & Bradley, K. (2014). Best practice recommendations for designing and implementing experimental vignette methodology studies. *Organizational Research Methods*, *17*(4), 351–371.

Alvesson, M., & Sveningsson, S. (2003). Good visions bad micro-management and ugly ambiguity: Contradictions of (non-)leadership in knowledge-intensive organization. *Organization Studies*, *24*, 961–988.

Antonakis, J., Bastardoz, N., Liu, Y., & Schriesheim, C. A. (2014). What makes articles highly cited? *Leadership Quarterly*, *25*(1), 152–179.

Antonakis, J., Bendahan, S., Jacquart, P., & Lalive, R. (2010). On making causal claims: A review and recommendations. *Leadership Quarterly*, *21*(6), 1086–1120.

Antonakis, J., & Day, D. (2018). Leadership: Past, present, and future. In J. Antonakis & D. V. Day (Eds.), *The Nature of Leadership* (3rd edn, pp. 3–26). Sage.

Bandura, A. (1977). *Social Learning Theory*. Prentice-Hall.

Barnes, C. M., Dang, C. T., Leavitt, K., Guarana, C. L., & Uhlmann, E. L. (2018). Archival data in micro-organizational research: A toolkit for moving to a broader set of topics. *Journal of Management*, *44*(4), 1453–1478.

Beck, T., Clarke, G., Groff, A., Keefer, P., & Walsh, P. (2001). New tools in comparative political economy: The database of political institutions. *World Bank Economic Review*, *15*(1), 165–176.

Bernerth, J., & Aguinis, H. (2016). A critical review and best-practice recommendations for control variable usage. *Personnel Psychology*, *69*(1), 229–283.

Betton, J., & Dess, G. (1985). The application of population ecology models to the study of organizations. *Academy of Management Review*, *10*, 750–757.

Bligh, M. C., & Hess, G. (2007). The power of leading subtly: Alan Greenspan, rhetorical leadership, and monetary policy. *Leadership Quarterly*, *18*, 87–104.

Boyatzis, R. (1982). *The Competent Manager: A Model for Effective Performance*. John Wiley & Sons.

Carpini, J., Parker, S., & Griffin, M. (2017). A look back and a leap forward: A review and synthesis of the individual work performance literature. *Academy of Management Annals*, *11*, 825–885.

Chen, J., & Nadkarni, S. (2017). It's about time! CEOs' temporal dispositions, temporal leadership, and corporate entrepreneurship. *Administrative Science Quarterly*, *62*, 31–66.

Chen, Z., Zhu, J., & Zhou, M. (2015). How does a servant leader fuel the service fire? A multilevel model of servant leadership, individual self identity, group competition climate, and customer service performance. *Journal of Applied Psychology*, *100*(2), 511–521.

Chizema, A., Kamuriwo, D. S., & Shinozawa, Y. (2015). Women on corporate boards around the world: Triggers and barriers. *Leadership Quarterly*, *26*(6), 1051–1065.

Chung, C., & Luo, X. (2008). Institutional logics or agency costs: The influence of corporate governance models on business group restructuring in emerging economies. *Organization Science*, *19*(5), 766–784.

Crawford, J., & Bolas, S. (1996). Sick building syndrome, work factors and occupational stress. *Scandinavian Journal of Work, Environment and Health*, *22*(4), 243–250.

Davis, K., & Gardner, W. (2012). Charisma under crisis revisited: Presidential leadership, perceived leader effectiveness, and contextual influences. *Leadership Quarterly*, *23*, 918–933.

Day, D., & Antonakis, J. (2012). Leadership: Past, present, and future. In D. V. Day & J. Antonakis (Eds.), *The Nature of Leadership* (2nd edn, pp. 3–25). Sage.

DeRue, S., & Ashford, S. (2010). Who will lead and who will follow? A social process of leadership identity construction in organizations. *Academy of Management Review*, *35*(4), 627–647.

Dorfman, P., Howell, J., Hibino, S., Lee, J., Tate, U., & Bautista, A. (1997). Leadership in Western and Asian countries: Commonalities and differences in effective leadership processes across cultures. *Leadership Quarterly*, *8*, 233–274.

Eagly, A., & Karau, S. (1991). Gender and the emergence of leaders: A meta-analysis. *Journal of Personality and Social Psychology, 60*, 685–710.

Eagly, A., Makhijani, M., & Klonsky, B. (1992). Gender and the evaluation of leaders: A meta-analysis. *Psychological Bulletin, 111*, 3–22.

Ellis, C., Horowitz, M., & Stam, A. (2015). Introducing the LEAD data set. *International Interactions, 41*(4), 718–41.

Ensari, N., & Murphy, S. (2003). Cross-cultural variations in leadership perceptions and attribution of charisma to the leader. *Organizational Behavior and Human Decision Processes, 92*, 52–66.

Fiedler, F. (1978). The contingency model and the dynamics of the leadership process. In L. Berkowitz (Ed.), *Advances in Experimental Social Psychology* (Vol. 11, pp. 59–96). Academic Press.

Fu, P., & Yukl, G. (2000). Perceived effectiveness of influence tactics in the United States and China. *Leadership Quarterly, 11*, 251–266.

Gabriel, A., Daniels, M., Diefendorff, J., & Greguras, G. (2015). Emotional labor actors: A latent profile analysis of emotional labor strategies. *Journal of Applied Psychology, 100*, 863–879.

Gennetian, L. A., Magnuson, K., & Morris, P. (2008). From statistical associations to causation: What developmentalists can learn from instrumental variables techniques coupled with experimental data. *Developmental Psychology, 44*(2), 381–394.

Goemans, H., Gleditsch, K., & Chiozza, G. (2009). Introducing Archigos: A data set of political leaders. *Journal of Peace Research, 46*(2), 269–183.

Hackman, J., & Oldham, G. (1976). Work redesign and motivation. *Professional Psychology, 11*(3), 445–455.

Hannah, S., Uhl-Bien, M., Avolio, B., & Cavaretta, F. (2009). A framework for examining leadership in extreme contexts. *Leadership Quarterly, 20*, 897–919.

Hannan, M., & Freeman, J. (1977). The population of ecology. *American Journal of Sociology, 82*, 929–964.

Hatch, J., & Cunliffe, A. (2013). *Organization Theory: Modern, Symbolic and Postmodern Perspectives*. Oxford University Press.

Hedge, A. (1982). The open-plan office: A systematic investigation of employees' reactions to their work environment. *Environment and Behavior, 14*, 519–542.

Hertwig, R., & Ortmann, A. (2001). Experimental practices in economics: A methodological challenge for psychologists? *Behavioral and Brain Sciences, 24*(3), 383–403.

Higgins, E. (1997). Beyond pleasure and pain. *American Psychologist, 52*, 1280–1300.

Highhouse, S. (2009). Designing experiments that generalize. *Organizational Research Methods, 12*(3), 554–566.

Holmberg, I., & Tyrstrup, M. (2010). Well then – what now? An everyday approach to managerial leadership. *Leadership, 6*, 353–372.

House, R. (1971). A path–goal theory of leadership effectiveness. *Administrative Science Quarterly, 16*, 321–328.

House, R., & Mitchell, T. (1974). Path–goal theory of leadership. *Journal of Contemporary Business, 3*, 81–98.

Howell, J., Neufeld, D., & Avolio, B. (2005). Examining the relationship of leadership and physical distance with business unit performance. *Leadership Quarterly, 16*, 273–285.

Johns, G. (2006). The essential impact of context on organizational behavior. *Academy of Management Review, 31*, 386–408.

Kelley, R. (1988). In praise of followers. *Harvard Business Review, 66*, 142–148.

Kerr, S., & Jermier, J. (1978). Substitutes for leadership: Their meaning and measurement. *Organizational Behavior and Human Performance, 22*, 375–403.

Liden, R., & Antonakis, J. (2009). Considering context in psychological leadership research. *Human Relations, 62*(11), 1587–1605.

Liu, Y., Wu, A., & Zumbo, B. (2010). The impact of outliers on Cronbach's coefficient alpha estimate of reliability: Ordinal/rating scale item responses. *Educational and Psychological Measurement, 70*, 5–21.

Lord, R., & Brown, D. (2001). Leadership, values, and subordinate self-concepts. *Leadership Quarterly, 12*(2), 133–152.

Ma, L., Tunney, R., & Ferguson, E. (2017). Does gratitude enhance prosociality? A meta-analytic review. *Psychological Bulletin, 143*, 601–635.

Marks, M., Mathieu, J., & Zaccaro, S. (2001). A temporally based framework and taxonomy of team processes. *Academy of Management Review, 26*, 356–376.

Mattes, M., Leeds, B., & Matsumura, N. (2016). Measuring change in source of leader support: The CHISOLS dataset. *Journal of Peace Research, 53*(2), 259–267.

Meindl, J. (1995). The romance of leadership as a follower-centric theory: A social constructionist approach. *Leadership Quarterly, 6*, 329–341.

Mohammed, S., & Nadkarni, S. (2011). Temporal diversity and team performance: The moderating role of team temporal leadership. *Academy of Management Journal, 54*, 489–508.

Morin, A., Morizot, J., Boudrias, J., & Madore, I. (2011). A multi-foci person-centered perspective on workplace affective commitment: A latent profile/factor mixture analysis. *Organizational Research Methods, 14*, 58–90.

Oc, B. (2018). Contextual leadership: A systematic review of how contextual factors shape leadership and its outcomes. *Leadership Quarterly*, *29*, 218–235.

Oc, B., & Bashshur, M. (2013). Followership, leadership, and social influence. *Leadership Quarterly*, *24*(6), 919–934.

Oc, B., Daniels, M., Diefendorff, J., Bashshur, M., & Greguras, G. (2020). Humility breeds authenticity: How authentic leader humility shapes follower vulnerability and felt authenticity. *Organizational Behavior and Human Decision Processes*, *158*, 112–125.

Osborn, R., Hunt, J., & Jauch, L. (2002). Toward a contextual theory of leadership. *Leadership Quarterly*, *13*, 797–837.

Porter, L., & McLaughlin, G. (2006). Leadership and the organizational context: Like the weather? *Leadership Quarterly*, *17*, 559–576.

Rousseau, D., & Fried, Y. (2001). Location, location, location: Contextualizing organizational research. *Journal of Organizational Behavior*, *22*, 1–13.

Rubin, D. (2008). For objective causal inference, design trumps analysis. *Annals of Applied Statistics*, *2*(3), 808–840.

Ruiz-Ortega, M., Parra-Requena, G., Rodrigo-Alarcón, J., & García-Villaverde, P. (2013). Environmental dynamism and entrepreneurial orientation. *Journal of Organizational Change Management*, *26*, 475–493.

Sajons, G., (2020). Estimating the causal effect of measured endogenous variables: A tutorial on experimentally randomized instrumental variables. *Leadership Quarterly*, *31*(5), 101348.

Scully, J., Sims, H. Jr, Olian, J., Schnell, E., & Smith, K. (1994). Tough times make tough bosses: A meso analysis of CEO leader behavior. *Leadership Quarterly*, *5*, 59–83.

Shamir, B., & Howell, J. (1999). Organizational and contextual influences on the emergence and effectiveness of charismatic leadership. *Leadership Quarterly*, *10*, 257–283.

Spencer, S., Zanna, M., & Fong, G. (2005). Establishing a causal chain: Why experiments are often more effective than mediational analyses in examining psychological processes. *Journal of Personality and Social Psychology*, *89*, 845–851.

Sy, T. (2010). What do you think of followers? Examining the content, structure, and consequences of implicit followership theories. *Organizational Behavior and Human Decision Processes*, *113*, 73–84.

Tajfel, H. (1974). Social identity and intergroup behavior. *Social Science Information*, *13*, 65–93.

Thornton, P., & Ocasio, W. (1999). Institutional logics and the historical contingency of power in organizations: Executive succession in the higher education publishing industry, 1958–1990. *American Journal of Sociology*, *105*, 801–844.

Uhl-Bien, M., & Marion, R. (2009). Complexity leadership in bureaucratic forms of organizing: A meso model. *Leadership Quarterly*, *20*, 631–650.

Uhl-Bien, M., Riggio, R., Lowe, K., & Carsten, M. (2014). Followership theory: A review and research agenda. *Leadership Quarterly*, *25*, 83–104.

Vroom, V., & Yetton, P. (1973). *Leadership and Decision-Making*. Wiley.

Whiteley, P., Sy, T., & Johnson, S. (2012). Leaders' conceptions of followers: Implications for naturally occurring Pygmalion effects. *Leadership Quarterly*, *23*(5), 822–834.

Williams, E., Pillai, R., Deptula, B., & Lowe, K. (2012). The effects of crisis, cynicism about change, and value congruence on perceptions of authentic leadership and attributed charisma in the 2008 presidential election. *Leadership Quarterly*, *23*, 324–341.

Williams, E., Pillai, R., Lowe, K., Jung, D., & Herst, D. (2009). Crisis, charisma, values, and voting behavior in the 2004 presidential election. *Leadership Quarterly*, *20*, 70–86.

Zalesny, M., & Farace, R. (1987). Traditional versus open offices: A comparison of sociotechnical, social relations, and symbolic meaning perspectives. *Academy of Management Journal*, *30*, 240–259.

Leadership Within 'Alternatives'

Stephen Allen and Dermot O'Reilly*

INTRODUCTION: THE MEANINGS OF ALTERNATIVES AND IMPETUS FOR EXPLORING LEADERSHIP WITHIN THEM

In this chapter we examine how leadership has been conceptualised and applied in alternative forms of organising. We develop new understanding about leadership in alternatives (e.g., cooperatives, social movements, or militant organisations) by exploring how it is understood, produced and operates in different contexts of alternative organising. We consider what is focal to meanings of leadership, and how leadership (whether as a form, style, process, or practice) varies within alternatives. Based on our analysis we suggest some possibilities for developing studies of leadership in alternatives, as well as posing questions about studying leadership in general.

We focus on alternatives as part of a counter to the argument, or assumption, that 'there is no alternative'. This assumption, voiced by many ideologues of the past, is that there is a teleological unity behind organisational and social evolution, and thus no point or reason to consider other possibilities. The recognition of the existence of many varieties of alternatives, however, ruptures this assertion. Consequently, we believe that by exploring the dynamics that inform or shape alternatives, the potential for, and possibilities of, alternatives is renewed.

Our affinity for considering alternatives is not a romantic attachment to 'the road less travelled', but a critical-political positioning for heterogeneity in forms of leading and organising. Indeed, some have argued that 'alternative' forms of social organisation are numerically, geographically, socially and historically more extensive than the symbolically prominent organisational norm of the capitalist firm (Parker et al., 2014). Consequently, exploring alternatives enables the potential re-evaluation of what is considered 'normal' or mandatory.

Significantly, other than a minority interest in the solidarity economy (e.g., Gibson-Graham et al., 2013; Parker et al., 2014;), organisational theory largely ignores how coordination works in non-profit-oriented communities and forms of social organising. The focus of organisational theorists tends to be on profit-oriented organisations, such that even authors who have noted the importance of the 'informal' organisation or the forms of community within private organisations (Barnard, 1938; Mayo, 1949; Scott & Davis, 2007; Selznick, 1994)

*Both authors contributed equally, and are listed in alphabetical order.

have often treated this social phenomenon as a shadow of, or complement to, market and hierarchical relations.

To make comparisons between studies of alternatives requires us to make decisions about what organisational characteristics define what is and what is not 'alternative'. These decisions involve assumptions about what is mainstream, symbolically prominent, or 'normal'. We will explain our choices in the first section by outlining three different, but complementary, conceptual lenses (coordination arrangements, organisational purpose and value orientation) for identifying and contrasting 'symbolically prominent/normal', 'supporting' and 'alternative' organisational forms[1]. The second section presents an overview of explicit empirical studies of leadership in different types of alternatives, and identifies themes and issues across these different organisational forms and contexts. The third section reflects back on the extant literature on leadership within alternatives, in order to highlight questions and areas for future investigation, both for leadership in alternatives and for leadership.

Sense-making 'Alternatives': Three Lenses of Coordination Arrangements, Organisational Purpose and Value Orientation

Various authors have offered definitions about how 'alternatives' are distinctive (e.g., Parker et al. 2014; Reedy & Learmonth, 2009). We believe, however, that there are greater conceptual possibilities to build on these existing distinctions in order to appreciate the variety and nuances of organisational forms. Such appreciations are crucial for understanding leadership in 'alternatives'. Consequently, to help to explore the varieties of 'alternatives' we identify three categories of organisation: 'symbolically prominent/normal', 'supporting' and 'alternative'. They can be appreciated to be dialectically related because they are defined and understood in relation to each other. We consider these three categories through three conceptual lenses. The purpose of considering the three lenses is not only to express the complexity of 'alternatives', but also to be broadly inclusive in the representation of 'alternatives'.

Our *first lens* for understanding and distinguishing organisational and social relations is of the predominant *coordination arrangements* identified in organisational and social theory: the idealised organisational types of the market ('symbolically prominent/normal'), which coordinates via price; the top-down bureaucratic hierarchy ('supporting') which coordinates via authority; and the clan or community ('alternative') which coordinates via norms, values, solidarity, or trust (Adler, 2001; Durkheim, 1933; Ouchi, 1980; Ouchi, 1979; Scott & Davis, 2007).

Our *second lens* for understanding alternatives is of *organisational purpose/s*. 'Symbolically prominent/normal' organisations' foremost purpose is profit-growth (which may or may not be seen to lead to social development), pursued by market-oriented entrepreneurial organisations. 'Supporting' organisations' foremost purpose is social reproduction through economic reproduction – for example, in government or public service organisations where welfare goals and economic goals are considered together. 'Alternative' organisations' foremost purpose is the support, development and growth of social and cultural forms of living – for example, in various forms of lifestyle development, cultural endeavours and value-expression, or in modes of charity, mutual aid, or care which defend or preserve basic social as well as cultural reproduction.

The *third lens* for our three-way categorisation is of *value orientation*. The 'symbolically prominent/normal' value orientation in contemporary market-embedded organisations is of egocentrism – where the individual self is presumed as, or socialised into, having a focus on self-protection, -development and -expansion (Knights & O'Leary, 2006). The 'supporting' value orientation in contemporary society is group-centrism – where people are seen to value the group, whether for egocentric security or for more socialised motives, such as the private family, town or city councils, or mutual welfare groups. The 'alternative' value orientation is a universalist-orientation – where the locus of values is seen as ubiquitous and unlimited within, and potentially beyond, the organisational form, such as humanistic, religious, spiritual, or ecological communities.

Table 30.1 summarises our three lenses in relation to the three categories of organisation. The shading indicates the selected criteria for 'alternative' organisations and social relations, and of organisations that are part-alternative that will be included in our review. The two-dimensional representation of Table 30.1 means that it does not display all the potential combinations. For example, a hierarchical organisation may have a social development purpose and be universalist in value orientation; indeed, many charities have exactly this combination of form, purpose and value orientation. Also, the table could imply that these distinctions are mutually exclusive. This is not necessarily the case; rather there may be combinations of each of these dimensions, and varying degrees of each of them[2]. Although, the lenses and categories inevitably simplify organisational realities they allow us to express what we mean by 'alternatives' and so enable us to explain what is, and is not, in focus in our exploration of leadership within 'alternatives'.

Table 30.1 focuses on contemporary or modern forms of organisational and social relations, but traditional forms (e.g., actual clans or hunter-gatherer groups) are also covered in the second section. From reviewing across different fields of research we have found that there are a series of exclusions that we need to apply to make the project of overviewing leadership within alternatives manageable[3]. It is also important not to read any of these distinctions as logically or inherently either 'good' or 'bad'. Indeed, many community groups or organisations are significantly self-interested and some produce toxic behaviours, relations and results – for example, in some cults (see Tourish, 2011). Values that are group-centred, or universalist can shape groups and practices that are sectarian, exclusionary, or violent (including terrorist organisations; Blair et al., 2021) as well as egalitarian, pacifist, or inclusive, and are sometimes expressed in 'normal' organisations.

Table 30.1 thus summarises our selection criteria for identifying the types of 'alternatives' and part-alternatives within which leadership has been explicitly studied. As will become clear from our review of this literature, the types of 'alternative' organisation do not correspond to pre-existing categorisations of the leadership literature. Within and across the different types of 'alternatives' previously studied, various forms of leadership concepts and methodologies are apparent. The lenses we utilise in Table 30.1, however, help enable the sense-breaking and remaking of leadership through alternatives that we sketch in the third section.

SENSE-MAKING STUDIES OF LEADERSHIP WITHIN 'ALTERNATIVES'

In this section we review literature published in English which explicitly studies leadership through empirical research of the above-selected 'alternative' forms of organising. This literature is not significantly clustered within identifiable disciplinary areas or themes. Moreover, the literature is multidisciplinary and has not previously been brought together under the general framing of leadership within 'alternatives'.

From our searches we identified studies of leadership which can be associated with different framings of alternative organisations: egalitarian social organisation, including studies of

Table 30.1 Three lenses on types of organisations and social relations in contemporary society

Categorisations of organisations and social relations Lenses	Symbolically prominent/normal	Supporting	Alternative
Ideal organisational types (coordination arrangements)	Market (price) e.g., individual economic actor	Hierarchy (authority) e.g., state government	Organisational clan/ community (values, norms, trust) e.g., utopian communes
Economic/social purpose	Economic development e.g., profit-seeking private organisations	Economic/social reproduction e.g., public service organisations, professional associations, cooperatives, employee-controlled organisations, intentional communities, social enterprises	Social development e.g., social movements, developmental charities, hobby clubs, community interest companies
Value orientation	Ego-centrism e.g., profit-oriented 'platform' organisations	Group-centrism e.g., nuclear family, interest-based political parties, trade unions, indigenous movements, resistance movements, mutual welfare groups	Universalism e.g., eco-socialist-feminist collectivist movements; inclusive spiritual/religious movements

acephalous groups in hunter-gatherer societies (Boehm et al., 1993; Edwards, 2015; Glowacki & von Rueden, 2015; von Rueden et al., 2014; von Rueden & van Vugt, 2015) and studies of egalitarian communities in modern settings (Yngvesson, 1978); civic associations (Andrews et al., 2010; Buzzanell et al., 1997); community-based labour organisations (Fu, 2021; Rosile et al., 2021); women-centred forms of organising (Brown & Hosking, 1986; Freeman, 2013 [1972]); cooperatives (Buzzanell et al., 1997; Goldberg, 1969); utopian communes and gatherings (Brumann, 2000; MacGill, 2014); social change/social movement organising[4] (Bligh & Robinson, 2010; Carson, 1987; Ganz, 2010; Gerbaudo, 2012; Kallman, 2022; Keshtiban et al., 2021; Ospina & Su, 2009; Sutherland et al., 2014; Tranter, 2009; Western, 2014), including protest and resistance groups (Einwohner, 2007; Eslen-Ziya & Erhart, 2015; Zoller & Fairhurst, 2007); vanguard groups (Marcy, 2020); and terrorist groups (Grint, 2005).

The disciplines used to research leadership in alternatives vary widely, and are variously combined – from anthropology (Boehm et al., 1993; Brumann, 2000), to communication studies (Buzzanell et al., 1997; Moon & Kim, 2019), social psychology (Brown & Hosking, 1986), organisation studies (Andrews et al., 2010; Zoller & Fairhurst, 2007), leadership studies (Allen, 2019; Bligh & Robinson, 2010; Edwards, 2015; Simsa & Totter, 2020; Sutherland et al., 2014; Tranter, 2009; Western, 2014; Zoller & Fairhurst, 2007), history and historiography (Carson, 1987; Edwards, 2015), evolutionary theory (Glowacki & von Rueden, 2015; von Rueden et al., 2014; von Rueden & van Vugt, 2015), social movement studies (Andrews et al., 2010; Ganz, 2010; Ganz & McKenna, 2018) and sociology (Andrews et al., 2010).

The conceptions of leadership are also diverse – from leadership concepts that are focused more on leaders – such as charismatic leadership (Bligh & Robinson, 2010; Carson, 1987) and leaders' styles and actions (Marcy, 2020; Ganz, 2010) to more distributed conceptions of leadership such as post-heroic leadership (Eslen-Ziya & Erhart, 2015), distributed leadership (Brown & Hosking, 1986; Edwards, 2015), relational leadership (Allen, 2019), decolonial leadership (Jimenez-Luque, 2021), place leadership (Rees et al., 2021), ensemble leadership (Rosile et al., 2021), invitational and dramaturgical leadership (Buzzanell et al., 1997) and complexity leadership (MacGill, 2014). These different disciplines and conceptions of leadership similarly reflect substantially different research purposes – from functionalist approaches to leadership (Andrews et al., 2010; Ganz, 2010; von Rueden & van Vugt, 2015) and interpretive and hermeneutic approaches to leadership (Brown and Hosking, 1986; Buzzanell et al., 1997; Edwards, 2015), to critical approaches to leadership (Kallman, 2022; Sutherland et al., 2014; Zoller and Fairhurst, 2007). The following sub-sections identify some key themes across the literature.

Leaders, Leadership

One of the most obvious distinctions between the various studies is how while some studies focus on individuals as leaders, others stress de-centring leadership by focusing on the distributed practices (see Chapter 2, Leadership and practice theories), interactions (see Chapter 3, Leadership in interaction) and processes (see Chapter 23, Process theory approaches to leadership) that comprise various forms of 'plural' leadership (see Chapter 1, Pluralism in studies on plural leadership).

Von Rueden and von Vugt (2015), for example, focus on leaders in hunter-gatherer groups from an evolutionary perspective – their functions and roles; the traits and behaviours conducive to their emergence and effectiveness, and the motivations and incentives to assume leadership positions (p. 978). In contrast, Edwards (2015) distils more pluralist views of leadership processes from a review of anthropological literature, arguing that there is significant evidence for both individual-based and distributed forms of leadership. In civic associations, Andrews et al. (2010) argue that leader development is particularly important owing to their decentralised structure entailing significant numbers of leader positions. In contrast, in their study of a US quilting guild and a food cooperative Buzzanell et al. (1997) stress not the person of the leader, but the performances that enact leadership through the notion of 'dramaturgical' leadership. For some authors, leadership is something that a leader does, whereas for Buzzanell et al. leadership is understood as *the process of collective action* (p. 287).

Similarly, some studies of social movements/ social change organisations focus on charismatic leadership, either on particular movement leaders (Bligh & Robinson, 2010; Carson, 1987), or on exploring how charisma exists in different forms after the routinisation of the social movement (Tranter, 2009). Tranter (2009) broadens the perspective from individual leaders or movements and also explores some of the relations between different types of movement organisation, and questions of leader succession in movement organisations. In contrast, other social movement studies explicitly take a constructionist perspective of leadership to consider it as a process of how communities make meanings and take action together (e.g., Ganz & McKenna, 2018; Keshtiban et al., 2021; Ospina & Su, 2009; Sutherland et al., 2014). They sometimes focus on *identifying and exploring 'leadership practices' that set the stage for explicit collaborative work* (Ospina & Foldy, 2010, p. 295), or on how *leadership shifts amongst multiple leadership actors* through *distributed meaning-making* and processes of role rotation (Sutherland et al., 2014, p. 772).

Leaderlessness, Leadershiplessness and Dominance

One of the most striking features of these studies is the stress on leaderlessness within many groups, and the differing interpretations as to what this means, whether it is possible and whether it is desirable.

There is a broad consensus among archaeologists and anthropologists that hunter-gatherer societies both were, and are, largely acephalous (literally, 'without head'), in that there are limited formal leader roles and significant norms and practices for reproducing relative social equality (Boehm et al., 1993; von Rueden & van Vugt, 2015), and that leadership appears to be significantly influenced by the context or situation as well as the culture of the group (von Rueden et al., 2014; Edwards, 2015). For most of human existence the dominant social form was largely egalitarian in form and practice (von Rueden & van Vugt, 2015). Some anthropologists argue that in egalitarian acephalous societies group members exert a form of bottom-up 'dominance' in that they are seen to exert collective pressure on informal and temporarily formal leaders (via various forms of sanction, ostracism, or in extreme cases, killing) (Boehm et al., 1993).

Since the 1960s, a recurrent theme has been the critique of the idea that leaderlessness is possible in organisation, and a concomitant focus on the tension between an ideal of leaderlessness and actual or hidden forms of social ordering. Goldberg (1969) explores tensions between egalitarianism and autocratic organisation in a smallholders' farming cooperative ('moshav') in Israel. The aims of the group involve *levelling those who are getting ahead* as well as *the sharing of wealth with those who might otherwise slip back into dire poverty* (Goldberg, 1969, p. 72). He describes how *the various households* [99 families] *are bound together by mutual aid as well as by common agricultural credit, supply, and marketing services* (Goldberg, 1969, p. 55). Control over decision-making power is highly contested within the community, involving a complex mix of: deference to the leader ('the mazkir'); an annoyance from the community when elected committee members are not vocal in expressing their views in public; that only more wealthy community members are more willing to challenge the mazkir; and that the mazkir *should be 'quiet' and modest by conducting himself with dignity* (Goldberg, 1969, p. 71).

Yngvesson (1978) considers the nuances of leaderlessness in egalitarian group processes of Swedish fishing boats, arrangements which are also reflected within general community organisation. There are role distinctions but none are understood to have more prestige than others. The boat team is suggested to function based on voluntary cooperation, with role rotation, no orders given by one member to another, and decisions reached on a consensus basis. As Yngvesson describes *team decision-making, taken at face value, is a simple operation involving a suggestion by one person, which is generally accepted (tacitly or overtly) by other members of the team, following a period of silence or informal discussion* (1978, p. 80). In this context she draws on ideas of leadership by considering how *a facade of 'leaderless unity' can be maintained while in fact the need for a leader is met* (Yngvesson, 1978, p. 74). She describes *masking processes* whereby individuals disguise taking action in their own (and potentially team and/or communities) best interest to avoid confrontation. In particular, the masking of leaders is explored in crisis situations where immediate action must be taken. She describes how *this mask may be provided not only by a person but by a process, which instead of removing the source of a controversial decision from the group, distributes responsibility for it among the members of the group in such a way that no one person or faction can be held accountable* (Yngvesson, 1978, p. 88).

A key study – it is heavily referenced in many of the articles we reviewed – exploring leaderlessness is by Freeman (2013 [1972]) who studies the women's liberation movement in the US. Freeman's (2013 [1972]) framing of *leaderlessness* emerges from ideas of *structurelessness* which involves considering the potential limitations of structureless organising (e.g., no official spokespeople nor any defined decision-making process). Freeman suggests that structurelessness, with an *informal structure [...] becomes a way of masking power [...] usually most strongly advocated by those who are the most powerful* [or those who] *know the rules* (2013 [1972], p. 152). In the women's liberation movement, Freeman highlights the potential for *elitist and exclusive [...] informal communication networks of friends* (2013 [1972],

p. 155) to informally exert power. Those who can be regarded as *elites* are suggested to be identifiable by certain characteristics such as a person's background, personality, or amount of time allocated to the movement. It is these informal elites which are seen to hold power in which the leaders, and any connected notions of leadership, reside. Freeman's (2013 [1972]) writing is a provocation to creating forms of *democratic structuring* for greater political effectiveness within the women's liberation movement. Such structure is proposed to involve formalising how authority is democratically given (and taken away) via roles and task assignment, alongside equal access to resources and organisational information. Consequently, although a theory of leadership is not specifically engaged with, leaders as formal holders of (temporary) authority via roles is suggested to be an antidote to an imaginary of leaderlessness which is argued to mask who holds power.

Subsequent studies engage with Freeman's arguments against ideals of leaderlessness and structurelessness. Gerbaudo (2012) explores the difficult relations that social movements in a number of countries have with associating their ways of organising with *leadership* of any form. He argues that despite claims to leaderlessness there are identifiable forms of *soft*, *emotional* and *dialogical* leadership, which *are by and large indirect as well as invisible but nonetheless effective in giving collective action a certain degree of coherence and a sense of direction* (Gerbaudo, 2012, p. 157). In particular he considers how uses of social media by people active in social movements cannot be blindly regarded as bringing *horizontality*, as his ethnographic research highlights, often a *handful of people control most of the communication flow* (Gerbaudo, 2012, p. 135). Similarly, Allen (2019) suggests in his study of Quakers that relations of power and associated influence within the group can become ignored, since they are understood to be obviated by consensus based organisational processes; and that the appreciations of leadership being fluid within the group, or that any possibility for leaders(hip) is denied, can obscure how many patterns of influencing can be quite static and become ingrained.

Sutherland et al. (2014) explore social movement organising in the UK by engaging with ideas of leaderlessness or 'anti-leadership'. They draw on critical leadership studies and earlier work about anarchism (e.g., Fyke and Sayegh, 2001) to consider how the refusal to acknowledge any kind of leadership can be detrimental to possibilities for egalitarian organising. In particular, they explore how *leadership shifts amongst multiple leadership actors* [through] *distributed meaning-making and processes of role rotation* (Sutherland et al., 2014, p. 772). In particular, they argue that even if a group is leaderless, in terms of having no formal leaders, there is nonetheless necessarily leadership. Western makes a related point by suggesting that a key reason why social movements do not develop beyond protest is because *their agency is diluted and constrained by the continued disavowal of leadership* (2014, p. 692). He develops a notion of *autonomist leadership* which is described as an *anti-hierarchical, informal and distributed leadership that is distinctive to emancipatory social movements* (Western, 2014, p. 676). His work maintains that within social movements other forms of leadership are constructed and that it is by exploring these, and disengaging a resolute idea of leaderlessness, that there are opportunities for more effective social movement organisation. Likewise, Fotaki and Foroughi (2021) engage with notions of leaderlessness by using the Lacanian concept of fantasy to explore how debates about leadership are avoided in the Extinction Rebellion movement in the UK, which helps to thwart the potential for democratic politics and social change. They suggest that acknowledging psychic conflicts and tensions in relation to leaders and leadership is key for developmental governance and 'leaderfull-ness' in social movements.

While the authors involved in these studies concur with Freeman that there are dangers in an ideal of leaderlessness, and that such an ideal does not obviate power asymmetries, others take a more positive view of the ideal of leaderlessness. From the angle of post-heroic leadership in their study of the Gezi Park protests in Turkey, Eslen-Ziya and Erhart (2015) see leaderlessness as offering possibilities, rather than seeing it as a barrier for the ongoing development of social movement organising. From a prefigurative angle, Simsa and Totter (2020) explore how members of the Spanish protest movement 15M *stress the necessity of collective reflection to understand organizational dynamics, and to learn to ensure efficient organization without hierarchies* (Simsa & Totter, 2020, p. 236). They suggest that modes of reflexive organising are in operation, such that attention is given to power, and potential hidden hierarchies are engaged with in the social movement. Such engagement is visible by members experimenting with ways of organising and processes of doing leadership. Their study suggests that some movements take the question of asymmetric power seriously and thus try to avoid an ideal of leaderlessness detracting from dealing with the possible problems of informal hierarchy or structure.

Related to this theme of leaderlessness, there are also some salutary findings from utopian communes and temporary groups that relate back to questions of dominance identified in acephalous hunter-gatherer groups. Utopian communes are *groups that voluntarily live together and share all their property* (Brumann, 2000, p. 425). Brumann (2000) analyses historical and contemporary utopian communes to identify the characteristics that enable some of these communes to be socially vibrant for a considerable period of time. His key findings are that individual communes where there is a leader displaying 'high' dominance, or federations of communes where a particular branch has high dominance, tend to have a limited active lifespan. In contrast, those communes which are active for longer periods are often of a federative branch structure – that is, they are based over multiple locations without one being overly dominant, and charismatic leaders within these communes display 'mild' as opposed to 'high' dominance. MacGill's (2014) study of a five-day co-located event experimenting in alternative lifestyles in New Zealand focuses on how it has reproduced itself for approximately 30 years without formal hierarchies, roles, or rules. While not without practical problems, MacGill argues that the longevity of 'Convergence' indicates that acephalous organisation is possible for particular types of medium-scale groups, and he questions assumptions about the maximum size of egalitarian groups and the *iron law of hierarchy* (Boulding, 1968).

Leadership: For and Against

There are significant elements of the literature on leadership within alternatives, similar to much of the leadership literature, that point to how leadership is aimed towards, or *for*, some goal or purpose. This is seen in the studies where leadership is identified as occurring in the accomplishment of various tasks – for example, in hunting, fishing, or in conflict-mediation in hunter-gatherer groups (Edwards, 2015) or egalitarian community relationships (Yngvesson, 1978), and in coordinating civic associations (Andrews et al., 2010; Buzzanell et al., 1997) or social movements (Kallman, 2022; Sutherland et al., 2014; Western, 2014).

There are also significant indications of leadership as operating *against* something, as oppositional. This feature of opposition is most evident in particular types of social change/movement organisations such as protest or resistance organising, vanguard groups, or revolutionary/terrorist groups. Leadership in resistance has been theorised in terms of *resistance leadership* (Zoller and Fairhurst, 2007), which they specify as being oriented towards changing structural arrangements rather than involving simply individual, covert, or discrete acts of resistance. Zoller and Fairhurst (2007) consider how leadership relationships develop among resisters, which variously involves perceived injustice or 'hidden transcripts' of injustice, the handling of shared emotions, the use of instrumental arguments, relational attributes, attributions, charisma and *crucibles* of experience.

Einwohner's (2007) study of resistance in Jewish Ghettos in World War II, for example, highlights the importance of resistance leaders establishing and maintaining their credibility and legitimacy as leaders. Zoller and Fairhurst (2007) also note the instrumentalisation of this oppositional consciousness into the mobilisation of collective action. Such processes are identified via symbolic actions and material practices such as *massing* which involves bringing people together to both facilitate and display collective power (Scott, 1990). In turn, Zoller and Fairhurst (2007) address the issue of how resistance leadership involves *continued redrafting of an emerging story* (Weick et al., 2005, p. 415) in order to make the discourse of change *stick*, and embedding it into material codes, forms, or practices. Zoller and Fairhurst's (2007) analysis of resistance leadership points to the dialectical tensions and processes evident in resistance leadership as it shifts between being 'against' a status quo, prominent symbol, or structural arrangement, and 'for' an alternative vision, symbol, or structure.

A particular type of oppositional social change organisation are socio-political *vanguards* (Marcy, 2020) – groups or organisations that aim at disrupting accepted social consciousness and that attempt to insert, or at least enable, alternative meanings or social ordering. Marcy (2020) locates both overlaps and distinctions between vanguard organisations and social movement and revolutionary organisations. Social movements seek to actively organise and mobilise people and revolutionary groups seek to overthrow the status quo. In contrast, vanguard groups seek to disrupt thought and habit. Marcy (2020) identifies various vanguard organisations that lie on both the political 'right' (e.g., alt-Right) and political 'left' (e.g., the Situationist International). By focusing particularly on their traits, skills and outcomes he studies what vanguard leaders do – as individuals, within their groups and in relation to the wider society that they seek to influence. There is relatively little on leadership in revolutionary or terrorist forms of social change organisations, but Grint (2005) notes the *Hydra-like* (as in multi-headed) organisational and leadership structure of Al-Qaeda. He notes that the distributed leadership evident in such a structure can be positive in terms of inhibiting authoritarian leaders, but that it also potentially enables unrepresentative or undemocratic groups to destabilise liberal democratic societies, potentially resulting in a type of *leaderless authoritarianism*.

SENSE-BREAKING AND REMAKING LEADERSHIP THROUGH ALTERNATIVES

Questions About Leadership in Alternatives

Our review of leadership within alternatives raises a variety of questions. We start with the obvious task of 'gap-spotting'. First, there appears to be a serious dearth of studies of leadership in cooperatives, in intentional communities (those which are not utopian communes), mutual aid groups, or common interest groups (where the interests are non-economic). There is potential to examine extant studies of these types of organisations and social relationships for implicit accounts of leadership in these contexts in order to lay the ground for more explicit studies of leadership. Second, as noted above, most of the studies reviewed tend to be of single cases, with only a small number of comparative analyses undertaken. The comparative studies reported (e.g., Brumann, 2000; Buzzanell et al., 1997; Ospina & Su, 2009), though, are particularly informative about some key features of the type of alternative that they examined, suggesting that there is much greater scope for comparative analysis across alternatives of the same and different types. However, for comparative analysis it is important that a recognition of the different sociocultural contexts and worldviews that animate different alternatives is retained. This is because these empirical features, which can be highly significant, can become obscured in cross-cultural analysis (Edwards, 2015). Significantly, our searching was in English which means that studies in all other languages were excluded; this is a potentially very significant 'gap' that can be addressed.

There are also questions about leadership in alternatives that are generated by reflecting on the lenses noted in the first section. For example, the organisational theory literature on coordination arrangements seems strongly focused on the 'positive' modes of coordination through provisioning or accumulation. For example, markets are seen as providing positive economic incentives, hierarchies are seen as allocating positive resources or rewards and clans or communities are seen as expressing or actualising positive joint values. However, the empirical literature on leadership in alternatives implies that coordinating arrangements are composed of both accumulative modes and punitive modes. While the punitive mode of the market is economic deprivation and the punitive modes of the hierarchy are, variously, punishment, resource deprivation, or marginalisation, the punitive modes of the clan/community are exclusion or marginalisation (evident in Freeman's, 2013 [1972]) account of the negative sides of structurelessness and leaderlessness), or denigration, or, occasionally, killing – which is evident in anthropological accounts of acephalous communities (Boehm et al., 1993). There is significant scope for the future exploration of the interplay between 'accumulative' and 'punitive' modes of coordination.

As well as using more comparative analysis to understand alternatives and leadership within them, there would also be value in taking a more 'cultural-ecological' approach (which would include a historical sensibility; see Chapter 26, Leadership through history) to understanding alternative organisations, their contexts and values, and the roles and forms of leadership within them. Taking such a cultural-ecological approach might suggest that accumulative modes of coordination are ascendant in periods of growth, whereas punitive modes of coordination may predominate in periods of stagnation or decline. There is also circumstantial evidence that the mix of coordinating arrangements may fluctuate according to social conditions – with the suggestions of community being strong in times of stress or crisis, such as depressions, pandemics, or wars (e.g., Solnit, 2010). Indeed, it has long been hypothesised that economic recessions and other forms of societal crises give an impetus to the generation of 'alternative' modes of organisation and social relationships. There is, thus, a rich series of potential studies into the cultural-ecology of the rise and fall of 'alternatives', and of the differing roles and processes of leadership within this cultural-ecology.

Another question posed to leadership in alternatives from our review relates to the dynamics of leadership in alternatives. As noted above, a key theme in the literature on leadership in 'alternatives' relates to processes of working through tensions and oppositions that are seen to be inevitable within (alternative) organising (Brumann, 2000; Buzzanell et al., 1997). In particular, it has been argued that the particularities of leadership in 'alternatives' require different ways of conceptualising how leadership and collective action emerges in connection with certain people and at certain moments (Buzzanell et al., 1997). It is clear from our review that leadership within 'alternatives' is variously in tension with values about leaderlessness, formal and informal practices and structures of authority, and is bound up in questions of, and tensions between, instrumental efficacy and valued ways of being. Sutherland et al. (2014) and Western (2014) suggest that what is perhaps most important in 'alternatives' is not so much whether there are or are not leaders or leadership, but the types of roles and processes of leaders and leadership that there are, and the types of effects that they have in their particular cultural-ecological location and time. This suggests that the study of leadership in 'alternatives' needs to continue focusing ever more closely on the variety within different modes of leadership and different modes of 'alternatives' and the dialectics of their modes, roles, processes, practices and their effects in their cultural and material contexts over time.

A final question posed relates to the broad themes and issues associated with gender and race, and how these relate to leadership in 'alternatives'. There are very few studies which specifically address these themes; on race there is one study (Ospina & Su, 2009), and also only one which specifically considers gender constructions and dynamics (Moon & Kim, 2019), despite feminist organising being a prominent focus of some of these studies. Indeed, we notice in some historical accounts of 'egalitarian' groups and communities that they appear to be patriarchal is taken-for-granted (e.g., Goldberg, 1969; Yngvesson, 1978). Consequently, how leadership in 'alternatives' can be (counter) productive in relation to these themes is ripe for investigation. Also, although ecological sustainability is engaged with as an agenda, particularly in the social movement contexts (e.g., Fotaki & Foroughi, 2021), how 'alternatives' show forms of leadership on, for example (non-) consumption practices and the influence dynamics involved in the creation of these organisational practices has not yet been explored.

Questions from Alternatives to Leadership Research

There are also a few deeper questions that this exploration of research on leadership within alternatives asks of leadership studies. The first question is perhaps the simplest and also the most complex – how, and in what ways, does sociocultural context lead? The majority of studies reviewed tended to oscillate between viewing leadership as an individual or as a collective phenomenon, but there were instances where the sociocultural context was apparent as a perceived force. Sahlins (2017) argues that even egalitarian acephalous societies operate within a hierarchical cosmology of various divinities or spirits; similarly, Allen (2019) notes that in Quaker organising the ultimate authority is *the will of God*. Abélès (2017), disputes what Sahlins infers from this, arguing that even if people in these groups see themselves as existing within these cosmological hierarchies, it is another thing altogether to suggest that these cosmological hierarchies actually act upon them. That is, Abélès appears to be arguing that cosmological hierarchies lack agency, and so cannot be said to be actually exercising leadership or authority upon their believers, even if their believers fervently believe that they do and these beliefs impact on what they do.

These contexts may seem like purely animistic, spiritual, or religious circumstances, but consider how resistance leaders react to feelings of injustice, or vanguard leaders react to what they consider to be misbegotten in 'mainstream' society – they are led by their beliefs, and their beliefs are necessarily socially, culturally, historically and situationally shaped. In some manner, therefore, all the various protagonists of leaders, and all the various processes of leadership, are led, given a form of direction, by their sociocultural context. Our review suggests that leadership scholars could usefully enquire into how it does so (see Chapter 31, Leadership and culture).

The second question is raised by the observation of the oppositional thrust of much of the leadership in alternatives; many of the social movements mentioned – 15M in Spain, the Gezi Park protests in Turkey, Extinction Rebellion in the UK, women's movements in South Korea – are explicitly premised against economic, social and political processes and orderings. The very concept of resistance leadership is founded on the observation of the oppositional mobilisation of injustice against social arrangements, and many utopian communes are predicated as a way to live differently to what is considered 'normal', mainstream, or lacking in their surrounding society. Yet, the mainstream of leadership research is founded on a unitary assumption – that leadership is functional to achieving some common goal or objective; for example, in their discussion of leadership in egalitarian small-scale societies, von Rueden and von Vugt (2015) define leadership thus:

Leadership is a primary mechanism by which groups resolve coordination and motivation problems. We define leaders as individuals who have differential influence within a group over the

> *establishment of goals, logistics of coordination, monitoring of effort, and reward or punishment strategies.*
> (Bass, B. M., 1990, Day, D. and Antonakis, J., 2012, cited in von Rueden and von Vugt, 2015, p. 978)

These unitary assumptions are undercut, or at least problematised, when one considers the oppositional nature of resistance indicated in many forms of 'alternatives'. The mainstream literature appears to assume that leadership is concertive direction *towards* something, whether that something is a goal, a community, a purpose, a value, or an identity. But leadership can also be *against* a goal, community, identity and so on. Nor does being against something even entail or necessarily require organised concertive coordination of those opposing or resisting (such a conception would 'smuggle in' a unitary moment into resistance or protest). The idea of *massing*, noted by Zoller and Fairhurst (2007), suggests there are moments of uncoordinated and spontaneous synchronous interaction of individuals and collectives where direction is emergent rather than given or taken, and any perceived unity is imposed on empirical plurality. In these instances, such self-coordinated emergent direction is a product of an intersubjective or extra-individual awareness, attention, or presence. And it may not even be that rare; surely it is just such a phenomenon that animates most collective endeavours – for example, in sports teams – and has been previously termed *collective mind* or *heedful interrelating* (Weick and Roberts, 1993). However, there is no need to romanticise or over-valorise such a phenomenon which is suggested by Sutherland et al.'s (2014) and Western's (2014) accounts of the desire for leaderlessness in social movement and anarchist organising.

Finally, from our review of leadership within alternatives, we notice how conceptualisations of leadership overlap with, and are distinct from, other related concepts, including in terms of its (and their) formal, informal, material and ideational forms. For example, if our review had considered explicit accounts of authority, or of power, as well as explicit accounts of leadership in alternatives, the number of studies to review would have multiplied significantly. Interestingly, a number of studies encountered in the review equated leadership with authority. More interestingly, a number of studies encountered did not distinguish either between formal and informal leadership, or between formal and informal authority. It has to be acknowledged that these distinctions are both tricky and fluid. When informal authority becomes recognised as such, it can either take on a degree of formality, or have its legitimacy questioned. When informal leadership is recognised as such, it too can be either buttressed or eroded. The dynamics and inter-relations of these different phenomena would bear much greater conceptual enquiry from leadership scholars, suggesting that the future study of leadership needs to return to more fully considering the relations between leadership (formal, informal, material and ideational) with authority, power, legitimacy, culture and symbolism (see Chapter 32, From 'leadership' to 'leading') and social and organisational forms and processes, and the different alternative concepts available for theorising and studying them (see Chapter 37, Leadership and its alternatives, and Chapter 39, Leadership dialectics, for complementary discussions).

Notes

1. The 'scare quotes' are deliberate in order to highlight the contested and contestable nature of these labels, and the dialectical relations between what might be considered 'symbolically prominent/normal', 'supporting', and 'alternative' (see Chapter 39 for more on dialectics).
2. Within theorising on alternative organisation, autonomy and solidarity, i.e., allowing individuals' freedom and acting collectively, have been suggested to be in tension or even contradictory (Parker et al., 2014), whereas Adler (2001) argues that egocentric and universal motives are not necessarily opposed to each other.
3. Intentional exclusions from the review: public service organisations (for example, see Chapter 35), mainstream political parties (because there are significant literatures on leadership in these types of organisations already); professional associations, the nuclear family (because of their primarily group-centred reproduction character); the 'platform economy' (because such organizations are primarily economically focused); informal groups in experiments (since this is experimental research, and the value-orientation is potentially skewed towards self- or group-centricity owing to this feature); formal labour organising or trade unions (Ganz 2000, Kirton and Healy 2012) (since there is a sizeable literature on these); (economic) interest groups (since by definition these groups are economically group- or self-oriented); non-profit organisations (since there is a very large literature on this in the journal 'Nonprofit management and leadership'; cults (since these are a particular form of intentional community or commune, and are examined in depth in Tourish (2011)); alternative philosophies, ideas, or fictions (although the consideration of alternative

philosophies, ideas, and fictional worlds is of importance in its own right, see Chapter 28, we focus on empirically based studies of alternatives); indigenous communities (there is a recent and growing literature on leadership in various indigenous communities that are at least part-embedded in modern society and that often resist particular processes and effects of modern society, see Chapter 25).
4. In different geographical and disciplinary contexts these organisations are sometimes referred to as 'social change' organisations, or as 'social movement organisations' or 'social movements'.

REFERENCES

Abélès, M.(2017). The virtues of cosmopolitics. *HAU: Journal of Ethnographic Theory*, 7, 129–132.

Adler, P. S. (2001). Market, hierarchy, and trust: The knowledge economy and the future of capitalism. *Organization Science*, 12, 215–234.

Allen, S. (2019). Exploring Quaker organising to consider the possibilities for relational leadership. *Quaker Studies*, 24, 249–269.

Andrews, K. T., Ganz, M., Baggetta, M., Han, H., & Lim, C. (2010). Leadership, membership, and voice: Civic associations that work. *American Journal of Sociology*, 115, 1191–1242.

Barnard, C. (1938). *The Functions of the Executive*. Harvard University Press.

Blair, C. W., Chenoweth, E., Horowitz, M. C., Perkoski, E., & Potter, P. B. K. (2022). Honor among thieves: Understanding rhetorical and material cooperation among violent nonstate actors. *International Organization*, 76(1), 164–203.

Bligh, M. C., & Robinson, J. L. (2010). Was Gandhi 'charismatic'? Exploring the rhetorical leadership of Mahatma Gandhi. *Leadership Quarterly*, 21, 844–855.

Boehm, C., Barclay, H. B., Dentan, R. K., Dupree, M.-C., Hill, J. D., Kent, S., Knauft, B. M., Otterbein, K. F., & Rayner, S. (1993). Egalitarian behavior and reverse dominance hierarchy [and comments and reply]. *Current Anthropology*, 34(3), 227–254.

Boulding, K. E. (1968). *The Organizational Revolution: A Study in the Ethics Of Economic Organization*. Quadrangle.

Brown, M. H., & Hosking, D. M. (1986). Distributed leadership and skilled performance as successful organization in social movements. *Human Relations*, 39, 65–79.

Brumann, C. (2000). The dominance of one and its perils: Charismatic leadership and branch structures in utopian communes. *Journal of Anthropological Research*, 56, 425–451.

Buzzanell, P. M., Ellingson, L., Silvio, C., Pasch, V., Dale, B., Mauro, G., Smith, E., Weir, N., & Martin, C. (1997). Leadership processes in alternative organizations: Invitational and dramaturgical leadership. *Communication Studies*, 48, 285–310.

Carson, C. (1987). Martin Luther King, Jr.: Charismatic leadership in a mass struggle. *Journal of American History*, 74, 448–454.

Durkheim, E. (1933). *The Division of Labor in Society*. Free Press.

Edwards, G. (2015). Anthropological accounts of leadership: Historical and geographical interpretations from indigenous cultures. *Leadership*, 11, 335–350.

Einwohner, R. L. (2007). Leadership, authority, and collective action: Jewish resistance in the ghettos of Warsaw and Vilna. *American Behavioral Scientist*, 50, 1306–1326.

Eslen-Ziya, H., & Erhart, I. (2015). Toward postheroic leadership: A case study of Gezi's collaborating multiple leaders. *Leadership*, 11, 471–488.

Fotaki, M., & Foroughi, H. (2021). Extinction Rebellion: Green activism and the fantasy of leaderlessness in a decentralized movement. *Leadership*, 18(2), 224–246.

Freeman, J. (2013 [1972]). The tyranny of structurelessness. *Women's Studies Quarterly*, 41, 231–246.

Fu, H. (2021). Social action as 'a total social phenomenon': Comparing leadership challenges facing community-based labour organizations in China and Japan. *Human Relations*, 74, 1396–1420.

Fyke, K., & Sayegh, G. (2001). Anarchism and the struggle to move forward. *Perspectives on Anarchist Theory*, 5, 30–38.

Ganz, M. (2010). Leading change: Leadership, organization, and social movements. In N. Nohria & R. Khurana (Eds.), *Handbook of Leadership Theory and Practice: An HBS Centennial Colloquium on Advancing Leadership* (pp. 527–568). Harvard Business Review Press.

Ganz, M., & McKenna, E. (2018). Bringing leadership back in. In D. A. Snow, S. A. Soule, H. Kriesi & H. J. McCammon (Eds.), *The Wiley Blackwell Companion to Social Movements* (pp. 185–205). John Wiley & Sons.

Gerbaudo, P. (2012) *Tweets and the Streets: Social Media and Contemporary Activism*. Pluto Press.

Gibson-Graham, J., Cameron, J., & Healy, S. (2013). *Take Back The Economy: An Ethical Guide for Transforming Our Communities*. University of Minnesota Press.

Glowacki, L., & von Rueden, C. (2015). Leadership solves collective action problems in small-scale societies. *Philosophical Transactions of the Royal Society B: Biological Sciences*, 370, 20150010.

Goldberg, H. E. (1969). Egalitarianism in an autocratic village in Israel. *Ethnology*, 8, 54–75.

Grint, K. (2005). *Leadership: Limits and Possibilities.* Palgrave.

Jimenez-Luque, A. (2021). Decolonial leadership for cultural resistance and social change: Challenging the social order through the struggle of identity. *Leadership, 17*, 154–172.

Kallman, M. (2022). Autonomist leadership and organizational practices in leaderless street bands. In M. Godwyn (Ed.), *Research Handbook on the Sociology of Organizations.* Edward Elgar.

Keshtiban, A. E., Callahan, J. L., & Harris, M. (2021). Leaderlessness in social movements: Advancing space, symbols, and spectacle as modes of 'leadership'. *Human Resource Development Quarterly*, October.

Knights, D., & O'Leary, M. (2006). Leadership, ethics and responsibility to the other. *Journal of Business Ethics, 67*, 125–137.

MacGill, V. (2014). Convergence gathering as an example of a medium-scale acephalous group. *Systems Research and Behavioral Science, 31*, 606–613.

Marcy, R. T. (2020). Leadership of socio-political vanguards: A review and future directions. *Leadership Quarterly, 31*, 101372.

Mayo, E. (1949). *The Social Problems of an Industrial Civilization.* Routledge.

Moon, Y. E., & Kim, H. H. (2019). Unnie 1 comes out 2: Conceptualizing egalitarian leadership among South Korean women. In C.-C. Chao & L. Ha (Eds.), *Asian Women Leadership: A Cross-National and Cross-Sector Comparison.* Routledge.

Ospina, S., & Foldy, E. (2010). Building bridges from the margins: The work of leadership in social change organizations. *The Leadership Quarterly, 21*(2), 292–307.

Ospina, S., & Su, C. (2009). Weaving color lines: Race, ethnicity, and the work of leadership in social change organizations. *Leadership, 5*, 131–170.

Ouchi, W. G. (1979). A conceptual framework for the design of organizational control mechanisms. *Management Science, 25*, 833–848.

Ouchi, W. G. (1980). Markets, bureaucracies, and clans. *Administrative Science Quarterly, 25*, 129–141.

Parker, M., Cheney, G., Fournier, V., & Land, C. (2014). *The Routledge Companion to Alternative Organization.* Routledge.

Reedy, P., & Learmonth, M. (2009). Other Possibilities? The Contribution to Management Education of Alternative Organizations. *Management Learning, 40*(3), 241–258.

Rees, J., Sancino, A., Jacklin-Jarvis, C., & Pagani, M. (2021). 'You can't Google everything': The voluntary sector and the leadership of communities of place. *Leadership, 18*(1), 102–119.

Rosile, G. A., Boje, D. M., Herder, R. A., & Sanchez, M.(2021). The coalition of Immokalee workers uses ensemble storytelling processes to overcome enslavement in corporate supply chains. *Business & Society, 60*(2), 376–414.

Sahlins, M. (2017). The original political society. *HAU: Journal of Ethnographic Theory, 7*, 91–128.

Scott, J. C. (1990). *Domination and the Arts of Resistance: Hidden Transcripts.* Yale University Press.

Scott, W. R., & Davis, G. F. (2007). *Organizations and Organizing: Rational, Natural, and Open Systems Perspectives.* Pearson Prentice Hall.

Selznick, P. (1994). *The Moral Commonwealth: Social Theory and the Promise of Community.* University of California Press.

Simsa, R., & Totter, M. (2020). The struggle for good leadership in social movement organizations: Collective reflection and rules as basis for autonomy. *Ephemera, 20*, 223–249.

Solnit, R. (2010). *A Paradise Built in Hell: The Extraordinary Communities that Arise in Disaster.* Penguin.

Sutherland, N., Land, C., & Böhm, S. (2014). Anti-leaders(hip) in social movement organizations: The case of autonomous grassroots groups. *Organization, 21*, 759–781.

Tourish, D. (2011). Leadership and cults. In A. Bryman, D. Collinson, K. Grint, B. Jackson & M. Uhl-Bien (Eds.), *The SAGE Handbook of Leadership* (pp. 215–229). Sage.

Tranter, B. (2009). Leadership and change in the Tasmanian environment movement. *Leadership Quarterly, 20*, 708–724.

von Rueden, C., Gurven, M., Kaplan, H., & Stieglitz, J. (2014). Leadership in an egalitarian society. *Human Nature, 25*, 538–566.

von Rueden, C., & van Vugt, M. (2015). Leadership in small-scale societies: Some implications for theory, research, and practice. *Leadership Quarterly, 26*, 978–990.

Weick, K. E., & Roberts, K. H. (1993). Collective mind in organizations: Heedful interrelating on flight decks. *Administrative Science Quarterly, 38*, 357–381.

Weick, K. E., Sutcliffe, K. M., & Obstfeld, D. (2005). Organizing and the process of sensemaking. *Organization Science, 16*, 409–421.

Western, S. (2014). Autonomist leadership in leaderless movements: Anarchists leading the way. *Ephemera, 14*, 673–698.

Yngvesson, B. (1978). Leadership and consensus: Decision-making in an egalitarian community. *Ethnos, 43*, 73–90.

Zoller, H. M., & Fairhurst, G. T. (2007). Resistance leadership: The overlooked potential in critical organization and leadership studies. *Human Relations, 60* 1331–1360.

31

Leadership and Culture

Vanessa Iwowo, Peter Case and Samantha Iwowo

INTRODUCTION

Interest in the relationship between leadership and culture first garnered attention during the 'cultural turn' in management and organisation studies in the 1980s (Morgan, 1986; Peters & Waterman, 1982; Smircich & Morgan, 1982) and has grown considerably in subsequent decades. We now stand at a point where there is a substantive body of literature on how leadership manifests itself within organisational cultures as well as across diverse national cultural contexts. In this chapter, we begin by introducing the reader to literature on leadership from various extant perspectives paying particular critical attention to social psychological and psychological approaches that currently dominate the field of leadership studies. We then proceed to explore new thought and emerging directions for culturally alert and sensitive research into relationships between culture and leadership. In so doing, we make no apology for privileging interpretative and critical approaches to the study of leadership and culture – particularly those drawn from disciplines of anthropology and postcolonial studies – as we contend that these offer means of addressing the most pressing issues faced in this area. We draw selectively on our own scholarship and empirical research to propose and illustrate possibilities for fresh research agendas. What follows is an outline of the chapter.

The first part of this chapter provides an overview of extant literature on leadership and culture, including main perspectives that foundationally established the field and various critiques which have over time shaped the debate. In this, we engage with the sense-making that has informed current understanding in this area. Early preoccupations with leadership and culture gave rise to what we now know as the field of cross-cultural leadership, which from the 1980s began to emerge as one worthy of research endeavour. From Hofstede (1980, 1991) – whose work, though heavily criticised, provided an early template for observing cultural dimensions in organisations and, arguably, a basis for subsequent investigations into the relationship between culture and leadership (Hampden-Turner & Trompenaars, 1997; House et al., 1999; House et al., 2004; Schwartz, 1999; Smith et al., 1996) – until now, the field of cross-cultural leadership has evolved as a legitimate domain of enquiry in its own right. In this early period of development, there were also explorations of the arguably instrumental relationship between *organisational culture* and leadership (Case, 2008).

The attempt to understand leadership from a cultural standpoint has not been without its critics as many scholars have argued that research on cross-cultural leadership – dominated largely by social psychology – remains mainly predicated on dimensionalisation of culture which presents a narrow view of the phenomena and occasions loss of the bigger picture (Dansereau & Yamarino, 2006; Jepson, 2009; Tayeb, 2001). Others note heterogeneity and complexity of societal culture (Iwowo, 2012, 2015; Nkomo, 2011), its fluidity and instability (Bhabha, 1994) and importance of power, positionality and cultural symbolism (Ailon, 2008; Eyong, 2017) – all of which call for a more holistic and interpretively sensitive appreciation of the leadership–culture nexus.

The second part of the chapter considers contemporary strands of research into culture that are informing the field of leadership studies, including those serving to break convention with established thinking. We hope this sense-breaking might help identify, articulate and establish new directions for the debate. For instance, we foreground growing interest in anthropologically informed research into *leadership practices* that try to escape some of the heretofore ethnocentric, corporatist and instrumental proclivities of leadership studies (Case & Śliwa, 2020; Guthey & Jackson, 2011; Jones, 2005, 2006; Warner & Grint, 2006). Such research calls for paying close and culturally sensitive attention to leadership practices in non-Anglophone contexts (Case et al., 2017; Jepson, 2009, 2010; Schedlitzki et al., 2017). We also pay attention to postcolonial critiques of leadership studies which offer a more fundamental challenge to the status quo – a challenge that, we contend, is now overdue in light of the dominance that Western corporatist views of leadership have long enjoyed. Drawing on the work of pioneering scholars such as Achebe (1958), Fanon (1963), Said (1978), Spivak (1988) and Bhabha (1994) who have supplied the language with which to problematise mainstream knowledge frameworks originating from the Global North, we offer some alternative heterodox research agendas.

TOWARDS CULTURAL UNDERSTANDING OF LEADERSHIP: *WHAT WE KNOW*

It is widely acknowledged that cultural forces play a significant role in shaping leadership perception, understanding and practice (Gill, 2006; House et al., 2004; Hunt & Yan, 2005; Lord & Maher, 1991; Meindl, 1995; Northouse, 2004; Smircich & Morgan, 1982). As Smircich and Morgan (1982) argued in their seminal paper, leadership in organisations is intimately related to processes of *meaning management* – that is, the ways those in positions of authority (typically managers) seek explicitly or implicitly to shape perceptions of colleagues and subordinates. More recently, Schnackenberg et al. (2019) have provided a comprehensive review of symbolic management research, revealing how this area of interest has developed in the years following the formers' ground-breaking work (see also Chapter 30, Leadership within 'alternatives', on the role of symbolism with respect to leadership in a post-truth world). Viewed from this perspective, leadership entails a process by which others *perceive* someone to be a leader, the logical corollary being that such perceptions will vary widely across cultures (Lord & Maher, 1991). The leadership relationship, moreover, exposes values and beliefs of both leaders and followers (Northouse, 2004). Against the backdrop of different cultures, *leadership means different things to different people* (Gill, 2006, p. 7) and should therefore be studied in the context of how it is perceived by those involved in leading and following because, among other things, it is culturally contingent (House et al., 2004). In this view, leadership is enacted within social space and its *meaning* constructed based on individual accounts of experience occurring in social reality – one that is itself steeped in cultural norms, values and practices. Given the all-important role that cultural forces play in shaping understanding and practice of leadership, the need for leadership to be understood in terms of cultural composition and complexity across culturally bounded spheres of meaning, as well as how the latter informs practice, is what gave rise to cross-cultural leadership research.

Mainstream Cross-Cultural Studies of Leadership

In 1980, Hofstede published *Culture's Consequences*, a treatise on manifestations of national culture in IBM across 53 countries which went on to become a foundational text in the study of national culture in organisations. He examined the impact of cultural differences on management practice and identified four components of culture: *power distance* – degree of inequality among a country's people deemed acceptable within that culture; *individualism/collectivism* – value placed on individual versus group relations/orientation; *masculinity/femininity* – how a society views goals and achievement; and *uncertainty avoidance* – a people's risk appetite and approach to uncertainty. He subsequently expanded this to include a fifth dimension: *Confucian dynamism* or *long-term orientation* (1991) – a concept of time-orientation derived from Confucius's ideas. Hofstede argued that the degree to which these components are present within any national culture would influence management/leadership practices within those societies.

The GLOBE study of *Culture and Leadership* (House et al., 2004) was another influential text that shaped contemporary thinking on cross-cultural leadership. In this, the authors argued that leader-effectiveness within a given society was inextricably tied to its cultural perceptions of leadership and embedded within its values/belief systems, with such perceptions and status/influence of leaders varying across cultures. Leadership was studied across 62 countries and, building on the Hofstedian analysis, five additional cultural dimensions were developed. These included: *assertiveness* – the degree to which individuals are decisive and willing to be confrontational/aggressive in their relationships with others; *gender-egalitarianism* – the extent to which a collective minimises gender inequality; *future orientation* – how individuals engage in future-oriented behaviours; *humane orientation* – the degree of collective altruism; and *performance orientation* – how a collective rewards members for performance (House et al., 2004). Furthermore, the work of Smith et al. (1996), Hampden-Turner and Trompenaars (1997) and Schwartz (1999) all offer perspectives that have helped shape the discourse. Other studies include Gerstner and Day (1994), Mendonca and Kanungo (1996), Jung and Avolio (1999), Mellahi (2000), Martin et al. (2009) and Resick et al. (2011) to mention a few.

As much as they helped further understanding of leadership across cultures, these studies have not been without their drawbacks. Chief of these was the tendency to make sweeping categorisations and unduly homogenise culture across diverse geographical spaces and human subjectivities. This led to unwarranted and implicitly ethnocentric generalisations whereby the cultural identity of one country/group of countries is taken to be representative of a much wider whole. For instance, a major critique of Hofstede's work lay in its tendency to portray Africa and, later, sub-Saharan Africa as culturally homogeneous, even while arguing for the uniqueness and particularism of national cultures. There was equally an inability of this study to distinguish between whether West Africa was a region or just a country (see Nkomo and Ngambi 2009). Sub-Saharan Africa was grouped into West, East and South, and listed alongside countries such as the US, Germany and the Netherlands. In contrast to the standard country listing, Africa was broadly studied on a continental, rather than on a country level. This connotes a sweeping generalisation and culturally homogenises an entire sub-region. For example, it presents certain findings as being from 'West Africa', implying that such findings are representative of all countries in that sub-region; culture (and subsequently, management practice) in Francophone Senegal is rendered as being same as in Anglophone Ghana. As with Hofstede, though to a lesser degree, the GLOBE study advanced an inaccurate portrayal of Africa, presenting culture as homogeneous in its sweeping classification of the Continent. For instance, findings from five different African countries – Namibia, Nigeria, South Africa, Zambia and Zimbabwe – are presented as representative of the entire sub-Saharan Africa region. From this, it would seem that leadership in Africa is uniformly characterised by high uncertainty avoidance, high power distance and high collectivism, which, despite the existence of shared cultural symbolism across many parts of African society, is certainly *not invariably the case*.

A further criticism lay in the contention that dimensionalisation of national culture was fundamentally reductionist. Proponents of this view contended that such categorisation tended to narrow the purview of phenomena under study and, more often than not, occasioned a loss of the bigger picture (Tayeb, 2001) – a situation that undermines the complexity of the leadership–culture nexus and is ultimately detrimental to a more nuanced appreciation of contextual practices.

Organisational Culture and Leadership

In addition to interest in cross-cultural leadership phenomena, there were also explorations of the rather instrumental relationship between *organisational culture* and leadership (Case, 2008). According to Peters and Waterman (1982), for instance, successful companies possessed *strong cultures* in which employees were committed to a clear set of values that united and motivated them. *Good managers*, they claimed, *make meanings for people, as well as money* (1982, p. 29). In their winning formula, it was the leader's duty and prerogative to persuade employees to sign up to corporate values and thereby exact a commitment to work that transcended the mere compliance that could be secured through paid employment. In other words, by contracting normatively with their organisation (Etzioni, 1961), employees would always be willing to go the extra mile for that employer. Similarly, Deal and Kennedy argued that companies with so-called strong cultures *can gain as much as one or two hours productive work per employee per day* (1982, p. 15). They asserted that leaders not only had the right but also the obligation to change organisational culture through manipulation of symbols, stories, myths, rituals and ceremonies in order to secure greater productivity from the workforce.

The 'cultural excellence' movement enjoyed popularity at the time and can lay claim to having significantly influenced corporate leadership and change methodologies. Indeed, it spawned an entire consultancy industry in its own right. Nonetheless, it certainly was not without its detractors. Critics at the time included, *inter alia*, Kunda (1992), Parker (2000), Willmott (1993) and Wilson (1992). These authors mounted critiques on a variety of grounds, including: *conceptual inadequacy*; *questionable ethics*; and *lack of practical feasibility* to control cultural change implementation. Indeed, Willmott (1993) coined the disparaging term *corporate culturism* to apprehend the way in which managerial consumers of cultural excellence were being ideologically duped into accepting views and pursuing practices that were inherently deceptive, misleading and ethically compromised.

EMERGING THOUGHT AND NEW DIRECTIONS: *WHERE WE GO*

Leadership in 'Our' image and Likeness? African Philosophy and Knowledge Politics

While sustained progress appears to have been made towards greater understanding of leadership phenomena, much of the discourse remains dominated by Western-centric perspectives, to the exclusion of the diverse range of alternatives hailing from the Global South. Many scholars contend that despite the existence of other views as to the nature of these variegated social phenomena, the former have been systemically privileged as mainstream, with the rest othered in wider contemporary debate (Iwowo, 2015; Mbigi, 2005; Nkomo and Ngambi, 2009; Obiakor, 2004). This knowledge positioning is seen as not only intellectually ethnocentric but as a fallout of Western knowledge hegemony and systemically pervasive, having positioned itself on the back of colonial power and authority in the wake of Empire (Bhabha; 1994; Said, 1978; Spivak, 1988).

A few critical perspectives speak to this issue of knowledge politics, most prominent of which lies within the field of *postcolonial critique* (PCT). As a body of knowledge, it challenges established ways of knowing and contends for the deconstruction of dominant hegemonic ways of understanding the world. It is defined broadly as the critique of social, economic and political conditions, as well as of ways of thinking and representing Empire that persist long after its dismantling (Brett, 2007). Its proponents argue that the world has long been viewed through the narrow ethnocentric lens of the coloniser to the detriment and exclusion of the equally significant worldviews of the colonised – with systemic production and representation of Western knowledge not only legitimising its privileged positioning as mainstream, but creating an uneven dichotomy in which other knowledge forms were cast in the periphery. Knowledge has thus been and, to a large extent, is still produced and controlled by the West, with its real power lying not in the political, economic or technological, but in its assumed authority to define, represent and theorise Other's subjectivities (McEwan, 2001). This privileging tendency (Dutton et al., 1998) not only sponsors the universalising assumptions of Western knowledge, but also its authority to legitimise them. In challenging this, postcolonialism cites the insufficiency of Western epistemological frameworks in grappling with the totality and complexity of the rest of the world, calling for recognition and respectful acknowledgement of knowledge pluralism. Mainstream knowledge is thus considered an off-shoot of historical European expansionism and challenged on the basis that it unduly universalises a narrow ethnocentric worldview.

Leadership Theory Through a Postcolonial Lens

This argument has significant implications for what we say leadership *is* (its ontological status) and for how we say it *should* be practised (the normative ethics associated with leadership). In other words, if leadership means different things to different people, then it follows that it will inevitably be a contested concept (Grint, 2005) which will resist facile 'mainstream' appropriation/representation. If we say that Western knowledge frameworks are epistemologically unaligned with non-Western subjectivities, for example, what then does this mean for our understanding and practice of a putatively 'mainstream' representation of leadership, which is itself arguably informed by partial and culturally attenuated conceptual frameworks?

It has been argued that mainstream leadership discourse is indeed part and parcel of an enduring

Western knowledge hegemony (Banerjee, 2004; Banerjee & Linstead, 2004; Prasad, 1997; Chapter 37, Leadership and its alternatives). For instance, the paradigm of 'transformational leadership' has remained one of the most widely adopted approaches in management learning, despite its many detractors (Blunt and Jones, 1997). It is further argued that mainstream leadership theory is culturally dissonant and often philosophically inconsistent with the sociocultural fabric of many African societies. Because of this, it is grossly ineffective for addressing the unique sociocultural and socioeconomic problems of African national contexts (Eyong, 2017; Mbigi, 2005; Nkomo and Ngambi, 2009 Obiakor, 2004) – a reality that is all too infrequently taken into account with respect to leadership education (Iwowo, 2015). If this is the case, why then does Western leadership theory continue to dominate contemporary discourse? Why is it continually positioned as mainstream and to what end?

One might imagine that it is because alternative perspectives, such as, indigenous accounts of leadership, either do not exist or, if and where they do, have been deemed inferior and occluded by powerful hegemonic forces. PCT contends the latter is the case and we believe it is important to keep this in mind when appraising mainstream leadership and, not least, *cross-cultural* leadership. Within the critical gaze on leadership and culture, the role of knowledge politics in shaping the field has given further rise to discourses of resistance. The critique of Western knowledge hegemony with respect to the above remains a subject of growing interest, gaining prominence in the debate. Such prominence ensures that we maintain a critical gaze and thus sustain the interest generated thus far. We believe the voices that speak to this are on the rise and will continue to be for the foreseeable future.

ANTHROPOLOGICAL PERSPECTIVES ON LEADERSHIP AND CULTURE

We have thus far implicitly assumed the meaning of two key terms – *leadership* and *culture* – that we are exploring in cross-cultural context in this chapter. It is now time to pay closer attention to these concepts in ways that are alert to the postcolonial critique that we are trying to advance. This is not the place to engage in a detailed definitional debate with respect to either concept and, indeed, others have already undertaken this daunting task and provided comprehensive reviews (see, e.g., Bryman, 2013; Burns, 1978; Burns, 1996; Goldstein, 1957; Grint, 2005; Heifetz, 1994; Katan 2018).

Nonetheless, as they lie at the core of the various academic positions we are exploring and arguments we wish to advance, it is helpful to outline some of our thoughts on these notions.

The discipline of anthropology (in all its forms) takes the exploration and understanding of human culture as its main purpose and *raison d'être*. So, it is appropriate that we look for definitional insight and inspiration from this field of study. When turning our gaze towards leadership practices, we would argue strongly that these are best understood in *cultural terms*. In other words, we need to approach leadership phenomena reflexively from a theoretical position culturally nuanced in terms of the dimensions and sensitivities (Brown, 2004). This means viewing leadership through a hybrid lens that permits and accommodates interaction of the social, psychological and physical. Certain recent theoretical innovations in the discipline of leadership studies, in particular, the *leadership-as-practice* (LAP) movement, are well suited to facilitating socio-material explorations of leadership phenomena (Crevani and Endrissat, 2016; Raelin, 2016; Raelin et al., 2018; Sergi, 2016; Chapter 2, Leadership and practice theories, Chapter 21 Problematising communication and providing inspiration). Indeed, this theoretical perspective on leadership practices can be employed usefully to examine leadership phenomena *empirically* in postcolonial cultural contexts and we shall shortly outline some studies that illustrate its fecundity in this regard. Before doing so, however, it may be helpful to consider a little more what anthropology has to say about leadership.

From inception as an academic discipline, anthropology has been interested in highlighting and accounting for leadership phenomena in human communities (e.g., Mumford, 1909). Early ethnographic work, for example, focused on chieftains – or what Mead (1935) referred to as 'Big Men' – and patterns of authority in small-scale traditional societies. In this regard, the writings of Margaret Mead on Papua New Guinea, Raymond Firth with respect to Melanesia, Marshal Sahlins on Polynesia and the Amazonian research reported by Claude Lévi-Strauss come immediately to mind as seminal accounts of the dynamics of leadership, authority, social organisation and culture (Mead, 1935; Firth, 1949; Sahlins, 1958, 1963; Lévi-Strauss, 1944). While these accounts of relationship between leadership and culture privilege the *social*, developments of evolutionary anthropology have sought to place greater emphasis on the physiological, genetic, sexual and neurological dimensions of leader–follower relations and influence. This diverse field of study finds parallels between authority patterns in the behaviour of other mammals, such as dominance hierarchies in social carnivores (wolves, lions, wild dogs, etc.) and primates (chimpanzees, gibbons, bonobos, etc.) and contemporary human social organisation. It also explores evolutionary links to hominin and archaic *homo sapiens* communities (Garfield et al., 2019; Graeber & Wengrow, 2021).

In light of our concern that leadership studies in cross-cultural context should be alert and sensitised to postcolonial critique, it is important that we acknowledge the way in which the discipline and sub-disciplines of anthropology have been strongly implicated historically in colonial ambitions and exploits (Banerjee & Linstead, 2004). For example, Brelsford (1944) set out to 'advise' British colonial district officers in Zambia on authority relations among the Bemba, to better predict and manage these peoples. On a related theme, Mamdani (2012) points out how the anthropological notion of 'tribe' was used instrumentally by colonial states to impose certain forms of group identity on individual subjects. Organising populations in terms of putative tribal affiliation helped subjugate and render them more malleable to colonial regulation and government. There are many such examples in the anthropological record that make clear the 'facilitative' role this discipline often played in terms of supporting and strengthening colonial administration. In short, anthropology has a chequered history and has bestowed a legacy of academic guilt (Rosaldo, 1989) that contemporary scholars working in the field have had to contend with. Anthropologists writing and researching in a postcolonial context have taken this to heart and made a concerted effort, reflexively, to redress the problem both in terms of retrospective evaluation of past practices and methodological prescriptions intended to avoid future research relations with 'subjects' that could be damaging or exploitative (Clifford & Marcus, 1986; Marcus & Fischer, 1986; Rosaldo, 1989; Sedgwick, 2017).

We hope to have made clear that, as a discipline, anthropology has taken – and continues to take – an active and explicit interest in leadership phenomena. However, one might reasonably ask what, precisely, is the *subject of study*? What do anthropologists, or anyone else for that matter, mean by leadership? This question brings us roundly back to the problematic and seemingly elusive matter of how to define or otherwise circumscribe leadership phenomena.

Perhaps the first and most obvious thing to point out is that *leadership* is an abstract noun found within the English language. It is *one* word in a *one* particular language. As Jepson (2009) and Case et al. (2011) have pointed out, it is rare to find a nounal term for *leadership* in languages other than English. It would seem that the historical 'slippage' of the verb *lead* to the role *leader* and abstract noun *leadership* is something peculiar to the English language (Case et al., 2011).

From the anthropological record, it might reasonably be concluded that there is a set of phenomena manifesting universally – or, perhaps to be more precise, near universally (Brown, 2004) – that can be connoted by terms that signify ways in which individuals exercise agency in mobilising socio-material resources within a given time-specific setting that, in turn, motivate others to be moved, or permit themselves to be persuaded to pursue a particular end or set of ends. An innovation that the English language – a language that has become so globally ubiquitous in large measure as a result of Empire – alighted upon was to generate a single abstract noun to represent these patterns of conduct in human communities and organisations. It is critically important to recognise, however, that this is a relatively unusual linguistic invention and that different constellations of terms relating to leadership phenomena are found in non-Anglophone settings. Moreover, the fact that there is a word in English that serves as both metonym and synecdoche for leadership phenomena in no way 'solves the problem of representation', as it were. Difference, variation, ambiguity and mutual misapprehension seem to abound. Indeed, at the limit, it has been claimed that the English word *leadership* is little more than an empty signifier that is open to multiple uses and interpretations (Spoelstra, 2013).

So, if simple definition and agreement about what *leadership* connotes remains elusive, what might researchers interested in such phenomena usefully explore? This is a question that, on the one hand, we would want to leave open because nobody can be sure what future creativity and innovation might be possible, yet, on the other, we would like to suggest some lines of enquiry that could be fruitful to other researchers. For example, we have found significant inspiration in Keith Grint's treatment of *leadership* as an *essentially contested concept* (Grint, 2005, *pace* Gallie, 1955/56). In other words, rather than *expecting* to be able precisely and incontestably to *define* leadership, for all practical purposes it makes sense to view leaders and leadership as socio-material assemblages – a notion that Grint draws from actor network theory (Latour, 1996, 2005) – that lack intrinsic *essence* and can be recovered in scientific, professional or lay terms in multiple ways.

Rather than define terms in abstract, we might instead map the empirical terrain by finding out what concepts are invoked and what socio-material conduct takes place in the name of leadership and related terminologies *in any given culture and language*. Based on his own enquiries in this regard, Grint suggests that the empirical field can be organised by answering a series of questions relating to the 'who', 'what', 'where', 'how' and 'why' of the phenomenon. Elements of the resulting nomenclature correspond respectively to leadership as person (who), result (what), position (where), process (how) and purpose (why). In other words, in historical and contemporary studies of leadership a certain structural *grammar* seems to inform scientific, professional and lay accounts (Case, 2013). These, in turn, reflect particular explanatory dispositions, preferences and assumptions. For instance, according to some person-centric narratives, *who* leaders are makes them leaders, in others it is *what* leaders achieve, *where* they are located, or *how* they get things done that qualifies them as leaders. Forms of explanation can be located within this conceptual alembic, some focusing exclusively on one dimension and others proposing an admixture of the who, what, where, how and why motives.

We would like cautiously to suggest that this heuristic approach to exploring patterns of explanation and understanding in relation to leadership provides a nuanced and sensitive way of investigating the relationship between leadership and culture that is linguistically mobile.

In this subsection we have thus far attempted to offer insight into how anthropological and linguistic sensitivity, informed by postcolonial critique, offers an emerging way forward for research into the relationship between leadership and culture. We now move to demonstrating how these ideas and the research platform we argue for may be applied empirically. To this end we draw on the authors' studies of leadership practices in two postcolonial contexts: a) Official Development Assistance interventions in Lao People's Democratic Republic (a former French colony); and b) the Nollywood film industry in Nigeria (a former British colony).

STUDYING LEADERSHIP FROM INDIGENOUS PERSPECTIVES: TWO ILLUSTRATIONS

The Language and Practice of Leadership in Laos

To illustrate some arguments and proposals we have made thus far, we draw attention to some anthropological-linguistic research into leadership one of the authors undertook in the postcolonial context of Lao People's Democratic Republic between 2011 and 2016. Laos did not exist as a nation state until it was colonised by the French and its borders formally demarcated in a treaty of 1893. The country formed part of what became known as French Indochina alongside other colonial acquisitions of Vietnam and Cambodia. Aside from a slight interregnum during World War II when the Japanese conquered and occupied Laos, the French remained colonial masters until the victory in 1975 of the communist Lao People's Revolutionary Party (LPRP) at the end of what, in local parlance, was termed 'the American war'. The LPRP created a single-party socialist state informed by a broadly Marxist–Leninist ideology that remains in power to this day. It was in this setting, while working on a series of rural development Official Development Assistance (ODA) projects, that Case et al. (2017) undertook an ethnographic study of leadership practices in formal meetings (typically attended by state civil servants, agricultural professionals and members of farming communities). They also report on some of the challenges faced politically by smallholder farmers working in the field (both literally and metaphorically) in trying to represent or describe *their understanding* of leadership, given that there is no translational equivalent for this abstract noun in the Lao language. What Case et al. (2017) concluded from their empirical investigations is that leadership in Laos is highly person-centric and intimately related to personal position or placement within situated social and political hierarchies. In other words, leadership practices closely and predominantly coalesce around what Grint (2005) proposed as the *who* and *where* of leadership. Of course, other leadership-related motives – the whats, whys and hows – were present in the narratives they recorded but these were significantly less prominent.

Case et al. (2017) also point to the way that leadership and authority relations need to be understood as the outcome of complex historical and socio-material conditions. Many leadership-related patterns of conduct, such as systems of patronage and the terminology used to designate leaders, have been inherited by the LPRP from the precolonial period, a time when the region now occupied by Laos, northern Thailand, southern Myanmar and southern China was characterised by rule of *mandala* states (Evans, 2002). Kinship relations found in villages to this day, but dating back millennia, as well as systems of property rights, patronage, inheritance, etc., also feed into the contemporary leadership nexus. These ancient patterns of conduct have been overlaid by an admixture of colonial influence stemming from the period of French rule, Communist Party ideology, Russian-influenced politburo political organisation and, not least, the language of ODA intervention (much of it 'English') that has come into play since 1986 when the LPRP began a programme of relative liberalisation and general 'opening up' to the outside world. These historical and contemporary conditions give rise to a rich palimpsest of leadership-related terms and practices.

The Case of Nollywood New Media

A poignant illustration of the all-important role that contextual and sociocultural spaces play in shaping and impacting our understanding/practice of leadership may also be found in Nigeria's mainstream film industry. We focus here on traditional Nollywood, its earliest sphere characterised by home-video and DVD movies made in the English and/or Igbo language (Iwowo, 2018, 2020). We draw on the example of how the enactment of indigenous leadership frameworks (in this case, the particular African leadership philosophy of *ubuntu*) in lived experience are used to defy the hegemonic capitalist structures of Hollywood. This lived enactment of *ubuntu* is presented as a radical alternative to the hegemonic demands of Hollywood capitalism.

The capitalist leadership structures of Hollywood (Gomery 1978, Ross 2021; Sklar 1975) are supported by its history of the monopolistic 'system'. In contrast, traditional Nollywood leadership stems from a sustained defiance to the capitalist British (neo)colonial legacy of paternalism. This defiance subconsciously relied on the cultural values of *collective survival*, *shared ownership*, *reciprocal respect* and *humaneness* – these being manifestations of *ubuntu*. *Ubuntu* is that African leadership philosophy meaning 'personhood' or 'humanity' in the Bantu languages of Southern African regions, and also enunciated in iziXhoxha as '*umuntu ngumuntu ngabantu*'. Tutu (1999, p. 31) unbundles this as, *my humanity is inextricably bound up in yours*. Broadly constituting an existential philosophy of most African traditions, which prioritise the indispensability of community, hospitality, care, respect and reciprocity to interpersonal relations (Mangaliso, 2001, p. 24; Ncube, 2010, p. 78), this worldview centralises collective survival, commonwealth, interconnectedness and dignity, condensed in the proverb: *I am because, you are*. Common parlance among Nigerians also illuminates this philosophy: *What affects the eyes affects the nose*. At the commencement of traditional Nollywood in 1992, this *ubuntu* character was reinforced by attempts of Nigerian filmmakers to circumvent prohibitive costs of filmmaking. By this negotiation, they trammelled the colonial legacy of dependence hitherto installed by the British to forestall the flourishing of an independent Nigerian film industry.

At the time of Nigeria's independence in 1960, its cinema was confronted by a dearth of professionally skilled filmmakers (Olusola, 1965). This resulted from the paternalistic policies of the Colonial Film Unit (CFU), informed by its stereotyping of the colonised as mentally inferior. At its inception in 1939, the CFU instituted a policy of *specialised techniques* for films made for *primitive people* (*Colonial Cinema* 1943). These specified that sophisticated scripting, cinematography and editing be *rigidly eschewed* in films made for the British colonies (Iwowo, 2018, p. 37) and were perpetuated through the CFU *Africanisation* drive, in which indigenous filmmakers were taught substandard filmmaking. However, the latter were further disadvantaged by lack of opportunities, as the CFU commissioned only British filmmakers for productions involving complex technologies and critical practice. As such, early Nigerian filmmakers were ill-equipped to tell their stories using the international conventions of cinematic vocabulary (Diawara, 1992; Iwowo, 2018; Obiaya, 2011; Olusola, 1965). Post-independence, Nigerian cinema subsequently sought skilled resources from the UK. This was a deliberate neocolonial structure of leadership dependency, which crippled the cinema when Nigeria's economy collapsed in the 1980s (Obiaya, 2011).

In 1992, Nigerian filmmaking enterprise was reactivated as 'traditional Nollywood' by some young Nigerian theatre and film graduates who, seeking to mediate their unemployment through productions, relied on inherited cinematic naiveté and scant equipment. Unlike their predecessors, however, these filmmakers did not look to the West for technical leadership – that is, postproduction skills, funding, or distribution – but they developed a minimalist budgetary template, combining goodwill and communal approaches to living via *ubuntu*. In demonstrating this, relatives and friends offered their homes as film locations for little or no fee, with costumes often borrowed for free. Producer Bond Emerua recalls that communities sometimes fed cast and crew for free, and sent out town-criers to solicit for extra cast members – with Nigerian retirees often happy to be cast as elders in films (Haynes, 2016, p. 142). Reciprocally, producers were expected to respectfully utilise such goodwill and show gratitude to benefactors in film credits. This worldview equally gained expression in the general non-necessity of written contracts. Collaborators, guided by the *ubuntu* spirit and the belief in the African metaphysical laws that 'you reap what you sow', usually trusted that verbal agreements would be honoured. Consequently, product turnaround was typically swift and producers satisfied with making slight returns on a film before moving on to the next production. With this affordable style, indigenous moviemakers – leading collective action to harness resources – proliferated narratives addressing myriad socioeconomic issues in Nigeria and quickly amassed audiences across Africa, Caribbean and Western diasporic communities. Indeed, traditional Nollywood is the metaphoric child of *ubuntu*.

Thus, the industry's popularity soon displaced what was termed *African cinema* (Iwowo, 2020, p. 96) – that postcolonial film genre ironically hamstrung by its fidelity to (neo)colonial, production-budget standards. In this contextualisation, *ubuntu* thus challenges the predatory capitalism of colonialism, demonstrating that wealth can be collectively made and owned if sincerity, respect and reciprocity are prioritised. In postcolonialism one can read this as dislodging (neo)colonial leadership.

Thus, we not only see the lived embodiment of non-Western leadership philosophy in a non-Western context but, more importantly, how this underscores anticolonial/postcolonial resistance to Western hegemonic thought – that is, capitalism and knowledge imperialism within this particular context of African filmmaking. We also see how the enactment of indigenous leadership practices unconsciously becomes a site of anti-hegemonic resistance in this context. In addition, the community action of *ubuntu* undermines the colonial idea of the 'great man'/heroic forms of leadership in the way it harnesses collective energies within this sociocultural context to achieve objectives. In terms of Grint's (2005) typology, this marks a shift from the colonial emphasis on the person – the 'who' of leadership – to process and purpose – that is, the 'how' and 'why' of leadership afforded by *ubuntu* philosophy. Furthermore, the harnessing of collective economic resources is resonant of what we might frame in terms of leadership-as-practice (LAP) as socio-material endeavour (Carroll et al., 2008; Raelin, 2016; Raelin et al., 2018), this approach – in its espoused ethics – arguably being consistent with the philosophical underpinnings of *ubuntu*.

CONCLUSION

In this chapter we began by offering an overview of the field of cross-cultural leadership studies and its emergence as a domain of enquiry in the 1980s to 1990s, paying particular attention to how its study has been shaped over time by the various scholarly perspectives that speak to it. Moving on to its critique, we noted how the cultural turn in leadership studies was fundamentally reductionist and sweepingly ethnocentric in its dimensionalisation, categorisation and simplification of leadership culture. We then sought to present alternatives that challenge accepted wisdom and mainstream hegemonic thought. Our postcolonial critique set the stage for a closer consideration of anthropological perspectives that attend to the contextual relationship between leadership and culture. In so doing, however, we were also at pains to acknowledge the darker role anthropology played in the ethnocentrism and colonial exploitation of Empire. In short, anthropology is burdened by postcolonial guilt and has sought to distance itself from its earlier positions by offering alternative and more reflexive approaches that counteract the dangers of ethnocentrism. Having made a strong case for the inexorable and intimate interrelationship between leadership and culture, we presented two cases that demonstrated how anthropologically and linguistically nuanced interpretative methods can be applied to empirical understandings of leadership phenomena. One example drew on our studies of the language and practices of leadership in Laos; the other, our research into postcolonial and anticolonial filmmaking in Nigeria. Exemplifying *ubuntu* philosophy, the latter showcased distributed leadership and the egalitarian harnessing of collective action. In both illustrations, we attempted to foreground the importance of approaching leadership phenomena from a socio-material perspective and the potential value of applying leadership-as-practice theory in understanding situated leadership processes (see also Chapter 2, Leadership and practice theories, Chapter 21 Problematising communication and providing inspiration).

These examples sought to exemplify an alternative, heterodox and critical agenda that contrasts with extant mainstream approaches to the study of cross-cultural leadership: approaches which, we argued in our earlier critique, exhibit hegemonic, corporatist and Western-centric dispositions inherited from the days of Empire. Future studies of leadership, we contend strongly, should eschew extant intellectual chains that bind them to Empire in implicit and explicit ways. Instead, when studying leadership in cultural context, perspectives need to shift radically away from the inherited gaze of the coloniser and towards indigenous sensibilities and understandings. The contemporary interpretative modes of enquiry offered by social and cultural anthropology offer the appropriate methodological equipment, linguistic sophistication and analytical nuance to redress the imbalances in research orientation that we have been at pains to point out. We trust our critical review of the current state of cross-cultural leadership studies combined with thoughts on some possible future directions and programmes of research that might be taken up within the field provides a stimulus for fresh work on the part of interested readers.

REFERENCES

Achebe, C. (1958). *Things Fall Apart*. Astor-Honor.
Ailon, G. (2008). Mirror, mirror on the wall: Culture's consequences in a value test of its own design. *Academy of Management Review*, 33(4), 885–904.
Banerjee, S. B. (2004). Reinventing colonialism: Exploring the myth of sustainable development. *Situation Analysis*, 4(Autumn), 95–110.
Banerjee, S. B., & Linstead, S. (2004). Masking subversion: Neo-colonial embeddedness in anthropological accounts of indigenous management. *Human Relations*, 57(2), 221–258.
Bhabha, H.K. (1994). *The Location of Culture*, Routledge.
Blunt, P. and Jones, M. (1997). Exploring the limits of Western leadership Theory in East Asia and Africa. *Personnel Review*, 26. (1).
Brelsford, W. (1944). *Succession of Bemba Chiefs: A Guide for District Officers*. Government Printer.
Christophers, B. (2007). Ships in the night: Journeys in cultural imperialism and postcolonialism. *International Journal of Cultural Studies*, 10(3), 283-302.
Brown, D.E. (2004). Human universals, human nature and human culture. *Daudelus*, 133(4), 47–54.
Bryman, A. (2013). *Leadership and Organizations*. Routledge.
Burns, J. M. (1978). *Leadership*. Harper and Row.
Burns, J. S. (1996). Defining leadership: Can we see the wood for the trees? *Journal of Leadership and Organizational Studies*, 3(2), 148–157.
Carroll, B., Levy, L., & Richmond, D. (2008). Leadership as practice: Challenging the competency paradigm. *Leadership*, 4(4), 363–379.
Case, P. (2008). Organizational culture. In J. Gosling and A. Marturano (Eds.), *Key Concepts in Leadership Studies*. Routledge.
Case, P. (2013). Book review: Keith Grint, *The Arts of Leadership* (Oxford University Press, Oxford, UK 2001) 454 pp. and Keith Grint, *Leadership: Limits and Possibilities* (Palgrave Macmillan, Houndmills, Basingstoke, UK and New York, NY, USA 2005) 192 pp. *Leadership and the Humanities*, 1(1), pp. 59–62.
Case, P., French, R., & Simpson, P. (2011). Philosophy of leadership. In A. Bryman, D. Collinson, K. Grint, B. Jackson & M. Uhl-Bien (Eds.), *Sage Handbook of Leadership* (pp. 242–254). Sage.
Case, P., Connell, J.G. & Jones, M.J. The language of leadership in Laos. *Leadership*, 13(2), 173–193.
Case, P., & Śliwa, M. (2020). Leadership learning, power and practice in Laos: A leadership as-practice perspective. *Management Learning*, 51(5), 537–558.
Clifford, J., & Marcus, G. E. (Eds.) (1986). *Writing Culture: The Poetics and Politics of Ethnography*. University of California Press.
Colonial Cinema (1943). Mass education in African society. *Colonial Cinema*, 2(2), 2–7.
Crevani, L., & Endrissat, N. (2016). Mapping the leadership-as-practice terrain: Comparative elements. In J. Raelin (Ed.), *Leadership-As-Practice: Theory and Application* (pp. 21–49). Routledge.
Dansereau, F., & Yammarino, F. (2006). Is more discussion about levels of analysis really necessary? When is such discussion sufficient? *Leadership Quarterly*, 17(5), 537–552.
Deal, T., & Kennedy, A. (1982). *Corporate Cultures: The Rites and Rituals of Corporate Life*. Addison-Wesley.
Diawara, M. (1992). *African Cinema: Politics and Culture*. Indiana University Press.
Dutton, M.; Gandhi, L. and Seth, S. (1998) Postcolonial Studies: A Beginning: *Postcolonial Studies*, 1(1), 7–11
Etzioni, A. (1961). *Comparative Analysis of Complex Organizations*. Collier-Macmillan.
Evans, G. (2002). *A Short History of Laos: The Land In Between*. Allen & Unwin.
Eyong, J. E. (2017). Indigenous African leadership: Key differences from Anglo-centric thinking and writings. *Leadership*, 13(2), 133–153.
Fanon, F. (1963). *The Wretched of the Earth*. Grove Press.
Firth, R. (1949). Authority and public opinion in Tikopia. *Social Structure: Studies Presented to A. R. Radcliffe-Brown* (pp. 168–188). Clarendon Press.
Gallie, W. B. (1955/56). Essentially contested concept. *Proceedings of the Aristotelian Society*, 56, 167-98.
Garfield, Z. H., von Rueden, C., & Hagen, E. H. (2019). The evolutionary anthropology of political leadership. *Leadership Quarterly*, 30(1), 59–80.
Gerstner, C. R., & Day, D. V. (1994). Cross-cultural comparison of leadership prototypes. *Leadership Quarterly*, 5(2), 121–134.
Gill, R. (2006). *Theory and Practice of Leadership*: SAGE.
Goldstein, L. J. (1957). On defining culture. *American Anthropologist*, 59(6), 1075–1081.
Gomery, D. (1978). The picture palace: Economic sense or Hollywood nonsense? *Quarterly Review of Film & Video*, 3(1), 23–36.
Graeber, D., & Wengrow, D. (2021). *The Dawn of Everything: A New History of Humanity*. Allen Lane.

Grint, K. (2005). *Leadership: Limits and Possibilities*. Pagrave Macmillan.

Guthey, E., & Jackson, B. (2011). Cross-cultural leadership revisited. In A. Bryman, D. Collinson, K. Grint, B. Jackson & M. Uhl-Bien (Eds.), *The SAGE Handbook of Leadership* (1st edn, pp. 165–178). Sage.

Hampden-Turner, C., & Trompenaars, F. (1997). Response to Geert Hofstede. *International Journal of Intercultural Relations, 21*(1), 149–159.

Haynes, J. (2016). *Nollywood: The Creation of Nigerian Film Genres*. University of Chicago Press.

Heifetz, R. A. (1994). *Leadership Without Easy Answers*. Belknap Press of Harvard University Press.

Hofstede, G. (1980) *Culture's Consequences: International Differences in Work Related Values*. SAGE.

Hofstede, G. (1991). *Culture's Consequences* SAGE.

House, R. J., Hanges, P. J., Javidan, M., Dorfman, P. W., & Gupta, V. (Eds.) (2004). *Culture, Leadership, and Organizations: The GLOBE Study of 62 Societies*. Sage.

House, R. J., Hanges, P. J., Ruiz-Quintanilla, S. A., Dorfman, P. W., Javidan, M., Dickson, M., & Gupta, V. (1999). Cultural influences on leadership and organizations: Project GLOBE. *Advances in Global Leadership, 1*(2), 171–233.

Hunt, J. & Yan, J. (2005) A Cross-Cultural Perspective on Perceived Leadership Effectiveness: *International Journal of Cross-Cultural Management,* 5, 49–66

Iwowo, S. (2018). *Colonial continuities in Neo-Nollywood: A postcolonial study*. Doctoral dissertation, University of Bristol.

Iwowo, S. (2020). The problematic mise en scène of neo-Nollywood. *Communication Cultures in Africa, 2*(1). Available at: https://communication-culturesinafrica.com/articles/abstract/10.21039/cca.34/

Iwowo, V. (2012). The internationalization of leadership development. In S. Turnbull, P. Case, G. Edwards, D. Schedlitski & P. Simpson (Eds.), *Worldly Leadership* (pp. 52–67). Palgrave Macmillan.

Iwowo, V. (2015). Leadership in Africa: Rethinking development. *Personnel Review, 44*(3), 408–429.

Jepson, D. (now Schedlitzki, D.) (2009). Studying leadership at cross-country level: A critical analysis. *Leadership, 5*(1), 61–80.

Jepson, D. (now Schedlitzki, D.) (2010). The importance of national language as a level of discourse within individuals' theorising of leadership: A qualitative study of German and English employees. *Leadership, 6*(4), 425–445.

Jones, A. (2005). The anthropology of leadership: Culture and corporate leadership in the American south. *Leadership, 1*(3), 259–278.

Jones, A. (2006). Developing what? An anthropological look at the leadership development Process. *Leadership, 2*(4), 481–498.

Katan, D. (2018). Defining culture, defining translation. In S. A. Harding & O. Carbondell Cortés (Eds.), *The Routledge Handbook of Translation and Culture*. Routledge.

Kunda, G. (1992). *Engineering Culture*. Temple University Press.

Latour, B. (1996). On actor-network theory: A few clarifications plus more than a few complications. *Soziale Welt, 47*, 369–381.

Latour, B. (2005). *Reassembling the Social: An Introduction to Actor-Network-Theory*. Oxford University Press.

Lévi-Strauss, C. (1944). The social and psychological aspects of chieftainship in a primitive society: The Nambikwara. *Transactions of the New York Academy of Sciences, 2*.

Lord, R. and Maher, K.J. (1991) *Leadership and Information Processing*. Boston: Unwin Hyman.

Mamdani, M. (2012). What is a tribe? *London Review of Books, 34*(17), 13.

Mangaliso, M. (2001). Building competitive advantage from Ubuntu: Management lessons from South Africa. *Academy of Management Executive, 15*(3), 23–33.

Marcus, G., & Fischer, M. M. J. (1986). *Anthropology as Cultural Critique: An Experimental Moment in the Human Sciences*. University of Chicago Press.

Martin, G. S., Resick, C. J., Keating, M. A., & Dickson, M. W. (2009). Ethical leadership across cultures: A comparative analysis of German and US perspectives. *Business Ethics: A European Review, 18*(2), 127-144.

Mbigi, L. (2005). *The Spirit of African Leadership*: Knovres, South Africa.

McEwan, C. (2001). Postcolonialism, Feminism and Development: Intersections And Dilemmas: *Progress in Development Studies 1*(2), 93–111.

Mead, M. (1935). *Sex and Temperament*. Routledge and Kegan Paul.

Meindl, J.R. (1995). The Romance Of Leadership As A Follower-Centric Theory: A Social Constructionist Approach, *Leadership Quarterly, 6*(3), 329–341.

Mellahi, K. (2000). The teaching of leadership on UK MBA programmes: A critical analysis from an international perspective. *Journal of Management Development, 19*(4), 97–308.

Mendonca, M., & Kanungo, R. N. (1996). Impact of culture on performance management in developing countries. *International Journal of Manpower*.

Morgan, G. (1986). *Images of Organization*. Sage.

Mumford, E. (1909). *The Origins of Leadership*. University of Chicago Press.

Ncube, L. (2010). Ubuntu: A transformative leadership philosophy. *Journal of Leadership Studies, 4*(3), 77–82.

Nkomo, S. M., & Ngambi, H. (2009). African women in leadership: Current knowledge and a framework for future studies. *International Journal of African Renaissance Studies*, 4(1), 49–68.

Nkomo, S. M. (2011). A postcolonial and anti-colonial reading of 'African' leadership and management in organization studies: Tensions, contradictions and possibilities. *Organization*, 18(3), 365–386.

Northouse, P. (2004). *Leadership: Theory and Practice* 3rd edition. Thousand Oaks, CA: Sage.

Obiakor, F. (2004). *Building Patriotic African Leadership through African-Centred* Education. *Journal of Black Studies* 34(3), 402-420.

Obiaya, I. (2011). A break with the past: The Nigerian video-film industry in the context of colonial filmmaking. *Film History: An International Journal*, 23(2), 129–146.

Olusola, S. (1965). Shooting for live television under difficult conditions in Nigeria. UNESCO Documents and Publications. http://unesdoc.unesco.org/images/0014/001437/143703eb.pdf

Parker, M. (2000). *Organizational Culture and Identity*. Sage.

Peters, T., & Waterman, R. (1982). *In Search of Excellence: Lessons from America's Best Run Companies*. Harper & Row.

Prassad, P., Prassad, P., Mills, A., Elmes, M.B. and Prasad, A., (1997). The protestant ethic and the myths of the frontier. In P. Prassad, A. Mills, M. Elmes, & A. Prasad (Eds.) *Managing the Organizational Melting Pot: Dilemmas of Workplace Diversity* (pp. 129–149). SAGE.

Raelin, J. A. (Ed.) (2016a). *Leadership-As-Practice: Theory and Application*. Routledge.

Raelin, J. A., Kempster, S., Youngs, H., & Carroll, B. (2018). Practicing leadership-as-practice in content and manner. *Leadership*, 14(3), 371–383.

Resick, C. J., Martin, G. S., Keating, M. A., Dickson, M. W., Kwan, H. K., & Peng, C. (2011). What ethical leadership means to me: Asian, American, and European perspectives. *Journal of business ethics*, 101(3), 435–457.

Rosaldo, R. (1989). *Culture and Truth: The Remaking of Social Analysis*. Beacon Press.

Ross, S. J. (2021). *Working-class Hollywood*. Princeton University Press.

Sahlins, M. D. (1958). *Social Stratification in Polynesia, Vol.29*. University of Washington Press.

Sahlins, M. D. (1963). Poor man, rich man, big-man, chief: Political types in Melanesia and Polynesia. *Comparative Studies in Society and History*, 5, 285–303.

Said, E. (1978). *Orientalism*. Pantheon.

Schedlitzki, D., Case, P., & Knights, D. (2017). Ways of leading in non-Anglophone contexts: Representing, expressing and enacting authority beyond the English-speaking world. *Leadership*, 13(2), 1–6.

Schnackenberg, A. K., Bundy, J., Coen, C. A., & Westphal, J. D. (2019). Capitalizing on categories of social construction: A review and integration of organizational research on symbolic management strategies. *Academy of Management Annals*, 13(2), 375–413.

Schwartz, S. H. (1999). A theory of cultural values and some implications for work. *Applied Psychology*, 48(1), 23–47.

Sedgwick, M. W. (2017). Complicit positioning: Anthropological knowledge and problems of 'studying up' for ethnographer/employees of corporations. *Journal of Business Anthropology*, 6(1), 58–88.

Sergi, V. (2016). Who's leading the way? Investigating the contributions of materiality to leadership-as-practice. In J. Raelin (Ed.), *Leadership-As-Practice: Theory and Application* (pp. 110–131). Routledge.

Sklar, R. (1975). *Movie-made America: How the Movies Changed American Life*. Random House.

Smirchich, L., & Morgan, G. (1982). Leadership: The management of meaning. *Journal of Applied Behavioral Science*, 18(3), 257–273.

Smith, P. B., Dugan, S., & Trompenaars, F. (1996). National culture and the values of organizational employees: A dimensional analysis across 43 nations. *Journal of Cross-Cultural Psychology*, 27(2), 231–264.

Spivak, G. (1988). *Can the Subaltern Speak?* Macmillan.

Spoelstra, S. (2013). Is leadership a visible phenomenon? On the (im)possibility of studying leadership. *International Journal of Management Concepts and Philosophy*, 7(3–4), 174–188.

Tayeb, M. (2001). Conducting research across cultures: Overcoming drawbacks and obstacles. *International Journal of Cross-Cultural Management*, 1(1), 91–108.

Tutu, D. (1999). *No Future Without Forgiveness*. Doubleday Unwin.

Warner, L. S., & Grint, K. (2006). American Indian ways of leading and knowing. *Leadership*, 2(2), 225–244.

Wilmott, H. (1993). Strength is ignorance, slavery is freedom: Managing culture in modern organizations. *Journal of Management Studies*, 30, 515–552.

Wilson, D. C. (1992). *A Strategy of Change*. Routledge.

32
From 'Leadership' to 'Leading': Power Relations, Polyarchy and Projects

Stewart Clegg, Ace V. Simpson, Miguel Pina e Cunha and Arménio Rego

INTRODUCTION

There have been very few theories of power in leadership studies; generally, power is referred to only in the small sub-discipline of critical leadership studies. Surprisingly, scholarship often fails to identify and discuss the power relations embedding leadership. In principle, power can be *over* someone or something. It can also be power to do something ('power *to*'), where others are empowered to do things that they might not otherwise be able to do (Clegg & Haugaard, 2009). Power is also engendered when actors collaborate to exercise 'power *with*' each other as a team. In leadership, however, the focus has traditionally largely been on 'power *over*', usually thought of one dimensionally in terms of an assumption that power is something someone 'has' through the control of resources, expertise, information, decisional authority, or coercive control, by virtue of being a leader (Pierro, et al., 2013; Raven, 1993), rather than being a relational quality of how leading is done.

In this chapter, we discuss the co-evolution of leadership and power, pivoting to a consideration of leading in a digitally enabled organisational democracy. We start by reviewing the sense made by past theorising, discussing the rational mode of organising (the default mode of organising in bureaucracies) which, as suggested by Weber, represents a mode of power *over*. Next, we discuss other aspects of power, including power *to* and power *with*. Power *to* is manifest in notions of empowerment, where a leader devolves some elements of decisional power, authority and accountability to teams as a more motivating and efficient form of power than the exercise of power *over*. The motivational and efficiency aspects reside in the way that such devolution situates responsibility in the team. The process of responsibilisation makes individual subjects responsible for the efficient and effective dispatch of tasks that would have previously been under the scrutiny of supervision, exercising power *over*. As individual subjects working in a team, each member becomes responsible not only for the good conduct of their self but also for managing that of other team members. In some situations, this 'giving away' of power constitutes what is known as servant leadership constituting a way of leading by empowering others with the power *to* exercise agency. Power *with* is at the core of understanding leadership as a process co-created by both leaders and followers (Uhl-Bien et al., 2014), first conceived in the circular theory of power suggested a century ago by Mary Parker Follett (1868–1933). Subsequently, in our final section, we break with the conventions of past sensemaking by considering an emerging future in which there is growing reliance on distributed leading, mostly focused on project work aided by digital technologies, reliant on power *within* a networked system of social relations. Overall, we argue that power and leadership, leading and organising, are intertwined – or, better, modes of organising representing different frameworks of power in action (Clegg, 1989; Cunha et al., 2021), where power, leadership and design are related and co-evolve in new organisational forms (see Table 32.1). Of course, the different types are not mutually exclusive, in fact they may well coexist, but different designs give more prominence to some expression of power than to others.

POWER *OVER*: LEADERSHIP AS HIERARCHICAL CONTROL

The conventional point of departure for a discussion of power and leadership is the work of Max Weber (1922/1978), who used several concepts to discuss power relations in organisations, mainly bureaucracies. These concepts included domination, legitimacy, authority and power, which he defined as *the probability that one actor within a social relationship will be in a position to carry out his or her own will despite resistance, regardless of the basis on which this probability rests* (Weber, 1922/1978, p. 53). In Weber's (1922/1978) theory of bureaucracy, the focus was on relations of domination and power, especially the conditions that could sustain them through legitimation as authority.

Domination, when acceded to by those subject to it, is taken to be legitimate, enacted through an individual's voluntary consent to what is thus titled authority. The essence of leadership is the requirement of legitimacy. Weber described three forms of authority premised on the legitimacy of charisma, tradition and rational legality. Of these three forms of leadership, Weber (1922/1978) held reliance on rational-legal power to be the most stable and efficient. Being founded on systems of rational rules that transcend individual authority, it could most easily handle succession of authority; it depended neither on the vagaries of fertility nor genetic inheritance nor on the promotion of extraordinary qualities whose extinction might lead to problems with the routinisation of charisma. Charismatic leadership might be routinised based on tradition, as has happened with the heirs of the Murdoch family (Graham, 2015), the second generation of whom, in the form of Rupert Murdoch, is handing over the reins to the third generation – the dynastic principle thus forming the basis of monarchies globally as well as of family firms. In perhaps the strangest case of the dynastic principle, the heirs of Kim il Jung in North Korea have ruled the nation since his death, fusing the dynastic principle with some precepts of communism as a tradition.

Weber recognised that, despite its benefits, the limitations of bureaucratic power included the stifling of individual autonomy, freedom and creativity. Later writers added to its offences *rule tropism*, where rules are followed for their own sake while forgetting their originally intended purpose (Merton, 1936), creating labyrinthine organisational forms (Clegg et al., 2016). These tensions arise from bureaucracy as a system of

Table 32.1 How power, leadership and designs co-evolve

	Leadership characterisation	Habitual designs in which each type prevails	Exemplars
Power *over*	Leaders impose and command control through instruction, rules, mandated digital training	Organisational hierarchies	Weber (1922/1978)
Power *to*	Leaders engender commitment by empowering followers with relative autonomy, reinforced by group norms rather than central control	Hierarchical forms with autonomous working groups	Barker (1993)
Power *with*	Leaders and followers co-actively enact power, not as power sharing, but to increase circular power	A stakeholder orientation, worker representation on boards, workers councils, profit sharing	Follett (1941/2003)
Power *within*	Emphasis placed on distributed leadership and the emergent power *within* a system of relations	Creative compartments formally democratised, expert teams, collaborative projects	Fairtlough (1994)

power over those subject to it. The more effective any bureaucracy is as a system of control and productivity, the more it is likely to undermine its prospects due to stifling individual autonomy, creativity, motivation and well-being on the part of rule-followers (as recently discussed by Hamel & Zanini, 2020). Control mechanisms in the past sought to ensure employees observed formal policies and procedures (Tyler & Blader, 2005) put in place by an organisational hierarchy that operated as a complex dynamic command and control system. In modern organisations, power *over* employees was originally embedded in the files and the bureau of an organisation, where they were written down, initially in longhand, later mechanically by typewriters and today, digitally and virtually. The bureau is increasingly enacted through technologies that seek to optimise workforce performance by monitoring, directing, evaluating and rewarding employee behaviours through a *digitocracy* (Ballesteros, 2020) or *algocratic* system (Malhotra, 2021) leading increasingly towards a *surveillance capitalism* (Zuboff, 2019).

Simons (1995) describes four levers of control operated by managers across varied situations: systems of belief, boundaries, diagnosis and interaction. Lewis et al. (2019, p. 488) note that *an over reliance on the direct control of employee behaviour only emphasises the need for employee empowerment*, an observation supported by evidence. External control forced on individuals potentially diffuses responsibility, followed by decline in trust levels and subsequent performance. Despite this, payoffs from tighter control tend to be achieved more quickly, more easily and with greater certainty, at least in the short run while the 'cogs' are energised with a reasonable level of commitment. Consequently, organisations have tended to favour control over autonomy, even when the narrative suggests otherwise (i.e., an alleged autonomy is used to control). This is the case of several platforms operating in the gig economy (Prassl, 2018): a narrative full of terms such as 'autonomy', 'freedom', 'entrepreneurship', 'independence', ' freelancers', 'independent suppliers' and 'sharing economy' often conceals an algorithmic hyper-control. Illustrative is the case of Deliveroo, accused of *creating vocabulary* to avoid calling couriers employees (e.g., *Supplier agreement review* means *Performance management/disciplinary meeting/(final) warning*; see Butler, 2017). Even when it appears otherwise, leadership as bureaucratic control is often used as a default management approach, despite its being often experienced by employees, cast as rule-followers, as rigid, stifling, coercive and suffocating (Adler & Borys, 1996; Ritzer, 1998).

POWER *TO*: LEADERSHIP AS EMPOWERMENT

The literature on power recognises at least two more basic conceptions of power than power over: power *to* and power *with*. Power *to* is facilitative rather than prohibitive. Rather than being based on getting someone to do what they would otherwise not do or having them refrain from doing what they prefer to do, the concept of power *to* taps into the concept of power as a creative capacity. Facilitative power *to* as a social science conception was first elaborated in the work of Talcott Parsons (1963), who represented power as systematically property of the political system. Parsons argued that the creation of power normally *presupposed consensus on system goals* (Haugaard, 2003, p. 90), providing a framework within which facilitative power can operate. The leadership task is to frame this consensus.

Critics of Parsons argue that although power might be positive for those aligned with collective managerial goals, as authority, for those with values and objectives that differ from the prevailing majority, power will be experienced as less legitimate (Clegg et al., 2006). That is why the leadership task is seen to be so focused on framing consensus. Where this framing is not achieved, the lack of a consensual basis of legitimate authority undermines Parsons' notion of leadership enabling power *to* as creative and dynamic. People are likely not to feel empowered when they understand there are structural mechanisms at work that put some people, the leaders, in a position to empower others but only if they first accept the consensual frame that is being subtly imposed by the leadership's framing. Howcroft and Wilson (2003, p. 10) observe that one does not have power where it is given but can be taken away if the agency granted is not channelled in the frame that the leader has prepared.

In organisational terms, the classic study of giving power to people is that of Barker (1993), who details an ethnography of a transition in power relations. The transition is from a situation in which power was exercised unambiguously over employees in terms of hierarchical bureaucratic control to one empowering teams, giving them the power to self-manage. All was not what it might appear to be, however. The power of a direct supervisor over the employees was replaced by a strongly normative control embedded in the team whereby they exercised what Barker termed *concentrative control of each other*. They established and policed a system of normative controls that proved to be more binding and encompassing than the relatively remote control of supervision over them. What had previously been control by exercises of power *over* was replaced by their ability to exercise power *to* do things in ways that the team approved; however, team approval became the key control. It was not so much an overt control, premised on exercises of power of some over others; instead, it was a tacitly agreed set of normative principles premised on 'mateship' among team members who, as a principle, would not let each other down. Control became increasingly rationalised in terms of these norms and their self-management as power *to* become a most effective and more disciplined substitute for the power *over* of the frontline supervisor.

In a more inclusive, if somewhat paternalistic vein, is the notion of servant leadership. A central feature of servant leadership is placing *the good of those led over the self-interest of the leader, emphasizing leader behaviours that focus on follower development, and de-emphasizing glorification of the leader* (Hale & Fields, 2007, p. 397). Leaders remain, however – albeit, somewhat reduced in hubris and power *over* others. Servant leadership contradicts the assumption of leadership as top-down and considers instead that leading can be simultaneously both a service *and* a guide (Van Dierendonck, 2011). Servant leadership does not assert a *right* or claim a *freedom* (Hutson, 2017) to act denied to others. The expression 'servant leadership' was coined by Greenleaf (1970, p. 15). According to the Greenleaf Center for Servant Leadership (initially called the Center for Applied Ethics, founded in 1964), servant leadership *is a philosophy and set of practices that enriches the lives of individuals, builds better organizations and ultimately creates a more just and caring world*. Spears (2002) studied Greenleaf's original writings and identified ten critical characteristics of servant leading: 1) listening, 2) empathy, 3) healing, 4) awareness, 5) persuasion, 6) conceptualisation, 7) foresight, 8) stewardship, 9) commitment to the growth of people, 10) building community. These principles, in various forms and combinations, have been adopted as a guiding philosophy in companies including Herman Miller, ServiceMaster, Synovus Financial Corporation, Southwest Airlines and TDIndustries (Spears, 2002). Except for an article by Graham (1991) in the inaugural issue of *Leadership Quarterly*, servant leadership attracted little interest from the academic community until the 2000s. Since then (mainly after the seminal work of Ehrhart, 2004), researchers have examined the conceptual underpinnings of servant leadership, developed theory and carried out a significant number of empirical studies (e.g., Chiniara & Bentein, 2016; Donia et al., 2016; Hu & Liden, 2011; Liden et al., 2014a, 2014b; Neubert et al., 2008; Peterson et al., 2012; Sousa & Van Dierendonck, 2017) and meta-analyses (e.g., Lee et al., 2020; Zhang et al., 2021).

Servant leadership serves the interests of contemporary leaders well, appearing to be, as Donia et al. (2016, p. 722) argue, *particularly relevant in today's business world*. The *interests of all stakeholders* will be taken into consideration and employees will *experience greater wellbeing, more positive attitudes, and, as they themselves adopt a serving orientation akin to that of their leader, exhibit behaviors which are beneficial to the organization, its members, and the greater community*. The key theme is that of the leader as a benign and caring guide, guiding others that are not blessed with being leaders through the legitimacy of leaders' provision of service to their followers. Servant leadership suggests the notion of power being shared across an organisation; however, individual leaders still lead. What is missed is an essential insight from Follett (1924): any claims to lead always imply relations of power; where these are vested in the superordinate claim of specific individuals, power *over* is implied.

POWER *WITH*: LEADERSHIP AS PARTNERSHIP

A further conception of power involves power *with*. This conception differs from power *to* in that it involves the capability to achieve a jointly desired outcome working together with others towards the common objective. Its key conceptualisation is its system-expanding capabilities which are based in the efforts of the many joined in a common intended outcome (Reed, 2012; Zald & Lounsbury, 2010). The classic proponent of this view was Mary Parker Follett (1924; see Boje & Rosile, 2001; Carlsen et al., 2020; Melé & Rosanas, 2003). An American political scientist sometimes described as the mother of organisation studies (Clegg et al., 2021), Follett was a person ahead of her time (Graham, 1995). Writing in the 1920s and 1930s, Follett (1924, 1995) saw enterprise as a social setting rather than merely an economic one. In some respects, it has been argued, there were some continuities between her arguments and those deployed much later by Foucault (Carlsen et al., 2020) as well as by Clegg (Boje & Rosile, 2001).

Follett sought to manage tensions in the perennial conflict between owners of capital (shareholders and managers employed to represent their interests) and labour (workers) by harmonising power relations, writing: *What is the central problem of social relations? It is the question of power;*

this is the problem of industry, of politics, of international affairs (Follett, 1924, p. xii). Follett described genuine power not as coercive power *over*, but as co-active power, writing: *This kind of power, power-with, is what democracy should mean in politics or industry* (p. 187). Follett held that power cannot be delegated by leaders within organisations as genuine power is not a 'thing' that the powerful can bestow upon the powerless. Power cannot be given or seized because it is not a material possession but a social relation. Managers and workers in conflict seek outcomes where a single side wins, producing a loss for both sides in which the whole has been depleted rather than enriched, she maintained.

Follett's (1941/2003) circular theory of power describes managers and workers, influencing one another in a complex social relational web. She espoused democratic authority in which bureaucratic institutions are replaced with networks of people analysing, producing and taking responsibility for outcomes at each stage of organisational processes. Circular power updates the facts accounted for in an evolving context, accommodating new interpretations, experiences and insights across time; as interpretations of the realities constructed change, so do the relations inscribed in this changing reality. Follett conceptualises power as a democratic accomplishment that organisational leaders can facilitate workers in growing. Conditions allowing a single individual or group to empower others, as in power *to*, can be just as likely to undermine empowerment (Gruber & Trickett, 1987; Simon, 1990). Empowerment can arise only through democratic participation of all on premises all can accept, all can follow, to conclusions that all can agree. At the organisational level, the objective of circular co-active power *with* is not power sharing but to increase power: *our task is not to learn where to place power; it is how to develop power [...] Genuine power can only be grown, it will slip from every arbitrary hand that grasps it* (Follett, 1941/2003, pp. xii–xiii). Authentic democracy is what grows power.

Follett's writings anticipate more contemporary discussions on empowerment (Eylon, 1998). She believed that a definitive driver of human behaviour is the desire for self-governance in directing one's own affairs, yet this desire is incompatible with collective participation necessary for realising an individual's full potential. In the view of Follett, genuine empowerment will only occur when all parties perceive one another as equal partners. Under these conditions, individuals can contribute their unique knowledge, abilities and experiences to the collective. Leaders should manage by seeking to be and remaining adaptive to member contributions. Management has a responsibility to orchestrate a collaborative environment that is adaptive to *the law of the situation* (Follett, 1924, p. 152) – something that is incompatible with exercising power *over*, something requiring mutuality and collaborative framing in social relations.

The intention to collaborate and integrate is insufficient, in Follett's (1924) view, for the transfer of formalised power, as is the notion of 'giving' power to people. Rather, the removal of all structural impediments to the full participation of the organisation's members in all activities responding to the law of the situation is the only means of achieving true democratic power. Follett (1924) wrote: *Many persons' idea of increased democracy within the cooperative movement is to democratize the organization: to have it less hierarchical than at present, to have more democratic elections, etc. This is not enough, to elect the officials and then to listen to their policy and consent. The farmers must also contribute* (p. 215). Follett's conceptualisation is not the action of authorising but rather a concerted action to build, develop and increase power through the coordination of relationships (Murrell, 1985; Thomas & Velthouse, 1990).

In the process of developing and increasing co-active power, Follett (1995) paid due attention to language. She argued that words such as 'higher' and 'lower' or 'over' and 'under' were unhelpful in the organisational context. They denote hierarchical relational constructs of power such as overseeing, super(ordinate)vision, subordination and so on. These words and the practices that they represent and legitimise undermine specific individual contributions by placing some in positions where their contributions may be overlooked (p. 142) – in both senses of the word. In contrast, words such as 'persuade' rather than 'convince' (p. 104) seek to clarify differences between management based on power *over*, opposed to what she espoused as the only beneficial mode of organisational power, power *with*. For Follett, organisations provide the context for such coordination and expansion of people sharing power with others.

Follett's concept of growing co-active power *with* also bears a close relationship with her ideas concerning conflict, where she sees the most sustainable solutions as being those obtained by understanding and satisfying the needs of both parties. *A business should be so organized*, Follett (1995, p. 76) writes, *that full opportunity is given in any conflict, in any coming together of different desires, for the whole field of desire to be viewed*. Unless power is understood as co-active, it will involve zero-sum perceptions of one party's winning depending on another party losing. Achieving power *with* outcomes, however, requires all parties putting aside the expectation that 'their' perspective on an issue must prevail. Instead, relationships must be understood in terms of commonality, integration and circularity:

> Circular behaviour is the basis of integration. If your business is so organized that you can influence a co-manager while he is influencing you, so organized that a workman has an opportunity of influencing you as you have of influencing him, if there is an interactive influence going on all the time between you, power-with may be built up.
> (Follett, 1995, p. 107)

Follett also further advocated the need for a free flow of information as vital to growing co-active power. Her notion of information flow goes beyond open communication by being associated with a notion of establishing respectful ongoing dialogue between all organisational members. To her credit, Follett acknowledges that her proposed dynamic approach to collective organisation is not simple or easy. Rather, in correspondence with contemporary findings, she recognises empowerment as a cyclical process (e.g., Thomas & Velthouse, 1990) where, despite the challenges involved, it is the cycle itself that facilitates success within the process. Achieving co-active power requires leaders recognising empowerment as a dynamic and dialectic process in which they cease to be 'leaders' per se, where the leader is considered a more powerful being. It is an iterative process of ongoing adaptation and adjustment between individual members, in which leadership is a collective and democratic responsibility defining the essential characteristics and functions of organisational practices and work.

To summarise, Follett differs from the power *over* response of denying the need for autonomy of power *to* in offering a rhetoric of empowerment to disguise more subtle technologies of disempowerment and control. Follett (1995) describes genuine power not as the zero-sum game of power *over* or even power *to* but as the self-developing capacity of power *with*. Leadership that is premised on being able to exercise power *over* others or that presumes it can 'give' power *to* others is premised on a fundamental flaw. As Marcus Garvey (1938) knew well from the experience of being black in a white America, only oneself can free one's mind, a sentiment that Bob Marley (1979) channelled in his 'Redemption Song': *Emancipate yourself from mental slavery, none but ourselves can free our minds*. Follett (1995, p. 222) acknowledged that power over will never be eliminated entirely:

> What we need is some process for meeting problems. When we think we have solved a problem, well, by the very process of solving, new elements or forces come into the situation and you have a new problem on your hands to be solved. When this happens, men are often discouraged. I wonder why; it is our strength and our hope. We don't want any system that holds us enmeshed within itself.

Follett's insights concerning co-active power inform modern management approaches acknowledging stakeholder needs, the representation of workers on organisational leadership boards, co-determination and participative management, where management consult with workers councils on decisions relating to employee rights and status (Logue et al., 2015) and profit-sharing initiatives. Strictly speaking, no followers feature in Follet's co-active vision of power because she does not presume an a priori ascribed leader for whom there might be followers. In this respect, she is an iconoclastic voice in debates linking power and leadership, as, for her, authentic power comes from sharing, not following. She assumes a leader's confidence and independence in their own power, power *within, power shared with others*.

POWER *WITHIN*: EMPOWERING LEADING (NOT LEADERS)

Looking to the future of power and leadership, as the boundaries between leaders and followers continue to blur, the focus on 'the leader' in more traditional theories is becoming increasingly problematic – especially as technology, artificial intelligence and deep learning, simplification and automation advance. Where is 'the leader' in Apple's or Google's algorithms? When skills and responsibilities are distributed and shared throughout an organisation, enabled by technology, an emphasis is placed on the process and practice of leading and not on the attributes or style of a unique person or set of persons – the 'leaders'. Leadership as power *over* or as power given *to* others by empowerment no longer makes sense in this scenario. In short, *dispersed leadership theories* – theories that move leadership away from an individual person (Gordon, 2002, 2010; Konradt, 2014; Rosile et al., 2018) – see leadership as emergent and not a property of individuals. Leading as a relational process suggests that the leader–follower relationship is no longer of central importance to the study of leadership. More important, we argue, is the ability for agents to be critically reflexive about how power *within* a system of relations informs practices and how these practices relate to and impact on oneself and others (Gambrell et al., 2011; Ladkinn & Probert, 2021), which is a different take on power *within* as inner personal strength expressed through self-creation (Cunha et al., 2020).

If we shift from the reification of leadership as a noun, as something invested in a person, to consider leading as a practice that can be distributed among people equally but differentially capable of guiding on specific issues, in specific directions, collectively agreed, then we can begin to appreciate the potency of Follett's democratic thought. Researchers such as Raelin (2012) describe this as *leaderful practice*, something that, in an organisation of excellence and difference, can produce a *creative compartment* (Fairtlough, 1994) in which something akin to an *ideal speech situation* (Habermas, 1971) might flourish in a democratic organisation of science and technology. In Fairtlough's (1994) practice, highly skilled research chemists collaborated freely in exchanging ideas and forging innovation. Fairtlough termed these conditions that of a *creative compartment* in which a close-knit group of up to a few hundred people were working together with enough resources to tackle significant projects yet were able to maintain face-to-face communications. Each compartment within an organisation must have a clear boundary, a well-understood and shared common purpose and common understanding in which members support each other and engage in open communications about personal as well as task issues. It would be a mistake to assume that this design was one of communitarian and egalitarian socialism. Far from it; Fairtlough was a distinguished bio-chemist who had held executive-level positions with Royal Dutch Shell prior to founding an innovative biotechnology company, Celltech, where he was CEO for ten years and it was on the basis of this experience that his ideas were formed.

The political philosopher Carole Pateman (2002) comes close to capturing the essence of the vision that characterised Fairtlough's (1994) work:

> *In a democratized firm all participants are legally responsible for their joint activities, although they may delegate some authority to managers (representatives). [...] The participants in a democratized firm are not employees. They are self-governing (autonomous) members and partners in the firm, with the rights of citizens.*
>
> (p. 48)

Collaborative and democratic teams – employing power *within* and from each participant rather than a single leader – are being recognised as necessary for delivering projects planned to add value through a product, service or event in a specified time in which the project will start and end. Essential to the autonomy of members is their character and ethos fused in the design of a democracy of projects for which collaborative *idea work* (Carlsen et al., 2012; Coldevin et al., 2019) is the context. In organisation studies, it is design prescriptions such as heterarchy and responsible autonomy (Fairtlough, 2005) that define these contexts, to which we wish to add a third element: that of polyarchy (Courpasson and Clegg, 2012). Heterarchy (Ogilvy, 2016) characterises partnerships in professional organisations, such as law firms in which any unit can govern or be governed by others, depending on circumstances. No one group dominates the rest and authority is distributed. Heterarchy's close conceptual stablemate, responsible autonomy, describes an organisational situation in which control resides in professional experts open to critique and regular audit (Fairtlough, 2005, pp. 31–33). Combined, heterarchy and responsible autonomy comprise a form of polyarchy as Dahl (1971, p. 8) defined it: a form of organisation that is *highly inclusive and extensively open*. Members have a *de facto* informal right creatively to contest and make decisions despite being embedded in a host system of hierarchical authority. Temporary in duration, Clegg et al. (2006, p. 338) characterise a polyarchic project as *soft and decentralized with strict and relatively insuperable social and symbolic boundaries*, constituting *strong intermediate bodies often articulated around internal professions and sub elites* – creative compartments. Such structures allow for highly individualised forms of action to generate high levels of internal creative debate.

Nieto-Rodriguez (2021) argues that projects increasingly characterise both short-term performance and long-term value creation of organisations as a global phenomenon whose projected value will be $20 trillion in 2027. Projects are concerned with innovation, transformation, agility and long-term value creation achieved by flat structures, organised as democratically open, entrepreneurial and collaborative. In a project-based organisational world, the old habits of command and control (power *over*) or giving away a little power to enhance normative control (power *to*) will not be adequate or appropriate. To call projects collaborative and democratic processes has a precise meaning. As Frega (2020) argues, it is important to distinguish democracy as an institutional arrangement dependent on processes of voting, decision-making and so on, from democratic processes dependent on the values, attitudes and activities of people. Normatively, these are underlain by three principles that have significant implications for leading in organisations. These principles are relational parity, inclusive authority and social involvement.

A relation is asymmetric whenever external conditions impose on a given category of individuals by, for instance, specialising duties of care on a gendered basis thus bestowing comparatively higher interaction costs; hence relational parity strives to eliminate these (Frega, 2020). Inclusive authority is furthered by practices such as quality circles, lean organisation and other solutions that promote a shared exercise of authority and deliberative competence. Leading becomes a shared and distributed practice. Social involvement entails fusing instrumental and expressive value. The former is efficacious; the latter entails social recognition that one is more than a cog in a machine but a valued member free to speak up and participate fully, one who is socially bonded and included in the expressive life of an organisation guided by principles of tolerance, diversity and constructive conflict resolution when differences surface. Efficaciously, members of project teams need a flexible approach to project management skills as a toolbox from which they might select or discard as they fit project issues, working adeptly with collaborators and contributors in defining scope, managing risk, monitoring progress, marshalling expertise, strategising, managing democratically and ethically. As we shall argue next, digitally enabled organisation goes some way to accommodating these various principles.

Digital instruction, premised on relational parity, inclusive authority and social involvement, is a means of informing and securing consent to a form of leading and serving that is mutually constitutive. Typically, digitalisation in the workplace is seen as an example of 'veillance' (Zorina et al., 2021). Could the veillance that is deployed be used not as a power tool for centralising and hierarchising surveillance but as a tool to instil democracy in organisations? Many people working within universities will be familiar with the digital quizzes that HR often insists we take to be informed about policies. Organisation members must consent to complete these quizzes; consent and completion ensures that the organisation's norms are formally instituted as a shared practice. They are a governmental device formally positioning subjects as responsible to various norms. Explicitly constructed quizzes that strive to expunge illegitimate breaches of civil democracy at work could be devices for translating organisations into normative democracies in which distributed leading on various projects became the norm, as various types of expertise play leading roles at different moments in the evolution of projects. Typically, with such quizzes a substantial internalisation of (or at least high sensitivity towards) the goals and values of those engaged in leading the organisation is assumed (Levay & Waks, 2009; Rhodes, 2007). The focus is on the subject's commitment being realised as a part of team, peer scrutiny and (digital) self-monitoring.

Digital self-monitoring need not only be constructed in an interest in control (Habermas, 1971); it could also be designed with an interest in fostering democratic critique of leadership autocracy embedded in organisation rank and status. These presumptions and practices run counter to the notion of the organisation as composed of various projects, in which democratic principles are valued, in which leadership is eschewed and leading as a process is assumed by different expertise at different stages in the evolution of the project. The democratic principles of organising and leading can be worked out together by employees, with the advice of expert organisational researchers best able to guide on how to frame what is wanted and to assist in devising digital frameworks defining membership, frameworks that can be subject to periodic review and updating.

CONCLUSION

Leadership and power co-evolve. As organisational designs change, leadership roles, practices and expectations change with them. The move from organisational command and control to organisations as projects and employees as project managers requires different forms of power, a move from organisational leadership to leading in projects. We have discussed how leadership is evolving from hierarchical bureaucracies to fluid networks in which what is differential but equal membership is organised along the lines of democratic parity, inclusivity and involvement. Leadership *becoming* a relational process of leading rather than a positional status of *being* a leader is a key means of breaking the conventions of the leadership literature as well as leadership practice.

Scientific research organisations, such as Fairtlough (1994) studied as creative compartments, provide a blueprint. As organisations become increasingly projectified in an adaptive mode, reliant on multi-scalar networks for the coordination of project activities and knowledge (Munck af Rosenschöld, 2019) there is no necessary congruence between status ascription and power. Leading projects can be conceived as process in which different people's expertise will lead different phases of the project. Organisationally, these people will be normatively constituted and constrained by local articulations of the democratic principles discussed. Leading will be permeated by open, fluid and dynamic power networks, with leading being shaped by social relations that are democratically framed and limited. Leading will be pervasively present; leadership will be situationally shared rather than being an exalted status.

One must not, however, be naive enough to believe power *over* was an historic relic that can be transformed by introducing digital means into organisations that transforms relics into harbingers of a future. Digitocracy (Ballesteros, 2020), in which digital black-boxed algorithms replace the files of the bureau, is not democracy. On the contrary: leading through exercising power *over* is an essential feature of several organisations of our digitalised world, often concealed by appealing narratives suggesting otherwise. As Prassl (2018, p. 52) has stated: *Today, Taylorism is back in full swing, resurrected under the guise of the on-demand economy, with technology and algorithms providing a degree of control and oversight of which even Frederick himself could not have dreamed.* It is not the technology that makes democracy a possibility but a design imperative, as well as an ethos and character that is formally inscribed, which digital means can distil individually and entrain collectively. Any such organisation will necessarily not be egalitarian in rank so much as in ethos and character, such that leading, rather than leadership, becomes the dominant practice of polyarchic creative compartments.

REFERENCES

Adler, P. S., & Borys, B. (1996). Two types of bureaucracy: Enabling and coercive. *Administrative Science Quarterly*, *41*(1), 61–89.

Ballesteros, A. (2020). Digitocracy: Ruling and being ruled. *Philosophies*, *5*(2), 9. https://doi.org/10.3390/philosophies5020009

Barker, J. R. (1993). Tightening the iron cage: Concertive control in self-managing teams. *Administrative Science Quarterly*, *38*(3), 408–437.

Boje, D. M., & Rosile, G. A. (2001) Where's the power in empowerment? Answers from Follett and Clegg. *Journal of Applied Behavioral Science*, *37*(1), 90–117.

Butler, A. (2017). Deliveroo accused of 'creating vocabulary' to avoid calling couriers employees. *Guardian*, 5 April. https://www.theguardian.com/business/2017/apr/05/deliveroo-couriers-employees-managers

Carlsen, A., Clegg, S. R., & Gjersvik, R. (2012). *Idea Work*. Cappellen Damm.

Carlsen, A., Clegg, S. R., Pitsis, T. S., & Mortensen, T. F. (2020). From ideas of power to the powering of ideas in organizations: Reflections from Follett and Foucault. *European Management Journal*, *38*(6), 829–835.

Chiniara, M., & Bentein, K. (2016). Linking servant leadership to individual performance: Differentiating the mediating role of autonomy, competence and relatedness need satisfaction. *Leadership Quarterly*, *27*(1), 124–141.

Clegg, S. R. (1989). *Frameworks of Power*. Sage.

Clegg, S. R., Courpasson, D., & Phillips, N. (2006). *Power and Organizations*. Sage.

Clegg, S., Cunha, M.P. Munro, I., Rego, A., & Sousa, M. O. (2016). Kafkaesque power and bureaucracy. *Journal of Political Power*, *9*(2), 157–181.

Clegg, S. R., & Haugaard, M. (Eds.). (2009). *The SAGE Handbook of Power*. Sage.

Clegg, S. R., Pitsis, T. S., & Mount, M. (2021). *Managing and Organizations: An Introduction to Theory and Practice*. Sage.

Coldevin, G., Carlsen, A., Clegg, S., Pitsis, T. S., & Antonacopoulou, E. P. (2019). Organizational creativity as idea work: Intertextual placing and legitimating imaginings in media development and oil exploration. *Human Relations*, *72*(8), 1369–1397.

Courpasson, D., & Clegg, S. (2012) The polyarchic bureaucracy: Cooperative resistance in the workplace and the construction of a new political structure of organizations. *Research in the Sociology of Organizations*, *34*, 55–79.

Cunha, M. P., Clegg, S., Rego, A., & Berti, M. (2021). *Paradoxes of Power and Leadership*. Routledge.

Cunha, M. P., Rego, A., Simpson, A. V., & Clegg, S. (2020). *Positive Organizational Behaviour: A Reflective Approach*. Routledge.

Dahl, R. (1971). *Polyarchy: Participation and Opposition*. Yale University Press.

Donia, M. B., Raja, U., Panaccio, A., & Wang, Z. (2016). Servant leadership and employee outcomes: The moderating role of subordinates' motives. *European Journal of Work and Organizational Psychology*, *25*(5), 722–734.

Eylon, D. (1998). Understanding empowerment and resolving its paradox: Lessons from Mary Parker Follett. *Journal of Management History*, *4*(1), 16–28.

Fairtlough, G. (1994). *Creative Compartments: A Design for Future Organizations*. Adamantine Press.

Fairtlough, G. H. (2005). *The Three Ways of Getting Things Done: Hierarchy, Heterarchy and Responsible Autonomy in Organizations*. Triarchy Press.

Follett, M. P. (1924). *Creative Experience*. Longmans, Green, and Co.

Follett, M. P. (1941/2003) *Dynamic Administration: The Collected Papers of Mary Parker Follett: Early Sociology of Management and Organizations*. Routledge.

Follett, M. P. (1995). *Mary Parker Follett: Prophet of Management*. Harvard Business School.

Frega, R. (2020). Democratic patterns of interaction as a norm for the workplace. *Journal of Social Philosophy*, 5(1), 27–53.

Gambrell, K. M., Matkin, G. S., & Burbach, M. E. (2011). Cultivating leadership: The need for renovating models to higher epistemic cognition. *Journal of Leadership & Organizational Studies*, 18(3), 308–319.

Garvey, M. (1938). The work that has to be done. *Black Man Magazine*, 3(10), 7–11.

Gordon, R. D. (2002). Conceptualizing leadership with respect to its historical–contextual antecedents to power. *Leadership Quarterly*, 13(2), 151–167.

Gordon, R. D. (2010). Dispersed leadership: Exploring the impact of antecedent forms of power using a communicative framework. *Management Communication Quarterly*, 24(2), 260–287.

Graham, D. A. (2015). A short history of Rupert Murdoch's heirs apparent. *The Atlantic*. https://www.theatlantic.com/business/archive/2015/06/history-of-rupert-murdoch-successor-intrigue/395678/

Graham, J. W. (1991). Servant-leader in organizations: Inspirational and moral. *Leadership Quarterly*, 2, 105–119.

Greenleaf, R. (1970). *The Servant as Leader*. Robert K. Greenleaf Center.

Gruber, J., & Trickett, E. J. (1987). Can we empower others? The paradox of empowerment in the governing of an alternative public school. *American Journal of Community Psychology*, 15(3), 353–371.

Habermas, J. (1971). *Knowledge and Human Interests*. Heinemann.

Hale, J. R., & Fields, D. L. (2007). Exploring servant leadership across cultures: A study of followers in Ghana and the USA. *Leadership*, 3(4), 397–417.

Hamel, G., & Zanini, M. (2020). *Humanocracy*. Harvard Business Review.

Hu, J., & Liden, R. C. (2011). Antecedents of team potency and team effectiveness: An examination of goal and process clarity and servant leadership. *Journal of Applied Psychology*, 96(4), 851–862.

Haugaard, M. (2003). Reflections on seven ways of creating power. *European Journal of Social Theory*, 6(1), 87–113.

Howcroft, D., & Wilson, M. (2003). Participation: 'Bounded freedom' or hidden constraints on user involvement. *New Technology, Work and Employment*, 18(1), 2–19.

Hutson, M. (2017). When power doesn't corrupt. *New York Times*, 21 May, BU11.

Konradt, U. (2014). Toward a theory of dispersed leadership in teams: Model, findings, and directions for future research. *Leadership*, 10(3), 289–307.

Ladkin, D., & Probert, J. (2021). From sovereign to subject: Applying Foucault's conceptualization of power to leading and studying power within leadership. *Leadership Quarterly*, 32(4), 101310.

Lee, A., Lyubovnikova, J., Tian, A. W., & Knight, C. (2020). Servant leadership: A meta-analytic examination of incremental contribution, moderation, and mediation. *Journal of Occupational and Organizational Psychology*, 93(1), 1–44.

Levay, C., & Waks, C. (2009). Professions and the pursuit of transparency in healthcare: Two cases of soft autonomy. *Organization Studies*, 30(5), 509–527.

Lewis, R. L., Brown, D. A., & Sutton, N. C. (2019). Control and empowerment as an organising paradox: Implications for management control systems. *Accounting, Auditing & Accountability Journal*, 32(2), 483–507.

Liden, R. C., Panaccio, A., Meuser, J. D., Hu, J., & Wayne, S. (2014a). Servant leadership: Antecedents, processes, and outcomes. In D. V. Vay (Ed.), *The Oxford Handbook of Leadership and Organizations* (pp. 357–379). Oxford University Press.

Liden, R. C., Wayne, S. J., Liao, C., & Meuser, J. D. (2014b). Servant leadership and serving culture: Influence on individual and unit performance. *Academy of Management Journal*, 57, 1434–1452.

Logue, D. M., Jarvis, W. P., Clegg, S., & Hermens, A. (2015). Translating models of organization: Can the Mittelstand move from Bavaria to Geelong? *Journal of Management & Organization*, 21(1), 17–36.

Malhotra, A. (2021). The postpandemic future of work. *Journal of Management*, 47(5), 1091–1102.

Marley, B. (1979). Redemption Song, *Uprising* (Bob Marley and the Wailers LP). Island Records.

Melé, D., & Rosanas, J. M. (2003). Power, freedom and authority in management: Mary Parker Follett's 'power-with'. *Philosophy of Management*, 3(2), 35–46.

Merton, R. K. (1936). The unanticipated consequences of purposive social action. *American Sociological Review*, 1(6), 894–904.

Munck af Rosenschöld, J. (2019). Inducing institutional change through projects? Three models of projectified governance. *Journal of Environmental Policy & Planning*, 21(4), 333–344.

Murrell, K. L. (1985). The development of a theory of empowerment: Rethinking power for 91 organization development. *Organizational Development Journal*, 34, 34–38.

Neubert, M. J., Kacmar, K. M., Carlson, D. S., Chonko, L. B., & Roberts, J. A. (2008). Regulatory focus as a mediator of the influence of initiating structure and servant leadership on employee behavior. *Journal of Applied Psychology*, *93*(6), 1220–1233.

Nieto-Rodriguez, A. (2021). The project economy has arrived. *Harvard Business Review*, *99*(6), 38–45.

Ogilvy, J. (2016). *Heterarchy: An idea finally ripe for its time*. http://www.forbes.com/sites/stratfor/2016/02/04/heterarchy-an-idea-finally-ripe-for-its-time/

Parsons, T. (1963). On the concept of political power. *Proceedings of the American Philosophical Society*, *107*(3), 232–262.

Pateman, C. (2002). Self-ownership and property in the person: Democratization and a tale of two concepts. *Journal of Political Philosophy*, *10*(1), 20–53.

Peterson, S., Galvin, B. M., & Lange, D. (2012). CEO servant leadership: Exploring executive characteristics and firm performance. *Personnel Psychology*, *65*, 565–596.

Pierro, A., Raven, B. H., Amato, C., & Bélanger, J. J. (2013). Bases of social power, leadership styles, and organizational commitment. *International Journal of Psychology*, *48*(6), 1122–1134.

Prassl, J. (2018). *Humans as a Service: The Promise and Perils of Work in the Gig Economy*. Oxford University Press.

Raelin, J. A. (2012). Dialogue and deliberation as expressions of democratic leadership in participatory organizational change. *Journal of Organizational Change Management*, *25*(1), 7–23.

Raven, B. H. (1993). The bases of power: Origins and recent developments. *Journal of Social Issues*, *49*(4), 227–251.

Reed, M. (2012). Researching organizational elites: A critical realist perspective. In D. Courpasson, D. Golsorkhi & J. J. Sallaz (Eds.), *Rethinking Power in Organizations, Institutions, and Markets* (*Research in the Sociology of Organizations*, Vol. 34, pp. 21–53). Emerald.

Rhodes, R. A. (2007). Understanding governance: Ten years on. *Organization Studies*, *28*(8), 1243–1264.

Ritzer, G. (1998). *The McDonaldization Thesis*. Sage.

Rosile, G. A., M Boje, D., & Claw, C. M. (2018). Ensemble leadership theory: Collectivist, relational, and heterarchical roots from indigenous contexts. *Leadership*, *14*(3), 307–328.

Simon, B. L. (1990). Rethinking empowerment. *Journal of Progressive Human Services*, *1*(1), 27–39.

Simons, R. (1995). *Levers of Control*. Harvard Business School.

Spears, L. C. (2002). Introduction: Tracing the past, present, and future of servant-leadership. In L. C. Spears & M. Lawrence (Eds.), *Focus on Leadership: Servant-Leadership for the Twenty-First Century* (pp. 1–16). John Wiley & Sons.

Sousa, M., & Van Dierendonck, D. (2017). Servant leadership and the effect of the interaction between humility, action, and hierarchical power on follower engagement. *Journal of Business Ethics*, *141*(1), 13–25.

Thomas, K. W., & Velthouse, B. A. (1990). Cognitive elements of empowerment: An 'interpretive' model of intrinsic task motivation. *Academy of Management Review*, *15*(4), 666–681.

Tyler, T. R., & Blader, S. L. (2005). Can businesses effectively regulate employee conduct? The antecedents of rule following in work settings. *Academy of Management Journal*, *48*(6), 1143–1158.

Uhl-Bien, M., Riggio, R. E., Lowe, K. B., & Carsten, M. K. (2014). Followership theory: A review and research agenda. *Leadership Quarterly*, *25*(1), 83–104.

Van Dierendonck, D. (2011). Servant leadership: A review and synthesis. *Journal of Management*, *37*(4), 1228–1261.

Weber, M. (1922/1978). *Economy and Society: An Outline of Interpretive Sociology*. University of California Press.

Zald, M. N., & Lounsbury, M. (2010). The wizards of Oz: Towards an institutional approach to elites, expertise and command posts. *Organization Studies*, *31*(7), 963–996.

Zhang, Y., Zheng, Y., Zhang, L., Xu, S., Liu, X., & Chen, W. (2021). A meta-analytic review of the consequences of servant leadership: The moderating roles of cultural factors. *Asia Pacific Journal of Management*, *38*(1), 371–400.

Zorina, A., Belanger, F., Kumar, N., & Clegg, S. R. (2021). The web of veillance: Enacting visibility in the digital age. *Organization Science*, Articles in Advance, pp. 1–26

Zuboff, S. (2019). *The Age of Surveillance Capitalism: The Fight for a Human Future at the New Frontier of Power*. Public Affairs.

33

In Defence of Hesitant Leadership: An Ancient Chinese Perspective

Ralph Bathurst and Michelle Sitong Chen

WHAT'S ON THE TABLE?

In this chapter we offer an alternative to the leader construct of a person atop an organisation with superior knowledge and skills capable of directing their enterprise. Our discussion draws on the ancient Chinese text the *Tao Te Ching* attributed to Lao Tzu, a 4th-century BCE sage, who was perhaps a contemporary of another well-known scholar, Confucius. The set of teachings contained in the text remain interesting today because of their difference to contemporary ideas generated by Western leadership scholars and practitioners.

The *Tao Te Ching* has spawned numerous spin-off texts including those of a spiritual orientation, such as Wu's (2021) *Vital Breath of the Dao*; economics in Spitznagel's (2013) *Dao of Capital*; science in Kohn's (2016) *Science and the Dao*; sport in Nandy's (2001) *Tao of Cricket*; and Heider's (2005) *Tao of Leadership*. Although not an extensive list, these few cited texts demonstrate attempts to capture ancient ideals and practices, making them relevant to this age as we seek to overcome the more deleterious effects of life as we have come to live it in the 21st century.

Our chapter offers a view of leadership based on a core skill of *hesitancy*. We are cognisant that on first blush, this competency is counter-intuitive.

The extant literature tends to privilege leaders that are strong and directive, willing to stand and fight, against the odds if called on, to achieve greatness for themselves and their followers. We argue, however, that this prevailing ideology is ending badly for humanity. Two global conflagrations in the 20th century and the climate emergency that we are now struggling to address are achievements of commanding leaders and their followers driven more by hubris and less by humility. Whether or not Albert Einstein claimed that doing the same thing repeatedly while expecting a different result is madness, we humans appear unwilling to operationalise other forms of leadership that eschew the dominating figure at the sharp end of the hierarchy.

Hesitancy, we argue, is foundational to alternative constructs and can be found in the contemporary literature in the notions of *negative capability* and *paradox*. These two ideas are attempts at redefining leadership beyond the great man, single leader syndrome.

First, negative capability emerged in the letters of John Keats to his brothers in 1817 and relates to his poetic insights, particularly in embracing doubt and uncertainty. Simpson et al. (2002) note in their application of the construct to leadership that 'negative' conveys an inaccurate idea, for, as they argue, negative capability is a positive quality because it allows leaders to *not* know, thereby opening space for alternative solutions. On the basis of this uncertainty, leaders can be present to each moment as it occurs (Simpson & French, 2006) thereby avoiding the trap of relying on prior knowledge and assumptions. Despite its appeal, these scholars limit their scope to psychoanalysis and find application within the arts sector, both of which are worthy pursuits though neither appear to be embraced wholeheartedly by the broader leadership community.

These reservations notwithstanding, negative capability has a growing corpus of publications, notable among them Broeng (2018) who explores *provisional indecision* (p. 432) as a necessary leadership skill, Hay and Blenkinsopp (2019) who promote the concept in the human resources domain and Saggurthi and Thakur (2016) who amplify Simpson and colleagues' (2002) exhortation for slowing the pace of decision-making in managing risk.

Second, embracing paradox enables leaders to hold *"contradictory yet interrelated elements that exist simultaneously and persist over time"* (Smith & Lewis, 2011, p. 382). The literature describes three core tenets of paradox, namely *holism*, *dynamism* and *duality* (Li, 2016; Schad et al., 2016). Holism shows that systems operate with multiple variables and that if one element is moved, the entire system is impacted. Dynamism draws on the ancient Chinese *yin* and *yang* model where there is an interplay of elements, with opposite energies transforming each other in a balancing process (Fang, 2011). Further, Li et al. (2012) claim that duality posits the interdependence and interpenetration between opposite elements as related to the holistic tenet as well as the interaction and inter-transformation between opposing variables as related to the dynamic tenet.

Both negative capability and paradox play into our explorations of hesitancy in several ways. They overcome the need for a single all-knowing leader driving the action. Leaders who don't know are capable of working with the dynamism that paradox invites. We acknowledge that these are but small steps towards recasting forms of leadership that may achieve sustainable life for humans on Planet Earth. Yet infant stumbling is a necessary precursor to this revisionary agenda, as other chapters in this volume attest, such as Chapter 16, Leadership beyond the leader to relational quality, Chapter 19, Self-regulatory focus and leadership, Chapter 31, Culture and symbolism, Chapter 31, Post-colonial perspectives, and, Not becoming a leader.

In this chapter, our foray into hesitancy and leadership through the *Tao Te Ching* is motivated by a fascination with ancient Chinese philosophies. However, we also acknowledge the disconnection between the China of yesterday and ambivalence towards China today. Although some prognosticators declare the 21st century to be 'Chinese', Scott (2008) explores uncertainties towards this notion by questioning motives behind China's expansionary agenda. Reservations notwithstanding, Kirby (2014) notes that higher education follows changing political orientations away from former world powers such as France, the UK and the USA towards China. This means, according to Fogel et al. (2019), that Chinese ideas, both ancient and modern, will impact on Western ways of organising.

The Chinese dragon and its impact on the West has a long tail that reaches back to the post-Mao Zedong era. The opening of China to international trade in 1978 under Deng Xiaoping's tutelage has seen that country outstrip its Western counterparts in economic growth and development. Business leaders have looked on with envy at China's ability to corral its internal resources of people and product to compete as an equal player on the global stage. The institution of the Belt and Road Initiative (*Yí Dài Yí Lù*) in 2013 with its inseparable links to the Communist Party of China and Xi Jinping's presidency has confirmed China as a determined and significant global actor.

This growing influence on the world stage of politics and business has inspired curiosity as to how China has achieved this in such a short period of time. Leadership scholars have also turned with growing fascination towards ancient Chinese philosophies, exploring their potential impact on leadership practice (Bathurst & Chen, 2018; Lin et al., 2018; Pheng & Lee, 1997; Wang & Chee, 2011), particularly Lao Tzu's classic text *Tao Te Ching*. These enquiries are driven by a desire to understand if there are historical reasons that could account for China's position today. Accompanying the quest to tread these ancient paths is a disquiet about the role of China in this age (Wang, 2016), and that its expansionary agenda mirrors European colonising of past eras with all its accompanying abuses.

On the international stage, resistance to China's expanding interests have played out in the trade war initiated by the United States of America (USA) in 2018. Although then President Donald Trump's intention was protectionist, paradoxically it resulted in job losses and slowing investment capital (Lobosco, 2019) into the USA. Animosity towards China and its leaders spread across the Pacific (Walker, 2020) to the point where attempts at open dialogue have been thwarted. Notwithstanding outward expressions of hostility, global trade is dependent on Chinese investment – former USA President Donald Trump being a prime example of these contradictory logics at work (Caputo et al., 2020). Perhaps then, it is the role of leadership scholars to cut pathways through these thickets of claims and counter-claims, and to find ways of ending this intransigence.

LIFE IN THE SOUP

In the hope that dialogue between Eastern and Western ideas is possible, at least at a conceptual level, in this chapter we explore how leaders can learn from China's founding ancient philosophies. Alternatively, perhaps these ideas from the past are merely objects of fascination which have since lost their potency and are no longer apt to guide our contemporary leadership theorising.

In this chapter we discuss these propositions by exploring the statement from the *Tao Te Ching* about leadership. Before proceeding any further, we quote the passage in full:

> 39 The best of all rulers is but a shadowy presence to his subjects.
> Next comes the ruler they love and praise;
> Next comes one they fear;
> Next comes one with whom they take liberties.
>
> 40 When there is not enough faith, there is lack of good faith.
>
> 41 Hesitant, he does not utter words lightly.
> When his task is accomplished and his work done
> The people all say, 'It happened to us naturally.'
> (Lao Tzu, 4thC BCE/1988, Book I Chapter XVII: 39–41)

After analysing key words, in particular the word 'ruler', and phrases from this text from various sources, we show how the ideas within them might be salient through a discussion of propensity following François Jullien's insights. We conclude the chapter by suggesting that the leadership notions derived from the *Tao Te Ching* may no longer be available to us in these times, whether we are Chinese or not. Cultural values, mores and assumptions that underpin the *Tao Te Ching* appear to be out of sync with how we do things in this age, especially when it comes to leading.

We illustrate our conclusions with two speeches by contemporary leaders: Florida State Governor Ron DeSantis and Chinese President Xi Jinping. We choose these two as representatives of the problems we face when reconceptualising leadership by incorporating ancient philosophies. The two men appear in news broadcasts regularly and as representatives of the West–East political divide, they are similar in that they are both titular leaders who make public pronouncements that declare a strong, immovable position. DeSantis has also made known his intention to run as a candidate for the role of Commander-in-Chief of the USA in 2024, while Xi holds the top job in the world's most populated country. We show that their concepts of leadership are derived from the lingering impact of Carlyle's (1841) great man theory and his puffery of Napoleon as exemplary.

Before embarking on an analysis of these few influential verses from Chapter XVII, we first need to clarify authorship. Although attributed to a person, Lao Tzu is himself a shadowy figure who may have lived contemporaneously with Confucius in 6th century BCE or later in the Warring States period of 4th century BCE China. According to Barbalet (2014) the text, also named the *Daodejing* in pinyin, *"is a collection of sayings developed in and applied by a group, community, or college of moral-political thinkers and practitioners"* (p. 14). The ideas originated with a political and practical orientation but have since been appropriated and used by Taoist religious communities, who, in their observances, have deified the nominal author. Despite attempts to identify his history, an alternative reading is that Laozi simply means the 'old master'.

Our interest is not religious but, rather, to return to the original intent of the text as a guide for social action on the business and political stage. Therefore, a discussion of translation from ancient Chinese into English is not our concern, and we take as given the several English versions we have to hand: D. C. Lau's translation cited above, and Ames and Hall's (2003) philosophical work. We also refer to other interpretations of the text, namely Kaltenmar's (1969) book which was translated from French, and Callahan's (1989) dissenting interpretations.

Several further background issues are worth noting. Ames and Hall (2003) write in the introduction to their translation of the *Daodejing* the two crucial words in the title: *de* (德) and *dao* (道). They state that *de* embraces a sense of *"the ceaseless and usually cadenced flow of experience"* (p. 14), and *dao* "the discernible rhythm and regularly of the world as it folds around and through us" (p. 23), often reduced to the single notion of the *Way*.

The basic assumption of the text is that humans are participants and actors in the world, within a specific context, which is in a constant state of change that cannot be manipulated or forced. The essence is the *dao* and this governs behavior. Again, as Ames and Hall (2003) note, the *dao* "is non impositional" (p. 23).

In sum, the two words, *dao* and *de*, indicate that as we walk life's path, we cultivate our place in the world, a process more akin to the way water moves. Thus, Lao Tzu wrote:

> Nothing in the world
> is as soft and yielding as water.
> Yet for dissolving the hard and inflexible,
> nothing can surpass it.
> [...]
> True words seem paradoxical.
> (Lao Tzu, 4thC BCE/1988, Book II Chapter LXXVIII)

Paradox indeed, or, as Ames and Hall (2003) note, the ancient Chinese cosmological sense is bound by lived experience.

> There is no view from nowhere, no external perspective, no decontextualized vantage point. We are all in the soup. The intrinsic, constitutive relations that obtain among things make them reflexive and mutually implicating, residing together within the flux and flow.
> (p. 18)

The *soup* (tāng 汤) that was their daily experience in ancient times, is ours today; it is an indeterminate and complex consommé, replete with flavour, not easily bound by the formalities of title and position.

However, before accepting that we can discuss 'them' and 'us' as though historical ideas are consonant with ours, we need to address the problem of historical distance. Issues of fact and evidence-based truth-claims can be tamed by adopting a post-foundational stance. In this way, says Bevir (2011), the gap between the us and past is overcome by acknowledging that we are part of a *"web of beliefs"* (p. 34) where traces of the ancient are found in our present.

To return, then, to our analogy, knowing that we live in this undefinable and often unclear soupy world akin to the world of the ancients, is of little comfort to leaders seeking recipes to inspire action among staff members and followers. However, guidance is at hand in two essential base ingredients that animate life in the soup: namely, the daoist elements of *ziran* and *wuwei*.

ESSENTIAL INGREDIENTS

The complex and seemingly contradictory *dao*, or way, embraces two constructs of *ziran* (自然) and *wuwei* (無為) as its base: *ziran* ("ruler" in D. C. Lau's translation) describing the identity of people, and *wuwei* ("naturally" D. C. Lau's translation) in articulating the kinds of actions that people take.

Ziran is a compound word combining *zi* and *ran*. *Zi* can be used to describe the self and literally means 'nose,' and as Callahan (1989) notes: "It refers to one's point of view" (p. 173). *Ran*, Callahan claims, involves being able to make distinctions between 'this' and 'that' thing, and to declare something is 'like this.' He writes, "For if there is `like this,' then there must also be `like that.' Hence ran represents the ability to distinguish and assign names and to act from them" (p. 174). Taken together *ziran* indicates the abilities to see and discern, a state Callahan translates as "perspectival action-discrimination" (p. 176). This definition will be crucial when we return to the focal passage later in our discussion.

Wuwei has been described as *non-action*, but Slingerland (2003) claims that it is better understood as a state of *effortless action* and:

> represents the most general of a whole set of families of conceptual metaphors that convey a sense of effortlessness and unself-consciousness. These metaphor families include those of 'following,' or 'flowing along with,' being physically 'at ease,' enjoying a perfect 'fit' with the world, and 'forgetting' the self – the last quality also often being expressed literally as unself-consciousness or forgetfulness that comes from strong emotions such as joy.
> (p. 11)

From a Western individualistic perspective, *ziran* and *wuwei* can play together. The individual as leader has a particular perspective on the world (*ziran*) and responds by making some moves with *wuwei* in the softness of water, to address the focal issue. Such a position harmonises well with servant (Greenleaf, 1991) and transformational (Bass, 1990) leadership styles, for their espoused democratic values and leader-centric orientation.

A complicating factor is defining what is meant by a 'person' or 'individual'. Callahan (1989) explains that when referring to themselves, Chinese people point to their nose, rather than gesture to their chest or heart region as would Westerners. Further, in ancient China, a criminal may have had their nose amputated as punishment, signalling their disqualification from the community and their now less-than-human status. But what is intended by this nose-pointing gesture?

A self as a singular individual with intentions and passions, free to express and authentically represent their identity is, according to Bloom (1992) a peculiarly *American* invention. The self's fragility, Bloom argues, restricts a communitarian perspective, making people *"worse citizens"* (p. 21) despite claims to national pride and patriotism. This isolated self whose moral and ethical compass is the self-same self, has found its home throughout the Western world, spurred on by the neoliberal turn (Harvey, 2005) and its attendant narcissistic tendencies.

For the ancient Chinese, the self is a more complex, socially situated being. In their philosophical translation of the Confucian *Analects* Ames and Rosemont (1998) note that the word *ren* (仁), used today to describe benevolence and kindness, in Confucius's time was the preferred character for 'person'. The ideogram, they note, is a compound of two elements, person (人) and the number 2, *èr* (二). They write in conclusion, drawing on philosopher Fingarette's (1972) perspectives, that:

> This etymological analysis [of ren] underscores the Confucian assumption that one cannot become a person by oneself – we are, from our inchoate beginnings, irreducibly social. Herbert Fingarette has stated the matter concisely: 'For Confucius, unless there are at least two human beings, there can be no human beings.'
> (Ames & Rosemont, 1998, p. 48)

Callahan (1989) concurs, saying that *"images of ego as residence for autonomous individuality"* (p. 174) are not consonant with ancient Chinese worldviews. He explains further, writing:

> In classical Chinese all things are 'parts,' and all things are composed of parts which extend in an unbounded way large and small, qualitatively and quantitatively. For example, the term *ren*, which stands for human, refers to all things that are human, ranging from the human population of the Earth, to the human society of China, to an individual human being, to a human toenail, to a molecule within that toenail.
> (p. 174)

The nose-pointing gesture, therefore, results in a thickened meaning of 'self' and 'person' which implicates others beyond a solitary individual, but a more elusive sense of 'leader' and 'leadership'. For, whether it is action, non-action, or effortless action, the problem remains: how can we identify the person or people taking the action/non-action? Or, to remain with the metaphor, who stirs the pot to infuse flavour from the ingredients?

WHO STIRS THE POT?

Often the leadership agenda is to locate the person with whom the buck stops and equip them with the skills necessary to ensure the success of the given enterprise. Therefore, returning to the focal text from the *Tao Te Ching* (Book I Chapter XVII: 39 -41) D. C. Lau's translation begins "The best of all rulers is but a shadowy presence to his subjects." Kaltenmark (1969) in an English version taken from his translation into French, writes "The best [of all rulers] is he whose existence is unknown" also translated synonymously as "the Holy Man" (p. 54). Ames and Hall (2003) adopt a similar translation: "With the most excellent rulers, their subjects only know that they are there" (p. 103). In both, a clearly identifiable person, "ruler," is an absent presence, but with hands firmly grasping the ladle.

The *shadowy presence* of the ruler and/or sage, however, obscures more than it reveals, and opens questions about the nature of reality. Who is this person, this ghostly tenebrous chieftain who influences people and events but can never be known? At first blush, it appears that he or she manipulates events with a pretence of engaging the people in the work.

An example perhaps familiar to contemporary Chinese people is the unlikely rise of Empress Dowager Cixi who ruled during the final years of the Qing dynasty (from around 1861 to 1908). Over time and with an astute understanding of palace routines, Cixi entered the inner circle of Chinese politics as a concubine to Emperor Wenzong of Qing. When the emperor died, Cixi assumed control of the Qing dynasty, exercising considerable power, while being unseen. Chang (2014) writes that Cixi would discuss affairs of state from behind a curtain, meaning that ministers and dignitaries would never see her face.

However, Cixi's despotic powers and appropriation of public funds for her self-aggrandisement were far from the ego-less ruler of the *Tao Te Ching*. We can conclude, then, that D. C. Lau's shadowy figure is either an idealised image of a preferred leader-type or is a metaphysical invocation of a leader presence that can and does threaten punishment if their will is not fulfilled. Such regimes which turn tyrannical through the use of torture and the acquisition of public resources for private use are in direct contravention of the ideals laid out in the *Tao Te Ching*.

How is it then, that leaders down the centuries, and across the globe, have assumed positions of such authority and power, and then used their status to turn on their own citizenry inhumanely? Certainly, political analysis is beyond our mandate here, but it is worth noting that totalitarianism is no respecter of national or business cultures, Chinese included. For, as Cherniss (2006) notes in his commentary on Isaiah Berlin's insights, "managerialism, whether progressive or corporate" is as abusive a doctrine as Fascism, Communism and Nazism (p. xxiv). One explanation for an orientation where leaders assume sovereign power over followers while championing ancient works like the *Tao Te Ching* is one of textual translation.

Liu (2008) argues that our approaches to ancient texts like the *Tao Te Ching* are informed by our hermeneutic horizons. For example, contemporary beliefs in the importance of titular leaders may determine how words like *dao* and *ziran* are translated.

Fox (2017) is alert to this problem in his discussion of the main differences between ancient Chinese and English and even Modern Chinese. He notes that,

> in the ancient [Chinese] language there are no definite or indefinite articles ('the' or 'a'), plurals, gender, person, case, tense, or parts of speech, since words can serve as nouns or verbs. What this means is that so much of the meaning of the text will be completely dependent on context – that is, on the words and topics immediately surrounding any given word or phrase.
>
> (p. 31)

The implications of this are widespread because if a word cannot name a thing as a noun exclusively, then that word may also function as a verb. The argument here is between abstractions and living processes. Fox (2017) notes that "monolithic" (p. 31) and "ineffable" (p. 33) interpretations of *dao* rely on defining the construct as an actual thing that is eternal and precedes creation. If, however, *dao* is a process evident moment-by-moment, then our orientation towards time changes from "a diachronic [to a] synchronic cosmology" (p. 33). Furthermore, Fox claims that by reorienting our horizon around concepts of time and place, apparent paradoxes and non sequiturs within the *Tao Te Ching* are more readily resolved.

Liu (2008) notes that *ziran* can be translated as "humanistic naturalness" (p. 69), a state accessible to all citizens. Indeed, he argues that social order based on humanistic naturalness, is an ethical position "superior to social order based on coercion" and that "*humanistic naturalness* takes precedence over other principles, such as justice, correctness, and sanctity" (p. 84, emphases in the original). Where justice is the highest and guiding principle, says Liu, "all sorts of extraordinary, and even cruel, measures will be considered appropriate or legitimate" (p. 84). Therefore, the *Tao Te Ching* advocates for a social project far beyond minimal ethical and moral standards to which even today's national and organizational leaders adhere.

However, there is a possible resolution to this problem of identifying the presence of leadership. A way forward is to revisit the idea of *ziran*, a word that we have noted refers to individual identity. Lai (2007) translates *ziran* as *self-so-ness*, which highlights the spontaneous lifeworld in which humans live. This self does not float freely but is located within her or his locale. She writes that:

> We must also note that the 'unconditioned' self in Daoist philosophy is not one that is entirely free from all encumbrances and conditions. It is a self, as it exists, within the parameters of its existence. This interpretation captures a nascent dual polarity in the notion of self both situated within its environing conditions and free – spontaneous – within those boundaries.
>
> (p. 330)

Therefore, rather than being an absent, unreachable figure, Lai's interpretation of *ziran* invokes a political orientation that sees people actively participating in their world, sensitised to the natural energies of the environment. The self-so-ness of *ziran*, then, is the individual acting freely in their world. Li (2020) concurs, writing that, "Typically, the Daoist adopts a *laissez-faire* way on government, which is based on its fundamental principle of acting in accordance with the law of `self-so-ness'" (p. 764), a posture available to all.

Callahan (1989) strengthens these perspectives on *ziran* by reinterpreting the context as 'organic' rather than 'natural'. He understands the organic orientation to move us beyond a quietist disengagement to a much more *"an active critique of the society"* (p. 186), with its implied political focus. He argues that,

> there can be order without an orderer, a ruler. Each part has its own unique basis of judgment and action, yet this does not lead to chaos. It leads to a form of anarchism in which there is human–human and human–nature interrelation, not atomization and separation: all the parts coexist and cooperate within the gradations of composite wholes. This is not politics in the colloquial sense of elections and laws, but politics in the more basic sense of harmonious interrelation and interdependence of parts in human society as well as in the larger compound of nature.
>
> (p. 186)

It is worth lingering over Callahan's (1989) views, for, if *ziran* refers to self-so-ness, of being-in-the-world, then using the word 'ruler' in our focal passage creates a misinterpretation of the *Tao Te Ching*'s intent. Callahan notes that if *ziran* is translated as "perspectival action-discrimination" then the passage remains deliciously ambiguous, and the need to identify a ruler to stir the pot and ensure a flavoursome dish is obviated. Therefore, the people as a collective have sagacity, and can make decisions unfettered and unconstrained by a nominal ruler. Thus, Callahan offers an alternative translation:

> 39 The highest – is to not know you have it;
> Next one – love and praise it;
> Next one – fear it;
> Next one – ridicule it;
> When trust is insufficient in it,
>
> 40 There will be [those] who do not trust in it.
>
> 41 Relaxed, they treasure their words.
> Accomplishments completed, affairs ordered,
> The common people all say: 'We have perspectival action-discrimination.'
>
> (Callahan, 1989, p. 178)

Taking this approach encourages a re-description that shifts focus away from a wise ruler to the leadership of everyone. Or, to put this in contemporary parlance, towards what Raelin (2003) calls a *leaderful* organisation. Achieving this state of collective intelligence, however, requires a counter-intuitive disinterestedness where those with perspectival action-discrimination, or humanistic naturalness, do not know they have it. Rather, and in agreement with Simpson and colleagues' (Simpson, 2006; Simpson et al., 2002) discussions of negative capability, they act organically together in accordance with the needs of the moment, and within ethical constraints.

What, though, accounts for the gradual perspectival tightening of the first stanza, where disinterest turns progressively towards love, fear, ridicule and distrust? Or, put differently, what is required for the elements to retain their integrity and not turn into an indistinguishable mush of elements, which then calls for a leader to sort out the mess? The French sinologist François Jullien explores this conundrum through his examination of the propensity for movement within systems, as understood by the ancient Chinese.

POTENTIAL IN RECIPES

Born in 1951 in Embrun, France, François Jullien is a useful companion in navigating through the complexities of our focal passage from the *Tao Te Ching*. Between 1975 and 1977 he studied Chinese language at Peking and Shanghai universities respectively and has followed the trajectories of Durkheim (1858–1917), Mauss (1872–1950), Granet (1884–1940) and Lévi-Strauss (1908–2009) in seeking to understand anthologically the differences and intersections between Greek and Chinese philosophical thought. Jullien uses his understandings of Chinese constructs as an outsider, to identify taken-for-granted ideas. Thus, the foundations of Greek and Chinese philosophical enquiry inform contemporary understandings of the 'Western' lifeworld. We narrow this focus to leadership through this process of exploring Chinese alterity.

In his (1995) work, *The Propensity of Things*, Jullien discusses the ancient Chinese concepts of 'potential' and 'movement' through the notion of *shi* (勢). He notes that this term *shi* was so ubiquitous that its role in explaining social affairs was assumed. Jullien describes this compound word as a combination of elements, which, if distilled, imply power, or 'force', paradoxically as static and active. *Shi* has also been translated as 'energy' but as Xiongbo Shi (2015) notes, this is too esoteric and, therefore, its source is difficult to identify.

Jullien's (1995) etymological discussion of *shi* demonstrates how a tendency towards enigmatic, if not metaphysical attributions are overcome by noting that the pictogram depicts a hand holding a clod of earth. Thus there is a positioning of a thing which embraces both "spatial…[and] temporal associations in the sense of 'opportunity' or `chance'" (p. 267).Therefore, it is both *static* and *active*; is *actual* and has *potential*, while being situated in time and space.

Jullien (1995) claims that this notion of *shi*, which appeared in the ancient Chinese lexicon around the time of the *Tao Te Ching*, is evident throughout all affairs whether those of the State or of people in community. Three elements coalesce to reveal propensity in the environment, namely, "an *inherent potentiality at work in configuration…a functional bipolarity…*and a *tendency* generated sponte sua simply through *interaction*, which proceeds to develop through *alternation*" (p. 14, emphases in the original). Therefore, systems are generative and fecund, sustained through their propensity and potentiality, a process similar to the ideas on paradox discussed above.

The idea of continual renewal and movement within systems (Latin, *sponte sua*) has important implications for Western understandings of leadership, particularly in its apparent stasis. Typically, today's leaders are identified by their position and then held to account for decisions. The oft-invoked aphorism attributed to USA President Harry Truman that the *buck stops* with the nominal leader (National Archives, 1951), demonstrates such an inert construct. Jullien's (1995) discussion helps us see beyond this impasse, for an environment infused with *shi* resists this drive towards closure and finality. Truman's closed buck-stopping injunction lacks perpetual motion and tends towards an idea that power is somehow grasped.

Whether a president, CEO or sports coach, to adopt this closed construct imposes an impossible burden of responsibility on the leader, while releasing followers from accountability. This could not be further from the ancient Chinese, for *shi* grounds people to the here-and-now and is available to everyone.

Jullien's insights into *shi* can help us identify leadership beyond de-contextualised theories and to observe occurrences of it being embodied in time and space. Furthermore, the temptation to make extra-temporal, if not metaphysical associations is mitigated with this embodiment. For example, in his book *The Impossible Nude* (2007) Jullien explores the observable artistic and aesthetic differences between style in China and the West. He notes that for the Chinese artist the human body does not stand alone as an admirable object, but rather as an organic whole connected to the world. He writes:

> The body is conceived of in exact correspondence to the external world, with which it is in permanent communication. It is itself a universe that is both closed and open, permeated by breaths flowing through a system of channels or 'meridians' which run through the body and circulate vitality.
> (Jullien, 2007, p. 34)

Again, the leadership implications are intriguing. Specifically, the human body is connected to other bodies, who, in community, have potential and propensity. Stated differently, *shi* is present in all human interactions, encouraging responsive social interactions, which negates the necessity for a single person (leader, ruler, or sage) to take control. Furthermore, when an individual assumes sovereignty, this vibrant environment is inhibited.

This, then, enlightens our interpretation of the latter verse of the focal passage. To reprise, D. C. Lau's translation is "Hesitant, he does not utter words lightly" (Lao Tzu, 4thC BCE/1988, Book I Chapter XVII: 41), whereas Callahan prefers "Relaxed, they treasure their words" (Callahan, 1989, p. 178). And to further clarify the differences in approach, D. C. Lau's "he" refers to the "best of all rulers" while Callahan's "they" are those with "perspectival action-discrimination." For D. C. Lau, the common people respond to the leader's shadowy presence by their actions, whereas for Callahan, the common people and those who make decisions are synonymous.

However, this apparently easy solution presents a further problem, namely, the meanings of the words themselves. This issue is compounded by the distance between the emergence of the text, which we identify as the *Tao Te Ching* in ancient China, and us in the 3rd millennium of the Common Era. How might we understand the complexities of the text given that our thinking about leadership is constrained by our experience of and our ontological assumptions about the world?

LOSING OUR WAY

Continuing with our adopted soup metaphor from Ames and Hall (2003), we are now confronted with the nature of the leadership and what happens when social ingredients are mixed. If we can identify language differences between then and now, we might be better equipped to understand the substantive differences between Ames and Hall (2003) and D. C. Lau's (1988) translations compared with Callahan's (1989) dissenting views.

The question remains, therefore, as to the salience of ancient texts in our contemporary world their impacts, if any, on leadership as it is theorized and practiced. This question applies also to religious texts such as the Bible and Qur'an, whose combined adherents total to over half the world's population. For, despite the injunctions to "Love your neighbor as yourself" (Mathew 12:31 NIV) and to "give wealth, for love of Him, to kinsfolk and to orphans and the needy and the wayfarer, and to those who ask, and who set slaves free" (Al-Baqarah - the Cow - 2:177), we live in a world where love of neighbours locally and internationally, and active support of the needy, are rare commodities. So too with the insights from Lao Tzu.

The resources available to the ancient Chinese appear to be unavailable to us today. Weak signals appear on the horizon, such as Frédéric Laloux's proposed 'teal' organisations (Laloux, 2014), but these are fleeting glimpses of a world of organising not known or wanted by communities. Even the oft-invoked claim by Abraham Lincoln at Gettysburg (1863/2020) that those who perished in that bloody Civil War would not "have died in vain - that this nation, under God, shall have a new birth of freedom - and that government of the people, by the people, for the people, shall not perish from the earth" (Lincoln, 1863/2020) struggles until today to find its fulfilment in the USA.

It is no surprise, then, that Lau Tzu's implications that a leader is gentle, who has few words and performs without actions does not sit well with our current need for leaders to show strength, to intervene and to declaim their position with clarity. It is barely imaginable that Lao Tzu would find his way into a corporation's board room or nation's cabinet table with what appears to be insipid, if not obtuse, ideologies such as:

> 43 The gentlest thing in the world
> overcomes the hardest thing in the world.
> That which has no substance
> enters where there is no space.
> This shows the value of non-action.
> Teaching without words,
> performing without actions:
> that is the Master's way.
>
> (Lao Tzu, 4thC BCE/1988, Book II Chapter XLIII)

A leader's non-action in today's world would send journalists and commentators scurrying for their keyboards to write op-eds denouncing such weakness. For, strong and resolute leadership defines our age.

Witness, for example, the Florida Governor Ron DeSantis in August 2021 steadfastly refusing to permit schools to mandate mask-wearing by students at a time when the Covid-19 pandemic was ravaging that state. His executive order (DeSantis, 2021b) prohibiting such mandates was accompanied by a strident speech in reference to Federal interference, and in particular that of USA President Joe Biden, where he declared to cheers from the assembled crowd, "I am standing in your way" (DeSantis, 2021a). Declaring this position and then backing it up with threats of withholding salaries of school administrators (Romo, 2021) evidences a type of strong leadership that would undergird his supposed run for the Republican presidential nomination in 2024 (Oliphant et al., 2021). Yet such leadership is void of moral and ethical considerations that might protect the very people he hopes will support his political ambitions. Hesitancy appears to be anathema to this ambitious leader.

Witness too, President Xi Jinping's speech to mark the 100th anniversary of the Communist Party of China (CPC), and his affirmation of the strength of the economy and military prowess in maintaining the country's status as an active player on the world stage. His references to the resilience of the CPC in its 70 years of governing the nation play well to the party faithful, numbering 95 million, and the entire nation of 1.4 billion inhabitants. He represents to them a steady hand on the nation: a 'head chef' who can stir the soup pot with wisdom.

His speech was a celebration of the CPC's history. However, within his triumphalism is couched warnings to insiders seeking to destabilise the nation: *"Any attempt to divide the Party from the Chinese people or to set the people against the Party is bound to fail;"* and to outsiders who would interfere:

> We Chinese are a people who uphold justice and are not intimidated by threats of force. As a nation, we have a strong sense of pride and confidence. We have never bullied, oppressed, or subjugated the people of any other country, and we never will. By the same token, we will never allow any foreign force to bully, oppress, or subjugate us. Anyone who would attempt to do so will find themselves on a collision course with a great wall of steel forged by over 1.4 billion Chinese people.
>
> (Xi, 2021)

Yet, Xi's claims to justice and his implied turn to force are as far from the *dao* as DeSantis's rejection of mandates that would maintain the safety of Florida State's most vulnerable, its children.

Both Ron DeSantis's and Xi Jingping's claims to strong leadership rest more on governance for and by the *person*, rather than for and by the *people*, despite both jurisdictions asserting democracy as their founding governing logic. In both cases, their leadership appears to lack insights into the profundity of the ideas within the *Tao Te Ching*.

Our brief summary of recent events in 21st-century political leadership reveals an inability to appropriate wisdom from the past. This is not at all surprising given the lingering influence of Thomas Carlyle's so-called 'great man theory' of leadership (Carlyle, 1841) and his belief that Napoleon alone was responsible for bringing order to revolutionary France (Carlyle, 1896). Napoleon's use of deadly force against his own citizenry in Paris on 13 Vendémiaire (5 October 1795) not only cemented his position as an aspiring leader, it also became a model he later deployed as he expanded his empire into Italy and beyond. As Jordan (2012) notes, "Napoleon intended to impose the French revolution on Italy in its Bonapartist form, with the people reduced to passive participation under an authoritarian, efficient government, set in motion and sustained by Paris" (p. 44). Perpetuating such claims of strength rewards the egos of men and women who wrest control groups as small as the board room and as large as the nation state through political manipulation, threats and brute force. This model of leadership has been slow to yield its influence despite two devastating global wars in the 20th century and the concomitant questionable actions of those dictating events. This form of authoritarian leadership continues in this century, notable in a reluctance of world leaders, political and corporate, to tackle the effects of our changing climate.

It is not surprising, then, that the ideals of the *Tao Te Ching* are unrealisable in our current political and business worlds. Today we operate with a different hermeneutic horizon and more diverse cultural experiences. Even something as basic as defining the self does not square with Lao Tzu's understandings. Our private, buffered selves (Smith, 2009; Taylor, 2007) would be unrecognisable in ancient China, just as Lao Tzu's *ziran* is to us today.

It appears that we are afraid of the kind of business and society comprising politically involved citizens who act for the benefit of all, rather than preserving the status of a few powerful elites. Stated more bluntly and following Lachmann (2020), leaders, following Lachmann (2020), leaders would rather preserve would rather preserve their position than the Planet even in the face of pending catastrophe.

To lay the responsibility at the feet of our leaders alone, though, is to deny the importance of communitarian import of *ziran*. If the self is a compound of you and me, then we are responsible for our world and how we enact our leaderly behaviours. Despite Lao Tzu's statement quoted above that "Everyone knows this is true, but few can put it into practice" (Lao Tzu, 4thC BCE/1988, Book II Chapter LXXVIII), we think that we can turn what we know into wise action, and together we can become more sensitised to the moment.

Lao Tzu's vision outlined in our focal chapter of the *Tao Te Ching* is radical. It calls us to have the courage to examine the roots of our leadership practices and to revise our preferred behaviours so that we can say in our age, "We have perspectival action-discrimination and things happened organically."

REFERENCES

Ames, R. T., & Hall, D. L. (2003). *Daodejing 'making this life significant': A philosophical translation*. Ballantine.

Ames, R. T., & Rosemont, H. (1998). *The Analects of Confucius: A Philosophical Translation*. Ballantine.

Barbalet, J. (2014). Laozi's Daodejing (6th century BC). In J. Helin, T. Hernes, D. Hjorth & R. Holt (Eds.), *The Oxford Handbook of Process Philosophy and Organisation Studies* (pp. 17–31). Oxford University Press.

Bass, B. M. (1990). From transactional to transformational leadership: Learning to share the vision. *Organizational Dynamics*, 18(3), 19–31.

Bathurst, R. J., & Chen, M. S. (2018). A smile and a sigh: Leadership insights from the East. In C. Neesham & S. Segal (Eds.), *Handbook of Philosophy of Management* (pp. 1–18). Springer. https://doi.org/10.1007/978-3-319-48352-8_21-1

Bevir, M. (2011). Why historical distance is not a problem. *History and Theory*, 50(4), 24–37. https://www.jstor.org/stable/41342619

Bloom, H. (1992). *The American Religion: The Emergence of the Post-Christian Nation*. Simon & Schuster.

Broeng, S. (2018). Action research on employee silence: The need for negative capability in leadership. *Management Revue*, 29(4), 432–448. https://10.5771/0935-9915-2018-4-432

Callahan, W. J. (1989). Discourse and perspective in Daoism: A linguistic interpretation of ziran. *Philosophy East and West*, 39(2), 171–189.

Caputo, M., McGraw, M., & Kumar, A. (2020). Trump owed tens of millions to Bank of China. *Politico*, 28 April. https://www.politico.com/news/2020/04/24/trump-biden-china-debt-205475

Carlyle, T. (1841). *On Heroes, Hero-Worship, and the Heroic in History*. James Fraser.

Carlyle, T. (1896). *The French Revolution: A History*. Chapman and Hall.

Chang, J. (2014). *Empress Dowager Cixi: The Concubine Who Launched Modern China*. Vintage.

Cherniss, J. L. (2006). Isaiah Berlin's political ideas: From the twentieth century to the Romantic age. In H. Hardy (Ed.), *Political Ideas in the Romantic Age: Their Rise and Influence on Modern Thought* (pp. xxi–lx). Princeton University Press.

DeSantis, R. (2021a). DeSantis blasts Biden: 'I am standing in your way'. *Fox 13 Tampa Bay*, 5 August. https://www.youtube.com/watch?v=wuAbLlexkAw

DeSantis, R. (2021b). Executive Order number 21-175. *State of Florida Office of the Governor*, 30 July. https://www.flgov.com/wp-content/uploads/2021/07/Executive-Order-21-175.pdf

Fang, T. (2011). Yin yang: A new perspective on culture. *Management and Organization Review*, 8(1), 25–50. https://dx.doi.org/10.1111/j.1740-8784.2011.00221.x

Fingarette, H. (1972). *Confucius: The Secular as Sacred*. Harper & Row.

Fogel, J. A., Cheek, T., & Ownby, D. (2019). *Voices from the Chinese Century: Public Intellectual Debate*. Zookal.

Fox, A. (2017). A process interpretation of Daoist thought. *Frontiers of Philosophy in China*, 12(1), 26–37. https://10.3868/s030-006-017-0003-2

Greenleaf, R. K. (1991). *Servant Leadership: A Journey into the Nature of Legitimate Power and Greatness*. Paulist Press.

Harvey, D. (2005). *A Brief History of Neoliberalism*. Oxford University Press.

Hay, A., & Blenkinsopp, J. (2019). Anxiety and human resource development: Possibilities for cultivating negative capability. *Human Resource Development Quarterly*, *30*(2), 133–153. https://10.1002/hrdq.21332

Heider, J. (2005). *The Tao of Leadership: Lao Tzu's Tao Te Ching Adapted for a New Age*. Green Dragon.

Jordan, D. P. (2012). *Napoleon and the Revolution*. Palgrave Macmillan.

Jullien, F. (1995). *The Propensity of Things: Toward a History of Efficacy in China*. Trans. J. Lloyd. Zone Books.

Jullien, F. (2007). *The Impossible Nude: Chinese Art and Western Aesthetics*. Trans. M. de la Guardia. University of Chicago Press.

Kaltenmark, M. (1969). *Lao Tzu and Taoism*. Trans. G. Roger. Stanford University Press.

Kirby, W. C. (2014). The Chinese century? The challenges of higher education. *Daedalus*, *143*(2), 145–156.

Kohn, L. (2016). *Science and the Dao: From the Big Bang to Lived Perfection*. Three Pines Press.

Lachmann, R. (2020). *First Class Passengers on a Sinking Ship: Elite Politics and the Decline of Great Powers*. Verso.

Lai, K. (2007). Ziran and wuwei in the *Daodejing*: An ethical assessment. *Dao: A Journal of Comparative Philosophy*, *6*(4), 325–337. https://doi.org/10.1007/s11712-007-9019-8

Laloux, F. (2014). *Reinventing Organizations: A Guide to Creating Organizations Inspired by the Next Stage of Human Consciousness*. Nelson Parker.

Lao Tzu (4thC BCE/1988). *Tao Te Ching*. Trans. D. C. Lau. Chinese University Press.

Li, L. (2020). Teaching beyond words: 'Silence' and its pedagogical implications discoursed in the early classical texts of Confucianism, Daoism and Zen Buddhism. *Educational Philosophy & Theory*, *52*(7), 759–768. https://10.1080/00131857.2019.1684896

Li, P. P. (2016). Global implications of the indigenous epistemological system from the east: How to apply Yin–Yang balancing to paradox management. *Cross Cultural & Strategic Management*, *23*(1), 42–77. https://10.1108/CCSM-10-2015-0137

Li, P. P., Leung, K., Chen, C. C., & Luo, J.-D. (2012). Indigenous research on Chinese management: What and how. *Management and Organization Review*, *8*(1), 7–24. https://dx.doi.org/10.1111/j.1740-8784.2012.00292.x

Lin, L., Li, P. P., & Roelfsema, H. (2018). The traditional Chinese philosophies in inter-cultural leadership: The case of Chinese expatriate managers in the Dutch context. *Cross Cultural & Strategic Management*, *25*(2), 1–38. https://doi.org/10.1108/CCSM-01-2017-0001

Lincoln, A. (1863/2020). The Gettysburg address. *Abraham Lincoln Online*. http://www.abrahamlincolnonline.org/lincoln/speeches/gettysburg.htm

Liu, X. (2008). Transition and articulation between two orientations: An experimental analysis of a new interpretation of *ziran*. *Contemporary Chinese Thought*, *40*(2), 67–88. https://10.2753/CSP1097-1467400204

Lobosco, K. (2019). This one business shows exactly how Trump's China tariffs are hurting the economy. *CNN Politics*, 29 August. https://edition.cnn.com/2019/08/29/politics/tariffs-trump-economy-business-uncertainty/

Nandy, A. (2001). *The Tao of Cricket: On Games of Destiny and the Destiny of Games*. Oxford University Press.

National Archives (1951). 'The buck stops here' desk sign. *US National Archives*. https://www.trumanlibrary.gov/education/trivia/buck-stops-here-sign

Oliphant, J., Layne, N., & Borter, G. (2021). Florida's DeSantis rises as possible 2024 alternative to Trump. *Reuters*, 2 July. https://www.reuters.com/world/us/floridas-desantis-rises-possible-2024-alternative-trump-2021-07-01/

Pheng, L. S., & Lee, B. S. K. (1997). East meets west: Leadership development for construction project management. *Journal of Managerial Psychology*, *12*(5/6), 383–400. https://10.1108/02683949710176133

Raelin, J. A. (2003). *Creating Leaderful Organizations: How to Bring Out Leadership in Everyone*. Berrett-Koehler.

Romo, V. (2021). Florida's governor says school leaders' salary may be withheld if they require masks. *NPR*, 9 August. https://www.npr.org/sections/coronavirus-live-updates/2021/08/09/1026299001/florida-governor-desantis-school-superintendent-salary-masks

Saggurthi, S., & Thakur, M. (2016). Usefulness of uselessness: A case for negative capability in management. *Academy of Management Learning & Education*, *15*(1), 180–193. 10.5465/amle.2013.0250

Schad, J., Lewis, M. W., Raisch, S., & Smith, W. K. (2016). Paradox research in management science: Looking back to move forward. *Academy of Management Annals*, *10*(1), 5–64. https://dx.doi.org/10.1080/19416520.2016.1162422

Scott, D. (2008). *'The Chinese Century'? The Challenge to Global Order*. Palgrave Macmillan.

Shi, X. (2015). *Writing forces: Revisiting the aesthetic concept of shi* 勢 *in Chinese calligraphy criticism*. Paper presented at the Asian Conference on Arts & Humanities, Osaka.

Simpson, P. F., & French, R. (2006). Negative capability and the capacity to think in the present moment: Some implications for leadership practice. *Leadership*, *2*(2), 245–255. https://10.1177/1742715006062937

Simpson, P. F., French, R., & Harvey, C. E. (2002). Leadership and negative capability. *Human Relations*, *55*(10), 1209–1226.

Slingerland, E. (2003). *Effortless Action: Wu-wei as Conceptual Metaphor and Spiritual Ideal in Early China*. Oxford University Press.

Smith, K. E. (2009). Meaning and porous being. *Thesis Eleven*, *99*, 7–26.

Smith, W. K., & Lewis, M. W. (2011). Toward a theory of paradox: A dynamic equilibrium model of organizing. *Academy of Management Review*, *36*(2), 381–403. https://dx.doi.org/10.5465amr.2009.0223

Spitznagel, M. (2013). *The Dao of Capital: Austrian Investing in a Distorted World*. Wiley.

Taylor, C. (2007). *A Secular Age*. Belknap Press.

Walker, T. (2020). China and Australia went from chilly to barely speaking. That could have been avoided. *Channel News Asia*, 13 December. https://www.channelnewsasia.com/news/commentary/australia-china-relations-trade-wine-tariff-morrison-xi-diplomac-13751260

Wang, B. X., & Chee, H. (2011). *Chinese Leadership*. Palgrave Macmillan.

Wang, Y. (2016). Offensive for defensive: The Belt and Road initiative and China's new grand strategy. *Pacific Review*, *29*(3), 455–463. https://10.1080/09512748.2016.1154690

Wu, Z. (2021). *Vital Breath of the Dao: Living with the Heavenly Thread*. Singing Dragon.

Xi, J. (2021). Speech by Xi Jinping at a ceremony marking the centenary of the CPC. *Xinhua*, 1 July. http://www.xinhuanet.com/english/special/2021-07/01/c_1310038244.htm

Popular Culture and Leadership

Brigitte Biehl and Suvi Satama

INTRODUCTION

Henry V, *Game of Thrones* and *The Wolf of Wall Street* are not just fictional stories, but stories about people. Popular culture can be seen as a serious exploration of leaders and their human nature. Protagonists such as Harry of Lancaster, Daenerys Targaryen and Jordan Belfort struggle to gain and hold power and to align with their followers. These issues resonate with audiences who are turning towards popular culture to make sense of their lives, including those asking questions of leadership. 'Leadership' currently is everywhere in public discourse (Learmonth & Morrell, 2017) and management research has, for many decades, acknowledged that popular culture provides dramatic representations of a 'reality' of working life (Hassard & Holliday, 1998) that differs from the more 'dry', intellectual, or abstract accounts in scholarly management books (Taylor & Hansen, 2005). Films, books and stories are emotional, visual and illustrative. They express and reveal many ideologies of contemporary leadership (Bell, 2008), reflect misogyny, hetero- and cissexism, and toxic masculinity (Askey, 2018), but also offer critique, inspiration and new perspectives on leadership (Pullen & Rhodes, 2013; Rhodes, 2016).

Pop culture includes various forms of media and entertainment, such as film, music, television, social media, even sport and fashion, and arts such as theatre, dance and the fine arts. Pop culture can be entertainment and amusement, fiction and fantasy, but always is a source of knowledge about the world (Clapton & Shepherd, 2017; Kuhn et al., 2013). Popular culture, or entertainment media more broadly, is an important source for us to make sense of ourselves, our work, management and leadership. It also critiques and refreshes our understanding of these issues (see also Chapter 14, Leadership development, and Chapter 31, Leadership and culture).

In this chapter, we consider popular culture as a representation of leadership that also includes many opportunities for reflection, critique and learning, and thus impacts our understanding of leadership. In this chapter, we do not attempt to 'measure' the impact of the mass media on leadership in business organisations or in politics. Also, we do not write about leadership in the media industry or in the creative industries (Biehl, 2020) – which, however often, is represented in popular media, along with all other kinds of leadership models.

Popular culture as a representation of reality addresses and shows a variety of possible approaches to leadership, including leader-centric, follower-centric, relational, role-based and constructionist views that are discussed in leadership studies (Uhl-Bien et al., 2014). Common leadership archetypes – for example, the charismatic leader, the authentic leader, the masculine leader, the feminine leader, the mother type, the disabled leader and many more – can be found in countless popular books (Badaracco, 2006), blockbuster films (Carroll et al., 2015; Urick, 2021a, b) and TV series (Biehl, 2021b; Craven, 2019). Films, books and stories are products of multiple voices and creative collaboration, are symbolic and experiential (Townley et al., 2009), a 'social dream' (if one were to use a psychoanalytic vocabulary) that soaks up all kinds of contemporary influences. Protagonists can be historical, realistic and fictional, are far from perfect, under tremendous pressure and must make decisions with great uncertainty, uneasy feelings and uncertain outcomes. We follow them with emotional close-ups, captivating lines and through tense situations, and can experience the complexity of these leaders. Scholars writing about these topics agree that people learn about leadership not (solely or even mostly) from management textbooks, but from popular culture when audiences draw conclusions about how to behave in the workplace in part from what they see on the television screen (Towers, 2018).

This chapter is structured as follows. We will outline the value of popular culture for leadership, as it can convey the essence and emotions in leadership differently from academic works. Working from the assumption that popular culture is a vivid representation of reality, we also show how scholars have criticised mass media as vehicles for ideology that dupe people into accepting the status quo. At the same time, scholars have also valued its critical potential. After this exploration of the current structures and themes (sense-making), we refresh and develop this topic (sense-breaking) by illustrating newer epistemological and methodological positions and developments, where popular culture is not primarily valued for its content, but for its experience. The focus on the experience makes popular culture well suited for leadership education and development, also stretching deep into popular culture to include formats that are not realistic, but scripted-reality, fictional and even fantasy. Popular culture challenges charismatic leaders and shows struggling, disabled, diverse and female leaders, along with new leadership role models. With examples, we discuss ideology and critical potential, emphasising the role of emotions and the aesthetic experience.

EMOTIONS AND ESSENCE OF LEADERSHIP

While the transfer of management and leadership knowledge is usually seen as a formal process involving business schools, training courses and books, leadership knowledge can also be diffused through the media (Towers, 2018). Popular culture and the arts offer insights into leadership that are different from management textbooks (see Chapter 22, Leadership as aesthetic and artful practice). Popular culture provides more emotions and entertainment and tells us stories, while academic texts tend to delineate, parcel out, dig deep and produce knowledge within their disciplines (Clapton & Shepherd, 2017). Popular culture is not only an entertainment or escape from everyday life, but also offers various forms of knowledge that are *different, and value-adding, to more conventional academic knowledge* (Rhodes, 2016, p. 129).

Business schools, in particular, have received criticism for their positivist, quantitative orientation that emphasises formal management tools and models at the expense of emotional and sensuous questions of leadership, decision-making and moral judgement. Leadership studies have turned to the world of arts and popular culture to bring ethical discussions, reflection and emotional inspiration into the discipline (Adler, 2006; Ladkin & Taylor, 2010; Taylor & Hansen, 2005). Issues revolving around power, leading and following are widely covered in films, books and dramas. The subject matter of popular culture and the subject matter of leadership studies in this sense are closely related.

Products in popular culture are symbolic, aesthetic and experiential (Townley et al., 2009), and thus are well suited to convey tacit and embodied forms of knowing (Taylor & Hansen, 2005; see also Chapter 22, Leadership as aesthetic and artful practice). These works can show us the *essence* of leadership (Ladkin & Taylor, 2010) as they embody universally recognised qualities, emotional responses, or ways of being that we do not easily find in academic research based on information, surveys, data and cases.

IDEOLOGY AND CRITIQUE

Research in leadership and management studies traditionally has assumed two opposing possibilities of popular culture. One is that popular culture carries ideological persuasions, *ensuring that their audiences accept and conform to the values* that are suggested (Hassard & Holliday, 1998, p. 1); the other one puts an emphasis on the critical potential of popular culture.

The first view stands in the critical tradition of the *Kulturindustrie* or *culture industry* by Theodor W. Adorno and Max Horkheimer (1947) that sees popular culture and entertainment media as transmitters of false consciousness, numbing the minds of the passive masses. So-called *capitalist media* (Fuchs, 2014, p. 22) perpetuate many ideologies. For example, *Star Trek* has been criticised for its imperialist impetus (Weldes, 1999), and Hollywood films reduce disabled people to jokes and clichés (Ellis, 2014) and suggest neoliberal ideas of success. Women in general are objectified in front of the camera and turned into an object of the male gaze (Mulvey, 1975). Many film products on work life show mostly white men and white male leaders (e.g., *The Office*). For example, there are few openly gay leaders in films. *Star Trek* did not dare to show queerness, although it is a topic in fan fiction and even though the writers could vividly imagine beings 'from a different planet'. The journalist Laurie Penny (2012) made a point when considering other TV series: *If the creator of a fantasy series can dream up an army of self-resurrecting zombie immortals he can damn well dream up equal marriage rights, and if he chooses not to do so then that choice is meaningful.* The only gay commander of a battle ship, for example, is 'Captain Cock' (sic) in the German box-office hit *(T)Raumschiff Surprise – Periode 1* (2004). For commercial return, the cis male, heterosexual, white director Bully Herbig reduced gay identity to sexuality, turning the space ship into a big penis and degrading black people and women; therefore his work has been recognised as racist, misogynist and homophobic (Volkmann, 2020). Representations like these have implications on how we understand leadership, whom we can imagine as possible leaders and whom we do not.

This view has developed and expanded in scholarship on popular culture, while the ideological potential of mass media is always present (Rhodes, 2016; Towers, 2018). Management and leadership researchers have discussed the critical potential of entertainment media, for example, with regard to undoing gender (Pullen & Rhodes, 2013) and questioning systems of power. Popular culture scholars identify the potential of popular culture in allowing people to make sense of their lives, criticising established identities, raising doubt, showing the dark side of things and offering new ideas of how to change our society, also specifically with regard to leaders, leader role models and leadership (e.g., Acevedo, 2011; Biehl, 2020b). More generally, popular culture and the arts have been heralded as a source of newness and inspiration not only for our society, but also for leadership and management studies (Adler, 2006; Taylor & Hansen, 2005).

EXPERIENCE

When popular culture is not considered merely ideological, but afforded a critical potential and an opportunity for experience, it is well suited for leadership education and development. The viewers are not seen as mere passive receivers of ideology, but actively engage in an experience. In this vein, some leadership researchers start from the notion of the *aesthetic experience* (e.g. Chapter 22, Leadership as aesthetic and artful practice; Ropo & Sauer, 2008; Satama, 2020; see also Strati, 1992) to explain the importance of sensual perception and experiential knowing for leadership education. Recipients of popular culture – film, for example – do not *have* an experience passively, but rather *make* an experience (such as in German language: 'Eine Erfahrung machen') (Stadler, 1990, p. 40). Viewers respond to the moving film image, or the dance and performance situation or the canvas, and enter into an experiential dialogue with the material (e.g., Biehl, 2021a; Chapter 42, Leadership as (new) material(ities) practices). This means that the theatre play, film, or art work and its content are not the only source of meaning; rather, these products speak to the life-worldly experience and the context of the recipient who *constitutes her or his own experience* (Stadler, 1990, p. 41), rather than being a passive receiver.

To explain how individuals connect to popular culture, media theorists use the concept of *emotional realism* (Ang, 1985, p. 43): audiences can identify with the emotional substance or psychological reality of a media text, and may derive pleasure from watching, use experiences towards their own lives and give meaning to them. Emotional realism is what viewers *recognize as realistic* in *fictional worlds* (Ang, 1985, p. 43). Protagonists and personas in popular culture are still based on ordinary individuals going through actual situations and this makes popular culture valuable for leadership research and education. In this sense, protagonists in popular media serve as role models, inviting followers to emulate their example (Duffy & Pooley, 2019). In the management field, the notion of identity work includes incorporating, adapting, or refusing to accept established ideas of 'the leader' into one's identity (Corlett et al., 2019).

To be of value for leadership theory and also learning, media content hence does not need to stand in a direct relationship to social reality, as commonly suggested by the tropes of 'mirror'. Many works of popular culture have been widely discussed with regard to their striking analogies and the interpretations of our reality, as they can be read as an accurate reflection of the most contemporary, up-to-date management theories (Towers, 2018). Among the well-known examples is the film biography *The Wolf of Wall Street* which presents a strongly masculine leader, Jordan Belfort, fuelled by alcohol, cocaine, greed and the desire for excess (Hartz & Kötschau, 2019). These illustrative works with strong images and emotional content in a learning context provoke *aha moments*, furthering the understanding and retention of abstract leadership theories and concepts (Champoux, 1999, p. 206).

Works of popular culture use fictional elements and may be more or less 'realistic', but all of them speak to our contemporary experience, even if they are fantasy or a-historical. Only on this basis, the fantasy series *Game of Thrones*, for example, has been widely investigated with regard to leadership issues (Biehl, 2021a, b; Clapton & Shepherd, 2017; Craven, 2019); validating fantasy-fiction as a *thought-provoking medium* that provides inspiration and ideas to organisational studies (Savage et al., 2018, p. 3). Buchanan and Hällgren (2019) have used zombie movies to explore leadership in extreme situations that otherwise cannot be easily studied (e.g., a sudden catastrophe), arguing that these films provide implicit theories on how leadership configurations work or do not work. By using fictional plots, exaggeration, parody and a broad range of artistic expressions, popular media are promising for insights into the *messy*, unordered side of leadership and management (Taylor & Hansen, 2005, p. 1224), into ill-defined, emotive and complex issues, into real-world untidiness as opposed to text-book orderliness that is important for leadership.

LEARNING

The focus on the experience, rather than the content, entails an epistemological change in leadership studies. Aesthetic forms mean more emotional engagement and more emotional engagement means more learning (Taylor & Statler, 2014; Vince, 2015). Aesthetic forms enable participants to connect knowing, experience and emotions, and achieve a better understanding of who they are and how to relate to their surroundings (Taylor & Ladkin, 2009; see also Chapter 22, Leadership as aesthetic and artful practice). Scholars suggest that management and leadership practice are as much based on intuition, perception and tacit or aesthetic knowing as they are on rational decision-making (Chapter 22, Leadership as aesthetic and artful practice; Ladkin & Taylor, 2010; Ryömä & Satama, 2019).

The shift towards relational understanding of leadership (Uhl-Bien & Ospina, 2012) and learning is well-established and can be realised, for example, through subtle movement characterised by dancers' attitudes towards their own and others' bodies (Figure 34.1) and through all the materialities they are surrounded by (see also Chapter 42, Leadership as (new) material(ities) practices). Even if – or perhaps *because* – contemporary work happens largely in our heads, we must pay attention to how our bodies generate communicative meanings, messages and hidden qualities that explain a lot about ourselves and others, even if we are not aware. In Figure 34.1, bodily movements express humour, but learning and concentration are also fully embodied, as the dancers focus solely on each other and the music. Here, leadership is illustrated as a relational phenomenon defined by bodily reflexive actions (Ryömä & Satama, 2019). In this way, dance provides novel insights into leadership and learning.

Efforts are made to describe how the arts and entertainment media can be used for learning. The general position is that these formats need to be embedded in a training context with guided reflection (e.g., leadership seminar with film material). Dozing in front of the television watching a movie or TV series will not lead to some sort of individual transformation or change in organisational leadership.

An approach to use film for management learning includes the following three steps (Biehl, 2021a): 1) making a film experience; 2) processing the experience; 3) cultural aesthetic reflexivity. Process steps and teaching strategies have been identified that help move management learners along in the process towards specific learning outcomes. For example, in order to 1) *make* (not *have*) a film experience, the film is framed accordingly – that is, related to 'leadership', also with further readings on leadership styles for example, and students are encouraged to speak about their experience with regard to film sequences that evoke emotions and embodied understandings in viewers. For 2) processing the experience, simple film analysis tools can be used that help to identify

Figure 34.1 Dance practice. Photographer: Sakari Viika

which emotions and understandings are created through film techniques (e.g., camera movements, editing, composition, style). This helps to start an emotional and moral dialogue with characters. Learners also include theoretical questions when comparing, relating and valuing characters, and propose judgements. For 3) aesthetic cultural reflexivity, the management concept (e.g., leadership) is linked to history and culture, and evaluated individually or in a group. It is about revising judgements and mobilising aesthetic experience and cultural knowledge for personal growth and to create new ideas of leadership.

In a broader context, products, processes and people from the arts and the realm of popular culture are increasingly used for leadership education and development (Adler, 2006; Taylor & Hansen, 2005) – for example, in workshops with poetry or literature (Badaracco, 2006), theatre and dance (Satama et al., 2021), art and film workshops or student seminar sessions. Popular culture, of course, can also be used for individual and scholarly exploration. In the subsequent section, we discuss examples from different areas of popular culture with regard to their possible influence on leadership, emphasising the role of the aesthetic experience. We start with charismatic leadership as one of the leader-centric models that have long dominated leadership research. This is followed by leaders who are still marginalised in organisations – for example, disabled people, queer people and women. We then turn to reality TV and social media for new leader models.

LEADERS IN POPULAR CULTURE

Struggling Charismatic Leaders

Leaders are the epitome of drama and, over the millennia, the theatre stages have made fools of kings, capitalists and communists rather than praising them. Other forms of popular culture also denounce the strong man, the charismatic woman and insecure protagonists (Hamlet: 'To be or not to be'). Unlike management literature with its widespread leader-centric, charismatic and heroic leadership models, these protagonists do not appear as heroes, but show their unheroic sides.

Charisma has been an influential concept from sociology in leadership studies for many decades and was often understood as some sort of gift, charm or aura that gives authority to leaders (House, 1977). As charisma is not easy to define, but from a sociological perspective is seen as socially constructed and influenced by emotions (Conger & Kanungo, 1987), film as an emotional and aesthetic medium can further viewers' attributions of a person being visionary, exceptional and charismatic. This view also links to more recent management studies approaches to charismatic leadership that speak of a more domesticated version of charisma that can be observed in various settings and operationalised to predict various outcomes. In this view, charisma is a *gift* that leaders can receive via well-designed interventions (Antonakis et al., 2016, p. 312). Many of these efforts are undertaken by films which use compositions, camerawork such as close-ups, light and many other techniques. Films make us experience how charisma is constructed and deconstructed, when certain variables are alternated.

Protagonists in popular culture often struggle with charismatic leader images. Examples include anti-heroes Tony Soprano (*The Sopranos*) and the head of the Lebanese mafia clan Ali 'Toni' Hamady (*4 Blocks*) who are trapped in male clichés and toxic masculinity, brutality and emotional reduction. Their TV series show them talking to their shrinks and being deprived of their own sexuality. Mob boss Tony Soprano struggles, and has identified Gary Cooper as a strong and determined masculine role model that he becomes increasingly frustrated with (The Sopranos: Gary Cooper Compilation, 2019). In other areas of popular culture, however, such as in rap music and rappers' social media accounts, a more one-dimensional interpretation is promoted of strong, toxic masculinity, often racist and misogynist, with only few role models for women (Sahin, 2019), brutal and powerful, with a strong penchant for luxury watches, cars and jewellery.

The ambiguous nature of charismatic personalities has also been discussed in the area of serious fiction (Badaracco, 2006) and management researchers have read Shakespeare through the leadership lens (Burnham et al., 1999). Henry V, for example, has been described not as a moral ideal by any means, rather as a sinister character and master dissembler with different faces. The entire Henriad can be seen as a piece on the pursuit and maintenance of power as a *matter of becoming a consummate actor* (Mangham, 2001, p. 302). The theatre play poses the question: has the leader already succumbed to the image of the invincible self?

Similar questions are negotiated in other media as well, like in TV series. *Game of Thrones* presents a highly charismatic leader, Daenerys Targaryen, who amasses a long range of titles: Daenerys Stormborn of House Targaryen, rightful heir to the Iron Throne, rightful Queen of the Andals and the First Men, Protector of the Seven Kingdoms, the Mother of Dragons, the Khaleesi of the Great Grass Sea, the Unburnt, the Breaker of Chains. After eight glorious seasons, however, she becomes lost in her theatricality. For a final victory speech (S08E06) she appears in seemingly charismatic style with an elevated speaker position, impressive outfit, cheering soldiers and her mighty dragon backing her visually. She is placed in the centre of the frame, her dark leather outfit contrasts the lighter surroundings, the wings of the dragon behind her merge with her figure to create a hybrid persona, simultaneously a human being and a mystical, dangerous creature (Figure 34.2).

The film provides viewers with an experience that starts off as charismatic and then turns sour (Biehl, 2021a, p. 17; 2021b, p. 88). Editing techniques are used that interject the doubtful gaze of followers. Camera movements show her strained face in emotional and revealing close-ups. The style evokes the historical and aesthetic phenomenon of fascism that has been widely picked up in popular culture: uniforms and power attributes perpetuate stereotypes and psychological interpretations of mostly German national socialism and terror. Global audiences typically respond to interrelated cultural clichés of the cold-hearted and merciless SS-tyrant (Stiglegger, 2015, p. 15), as also expressed in social media comments on YouTube: *Jesus they had her looking like some medieval Adolf Hitler there she might as well have been speaking German.*

Figure 34.2 **Charismatic leader (*Game of Thrones*, US, S08E08, 2019, HBO, YouTube)**

The once charismatic leader becomes a tyrant and followers turn away from her. In such a moment, one can link to a philosophical critique that suggests to distance oneself from an aesthetic of power when it is void of purpose and exists only for its own spectacle (Böhme, 1995). One can also link to issues of follower empowerment: challenging charismatic leaders to avoid negative relationships based on blind faith (Howell & Shamir, 2005), among other theories. The scene aroused heated public debate (Tucker, 2019), evidencing how viewers are emotionally involved and struggle to evaluate the episode. This outlines the potential of popular culture for pointing out the 'dark' sides of leadership and training viewers to be apprehensive of them.

On a more general level, in film, theatre and other media, the actor (in Greek: *hypocrites*) as a medium is always the message, speaking to us as the proverbial 'role-player'. Popular culture cannot be expected to provide ideal leadership models, but shows how the 'hero takes a fall', exposing weaknesses, the constraints of role-playing and the fact that appearances are deceiving, thus encouraging audiences to question and *possibly reject charismatic leaders and the organizational systems that surround them* (Biehl-Missal, 2010, p. 280). The playwright Bertolt Brecht has used the phrase: *To see the curtain down and nothing settled (Der Vorhang zu und alle Fragen offen)*. Literature scholars suggest that novels that passed the test of time raise more questions than they answer and constitute an indispensable source for reflection (Badaracco, 2006).

The 'charismatic leader' also has a critical history in the fine arts. Portrait paintings have been widely used to show powerful people, furthering their reputation and charisma. They provide an emotional component to leadership (Bass, 1985). Paintings are an aesthetic expression that can be used as a means of enquiring into certain aspects of leadership (Taylor & Hansen, 2005). For example, Francis Bacon's interpretation of the Portrait of Pope Innocent X (1650) by Velázquez can be seen as an exemplary way of revealing the complex dilemmas incorporated within a charismatic leader. *Velázquez [...] shows an efficient and cruel leader while offering his personal interpretation of the politics of his time. Bacon's interpretation goes further, by representing a powerful yet isolated leader, whose excessive individuality has produced a cage in which he remains trapped* (Acevedo, 2011, p. 27). Images of leaders as depicted by portraiture contribute to our understanding of leadership by showing how representations are socially constructed and can also challenge and contort leadership.

Popular culture uses many variations and quotations of established themes and visuals, which is termed intertextuality. Bacon's *Pope Innocent X* can, for example, be found as an intertextual reference in the depiction of Cersei Lannister at the end of season 6 in *Game of Thrones*, when she becomes the head of the state and the church after having eliminated all her enemies in other positions of power. She also has lost family members and social allies. As the painter Bacon shows a powerful leader isolated from all other people (see here for a picture: https://en.wikipedia.org/wiki/Study_after_Velázquez%27s_Portrait_of_Pope_Innocent_X), Cersei in this view must feel very similar, having climbed up into a position that has produced a cage in which she is trapped (Biehl, 2021b, p. 75). The still image from the film bears similarities to the famous painting, echoing the play of light and vertical structures and diagonal lines which, with their metallic materiality in contrast to some warm and golden lines, can be imagined as a cage. Her face is firm, almost desperate, a silent scream (Figure 34.3). Popular culture, via artworks and filmic compositions, endows individuals with charisma, but also inverts the power instrument of leader portraits, providing what can be seen as an aesthetic warning of charismatic and person-centred leader models. In lieu of socially constructed and imagined charisma, one sees isolation and loneliness and may imagine that leadership is not only a position, but a social process that also depends on followers.

Disabled Leaders

Popular culture not only represents, but can make us experience protagonists that are 'unusual' leaders and divert from dominant, 'abled' body images and reveal managerial vulnerabilities (Corlett et al., 2019). Historically, it is rare that we see disabled people in film and television – outside documentaries – in a story that is not cheesy or made to motivate able-bodied people into appreciating their reality (Ellis, 2014). However, film, television and other media may effectively depict and promote disability as a part of everyday life, making it visible to audiences in ways that are accurate, inclusive and multifaceted. The Media Access Award in this spirit has honoured TV series such as *The Sopranos* and *Breaking Bad* that challenge entrenched cultural views of normality. Tony Soprano, as one of the first anti-heroes in TV series (alongside Don Draper on *Mad Men*, Dexter and Walter White on *Breaking Bad*), a global audience witnessed him addressing

Figure 34.3 Leadership and loneliness (*Game of Thrones*, US, S06E10, 2014, HBO, YouTube)

his mental health issues and moral confusion onscreen with his therapist, Dr Melfi. On *The Sopranos*, disability is portrayed in several supporting roles as 'just another fact of life', and the ideology of the supposedly normal is inverted when the supposedly disabled person appears normal in contrast to the others. Similarly, *Game of Thrones* was lauded not only as a show that *deals with* disability, but as *something even better: a show that embraces the reality that no one is easily definable* (Martin, 2013).

One of the persistent and most effective leader figures is Tyrion, 'the dwarf', who serves as an advisor to many kings and rules for them (performed by Peter Dinklage). People of short stature commonly are either trivialised as Disney dwarves or shown as stubborn and greedy in Tolkien's *Hobbit* and C. S. Lewis' *Chronicles of Narnia*. Deformed, monstrous, or disabled individuals traditionally are chosen to represent evildoers and villains, playing on negative archetypes associated with disability, as if physical deformity expresses the distorted soul (Donnelly, 2016). Tyrion was treated in this way and eventually faces trial for a crime he did not commit. In this scene (S04E06, available on YouTube), he actively claims *dis-ability* for himself, presents himself as a target and exposes social prejudice. The film creates an emotional experience with strong cuts in a series of continuous editing that marks the different positions, the camera is zooming in on one of the bigot agents after the other, framing and thereby judging them, giving Tyrion relevance and screen space with emotional and personalising close-ups, his voice raising, music supporting the tension, until the crowd, disloyal to the king, is cheering in expectation of further public embarrassment. The character is visually backed by the crowd behind him, the close frame emphasises his mimics, his face and mouth distorted by anger, the body language expressing hate and resistance (Figure 34.4).

Tywin: Tyrion, do you wish to confess?
Tyrion: Yes, father. I'm guilty. Guilty. Is that what you want to hear?
Tywin: You admit you poisoned the king?

Figure 34.4 'Guilty of being a dwarf'. (GoT, USA, S04E06, 2014, HBO, YouTube)

Tyrion:	No. Of that, I'm innocent. I'm guilty of a far more monstrous crime. I'm guilty of being a dwarf.
Tywin:	You are not on trial for being a dwarf.
Tyrion:	Oh, yes I am. I've been on trial for that my entire life.

Dinklage won an Emmy for his performance as Tyrion, who is not a cliché media-dwarf but one of the show's most complex characters, acting less 'impaired' than most of the others. Many of these *cripples, bastards, and broken things* (title of S01E04, *Game of Thrones*) lead successfully, not choosing a charismatic approach, as they know how society ticks: *People follow leaders, and they will never follow us. They find us repulsive*, says Varys as a queer advisor who is victim to forced genital mutilation (S05E02). Rather, these leaders work with others, using 'smart power' rather than 'hard power' and coercion, reinforcing a relational view on leadership: leadership is co-created between people (Uhl-Bien & Ospina, 2012) and not something that belongs to an 'able-bodied' person only.

Eventually, in *Game of Thrones*, 'Bran The Broken' is chosen as the ultimate leader. Bran no longer identifies as a man, but as a medium, the 'Three-Eyed Raven', the people's *memory, the keeper of all our stories* (S08E06). His disabled body in a wheelchair, emotionless face and impersonal gaze are in stark contrast to common leader-centric models. The global audience is at a loss, which is promising for leadership learning and development that encourages reflection and personal competence. Apart from individual moral reflection, this topic can be linked to legal efforts that are made across the globe (e.g., the Americans with Disabilities Act [ADA], the German Allgemeines Gleichbehandlungsgesetz [AGG]) that are intended to protect people who experience discrimination on the basis of their ethnic origin or on racist grounds, on the basis of their gender, religion, or ideology and on the basis of a disability, their age, or their sexual identity.

Women in Leadership

Popular culture represents and negotiates various explanations for women's leadership disadvantage and their marginalisation that scholars have outlined (Höpfl, 2007). Scholars have debated that media culture serves to patriarchal cultural norms and structures, and may also provide valuable critiques of gender relations (e.g., Pullen & Rhodes, 2013). An example for the illustration of women that may be complicit in fostering inequality and oppression is *Disclosure*, with Demi Moore, where the female boss sexually harasses a male victim, giving a reason to hostility to women at work (Brewis, 1998; see Chapter 20, Critiquing leadership and gender research through a feminist lens, Chapter 43, Leadership representation). In *Hunger Games,* the rebellion leader Katniss Everdeen (played by Jennifer Lawrence) is, according to the *New York Times*, *one of the most radical female characters to appear in American movies* (Scott & Dargis, 2012), yet reaffirms racialised and gendered tropes by a *performance of not-performing* as a gender ritual that naturalises her femininity, thereby producing an ideal of whiteness and femininity (Dubrofsky & Ryalls, 2014). While Katniss eschews masculine aggressiveness and presents maternal instincts as stereotypical feminine qualities, the female elite soldier *G. I. Jane* (played by Demi Moore) cancels her femininity to succeed in a military organisation, looking and behaving like a man, signalling that there is no other way for a woman to become part of a masculine organisation (Höpfl, 2003). The same story again is open to several readings and has been heralded as a tale of the *triumph of the female character despite her sex* (Youngs, 1999, p. 476), where female embodiment can be transformed and thereby expresses a critique of political and social structures.

Popular culture remains a forum for contemporary debates about leadership. Reflecting our times, women are shown in the top echelons of business and politics. The *Economist*, for example, states: *Women rule Westeros. How strange* (Prospero, 2016), responding to the heated public discussion of misogyny in the popular series *Game of Thrones* that may have caused the screenwriters to change their approach and put women in power positions, acting as queens, military strategists and rebellion leaders. Novels, Broadway productions and other TV series mirror contemporary anxieties; for example, the animated series *Tuca and Bertie* and the women wrestling drama *GLOW feel like a direct response to the #MeToo movement [...] not merely to comfort or inspire but to unsettle* (Nussbaum, 2019).

Popular media can make viewers experience with their senses how some of these mechanisms work socially and aesthetically. For example, the use of gendered language can be presented powerfully. Scholars have theorised that organisation leadership expresses itself with phallic and testicular metaphors (Linstead & Maréchal, 2015). This can be experienced vividly in a scene in *Game of Thrones* (S06E05, available on YouTube), where a woman and a man compete for the leader position (Biehl, 2021b, pp. 43–45). Yara Greyjoy of the Iron Islands (played by Gemma Whelan) appears with whopping credentials, highly qualified, giving a dynamic battle speech and ticking all boxes (commitment, qualifications, achievements) in an impressive perfect setting. Then the energy shifts and she is outmanoeuvred by a man (Euron Greyjoy, played by Pilou Asbæk), who does not have any achievements, but explicitly distinguishes himself by having 'a dick'. The woman fails because she is not a man, reminding us of the presidential race between Hillary Clinton and Donald Trump that has been interpreted by leadership scholars (Ladkin, 2017; see also Chapter 43, Leadership representation). 'Hillary' (who the press and opponents commonly named by her first name only) argued with facts, economic figures and social implications; Trump reiterates simple 'man things': *I will build the wall. I will build the wall.* And he won. Euron gives a short speech with a decidedly satirical quality: there's talk of his 'big penis', of building a 'huge fleet,' of 'seducing' another queen (*I am going to give* [her] *my big cock*). He ends with another phallogocentric metaphor: *Here I staaaand!* The troupe of men responds by euphorically chanting his name and nominating him as the leader. Yara, as a woman without a penis, loses the symbolic confrontation, making viewers experience how gender limits leader career possibilities, when in social reality, it is an obvious divergence to rational analysis (Biehl, 2021b, p.45).

Media scholars suggest using the films to undertake repeated viewings and reflection of personal and social positions, particularly with regard to gender topics (Kamir, 2006). Films can be used for personal reflection and in leadership education for teaching, but also as a starting point for participation in public discourse on topics – such as women in leadership – that refer to TV series and find its arena on Twitter (Robinson, 2015). Audiences and scholars can debate popular culture out of a political or academic motivation to unravel and unsettle gendered norms and drive forward change in the area of gender and leadership.

New Leader Role Models in Reality TV and Instagram

Reality TV as a facet of popular culture has gained increasing popularity and presents us with new role models, offering many forms of identification for audiences (Psarras, 2020). Famous reality TV stars are big in business and stand in a strong contrast to traditional business leaders, entrepreneurs, or managers, who are correct, knowledgeable, in control and mostly white and cis male. For example, business mogul Bethenny Frankel televised her emotional breakdowns (*I need to start drinking alcohol*) and the Kardashians are strong on affective display, emotionality and drama. Frankel is known from Bravo's *The Real Housewives of New York City*, *Bethenny Getting Married?*, *Bethenny Ever After*, as a former runner-up on *The Apprentice: Martha Stewart* and subsequently leading HBO Max's *The Big Shot with Bethenny*, where contestants compete to work for Frankel's lifestyle brand, Skinnygirl. Women in these shows use emotional self-presentation behaviours as *affective entrepreneurship* (Arcy, 2015, p. 82) or *emotional camping* (Psarass, 2020): a mix of 'emotional labour' whereby emotions are produced as a necessary part of the media job, and 'camping', which exaggerates these emotions. Examples include personal misfortunes, trauma from childhood neglect, pain of romantic misadventures, social degradation through business failures, struggles and breakdowns (Frankel, 2011).

These impression management strategies also entail a gendered feminine emotionality that, in popular media, is often close to, or convergent with, anti-feminist thinking, misogyny (the 'hysteric' woman), female degradation (Oulette, 2016), post-feminism and neoliberal ideologies (Arcy, 2015, p. 88). However, these women receive lots of empathy and sympathy, particularly on social media. They serve as role models, inviting fans and followers to emulate their example (Duffy & Pooley, 2019, p. 41).

Other role models include influencers who assertively, emotionally and openly communicate about their feelings and social experiences, including misogyny directed against black women ('misogynoir') and fatphobia. For example, the artist Lizzo may not be a corporate leader, but she is a social leader for many with a huge following. On Instagram, she uses symbols of power from corporate and masculine contexts (jet, Rolls Royce) and asserts herself, occupying a visual space in the public discourse in which people like her are marginalised traditionally (Figure 34.5).

Performances in the media can still be self-directed and calculated as forms of female resistance (Psarras, 2020), and can become potential resources that all viewers can use, when role models change and new available identities emerge. If we are influenced by the media and by how they show 'leadership', all kinds of people who do not correspond to a dominant leader role model can take inspiration from these formats, to interact and connect in new ways that are different from – and critical and subversive against – traditional types of 'leader'.

Figure 34.5 A new role model @Lizzobeeating https://www.instagram.com/p/COGJr33MH7h/

This example also stands up against dominant norms and points to criticisms of mass media productions that often include a discussion of how women and minorities are systematically ignored or relegated to minor roles, or roles that match traditional stereotypes. In leading roles, minorities are still under-represented, and their portrayals are often consistent with traditional stereotypes (Eschholz et al., 2002). This 'cultural typecasting' includes, for example, the (black) criminal, the (Italian) mafia boss, the (Arab) clan boss and the (Turkish) terrorist (German actor Numan Acar as Muslim extremist Haqqani in *Homeland*).

The imagery Lizzo presents helps to situate herself in a white and male-dominated environment as a business leader, but resembles what is trending on social media and Instagram (e.g., @richrussiankids). Individuals show off their wealth, their yachts, their car, their status symbols, go shopping at Louis Vuitton, fly private jets and look down on others (Tams et al., 2021). This is part of the commodity market in late capitalism which thrives off narrations and valuations of luxury products, and benefits from this discourse as a form of 'enrichment' (Boltanski and Esquerre, 2020). Again, this shows both the potential of new imagery and its ambivalent nature, operating within a social discourse that is culturally constituted but always in flux.

CONCLUSIONS

This chapter explored how leaders are represented in popular culture. Many media formats, including film and TV, reproduce misogyny, racism, sexual and political discrimination, while they also unfold a critical potential and offer new leader role models. We have illustrated these debates and also pointed to an important epistemological development in management and leadership studies: it is not only about the intellectual appreciation of the media content and the story, but about the experience of popular culture that reaches people's hearts and minds and influences how we lead and follow. Popular culture is experiential, emotional and aesthetic, offering particular opportunities for leadership theory and education. More specifically, we often do not know what our bodies show to each other. The nuances of gesture, movement, intimacy and performativity visible in popular culture tell us much about the emotions, power and inter-corporeal dynamics that people perceive in different work contexts.

Experiential learning with popular culture also works with fictional and fantasy works, but it requires a framing. For example, the action on screen, on stage, or in a novel, needs to be framed 'as leadership', possibly, but not necessarily, with regard to a defined leadership model.

In a teaching context, the subsequent reflection is guided through readings and group discussion, but can also be done individually in a research situation or for personal development.

Scholars have to accept that transfer of leadership knowledge is not only a formal process involving business schools and corporate work experience, but also happens through (social) media. Famous celebrities in popular media, for example, may shape the ways their target groups (millennials) see and understand leadership and management. This is a thought that is obvious to media scholars, but still alien to most business school leadership research.

Another important conclusion from our chapter is that popular culture potentially enables different ways of thinking about leadership in organisations that subvert both the disciplinary mechanisms that divide up knowledge and the related marginalisation of various knowledge claims. An interdisciplinary perspective that takes seriously popular culture as a form of leadership knowledge can unsettle and enrich the disciplinary organisation of leadership theory. This seems a moral and social imperative today when business school theory 'disciplines' knowledge and has often done a poor job for inclusion and diversity, while popular culture gives screen time to people that have been marginalised in organisations, including women in power, people of colour, queer people and disabled leaders. It is about time to embrace the idea that popular culture and the media can provide new leader models and insightful ideas to the future of leadership.

REFERENCES

Acevedo, B. (2011). The screaming pope: Imagery and leadership in two paintings of Pope Innocent X. *Leadership*, 7(1), 27–50.

Adler, N. (2006). The art of leadership: Now that we can do anything, what will we do? *Academy of Management Learning and Education Journal*, 5(4), 486–499.

Adorno, T. W., & Horkheimer, M. (1947). *Dialektik der Aufklärung*. Querido.

Ang, I. (1985). *Watching Dallas: Soap Opera and the Melodramatic Imagination*. Routledge.

Antonakis, J., Bastardoz, N., Jacquart, P., & Shamir, B. (2016). Charisma: An ill-defined and ill-measured gift. *Annual Review of Organizational Psychology and Organizational Behavior*, 3, 293–319.

Arcy, J. (2015). Affective enterprising: Branding the self through emotional excess. In R. Silverman (Ed.), *The Fantasy of Reality: Critical Essays on The Real Housewives* (pp. 75–92). Peter Lan.

Askey, B. (2018). 'I'd rather have no brains and two balls': Eunuchs, masculinity, and power in Game of Thrones. *Journal of Popular Culture*, 51(1), 50–67.

Badaracco, J. (2006). *Questions of Character: Illuminating the Heart of Leadership Through Literature*. Harvard Business School.

Bass, B. M. (1985). *Leadership and Performance Beyond Expectations*. Free Press.

Bell, E. (2008). *Reading Management and Organization in Film*. Palgrave Macmillan.

Biehl, B. (2020). *Management in der Kreativwirtschaft*. Springer.

Biehl, B. (2021a). 'Dracarys' for all: TV series and experiential learning. *Management Learning*, November https://doi.org/10.1177/13505076211053327

Biehl, B. (2021b). *Leadership in Game of Thrones*. Palgrave Macmillan.

Biehl-Missal, B. (2010). Hero takes a fall: A lesson from theatre for leadership. *Leadership*, 6(3), 279–294.

Boltanski, L., & Esquerre, A. (2020). *Enrichment: A Critique of Commodities*. Trans. C. Porter. Polity.

Brewis, J. (1998). What is wrong with this Picture? Sex and gender relations in disclosure. In J. Hassard & R. Holliday (Eds.), *Organization Representation: Work and Organization in Popular Culture* (pp. 83–100). Sage.

Buchanan, D., & Hällgren, M. (2019). Surviving a zombie apocalypse: Leadership configurations in extreme contexts. *Management Learning*, 50(2), 152–170.

Böhme, G. (1995). Kant's Aesthetics: a New Perspective. *Thesis Eleven*, 43(1), 100–119.

Burnham, J. Augustine, N., & Adelman, K. (1999). *Shakespeare in Charge: The Bard's Guide to Leading and Succeeding on the Business Stage*. Hyperion.

Carroll, S., Kinney, A., & Sapienza, H. (2015). *Effective Teaching for Managers: Lessons from Films*. Emerald.

Champoux, J. (1999). Film as a teaching resource. *Journal of Management Inquiry*, 8(2), 206–217.

Clapton, W., & Shepherd, L. (2017). Lessons from Westeros: Gender and power in Game of Thrones. *Politics*, 37(1), 5–18.

Conger, J. A., & Kanungo, R. N. (1987). Toward a behavioral theory of charismatic leadership in organizational settings. *Academy of Management Review*, 12(4), 637–647.

Corlett, S., Mavin, S., & Beech, N. (2019). Reconceptualising vulnerability and its value for managerial identity and learning. *Management Learning*, 50(5), 556–575.

Craven, B. (2019). *Win Or Die: Leadership Secrets from Game of Thrones*. Thomas Dunne.

Donnelly, C. E. (2016). Re-visioning negative archetypes of disability and deformity in fantasy:

Wicked, Maleficent, and Game of Thrones. *Disability Studies Quarterly*, *36*(4). https://dsq-sds.org/article/view/5313/4470

Dubrofsky, R., & Ryalls, E. (2014). The Hunger Games: Performing not-performing to authenticate femininity and whiteness. *Critical Studies in Media Communication*, *31*(5), 395–409.

Duffy, B., & Pooley, J. (2019). Idols of promotion: The triumph of self-branding in an age of precarity. *Journal of Communication*, *69*(1), 26–48.

Ellis, K. M. (2014). Cripples, bastards and broken things. Disability in Game of Thrones. *M/C Journal*, *17*(5). https://doi.org/10.5204/mcj.895

Eschholz, S., Bufkin, J., & Long, J. (2002). Symbolic reality bites: Women and racial/ethnic minorities in modern film. *Sociological Spectrum*, *22*(3), 299–334.

Frankel, B. (2011) *A Place of Yes. 10 Rules for Getting Everything You Want Out of Life*. New York: Touchstone.

Fuchs, C. (2014). *Social Media: A Critical Introduction*. Sage.

Hartz, R., & Kötschau, S. (2019). Zur Ästhetisierung der Finanzmärkte. Eine explorative Analyse des Films The Wolf of Wall Street. In R. Hartz, W. Nienhüser & M. Rätzer (Eds.), *Ästhetik und Organisation* (pp. 161–188). Springer.

Hassard, J., & Holliday, R. (Eds.) (1998). *Organization-representation: Work and Organizations in Popular Culture*. Sage.

Höpfl, H. (2003). Becoming a (virile) member: Women and the military body. *Body and Society*, *9*(4), 13–30.

Höpfl, H. (2007). The codex, the codicil and the codpiece: Some thoughts on diminution and elaboration in identity formation. *Gender, Work & Organization*, *14*, 619–632.

House, R. J. (1977). A 1976 theory of charismatic leadership. In J. Hunt & L. Larson (Eds.), *The Cutting Edge* (pp. 189–207). Southern Illinois University Press.

Howell, J., & Shamir, B. (2005). The Role of Followers in the Charismatic Leadership Process: Relationships and Their Consequences. *The Academy of Management Review*, *30*(1), 96–112.

Kamir, O. (2006). *Framed: Women in Law and Film*. Duke University Press.

Kuhn, J., Kleiner, M., & Wilke, T. (Eds.) (2013). *Performativität und Medialität Populärer Kulturen*. VS.

Ladkin, D. (2017). How did that happen? Making sense of the 2016 US presidential election result through the lens of the 'leadership moment'. *Leadership*, *13*(4), 393–412.

Ladkin, D., & Taylor, S. (2010). Leadership as art: Variations on a theme. *Leadership*, *6*(3), 235–241.

Ladkin, D., & Taylor, S. (2010) Enacting the 'true self': towards a theory of embodied authentic leadership. *Leadership Quarterly*, 21(1), 64–74.

Learmonth, M., & Morrell, K. (2017). Is critical leadership studies 'critical'? *Leadership*, *13*(3), 257–271.

Linstead, S., & Maréchal, G. (2015). Re-reading masculine organization: Phallic, testicular and seminal metaphors. *Human Relations*, *68*(9), 1461–1489.

llis, K. (2016) *Disability and Popular Culture: Focusing Passion, Creating Community and Expressing Defiance*. Routledge: London.

Mangham, I. (2001). Afterword: Looking for Henry. *Journal of Organizational Change Management*, *14*(3), 295–304.

Martin, G. R. R. (2013). *Media access award for Game of Thrones*. http://www.georgerrmartin.com/media-access-award-for-game-of-thrones/

Mulvey, L. (1975). The male gaze and narrative cinema. *Screen*, *16*(3), 6–18.

Nussbaum, E. (2019). TV's reckoning with #MeToo. *New Yorker*, 3 June. https://www.newyorker.com/magazine/2019/06/03/tvs-reckoning-with-metoo

Oulette, L. (2016). *Lifestyle TV*. Routledge.

Penny, L. (2012). Laurie Penny on Game of Thrones and the good ruler complex. *New Statesman*, 4 June. https://www.newstatesman.com/blogs/tv-and-radio/2012/06/game-thrones-and-good-ruler-complex

Psarras, E. (2020). 'It's a mix of authenticity and complete fabrication'. Emotional camping: The cross-platform labor of the Real Housewives. *New Media & Society*, *24*(6), 1382–1398. doi: 1461444820975025

Pullen, A., & Rhodes, C. (2013). Parody, subversion and the politics of gender at work: The case of Futurama's Raging Bender. *Organization*, *20*(4), 512–533.

Prospero, (2016). Game of Thrones. Women rule westeros. How strange. The Economist, 27. Juni. https://www.economist.com/prospero/2016/06/27/women-rule-westeros-howstrange

Rhodes, C. (2016). Popular culture and management: The provocation of SpongeBob SquarePants. In B. Czarniawska (Ed.), *A Research Agenda for Management and Organization Studies* (pp. 126–135). Edward Elgar.

Robinson, J. (2015). Outcry over rape in Game of Thrones causes creators to change their approach for season. *Vanity Fair*, December. https://www.vanityfair.com/hollywood/2015/12/game-of-thrones-rape-season-6

Ropo, A., & Sauer, E. (2008). Dances of leadership: Bridging theory and practice through an aesthetic approach. *Journal of Management and Organization*, *14*(5), 560–572.

Ryömä, A., & Satama, S. (2019). Dancing with the D-man: Exploring reflexive practices of relational leadership in ballet and ice hockey. *Leadership*, *15*(6), 696–721.

Sahin, R. aka Dr Bitch Ray (2019). *Yalla, Feminismus!* Tropen.

Satama, S. (2020). Researching through experiencing aesthetic moments: 'Sensory slowness' as my methodological strength. In A. Pullen, J. Helin & N. Harding (Eds.), *Writing Differently: Dialogues in Critical Management Studies*, 4, 209–230. Emerald.

Satama, S., Blomberg, A., & Warren, S. (2021). Exploring the embodied subtleties of collaborative creativity: What organisations can learn from dance. *Management Learning*, 53(2), 167–189.

Savage, P., Cornelissen, J., & Franck, H. (2018). Fiction and organization studies. *Organization Studies*, 39(7), 975–994.

Scott, A.O., & Dargis, M. (2012, April 4). A radical female hero from dystopia. *New York Times*. Retrieved from https://www.nytimes.com/2012/04/08/movies/katniss-everdeen-a-new-type-of-woman-warrior.html

Shepherd, L. (2013). *Gender, Violence and Popular Culture: Telling Stories*. Routledge.

Stadler, H. (1990). Film as experience: Phenomenological concepts in cinema and television studies. *Journal Quarterly Review of Film and Video*, 12(3), 37–50.

Stiglegger, M. (2015). *SadicoNazista. Geschichte, Film und Mythos*. Hagen-Berchum: Eisenhut Verlag.

Strati, A. (1992). Aesthetic understanding of organizational life. *Academy of Management Review*, 17(3), 568–581.

Tams, S., Biehl, B., & Eliseev, N. (2021). The inner Louis-Vuitton-circle: An arts-based inquiry into luxury in Russia. *Society*, 58, 406–412. https://doi.org/10.1007/s12115-021-00611-w

Taylor, S., & Hansen, H. (2005). Finding form: Looking at the field of organizational aesthetics. *Journal of Management Studies*, 42(6), 1211–1231.

Taylor, S., & Ladkin, D. (2009) Understanding arts-based methods in managerial development. *Academy of Management Learning and Education*, 8(1), 55–69.

Taylor, S., & Statler, M. (2014). Material matters: Increasing emotional engagement in learning. *Journal of Management Education*, 38(4), 586–607.

The Sopranos: Gary Cooper Compilation (2019). https://www.youtube.com/watch?v=yMqoVxR_mA

Towers, I. (2018). Learning how to manage by watching TV. *International Journal of Organizational Analysis*, 25(2), 242–254.

Townley, B., Beech, N., & McKinlay, A. (2009). Managing in the creative industries: Managing the motley crew. *Human Relations*, 62(7), 939–962.

Tucker, K. (2019). *Best Twitter Reactions about Daenerys Targaryen's Fate in Game of Thrones*. Elle, 20 May. Available at: https://www.elle.com/culture/movies-tv/a27521172/game-of-thrones-finale-daenerys-targaryen-death-best-twitter-reactions/ (accessed 26 September 2022).

Uhl-Bien, M., & Ospina, S. (Eds.) (2012). *Advancing Relational Leadership Research: A Conversation among Perspectives*. Information Age.

Uhl-Bien, M., & Ospina, S. (Eds.) (2012). *Advancing Relational Leadership Research: A Conversation among Perspectives*. Charlotte, NC: Information Age.

Uhl-Bien, M., Riggio, R., Lowe, K., & Carsten, M. (2014). Followership theory: A review and research agenda. *The Leadership Quarterly*, 25(1), 83–104.

Urick, M. J. (2021a). *A Manager's Guide to Using the Force: Leadership Lessons from a Galaxy Far Far Away*. Emerald.

Urick, M. J. (2021b). *Leadership in Middle-Earth: Theories and Applications for Organizations*. Emerald.

Vince, R. (2015). Emotion and learning: An Introduction to the JME curated collection. *Journal of Management Education*, 40(5), 538–544.

Volkmann, L. (2020). 10 Dinge, die ich beim Rewatch von '(T)Raumschiff Surprise' gelernt habe – Volkmanns Popwoche im Überblic. *MusikExpress*, 86. https://www.musikexpress.de/10-dinge-die-ich-beim-rewatch-von-traumschiff-surprise-gelernt-habe-volkmanns-popwoche-im-ueberblick-1619961/

Weldes, J. (1999). Going cultural: Star Trek, state action and popular culture. *Millennium: Journal of International Studies*, 28(1), 117–134.

Youngs, G. (1999). Three readings of GI Jane. *International Feminist Journal of Politics*, 1(3), 476–481.

35

The Impact of Context on Healthcare Leadership

Lester Levy and Kevin B. Lowe

INTRODUCTION

The novel coronavirus pandemic has intensified the unavoidable complexity inherent in health systems. While the pandemic may have unified global health *attention* it has not unified the global health *agenda*. Profoundly different perspectives about what are the most significant global health challenges and how they should be tackled persist. These different perspectives are contingent on the particular lens applied and vary considerably based on a kaleidoscope of contextual factors such as a country's economic prosperity, level of development, nature of governance, philosophy towards social infrastructure and geographical location. An example of these contextual differences can be found in the principal drivers of health morbidity and mortality. In sub-Saharan Africa communicable disease, gastro-intestinal diarrheal disease, respiratory infection and protein-energy malnutrition are the principal causes while in more developed countries non-communicable disease, obesity and addictions are the primary drivers.

Even where common drivers are present and intersect such as epidemic preparedness and response, climate crisis and its health consequences, and antimicrobial resistance the approach to resolution is far from shared. Paradoxically in some parts of the globe health issues arise from malnourishment because of food scarcity while in other parts of the world major health issues such as obesity are a result of food abundance (and poor choices). Likewise in some parts of the world inadequate access to essential, appropriate and safe investigations and treatments is a significant cause of health deficit and death while at the same time other parts of the globe experience problems of overservicing patients with unwarranted investigations and treatments.

Differences in access to and the outcomes from healthcare services are not limited to *between*-country differences. Striking differences in approaches are also prevalent *within* countries resulting in significant inequity of health service access and delivery to specific populations, who consequently experience soberingly divergent health outcomes. These obvious differences form the backdrop as to why it is important to understand the impact of context on health leadership.

In this chapter we seek to establish the importance of understanding contextual issues for those seeking a better understanding of the challenges and possibilities faced by healthcare leaders. As alluded to earlier this may be especially challenging in healthcare as what may be rational behaviour for achieving certain outcomes within a given health subsystem may result in seemingly irrational (or at least highly inefficient) behaviours at the system level. Having established the importance of studying leadership in a healthcare context we next move to a brief review of the broader context literature highlighting aspects of research on context which are highly relevant to healthcare. Next, we seek to situate our discussion of healthcare context within the broader research literature on context. Following this integration, we identify the increasing pace of change in the healthcare context driven by several factors including technological advancement, and further identify how the coronavirus pandemic has tipped the rate of change into what may be regarded as an extreme context in the intermediate term. We conclude by discussing some responses to the accelerating contextual challenges including the need to purposefully recentre leadership development in healthcare away from the specialist leader-centric model to more collective, relationally oriented and contextually connected forms of leadership.

THE IMPORTANCE OF STUDYING LEADERSHIP IN THE HEALTHCARE CONTEXT

It is important to clarify more explicitly what is meant by context in healthcare. A definition with the potential to connect well with healthcare and its bio-science identity is that context denotes an arrangement of all the active variables that could or do influence the independent and dependent variables (Dopson et al., 2008). Within healthcare systems these active variables include a combination of social determinants of health, environmental influences, behavioural patterns and genetic disposition which determine health outcomes for individuals and populations. Healthy populations are typically characterised as having higher well-being indices and are more productive and thereby stimulate stronger and more stable economies. The two primary measures of healthier populations are longevity and quality of life. In this context the global health system is disconcertingly underperforming compared to system potential, with wide health outcome disparities between developed and less developed countries; stagnation of health system performance; high levels of system waste; inappropriately high levels of non-evidence-based practice and stubbornly high rates of adverse events (Berwick & Hackbarth, 2012; Dixon-Woods, 2019; Kitson et al., 2018; Morgan et al., 2019; OECD, 2017; Saini et al., 2017).

Given that accessible, safe, effective and affordable healthcare is so critical to individuals and populations it is essential to understand why health system progress has been so modest.

The main reason health system progress has not transpired, despite active and pervasive interest in improvement across the wider health system, is that healthcare systems are complex adaptive systems (Belrhiti et al., 2018; Stevens et al., 2020). Complex adaptive systems are for the most part non-deterministic and responses cannot be consistently or easily anticipated or predicted. The fundamental mindset shift is from the metaphorical depiction of health systems as mechanical to their characterisation as eco-systems, with unclear and porous boundaries, innate non-linearity, manifold interdependencies and numerous points of control (Petrie & Swanson, 2018; Plsek & Greenhalgh, 2001). The argument advanced for the elusiveness of system improvement is that as a complex adaptive system healthcare does not respond predictably like a machine would and therefore rather than repeatedly pressing on with linear, simplistic, structural and hierarchical performance improvement and change initiatives a more nuanced complexity science approach is required (Belrhiti et al., 2018; Plsek & Greenhalgh, 2001).

Complexity science in healthcare provides a means of understanding non-linearity and is based on the notion that organisations as complex adaptive systems offer new and different ways to think about healthcare leadership (Churruca et al., 2019). It draws on the study and understanding of systems sciences describing the core features and behaviours of complex adaptive systems and how to best deal with them. Advancing a more nuanced complexity science approach will require additional in-depth research about the application of a social complexity perspective to leadership in healthcare settings. In fields outside healthcare there is a comprehensive research agenda into complex leadership but within the healthcare domain the research experience using a complexity leadership lens is limited (Belrhiti et al., 2018). This is despite healthcare systems being recognised as being the most complex of all systems with their undeniable criticality, scale and scope, complex funding and operating models, increasing and uneven demand, disparate outcomes and wide array of stakeholders with widely divergent and frequently conflicting interests (Braithwaite, 2018). In drawing the contrast between making change to a health system's 'hardware' (institutional arrangements, infrastructure and funding models) and 'software' (leadership, culture and operating models) Braithwaite (2018) makes a case for the latter, a perspective we adopt.

Accordingly, our emphasis in this chapter is on the role of shifting the leader's worldview and building additional capabilities and capacities in the leadership development of healthcare governors, managers and professionals.

This appeal for a paradigm shift in the approach to leadership in healthcare contexts is not novel and has been made previously by the leadership scholars Uhl-Bien and Marion (2011). They identify that new foundations for leadership are needed in healthcare settings as the existing model and constructs of leadership are not well aligned to contexts that are especially complex, challenging and subject to relentless change. Given the critical nature of health to all individuals and societies there is an unequivocal global need for high-performing, accessible, safe, modern and financially sustainable health systems, which is currently not the case by a very substantial margin. The level of underperformance of the wider health system coupled with the repetitive tendency to turn to the health system's 'hardware' rather than 'software' for the fix, provides compelling reason for the study of leadership in healthcare. When the research deficit into the relationship between complexity theories and health leadership is carefully considered the importance of studying leadership in healthcare contexts simply becomes intensified.

THEORETICAL PERSPECTIVES OF CONTEXT

While the characteristics of leadership such as clear sense of purpose, authenticity, empathy, influencing, judgement, communication, connection and courage are important so is the context for leadership. Context is vital to leadership and who is seen as providing leadership, the nature of their leadership, the efficacy of that leadership and the wider commitment to it by others will change depending on the context in which that leadership is taking place (Lord & Dinh, 2014). The notion that leadership does not occur in a void was initially promoted by Fiedler (1978) who postulated that better organisational performance outcomes were a result of the balance between a leader's characteristics and situational factors, rather than the characteristics of the leader alone. As noted above using a contextual lens to evaluate leadership is neither new or fresh thinking, but while the need to build context into the development of concepts of leadership has been identified as an important and incomplete area of research, it has not been acted on to the degree called for by leadership scholars (Osborn et al., 2002). This dearth of attention to context in leadership research was highlighted in a comprehensive review by Porter and McLaughlin (2006) which revealed only a modest body of relevant investigation and evaluation of the relationship between context and leadership. While the problematic nature of the leader-centric approach has become better appreciated and interest in context has recently increased within the field of leadership research, the interplay between the constructs of context and leadership remains a significant and incomplete area of research (Gardner et al., 2020).

There is a perspective that in knowledge-intensive environments like health systems the normative or conventional approach to system change and improvement by top-down prescription falls well short of being able to deal with the contextual complexity (Kitson et al., 2018; Uhl-Bien et al., 2007). In this setting a complexity leadership approach is thought to be necessary. Complexity leadership theory is essentially a meta-framework for adaptive leadership and the complexity leadership approach is identified as being necessary because context is integral to shaping leadership (Uhl-Bien et al., 2007; Uhl-Bien & Arena, 2018). Consequently, if those responsible for health system performance are genuinely striving for system improvement they should as a matter of course assume a leadership style and perspective that is more collaborative, connected, attentive, mentoring and generative (Kitson et al., 2018; Uhl-Bien et al., 2007; Uhl-Bien & Arena, 2018). This distinctive contextual leadership approach is far more likely to effectively deal with cornerstone characteristics of complex adaptive systems such as system reluctance to change, ingrained stakeholder philosophies and unyielding cultural characteristics, than a more conventional leadership-centric top-down approach where the mode of change is most frequently structural and mandated (Coiera, 2011, Nugus et al., 2010). Curiously, the research community has not paid enough attention to how health system leaders should tackle complexity which is a key reason why the impact of context in this domain specifically needs deeper consideration and more research (Belrhitietal et al., 2018). In the long run a profound step up in the nature and quantum of research into particularly complex contexts such as healthcare will be required if the knowledge base and understanding of leadership in this crucial area is to be effectively cultivated. Without putting too fine a point on it, this is the context where leadership efficacy may well be the most crucial as healthy individuals and societies are so indispensable to well-being and economic prosperity as has been so plainly revealed by the coronavirus pandemic.

CONTEXT IN HEALTHCARE

It is not really possible to fully understand notions and concepts that have been uncoupled from their context as context confers meaning to what we think and do. A contextual approach to leadership has an insightful understanding and appreciation that leadership is socially constructed and derived from its context and therefore when the context changes, leadership will need to adapt and change as well (Bate et al., 2007; Osborn et al., 2002). In turning to the healthcare literature specifically, research on the impact of context on health leadership lacks depth and according to Porter and McLaughlin (2006) research into the relationship between context and leadership has scarcely touched on the healthcare field. Independent of this, the notion of the interaction of leadership with external and organisational contexts to achieve more effective health system change and performance is gradually becoming better appreciated. Inherent in this notion is the principle that the more context-sensitive healthcare governance and management become, the closer they will get to developing the necessary insights and ideas to facilitate the health system change and improvement they aspire to.

HEALTHCARE AS A COMPLEX AND OPEN SYSTEM

Following on from the argument by Dopson et al. (2008) that context is an arrangement of all the intervening variables, Bate (2014) noted the positivist connotations of this interpretation as having the advantage of helping to move away from a linear, causal, closed system paradigm to one that is more multifaceted, complex and open. Bate (2014) is thoughtful about further considerations about what may be ascribed to the definition of context to give it richer texture and meaning. By way of example, a contextual determinant creates a sense of more strength than a contextual influence and a contextual frame does not signify the same impetus as a contextual force. Language matters as leadership is mediated through culture and symbolism and *change-facilitating language* is intrinsic to culture (Alvesson & Svenigsson, 2015). While the definition of context proposed by Dopson et al. (2008) may be reassuring and accepted in a healthcare environment, it is nonetheless rather literal, austere and less intuitively appealing than a metaphorical depiction of context (Bate, 2014). A prevalent metaphor relating to innovation in social and organisational science is the concept of context as fertile soil and interventions as seeds which when planted in the fertile soil flourish and bloom (Kanter, 1988). The process of cultivation of the flowers realistically depends on aspects of context other than only soil, such as sunlight, water and carbon dioxide for photosynthesis and consistent care and attention to prevent damage from insects, birds and wind, pertinently describing the complex interconnectedness of context (Bate, 2014). In this scenario a whole-systems approach is very helpful as it integrates systems thinking methods and practices to understand healthcare challenges more deeply. Systems thinking is an analytic approach that centres on the interrelation of a system's component parts and helps to develop the whole-systems view of the context of healthcare with its many and diverse influences on leadership. This requires an intricate understanding of the multi-layered internal and external variables as well as their points of intersection and with leadership contingent on context, when context changes leadership will also need to adapt and change (Bate et al., 2007; Hartley & Benington, 2010).

UNSHACKLING LOCAL KNOWLEGDGE AND SOCIAL CAPITAL

These external and internal healthcare contextual variables which present in multiple different combinations include socioeconomic and environmental conditions, natural disasters, legislation and regulation, health policy, markets, funding mechanisms, supply and demand, system design and planning, structure, leadership and culture, care standards, the role of the professions and trade unions, technology and equipment, partnerships and social activism (Hartley & Benington, 2010). Care should be exercised when using the fertile soil metaphor as it is important not to think about context only as a physical space, ignoring the importance of temporal context which is very pertinent in how healthcare organisations operate and evolve (Bate et al., 2007; Dopson et al. 2008; Alipour & Mohammed, 2023; Oc & Carpini, 2023). The soil, macro-climatic factors and intervention metaphor is a very useful reminder of the vital need to turn to local knowledge when dealing with context. This is described by Dixon-Woods (2014) as *practical wisdom* and is replete with important lessons from the past that if considered with an open mind may validate or redirect interventions. This is generally not the case in top-down all-encompassing initiatives which tend to overlook or discount both local knowledge and social capital. Local knowledge and social capital is typically composite and tacit and therefore not able to be easily accessed and shared, but with relational trust and patience it is entirely possible to access these critical local assets (Dixon-Woods, 2014). Despite the metaphorical possibilities the more conventional way of thinking about context in healthcare settings is through a primarily analytic lens with context described in very objective and tangible terms creating a comfortable (but impracticable) sense of being able to deal with it in mechanical and systematic ways.

SENSE-MAKING IN THE HEALTHCARE CONTEXT

There are alternative lenses through which context can be viewed which are aligned to a more constructionist perspective with context being thought of as more of a personal mental image (Van Dijk, 2009). This is an important reflection as the interpretation of context from a leadership perspective is not just to simply focus on what is observable and tangible but rather to integrate the objective with the subjective as a process of sense-making. Counter-intuitively, the reading of context quite conceivably begins with what a leader thinks rather than what they see. Understanding the context is more akin to synthesis than it is to analysis and requires an adaptive rather than technical leadership approach which has material consequences for recruitment, promotion and leadership development within the healthcare sector (Heifetz et al., 2009). They propose that the technical leadership approach is the application of existing understanding and knowledge within the current problem-solving process as opposed to the adaptive leadership approach where the people with the problem find and learn new ways of problem-solving. Appreciation of the more constructionist view of context has further implications as this subjective nature of interpretation will likely mean different actors have different perspectives of the same contextual configuration based on the weights they ascribed to various contextual factors. This reinforces the importance of diversity to resolve the complex paradoxical issues of contemporary healthcare systems. In their work on contextual change Dopson et al. (2008) propose that context is integral to change in healthcare systems and should not be seen as a *back-cloth to action* (p. 213) but as an *interacting element in the diffusion process* (p. 213). This creative depiction of context clarifies that it should be perceived as dynamic rather than static with the point of deeply understanding context in healthcare settings being able to successfully lead improvement and change interventions (Coles et al., 2020; May et al., 2016). The research on context pertinent to intervention identifies two elements that either act as barriers to intervention or facilitators of intervention (May et al., 2016). These elements, known as 'contextual confounders' form part of the everyday nature of practice but are not readily recognised or taken into active consideration as the interventions are planned (May et al., 2016). These contextual confounders play out by being a barrier in certain circumstances and then a facilitator in others, which has important implications for interventions relating to change and improvement in healthcare settings. In particular this level of insight into context creates a practical understanding of how interventions can be successfully scaled, how they fail to embed and why changing established practice is so difficult (May et al., 2016).

SPEED AND EXTENT TO WHICH HEALTHCARE CONTEXTS ARE CHANGING

Contemporary healthcare contexts are increasingly and frequently changing at very rapid rates. The speed and extent to which the complexity of contexts are changing is a critical intensifier of the leadership challenges faced, with health system's leaders having to effectively respond, learn and adapt in progressively shorter time periods. These rapidly changing and complex healthcare contexts are mainly a result of rapid technological advances, new and menacing communicable diseases, severe and worsening environmental impacts and escalating socioeconomic inequities. The concern is that these complex contexts (particularly extreme healthcare contexts) are changing much more quickly than health systems can respond with effective change.

The speed and degree of health system contextual complexity is evidenced by the global coronavirus pandemic, severe impacts of climate crisis, major natural disasters, geopolitical conflicts and socioeconomic failures. Collectively these challenges should serve as a grave warning as well as a catalyst for healthcare practitioners and researchers to significantly step up and become more searching and perceptive about the reality of leading health systems in times of compounding complexity (Uhl-Bien, 2021). There is a persuasive and credible call by Uhl-Bien (2021) for health system leaders and scholars to work together to create an environment where deeper and more meaningful insights into complexity and adaptive leadership can be uncovered and put into practice. In the healthcare context an example of this deeper and more complex perspective is the irony that the most common and costly health conditions (chronic or non-communicable diseases) are the most preventable, yet the health system continues to privilege treatment ahead of prevention. Realistically, the effects of prevention take time to embed and therefore over the next two decades the healthcare system funding landscape needs to progressively shift to a greater emphasis on prevention as the system totally rebalances. The urgent understanding and acceptance of complexity leadership needs to be prioritised as the global health system and its leadership mobilise to create the momentum to effectively deal with this new abnormal. The words of Uhl-Bien (2021) *that things are not and never will be exactly the same* (p. 159) should resoundingly echo throughout the global health system.

EXTREME HEALTHCARE CONTEXTS AS FORMIDABLE CONTEXTUAL LEADERSHIP CHALLENGES

The scale and scope of the coronavirus pandemic has created one of the most complex healthcare contexts and leadership challenges at every level and across multiple dimensions. Curiously, leadership in extreme contexts which requires one of the most sophisticated and fearless adaptive leadership responses happens to be one of the more under-researched topics in leadership (Gladstein & Reilly, 1985; Heifitz & Heifitz, 1994). From a contextual leadership perspective it is important to understand that virtually any context can suddenly and with little or no warning become an extreme context (Buchanan and Hällgren, 2019). According to Hannah et al. (2009) extreme contexts are when there are one or more extreme events happening or likely to happen which could outstrip the organisation or country's capacity to prevent massive physical, psychological and material consequences from known unknowns and unknown unknowns.

Because of their scale, ubiquity and criticality healthcare systems have been subject to a range of very challenging, sudden, extreme and frightening contextual changes including pandemics, critical weather events, cyberattacks, geopolitical conflicts and financial crises. While the coronavirus pandemic is the most evident current example of an extreme healthcare context, particularly in the way it has profoundly disrupted and disabled multiple global systems, there have been other examples of serious communicable disease extreme contexts such as the deadly 1918 Spanish flu pandemic and the HIV/AIDS pandemic that started in the early 1980s. There have also been epidemics that are examples of extreme healthcare contexts such as the polio epidemic of the early 1900s. Perhaps the most devastating example of extreme healthcare contexts will be those caused by the climate crisis and will likely include extreme weather-related injury and death; heat-related new and worsening illnesses; changing patterns of infectious diseases particularly related to waterborne, vector and zoonotic infections such as cholera, malaria and Ebola; as well as the adverse physical and mental health impacts of food and water shortages, mass loss of employment, forced migration and conflict.

It is crucial to make the distinction between an extreme context and a crisis. Although they are related by a shared sense of urgency, uncertainty and a threat to high-priority goals, crisis is more prosaic than an extreme context. While crises and extreme contexts are not the same, it is not only possible but quite likely that the two interact so that a crisis evolves into an extreme context or the converse (Hannah et al., 2009).

Leadership in extreme contexts is the arena where the most compelling and effective leadership needs to be revealed with it being very likely that quite different types of leadership may be required before, during and after an extreme healthcare context event (Hannah et al., 2009). Having said that, the depth of understanding of leadership in extreme contexts is underdeveloped. Leadership in extreme contexts is characteristically contextualised and is not only influenced by the context but also interacts with the context, which has the potential to amplify the degree of extremity (Hannah et al., 2009). Complexity also has a multiplier effect in extreme contexts and may result from few or many elements coalescing into an exceptional blend of unanticipated, simultaneous misadventures (Weick, 1988). The importance of complexity to extreme events should stimulate further and deeper investigation of leadership in extreme and complex contexts (Hannah et al., 2009). The ominous nature of the coronavirus pandemic has placed the entire globe in a very challenging position where sound, perceptive and thoughtful leadership is fundamental to navigate through a very threatening medium-term extreme healthcare context.

THE ACCELERATION OF VIRTUAL LEADERSHIP IN THE HEALTHCARE CONTEXT

The pandemic-induced extreme context has profoundly accelerated the availability and uptake of virtual healthcare and this section considers the particular challenges of virtual healthcare leadership. One of the more immediate and evident changes of the coronavirus pandemic has been the different way large numbers of patients have accessed the healthcare system. Telehealth (virtual consultation) is the more obvious and ubiquitous example of virtual healthcare where patients have been able to be safely treated at home through video-enabled contact. Other virtual healthcare examples that have seen significant uptake include digitally remote monitoring of patients' physiological and physical parameters by a variety of wireless-enabled smart medical devices; virtual intensive care unit and ward rounds; virtual at home postnatal support; virtual prescribing and medication dispensing; and remote triage. There are many advantages of virtual healthcare including decreased exposure of patients, health professionals and support staff to communicable diseases, balancing workload and scaling expertise and capacity. It is unlikely that patients and health professionals will completely return to the non-virtual environment now that they have experienced the ease and convenience of the virtual healthcare models. Therefore, the contextual challenge of leading in the virtual healthcare environment will persist and grow.

The focus is on how leadership is socially constructed in a virtual environment, how information is processed by leaders in virtual healthcare contexts, the required leadership behaviours for indirect leadership effects and how to lead workforces that will continue to change in nature, composition and approach (Schmidt, 2014). The combination of the speed of contextual change in healthcare domains as well as extreme healthcare contexts has promoted the importance of a new contextual feature which is the virtual healthcare team. Virtual teams are a new contextual feature of increasing interest and importance in healthcare, with these communication technology-enabled teams potentially spanning different geographies, time zones, organisations and cultures at the macro- and meso-level and different locations, departments, functions and approaches at the micro-level (Huang et al., 2010).

This new paradigm of working has created a need for effective virtual healthcare leadership and although the existing research base has facilitated some understanding, there is little empirical evidence about the characteristics of effective virtual healthcare leadership (Saltman, 2020). Although virtual teams are now a global phenomenon, substantially accelerated by the coronavirus pandemic, their presence was already slowly but progressively being felt prior to the pandemic (Saltman, 2020). The emergence of the virtual context has had a strong influence over who identifies or is identified as the leader and the manner in which they give effect to their leadership (Lord & Dinh, 2014). Research into virtual leadership has uncovered that the effects of the key elements found in conventional face-to-face leadership are not the same in the virtual context and by way of an example the effect of the hierarchical leadership style is diluted by the virtual context and furthermore, generational and experience differences may manifest in very different ways (Huang et al., 2010; Hoch & Kozlowski, 2014). The regularity and cadence of contact and communication between leaders and followers in the virtual team context has predictably been identified as one of the essential variables (Gajendran & Joshi, 2012; Schmidt, 2014). Another governing variable of the virtual context is the disposition of virtual leadership which will need to adapt as technologies emerge, change and transform. Understanding leading and leadership in the virtual context can be improved by more empirical investigation into how leaders enhance closer and less formal interfaces between virtual team members. More meaningful personal relationships within the virtual context are identified by Hart and McLeod (2003) as an important basis for productivity in this way of working. The fact that the currently available research points to virtual leadership having a number of major differences to face-to-face leadership reinforces the material impact context has on leadership (Lord & Dinh, 2014).

The virtual health context has created a new model for health delivery that needs to be understood in much greater depth in order to more completely uncover the critical nature of this contemporary working context. The speed at which the virtual work environment has become acceptable in healthcare is described as an adaptive response to complexity, with the reason for this rapid response to such a markedly different way of working being identified as generative emergence (Lichtenstein, 2014; Uhl-Bien, 2021; Uhl-Bien & Arena, 2018). The concept of generative emergence is essentially the establishment of novel and different arrangements as a result of the enterprise, creativity, intentionality and collective action of individuals independent of their positional authority (Eva et al., 2021; Lichtenstein, 2016). It is the blend of complexity leadership and generative emergence that enables the rapid response to this new way working with leaders and followers acting in synchrony in response to the forces of complexity (Uhl-Bien, 2021). Leadership in the virtual health context will need to have a very strong, intentional focus on delivering an effective workforce and the development of both theory and research on virtual teams and how they operate in a healthcare context needs to be given a high priority (Huang et al., 2010).

IMPLICATIONS FOR LEADERSHIP DEVELOPMENT IN CHANGING HEALTHCARE CONTEXTS

This section considers the leadership development factors that need to be taken into account in the design of healthcare leadership development programmes that shape leaders with the enhanced capacity to effectively deal with emerging, complex and rapidly changing contexts. A greater understanding of contextual leadership in the healthcare domain will inevitably lead to a number of important implications for and new approaches to leadership development. One of the more important is that the focus of leadership development in healthcare should not be limited to leader-centric development and embraces contextual leadership development (Dinh et al., 2014; Gardner et al., 2010; Oc, 2018). In the leader-centric development model leadership is described as the property of the leader alone, uncoupled from the context in which it takes place. It is doubtful that an uncritical and poorly evaluated perspective of leadership development in the rapidly changing healthcare context will lead to the equipoise required for the effective leadership development needed in these environments (Grint et al., 2009).

This recalibration from *leader* development to *leadership* development is fundamental to leading through the rapid and complex changes associated with extreme, digital and virtual healthcare contexts (Bolden, 2007). A shift in emphasis away from leader-centric development in healthcare hierarchies is recommended on the basis that leadership within health systems cannot be realistically developed without the appropriate consideration of local context and culture (Edmonstone, 2011). The more typical and prevailing leadership development model in the healthcare system places the emphasis on behavioural competencies with the proponents of this method arguing that it provides the necessary structure to develop leaders through the enrichment of their existing personal qualities and behaviours.

There are perspectives that contrast sharply with the competency approach to leadership development, arguing that competencies fragment rather than integrate leadership and consequently subvert the importance of context, thereby strengthening rather than challenging the conventional approach to leadership (Carroll et al., 2008; Edmonstone, 2011). Competencies are described by Carroll et al. (2008) as being unanchored in relationships and context while leadership conceived as practice is located in context, discouraging individuals from acting and performing in isolation of both others and context. This counterpoint to the competency framework approach to leadership in healthcare is supported by the work of Bolden and Gosling (2006) and Bolden (2007), who challenge the simplistic approach of leadership competencies, particularly the way in which they fail to recognise the true importance of context in leadership and also the way in which they tend to diminish nuanced interfaces and contextual factors. The leadership as practice alternative places emphasis on the dimensions of leadership that are more relevant to context and essentially invalidates the competency paradigm as a machine-like constraint (Bolden, 2007; Bolden & Gosling 2006; Carroll et al., 2008). If the leadership that is necessary to meet the contextual challenges in healthcare is to become a lived experience, then a consideration of the leadership as practice perspective or some other more context aligned approach to leadership development should be seriously and urgently contemplated. The approach to leadership and leadership development by Raelin (2004) and also Bolden and Kirk (2006) support this approach by maintaining that the development of a small cohort of individuals in relative isolation is most unlikely to result in successful leadership outcomes in very challenging circumstances. This alternative approach to leadership places the development emphasis on the leadership process as highly relational, socially constructed, collective and context-sensitive with an acceptance that these contexts are not only complex but also uncertain where not everything can and will be known (Bolden, 2004; Day, 2001; Edmonstone, 2011).

The nature of leadership development required for complex health contexts which are undergoing rapid change will require the development of refined influencing capacities, including consummate political awareness to allow situations and contexts to be understood and uncoded so that the required alliances and social networks can be constructed (Hartley et al., 2008). When reflecting on the evolving analysis and appraisal of leader-centric development, Edmonstone (2011) highlighted how this has created an asymmetrical emphasis on a mode of leadership development that, particularly in the context of radical healthcare change, is unlikely to create successful comes. An unfortunate consequence of the lack of balance between leader and leadership development has been the under-development of social capital which is a practice and research issue that should have a higher profile than it does. The assumption that developing individual leaders will in time also lead to the enhancement of social capital does not appear to be well founded. Rather than creating a rift between leader development and leadership development in healthcare, Edmonstone (2011) suggests taking a balanced approach with the acknowledgement that by developing leadership in an embracing way, individual leaders will also be cultivated and through the development of social capital, individual human capital will also be generated.

THE NEED FOR FRAME-BREAKING

Health systems have been so impervious to change it seems conceivable that the quote, *Every system is perfectly designed to get the results it gets* originated in the domain of healthcare. While this quote has been attributed to many thought leaders in the world of quality improvement (including healthcare), it turns out to have originated in 1982 from a United Kingdom-based Procter and Gamble executive, Arthur Jones; in its original form it was, *All organizations are perfectly designed to get the results they get* (p. 36). With this perceptive quote in mind the languid pace of effective health system change and improvement has been proposed to be the net effect of system-induced inertia which translates as the tendency for the system to continue doing what it did before, irrespective of changing conditions (Coiera, 2011). It is clearly spelt out by Coiera (2011) that complex systems do not simply change as a result of a top-down predetermined scheme of reform or change. This is because a system that is overly constrained by contesting and even opposing demands has very limited adaptive capacity to accommodate successful change interventions, no matter how rational and well-intentioned they are.

It seems inevitable that in the absence of a frame-breaking change the past will continue to repeat itself and the wider health system will be unlikely to be liberated and reinvented in a form with more potential to deliver on the widely held aspiration for change and improvement. We suggest that a refined and composite understanding, appreciation and implementation of contextual leadership in healthcare is key to overcoming the current healthcare system stasis and releasing it from the particular recurring and unhelpful pattern it has become stuck in. The essence of this contextual leadership in healthcare is a changed mindset where things are seen as they are rather than how the healthcare actors would like them to be. A cognitive grasp of the importance and relevance of contextual leadership to healthcare is entirely insufficient on its own and needs to be tightly complemented with an equally refined capacity for implementation. As a thought experiment, we propose a potential frame-break which is the overlapping concept of deeply understanding contextual leadership in a healthcare setting and then implementing it effectively. While this potential frame-break may appear overly simple it could conceivably act as a critical enabler to break from the prevailing conventional leadership approach in healthcare which for the most part is context-insensitive and its adoption would be likely to profoundly change the healthcare system for the better. In suggesting this frame-break as a thought experiment we are guided by the words of Oscar Wilde, *Life is not complex. We are complex. Life is simple and the simple thing is the right thing* (p. 66).

An authentic contextualised leadership frame-breaking approach in healthcare will likely result in more genuine, pragmatic and effective approaches to change and improvement as exemplified by a thoughtfully constructed; co-designed; appropriately resourced; locally derived and delivered micro-reform backed by patience and endurance. This is in contrast to the more currently pervasive, conventional, top-down, somewhat impractical macro-reform or imposed change programme characterised by unrealistically short implementation time frames and a contest for resources. This theoretical micro-reform approach in healthcare represents an inverted or flipped approach compared to the more conventional top-down or pre-scribed approach. From a purely conceptual point of view this would not be too unlike the flipped classroom approach in education which aims to promote student engagement, self-directed learning and prioritisation of teaching time to where it can add the most value. In the healthcare context the objective of the flipped model would be to engage with local knowledge and social capital, create the conditions for locally generated and implemented solutions and prioritise governance and senior management time to where they could add the most value. In this flipped model the likely outcome for health governors and managers is that they uphold rather than hold up the forces for change and innovation by promoting insight above oversight and generativity over scrutiny.

The inverted or flipped model in healthcare as a frame-breaker has wider possibilities in solving other deeply entrenched problems in healthcare. Medical doctors are taught and acculturated to act as the patient's (singular) advocate whereas the healthcare system acts for the greatest good for the most people and therefore acts as the patients' advocate (plural) (Bujak, 2003). This *problem of the apostrophe* exemplifies the pivotal and powerful ethical dilemma that inadvertently tends to separate doctors from the healthcare system. It appears logical from a health system perspective to think more systematically about resources and that those allocated to one area are resources no longer available to be allocated elsewhere (Bujak, 2003). Frequently, well-meaning system approaches and new initiatives are perceived as wanting the doctor to serve as the patients' (plural) advocate rather than the patient's advocate (singular). Each of these positions is attended by a separate and equally valid set of ethics but it is not easy to operate in both systems simultaneously, especially when doctors are held individually accountable and liable for an individual patient's outcome (Bujak, 2003). They are also responsible for their own liability insurance which further reinforces the *problem of the apostrophe*. This dilemma, typified by the placement of the apostrophe, is at the root of many difficult choices that confront doctors in times of limited resources, crises and extreme contexts and is a critical reason that doctor engagement is so challenging for health systems. Conceivably in a flipped model the system can take full responsibility for the liability insurance and share much more in the responsibility for patient outcomes. Instead of a somewhat limited either/or approach it can become a more purposeful both/and approach with the problem of the apostrophe being resolved by both doctors and the system acting together as the patient's (singular) and patients' (plural) advocate.

In reference to the point previously made about the under-development of social capital in healthcare contexts, it is interesting to note that the power of health professional cultures as a critical contextual factor has a curiously lower research profile in this domain than would be expected. Due to very strong professional cultures in healthcare systems power has traditionally been ascribed to those holding the deepest level of person specific technical knowledge rather than the deepest level of relational capital from which system-level knowledge can be drawn. Dopson et al. (2008) describes genuine authority in health systems as residing more with health professionals than with management. If there is to be a frame-breaking shift to a more collective, relationally oriented and contextually connected form of leadership in healthcare to overcome the inertia to change then, as Dopson et al. (2008) suggest, the substantial *power of the professional subsystem* (p. 229) should be acknowledged, well understood and *handled explicitly* (p. 229). This clinical subsystem within the health system is not homogeneous and conspicuous differences in the perception and distribution of occupational power between different occupational healthcare groups have been revealed, with a distinctive pattern of power by medical doctors over other occupational groups (Nugus et al., 2010). The latter is a result of a combination of characteristics that are somewhat unique to health systems. Nugus et al. (2010) describe the presence of both competitive and collaborative power in the interplay between health professional groups and also management. Building on an earlier theme we suggest that new models and approaches to collaborative power and power dynamics more generally be considered as potential frame-breaking opportunities to overcome health system inertia through more collective and relational approaches. The under-examined contextual role of professional (clinical) power within the health system, its social structure and the degree to which its underlying philosophy and approach is responsible for healthcare system stasis is another fertile avenue to be prioritised for further research.

These theoretical frame-breaking concepts along with others will need to be subject to investigation and trial to develop an informed and empirical basis for health system governors and managers to integrate into their health system leadership. It is axiomatic that it will be important for health system governors and managers to have an enriched insight into the value of contextual leadership which explicitly includes an advanced understanding and application of the constructs of complex adaptive systems, complexity science, complexity leadership and generative emergence.

CONCLUSION

In drawing the various themes of this chapter together it is clear that context matters for leadership in all systems and with healthcare systems identified as the most complex of all systems it is logical that healthcare contexts matter a great deal for healthcare leadership. Notwithstanding the worldwide criticality of healthcare systems to people and populations, health system change has not been anywhere near fast or effective enough to keep up with the speed of contextual change resulting in regrettable system underperformance (Berwick & Hackbarth, 2012; Dixon-Woods, 2019; Kitson et al., 2018; Morgan et al., 2019; OECD, 2017; Saini et al., 2017).

Understanding the mode of leadership that does not work for health system change is helpful but what is more important is knowing what type of contextual leadership mode is likely to work. Dopson and Mark (2003) have proposed a plausible 'pluralistic' notion of effective healthcare system leadership where the leadership paradigm is collective; covenants explicitly with professional (clinical) power; surfaces and works with the complex social relationships; embraces talents from all dimensions; and fosters different perspectives. This concept of pluralism has been further developed by Uhl-Bien (2021) who proposes that effective contextual leadership is generated through the joint actions of leaders and followers, reinforcing the point made earlier that a leader-centric approach in the increasingly complex healthcare context will not deliver the results necessary for health system change and improvement. These approaches of Dopson and Mark (2003) and Uhl-Bien (2021) recognise and integrate the criticality of contextual confounders; local knowledge and social capital; diversity and inclusion; professional (clinical) engagement; adaptive leadership; a 'software' rather than a 'hardware' fix and a development model focused on leadership rather than the leader (Bolden and Gosling, 2006; Braithwaite, 2018; Carroll et al., 2008; Dixon-Woods, 2014; Dopson & Mark, 2003; Heifitz et al., 2009; May et al., 2016; Uhl-Bien, 2021). The conventional non-contextual health system leadership model generally does not privilege the elements that constitute the approaches proposed by Dopson and Mark (2003) and Uhl-Bien (2021). By way of example we interpret the conceptualisation by Uhl-Bien (2021) that effective contextual leadership is generated through the joint actions of leaders and followers as leaders leading and followers following admixed with followers leading and leaders following. Effectively who leads and who follows at a particular point in time is based on whatever make sense contextually and not on what is predicated by hierarchy.

Context has a very important impact on healthcare leadership and with changed paradigms and approaches to health system leadership, leadership development and culture it is possible to start to close the gap between the health system speed of change and the contextual speed of change. This appears unlikely without global health system governance and management as well as the leadership scholarly community jointly addressing the limited and inconsistent literature about the relationship between healthcare contexts and healthcare leadership (Coles et al., 2020). More advanced investigation to deconstruct the role of context in healthcare leadership and more deeply investigate its qualities is recommended as a research imperative to be progressed widely and with resolve.

The pressure on and in the healthcare system is building and intensifying as it faces a likely future of aging populations and their impact on both patient load and health workforce availability, more intimidating communicable diseases, potentially devastating antimicrobial resistance, threatening health effects of the climate crisis and distressing health impacts of socioeconomic inequities. It is fairly clear what outcomes are needed from the global healthcare system and that these have not been delivered. This is the time to break the mould and reconceptualise the system by way of a frame-breaking effective contextual leadership.

Health system governors, managers and professionals are not powerless and should not simply be passive recipients of their healthcare context. They need to be alert to it, observant of it, understand it deeply and respond strategically and adaptively to it. Furthermore, by acting collectively and collaboratively with creativity and innovation they can modify and modulate critical aspects of their specific healthcare context. If context continues to be a leadership blind spot for healthcare governors, managers and professionals then their prevailing paradigms will prevent them from having the most relevant, informed and open-minded perspective of how to lead in the most effective way and that would be a tragedy of the commons for the global health system and the people and populations that depend on it.

REFERENCES

Alipour, K.A., & Mohammed, S. (2023). Temporal considerations in leadership and followership. Sage Handbook of Leadership. In Schedlitzki, D., Bligh, M., Carroll, B., Epitropaki, O. & Larsson, M. (Eds.), California, Sage.

Alvesson, M., & Sveningsson, S. (2015). *Changing Organizational Culture: Cultural Change Work in Progress*. Routledge.

Bate, P. (2014). Context is everything. *Perspectives on Context*. Health Foundation, November, 3–29.

Bate, P., Mendel, P., & Robert, G. (2007). *Organizing for Quality: The Improvement Journeys of Leading Hospitals in Europe and the United States*. CRC Press.

Belrhiti, Z., Nebot Giralt, A., & Marchal, B. (2018). Complex leadership in healthcare: A scoping review. *International Journal of Health Policy and Management*, 7(12), 1073–1084.

Berwick, D. M., & Hackbarth, A. D. (2012). Eliminating waste in US health care. *Journal of the American Medical Association*, 307(14), 1513–1516.

Bolden, R. (2007). *A Yearning for the Vast and Endless Sea: From Competence to Purpose in Leadership Development*. Centre for Leadership Studies, University of Exeter.

Bolden, R., & Gosling, J. (2006) 'Leadership competencies: Time to change the tune?', *Leadership*, 2(2), 147–63.

Bolden, R., & Kirk, P. (2006), From 'leaders' to 'leadership'. *Effective Executive*, October.

Braithwaite, J. (2018). Changing how we think about healthcare improvement. *British Medical Journal*, 361.

Buchanan, D. A., & Hällgren, M. (2019). Surviving a zombie apocalypse: Leadership configurations in extreme contexts. *Management Learning*, 50(2), 152–170.

Bujak, J. S. (2003). How to improve hospital–physician relationships. *Frontiers of Health Services Management*, 20(2), 3.

Carroll, B., Levy, L., & Richmond, D. (2008). Leadership as practice: Challenging the competency paradigm. *Leadership*, 4(4), 363–379.

Churruca, K., Pomare, C., Ellis, L. A., Long, J. C., & Braithwaite, J. (2019). The influence of complexity: A bibliometric analysis of complexity science in healthcare. *BMJ Open*, 9(3).

Coiera, E. (2011). Why system inertia makes health reform so difficult. *British Medical Journal*, 342.

Coles, E., Anderson, J., Maxwell, M., Harris, F. M., Gray, N. M., Milner, G., & MacGillivray, S. (2020). The influence of contextual factors on healthcare quality improvement initiatives: A realist review. *Systematic Reviews*, 9(1), 1–22.

Day, D. (2001), Leadership development: A review in context. *Leadership Quarterly*, 11(4), 581–613.

Dinh, J. E., Lord, R. G., Gardner, W. L., Meuser, J. D., Liden, R. C., & Hu, J. (2014). Leadership theory and research in the new millennium: Current theoretical trends and changing perspectives. *Leadership Quarterly*, 15, 36–62.

Dixon-Woods, M. (2014). The problem of context in quality improvement. *Perspectives on Context*. Health Foundation, 87–101.

Dixon-Woods, M. (2019). How to improve healthcare improvement: An essay by Mary Dixon-Woods. *British Medical Journal*, 367.

Dopson, S., Fitzgerald, L., & Ferlie, E. (2008). Understanding change and innovation in healthcare settings: Reconceptualizing the active role of context. *Journal of Change Management*, 8(3–4), 213–231.

Dopson, S., & Mark, A. (Eds.) (2003). *Leading Healthcare Organisations*. Palgrave Macmillan.

Edmonstone, J. (2011). Developing leaders and leadership in health care: A case for rebalancing? *Leadership in Health Services*, 24(1), 8–18.

Eva, N., Cox, J. W., Herman, H. M., & Lowe, K. B. (2021). From competency to conversation: A multi-perspective approach to collective leadership development. *Leadership Quarterly*, 32(5), 101346.

Fiedler, F. E. (1978). The contingency model and the dynamics of the leadership process. In L. Berkowitz (Vol. Ed.), *Advances in Experimental Social Psychology. Vol. 11.* (pp. 59–96). Academic Press.

Gajendran, R. S., & Joshi, A. (2012). Innovation in globally distributed teams: The role of LMX, communication frequency, and member influence on team decisions. *Journal of Applied Psychology*, 97(6), 1252.

Gardner, W. L., Lowe, K. B., Meuser, J. D., Noghani, F., Gullifor, D. P., & Cogliser, C. C. (2020). The leadership trilogy: A review of the third decade of the leadership quarterly. *Leadership Quarterly*, 31(1), 101379.

Gardner, W. L., Lowe, K. B., Moss, T. W., Mahoney, K. T., & Cogliser, C. C. (2010). Scholarly leadership of the study of leadership: A review of the *Leadership Quarterly*'s second decade, 2000–2009. *Leadership Quarterly*, 21, 922–958.

Gladstein, D. L., & Reilly, N. R. (1985). Group decision-making under threat: The tycoon game. *Academy of Management Journal*, 28, 613–627.

Grint, K., Martin, G., Wensley, R., Doig, G., Gray, P., & Martlew, C. (2009). *Leadership in the Public Sector in Scotland*. Economic & Social Research Council.

Hanna, D. P. (1988). *Designing organizations for high performance* (Vol. 12693). Prentice Hall.

Hannah, S. T., Uhl-Bien, M., Avolio, B. J., & Cavarretta, F. L. (2009). A framework for examining leadership in extreme contexts. *Leadership Quarterly*, 20(6), 897–919.

Hart, R. K., & McLeod, P. L. (2003). Rethinking team building in geographically dispersed teams: One message at a time. *Organizational Dynamics*, 4(31), 352–361.

Hartley, J., & Benington, J. (2010). *Leadership for Healthcare*. Policy Press.

Hartley, J., Martin, J., & Benington, J. (2008). *Leadership in Healthcare: A Review of the Literature for Health Care Professionals*. Managers and Researchers, Institute of Governance & Public Management, University of Warwick.

Heifetz, R. A., & Heifetz, R. (1994). *Leadership Without Easy Answers* (Vol. 465). Harvard University Press.

Heifetz, R. A., Heifetz, R., Grashow, A., & Linsky, M. (2009). *The Practice Of Adaptive Leadership: Tools and Tactics for Changing your Organization and the World*. Harvard Business Press

Hoch, J. E., & Kozlowski, S. W. (2014). Leading virtual teams: Hierarchical leadership, structural supports, and shared team leadership. *Journal of Applied Psychology*, 99(3), 390.

Huang, R., Kahai, S., & Jestice, R. (2010). The contingent effects of leadership on team collaboration in virtual teams. *Computers in Human Behavior*, *26*, 1098–1110.

Kanter, R. M. (1988). When a thousand flowers bloom: Structural, collective, and social conditions for innovation in organizations. *Knowledge Management and Organisational Design*, *10*(1), 93–131.

Kitson, A., Brook, A., Harvey, G., Jordan, Z., Marshall, R., O'Shea, R., & Wilson, D. (2018). Using complexity and network concepts to inform healthcare knowledge translation. *International Journal of Health Policy and Management*, *7*(3), 231.

Lichtenstein, B. B. (2014). *Generative Emergence: A New Discipline of Organizational, Entrepreneurial and Social Innovation*. Oxford University Press.

Lichtenstein, B. B. (2016). Complexity science at a crossroads: Exploring a science of emergence. *Academy of Management Proceedings* (1, p. 12259). Academy of Management.

Lord, R. G., & Dinh, J. E. (2014). What have we learned that is critical in understanding leadership perceptions and leader-performance relations? *Industrial and Organizational Psychology: Perspectives on Science and Practice*, *7*(2), 158–177.

May, C. R., Johnson, M., & Finch, T. (2016). Implementation, context and complexity. *Implementation Science*, *11*(1), 1–12.

Morgan, D. J., Dhruva, S. S., Coon, E. R., Wright, S. M., & Korenstein, D. (2019). 2019 update on medical overuse: a review. *JAMA Internal Medicine*, *179*(11), 1568–1574.

Nugus, P., Greenfield, D., Travaglia, J., Westbrook, J., & Braithwaite, J. (2010). How and where clinicians exercise power: Interprofessional relations in health care. *Social Science & Medicine*, *71*(5), 898–909.

Oc, B. (2018). Contextual leadership: A systematic review of how contextual factors shape leadership and its outcomes. *Leadership Quarterly*, *29*(1), 218–235.

Oc, B., & Carpini, J.A. (2023). How and why is context important in leadership? Sage Handbook of Leadership. In Schedlitzki, D., Bligh, M., Carroll, B., Epitropaki, O. & Larsson, M. (Eds.), California, Sage.

OECD (2017). *Tackling Wasteful Spending on Health*. OECD.

Osborn, R. N., Hunt, J. G., & Jauch, L. R. (2002). Toward a contextual theory of leadership. *Leadership Quarterly*, *13*(6), 797–837.

Petrie, D. A., & Swanson, R. C. (2018). The mental demands of leadership in complex adaptive systems. *Healthcare Management Forum*, *31*(5), 206–213.

Plsek, P. E., & Greenhalgh, T. (2001). The challenge of complexity in health care. *British Medical Journal*, *323*(7313), 625–628.

Porter, L. W., & McLaughlin, G. B. (2006). Leadership and the organizational context: Like the weather? *Leadership Quarterly*, *17*(6), 559–576.

Raelin, J. (2004), Don't bother putting leadership into people. *Academy of Management Executive*, *18*, 131–135.

Saini, V., Garcia-Armesto, S., Klemperer, D., Paris, V., Elshaug, A. G., Brownlee, S., Ioannidis, J. P. & Fisher, E. S. (2017). Drivers of poor medical care. *The Lancet*, *390*(10090), 178–190.

Saltman, D. C. (2020). Is Covid-19 an opportunity to improve virtual leadership. *Australian Journal of General Practice*, *49*, 12.

Schmidt, G. B. (2014). Virtual leadership: An important leadership context. *Industrial and Organizational Psychology*, *7*(2), 182–187.

Stevens, J. P., O'Donoghue, A., Horng, S., Tandon, M., & Tabb, K. (2020). Healthcare's earthquake: Lessons from complex adaptive systems to develop Covid-19-responsive measures and models. *NEJM Catalyst Innovations in Care Delivery*, *1*(5).

Uhl-Bien, M. (2021). Complexity leadership and followership: Changed leadership in a changed world. *Journal of Change Management*, *21*(2), 144–162.

Uhl-Bien, M., & Arena, M. (2018). Leadership for organizational adaptability: A theoretical synthesis and integrative framework. *Leadership Quarterly*, *29*(1), 89–104.

Uhl-Bien, M. & Marion, R. (2011). Complexity leadership theory. In A. Bryman, D. Collinson, K. Grint, B. Jackson & M. Uhl-Bien (Eds.), *The SAGE Handbook of Leadership* (pp. 468–482). Sage.

Uhl-Bien, M., Marion, R., & McKelvey, B. (2007). Complexity leadership theory: Shifting leadership from the industrial age to the knowledge era. *Leadership Quarterly*, *18*(4), 298–318.

Van Dijk, T. A. (2009). Critical discourse studies: A sociocognitive approach. *Methods of Critical Discourse Analysis*, *2*(1), 62–86.

Weick, K. E. (1988). Enacted sensemaking in crisis situations [1]. *Journal of Management Studies*, *25*(4), 305–317.

Wilde, O. (2007). *Epigrams of Oscar Wilde*. Wordsworth Editions.

PART 5

But: A Critical Examination of Leadership

36

On Destructive Leadership

Laura G. Lunsford and Art Padilla

INTRODUCTION

All leaders try to shape their environments, of course, and many succeed. In fact, important markers of effective leaders include three items:

- ability to adapt to their environments but also to change them;
- skill in building and retaining effective teams; and
- inclination to persist and persevere (often in extraordinary ways) in the face of great odds, in achieving their organisational goals.

It is in the nature and form of these goals, and in the absence or presence of checks and balances, that the difference between destructive and constructive lies. Destructive leaders have personalised goals, consistent with their spiteful and negative worldviews. Their objectives are developed in the absence of appropriate group consensus and without countervailing influences or without the vibrant participation of empowered followers (Buchholz et al., 2020; Conger, 1990). Coercion and force are invariably necessary and present in destructive leadership episodes. Contrariwise, constructive leaders tend to have socialised goals, developed in consonance with followers and in the presence of effective organisational controls and balances. Motivation and persuasion ultimately control in constructive episodes (Gottfredson & Aguinis, 2017).

The roles of colluding and conforming followers are also clear in destructive leadership episodes (Offerman, 2004). No matter how clever or devious, destructive leaders alone cannot cause organisational harm. To be sure, an abusive manager or leader can harm employees in the short term. But such abuse begs the question of why such individuals are allowed to remain in their positions. Is it a failure of a board of directors? Is it a hiring problem? Are the checks and balances that would offset or get rid of a despot too weak? Why are toxic leaders allowed to victimise followers in certain organisations but not in others? In spite of these universal questions, traditional leadership studies largely ignore both the colluding and conforming followers and the conducive environments that permit lousy leaders to persist.

As important as it is, the environment is perhaps the least studied area of destructive leadership and of leadership more generally (Avolio, 2007). Political science scholars have paid the most attention to environmental factors in leadership, generally in the context of individual political power

(Burns, 1978, 2003). Organisational behaviour scholars have at times examined the environment, but they generally have paid much more attention to the 'behaviour' and much less to the 'organisation' (Mackey et al., 2019). Most research has been quite leader-centric, focusing principally on leader behaviours and traits. To a lesser extent, some research has looked at followers, but generally this research on followers derives because of what leaders do (Craig and Kaiser, 2013).

Given these prefatory observations, we attempt in this chapter to do four things. We first review recent literature to summarise the different approaches in defining and studying destructive leadership. The ideas that leadership is person rather than a process, and that leadership is always a positively valued activity are examined in this review. Second, we make sense of destructive leadership by identifying its unique characteristics using the toxic triangle approach. Third, previous approaches used to study leadership are examined and areas for future investigation are suggested. Finally, implications for individuals and organisations are discussed.

LITERATURE

The content of review articles on destructive leadership has not changed much in recent years. When authors use the term 'destructive leadership', they are still mostly referring to behavioural constructs, such as abusive supervision, petty tyranny, or supervisor undermining (Mackey et al., 2021). In this section we highlight influential definitions of destructive leadership before proceeding to address two key themes that warrant clarification in the destructive leadership literature: leader-centrism and leadership as a positively valued concept.

Much of the recent literature on destructive leadership can be traced to Einarsen and colleagues' (2007) conceptual model of destructive leadership (DL). They defined DL as leader behaviour that undermines the organisation and or their subordinates. This model focused on leader and subordinate behaviours.

A theoretical review of DL built on this work by adding *intentionality* to the definition, such that destructive leadership referred to volitional leader behaviours that interfere with the organisation's goals (Krasikova et al., 2013). These scholars acknowledged that leadership is a process between leaders and followers that unfolds over time. Mackey and colleagues' (2019) also endorsed this definition of DL in their meta-analysis of destructive leadership. They found evidence that destructive leaders had a linear rather than curvilinear influence on followers.

The distinction about intentionality is important and not universally accepted. For example, Fraher's case study (2016) of the Bristol Royal Infirmary in the United Kingdom finds that well-intentioned leaders engaged in behaviours that contributed to destructive leadership.

Schyns and Schilling (2013) argued that destructive leader behaviour should be differentiated from destructive leadership. Their meta-analysis on destructive leadership found that destructive leader behaviour is associated with counter-productive work behaviour and other negative outcomes. They specifically noted that they could not consider the environment in their analysis as none of the available studies included the organisational context.

Krasikova and colleagues later highlighted a need for research to address the *broader social contexts* (2013, p. 1330) of DL and a lack of consensus that DL involves intentional behaviour (Krasikova et al., 2013). Mackey and colleagues (2021) sought to clarify the nomological net of DL constructs. They reported that abusive supervision was the most studied of the 13 styles of DL identified in the literature. Their comprehensive meta-analysis provided evidence that most studies examine follower perceptions rather than the effect leaders have on followers and organisations.

To this later point, Schilling (2009) interviewed 42 mostly male managers to identify how followers perceive negative leadership. Similarly, but notably in a non-Western context, Shaw and colleagues (2014) examined follower perceptions of leaders in Iran to develop a typology of destructive leaders. Pelletier (2010) also examined follower perceptions to identify the set of behaviours performed by leaders perceived as destructive. All of these studies focused on follower perceptions rather than leader behaviours or the effect of destructive leaders on organisational outcomes.

We agree with Mackey and colleagues' recommendation that future research needs to consider the *full experience of destructive leadership, which encompasses leaders, followers, and organizations* (2021, p. 715). Destructive leadership is, we suggest, best understood as a process that involves a flawed leader and susceptible followers interacting in a facilitating context or environment and resulting in relatively poor outcomes for the group (Padilla et al., 2007; Padilla & Lunsford, 2013). The response of some categories of followers may be entirely different from those belonging to another type of followers. Certain leader behaviours may be well suited to particular environments or followers but not to others – for example, decisive or autocratic leader actions may be useful in a firefight; followers in transparent and empowering environments are much less likely to submit to or tolerate a flawed leader's abuse. Further, destructive leadership is ultimately discerned by examining organisational outcomes that leave the organisation worse off than its peers, including in extreme cases the total destruction of the group or organisation.

Leader-centrism

Semantics are relevant in appreciating the process of leadership. People struggle to understand the difference between leader and leadership, but they seem to understand the distinction between a manager and the process of management.

Despite increasing calls to view leadership as a process (Avolio, 2007; Williams, 2014), there continues to be confusion between a leader and leadership. Landay and colleagues (2019) provide an illustrative example of this semantic confusion where they examined psychopathy in relationship to *leadership emergence, leadership effectiveness* (p. 183) rather than to *leader* emergence or effectiveness. Using the word 'leadership' for the term 'leader' complicates the understanding of leadership as a broader process.

Most of the scholarly destructive leadership literature, despite calls for broader approaches, also remains primarily leader-centric, whether it's about abusive supervision, petty tyranny, or supervisor undermining (Kant et al., 2013; Mackey et al., 2021; Tepper et al., 2017). It's about what leaders do. Even within this narrow focus of analysis, few studies have even tried to examine why some workers are affected while others have not apparently been affected or why some organisations permit the abuse while others don't seem to allow it as a matter of course. The literature is largely silent on differences in search processes and on organisational or cultural differences that allow the abuse to persist. When authors use the term 'destructive leadership', they're still mostly referring to behavioural constructs, such as abusive supervision, petty tyranny, supervisor undermining, etc. as noted above.

The dark triad

There has been interest in the relationship between the three dark triad traits of narcissism, psychopathy and Machiavellianism and destructive leaders. Some scholars report there is a bright side to these dark traits that yield benefits to followers (Mackey et al., 2021) or are rated positively (Furhnam et al., 2012). For example, leader narcissism (a dark triad trait) has been associated with increased follower career success in the form of more promotions and increased salary (Volmer et al., 2016).

Abusive supervision

Aryee and colleagues (2008) consider abusive supervision, as the one concept that has dominated empirical research in this area, as a *low base rate phenomenon* (p. 394). Others, analysing more limited and restricted settings, report higher rates of abuse: in the Netherlands, Hubert and van Veldhoven (2001) report a prevalence rate of about 11 per cent. Even higher prevalence rates have been found in a Norwegian study (Aasland et al., 2010) where about a third of employees reported some form of abuse. In the US, abusive supervision has been estimated by one study to affect 14 per cent of workers (Tepper, 2007). Yet, perception matters. For example, Pelletier (2012), using a leader–member exchange lens, found that out-group members were more likely to perceive their leader as toxic than were in-group members.

These leader-centric studies thus show three things: a) 'abuse' exists and appears to affect self-reported worker productivity and absenteeism even if these effects are self-reported; b) the levels of self-reported abuse seems to affect 10 per cent of workers and may be even lower; and c) the studies beg the questions of how the remaining 90 per cent of the workforces are faring (no abuse, no abuse worth mentioning?) and whether the organisations as a whole are actually underperforming relative to their competitors and peers. Some employees who feel abused may justifiably tend to underperform at their jobs, but does this mean the organisation as a whole is underperforming? Are there 'perfect' organisations where no one feels abused? Abusive leader literature remains a function of what leaders do, and their ultimate organisational impacts are problematically defined. The overall, ultimate performance of the organisation writ large is typically not even considered, even if performance is what interests boards of directors and stockholders.

The studies, as noted earlier, typically rely on surveys of employees that ask confidential questions about behaviours and traits of their managers or supervisors. There are no controls on the reliability or veracity of the respondents. Some scholars assert that a defining feature of the construct is that others may not be able to witness or verify it, for example, as in the case of abusive supervision. Further, it may be the case that the recipients of seemingly abusive behaviours do not perceive them as such (Tepper et al., 2017).

Future research could develop a more nuanced understanding of how much of destructive leader behaviour is in the eye of the beholder, especially if such perceptions about a leader are not widely held either by subordinates or upper management. Some subordinates' personality traits may predispose them to perceive destructive leader behaviour in the first place and to affect their perceptions about it. Some studies have found that the Big Five personality factors were generally very weak predictors of destructive leader comportment ($-0.18 \leq \rho \leq 0.20$) (Mackey et al., 2021).

Leader-centric perspectives discount the influence of organisational contexts in destructive leadership episodes. There is a need to examine leader behaviours, of course, but their independent predictive value is unclear when the organisational context is neglected (Collins & Jackson, 2015; Schmid et al., 2019). Isolated considerations of behaviours and neglect of the influence of the environments and follower characteristics may have difficulty in accounting for successful leaders like Steve Jobs at Apple. Jobs was widely perceived by some followers (not all) as an abusive and very difficult manager or, more bluntly, as a world-class jerk (Coursey, 2011) yet the organisational outcomes for Apple during his tenure were widely viewed as highly successful.

Leadership as a Positive Construct

The terms 'leader' or 'leadership' tend to apply only to well-liked people or to positive episodes. The view that leadership is a positive, value-laden concept is problematic and laden with theoretical and measurement flaws (Alvesson & Einola, 2019). Adolf Hitler was a tyrant and dictator and because of this people have been reluctant to call him a leader (e.g., Burns, 2003). Castro was equally or even more ruthless than Hitler in proportion to Cuba's population, yet many have referred to him as a leader who improved the educational and health conditions in Cuba.

The scholarly work in general reflects this inclination towards the positive. For example, an analysis of leadership approaches over 14 years in the top leadership journals found that the commonly used theories focused on constructive leadership, and none were destructive (Meuser et al., 2016). Some scholars assert that the term 'leadership' is applicable only in the positive and that the term *'negative leadership'* be reserved for ineffective or disliked leaders (Schyns and Schilling, 2013). Other scholars assert this focus on the positive emerges in leader behaviours – that is, they engage in *excessive positivity* in their speeches and demeanours (Collinson, 2012, p. 88), which ironically may lead to follower resistance.

The larger point is that destructive leadership merits study as part of the scholarship on leadership because it forces a broader perspective and because it points to more nuances and distinctions in leadership episodes. Viewing leadership as a value-positive process moves it out of the leadership realm where it belongs.

In summary, recent theoretical, conceptual and meta-analytic examinations of destructive leadership focus on leader behaviours or subordinate perceptions of leaders. Follower outcomes rather than organisational outcomes are usually considered. Some scholars view destructive leadership as a process that should include a consideration of outcomes. The environment or organisational context is not included in meta-analytic reviews as none of the empirical literature addresses this feature of destructive leadership. The leader-centric focus is tied to work on the dark triad and abusive supervision. In addition, viewing leadership as a positive construct rather than a neutral one would place work on destructive leadership outside the leadership umbrella.

TOXIC TRIANGLE

An epistemology of destructive leadership must account for how leaders, followers and environments influence one another, over time, in ways that result in poor organisational outcomes. The toxic triangle makes sense of destructive leadership episodes by identifying all of its unique characteristics (Padilla et al., 2007). Below we examine each element of the toxic triangle and align it with the extant literature. A more comprehensive analysis of destructive leadership requires attention to all these elements.

Destructive Leaders

There is a substantial research stream focused on leader behaviours and traits (see, for example, Lord et al., 1986, or Judge et al., 2002). Indeed, it is useful to know more about the traits associated with leaders. However, it is important to distinguish the traits of constructive versus destructive leaders. Some scholars have attempted to do so by identifying the bright side and dark side of personality (Kaiser et al., 2015). According to this perspective, destructive leaders express the dark side of personality traits. Yet, there is little agreement on the constellation of the dark side traits or even when they are expressed. Kaiser and colleagues report that the dark side traits are an under- or over-expression of traits. Other scholars have suggested that increased self-awareness and self-regulation may limit the expression of dark side traits (Harms et al., 2011). Zeitoun and colleagues (2019) have expanded on these destructive leader traits to examine if hubris is a dark trait that emerges when environmental factors do not constrain it.

An analysis of destructive leaders needs to consider leader emergence as well as the constellation of traits that are associated with a destructive leader. According to the toxic triangle model, destructive leaders tend to be charismatic, have a personalised need for power, are narcissistic, advance an ideology of hate and have a childhood marked by negative life themes (Padilla et al., 2007). The scholarship mentioned earlier on the dark triad and abusive supervision are attempts to understand destructive leader traits.

Susceptible Followers

Susceptible followers either conform (acquiesce) to or collude (actively participate) with the destructive leader. Scholars have expanded this typology by identifying three types of conformers and two types of colluders (Thoroughgood et al., 2012). Conformers might be authoritarians, lost souls, or bystanders. Authoritarians have rigid attitudes that make them loyal to a leader. In contrast, lost souls are needy followers with an ill-defined sense of self. Bystanders are afraid to lose their job or suffer some other reprisal and silently go along with a destructive leader.

Colluders might be acolytes or opportunists. Opportunists support the destructive leader's agenda to accrue personal benefits. Acolytes are 'true believers' who share the destructive leader's values.

Other scholars have examined the assumption that it is destructive leaders who influence susceptible followers. But the direction of causation may work both ways; it is not always the leader who precipitates destructive leadership. Susceptible followers often influence destructive leaders, through cognitive and emotional process, in a manner that leads to destructive leadership outcomes (Tee et al., 2013).

Conducive Environments

Conducive environments are marked by instability, perceived threat, a lack of checks and balances, and cultural values that enable destructive leadership. Chapter 29, How and why is context important in leadership?, highlights the importance of contexts. Given the importance of conducive environments, one wonders why there is so little scholarly attention paid to environments.

In part, organisations are reluctant to share information when a destructive leadership episode has taken place. The lack of information makes it difficult to analyse some aspects of the environment or organisational culture. Private companies, and even public ones, do not freely share information about destructive leadership events. The press is an important source of organisational wrongdoing or misdeeds. Yet, destructive leaders seek to control journalists and their access to information. Freedom of the press is not a right under totalitarian regimes like South Korea, Russia, or Cuba.

Another reason for the relative disinterest in environments may be because the environments in constructive leadership episodes are taken for granted, especially in Western societies with rule of law, stable political and economic institutions, and empowered followers. Thus, scholars would have little interest in environmental factors if they were not associated with political crises or variability in leader behaviours or leadership outcomes. Effective organisations have transparent policies and procedures; operate in a relatively predictable environment; and have effective oversight over top leaders (Hogan and Kaiser, 2005).

The importance of conducive environments is highlighted by athletic scandals like Lance Armstrong's drug doping in the Tour de France (Erickson et al., 2015; Lunsford & Padilla, 2015). In the case of the Tour de France, the innovations in drug doping were not matched by the testing agencies' ability to detect new performance-enhancing drugs. There were insufficient checks and balances, along with a sport culture driven by an attitude of win at any cost, to prevent or catch winners who were using illegal, performance-enhancing drugs. Ultimately, the winners in the Tour de France were vacated for seven years, from 1999 to 2005, as the runners-up could not be cleared of drug use.

Thus, in destructive leadership episodes, there is evidence that conducive environments may be the most important factor, over destructive leaders or susceptible followers. Weak environments may allow destructive leaders to emerge and to persist. Weak environments also do not check ambitious and colluding followers or protect the conformers.

Destructive Outcomes

Destructive leadership ultimately results in bad outcomes for the group or organisation. Here we distinguish between leader derailment on the one hand and destructive leadership on the other. A destructive leader may be ejected from an organisation that has empowered followers and vibrant checks and balances in what might be termed a 'leader derailment'. Such derailments may be seen as misfits between the organisation and its leader. The followers or the organisational checks and balances, in such cases, prevent longer-term destructive leadership; the organisation continues on its course without greater disruption after the flawed leader is replaced. In contrast, a destructive leadership episode would entail an organisation in persistent decline relative to its peers due to the influence of a bad leader, susceptible followers, or weak, ineffective environments. The decline could be the total breakdown or dissolution of the organisation, as in the case of Enron or Hitler's regime, or less dramatically, in terms of outcomes such as long-term stock value or organisational reputation that leaves the entity at a major, ongoing disadvantage relative to its peers.

Few organisational outcomes are purely bad or exceptionally great. Most are average. But are positive organisational outcomes possible under destructive leaders? An entire book could be written on this and related questions such as the difference between managerial ineptness or bad luck or malevolent intent, perhaps on another occasion. Nonetheless, Rizio and Skali (2020) disprove the benevolent dictator hypothesis in their examination of economic growth and political regimes. There is little evidence that destructive leaders are ultimately associated with positive organisational outcomes and plenty of evidence that they are associated with negative ones (Kets de Vries et al., 2016; Lunsford et al., 2021). In the short term and in certain situations, a largely destructive leader can be associated with positive outcomes, just as a leader widely viewed as constructive might be associated with poor outcomes or costly mistakes in the short term. Even though cycling and university sports are quite enduring and resilient, the vacated winners in the Tour de France hurt the sport of cycling in terms of loss of revenue and credibility. Lance Armstrong's foundation Livestrong suffered financial losses when Lance was found guilty, and Armstrong had to resign from its board of directors.

These outcomes suggest a related point. It takes time for these outcomes to occur or fully manifest themselves; sometimes it takes decades (Thoroughgood et al., 2018). Thus, the study of destructive leadership presents temporal challenges to scholarly efforts. Pelletier and colleagues (2019) make this point in applying the toxic triangle framework to a destructive leadership episode at a public university. They found the toxic triangle to be a comprehensive framework for analysing a destructive leadership episode. Destructive leadership may take a long time to emerge and often can only be identified retrospectively through its outcomes. Further, the presence of multiple individuals in combination with varied organisational cultures makes it a complex area of study.

APPROACHES

As noted, destructive leadership requires broader approaches to understand the phenomena. Below we highlight three areas that warrant methodological attention. First, the theory highlights a greater need for longitudinal study. Second, qualitative methods are needed to understand conducive environments. Third, the toxic triangle suggests that interdisciplinary work is needed to understand destructive leadership.

Longitudinal Studies

Destructive leadership usually takes time to occur and develop. Thus, cross-sectional studies are insufficient to capture the time dimension (Thoroughgood et al., 2012) and therefore to detect or predict such events. A destructive leader in their first year is not the same as an entrenched destructive leader. Qualitative approaches, described below, can examine how destructive leadership episodes unfold over time (Klenke, 2016).

For example, Carlos Ghosn was initially viewed favourably by some when he took over Nissan, even as he faced tremendous cultural challenges and criticisms. He was not as favourably viewed by the Japanese employees or Japanese press – who harboured resentment that the organisation brought in an outsider. Ultimately, one of his Japanese executives worked with the police to arrange for his arrest. Ghosn later arranged an implausible escape from prison in Japan (Chozick and Rich, 2018), fleeing to Lebanon, which does not have extradition with Japan. The eventual decline of Nissan (for which Ghosn denies responsibility) suggests temporary accounting solutions that papered over deeper organisational problems; destructive leadership eventually occurred at Nissan. Yet, the Nissan early in Ghosn's tenure might have looked like a constructive leadership episode, a dramatic turn-around of a company that was important to Japan's economic success (Donnelly et al., 2005; Ghosn, 2002; Millikin and Fu, 2005).

Qualitative Approaches

Broader views on destructive leadership may be best accomplished through carefully documented, qualitative analysis. Despite an increase in qualitative articles on leadership, quantitative studies continue to characterise most of the published work (Bryman et al., 1996; Klenke, 2008; Klenke, 2016). In part, the emphasis on quantitative approaches has occurred as a function of the methodological preference of psychologists for experimental methods. Psychologists are frequent contributors to leadership journals. Thus, leadership scholars have embraced qualitative methods later than did scholars in disciplines such as anthropology, political science, or sociology (Bryman, 2004). Klenke (2016) records continued obstacles to conducting qualitative work on leadership, including having such work accepted at the top journals and a lack of qualitative methods courses in doctoral studies. Yet, qualitative methods give distinctive attention to the influence of environments on human behaviour and tend to acknowledge the process of leadership is context-dependent (Bryman, 2004; Klenke, 2016).

Ghosn's destructive leadership episode also highlights the problem with the monochromatic lens used in most leadership research. Why did some followers like Ghosn while others reacted poorly to him? Scholarship on abusive leadership assumes that there is uniformed unanimity in the reaction to abusive leaders. It seems more credible that some followers will acquiesce to destructive leaders while other followers will react visibly and perhaps even violently to them.

Klenke (2016, p. 5) notes that qualitative approaches allow for an examination of the processes of leadership by answering *why* rather than *how* and *what* questions by quantitative research. It has been decades since Conger (1990) called qualitative approaches a cornerstone to understand leadership. We need more scholars to heed his call to understand the complexity of leadership. In addition to case studies, the field would benefit from a variety of qualitative approaches such as observational research and ethnographic research (Conger, 1990; Deckers, 2021).

Data from converging qualitative approaches may assist in identifying how conducive environments influence destructive leadership. One approach would be to study one organisation at a time, like the military (Gallus et al., 2013) or a specific country such as Lebanon (Neal & Tansey, 2010). A second approach would be to compare organisations in existing cross-sectional studies of destructive leadership.

Interdisciplinary Approaches

Scholarship on destructive leadership would benefit from greater interdisciplinary efforts with scholars in social sciences like anthropology, history and political science, and not just from psychology, management and organisational behaviour.

Political science scholars focus on the environment and usually on power. It is rare to find research on the environment because it is not amenable to quantitative methods, which is usually emphasised by the top journals in management and psychology. Scholars of history examine the actors and the environments of the relevant time period. Conger (1990) notes the importance of anthropology in his thinking about leadership.

More work on conducive environments may identify what combinations of factors are likely to lead to emergence of destructive leaders. More importantly, being able to create environments that are not conducive to destructive leadership may eliminate or prevent destructive leaders or susceptible followers while minimising negative organisational outcomes.

Additional study is needed on how certain factors destabilise organisations. The fast pace of technological innovation can contribute to significant disruption, as can financial upheavals. What threats to organisations might turn environments more conducive to destruction? Lack of transparency is a cultural value often associated with ineffective checks and balances. What are other relevant cultural values that make destructive leadership more likely?

The methods usually employed to study destructive leadership episodes are not equipped to answer the broader questions about conducive environments. We attempt to use quantitative results to answer qualitative questions. Scholarly journals need to be more open to broader qualitative work.

EMERGING IDEAS

In certain conducive environments – for example, times of crisis or instability and lack of oversight – the combination of destructive leaders and susceptible followers make destructive leadership likely. In addition to the approaches we describe above, a broader conceptualisation of destructive leadership suggests there are implications related to leader emergence, leader effectiveness and organisational checks and balances.

Leader Emergence

The selection of leaders is surely an under-studied topic as it relates to leadership and successful leader transitions. Some scholars have examined leader emergence (Acton et al., 2019) and have proposed a multi-level framework to understand the process of who emerges as a leader and why. Some scholars are examining the contexts in which certain leaders emerge (Dinh et al., 2014).

It has been suggested that the best predictor of future behaviour may be past behaviour. However, organisations fail to investigate fully relevant past behaviour (Hogan et al., 1994). Past behaviour is often neglected by search committees or may be hard to discern – for example, as in the case of young leaders. But some of the hiring failures have to do with a lack of investigation or checking up on the candidate (Hogan & Kaiser, 2005).

There seems to be a great deal of interest at the corporate level to adopt better methods and processes. Yet interviews continue to be principal source of information about candidates. We trust our intuition when we should not. Interviews are notoriously poor selection tools and efforts to improve them, in the form of behavioural interviews or situational judgement tasks, have been slow to be embraced by search committee members (Highhouse, 2008).

Search committees have delegated much of their work to select leaders to search firms. There is an argument that search firms may be more efficient yet there is limited research on the effectiveness of leaders selected with the help of search firms (Hamori, 2010). Executives at well-functioning organisations are less likely to leave. Does this mean that leaders may be more likely to selected from organisations with problems or cultures more conducive to destructive leadership? More attention on leader emergence might reduce advancement of individuals who become destructive leaders.

In some cases, however, destructive leaders are not selected but they persuade susceptible followers to their cause to take over, such as in the case of totalitarian regimes like North Korea or Cuba. The literature is silent on the question of why some children, with negative life themes, become destructive leaders, while others do not.

Leader Effectiveness

In the political context we seem to believe that if despots in totalitarian regimes are shown the democratic way, then they will be encouraged towards more transparent ways of governing. There is a belief that we can change the leader and their effectiveness. Yet, this approach does not seem to be working. Regimes like Cuba, North Korea, Iran, Russia and China continue to repress and eliminate dissension despite the best efforts of Western governments to show them 'the right way' through controls such as sanctions. What implications does this have for policy, not just foreign policy at a national level, but also at a more local level and in corporations and organisations of various sorts?

It can be difficult to assess leader effectiveness. The trait approach might examine if followers like the leader or assess leader personality traits. Schyns and Shilling (2013), for example, take a process view of destructive leadership that involves leader–follower interactions over time. The outcomes they examined were perceptions of leader behaviours rather than organisational outcomes or conducive environments.

As noted above, the time dimension is relevant. Jack Immelt, former CEO of General Electric (GE), tried to discredit Jack Welch, his predecessor, when he said that *even a dog could have run GE* (Collingwood, 2009). Immelt's implication of course is that Welch was lucky and that conditions had worsened dramatically during Immelt's tenure. Regardless of how one views the Welch versus Immelt question, is leader effectiveness to be judged at the time when the leader departs? If so, Welch was clearly an effective leader. Relatedly, if a leader inherits a great team, then is the prior leader responsible for the organisation's success and for how long?

At times organisations attempt to improve leaders. An entire industry has flourished around executive coaching, which emerged in part to improve poor executive leadership (Kampa-Kokesch & Anderson, 2001). Certainly, some leaders may wish to develop their skills. But it is unlikely that destructive leaders wish to change their behaviours. It is also difficult to curb bad behaviours despite exhortations that you can do so (Riggio, 2018). Further, it is challenging to change values of adults to avoid autocratic leaders (Harms et al., 2018). Better metrics are needed to assess organisational outcomes as a function of leader effectiveness. These metrics may also change over the leader's tenure.

Organisational Checks and Balances

Examining more closely those organisations that resist bad leaders versus those that tolerate bad behaviours seems warranted. Are there differences among follower behaviours and characteristics?

What are the differences among such organisations in checks and balances and managerial controls?

Internal checks and balances refer to processes and procedures that can recognise and deal with destructive leadership that emerges over time. For example, in the Tour de France example above, team-mate Floyd Landis reported Lance Armstrong to USA Cycling in 2010. It took two years for a full investigation to be completed that identified blood doping had been going on for over a decade (Cohen, 2020). Yet, no one had reported any wrongdoing during that decade long period.

Clear policies that protect whistleblowers may provide another internal check and balance. Organisations with more reports from internal whistleblowers suffered fewer lawsuits and governmental fines (Stubben and Welch, 2020). Yet many organisations do not have whistleblower policies and there are great costs to those who blow the whistle (Lunsford et al., 2021). Research on the most effective whistleblower policies and protections may help limit destructive leadership.

External checks and balances might include independent boards of directors who are not appointed or anointed by the leader. Yet, even independently appointed boards, such as those for universities, are often filled with university boosters who may be reluctant to be critical of institutional wrongdoing. Some scholars find limited support for independently appointed boards, which were not associated with a reduction in scandals for mutual funds (Ferris and Yan, 2007). More research is needed on how organisations can establish external checks and balances that will reduce the possibility of destructive leadership.

CONCLUSION

In this chapter we reviewed how scholars define and study destructive leadership. We support Mackey and colleagues' (2021) call for scholars to attend to leaders, followers *and organisations* (emphasis added) to understand *the full experience of destructive leadership* (p. 715). We make sense of destructive leadership by offering the toxic triangle model as a foundation to invite interdisciplinary work that might lead to broader, more comprehensive study. More attention to the conducive environments is needed as well as to longitudinal, qualitative and interdisciplinary approaches.

The prototypical examples of destructive leaders are those who operate in weakened environments and with cultures of repression and coercion.

A paradox emerges here. If organisations wish to reduce the likelihood of destructive leadership, then more transparency and oversight is required. More importantly, the leader has to be willing to give up power and control. Constructive leadership is more likely to occur when leaders are open to helpful criticism and are comfortable operating with someone looking over their shoulders. Alas, this is harder done than said for many leaders. The fact remains that flawed leaders exist everywhere and in the right mixture with susceptible followers and conducive environments, it will be likely that destructive leadership will occur.

REFERENCES

Aasland, M. S., Skogstad, A., Notelaers, G., Nielsen, M. B., & Einarsen, S. (2010). The prevalence of destructive leadership behaviour. *British Journal of Management*, 21(2), 438–452. https://doi.org/10.1111/j.1467-8551.2009.00672.x

Acton, B., Foti, R., Lord, R., & Gladfelter, J. (2019). Putting emergence back in leadership emergence: A dynamic, multilevel, process-oriented framework. *Leadership Quarterly*, 30(1), 145–164. https://doi.org/10.1016/j.leaqua.2018.07.002

Alvesson, M., & Einola, K. (2019). Warning for excessive positivity: Authentic leadership and other traps in leadership studies. *Leadership Quarterly*, 30(4), 383–395.

Aryee, S., Sun, L. Y., Chen, Z. X. G., & Debrah, Y. A. (2008). Abusive supervision and contextual performance: The mediating role of emotional exhaustion and the moderating role of work unit structure. *Management and Organization Review*, 4(3), 393–411. https://doi.org/10.1111/j.1740-8784.2008.00118.x

Avolio, B. J. (2007). Promoting more integrative strategies for leadership theory-building. *American Psychologist*, 62(1), 25–33. https://doi.org/10.1037/0003-066X.62.1.25

Bryman, A. (2004). Qualitative research on leadership: A critical but appreciative review. *Leadership Quarterly*, 15(6), 729–769. https://doi.org/10.1016/j.leaqua.2004.09.007

Bryman, A., Stephens, M., & a Campo, C. (1996). The importance of context: Qualitative research and the study of leadership. *Leadership Quarterly*, 7(3), 353–370. https://doi.org/10.1016/S1048-9843(96)90025-9

Buchholz, F., Lopatta, K., & Maas, K. (2020). The deliberate engagement of narcissistic CEOs in earnings management. *Journal of Business Ethics*, 167(4), 663–686. https://doi.org/10.1007/s10551-019-04176-x

Burns, J. M. (1978). *Transformational Leadership*. Harper & Row.

Burns, J. M. (2003). *Leaders who Changed the World*. Penguin Viking.

Chozick, A., & Rich, M. (2018). The rise and fall of Carlos Ghosn. *New York Times*, 30 December. https://www.nytimes.com/2018/12/30/business/carlos-ghosn-nissan.html

Cohen, K. (2020). The rise and fall of Lance Armstrong: What you need to know before watching 'LANCE'. 21 May. ESPN. https://www.espn.com/olympics/story/_/id/29177242/the-rise-fall-lance-armstrong-need-know-watching-lance

Collingwood, H. (2009). Do CEO's matter? *The Atlantic*, June. https://www.theatlantic.com/magazine/archive/2009/06/do-ceos-matter/307437/

Collins, M. D., & Jackson, C. J. (2015). A process model of self-regulation and leadership: How attentional resource capacity and negative emotions influence constructive and destructive leadership. *Leadership Quarterly*, 26(3), 386–401.

Collinson, D. (2012). Prozac leadership and the limits of positive thinking. *Leadership*, 8(2), 87–107.

Conger, J. A. (1990). The dark side of leadership. *Organizational Dynamics*, 19(2), 44–55. https://doi.org/10.1016/0090-2616(90)90070-6

Coursey, D. (2011). Steve Jobs was a jerk, you shouldn't be. *Forbes*, 12 October. https://www.forbes.com/sites/davidcoursey/2011/10/12/steve-jobs-was-a-jerk-you-shouldnt-be/?sh=7ed37be44045

Craig, S. B., & Kaiser, R. B. (2013). Destructive leadership. *The Oxford Handbook of Leadership* (pp. 439–454). Oxford University Press.

Deckers, J. (2021). The value of autoethnography in leadership studies, and its pitfalls. *Philosophy of Management*, 20, 75–91. https://doi.org/10.1007/s40926-020-00146-w

Dinh, J. E., Lord, R. G., Gardner, W. L., Meuser, J. D., Liden, R. C., & Hu, J. (2014). Leadership theory and research in the new millennium: Current theoretical trends and changing perspectives. *Leadership Quarterly*, 25(1), 36–62. https://doi.org/10.1016/j.leaqua.2013.11.005

Donnelly, T., Morris, D., & Donnelly, T. (2005). Renault–Nissan: A marriage of necessity? *European Business Review*, 17(5), 428–440. https://doi.org/10.1108/09555340510620339

Einarsen, S., Aasland, M. S., & Skogstad, A. (2007). Destructive leadership behaviour: A definition and conceptual model. *Leadership Quarterly*, 18(3), 207–216. https://doi.org/10.1016/j.leaqua.2007.03.002

Erickson, A., Shaw, B., Murray, J., & Branch, S. (2015). Destructive leadership. *Organizational Dynamics*, 4(44), 266–272.

Ferris, S. P., & Yan, X. S. (2007). Do independent directors and chairmen matter? The role of boards of directors in mutual fund governance. *Journal of Corporate Finance*, 13(2–3), 392–420. https://doi.org/10.1016/j.jcorpfin.2006.12.004

Fosse, T. H., Skogstad, A., Einarsen, S. V., & Martinussen, M. (2019). Active and passive forms of destructive leadership in a military context: A systematic review and meta-analysis. *European Journal of Work and Organizational Psychology*, 28(5), 708–722.

Fraher, A. L. (2016). A toxic triangle of destructive leadership at Bristol Royal Infirmary: A study of organizational Munchausen syndrome by proxy. *Leadership*, 12(1), 34–52.

Furnham, A., Trickey, G., & Hyde, G. (2012). Bright aspects to dark side traits: Dark side traits associated with work success. *Personality and Individual Differences*, 52(8), 908–913.

Gallus, J. A., Walsh, B. M., van Driel, M., Gouge, M. C., & Antolic, E. (2013). Intolerable cruelty: A multilevel examination of the impact of toxic leadership on US military units and service members. *Military Psychology*, 25(6), 588–601. https://doi.org/10.1037/mil0000022

Ghosn, C. (2002). Saving the business without losing the company. *Harvard Business Review*, 80(1), 37–45.

Gottfredson, R. K., & Aguinis, H. (2017). Leadership behaviors and follower performance: Deductive and inductive examination of theoretical rationales and underlying mechanisms. *Journal of Organizational Behavior*, 38(4), 558–591. https://doi.org/10.1002/job.2152

Hamori, M. (2010). Who gets headhunted – and who gets ahead? The impact of search firms on executive careers. *Academy of Management Perspectives*, 24(4), 46–59. https://doi.org/10.5465/amp.2010.24.4.3654611.a

Harms, P. D., Spain, S. M., & Hannah, S. T. (2011). Leader development and the dark side of personality. *Leadership Quarterly*, 22(3), 495–509. https://doi.org/10.1016/j.leaqua.2011.04.007

Harms, P. D., Wood, D., Landay, K., Lester, P. B., & Lester, G. V. (2018). Autocratic leaders and authoritarian followers revisited: A review and agenda for the future. *Leadership Quarterly*, 29(1), 105–122. https://doi.org/10.1016/j.leaqua.2017.12.007

Highhouse, S. (2008). Stubborn reliance on intuition and subjectivity in employee selection. *Industrial and Organizational Psychology*, 1(3), 333–342. https://doi.org/10.1111/j.1754-9434.2008.00058.x

Hogan, R., Curphy, G. J., & Hogan, J. (1994). What we know about leadership: Effectiveness and personality. *American Psychologist*, 49(6), 493.

Hogan, R., & Kaiser, R. B. (2005). What we know about leadership. *Review of General Psychology*, 9(2), 169–180.

Hubert, A. B., & van Veldhoven, M. (2001). Risk sectors for undesirable behaviour and mobbing. *European Journal of Work and Organizational Psychology*, *10*(4), 415–424. https://doi.org/10.1080/13594320143000799

Judge, T. A., Bono, J. E., Ilies, R., & Gerhardt, M. W. (2002). Personality and leadership: A qualitative and quantitative review. *Journal of Applied Psychology*, *87*(4), 765–780. https://doi.org/10.1037//0021-9010.87.4.765

Kaiser, R. B., LeBreton, J. M., & Hogan, J. (2015). The dark side of personality and extreme leader behavior. *Applied Psychology*, *64*(1), 55–92. https://doi.org/10.1111/apps.12024

Kampa-Kokesch, S., & Anderson, M. Z. (2001). Executive coaching: A comprehensive review of the literature. *Consulting Psychology Journal: Practice and Research*, *53*(4), 205. https://doi.org/10.1037/1061-4087.53.4.205

Kant, L., Skogstad, A., Torsheim, T., & Einarsen, S. (2013). Beware the angry leader: Trait anger and trait anxiety as predictors of petty tyranny. *Leadership Quarterly*, *24*(1), 106–124. https://doi.org/10.1016/j.leaqua.2012.08.005

Kets de Vries, M. F., Sexton, J. C., & Ellen III, B. P. (2016). Destructive and transformational leadership in Africa. *Africa Journal of Management*, *2*(2), 166–187. http://dx.doi.org/10.1080/23322373.2016.1175267

Klenke, K. (Ed.). (2008). *Qualitative Research in the Study of Leadership*. Emerald.

Klenke, K. (2016). *Qualitative Research in the Study of Leadership*. 2nd Edn. Emerald.

Kozlowski, S. W., Watola, D. J., Jensen, J. M., Kim, B. H., & Botero, I. C. (2009). Developing adaptive teams: A theory of dynamic team leadership. In E. Salas, G. F. Goodwin & S. C. Burke (Eds.), *Team Effectiveness in complex Organizations: Cross-Disciplinary Perspectives and Approaches* (pp. 113–155). Psychology Press Taylor & Francis Group.

Krasikova, D. V., Green, S. G., & LeBreton, J. M. (2013). Destructive leadership: A theoretical review, integration, and future research agenda. *Journal of Management*, *39*(5), 1308–1338. https://doi.org/10.1177/0149206312471388

Landay, K., Harms, P. D., & Credé, M. (2019). Shall we serve the dark lords? A meta-analytic review of psychopathy and leadership. *Journal of Applied Psychology*, *104*(1), 183–196. https://doi.org/10.1037/apl0000357

Lord, R. G., DeVader, C. L., & Alliger, G. (1986). A meta-analysis of the relation between personality traits and leader perceptions. *Journal of Applied Psychology*, *71*(3), 402–410. https://doi.org/10.1037/0021-9010.71.3.402

Lunsford, L. G., & Padilla, A. (2015). Destructive and toxic leadership. In I. O'Boyle, D. Murray & P. Cummins (Eds.), *Leadership in Sport* (pp. 63–78). Routledge.

Lunsford, L., Padilla, A., & Mulvey, P. (2021). Destructive leadership episodes: Why can't we learn from them? In J. H. Dulebohn, B. Murray & D. L. Stone (Eds.), *Leadership: Leaders, Followers, and Contexts. Research in Human Resource Management*. Information Age.

Mackey, J. D., Ellen III, B. P., McAllister, C. P., & Alexander, K. C. (2021). The dark side of leadership: A systematic literature review and meta-analysis of destructive leadership research. *Journal of Business Research*, *132*, 705–718. https://doi.org/10.1016/j.jbusres.2020.10.037

Mackey, J. D., McAllister, C. P., Maher, L. P., & Wang, G. (2019). Leaders and followers behaving badly: A meta-analytic examination of curvilinear relationships between destructive leadership and followers' workplace behaviors. *Personnel Psychology*, *72*(1), 3–47. https://doi.org/10.1111/peps.12286

Meuser, J. D., Gardner, W. L., Dinh, J. E., Hu, J., Liden, R. C., & Lord, R. G. (2016). A network analysis of leadership theory: The infancy of integration. *Journal of Management*, *42*(5), 1374–1403. https://doi.org/10.1177/0149206316647099

Millikin, J. P., & Fu, D. (2005). The global leadership of Carlos Ghosn at Nissan. *Thunderbird International Business Review*, *47*(1), 121–137.

Neal, M. W., & Tansey, R. (2010). The dynamics of effective corrupt leadership: Lessons from Rafik Hariri's political career in Lebanon. *Leadership Quarterly*, *21*(1), 33–49. https://doi.org/10.1016/j.leaqua.2009.10.003

Offerman, L. R. (2004). When followers become toxic. *Harvard Business Review*, *82*(1), 54–60.

Padilla, A., Hogan, R., & Kaiser, R. B. (2007). The toxic triangle: Destructive leaders, susceptible followers, and conducive environments. *Leadership Quarterly*, *18*(3), 176–194.

Padilla, A., & Lunsford, L. G. (2013). The leadership triangle: It's not only about the leader. *European Business Review*, 9 May.

Pelletier, K. L. (2010). Leader toxicity: An empirical investigation of toxic behavior and rhetoric. *Leadership*, *6*(4), 373–389.

Pelletier, K. L. (2012). Perceptions of and reactions to leader toxicity: Do leader–follower relationships and identification with victim matter? *Leadership Quarterly*, *23*(3), 412–424.

Pelletier, K. L., Kottke, J. L., & Sirotnik, B. W. (2019). The toxic triangle in academia: A case analysis of the emergence and manifestation of toxicity in a public university. *Leadership*, *15*(4), 405–432.

Riggio, R. E. (Ed.) (2018). *What's Wrong with Leadership? Improving Leadership Research and Practice*. Routledge.

Rizio, S. M., & Skali, A. (2020). How often do dictators have positive economic effects? Global evidence, 1858–2010. *Leadership Quarterly*, *31*(3), 101302. https://doi.org/10.1016/j.leaqua.2019.06.003

Schilling, J. (2009). From ineffectiveness to destruction: A qualitative study on the meaning of negative leadership. *Leadership*, *5*(1), 102–128.

Schmid, E. A., Pircher Verdorfer, A., & Peus, C. (2019). Shedding light on leaders' self-interest: Theory and measurement of exploitative leadership. *Journal of Management*, *45*(4), 1401–1433. https://doi.org/10.1177/0149206317707810

Schyns, B., & Schilling, J. (2013). How bad are the effects of bad leaders? A meta-analysis of destructive leadership and its outcomes. *Leadership Quarterly*, *24*(1), 138–158. https://doi.org/10.1016/j.leaqua.2012.09.001

Sergiovanni, T. J. (1982). Ten principles of quality leadership. *Educational Leadership*, *39*(5), 330–336.

Shaw, J. B., Erickson, A., & Nassirzadeh, F. (2014). Destructive leader behaviour: A study of Iranian leaders using the Destructive Leadership Questionnaire. *Leadership*, *10*(2), 218–239.

Stubben, S. R., & Welch, K. T. (2020). Evidence on the use and efficacy of internal whistleblowing systems. *Journal of Accounting Research*, *58*(2), 473–518. https://doi.org/10.1111/1475-679X.12303

Taylor, B. J., Cantwell, B., Watts, K., & Wood, O. (2020). Partisanship, white racial resentment, and state support for higher education. *Journal of Higher Education*, 1–30. https://doi.org/10.1080/00221546.2019.1706016

Tee, E. Y., Paulsen, N., & Ashkanasy, N. M. (2013). Revisiting followership through a social identity perspective: The role of collective follower emotion and action. *Leadership Quarterly*, *24*(6), 902–918. https://doi.org/10.1016/j.leaqua.2013.10.002

Tepper, B. J. (2007). Abusive supervision in work organizations: Review, synthesis, and research agenda. *Journal of Management*, *33*(3), 261–289.

Tepper, B. J., Simon, L., & Park, H. M. (2017). Abusive supervision. *Annual Review of Organizational Psychology and Organizational Behavior*, *4*, 123–152. https://www.annualreviews.org/doi/10.1146/annurev-orgpsych-041015-062539

Thoroughgood, C. N., & Padilla, A. (2013). Destructive leadership and the Penn State scandal: A toxic triangle perspective. *Industrial and Organizational Psychology*, *6*(2), 144–149. https://doi.org/10.1111/iops.12025

Thoroughgood, C. N., Padilla, A., Hunter, S. T., & Tate, B. W. (2012). The susceptible circle: A taxonomy of followers associated with destructive leadership. *Leadership Quarterly*, *23*(5), 897–917. https://doi.org/10.1016/j.leaqua.2012.05.007

Thoroughgood, C. N., Sawyer, K. B., Padilla, A., & Lunsford, L. (2018). Destructive leadership: A critique of leader-centric perspectives and toward a more holistic definition. *Journal of Business Ethics*, *151*(3), 627–649. https://doi.org/10.1007/s10551-016-3257-9

Volmer, J., Koch, I. K., & Göritz, A. S. (2016). The bright and dark sides of leaders' dark triad traits: Effects on subordinates' career success and well-being. *Personality and Individual Differences*, *101*, 413–418. https://doi.org/10.1016/j.paid.2016.06.046

Williams, M. J. (2014). Serving the self from the seat of power: Goals and threats predict leaders' self-interested behavior. *Journal of Management*, *40*(5), 1365–1395. https://doi.org/10.1177/0149206314525203

Zeitoun, H., Nordberg, D., & Homberg, F. (2019). The dark and bright sides of hubris: Conceptual implications for leadership and governance research. *Leadership*, *15*(6), 647–672. https://doi.org/10.1177/1742715019848198

Leadership and Its Alternatives

Mats Alvesson, Martin Blom and Thomas Fischer

INTRODUCTION

The idea of leadership as both a vital and indefeasible aspect of modern working life is firmly rooted in both management studies and practice. Organisational success and individual well-being at work are often explained as a result of proper leadership. There is an almost endless long list of good things that are said to follow from, for example, transformational or authentic leadership. The solution to many organisational and social problems is also frequently spelt out as requiring new, more or better leadership. New leadership concepts and formulas are regularly launched. Therefore, one easily gets the impression that there are no alternatives to leadership. In this chapter we depart from a different assumption: alternatives to leadership do exist, and once we drop the blinders of the paradigmatic leader–follower distinction, we see that these alternatives to leadership are numerous. As Hirschman (1970) put it, paradigms can be a hindrance to understanding and foster a *tendency toward compulsive and mindless theorizing* (p. 329). We invite the reader to leave behind the paradigmatic leader–follower distinction to see empirically pertinent and conceptually meaningful alternatives to leadership.

In order to be able to talk about alternatives it is necessary to first define or at least try to delimit the notion of leadership. In this chapter, we are mainly concerned with managerial leadership in organisations. That means that we do not, for example, include political leadership (Hartley & Benington, 2011), the impact of social media influencers on anonymous followers, parents' influence on their children, teachers' influence on their students, or 'leaders' without followers (Lovelace et al., 2007; Manz, 1986). Nor do we address 'informal leadership' that arises, for instance, in otherwise egalitarian groups. Of course, much of what we say is relevant also for other issues than managerially based leadership, but we concentrate on leadership in organisation within formal hierarchies and with employment contracts.

Leadership, as we refer to it in this chapter, is understood as *the intentional influencing of ideas, meanings and emotions of others within an asymmetrical, yet mainly voluntary relational context, primarily through interpersonal interactions* (Alvesson et al., 2017; Blom & Lundgren, 2020; Ladkin, 2010; Seers & Chopin, 2012; Smircich & Morgan, 1982; Zaleznik, 1977). Such a view of leadership is distinct from two other phenomena in organisations: relationships based on egalitarian influence and hierarchy-based compliance involving force and coercion. First, if influence is more or less equally distributed among actors in an organisation, there is, as we see it, less meaning to describe it in terms of leadership (cf. Gronn, 2002; Pearce & Conger, 2003). The terms simply lead to confusion and mystification. Second, if compulsion, obligation and/or ignorance dominate the relationship, we see less point in describing the actors in terms of 'leaders' and 'followers' (Blom & Lundgren, 2020). Influential textbooks of leadership as well as underlying primary research distinguish leadership from management such that the former rests on informal interpersonal influence whereas the latter rests on formal decision-making (Antonakis & Day, 2017; Yukl & Gardner, 2019). Hence, a leader is different from a manager who is seen as an administrator or 'boss'. Management seems to be practised more commonly than leadership and, for this reason, the perhaps most common way for subordinates to relate to their superiors is regarding them more as managers and less as leaders (Blom & Alvesson, 2014; Learmonth & Morrell, 2017). Of course, even a superior who is mostly seen as a manager can engage in some elements of leadership. However, if the leadership elements are not dominant, then referring to superiors as leaders and referring to their work activities as leadership is misleading and mystifying.

The remaining parts of the chapter are as follows. First, we describe alternative theoretical concepts to leadership. Then, we describe alternatives from a more practical perspective, both within and outside the leadership domain. We conclude with a summary of our main message: that the success and popularity of leadership as a signifier has crowded out other, perhaps more relevant alternative concepts. We argue that leadership should be used as something more distinctive in theory as well as practice.

ALTERNATIVES FROM A THEORETICAL PERSPECTIVE

In this section, we provide an overview of three theoretical perspectives that offer alternatives to thinking about leadership. First, we synthesise the work of mainstream leadership scholars who identified boundary conditions to the necessity of leadership. Second, we review selected work of critical leadership scholars who argue that leadership writings are rather an artefact of managerial ideology that involves locking people at work into constrained subject (identity) positions than a reflection of organisational practice. Third, we discuss an alternative conception of workplace relationships that promises to retain core concerns of mainstream leadership as well as critical leadership scholars, yet which disposes of ideological overtones that are so endemic to contemporary leadership writings.

Boundary Conditions to the Necessity of Leadership: When Leadership Might Not be Called for

More than four decades ago, Kerr and Jermier (1978) wrote their well-cited theory on *substitutes for leadership*. According to this work, contextual variables such as subordinate characteristics, organisational characteristics and task characteristics can substitute for, neutralise, or enhance the effects of leadership interventions (Dionne et al., 2005; Howell et al., 1986; Jermier & Kerr, 1997; Keller, 2006; Kerr & Jermier, 1978; Podsakoff et al., 1996; Schriesheim, 1997). The threefold key idea is as simple as powerful. First, independent and high-skilled professionals need less leadership than low-skilled amateurs. Second, in highly formalised organisations with rigid rules and well-functioning work groups there is a lower need for active supervisor intervention than in more informal, evolving and unstable work settings. Third, for clear routine tasks that require the application of the ever-same work procedures there is a lower need for feedback and leadership than for ambiguous and ever-evolving tasks. Taken together, research on substitutes for leadership has identified several factors outside the control of the 'leader' that render managerial leadership interventions superfluous (Kerr & Jermier, 1978). Similar ideas on important contingencies can also be found in the literature on *situational leadership* (Hersey & Blanchard, 1977), where the subordinates' 'development levels' are seen as pivotal for the type of – if any – managerial leadership interventions they are in need of. However, these authors seem mainly to have supervision and management rather than leadership, at least as defined in this chapter, in mind.

Substitutes for leadership (as the term is used in the reviewed texts) are a special lens emanating from a more comprehensive theoretical framework: House's path–goal theory (1971). This theory takes an explicitly functional view and describes the responsibility of a managerial person (leader) as enabling followers (or, perhaps more accurately, his/her subordinates) to perform. House (1971) combines this functional view with a need–satisfaction logic: the managerial leader has to give followers what they need to perform (House, 1996). Following the precepts of path–goal theory, we can see that there are many alternatives to leadership: having high-skilled professionals, well-functioning teams and/or a supportive organisational environment. Whereas House's (1971) original theory as well as its extension and refinement (House, 1996) is a theory of leadership, the same conceptual arguments can be used to identify that leadership is often superfluous. Knowledge-workers embedded in teams governed by peer-to-peer relations are both a classical and modern example for not needing regular managerial leadership interventions (see, e.g., Blom & Alvesson, 2014).

Leadership scholars should be well equipped to identify alternatives to leadership if they are willing to drop the blinders of 'typical leadership studies', such as that followers innately desire leadership and that there is a fixed set of leadership behaviours that is consistently satisfying such a need (Hunter et al., 2007). Typical leadership research postulates certain leadership behaviours or styles as a solution – even if these scholars did not yet identify a problem (e.g., a need to cover the absence of leadership). Although rarely acknowledged as such, House's path–goal theory (1971, 1996) offers a valuable lens for thinking beyond the manifold blinders in leadership research.

Leadership as a Tool of Managerial Ideology

When we recognise that in many settings professionals are motivated and well equipped for doing their job even without regular leadership interventions, the question arises if the practical relevance of leadership meets the omnipresent status of leadership in current writings about management. The practical value of leadership might be more narrowly circumscribed and the widespread reference to leadership might to a large extent be the result of ideology. Consequently, the 'need' for managerial leadership can – and should – also be discussed in the light of ideology.

Gemmill and Oakley (1992, p. 115), partly based on the work by Bennis (1989), argue that the whole idea of a need for leadership should be regarded as a dangerous social myth:

> The idea of a leadership elite explains in a Social Darwinistic manner why only certain members of a social system are at the apex of power and entitled to a proportionably greater share of the social wealth [...] It is our contention that the myth making around the concept of leadership is [...] an unconscious conspiracy, or social hoax, aimed at maintaining the status quo.

Similar ideas, even if the degree of indignation and radicalism varies, can frequently be found within the broad and diverse research stream sometimes referred to as *critical leadership studies* (see, e.g., Calas & Smircich, 1991; Collinson, 2011; Gordon, 2002; Learmonth & Morrell, 2019, as well as Chapter 36, On destructive leadership). Learmonth and Morrell (2017, p. 257) claim that *The term 'leader' and 'follower' are increasingly replacing expressions like 'manager' and 'worker' and becoming routine ways to talk about hierarchical groups within organizations.* In a similar vein, Alvesson and Kärreman (2016, p. 142) warn us that the concepts of leaders and followers are used *to build and maintain a positive, celebrating, even glamorous view of organizational relations* [while] *naturalizing and freezing (asymmetrical) social relations.* How we label a certain empirical phenomenon is important since it frames how we think about it. Few leadership scholars would, for example, refer to their dean as their 'leader', unless joking, but we routinely use this signifier when we try to make sense of other peoples' organisations and relationships. If we call a faculty member a 'university professor' or a 'follower' would lead to rather different connotations.

As scholars we should think carefully about what concepts we use. It is tempting to use popular terms very broadly. Instead of just routinely picking the favourite position (or identity)-defining terms, the well-read student of organisations makes use of a broad set of potential concepts and theories in order to make sense of the world out there. Many human relations conceptualised as leadership/followership could, for example, as well be described by the closely related concepts of *power* (Gordon, 2002, 2011; Lukes, 1978) or *authority* (Sennett, 1980). Additional theoretical alternatives could also be *sense-giving* (Gioia & Chittipeddi, 1991) followed by *sense-making/ breaking* (Pratt, 2000, p. 464; Weick, 1995; Weick et al., 2005). Obviously, 'management', 'managerial work' or 'supervision' are often more appropriate although less sexy terms than leadership. The suggested terms are all partly overlapping alternatives to the concept of leadership but with different connotations and aspects in focus.

When thinking about theoretical alternatives to leadership it is important to avoid the temptation of thinking in terms of *variants* of leadership. Examples of the latter include self-leadership, post-heroic leadership, servant leadership, shared leadership, distributed leadership, delegated (situational) leadership, transactional leadership etc. They all provide valuable counter-pictures to the mainstream conception of leadership but still keep us caught within the framework and discourse of leadership/followership (see for example Alvesson, 2019; Blom, 2016; Learmonth & Morrell, 2017). However, the leadership/followership framework rests on its own questionable set of assumptions (Hunter et al., 2007). Going beyond *compulsive and mindless theorizing* (Hirschman, 1970, p. 329) and conceiving of alternatives to leadership calls for dropping the paradigmatic blinders of leadership writings that only add to conceptual confusion:

> Many researchers find a market for work using the popular signifier 'leadership' because [...] mainstream approaches have made leadership fashionable. Many efforts to develop 'alternative' views thus at the same time partly break with and reinforce the domination of 'leadership' [...] Nuances involved in the efforts to revise 'leadership' are easily lost as the major framing reinforces a dominating 'mega-discourse,' weakening others. For example, this reinforces an understanding that the alternative to leadership is leadership, not peer relations, professionalism, autonomy, co-workership, organising processes, or mutual adjustment offering alternative framings and understanding than what the leadership vocabulary invites.
> (Alvesson & Kärreman, 2016, p. 142)

The very use of the word *leadership* – even if shared, collective, social etc. – probably leads most people to think about the leader somehow being a centre of influencing.

Learmonth and Morrell (2017, p. 266) advocate the use of terms such as 'worker' and 'management' as they encourage scholars to keep an eye on the structured antagonism between capital and labour – that is, between those owning an enterprise and those working for it, while [T]*he leader/follower dualism is hard to read as anything other than a denial of the central tenet of Marxian-infected organization analyses*, thereby serving the capitalist elite's interest to produce an image of a rather harmonious relationship between superiors and subordinates. There is no apparent class-solidarity between followers in relation to their leader. But also within less antagonistic relations, where managers and subordinates feel that they are broadly on the same side, the employment relation and the expectations associated with the manager's formal role, with its privileges and responsibilities, may be better understood in manager/subordinate than leader/follower terms or even in more collegial or group-based terms ('we in this department', where the manager is rather seen as group member with some administrative/coordinating duties than as manager in relationship to subordinates).

Where does the ideologically charged nature of contemporary leadership research come from? We suppose that the confound of ideology and supervision stems from a double legacy of contemporary leadership research: 1) studying supervisors and 2) studying grandiosely influential persons. On one hand, leadership research stands in the tradition of scholars who sought to describe accurately the behaviour of supervisors (see Dinh et al., 2014; Schriesheim & Bird, 1979). Such scholarship equates leadership with the position of being a supervisor and is explicitly functional by seeking to examine how supervisors can make subordinates contribute better to organisational goals (Fleishman et al., 1991). On the other hand, from the 1970s and onwards leadership scholars have drawn from research in sociology and political science to go beyond functional notions and study how single people, typically in senior positions, can wield extraordinary influence. Formulations of charismatic and transformational leadership are the most prominent exemplar of this trend (House, 1977; Bass, 1985) and are jointly referred to as the *neocharismatic* school (House & Aditya, 1997).

This double legacy combines the mundane work of supervision with the grandiosely sounding lure of outstanding historical figures. Neocharismatic leadership studies commonly claim to build on Max Weber. It seems questionable, however, if all leadership scholars who portray themselves as standing in a Weberian tradition have ever read the work of Max Weber. Drawing on adjacent disciplines such as sociology and their brightest minds such as Weber can indeed pave the way to increased understanding. Drawing on the work of other disciplines without bothering about the foundation of these disciplines' reasoning, by contrast, can lead to intellectual impoverishment in conjunction with excessive claims about the value of one's own work. For Weber, the origins of charisma lay as much in a social process of other people mystifying a person as a leader as in the acts of the leader themselves. For mainstream charismatic leadership scholars, by contrast, the origins of charisma are searched for in the leader's usage of words, often coded and quantified with software packages (e.g., Shamir et al., 1994). Charisma is perceived as being a bit more inspirational than the average manager. Answering if neocharismatic leadership indeed stands on the shoulders of Max Weber – as commonly claimed (e.g., House & Aditya, 1997) – or if it misuses the grandeur of Weber to boost the alleged merit of the own work is beyond the scope of this chapter. It is within the scope of this chapter, however, to note that since the 1970s leadership scholars mess up the mundane work of supervision at the workplace with grandiose cases of leadership in society at large. A similar critique about poor scholarship can be directed against authentic leadership, where the concept of authenticity tends to be trivialised into a measurement of subordinates' perception of their manager (Alvesson & Einola, 2019).

An Alternative Conception to Overcome the Blinders of the Leader–Follower Distinction

Another alternative vocabulary that goes beyond the framing of human relations in terms of leadership/followership is suggested by Alvesson et al. (2017), trying to bypass the static and ideologically loaded terms 'leader' and 'follower' as well as 'leadership' and 'followership'. They talk about high-, medium- and low-level influence. The term 'high influential person (position or process)' (HIP) captures both leaders and formal managers (and other holders of authority and/or power) – that is, when the manager has some influence. This is something which we cannot take as given, as many managers may actually have a rather limited impact, particularly in strongly constrained organisations and situations, and when subordinates have a strong position. Think of a manager in a machine-like distribution system or a highly automated factory, or a head of department at a university with mainly autonomous faculty members. Standardised processes and systems and academic culture respectively will limit the space for the manager to be a HIP, including acting as a leader.

The concept of HIP covers a variety of vertical/hierarchical exercises of influence, including leadership, management and coercive power. In many cases it is difficult to separate these three types of influencing. They also often work in tandem. HIP may then be a useful term, but the main purpose here is to encourage thought and action based on alternative ways of organising work. Following this we often draw upon and talk about leadership – our focus in this handbook – but sometimes other labels (including the broader concept HIP) are more enlightening and relevant. As an example, the HIP concept may capture the specific combination of some managerially based legitimate authority, some leadership acts and some use of blunt (or other forms of) power that a clear distinction between manager, leader and power holder tends to miss.

Leadership studies often frame (sometimes even ex ante in relation to the empirical study) those not regarded as leaders as followers – they are portrayed as a pendant and partner to leaders – but it frequently makes more sense to refer to 'non-managers' or 'non-leaders' as employees, workers, organisational citizens, members, or professionals (or a particular type of such, e.g., teachers, engineers etc.). Precision in categorisation is crucial for any decent academic enterprise. The routinised attribution of people as 'followers' (see also Chapter 6, Romance of leadership) without careful investigation and thinking about the group targeted is bad practice. Sometimes it is more precise to see them as subordinates, thereby emphasising their formal subordination to managers within the constraints of the employment contract and legitimate, formal authority (Alvesson et al., 2017). You follow your leader because you are convinced, but comply with your manager mainly because of rights and responsibilities associated with the employment contract and formal organisational structure. When coercive power is at stake, low-powered individuals or targets for power make more sense than the label 'follower', since people 'follow' less as 'leader-followers' but are 'pushed' by the force of more politically resourceful actors. A common label for all these positions or roles is 'low-influence persons' (LIPs, or people in low-influencing positions or, more dynamically, low-influencing process). This term works in tandem with HIPs. 'Low' is relevant as most organisational relationships involve influencing – followers/subordinates/targets of power also exercise influence, but that influence is relatively weak compared to the HIP. Not always and in all respects but most of the time and in key respects.

While formal positions like middle manager or senior manager are 'fixed' positions and leader and follower tends to favour thinking in a 'semi-fixed' way (assuming a somewhat stable relation), HIP and LIP are always within a relation and more fluid. Almost no one is always a HIP. A vice-president may be a HIP in most work relations but may be a LIP in relation to the CEO or another more influential vice-president.

In horizontal modes of organising, the presence of HIPs and LIPs is not that salient. Of course, even in an egalitarian group working together some people might be more influential and dominant than others (by some viewed as 'informal leaders') and this position might also change/rotate over time (sometimes referred to as 'distributed leadership'; see Gronn, 2002). The same can perhaps also be said about collaborations between peers in an extra-organisational network, where a few individuals seem to dominate more than others. Here we may have issues bordering on leadership or use of power. However, in group work and in networks of peers organising means that horizontal influence dominates. People remind each other about norms, provide arguments and counter-arguments, give advice and support and coordinate their work mainly based on mutual adjustment, not followership, formal subordination or as an effect of coercive power in use. We can talk about 'medium-influencing people' (MIPs) taking care of the process of organising.

In group work it is the team that is crucial. There is close-range influencing, sometimes leading to rather strong and even harsh norm-setting from which it is much more difficult to escape (concertive control; Barker, 1993). A united and tight group is often a much more powerful source of influence and control than a single HIP. In some cases, where a team has a common purpose and works on a project that is distinct, the group tends to be crucial for support, coordination and influencing. In many cases, groups are not that united and the impact of colleagues is fairly loose, but still people may rely on the group's resources as much or more than on any HIP. Often group-norms for, for example, effort matter more than a manager trying to increase work pace.

The idea with the 'HIP', 'MIP' and 'LIP' terms is to encourage thinking that facilitates a different and possible empirically and analytically more thoughtful way of addressing what is often termed leadership and followership. Terms like HIP, MIP and LIP are as broad as leadership and followership but can be used to reflect on what is involved in the HIP, whether a high-impact person, position or process. Sometimes this involves leadership, sometimes management, sometimes using power (in a forceful or manipulative way). What authors like Kerr and Jermier refer to as alternatives to leadership, for example, is perhaps better seen as HIP than leadership. The alternative vocabulary can thus encourage the zooming in and out of what is happening in social relations involving organising, guidance, control etc. at work. Authors interested in moving away from traditional notions of leadership and eager to promote practice, relational, shared and other 'non-heroic' and more socially shared views of leadership are probably wise to develop and at least occasionally use alternative concepts that are not so easily confused with leadership vocabulary. Leadership too easily becomes everything and nothing.

A scholarly rich yet practically problematic example is the work of DeRue and Ashford (2010). Their conceptual model describes how people claim and grant social influence, and the model emphasises the dynamic nature of these processes. However, DeRue and Ashford do not use a descriptive terminology centred on social influence – such as HIP, MIP and LIP – but call the dynamic social influence process 'claiming and granting leadership'. The work of DeRue and Ashford shows how social influence can dynamically switch in otherwise stable relationships, and the described dynamic relationships might be rather peer-based than requiring a leader–follower distinction. In this way, their work could have become a foundational article for rethinking alternatives to leadership. However, supposedly due to the leadership label, the article is mostly cited by leadership scholars and is commonly referred to as an exemplar for the progress of knowledge about leadership (cf. Dinh et al., 2014). Inadvertently – and unnecessarily – DeRue and Ashford might reinforce the leader-centrism that their work is supposed to challenge as they leave little space for other constructions than leader/follower and use key term 'leader' quite broadly.

As we have seen there are plenty of alternative framings for asymmetrical human relations besides the leader–follower distinction. By returning to many of the classic – but today perhaps less fashionable – texts on work organisations, we can find many useful concepts and the ones we have touched upon in this section are of course just a small sample. Being clear about theoretical concepts and working with differentiations within and outside leadership language makes it also easier to see practical alternatives, which we will explore now.

ALTERNATIVES FROM A PRACTICAL PERSPECTIVE

The difference in the section below compared to our more theoretical outlook above should not be exaggerated; also practitioners need to be careful about what concepts to use and when, even if expectations often are higher for scholarly use of leadership vocabulary. However, the reflexive practitioner is also well served with a broader linguistic 'toolbox' than one that only contains a limited number of alternatives. This may inform decision-making and action about when to use instruction (management), sweet talk (leadership) and the whip (power).

Instead of leadership development specialists and managers working with their own pet solution – typically a favoured, upbeat version of leadership – as the answer to all (and even non-existing) problems, practitioners are wise to start with identifying an organisational problem first and thinking about a range of solutions before adapting one. If leadership is not postulated as the solution ex ante, managers have the chance to identify that a certain problem (e.g., lack of employee performance, motivation or satisfaction) can be overcome better by alternatives to leadership than by leadership itself. For instance, offering suitable seminars for training and development, or offering good work conditions, might better meet people's and organisations' needs than regular managerial leadership interventions. In fact, good work conditions might be characterised by the very absence of having a boss who constantly interferes with the work in an attempt to 'inspire' or 'transform' an employee or having long meetings allowing the demonstration of leadership. A manager not immediately being involved, present and available may foster independence among employees. Sometimes laissez faire orientations from management may actually be a good idea. It should be on a spectrum of possibilities that managers, HR, educators and others interested in organisational practice consider. Thus, for those who seek to improve work processes and outcomes instead of reaffirming managerial ideology with fashionable leadership lingo, adopting a more problem-oriented and less leadership-is-the-solution type of logic is advisable.

Of course, there are endless alternatives within what is categorised as leadership (as defined above). First, we briefly summarise alternatives *within* leadership. This is not our main point in this chapter, but helps to clarify what we (and many others) mean by leadership and then we can easier clarify *alternatives outside* (or *alternatives to*) leadership. Concept confusion is a major problem in this domain, so we need to work with both what we mean by leadership and what leadership is not – that is, what is better addressed through other terms (Alvesson & Blom, 2022). Finally, we outline in more detail one outside alternative – that is, how managers can re-envision coordination at work by assuming a middle ground between regarding people as innately desiring leadership or as innately governing themselves.

Perhaps needless to say, the theoretical and the practical hang together, there is no practice not informed by some theoretical notion, but of course academics trying to theoretically account for alternatives to leadership is different from managers and subordinates (or people in more open and sometimes fluctuating HIP–MIP–LIP relations) trying to deal with practical problems. Our emphasis below is more on the ways in which organisational practitioners can address the alternatives to leadership issue.

Alternatives Within the Leadership Domain

Even if we manage to define leadership in a fairly precise way that does not cover every aspect of organisational everyday life in terms of hierarchy, influence and collaboration, it tends to entail fairly different elements and activities. Within the leadership concept as defined in the very beginning of this chapter we can still find several rather different ways of exercising influence: leadership as *prophesy* (vision, charisma), *preaching* (values, ideals, ethics), *pedagogy* (developing, learning, personal growth), *psychotherapy* (support, emotional labour) and *party hosting* (keeping up the good spirit, creating team feelings etc.) (see Alvesson et al., 2017 for a more detailed description of these five key elements). From a practical perspective, as manager or other authority, it is useful to think about which of the five key elements of leadership the supposed followers and the organisation and those it serves need most. Usually, not all five key elements are equally important in a given situation. For instance, some situations rather call for instructing and fostering learning whereas others call for emotional support.

Other ways of describing the key elements of leadership could be in terms of influencing cognitive, emotional or axiological meanings: addressing both head and heart. It may be conducted through sense-giving (Gioia & Chittipeddi, 1991), role-modelling behaviour (being first, eating last) and through narratives, storytelling, slogans, aesthetics, material arrangements, rituals etc., expressing meanings and values (Alvesson, 1995) or trying to work with the unconscious or taken for granted (Schein, 1985).

Alternatives Outside the Leadership Domain

We just discussed alternatives within leadership (as defined here and by many other scholars). However, we focus on alternatives to (or outside) leadership in this chapter. Outside the leadership domain, we can point at the following practical alternatives, grouped in three broad categories.

Hierarchical: For example, management (here understood as direction and control based on formal rights and hierarchy, such as planning, budgeting, scheduling, guidelines, supervision, performance control: see, e.g., Mintzberg, 2009; Tengblad, 2006), coercive power (Alvesson et al., 2017) and bureaucracy (Adler & Borys, 1996).

Automatic: For example, market feedback and performance management systems (see, e.g., Kerr & Jermier, 1978, on task feedback).

Horizontal: For example, processes (coordination mechanisms concerning standardisation of processes and/or outputs; Howell & Dorfman, 1981), professionalism, teams (Bass, 1990; Villa et al., 2003), adhocracy/mutual adjustment and autonomy (e.g., for people less interested in extrinsic rewards provided by their 'leader'; Kerr & Jermier, 1978). Also organisational cultures may provide meaning, direction and cohesion through horizontal processes in the form of broadly shared meanings (Alvesson, 2013).

These modes of organising are not mutually exclusive but may work in tandem with each other, some also with leadership. For instance, management may be softened or supplemented with leadership. Likewise, wielding coercive power might be softened too – for example, when a manager punishes a subordinate after a wrongdoing and does 'leadership' by explaining why she kicked ass and underscores values and norms so that the subordinate understands why the butt hurts; leadership can promote understanding or even acceptance of coercion. So alternatives are seldom categorical, it is not a matter of strict either–or, at least not over longer time periods.

Departing From the Subordinates' Perspectives

There are two opposing assumptions that people can make about leadership. First, that organisations and people in them have an innate need of leadership. According to such a view, alternative modes of organising are exceptions. Second, the counter-assumption is that most organisations call for some management and structure for planning and coordination in combination with competent employees, and that leadership is the exception. According to such a view, most employees can handle most of their work tasks and their relations through own initiatives, problem-solving and peer support in well-structured organisations without any need for managerial leadership interventions.

One does not need to buy firmly into either of the two assumptions about a) there being an innate individual/organisational need for leadership, or b) the majority of people being self-governing and drawing upon other social resources than managerial leadership. Instead, we can keep in mind that both tendencies exist and that in real life many people are between the two extremes. We do, however, believe that most leadership researchers and practitioners (educators, HR people, consultants, managers) are too strongly attached to the first assumption – and would call for a much more multidimensional and reflexive approach to leader-centric thinking and practical interventions. There is a serious 'over-selling' of leadership in business schools, by media, consultants and organisations that may foster immaturity, passivity, dependence and even learned helplessness by people. Arguably, idealistic notions promising both much leadership and *star followership* (Kelley, 1988) are paradoxical, confusing and not helpful. Leadership calls for the taking of a followership position, and by that the recognition and acceptance of a clear asymmetrical relation. Initiatives and autonomy are then to a certain extent limited and constrained.

Instead of habitually relying on some leadership model from the latest attended executive education sessions, managers could depart from what the subordinates really need – and want – from their superior in terms of support and interventions. Often employees are more concerned with mundane managerial issues regarding how to get the job done rather than asking for bold new visions, inspiration or groundbreaking cultural change (Blom & Alvesson, 2014). Sometimes subordinates see leadership as interference at work, involving time-consuming meetings. Of course, leadership interventions that are not demanded might still be helpful because subordinates may be wrong, opportunistic or short-sighted in terms of their needs, and sometimes a degree of force (use of bureaucracy, management or coercive power) may be necessary. However, managers may be wrong too, be overambitious or insensitive to subordinates' situation and responses, and sometimes subordinates know better what has to be done than managers. Often a dialogue and mutual consideration of managerial and subordinates' assessments and wants may be motivated (Fryer, 2011). When it comes to leadership – more than management and 'transactional issues' (wages, work tasks, schedules, performance assessment) – the inclinations of subordinates to take a receptive role are, as said, crucial, so a significant grounding in the subordinates' experiences, views and responses are important here. Blom and Alvesson (2014) talk about *leadership on demand* as a possibly relevant view and working principle.

The relative need or demand for leadership can be framed in terms of *why, what, how* or *when* something should be done. It is suggested that there is a declining need for leadership along the four interrogatives. That is, questions around 'why' we do a certain activity are generally more suitable for leadership activities (e.g., providing meaning by addressing both heart and mind) than questions on 'when' something should be done (e.g., timing of an activity and/or deadlines, which is typically more a matter of management). 'What' and 'how' things are done is somewhere between 'why' and 'when', as illustrated in Figure 37.1 below. This heuristic model based on the fourfold typology above illustrates that the need for leadership varies

```
Why?    ──▶  ┌─────────────┐
             │  Leadership │
What?   ──▶  │             │
             │             │
How?    ──▶  │             │
             │  Management │
When?   ──▶  └─────────────┘
```

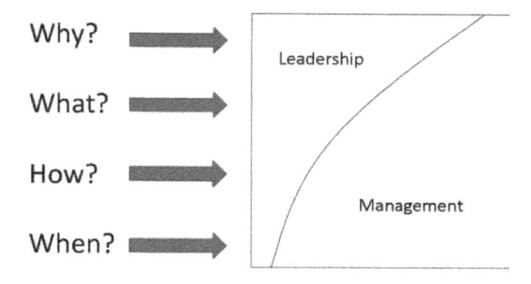

Figure 37.1 The usefulness of leadership as a managerial response to subordinates' task related issues

across situations and might be a simple yet powerful tool for managers and other superiors but also consultants, HR people and educators as well as subordinates thinking about appropriate support or interventions.

As said, leadership is of course not isolated from the alternatives, and one should always be careful with clean-cut dichotomies in leadership studies (Collinson & Tourish, 2015), but still, it makes much sense to not drown too much in a vague and all-embracing concept of leadership, obstructing clear thinking and discussions about alternative ways of organising.

SUMMARY AND CONCLUDING WORDS

We suggest that it is important to think about a set of alternatives within as well as outside leadership. In this chapter, we have mainly addressed the latter. With the explosion of perspectives, definitions and vocabularies addressing 'leadership' in one or another, sometimes wild-eyed sense, it may be difficult to think about alternatives to leadership as there is a surplus of people suggesting an alternative view of – and not an alternative to – leadership; the only alternative to leadership type A may be leadership type B. Sometimes this appears progressive such as post-heroic leadership, but it still reinforces the domination of leadership vocabulary and the practical effect may be that theoretical nuances are lost and the dominant discourse of the centrality of leadership is maintained rather than softened. Even if participatory, coaching, delegating, supportive, shared, distributed, servant and other post-heroic views of leadership are popular, there is still an emphasis on 'leadership' playing an important role, guiding most people's thinking into leadership/followership and away from *real* alternatives to leadership.

The entire idea of alternatives to leadership is in a sense problematic as it still frames the issue around leadership. Alternatives seem to call for deviations from the normal case. The framing indicates that leadership is normal and significant, and that its alternatives such as autonomy or professionalism are exceptions. Inadvertently, such a framing imposes an order of importance that puts leadership above its alternatives, but this order is only assumed instead of empirically grounded. Instead of thinking about alternatives to leadership, we need to move away from a leadership-focused framing and switch the perspective. For instance, we could search for alternatives to competence, professionalism, autonomy and group support, and identify leadership as one possible option. Until now, such alternative perspectives are rarely taken, which is testified by the preponderance of leadership handbooks and the relative absence of handbooks on autonomy or self-directed workers – where a chapter could be alternatives to autonomy and include leadership/followership as one option.

Leadership scholars claim an extreme significance of leadership, which motivates the centrality of the topic (e.g., Avolio et al., 2009). But significance is easily an outcome of how much a vocabulary covers – if leadership is addressed broadly and variedly enough, then it is of course very significant; and if a concept covers everything, it tells us nothing. Leadership studies bear strong imprints of this problem. Leadership as a 'hembig' – a hegemonic, ambiguous, big term used without precision or discrimination – should be avoided as far as possible (Alvesson & Blom, 2022). Geertz (1973) suggests that we cut concepts down in size so they cover less and reveal more. The leadership field has moved in the other direction. A more limited and precise understanding opens up for alternatives – intellectually and practically. It might therefore be seen as a paradox that we suggest the broader and more abstract terms HIP/LIP/MIP above. Are they not more 'vague' than leader, manager, etc.? To a certain extent they are but should be seen as less ideologically loaded tools for stimulating reflexivity and new thinking and they can serve as a preliminary starting point for the curious researcher exploring how work is directed and supported in an empirical context without locking themselves in a narrower – and perhaps overhasty – vocabulary a priori. In some cases it may be difficult to empirically uphold the distinction management/leadership – the theoretical definitions are reasonably clear, but sometimes empirical examples may at first be hard to define in terms of management or leadership and here HIP may signal something more open than a premature categorisation such as leadership. Furthermore, the idea is to use HIP/LIP/MIP *together* with the vocabulary of leadership, management, power, group work, peer work, autonomy etc. (Alvesson et al., 2017).

Vital is of course to recognise that a non-leader is not per definition the same as a follower. We need alternatives to followership. People can do work, organisation and employment in many different ways, many of them not falling into a leader–follower categorisation. A reflexive research practice calls for working with distinctions – as pedagogical and clear as possible. An all-embracing and ambiguous leadership concept clouds both theoretical thinking and practical interventions. Thinking of alternatives to leadership – and seeing leadership as just one option of many on how to organise people at work – is a possibility worth taking seriously.

REFERENCES

Adler, P. S., & Borys, B. (1996). Two types of bureaucracy: Enabling and coercive. *Administrative Science Quarterly*, 61–89.

Alvesson, M. (1995). *Management of Knowledge-Intensive Firms*. de Gruyter.

Alvesson, M. (2013) *Understanding Organizational Culture*. Sage.

Alvesson, M. (2019). Waiting for Godot: Eight major problems in the odd field of leadership studies. *Leadership*, 15(1), 27–43.

Alvesson, M., & Blom, M. (2022). The hegemonic ambiguity of big concepts in organization studies. *Human Relations*, 75(1), 58–86.

Alvesson, M., Blom, M., & Sveningsson, S. (2017). *Reflexive Leadership*. Sage.

Alvesson, M., & Einola, K. (2019) Warning for excessive positivity: Authentic leadership and other traps in leadership studies. *Leadership Quarterly*, 30(4), 383–395.

Alvesson, M., & Kärreman, D. (2016). Intellectual failure and ideological success in organization studies: The case of transformational leadership. *Journal of Management Inquiry*, 25(2), 139–152.

Antonakis, J., & Day, D. V. (2017). *The Nature of Leadership*. Sage.

Avolio, B. J., Walumbwa, F. O., & Weber, T. J. (2009). Leadership: Current theories, research, and future directions. *Annual Review of Psychology*, 60, 421–449.

Barker, J. R. (1993). Tightening the iron cage: Concertive control in self-managing teams. *Administrative Science Quarterly*, 38, 408–437.

Bass, B. M. (1985). *Leadership and Performance Beyond Expectations*. Collier Macmillan.

Bass, B. (1990). *Bass & Stogdill's Handbook of Leadership: Theory, Research, and Managerial Applications* (3rd edn). Free Press.

Bennis, W. (1989). *Why Leaders Can't Lead: The Unconscious Conspiracy Continues*. Jossey-Bass.

Blom, M. (2016). Leadership studies: A Scandinavian inspired way forward? *Scandinavian Journal of Management*, 32(2), 106–111.

Blom, M., & Alvesson, M. (2014). Leadership on demand: Followers as initiators and inhibitors of managerial leadership. *Scandinavian Journal of Management*, 30(3), 344–357.

Blom, M. & Lundgren, M. (2020). The (In)voluntary follower. *Leadership*, 16(2), 163–179.

Calas, M., & Smircich, L. (1991). Voicing seduction to silence leadership. *Organization Studies*, 12(4), 567–602.

Collinson, D. (2011). Critical leadership studies. In A. Bryman, D. Collinson, K. Grint, B. Jackson, B. & Uhl-Bien, M. (Eds.). *The Sage Handbook of Leadership* (pp. 181–194). Sage.

Collinson & D. Tourish (2015). Teaching leadership critically: New directions for leadership pedagogy. *Academy of Management Learning and Education*, 14(4), 576–594.

DeRue, S., & Ashford, S. (2010). Who will lead and who will follow? A social process of leadership identity in organizations. *Academy of Management Review*, 35(4), 627–647.

Dinh, J. E., Lord, R. G., Gardner, W. L., Meuser, J. D., Liden, R. C., & Hu, J. (2014). Leadership theory and research in the new millennium: Current theoretical trends and changing perspectives. *Leadership Quarterly*, 25(1), 36–62.

Dionne, S., Yammarino, F., Howell, J., & Villa, J. (2005). Substitute for leadership, or not. *Leadership Quarterly*, 16(1), 169–193.

Fleishman, E. A., Mumford, M. D., Zaccaro, S. J., Levin, K. Y., Korotkin, A. L., & Hein, M. B. (1991). Taxonomic efforts in the description of leader behavior: A synthesis and functional interpretation. *Leadership Quarterly*, 2(4), 245–287.

Fryer, M. (2011). Facilitative leadership: Drawing on Jürgen Habermas' model of ideal speech to propose a less impositional way to lead. *Organization*, 19(1), 25–43.

Geertz, C. (1973). *The Interpretation of Cultures*. Basic Books.

Gemmill, G., & Oakley, J. (1992). Leadership: An alienating social myth? *Human Relations*, 45(2), 113–129.

Gioia, D., & Chittipeddi, K. (1991). Sensemaking and sensegiving in strategic change initiation. *Strategic Management Journal*, 12(6), 433–448.

Gordon, R. (2002). Conceptualising leadership with respect to its historical-contectual antecedents to power. *Leadership Quarterly*, 13(2), 151–167.

Gordon, R. (2011). Leadership and power. In A. Bryman, D. Collinson, K. Grint, B. Jackson & M. Uhl-Bien (Eds.). *The Sage Handbook of Leadership* (pp. 195–202). Sage.

Gronn, P. (2002). Distributed leadership as a unit of analysis. *Leadership Quarterly*, *13*(4), 423–451.

Hartley, J., & Benington, J. (2011). Political leadership In A. Bryman, D. Collinson, K. Grint, B. Jackson & M. Uhl-Bien (Eds.). *The Sage Handbook of Leadership* (pp. 203–214). Sage.

Hersey, P., & Blanchard, K. (1977). *Management of Organizational Behavior: Utilizing Human Resources* (3rd edn). Prentice Hall.

Hirschman, A. O. (1970). The search for paradigms as a hindrance to understanding. *World Politics*, *22*(3), 329–343.

House, R. J. (1971). A path goal theory of leader effectiveness. *Administrative Science Quarterly*, *16*(3), 321–339.

House, R. J. (1977). *A 1976 Theory of Charismatic Leadership*. Faculty of Management Studies, University of Toronto.

House, R. J. (1996). Path-goal theory of leadership: Lessons, legacy, and a reformulated theory. *Leadership Quarterly*, *7*(3), 323–352.

House, R. J., & Aditya, R. N. (1997). The social scientific study of leadership: Quo vadis?. *Journal of Management*, *23*(3), 409–473.

Howell, J., & Dorfman, P. W. (1981). Substitutes for leadership: Test of a construct. *Academy of Management Journal*, *24*(4), 714–728.

Howell, J., Dorfman, P. W., & Kerr, S. (1986). Moderator variables in leadership research. *Academy of Management Review*, *11*(1), 88–102.

Hunter, S. T., Bedell-Avers, K. E., & Mumford, M. D. (2007). The typical leadership study: Assumptions, implications, and potential remedies. *Leadership Quarterly*, *18*(5), 435–446.

Jermier, J., & Kerr, S. (1997). Substitutes for leadership: Their meaning and measurement – contextual recollections and current observations. *Leadership Quarterly*, *8*(2), 95–100.

Keller, R. T. (2006). Transformational leadership, initiating structure, and substitutes for leadership: A longitudinal study of research and development project team performance. *Journal of Applied Psychology*, *91*(1), 202–210.

Kelley, R. (1988). In praise of followers. *Harvard Business Review*, *66*(6), 141–148

Kerr, S., & Jermier, J. M. (1978). Substitutes for leadership: Their meaning and measurement. *Organizational Behavior and Human Performance*, *22*, 375–403.

Ladkin, D. (2010). *Rethinking Leadership*. Edward Elgar.

Learmonth, M., & Morrell, K. (2017). Is critical leadership studies 'critical'? *Leadership*, *13*(3), 257–271.

Learmonth, M., & Morrell, K. (2019). *Critical Perspectives on Leadership*. Routledge.

Lovelace, K. J., Manz, C., & Alves, J. C. (2007). Work stress and leadership development: The role of self-leadership, shared leadership, physical fitness and flow in managing demands and increasing job control. *Human Resource Management Review*, *17*(4), 374–387.

Lukes, S. (1978). Power and authority. In Bottomore, T. & Nisbet, R (Eds.) A History of Sociological Analysis. (pp 633-76) Heinemann.

Manz, C. (1986). Self-leadership: Toward an expanded theory of self-influence processes in organizations. *Academy of Management Review*, *11*(3), 585–600.

Mintzberg, H. (2009). *Managing*. Berrett-Koehler.

Pearce, C., & Conger, J. (Eds.). (2003). *Shared Leadership*. Sage.

Podsakoff, P., MacKenzie, S., & Bommer, W. (1996). Transformational leader behaviors and substitutes for leadership as determinants of employee satisfaction, commitment, trust, and organizational citizenship behaviors. *Journal of Management*, *22*(2), 259–298.

Pratt, M. (2000). The good, the bad, and the ambivalent: Managing identification among Amway distributors. *Administrative Science Quarterly*, *45*(3), 456–493.

Schein, E. (1985). *Organizational Culture and Leadership*. Jossey-Bass.

Schriesheim, C. A. (1997). Substitutes-for-leadership theory: Development and basic concepts. *Leadership Quarterly*, *8*(2), 103–108.

Schriesheim, C. A., & Bird, B. J. (1979). Contributions of the Ohio state studies to the field of leadership. *Journal of Management*, *5*(2), 135–145.

Seers, A., & Chopin, S. (2012). The social production of leadership. In M. Uhl-Bien & S. Ospina (Eds.), *Advancing Relational Leadership* (pp. 43–81). Information Age.

Sennett, R. (1980). *Authority*. Knopf.

Shamir, B., Arthur, M. B., & House, R. J. (1994). The rhetoric of charismatic leadership: A theoretical extension, a case study, and implications for research. *Leadership Quarterly*, *5*(1), 25–42.

Smircich, L., & Morgan, G. (1982). Leadership: The management of meaning. *Journal of Applied Behavioral Science*, *18*(3), 257–273.

Tengblad, S. (2006). Is there a 'new managerial work'? A comparison with Henry Mintzberg's classic study 30 years later. *Journal of Management Studies*, *43*(7), 1437–1461.

Villa, J. R., Howell, J., Dorfman, P. W., & Daniel, D. L. (2003). Problems with detecting moderators in leadership research using moderated multiple regression. *Leadership Quarterly*, *14*(1), 3–23.

Weick, K. E. (1995). *Sensemaking in Organizations*. Sage.

Weick, K. E., Sutcliffe, K. M., & Obstfeld, D. (2005). Organizing and the process of sensemaking. *Organization Science*, *16*(4), 409–421.

Yukl, G., & Gardner, W. L. (2019). *Leadership in Organizations* (9th edn). Pearson Education.

Zaleznik, A. (1977). Managers and leaders: Are they different? *Harvard Business Review*, *55*(May–June), 67–78.

38

Paradoxes in Agentic and Communal Leadership

Jennifer L. Sparr, David A. Waldman and Eric Kearney

INTRODUCTION

Leadership in organisations – the process of *influencing and facilitating individual and collective efforts to accomplish shared objectives* (Yukl, 2012, p. 66) – is a phenomenon that has fascinated researchers for more than a century (Day & Antonakis, 2012). Scholars and practitioners alike have attempted to define a core of characteristics and behaviours associated with effective leadership, but in the ever-changing world of work this core also seems to be shifting and changing. The increasing level of complexity seems to require more complexity in leadership as well (Uhl-Bien & Arena, 2018; Waldman & Bowen, 2016).

Unfortunately, predominant paradigms in leadership research are ill-equipped to represent this complexity. The leadership literature presents itself in a rather fragmented state, which is due to the longstanding focus on single or unidimensional aspects of leadership (e.g., single traits like humility, or styles like empowering leadership). This has led to a long list of positive leadership concepts, albeit a lack of a clear understanding of effective leadership (Ashford & Sitkin, 2019; DeRue et al., 2011; Dinh et al., 2014; Zhu et al., 2019).

Fortunately, the nascent paradox perspective on leadership offers an integrative approach to help capture the complexity of leadership.

In this chapter, we build on the notion that an important aspect of effective leadership in a complex and dynamic world is to constructively manage paradoxes. Following Schad et al. (2016, p. 6), we define paradox as *persistent contradictions between interdependent elements.* The core idea of paradox theory is that whenever one is facing a paradox, *both-and* approaches are more effective than *either/or* strategies (for an overview see Schad et al., 2016). A both-and approach acknowledges the seeming contradictions that are inherent in a paradox. But it also recognises the interdependence between and persistence of the conflicting elements of a paradox. It is the ongoing reconciliation of this interdependence that is key to what has become known as paradoxical leadership (Zhang et al., 2015).

In this chapter, we first provide a short overview of the literature on paradox and leadership. We then discuss agency and communion as meta-categories from which to draw paradoxes in leader traits, orientations and behaviours (Kearney et al., 2019; Waldman & Bowen, 2016; Zheng et al., 2018a). We chose agency and communion because they have been described as *two fundamental dimensions of social judgment* (Abele et al., 2008, p. 1202) and leadership is an inherently social process. Agency refers to how leaders assert themselves, whereas communion is about how leaders attend to the needs of others (Waldman & Bowen, 2016). As we argue, some leaders feel torn between agentic and communal elements, and thus choose an either/or approach to address them. In contrast, other leaders will embrace the seemingly contradictory yet interdependent elements in a paradox (i.e., both-and approach), thereby leveraging the energy of the tensions between them (Miron-Spektor et al., 2018).

We introduce paradoxical examples of agency and communion in leaders' traits, orientations and behaviours for illustration. Further, we compare three typical leadership approaches to agency and communion, namely the unidimensional one-best-way approach, a situational switching approach and the paradoxical approach. Since leadership is a process that is co-created between leaders and followers (DeRue & Ashford, 2010; Uhl-Bien et al., 2014), we juxtapose leader agency and communion with follower alignment and initiative as the paradoxical building blocks of follower performance (Uhl-Bien et al., 2014). We elaborate on the sense-making–sense-giving process as the core of paradoxical leadership before we discuss how paradoxes are co-constructed, not only between leaders and followers in organisations but importantly also between researchers to integrate the extant leadership research.

PARADOX AND LEADERSHIP

Paradox research has a tradition of more than 30 years, with its roots going back to both Eastern and Western ancient philosophy (Schad et al., 2016). The paradox perspective has informed various fields of research over time, thus serving as a meta-theory that *deals with principles of tensions and their management across multiple contexts, theories, methodological approaches, and variables* (Schad et al., 2016, p. 9).

One of those fields informed by paradox theory is leadership. Scholars have studied paradox in leaders' roles and interactions, with the idea that effective leaders demonstrate more behavioural complexity, as manifested in paradoxical behaviours, than ineffective leaders (Denison et al., 1995). Others have focused on leadership dealing with stability and adaptability in organisational change, suggesting that effective leaders shift between forceful and approval-oriented leadership (Denis et al., 2001). In the context of team innovation, Gebert et al. (2010) illustrated that the opposing action strategies of delegation and directiveness need to be combined to draw on the positive effects of each of these strategies, while neutralising their respective potential downsides. The relevance of paradox management has been discussed for senior leaders who face strategic paradoxes (Smith, 2014; Smith et al., 2012) and middle managers dealing with change and complexity (Lüscher & Lewis, 2008; Sparr, 2018), as well as for leaders at all levels engaging in people-focused leadership (Zhang et al., 2015). Thus, learning to be paradox-savvy (Waldman & Bowen, 2016) is an important challenge for leaders at all levels in an organisation (Waldman et al., 2019).

These studies provide important insights, based on conceptual (e.g., Gebert et al., 2010, Smith, 2014; Smith et al., 2012; Sparr, 2018; Waldman & Bowen, 2016) and empirical work, both qualitative (e.g., Lüscher & Lewis, 2008) and quantitative (e.g., Zhang et al., 2015). However, there are still blind spots in our understanding of paradox and leadership. For example, scholars have only recently begun to study mediators and moderators in the relationship between paradoxical leadership and outcomes such as creativity, innovative behaviour and performance in general. This research highlights the importance of leader vision and team and individual ambidexterity (Zhang et al., 2021), workload pressure and employee integrative complexity (Shao et al., 2019) and change readiness (Sparr et al., 2022) for paradoxical leadership effectiveness.

Another blind spot in the extant literature on paradox and leadership involves outcomes other than performance, creativity and innovation, such as follower well-being. Furthermore, the potential dark side of paradoxical leadership is not yet well understood. For example, Berti and Simpson (2021) argue that an implicit assumption in paradox theory is that actors have full agency in responding to paradoxes, which might not be true in asymmetric power relationships, such as leader–follower relationships.

While the field of paradox and leadership studies is expanding, a framework to integrate the different models and empirical findings is missing. Therefore, we continue this chapter with presenting agency and communion as meta-categories of leadership that allow us to comprehensively capture paradoxical tensions between seemingly contradictory, yet interdependent and persistent leader traits, orientations and behaviours. We argue that these meta-categories can serve as a basic framework for theorising on paradox and leadership with regard to multiple desirable outcomes.

Agency and Communion as Meta-Categories of Leadership

More than a century of research has examined leader traits, orientations and behaviours in different contexts (e.g., Day & Antonakis, 2012). The heterogeneity of the resulting leadership literature is illustrated in the comprehensive review conducted by Dinh et al. (2014), who identified 66 different leadership theory domains. These authors, together with others (e.g., Ashford & Sitkin, 2019; DeRue et al., 2011; Zhu et al., 2019), call for future research to *develop integrative perspectives that consider how disparate leadership theories relate or operate simultaneously to influence the emergence of leadership phenomena* (Dinh et al., 2014, p. 55). Extant frameworks either focus on leader behaviour to the exclusion of leader traits and orientations (Borgmann et al., 2016; Yukl, 2012), or on leader characteristics but not leader behaviour (Zaccaro et al., 2018). Moreover, if studies focus on behaviours (or traits or orientations), they tend to investigate one particular variable and not others in the same category (Yukl, 2012). Or alternatively, they study two variables within the same category (e.g., behaviours), but frame them as distinct, without addressing potential benefits of their combination (e.g., Lorinkova et al., 2013; Martin et al., 2013).

We propose that agency and communion are meta-categories that, in combination with paradox theory, are useful to foster an integration of the extant literature on leaders' traits, orientations and behaviours. From a paradox perspective, there is an inherent tension between agency and communion in leadership, as agency describes how leaders assert themselves, their goals and self- or organisational interests in their interactions with followers. In contrast, communion refers to leaders attending to the needs and interests of followers (Waldman & Bowen, 2016). Waldman and Bowen (2016) discussed the agency and communion framework as a means of considering paradoxes associated with combinations of a strong sense of self versus humility, and of maintaining control versus letting go of control. Further, Kearney et al. (2019) framed visionary and empowering leadership as manifestations of agency and communion, respectively. These leader qualities have in common that they seem reasonable when considered in isolation, but contradictory when imagined simultaneously within the same leader at the same time.

To illustrate this notion, we provide three examples pertaining to leader traits, orientations and behaviours, respectively. Each of these examples reveals how agency and communion can form the basis of leadership paradoxes. Figure 38.1 summarises the framework of agency and communion as meta-categories in leadership.

Trait Example: Narcissism and Humility

(Non-pathological) narcissists are self-centred, feel superior and strive for personal power (Galvin et al., 2010). Narcissistic leaders are agentic because they clearly assert themselves – for example, their own goals and interests – in their interactions with followers (Nehrlich et al., 2019). Narcissism is positively related to leader emergence. However, narcissism is also associated with leadership problems, and when viewed in isolation its effectiveness as a leader quality is not sustainable over time (Braun, 2017).

Humility is seemingly the opposite: *(a) a willingness to view oneself accurately, (b) an*

	Traits	Orientations	Behavior
Agentic Leadership	e.g., Narcissism	e.g., Determination	e.g., Directive
Communal Leadership	e.g., Humility	e.g., Ambivalence	e.g., Empowering

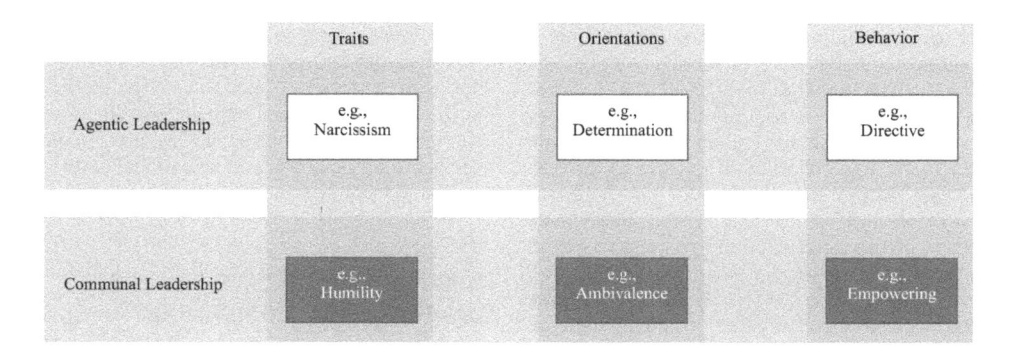

Figure 38.1 The meta-paradox of agency and communion in leadership with examples of leader traits, orientations and behaviours

appreciation of others' strengths and contributions, and (c) teachability (Owens & Hekman, 2016, p. 1088). Humble leaders are indeed perceived as communal (Zapata & Hayes-Jones, 2019). They foster communal processes, such as perspective-taking (Wang et al., 2018) or team-learning orientation (Owens et al., 2013) and thus facilitate positive outcomes (Owens et al., 2013). Nevertheless, leader humility may reduce one's identification with the leader role or desire to take charge (Waldman et al., 2012).

Narcissism and humility are examples of seemingly contradictory leader traits that have been studied mostly in isolation. However, they are also interdependent as humility keeps a narcissist grounded over time in terms of a sense of self in relation to others, while a tendency towards narcissism helps the humble person to maintain a sense of identification as a leader (Owens et al., 2015; Waldman et al., 2012; Zhang et al., 2017).

Orientation Example: Determination and Ambivalence

Prototypical leaders are expected to be determined – that is, having a clear understanding of where the organisation is going (e.g., Epitropaki et al., 2013; Podsakoff et al., 1996). Determined leaders provide stability and direction to followers and thus get things done (Podsakoff et al., 1996), which is clearly agentic. However, leaders who are overly determined may also risk losing followers along the way (e.g., Ames, 2009).

Conversely, ambivalence is defined as *simultaneously positive and negative orientations towards an object* (Ashforth et al., 2014, p. 1454). Ambivalence is triggered by complexity and invites collaborative contextual interpretation between leaders and followers (Guarana & Hernandez, 2014). Therefore, we consider ambivalence as communal. Positive outcomes include adaptation, proactivity and creativity (Ashford & Sitkin, 2019; Rothman & Melwani, 2017). On the downside, ambivalent leaders might also cause stress (Herr et al., 2019) and dysfunctional outcomes due to uncertainty and inaction (Ashforth et al., 2014; Rothman et al., 2017).

Leader determination and ambivalence are examples of seemingly contradictory leader orientations that have been studied in separate literatures. While leaders are likely to experience a tension between determination and ambivalence, these orientations are also interdependent and persistent as leaders pursue goals. That is, in order to effectively show determination (i.e., confidence in structures and directions), leaders may also need to allow for ambivalence (i.e., willingness to see both the pros and cons of an issue, question their direction based on new information and so forth) and vice versa.

Behaviour Example: Directive and Empowering Leadership

Directive leadership can be defined as *leader behaviors that provide followers with specific guidance regarding goals, means of achieving goals, and performance standards* (Martin et al., 2013, p. 1374). Directive leaders allow for very limited, if any, follower input on decisions (Lorinkova et al., 2013). Empirical results corroborate the agentic nature of directive leadership, which is positively related to task, process and role clarity (Lorinkova et al., 2013), but not proactive follower behaviour (Martin et al., 2013).

Conversely, empowering leadership is a set of leader behaviours that involve sharing power, responsibility and decision-making authority, as well as motivational and development support (Lee et al., 2017; Martin et al., 2013: Sharma & Kirkman, 2015). As such, it can be considered a communal leadership style. Empowering leadership is associated with a range of positive outcomes, such as follower proactive behaviour (Martin et al., 2013), team learning and performance (Lorinkova et al., 2013). However, empowering leadership seems to take time to engender positive effects on performance in teams (Lorinkova et al., 2013), and it can burden followers (Cheong et al., 2016).

Directive and empowering leadership behaviours have been studied extensively, but largely in isolation or in direct comparison (Lorinkova et al., 2013; Martin et al., 2013). However, they are also interdependent and persistent because for most jobs it is impossible for leaders to predefine every action of the followers. Thus, while providing direction, the leader may need to also empower followers to make their own decisions. At the same time, empowerment may be dependent on leader directiveness in order to maintain follower alignment with organisational goals.

THREE APPROACHES TO PARADOXES IN AGENCY AND COMMUNION

In the previous section, we established agency and communion as meta-categories in leadership, which provide an organising framework for key paradoxes in leadership traits, orientations and behaviours. Based on the assumption that: 1) agency and communion are the basic building blocks of leadership and 2) agency and communion often result in leadership paradoxes, we now compare three approaches to addressing paradoxes. We argue that when leaders face agentic and communal elements in their traits, orientations and behaviours, their approach to dealing with paradoxical tensions depends on the way that they frame and interpret the paradox. If they recognise and accept the tension between the seeming opposites but acknowledge their joint contribution to leadership effectiveness, they are likely to choose a both-and approach that combines the elements of the paradox. However, if leaders frame agency and communion as a dilemma, where competing choices come with fixed and inevitable advantages and disadvantages, they are more likely to choose an either/or approach (Miron-Spektor et al., 2018; Smith & Lewis, 2011; Waldman & Bowen, 2016). In the following sections, we describe and evaluate the three main approaches to paradoxes based in agency and communion, namely one-best-way (i.e., consistent choice of either/or), situationally flexible (i.e., flexible choice of either/or) and paradoxical (i.e., simultaneous choice of both-and) approaches.

One-best-way Approach

In a one-best-way approach, leaders clearly and consistently favour either agentic or communal leadership. The quest for identifying the one-best-way approach is a common tendency in the leadership literature (e.g., Ashford & Sitkin, 2019; Dinh et al., 2014). For example, in the early research on empowering leadership, these leader behaviours were viewed as superior to directive leadership. However, research shows that empowering leadership can be burdening for employees (Cheong et al., 2016; Sharma & Kirkman, 2015), which might indicate a lack of guidance and direction.

We suggest that agentic leadership primarily elicits follower alignment because leaders who assert themselves require followers to defer to them (cf. DeRue & Ashford, 2010). This might work well in a given situation, but over time the agentic-only leader risks rigidity in followers' responses because followers will increasingly be discouraged from taking their own perspective and initiative. By contrast, communal leadership is likely to stimulate follower initiative because the leader encourages followers to contribute their own ideas and capabilities. This also might work well in a given situation, but without clear direction there is the risk of confusion and chaos due to the lack of alignment. Paradox theory explains why tending to only one of the elements of a paradox results into such vicious cycles (Smith & Lewis, 2011).

Consider the difficulties of Steve Jobs in his early years at Apple as example (Isaacson, 2011). Essentially, Jobs was highly determined in his vision for the Macintosh computer as the predominant product for the firm. Jobs' determination and directive leadership style were essential to realise the creation of the Macintosh, which at the time in 1984 was truly innovative. However, the narcissistic Jobs was not able to simultaneously demonstrate humility, ambivalence and an empowering leadership style by pausing and taking into account the countervailing views of others on Apple's board of directors, especially the CEO at the time, John Sculley. In the end, the alignment that Jobs demanded from board members, coupled with his lack of communion – that is, his lack of willingness to question his own assumptions and consider other perspectives – led to rigidity and facilitated his ouster during his initial tenure at Apple.

Situationally Flexible Approach

The second option that leaders have when addressing agency and communion from an either/or perspective is to take a situationally flexible approach, in which they choose to display either agentic or communal traits, orientations, or behaviours, depending on what they decide is appropriate in a given situation. They switch back and forth between opposites, guided by their interpretations of situations and follower needs. This approach is well known in the literature; for example, in Hersey and Blanchard (1996)'s situational leadership theory.

The situationally flexible approach shares similar benefits and limitations as the one-best-way approach within a given situation because it encourages either follower alignment or initiative, but not both at relatively the same time. However, this approach is more flexible in the sense that the choice of agency and communion can be adapted to situational conditions. For example, if a leader whose natural tendency is to be agentic recognises that followers become rigid, that leader might choose to switch to communal leadership in some situations to stimulate follower initiative. Over time, the leader switches back and forth based on the followers' responses. Thus, a major advantage to the situationally flexible approach is that the leader potentially adapts to follower responses over time.

That said, this approach is still limited because it is, in essence, a rather bumpy sequence of successive one-best-way approaches in which the leader may attempt to engage in the 'one right leadership' for the respective situation. In some situations, followers' alignment is promoted through agentic leadership, but follower initiative is discouraged. In other situations, followers' initiative is elicited through communal leadership, but follower alignment is impeded. Thus, there is no situation in which the benefits of follower alignment and initiative are brought together, and this lost potential in each situation is likely to cumulate to less-than-optimal outcomes over time.

Moreover, diagnosing what is called for in a particular situation is a difficult task. For example, it has been suggested that followers with low experience should be led in a directive manner, while those with more experience should be empowered (Thompson & Vecchio, 2009). But other work would suggest the exact opposite (Ahearne et al., 2005). Indeed, this inconclusiveness could be a key reason for why it has been difficult to find supporting evidence for the effectiveness of situational leadership approaches (Johansen, 1990; Thompson & Vecchio, 2009).

Finally, such ways of approaching leadership can lead to attributions of leader inauthenticity due to perceived inconsistency, which can undermine leader effectiveness (Gardner et al., 2011). Leaders who frame agency and communion as a dilemma are likely to have relatively stable preferences for certain elements over their respective opposites (Zaccaro, 2007; Zaccaro et al., 2018). For example, a natural narcissist is likely to experience difficulties when attempting to be genuinely and exclusively humble under some conditions.

The Both-and Approach

Besides the described either/or approaches, leaders may choose a both-and approach to the contradictory, yet interdependent, elements of agency and communion in their traits, orientations and behaviours (Smith & Lewis, 2011; Zhang et al., 2015). We argue that, ultimately, the both-and approach can reveal the full benefits of agentic and communal leader qualities over time. Combining agency with communion leverages the virtues of both follower alignment and initiative, while neutralising potential disadvantages of one-sided agency or communion (for a similar argumentation, see Gebert et al., 2010). It allows leaders to fully utilise a broader repertoire of traits, orientations and behaviours. It does not favour one side, nor make compromises. Further, there is no such thing as an optimal level of certain traits, orientations and behaviours. Rather, leaders who pursue this approach will realise the positive sides of both elements, which neutralises the downsides of the respective opposite element. As such, the both-and approach is a *consistently inconsistent* strategy (Smith et al., 2016). It is consistent because the leader shows both agency and communion in a general sense over time. However, it is also inconsistent because the momentary manifestations of leading with both agency and communion can vary over time.

For example, leaders who combine directive and empowering leadership simultaneously take control, while sharing control with their followers (Waldman & Bowen, 2016; Zhang et al., 2015). They do not understand control as a zero-sum game in which sharing control means less control (Smith et al., 2016). Rather, they make suggestions for a certain direction and invite followers to discuss and decide together (Lüscher & Lewis, 2008). Such leaders encourage and fully support the development of their followers, and they do so in a directed manner that enables followers to have more structure as they pursue their empowerment in ways that serve the goals of both the employee and the company. In short, the paradoxical leader consistently, yet flexibly, employs both directive and empowering leadership – *relatively* simultaneously and over time. The term 'relative' is important here, since at any one moment in time the leader may be emphasising a particular pole (e.g., directiveness) of a leadership paradox. However, for various endeavours (e.g., making a decision on a task) and over time, the leader is careful to integrate both poles (e.g., both directiveness and empowerment) of the agency–communion paradox.

SENSE-MAKING: SENSE-GIVING PROCESSES AT THE CORE OF PARADOXICAL LEADERSHIP

Combining agency and communion is a complex task for leaders, as is combining alignment and initiative for followers. We argue that due to this complexity, leaders and followers need to co-create a reality in which they can thrive with the seemingly contradictory, yet interdependent, demands. To better understand this ongoing process, we draw on recent research on the paradox mindset (Miron-Spektor et al., 2018) and the notion that leader sense-giving about paradox is at the core of paradoxical leadership (Sparr, 2018; Waldman & Bowen, 2016). In the following, we summarise the model illustrated in Figure 38.2.

Leader Paradox Mindset and Sense-making of Agency and Communion

The concept of the paradox mindset describes the propensity of individuals to accept paradoxes, see the value in paradoxical tensions and feel comfortable (even energised) in dealing with them (Miron-Spektor et al., 2018). We argue that the acceptance of agency and communion as opposing yet complementary elements in their traits, orientations and behaviours helps leaders to explore the opportunities of a both-and approach. Instead of trying to avoid the tensions that are inherent in agency and communion, they will attempt to realise the advantages of combining the opposite elements in their traits, orientations and behaviours (Miron-Spektor et al., 2018; Smith & Lewis, 2011).

The process of working through paradox (Lüscher & Lewis, 2008) involves sense-making, namely a *process through which individuals work to understand novel, unexpected, or confusing events* (Maitlis & Christianson, 2014, p. 58). We suggest that leaders' paradox mindset helps them to stay positive and to continue the above described both-and sense-making process about how to leverage the potential of both agency and communion in an ever-changing, complex world. This will help them to find creative approaches (Miron-Spektor et al., 2018) and to acquire behavioural complexity in their leadership (Zheng et al., 2018b).

Leader Sense-giving and Follower Sense-making About Alignment and Initiative

Followers of a paradoxical both-and leader will experience both agency and communion in ongoing interactions with their leader and will experience those interactions as the paradoxical request for both alignment and initiative in their own responses. Like their leader, followers basically have two options when trying to make sense of these paradoxes. First, they can frame those tensions as a dilemma, classifying the leader's demands as either agentic or communal – that is, asking for either alignment or initiative. However, in this either/or framing, both-and signals are inconsistent and will leave the follower potentially confused, frustrated, or even behaviourally paralysed.

The second option that followers have is to understand their leaders' agency and communion, as well as the resulting demands for alignment and initiative, as contradictory but mutually enabling elements, which require a combination (see also Smith & Lewis, 2011; Zheng et al., 2018a). The both-and sense-making will result in combined actions because sense-making serves as the basis

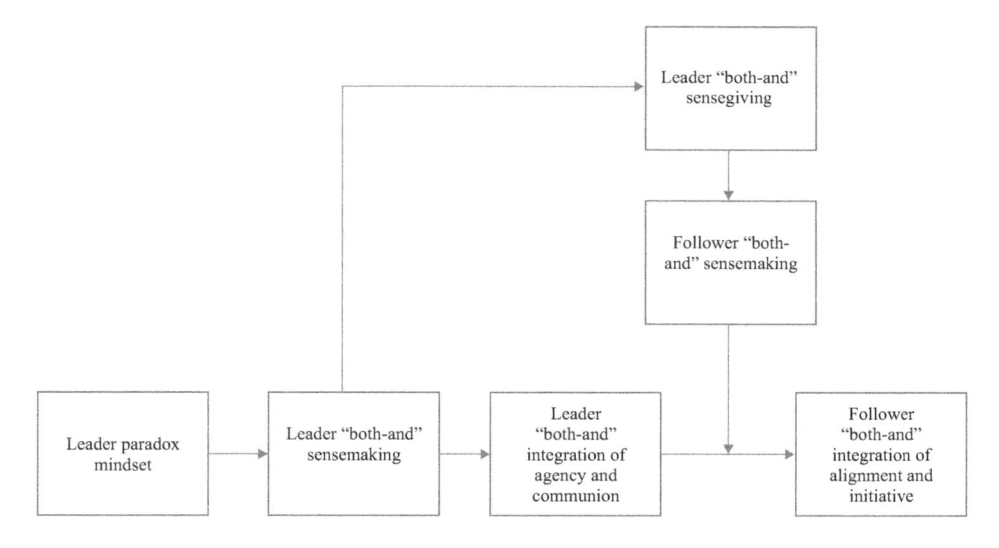

Figure 38.2 Model of 'both-and' leadership and followership

for action (Lüscher & Lewis, 2008; Weick et al., 2005). We claim that the followers' active both-and sense-making of the implications and expectations for their own behaviour will facilitate the relationship between both-and leadership and both-and followership. Empirical support for the facilitating role of follower both-and sense-making about paradoxical demands comes from research on follower paradox mindset, which has been shown to moderate the relationship between paradoxical tensions and follower in-role performance (i.e., alignment), as well as innovative behaviour (i.e., initiative; Miron-Spektor et al., 2018).

Sense-making is a social process that does not take place in isolation (Weick et al., 2005). Leaders are in a privileged position to influence their followers' sense-making through their own sense-giving regarding paradox, which is the process in which leaders convey their interpretation of paradoxes to followers and persuade them to adopt this interpretation (Maitlis & Lawrence, 2007; Sparr, 2018). Leaders' sense-giving pertaining to their own agency and communion ensues because the leader anticipates a gap in follower sense-making (Maitlis & Lawrence, 2007). As such, leader sense-giving is one of the most important leadership tasks in complex and ambiguous situations (Foldy et al., 2008; Gioia & Chittipeddi, 1991; Kraft et al., 2016). In other words, sense-giving is at the core of both-and leadership.

For example, a leader might explain to followers why they are empowering (i.e., to develop followers by providing them with freedoms and challenging them to be proactive), while at the same time directive (i.e., to ensure that whatever ideas and solutions followers develop are in line with the leader's expectations and specified objectives). Explaining the leader's actions should help followers understand that paradoxical leadership is not erratic, but that combining opposites follows a clear logic. It is intended to promote both follower initiative and alignment. We draw on earlier theorising on the importance of leader sense-giving about paradox (Sparr, 2018; Waldman & Bowen, 2016) to propose that leader both-and sense-giving facilitates follower both-and sense-making.

Implications for Sustainable Well-being and Performance

As argued above, one-best-way approaches to the agency–communion meta-paradox can create vicious cycles. That is, these approaches can engender downward spirals of increasing follower rigidity or confusion, which are the respective downsides of a consistent choice of either leader agency or communion. While both the one-best-way and situationally flexible approaches might work well within a given situation or in the short term, they are likely to engender inferior results over time – not only in terms of performance, but also with regard to well-being, as we have seen in the downsides of our examples (e.g., Cheong et al., 2016; 2019; Sharma & Kirkman, 2015). In contrast, the simultaneous both-and approach to leader agency–communion creates virtuous cycles – that is, upward spirals of leader agency and communion mutually complementing each other to stimulate both follower alignment and initiative, thus enabling sustainable outcomes over time (Smith & Lewis, 2011).

Ultimately, an important goal of effective leadership is to ensure both short- and long-term performance (Andriopoulos & Lewis, 2009) or, more generally, sustainable performance (Smith & Lewis, 2011). Long-term performance is dependent on short-term performance, because without the latter neither the individual nor the team or the organisation will realise a sustainable future. Similarly, long-term performance enables better short-term performance over time due to an accumulation of experience and resources. We propose that short- and long-term/sustainable performance at the individual, team and organisation levels is the cumulative, paradoxical outcome of simultaneous both-and leadership in dyadic leader–follower relationships, team-leadership and strategic leadership (see also Waldman & Bowen, 2016).

Future Directions and Conclusions

Co-construction of paradoxes between leaders, followers and researchers

In our discussion of the sense-making–sense-giving process at the core of both-and leadership and followership, we described this process as a co-construction of leader agency and communion and follower alignment and initiative. Both leaders and followers need the ability and motivation to adopt the paradoxical perspective, and this process is easier for individuals with a paradox mindset. With our reasoning in this chapter, we hope to encourage the leadership research community to also adopt a paradox mindset when framing their own research. With the notion of agency and communion as a meta-framework for leader traits, orientations and behaviours, we offer leaders and scholars alike a concrete way of framing both-and leadership.

Thus, researchers and practitioners can contribute to collective paradoxical frames (Miron-Spektor & Paletz, 2020), resulting in the valuing of both agency and communion in leadership processes. In the long term, this might even have consequences for implicit leadership and followership theories at the larger, societal level. That is, societies might move from predominantly agentic expectations of leaders to a more balanced view of agency and communion. This issue has been highlighted in discussions about gender and leadership (Zheng et al., 2018a; Zheng et al., 2018b).

At the same time, we caution organisational researchers and practitioners to be cognisant of their own potential biases regarding one particular pole of a paradox, or how exactly a pole might be operationalised in practice. Three examples come to mind. First, we have already mentioned the paradox of narcissism and humility, fully recognising that the former concept is often met with scepticism, or even disdain, by researchers and practitioners alike. Yet both theory and research point to the notion that narcissism and humility can potentially work in harmony to produce better leadership (e.g., Owens et al., 2015).

Second, Waldman and Javidan (2020) considered how the paradox of nationalism and globalism pertains to effective leadership. Among the two poles of this paradox, nationalism is obviously the more controversial in modern times. Nevertheless, Waldman and Javidan (2020) described how both nationalism and globalism can work in harmony for strategic/global leaders. In a way, this example underlines the ethical aspect in both-and leadership, because nationalism and globalism are only harmful if pursued in isolation, assuming one of them to be superior to the other. However, the both-and approach enables the benefits of both nationalism (e.g., good local citizenship) and globalism (e.g., embracing other cultures) at the same time, while neutralising their downsides (e.g., xenophobia, loss of national opportunities).

Third, also in line with current events, we recognise diversity and inclusion as important issues for organisations and their leaders. Diversity can be viewed in paradoxical terms by juxtaposing it with its opposite – homogeneity or unity (i.e., a belonging paradox according to Smith & Lewis, 2011; see also Zhang et al., 2015). While diversity and homogeneity/unity are seeming opposites, they are nevertheless interdependent in order to ensure effectiveness. For organisations, the paradoxical challenge is how to pursue diversity, while simultaneously maintaining and even strengthening unity. This is achieved by inclusion, the process of enabling people of different identities to be themselves, while also contributing to the collective sense of purpose or mission (Ferdman, 2017). Indeed, although diversity benefits organisations, a cohesive and strong or unified organisational culture is likely to also be necessary to achieve organisational effectiveness (cf. Nishii, 2013). In paradoxical leadership terms, the question becomes how organisational leaders can pursue diversity, while simultaneously pursuing unity (e.g., in terms of cultural values and beliefs).

The paradox perspective as a means to advance leadership research

The notion of agency and communion as organising meta-categories in leadership can guide researchers to classify and integrate patterns of leadership traits, orientations, behaviours and other concepts that have been the targets of research for years. To date, we have largely seen a focus on individual traits, orientations, or behavioural components of leadership. However, our paradoxical approach, which is centred around agency and communion, proposes that focusing on a unitary concept (e.g., humility, ambivalence, empowerment) misses the value of considering its respective conceptual opposite (e.g., narcissism, determination, directiveness). Further, we challenge some current thinking that dismisses the potential value of a trait like narcissism, or a behavioural tendency like directiveness. When examined in isolation, such traits or behaviours might seem problematic and less desirable than their seeming opposites, but in paradoxical combinations, they can make important contributions to leader effectiveness.

With our three examples of narcissism and humility, determination and ambivalence, and directive and empowering leadership, we have illustrated how a consideration of both the agentic and the communal elements of paradoxes contributes to our understanding of effective leadership. Nevertheless, we recognise that other paradoxical combinations exist, which could be incorporated into theoretical extensions of our meta-category of agency and communion paradoxes. They include, for example, the combination of distance and closeness (Zhang et al., 2015), collaboration and competition (Lavine, 2014) and vertical and shared leadership (Pearce et al., 2019).

In future research, we encourage experimental designs that manipulate traits, orientations and behaviours associated with agency and communion and, in a series of different scenarios, examines and compares one-sided, situationally switching and paradoxical leadership. This needs to be supplemented by qualitative and field research that helps us to better understand *how* leaders and followers actually address the type of paradoxes considered in this chapter. Furthermore, to study dynamics in the both-and leadership and followership process, methods including real-time observation for micro-scale dynamics and social network analysis for meso-scale dynamics could be considered (cf. Dooley & Lichtenstein, 2008). This will help us to better understand reciprocal effects in sense-giving and sense-making (Maitlis & Christianson, 2014; Weick et al., 2005), in particular between leader sense-giving and follower paradox mindset, and vice versa (Miron-Spektor et al., 2018), as well as between leadership and followership (DeRue & Ashford, 2010). Note that our assumptions may not be restricted to formal leadership. Indeed, the same assumptions may hold when leadership is shared, and leaders and followers flip their roles on a frequent basis.

REFERENCES

Abele, A. A., Uchronski, M., Suitner, C., & Wojciszke, B. (2008). Towards an operationalization of the fundamental dimensions of agency and communion: Trait content ratings in five courtries considering valence and frequency of word occurrence. *European Journal of Social Psychology*, 38, 1202–1217. https://www.doi.org/10.1002/ejsp.575

Ahearne, M., Mathieu, J., & Rapp, A. (2005). To empower or not to empower your sales force? An empirical examination of the influence of leadership empowerment behavior on customer satisfaction and performance. *Journal of Applied Psychology*, 90(5), 945–955. https://doi.org/10.1037/0021-9010.90.5.945

Ames, D. (2009). Pushing up to a point: Assertiveness and effectiveness in leadership and interpersonal dynamics. *Research in Organizational Behavior*, 29, 111–133. https://doi.org/10.1016/j.riob.2009.06.010

Andriopoulos, C., & Lewis, M. W. (2009). Exploitation–exploration tensions and organizational ambidexterity: Managing paradoxes of innovation. *Organization Science*, 20(4), 696–717. https://doi.org/10.1287/orsc.1080.0406

Ashford, S. J., & Sitkin, S. B. (2019). From problems to progress: A dialogue on prevailing issues in leadership research. *Leadership Quarterly*, 30(4), 454–460. https://doi.org/10.1016/j.leaqua.2019.01.003

Ashforth, B. E., Rogers, K. M., Pratt, M. G., & Pradies, C. (2014). Ambivalence in organizations: A multi-level approach. *Organization Science*, 25(5), 1453–1478. https://doi.org/10.1287/orsc.2014.0909

Berti, M., & Simpson, A. V. (2021). The dark side of organizational paradoxes: The dynamics of disempowerment. *Academy of Management Review*, 46(2), 252–274. https://doi.org/10.5465/amr.2017.0208

Borgmann, L., Rowold, J., & Bormann, K. C. (2016). Integrating leadership research: A meta-analytical test of Yukl's meta-categories of leadership. *Personnel Review*, 45(6), 1340–1366. https://doi.org/10.1108/pr-07-2014-0145

Braun, S. (2017). Leader narcissism and outcomes in organizations: A review at multiple levels of analysis and implications for future research. *Frontiers of Psychology*, 8, 773. https://doi.org/10.3389/fpsyg.2017.00773

Cheong, M., Spain, S. M., Yammarino, F. J., & Yun, S. (2016). Two faces of empowering leadership: Enabling and burdening. *Leadership Quarterly*, 27(4), 602–616. https://doi.org/10.1016/j.leaqua.2016.01.006

Day, D. V., & Antonakis, J. (2012). Leadership: Past, present, and future. In D. V. Day & J. Antonakis (Eds.), *The Nature of Leadership* (2nd edn, pp. 3–28). Sage.

Denis, J. L., Lamothe, L., & Langley, A. (2001). The dynamics of collective leadership and strategic change in pluralistic organizations. *Academy of Management Journal*, 44(4), 809–837. https://doi.org/10.5465/3069417

Denison, D. R., Hooijberg, R. & Quinn, R. E. (1995). Paradox and performance: Toward a theory of behavioral complexity in managerila leadership. *Organization Science*, 6(5), 524–540. https://www.jstor.org/stable/2634960

DeRue, D. S., & Ashford, S. J. (2010). Who will lead and who will follow? A social process of leadership identity construction in organizations. *Academy of Management Review*, 35(4), 627–647. https://doi.org/10.5465/amr.35.4.zok627

DeRue, D. S., Nahrgang, J. D., Wellman, N. E. D., & Humphrey, S. E. (2011). Trait and behavioral theories of leadership: an integration and meta-analytic test of their relative validity. *Personnel Psychology*, 64(1), 7–52. https://doi.org/https://doi.org/10.1111/j.1744-6570.2010.01201.x

Dinh, J. E., Lord, R. G., Gardner, W. L., Meuser, J. D., Liden, R. C., & Hu, J. (2014). Leadership theory and research in the new millennium: Current theoretical trends and changing perspectives. *Leadership Quarterly*, 25(1), 36–62. https://doi.org/10.1016/j.leaqua.2013.11.005

Dooley, K. J., & Lichtenstein, B. (2008). Research methods for studying the complexity dynamics of leadership. In M. Uhl-Bien & R. Marion (Eds.), *Complexity and Leadership Volume I: Conceptual Foundations*. Information Age.

Epitropaki, O., Sy, T., Martin, R., Tram-Quon, S., & Topakas, A. (2013). Implicit leadership and followership theories 'in the wild': Taking stock of information-processing approaches to leadership and followership in organizational settings. *Leadership Quarterly*, *24*(6), 858–881. https://doi.org/10.1016/j.leaqua.2013.10.005

Ferdman, B. M. (2017). Paradoxes of inclusion: Understanding and managing the tensions of diversity and multiculturalism. *Journal of Applied Behavioral Sciences*, *53*(2), 235–263. https://doi.org/10.1177/0021886317702608

Foldy, E. G., Goldman, L., & Ospina, S. (2008). Sensegiving and the role of cognitive shifts in the work of leadership. *Leadership Quarterly*, *19*(5), 514–529. https://doi.org/10.1016/j.leaqua.2008.07.004

Galvin, B. M., Waldman, D. A., & Balthazard, P. (2010). Visionary communication qualities as mediators of the relationship between narcissism and attributions of leader charisma. *Personnel Psychology*, *63*, 5009–5537. https://doi.org/10.1111/j.1744-6570.2010.01179.x

Gardner, W. L., Cogliser, C. C., Davis, K. M., & Dickens, M. P. (2011). Authentic leadership: A review of the literature and research agenda. *Leadership Quarterly*, *22*(6), 1120–1145. https://doi.org/10.1016/j.leaqua.2011.09.007

Gebert, D., Boerner, S., & Kearney, E. (2010). Fostering team innovation: Why is it important to combine opposing action strategies? *Organization Science*, *21*(3), 593–608. https://doi.org/10.1287/orsc.1090.0485

Gioia, D. A., & Chittipeddi, K. (1991). Sensemaking and sensegiving in strategic change initiation [https://doi.org/10.1002/smj.4250120604]. *Strategic Management Journal*, *12*(6), 433–448. https://doi.org/https://doi.org/10.1002/smj.4250120604

Guarana, C. L., & Hernandez, M. (2014). Building sense out of situational complexity: The role of ambivalence in creating functional leadership processes. *Organizational Psychology Review*, *5*(1), 50–73. https://doi.org/10.1177/2041386614543345

Herr, R. M., Van Harreveld, F., Uchino, B. N., Birmingham, W. C., Loerbroks, A., Fischer, J. E., & Bosch, J. A. (2019). Associations of ambivalent leadership with distress and cortisol secretion. *Journal of Behavioral Medicine*, *42*(2), 265–275. https://doi.org/10.1007/s10865-018-9982-z

Hersey, P., & Blanchard, K. (1996). Great ideas revisited: Revisiting the life-cycle theory of leadership. *Training & Development*, *50*(1), 42–47.

Isaacson, W. (2011). *Steve Jobs: The Exclusive Biography*. Little, Brown.

Johansen, B.-C. (1990). Situational leadership: A review of the research. *Human Resource Development Quarterly*, *1*(1), 73–85. https://doi.org/10.1002/hrdq.3920010109

Kearney, E., Shemla, M., van Knippenberg, D., & Scholz, F. A. (2019). A paradox perspective on the interactive effects of visionary and empowering leadership. *Organizational Behavior and Human Decision Processes*, *155*, 20–30. https://doi.org/10.1016/j.obhdp.2019.01.001

Kraft, A., Sparr, J. L., & Peus, C. (2016). Giving and making sense about change: The back and forth between leaders and employees. *Journal of Business and Psychology*, *33*(1), 71–87. https://doi.org/10.1007/s10869-016-9474-5

Lavine, M. (2014). Paradoxical leadership and the competing values framework. *Journal of Applied Behavioral Science*, *50*(2), 189–205. https://doi.org/10.1177/0021886314522510

Lee, A., Willis, S., & Tian, A. W. (2017). Empowering leadership: A meta-analytic examination of incremental contribution, mediation, and moderatoin. *Journal of Organizational Behavior*, *39*, 306–325. https://doi.org/10.1002/job.2220

Lorinkova, N. M., Pearsall, M. J., & Sims, H. P. (2013). Examining the differential longitudinal performance of directive versus empowering leadership in teams. *Academy of Management Journal*, *56*(2), 573–596. https://doi.org/10.5465/amj.2011.0132

Lüscher, L. S., & Lewis, M. W. (2008). Organizational change and managerial sensemaking: Working through paradox. *Academy of Management Journal*, *51*(2), 221–240. https://doi.org/https://doi.org/10.5465/AMJ.2008.31767217

Maitlis, S., & Christianson, M. (2014). Sensemaking in organizations: Taking stock and moving forward. *Academy of Management Annals*, *8*(1), 57–125. https://doi.org/10.1080/19416520.2014.873177

Maitlis, S., & Lawrence, T. B. (2007). Triggers and enablers of sensegiving in organizations. *Academy of Management Journal*, *50*(1), 57–84. https://doi.org/amj.2007.24160971

Martin, S. L., Liao, H., & Campbell, E. M. (2013). Directive versus empowering leadership: A field experiment comparing impacts on task proficiency and proactivity. *Academy of Management Journal*, *56*(5), 1372–1395. https://doi.org/10.5465/amj.2011.0113

Miron-Spektor, E., Ingram, A., Keller, J., Smith, W. K., & Lewis, M. W. (2018). Microfoundations of organizational paradox: The problem is how we think about the problem. *Academy of Management Journal*, *61*(1), 26–45. https://doi.org/10.5465/amj.2016.0594

Miron-Spektor, E., & Paletz, S. B. F. (2020). Collective paradoxical frames: Managing tensions in learning and innovation. In L. Argote & J. M. Levine (Eds.), *The Oxford Handbook of Group and Organizational Learning*. Oxford University Press. https://doi.org/10.1093/oxfordhb/9780190263362.013.32

Nehrlich, A. d., Gebauer, J. E., Sedikides, C., & Schoel. C. (2019). Agentic narcissism, communal narcissism, and prosociality. *Journal of Personality* and *Social Psychology, 117*(1), 142–165. https://doi.org/10.1037/pspp0000190

Nishii, L. H. (2013). The benefits of climate for inclusion for gender-diverse groups. *Academy of Management Journal, 56*(6), 1754–1774. http://dx.doi.org/10.5465/amj.2009.0823

Owens, B. P., & Hekman, D. R. (2016). How does leader humility influence team performance? Exploring the mechanisms of contagion and collective promotion focus. *Academy of Management Journal, 59*(3), 1088–1111. https://doi.org/10.5465/amj.2013.0660

Owens, B. P., Johnson, M. D., & Mitchell, T. R. (2013). Expressed humility in organizations: Implications for performance, teams, and leadership. *Organization Science, 24*(5), 1517–1538. https://doi.org/10.1287/orsc.1120.0795

Owens, B. P., Wallace, A. S., & Waldman, D. A. (2015). Leader narcissism and follower outcomes: The counterbalancing effect of leader humility. *Journal of Applied Psychology, 100*(4), 1203–1213. https://doi.org/10.1037/a0038698

Pearce, C. L., Wassenaar, C. L., Berson, Y., & Tuval-Mashiach, R. (2019). Toward a theory of meta-paradoxical leadership. *Organizational Behavior and Human Decision Processes, 155*, 31–41. https://doi.org/10.1016/j.obhdp.2019.03.003

Podsakoff, P. M., MacKenzie, S. B., & Bommer, W. H. (1996). Transformational leader behaviors and substitutes for leadership as determinants of employee satisfaction, commitment, trust, and organizational citizenship behaviors. *Journal of Management, 22*(2), 259–298. https://doi.org/10.1177/014920639602200204

Rothman, N. B., & Melwani, S. (2017). Feeling mixed, ambivalent, and in flux: The social functions of emotional complexity for leaders. *Academy of Management Review, 42*(2), 259–282. https://doi.org/10.5465/amr.2014.0355

Rothman, N. B., Pratt, M. G., Rees, L., & Vogus, T. J. (2017). Understanding the dual nature of ambivalence: Why and when ambivalence leads to good and bad outcomes. *Academy of Management Annals, 11*(1), 33–72. https://doi.org/10.5465/annals.2014.0066

Schad, J., Lewis, M. W., Raisch, S., & Smith, W. K. (2016). Paradox research in management science: Looking back to move forward. *Academy of Management Annals, 10*(1), 5–64. https://doi.org/10.1080/19416520.2016.1162422

Shao, Y., Nijstad, B. A., & Täuber, S. (2019). Creativity under workload pressure and integrative complexity: The double-edged sword of paradoxical leadership. *Organizational Behavior and Human Decision Processes, 155*, 7–19. https://doi.org/10.1016/j.obhdp.2019.01.008

Sharma, P., & Kirkman, B. L. (2015). Leveraging leaders: A literature review and future lines of inquiry for empowering leadership research. *Group and Organization Management, 40*, 193–237. https://doi.org/10.1177%2F1059601115574906

Smith, W. K. (2014). Dynamic decision making: A model of senior leaders managing strategic paradoxes. *Academy of Management Journal, 57*(6), 1592–1623. https://doi.org/10.5465/amj.2011.0932

Smith, W. K., Besharov, M. L., Wessels, A. K., & Chertok, M. (2012). A paradoxical leadership model for social entrepreneurs: Challenges, leadership skills and pedagogical tools for managing social and commercial demands. *Academy of Management Learning and Education, 11*(3), 463–478. https://dx.doi.org/10.5465/amle.2011.0021

Smith, W. K., & Lewis, M. W. (2011). Toward a theory of paradox: A dynamic equilibrium model of organizing. *Academy of Management Review, 36*(2), 381–403. https://doi.org/10.5465/amr.2011.59330958

Smith, W. K., Lewis, M. W., & Tushman, M. L. (2016). 'Both/and' leadership: Don't worry so much about being consistent. *Harvard Business Review* (May), 63–70.

Sparr, J. L. (2018). Paradoxes in organizational change: The crucial role of leaders' sensegiving. *Journal of Change Management, 18*(2), 162–180. https://doi.org/10.1080/14697017.2018.1446696

Sparr, J. L., van Knippenberg, D., & Kearney, E. (2022). Paradoxical leadership as sensegiving: Stimulating change-readiness and change-oriented performance. *Leadership & Organization Development Journal, 43*(2). https://doi.org/10.1108/LODJ-04-2021-0161

Thompson, G., & Vecchio, R. P. (2009). Situational leadership theory: A test of three versions. *Leadership Quarterly, 20*(5), 837–848. https://doi.org/https://doi.org/10.1016/j.leaqua.2009.06.014

Uhl-Bien, M., & Arena, M. (2018). Leadership for organizational adaptability: A theoretical synthesis and integrative framework. *Leadership Quarterly, 29*(1), 89–104. https://doi.org/10.1016/j.leaqua.2017.12.009

Uhl-Bien, M., Riggio, R. E., Lowe, K. B., & Carsten, M. K. (2014). Followership theory: A review and research agenda. *Leadership Quarterly, 25*(1), 83–104. https://doi.org/10.1016/j.leaqua.2013.11.007

Waldman, D. A., & Bowen, D. E. (2016). Learning to be a paradox-savvy leader. *Academy of Management Perspectives, 30*(3), 316–327. https://doi.org/10.5465/amp.2015.0070

Waldman, D. A., Galvin, B. M., & Walumbwa, F. O. (2012). The development of motivation to lead and leader role identity. *Journal of Leadership & Organizational Studies, 20*(2), 156–168. https://doi.org/10.1177/1548051812457416

Waldman, D. A., Putnam, L. L., Miron-Spektor, E. & Siegel, D. (2019). The role of paradox theory in decision making and management research. *Organizational Behavior and Human Decision Processes, 155*, 1-6.

Waldman, D. A., & Javidan, M. (2020). The false dichotomy between globalism and nationalism. *HBR.org*. https://hbr.org/2020/06/the-false-dichotomy-between-globalism-and-nationalism

Wang, L., Owens, B. P., Li, J., & Shi, L. (2018). Exploring the affective impact, boundary conditions, and antecedents of leader humility. *Journal of Applied Psychology, 103*(9), 1019–1038. https://doi.org/10.1037/apl0000314

Weick, K. E., Sutcliffe, K. M., & Obstfeld, D. (2005). Organizing and the process of sensemaking. *Organization Science, 16*(4), 409–421. https://doi.org/10.1287/orsc.1050.0133

Yukl, G. (2012). Effective leadership behavior: What we know and what questions need more attention. *Academy of Management Perspectives, 26*(4), 66–85. https://doi.org/10.5465/amp.2012.0088

Zaccaro, S. J. (2007). Trait-based perspectives of leadership. *American Psychologist, 62*(1), 6–16; discussion 43-17. https://doi.org/10.1037/0003-066X.62.1.6

Zaccaro, S. J., Green, J. P., Dubrow, S., & Kolze, M. (2018). Leader individual differences, situational parameters, and leadership outcomes: A comprehensive review and integration. *Leadership Quarterly, 29*(1), 2–43. https://doi.org/10.1016/j.leaqua.2017.10.003

Zapata, C. P., & Hayes-Jones, L. C. (2019). The consequences of humility for leaders: A double-edged sword. *Organizational Behavior and Human Decision Processes, 152*, 47–63. https://doi.org/10.1016/j.obhdp.2019.01.006

Zhang, H., Ou, A. Y., Tsui, A. S., & Wang, H. (2017). CEO humility, narcissism and firm innovation: A paradox perspective on CEO traits. *Leadership Quarterly, 28*(5), 585–604. https://doi.org/10.1016/j.leaqua.2017.01.003

Zhang, Y., Waldman, D. A., Han, Y.-L., & Li, X.-B. (2015). Paradoxical leader behaviors in people management: Antecedents and consequences. *Academy of Management Journal, 58*(2), 538–566. https://doi.org/10.5465/amj.2012.0995

Zhang, M. J., Zhang, Y., & Law, K. S. (2021). Paradoxical leadership and innovation in work teams: The multilevel mediating role of amidexterity and leader vision as a boundary condition. *Academy of Management Journal.* https://doi.org/10.5465/amj.2017.1265

Zheng, W., Kark, R., & Meister, A. L. (2018a). Paradox versus dilemma mindset: A theory of how women leaders navigate the tensions between agency and communion. *Leadership Quarterly, 29*(5), 584–596. https://doi.org/10.1016/j.leaqua.2018.04.001

Zheng, W., Surgevil, O., & Kark, R. (2018b). Dancing on the razor's edge: How top-level women leaders manage the paradoxical tensions between agency and communion. *Sex Roles, 79*(11–12), 633–650. https://doi.org/10.1007/s11199-018-0908-6

Zhu, J., Song, L. J., Zhu, L., & Johnson, R. E. (2019). Visualizing the landscape and evolution of leadership research. *Leadership Quarterly, 30*(2), 215–232. https://doi.org/10.1016/j.leaqua.2018.06.003

39

Leadership Dialectics

Gail T. Fairhurst and David L. Collinson

Organisational researchers have moved increasingly towards the analysis of process (Langley & Tsoukas, 2017), and nowhere is this more evident than in the shift to study leadership dialectically (Collinson, 2005, 2014; Fairhurst et al., 2020; Zoller & Fairhurst, 2007). A dialectic perspective eschews simple binaries like leader–follower, leader–manager, transformational–transactional and so on, asserting that they oversimplify complex relationships (Collinson, 2014). Instead, dialectics focuses on *interdependent opposites aligned with forces that push–pull on each other like a rubber band and exist in an ongoing dynamic interplay as the poles implicate each other* (Putnam et al., 2016, p. 7). Dialectics focuses on this interplay and the forces or processes that connect them. Collinson (2005) was among the first to suggest reframing traditional leadership binaries such as control–resistance, dissent–consent, male–female – to which others have added individual–collective, informal–formal, fixed–fluid meaning potentials and many more – as multiple, intersecting dialectics (Collinson, 2005; Zoller & Fairhurst, 2007).

Mainstream leadership research tends to construct and rely on either–or binaries, which oversimplify and sometimes ignore complex interrelations (Fairhurst, 2001; Collinson, 2005, 2019, 2014). As Harter (2006, p. 90) observed, in the study of leadership *dualisms pop up everywhere*, such as born–made leaders, task–people, theory X–theory Y, organic–mechanistic, autocratic–participative and rational–emotional. This *bi-polar shopping list approach* (Grint, 1997, p. 3) is particularly prevalent in mainstream studies where leaders' personas and practices tend to be privileged and psychological perspectives predominate (Fairhurst, 2007; Jackson & Parry, 2018). One of the most intractable dichotomies is that between leaders and followers (Burns, 2008). Much of the mainstream literature privileges and elevates leaders and neglects the active role of followers. It typically assumes that 'leaders' are in charge and make decisions and 'followers' simply carry out orders from 'above'. Relations between them are often ignored or taken for granted and, even when addressed, they tend to be (mis)understood as largely static, stable and predictable, while their dynamic, shifting character is underplayed.

This chapter reviews the recent work on leadership dialectics of the last 20+ years. It argues that rethinking deeply embedded dichotomies in dialectical terms can enrich and deepen the study of leadership, open new approaches to theory and practice, and address important ontological, epistemological and methodological implications for research and analysis. In relation to ontology, dialectics refers to a view of reality as the dynamic interplay of opposing forces. Dialectically evolving interactions and their consequences are *the very stuff of leadership attributions – or lack thereof* and deepen our understanding of the ontologies of leadership whether in individual or collective forms (Fairhurst et al., 2020, p. 608). From an epistemological standpoint, dialectics describes a method of reasoning that searches for understanding through the clash of opposing arguments. With respect to methodology, dialectical analysis raises important questions about causality, temporality and the limitations of the natural science methods that tend to inform mainstream leadership studies.

The chapter begins by briefly considering the origins and historical evolution of the term 'dialectics' in philosophy and social science, followed by a discussion of the appropriation of dialectics in contemporary paradox research. The next section draws on critical leadership theory to challenge this appropriation to consider critical dialectical research. This is followed by a review of 35 dialectical studies published since 2000 that examine issues of power and performativity in leadership and followership relationships (Table 39.1). The chapter concludes by addressing why dialectical research fits squarely within a critical leadership studies framework (Collinson, 2020; Fyke & Buzzanell, 2013), as well as discussing theory–method implications of a dialectical research agenda.

DIALECTICS

The notion of 'dialectics' has a long conceptual history in the humanities (Clegg & Cunha, 2017), with its intellectual roots dating back to the ancient Greek philosophers like Aristotle, Socrates and Plato (Bhaskar, 1993). Indeed, the term is almost as old as the practice of philosophy itself (Hook, 1939). Writers from various intellectual disciplines have defined and used dialectics in different ways (Zeitz, 1980). Derived from the Greek word *dialektikē*, meaning the art of discussion or debate (Hall, 1967), the term itself has been hotly contested. Greek scholars tended to view dialectics as a form of reasoning and search for truth through dialogue: a method for resolving disagreement and contradictory viewpoints. This might lead to the refutation of an argument, the development of a synthesis, a combination of the opposing assertions, or a qualitative improvement of the dialogue.

Dialectical thinking is also central to ancient Buddhist philosophies. Viewing 'reality' itself as a dialectic, Tao and Zen Buddhism, for example, highlight the importance of interrelatedness, polarity and continuous flux and change (Lao Tzu, 2020). While reality is ultimately understood as a unified whole where everything is connected to everything else, it may be experienced and perceived in fragmented, dualistic ways, as apparent polarities such as: subject–object, life–death, black–white and yin–yang (Watts, 2017). Emphasising the importance of existential ironies, Eastern philosophies also attend to the paradoxical, unintended consequences of human action, pointing out, for example, how an excessive search for security can increase insecurity and how the pursuit of order may create chaos (Watts, 1973, 2021). The insights of Buddhism continue to be drawn on in humanistic psychology (Wheeler, 2021), 'dialectical behaviour therapy' (Robins, 2002; Limandri, 2022) and leadership studies (Heider, 1996; Prince, 2005).

Hegel's (1969) view of dialectical thinking attends to the conflictual processes of thesis, antithesis and synthesis: the tensions between thesis and antithesis would be resolved, he argued, through the emergence of a new synthesis that in turn would lead to a better future. While Hegel focused on the consciousness of mind, his student Marx (1906/2010) shifted dialectics out of the cognitive domain into the concrete economic processes of society, ascribing a more revolutionary meaning. In dialectical materialism, Marx developed the idea of class struggle to describe the contradictions between owners of capital and commodified labour, mental and manual workers, and town and country. For Marx, economic forces drive the dialectic. He argued that once they become fully aware of the material conditions of their exploitation, the working class would organise collectively to overthrow capitalism. In the *Dialectics of Nature*, Engels (2012) built on Marx's ideas to highlight three laws of dialectics: the transformation of quantity into quality (and vice versa); the interpenetration of opposites; and the negation of the negation. Subsequent writers within the Frankfurt School (e.g., Adorno, Marcuse, Horkheimer) have sought to build on this focus on worker emancipation from forms of alienation produced by capitalism and class-structured societies.

These (r)evolutionary interpretations have been questioned theoretically and empirically, and historical events have not supported the mechanistic and law-like predictions of either linear progress or working-class emancipation. Although the term is often associated with Hegel and Marx, recent suggestions of an essential link with these two

Table 39.1 Dialectical leadership/followership empirical research

Dialectical tensions	Leadership/followership Implications	Study (ordered by year)/topic/method
Multiple: Distributed–directive leadership Pluralism–consensus Stability–change	Collective (strategic) leadership emerges from a fragile mix of oppositional forces constantly in tension. Change occurs in a cyclical fashion in which opposing forces are reconciled sequentially rather than simultaneously	Denis et al., 2001: collective senior leadership in healthcare settings (five multi-method case studies)
Primary: Profits–people **Secondary:** Control–resistance Voluntary–involuntary	Giddens' (1984) dialectic of control explains legacy workers who refused to 'volunteer' to be downsized as prescribed by management, but also a management team unbowed by the push for more humane downsizings	Fairhurst et al., 2002: successive downsizings of a legacy workforce at an environmental remediation site (multi-method case study)
Multiple: Autonomy–connection Predictability–novelty Open–closed Team–individual Dominance–submission Competence–incompetence	Two of six dialectical tensions were important drivers of team development: team–individual and competence–incompetence. The (presumed) presence of shared leadership in the teams led to significantly lower ratings for dominance–submission	Erbert et al., 2004: perceptions of turning points and dialectics in organisational team development (mixed methods)
Multiple: Respect–suspect Nurture–discipline Consistency–flexibility Solidarity–autonomy	Framing tensions as complementary edicts upheld multiple organisational norms simultaneously	Tracy, 2004: prison officers' treatment of inmates (ethnography)
Control–resistance	Airline pilots' identity shift from infallible captains to empowering managers is an unhelpful dichotomy when pilots use the latter discourse to resist their declining control through apparent consent	Ashcraft, 2005: airline pilots' gendered identity shifts (interviews, discourse analysis)
Symbolic–material	The limits of discourse for strike workers without economic or other structural forms of power are clear. Identity narratives shift from warrior to victim to martyr to reflect increasing powerlessness vis-à-vis management	Cloud, 2005: dialectical materialism in a management-labour conflict (discourse analysis)
Control–resistance	Managers were constrained by the control systems they created. Employees found space to resist within managers' ambivalence to proposed change	Larson & Tompkins, 2005: concertive control in the aerospace industry in response to organisational change (multi-method longitudinal case study)
Control–resistance	Self-help groups' discourse regulates the identities of employees and managers, while employees also used it to resist organisational demands	Carlone & Larson, 2006: self-help programmes as instruments of organisational control and resistance (multi-method case study)
Control–resistance	Resistance to workplace abuse and bullying assumes individual and collective forms, especially when organisational leadership delays responding	Lutgen-Sandvik, 2006: workers subject to or those who witnessed workplace bullying (interview study)
Multiple: Autonomy–accountability Differentiation–integration Regulation–openness	Leadership structures have 'tensegrity' if they simultaneously balance the contradictory yet beneficial forces of socio-political conditions	Martin, 2006: dialectical leadership structures in medium-sized industrial firms (surveys)

(Continued)

Table 39.1 Dialectical leadership/followership empirical research (*Continued*)

Dialectical tensions	Leadership/followership Implications	Study (ordered by year)/topic/method
Closeness–distance	'Paradoxing the dialectic' occurs when operating within (the fluid choices of) a dialectic is blocked by the fixed and mutually contradictory choices of a paradox	McGuire et al., 2006: sexual harassment of nurses by their patients (interview study)
Heroic–post–heroic Delegation–direction Proximity–distance Internal–external engagement	Employees in UK Further Education viewed a 'blended' approach as comprising the most effective form of leadership. 'Blended leadership' redefines (perceived) leadership tensions not as separate and incompatible dichotomies but as interrelated and mutually necessary	Collinson & Collinson, 2009: the value of dialectical approaches to leadership in Further and Higher Education (case studies, interviews)
Assert–challenge–overcome	Endorsement of leaders (or lack thereof) by team members occurred via oppositional interactions with problematic team members. In Hegelian fashion, a foil became a contrast that helped groups endorse the leaders and values advocated	Garner & Poole, 2009: leader–foil interactions over time in quality improvement teams. (three longitudinal case studies)
Multiple families: Autonomy–connection Inclusion–exclusion Empowerment–disempowerment	Managers were better able to transcend dialectical tensions than team members	Gibbs, 2009: boundary spanning dialectics in global virtual teams (ethnography)
Control–resistance	Managers used humour to exert authority and mask power differences. Chefs used humour to maintain professional identities, creative input, and control	Lynch, 2009: use of humour in the kitchen labour process in the restaurant industry. (ethnography)
Stabilisation–destabilisation	Leaders' discourses of transcendence to resolve contradictions failed over time. A Hegelian view of contradictions' stabilisation by synthesis appears much less likely than Benson's view of their ongoingness	Abdallah et al., 2011: discourses of transcendence during organisational change (three multi-method case studies)
The said/sayable–unsaid/unsayable	Leaders stir homoerotic desires in followers, so followers are seduced into achieving organisational goals. Yet, a leader's body is absent from the scene of seduction, so organisational heteronormativity remains unchallenged	Harding et al., 2011: charismatic leadership in queer theory (interview study)
Mindfulness–mindlessness	Collective minding by architectural partners and its contractors involved simultaneous mindfulness and mindlessness. The same information technologies were enacted as multiple, contradictory technologies-in-practice	Carlo et al., 2013: collective minding in technology use in a high-risk context (longitudinal, multi-method case study)
Multiple: Centralisation–decentralisation Planning–action Directive–participative style	Improvisational leadership involved simultaneously integrating opposite leadership behaviours for important tasks in turbulent environments with flexible resources	Cunha et al., 2013: organisational improvisation (two longitudinal, multi-method case studies)
Multiple: Pragmatics–idealism Mindfulness–mindlessness	The discourse of conscious capitalism is a mindful way to train ethical leaders dealing with the wicked problems to alternately counter the mindlessness of capitalist discourse	Fyke & Buzzanell, 2013: ethical leadership development (longitudinal, multi-method case study)

(*Continued*)

Table 39.1 Dialectical leadership/followership empirical research (*Continued*)

Dialectical tensions	Leadership/followership Implications	Study (ordered by year)/topic/method
Control–resistance	Control and resistance sparked each other as asymmetric power imbalances retained their hold until crucible moments in leadership training, which demonstrated the simultaneity of consent and resistance	Carroll & Nicholson, 2014: leadership development (multi-method case study)
Control–resistance	Identity regulation processes in global leadership development programmes may lead to overt or disguised resistance	Gagnon & Collinson, 2014: a critical identity lens regarding the regulatory practices that constitute an idealized (global) leader (ethnographic interviews)
Multiple: Attraction–adjustment Ownership–oversight Formalization–flexibility Intimacy–distance	Successful volunteering hinged on recognising the dialectics in ongoing volunteer–manager communication and then reframing them as complementary and 'professional'; meta-communicating about them in micro-practices around values; and highlighting them through connecting volunteers in role-related activities	McNamee & Peterson, 2014: volunteering as an ambiguous 'third space' of organisational spatiotemporal enactment (three longitudinal, multi-method case studies)
Primary: Expanded–constricted identity **Secondary:** Core–peripheral identities Continuity–change Enhance–loss	Leaders and members dialectically created identity elasticity through a unified diversity of identity interpretations in response to change	Kreiner et al., 2015: organisational identity in response to first openly gay bishop (longitudinal, multi-method case study)
Control–resistance	Role of identity work as both resistance and compliance in response to dominant organisational ideology; narratives reflected distinct modes of reworking dialectical tensions	Bristow et al., 2017: early career academics' dialectics of resistance and compliance with business school neoliberalism (interview study)
Control–resistance	Through oppositional practices of 'resistance through difference', managers' dissent challenges the hegemonic cultural disciplinary practices embedded in a global leadership development programme	Gagnon & Collinson, 2017: the discursive construction of (cultural) difference can shape resistance in international teams. Team members' dissent expresses their heterogeneity while simultaneously reinforcing group solidarity. (ethnographic interviews)
Multiple: Structure–flexibility (Fixed–fluid identities, practices) Integration–differentiation Stability–change	Dialectical processes nested within a strategic paradox enabled leaders to maintain commitments to competing missions. Leaders held paradoxical frames to promote adaptive enactment and guard rails to keep from veering too heavily towards one side over another	Smith & Besharov, 2019: organisational hybridity due to competing social and business missions (longitudinal, multi-method case study)
Multiple Women as leaders–women as feminine women as credible leaders–women as lacking credibility, women as victims–women as their own worst enemies	Reveals how UK media employs feminine capital to promote women's positioning as leaders yet also leverages female capital as a constraint	Elliott & Stead, 2018: the gendering of women's leadership in the popular press during the global financial crash 2008–2012, mediated through three dialectical, gendered tensions. (multimodal, textual, visual discursive analysis)

(*Continued*)

Table 39.1 Dialectical leadership/followership empirical research (*Continued*)

Dialectical tensions	Leadership/followership Implications	Study (ordered by year)/topic/method
Multiple Control–resistance Hierarchical–shared leadership Individual–collective	Time and timing of authoritative moves explain the dialectical interplay between hierarchical and shared leadership in implementing teams. Yet, follower attributions of successful leadership were lacking due to the absence of specifically timed leader moves	Holm & Fairhurst, 2018: interplay between shared and hierarchical leadership in strategic change to a team-based system (ethnography, discourse analysis)
Multiple: Truth–post-truth Popular–elite Unity–disunity	Two world leaders used Twitter and speeches to demonstrate the seeds of democracy in a historically autocratic organisation and roots of authoritarianism in a historically democratic one	Deye & Fairhurst, 2019: post-truth leadership (two multi-method case studies)
Multiple: Leader–follower Formal–informal authority	Leader authoritative moves, mediated by objects and bodies, require followers' consent. Shared leadership entailed conflict between formally and informally authored moves	Van De Mieroop et al., 2020: interplay between formal and informal leadership in shared leadership configuration (multimodal conversation analysis case study)
Multiple: Positive–negative Self–other Short-term–Long-term Engaged–disengaged	Leaders and followers can achieve resilience due to job insecurity by maintaining dialectical tensions with a both-and stance over either-or	Wieland, 2020: leader-follower resilience (interview study)
Multiple: Coercion–empowerment Compliance–resistance	The politics of organisational learning in a hierarchical environment is neither liberating empowerment nor disciplinary control but a contradictory interplay of modalities	Bristow et al., 2021: a dialectical approach to the organisational politics of learning in a police organisation (ethnography)
Multiple Equality–integration Private–corporate agency Reproduction–learning	Unequal power arrangements between managers and migrant followers creates variety in assimilation and integration practices	Omanović & Langley, 2021: migrant socialisation practices (meta-synthesis of qualitative research)
Multiple: Control–resistance Researcher–subject Language–materialities	Workers problematise power asymmetries in the dialectical production of leadership through exposing capital's practices to control space/place from afar, then 'replacing' with potentially emancipatory alternative	Smolović Jones et al., 2021: a Marxist account of space and place in exploitative employment and the (uneven) agency of workers (workers' inquiry approach)

writers (e.g., Knights, 2021) seem to underestimate or ignore debates about dialectics that both pre-date and post-date their writings. Dialectical materialism is only one way of thinking about dialectical processes. Indeed, subsequent theorists of society and organisation have reinterpreted dialectics in less dogmatic and more open-ended ways to examine economic, social and organisational tensions and contradictions (e.g., Benson, 1977; Calori, 2002). As Zeitz (1980, p. 73) argued, *in its most general and loosest sense, dialectics refers to any aspect of social processes having to do with conflict, paradox, mutual interaction, unintended consequence, and the like.*

Dialectical perspectives continue to be influential in philosophy (Bhaskar, 1993). Hook (1939) distinguished between two generic conceptions of dialectic: a pattern of existential change in nature and/or society or a special method for analysing these changes. Dialectics has also been used in sociology, for example, as a way of reconciling the dualism between theories of human agency and structure (Giddens, 1979, 1984). In their classic text on the social construction of reality, Berger and Luckmann (1967) examined the social dialectic through which humans construct reality and reproduce themselves in a mutually formative relationship with society. For Berger and

Luckmann, society exists as both objective and subjective reality, and is best understood in terms of an ongoing dialectical process composed of the three moments of externalisation, objectivation and internalisation.

Bakhtin's (1981) dialogic perspective resonates with these themes and departs from Hegel and Marx by focusing on ongoing sense-making, speaking and communicating. He views social life as an open-ended dialogue characterised by utterances and responses, agreements and disagreements: the simultaneous fusion and differentiation of multiple voices in which participants partially integrate and/or sustain their own perspectives. Within these dialogical processes, Bakhtin highlighted the recursive and indeterminate dynamics and contradictions of differences and unities.

Drawing from Bakhtin, Baxter (2011) and Baxter and Montgomery (1996) argued that dialectics is best understood as a meta-theory describing a set of conceptual assumptions that revolve around contradiction, change, praxis and totality. They view social life as a *dynamic knot of contradictions, a ceaseless interplay between contrary or opposing tendencies* (1996, p. 3). Baxter's (2011) relational dialectics examine how social life is reproduced in and through discursive practices that give voice to multiple opposing tendencies. In addition to Baxter, Bakhtin's view of dialectics as recursive cycling has also become influential in the growing literature on organisational paradoxes (e.g., Costanzo & Domenico, 2015; Farjoun, 2017; Lewis et al., 2017; Smith & Lewis, 2011), to which we now turn.

PARADOX AND DIALECTICS RESEARCH AND CRITICAL LEADERSHIP STUDIES

The study of organisations from a paradox perspective has encapsulated modern-day versions of dialectical theory so much so that the two bodies of work are often reviewed together (Clegg et al., 2002; Farjoun, 2017; Hargrave, 2021; Hargrave & Van de Ven, 2017; Putnam et al., 2016; Schad et al., 2016). Both concern themselves with the irrational, irreconcilable and disorganising aspects of organisational life, not as anomalies but the new normal. Leadership scholars have not been immune to this trend because paradox research tends to treat organisational paradoxes as problems (Farjoun, 2016), and managers are typically expected to solve them. For example, Storey and Salaman (2009, p. 22) hold that the management of dilemma and paradox is *the essence of leadership*, while paradoxical (both–and) thinking is often deemed to be the ultimate best practice for discerning leaders (Cameron et al., 2006; Collins, 2001; Cunha et al., 2021; Kaplan & Kaiser, 2013; Lüscher & Lewis, 2008; Waldman & Bowen, 2016).

Historically, much of the paradox literature has focused on sense-making and solving problems in micro-level interactions (Farjoun, 2016; Putnam et al., 2016). Simple solutions to isolated tensions or *singular grand responses* (Lê & Bednarek, 2017, p. 495) to primary tensions often followed, which underrepresented underlying dialectical tensions, how they intersected and the responses they evoked. The paradox literature also naively presumed that all actors have agency (Berti & Simpson, 2021; Hargrave, 2021) or remain uninfluenced by socio-historical forces (Putnam et al., 2016), suggesting power-laced dialectical tensions (e.g., control–resistance, domination–subordination, overt–covert, sayable–unsayable [responses to power]) require more attention. A heavy cognitive emphasis also tended to usurp the performativity of paradox in socio-material practices, diminishing the role of material artefacts (e.g., objects, sites, spaces, bodies) in instigating and responding to paradox (Benson, 1977; Fairhurst & Putnam, forthcoming).

The neglect of power and performativity in much of the paradox literature is a particular concern of critical leadership studies (CLS), given the number of leadership scholars turning to a paradox lens. CLS examines how power asymmetries and control practices are often implicated in the conditions, processes and consequences of leadership dynamics (e.g., Alvesson & Spicer, 2012; Collinson, 2005, 2011, 2014; Fairhurst, 2007; Fairhurst & Connaughton, 2014). CLS is a loose umbrella term for a diverse and heterogeneous set of perspectives (from labour process theory, critical management studies, theories of communication, post-colonialism and feminism to post-structuralism, radical psychology and psychoanalysis). Sometimes competing and in tension, these perspectives critique the situated power relations and identity constructions through which leadership and followership dynamics are frequently rationalised, sometimes resisted and occasionally transformed (Ford, 2010; Ford & Harding, 2011; Spector, 2014, 2019; Wilson, 2016).

Critical dialectical studies suggest that it can be helpful to rethink leadership power dynamics as dialectical processes: typically taking multiple simultaneous forms, often interconnecting in ways that are mutually reinforcing, but sometimes in tension. Acknowledging that power can be productive as well as oppressive, covert as well as overt, dialectical studies seek to show

how different forms of (leaders') control may produce (un)intended and (un)anticipated effects such as followers' resistance or emergence as leaders themselves in shifting interaction dynamics (Collinson, 2020). Highlighting the importance of 'worker enquiry', Smolović Jones et al. (2021) reaffirm the conceptual importance of class antagonisms, conflicts of interest and asymmetrical power relations in leadership dialectics. They argue that research on worker experience and agency can reveal the oppressions, absurdities and contradictions of some leadership discourses and practices of capital.

Several scholars have also studied leadership dialectically and empirically over the past 20+ years; we summarise a representative sample of those findings in Table 39.1. These studies come from a variety of theoretical traditions including many that inform CLS (critical, postmodern, Hegelian and Bakhtinian approaches). Not only do most concern themselves with issues of power, but they also suggest a growing emphasis on studying processes through analysing the performativity of leadership and followership in and through a socio-material world.

EMPIRICAL STUDIES OF DIALECTICAL LEADERSHIP

Space does not permit an intensive literature review, but we can draw a few conclusions from the 35 empirical studies described in Table 39.1. An overwhelming majority were heavily qualitative, and several were multi-method and longitudinal; most were published in interdisciplinary organisational journals (e.g., *Academy of Management Journal*, *Administrative Science Quarterly*, *Human Relations*, *Leadership*, *Management Communication Quarterly*, *MIS Quarterly*, *Organization* and others) since 2000. We found two major themes, the most dominant of which was power.

A power theme is perhaps the most obvious observation of Table 39.1 since 13 papers examine control–resistance as a dialectic. Some of these studies draw from Giddens' (1979, 1984) dialectic of control, which suggests that while leaders' power may be extensive, it also depends on followers who thus retain a degree of autonomy and discretion. More broadly, Giddens' arguments suggest the importance of follower-related questions of conformity, consent, disguised dissent and overt resistance (Collinson, 2020). For example, Carroll and Nicholson's study (2014) demonstrated how actors in a leadership development programme simultaneously portrayed consent and resistance to power. Similarly, Gagnon and Collinson (2014, 2017) explored how international team members explicitly resisted strong normalising controls in two global leadership development programmes. They opposed prevailing idealised models of the global leader prescribed in the programmes and by expressing their difference and heterogeneity in ways that simultaneously reinforced group solidarity and inclusion. Their 'resistance through difference' challenged disciplinary practices embedded in the leadership programmes.

Ashcraft (2005) concluded that airline pilots' identity shift from (historically) infallible captains to empowering managers in the cabin is an unhelpful dichotomy when pilots use the latter discourse to resist their declining control through apparent consent. Lynch's (2009) study of a professional kitchen revealed how chefs used humour to influence the labour process to maintain their professional autonomy and identity and to resist managerial control of their craft. Carlone and Larson (2006) also found identity to be a key point of resistance, finding the polysemy of ideas in organisational change programmes allows followers to appropriate them in self-interested ways.

Thus, far from always being passive and unquestioning, followers (broadly defined) can express opposition in multiple forms, using knowledge, information and self-protective practices in ways that blur boundaries to simultaneously enact, yet conceal their resistance. Emphasising the mutually reinforcing nature of leaders' power and followers' resistance, dialectical studies also show how leaders' control can have unintended and contradictory consequences that leaders do not always understand or anticipate. For example, Fairhurst et al.'s (2002) study of the unintended consequences of successive downsizings revealed a leadership team at the mercy of the waves of contradictions they created. This is not to suggest that followers will invariably engage in dissent, or that opposition is necessarily always effective (e.g., Cloud, 2005); leaders' control may produce compliance and even conformity, while resistance can also have unintended and contradictory consequences (e.g., Ashcraft, 2005).

Moving away from an emphasis on control–resistance as a dialectical tension, other dialectical studies in Table 39.1 show power and control assuming multiple forms. Power can be conferred by hierarchical position, as well as enacted more informally through processes, relationships, networks and personal agency. While leadership and power are often associated with those in positions of formal authority, these dialectical studies emphasise that leadership can also emerge informally in more subordinated and dispersed relationships. For example, Denis et al. (2005) drew on five case studies in healthcare organisations to study the emergence of collective leadership when control by fiat was not possible. While members of collective leadership groupings played complementary (i.e., dispersed power) roles critical to achieving organisational change, they were a fragile mix of oppositional forces: distributed–directive leadership; pluralism–consensus; and stability–change. Elliott and Stead's (2018) study of media representations of women leaders during the global financial crash reveals how power in leadership dynamics can often reflect and reinforce deeply held gendered assumptions. They found that gendered media representations were mediated through three dialectical tensions: women as leaders–women as feminine; women as credible leaders–women as lacking credibility; and women as victims–women as their own worst enemies.

Several studies demonstrate the discursive practices through which leaders and followers hold together (or fail to hold) fragile coalitions or other power-sharing arrangements by dialectically responding to tensional push–pulls. Tracy (2004) showed how prison guards framed dialectical tensions as complementary edicts to uphold organisational norms with respect to inmates (e.g., respect for inmates yet suspicion of them; nurturance yet discipline). Cunha et al. (2013) found that improvisational leadership promoted innovation in computer-mediated settings when it simultaneously integrated opposite leadership behaviours (centralising–decentralising; planning–action; directive–participating) for important tasks. Similarly, Collinson and Collinson (2009) explored employees' views about what constitutes effective leadership in the UK Further Education sector. Their research found that followers preferred a 'blended leadership' approach that redefined (perceived) leadership tensions not as separate and incompatible dichotomies but as interrelated and mutually necessary, especially in relation to the apparent tensions between delegation–direction, proximity–distance and internal–external engagement.

Smith and Besharov's (2019) study of a hybrid organisation with dual social and business missions found leaders enacting guard rails to keep from favouring one mission over another. Kreiner et al. (2015) described how leaders and members of the Episcopal Church created identity elasticity to achieve a unified diversity of identity interpretations in response to how the Church would handle its first openly gay bishop. They did this through dialectical category work – that is, the modification of categories through talk so they contain their opposites (Fairhurst & Putnam, forthcoming). Finally, Holm and Fairhurst (2018) found that shared leadership could not be sustained in a Danish municipality due to the time and timing of expected authoritative moves in the dialectical interplay between hierarchical and shared leadership in team interactions. This study challenges the view that leaders may be more skilled in transcending dialectical tensions than followers (cf. Gibbs, 2009).

A second major theme from Table 39.1 concerns the performativity of leadership vis-à-vis the embodied, physical, or spatiotemporal materialities beyond the realm of language use. 'Performativity' is a term that gets passed around a lot (Butler, 1990, 1999; Goffman, 1959; Gond et al., 2015; Spicer et al., 2016), but it generally answers the question of *how* something is enacted in practice. Regarding leadership, we must also speak of its effects as they are enacted in social and organisational settings. Specifically, how is leadership/followership performed vis-à-vis a fuller understanding of the socio-material actants informing the relationalities involved? Compared to the theme of power, performativity studies are fewer, but we believe they represent an important potential path forward for CLS and dialectical leadership research (see also Simpson et al., 2021).

Deye and Fairhurst's (2019) study comparing Twitter and the public-speaking performances of former President Donald Trump and Pope Francis demonstrated the seeds of democracy in a historically autocratic organisation and roots of authoritarianism in a historically democratic society. Twitter's truncated, drive-by messaging format heightened the mockery, inuendo, criticism and autocratic (charismatic?) presence that Trump was so adept at delivering through that medium. Carlo et al. (2012) studied collective minding in a large architectural building project, which required organisational actors to simultaneously exhibit aspects of being both mindful and mindless as they struggled with technological and environmental contradictions. As a result of such struggles, the same information technologies were flexibly appropriated to perform multiple, contradictory technologies-in-practice. Van De Mieroop et al. (2020) demonstrated the dialectical interplay of formal and informal leadership as mediated by a host of materialities beyond talk: objects, gaze and use of space. Leader authoritative moves, mediated by objects and bodies, required followers' consent, while shared leadership entailed conflict between formally and informally authored moves. Finally, Harding et al. (2011) used queer theory to explore what is sayable and unsayable in lay theories of leadership. They argued that leaders stir homoerotic desires in followers in which the latter are seduced into attaining organisational goals. However, the actual body of the leader is an absent presence from the scene of seduction, reinforcing heteronormativity – and the black-boxing of leaders' physicality, all the while the (unsayable) desire remains to lead and be led by others in seductively embodied ways.

The performative aspects of leadership come into fuller view when actors are not viewed solely (and simply) as having strong inner motors (Fairhurst, 2007). Leadership emerges as role behaviour but also influential acts of organising that advance the task (Carlo et al., 2012; Cunha et al., 2013) or dupe converts (Deye & Fairhurst, 2019); leadership as an advanced skill set (Kreiner et al., 2015; Smith & Besharov, 2019) that not all possess (Holm & Fairhurst, 2018; Tracy, 2004); leadership as a relationality that requires consent (Van De Mieroop et al., 2020) and attribution (Holm & Fairhurst, 2018); leadership as shared, fragile and more collective than individually based (Denis et al., 2005); and leadership as embodied power (Harding et al., 2011; Van De Mieroop et al., 2020).

Followership performativity likewise reveals the relationality and embodiment of followers (Harding et al., 2011; Van De Mieroop et al., 2020); the preservation of the dialectic of control (Larson & Tompkins, 2005; Lynch, 2009; Smolović Jones, et al., 2021); the simultaneity and masking of consent and resistance (Ashcraft, 2005; Carlone & Larson, 2006; Carroll & Nicholson, 2014; Gagnon & Collinson, 2017); an advanced skill set (Carlone & Larson, 2006; Lynch, 2009), the deployment of which is not always successful (Cloud, 2005); and the shared, fragile and more collective view of followership that does not necessarily reside in compliant expectations or strict role assignments (Denis et al., 2005; Garner & Poole, 2009).

Thus, we see why some CLS writers embrace a critical dialectical approach given the ability of the above studies to marry power and performativity; indeed, Table 39.1 emphasises the performative aspects of leadership/followership cannot divorce issues of power from their materialised enactments and effects (e.g., Harding et al., 2011; Holm & Fairhurst, 2018; Van De Mieroop et al., 2020). Table 39.1 also reflects the trend to borrow from several theoretical bodies (e.g., Marxism, queer theory, communicative constitution of organisations, structuration) to study multiple dialectical tensions. This enables researchers to move beyond power and control to see how multiple tensions may play off one another and/ or to intersect in mutually reinforcing ways to weave the very fabric of localised enactments of leadership and followership (Collinson, 2014). If leadership and followership represent a family resemblance among language games (Kelly, 2008, 2014; Wittgenstein, 1953), we understand better the resemblances and departures from the family tree. Finally, Table 39.1 marks a decided departure from the surveys and seven-point scales marking the history of (US) leadership research (Fairhurst, 2007), towards more qualitative, longitudinal and materially sensitive research that gives us multiple and more nuanced angles with which to view the shape-shifting of leader–follower roles, especially in today's power-sharing environments.

Alvesson and Spicer (2012) and Spicer et al. (2016) have extended this interest with performativity to advocate a more interventionist and direct engagement with practitioners and greater theoretical and empirical focus on influencing practices (see also Jones et al., 2021). Alvesson and Spicer (2012) propose the value of a critical performativity perspective for understanding and researching leadership. Building on emerging interest in critical leadership studies that examine the dialectics of control and resistance and the ideological aspects of leadership, they posit a more affirmative performative engagement. This emphasises the need for tactics of *circumspect care* (taking respondents' views seriously, but also critically interrogating them), *progressive pragmatism* (pragmatically but also critically working with already accepted discourses) and *searching for present potentialities* (moving beyond a critique of existing practices of leadership to create a sense of what could be). Alvesson and Spicer conclude by advocating that critical leadership approaches require a *constant dialectical movement between pragmatic engagement **and** emancipatory critique* (2012, p. 385, emphasis original).

More recently, Spicer et al. (2016) elaborate their perspective on dialectics. Advocating a return to a longstanding tradition of dialectics-based organisational interventions (for a review, see Fairhurst, 2019), they introduce *dialectical reasoning* into a model of critical performativity that highlights the value of public engagement. For Spicer et al., dialectical reasoning involves recognising and exploring tensions between opposing concepts. Acknowledging that dialectical tensions can take many different forms and are likely to be specific to the research site, the authors recast circumspect care, progressive pragmatism and searching for present potentials as general and generative dialectical tensions.

Their point is not to try to resolve each of these tensions, but to use them as a springboard for new and imaginative ways of conceiving and enacting leadership and followership. They argue that this extended conception of critical performativity offers an alternative approach for doing critical work and public-facing critique. As such, critical performativity requires different skills of public engagement including an ability to think dialectically. Contra-paradoxical thinking with its focus on problems and both–and solutions; dialectical thinking has a historical, contextual, contrarian and narrative quality to it (Farjoun, 2017). It means being more reflexively aware of the pushing and pulling tensions that characterise a specific research and praxis field. It also means developing more nuanced and sophisticated analyses than the one-dimensional or oppositional critiques that, they argue, have often characterised critical management studies and organisation studies more generally. Suffice it to say that for critical leadership researchers, a critical performativity lens advocates a serious commitment to praxis and a return to dialectical interventionist methods.

CONCLUSION

This chapter has explored the value of rethinking leadership studies in terms of dialectical theorising, highlighting the neglected importance of power and performativity in leader–follower dynamics. In doing so, it has considered the emergent field of critical dialectical leadership studies, which addresses the relational, (a)symmetrical and push–pull character of ongoing leadership–followership dynamics. Dialectical perspectives challenge dichotomised understandings of leaders, followers and leader-led relations that persist in much of the mainstream literature. They question either–or polarities that downplay or neglect leader–follower interrelations, tensions, asymmetries, contradictions and ways of morphing so that tensional poles can evolve – for example, leaders can follow and followers can lead. Critical dialectical perspectives acknowledge that leaders' and followers' power(s) can take multiple forms, and have contradictory and unintended outcomes, which they may not understand or realise. Leadership and followership processes are ripe with the potential for conflict and dissent; leaders cannot simply assume followers' assent, obedience, or loyalty. Critical dialectical studies view control and resistance as inextricably linked, mutually reinforcing processes that are also inherently ambiguous and potentially contradictory.

While this chapter has argued that leadership and power are frequently closely connected, this is not to imply that leadership issues can be reduced to questions of power. Rather, the broader goal of CLS is to understand leadership–followership performativity *and* power, as the latter has been so often ignored in leadership studies. Accordingly, the chapter has highlighted the value of connecting leadership studies (where questions of power have been largely neglected) with the socio-material, social theory, CMS and labour process analysis (where power has been examined but leadership issues have rarely been considered). Furthermore, our chapter has suggested that both in theory and in practice, power typically takes a plurality of dialectical, simultaneous and intersecting forms, and is therefore likely to require multiple interwoven theoretical and methodological frameworks. Critical dialectical analyses of leadership dynamics are suggestive of important new lines of research that can further enhance and integrate theory and practice. Indeed, Spicer et al.'s (2016) emphasis on dialectical reasoning within critical performativity encourages critical researchers to engage in more direct interventions with practitioners to influence and shape the everyday practices of leaders and followers.

Future research on leadership power dialectics could surface additional important issues about conflict, tensions, paradoxes and contradictions, and engage with popular distinctions between 'power over', 'power to' and 'power with' (e.g., Salovaara & Bathurst, 2018). The resurgence of authoritarian and autocratic political leadership on a global scale also raises significant questions about the exercise of power in organisations. So too does the crucial connections between leadership dialectics and climate change. In addition, researchers need to consider the multiple and intersecting nature of leadership dialectics. When addressing leader/follower dialectics, how these dynamics are shaped by inequalities such as gender, ethnicity, race and class are important questions. For example, focusing on the barriers to advancement for white, middle-class women can neglect how women of colour predominate in lower-paid, insecure and dead-end jobs. Critical studies therefore need to develop sophisticated understandings of how leadership dialectics may connect and intersect.

Finally, in embracing dialectical thinking, we should also address the theory–method implications of doing empirical research. First, instead of thinking dichotomously and reifying categories like leader–follower, individual–collective and power (bad)–influence (good), treat them as tensional poles and focus on their interplay to better capture the colour, shadings and spaces in between (Collinson, 2005, 2014). For example, *precisely* how, why, in what contexts, and with what consequences do leaders become followers and followers become leaders? Second, incorporate time and history into leadership–followership research design and collect multiple types of data. Then zoom in to look for 'hot spots' of tensions and contradictions in actors' problematisations of their circumstances and zoom out to gain historical perspective, a sense of their evolution and their (un)intended consequences (Jarzabkowski et al., 2019). Third, take advantage of the still-emerging methodologies for doing paradox and dialectics research for more nuanced approaches to data analysis beyond general qualitative methods (Andriopoulos & Gotsi, 2017; Fairhurst & Putnam, 2019). Finally, read widely in the leadership, paradox and dialectics literatures because, as this chapter suggests, a growing number of theoretically informed empirical studies are helping to realise the promise of a critical dialectical approach.

SELECTED REFERENCES (FOR A FULL LIST, PLEASE EMAIL FAIRHUG@UCMAIL.UC.EDU)

Alvesson, M., & Spicer, A. (2012). Critical leadership studies: The case for critical performativity. *Human Relations*, 65(3), 367–390.
Bakhtin, M. (1981). *The Dialogical Imagination*. University of Texas Press.
Baxter, L. A. (2004). A tale of two voices: Relational dialectics theory. *Journal of Family Communication*, 4(3–4), 181–192.
Baxter, L. A. (2011). *Voicing Relationships: A Dialogic Perspective*. Sage.
Baxter, L. A. & Montgomery, B. M. (1996). *Relating: Dialogues and Dialectics*. Guilford.
Benson, J. K. (1977). Organizations: A dialectical view. *Administrative Science Quarterly*, 22(1), 1–21.
Berger, P. and Luckmann, T. (1967) *The Social Construction of Reality*. Penguin.
Berti, M., & Simpson, A.V. (2021). The dark side of organizational paradoxes: The dynamics of disempowerment. *Academy of Management Review*, 46(2), 252–274.
Bhaskar, R. (1993). *Dialectic*. Verso.
Bristow, A., Robinson, S., & Ratle, O (2017). Being an early-career CMS academic in the context of insecurity and 'excellence': The dialectics of resistance and compliance. *Organization Studies*, 38(9), 1185–1207.
Bristow, A., Tomkins, L., & Hartley, J. (2021). A dialectical approach to the politics of learning in a major city police organization. *Management Learning*, 53(2), 223–248. https://journals.sagepub.com/home/mlq
Butler, J. (1999). *Gender Trouble: Feminism and the Subversion of Identity* (2nd edn). Routledge.
Calori, R. (2002). Organizational development and the ontology of creative dialectical evolution. *Organization*, 9(1), 127–150.
Cameron, K. S., Quinn, R. E., & Degraff J, (2006). *Competing Values Framework*. Edward Elgar.

Carlo, J. L., Lyytinen, K., & Boland, R. J. Jr (2012). Dialectics of collective minding: Contradictory appropriations of information technology in a high-risk project. *MIS Quarterly*, 36(4), 1081–1108.
Carlone, D., & Larson, G. S. (2006). Locating possibilities for control and resistance in a self-help program. *Western Journal of Communication*, 70(4), 270–291,
Carroll, B., & Nicholson, H. (2014). Resistance and struggle in leadership development. *Human Relations*, 67(11), 1413–1436.
Clegg, S. & Cunha, M. P. (2017). Organizational dialectics. In M.W. Lewis, W. K. Smith, P. Jarzabkowski & A. Langley (2017) (Eds.), *Oxford Handbook of Organizational Paradox: Approaches to Plurality, Tensions, and Contradictions* (pp. 105–124). Oxford.
Clegg, S. R., Cunha, J. V., & Cunha, M. P. (2002). Management paradoxes: A relational view. *Human Relations*, 55(5), 483–503.
Cloud, D. L. (2005). Fighting words: Labor and the limits of communication at Staley, 1993 to 1996. *Management Communication Quarterly*, 18(4), 509–542.
Collins, J. (2001). *Good to Great*. Random House.
Collinson, D. L. (2003). Identities and insecurities: Selves at work. *Organization*, 10(3), 527–547.
Collinson, D. (2005). Dialectics of leadership. *Human Relations*, 58(11), 1419–1442.
Collinson, D. (2014). Dichotomies, dialectics and dilemmas: New directions for critical leadership studies? *Leadership*, 10(1), 36–55.
Collinson, D. (2020). 'Only Connect!': Exploring the critical dialectical turn in leadership studies' *Organization Theory*, 1(2), 1–22. https://doi.org/10.1177/2631787720913878
Collinson, D., & Collinson, M. (2009). 'Blended leadership': Employee perspectives on effective leadership in the UK Further Education sector. *Leadership*, 5(3), 365–380.
Cunha, M. P. C., Clegg, S. R., Rego, A., & Berti, M. (2021). *Paradoxes of Power and Leadership*. Routledge.
Engels, F. (2012). *Dialectics of Nature*. Wellred.
Erbert, E. A., Mearns, G. M., & Dena, S. (2005). Perceptions of turning points and dialectical interpretations in organizational team development. *Small Group Research*, 36(1), 21–58.
Deye, J. M., & Fairhurst, G. T. (2019). Dialectical tensions in the narrative discourse of Donald J. Trump and Pope Francis. *Leadership*, 15(2), 152–178.
Elliott, C., & Stead, V. (2018). Constructing women's leadership representation in the UK press during a time of financial crisis: Gender capitals and dialectical tensions. *Organization Studies*, 39(1), 19–45.
Fairhurst, G. T. (2007). *Discursive Leadership: In Conversation with Leadership Psychology*. Sage.

Fairhurst, G. T. (2019). Return paradox to the wild? Paradox interventions and their implications. *Journal of Change Management*, *19*(1), 6–22.

Fairhurst, G. T. & Connaughton, S. L. (2014). Leadership: A communicative perspective. *Leadership*, *10*(1), 7–35.

Fairhurst, G. T., Cooren, F., & Cahill, D. (2002). Discursiveness, contradiction, and unintended consequences in successive downsizings. *Management Communication Quarterly*, *15*(4), 501–540.

Fairhurst, G. T., Jackson, B., Foldy, E. G., & Ospina, S. M. (2020). Studying collective leadership: The road ahead. *Human Relations*, *73*(4), 598–614.

Fairhurst, G. T., & Putnam, L. L. (forthcoming). *Organizational Paradoxes: A Constitutive Approach*. Routledge/Taylor & Francis.

Farjoun, M. (2017). Contradictions, dialectics and paradoxes. In A. Langley & H. Tsoukas (Eds.), *The SAGE Handbook of Process Organization Studies*. Sage. 87–109.

Ford, J. (2010). Studying leadership critically: A psychosocial lens on leadership identities. *Leadership*, *6*(1), 1–19.

Ford, J., & Harding, N. (2011). The impossibility of the 'true self' of authentic leadership. *Leadership*, *7*(4), 463–479.

Ford, J., Harding, N., Gilmore, S., & Richardson, S. (2017). Becoming the leader: Leadership as a material presence. *Organization Studies*, *38*(11), 1553–1571.

Fyke, J. P., & Buzzanell, P. M. (2013). The ethics of conscious capitalism: Wicked problems in leading change and changing leaders. *Human Relations*, *66*(12), 1619–1644.

Gagnon, S., & Collinson, D. (2014). Rethinking global leadership development programmes: The interrelated significance of power, context and identity. *Organization Studies*, *35*(5), 645–670.

Gagnon, S., & Collinson, D. (2017). Resistance through difference: The co-constitution of dissent and inclusion. *Organization Studies*, *38*(9), 1253–1276.

Garner, J. T., & Poole, M. S. (2009). Opposites attract: Leadership endorsement as a function of interaction between a leader and a foil. *Western Journal of Communication*, *73*(3), 227–247.

Gibbs, J. (2009). Dialectics in a global software team: Negotiating tensions across time, space, and culture. *Human Relations*, *62*(6), 905–935.

Giddens, A. (1979). *Central Problems in Social Theory*. Macmillan.

Giddens, A. (1984). *The Constitution of Society*. Polity Press.

Goffman, E. (1959). *The Presentation of Self in Everyday Life*. Doubleday.

Hall, R. (1967). Dialectic. In P. Edwards (Ed.), *Encyclopedia of Philosophy* (vol. 2, pp. 385–389). Macmillan.

Harding, N., Lee, H., Ford, J., & Learmonth, M. (2011). Leadership and charisma: A desire that cannot speak its name? *Human Relations*, *64*(7), 927–949.

Hargrave, T. J., & Van de Ven, A. H. (2017). Integrating dialectical and paradox perspectives on managing contradictions in organizations. *Organization Studies*, *38*(3–4), 319–339.

Hegel, G. W. F. (1969). *Hegel's Science of Logic*. Allen & Unwin.

Holm, F. & Fairhurst, G. T. (2018). Configuring shared and hierarchical leadership through authoring. *Human Relations*, *71*(5), 692–721.

Hook, S. (1939). Dialectic in social and historical inquiry. *Journal of Philosophy*, *36*(14), 365–378.

Jones, O., Briley, G., & Woodcock, J. (2021). Exposing and replacing leadership through workers inquiry. *Leadership*, *18*(1), 61–80.

Kanter, R. M. (1977). *Men and Women of the Corporation*. Basic Books.

Kaplan, R., & Kaiser, R. (2013). *Fear Your Strengths*. Berret-Koehler.

Kelly, S. (2008). Leadership: A categorical mistake? *Human Relations*, *61*(6), 763–782.

Kelly, S. (2014). Towards a negative ontology of leadership. *Human Relations*, *67*(8), 905–922.

Knights, D. (2021). *Leadership, Gender and Ethics: Embodied Reason in Challenging Masculinities*. Routledge.

Langley, A., & Tsoukas, H. (eds). (2017). *The SAGE Handbook of Process Organization Studies*. Sage.

Lao Tzu (2020). *Tao Te Ching*. Penguin.

Larson, G. S., & Tompkins, P. K. (2005). Ambivalence and resistance: A study of management in a concertive control system, *Communication Monographs*, *72*(1), 1–21.

Lewis, M. W., Smith, W. K., Jarzabkowski, P., & Langley, A. (Eds.) (2017). *Oxford Handbook of Organizational Paradox: Approaches to Plurality, Tensions, and Contradictions*. Oxford University Press.

Lüscher, L. S., & Lewis, M. W. (2008). Organizational change and managerial sensemaking: Working through paradox. *Academy of Management Journal*, *51*(2), 221–240.

Lutgen-Sandvik, P. (2006). Take this job and … : Quitting and other forms of resistance to workplace bullying. *Communication Monographs*, *73*(4), 406–433.

Lynch, O. H. (2009). Kitchen antics: The importance of humor and maintaining professionalism at work. *Journal of Applied Communication Research*, *37*(4), 444–464.

Martin, A. (2006). Dialectical conditions: Leadership structures as productive action generators. *Management Revue*, *17*(4), 420–447.

Marx, K. (1906/2010). *Capital: A Critique of Political Economy. Volume I: The Process of Capitalist Production*. CreateSpace Independent Publishing Platform.

Mumby, D. K. (2005). Theorizing resistance in organizational studies: A dialectical approach. *Management Communication Quarterly*, *19*(1), 1–26.

Nonaka, I., & Toyama, R. (2002). A firm as a dialectical being: Towards a dynamic theory of the firm. *Industrial and Corporate Change*, *11*(5), 995–1009.

O'Reilly, C. A., & Tushman, M. (2013). Organizational ambidexterity: Past, present and future. *Academy of Management Perspectives*, *27*(4), 324–338.

Omanović, V., & Langley, A. (2021). Assimilation, integration or inclusion? A dialectical perspective on the organizational socialization of migrants. *Journal of Management Inquiry*, December.

Putnam, L. L., Fairhurst, G. T., & Banghart, S. G. (2016). Contradictions, dialectics, and paradoxes in organizations: A constitutive approach. *Academy of Management Annals*, *10*(1), 65–172.

Robins, C. J. (2002). Zen principles and mindfulness practice in dialectical behavior therapy. *Cognitive and Behavioral Practice*, *9*(1), 50–57.

Salovaara, P., & Bathurst, R. (2018). Power-with leadership practices: An unfinished business. *Leadership*, *14*(2), 179–202.

Schad, J., Lewis, M. W., Raisch, S., & Smith, W. K. (2016). Paradox research in management science: Looking back to move forward. *Academy of Management Annals*, *10*(1), 5–64.

Smith, W., & Besharov, M. (2019). Bowing before dual gods: How structured flexibility sustains organizational hybridity. *Administrative Science Quarterly*, *64*(1), 1–44.

Smith, W. K. & Lewis, M. W. (2011). Toward a theory of paradox: A dynamic equilibrium model of organizing. *Academy of Management Review*, *36*(2), 381–403.

Smolović Jones, O., Briley, G., & Woodcock, J. (2021). Exposing and re-placing leadership through workers inquiry. *Leadership*, *18* (1).

Spector, B. (2019). *Constructing Crisis: Leaders, Crises and Claims of Urgency*. Cambridge University Press.

Spicer, A., Alvesson, M., & Kärreman, D. (2016). Extending critical performativity. *Human Relations*, *69*(2), 225–249.

Storey, J., & Salaman, G. (2009). *Managerial Dilemmas*. John Wiley & Sons.

Tracy, S. J. (2004). Dialectic, contradiction, or double bind? Analyzing and theorizing employee reactions to organizational tension. *Journal of Applied Communication Research*, *32*(2), 119–146.

Waldman, D. A., & Bowen, D. E. (2016). Learning to be a paradox-savvy leader. *Academy of Management Perspectives*, *30*(3), 316–327.

Watts, A. (1973). *This Is It*. Random House

Watts, A. (2017). *Psychotherapy East and West*. New World Library.

Watts, A. (2021). *The Wisdom of Insecurity*. Penguin.

Wieland, S. M. B. (2020). Constituting resilience at work: Maintaining dialectics and cultivating dignity throughout a worksite closure. *Management Communication Quarterly*, *34*(4), 463–494.

Wilson, S. (2016). *Thinking Differently About Leadership*. Edward Elgar.

Wittgenstein, L. (1953). *Philosophical Investigations*. Trans. G. E. M. Anscombe. Blackwell.

Zeitz, G. (1980). Interorganizational dialectics. *Administrative Science Quarterly*, *25*(1), 72–88.

Zoller, H. M., & Fairhurst, G. T. (2007). Resistance leadership: The overlooked potential in critical organization and leadership studies. *Human Relations*, *60*(11), 1331–1360.

Care and Caring Leadership: Positive Attractions and Critical Asymmetries

Leah Tomkins

INTRODUCTION

This chapter provides an overview of the topic of caring leadership. I sketch out the key themes of the modern care ethics movement and consider how they have inspired a range of theorisations of the caring leader and, by extension, what it means to be cared-for as a follower. While these theories have different emphases, I crystallise the notions of care and caring leadership as involving:

- a commitment to relationship and an empathic attunement to another person's needs;
- a shift in perspective which enables us to see things through another person's eyes;
- a focus on the particular (what matters here) more than the universal (what matters everywhere);
- a practice traditionally associated with women, but ethically applicable to all humans;
- an extrapolation of the dynamics of family and home into the wider social, institutional and organisational landscape, with leaders usually conceived as care-givers and followers as care-recipients.

In line with the overall schematic for this handbook, I structure the chapter along lines of sense-making and sense-breaking. From a sense-making perspective, I consider how caring leadership can encourage more ethically and emotionally satisfying organisational relations. From a sense-breaking perspective, I then explore caring leadership more critically, namely, as the site of complex, often hidden, dynamics of power, exploitation and sacrifice, which can afflict leaders and followers alike. Bringing these dynamics to the surface offers the possibility of fostering more authentically supportive relationships both in the workplace and in society at large.

CARING LEADERSHIP: A PATH TO SUCCESSFUL LEADERSHIP RELATIONS

In this section, I focus on some of the positive aspects of care and caring leadership. I trace contemporary enthusiasm for this approach to the modern care ethics movement, which arose in the 1970s and 1980s as a way of highlighting the societal value of relationship and the significance of what was being produced and reproduced in the home through care as a 'labour of love' (Finch & Groves, 1983; Kittay, 2013). When applied to the phenomenon of leadership, the notion of care seems to capture and express an authentic interest in, and concern for, other people's well-being. It is not surprising, therefore, that care has been associated with a range of organisational benefits, including enhanced employee commitment, loyalty and performance.

This section addresses two of the most positive associations between leadership and care:

- leadership ethics, highlighting the role of care in the ethics of transformation, contractualisation and sustainability;
- positive effects on follower well-being, focusing on compassion, psychological containment and self-esteem.

FROM CARE ETHICS TO LEADERSHIP ETHICS

The growing impact of care on leadership studies is due more to its conceptualisation as a system of ethics than to its associations with emotion (even though care often does involve emotion). While care relations originate in the domestic sphere, the construction of care as a framework for moral reasoning – that is, as *care ethics* – gives it a much broader relevance and application. This broader approach informs a range of issues in leadership ethics – in particular, the ethics of transformation, contractualisation and sustainability.

Gilligan (1982), one of the most influential figures in the modern care ethics movement, portrays an ethics of care as a distinctly female moral voice. She differentiates this from an ethics of justice, which involves a specifically male moral voice. Through the prism of Gilligan's care ethics, actions and decisions are motivated and evaluated by a concern for how they affect particular people in particular circumstances, rather than whether they are universally right or wrong. Care ethics is therefore as much about the logics of reasoning, problem-solving, priority-setting and decision-making as about sentiment. It is a mode of thinking that rejects associations of moral and intellectual maturity with the capacity for abstraction. Instead, it prioritises the particularist knowledge and values that are experienced – and contested – within concrete human relationships.

Building on these foundations, leading care scholars approach care as an ethical system that can inform, motivate and moderate our behaviour as a general theory of moral and social obligation. This highlights one of the paradoxes of care, namely that it unfolds as a *general* theory which focuses on the *particular*. As such, care is extrapolated from intimate, familial relationships, where care-givers are traditionally assumed to be women, and developed as a logic of mutual recognition, concern and responsibility which is equally applicable to all human beings. Thus, *while we can fulfil some of our obligations to others through personal caring relationships, we can fulfil many others only through collective caring institutions and policies* (Engster, 2007, p. 2). Relatedly, Held (2006) argues for care as a public, not just a private, commitment, because honouring interpersonal relationships of care without attending to the broader question of social justice can reify patriarchal structures that place the burden of care primarily on women.

If care is conceived as a moral theory of mutual obligation, then it might be the foundation, not the opposite, of justice. Noddings' (2002) elaboration of the kind of 'justice' that can be delivered through the template of familial care bears a considerable resemblance to what we might consider good leadership. Care ethics takes the best of what works well at home to see how this might guide what happens in institution, organisation and society, for:

> All good homes put an emphasis on shifting the locus of control from the stronger and more mature to the weaker or less mature, but the best homes retain and promote the idea of shared responsibility [...] When one person hurts another, the conversations and decisions that follow are aimed at restitution, at understanding what happened, how each party might have behaved differently, and how similar future events might be prevented. Healthy guilt is encouraged; unhealthy guilt and shame are minimised.
> (Noddings, 2002, p. 228)

As a logic of reasoning, then, care ethics prioritises actual over abstract issues; acknowledges different perspectives and interests; and gauges success in relation to safeguarding and restitution. From here, there is an easy segue from care ethics to leadership ethics, an area of leadership studies attracting burgeoning interest in recent years. Much of this interest is inspired by Brown & Treviño's (2006) exploration of ethical leadership as both overlapping with, and distinct from, other approaches with an overt moral dimension, principally authentic, transformational and spiritual leadership. Leadership ethics demands that we look beyond a leader's vision, skills and effectiveness to consider the fundamental question of leadership morality (Ciulla & Donelson, 2011; Lemoine et al., 2019). This means reflecting on whether leadership actions are right or wrong, and on which criteria, standards or values we are using, whether implicitly or explicitly, to make such judgements.

Through just such a lens, Simola et al. (2010) examine different perceptions of leadership by contrasting care ethics with justice ethics. Their analysis concludes that leaders who demonstrate a care-ethical problem-solving style are perceived by followers as transformational (not transactional) leaders; whereas those enacting a justice-ethical approach are more likely to be perceived as transactional (not transformational) leaders. This is an intriguing finding, not least because transformational leadership tends to be considered a more effective and inspirational way of tackling the challenges of contemporary organisational life than its transactional counterpart. It suggests that transformational leaders may have the ability to work with actual rather than abstract moral dilemmas, and to find creative and constructive ways to acknowledge the ongoing tensions and paradoxes of organising, rather than aiming to remove all conflict and/or ambiguity. This chimes with Robinson's (2019) analysis of care ethics as a reasoning style that rejects splitting and binaries in favour of more integrative ways of approaching our organisational world.

Exploring a complementary aspect of leadership ethics, Brophy (2011) examines the issues and implications of contract ethics. He argues that traditional business ethics is founded on a number of false and potentially harmful assumptions, including that people entering into work contracts are doing so as fully free and autonomous agents – that is, that even overtly shameful terms and conditions are simply 'what they signed up for'. He suggests that care ethics can tease out alternative ways of constructing and conducting contractual relationships, focusing on the different perspectives and interests among organisational members. While contract ethics deems leadership behaviour broadly acceptable if it stays within the bounds of the law, is free from overt fraud and deception and can claim to be 'in the interests of the organisation', care ethics evaluates behaviour based on a non-exploitative recognition of any vulnerability in one or both of the contracting parties. Such an approach exposes the ways in which contractual relationships are sometimes based on the need for psychological as well as fiscal relief from anxiety and uncertainty. They are not, therefore, always the marker of an ethical relationship between equally sovereign parties.

The ethical complexities of corporate versus environmental sustainability have also been examined through the lens of care ethics. Simola (2007) argues that tensions between business profitability, environmental protection, globalisation and social responsibility are unlikely to be resolved within traditional paradigms of business ethics. In particular, she focuses on the value of a care-ethical approach to conducting business in the developing world. Drawing on the notion of *native capabilities*, she posits powerful connections between the relational sensitivity of care ethics and the skills required to develop *authentic, culturally sensitive, and mutually beneficial relationships with cautious or distrustful indigenous groups* (Simola, 2007, p. 132). Interestingly, the application of care ethics to environmental sustainability is an example of care breaking free of its bonds of family and familiarity. Taking care of the planet means looking out for the needs and interests of people we do not and may never know in person; and without an expectation of any immediate feedback or reciprocity.

POSITIVE EFFECTS ON FOLLOWER WELL-BEING

It makes considerable sense that care and caring leadership might be beneficial for follower well-being through fostering feelings of commitment, community and belonging. In this vein, there is a rich literature from a broadly 'positive organisational perspective' that blends care with notions of compassion (Cameron et al., 2003; Rynes et al., 2012). This combination invokes an organisational world in which human factors are brought to the fore in leadership relations. In a landmark article in this field, Frost (1999) proposes that:

> Compassion counts as a connection to the human spirit and to the human condition. In organizations there is suffering and pain, as there is joy and fulfillment. There is a need for dignity and self-respect in these settings, and to the extent that our theories, models, and practices ignore these dimensions, so do they distort our understanding of life in these enterprises. Looking at organizations through the compassion lens [...] takes us to empathy, to emotion, to aesthetics.
> (Frost, 1999, p. 131)

The importance of care and compassion is especially marked in times of trouble. Petriglieri (2020) considers the duties of leadership to involve two types of holding: institutional holding and interpersonal holding. The former, on the one hand, means introducing or reinforcing policies and procedures which give or restore feelings of security and reassurance. It encourages a kind of collective sense-making based not on predictions or guarantees about the future but on participation in discussions about how decisions will be reached and what criteria will be deployed to balance competing organisational priorities. Interpersonal holding, on the other hand, involves a more intimate kind of leadership work. It is more than simply being attentive and/or supportive to other people. Rather, it is *a mixture of permission (to feel whatever it is that we are feeling without being shamed or overwhelmed) and curiosity (to consider different ways to understand our circumstances and, eventually, to imagine our future)* (Petrigilieri, 2020, p. 5). In this way, leaders exercise their duty of care by acknowledging distress and role-modelling ways not to be crushed by it.

In a related vein, Petriglieri and Maitlis (2019) reflect on the phenomenon of mourning in organisations, suggesting that a crucial duty and skill of leadership is to be able to cope with and contain grief. They suggest that this aspect of organisational leadership has become more significant in recent decades, as the traditional institutions of church and extended family have given way to the workplace as the primary source of meaning. Organisations and other work-based institutions are increasingly expected to foster a sense of identity as well as (perhaps even more than) providing financial remuneration. Thus, when misfortune strikes, caring leadership must first bear witness to the other person's pain. It then involves helping those in mourning gradually to rediscover meaning, purpose and re-anchoring in their work and work affiliations. From this perspective, the caring leader is both sense-maker and sense-making facilitator.

The significance of sense-making in caring leadership is emphasised by Lawrence and Maitlis (2012), who consider care as a discursive and narrative practice as much as a value or emotion. They emphasise that discourses of organisational care encourage and comprise multiple perspectives and multiple voices, *for polyphonic narratives exemplify an ethic of care [...] by emphasizing ongoing interdependent relationships [...] by rejecting standard, universal plots in favour of particular and uncertain life paths; and by acknowledging the power of external forces, such as politics and broader discourses, on any future path* (Lawrence & Maitlis, 2012, p. 650). Successful care narratives therefore contextualise the personal struggles of organisational life so that they are not individually pathologised, but instead experienced as features of the wider institutional landscape with which all members – leaders and followers alike – must deal. This commits the caring leader to communication and dialogue, thereby overlapping with several other leadership approaches, including relational leadership (Cunliffe & Eriksen, 2011; Fairhurst & Uhl-Bien, 2012), dialogical leadership (van Loon, 2017) and various forms of *leadership in the plural* (Denis et al., 2012).

Care is also said to exert a positive influence on work-based self-esteem. McAllister and Bigley (2002) highlight the significance of whether organisational members feel cared-for at an individual level ('my leader cares for me') and at an organisational level ('leadership here is about caring for all of us'). They suggest that care creates an overall value system which has a greater and more sustainable influence over employee self-esteem than individual initiatives such as counselling, job enrichment, promotion, etc. In other words, care is the wood within which individual policies and practices can be successful as trees. Such arguments hold considerable intuitive appeal, for when people feel cared-for, both by leaders and by colleagues, they are more likely to enjoy feelings of security, higher levels of motivation and a greater readiness to engage in creative and innovative behaviour (Vinarski-Peretz & Carmeli, 2011). Furthermore, McAllister and Bigley (2002) argue that organisational care is deeply enmeshed with perceptions of organisational fairness. This seems to reinforce arguments for care as a prerequisite or an accompaniment to justice, rather than its opposite.

CARING LEADERSHIP: THE SITE OF COMPLEX WORKINGS OF POWER

So far, care and caring leadership have emerged as largely positive forces for organisational relations, often exerting a motivational and inspirational influence that makes intuitive sense. Turning from sense-making to sense-breaking, I now focus on how the positive associations of care can mask some of its less positive features. I reflect critically on the intersections of care and power, especially the unequal or asymmetrical power relations between leaders and followers.

As highlighted at the start of this chapter, when we talk about the connections between leadership and care, we tend to conceive of leaders as care-givers and followers as care-recipients. This allows us to draw parallels between a power asymmetry in leader/follower relations and an equivalent power asymmetry in care-giver/care-recipient relations. Such parallels can be highly productive for our understanding of the tensions of leadership, and for the prospects of reimagining the leader/follower relationship in more mutually supportive ways.

In this section, I reflect critically on three aspects of the asymmetry of care:

- the risk of dependency and disempowerment for followers;
- the appeal of self-care for both leaders and followers;
- the risk of self-sacrifice for leaders.

DEPENDENCY AND DISEMPOWERMENT FOR FOLLOWERS

Asymmetries between leaders/followers and care-givers/care-recipients are usually depicted as bestowing power, influence and agency to leaders as care-givers and relative impotence, disadvantage and dependency to followers as care-recipients. In other words, leaders are said to be in control; followers are seen as being in need. Explorations of the power dynamics of caring leadership have, therefore, tended to position asymmetry as a particular problem for followers, who risk having their autonomy and agency curtailed or even denied.

For instance, Munro and Thanem (2018, p. 55) argue that the permeation of care ethics into leadership relations *actualizes a sense of pastoral care that is deeply invested with power [...] Today the priest has been replaced by the figure of the manager-leader in current expressions of pastoral care*. In such an actualisation, the well-being of followers involves having their needs and desires anticipated and met (or refused) by their leaders and other powerful organisational players. The individual employee is cast as someone in need of care – that is, as weak, inferior or deficient in some sense. Seen this way, the notion of the caring leader reinforces an inequality among organisational members. It can become an exploitation of the powerless by the powerful, all in the name of care (Munro & Thanem, 2018).

The asymmetries of care are brought to the fore in psychoanalytical explorations of caring leadership which are developed from the original template of the family. Gabriel (2015) proposes that our expectations of leaders are moulded from familial archetypes, as well as our early childhood experiences of authority, which get re-triggered in adulthood. Based on the primal templates of father and mother, leaders in our adult life are experienced as the all-mighty father-figure and/or the all-loving, all-caring mother-figure. The paternal archetype is easily discernible in discourses of heroic leadership, which continue to resist efforts to displace them with a 'post-heroic' perspective, at least in the popular imagination. Despite recent enthusiasm for theories of caring leadership, the maternal archetype still receives less attention than its heroic, paternal counterpart (Gabriel, 2015).

Gabriel's (2015) maternal caring leader archetype emphasises that leaders are expected – both consciously and unconsciously – to be nurturing, accessible and reliable in their support for their followers and their containment of their followers' anxieties and fears. This helps to explain why experiencing one's leader as *uncaring* can have such a devastating effect on followers' feelings of security. If a leader does not care enough about his/her followers to put effort into reassuring and bolstering them, this can trigger a primal fear of abandonment and betrayal, and inflict immense damage on their sense of safety and well-being, especially in times of crisis. A perceived absence of care in a leader can be very damaging indeed (Gabriel, 2015).

However, the flip-side – the presence of care – can also be harmful when it is too cloying, interventionist or indeed, infantilising. Because caring leaders supposedly know and can provide what followers need, there is a risk that followers will be denied the space to develop their *own* answers to their *own* questions. Thus, the independence and autonomy of both follower and child are at risk when care becomes too knowing and smothering for, *as every caring parent knows, excessive caring can seriously inhibit the autonomy of followers, instilling dependence and inertia [...] At what point does caring turn into overprotection and cosseting?* (Gabriel, 2015, p. 329).

The challenge for caring leaders is to find some sort of middle ground between excessive care (depriving followers of their independence) and insufficient care (triggering followers' primal terrors of abandonment). This balancing act has been exercising philosophers of human relations for millennia; it is arguably one of the oldest dilemmas of leadership. For instance, Atack (2020) explores caring leadership in Plato and Xenophon, where the analogy of the shepherd king and his flock exposes the crucial difference between *assuming* and *ascertaining* what followers really need and, indeed, are prepared to tolerate from their leaders. Tomkins and Simpson (2015) use Heideggerian philosophy to develop different styles of caring leadership depending on whether the leader is intervening to fix things (risking a loss of follower autonomy) or trying to give space and encouragement to others to work things out for themselves (risking laissez-faire associations). They connect this challenge to the issue of authenticity, emphasising that a Heideggerian *authentic leadership* has as much to do with the authenticity of followers as with the authenticity of leaders.

So far, our discussion has allowed for the possibility that these power dynamics might not be conscious or deliberate. The caring leader who infantilises his/her followers and tries to anticipate their every need and desire could easily be acting from the best of intentions – that is, 'just trying to help'. It might not always be obvious that casting a follower – or indeed, any other human being – as being *in need of care* could potentially be damaging to them. However, in some cases, such power manoeuvres might be very conscious and deliberate, for the desire to feel loved and nurtured can easily be exploited by unscrupulous leaders. For instance, Capriles (2012) discusses how former Venezuelan President Hugo Chavez systematically cultivated dependency in his people, stirring up their resentment and encouraging them to feel that only he truly understood and cared about their aspirations and frustrations. This kind of 'caring leadership' manipulates followers' need and/or desire to belong, whether to an organisation, a community or a nation. It makes strategic use of an *engineered* dependency in what Chatzidakis et al. (2020) call the reactionary type of caring leadership.

It is instructive to look to the care ethics literature to see how dependency issues might be approached more constructively – that is, in ways which *acknowledge* asymmetry and recognise differences of capability, experience and expertise, but without disempowering or exploiting the care-recipient and, by extension, the follower. Notably, Tronto (2015) sees care as a political philosophy of symmetry, not asymmetry: Since care is something we *all* need and receive at certain points in our lives, it is precisely through care that we should approach the issue of democracy. Tronto tackles the apparent paradox of democracy's emphasis on equality and opportunity and care's emphasis on inequality and need by arguing that any *specific* act of care is necessarily unequal between caregiver and care-recipient. Our moral challenge is not to deny this, but to commit to rectifying this imbalance over time, for:

> What makes care equal is not the perfection of an individual caring act, but that we can trust that over time, we will be able to reciprocate the care we received from fellow citizens, and that they will reciprocate the care we've given to them. In such an ongoing pattern of care, we can expect moral virtues to deepen: We will trust in one another and in our social and political institutions.
> (Tronto, 2015, p. 14)

Kittay (2013) argues that strategies based on principles of equality have not actually managed to reduce injustice in either society or institution, and that we should interrogate our fear of human dependency rather than trying to deny it or wish it away. She proposes the concept of *dependency work* to capture the experience of attending to those who need or rely on us. Dependency work is less romanticised than 'care', and it highlights the difficult as well as the wonderful emotions that are evoked in our relationships with others. It involves a deep sense of responsibility towards another person or other people, but within the context of a relationship which differentiates between power and domination. Rather than addressing the problems of asymmetry by simply asserting (or hoping for) symmetry, Kittay argues that we should hone our ability to differentiate between those aspects of dependency that are inevitable and potentially productive, and those which are not inevitable and potentially exploitative.

Thus, both Tronto and Kittay seek to develop an ethics of care which does not shy away from dependency. They highlight that the power relations of care do not have to either assume or emphasise the inferiority or vulnerability of the care-recipient. They offer organisational scholars an impetus to move past a simplistic binary assumption that leaders have all the power and followers have all the disadvantage. Challenging this binary is an important focus for critical leadership studies, for ultimately such binary thinking diminishes everyone involved in our organisational relationships. Acknowledging one's own desire for care does not have to be equated with an unhealthy neediness although, as the next section highlights, it is not without its own complications.

THE APPEAL OF SELF-CARE

Another way in which care is invoked as a form of power is via connections between care and health. These are especially marked in discourses of self-care. Only a few years ago, the concept of self-care was almost unheard of in organisational life, except in the context of looks and appearance, where it was mostly used to criticise women who failed to invest sufficient effort in making themselves attractive as organisational mascots (Tomkins & Pritchard, 2019). Now, however, the rhetoric of self-care has been absorbed almost seamlessly into what Cederström and Spicer (2015) call the *wellness syndrome*. In this paradigm, emotional, corporeal and spiritual self-development are added to the more traditional skills-development duties of the responsible, career-minded employee. Self-care is thus associated with a project of self-enhancement which takes on a moral, even existential dimension, turning life both in and out of work into a campaign of self-optimisation.

Organisations which use the rhetoric of self-care may sound progressive, indeed, caring, but the implications of this discourse for the power relations of leadership can be more problematic. If wellness is constructed as a lifestyle choice, and considered achievable as long as one engages in the discipline of routinised self-care, then there is nobody else to blame if one experiences ill health, disappointing performance or simply common-or-garden dissatisfaction. The responsibility for wellness is thereby shifted away from the organisation or institution and onto the individual. Indeed, when one looks at the rhetoric of self-care (often in corporate materials offering advice on exercise, healthy eating, mindfulness, etc.), it is difficult to resist the interpretation that what they are really saying is, 'look after your own health, or you only have yourself to blame'. From this critical perspective, the language of self-care can be deployed to let organisations, employers and leaders off the hook.

Within the neoliberal paradigm of the wellness syndrome, devoting inadequate time and resources to perfecting oneself can create a deep sense of guilt and inadequacy. Failures of self-care can trigger an excoriating self-loathing, in which *stress, anxiety and feelings of depression are not seen as a creation of the external work environment. Instead, they are a creation of your own lazy and unfocused mental habits* (Cederström & Spicer, 2015, p. 25). Through the rhetoric of self-care, leaders become coaches for their workers' campaigns of self-enhancement, fostering dissatisfaction with their previous selves to spur them to work harder at becoming better, healthier and more successful selves.

Discourses of self-care can thus have a significant influence on leadership relations. A recent study by Johansson and Edwards (2021) argues that leaders' own projects of self-care can be used as a way of regulating their followers' identities. By role-modelling self-care – that is, a health-oriented, self-disciplining and self-improving lifestyle – leaders send a message to their subordinates that self-care is one of the key criteria by which they too will be judged. The authors showcase one particular leader, Adam, who frequently uses the language of care and health to exercise such an influence over his followers. His role-modelling of self-care seems to be fuelled by good intentions – that is, he sees it as a way of demonstrating how much he cares for those who work for him and how he wants the best both for them and – by extension and implication – for the company. As the authors argue, however, this is not care in its relational, care-ethical sense, for it is a leader's unilateral prescription for the optimal identity and lifestyle. Irrespective of Adam's apparently good intentions, his followers do not experience him as genuinely caring, but as highly and inappropriately intrusive. His literal and metaphorical hugs do not bring them closer, but rather, emphasise and intensify the distortions and asymmetries of their relationship.

In Johansson and Edwards' (2021) analysis, the power effects of self-care are explored as explicit features of masculine leadership and are contrasted with a feminist care ethics. Thus, Adam's project of self-care invokes a specifically male model of perfection, based on athleticism and ruthless competitive performance (Collinson & Hearn, 1994). However, role-modelling the pursuit of perfection via self-care is something that women leaders engage in, too. One might consider, for instance, the example of Gwyneth Paltrow, a leader in the sense of being a social influencer. She similarly role-models a devotion to the project of self-care, setting the tone for a constant self-vigilance and occasionally giving her followers permission to loosen the reins a little and permit themselves the odd glass of wine or a cheeky slice of pizza. Here, too, self-care is used as a mechanism of identity regulation.

In short, the apparently benign notion of self-care can be seen as an instrumental fashioning of the leader persona in order to influence and manipulate others, and hence connects to broader critiques of transformational and charismatic leadership (e.g., Bass & Steidlmeier, 1999; Tourish, 2013). What unfolds in the name of care can thus be experienced and perceived by others as an abuse of power and/or a manifestation of leader narcissism. Such a distortion of care is a reminder that it is precisely when something seems to be unequivocally and unimpeachably good that we should probably gird our critical loins to challenge it (Haunschild, 2003).

Finally, it is interesting to see how far the notion of self-care has travelled from its philosophical and historical roots. There are variants of the idea in classical philosophy from Socrates, Plato and Xenophon, through the Stoics, Epicureans and Cynics, via the arrival and influence of Christianity, and towards modernist and postmodernist notions of selfhood and identity. At the source of this philosophical trajectory is Socrates, whose elaborations of self-care – *epimeleia heautou* – have been interpreted, challenged and refashioned for millennia (Tomkins, 2020). A major Socratic motif is the quality and quantity of self-*work* required to ensure that one plays a fully meaningful role as a leader, whether formal or informal, in society.

It is through Foucault's eyes that Socratic self-care has attracted the attention of contemporary leadership scholars (Ladkin, 2018; Randall & Munro, 2010). Foucault's later works draw on classical philosophy to explore how power can be challenged and a degree of personal freedom attained via technologies of the self (Foucault, 1986, 1997). He argues that our modern interpretations of the classics have privileged self-knowledge (as in the famous 'Know Thyself' at the temple of Apollo at Delphi) over a more fundamental creed of self-care. Tracing a number of common themes across antiquity's various philosophical schools of care, Foucault summarises self-care as the conscientious scrutiny of truth claims, both one's own and other people's; the unlearning of bad habits, including the habit of taking said truth claims as givens; a commitment to rigorous and critical self-reflection; and the cultivation of the courage to speak out and speak up. As he explains (1997, p. 95), *in all of ancient philosophy the care of the self was considered as both a duty and a technique, a basic obligation and a set of carefully worked-out procedures.*

Somewhere in the translation from Socratic and Foucauldian philosophy to the wellness syndrome, we seem to have lost the critical and emancipatory force of self-care. We have also lost the Foucauldian paradox in the connection between care and health, whereby wellness can unfold in 'illness' as much as in 'health', insofar as self-care involves finding ways to tell one's *own* story in the *practice of reclaiming a voice that bodily trauma and institutional treatment have caused to be silenced* (Frank, 1998, p. 336). Returning to the case of Adam (Johansson and Edwards, 2021), a philosophically healthy self-care for Adam's followers would involve their resisting his identity and lifestyle mandates, and speaking up about their potentially damaging effects. A philosophically healthy self-care for Adam himself would mean resisting the role-modelling impulse, for both Socratic and Foucauldian self-care mean controlling one's own desires so that they do not harm or disadvantage others (Foucault, 1997).

THE RISK OF SELF-SACRIFICE

For most of this chapter, the problems with care have largely been those affecting followers – that is, they are associated with having one's scope for personal agency and choice curtailed by overly 'caring' or 'self-caring' leaders. I now turn to a perhaps less obvious form of power disadvantage, namely, the ways in which care can foster and reinforce impotence for leaders. Here, it is especially fruitful to connect with the sociological, political and feminist literatures on care ethics, where the impotence, self-sacrifice and potential abuse of care-*givers* has long been a crucial concern (Sander-Staudt & Hamington, 2011; van Nistelrooij, 2014).

Gilligan (1982) makes an important distinction between a *feminine* care ethics and a *feminist* care ethics. On the one hand, the former equates moral virtue with self-sacrifice – that is, with relating to other people solely on their terms and in the service solely of their needs. This kind of submissive care casts commitment to others as subservience to others, and hence as the opposite of moral maturity and agency. A *feminist* ethics, on the other hand, sees all human lives as interwoven and interdependent within a social, political and moral web of relationship. Gilligan's work helps to frame a key challenge for all relationships of care, namely how to ensure that care fosters a mutually enriching intersubjectivity and not a cringing, submissive self-sacrifice.

Returning to the theme of dependency, those who care for others face the possibility of two kinds of dependency. First, there is the risk of dependency for the care-recipient, as discussed earlier. But there is also a secondary dependency which affects the care-*giver*, because the responsibilities of care – both practical and emotional – can be so absorbing, even overwhelming, that they trap the care-giver in the care relationship. Kittay's (2013) concept of dependency work therefore encompasses the potential dependency of the care-giver (aka leader) as well as that of the care-recipient (aka follower), suggesting that the former can be as exploitative and disempowering as the latter. Thus, a care-giver's commitment to the relationship and attachment to the care identity can easily morph into a loss of independence and a diminished capacity to safely express his/her own needs and feelings (Kittay, 2013). This shifts the locus of power from the care-giver to the care-recipient, no matter how unintentional this may be. From this perspective, the idea of care-giving as an attunement which enables us to see the world through another person's eyes – and thus both predict and respond to his/her needs – does not feel like the sign of healthy empathy or intersubjectivity. It is a warning that:

> We can take up the perspective of others out of sheer necessity for survival, the necessity to anticipate others' needs in order to be a good servant or slave, for example. Women learn well to do this with men; slaves have learned well to do it with masters.
>
> (Card, 1990, p. 106)

Therefore, when we extrapolate care ethics from familial/domestic relations into the world of organisational and leadership relations, we should not assume that the power dynamics of care necessarily privilege leaders/care-givers and disadvantage followers/care-recipients. Just like Card's (1990) slave-like victim of abuse above, caring leaders risk being pulled into relationship dynamics that equate responsiveness to their followers' needs and perspectives with the denial or deprioritisation of their own.

Recent leadership scholarship has picked up this baton from the care ethics literature, highlighting that caring leadership might involve leader self-sacrifice and hence be a sign of impotence not strength. Abreu Pederzini (2019) explores caring leadership through the prism of evolution theory, constructing care as a matter of survival rather than moral virtue or authentically warm feelings towards others. In this view, caring leaders – based on the archetypal care-giver, the parent – care for their followers/offspring not because care-giving is righteous, but because it is a behavioural trait selected for its strategic evolutionary advantage. Self-sacrifice from the care-giver is thereby seen as a way to ensure that the gene can survive, whether literally in biology or analogously in organisational relations. In other words, the caring gene does not emerge or endure because it is a wonderful thing, but because it can and it must in order to survive.

The theme of self-sacrifice for the caring leader is also approached through the philosophy of Nietzsche in one of my own recent papers (Tomkins, 2021). This uses the Nietzschean concept of slave morality to expose one of the key tensions of organisation, namely a disconnect between the rhetoric of empowerment and the experience of impotence. At the heart of Nietzsche's critique of care and compassion is an inversion of values in which those who are guided by slave morality (even the overtly powerful) find ways to transform their impotence and submission into virtue, accomplishment and subject-position. This recalls Kittay's (2013) work on the risks of the caring identity, namely that seeing oneself as defined and valued only – or at least, principally – through subservience to others can become a powerful form of exploitation of the care-giver. It also recalls Card's (1990) analogy of the care-giver as slave. When discourses of caring leadership trigger the Nietzschean slave-within, the leader is effectively ceding control of the self to forces beyond the self. This is a useful reminder of what Burns (1978, p. 15) argued many decades ago, namely that we should not fall into the trap of thinking that leaders' actual power equals their reputed power, for *'power wielders are not free agents. They are subject – even slaves – to pressures working on them and in them'*.

RESEARCHING CARING LEADERSHIP

Over the course of this chapter, care and caring leadership have emerged as rich, multifaceted and sometimes contentious phenomena. Caring leadership involves and affects both leaders and followers, and can operate in a range of cognitive, emotional, ethical, behavioural and relational dimensions. This makes it a fascinating but complex topic to research empirically. In its current stage of evolution as a leadership approach, it does not lend itself to being operationalised into any sort of survey or questionnaire. Indeed, I would suggest that any attempt to create a Caring Leadership Questionnaire would suffer from many of the same problems as the Authentic Leadership Questionnaire (see, for instance, Alvesson & Einola, 2019).

Those looking to study caring leadership *a-priori* have to decide which particular elements of care they want to turn into research questions for participants. For instance, researchers might be most interested in care as a style of reasoning (Gilligan, 1982; Robinson, 2019); a style of problem-solving (Simola et al., 2010); a style of leadership intervention (Tomkins & Simpson, 2015); a style of critical reflection (Ladkin, 2018); an ability to contain other people's emotions (Petriglieri & Maitlis, 2019); a willingness to be visible and available in times of trouble (Gabriel, 2015), etc. Developing realistic research designs usually requires a narrowing down of this broad range of potential meanings and definitions and prioritising one particular aspect.

The relationality of care throws up a number of challenges for the researcher. A key question is whether caring leadership is experienced consistently by the range of different parties to the relationship. This dilemma is exposed by Johansson and Edwards (2021), where what is intended as care on the part of a leader is actually felt to be something quite different and indeed inappropriate by those on the receiving end. One implication of this is that researchers should talk both to leaders and to those who answer to them about how care is truly being experienced, mindful, of course, that power asymmetries might make it difficult for subordinates to speak up about any downsides or inconsistencies between intentions and results.

In my experience, the most rewarding research projects on caring leadership are inductive and exploratory in orientation – that is, care is not always the *a-priori* focus of the research. Instead, the research question is often something like 'what are the challenges of being a leader in this organisation?' or 'what are the main drivers of success and/or failure in this change initiative?' When the questions are framed as openly and curiously as this, there is space for a rich and diverse set of experiences to emerge; and these have often, to my mind, lent themselves well to being theorised using care ethics. A recent example is Tomkins and Bristow (2021), where we conducted an inductive analysis of qualitative data from an action research project on evidence-based practice, and used care ethics to theorise the limitations of its seductive catch-phrase of 'what works', with its often mechanistic, one-size-fits-all connotations. Building from our data, we developed a care-ethical approach to evidence-based practice, suggesting that 'what matters' is needed to counterbalance 'what works' if leaders are to role-model relational sensitivity, practical reasoning and a commitment to the particular. In this way, caring leadership became the/an answer, rather than the question.

FINAL WORDS

Caring leadership is appealing because it prioritises the human values of relationship, empathy and dialogue. It can, however, also mean infantilisation, subjugation and exploitation – both intended and unintended, both conscious and unconscious. Perhaps counter-intuitively, the power asymmetries of caring leadership do not automatically privilege leaders and disempower followers. Pushing past the surface appeal of this leadership approach is valuable, therefore, because the more alert we are to its hidden power dynamics, the greater our chances of *realistically* embedding care in our relations with self, others and organisation.

Whenever care is offered or withheld, leadership unfolds in an emotionally and ethically complex labyrinth of give and take; strength and vulnerability; capability and need. In such a labyrinth, power is never one-sided or easy to either consolidate or challenge. But to prioritise care is to attempt to come to terms with power and its limitations; and thus to:

> Recognise for both sexes the importance throughout life of the connection between self and other, the universality of the need for compassion and care. The concept of the separate self and of moral principles uncompromised by the constraints of reality is an adolescent ideal, the elaborately wrought philosophy of a [...] Daedalus whose flight we **know** to be in jeopardy.
>
> (Gilligan, 1982, p. 98, my emphasis)

REFERENCES

Abreu Pederzini, G. D. (2019). Realistic egocentrism: Caring leadership through an evolutionary lens. *Culture and Organization*, 26(5–6), 372–387.

Alvesson, M., & Einola, K. (2019). Warning for excessive positivity: Authentic leadership and other traps in leadership studies. *Leadership Quarterly*, 30(4), 383–395.

Atack, C. (2020). The shepherd king and his flock: Paradoxes of leadership and care in classical Greek philosophy. In L. Tomkins (Ed.), *Paradox and Power in Caring Leadership: Critical and Philosophical Reflections* (pp.75–85). Edward Elgar.

Bass, B. M., & Steidlmeier, P. (1999). Ethics, character, and authentic transformational leadership behavior. *Leadership Quarterly*, 10(2), 181–217.

Brophy, M. (2011). Bumfights and care ethics: A contemporary case study. In M. Hamington & M. Sander-Staudt (Eds.), *Applying Care Ethics to Business* (pp. 201–218). Springer.

Brown, M. E., & Treviño, L. K. (2006). Ethical leadership: A review and future directions. *Leadership Quarterly*, 17(6), 595–616.

Burns, J. M. (1978). *Leadership*. Harper Perennial Political Classics.

Cameron, K. S., Dutton, J. E., & Quinn, R. E. (2003). *Positive Organizational Scholarship: Foundations of a New Discipline*. Berrett-Koehler.

Capriles, R. (2012). *Leadership by Resentment: From Ressentiment to Redemption*. Edward Elgar.

Card, C. (1990). Caring and evil. *Hypatia*, 5(1), 101–108.

Cederström, C., & Spicer, A. (2015). *The Wellness Syndrome*. Polity Press.

Chatzidakis, A., Hakim, J., Littler, J., Rottenberg, C., & Segal, L. (2020). From carewashing to radical care: The discursive explosions of care during Covid-19. *Feminist Media Studies*, 20(6), 889–895.

Ciulla, J. B., & Donelson R. F. (2011). Leadership ethics. In A. Bryman, D. Collinson, K. Grint, B. Jackson & M. Uhl-Bien (Eds.), *The SAGE Handbook of Leadership* (pp. 229–241). Sage.

Collinson, D., & Hearn, J. (1994). Naming men as men: Implications for work, organization and management. *Gender, Work & Organization*, 1(1), 2–22.

Cunliffe, A. L., & Eriksen, M. (2011). Relational leadership. *Human Relations*, 64(11), 1425–1449.

Denis, J. L., Langley, A., & Sergi, V. (2012). Leadership in the plural. *Academy of Management Annals*, 6(1), 211–283.

Engster, D. (2007). *The Heart of Justice: Care Ethics and Political Theory*. Oxford University Press.

Fairhurst, G. T., & Uhl-Bien, M. (2012). Organizational discourse analysis (ODA): Examining leadership as a relational process. *Leadership Quarterly*, *23*(6), 1043–1062.

Finch, J., & Groves, D. (1983). *A Labour of Love: Women, Work and Caring*. Routledge.

Foucault, M. (1986). *The History of Sexuality, Vol. 3: The Care of the Self*. Trans. R. Hurley. Random House.

Foucault, M. (1997). The hermeneutic of the subject. In P. Rabinow (Ed.), *Ethics, Subjectivity and Truth*. Trans. R. Hurley (pp. 93–106). Penguin.

Frank, A. W. (1998). Stories of illness as care of the self: A Foucauldian dialogue. *Health*, *2*(3), 329–348.

Frost, P. J. (1999). Why compassion counts! *Journal of Management Inquiry*, *8*(2), 127–133.

Gabriel, Y. (2015). The caring leader: What followers expect of their leaders and why? *Leadership*, *11*(3), 316–334.

Gilligan, C. (1982). *In a Different Voice*. Harvard University Press.

Haunschild, A. (2003). Humanization through discipline? Foucault and the goodness of employee health programmes. *Tamara Journal of Critical Organization Inquiry*, *2*(3), 46–59.

Held, V. (2006). *The Ethics of Care: Personal, Political, and Global*. Oxford University Press.

Johansson, J., & Edwards, M. (2021). Exploring caring leadership through a feminist ethic of care: The case of a sporty CEO. *Leadership*, *17*(3), 318–335.

Kittay, E. F. (2013). *Love's Labor: Essays on Women, Equality and Dependency*. Routledge.

Ladkin, D. (2018). Self-constitution as the foundation for leading ethically: A Foucauldian possibility. *Business Ethics Quarterly*, *28*(3), 301–323.

Lawrence, T. B., & Maitlis, S. (2012). Care and possibility: Enacting an ethic of care through narrative practice. *Academy of Management Review*, *37*(4), 641–663.

Lemoine, G. J., Hartnell, C. A., & Leroy, H. (2019). Taking stock of moral approaches to leadership: An integrative review of ethical, authentic and servant leadership. *Academy of Management Annals*, *13*(1), 148–187.

McAllister, D. J. & Bigley, G. A. (2002). Work context and the definition of self: How organizational care influences organization-based self-esteem. *Academy of Management Journal*, *45*(5), 894–904.

Munro, I., & Thanem, T. (2018). The ethics of affective leadership: Organizing good encounters without leaders. *Business Ethics Quarterly*, *28*(1), 51–69.

Noddings, N. (2002). *Starting at Home: Caring and Social Policy*. University of California Press.

Petriglieri, G. (2020). The psychology behind effective crisis leadership. *Harvard Business Review*, April.

Petriglieri, G., & Maitlis, S. (2019). When a colleague is grieving. *Harvard Business Review*, *97*(4).

Randall, J., & Munro, I. (2010). Foucault's care of the self: A case from mental health work. *Organization Studies*, *31*(11), 1485–1504.

Robinson, F. (2019). Resisting hierarchies through relationality in the ethics of care. *International Journal of Care and Caring*, *4*(1), 11–23.

Rynes, S. L., Bartunek, J. M., Dutton, J. E., & Margolis, J. D. (2012). Care and compassion through an organizational lens: Opening up new possibilities. *Academy of Management Review*, *37*(4), 503–523.

Sander-Staudt, M., & Hamington, M. (2011). Care ethics and business ethics. In M. Hamington & M. Sander-Staudt (Eds.), *Applying Care Ethics to Business* (pp. vii–xxii). Springer.

Simola, S. K. (2007). The pragmatics of care in sustainable global enterprise. *Journal of Business Ethics*, *74*(2), 131–147.

Simola, S. K., Barling, J., & Turner, N. (2010). Transformational leadership and leader moral orientation: Contrasting an ethic of justice and an ethic of care. *Leadership Quarterly*, *21*(1), 179–188.

Tomkins, L. (2020). Autoethnography through the prism of Foucault's care of the self. In A. F. Herrmann (Ed.), *The Routledge International Handbook of Organizational Autoethnography* (pp. 54–68). Routledge.

Tomkins, L. (2021). Caring leadership as Nietzschean slave morality. *Leadership*, *17*(3), 278–295.

Tomkins, L., & Bristow, A. (2021). Evidence-based practice and the ethics of care: 'What works' or 'what matters'? *Human Relations*, September. https://doi.org/10.1177/00187267211044143

Tomkins, L., & Pritchard, K. (2019). *Health at Work: Critical Perspectives*. Routledge.

Tomkins, L., & Simpson, P. (2015). Caring leadership: A Heideggerian perspective. *Organization Studies*, *36*(8), 1013–1031.

Tourish, D. (2013). *The Dark Side of Transformational Leadership: A Critical Perspective*. Routledge.

Tronto, J. C. (2015). *Who Cares? How to Reshape a Democratic Politics*. Cornell University Press.

van Loon, R. (2017). *Creating Organizational Value Through Dialogical Leadership*. Springer.

van Nistelrooij, A. A. M. (2014). *Sacrifice: A Care-Ethical Reappraisal of Sacrifice and Self-sacrifice*. Peters.

Vinarski-Peretz, H., & Carmeli, A. (2011). Linking care felt to engagement in innovative behaviors in the workplace: The mediating role of psychological conditions. *Psychology of Aesthetics, Creativity and the Arts*, *5*(1), 43.

41

Politicising the Leader's Body: From Oppressive Realities to Affective Possibilities

Celina McEwen, Alison Pullen and Carl Rhodes

INTRODUCING EMBODIED LEADERSHIP

One of the most promising directions in contemporary leadership research concerns the ways leadership emerges through bodies, recognising not only their materiality, but also their intercorporeality. In this chapter, we present an integrative review of leadership thought focusing on how attention to the body can lead to a politicisation of leadership, as well as to new forms of emergent communal practice. The bodies we speak of are not understood in abstract and generalised terms, they relate directly to the lived and felt experiences of living breathing bodies, equally capable of joy, pain, pleasure and sorrow. Acknowledging lived bodies in leadership constitutes a move towards greater recognition of the ways in which leadership can be contested by unequal bodies in both proximity and relationality.

Historically, leadership theory has, by and large, not fully considered the role of the body and embodiment in practice (Hansen et al., 2007; Ford et al., 2017; Knights, 2021b), taking the leader's body for granted. Instead, cognitive and behavioural appreciations of leadership practice, whether they come in the form of traits, actions, values or effects, are the focus of mainstay leadership research and presented as the foundations of leadership practice. Critical leadership scholars have sought to theorise and practise leadership in ways that consider the unequal and increasingly complex world we live in, arguing that bodies and emotions have been largely omitted or negated from conceptualisations of leadership. They posit that this has been the case because of science's primacy of Cartesian thought that separates the mind from the body and presumes the mind to be rational (Knights, 2021b; Pullen & Rhodes, 2015).

In this chapter, we draw on critical leadership theories that focus on leadership as a process that emerges through daily interactions, rather than the traits, behaviours or individual practice of an extraordinary leader (cf., Crevani et al., 2010; Cunliffe & Eriksen, 2011). Although the concept of relationship-oriented behaviour has been around since the earliest formal studies of leadership in organisations (Stogdill & Coons, 1957), the term 'relational leadership' is surprisingly new (Brower et al., 2000; Drath, 2001; Murrell, 1997; Uhl-Bien, 2003, 2005) (Uhl-Bien, 2011, p. 75). Relational leadership is a non-traditional approach at the forefront of advancing leadership theory. Whereas trait-, style- or contingency-based leadership approaches attended to leadership in terms of different attributes of leaders themselves, relational leadership sees leadership as primarily happening between leaders and others that they lead in the context of social interaction and dialogue (Uhl-Bien, 2006). Understanding leadership as situated and relational sits for us within the body of work on relational leadership.

As a relational practice, leadership can be thought about and experienced as socially constructed and dynamic processes created between people as they interdependently interact with each other in routine or ordinary day-to-day activities (cf. Fairhurst & Uhl-Bien, 2012). Relationally, leadership is a process of social influence through which organising and coordination emerge, and through which practical, behavioural, ideological and cultural changes can be enacted and produced in organisations (Uhl-Bien, 2006); it is an ongoing accomplishment that is framed within and by the relationships between people. Relational leadership moves beyond considering leaders and followers as fully formed subjects whose existence precedes their relationships, towards the relationships themselves creating subjects (Hosking, 2011). Relational leadership is not assessed simply in terms of task effectiveness, but on the nature and quality of the relationships that it sustains and from which it emerges. Leaders and followers are interdependent, both in practical terms of having to rely on one another and in ontological terms of leadership identity and practice emerging out of relationships rather than preceding them. This enables leadership to be studied as the *human social constructions that emanate from the rich connections and interdependencies of organizations and their members* (Uhl-Bien, 2006, p. 655).

Relational leadership assumes a collective dimension to the practice of leadership as it is constructed through social interactions *with* others. This approach gives leadership a moral dimension where the practice is seen as being *for* others and, thus, those in leadership positions as being accountable to others for their actions and decisions (Cunliffe & Eriksen, 2011). As a moral and ethical dimension of leadership as relational, it assumes a caring stance where leadership is grounded in a genuine engagement with staff's well-being and fostering of a thriving organisational culture (Nicholson & Kurucz, 2019; Rhodes & Badham, 2018).

In addition to being dialogical, relational leadership is a *reflexive activity that comprises the subtle interplay between the verbal and bodily acts of people at work* (Ryömä & Satama, 2019, p. 696). Despite drawing on different philosophical perspectives, relationality in leadership is linked to studies on embodied leadership. In some cases, embodiment is considered as part of a focus on relationality in leadership, which presupposes a hierarchical relationship between the two concepts (Hansen et al., 2007). In other cases, relationality emerges from the subject's materiality and interactions with others. This is particularly the case when intercorporeality (emerging from inter and intra-actions with other bodies) is emphasised (Pullen & Vachhani, 2020). The lived body is thus a site that bridges the personal and the political (relational) as well as the individual and the collective, and the private and the public (Pullen et al., 2017). Because of that, embodied leadership is concerned with both leadership as a relational practice and leaders interacting with and through their body with others.

The chapter is especially concerned with how research into embodied leadership reflects a politicisation of the leader's body and the practice of leadership, recognising it as a site on which power is written, exercised and potentially resisted. In reviewing the extant literature on embodied leadership, we developed the idea that an embodied approach can undermine the assumption of masculinity in leadership, and what this might mean for a renewed appreciation of leadership itself as an embodied practice that can positively address discrimination and disadvantage in organisations. This points to the possibilities of reimagining leadership differently such that the feminine need no longer be castigated as the other of the masculine-rational leadership ideal in theory and practice that organisations have been shackled with for too long. As Genevieve Lloyd (1984, p. 1) describes in relation to Western cultures, *rational knowledge has been constructed as a transcending, transformation or control of natural forces; and the feminine has been associated with what rational knowledge transcends, dominates or simply leaves behind.* Nowhere is this more the case than in leadership and management, where gendered substructures are obscured by the *normalization of the masculine-rational ideal* (Rhodes & Pullen, 2018, p. 8). More problematically, this cultural normalisation obfuscates non-rational masculine desire for power, which is central to actual leadership practices.

This chapter contributes to that body of work on leadership as relational, embodied practices. Relationality in leadership studies can be associated with the emergence of critical leadership studies and the adoption of practice theories in the field. It has been the theoretical focus of studies seeking to understand leadership as a dynamic relational process as well as reciprocal and ethical practices concerned with equality between leaders and followers. Further, it has been the attention of methodological enquiries in organisational studies exploring relational processes in the doing of ethnographic research (cf., Mosleh & Larsen, 2020).

The chapter begins by providing an overview of the key debates in the study of embodied leadership from a critical leadership perspective. We show how critical and feminist leadership theorists have sought to problematise the common dichotomies in leadership thought. In particular, the chapter reviews the mind–body dichotomy of the earlier leadership theories and problematises the masculine-rational ideal in leadership, which rests on a long tradition in Western culture that denigrates the feminine as being emotional. Then, we consider what it means to explore the body in leadership as a site of power and gendered politics. We conclude with a discussion about the productive possibilities arising from the politics of embodied leadership, showing how an acknowledgement of this politics can serve to redirect leadership as an affective and affirmative practice.

CHALLENGING THE MIND–BODY DICHOTOMY

Many authors writing about embodied leadership practices draw on Maurice Merleau-Ponty's philosophy, which counters René Descartes' idea of the dichotomy between mind and body (Ladkin, 2013). Descartes studied the body as an objective entity composed of fragmented anatomical elements. In doing so, the mind is separated from, and superior to, the body because of its capacity to reason. This reflects the ideas of the enlightenment era within which these theories were formed (Dale, 2000). Merleau-Ponty rejected this dualism proposing that bodies and minds could both be sites of consciousness and intentions. The French philosopher proposed the ideas that bodies are at once natural elements and social constructs; sensory and experiential entities that help us understand the world we encounter on a daily basis; and sites of historical and spatial happening. He argued that the body enables us to visible perceive/experience things and act and make sense of the world as one. He also posited that bodies hide and render many processes invisible (cf. Küpers, 2014).

This critique of Descartes' thinking of the body versus the mind is quite different to that of Gilbert Ryle (2009), a British philosopher and contemporary to Merleau-Ponty, who was also refuting what he called *the dogma of the Ghost in the Machine*. Ryle's argument against the false mind–body dichotomy rests on what he saw as Descartes' desire to elevate the mind (as a proxy of the soul) beyond Galileo's laws of mechanical causation; to account for the mental as a spiritual activity that is more than belonging to the simple physical realm – mistakenly associated with non-intelligence. Different to Merleau-Ponty's critique of the dualism that led to theorising the body as subject (Crossley, 1995) or Ryle's (2009) that resulted in discussions about intelligence and dispositions, Michel Foucault's (1980) subsequent critique of the mind–body dichotomy introduced the idea of the body as a site of power struggle. Foucault is another key theorist of the lived body often cited in embodied leadership literature. Foucault theorised about the body as an expression of power to be controlled as part of normative processes. He explored the relationship between the mind and body and what it means to not only overcome the dichotomy, but also to experience the constraints of being confined inside our bodies.

Embodiment scholars have drawn on these philosophers to challenge, mind–body dualisms – still observed in modern-day Cartesian-inspired work – that focus on understanding *the* body as a mechanistic, inanimate object capable of being separated from the mind under the premise that it does not think. These scholars developed an understanding of the body beyond being and doing to explore ideas of the body as knower and knowing of *what* and *how*. In doing so, they have breached the divide between the body as subject and object of enquiry (Dale, 2000; Dale & Burrell, 2014). Consequently, in the leadership literature, this translated into a shift away from accounting for the notion of the body as an isolated and contained sense-making entity towards reciprocal meaning-making or making sense of and through bodies together.

Studies of leadership and organisations have drawn on theories of the lived body and embodiment to challenge the taken-for-granted assumptions that judgement and skills occur in/through the mind. Therefore, the mind–body dichotomy at the heart of the notions of the leader as the rational individual is troubled, and the omission of non-rational ways of doing, being and relating is addressed. By drawing on embodiment theories, leadership and organisational studies scholars have demonstrated the impact corporeality has on so-called rational thought processes and practices (Gherardi et al., 2019; Pullen & Rhodes, 2015; Pullen & Vachhani, 2013).

For example, some researchers have sought to theorise embodied knowledge and practices, rather than focusing on the role of the body as an added value to the mind. Some of the questions they explore are: *Can we study somebody else's knowledgeable working practices and at the same time our own (working) practices when we, as embodied beings, encounter other bodies?* […] *What happens to us, as persons and researchers, when we put ourselves inside the practices we study?* (Gherardi et al., 2019, p. 295). Other studies on embodied leadership investigate what it means to perceive with or through the body the experience of being part of a leadership relation or dynamic and/or to conceptualise leadership as being constructed through the senses (e.g., by seeing and hearing). Further studies theorise the role of the body as materiality, realisation or performativity of practices, the self or a group; where the body is positioned as a corporeal materiality (inside and outside) and where *leadership is practised through and between bodies, where matter matters* (Pullen & Vachhani, 2013, p. 315).

Embodiment has also been used as a methodology in the field of organisational studies to help researchers make sense of data generated about and through perception, judgements and affect. For instance, Marcelo de Souza Bispo and Silvia Gherardi (2019) offer an analytical approach to what they call *embodied practice-based research*. Their work is underpinned by Loïc Wacquant's (2015) framework of six 'S' of carnal sociology to capture embodied practical knowledge – sentient, suffering, skilled, sedimented and situated – and Gherardi et al.'s (2019) work on affect.

Still, some researchers within the fields of management and organisational studies seek to impose the mind on embodied analyses. This is the case, for example, when scholars examine leadership in terms of dress codes and leaders' aesthetic of appearances (Ladkin, 2013) or the body as a representation of the mind or self (Lipton, 2020). These latter studies displace the body seeking to validate the bodily experience and performance as they relate to sense-making (the mind). Thus, we ask: can we think ourselves out of this problematic dichotomy?

David Knights (2021b) maintains that the attempts to disrupt the polarised binary split between mind and body will not have the intended outcome of tackling the disembodied fallacy in theory. This is because such a disruption is always already rational and cognitive. Moreover, it is achieved from the centrality of individual identity, still located in the mind and separate from others. So how might we escape from the confines of masculine-rational conception of leadership? Knights follows Elizabeth Grosz (1994) in proposing that *the mind and body are understood as in a process of continually becoming one another such that the inside or psychic aspects drift into the outside corporeal self and vice versa* (Knights, 2021b, p. 133). Further, it is with Karen Barad (2007) that Knights (2021b, p. 134) reminds us that *matter and meaning, nature and culture, body and mind, and emotion and cognition* [are] *performatively entangled as agents and products of one another*.

Considering mind and body as entangled has offered an initial way out of assuming the primacy of rationality in leadership. It is the same inspiration that Jackie Ford, Nancy Harding and Sarah Gilmore (2017) draw on to discuss leadership as a *material presence*. They extend the notion that to consider inter-human relations as forms of entanglement. Bodies together affect each other such that neither can be regarded as distinct when relating with others or objects. Barad (2007) refers to this process as *inter-action*, with Ford et al. (2017) building on this conceptualisation of practice to insist that leadership is always embodied and contextually embedded in its physical environment to be structured by embodiment, affect, materiality and discourse. They also point out that this material inter-action is present even when leaders themselves articulate an understating of leadership as disembodied; the discursive transcendence of the body does not constitute material disembodiment.

PROBLEMATISING THE MASCULINE-RATIONAL LEADER

Critics have asserted that a central reason for the traditional Western understanding of leadership centred on the mind and psychology of actions is because of its development as a masculine construct. The situation is that *while within leadership, there is a considerable emotional or bodily content as well as strong masculine rationalities, research fails to examine them largely because the cerebral norm takes precedence* (Knights, 2022, p. 3). This follows a long tradition in Western thought that not only makes a distinction between the mind and the body, but, moreover, associates the rational mind with masculinity and privileges the masculine-rational over the emotive body associated with femininity (Lloyd, 1984). This distinction is not neutral, and is applied to leadership, rendering the concept disembodied, while surreptitiously making the leadership body by default virile, able and male (cf. Gherardi et al., 2019; Knights, 2021b; Pullen & Vachhani, 2013; Höpfl & Matilal, 2007).

The masculine-rational leadership ideal is, therefore, not natural to practice, but culturally reproduced through norms, not the least in leadership research. Knights (2021b) illustrates this point through a series of vignettes about personal experiences where he reflects on the methodological tendency of analytical focus on emotionless facts. He problematises the assumption that leadership is a rational-cognitive and masculine discursive process. Even though this approach might aid abstract theory building, it is achieved by containing uncertainty and suppressing the realities of bodies as sites of un-namely desires and repulsive emanating fluids and leakage. The resulting masculine-rational scientific process also serves to reinforce the social construct that identifies men as objective, instrumental, logical leaders and women as subjective, passive, emotional followers and, thus, gives rigour and validity to the 'men versus women' gender binary.

Although research on the embodied politics of leadership has developed considerably, by and large, Amanda Sinclair's (2004, p. 17) assertion that *leadership, as we understand it in contemporary societies and organizations, is undoubtedly a white, male idea, a motif manufactured and embroidered by managerial elites to legitimize habits and advance their interests* still holds, with the body being *important yet neglected in leadership* (Knights, 2017, p. 75; cf. Pullen & Vachhani, 2013, 2020).

It is the case that *most leadership theorizing and practice continues to legitimize the overwhelming concentration of power among elite white men, reinforcing white masculinities as norm and exemplar* (Pullen et al., 2019, p. 2555). Feminist approaches have been central in forging new directions that not only trouble the separation between mind and body, but also the attendant privileging of a disembodied male and rationalised idea of leadership, challenging the notion that leadership is formal and ideally embodied by a white male body with 'heroic' features (Collinson, 2020).

Feminist research in management and organisation studies has shown how organisations do little to question the male body, while at the same time objectifying women's bodies as being leaky and vulnerable, the object of heterosexual male desire and harassment, or judged according to beauty norms (Thanem & Knights, 2019). Claire O'Neill (2019) studied how women's bodies are othered through masculine discourses of leadership. O'Neill uses the idea of *dys-appearance* – developed from Leder (1990) – to understand *the unique or different experiences of leadership for women, and the impact of the problematising of the female body on their self-perceptions* (O'Neill, 2019, p. 296). Dys-appearance is a *dysfunctional condition as a source of bodily visibility* (Leder, 1990, cited in O'Neill, 2019, p. 301). O'Neill seeks to problematise the emphasis placed on the mind, which leads to the disembodiment of leadership, and the neutrality and invisibility of the body, presumed to be masculine, with her study of self-identified women in leadership positions and their experiences of being 'othered' from the dominant masculine norm. O'Neill writes (2019, p. 299):

The visible body highlights the futility of talking about gender as a purely abstracted concept, which exists beyond, above or before the material. The body plays a crucial role in the determination and perpetuation of gender discourses and power relations, and so is a crucial analytical focus in developing an understanding of women's experiences of leadership.

O'Neill contends that the body becomes aware of itself when it performs badly not just as a physical entity but when it enacts this performance in a social context. The experience of the sexed/gendered body includes being seen as disruptive, different or even threatening to the norm, attending also to the possible painfulness of this experience. It is this pain that can make us aware of our bodies.

Although some researchers may resist the othering processes of the female body, O'Neill finds that more commonly it results in a transformation towards respectability as invisibility. For the public performance of leadership, however, this adds further complications for women. When women's bodies are cast as problems to be 'fixed' or 'removed' in leadership (cf. Höpfl & Matilal, 2007) they lose the desired absence of the body within their intentional field, a state that accompanies the unproblematically functioning body. The body becomes a visible object within their perception of self, something that stands opposed to the self and is regarded as a recalcitrant and undesirable accompaniment; something that requires change (O'Neill, 2019).

Pullen and Vachhani (2013) posit that it is the relations between the body's inside and outside that enable power to be exercised on women's bodies, rendering them other, invisible and out-of-place in the masculine organisational world. For women, this leads to tensions between visibility and invisibility as they feel the need to constantly monitor, adjust, change and censor their bodies to be unseen.

Under the veneer of scientific enquiry, we find deep cultural tensions and oppressions between the masculine and the feminine, and the rational and the affective, in all cases sublimating the feminine affective as inferior within a patriarchal social context. This is the oppressive gendered politics that one finds crawling underneath the rock of scholarly legitimacy once it is lifted.

POLITICISING THE BODY

Looking at leadership thought and practice through embodied approaches has not only developed more accurate perceptions of what leadership is, it has also made visible the repressed inequalities and injustices located in and imposed on bodies, which are inherent to organisational and institutional life. Rita Gardiner (2018, p. 294) explains:

> By attending to embodied responses, leadership researchers are able to understand how spatial surroundings privilege some bodies while marginalizing others [...] Attending to how relationships exist within particular, organizational contexts offers insight into organizational norms that structure our spatial environment, and influence how some bodies are marginalized while others are privileged.

Bringing the body to bear on leadership theory and practice as a means of examining leadership politics does not, however, mean that we can simply take bodies for granted as if they were just a matter of material facticity. Drawing on Foucault (2003), we understand that bodies are disciplined around particular norms embedded in discourses that determine what counts as normal, desirable and dominant, at the level of the individual, the population and the organisation. This alerts us to how theorising leadership as an embodied practice is an engagement with the power relations that determine the social value and worth of some bodies over others, both in general and at the specific sites where different bodies interreact in practice (Randall & Munro, 2010).

Care needs to be taken here not to instate a new structure of privilege that prizes the body's 'flesh' over its appearance; its inside over its outside (Pullen & Vachhani, 2013). Indeed, the experience of one's body is as much in the mirror and the gaze as it is in the gut and the punch. To this point, Ford et al. (2017) report on a study that asked *how do participants make themselves visible and recognizable as leaders?* (p. 1555) and explored *how leaders manifest themselves as leaders by and through their physical appearance* (p. 1557). They found that situated and shared understandings of leadership as presence/visible does not support theories of leadership as purely disembodied cognitive process or rational disposition. Ford et al.'s (2017) analysis highlights the material micro-dynamics of leadership and reveals lay understandings of the materiality and corporeality of leadership. Ford et al.'s (2017) study elicited three salient themes. The first theme analysed is that of *reading appearances*, where participants made judgements about character and leadership qualities (e.g., authority) of people represented in photographs. The second theme, *work on the self*, is about how leaders apply the same judgement based on appearance to themselves, believing that if they dress (and pose) the part, they will be perceived as intended or influence a particular response from others (e.g., accept or recognise that change is coming). The authors suggest that this indicates that leaders have their own (colloquial and local) understanding. They refer to this as a lay or *endogenous theory* of leadership of the impact of appearances on judgement of character and how to manipulate impressions through (re) presentation; a 'theory-in-practice' as opposed to exogenous theory proposed by expert scholars. The third theme is *the self as ideal leader* because of how participants tended to compare excellent and poor leaders with themselves, but also describe ideal leaders as extensions of themselves.

For Ford et al. (2017), these themes highlight how the people they research enacted *a morphology of the material self as something that can be manipulated through working on one's appearance* (p. 1564). They conclude that *tasks of preparing for work through showering, dressing and making the self presentable can be understood as complexly coded acts of materialization of norms, codes, cultures, histories, economics, legal systems and so on, all of which coalesce as rules about how 'the leader' should look* (p. 1567). It is in this sense that the apparently superficial and exterior dimensions of the body are in fact not superficial or meaningless at all because they represent the very *location* where power operates on 'leaders' and how particular, often oppressive, norms are routinely and daily reproduced.

EMBODYING RESISTANCE

With a particular focus on issues of power and inequality feminist studies on embodied leadership have been inspired by Judith Butler's notion of the vulnerability of the body as a source of resistance and feminist solidarity building (Butler, 2016). Butler attends to how bodily vulnerability, as much as it might be conceived as dangerous, is also the basis for responsibility for the lives of others and what binds us to that other. Butler argues that an acknowledgement of vulnerability can also be a precursor to resistance and feminist solidarity building. Vulnerability is both political and ethical: political in the sense that it involves an exposure to violence that is geographically and demographically allocated; ethical in the sense that it focuses on humanity's common mortality as well as stirring a sense of ethical responsibility for the needs and rights of others. That vulnerability might itself be the basis of collective human responsibility informs Sanela Smolović Jones, Nick Winchester and Caroline Clarke's (2021) discussion of feminist solidarity building. They theorise about how solidarity can be built with and across tensions expressed through differences in language and embodied ontology and epistemology, including shared vulnerability. Embodiment brings an additional level of nuance to relationality, which is by nature experiential and affective, as much as it involves the strain of human difference and the potential for violence inherent in it. By contrast, feminist solidarity *"can foreground conflict in a way that enacts and seeks to enshrine equal voice and participation, thus viewing difference as generative rather than inhibiting"* (Smolović Jones et al., p. 921).

For Smolović Jones et al., embodied solidarity is a democratic practice that harnesses difference, and conflict, to develop collective agency. More specifically, it is defined as *a participative and inclusive endeavour driven by conflictual encounters, constituted through the bodies, language and visual imagery of assembling and articulating subjects* (p. 917). This modus operandi is characterised by the three dimensions of sensory experiences of exposing, citing and inhabiting:

> First, the **exposing** of one's body to the hardship of others to enable alliances between unlikely allies to form. Second, **citing** as a means of drawing in the symbolic resources of others and publicly affirming them. Third, creating a new political subject through **inhabiting**, which strengthens solidarity and enables assembly to grow and persist.
> (Smolović Jones et al., p. 932, my emphasis)

This analytical framework was applied to an ethnographic study conducted by Smolović Jones of the 2016 Montenegro mothers' protest to demonstrate how women who disagreed on political views came together in solidarity to support those in hardship and deceived by the government. While this study is not explicitly about leadership, it implicitly demonstrates a form of collective leadership that directly defies the masculine-rational model discussed earlier. Through protest, the authors showed how women worked together despite their differences to form a collective leadership based on embodied interaction and negotiation.

Emmanouela Mandalaki and Marianna Fotaki (2020) read the body as a political actor, a site of vulnerabilities and precariousness, and as knowledge and resistance, at the heart of the processes and practices of communal living. The body is weak, yet strong, as it produces, maintains and solidifies shared experiences and relationships that are inclusive, collaborative and interdependent and resistant to capitalisms' attempts to constrain it to a manufacturing tool. To advance their conceptualisation of embodied ethics, the authors work with feminist ethics based on shared responsibility and reciprocity to the body to conceptualise ethical practices as embodied and relational. Their analysis surfaces *the social and participative processes of organizing and reproducing the commons* (Mandalaki & Fotaki, p. 746). This relational embodied ethics draws on Valerie Fournier's (2013) social organisation of the commons as involving a three-tiered process:

> commoning evolves around three interdependent axes of social organizing: (i) organizing in common, denoting users' responsibilities for and collective allocation of common resources; (ii) organizing for the common, denoting shared consumption and use of the commons; and (iii) organizing of the common, denoting how the commons are constantly reproduced through collective use and reciprocal exchanges.
> (Mandalaki & Fotaki, 2020, p. 747)

It is with this fully developed idea of a *relational ethics of the commons* that [e]*thical processes of commoning based on actors' shared corporeal experiences put community benefit beyond individual benefit to encompass communal processes of social organizing in common, of the commons and for the commons* (Mandalaki & Fotaki, p. 753). We see an affinity with forms of collective leadership that defy the assumption that leadership is the role of a single person, or a 'great man', who leads while others follow. Inter-corporeality, thus, starts to lend itself to a new mode of leadership unshackled from the ego of any singular person and embedded in the collective life of a community.

For Laura Dobusch (2020, p. 382) there is a *fundamental vulnerability and inter-/dependence of human life in general.* [and] *human existence is dependent on its actual embodiment; an embodiment that needs to be constantly nurtured – actively produced – and is thus always confronted by the possibility of unexpected changes and 'failures'*. Writing about people with degrees of ability, Dobusch maintains that instead of denying human vulnerability, it is important to welcome body differences that have traditionally been seen as flawed or broken so as to undermine *phallic fantasies* of unity, consistency and rationality. Dobusch brings this argument to a discussion about relational leadership practices ostensibly committed to inclusion:

> For inclusion approaches to live up to their own standards, it is necessary to explicitly acknowledge

their constitutive relationship with forms of exclusion. Only then does it become possible to discuss the legitimacy of certain ways of drawing boundaries and their inclusionary and exclusionary consequences.

(Dobusch, 2020, p. 380)

On these grounds, Dobusch contends that instead of basing relational leadership practices around inclusion, a combination of alternative experiential and practice-based approaches is preferred. Drawing on Melissa Tyler's (2019) articulation of *embodied recognition* and *liveable interdependency* Dobusch develops a way for *unconditional inclusion*. This involves a recognition that all bodies are inherently vulnerable and dependent on others, and that the assumption that so-called able-bodied people are 'independent' is a normalising myth that reinforces exclusions. In contrast, an embodied ethics embraces inclusion *as the affirmative experience of being part of a social whole* (Dobusch, 2020, p. 12). Once more, we see the politicisation of the body leading to a communal ethos that works through identification and difference so as to assert our social foundation on bodily vulnerability and mortality. These ideas align with Lori Knutson's (2015) discussion of how the embodied health movement can develop an integrative and transformative leadership practice based *on a shared consciousness and shared physical experience that impassions people to transform not only themselves but also society* (p. 407).

An awareness of the embodied realities of communal life is captured well by Erin Ellison and Regina Langhout's (2020) exploration of *corporeal literacy*. Corporeal literacy is defined as *the ability to recognize and attend to information created through the body* [that] *occurs viscerally through knowledge of the self, another, and the sociocultural context* (Ellison & Langhout, p. 954). The value of developing such literacy, they aver, is to enable people to act in solidarity despite, and across, their differences. Although Ellison and Langhout's work is specific to the practice of union organising, their insights are of value much more broadly to the practice of leadership. In their case, they report on how union members have become disaffected by traditional centralised and hierarchical modes of leadership, showing how a relational approach based on corporeal literacy is much more effective in building solidarity and countering oppression. What we called earlier masculine-rational approaches to leadership can, thus, be superseded by *a relational–corporeal praxis process of intersectional solidarity as an organizing framework* (Ellison & Langhout, p. 965).

BRINGING AFFECTIVE EMBODIMENT TO BEAR ON LEADERSHIP THEORY AND PRACTICE

Embodiment theory and practice harbour the potential for contemporary forms of leadership. Considering leadership as an embodied phenomena and/or practice is a way of affirming the positive possibilities of collective life. This collective life is a more liveable life than that offered by the individualism inherent in neoliberal organisations. Such affective, embodied leadership could be seen as constituting an assembly as communal organising to affect change. Assembly, following Butler (2015), entails the mutual recognition of bodies in a shared space and in recognition of each other. With assembly *showing up, standing, breathing, moving, standing still, speech, and silence are all* […] *an unforeseen form of political performativity* (Butler, 2015, p. 18). Is it then possible that the intercorporeal connections that constitute embodied leadership are inherently necessary and productive of assembly? Does this leadership share with assembly a form of mutual respect, recognition and respect for difference? The discussion engaged with in this chapter suggests that this is the very defining feature of embodied leadership. This leadership of assembled bodies is one that:

> moves from an individual desire for recognition, to one that becomes collective and focuses on the recognition of, and care for, others as is only possible through a larger collective struggle. For the marginalized and minoritized, the abject and erased, this collective demand becomes central to living a liveable life. Collective struggle operates beyond ego-centric self-satisfaction in the hope that collective recognition of the many can be gained against economic and political injustices.
>
> (Pullen & Rhodes, 2022, p. 70)

However, this means decentring leadership from an association with a singularly embodied person, drawing attention to how leadership operates through the collective based on both its unity and its difference. It is in this sense that the body is relational, a site that bridges the personal and the political as well as the individual and the collective, and the private and the public (Pullen et al., 2017). There is more to embodied leadership than individual leaders' acknowledgement of their bodies. As Knights (2021a, p. 675) puts it: *while embodiment may be necessary, it is not a sufficient condition, because the ethical leader has also to want others to be as embodied and engaged in the leadership process as they are themselves*. Such leadership involves a *collective, embodied engagement [...] that embrace inclusion and unification rather than exclusion and division.*

An important part of thinking of the leadership body as communal is countering the individualisation and tendency to see leadership as the property of one person. Therefore, we can *re-envisage leadership [...] not only more about a collectively shared experience but also concerned with making a difference through embodied energy* (Knights, 2021b, p 120). It is important to remember here that such forms of leadership need not be excessive or remarkable, but rather more importantly operate through the mundane practices of everyday life as they are collectively constructed and sensed through the bodily acts and experiences of thinking, saying and doing from self and with other members of an organisation (Ryömä & Satama, 2019).

We are, however, well aware that leadership is too easily associated with autocracy, or even demagoguery, and the normalisation of inequality. Indeed, as the literature and debates reviewed above show, the body can be a site of repressive power and oppressive gender politics. Knights (2018, p. 82) illustrates this by proposing affective leadership as a form of ethical leadership practice, highlighting how *embodied leadership is distributed socially such that we lead one another through affecting one another in different ways.*

Affective leadership is a way to counter practices that seek to reinforce compliance, and to build and strengthen leadership capacity for action that is not just ethically informed, but reasoned and undertaken with others (Knights, 2019; Munro & Thanem, 2018). Affective leadership as a practice can liberate the notion of *leadership from the belief in techniques or prescriptions to be imposed in interventionist ways on practice [...] Affect does not have to be invented; it just has to be nurtured rather than denied or neglected. All leadership is affective but prescriptive and technical interventions invariably distort its effects* (Knights, 2017, p. 88).

Expanding on the work on vulnerable bodies, Alison Pullen, Carl Rhodes and Torkild Thanem (2017, p. 112) discuss how researching embodiment at work means considering *how affects bring people together by passing between us, without ignoring the nuanced and differential ways in which the gendered organization affects us, and is affected by us, across the corporeal and political registers of social and organizational life.* This is an affective politics as well as an affirmative politics mobilising resistance and activism through joy. Focusing specifically on the gendered organisation, such a politics recognises the sedimentation of gender inequality into the practices and structures of work that create and maintain advantages and disadvantages. Furthermore, it attends to the point that if embodied affect is merely considered as a critically descriptive exercise, resulting only in clever insights into inequality and prejudice, it falls short of anything but benign spectatorship that does little to change anything.

To materially improve the lives of those who have been rendered abject and disadvantaged by resisting or co-opting the disadvantages that arise out of the dominance of the masculine-rational ideal in organisations requires an affective politics, as it can be exercised through communal and embodied leadership:

> *The gendered organization [...] demands continuous elaboration of how people can respond to the inequities that it breeds. Even though affect enables us to rethink how the oppression of gendered organization is felt, analyzing the gendered organization also allows us to start thinking about how, through an affective politics, we can resist it and craft ways of living and working that transgress and subvert its limits.*
> (Pullen et al., 2017, p. 108)

The embodied leadership that might yield such subversion manifests through a radical politics that enacts change as much as it demands it. This leadership is a social process rather than the result of individual action. It attests to how affective experiences sensed through our bodies (e.g., discomfort, shame), once interpreted, can be used to enact change (cf. Ellison & Langhout, 2020).

Bringing affective embodiment to bear in theorising about leadership practice is not just a politicisation of the leadership body, but also of the researchers' work. As researchers, to understand leadership as a relational practice that affects and is affected by bodies also requires taking up the reflexive challenge of questioning the impact of the researchers' body on their study and theorising of leadership. If embodiment is a central part of leadership practice, then surely the same insights hold relevance to doing research. Perhaps even more than leadership, the scientific process is, by and large, understood as a rational-cognitive process, as well as masculine (Phillips et al., 2014), but also, that we may forget our own bodies as researchers and their role in conducting research, thus creating another problematic dichotomy. Silvia Gherardi (2019, p. 295) asks: *Can we study somebody else's knowledgeable working practices and at the same time our own (working) practices when we, as embodied beings, encounter other bodies? [...] What happens to us, as persons and researchers, when we put ourselves inside the practices we study?*

These are important questions that need to be further explored if we are to better deal with the entrenched dichotomies inherent in leadership research. Only then, can we develop a more robust understanding of, on the one hand, how a shared, communal and relational practice that affects bodies that affect practices is a necessary part of a politically aware and ethical leadership practice, as well as, on the other hand, how shared vulnerability can serve as a unifying force that enables people to identify collectively while at the same time preserving and valuing their differences. To pursue such research, we recommend exploring affective leadership based on affective solidarity, such as that exists in the social movement organising, from Black Lives Matter to the Women's Marches (Vachhani & Pullen, 2019). Further studies could also examine the everyday and mundane practices of working collectively without the presence of a formal leader in organisational teams.

If leadership is thought of as the heroic act of a disembodied masculine-rational individual, then the vibrancy and potential of human interaction are side-lined in favour of either hubris or deference. Embodied and affective leadership offers the possibility to understand leadership as a political and social process that transcends the body of any individual to bring sameness or difference together in a manner that affirmatively resists inequality and oppression. This is the possibility and promise of the politics of the leader's body.

REFERENCES

Barad, K. (2007). *Meeting the Universe Halfway: Quantum Physics and the Entanglement of Matter and Meaning*. Duke University Press.

Bispo, M. S., & Gherardi, S. (2019). Flesh-and-blood knowing: Interpreting qualitative data through embodied practice-based research. *RAUSP Management Journal*, 54(4), 371–383.

Brower, H. H., Schoorman, F. D., & Tan, H. H. (2000). A model of relational leadership: The integration of trust and leader–member exchange. *Leadership Quarterly*, 11(2), 227–250.

Butler, J. (2015). *Notes Toward a Performative Theory of Assembly*. Harvard University Press.

Butler, J. (2016). Rethinking vulnerability and resistance. In J. Butler, Z. Gambetti & L. Sabsay (Eds.), *Vulnerability in Resistance* (pp. 12–27). Duke University Press

Collinson, D. L. (2020). 'Only connect!': Exploring the critical dialectical turn in leadership studies. *Organization Theory*, 1(2), 1–22. doi.org/10.1177/2631787720913878

Crevani, L., Lindgren, M., & Packendorff, J. (2010). Leadership, not leaders: On the study of leadership as practices and interactions. *Scandinavian Journal of Management*, 26(1), 77–86.

Crossley, N. (1995). Merleau-Ponty, the elusive body and carnal sociology. *Body & Society*, 1(1), 43–63.

Cunliffe, A. L., & Eriksen, M. (2011). Relational leadership. *Human Relations*, 64(11), 1425–1449.

Dale, K. (2000). *Anatomising Embodiment and Organisation Theory*. Palgrave Macmillan.

Dale, K., & Burrell, G. (2014). Being occupied: An embodied re-reading of organizational 'wellness'. *Organization*, 21(2), 159–177.

Dobusch, L. (2020). The inclusivity of inclusion approaches: A relational perspective on inclusion and exclusion in organizations. *Gender, Work & Organization*, 28(1), 379–396.

Drath, W. (2001). *The Deep Blue Sea: Rethinking the Source of Leadership*. Jossey-Bass.

Ellison, E. R., & Langhout, R. D. (2020). Embodied relational praxis in intersectional organizing: Developing intersectional solidarity. *Journal of Social Issues*, 76(4), 949–970.

Fairhurst, G. T., & Uhl-Bien, M. (2012). Organizational discourse analysis (ODA): Examining leadership as a relational process. *Leadership Quarterly*, 23(6), 1043–1062.

Ford, J., Harding, N. H., Gilmore, S., & Richardson, S. (2017). Becoming the leader: Leadership as material presence. *Organization Studies*, 38(11), 1553–1571.

Foucault, M. (1980). *Power/Knowledge: Selected Interviews and Other Writings, 1972–1977*. Vintage.

Foucault, M. (2003) *Society Must be Defended: Lectures at the Collège de France 1975–76*. Penguin.

Fournier, V. (2013). Commoning: On the social organisation of the commons. *M@n@gement*, 16(4), 433–453.

Gardiner, R. A. (2018). Hannah and her sisters: Theorizing gender and leadership through the lens of feminist phenomenology. *Leadership*, 14(3), 291–306.

Gherardi, S. (2019). Theorizing affective ethnography for organization studies. *Organization*, 26(6), 741–760.

Gherardi, S., Murgia, A., Bellè, E., Miele, F., & Carreri, A. (2019). Tracking the sociomaterial traces of affect at the crossroads of affect and practice theories. *Qualitative Research in Organizations and Management: An International Journal*, 14(3), 295–316.

Grosz, E. (1994). *Volatile Bodies: Toward a Corporeal Feminism*. Indiana University Press.

Hansen, H., Ropo, A., & Sauer, E. (2007). Aesthetic leadership. *Leadership Quarterly*, 18(6), 544–560.

Höpfl, H., & Matilal, S. (2007). 'The lady vanishes': Some thoughts on women and leadership. *Journal of *Organizational Change Management*, 20(2), 198–208.

Hosking, D. M. (2011) Telling tales of relations: Appreciating relational constructionism. *Organization Studies*, 32(1), 47–65.

Knights, D. (2017). What's more effective than affective leadership? Searching for embodiment in leadership research and practice. In C. Mabey & D. Knights (Eds.), *Leadership Matters: Finding Voice, Connection and Meaning in the 21st Century* (pp. 75–87). Routledge

Knights, D. (2018). Leadership Lives?: Affective Leaders in a Neo-Humanist World. In B. Carroll, J. Firth, & S. Wilson (Eds.), *After leadership* (pp. 81-94). Routledge.

Knights, D. (2019). Epilogue: Embodied leadership, ethics and its affects. In B. Carroll, J. Ford & S. Taylor (Eds.), *Leadership: Contemporary Critical Perspectives*. Sage.

Knights, D. (2021a). Challenging humanist leadership: Toward an embodied, ethical, and effective neo-humanist, enlightenment approach. *Leadership*, 17(6), 674–692.

Knights, D. (2021b). *Leadership, Gender and Ethics: Embodied Reason in Challenging Masculinities*. Routledge.

Knights, D. (2022). Disrupting masculinities within leadership: Problems of embodiment, ethics, identity and power. *Leadership*, 18(2), 266–276. https://doi.org/10.1177/17427150211004053

Knutson, L. (2015). Integrative leadership: An embodied practice. *Explore (NY)*, 11(5), 407–409.

Küpers, W. (2014). *Phenomenology of the Embodied Organization: The Contribution of Merleau-Ponty for Organizational Studies and Practice*. Springer.

Ladkin, D. (2013). From perception to flesh: A phenomenological account of the felt experience of leadership. *Leadership*, 9(3), 320–334.

Leder, D. (1990) *The Absent Body*. University of Chicago Press.

Lipton, B. (2020). Academics' dress: Gender and aesthetic labour in the Australian university. *Higher Education Research & Development*, 40(4), 767–780.

Lloyd, G. (1984). *The Man of Reason: 'Male' and 'Female' in Western Philosophy*. Routledge.

Mandalaki, E., & Fotaki, M. (2020). The bodies of the commons: Towards a relational embodied ethics of the commons. *Journal of Business Ethics*, 166(4), 745–760.

Mosleh, W. S., & Larsen, H. (2020). Fieldworking the relational complexity of organizations. *Qualitative Research in Organizations and Management: An International Journal*, 15(4), 421–439.

Munro, I., & Thanem, T. (2018). The ethics of affective leadership: Organizing good encounters without leaders. *Business Ethics Quarterly*, 28(1), 51–69.

Murrell, K. L. (1997). Emergent theories of leadership for the next century: Towards relational concepts. *Organization Development Journal*, 15, 35–42.

Nicholson, J., & Kurucz, E. (2019). Relational leadership for sustainability: Building an ethical framework from the moral theory of 'ethics of care'. *Journal of Business Ethics*, 156(1), 25–43.

O'Neill, C. (2019). Unwanted appearances and self-objectification: The phenomenology of alterity for women in leadership. *Leadership*, 15(3), 296–318.

Phillips, M., Pullen, A., & Rhodes, C. (2014). Writing organization as gendered practice: Interrupting the libidinal economy. *Organization Studies*, 35(3), 313–333.

Pullen, A. & Rhodes, C. (2015). Ethics, embodiment and organizations. *Organization*, 22(2), 159–165.

Pullen, A., & Rhodes, C. (2022) *Organizing Corporeal Ethics: A Research Overview*. Routledge.

Pullen, A., Rhodes, C., McEwen, C., & Liu, H. (2019). Radical politics, intersectionality and leadership for diversity in organizations. *Management Decision*, 59(11), 2553–2566.

Pullen, A., Rhodes, C., & Thanem, T. (2017). Affective politics in gendered organizations: Affirmative notes on becoming-woman. *Organization*, 24(1), 105–123.

Pullen, A., & Vachhani, S. (2013). The materiality of leadership. *Leadership*, 9(3), 315–319.

Pullen, A., & Vachhani, S. (2020). Feminist ethics and women leaders: From difference to intercorporeality. *Journal of Business Ethics*, 173, 233–243. doi: 10.1007/s10551-020-04526-0

Randall, J., & Munro, I. (2010). Foucault's care of the self: A case from mental health work. *Organization Studies*, 31(11), 1485–1504.

Rhodes, C., & Badham, R. (2018). Ethical irony and the relational leader: Grappling with the infinity of ethics and the finitude of practice. *Business Ethics Quarterly*, 28(1), 71–98.

Rhodes, C., & Pullen, A. (2018). Critical business ethics: From corporate self-interest to the glorification of the sovereign pater. *International Journal of Management Reviews*, 20(2), 483–499.

Ryle, G. (2009). *The Concept of Mind*. Routledge.

Ryömä, A., & Satama, S. (2019). Dancing with the D-man: Exploring reflexive practices of relational leadership in ballet and ice hockey. *Leadership*, 15(6), 696–721.

Sinclair, A. (2004). Journey around leadership. *Discourse: Studies in the Cultural Politics of Education*, 25(1), 7–19.

Smolović Jones, S., Winchester, N., & Clarke, C. (2021). Feminist solidarity building as embodied agonism: An ethnographic account of a protest movement. *Gender, Work & Organization*, 28(3), 917–934.

Stogdill, R. M., & Coons, A. E. (Eds.) (1957). *Leader Behavior: Its Description and Measurement*. Ohio State University, Bureau of Business.

Thanem, T., & Knights, D. (2019). *Embodied Research Methods*. Sage.
Tyler, M. (2019). Reassembling difference? Rethinking inclusion through/as embodied ethics. *Human Relations*, 72(1), 48–68.
Uhl-Bien, M. (2003). Relationship development as a key ingredient for leadership development. In S. E. Murphy & R. E. Riggio (Eds.), *The Future of Leadership Development* (pp. 129–147). Lawrence Erlbaum.
Uhl-Bien, M. (2005). Implicit theories of relationships in the workplace. In B. Schyns & J. R. Meindl (Eds.), *Implicit Leadership Theories: Essays and Explorations* (pp. 103–133). Information Age.
Uhl-Bien, M. (2006). Relational leadership theory: Exploring the social processes of leadership. *Leadership Quarterly*, 17(6), 654–676.
Uhl-Bien, M. (2011). Relational leadership and gender: From hierarchy to relationality. In P. H. Werhane & M. Painter-Morland (Eds.), *Leadership, Gender, and Organization* (pp. 65–74). Springer.
Vachhani, S. J., & Pullen, A. (2019). Ethics, politics and feminist organizing: Writing feminist infrapolitics and affective solidarity into everyday sexism. *Human Relations*, 72(1), 23–47.
Wacquant, L. (2015). For a sociology of flesh and blood. *Qualitative Sociology*, 38(1), 1–11.

42

Leadership as (New) Material(ities) Practices: Intra-Acting, Diffracting and Agential-Cutting with Karen Barad

Nancy Harding

INTRODUCTION

Critical leadership thought has long been informed by constructionist/constructivist and poststructuralist theoretical perspectives. These perspectives, and the latter in particular, are now criticised for over-emphasising discourse's role in the constitution of 'realities' (Hekman, 2008). The challenge made is to the longstanding perspective that sees 'reality' as accessible and understandable only through discourse or, more narrowly, language (I may sit on a rock but the only ways in which I can understand that rock is by means of the language through which I describe it). However, that rock has a 'rockness' that is beyond language, a hard physical presence that in various ways influences the world (grass does not grow under it, toes that are stubbed on it hurt, walkers must move around it, moving it may require the hard work of various human and non-human actors and so on). This seemingly trivial example is not separate and distinct from important material affects including global warming, the environment and global pandemics, to name just a few. Profound questions follow: *Is all of reality socially constructed (through language), or does a reality exist outside of humans, a reality with its own ontologies and epistemologies? Are humans the only entities with agency? Does agency require language?* (Gullion, 2018, p. 3). Even more (Kuhn et al., 2017): should such distinctions be abandoned altogether? New materialities theories, and Karen Barad's work in particular, answer: 'the world' cannot be reduced solely to language; its materiality is inescapable; but this distinction between materialities and language is itself false. This, then, is the 'ontological turn' in which I locate leadership theory in this chapter.

Jessica Smart Gullion (2018) identifies three dominant ontologies in the history of the global north's social sciences. The first of these is a cause/effect prediction approach that analyses the macro level and understands the social as something that can be engineered. This is where the majority of leadership studies has been and continues to be positioned. The second is the linguistic, interpretivist ontological turn that understood existence to be located not in 'structures' but in discourses, with structures themselves, such as selves, laws, economies, organisations, etc., constituted within and through discursive processes. Many critical approaches to leadership draw on aspects of this tradition. The third, discussed in more depth below, is the current ontological turn towards *new materialities*. This does away with macro/micro distinctions and understands that what exists are relational assemblages. It involves turning away from human-centric thinking that has been so destructive of the planet, and towards what Jane Bennett (2010) calls *vibrant materialism* – that is, the agentive capacity of non-sentient things. I will argue that locating 'the leader' and 'leadership' within this new ontology implies, at the simplest level, that 'leadership' rather than an act carried out by an individual called 'the leader', as traditionally assumed (Ford et al., 2008), can be interpreted as a relational assemblage incorporating sentient and non-sentient actors.

There is a range of new materialities approaches, including actor-network theory, affect theory, complexity theory, object-oriented ontology, speculative realism, non-representational and assemblage theories, object-centred sociality, material sociology and others (Fox & Alldred, 2016; Orlikowski, 2007). Researchers who study work and organisations draw on a range of these influences. For example, Cnossen and Bencherki (2019), writing within the tradition of the communicative constitution of organisation, explore how organisations endure in time because of formations of artefacts into assemblages. These artefacts include space which they argue is an active and important actor in the endurance of emerging organisations. Kivinen and Hunter (2019) follow a line of thought through Celia Lury's work to explore the coming-into-being of gendered media brands through assemblages in which artefacts, including brands, are agentive. Illuminating though such studies are, my focus here is specifically on feminist new materialities. As a feminist theory it not only has explanatory power but is inherently political (Calás and Smircich, 1999); it entails a desire to identify and challenge the various forms of violence inherent in organisations, management, the conditions of working lives and, of course, leadership. This approach therefore incorporates politics and power in an understanding of leadership as a relational assemblage.

In this chapter I bring feminist new materialities theories, specifically the contribution of Karen Barad's (2007) theory of agential realism, to an understanding of leadership. A Baradian interpretation requires not only that we insert non-sentient as well as sentient actors into our analyses, but that we attend to the non-sentient actors that are there in the theories but ignored. My aim is to challenge leadership theories' long ignoring of physical existents and to say something more about imagination, understood here in its mundane, everyday sense, as the foundation on which leadership thought rests. This analysis will suggest how and why leadership theorists, although aiming to develop an applied body of theory, conceive of disembodied actors (leaders and followers) (Pullen and Vachhani, 2013; Ford et al., 2017) moving through immaterial spaces and places. In what follows I will read two influential theories of leadership through a Baradian lens. My task is to follow a non-sentient but agentive actor through a theory that has relegated that actor to its interstices from where, nonetheless, it haunts the theory. Arguably *all* leadership approaches do this, but I narrow my focus to two major theories: transformational leadership and leadership-as-practice. In each case I will focus on one representative paper. This results in undermining those theories but points towards the urgent necessity of developing new theories of leadership that include materialities.

I next outline the feminist new materialist approach I am using in this chapter before reading transformational leadership and leadership-as-practice through its terms.

FEMINIST NEW MATERIALITIES

Feminist new materialities starts from a recognition of the major, if not earth-shattering, environmental, technological and societal changes taking place in the 21st century. Poststructural theory has proved a highly productive explanatory force, but at the same time limited what could be said and known about a material world that is, as environmental change and the Covid-19 pandemic so memorably demonstrate, inescapably agentive and having effects in the world. What is needed are *ways of understanding the agency, significance, and ongoing transformative power of the world – ways that account for myriad 'intra-actions' (in Karen Barad's terms) between phenomena that are material, discursive, human, more-than-human, corporeal, and technological* (Alaimo and Hekman, 2008, p. 5). The neologism 'intra-action' is important because it shows the limitations of the concept of 'inter-action' that implies bodies may interact without materially affecting each other. Intra-action emphasises that entities emerge through entanglements within and through the numerous discourses/materialities/affects/etc. that facilitate their emergence. This understanding of the ontological inseparability of determinate entities (Alaimo and Hekman, 2008, p. 128), encapsulated in the term 'intra-actions', captures the idea that entities are not ontologically separable. This requires a major shift in perception towards an understanding of matter as something that is *not* mute and inert, but that has agency. Feminist new materialities therefore rethinks ontology, and it does this through developing an understanding of material 'objects' as immanent (understood as meaning within the limits of experience and thought rather than hovering above them) and lively rather than passive participants in social worlds.

What may appear on the face of it as an absurd statement is not so absurd when put in the history of intellectual thought and a positivist, empiricist tradition that is now widely critiqued. That is, Cartesian theory had differentiated between dumb and passive nature (body) and articulate, agentive culture (mind), and it is that heritage that has inhibited the ways in which materialities can be apprehended. New materialism rejects that Cartesian legacy through *attempt*[s] *to denaturalize nature and deculturalize culture, and thus decenter human intentionality* (Frost, 2011, p. 77). However, it does not abandon poststructuralism because the explanatory power of poststructural thought remains invaluable. Importantly, it does not reverse the discourse and privilege materialities. Rather, both baby and bathwater are regarded as equally privileged and, indeed, both language and matter are understood to be agentive, living energies (Colebrook, 2008). New materialities theories aim to reconcile the two through recognising not that realities are *both* discursive and material, but that 'the discursive' and 'the material' are irredeemably interwoven, so drawing a binary distinction between them is mistaken.

In feminist new materialities therefore the long-held, modernist belief in a definitive break between sentient and non-sentient subjects/objects is challenged, as is any distinction between nature and culture. The notion that clearly defined boundaries divide the sentient subject from the non-sentient object collapse as the focus becomes one of exploring the *emergent interplay* (Tuana, 2008, p. 189) through which 'realities' emerge. Indeed, all boundaries collapse so there could be no distinction between 'leader/ship' and 'follower/ship'. It is easy at this point to write that it would be an error to say that the two merge, not only because there are far more than 'two' in the leader/follower assemblage, but because the concepts of 'true' and 'false' are acts of boundary-making that should be challenged.

That is, new materialist theories understand that language, matter, technologies and other elements intra-act in the formation of subjects or 'reality' (Hekman, 2008). This entails a shift in perspective from working with human ideas about matter to working with material organisms and things themselves. Rather than understanding commodities, machines and the forces of production as solely human-made phenomena, as Marxist materialism had done, new materialism seeks to understand how the human emerges through intra-actions with commodities, machines, forces of production and so on because *the things we interact with are an inescapable part of who we are* (LeCain, 2017, p. 21). At the same time, commodities, machines, forces of production and so on do not precede these intra-actions but emerge within and through them.

Karen Barad Who Meets the Universe Halfway

Karen Barad's theory of agential realism is a major influence within this body of thought. She combines quantum mechanics with feminist and poststructuralist theory. Her inspiration is the work of the physicist Neils Bohr, who observed that measuring devices are not merely objects whose purpose is the measuring of something else, but agents that actively constitute that which they measure. That is, *experimental apparatus* (in which are included ways of thinking and seeing) face an indeterminate mess of potentiality (or *agentially intra-acting components* in Barad's [2007, p. 33] terms). The apparatus influences what, from that swirl of possibilities, shall be admitted into 'reality' and what excluded. It draws a sharp dividing line (an *agential cut*) that eliminates numerous possibilities and elevates (what appears to be) a singular object to the status of 'the real'. Thus representations of certain (what we call) 'objects' are privileged, and numerous other potentialities are unrepresented and erased from thought. In summary, what are assumed to be *individual entities with separately determinate properties* (Barad, 2007, p. 55) are, rather, condensations or traces of multiple practices that measuring devices, including the human 'observer', actively produce. As Barad (2007, p. 118) writes, the Cartesian distinction between *object* [and] *agencies of observation* breaks down.

Barad's work is inspired by Judith Butler's (1990, 1993) theory of performativity and aims to make good the supposed absence of materialities from Butler's (1990, 1993) approach. Barad argues that although there may not be an independent reality, there *are* real, material phenomena. *Phenomena* are Barad's primary ontological unit. Phenomena *do not merely mark the epistemological inseparability of observer and observed, or the results of measurements; rather, phenomena are the ontological inseparability/entanglement of intra-acting agencies* (Barad, 2007, p. 139). They are *condensations or traces of multiple practices of engagement* (Barad, 2007, p. 53). This challenges the Cartesian heritage in Western thought that assumes objects to be ontologically separate and distinct from each other, already existing before they meet any other object. The question that emerges is: how do 'things' come to be understood as separate and distinct objects? Barad provides a methodology for exploring this question: she argues that objects become perceived as objects through *boundary-drawing practices – specific material (re)configurings of the world – which come to matter* (Barad, 2007, p. 140).

These phenomena are, emphatically, NOT singular, static entities, as a metaphysics of individualism would have it. Barad (2007) argues that phenomena are to be understood as *entangled material agencies* (p. 56) that emerge through constitutive practices. This extends Foucault's genealogy of sex to other domains, as Barad points out (p. 60): Foucault had exposed the category of sex as a mechanism that unifies what are otherwise discontinuous elements and functions. But she also observes that although Foucault had emphasised the material nature of discourse, he was not clear about that material nature (p. 63). Butler (1990, 1993) had done some of the crucial work of elaborating Foucault's thesis, but her work appears similarly bedevilled, in Barad's account, by its inability to clarify the material nature of discursive practices. From this follows Barad's intention to develop a robust theory of how material forces, including the body, *actively matter to the process of materialization* (Barad, 2007, p. 65).

Barad's task becomes that of developing a theory of *intra-actions that reconstitute entanglements* (2007, p. 74). The neologism intra-action is important because it shows the limitations of the concept of inter-action that implies bodies may interact without materially affecting each other. Intra-action emphasises that entities emerge through entanglements within and through the numerous discourses/materialities/affects/etc. that facilitate their emergence. This understanding of the ontological inseparability of determinate entities (Barad, 2007, p. 128), encapsulated in the term 'intra-actions', captures the idea that entities are not ontologically separable. What should be emphasised here, in what Barad calls her theory of agential realism, is that boundaries of objects or subjects should not be presumed or taken-for-granted (the desk on which my keyboard rests should not be regarded as an entity called 'a desk' that has clearly demarcated boundaries); rather we should *investigate [...] the material-discursive boundary-making practices that produce 'objects' and 'subjects'* (Barad, 2007, p. 93). That is, what practices determine that something is a subject (understood in the simplest definition as having subjectivity) and something an object (that is presumed to lack subjectivity)? There may be violence in determining that something is an object, especially if it is a living, breathing sentient being that, if it is believed to lack subjectivity, can be treated without any respect, care or dignity. In Baradian terms, intra-actions within and between sub-systems and sub-systems' sub-systems, all of which are entangled within and through each other, performatively constitute what appear to be the 'boundaries', 'entities' or objects that I am calling 'my desk', 'its contents' and 'myself'.

Barad argues phenomena categorised as *cultural* and *natural* should be read through each other diffractively to understand the enactment of boundaries and their constitutive exclusions (2007, p. 135). By *diffractive* she refers to the need to avoid putting texts and thought against each other (my interpretivism against your positivism, for example) and instead reading them through each other to engender creativity and the unexpected. She exemplifies this in her own work, in a diffractive reading of quantum mechanics and feminist philosophy (2007). A diffractive analysis focuses on differences rather than similarities, something that is facilitated by bringing different research and theoretical perspectives to the task, or reading insights through each other, or thinking about more-than-human worlds (Barad, 2014). The 'findings' of research projects are thus achieved through agential cuts so those findings are always contingent, contextual and emergent (Lupton, 2019).

These are the aspects of Barad's theory of agential realism that I draw on here. As Visser and Davies (2021) summarise in their fine exposition of Barad's theory, all 'things' are processes of coming-into-being through fundamental entanglements within and through numerous other 'things'. Boundaries are similar: they too are not material realities but processes-of-becoming that reflect agential but not ontological separability (Visser & Davies, 2021, p. 1820).

In this approach, 'matter', by which is meant the material 'stuff' of the physical world, must be included as an active participant in performativity (Barad, 2007, p. 136); matter is *neither fixed nor given nor the mere end result of different processes. Matter is produced and productive, generated and generative. Matter is agentive, not a fixed essence or property of things. Mattering is differentiating, and which differences come to matter, matter in the iterative production of different differences* (p. 137). This is why in previous work (Ford et al., 2017; Harding et al., 2021) I have, with colleagues, argued that Butler takes us to the level of the iterated movements that constitute sentient actors from moment-to-moment-to-moment, but Barad invites us to analyse each of those re-iterated micro-movements and especially to include the influence of non-sentient actors.

Butler's theory of performativity takes us to the atomic level, to draw on Barad's analogies with quantum mechanics, and Barad's approach splits the atom and requires that we look inside it.

Note that discourse remains important in this approach to understanding materialities – that is, a specific body's *differential materialization is discursive – entailing causal practices reconfiguring boundaries and properties that matter to its very existence* (Barad, 2007, p. 370). Barad's attempt to summarise her thesis in a diagram (2007, p. 389) is well worth studying. The diagram illustrates how many intra-acting genealogies are entangled in the constitution of what appears as an entity. That is, attention is focused on multiple affects and intra-relationships (Lockwood Harris, 2016), alerting the researcher (who is inevitably entangled within that which she studies) to the necessity of avoiding falling into the familiar trap of dualism and binarism. Applied to leadership studies the distinction between leader and follower and indeed between leader and leadership and follower and followership cannot hold. Rather our attention is directed to the multiple agents intra-acting at the site of leader/ship and to identifying the agentive cut through which leader/ship and follower/ship emerge as, apparently, singular, inter-acting entities.

The next section of this chapter applies these ideas to two major theories of leadership, through an in-depth analysis of an exemplary paper from each approach.

Transformational Leadership

The influence of the theory of transformational leadership cannot be underestimated. Although originating in the work of Burns (1978), it owes its status as a globally influential theory to the work of Bernard Bass and colleagues who defined its components and developed a measurement tool, the Multifactor Leadership Questionnaire (MLQ), that is widely used in both studies of leadership effectiveness and in leadership development programmes (Wilson et al., 2021). The reach of the theory of transformational leadership can be seen in the 188,524 citations of Bass's work, while the manual for the MLQ has been cited 13,228 times since its publication in 1990. Transformational leadership theory, and thus the MLQ, were so thoroughly critiqued by van Knippenberg and Sitkin (2013) that it is surprising that they are still widely used, but the 69,649 citations to Bass's work since 2016 (statistics again from Google Scholar) suggests this is far from the case. Van Knippenberg and Sitkin showed, very persuasively, that the theory of transformational leadership and its related instrument, the MLQ, is based on a grounded taxonomy that *presumes* what factors constitute good leadership and then sets out to look for these in practice. It also suffers from a lack of conceptual definition and assumes, further, that particular behaviours cohere into a group simply because they have been clustered under a common label. Van Knippenberg and Sitkin (2013) conclude that research into transformational leadership is circular: it defines leadership in terms of what is thought to have desirable effects on followers, then defines effective leaders as those portraying those characteristics: *the MLQ and similar instruments study the effectiveness of leadership that is defined **a priori** as effective* (van Knippenberg and Sitkin, 2013, p. 15, original emphasis). However, transformational leadership cannot be dismissed because of the spurious foundations on which it rests. It is very widely circulated, with the MLQ having become almost ubiquitous (Day et al., 2014); conservative estimates suggest hundreds of thousands of people have been subjected to being measured by the MLQ or similar psychometric instruments (Markham et al., 2015). The MLQ is the most widely used, with alternative versions sharing many similarities with it (van Knippenberg and Sitkin, 2013). Its widespread use means that, through the power of performativity, it *does* things, but what it does may be very different from what it promises to do, as this chapter will argue (see also Meier and Carroll, 2020).

That is, a Butlerian (1990, 1993) interrogation of the theory of transformational leadership would explore the performative constitution of the identities of leaders and followers and how people become subjected and subjectified (Butler, 1997) within, through and by this discourse. It would argue that rather than transformational leaders pre-existing the concept and waiting to be discovered and developed by means of Bass and other's research, the term itself would *constitute* the identity and subject position of 'transformational leader'. Rather than measuring the characteristics and behaviours of people in leadership positions, therefore, transformational leadership and the MLQ interpellate people into the identity category of the leader and impose norms with which they must comply if they are to sustain that identity. This poststructural reading focuses on discourse but will be augmented by a new materialities approach.

The micropolitical focus of poststructuralism continues within feminist new materialism, but the analysis is not only on language but also on the onto-ethico-epistemological entanglements of matter and meaning (Barad, 2007). What is understood to come into existence through these entanglements of matter *and* discourse (onto-), what forms of knowledge inform those entanglements (epistemological) and what social justice and other political issues are intra-woven within them (ethico-). This requires, as Lupton (2019) explains, understanding and mapping ontologies of that difficult-to-define category, the *human*, understood here as a constantly changing *unstable and emergent knowing, sensing, embodied, affective assemblages of matter, thought, and language,* **part of and inseparable from more-than-human worlds** (Lupton, 2019, p. 2002, emphasis added). Power here is transitory, enacted within and between assemblages, and is both constraining and enabling. The researcher is part of the research assemblages they are addressing, and their analyses are always constitutively involved in 'producing' interpretations.

The paper on transformational leadership I am analysing, Seltzer and Bass (1990), entitled 'Transformational leadership: Beyond initiation and consideration', appeared quite early in the history of the development of transformational leadership theory. It discusses a study the authors carried out to refine the MLQ and is very similar in this aim to numerous studies published by Bass and colleagues. That is, it describes a quantitative study that tests aspects of Bass's transformational model of leadership. It does this through a survey, and analyses 138 subordinates' views of 55 managers. In many ways the Seltzer and Bass (1990) paper is quite traditional in its structure: an introduction and literature review that outline and justify the aims of the research, discussion of the methodology, analysis of data and a conclusion that includes the ubiquitous discussion of 'further research'. The paper is written in the scientific third person, so Seltzer and Bass hover above it, occupying the *view from nowhere* (Haraway, 1988), the *god position* of the impartial, objective, all-seeing researcher. At the same time as being transcendent to the paper, Bass (although not Seltzer) is immanent within it, or rather Bass's name is. Its reference list contains 26 publications, and in 16 of those Bass is an author – sole author of four and first author in a further five. The name (of the father of the MLQ) is thus omnipresent in this paper but as an invisible, immaterial, transcendent presence.

Human agency is excised from the paper; it is the paper itself that describes the study. In describing how to interview digital objects, Adams and Thompson (2016) discuss the value of anecdotes to research. Their definition of anecdotes encompasses methodologies, in that they *reassemble… and resemble… a possible human experience or observed moment of everyday life* (location 657 in Kindle edition). This reveals the fictive status of research texts that *involve a [...] creative reconstruction, selective cuts, and even poetic invention* (ibid). That is, these texts apparently account for their own creation ('This paper does the following') and in so doing obscure the intra-active generation and materialisation of the text. There is so much missing from a methodology's description of what actually took place during the research that authors and readers must *reassemble the eventing lifeworld* (op cit, location 686) to fill in the gaps, through bringing Bass and Seltzer back into their study, and it is fruitful to subject the language used by these living, breathing, very human authors to an analysis of that language's agency.

Bass and Seltzer (1990) indicate that as part of their participation in an MBA course, *managers were asked to give* MLQ forms to their *subordinates*. There is no indication in this statement of the agent who does the asking but the following sentence (p. 696) attributes agency to the survey instrument: it states that *The questionnaire indicated* how the results would be distributed. This reinforces the expunging of the human from the world (Pickering, 2010), such that the questionnaire arrives as something that has given birth to itself (its *measures* are drawn from other studies without any mention of human decision-making about what to include or exclude). It is to the survey instrument itself that agency is allocated: it does things. This is, of course, a familiar sleight of words in research that claims to rest on objectivity, but it directs our attention to Barad's (2007) insistence on the agency of research instruments and thus of the MLQ.

Barad (2007) illuminates how research instruments decide what shall be admitted into and what excluded from 'reality', and which objects become 'real' while others are unrepresented or rendered unrepresentable. The MLQ, it must be recognised, is a material object, printed on paper in the 1990s but now distributed online. It cannot be separated from other material objects that make it function, including printers, photocopiers, pens, computers, keyboards, desks, bodies and so on. These all intra-act, constituting an assemblage that, in the paper under examination, is labelled MLQ-Form 5.

The paper's Methods section describes how this form was used as follows: it asks respondents to rate the frequency of their immediate supervisor's display of described behaviours, including their transformational leadership behaviours (charisma, individualised consideration and intellectual stimulation), their effectiveness, their subordinate's extra effort (e.g., *My manager motivates me to do more than I originally expected I would do* [p. 697]), and the subordinate's satisfaction with the leader. Respondents are asked to rate the leader against a five-point scale: *frequently, if not always; fairly often; sometimes; once in a while; not at all* (p. 696). Thus, whether online or on paper, the material object, the MLQ-Form 5, cannot be separated from, and indeed is fundamentally entangled within and through, *the 98 full-time managers who were also part-time students in an advanced MBA elective* and the subordinates of each manager/student who were asked to distribute (the manager/student) and complete (the manager/student and three of his/her subordinates) the form (Bass and Seltzer, 1990, p. 696). The superior (the MBA student) would be given a summary of the *aggregated results*. The invisibilised researchers, Bass and Seltzer, are incorporated within this assemblage. So the process we are tracking is this: the researcher/lecturer hands the form (that is itself the product of previous work) to students/managers; students/managers will assess themselves against the measures on the form and also pass it to three of their colleagues; each person who fulfils their promise to complete the form does so; they then return it; the lecturers/researchers analyse the completed forms and write papers based on the results; individual feedback is given by the researchers to each student/manager.

This Baradian reading directs attention to what happens in that first moment, of the form being passed from lecturer to student. It can be seen that the form agentively constitutes the lecturer as researcher and the student as a leader with subordinates/followers. The form is both agentive and has power; in that single moment of passage from one person to another it constitutes identities, makes agential cuts (between identities) and confirms each in a position of power (lecturer) or powerlessness (student required to carry out this task as part of their MBA programme). But at the very same moment the form enacts another identity change in the student, from student to a leader with followers.

The next step in this process is usually written out of research studies: the period between a survey tool being distributed and its return. The first part of what happens here is when the leader passes the form to three subordinates, the latter are interpellated into the identity of follower by the form that makes an agential cut that distinguishes superior from subordinate. But what happens when recipients complete the survey? I will use a method developed by colleagues and myself in previous work (Ford et al., 2017; Harding et al., 2021) of analysing the performative moment as a micro-drama. We adopt a diffractive reading in which we interweave Butler's theory of performativity with that of Barad's theory of performativity and its development as agential realism. Butler theorises performativity as constituting identity through a process of constantly re-iterated movements, from moment-to-moment-to-moment, while Barad's approach enables analysis of the micro-drama occurring in each of those repeated moments.

The performative drama explored here is that which occurs in the moment of completing just one measure in the MLQ. The scene is one in which the form-filler, if they are completing the instrument as instructed, has read the descriptor and now has to assign a measure of how closely the leader aligns with that statement. This involves a hugely complex set of skills: interpreting abstract words such that meaning can be attached to them; transferring those abstract words from the page to the workplace; bringing to mind the person being evaluated even though they may not be present at that time; conjuring up memories of that person in action; positing that person as leader rather than their more familiar identity; moving the words from the page and attaching them to those memories of lived experience; carrying out a complex process of relating signifier to a newly conjured signified; and so on. All of these are taken-for-granted accomplishments that are quite miraculous when explored minutely. They are spurred by the MLQ's physical, material presence, albeit a presence that disappears from sight under the weight of the words it carries; we do not notice the page of a book when reading what is printed on it, just as we ignore the materiality of the pen or the computer screen and keyboard entailed in answering the MLQ's questions. In that moment of providing an assessment of just one of the many descriptors in the MLQ, materialities appear to disappear and abstract ideas are materialised.

Further, the now-disappeared physical entity (the form) does not vanish into thin air but remains as a material-discursive apparatus in which numerous phenomena are entangled and intertwined, so that dualities cannot be sustained; an agential cut is made that distinguishes leader from follower. The agency of that cut becomes clearer if we identify some of the many intra-acting entities coinciding in the assemblage that is 'the' person completing the MLQ. Thought processes cannot be separated from paper or computer screen, pen or keyboard. Rather these are all parts of an assemblage of printing press, electricity, an alphabet, bodies, a chair and desk, suits and shoes, an imagination that can make the connection between words on a page and an image, a mind that can conjure memories of working with that specific person they have been asked to bring to mind, literacy, a culture in which form-filling is a familiar action – all these and more, intra-act at the moment where the form-filler lifts the pen or presses the key to 'rate' someone. At that moment the MLQ (itself a melange of intra-acting actants) intra-acts with the object of the form (the person being rated, who is similarly an assemblage of multiple intra-acting actants) and with the subject (the self) who is completing the form (another complex and dynamic assemblage). They all are frozen for a performative moment in which the identities of MLQ, leader and follower are constituted and in which indefinable characteristics, such as charisma, are given a material presence through the sentences that claim to measure charisma. But an agential cut is made into this fluxing flow, and leadership is constituted as a series of personal characteristics and behaviours that are restricted to a pre-defined list, and other characteristics and behaviours are excluded from thought and at best regarded as 'not-leadership'. At worst they are expunged from the lexicon and so become unthinkable.

Finally, with the forms returned to the researchers and analysed, the student/leader can arrive to be given the results of how three subordinates have described them and how near or close those measures are to their self-assessment. In this dialogic encounter, the results emerge through the conversation (Meier and Carroll, 2020). Leaders will be told if they are charismatic enough, considerate enough, too uncaring, too focused on processes rather than people and so on. Areas in which they can develop themselves are 'revealed'. What is being discussed however is not the person but an imago, a reductionist representation that reduces an assemblage of bodies, texts and tests to something that is less than human.

To conclude this section, two things are given precedence in Bass and Seltzer's (1990) report on transformational leadership: the non-sentient but agentive questionnaire and the word 'Bass' that appears over and over throughout the paper. How can that repeated term be understood, torn away, as it were, from the human to which it refers? The repetition of the name Bass in the bibliography names Bass as a major researcher, a senior academic, of course, but the name Bass must refer to a complex human entangled within and through a host of intersecting and overlapping places, spaces and things. The family name, in its singularity, gives nothing away. We know nothing about Bass the person, save the number and topic of his publications and his place as author of this study. He is as immaterial and illusive as the leadership his research explored for many years. Curiously, a theory that requires we focus on materialities as well as discourses reveals the absence of the human actor from leadership theory. This is not a positive movement as it was in postmodern theories' decentring of the human to facilitate analysis of a complex world, because leadership, if it is anything, is concerned with people relating to other people. Taking the human out can therefore encourage inhuman behaviours.

Is this perhaps one of the most profound agential cuts that 'psychometric instruments' make? That is, designed to measure a human actor, they eradicate the putative human that is at the centre of their theorising from leadership. What is left in its place is a deracinated object that has been conjured up within imaginaries of leadership. This materialist interpretation suggests transformational leaders are lists of characteristics and behaviours untethered from persons. The human actor, whatever it is assumed to be, disappears. The measure by which the human actor in transformational leadership studies is assessed by the MLQ is therefore a measure of an imaginary/imagined object that would appear to have little relevance even within the theory's own terms.

Leadership-as-Practice

I turn next to a more recent theory of leadership that claims to focus on those everyday organisational practices and is garnering much attention: leadership-as-practice (LAP). My first task is to read LAP through the lens of Barad's theory of agential realism, before attempting to repeat following a material or non-sentient actor on a journey through the theory. I am focusing on a foundational paper (Raelin, 2011), entitled 'From leadership-as-practice to leaderful practice' that describes LAP as a *movement* that was then *emerging*. The paper aims to describe that movement and explore how it can be researched. It locates LAP in a thesis of the decline of bureaucracies and their replacement by 'adhocracy' in which managers become facilitators rather than controllers of workers who are regarded as self-managing (Raelin, 2011, p. 9).

LAP theorises leadership as something not carried out by individuals but that emerges within and through practices. That is, leadership is *connected to a practice rather than to the intersecting influence among individuals, namely between a leader and a group of followers*, such that leadership is as much a lateral as a vertical process (Raelin, 2011, p. 15). Here:

1. leadership is directly tied to the practices to which people are dedicated. Practices are *social sites in which temporary clusters of events, people, and meaning compose one another* (Raelin, 2011, p. 4);
2. through their practices, people decide on what they hope to accomplish;
3. participants organise the tasks that need to be performed to achieve their mission;

4. they commit to one another as a working body dedicated to a useful outcome;
5. they learn to adapt to exogenous changes; this may lead to healthy reappraisals of their mission.

That is, LAP is leadership where *we may find people talking together, acting together, and thinking together, all toward making the reality of their condition what it is* (Raelin, 2011, p. 22). Although the sense of this sentence breaks down under close analysis (there appears to be a tautology in the phrase *making the reality of their condition what it is*), it is an important statement when applying a new materialities perspective and I will come back to it after first using Baradian theory to help understand this formative account of LAP.

Raelin's first task in these early days of the emergence of LAP is to establish what LAP is *not* – that is, it is not a traditional model in which leadership is located in a person. He thus establishes a binary between leadership as, on the one hand, the traits and heroics of individual actors and, on the other, leadership in its activity. Barad's theory of the agential cut directs our attention to the work that this distinction does. Here, Raelin reduces and organises the multiple complexities of organisational behaviour into two types. There is either leadership understood as a singular person who practises the arts of leadership, or activities of leadership that emerge without the necessity of that singular person. However, this attempt to distinguish between individuals and practices is continually undermined, as seen in the brief summary above, by persons who repeatedly jump over the boundary and reinsert themselves into this leadership imaginary. The agential cut is unsteady, undermined it seems by the difficulty of theorising practices undertaken without persons. This returns us to the problems encountered above in understanding transformational leadership: can there be a theory of human interaction if the human is eradicated from it? Raelin has an answer to this: first analyse the practices and then the persons involved. That however results in the same dilemma because, in effect, an agential cut between material (human) practices and the materiality of those practices is needed if Raelin's guidance is to be followed, and that agential cut is impossible because the human is needed if the practices are to be observed.

The next point to explore is the performativity of the paradox of LAP's wish to jettison traditional leadership theories to history's dustbin but its retention of a longstanding description of leadership as consisting of the practice of certain functions. These functions remain unchanged: setting a mission, actualising goals, sustaining commitment and responding to changes (Raelin, 2011, p. 5). The use of such a traditional understanding of what leadership involves suggests perpetuation of the status quo rather than the intended innovations in practices that constitute leadership. Leadership remains the same, albeit carried out by different actors. This is supported by Raelin's (2011) argument, referred to briefly above, that in LAP attention should shift to the performance of these functions and that it is only when it is known how functions are performed that the focus should turn to who performs them. This is another agential cut, between functions and functionaries, so to speak, and its performative power is to transfer agency from persons to functions. But how can functions, or activities, have agency? Fortunately, Barad's perspective offers an answer: processes can and should be conceived of as *apparatuses*, and apparatuses, even though they may be non-sentient, have agency, just as the 360-degree survey instrument, discussed above, is agentive. If agency is not a possession but a relation, as Barad argues, then the conditions of possibility for the phenomena called leadership exist. It follows that these processes of setting a mission etc., *are constitutive of* leadership; through the enactment of these processes leadership materialises. It remains unchanged from previous theories save in the description of who it is that practises leadership.

That leadership is very narrowly defined is seen in a third agential cut within LAP theory, between those (traditional) functions defined as constitutive of leadership and other, un-named processes that are relegated to the outside of leadership and do not therefore engage in the constitution of leadership. Care, ethics, joy, laughter, compassion, equality, etc. are all omitted and are not agentive actors in the constitution of LAP.

This Baradian interpretation therefore points to the absence of new thought about leadership within LAP; leadership remains the same but it is now to be enacted by different people. This takes us back to that insistence of persons on continually interceding in a theory in which persons should be secondary. It is time to follow the material entity, the embodied person, through LAP. However, the high level of abstraction in this paper renders this desire futile; there is neither material person nor context to track on a journey through the theory. For example, LAP is described as encouraging reflective practitioners; there is no indication of what form the encouragement may take, who or what undertakes the encouraging, or what form these reflective practitioners may take. The theory also holds that participants will change their activities to the advantage of everyone involved, although the terms of that *everyone* remain vague, as do the forms that *advantage* may take. Participants, readers are told, will co-create a community in which there will be *true democratic participation in leadership* (Raelin, 2011, p. 3). These are both laudable aims; working with colleagues who practise vicious and negative politics, for example, is demoralising, while democratic participation is to be lauded. However, the high level of abstraction again gives us no foothold on which to work out how to proceed. This is therefore a theory of practitioners devoid of practitioners – of leadership without leadership – suggesting not only that the approach is not only *im*material but is located within the imagination, or as imaginary. In other words, the *cooperative effort among participants who choose through their own rules to achieve a distinctive outcome* (Raelin, 2011, p. 4) may be dearly desired, but desire is insufficient to ensure enactment. If democratic forms of leadership are to be enacted, then engagement in the materialities of organisational inter- and intra-actions is necessary. There is a need to understand what forms leadership may take when embodied actors, in all their complexities, engage in temporal/physical locations in intra-action with organisational paraphernalia. This requires understanding of those embodied actors, as well as other non-sentient material actors. Without such conceptualisation LAP outlines a normative aspiration and articulates a desire for what should be rather than a theory of leadership in/as practice.

But readers are encouraged by Raelin's paper to carry out research into LAP. This requires that *we must look to the practice within which it is occurring* (2011, p. 4) – that is, we should peer into the establishment of missions, achievement of goals, sustainment of commitment and responses to changes (p. 5). Such functions cannot take place in the ether: they require material actors, whether in online or face-to-face meetings. In other words, practices are impossible without bodies and numerous other materialities (spaces, places, furniture, electronics, clothes, bodies, etc., etc.). Any attempt to follow a material actor through the practices that constitute leadership in LAP is hobbled by the confusion regarding what is meant by 'practice'. It seems, on the one hand, to refer to day-to-day interactions, as seen in Raelin's argument that LAP replaces a dualist (Cartesian) ontology with a practice ontology that *conceives of practice as an ongoing recursive encounter among parties to a social interaction* and from which leadership emerges *as a contestation among mutual inquirers who share their intersubjective meanings* (2011, p. 6). It is, *therefore, a process of social construction that focuses not on the* **makers of processes** *but in the* **processes made** *within the concurrent undertaking* (2011, p. 6, emphasis in original), taking us back to the dilemma of how to study practices without agents.

That is, where transformational leadership uses surveys and psychometric instruments, LAP requires study of everyday interactions between persons (who have crept back in in the reference to the *inquirers who share their intersubjective meanings*) without actually studying persons. We have been warned against studying persons because of the danger of focusing attention on persons rather than practices. The researcher seems instructed to do the impossible. Indeed, the theory has difficulty in removing persons, as seen in a discussion of agency, which is defined as *the manner in which we make a difference in the world by mobilizing social actions* (Raelin, 2011, p. 8). Note the insertion of *we* in this definition: there is an actor that mobilises social actions. Further, agency in LAP is conceived of as *a process of influence* in which *one person may help others see their potential to actualize their own agency* (Raelin, 2011, p. 8). Altering the stance a little, readers are now warned that the focus should *not necessarily* be on either the initiator or recipient of this agentic relationship because that reproduces a passive/active dualism, so the researcher seems to be offered a way in to carry out studies. This is emphasised in the statement that agency can *be an intersubjective collaborative process that can reproduce and transform our social realities* (Raelin, 2011, p. 8) because intersubjective processes, collaborative or not, cannot occur without subjectivities and thus, of course, without persons. So, it seems that the claim that this theory *resolves* dualisms of subject/object and theory/practice in the reproduction of *generative structures* (Raelin, 2011, p. 8) cannot hold because the resolution relies upon removing agentive actors but agentive actors persist in making their presence known. In other words, wilfully removing the material in order to achieve theory's desires does not remove the material.

If this analysis suggests dismissal of LAP that is not what I intended. Rather, I am signalling disappointment because there is much to admire in LAP. It refocuses attention on teamwork, although now teamwork appears under the label of leadership. More fundamentally, it offers an organisational idyll in which control is *mutual* rather than top-down, and language is the medium for interactions rather than a means of establishing order (Raelin, 2011, p. 11). Its unrepentant advocacy of democratic values is thrilling, as is its desire for equality, collaboration and compassion (p. 16). Through its *offshoot, leaderful practice*, it encourages democracy, or the *free assembly of the commons* (Raelin, 2011, p. 17). I applaud its espoused ambitions and goals but I am concerned that it may do the opposite of what it intends. At a mundane level it offers little that is different from that advocated in self-managed teams designed to benefit profits rather than people (see, for example, Nicholls et al., 1999). At a more fundamental level, I am concerned that its high level of abstraction contains the seeds of the destruction of attempts to establish more democratic workplaces. This is because of what my reading of Raelin's foundational paper through the lens of Barad's theory of agential realism shows. That is:

1. the theory makes several agential (performative) cuts, and the first of these is between individual actors and activities;
2. in retaining an understanding of leadership as involving the traditionally recognised functions of leadership (setting a mission, actualising goals, sustaining commitment and responding to changes), another agential cut is made that distinguishes between what is and what is not leadership, consigning potentially revolutionary practices to the not-leadership category and valorising longstanding and arguably outdated perspectives.

This leads to the first caution regarding LAP achieving the opposite of what it intends. LAP perceives of leadership functions (setting a mission etc.) as agentive, in which case people do not perform those functions but are performed or constituted by them. Their humanity is removed in this sleight of hand: they must abandon egos, psyches, bodies, desires, needs, demands, activities, proclivities, ambitions, preferences, politics, freedom of thought, etc., and instead constitute themselves as deracinated objects that smile, and nod, and agree, and get on with the job of achieving organisational objectives. The marvellous complexities of the human being are set aside, making space for a one-dimensional person to be constructed.

The next caution arises from concerns about how LAP is to be researched.

3. Researchers' attention is directed towards the practices in which leadership functions will be enacted. This research will be aimed at understanding LAP in actual practice, but the researcher has been advised, albeit in passing, about what they should seek to identify: their focus should be on the traditional list of leadership functions. That is, the researcher should explore how missions are set, goals actualised, commitment sustained and changes responded to. This has two implications. First, alerted by van Knippenberg and Seltzer's (2013) (above) critique of the foundations of transformational leadership, there is a danger that LAP, like transformational leadership, defines in advance what leadership *is* and then sets out to find it. Second, instructed in what to seek, researchers perpetuate narrowly defined definitions of leadership, so leadership becomes ever-more outdated, the product of a very different era and unsuited to contemporary conditions.
4. Researchers' attention is also directed towards studying intersubjective processes but these appear to require subjects and there are no subjects in this theory, only practices carried out by objects. Despite the numerous references sprinkled throughout the paper to major thinkers who have pondered the nature of subjects and subjectivity (for example, to Bhaskar [p. 7], Goffman [p. 10], Mead [p. 10], Whitehead [p. 11], Foucault [p. 13], Bateson [p. 13], Dewey [p. 13], and Weick [p. 14]) there is no conceptualisation of the human subject nor of power, while agency is reduced to severely circumscribed forms required to achieve organisational desires.

In summary, this foundational paper directs researchers' attention to where *we may find people talking together, acting together, and thinking together, all toward making the reality of their condition what it is* (Raelin, 2011, p. 22). I have failed in my Baradian-inspired attempt to find a material entity whose passage I could follow through the paper into such meetings, suggesting that those 'people' are two-dimensional organisational characters devoid not only of bodies but of psyches, egos, desires, in short, of humanity. Their role is to practise a narrowly defined leadership. In these terms, LAP fails its democratic principles and becomes yet another attempt at improving organisational control.

This is a rather tired conclusion that joins numerous studies of innovations that are concluded to be something else to add to managers' (or leaders') arsenals of control.

A DISAPPOINTED AND DISAPPOINTING CONCLUSION

I had aimed, at this point, to draw together my interpretations of these two major theories of leadership and show how a new materialist approach could lead to their being conceived of differently, in ways that gave insights into the encounters between bodies, psyches, souls, rooms, furniture, technologies, dress, hair, nail varnish, brogues, posters, calendars, coffee mugs, packets of biscuits, window blinds, brief cases, rugs, etc., etc., to conceive of how leaders/leadership emerges within and through the complex entanglements of all these various actors in their intra-actions. I am frustrated in that aim by the realisation of how leadership theories not only eradicate the human and other sentient and non-sentient actors from their thinking, but also leave no space in which to introduce them. There are hints throughout of why this may be so. First, as van Knippenberg and Sitkin (2013) so ably showed of transformational leadership theory, and as seems plausible also of LAP, leadership theories tend to emerge from the normative dreams of thinkers who imagine *how* the organisational world should be and then look for that world in their research. This contradicts the rules of persuasive and reliable inductive research, that starts with the empirical world and theorises from that. Not much has improved since the early days of leadership research when insights were weakened by a tendency to ask leaders for their views and then uncritically analyse those views to identify the foundations of leadership. Second, contemporary leadership theory, if LAP is typical, is hidebound by its own long history and perpetuates old ideas in the guise of new ones. Thus leadership continues to be conceived of as specific practices and processes, and these have changed little in three-quarters of a century. Third, much leadership theory allies with the dominant aspiration within business schools of developing applied theories that are aimed to improve organisational practices. The politics of such an aim is debatable, but so long as theorists theorise from their imaginations rather than from empirical materials any theories they develop will work only in the imagination.

But new materialities theories require us, the researchers, to stop hovering over imaginary organisational encounters where leadership happens in our imaginations rather than in the phenomenological organisational world. We must engage in those encounters in all their complexities and avoid reducing actors to two-dimensional characters if we are to develop useful theory. The task is urgent. Right-wing populist leaders, corrupt leaders, CEOs whose salaries reach astronomical figures even as they drive down the wages and job security of their staff: the capacity of such people to remain in power is an issue for leadership theorists to explore. Leaders that are impotent in the face of climate change, unable to deliver the promises they make: why are they so weak? What inhibits their gathering people to the cause of net zero carbon omissions? Again, leadership theory should be able to provide insightful answers. However, answers are not to be found in existing theories because these changes in the world have been occurring while we leadership theorists had buried our heads in the sands of our preferred leadership theories rather than examining extant practices. New materialities theories require that we study assemblages of people/geography/space/time/materialities and such rich studies may guide us towards much better-informed understanding of leadership in these peculiar times. This chapter has shown how new materialities theories highlight what is wrong with existing theories: the next task is to use new materialities approaches to develop theories that influence practices in pursuit of the very desirable goals articulated in LAP. That endeavour is in its infancy, the necessary intellectual resources not yet developed, and the potential of using new materialities approaches to intervene in 'the world' not yet clear. That is the task of another paper.

REFERENCES

Adams, C., & Thompson, T. L. (2016). *Researching a Posthuman World: Interviews with Digital Objects*. Springer.

Alaimo, S., & Hekman, S. (2008). Introduction: Emerging models of materiality in feminist theory. In S. Alaimo & S. Hekman (Eds.), *Material Feminisms*. Indiana University Press.

Barad, K. (2007). *Meeting the Universe Halfway: Quantum Physics and the Entanglement of Matter and Meaning*. Duke University Press.

Bennett, J. (2010). *Vibrant Matter*. Duke University Press.

Burns, J.M. (1978) *Leadership*. New York: Harper and Row.

Butler, J. (1990). *Gender Trouble: Feminism and the Subversion of Identity*. Routledge.

Butler, J. (1993). *Bodies that Matter*. Routledge.

Butler, J. (1997). *Psychic Life of Power*. Stanford University Press.

Calás, M. B., & Smircich, L. (1999). From the 'woman's point of view': Feminist approaches to organization studies. In M. B. Calás, L. Smircich, S. R. Clegg, C. Hardy & W. R. Nord (Eds,), *Studying Organization: Theory and Method* (pp. 212–251). Sage.

Cnossen, B., & Bencherki, N. (2019). The role of space in the emergence and endurance of organizing: How independent workers and material assemblages constitute organizations. *Human Relations*, 72(6), 1057–1080.

Colebrook, C. (2008). On not becoming man: The materialist politics of unactualized potential. In

S. Alaimo, S. Hekman S.J. Hekman (Eds.) *Material feminisms*, pp. 52–84. Indiana: Indiana University Press.

Day, D. V., Fleenor, J. W., Atwater, L. E., Sturm, R. E. and McKee, R. A. (2014) Advances in leader and leadership development: A review of 25 years of research and theory. *Leadership Quarterly*, 25(1), 63–82.

Everett, D. (2010). *Don't Sleep, There are Snakes: Life and Language in the Amazonian Jungle*. Profile.

Ford, J., Harding, N., Gilmore, S., & Richardson, S. (2017). Becoming the leader: Leadership as material presence. *Organization Studies*, 38(11), 1553–1571.

Ford, J., Harding, N., & Learmonth, M. (2008). *Leadership as Identity: Constructions and Deconstructions*. Palgrave.

Fox, N. J., & Alldred, P. (2016). *Sociology and the New Materialism: Theory, Research, Action*. Sage.

Frost, S. (2011). The implications of the new materialisms for feminist epistemology. In H. E. Grasswick (Ed.), *Feminist Epistemology and Philosophy of Science. Power in Knowledge* (pp. 69–84). Springer.

Fullager, S., & Pavlidis, A. (2021). Thinking through the disruptive effects and affects of the coronavirus with feminist new materialism. *Leisure Sciences*, 43(1–2), 152–159.

Gullion, J. S. (2018). *Diffractive Ethnography: Social Sciences and the Ontological Turn*. Routledge.

Haraway, D. (1988). Situated knowledges: The science question in feminism and the privilege of partial perspective. *Feminist Studies*, 14(3), 575–599.

Harding, N., Gilmore, S., & Ford, J. (2021). Matter that embodies: Agentive flesh and working bodies/selves. *Organization Studies*, 43(5).

Hekman, S. (2008). Constructing the ballast: An ontology for feminism. In S. Alaimo, S. Hekman & S. J. Hekman (Eds.), *Material Feminisms* (pp. 85–119). Indiana University Press.

Hinton, P. (2014). 'Situated knowledges' and new materialism(s): Rethinking a politics of location. *Women: A Cultural Review*, 25(1).

Kivinen, N. H., & Hunter, C. (2019). 'Brand work': Constructing assemblages in gendered creative labour. *Human Relations*, 72(5), 910–931.

Kuhn, T., Ashcraft, K. L., & Cooren, F. (2017). *The work of communication: Relational perspectives on working and organizing in contemporary capitalism* (p. 232). Taylor & Francis.

LeCain, T. J. (2017). *The Matter of History: How Things Create the Past*. Cambridge University Press.

Lockwood Harris, K. (2016). Feminist dilemmatic theorizing: New materialism in communication studies. *Communication Theory*, 26, 150–170.

Lupton, D. (2019). Toward a more-than-human analysis of digital health: Inspirations from feminist new materialism. *Qualitative Health Research*, 29(14), 1998–2009.

Markham, S. E., Markham, I. S., & Smith, J. W. (2015) At the crux of dyadic leadership: self-other agreement of leaders and direct reports – analysing 360-degree feedback. *Leadership Quarterly*, 26(6), 958–977.

Meier, F., & Carroll, B. (2020). Making up leaders: Reconfiguring the executive student through profiling, texts and conversations in a leadership development programme. *Human Relations*, 73(9), 1226–1248.

Nicholls, C. E., Lane, H. W., & Brechu, M. B. (1999). Taking self-managed teams to Mexico. *Academy of Management Perspectives*, 13(3), 15–25.

Orlikowski, W. J. (2007). Sociomaterial practices: Exploring technology at work. *Organization Studies*, 28(9), 1435–1448.

Pickering, A. (2010). *The Mangle of Practice*. University of Chicago Press.

Pullen, A., & Vachhani, S. (2013). The materiality of leadership. *Organization*, 9(3), 315–319. https://doi.org/10.1177%2F1742715013486038

Raelin, J. (2011). From leadership-as-practice to leaderful practice. *Leadership*, 7(2), 195–211.

Seltzer, J., & Bass, B. M. (1990). Transformational leadership: Beyond initiation and consideration. *Journal of Management*, 16(4), 693–703.

Tepe-Belfrage, D., & Steans, J. (2016). The new materialism: Re-claiming a debate from a feminist perspective. *Capital & Class*, 40(2), 303–324.

Tuana, N. (2008). Viscous porosity: Witnessing Katrina. In S. Alaimo, S. Hekman & S. J. Hekman (Eds.), *Material Feminisms* (pp. 188–213). Indiana University Press.

Van Knippenberg, D., & Sitkin S. B. (2013). A critical assessment of charismatic-transformational leadership research: Back to the drawing board? *Academy of Management Annals*, 7(1), 1–60.

Visser, L. M., & Davies, O. E. (2021). The becoming of online healthcare through entangled power and performativity: A posthumanist agetial realist perspective. *Organization Studies*, 42(12), 1817–1837.

Wilson, S., Lee, H., Ford, J., & Harding, N. (2021). On the ethics of psychometric instruments used in leadership development programmes. *Journal of Business Ethics*, 172(2), 211–227.

43

Leadership Representation: A Critical Path to Equity

Suzanne Gagnon, Wendy Cukier and Mohamed Elmi
With acknowledgement to Tomke Augustin

INTRODUCTION

This chapter considers the 'who' of leadership, through the lens of representation for equity-seeking groups in positions of power in organisations. Representation has been a critical cornerstone of efforts to achieve equality for more than a century, including in the civil rights and feminist movements (Freedman, 2002; Nkomo & Ariss, 2014; Roberts & Mayo, 2019). Its central importance within the advancement of diversity, equity, and inclusion is underlined by recent research (Cukier et al., 2013; Gagnon et al., 2021a).

In leadership studies, however, a focus on representation risks becoming somewhat lost as scholars have rightly questioned traditional theories that centre on leadership as place in a hierarchy. Given the broad turn to leadership ontologies theorising its emergent, practice-based, non- or extra-individual and socially constructed character (e.g. Crevani, et al., 2007; Denis et al., 2012; Hazy & Uhl-Bien, 2013; Raelin, 2016), we raise a basic call that tracking, theorising, and extending questions around leadership representation remains critical to the scholarly work of promoting equity in leadership. Many organisations remain hierarchical with considerable power and authority resting 'at the top', but these positions are not accessible to all. Decades of research into gender and leadership from various streams helps to underline this ongoing 'fact', including analyses in other chapters of this book. We argue that larger questions of representation provide one essential lens into leadership for inclusion, equity and justice, bringing a structural and rights-based orientation to these questions. Seen as part of deep gender and racial hierarchies, representation is not a superficial nor surface-level concept, rather it is a central issue within the battle against systemic inequality (Gagnon et al., 2021a).

We recognise that the issue of representation has been problematised given limitations around how groups can be defined, and understandings of identity as fluid and socially constructed rather than singular or one-dimensional, and thus not 'measurable' in ways that representation studies would appear to require. It is here, however, that we wish to 'break sense' with the notion that because identities are multifaceted and not fixed nor essential, the concept of representation and its measurement is misguided (Cukier et al., 2013). We argue, in contrast, that despite ontological limitations and complexities, we can and must continue a focus on leadership representation to understand leadership equity and inclusion

(DiTomaso et al., 2007; Gagnon et al., 2021a). We also caution that definitional debates, while important, have also coincided with arguments that we can advance equity in leadership through pursuing 'diversity of thought', setting identity categories and attendant structural inequalities aside (DiTomaso et al., 2007). Such arguments sidestep historical and structural inequity and its links to representation (Gagnon et al., 2021a). Examining leadership diversity and equality through a positional/representational lens remains important to equity-seeking groups and, we contend, to drive change from the pro-white, pro-male bias in leadership, also labelled *whitestreaming* (Debassige & Brunette-Debassige, 2018).

The chapter is organised as follows. We first consider the historical context underlining links between leadership representation and social justice. We then present data on the current state of play of representation, examining how representation at the aggregate level is currently constituted, and showing that the battle for representation in leadership of women, racialised peoples and equity-seeking groups more broadly is by no means won. We draw on the Canadian case which has similarities to other jurisdictions where employment equity legislation was introduced several decades ago and how change, though evident, has been slow. We also present international data. Further, to make better sense of representation, we point to recent representation research that has added nuance to the question of identity categories, capturing the fundamental question of intersectionality (Crenshaw, 1989).

We title the next section 'The power of representation'. The 'fact' of representation has material, socioeconomic significance. Who does a society allow to populate its most senior decision-making positions, and with what benefits and outcomes? What is the impact on material outcomes for those who share identity group membership with those in leadership positions? The impact of greater leadership representation for organisations remains an important question, while inferences can be drawn from research on the business case for diversity in general. Other work considers leadership specifically. For example, research has found associations between more women in leadership and higher levels of innovation and the promotion and engagement of more women employees (Dezso & Ross, 2012), as well as the reduction of stereotyping in organisational language (Lawson et al., 2021). A growing stream of research also suggests that greater demographic diversity on corporate boards is connected to better decision-making in support of corporate social responsibility (Larrieta-Rubin de Celis et al., 2015; Rao & Tilt, 2016). Equally, representation has powerful social symbolic significance. Who holds leadership positions has signalling effects that reach beyond the organisation and those in the positions. We outline two such effects that we see as most important: the potential to erode stereotypes and mental models of who can lead; and the power to shape aspirations and actions of young people, or those in more junior positions. These signalling effects have considerable force and arguably hold potential to contribute to broader change in representation in the future.

At the same time, the 'doings' of leadership representation have also been studied, with compelling findings requiring attention and further research. In a subsequent section, we consider this research, asking: how do representative leaders experience their roles? The lived experience of 'representing' shows that it often comes with a range of challenges that require attention and action if change is to be realised. We consider phenomenological accounts of scholars such as Sarah Ahmed (2012, 2014) which show that 'inclusion' in leadership can be a conflictual experience, bringing both career risks and emotional demands. In this context, the doings of representation may best be understood as resistant performative acts by *wilful subjects* (Ahmed, 2014) in which racialised leaders act as purposeful agents against the normalised whiteness of institutions. Discrimination and subtle racism remain among the reasons that minority group members in leadership positions may be unable to exert influence to the same extent as their dominant-group (white, male) counterparts (Roberts & Mayo, 2019; Roberts et al., 2019). Token dynamics and the 'glass cliff' phenomenon for women in leadership roles also remain relevant (Ryan & Haslam, 2007).

These dynamics do not diminish the importance of what others have called descriptive representation and, indeed, may make the case for it even stronger (Childs & Krook, 2008). While the research is inconclusive, processes such as those outlined by scholars like Ahmed, and token dynamics and related themes on boards and in senior leadership, may recede with greater representation. This of course is the major argument of critical mass theory, much researched since its introduction following Kanter (1977) and Dahlerup (1988) several decades ago, including more recent applications (cf. Konrad et al., 2008) and the *power in numbers* thesis put forward by Cook and Glass (2015). Nevertheless, several questions around the doings of representation are important and we highlight these in this section.

Given both our arguments in this chapter and the questions that remain, the chapter calls for further theory development on leadership representation that integrates work on representation as 'presence' and its impact, and such doings of representation. We suggest that future work can usefully combine structural and phenomenological research to better understand and theorise the potential power for equity and inclusion of leadership representation.

LEADERSHIP REPRESENTATION: HISTORICAL CONTEXT AND THE CURRENT PICTURE

The murder of George Floyd in May 2020, seen around the world, accelerated the focus on racial justice, particularly for the black community; it precipitated new movements and momentum to advance leadership representation. In Canada, for example, the creation of Black North, a national advocacy group, quickly accumulated commitments from corporate leaders to advance opportunities for black people on boards of directors and in corporate leadership. However, the connection between social justice and leadership representation has a long history. Canada provides an illustrative case, and legislative histories in other countries with human rights frameworks show similarities to the Canadian case. The drive for the Employment Equity Act for 'designated groups' dates to the 1980s in Canada, and codified expectations for federally regulated corporations to set targets and track the representation of women, visible minorities, Indigenous peoples and persons with disabilities in leadership roles. Advancing women in leadership began with a focus on representation in politics in the early 20th century and spilt over into other sectors. In 1975, the government committed to the equitable representation of male and female employees in proportion to the availabilities of qualified persons of both sexes by organisation, occupational group and level. This laid the foundation for later affirmative action programmes aimed at improving representation at senior levels. The history in the US is somewhat different, dating back, arguably, to the Civil War and later civil rights movements for social justice, exemplified by Martin Luther King's 1963 March for Jobs and Freedom which made clear the importance of the distribution of opportunities, privileges and wealth within a society. As Nkomo and Ariss relay in their seminal article, 'The historical origins of ethnic (white) privilege in US organizations' (2014), it took the passage of Title VII of the Civil Rights Act in 1972 to seriously challenge white racial domination of organisations.

These movements had important impacts on subsequent legislation in the US, Canada and other countries, advancing policy and, arguably, the critical links between representation and social justice. Nonetheless, representation in leadership positions of women and people of colour remains weak in North America, with white males continuing to dominate disproportionately across all sectors, and most prominently in the corporate sector. In 2020, there were more CEOs named Michael or James than there were women chief executives in the US, with just 6 per cent of the top 500 public companies having a female CEO (Equileap, 2020). Recent data from Canada show that the proportion of racialised individuals in corporate sector board roles was 4.5 per cent in 2020, while racialised people represented 28.4 per cent of the population across the eight Canadian cities studied (Diversity Institute, 2020).

Current notions of leadership are highly gendered and raced. As Schein et al.'s (1996) influential 'Think manager – think male' revealed, gendered stereotypes of leadership in the media have a profound impact on how women are expected to behave in the workplace. Gündemir and colleagues (2014) pointed to parallel dynamics for people of colour. Societal factors shape the environment in which organisations operate, which coupled with organisational policies and practices have continued to limit opportunities on boards and in senior leadership roles (Campus, 2013; Trimble, 2013). Here, we are careful to specify that gender itself is a socially constructed category and wherever possible the category of 'women' should pertain to those who identify as women. Women are held to higher standards, and when men and women display similar behaviours, men are more likely to be labelled leaders, whereas women are described as 'bitches' (O'Loughlin, 2015). Research has examined women's representation in leadership across all sectors from financial services, to health care, to information technology (Cukier et al., 2002; Diversity Institute, 2020; Rosenbloom et al., 2008). Race is arguably an even more significant barrier to the attainment of positional leadership (Nkomo & Ariss, 2014). White men and women have significantly greater opportunities for career advancement and earnings compared to racial and ethnic minorities. While there have been breakthroughs both in politics and in corporate leadership, we are a long way from equality of opportunity or achievement of leadership positions, as the data presented below indicate.

Cultures and countries vary in the roles they assign to men and women in the private and public spheres as well as in their openness to change in relation to women and men taking up different roles. Socioeconomic conditions create opportunities for women to participate in the economy or pressures to withdraw from it, for example as seen in the disproportionate numbers of women who left the workforce in North America due to Covid-19 (Grandy et al., 2020). Other policies that can influence the participation of women in the labour market and in governing and leading organisations range from equal education, to childcare leaves and supports, to specific policies targeting the representation in governance and leadership. A recent analysis by the Diversity Institute in Toronto considered the MSCI World Index, which represents large and mid-cap equity performance across 23 developed market countries, against information on public policy in those countries (Diversity Institute, 2021). The study showed that there seem to be links between quotas and representation on corporate boards, but they have limited impact on corporate leadership representation. Please see Table 43.1.

However, there is more limited analysis on a global level of representation of racialised people on boards and in executive roles, in part because of differing definitions, reporting requirements and legislative frameworks. In the US, however, several advocacy organisations as well as policy bodies collect data, although reporting these data to the government is not required. A recent amalgamation of current indices found that black professionals in 2018 held just 3.3 per cent of all executive or senior leadership roles, defined as within two reporting levels of the CEO, according to the US Equal Employment Opportunity Commission (Sahadi, 2020). Among Fortune 500 companies, less than 1 per cent of CEOs are black and at the time of reporting, there were only four, down from a high of six in 2012; further, over the past two decades, there have only been 17 black CEOs in total in the US; of those, only one has been a woman (Sahadi, 2020).

In the Canadian context, it is clear that racialised people in general face more barriers than women in general, at an aggregate level. For example, in the city of Toronto, women are approximately half the workforce and racialised people are more than half but in the corporate sector, white women outnumber racialised women 12:1 in the most recent data (Diversity Institute, 2020). The same study also showed the differences within the broad

Table 43.1   Women on Boards and in CEO positions, 2020, world comparison

Rank	Country	% Cos with 3+ WOB	% Cos with 1-2 WOB	% Cos with 0 WOB	% Cos with W CEO	% Total WOB 2016/2020	Policy
1	Norway	100.0	0.0	0.0	30.0	39.4/42.3	Quotas
2	Belgium	100.0	0.0	0.0	7.7	27.7/38.5	Quotas
3	France	100.0	0.0	0.0	5.6	37.6/43.3	Quotas
4	Italy	100.0	0.0	0.0	0.0	33.1/36.5	Quotas
5	Portugal	100.0	0.0	0.0	0.0	9.1/22.0	Quotas
6	Sweden	91.2	8.8	0.0	11.8	35.6/38.0	Targets
7	Finland	90.9	9.1	0.0	9.1	30.2/37.4	Targets
8	Spain	90.0	10.0	0.0	5.0	20.6/31.2	Quotas
9	United Kingdom	84.8	15.2	0.0	8.7	25.3/34.3	Targets
10	Austria	83.3	16.7	0.0	0.0	20.9/24.8	Quotas
11	South Africa	78.4	21.6	0.0	5.4	18.7/28.8	Quotas (State-owned) Targets (Public)
12	Germany	77.6	19.0	3.4	1.7	19.5/25.2	Quotas
13	Denmark	76.5	23.5	0.0	11.8	20.9/26.5	Quotas
14	Canada	75.0	25.0	0.0	3.4	22.8/31.3	Comply-or-explain
15	Australia	71.0	27.4	1.6	6.5	26.0/34.0	Targets
16	Ireland	70.0	30.0	0.0	5.0	20.4/26.8	Targets
17	Netherlands	66.7	33.3	0.0	7.4	18.9/25.5	Targets
18	United States	66.0	33.4	0.2	5.7	20.3/28.2	Targets
19	New Zealand	57.1	42.9	0.0	14.3	29.6/42.3	Targets
20	Malaysia	57.5	42.5	0.0	0.0	15.3/28.1	Targets
-	MSCI World Index	57.6	36.9	5.3	4.9	19.1/26.2	

Note: Adapted from Milhomem, C. (2020).

category of racialised peoples. Of 1,600 corporate board members in all of Canada, there were 13 who were black (four women and nine men). Figure 43.1 provide summary results of this study.

INTERSECTIONALITY AND THE COMPLEXITY OF IDENTITY AND REPRESENTATION

Leadership scholars have begun to consider intersectionality in experienced discrimination, noting the importance of compounding barriers to leadership opportunities rooted in multiple and simultaneous dimensions of inequality, including gender, race, class and sexuality (Breslin et al., 2017; Richardson & Loubier, 2008). Such work and the foregoing analyses demonstrate the importance of recognising intersectionality within any determinations of leadership representation at the aggregate level. As first argued by Crenshaw (1989, 1991) in her theory of intersectionality, categories like gender, race, class and other sources of discrimination or marginalisation are best understood as mutually constitutive, operating in tandem rather than isolation. The figures introduced above give clear evidence of the significance of this concept within representation in leadership. Markers of social identity are *inextricably interconnected in the production of social practices of exclusion* (Crenshaw, 1997, p. 237). As such, studies of representation in leadership must strive to account for the compounded nature of barriers experienced by racialised, Indigenous and Lesbian, Gay, Bisexual, Transgender and Queer (LGBTQS+)-identified individuals, as well as persons with disabilities (e.g., Tolley & Young, 2011). Consequently, the notion and role of representation among specific groups is complex, and representation does not necessarily translate into legitimacy (Docherty, 2002). Analytical categories such as 'women' are heterogeneous both in terms of identity characteristics and lived experiences.

While at a policy level, most jurisdictions have delineated a small set of categories based on gender, race and other 'minority' identities through which equity in positional leadership may be tracked, a recent policy review process in Canada showed that such categories can be responsive to identity groups' preferences, recognising the limitations of binary identifiers, in particular regarding gender. Representation studies have in fact succeeded in taking this complexity into account, guided specifically by the concept of intersectionality and by scholarly work (Cukier et al., 2021). For example, through linking and disaggregating data from the Corporations Returns Act with those from the 2016 Census, a recent study of women board directors and senior corporate officers in Canada from an intersectional lens, found women executives earned 56 per cent less than men executives, but visible minority (racialised) women executives earned 32 per cent less than women executives who did not identify as visible minorities (Longpre-Verret & Richards, 2021). Further, women executives tended to be younger than men executives and were less likely to be in a relationship or to have children, and they were much less likely to hold the top position – for example, chair of the board.

Representation also raises questions around identity construction and disclosure. While some groups such as those identifying as women and many racialised peoples cannot avoid having identity characteristics ascribed to them based on their outward appearance, or in some cases other possible markers such as name or accent, others may have to decide whether or not to self-identify,

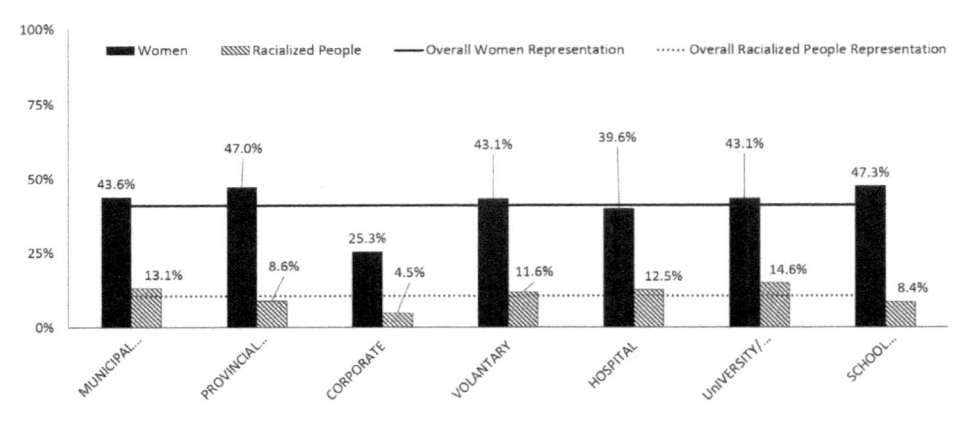

Figure 43.1 **Overall representation on boards of directors across sectors**

Note: Diversity Institute. (2020).

understanding the risks of discrimination and marginalisation if they do. Many prominent leaders – presidents of universities, chairs of boards of directors, high-profile corporate leaders – avoid sharing aspects of their identity; Indigenous peoples, some persons with disabilities and some who identify as LGBTQ2S+ may choose not to disclose (Diversity Institute, 2020). As one interviewee in a recent study said, *Most of the queer mentors I had early in my career shared the same 'wisdom' – hide who you are until you get promoted so high they can't get rid of you without people noticing* (Diversity Institute, 2020). So for some, the very decision to self-identify carries with it significant risks. An added layer of complexity comes from the identity groupings themselves. In Canada, for example, 'visibility minorities' is a term contained in the 1986 Employment Equity legislation but this has been critiqued and the recommended terminology has shifted to 'racialised peoples' (reflecting the social construction of race). However, that term also has limitations given the fact that there are substantial within-group differences between, for example, the experiences of Arab, South Asian, Chinese, black and Latin American groups. Additionally, many argue that such a blanket category perpetuates the othering of people who are not white (Diversity Institute, 2021).

There is also emerging complexity with efforts to clarify differences between sex (biological) and gender (socially constructed) in representation studies. An increasing proportion of the population now rejects binaries of man/woman or male/female altogether. Within LGBTQ2S+ communities there are also debates about which acronyms are appropriate. In Canada, there has been a shift by those wanting to show a commitment to Indigenous reconciliation to Two-Spirit or 2SLGBTQ+. Within disability communities there are also significant debates with some preferring to define themselves as 'mad' and others rejecting language of impairment and preferring to define difference (Diversity Institute, 2020). Identity and definitional issues create added complexity in attempting to understand issues of representation in leadership and efforts to advance gender parity, racial equality and increased diversity.

THE POWER OF REPRESENTATION: WHY DOES IT MATTER?

The 'fact' of representation of equity-seeking groups in leadership has material, socioeconomic significance both for the leaders themselves and more widely for employment, the economy and, by extension, a range of social outcomes. Equally important, leadership representation has powerful social symbolic significance or signalling effects to the broader society. We outline two such effects: the potential to erode stereotypes and mental models of who can lead; and the power to shape aspirations of young people and those in more junior positions. Such signalling effects of representation have considerable power and hold potential to contribute to sustained change.

Leadership Representation and Socioeconomic Power

Representation in leadership is tied to economic prosperity, a critical dimension of social justice (United Nations, 2021). The gender wage gap has been documented around the world and contributing factors to this gap comprise occupational segregation (e.g., the under-representation of women in high-paid sectors such as information communications and technology) as well as under-representation in leadership roles and the highest-paid positions. In Canada, the *Financial Times* top 100 companies include only two women in the CEO position. As above, data from Canada shows that even when they make it into the C-suite, women are paid significantly less than men and the pay gap is greater for racialised women (Longpre-Verret & Richards, 2021).

The 'business case' for diversity in governance, senior leadership and at all levels of the organisation has been increasingly well established by research and practical experience alike. Numerous studies have suggested organisations with more diversity in their leadership and on boards perform better, contributing to economic well-being (Buse et al., 2016; Diversity Institute, 2019, 2020; Hunt et al., 2020). Some research has pointed to a connection between increased firm value and boards that are more diverse. A 2020 study by McKinsey & Company finds that companies with diverse leadership outperform others in their industries by 30 per cent in terms of profitability, with higher levels of representation associated with greater returns (Hunt et al., 2020).

Other evidence suggests that diversity and inclusion including in leadership helps to broaden talent pools and overcome skill gaps in an increasingly volatile economy (Elias, 2020; Forbes Council, 2021). Attracting and retaining diverse talent is increasingly important in many jurisdictions, and diversity in organisations in general has been linked to increased levels of employee satisfaction, correlated with employee loyalty, productivity, performance and retention (Armstrong et al., 2010; Choi, 2009; Jauhari & Singh, 2013; McKay et al., 2007; Pitts, 2009). This is becoming increasingly important as organisations across sectors report skills and labour shortages, and worldwide competition for skilled immigrants increases with the aging population and low fertility rates in many high-income countries. For example, in Canada all labour market growth will come through immigration, and Statistics Canada estimates nearly 30 per cent of Canada's working-age population will be immigrants by 2036, and nearly 40 per cent will belong to a racialised group (Morency et al., 2017). Moreover, Indigenous youth are the fastest-growing demographic group in Canada (Statistics Canada, 2018). Leadership representation has also been connected to better responsiveness to increasingly diverse markets (Slater et al., 2008). Organisations may also benefit financially due to the positive impact of board diversity on support from diverse investors who prefer to support organisations that they feel represent and value them (Diversity Institute, 2019).

Globally, there is growing recognition that diversity and inclusion drive growth, innovation, creativity and problem-solving. Research has shown that increased leadership diversity is associated with an increase, for example, in patents production (TRIEC, 2010). In Canada, research suggests that $198 billion could be added to the GDP with a 10 per cent increase in women-owned small and medium-sized businesses (Cooper, 2013). Research also shows that diversity in leadership – representation – is associated with reduced groupthink and with that, reduced risk. As a result, diversity on boards may reduce the risks of financial misreporting and potential fraud, and is an effective strategy to mitigate legal and reputational costs (Diversity Institute, 2019). The same review of the research shows there are substantial reputational and legal risks for organisations that do not effectively address diversity and inclusion (Diversity Institute, 2019). There is also no shortage of examples of organisations facing public scrutiny or in some cases irreparable damage due to ineffective diversity and inclusion practices. In summer 2020, many organisations that came out in support of the Black Lives Matter movement were swiftly criticised for their poor track records in support of representation and equality and poor efforts to bring organisational change including in leadership representation (Glass & Cook, 2020; Jan et al., 2020; Wicks, 2017).

Representation and Social Symbolic Power

Beyond its important socioeconomic impacts, equity and inclusion in positional leadership has important social symbolic power, or signalling impacts.

Eroding stereotypes: Decades of research shows that gendered and culturally specific assumptions about leadership present barriers to women. Schein's research (1996) 'Think manager – think male' and subsequent work by others in different traditions has underscored how the dominance of white men in leadership has resulted in notions of leadership that exclude women and non-white male leaders (Elliott & Stead, 2018; Gagnon & Collinson, 2014; Grandy & Śliwa, 2017; Roberts et al., 2019). Stereotypes of women and men are deeply engrained in our societies. Women are seen as helpful, kind and compassionate, traits that are not congruent with the stereotypical traits of leaders or even ideal workers (Kalaitzi et al., 2017; Kossek et al., 2017; Lee & Huang, 2018). Societal beliefs and notions around masculinity and femininity, while not stable or fully static over time, are embedded in our culture and contribute to the expectations of gender roles (Chizema et al., 2015; Kossek et al., 2017). Starting at a young age, girls and boys are influenced by images they see, role models and the representation (or lack thereof) of women in the media (Cukier et al., 2016). Children are exposed to descriptive prejudice that results in them developing a (false) sense of what women are like and the ways in which women should behave (Soklaridis et al., 2017). Stereotypical images of women, discriminatory representation practices in the media and the lack of representation of women in politics and leadership positions influence the beliefs and behaviours of individuals and organisations that operate within society (Eagly & Karau, 2002; Gagnon et al., 2021b). Similarly, in 'Think leader, think white', Gündemir et al. (2014) found that notions of leadership exclude people who are black, outlining in detail how the predominant prototype of 'leader' in western societies is clearly biased, with so-called neutral leadership traits more strongly associated with white-majority group members.

While these associations and stereotypes present barriers to women and other groups who do not conform to the stereotypes, increasing the representation of women and other diverse leaders has the potential to help erode these stereotypes (c.f. Gagnon et al., 2021b). For example, research has shown that when women are exposed to other women in non-stereotypical gender roles, they have fewer negative self-perceptions and greater leadership aspirations, when compared to the impact of exposure to gender stereotypical roles (Simon & Hoyt, 2013). When women are exposed to negative gender stereotypes they are at risk of disengaging or having lowered participation (Simon & Hoyt, 2013). Gündemir et al.'s

(2014) study to examine the impact of recategorisation techniques involved placing racially diverse employees together in groups and teams, in leadership development or in decision-making roles. The study showed that at this micro level such recategorisation indeed eroded stereotypes.

Role models, shaping aspirations: The impact of stereotypes and the presence or absence of role models has also been explored. Representation in leadership sends strong signals about who belongs in the organisation and what the opportunities are for different groups. Many studies indicate that the symbolic or numeric representations of women are instrumental for instilling perceptions of legitimacy and fairness within our democratic institutions and signalling a commitment to gender equity (Dobrowolsky, 2000). Docherty (2002, 2017) draws on Bartsch et al. (2000) to suggest that individuals sharing characteristics with a specific group (e.g., shared gender) are better positioned to speak on behalf of this group.

Diversity in leadership is also found to positively impact the career advancement of under-represented groups by expanding their access to diverse role models and mentors and inspiring future leaders in their industries (Kilian, 2005). Female role models can inspire girls and women in male-typical domains such as STEM (Science, technology, engineering and math) (Cheryan et al. 2011; Dennehy & Dasgupta 2017), athletics (Greendorfer, 1977) and managerial and political leadership (Latu et al. 2013; Simon & Hoyt 2013; Singh et al. 2006; Wolbrecht & Campbell, 2007). Role models can improve women's increased sense of belonging and self-confidence (Dennehy & Dasgupta, 2017). Latu et al. (2019) propose specific behavioural mechanisms to explain how political female role models inspire women in leadership. Smooth and Richardson (2019) stress the importance of role models in the lives of black girls.

The notion that women in leadership roles help inspire other women is of course not simple and some have critiqued the neoliberal foundations on which this view appears to lie (Hoyt & Simon, 2011). Others have challenged assumptions that women should be encouraged to pursue leadership given the evidence of the unhealthy environments it will subject them to (Garcia-Collins & Lopez-Zafra, 2006) – for example, a 'chilly climate' found in academic leadership contexts (Britton, 2017). Still other research notes that the advantage of women role models in the political realm is important in the short term, but its impact may fade over time (Gilardi, 2015). Nonetheless, the balance of the research suggests that greater representation can serve to erode stereotypes and provide a wider range of role models for youth, shaping their aspirations.

THE 'DOINGS' OF LEADERSHIP THROUGH REPRESENTATION

While narratives of change through leadership representation abound in politics, there are fewer in organisation studies. Nonetheless, compelling accounts help in understanding the challenges and strategies that minority leaders confront in 'doing' representation. In this section, we ask, how do 'representative leaders' experience their roles? Evidence suggests that a 'burden of representation' can accrue to minority group members occupying leadership positions in white and male-dominated organisations. Accounts of leading for equality and diversity, for example, can be instructive here. The work of increasing representation through leadership of diversity and inclusion initiatives often falls on the shoulders of the minority leaders (Ahmed 2006, 2009, 2012), creating an emotional tax. They are often in less well-compensated positions. The burden includes emotional and performative tensions, as well as others' expectations that these actors will be grateful for the opportunity: *diversity becomes a commitment that requires that those who embody that diversity express happiness and gratitude. Our very arrival into organisations is used as evidence that the whiteness of which we speak no longer exists* (Ahmed, 2009, p. 41). Recent accounts of the experience of Indigenous peoples in academic leadership in Canada also point to this phenomenon (Debassige & Brunette-Debassige, 2018; Elson, 2019).

Thomas (2019) demonstrates how employees subject to historical othering but who have ascended to leadership positions encounter challenges that can put both their careers and their well-being at risk. Success depends on managing expectations and stereotypes through a layer of 'invisible labour' that may relate to stereotype threat (Steele, 1997). She describes a requirement to code-switch or behave differently in line with which identity one feels expected to enact at any given time, in order to manage intersecting identities. The risks of tokenism and of co-optation also make the work of minority leaders more onerous than others' work (Thomas, 2019). Dominant groups may bring minorities into the organisational leadership hoping to use the credibility of that group to their own benefit (e.g., Holdo, 2019). At the same time, to succeed these leaders must build diverse networks and support systems, a time-consuming process, to mitigate the personal and career risks associated with these processes.

Prejudice and micro-aggressions, such as being told you are not like others of your race or that you are 'articulate', have also been linked to a bigger risk of attrition for Black professionals, compounding the slower advancement they experience, with one study finding more than one-third intending to leave their companies within two years (Centre for Talent Innovation, 2019; see also Rosette et al., 2013). The experience of anti-Black racism and micro-aggressions produces physical as well as mental health harms.

Further, 'being there' – attaining positional leadership in organisations – does not guarantee voice: even when diverse groups are present, they may be treated inequitably. For example, gay men face gender penalties for non-conformance to gender stereotypes around masculinity that can limit their influence and voice (Wicks, 2017). Additional challenges experienced by gay men include that, like mental health/disability and religion, their sexuality is largely invisible. The need to outwardly share this fact repetitively and manage this process comes with psychological costs (e.g., Lyons et al., 2017).

Early work on tokenism demonstrated that a burden of representation for those in the minority also manifests in the form of discriminatory outcomes, in this case for women. According to Kanter's (1977) token theory, still influential today, token status in leadership brings a threefold burden. Women experience heightened visibility that creates performance pressures not experienced by men; they are often isolated by the majority who exaggerate their differences as they enter leadership; and they simultaneously face expectations to act within pre-defined gender roles (Kanter, 1977). While Kanter and many other researchers argue that the antidote to token dynamics is greater representation and, ultimately, gender parity in leadership, subsequent discussions of backlash as women gain power point to a continuing need to examine the processes as well as outcomes of attaining critical mass (Krook, 2015).

The glass cliff phenomenon further illustrates the dangers associated with representation, labelled a 'risk tax' for women and minority leaders (Glass and Cook, 2020; Ryan & Haslam, 2007). Theories of the glass cliff have focused on the penalties imposed upon women and minority leaders due to bias and discrimination at the time of appointment to top leadership positions. Finally, there is also no ironclad guarantee that those in positions of power will represent the interests of groups with whom they share an identity. Shared identity characteristics do not render automatic a leader's advocacy of the interests of that group: a woman in power does not make one a feminist, a type of 'Margaret Thatcher effect' after the famous British Prime Minister and first woman in the role, who openly rejected 'women's liberation' (Lakhani, 2013).

CONCLUSIONS AND QUESTIONS FOR FURTHER RESEARCH

Measuring representation at an aggregate level is central to tracking change for equality and inclusion in organisations; it is a measure of equity and inclusion and, while not perfect, research and policy rely on such measures. We have suggested that representation is not a unidimensional concept pertaining to presence alone – its doings are also critically important and multifaceted. At the same time, these undoubtedly relate to power in numbers albeit in complex ways that require further research to understand more fully. Further, leadership representation as presence has both structural, socioeconomic importance as a source of greater equality and signalling or social symbolic significance – for example, through the potential to erode powerful stereotypes that dictate behaviour and to shape aspirations.

Our chapter points to a number of important questions that call for more research. Two of the most immediate may be: when, where and how does representation lead to change in leadership practice? And, what is the relationship between leadership representation and inclusion of minority group members inside organisations? Both questions should be pursued in future research. The stream of research in *inclusive leadership* (Kuknor & Bhattacharya, 2020; Roberson & Perry, 2021) can provide some guidance here. We caution, however, following our arguments here about structural representation for advancement of equity and equality in organisations, this work must adopt a structural as well as a cultural-phenomenological orientation to inclusion (Gagnon et al., 2021a).

More generally, we would argue that leadership theory lags on these important questions. As Elliott and Stead have argued (2018), post-heroic models of leadership decreasingly associated with masculinity or seen as gender-neutral and thus viewed as more inclusive of women, and perhaps minority groups as well, do not offer women any particular advantage in the practice of leadership. Just why this is so and how representation may be part of the answer remain compelling questions. More research is required from leadership scholars, we contend, to unpack the ways in which diverse, non-white, non-cisgender male leaders are shifting prevailing normative notions about 'effective' leadership. Does increased representation change the practice of leadership itself, and where, when and how? This is a large research agenda, but one which several streams of extant research, several examined in this book, could inform.

More generally in leadership studies, as theorising has moved to understand leadership as socially constructed, a function of practice and processes that may be seen as connected to myriad actors, or as independent of actors (Denis et al., 2012; Hazy & Uhl-Bien, 2013), the fundamental question of who occupies positions of leadership should not be lost or under-valued. We suggest multi-paradigmatic approaches to future research that intertwine the structural and phenomenological to provide a greater understanding of both the impact and the experience of leadership representation. Indeed, one might separate these into 'leadership representation' and 'representative leadership', the latter informed by literature in political science but remaining an under-examined question in organisation studies. For organisations, studying leadership representation requires further work on the links between representation and what we have called cultural inclusion, or belonging. Understanding inclusion not as assimilation into the norm but as igniting change, under what conditions does representation garner these effects and when does it not? Questions of power are of particular importance in this regard.

Activists and equality advocates argue for the ongoing collection of data based on representation (e.g., Carter et al., 2003; Ontario Human Rights Commission, 2009) as important to effecting change, and indeed this is legislated in different international jurisdictions, while notably not in others (e.g., Canada versus Belgium). Important strides have been made in the research to examine impacts of intersectionality as well as the fluidity of categories, including the work by Longpre-Verret and Richards (2021) outlined earlier. Representation is not a guarantee of inclusion or equity. Nevertheless, it deserves our attention as scholars as we seek to inform policy and, further, to extend a rights- and justice-based approach to equality. A focus on representation recognises and addresses profound power imbalances among groups (Bonilla-Silva, 2010; DiTomaso et al., 2007; Nkomo & Ariss, 2014), aiming ultimately to counter those imbalances. Paraphrasing Acker (2006), this may not be so perfectly or completely, but of necessity. As Acker taught, inequality is present in the systematic disparities between participants of different social groups that may be manifest in several ways: for example, power and control over goals, resources and outcomes; workplace decisions such as how to organise work; opportunities for promotion and interesting work; security in the form of secure employment and benefits; and respect and satisfaction in work and work relations. 'Being there' in positions of power is a matter of justice and of change.

ACKNOWLEDGEMENT

The authors would like to acknowledge the support of the Social Sciences and Humanities Research Council of Canada.

REFERENCES

Acker, J. (2006). Inequality regimes: Gender, class, and race in organizations. *Gender & Society*, 20(4), 441–464.

Ahmed, S. (2006). Doing diversity work in higher education in Australia. *Educational Philosophy and Therapy*, 38(6), 745–768.

Ahmed, S. (2009). Embodying diversity: Problems and paradoxes for Black feminists. *Race Ethnicity and Education*, 12(1), 41–52.

Ahmed, S. (2012). *On Being Included: Racism and Diversity in Institutional Life*. Duke University Press.

Ahmed, S. (2014). *Willful Subjects*. Duke University Press.

Armstrong, C., Flood, P. C., Guthrie, J. P., Liu, W., MacCurtain, S., & Mkamwa, T. (2010). The impact of diversity and equality management on firm performance: Beyond high performance work systems. *Human Resource Management*, 49(6), 977–998.

Bartsch, R. A., Burnett, T., & Diller, T. R. (2000). Gender representation in television commercials: Updating an update. *Sex Roles*, 43, 735–743.

Bonilla-Silva, E. (2010). *Racism Without Racists: Color-Blind Racism and the Persistence of Racial Inequality in the United States*. Lanham.

Breslin, R. A., Pandey, S., & Riccucci, N. (2017). Intersectionality in public leadership research: A review and future research agenda. *Review of Public Personnel Administration*, 37(2), 160–182.

Britton, D. (2017). Beyond the chilly climate: The salience of gender in women's academic careers. *Gender and Society*, 31(1), 5–27.

Buse, K., Bernstein, R. S., & Bilimoria, D. (2016). The influence of board diversity, board diversity policies and practices, and board inclusion behaviors on nonprofit governance practices. *Journal of Business Ethics*, 133(1), 179–191.

Campus, D. (2013). *Women Political Leaders and the Media. Palgrave Studies in Political Leadership*. Palgrave Macmillan.

Carter, D. A., Simkins, B. J., & Simpson, W. G. (2003). Corporate governance, board diversity, and firm value. *Financial Review*, 38(1), 33–53.

Centre for Talent Innovation (2019). *Being Black in America: An Intersectional Exploration*. Centre for Talent Innovation.

Cheryan, S., Siy, J. O., Vichayapai, M., Drury, B. J., & Kim, S. (2011). Do female and male role models who embody STEM stereotypes hinder women's anticipated success in STEM? *Social Psychological and Personality Science*, 2(6), 656–664.

Childs, S. & Krook, M. L. (2008). Critical mass theory and women's political representation. *Political Studies*, 56(3), 725–736.

Chizema, A., Kamuriwo, D. S., & Shinozawa, Y. (2015). Women on corporate boards around the world: Triggers and barriers. *Leadership Quarterly*, *26*(6), 1051–1065.

Choi, S. (2009). Diversity in the US federal government: Diversity management and employee turnover in federal agencies. *Journal of Public Administration Research and Theory*, *19*(3), 603–630.

Cook, A., & Glass, C. (2015). The power of one or power in numbers? Analyzing the effect of minority leaders on diversity policy and practice. *Work and Occupations*, *42*(2), 183–215.

Cooper, L. (2013). Canadian women grabbing the baton. *RBC Economics*. http://www.rbc.com/economics/economic-reports/pdf/other-reports/canadianwomengrabbingthebaton.pdf

Crenshaw, K. (1989). Demarginalizing the intersection of race and sex: A black feminist critique of anti-discrimination doctrine, feminist theory and anti-racist politics. *University of Chicago Legal Forum*, *1*(8), 138–167.

Crenshaw, K. (1991). Mapping the margins: Intersectionality, identity politics, and violence against women of color. *Stanford Law Review*, *43*(6), 1241–1299.

Crenshaw, K. (1997). Intersectionality and identity politics: Learning from violence against women of colour. In M. L. Shanley & U. Narayan (Eds.), *Reconstructing Political Theory* (pp. 178–193). Polity Press.

Crevani L., Lindgren M., & Packendorff, J. (2007). Shared leadership: A postheroic perspective on leadership as a collective construction. *International Journal of Leadership Studies*, *3*(1), 40–67.

Cukier, W., Gagnon, S., & Latif, R. (2021). Changing the narrative: Shaping legislation to advance diversity on boards in Canada. *Equality, Diversity and Inclusion: An International Journal*, *40*(7), 770–800.

Cukier, W., Gagnon, S., Lindo, L. M., Hannan, C., & Amato, S. (2013) A critical ecological model to enable change: Promoting diversity and inclusion. In J. Murphy, M. Virpi & M. Siltaoja (Eds.), *Getting Things Done: Dialogues in Critical Management Studies, Vol. II* (pp. 245–275). Emerald.

Cukier, W., Jackson, S., Elmi, M. A., Roach, E., & Cyr, D. (2016). Representing women? Leadership roles and women in Canadian broadcast news. *Gender in Management*, *31*(5/6), 374–395.

Cukier, W., Shortt, D., & Devine, I. (2002). Gender and information technology: Implications of definitions, *SIGCSE Bulletin*, *34*, 142–148.

Dahlerup, D. (1988). From a small to a large minority: Women in Scandinavian politics. *Scandinavian Political Studies*, *11*(4), 275–297.

Dalhousie University & Canadian Centre for Diversity and Inclusion (2019). *National Diversity and Inclusion Benchmarking Study*. https://ccdi.ca/media/1979/20190715-research-national-diversity-and-inclusion-benchmarking-study.pdf

Debassige, B. & Brunette-Debassige, C. (2018). Indigenizing work as 'willful work': Toward indigenous transgressive leadership in Canadian universities. *Cultural and Pedagogical Inquiry*, *10*(2), 119–138.

Dennehy, T. C., & Dasgupta, N. (2017). Female peer mentors early in college increase women's positive academic experiences and retention in engineering. *Proceedings of the National Academy of Sciences*, *114*(23), 5964–5969.

Denis, J. L., Langley, A., & Sergi, V. (2012). Leadership in the plural. *Academy of Management Annals*, *6*(1), 211–283.

Dezso, C. L., & Ross, D. G. (2012). Does female representation in top management improve firm performance? A panel data investigation. *Strategic Management Journal*, *33*(9), 1072–1089.

DiTomaso, N., Post, C., & Parks-Yancy, R. (2007). Workforce diversity and inequality: Power, status, and numbers. *Annual Review of Sociology*, *33*(1), 473–501.

Diversity Institute (2019). *Diversity Leads: Women & Racialized People in Senior Leadership Positions*. https://www.ryerson.ca/diversity/reports/DiversityLeads_Montreal_EN.pdf

Diversity Institute (2020). *Diversity Leads: Diverse Representation in Leadership*. https://www.ryerson.ca/diversity/reports/DiversityLeads_2020_Canada.pdf

Diversity Institute (n.d.). *Brief Concerning: Bill C-25, Canada Business Corporations Act*. https://www.ourcommons.ca/Content/Committee/421/INDU/Brief/BR8803535/br-external/DiversityInstituteAtRyersonUniversity-e.pdf

Diversity Institute (2021). Background research for the 50–30 challenge seed document. Unpublished.

Dobrowolsky, A. (2000). The politics of pragmatism. Women, representation and constitutionalism in Canada. Toronto, Canada: Oxford University Press

Docherty, D. (2002). The Canadian Senate: Chamber of sober reflection or loony cousin best not talked about. *Journal of Legislative Studies*, *8*(3), 27–48.

Docherty, D. (2017). Citizens and legislators: Different views on representation. In N. Nevitte (Ed.), *Value Change and Governance in Canada* (pp. 165–206). University of Toronto Press.

Eagly, A. H., & Karau, S. J. (2002). Role congruity theory of prejudice toward female leaders. *Psychological Review*, *109*(3), 573–598.

Elias, H. (2020). *Diversity is the Bridge On Which We Can Cross the Skills Gap*. World Economic Forum. https://www.weforum.org/agenda/2020/01/diversity-tech-skills-gap-4ir-digital-revolution/

Elliott, C., & Stead, V. (2018). Constructing women's leadership representation in the UK press during a time of financial crisis: Gender capitals and dialectical tensions. *Organization Studies*, *39*(1), 19–45.

Elson, P. R. (2019). *University–Indigenous Relations: A Policy Assessment Framework in Four Dimensions*. In partial fulfilment of the Graduate Certificate in Indigenous Nationhood, University of Victoria.

Equileap (2020). *Gender Equality in the US: Assessing 500 Leading Companies on Workplace Equality Including Health Care Benefits. Special Report*. https://equileap.com/wp-content/uploads/2020/12/Equileap_US_Report_2020.pdf

Forbes Council (2021). Fourteen benefits of a more diversity leadership team. *Forbes Council Post*, 24 June.

Freedman, E. (2002). *No Turning Back: The History of Feminism and the Future of Women*. Random House.

Gagnon, S., Augustin, T., & Cukier, W. (2021a). Interplay for change in equality, diversity and inclusion studies. *Human Relations*, 23 April, 1–27.

Gagnon, S., Cukier, W., & Oliver, A. (2021b). Sexism, gendered deficits, and the gendered representation of entrepreneurship in Canadian print media. *Academy of Management Proceedings*, Annual Meeting, August.

Gagnon, S., & Collinson, D. (2014). Rethinking global leadership development programmes: The interrelated significance of power, context and identity. *Organization Studies*, *35*(5), 645–670.

Garcia-Collins, R., & Lopez-Zafra, E. (2006). Prejudice against women in male-congenial environments: Perceptions of gender role congruity in leadership. *Sex Roles*, *55*(1), 51–61.

Gilardi, F. (2015). The temporary importance of role models for women's political representation. *American Journal of Political Science*, *59*(4), 957–970.

Glass, C., & Cook, A. (2020). Pathways to the glass cliff: A risk tax for women and minority leaders? *Social Problems*, *67*(4), 637–653.

Grandy, G., & Śliwa, M. (2017). Contemplative leadership: The possibilities for the ethics of leadership theory and practice. *Journal of Business Ethics*, *143*, 423–440.

Grandy, G., Cukier, W., & Gagnon, S. (2020). (In)visibility in the margins: Covid-19, women entrepreneurs and the need for inclusive recovery. *Gender in Management: An International Journal*, *35*(7/8), 667–675.

Greendorfer, S. L. (1977). Role of socializing agents in female sport, Research Quarterly. American Alliance for Health. *Physical Education and Recreation*, *48*(2), 304–310.

Gündemir, S., Homan, A. C., de Dreu, C. K., & van Vugt, M. (2014). Think leader, think white? Capturing and weakening an implicit pro-white leadership bias. *PloS one*, *9*(1), e83915.

Hazy, J., & Uhl-Bien, M. (2013). Towards operationalizing complexity leadership: How generative, administrative and community-building leadership practices enact organizational outcomes. *Leadership*, *11*(1), 79–104.

Holdo, M. (2019). Cooptation and non-cooptation: Elite strategies in response to social protest. *Social Movement Studies*, *18*(4), 444–462.

Hoyt, C. L., & Simon, S. (2011). Female leaders: Injurious or inspiring role models for women? *Psychology of Women Quarterly*, *35*(1), 143–157.

Hunt, V., Prince, S., Dixon-Fyle, S., & Dolan, K. (2020). *Diversity Wins: How Inclusion Matters*, May. McKinsey & Co.

ISED (Innovation, Science and Economic Development Canada) (2021). The 50–30 Challenge, Participating Organizations. Government of Canada. https://www.ic.gc.ca/eic/site/icgc.nsf/eng/07712.html

Jan, T., McGregore, J., Merle, R., & Tiku, N. (2020). As big corporations say 'Black lives matter', their track records raise skepticism. *Washington Post*. https://www.washingtonpost.com/business/2020/06/13/after-years-marginalizing-black-employees-customers-corporate-america-says-black-lives-matter/

Jauhari, H., & Singh, S. (2013). Perceived diversity climate and employees' organizational loyalty. *Equality, Diversity and Inclusion: An International Journal*, *32*(3), 262–276.

Kalaitzi, V., Czabanowska, K., Fowler-Davis, S., & Brand, H. (2017). Women leadership barriers in healthcare, academia and business. *Equality, Diversity and Inclusion: An International Journal*, *36*(5), 457–474.

Kanter, R. M. (1977). *Men and Women of the Corporation*. Basic Books.

Kilian, C., Huaki, D., & McCarty, E. (2005). Building diversity in the pipeline to corporate leadership. *Journal of Management Development*, *24*(2), 155–188.

Konrad, A. M., Kramer, V., & Erkut, S. (2008). Critical mass: The impact of three or more women on corporate boards. *Organizational Dynamics*, *37*(2), 145–164.

Kossek, E. E., Su, R., & Wu, L. (2017). 'Opting out' or 'pushed out'? Integrating perspectives on women's career equality for gender inclusion and interventions. *Journal of Management*, *43*(1), 228–254.

Krook, M. L. (2015). Empowerment versus backlash: Gender quotas and critical mass theory. *Politics, Groups, and Identities*, *3*(1), 184–188.

Kuknor, S. C., & Bhattacharya, S. (2020). Inclusive leadership: New age leadership to foster organizational inclusion. *European Journal of Training and Development*, June, 1–28.

Lakhani, N. (2013). Margaret Thatcher: How much did the Iron Lady do for the UK's women? *Guardian*, 8 April.

Larrieta-Rubin de Celis, I., Velasco-Balmaseda, E., Fernández de Bobadilla, S., del Mar Alonso-Almeida, M., & Intxaurburu-Clemente, G. (2015). Does having women managers lead to increased gender equality practices in corporate social responsibility? *Business Ethics*, 24(1), 91–110.

Latu, I., Mast, M., Lammers, J. & Bombari, D. (2013). Successful female leaders empower women's behavior in leadership tasks. *Journal of Experimental Social Psychology*, 49(3). 444–448.

Latu, I., Mast, M., Lammers, J., & Hoyt, C. (2019). Empowering mimicry: Female leader role models empower women in leadership tasks through body posture mimicry. *Sex Roles*, 80(1–2), 11–24.

Lawson, M. A., Martin, A., Huda, I., & Matz, S. C. (2021). Hiring women into senior leadership positions is associated with a reduction in gender stereotypes in organizational language. *PNAS Proceedings of the National Academy of Sciences 2022*, 119(9), 1–11.

Lee, M., & Huang, L. (2018). Gender bias, social impact framing, and evaluation of entrepreneurial ventures. *Organization Science*, 29(1), 1–16.

Longpre-Verret, L. M., & Richards, E. (2021). *Diversity Among Board Directors and Officers: Exploratory Estimates on Family, Work, and Income*. Statistics Canada, Government of Canada.

Lyons, B., Pek, S., & Wessel, J. L. (2017). Toward a 'sunlit path': Stigma identity management as a source of localized social change through interaction. *Academy of Management Review*, 42(4), 618–636.

McKay, P. F., Avery, D. R., Tonidandel, S., Morris, M. A., Hernandez, M., & Hebl, M. R. (2007). Racial differences in employee retention: Are diversity climate perceptions the key? *Personnel Psychology*, 60(1), 35–62.

Milhomem, C. (2020). *Women on Boards: 2020 Progress Report*. MSCI. https://www.msci.com/documents/10199/9ab8ea98-25fd-e843-c9e9-08f0d179bb85

Morency, J.-D., Malenfant, E., & MacIsaac, S. (2017). *Immigration and Diversity: Population Projections for Canada and its Regions, 2011 to 2036*. https://www150.statcan.gc.ca/n1/pub/91-551-x/91-551-x2017001-eng.htm

Nkomo, S. M., & Ariss, A. A. (2014). The historical origins of ethnic (white) privilege in US organizations. *Journal of Managerial Psychology*, 29(4), 389–404.

O'Loughlin, V. (2015). I say assertive, you say bossy; I say leader, you say bi***: Gender bias in academia. *The FASEB Journal*, 29(1), Supplement, 9–4

Ontario Human Rights Commission (2009). Count Me In! Collecting Human Rights-Based Data. http://www.ohrc.on.ca/en/count-me-collecting-human-rights-based-data

Pitts, D. (2009). Diversity management, job satisfaction, and performance: Evidence from US federal agencies. *Public Administration Review*, 69(2), 328–338.

Regulations Amending the Canada Business Corporations Regulations, 2001 (2019). SOR/2019-258.

Raelin, J. (Ed.) (2016). *Leadership-as-Practice: Theory and Application*. Routledge.

Rao, K., & Tilt, C. (2016). Board composition and corporate social responsibility: The role of diversity, gender, strategy and decision making. *Journal of Business Ethics*, 138, 327–347.

Richardson, A., & Loubier, C. (2008). Intersectionality and leadership. *International Journal of Leadership Studies*, 3(2), 142–161.

Roberson, Q., & Park, H. J. (2007). Examining the link between diversity and firm performance: The effects of diversity reputation and leader racial diversity. *Group & Organization Management*, 32(5), 548–568.

Roberson, Q., & Perry, J. (2021). Inclusive leadership in thought and action: A thematic analysis. *Group & Organization Management*, 27 April.

Roberts, L. M., & Mayo, A. J. (2019). Toward a racially just workplace 2019: Diversity efforts are failing black employees. Here's a better approach. *Harvard Business Review*. The Big Idea Series/Advancing Black Leaders, 14 November.

Roberts, L. M., Mayo, A. J., & Thomas, D. (Eds.) (2019). *Race, Work, and Leadership: New Perspectives on the Black Experience*. Harvard Business Review.

Rosenbloom, J., Ronald, A., Dupont, B., & Coder, L. (2008). Why are there so few women in information technology? Assessing the role of personality in career choices. *Journal of Economic Psychology*, 29, 543–554.

Rosette, A. S., Carton, A., Bowes-Sperry, L., & Hewlin, P. F. (2013). Why do racial slurs remain prevalent in the workplace? Integrating theory on intergroup behavior. *Organization Science*, 24(5), 1402–1421.

Ryan, M. K., & Haslam, S. A. (2007). The glass cliff: Exploring the dynamics surrounding the appointment of women to precarious leadership positions. *Academy of Management Review*, 32(2), 549–572.

Sahadi, J. (2020). After years of talking about diversity, the number of black leaders at US companies is still dismal. *CNN Business*, 2 June.

Schein, V., Mueller, R., Lituchy, T., & Liu, J. (1996). Think manager – think male: A global phenomenon? *Journal of Organizational Behavior*, 17(1), 33–41.

Simon, S., & Hoyt, C. L. (2013). Exploring the effect of media images on women's leadership self-perceptions and aspirations. *Group Processes & Intergroup Relations*, 16(2), 232–245.

Singh, V., Vinnicombe, S., & James, K. (2006). Constructing a professional identity: How young female managers use role models. *Women in Management Review*, 21(1), 67–81.

Slater, S. F., Weigand, R. A., & Zwirlein, T. J. (2008). The business case for commitment to diversity. *Business Horizons*, 51(3), 201-209.

Smooth, W., & Richardson, E. (2019). Role models matter: Black girls and political leadership possibilities. In A. Halliday (Ed.), *The Black Girlhood Studies Collection* (pp. 131–156). Women's Press.

Soklaridis, S., Kuper, A., Whitehead, C. R., Ferguson, G., Taylor, V. H., & Zahn, C. (2017). Gender bias in hospital leadership: A qualitative study on the experiences of women CEOs. *Journal of Health Organization and Management*, 31(2), 253-268.

Statistics Canada (2017). *Immigration and Ethnocultural Diversity: Key Results from the 2016 Census*. https://www150.statcan.gc.ca/n1/daily-quotidien/171025/dq171025b-eng.htm?indid=14428-1&indgeo=0

Statistics Canada (2018). *First Nations People, Metis and Inuit in Canada: Diverse and Growing Populations*. https://www150.statcan.gc.ca/n1/pub/89-659-x/89-659-x2018001-eng.htm

Steele, C. M. (1997). A threat in the air: How stereotypes shape intellectual identity and performance. *American Psychology*, 52, 613–629.

Thomas, K. (2019). Leading as the 'other'. *Journal of Leadership and Organizational Studies*, 26(3), 402–406.

Tolley, E., & Young, R. (Eds.) (2011). *Immigrant Settlement Policy Canadian Municipalities* (Vol. 2011, pp. 3–49). McGill-Queen's University Press.

Toronto Region Immigrant Employment Council. 'Xerox Canada,' TRIEC (2010). 14 April. https://triec.ca/wp-content/uploads/2015/06/TRIEC_Annual_Report_2010.pdf

Trimble, L. (2013). *Gender, Political Leadership and Media Visibility: Globe and Mail Coverage of Conservative Party of Canada Leadership Contests*. Cambridge University Press.

United Nations (2021). *The Sustainable Development Goals Report 2021*. United Nations publication issued by the Department of Economic and Social Affairs. ISBN: 978-92-1-101439-6

Wicks, D. (2017). The consequences of outness: Gay men's workplace experiences. *Management Decision*, 55(9), 1868–1887.

Wolbrecht, C., & Campbell, D. (2007). Leading by example: Female members of parliament as political role models. *American Journal of Political Science*, 51(4), 921–939.

Index

Note: Page numbers followed by "*f*" indicate figure.

Aaker, J. L., 237
Abélès, M., 379
Abrahamson, E., 150
Abreu Pederzini, G. D., 506
Acker, J., 543
Acton, B. P., 166
Adams, C., 526
Adorno, T. W., 420
advocacy *versus* enquiry, 149–150
aesthetic leadership, 275, 277–282
aesthetic perception, 274–283
    6 January 2021 insurrection, U.S., 275–283
    analysis, leadership, 282
    field developed, Duke's work, 279–280
    implications, 282–283
    initial analysis, 276–277
    moral dimension, aesthetic leadership, 280–282
    relation to leadership, 277–278
affective embodiment, 517
    leadership theory and practice, 516–518
affective leadership, 132, 517, 518
agency, 17, 20, 21, 83, 287, 301, 472, 473, 476, 478, 502, 521, 522, 526, 529, 530
agential realism, 523, 524, 527, 528
agentic leadership, 471–480
    behaviour example, 474
    determination and ambivalence, 474
    directive and empowering leadership, 474
    meta-categories, 473
    narcissism and humility, 473–474
    orientation example, 474
    sense-making of, 477
    trait example, 473–474
agents, 11, 57, 85, 86, 123, 317, 318, 523, 526, 530, 535
Aime, F., 77
Algera, P. M., 147, 149
Alharbi, M., 194
Alipour, K. K., 339, 340
Allen, S., 376, 379
alternative organisations, 372, 373, 378
alternatives, leadership, 371–380, 459–468
    boundary conditions, 460–461
    coordination arrangements, organisational purpose and value orientation, 372–373
    departing from subordinates' perspectives, 466–467
    leader–follower distinction, 463–464

    leaderlessness, leadershiplessness and dominance, 375–377
    leaders and, 374–375
    leadership, for and against, 377–378
    meanings of alternatives and impetus, 371–372
    within and outside leadership domain, 465–466
    practical perspective, 464–467
    questions, 378–380
    sense-breaking and remaking, 378–380
    sense-making 'alternatives,' 372–373
    sense-making studies, 373–374
    theoretical perspective, 460–464
    tool of managerial ideology, 461–463
Alvarez, J.L., 7
Alvesson, M., 347, 353, 354, 461, 463, 466, 493
ambivalence, 43, 181, 348, 407, 474, 475, 479
Ames, R. T., 408–410, 413
ancient Chinese perspective, 406–415
Andrews, K. T., 374
anthropology, 131, 374, 383, 387, 388, 391, 453
Antonakis, J., 145, 365, 367
Archambault, D., 315
Aristotle, 205, 206, 208, 209, 326, 329, 485
Arnold, K. A., 130, 132
artful practice, 274–283
Arvedsen, L. D., 33, 35, 301
Aryee, S., 449
Ashcraft, K. L., 491
Ashford, S. J., 33, 36, 270, 464
Ashkanasy, N. M., 129–132
Ashman, I., 147
aspirational leadership, 149–150
aspiring leaders, 8, 11, 414
Atack, C., 502
Atkins, S., 31
authenticity, 142–145, 147–149, 214, 219, 279, 285, 353, 502
authentic leaders, 121, 143, 145–149, 282, 419
authentic leadership (AL) construct
    existentialist and psychodynamic critiques, 146–148
    historical background and emergence, 142–144
    problematising, 148–149
    state of evolution, 144–146
authoritarianism, 178, 180, 184, 186, 293, 492
Auvinen, T. P., 135
Avolio, B. J., 143, 302, 303

bad leaders, 349, 452, 454
Bailey, C., 219
Baker, C., 46
Bakhtin, M., 490
Balkundi, P., 122
Barad, K., 512, 522–526
Barad's theory, 524, 527–529, 531
Barbalet, J., 408
Barco, I. J., 194
Barker, J. R., 397
Barley, S. R., 17
Bartol, K. M., 171
Bartsch, R. A., 541
Bashshur, M., 362
Bass, B. M., 142. 144, 143, 526, 528
Bate, P., 435
Bathurst, R., 280, 301
Baumgarten, A. G., 274
Baxter, J., 30–32, 35
Baxter, L. A., 490
Bazerman, M. H., 218
beautiful leadership, 279
Benjamin, J., 254–256
Bennett, J., 522
Bennis, W., 289, 461
Bentham, J., 218
Berg, J. L., 194
Berger, P., 489
Bernerth, J. B., 46
Berson, Y., 233
Besharov, M., 492
better leadership, 69, 459, 479
Bevir, M., 409
Beyes, T., 347
Big Five, 100, 102–104, 106, 204–206, 292, 450
Bigley, G. A., 501
Bion, W. R., 181
Birmingham, C., 314, 315
Bispo, M. S., 512
Black, S. L., 314–315
Black Lives Matter (BLM), 303–304
Blair, A., 88
Blau, P. M., 45
Blenkinsopp, J., 407
Bligh, M. C., 65, 69, 367
Blom, M., 466
Bloom, P., 299, 304, 409
Boal, K. B., 317
body, politicising, 513–514
Boje, D. M., 300
Bolden, R., 439
Bono, J. E., 103
Booker Prize, 347, 350–354
Bourdieu, P., 17
Bourne, A., 103
Bowen, D. E., 473
Bowers, M. R., 234

Boyatzis, R. E., 193, 195–197
Braun, S., 121
Braverman, H., 297, 306
Breevaart, K., 107
Bristow, A., 507
Broeng, S., 407
Bromley, P., 9
Brophy, M., 500
Brown, M. E., 499
Brumann, C., 377
Buchanan, D., 421
bureaucracies, 395–397, 465, 466, 528
Burns, J. M., 506, 525
business contexts, 218, 364
business leader, 119, 300, 336, 407, 428
business organisations, 67, 418
business partners, 154, 156, 157, 160–162
business schools, 83, 90, 91, 299, 419, 429, 466, 532
Butler, A., 252
Butler, E. A., 136, 137
Butler, J., 516, 523, 524
Buzzanell, P. M., 374

Cairns, G., 347, 348
Cajete, G., 312–314, 317
Callahan, W. J., 408–411, 413
Campbell, C., 232
Capriles, R., 503
Card, C., 506
care ethics, 499–500, 502, 503, 505, 507
care-givers, 498, 499, 501–503, 505, 506
caring leaders, 498, 501–503, 506
caring leadership, 498–503, 505–507
    complex workings of power, 501–502
    researching, 506–507
    successful leadership relations, 498–499
Carlo, J. L., 492
Carlone, D., 491
Carlyle, T., 408
Carnabuci, G., 75, 122
Carnegie, D., 204
Carroll, B., 149, 265, 267, 302, 346, 350, 355, 439
Carroll, G. R., 18
Carson, J. B., 75
Carsten, M., 84, 90
Case, P., 20, 388, 389
Cederström, C., 503
Chaleff, I., 88, 90
Chalupnik, M., 31
Chamberlain, C., 315
charismatic entrepreneurs, 156–157
charismatic leaders, 154–156, 159–162, 276, 279, 419, 422–424
    in entrepreneurial organisations, 154–162
    as purveyor of growth opportunities, 160–161
    as 'scoop,' 159–160
    as wealth enhancer, 157–159

charismatic leadership, 67, 68, 103, 118, 154, 156, 162, 234, 235, 374, 422
Chatzidakis, A., 503
Cherniss, J. L., 410
Chia, R., 288, 289
Chizema, A., 364
Choi, S., 32
Chreim, S., 8
Christensen, L. J., 214
Chuang, A., 132
Chung, C., 367
Cicero, L., 56
Clark, D., 167
Clarke, C., 515
Clegg, S. R., 401
Clifton, J., 34, 265, 267
Cloutier, C., 11
Coats, M. R., 104, 119
coercive power, 399, 463–466
Coiera, E., 440
collective leadership, 4, 9, 32, 74–76, 166–168, 170, 305, 515
Collinson, D., 9, 88, 484, 491, 492
Collinson, M., 67, 68, 492
Colton, R. G., 349, 350
communal leadership, 471–480
　meta-categories, 473
　sense-making of, 477
communication, 28, 29, 166, 167, 262–269, 298, 305, 438
communicative constitution of organisation (CCO), 263
　concepts and studies, leadership, 266–268
　inspiration from, possibilities, 268–271
　main ideas, 263–266
communicative events, 263–268, 270
communities, 213, 214, 218–222, 313, 314, 317, 375, 378, 380, 390, 413
complex adaptive systems, 317, 318, 433, 434, 441
complexity leadership, 374, 437, 438, 441
Conger, J. A., 453
Connaughton, S. L., 263
conscientiousness, 102–109, 232
conscious adaptive system, 309–318
constructive leadership, 103, 450, 455
contagion effects, 158, 159, 161, 162, 303
contemporary leadership, 24, 408, 418
content overlap personality, leadership, 101
contextual factors, 43, 45, 78, 79, 227, 231, 359–367
contextualised leadership questionnaire, construction, 105
contextualised personality traits, 99–110, 214
contextual leadership, 360, 363, 364, 366, 439–441
Contractor, N. S., 72
Cook, A., 535
Cooper, C. D., 144, 146
Cooren, F., 264, 267–269
Costa, P. T. Jr, 102
Costas, J., 147

Courpasson, D., 10
Crenshaw, K., 538
Crevani, L., 6, 7, 18, 290
critical appreciation, 322–332
critical history perspective, 325
critical leadership studies, 10, 87, 88, 251, 263, 288, 376, 490, 493, 503, 510
critical theory, value, 252–253
cross-cultural leadership, 383–385, 391
Csikszentmihaly, M., 279
Cullen-Lester, K. L., 170
culture, 383–392
　African philosophy and knowledge politics, 386
　anthropological perspectives, 387–389
　indigenous perspectives, 389–391
　language and practice, Laos, 389–390
　mainstream cross-cultural studies, 384–385
　Nollywood new media, 390–391
　organisational culture, 385–386
　postcolonial critique, 386–387
Currie, G., 348
Czarniawska-Joerges, B., 348

Dahl, R., 401
Dahlerup, D., 535
Davies, O. E., 524
Day, D. V., 119, 164–168, 174
Dechawatanapaisal, D., 43
DeChurch, L. A., 301
De Cock, C., 347
de Luque, M.S., 216
Denis, J. L., 7, 8
De Paoli, D., 23
de Rivera, J., 132
DeRue, D. S., 33, 36, 89, 107, 464
DeRue, S., 270
destructive behaviours, 86, 87
destructive leaders, 87, 89, 447–455
destructive leadership, 87, 103, 292, 294, 447–455
　abusive supervision, 449–450
　conducive environments, 451
　dark triad, 449
　destructive leaders, 450–451
　destructive outcomes, 451–452
　interdisciplinary approaches, 453
　leader-centrism, 449
　leader effectiveness, 454
　leader emergence, 454
　literature, 448–450
　longitudinal studies, 452
　organisational checks and balances, 454–455
　positive construct, 450
　qualitative approaches, 453
　susceptible followers, 451
　toxic triangle, 450–452
DeVault, M. L., 348
De Vries, R. E., 101–103, 109
Deye, J. M., 492

dialectics, 305, 379, 484–491, 493
    critical leadership studies, 490–491
    paradox and, 490–491
Dienesch, R. M., 43
digital technology, 23, 25, 36, 297, 298, 301–306
Dinh, J. E., 473
D'Innocenzo, L., 75
directive leadership, 474, 475, 492
discrete context, 360–368
    methodological concerns, 364–368
    theoretical gaps, literature, 360–364
discrete contextual factors, 79, 360, 362, 366
disempowerment, 303, 400, 502
distributed leadership, 4, 7, 9, 10, 72–79, 374, 376, 378, 461, 463
    functionally distributed leadership, future research, 78–79
Dixon, N., 185
Dixon-Woods, M., 435
Do, M. H., 103
Dobusch, L., 515
Docherty, D., 541
Donia, M. B., 398
Dopson, S., 435, 436, 441, 442
Dovey, K., 22
Dragoni, L., 166, 167
Drath, W. H., 289
Drew, V., 34
Driscoll, C., 149
Durkheim, E., 276, 412
dynamic process, 87, 136, 286, 335, 510
dysfunctional leaders, 183–186
    authoritarianism, 184–185
    narcissistic leaders, 185–186

Eastman, K. K., 231
ecosystems, 219, 220, 312, 317
Edelman, P. J., 132
Eden, D., 116
Edmonstone, J., 439, 440
Edwards, G., 280, 374
Edwards, M., 504, 506
effective leadership, 56, 132, 173, 204, 286, 353, 437, 471, 478, 479, 492
Ehrlich, S. B., 65
Einarsen, S., 448
Einwohner, R. L., 377
Elfenbein, H., 89
Elliott, C., 300, 492, 542
Ellison, E. R., 516
embodied leadership, 509–511
Emerson, R.M., 77
emotional contagion, 129, 130, 132, 194, 195, 203
emotional experiences, 129, 133, 135, 136, 138, 191, 425
emotional intelligence, 129, 130, 132, 133, 135, 192, 197, 202–206
    critique, leadership research, 208–209
    and ethics, 208
    intelligence or knowledge, 204–205
    leadership studies, 204
    passion for, 203–204
emotionality, 104, 105, 137, 190, 196, 427
emotional labour, 130, 132, 133, 135, 148, 149, 181, 203, 306, 427, 465
emotional responses, 129, 195, 207, 208, 419
emotional stability, 103, 106, 107, 134, 137, 169
emotions, 89, 129–134, 136, 137, 179, 181, 192, 202–209, 419
    Aristotle on practising, 205–206
    emotion regulation and leadership research, 137–138
    extrinsic and intrinsic interpersonal emotion regulation, co-occurring, 136
    extrinsic interpersonal vs. intrinsic individual emotion regulation, 135–136
    interpersonal co-regulation, 136–137
    intrinsic versus extrinsic emotion regulation, 134
    and leadership, FLME, 131–137
    leadership and interpersonal emotion regulation, 133–134
    and power, 206
    regulation, 129, 130, 133, 135, 137, 192
    regulation and leadership, individual level, 133
    response-dependent emotion regulation, 134
    response-independent emotion regulation, 134
empathy, 207
empirical themes, 29–36
    concept of leadership, 35–36
    construction of leader and follower identities, 32–33
    influence and organising, action, 33–35
    roles and actions, 31–32
empowerment, 42, 296, 304, 395, 397, 399, 400, 474, 476, 479, 506
Emrich, C. G., 68
Endrissat, N., 7
Engels, F., 485
Ensari, N., 106
Ensley, M. D., 75
environmental dynamism, 227, 234–236
Eoyang, C., 278
epistemology, 316–317
Epitropaki, O., 87, 105, 117, 119
Erhart, I., 376
Eslen-Ziya, H., 376
essential ingredients, 409–410
ethical leadership, 103, 108, 109, 143, 144, 208, 331, 499
Eva, N., 167
Evans, M., 310
external stakeholders, motives, 156–157

Fairhurst, G. T., 32, 35, 263, 266, 269, 270, 377, 380, 492
Fairtlough, G., 401

Feldman, M. S., 17
Felfe, J., 66
feminist new materialities, 522–531
feminist psychoanalysis
    gendered thinking, leadership studies, 255–256
    intersubjectivity, 255–256
    recognition, 256
feminist theory, 252–253
Fiedler, F. E., 287, 359, 434
Fineman, S., 150
Fingarette, H., 410
Fischer, T., 46, 47, 287
Fisk, G. M., 132
Fitzsimons, D., 6
Flax, J., 254, 256
Fogel, J. A., 407
Follett, M. P., 398–400
follower-centric perspectives, 52, 55, 56, 67, 116, 154
followers, 42, 44, 85–87, 107, 134, 135, 180, 182, 196, 238, 339, 341, 359, 362, 448, 476, 478, 502
    business partners as, 160–161
    dependency and disempowerment, 502–503
    identities, 28, 29, 31–33, 35, 165, 270
    investors as, 157–159
    journalists as, 159–160
    outcomes, 41, 42, 44, 45, 107, 108, 450
    perceptions, 58, 59, 67, 286, 337, 448
    relationships, 35, 40–43, 46, 190–192, 217, 220, 228, 232
followership, 67, 75, 83–91, 154, 237, 335–343, 463, 478, 493
    across cultures, 88
    and/or leadership, 86–87
    balances leader(ship), 85–88
    challenging construal level, 89–90
    challenging dualism, 88
    challenging functionalism, 88–89
    challenging power symmetry, 89
    challenging rationalism, 89
    challenging universalism, 88
    destructive side of, 88–89
    developing followers, business schools, 90–91
    dialectical view on, 88
    differential followership, 89
    emotion-based followership, 89
    followers and following, 83–85
    manager Max and subordinate Sheila, hypothetical scenario, 336
    need for measures, 90
    prototypes, 88, 90, 122
    redefining, 154–162
    schemas, 116, 117, 119, 121
    theories, 78, 86, 115–124, 217
follower well-being
    positive effects, 500–501
Ford, J., 250, 512, 514
Fotaki, M., 515
Foucauldian-inspired critical history, 326–329

Foucault, M., 252, 325, 511, 514
Fournier, V., 515
Fox, A., 411
Fox-Kirk, W., 88
Fraher, A., 290
Fraser, T. N., 310, 314
Freeman, J., 375, 376
Frega, R., 401
Freitas, A. L., 231
Frenkel, R., 351
Freud, S., 179, 185
Fried, Y., 363
Friesen, J. P., 132
Frost, P. J., 500
Furnham, A., 204

Gabriel, Y., 502
Gagnon, S., 491
Galton, F., 104
Gambrell, K. M., 313
Gardiner, R. A., 149, 514
Gardner, H. E., 205
Gardner, W. L., 130, 143, 144
Garvey, M., 400
Gebert, D., 472
Geertz, C., 467
Gemmill, G., 252, 290, 461
gender, 66, 69, 116, 117, 121, 247–255, 538
    and domination, psychoanalytic theories, 254–255
    homosocial barriers, 251
    and leadership, new possibilities, 251–252
    and leadership, traditional perspectives, 249–251
    new directions and possibilities, 253–255
    and organisation theory, 248
    structural barriers, 250
    women's progression, barriers, 250
general intelligence, 203–207, 209
general organisational environment, 236–237
genetic overlap, 102
George, J. M., 129
George, W., 129, 143
Gerbaudo, P., 376
Gerstner, C. R., 119
Gherardi, S., 17, 512, 517
Gibeau, É., 7
Giddens, A., 17, 491, 499
Gilbert, G. R., 232
Gilligan, C., 505
Gilmore, S., 512
Gladstone, J. S., 315
Glass, C., 535
global cultural context, 236–237
Goldberg, L. R., 375
Goldman, B. M., 144
Goleman, D., 203, 206
Gooty, J., 131
Gosling, J., 439
Gottfredson, R. K., 45

Graen, G. B., 41
Graham, J. W., 398
Grand, J. A., 123, 124
Granet, 412
Greene, J., 218
Greenleaf, R., 398
Grint, K., 299, 377, 389, 391
Gronn, P., 7
Gross, D. M., 206
Gross, J. J., 133, 135, 142
Grosz, E., 512
group identity, 52, 53, 55–59, 388
group prototypes, 53–57, 59
group prototypicality, 56–57
Guillén, L., 117
Guillet de Monthoux, P., 279, 348
Gullion, J. S., 521
Gundemir, S., 536, 540
Guthey, E., 68, 143, 251
Gutmann, M., 331

Hackman, J. R., 78, 366
Hall, D. L., 408–410, 413
Hällgren, M., 421
Halme, M., 221
Halvorsen, K., 34
Hammond, M. M., 65, 166
Hampden-Turner, C., 385
Hannah, S., 363, 437
Hansen, H., 280
Harding, N., 492, 512
Harrington, A., 348
Hart, R. K., 438
Härtel, C. E. J., 132
Haslam, S. A., 66, 68, 119
Hassert, L. O., 33, 35, 301
Hatch, M. J., 230
Hawkins, B., 267
Hay, A., 407
healthcare, 7, 9, 155, 432–435, 438–441
    complex and open system, 435
    context, 435
    formidable contextual leadership challenges, 437
    leadership development, implications, 439–440
    sense-making, 436
    speed and extent, changing, 436–437
    unshackling local knowlegdge and social capital, 435–436
    virtual leadership acceleration, 438–439
healthcare leadership, 363, 432–442
    frame-breaking, 440–441
    importance of studying, 433–434
    theoretical perspectives, 434
Hegel, G. W. F., 485
Heider, J., 406
Heilman, M. E., 249
Held, V., 499
heritability, 100, 102, 108

Hernandez, M., 89
Herr, R. M., 43
hesitant leadership, 406–415
Hess, G., 367
HEXACO-Lead, 100, 105, 106, 108, 110
    self–other agreement, 105
    validity of, 105–106
Higgins, E. T., 229, 230, 232
Highhouse, S., 367
Hirschhorn, L., 184
Hirschman, A. O., 459
historical analysis, 322, 324, 325, 329–331
historical sensibility, 322–325, 330, 331, 378
historiographic considerations, 323–325
Hochschild, A., 181
Hofstede, G., 236, 383
Hogg, M. A., 55, 57
Hollenbeck, J. R., 77
Holm, F., 32, 35, 270, 492
Holmes, Elizabeth (founder of Theranos), 155
Holmes, J., 31
Homan, A. C., 76
Hook, S., 489
Hopkins, N., 42, 58
Horkheimer, M., 420
Hosking, D. M., 289
House, R. J., 236, 460, 461
Howcroft, D., 397
Hoyland, T., 117
Huambachano, M., 312, 316
Hubert, A. B., 449
Huggan, G., 351
Huisman, M., 34
humanistic naturalness, 411, 412
Humphrey, R. H., 209
Hunter, C., 522
Huxham, C., 7

Ilies, R., 106
implicit leadership, 115–124
implicit leadership and followership theories (ILTs/IFTs), 55, 63, 64, 67, 104, 115–124, 157, 166
    agents, 123
    bias and measurement error, 118
    collective context, 123–124
    common misconceptions, addressing, 118–120
    diversity and inclusion, 120–123
    ideal, typical, effective leader, 119–120
    implicit constructs, 118
    interactional rules, 123
    prototype–actual leader (follower) matching process, 118–119
    research, 117–118
    shared leadership schemas, 121–123
    studying dynamic, 123–124
    theoretical foundations, 116–117
    web of science core collection search, 120f
implicit organisational theory, 63, 64, 67

implicit theories, 67, 86, 87, 121, 122, 335, 339, 421
Indigenous leaders, 309, 311, 315
Indigenous leadership, 9, 221, 309–318
    activism, resistance and resilience, 315–316
    ancestral, cultural wisdom, 314–315
    co-evolution, symbiotic exchange and stewardship, 312–313
    key tenets of, 311–316
    place and community leadership, 313–314
Indigenous ontology, 316–317
Indigenous peoples, 309–313, 315, 317, 539, 541
individual differences, 40, 65, 76, 99, 100, 106, 116, 166, 169
individual identities, 8, 9, 33, 36, 411, 512
individualism, 236, 237, 516, 524
industry organisational environment, 234–236
informal leadership, 380, 459, 492
intelligence, 104–106, 118, 120, 202–206, 208, 209
intelligent emotions, 205, 207–208
interaction, 28–36
    empirical themes, 29–36
    leadership in, 28–29
    materiality of leadership, 35
    theoretical and methodological approaches, 29
interactional sociolinguistics, 29, 31
intergenerational leadership, 312, 313, 317
internal organisational environment, 230–234
    occupation type, 231–233
    organisational culture, 233–234
    task type, 230–231
interpersonal relationships, 43, 132, 170, 193, 263
intersubjectivity, 255, 256, 258, 505
investors, 154–162, 213
Iszatt-White, M., 149

Jack, A. I., 195
Jackson, B., 212, 219, 251
Jackson, E. M., 44
Jago, A., 287
Jakobsen, O. D., 281
Janson, A., 58
Javidan, M., 479
Jennings, R. E., 169
Jepson, D., 233, 388
Jermier, J., 366, 460
Johansson, J., 504, 506
Johns, G., 360, 362
Johnson, A. M., 102
Johnson, R. E., 44
Jordan, D. P., 414
Jordan, P. J., 132
Josephson-Storm, J. A., 310, 311, 317
Judge, T. A., 103
Jullien, F., 412
Junker, N., 90

Kaltenmark, M., 408, 410
Kanter, R., 251, 535, 542

Kark, R., 227, 229
Kärreman, D., 461
Kateb, G., 281
Katz-Buonincontro, J., 280
Kearney, E., 473
Kelan, E. K., 300
Kelley, R., 86, 90
Kelly, D., 313, 314
Kempster, S., 149, 212, 219, 221
Kendall, L. D., 194
Kenny, C., 310, 314
Kernis, M. H., 144
Kerr, S., 366, 460
Kersten, A., 281
Keshet, N. S., 105
Kets de Vries, M. F. R., 184
Khawaja, M. S., 196
Kilduff, M., 122
Kimmerer, R., 312, 314
Kirby, W. C., 407
Kirk, P., 439
Kittay, E. F., 503, 505, 506
Kivinen, N. H., 522
Klein, K. J., 77
Klenke, K., 453
Kluger, A. N., 231, 232
Knights, D., 512, 516, 517
Knutson, L., 516
Koenig, A., 249
Koestler, A., 118
Kohn, L., 406
Kohut, H., 182
Komives, S. R., 165
Kotter, J., 238
Kragt, D., 174
Krasikova, D. V., 448
Kuleshov Effect, 291, 292
Kwok, N., 169

Lacerenza, C. N., 171
Lachmann, R., 415
Ladegaard, H. J., 31
Ladkin, D., 68, 251
LaDuke, W., 313, 316
Lai, K., 411
laissez-faire way, 411
Land, C., 347
Landay, K., 449
Langhout, R. D., 516
Langley, A., 11
Larson, G. S., 491
Larson, L., 301
Larsson, M., 33–34, 46, 172, 266
Latif, K., 45
Latu, I., 541
Lau, D. C., 413
Lawler, J., 147
Lawrence, S. A., 133

Lawrence, T. B., 501
leader agency, 54, 58–59, 478
leader attributes, 55, 58, 323, 326, 330, 509
leader development, 164–166, 168–170, 172–175, 439, 440
leader effectiveness, 107, 110, 192, 204, 231, 363, 453, 454, 476, 479
leader fairness, 57–58
leader group prototypicality, 52–59
    core evidence, 54–55
    evidence and extensions, 54–59
leader identity, 32–35, 165, 166, 168, 169, 174, 175, 267, 268
leaderless movements, 68–69
    boundary conditions, 68–69
    gender, 69
leaderlessness, 375, 376, 378–380
leader–member exchange (LMX), 40–47, 90
    criticisms and future research directions, 45
    dyadic level, 44
    group level, 44–45
    individual level, 43–44
    longitudinal data, lack of, 47
    measurement issues, 45–46
    mediators, 41–42
    moderators, 42
    poor study design, 46–47
    quality, antecedents, 42–43
    quality, consequences, 41
    theoretical clarity, lack of, 45–46
leader qualities, 132, 255, 473
leader semiotics, 299–301
leadership-as-practice (LAP), 528–531
leadership concepts, 349, 373, 374, 465
leadership development, 90, 149, 150, 164–165, 167, 168, 171–175, 302, 439, 440
    additional recent research, 170
    evaluation, 171–172
    inclusiveness, 174–175
    leader identity, 165–166
    longitudinal studies and trajectories, 168–169
    practice concerns, 171–173
    research, 170–171
    science and practice of, 173–175
    sense-making and sense-breaking, 175
    sustainability of effects, 172–173
    team and collective, 167–168
    theoretical perspectives, 165–168
    trainers/developers effect, 173
leadership dialectics, 380, 484–495
    empirical studies, 491–494
leadership education, 346, 348–350, 387, 419, 420, 422, 427
leadership effectiveness, 52–58, 106, 108, 229–231, 236, 237, 525
leadership ethics, 499–500
leadership perceptions, 67, 120, 121, 166, 233, 500
Leadership Quarterly, 143, 279, 398

leadership representation, 426, 427, 534–543
    critical path to equity, 534–543
    'doings' of, 541–542
    historical context and current picture, 536–538
    identity and representation, 538–539
    intersectionality and complexity, 538–539
    power of representation, 539–541
    social symbolic power and, 540–541
    socioeconomic power and, 539–540
leadership research, 54, 55, 66, 99, 100, 108–110, 137, 142, 335, 350, 363, 379, 434
leadership studies, 5, 6, 11, 16, 18, 36, 204, 209, 213, 266, 267, 269, 271, 287, 306, 353, 354, 384, 419, 494
leadership theory
    Booker Prize, world of fiction, 350–352
    literary novel, leadership studies problems, 352–354
    novels in leadership studies, 348–350
    organisation studies and literary fiction, 347–348
    rebuilding through literature, 346–355
leadership through history, 322–332
    barriers and opportunities, 329–331
leadership traits, 100–102, 106
    follower outcomes/perceptions, 107
    leadership emergence and effectiveness, 106–107
    self–other agreement problem, 107–108
    structure of, 102–103
leader traits, 116, 286, 328, 359, 471, 473, 478
Leah, J., 194
Learmonth, M., 461–462
Leder, D., 513
LeDoux, J. E., 195
Lee, A., 43, 44
Lee, A. Y., 237
Leroy, S., 340, 341
Leviatan, V., 116
Lévi-Strauss, 412
Lewis, R. L., 397
Li, A. N., 41, 46, 102
Li, L., 411
Li, P. P., 407
Lichtenstein, B. B., 317
Liden, R. C., 43, 46
Lin, C. P., 214
Lipman-Blumen, J., 251
Lips-Wiersma, M., 147, 149, 214
Litano, M. L., 232
literary fiction, 346–350, 353, 354
Little, A. C., 135
Liu, X., 411
Liu, Z., 166
Livi, S., 101
Livingston, R. W., 120
Lloyd, G., 510
Loacker, B., 348
Loeffler, J., 312
Loignon, A. C., 44

London, M., 165
Longo M., 347
Longpre-Verret, L. M., 543
Lord, R. G., 116–119
Lorinkova, N. M., 171
Luckmann, T., 489
Lundholm, S. E., 33, 34, 266
Luo, X., 367
Lupton, D., 526
Luria, G., 173
Luthans, F., 143
Lynch, O. H., 491

Maak, T., 213, 214, 216, 220
MacGill, V., 377
MacIntyre, A., 218
Mackey, J. D., 99, 448, 455
mainstream leadership theories, 165, 213, 387
Maitlis, S., 131, 501
Mamdani, M., 388
managerial leadership, 123, 459, 461, 466
managers, 18, 19, 31, 46, 172, 231, 238, 341, 399, 441, 442, 449, 460, 462–467, 526
Mandalaki, E., 515
Marchioro, C. A., 121
Marcy, R. T., 377
Marion, R., 434
Mark, A., 442
Marley, B., 400
Marra, M., 31
Martela, F., 219
Martin, G. S., 385
Martin, L., 350
Martin, R., 105, 119, 172
Marx, K., 306, 485
masculine rational leader, 512–513
Maslow, A., 143
Maslyn, J. M., 46
materialisation, 264, 267, 268, 302, 526
materiality, 19–21, 23, 30, 31, 251, 252, 263, 268, 512, 521, 523, 527, 530
Maurer, T. J., 165
Mauss, 412
May, D. R., 143
Mayer, J. D., 133, 203
Mayo, M., 75, 154
McAllister, D. J., 501
McClean, S. T., 335
McCrae, R. R., 102
McGrath, J. E., 78
McLaughlin, G. B., 234, 434, 435
McLeod, P. L., 438
McMullen, J. S., 235
McPhee, R. D., 264
Mead, M., 387
Medvedeff, M. E., 116
Meier, F., 265, 267, 302
Meindl, J. R., 64–67, 154, 186

Melina, L., 251
Mellahi, K., 385
mental representations, 52–53, 55, 56, 116, 122, 179
Meschitti, V., 266
Mesinioti, P., 31, 35
messianic leaders, 182, 183
meta-categories, 471–474, 479
Meyer, J. W., 9
Meyer, M. A., 313, 318
Milgram, S., 293
Mill, J. S., 218
Miller, D., 184
Minbashian, A., 103
mind–body dichotomy, 511–512
Miscenko, D., 168
Mitchell, T. D., 106
moderators, 40–42, 45, 76, 118, 145, 146, 198, 215, 216
Mohammed, S., 366
Montgomery, B. M., 490
Morgan, G., 384
Morgeson, F. P., 76, 78, 79
Morrell, K., 461, 462
Morris, C. G., 78
Mumford, M. D., 231
Munro, I., 502
myth of passions, 202–209

Nadir, Asil, 142
Nadkarni, S., 366
Nandy, A., 406
narcissism, 36, 107, 178, 180, 184–186, 208, 473, 474, 479
national culture, 216, 230, 236, 237, 343, 363, 384, 385
negative emotions, 43, 132, 136, 197
Neumann, Adam (co-founder of WeWork), 155–156
neuroscience, leadership relationship
    coaching, role, 196
    coaching with compassion, followers impact, 197
    emotional contagion, 194–195
    organisational context, 195–196
    resonant leaders, developing, 196
    strategy, budgets and learning, 195–196
new materialities, 521–523
Nicholson, A., 313, 317
Nicholson, H., 149, 302
Nieberle, K. W., 122
Nielsen, M. B., 102
Nielsen, M. F., 33
Nieto-Rodriguez, A., 401
Niven, K., 135
Norris, S., 351
Northouse, P. G., 143
Nugus, P., 441
Nyberg, D., 149

Oakley, J., 252, 290, 461
objective reality, 178, 202, 206, 287
Oborn, E., 21

Oc, B., 360, 362
Offermann, L. R., 104, 119
Oldham, G., 366
Omilion-Hodges, L., 46
omnibus context, 360–368
    methodological concerns, 364–368
    theoretical gaps, literature, 360–364
O'Neill, C., 513
Oren, L., 232
organisational actors, 7, 8
organisational behaviour, 52–54, 192, 368, 453, 529
organisational change, 53, 56, 57, 59, 129, 136, 238, 262, 472, 492, 540
organisational commitment, 41, 54, 73, 107
organisational consciousness, four-level model, 221f
organisational context, 8, 11, 129, 131, 191–195, 198, 270, 271, 448, 450
organisational culture, 174, 184, 190, 191, 193, 227, 230, 233, 234, 383, 385
organisational leadership, 5, 72, 402, 421, 501, 541
organisational performance, 63–65, 67, 191, 204, 235, 363
organisational structures, 4, 6, 29, 230, 234, 251
organisation theory, 248, 348
Orlikowski, W. J., 17
Orr, J. E., 17
Osborn, R. N., 230, 363
Ostroff, C., 103
Overbeke, K. K., 193
Ozer, M., 42

Padilla, A., 292
paradoxes, 472–474
    advance leadership research, 479–480
    agency and communion, 474–476
    alignment and initiative, follower sense-making, 477–478
    alignment and initiative, leader sense-giving, 477–478
    both-and approach, 476
    leader paradox mindset, 477
    leaders, followers and researchers, co-construction, 478–479
    one-best-way approach, 475
    sense-giving processes, 476–477
    situationally flexible approach, 475–476
    sustainable well-being and performance, 478
paradoxical leadership, 471, 472, 477–479
Parker, M., 386
Parker Follett, M., 86, 396, 398
Parry, K., 36
Parsons, T., 397
passions, 207–208
Pastor, I., 154
Pateman, C., 401
Paterson, T. A., 55
Pawar, B. S., 231
Pearce, C.L., 4

Peat, F. D., 317
Pelletier, K. L., 448, 452
Penny, L., 420
Pepion, D. D., 315
personality, 42, 100–104, 106–110, 205, 206, 208, 289
    structure of, 103–104
    traits, 36, 100, 101, 103–109, 450
personal qualities, 285, 287, 291, 439
personal trajectories, 168, 169, 172
perspective action-discrimination, 409, 411–413, 415
Pessi, A. B., 219
Peters, T., 385
Petriglieri, G., 500, 501
Phillips, M., 347
physical traits, 86, 100
Pieratos, N. A., 315
Platow, M. J., 55
Pless, N., 220
Pless, N. M., 213–215
pluralism, 3–11, 442, 492
    self and plural leadership, 8–9
plurality, 3–6, 8, 9, 11, 494
plural leadership, 3–11, 19, 32, 374
    analysis and perspectives, 3–11
    combining representations, 6
    empirically driven studies, 6–8
    entitative perspective, 5
    novel ideas and promising perspectives, 8–10
    power and control, manifestation, 9–10
    relational perspective, 5–6
    representations, variations, 5–8
    resistors as actors, 10
    studies, 5–9, 269
    theoretically driven studies, 6–8
political contexts, 6, 66, 253, 454
polyarchy, 395–403
polychronicity, 336–341
popular culture, 418–429
    disabled leaders, 424–426
    emotions, 419
    experience, 420–421
    ideology and critique, 419–420
    learning, 421–422
    new leader role models, Reality TV and Instagram, 427–428
    struggling charismatic leaders, 422–424
    women in leadership, 426–427
Porter, L. W., 234, 434–435
positional leadership, 536, 538, 540, 542
postcolonial contexts, 388, 389
power, 8, 10, 206, 248, 275, 325, 327, 376, 395–402, 441, 463, 491, 494
    asymmetries, 10, 251, 256, 490, 501, 506, 507
power relations, 395–403, 503, 504, 513, 514
    empowering leading (not leaders), 400–402
    empowerment, leadership, 397–398
    hierarchical control, leadership, 396–397
    partnership, leadership, 398–400

practice theories, 16–25
    decentring leadership, 19
    differences, selected dimensions, 21–24
    expanding leadership, 19–20
    genealogy of, 17–18
    leadership and, 24–25
    in leadership studies, 18
    leadership studies building, 18–24
    redefining leadership, 20–21
Prassl, J., 403
Price, T. L., 143
process theory approaches, 285–294
    ideally isolated systems and fallacies, 287–289
    ontologies of leadership, 289–291
    rethinking property as process, 291–292
    shadow side of, 292–294
    understanding leadership, property or process, 286–287
promotion focus, 228, 229, 231–233, 237, 364
psychoanalysis, 178–181, 186, 187, 254, 255, 407, 490
psychoanalytic approaches, 178–187
    dysfunctional leaders, 183–186
    followership, 182–183
    Freud and Bion, 180–181
    managers of emotion, leaders, 181–182
Pullen, A., 513, 517

qualitative approaches, 64, 452, 453
quality of relationships, 40–47
queer theory, 252, 492, 493
Quigley, N. R., 169
Quinn, J. F., 196

Raelin, J. A., 167, 412, 439, 529
Randall, A. K., 136, 137
recipes, potential, 412–413
reciprocal care ethics, 256–257
    relational and transitional third, 257
Reckwitz, A., 17
regulatory fit theory, 229–230
regulatory focus theory, 227–229, 232, 238
Reicher, S., 42, 58
Reichers, A. E., 144–146
relational approaches, 5, 6, 8, 11, 178, 441, 516
relational energy, 191, 193, 194, 197
relational leadership, 252–254, 374, 501, 509, 510
relational process, 74, 122, 400, 402
relationship quality, 190–198
    compassion, 193–194
    emotional and social competencies (ESI), 192
    followers, fMRI studies, 196–197
    foundations, 192
    implications, 197–198
    performance constructs, impact, 193
    relational climate, 193
    relational climate, higher-order construct, 194
    relational energy, 194
    resonant relationships, 192–193
    shared vision, 193

representation studies, 534, 538, 539
Resick, C. J., 385
resistance, embodying, 514–516
resistance leadership, 299, 303, 304, 377, 379
Reskin, B., 250
responsibility, 19, 20, 25, 64–66, 208, 213, 215–217, 222, 399, 441, 515
responsible consciousness, 220–222
responsible leadership (RL), 24, 212–223
    making sense of, 213–217
    'Us with Them,' 217–220
Rhodes, C., 299, 300, 517
Richards, E., 543
Richardson, E., 541
Riggio, R., 83, 91
Rizio, S. M., 452
Robinson, F., 500
romance of leadership, 63–69
    archival studies, 65
    charisma, 67
    definition, 64
    empirical evidence, historical review, 64–66
    experimental studies, 65–66
    field studies, 66
    followership, 67
    implicit leadership theories, 67
    leaders as source, 66
    leadership research, influence, 66–68
    post-heroic leadership, 68
    succession, 67
Roos, P., 250
Ropo, A., 20
Rosemont, H., 410
Rosener, J., 249
Rosette, A. S., 120
Rousseau, D., 363
Rovelli, C., 318
Royal, C., 317
Rush, M. C., 116
Ryle, G., 511

Saggurthi, S., 407
Sahlins, M., 379
Sajons, G., 367
Salovaara, P., 20, 301
Salovey, P., 133, 203
Sarangi, S., 34
Savage, P., 347
Sayama, H., 73
Schad, J., 471
Schein, E. H., 234
Schein, V., 536
Schermerhorn, J. R., 143, 235
Schilling, J., 448, 454
Schnackenberg, A. K., 384
Schneider, B., 144–146
Schnurr, S., 32, 266
Schroeder, A., 266
Schultz, P. L., 317

Schwartz, S. H., 385
Schweiger, S., 170
Schyns, B., 66, 67, 118, 343, 448, 454
Scott, C. P. R., 122
Scott, D., 407
Sedgwick, E., 252
Seers, A., 75
self-care, 502–505
    appeal of, 503–505
self-managed teams, 77, 121, 531
self–other agreement
    HEXACO-Lead, 105
    problem, 103
self-regulatory focus, 227–238
self-sacrifice, 502, 505, 506
    risk of, 505–506
Seltzer, J., 526, 528, 532
senior leadership roles, 249, 250, 536, 537
sense-breaking, 108
    incremental validity of leadership, 110
    leader liking, role of, 110
    lifespan leadership research, 108–109
    person–supervisor fit, 109–110
    volitional leadership change, 109
sense-making, 100–102, 129–131, 133, 135–138, 170, 175, 310, 436, 477, 478, 501
    process, 134, 135, 137, 233, 477
Sergi, V., 7, 20
servant leadership, 68, 143, 213, 214, 216, 282, 395, 398, 461
Shamir, B., 130, 162
Shaw, J. B., 149, 448
Sheep, M. L., 222
Shi, X., 412
Shin, Y., 233
Shondrick, S. J., 116
signalling effects, 535, 539
Simola, S. K., 500
Simons, R., 397
Simpson, B., 22, 266, 302
Simpson, P., 502
Simpson, P. F., 406, 407
Simsa, R., 376
Sin, H. P., 44, 168
Sinclair, A., 310, 513
Sinha, P., 303
Sirén, C., 132
Sitkin S. B., 525
Skali, A., 452
Skogstad, A., 102
Slingerland, E., 409
Śliwa, M., 20, 347–348
Sluss, D. M., 42
Smircich, L., 384
Smith, P. B., 33, 385
Smith, T. J., 232
Smith, W., 492
Smolović Jones, O., 303, 491
Smolović Jones, S., 515

Smooth, W., 541
social capital, 167, 435, 436, 440–442
social exchanges, 41, 42, 46, 196
social identity, 52–54, 362
    of leadership and follower-centric theories, 55–56
social intelligence, 191, 194, 196, 203, 206
social movements, 10, 297, 371, 373, 374, 376, 377, 379, 380
social relations, 253, 372, 373, 396, 398, 399, 403, 461, 464
Solomon, R. C., 202
Spears, L. C., 398
Spears, R., 119
Spencer, S., 367
Spicer, A., 493, 494, 503
Spillane, J. P., 7
Spiller, C., 310, 314, 315, 317
Spitznagel, M., 406
Stahl, G. K., 216
stakeholders, 154, 156, 212–214, 217–221, 223, 398, 400
Stead, V., 300, 492, 542
Steffens, N. K., 54, 55, 57, 66
Steidlmeier, P., 142. 144
stereotypes, 541
    eroding, 540–541
Stogdill, R. M., 290
Storsletten, V. M. L., 281
structurelessness, 375, 376, 378
Sundstrom, E., 77
susceptible followers, 292, 293, 448, 451–455
Sutherland, N., 270, 376, 379, 380
Svejenova, S., 7
Sveningsson, S., 149
Sy, T., 89, 90, 120
symbiotic exchange, 311, 312

Taheri, A., 147
Taylor, F. W., 303
Taylor-Bianco, A., 235
team leadership, 72–74, 77, 78, 301
    collectively enacted team function, 73–78
    functional view of, 72–73
    people, 74–75
    people x roles, 75–77
    people x time, 77–78
team performance, 41, 45, 63, 72, 74–76, 171, 340
tech-driven (disruptive) leadership, 298–299
technological agency, 301, 302
technology, 296–306
    leaders and, 299–301
    leaders and gender, 299–300
    leader semiotics and value production, 299
    leadership, power and control, 302–303
    leadership and teams, 301–302
    making sense of, 297
    political leadership and, 303–304
Tee, E., 89
temporal characteristics, 78, 335, 336, 339, 341–343

temporal considerations, 335–343
    manager Max and subordinate Sheila, hypothetical scenario, 336
    practical implications, 343
    purpose, 336
temporal implicit theories, 338–340
temporal individual differences, 336–338
    leaders and followers, 340
    pacing style, 338
    polychronicity, 337–338
    time perspective, 337
    time urgency, 336–337
temporal leadership, 336, 339–343, 362, 367
temporal stability, 102
temporal themes
    additional, 342–343
    joint consideration of, 342
Thakur, M., 407
Thanem, T., 502, 517
theoretical gaps, literature, 360–364
Thielmann, I., 102, 109
Thomas, K., 541
Thompson, B. S., 42
Thompson, T. L., 526
Thoroughgood, C. N., 87
time-based inconsistencies
    leaders and followers, 338–341
    temporal fit, 339
    temporal implicit theories, 339
time pressure, 335–337, 340
time urgency, 336, 337, 340, 341, 343
Todd, R., 351
Tomkins, L., 502, 507
total management, 296, 298–299, 304
Totter, M., 376
Tracy, S. J., 492
trait variance, 101
transactional leadership, 102, 461
transformational leadership, 525–528
transitional space, 254, 256–258
Tranter, B., 374
Treviño, L. K., 499
Trompenaars, F., 385
Tronto, J. C., 503
Troth, A. C., 130, 133, 136, 137
Tse, B., 129, 131
Tse, H. H., 45
Tutu, D., 390
Tyler, M., 516

Uhl-Bien, M., 6, 7, 41, 83, 84, 86, 90, 266, 434, 437, 442
Ullrich, J., 58
unethical behaviour, 208, 209
Urbach, T., 88

Vachhani, S., 513
value orientation, 372, 373

Van de Mieroop, D., 32, 33, 35, 492
Van Dierendonck, D., 102
Van Dijk, D., 227, 229
Van-Dijk, D., 231, 232
Vangen, S., 7
Van Knippenberg, D., 55, 57, 132, 525, 532
van Veldhoven, M., 449
van Vugt, M., 374, 379
variance, 20, 44, 101, 102, 104, 110
Velasco, F., 171
Venus, M., 56
Vidyarthi, P. R., 45
Vine, B., 31, 266
Virno, P., 298
virtual teams, 35, 36, 438, 439
Visser, L. M., 524
Vizmuller-Zocco, I., 349, 350
Vogel, B., 165
Vollet-Neto, A., 85
von Rueden, C., 374, 379

Wacquant, L., 512
Wåhlin-Jacobsen, C. D., 34
Waldman, D. A., 234, 235, 473, 479
Waldo, D., 347
Wallace, D. M., 172
Walumbwa, F. O., 145
Wang, D., 76
Wang, L., 90
Waring, J., 9
Warner, N. O., 349
Warr, P., 103
Waterman, R., 385
Watson, C., 34
Weber, M., 67, 396
Weick, K. E, 131
Westcott, D., 121
Western, S., 379, 380
White, L., 7
Whiteley, P., 361
Wiebe, E., 149
Williams, M., 133, 135
Williams, W. C., 133, 136
Willmott, 386
Wilson, M., 397
Wilson, S., 317, 326
Winchester, N., 515
Winnicott, D. W., 256
Wodak, R., 31
Wolf, S., 219
women, 248–255, 426, 427, 492, 499, 513, 535–537, 539–542
    leaders, 69, 121, 249, 300, 350, 492, 504
    in leadership roles, 248–249
    liberation movement, 375, 376
Wood, M., 288, 289
workers, 297, 298, 300–306, 398–400, 449, 461, 462
Wren, J. T., 324

Yammarino, F. J., 7
Yang, Y., 90
Yeatman, A., 256
Yngvesson, B., 375
Youngs, G., 9
Yukl, G., 73, 130
Yunkaporta, T., 314, 316, 318
Zaccaro, S. J., 73
Zacher, H., 107
Zaki, J., 133, 136
Zaug, P., 264
Zeitoun, H., 451
Zeitz, G., 489
Zhang, H., 42
Zhou, W., 88
Zoller, H. M., 377, 380